$14.95 B74

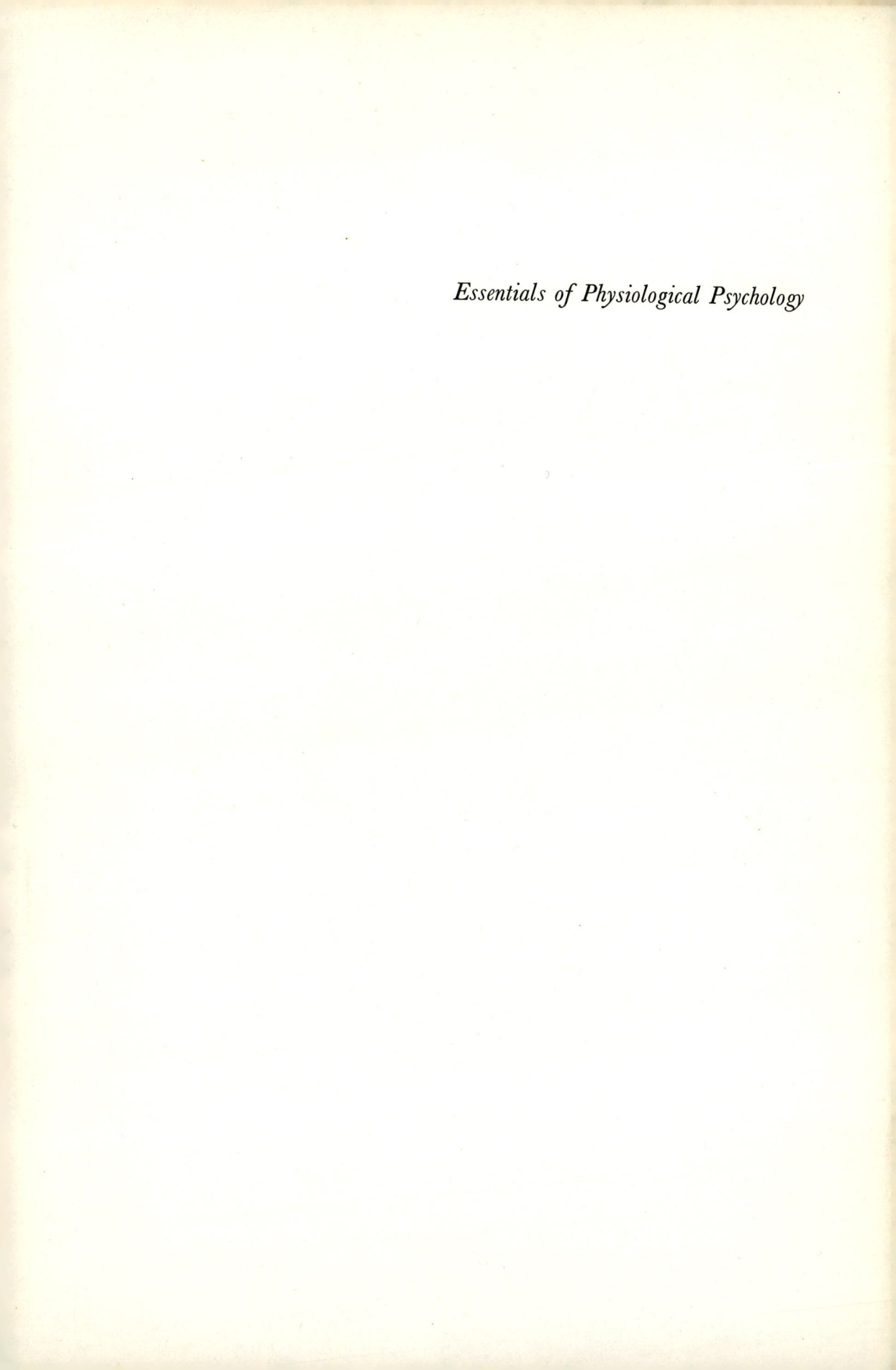

Essentials of Physiological Psychology

ESSENTIALS OF PHYSIOLOGICAL PSYCHOLOGY

Sebastian P. Grossman
DEPARTMENT OF PSYCHOLOGY
UNIVERSITY OF CHICAGO

John Wiley & Sons, Inc. New York · London · Sydney · Toronto

Copyright © 1973, by John Wiley & Sons, Inc.

All rights reserved. Published simultaneously in Canada.

No part of this book may be reproduced by any means, nor transmitted, nor translated into a machine language without the written permission of the publisher.

Library of Congress Cataloging in Publication Data

Grossman, Sebastian Peter.
  Essentials of physiological psychology.

Includes bibliographies.
1. Psychology, Physiological. I. Title. [DNLM:
1. Psychophysiology. WL 102 G878e 1973]
QP360.G76   152   72-1450
ISBN 0-471-32860-X

Printed in the United States of America.

10 9 8 7 6 5 4 3 2

PREFACE

In my *Textbook of Physiological Psychology*, published in 1967, I attempted to present a fair and thorough coverage of the available experimental literature and deliberately refrained from imposing on this material conclusions and generalizations that reflected my personal biases. I have found this type of presentation useful in my own graduate level courses because it invites synopsis and evaluation by the student instead of uncritical acceptance of predigested and biased opinions. However, this approach assumes a fair degree of prior preparation and sophistication and is not, in most instances, readily adaptable to an introductory course.

The present textbook, *Essentials of Physiological Psychology*, is specifically designed to fit the needs of an introductory course in physiological psychology. It covers the subjects that were included in the earlier version but emphasizes synopsis, synthesis, explanation, and conclusion. The principal developments in each area are presented in terms of key experimental findings and their theoretical implications. No attempt is made to present an exhaustive review of the literature.

The book has four sections. Section 1 contains a brief discussion of some of the techniques used in physiological psychology; a summary of a few of the neurophysiological principles that govern the actions of nerve cells and of the brain as a whole; and an outline of the neuroanatomical information needed to find one's way through the mammalian brain. These introductory chapters are not intended to take the place of expert treatises but seek to provide a suitable introduction for the typical undergraduate or graduate student in psychology.

The second section outlines the structure and function of some of the organism's primary input and output systems. It includes chapters on visual, auditory, and chemical sensory mechanisms, which are intended to provide appreciation of the processes that translate physical changes in the environment into proportional physiological signals. The rich and complex field of perceptual phenomena and their relationship to sensory events warrants separate treatment. The chapter on motor functions discusses how the central nervous system translates changes in its own state into overt actions. The material presented in the second section serves as background information for Sections 3 and 4, which constitute the topics of primary interest. It can be skipped if the course does not provide sufficient time for adequate coverage of all segments of this book.

Section 3 contains six chapters concerned with the biological basis of basic motivational processes such as hunger, thirst, sexual arousal, affective reactions, sleep, and the organism's response to reward and punishment. The final chapter integrates the principal observations from the diverse areas into a general model for simple motivational processes. In these chapters, the principal experimental observations on which our current knowledge of the phenomena in question rests are reviewed in detail and their implications and shortcomings are discussed. An attempt is made to provide critical synopses and to illuminate major trends and developments. Reviews and summaries are liberally used.

The fourth section is devoted to a discussion of the biological basis of learning and its end product, memory. The opening chapter presents some of the conceptual and practical problems that have made research in this important area very difficult. The following chapters discuss research and theory concerning the anatomical substrate of learning and memory; the electrophysiological, biochemical, and neuropharmacological changes that may accompany learning and/or recall; and the biochemical properties of the memory trace. The section ends with a brief discussion of the theoretical models that have been proposed to account for the functional or structural changes occurring in the nervous system as a result of learning. Many of the interpretations offered in this section are speculative because "hard" information is difficult to obtain in this area. Once again, I stress the principal developments and present frequent summaries and reviews of the often complex experimental findings.

I am deeply indebted to my wife, Lore, for her encouragement and patience during the gestation of this manuscript and to Rena Appel for her generous editorial, administrative, and clerical assistance with all phases of the manuscript. I also thank my students who, over the years, have contributed in many ways to the research and ideas presented here.

Sebastian P. Grossman

CONTENTS

Section 1: An Introduction to Neurophysiology and Neuroanatomy — 1
Chapter 1. Research Procedures in Physiological Psychology — 3
Chapter 2. Basic Units and Functions of Biological Organisms — 12
Chapter 3. Anatomy of the Nervous System — 36

Section 2: The Input and Output Channels of the Organism — 61
Chapter 4. Vision — 63
Chapter 5. Audition — 91
Chapter 6. The Chemical Senses — 120
Chapter 7. The Motor System — 150
Chapter 8. The Reticular Formation and Nonspecific Thalamic Projection System — 177

Section 3: The Biological Bases of Motivation — 187
Chapter 9. Hunger and the Regulation of Food Intake — 189
Chapter 10. Thirst and the Regulation of Water Intake — 225
Chapter 11. The Hormonal and Neural Basis of Sexual Behavior — 252
Chapter 12. Affective Behavior — 273
Chapter 13. Reward and Punishment — 306
Chapter 14. Sleep, Arousal, Attention, and Habituation — 326
Chapter 15. Theories of Motivation — 359

Section 4: Biological Bases of Learning and Memory — 373
Chapter 16. The Nature of Learning — 375
Chapter 17. Anatomical Substrate of Learning and Memory — 395
Chapter 18. Electrophysiology of Learning — 422
Chapter 19. Biochemistry and Neuropharmacology of Learning and Memory — 440
Chapter 20. Theories of Learning — 471
Author Index — 487
Subject Index — 499

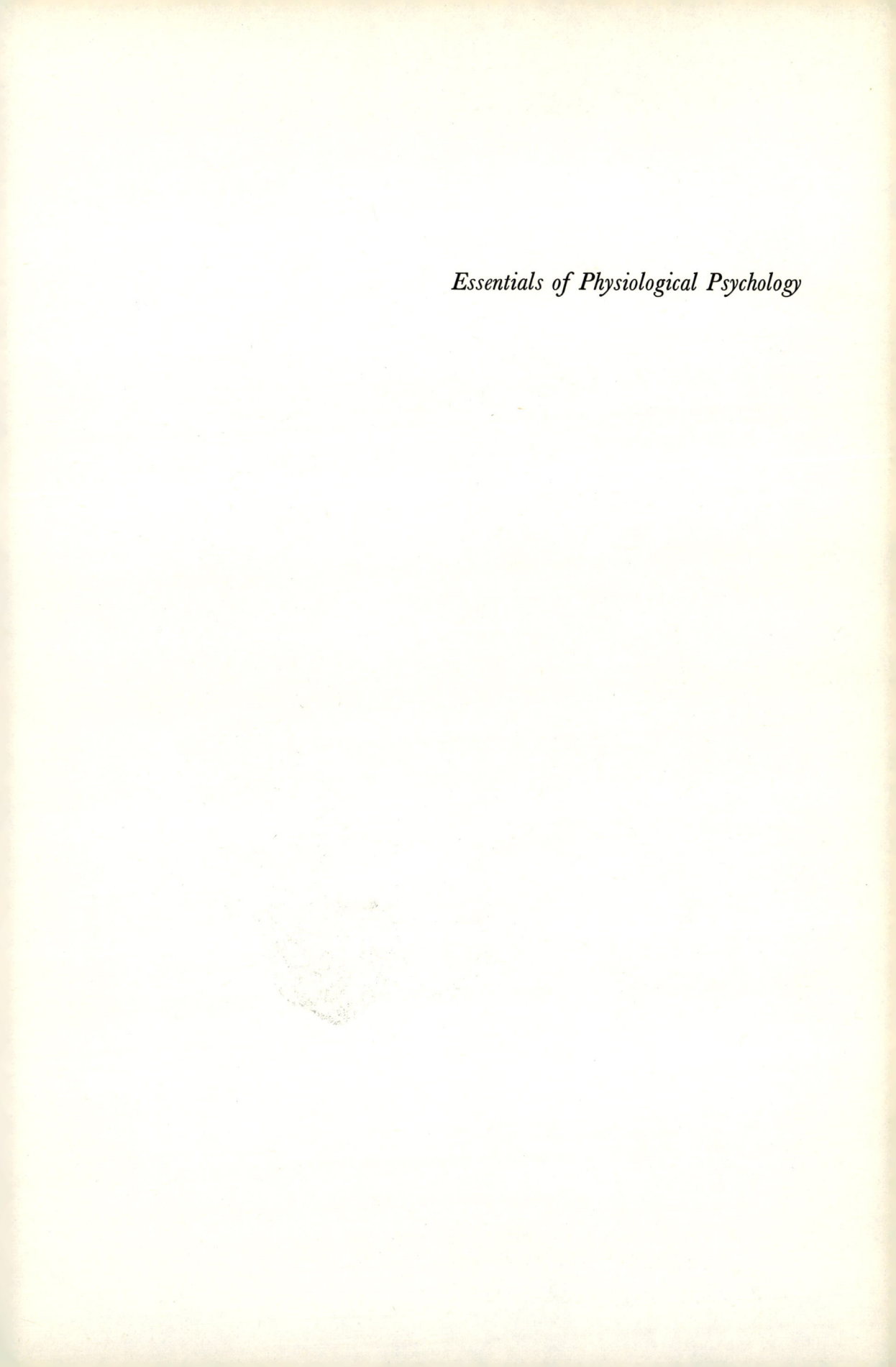

Essentials of Physiological Psychology

SECTION 1

An Introduction to Neurophysiology and Neuroanatomy

Physiological psychologists are concerned with the physiological events which correlate with psychological processes such as affective reaction, sexual arousal, or learning. Before we can begin to discuss these complex matters, it is necessary to acquire at least a rudimentary understanding of related fields that are more specifically concerned with the structure and function of biological organisms. Since psychological processes are most directly related to the activity of the brain and associated peripheral neural pathways, we can justify concentrating on two aspects of these complex fields—neurophysiology and neuroanatomy—for the purpose of our introductory discussions. It should be clear, however, that physiological psychologists cannot ignore nonneural aspects of the organism in their work.

The first section of this book contains condensed and simplified introductions to neurophysiology and neuroanatomy as well as a very brief description of some of the techniques used to obtain information about the structure and function of the brain. These chapters are intended to provide an overview of the geography of the central nervous system and an appreciation of some of the physicochemical events that occur in it. They will make difficult reading for the nonbiologist, particularly because the ancient discipline of anatomy relies extensively on Latin terminology. It may be best to skim this material to get a feel of the land and return to it later in the context of specific substantive issues that will be raised in subsequent sections of this book.

Chapter 1

RESEARCH PROCEDURES IN PHYSIOLOGICAL PSYCHOLOGY

Recording Techniques
Electrical and Chemical Stimulation
Ablation
Stereotaxic Procedures
Anatomical Procedures

The physiological psychologist is concerned with the relationship between physical and chemical events in the organism (particularly in its nervous system) and resultant psychological processes such as perception, motivation, or learning. There are two principal ways to investigate this relationship experimentally. Potentially the most satisfying but also the most difficult approach is to record the physical and chemical events and directly correlate them with behavior. An approximation to this ideal state can be attained by monitoring some of the electrical changes that occur when living tissue is active. We are only learning to obtain meaningful recordings of such bioelectric phenomena, but the approach is promising. The second principal approach to the study of the relationship between physical and psychological events consists of an attempt to interfere in some way with physiological processes and note the resulting behavioral changes. Here, too, our tools are still crude, as we shall see in a moment.

RECORDING TECHNIQUES

Only few attempts have so far been made to analyze chemical reactions in the intact organism, largely because the available procedures cannot do so without interfering with the very events they are trying to measure. Instead, we have concentrated on recording the electrical potentials that are generated by nerve cells as well as nonneural tissue during excitation or inhibition.

Single-Cell Activity

The activity of single cells can be recorded by

inserting the very fine (> 0.5 micron) tip of a wire electrode into the cell or into the extracellular spaces surrrounding it. Because of the size of its tip, such an electrode has a very high electrical resistance (impedance), and special amplifiers are required to record the electrical potential that is generated whenever the cell is active. When the electrode is outside the cell, this potential consists of a very brief (less than one millisecond) spike. The amplitude of this potential varies as a function of the distance between the recording electrode and the cell that generates it but rarely exceeds 500 microvolts. Intracellularly recorded potentials are much larger (often 100 millivolts) and complex (because slow potential changes that precede and follow the spike potential can be seen). (See Figure 1–1, line F).

Excitatory inputs to a cell shift the membrane potential and trigger a spike discharge when a threshold of positivity is reached. Inhibitory inputs shift the membrane potential in the opposite direction and reduce the probability of a spike discharge. The shifts in membrane potential cannot be seen in extracellular recordings.

In the awake unrestrained animal the brain moves continually, and it is impossible to obtain intracellular recordings. Recent technological advances have made it possible to obtain extracellular recordings from unrestrained animals, at least for a brief period of time. This is typically accomplished by inserting somewhat larger microelectrodes (tip diameter about 5 to 10 microns) into the brain until the spike discharges of a few cells can be recorded. Since the amplitude of the extracellularly recorded spike discharge is determined by the distance between the electrode and the cell, different cells can be identified on the basis of the amplitude of the spike discharge (see Figure 1–1, line E). This convenient feature is also the principal factor that limits the usefulness of this technique. As the brain moves with respect to the recording electrode, the distance between the electrode and a particular cell changes, and it becomes impossible to identify the cell in terms of previously obtained records.

Multiunit Activity

Still larger electrodes are used to record the spike potential of a large number of individual cells. Electrodes with a tip diameter of about 100 microns record the activity of so many cells that it becomes impossible to identify individual cells (see Figure 1–1, line D). Such population recordings may be more informative than recordings of the activity of a single cell because they reflect functional changes in the activity of significant numbers of neurons. To estimate the effect of a stimulus on a functional unit of the brain, it is necessary to either record many hundreds or thousands of single units (a tedious task at best) or to obtain a multiple-unit recording that reflects the average response of the relevant population of cells.

It is customary to use an electronic filter to remove slow potential changes below about 800 cycles per second or Hertz (Hz) from the multiple unit record and then integrate the total remaining electrical activity. Theoretically, this should provide a good estimate of the direction of the response of a fairly small number of cells (perhaps a few hundred) and give us an important measure of brain activity. The principal limitation of this method arises from the fact that the functional organization of the brain does not conform very closely to geographic boundaries so that it is difficult to obtain a multiple-unit recording from a homogeneous population of cells.

Electroencephalographic Recordings

Still larger macroelectrodes (with a tip diameter of several hundred microns) are used to record the rhythmic slow potential changes that are present in the brain even in the absence of particular stimulation. These electroencephalographic (EEG) recordings are thought to be related to the spike activity of single cells, but this relationship is clearly not a simple one. Concurrent recordings of EEG and single-cell activity from the same region of the brain have not yet revealed the principles that relate the two measures. An interpretation of the EEG in terms of functional changes is therefore difficult. EEG

Research Procedures 5

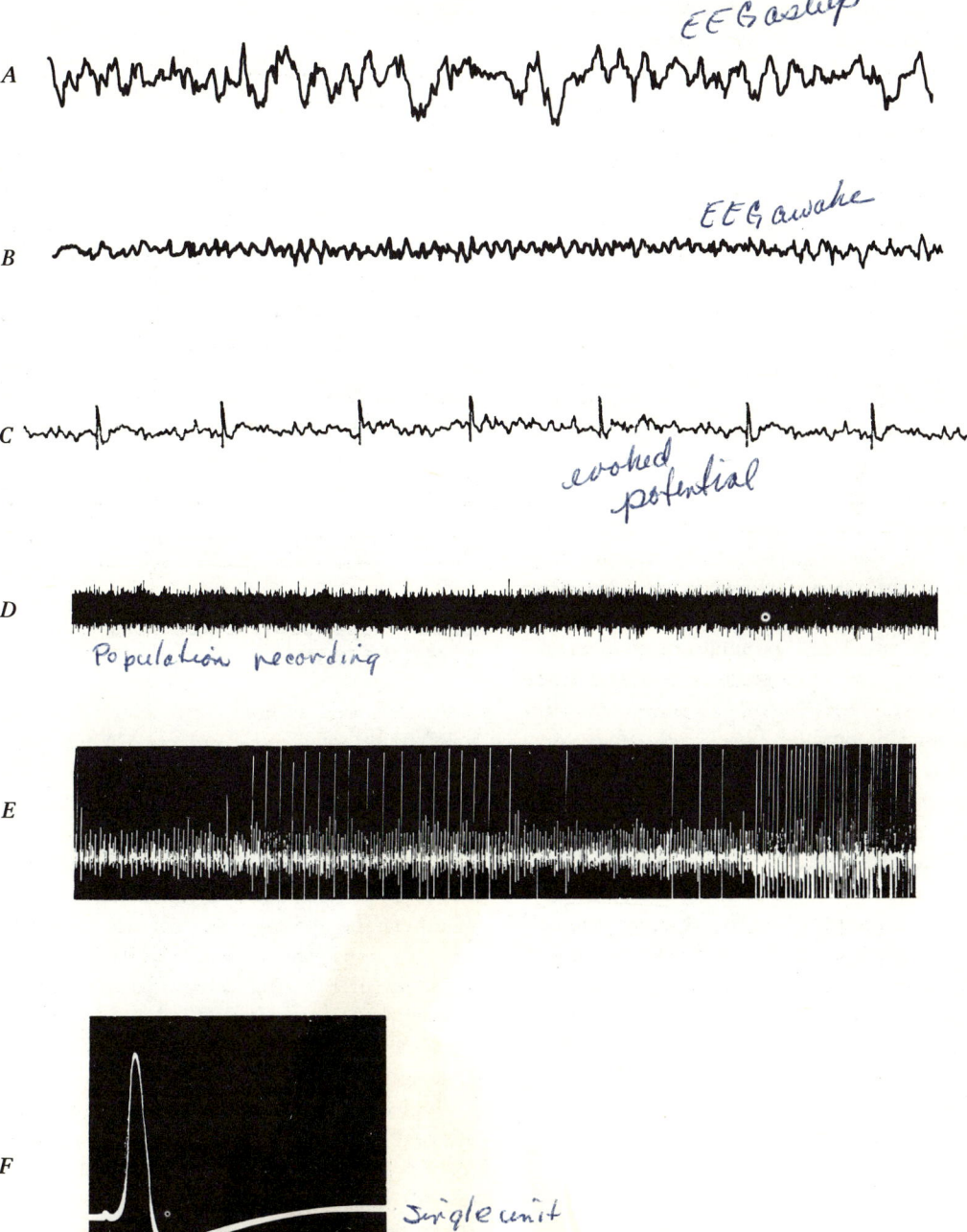

FIG. 1–1. Electrophysiological signals which are commonly recorded from the nervous system. (A) EEG of a quiet subject; (B) EEG of an aroused subject; (C) evoked potentials superimposed on the cortical EEG; (D) multiple unit activity; (E) single unit activity recorded extracellularly; (F) single unit activity recorded intracellularly. The EEG and evoked potentials are recorded from large electrodes, the single unit activity from very small microelectrodes.

Neurophysiology and Neuroanatomy

recordings are nevertheless used extensively, largely because they are easily obtained even from electrodes that are attached to the surface of the skull.

During sleep or inattentive wakefulness, the EEG record is dominated by slow (6 to 12 Hz), high-amplitude (200 to 500 microvolts) rhythmic waves (see Figure 1-1, line A). During attentive wakefulness, a much less regular, high-frequency (up to several hundred Hz) activity appears that is of much lower amplitude (20 to 200 microvolts) (see Figure 1-1, line B). Largely because of this correlation with sleep and wakefulness, it is customary to assume that the rhythmic slow waves reflect synchronous cellular activity that cumulates to produce the high amplitudes. This pattern of activity is thought to characterize a state of inactivity or inhibition. The irregular high-frequency activity that is found in the waking state, on the other hand, is believed to reflect the asynchronous firing of small cell populations that cancel each other and thus produce low amplitude discharges. There is little experimental support for this popular belief and some observations (such as periods of high frequency activity during deep sleep) that contradict it.

The EEG record contains some components that can be related to specific functional events and, in some instances, cellular activity. The best example of this is the *evoked potential*, which is recorded from the sensory projection areas of the cortex following the presentation of a novel stimulus (see Figure 1-1, line C). These relatively large potentials have been shown to be lawfully related to the response of single cells.

Slow Potentials

Even slower potential changes can be recorded, particularly from the cortical surface of the brain when direct-coupled (D.C.) amplifiers and nonpolarizing electrodes are used. Several negative and positive potentials are often seen following the presentation of a stimulus, and the entire response may last as long as a millisecond.

Electrical Potentials in Nonneural Tissues

All tissues develop bioelectric potentials during activation, and it is possible to record these potentials from a variety of sources. Muscle tissue, for instance, develops high-amplitude (several millivolts) spike potentials that can be recorded by placing wire electrodes into or on the surface of muscle. The resulting electromyogram (EMG) is an index of muscle tension that is sometimes used to monitor sleep or "tension." The activity of heart muscle is best recorded by placing large disk electrodes on the skin of the arms and legs (thus recording the potential across the heart). The resulting electrocardiogram (EKG) is volume conducted and sufficiently large that a clear record can be obtained if other muscle activity is discouraged.

ELECTRICAL AND CHEMICAL STIMULATION

Neural as well as nonneural tissues react to brief pulses of electric current. When such current is applied to the efferent motor pathways or central representations of the motor system, movements can be elicited. We have no way of ascertaining how "normal" the response to electrical stimulation is and whether the passage of electric currents always excites rather than inhibits the tissue on which it is acting. Electrical stimulation is nevertheless commonly used and has given us some insights into the functions of the nervous system.

Typically, two small wire electrodes are inserted into the brain, and a train of brief (0.1 to 10.0 millisecond) pulses of about 10 to 100 microvolts is applied between the electrodes. The response of individual cells is all or none. An increase in the amplitude of the stimulating current therefore cannot enhance its effects on a cell that is already responding. Increases in the amplitude of the stimulating current do, however, produce a more extensive spread of the current and thus affect larger areas of the brain.

The brain does not seem to be neatly organized in such a manner that all cells that contribute to a particular function cluster in a geographically defined area. A certain amount of anatomic organization fortunately obtains, but a great deal of intermingling occurs within these gross geographic boundaries. Because the spread of electric current is determined only by structural variables, its effects are limited geographically rather than on the basis of functional considerations.

To circumvent this shortcoming of the electrical-stimulation technique, attempts have been made to obtain a more selective activation of functionally defined populations of cells by microinjections of chemicals into the brain. This approach is based on the fact that many cells, neural as well as nonneural, respond selectively to some chemical substances and that these selective affinities are often closely related to the functional role of these cells. Anyone who consumes aspirins, coffee, tranquilizers, alcohol, or any medication does so in the expectation that this is true. The psychopharmacological approach to the study of brain functions is relatively novel, but important advances have already been made.

ABLATION

The simplest way to obtain some information about the function of a part of the body is to remove it and observe the resulting behavioral and physiological changes. When applied to the nervous system, this apparently simple and direct approach often gives ambiguous answers because the behavioral and physiological effects of localized damage merely reflect the organism's ability to operate without the structure that has been destroyed rather than its functions when it is present. This seemingly minor distinction is important because the nervous system appears to be constructed such that several geographically distinct mechanisms often interact to control a particular function. There is a good deal of duplication in such a system, and the degree of "overdetermination" seems to be greater the more important the function is. The ablation procedure has nevertheless given us a great deal of information and is widely used today.

Surgical ablation procedures have been used to transect the spinal cord or brainstem, to remove major sections of the brain, or to cut particular sensory or motor pathways. More restricted damage to surface portions of the brain are made by aspiration. Most current investigations are concerned with the effects of restricted damage to deep structures. These lesions are most easily made by passing a fairly strong (1 to 4 milliamperes) direct current through two implanted wire electrodes. This produces electrolytic reactions in the path of the current flow, which destroy the tissues. An alternative procedure uses high-frequency alternating current, which destroys by heating and is less likely to result in a transient stimulation of the tissues that surround the lesion.

Lesion procedures have two major drawbacks: (1) the effects of a lesion, like those of electrical stimulation, are geographically limited so that a selective effect on functionally defined pathways is difficult to achieve; (2) once the damage is done, it is impossible to obtain a sample of the organism's "normal" behavior—the effects are irreversible.

Pharmacological techniques have recently been developed that attempt to circumvent one or both of these objections. A reversible inhibition of cortical functions can be obtained by topical applications of potassium chloride. A reversible blockade of subcortical mechanisms may be obtained by microinjections of drugs, such as procaine, that temporarily interfere with neural functions. A more functionally selective blockade can be obtained by microinjections of drugs that selectively interfere with the transmission of information between some nerve cells.

STEREOTAXIC PROCEDURES

In order to place electrodes for recording, stimulation, or lesioning in specific parts of

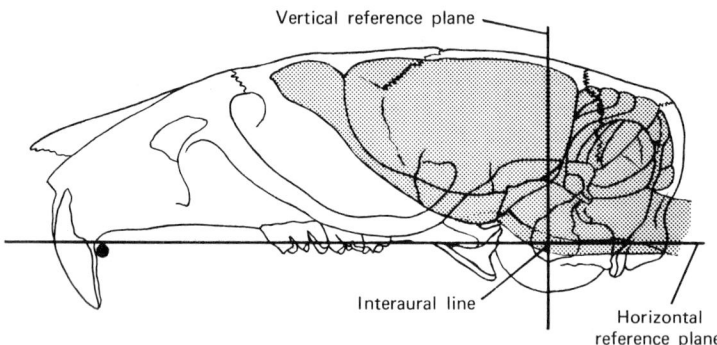

FIG. 1–2. Rat brain (shaded area) inside skull, showing the location of the commonly used reference points for stereotaxic surgery. The horizontal plane is an imaginary line extending from the external meatus of the ear to a point just behind the large incisor teeth, which are used to fix the animal's head in the stereotaxic instrument. The vertical reference plane is a line perpendicular to the first. It is customary to use an imaginary line between the external meatus of the two ears (the interaural line) as a convenient zero point for these two planes, and the middle of that line as a zero point for the lateral dimension. Any point in the brain can then be described as being some distance anterior or posterior to the interaural line, some distance above or below it, and some distance lateral to the center of it. The animal's head is fixed in the stereotaxic instrument such that the exact location of the interaural line and the slope of the horizontal line (and the slope of the vertical line) are known. It thus becomes possible to place the tip of an electrode precisely at a specified point in the brain without removing the tissues covering it.

(After *A stereotaxic atlas of the developing rat brain* by Nancy Sherwood and P. Timiras. Copyright © 1970. Originally published by the University of California Press; reprinted by permission of The Regents of the University of California.)

the brain, a system of coordinates has been developed that permits the localization of each point in the brain in three planes. By recording the extent and location of each anatomical subdivision of the central nervous system, an "atlas" has been constructed that locates each structure with respect to these planes which, in turn, are related to some constant landmark such as the imaginary line that connects the ears, or a plane perpendicular to the top of the skull. Each structure can then be identified as being x millimeters above landmark A; x millimeters ahead of landmark B; and x millimeters to the side of landmark C (see Figure 1–2).

The stereotaxic machine is simply a metal frame that fixes the position of the head with respect to these landmarks and is calibrated such that the electrode holder can be placed accurately with respect to them. The surgical procedure is not difficult (see Figure 1–3).

Once a set of coordinates has been selected from the atlas, an electrode is inserted into the electrode holder such that its tip has a known relationship to the three basic landmarks of the head in the stereotaxic instrument. The experimental animal is then anesthetized and its head fixed, by a system of clamps, in the stereotaxic instrument. Next, a small incision is made in the skin of the top of the head and a hole drilled through a point that has been fixed on the basis of the atlas coordinates. The wire electrodes are then inserted into the brain to the depth of the structure under investigation. The electrodes are fastened to the skull by a bit of dental cement, the incision is closed, and the animal is ready for stimulation or lesioning following a few days of postsurgical recuperation. Cannulas that permit injections of drugs into the brain are implanted in exactly the same way.

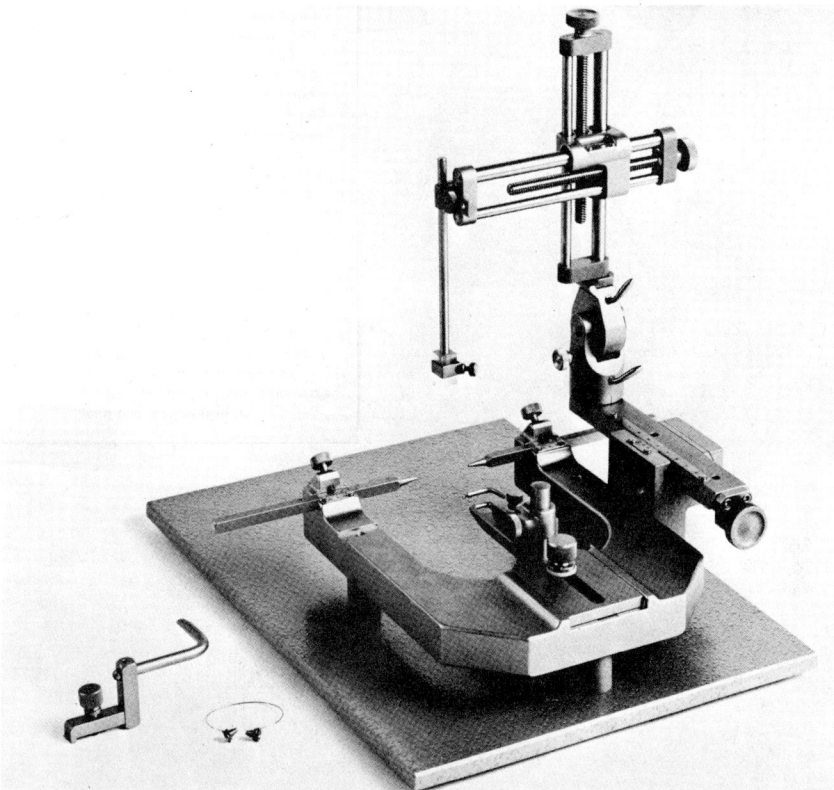

FIG. 1-3. Stereotaxic instrument for small rodents. The animal's incisor teeth are placed into the opening in the holder, which is affixed to the center of the front of the instrument. The small clamp is then lowered until it grips the animal's nose. The two ear bars are inserted into the external meatus of each ear. This establishes the three reference points discussed in Fig. 1-2. An electrode can then be placed into the movable carrier mounted on one side of the stereotaxic apparatus and the position of this carrier can be adjusted to permit accurate placement of the electrode into any portion of the brain.

(Reprinted by permission of David Kopf Instruments, Tujunga, California, 1970.)

ANATOMICAL PROCEDURES

Regardless of how one investigates the functions of the nervous system and its relationship to behavior, it is essential to determine precisely where the electrodes, lesions, or cannulas were placed. In some instances, it is sufficient to perfuse the brain with some hardening agent and to perform a gross dissection. More typically, it is necessary to analyze the affected region microscopically. A variety of anatomical procedures are available for this purpose.

In most cases, the brain tissue is hardened by perfusing it with some agent, such as formaline, and freezing it or embedding it in some gradually hardening substance, such as paraffin. The brain can then be cut into very thin (5 to 50 microns) slices, much as one would slice a salami. By a careful adjustment of the *microtome* that is used to perform this task, one can arrange the angles of this cut such that the slices duplicate the pattern of the stereotaxic atlas. The thin sections of brain tissue are then briefly submerged in various dyes that selectively stain cell bodies, or axons, or only abnormal tissues that have degenerated because of damage. The sections are then dried and mounted on glass slides

10 *Neurophysiology and Neuroanatomy*

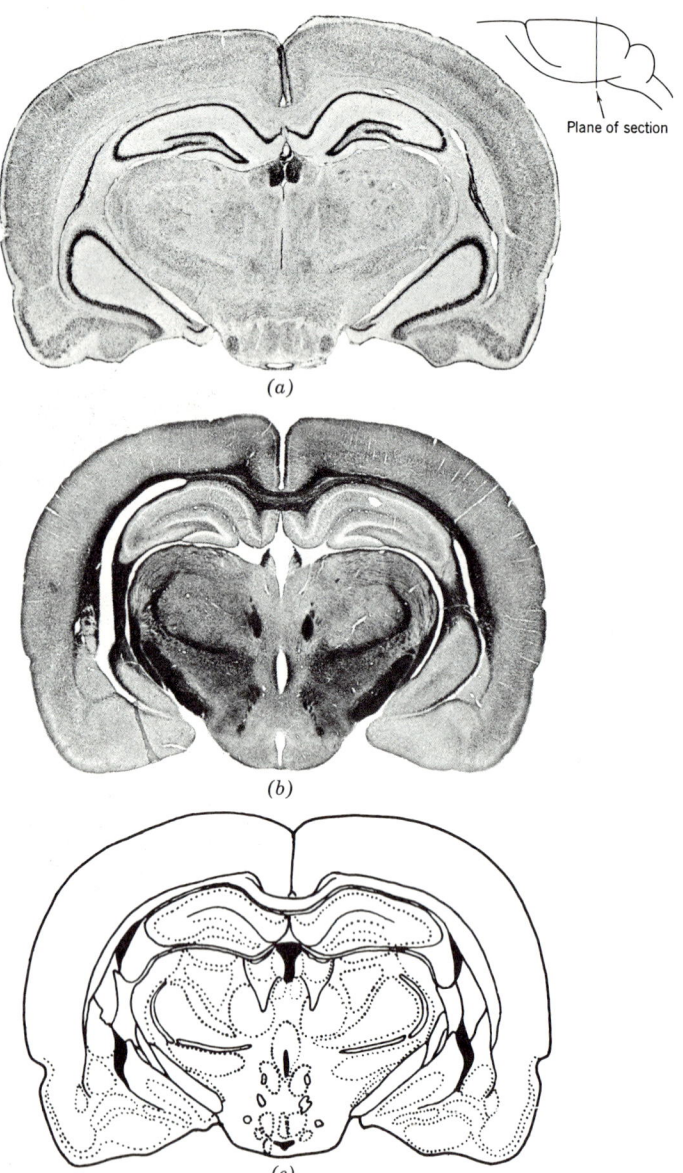

FIG. 1–4. A cross sectional "slice" of the rat brain at a point shown in the insert. (*a*) was exposed to a dye that selectively darkens the *bodies* of nerve cells. (*b*) was exposed to a dye that stains nerve *fibers* black. (*c*) is a corresponding section from a stereotaxic atlas giving the vertical coordinates on the sides and the lateral coordinates on the top and bottom. The notation in the lower right-hand corner indicates that this slice is 3.5 mm anterior to the interaural line.

(After *A stereotaxic atlas of the developing rat brain* by Nancy Sherwood and P. Timiras. Copyright © 1970. Originally published by the University of California Press; reprinted by permission of The Regents of the University of California.)

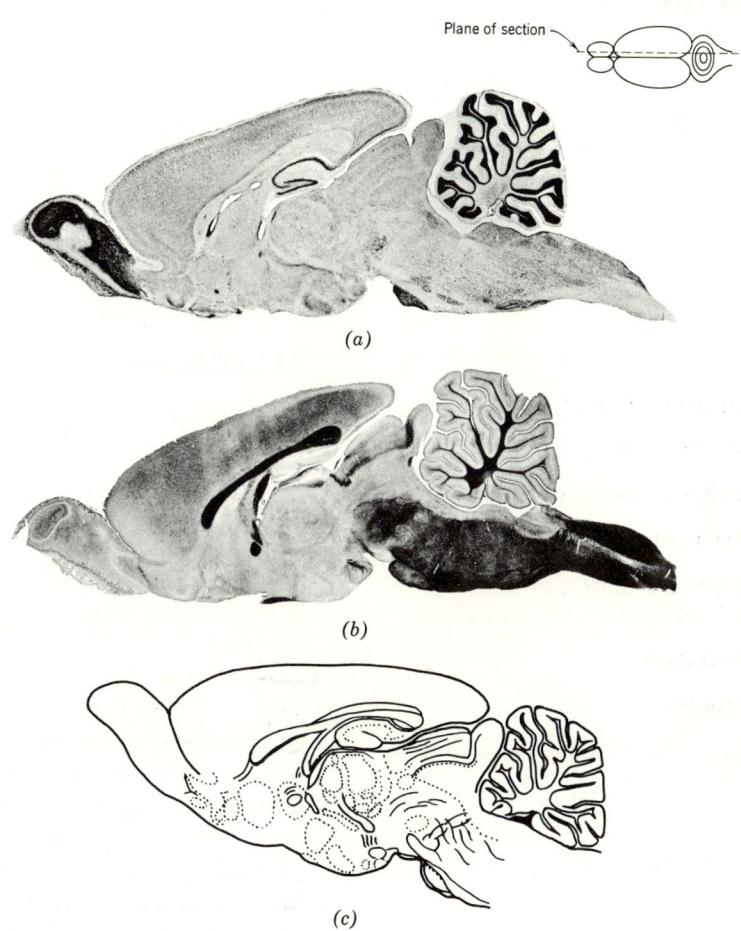

FIG. 1–5. Longitudinal (parasagittal) slice of the rat brain at a point indicated on the insert at top. (*a*) was exposed to a dye that selectively darkens the *bodies* of nerve cells. (*b*) was exposed to a dye that stains nerve *fibers* black. (*c*) is a corresponding section from a stereotaxic atlas (simplified) giving the vertical coordinates on the sides and the anterior-posterior coordinates at the top and bottom. The notation in the right-hand corner indicates that this slice is 1 mm from the center of the interaural line.

(After *A stereotaxic atlas of the developing rat brain* by Nancy Sherwood and P. Timiras. Copyright © 1970. Originally published by the University of California Press; reprinted by permission of The Regents of the University of California.)

and are ready for microscopic analysis. If everything was done just right, the localization of the electrode or lesion is easily performed by comparing the histological materials with the corresponding sections of the stereotaxic atlas (see Figures 1–4 and 1–5).

Bibliography

1. David Kopf Instruments. 1970 catalog. Box 636, Tujunga, California.
2. Sherwood, Nancy M., & Timiras, P. S. *A Stereotaxic Atlas of the Developing Rat Brain*. Berkeley: Univ. of California Press, 1970.

Chapter 2

BASIC UNITS AND FUNCTIONS OF BIOLOGICAL ORGANISMS

General Anatomy of Cells

Basic Constituents of Cells

Principal Activities of Cells

Types of Cells

Basic Functions of Some Specialized Cells

The Receptor

The Effector

GENERAL ANATOMY OF CELLS

Behavior is the end product of complex physiological processes that involve a vast number of individual cells. These basic building blocks of all biological organisms vary in size, shape, and function, depending on their location and the complexity of the host organism but have a basically similar structure that consists of (1) an outer *membrane*, which is selectively permeable to various chemical agents and maintains an equilibrium of electrochemical properties between the inside of the cell and its environment; (2) the *cytoplasm*, which makes up the main body of the cell and supports the metabolic processes that are responsible for all functions of the cell; and (3) the cell *nucleus*, which regulates the activities of the cell in accordance with information contained in the genetic code.

The Membrane

The membrane acts as a selective filter that permits certain chemicals (such as nutrients) to enter the cell and denies access to other substances that might be harmful. It contains the essential chemical constituents of the cell but permits the outward passage of waste products or of substances that some cells actively secrete.

Many chemicals (the *electrolytes*) are composed of molecules that dissociate into positively and negatively charged ions. The cell membrane maintains an equal number of ions on either side of itself. When a mechanical, chemical, or electrical disturbance removes some ions from the outer wall of the membrane, compensatory movements take place to restore this equilibrium. Most cell membranes normally separate an uneven distribution of positively and negatively charged ions (i.e., the membranes are *polarized*). A movement of ions disturbs this relationship between electrical charges, and the cell is said to be *irritated*. A compensatory movement of ions across the irritated membrane is then initiated, and this reestablishes the normal electrical potential between the inside and outside of the cell. This repair process may require a chain reaction along the membrane that results in the *conduction* of irritation to all parts of the cell membrane. Irritability and conductivity are important properties of all cells.

The Cytoplasm

The *cytoplasm* makes up the main body of the cell. The cytoplasmic material of all cells has common structural and functional properties, but its chemical composition and microstructure vary considerably, largely as a result of *differentiation* (the process by which cells develop one capability to the virtual exclusion of others).

One of the most important common functions of all cytoplasmic materials is the metabolism of nutrients. This results in the liberation of energy needed for the chemical reactions by which cells perform their varied functions. Metabolic processes also produce novel combinations of basic chemicals that are needed by the cell. Sometimes these new compounds are secreted through the cell membrane into the immediate environment or into the bloodstream.

The Nucleus

The *nucleus of a cell contains deoxyribonucleic acid* (DNA), which determines the basic functional properties of the cell in accordance with genetic information. Another nucleic acid (*ribonucleic acid* or RNA) carries the information from the nucleus to the cytoplasm where it can be implemented in terms of particular metabolic processes.

BASIC CONSTITUENTS OF CELLS

Water

The basic constituent of all cells is called *protoplasm*. Water makes up 60 to 99 percent of protoplasmic material. This assures that important chemicals can go into solution and become uniformly distributed in the cell. The high water content also makes possible a rapid and complete interaction between various other constituents of protoplasm, since chemical reactions occur more readily between substances in solution.

The presence of water also permits the splitting of certain molecules (called *electrolytes*) into smaller components, called *ions*, which possess electrical charges. Three basic classes of electrolytes can be distinguished: (1) *acids*, which in solution yield positively charged hydrogen ions; (2) *bases* or *alkalies*, which yield negatively charged hydroxyl ions; and (3) *salts*, which yield neither. Many of the important properties of cells, such as irritability and conductivity, depend on an unequal distribution of electrical charges inside and outside the cell membrane.

Inorganic Salts

Protoplasm contains, in addition to water, a variety of *inorganic salts*. The most common of these salts (in decreasing order of relative concentration) are chloride, sodium, potassium, calcium, and manganese. These salts exert important influences on cellular functions although they make up only about 0.9 percent of the total body weight.

Organic Compounds

Three major groups of organic compounds—carbohydrates, fats, and proteins—are found in cells.

The *carbohydrates* are composed of carbon, hydrogen, and oxygen. Three classes of carbohydrates are commonly distinguished. (1) The simplest sugars or *monosaccharides*, such as glucose, are plentiful and provide many of the nutriments used by all living organisms. (2) The double sugars or *disaccharides* are composed of two molecules of simple sugars.

(3) The *polysaccharides* or compound sugars make up the starches. Animal starches (*glycogens*) serve as a storage form of carbohydrates, particularly in liver and muscle cells, because they are readily converted into a glucose compound that is a necessary part of all combustion processes.

Carbohydrates not only serve this important "fuel" function but are also incorporated into the basic structure of the cell. Glucose normally makes up only about 0.1 percent of the total weight of mammalian cells, but even small deviations from this base-line level produce marked changes in the irritability of the cell. A number of closely cooperating mechanisms (mainly in the liver, pancreas, and adrenal glands) maintain the concentration of glucose in the blood within very narrow limits under all environmental conditions that permit survival.

The *fats* are also composed of carbon, hydrogen, and oxygen, but the proportion of oxygen to carbon and hydrogen is much smaller than that of the carbohydrates. Fats cannot be absorbed by complex cellular organisms until they are broken down by the enzymatic action of digestive juices into *glycerol* and *fatty acids.*

Fats contain twice as much energy per unit weight as carbohydrates and are therefore useful as energy stores. However, the conversion of fat to energy is a relatively slow process, and the organism typically exhausts all stores of the more readily available and convertible carbohydrates before drawing on its fat stores. Fats are incorporated into both intracellular and membrane components of cells and make up a greater fraction of all protoplasmic material than do carbohydrates.

The *proteins* are the last of the three major organic constituents of protoplasm. They consist of complex, large molecules that are made up of carbon, hydrogen, oxygen, nitrogen, and traces of sulfur and phosphorus. Protein molecules can be split into smaller molecules called *amino acids* that are, in a sense, the basic building blocks of all cells. More than 20 different amino acids are presently known, and an enormous variety of proteins can be created from the many possible combinations and permutations of these basic ingredients.

Proteins are the principal structural components of all animal tissues. They can also provide energy, but this mechanism comes into play only after an organism is starved to the point where all other energy stores have been exhausted. The cells then begin to burn themselves in a final effort to maintain essential life processes.

The *enzymes* are complex structures that are closely related to proteins. Enzymes promote chemical reactions without providing energy for these reactions—that is, they act as catalysts. They are indispensable for basic chemical reactions because they (1) speed up all cellular chemical reactions by facilitating essential oxidation processes that would otherwise occur much too slowly at normal body temperatures and (2) activate specific enzymatic processes that are needed to permit a reaction between otherwise inert chemical constituents of the cell. This second action is so selective that a specific enzyme may exist for every chemical reaction that occurs in protoplasm.

Two substances are functionally if not structurally related to the enzymes. *Hormones* are complex compounds that are manufactured and secreted by specialized gland cells. *Vitamins* cannot be produced by the organism and must constantly be supplied from external sources. Hormones and vitamins, like enzymes, are essential to many cellular processes although they do not form an important part of the structure of the cell and do not contribute energy to its reactions.

PRINCIPAL ACTIVITY OF CELLS

Energy Transformation

A cell is basically a container for complex chemical reactions that sustain the processes that are essential to life. All cellular activities as well as the complex reactions of multicellular organisms are the end products of such chemical reactions.

The term *metabolic processes* is used specifically to refer to the chemical reactions that occur in cells or within the cavities of complex organisms. *Anabolic* processes result in the manufacture of compounds that are essential to the survival of cells and organisms. *Catabolic* processes destroy cellular constituents. Cellular protoplasm is continually catabolized and replaced by anabolic processes.

The energy for these reactions is derived from oxidation (i.e., combustion). The basic mechanism is *aerobic oxidation*, a process which requires free oxygen normally obtained by respiration. A second type of combustive process, *anaerobic oxidation*, derives oxygen and energy from other compounds. Mammalian cells can extract only little energy from anaerobic reactions and are therefore dependent on a constant supply of air. Other cells, such as yeast, can maintain themselves indefinitely in the absence of free oxygen, and some (such as certain bacteria) even perish in its presence.

Exchange of Materials Across Membranes

The constant chemical activity of cells requires a continuous supply of raw materials as well as the speedy removal of potentially poisonous waste products of metabolic activity. Several transport mechanisms are available for this movement of molecules across the cell membrane.

Diffusion occurs because of the continuous motion that characterizes ions and molecules in solution. This motion produces collisions of particles and gives rise to a migration of molecules from regions of high concentration (and frequent collisions) to areas of relatively low concentration. Nutrients and other substances used in intracellular reactions are nearly always present in greater concentration outside the cell membrane and hence tend to diffuse into the cell. Waste products, on the other hand, are always more concentrated in the intracellular compartment and tend to diffuse out.

In multicellular organisms, diffusion also plays a role in getting essential materials into the vicinity of the cell and removing waste products from its immediate environment. For example, diffusion from the lungs transfers oxygen to the bloodstream. The oxygen then diffuses across the capillary walls into the extracellular spaces and finally crosses the cell membrane to be used in the many oxidation processes that sustain life. The waste product of this combustion, carbon dioxide, follows the same route in reverse and is finally expelled in the process of exhalation.

Filtration refers to the movement of molecules or ions across a membrane as a result of mechanical pressure differences. In vertebrates and some invertebrates, filtration is responsible for the movement of water and most metabolites through the capillary walls of the blood vessels into the extracellular spaces.

Osmosis refers to the movement of water across a membrane that is impermeable to a substance that exists in unequal concentrations on the two sides of the membrane.

Osmotic pressure gradients are common in multicellular organisms and are responsible for the regulation of the organism's fluid balance. They are also responsible for some of the difficulties that are encountered in the clinic and laboratory. Cells that are removed from an organism for the purpose of study must be maintained in an environment that avoids the development of osmotic gradients. For instance, a typical mammalian cell would balloon and burst if we tried to maintain it in pure water. If enough sodium chloride is added to its environment to make a 0.9 percent solution of NaCl, only little movement of water occurs and the cell can be maintained for long periods of time although other essential ions such as potassium are not present. This, of course, is the reason why drugs that are administered to an organism must be dissolved in such *physiological saline*.

Truly permeable membranes that do not provide a barrier to any molecule or ion are very rare in biological organisms. Truly impermeable membranes that do not permit the exchange of any particles are equally rare. Most biological membranes obstruct the passage of some materials and permit the transfer of others—that is, they are *semipermeable* or *selectively permeable*.

Not all cellular membranes are permeable to the same materials, and important differences in relative permeability exist. Many of the organism's most important functions depend on such selective permeability. For instance, ions readily pass through the walls of capillaries but may find a relative or absolute barrier at the cell wall. The resulting ionic concentration differences across the cell membrane are responsible for such important cellular properties as excitability and conductivity.

Various factors determine the permeability of a membrane to a particular substance. *Size* is one limiting factor—the size of the molecules may simply exceed the diameter of the available openings in the cell wall. This factor probably explains why complete protein molecules cannot enter most organic cells, whereas their constituents, the amino acids, typically do so with ease. *Solubility* is another important determinant of permeability. Substances easily soluble in fat generally pass through cellular membranes without difficulty because they can attack the fatty portions of the cell wall and, in effect, enlarge the available openings. The *electrical potential* that often exists across a cell membrane as a result of its selective permeability to some ions also affects the movement of some particles.

TYPES OF CELLS

Receptors (*see Figure 2–1*)

Cells that have selectively developed the property of irritability serve in multicellular organisms to transduce physical energy into electrochemical reactions that can be conducted to other cells. It is impractical for most organisms to respond in the same

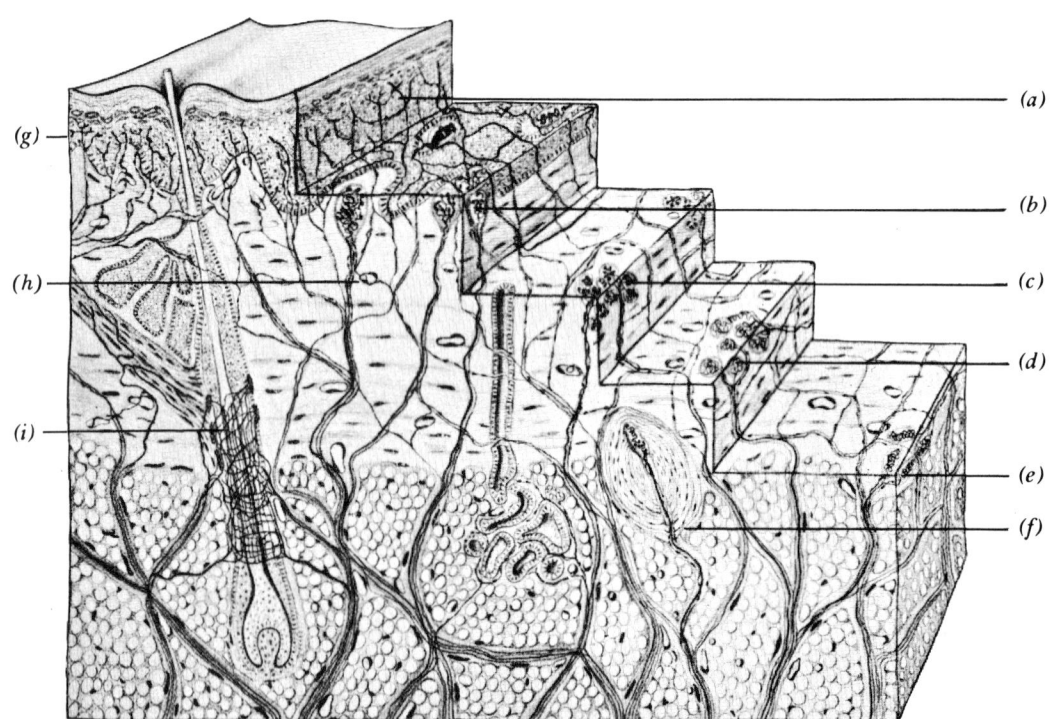

FIG. 2–1. Sensory receptors in the skin. (*a*) beaded nerve nets, subserving pain; (*b*) Meissner's corpuscle, subserving touch; (*c*) and (*d*) groups of Krause's end bulbs, subserving cold; (*e*) group of Ruffini endings, subserving warmth; (*f*) Pacinian corpuscle, subserving pressure; (*g*) Merkel's disks, subserving touch; (*h*) beaded nerve fibers. subserving pain; (*i*) nerve terminals about the sheath of a hair, subserving touch.

(From *The neuroanatomic basis for clinical neurology* (2nd ed.) by T. L. Peele. McGraw-Hill, 1961.)

fashion to all changes in their environment, and receptors consequently specialize to become preferentially sensitive to specific forms of physical energy.

Man and most of the animal species that are of interest to the physiological psychologist have developed four general classes of receptors preferentially sensitive to thermal, chemical, mechanical, and visual energies, respectively. This specialization is relative rather than absolute. All receptors remain sensitive, to a degree, to all forms of energy.

Some receptors (such as the rod and cone cells of the eye) serve almost exclusively as transducers of energy. Others (such as the mechanical and thermal receptors of the skin) combine the properties of receptors and conductors. Some receptors (such as the pressure receptors of the tectorial membrane of the ear) have accessory structures that amplify and channel the physical energy towards the receptor itself.

Conductors (see Figure 2-2)

Cells that specialize in the conduction of irritability are called *neurons* or *nerve cells*. They typically develop long thin processes that permit the transmission of irritation (excitation) over great distances. The main body of a neuron is called the *soma*. The processes of the cell are called *axons* and *dendrites*. The dendrites are typically short processes that conduct excitation *toward* the body of the cell (i.e., in an *afferent* direction in relation to the cell body). The axon conducts excitation *away* from the cell (i.e., in an *efferent* direction in relation to the cell body). Typically, a nerve cell has many diffusely branched dendrites but only a single, relatively long axon. At its peripheral end, an axon generally branches into *terminal arborizations* that relate to the dendrites or soma of other nerve cells or to the membrane of muscles via *end feet*. The junction between the end feet of an axon and the dendrites or soma of another cell is called a *synapse*.

Axons are surrounded by a fatty sheath (the *myelin sheath*). Large-diameter fibers typically are heavily myelinated and consequently

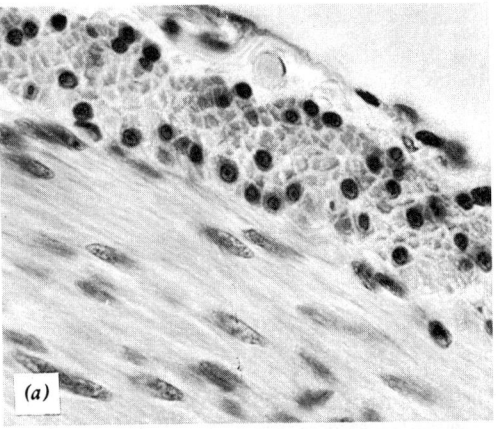

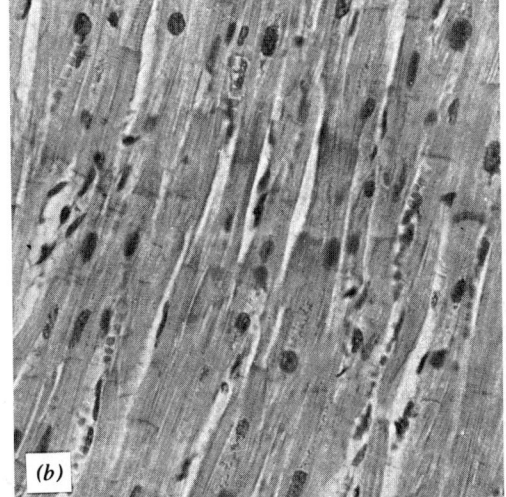

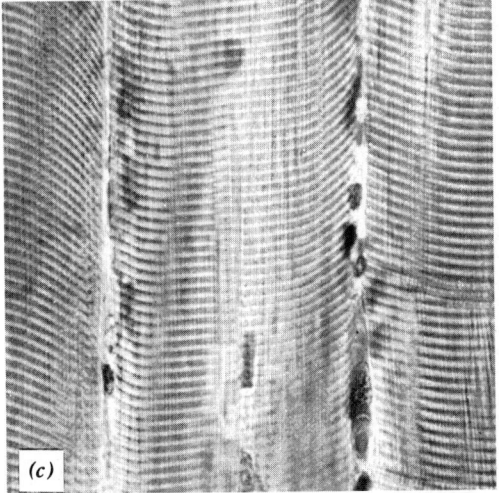

FIG. 2-2. Three types of muscle. (*a*) Smooth muscle; (*b*) cardiac muscle; (*c*) skeletal muscle.

(From *Human anatomy and physiology* by J. E. Crouch and J. R. McClintic. Copyright © 1971. John Wiley & Sons, Inc.)

appear white. Small fibers are poorly myelinated and appear grey.

The soma of nerve cells varies in diameter from 5 to about 100 microns. Their dendrites are typically short (in the order of a few hundred microns), but some cells in the somato-sensory system have dendritic processes several feet long. The axons of neurons range from a few microns to several feet in length.

Neurons are typically surrounded by *glial* cells. Some glial cells serve primarily supportive and protective functions. Others are phagocytes that remove the debris left after the disintegration of neurons. Some glial cells are connected to neighboring blood vessels. These vascular connections permit the secretion of materials into the bloodstream as well as the uptake of nutrients from it.

Effectors (*see Figure 2–3*)

Two basic classes of effectors—muscles and glands—are distinguished. *Muscle* cells have specialized in the property of contractility. They respond to stimulation by initiating chemical processes that change the configuration of the cell.

In vertebrates three varieties of muscle cells exist. The simplest *smooth* muscle has developed a special substance consisting of *fibrillae* that change in shape and produce the overall deformation of the cell. Smooth muscles are found primarily in the viscera. *Striated* muscles have developed two types of fibrillae, one dark and the other light. These are arranged in an orderly sequence, giving the muscle a striated appearance. Striated muscles make up all the skeletal musculature of the vertebrate organism. The third type of muscle contains the same light and dark fibrillae organized in what appears to be a random network. This muscle is found exclusively in the heart and has therefore been called *cardiac* muscle.

The second class of effector is the *gland* cell. This type of cell responds to irritating stimulation of its membrane by producing novel chemical substances that are eventually secreted. There are two types of gland cells. *Duct* glands discharge their secretions into body cavities such as the stomach or intestine. *Ductless* glands empty directly into the bloodsteam. The secretions of duct glands typically have a more localized effect than those of ductless glands.

Supporting Cells

Several types of cells have developed properties that are designed to support the more highly specialized cells discussed so far. *Connective* cells manufacture long fibrous strands that give the connective tissue a tough elastic consistency. Connective cells are found in all parts of the organism and provide a framework for other cells. A special type of connective cell is capable of manufacturing compounds that harden into rigid structural members—the bones and cartilage tissues of the organism. Other connective cells, called *epithelial* cells, line the exposed surfaces of the organism.

Fat cells have developed the ability to store large amounts of nutrients in the form of fats. The bulk of these cells is composed of inert fat.

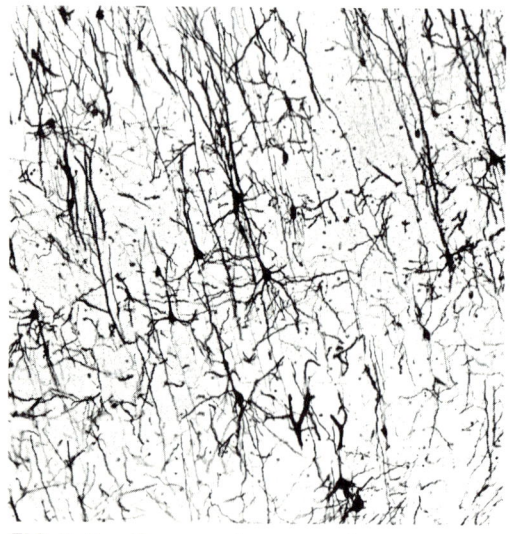

FIG. 2–3. Nervous tissue, cerebrum.

(From *Human anatomy and physiology* by J. E. Crouch and J. R. McClintic. Copyright © 1971. John Wiley & Sons, Inc.)

BASIC FUNCTIONS OF SOME SPECIALIZED CELLS

The Neuron (see Figure 2-4)
Ionic Mechanisms

Each cell of the organism is surrounded by *extracellular fluids*, which are similar in most respects to the *intracellular fluids*. Nutrient materials and waste products cross the cell membrane easily, but substances that are either essential or harmful to the metabolism of the cell are transported only with difficulty.

One of the most important differences between extracellular and intracellular fluids is a marked imbalance in the concentrations of certain ions. This imbalance is responsible for some of the electrochemical events that underly the important membrane properties of irritability and conductivity. The concentrations of sodium (Na^+) and chloride (Cl^-) are much higher in the extracellular fluids than inside the cell. The concentrations of potassium (K^+) and organic anions (A^-), on the other hand, are higher in the cytoplasm than in the extracellular fluids.

The ion imbalance between the interior and exterior of a cell creates an electrical potential across the cell membrane. This *steady* or *resting potential* in turn influences the transport of ions across the membrane. Since the inside of the cell is negative in relation to the extracellular environment, cations ($+$) tend to move into the cell and anions ($-$) out of it. Potassium tends to flow out of the cell because of its high initial concentration but also tends to diffuse *into* the cell because of the distribution of electrical charges on both sides of the membrane. These two tendencies almost cancel each other so that only a slight tendency remains for K^+ to move out of the cell. Chloride is subject to similar opposing forces. There normally is little or no net diffusion of Cl^- through the cell membrane; the tendency of chloride to diffuse into the cell because of excessive extracellular concentrations is exactly balanced by electrical opposition to the movement of negatively charged ions into the cell.

The situation is quite different for Na^+ and A^-. Here, the concentrations and the electrical differences act in concert. Sodium continually moves into the cell. The intracellular concentration of Na^+ nevertheless remains nearly constant because an active transport mechanism produces a compensatory outward movement of sodium ions. This active

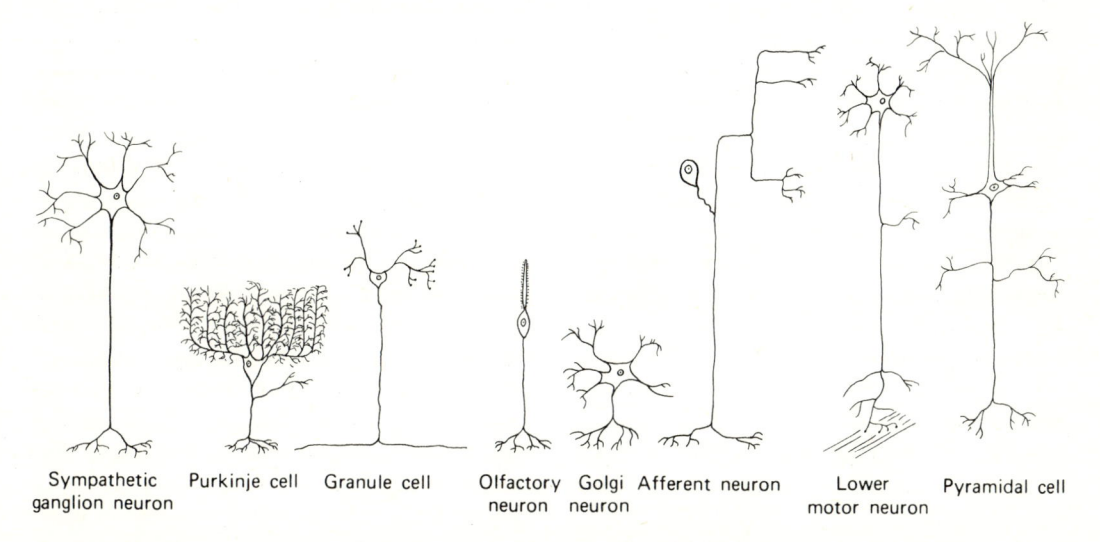

Sympathetic ganglion neuron   Purkinje cell   Granule cell   Olfactory neuron   Golgi neuron   Afferent neuron   Lower motor neuron   Pyramidal cell

FIG. 2–4. Some different forms of neurons from the human nervous system.
(From *Human anatomy and physiology* by J. E. Crouch and J. R. McClintic. Copyright © 1971. John Wiley & Sons, Inc.)

transport is usually accompanied by the uptake of potassium and has been called the *sodium-potassium pump*. The resting potential arises because the cell membrane is much more permeable to potassium than to sodium and because the active sodium transport maintains the intracellular sodium concentrations at a low steady value.

Propagation of Excitation in a Neuron

A cell at rest is said to be *polarized*. Any external or internal (metabolic) influence that changes the polarization of the cell membrane modifies its excitability. Changes in polarization produce momentary fluctuations in the transmembrane potential. These electrochemical changes are propagated along the cell membrane and may be transmitted to adjacent neurons across the synapse.

These transient electrochemical events carry all information in the nervous system. They are also responsible for the transduction of physical energies into information that is useful to the nervous system and for the transformation of neural signals into muscular contractions.

ACTION POTENTIALS

An electrochemical disturbance that is propagated in a nerve cell is called an *impulse* or *action potential*. The energy for the transmission of nerve impulses is derived from the metabolic activity of the nerve cell itself, not from the physical stimulus that originated the disturbance. As the action potential moves along a cell membrane, successive small sections of the neuron become electrically negative in relation to the surrounding portions of the cell. If one attaches two electrodes as in Figure 2-5, a sudden negative potential can be recorded that is followed by its positive mirror image as the traveling disturbance reaches the second electrode. The distance between the two portions of the observed wave is determined by the distance between the electrodes.

The ionic changes that underlie the development of the action potential are complex. Basically, stimulation (i.e., irritation) of a cell membrane produces a momentary increase in

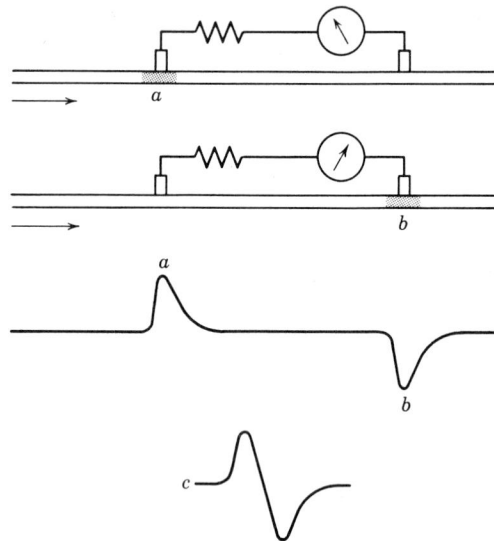

FIG. 2–5. The passage of a nerve impulse in a nonconducting medium. The record obtained when the two electrodes are close together, as shown at c, gives the appearance of a diphasic wave.

(From *The electrical activity of the nervous system* (3rd ed.) by Mary A. B. Brazier. Williams and Wilkins, 1968. Reprinted with permission of Pitman Publishing.)

membrane permeability to Na^+ that permits sodium to flow into the cell. This sets up a chain reaction that produces further depolarization. The cell returns to a polarized state because the increased permeability to sodium is transient and because the membrane permeability to potassium increases as the resting potential approaches zero.

The propagation of an action potential depends on the following ionic changes. When an action potential is initiated, the membrane potential in the active region is near the sodium equilibrium potential. The potential of neighboring inactive sections of the membrane is near the potassium equilibrium potential. Consequently, ions flow along the outside of the membrane from the inactive to the active region. Here, they enter the cell and return through the intracellular fluid to the inactive section, where they again flow out of the cell. The local circuit that is thus set up lowers the membrane potential in the inactive region. Eventually, the membrane potential decreases to the equilibrium potential of sodium, and the inactive region becomes active.

The propagation of action potentials is subject to the *all-or-none law*. This law states that once a neuron has been stimulated to the point where a traveling disturbance is created, the size of this response and the speed of its conduction are independent of the intensity of the stimulation. Neurons vary with respect to the size and conduction velocity of their action potentials, but the response of a given cell remains constant. (This law does not apply to the initiation and propagation of excitation at receptor terminals of nerve cells.) The size and conduction velocity of the action potential of a given cell depends, however, on the state of the cell at the time of stimulation. The size of the potential may be affected by fatigue, due to the recent passage of another action potential, or by a disturbance of cellular metabolism such as is produced by various drugs.

RESPONSE TO ELECTRICAL STIMULATION

Suprathreshold stimulation of a nerve depolarizes the cell membrane at one of the electrodes (the cathode) at the same time that the membrane under the other (the anode) becomes hyperpolarized. When the stimulating current is terminated, the membrane returns to its normal resting level. Most of the electrical current flows from the anode to the cathode along the low-resistance pathway that is provided by the extracellular fluid and has little effect on the fiber itself. Some of the current flows from the anode through the cell membrane into the cell and to the cathode. Since the membrane provides *resistance* to this current flow, a potential drop, opposite in sign to that of the resting membrane potential, occurs at the cathode (where the current flows out of the cell). This results in *hypopolarization* or *depolarization* of the cell membrane near the cathode. Current flows inward at the anode, producing an increase in the transmembrane potential or a state of *hyperpolarization*. If the membrane potential at the cathode is reduced to the threshold value for the cell, an action potential originates. The strength of an abruptly applied and terminated current required to exceed a cell's threshold and initiate an action potential is a function of the duration of current flow. When a stimulating current is maintained, a nerve fiber eventually ceases to respond because the excitation of the nerve depends on the *rate of change* in the transmembrane potential. A stimulus that increases only gradually in intensity fails to elicit an action potential in spite of clearly suprathreshold intensities.

Subthreshold stimulation of a nerve fiber does not evoke an action potential. It does, however, produce changes in the cell's threshold to subsequent stimulation. When a subthreshold stimulus is applied a few milliseconds before the presentation of a second test stimulus, the intensity of the test shock required to elicit an action potential will be lower than normal. This facilitation persists for a short time after the subthreshold stimulus is presented. The facilitatory effect decreases when subthreshold stimulation is repeated, a phenomenon referred to as *accommodation*.

Recovery from Suprathreshold Stimuli

Once the threshold of a cell is exceeded by stimulation, a complex series of electrochemical changes that produces an action potential occurs (see Figure 2-6). Following a brief buildup of subthreshold changes in the membrane potential (the local process), a very brief (typically less than 0.5 millisecond) *spike potential* arises. This represents the information-carrying portion of the action potential. During the propagation of this spike potential, the nerve fiber is in a state of *absolute refractoriness* (i.e., it cannot be excited by any stimulus, regardless of its intensity). The duration of this state puts an upper limit on the maximum number of impulses that can be conducted by a neuron. The upper limit has been calculated and demonstrated experimentally to be about 2000 impulses per second.

The absolute refractory period is followed by a more prolonged period of *relative refractoriness*, which corresponds to the transition period between the spike potential and a negative afterpotential that subsequently develops. During this 3 to 5 millisecond period of relative refractoriness, only very

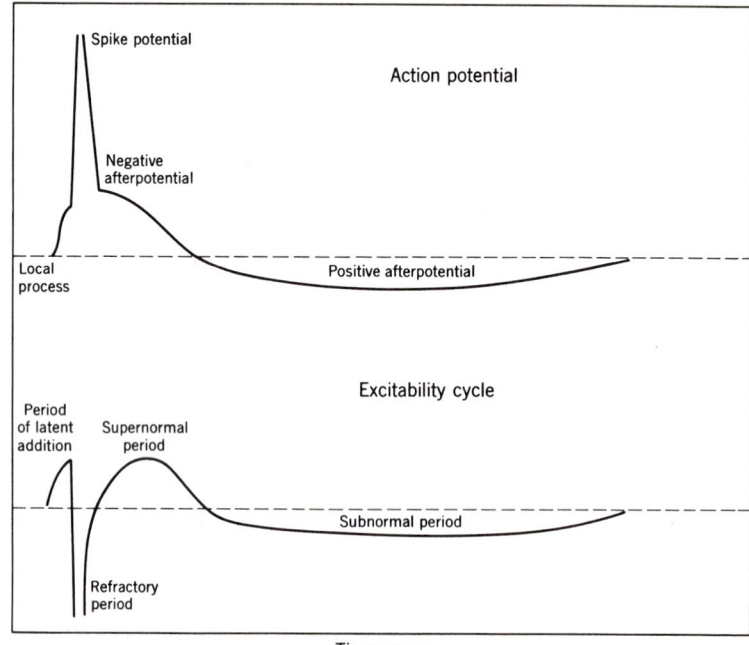

FIG. 2–6. The action potential and the excitability cycle of nerve fibers. The duration of the first two phases has been exaggerated in proportion to the second two phases in order to display all phases clearly. In the action potential, "local process" refers to the period when purely local changes, including the electronic potentials, occur at the site of stimulation. These changes are accompanied by a period of latent addition in the excitability of the fiber. The spike potential is the "nervous impulse" and corresponds to the refractory period. The negative and positive afterpotentials correspond, respectively, to the supernormal and subnormal periods of excitability.

(From *Physiological psychology* by C. T. Morgan and E. Stellar. Copyright © 1950. McGraw-Hill Book Company. Used with permission of McGraw-Hill Book Company.)

intense stimuli elicit a propagated action potential, and the size of the spike potential is smaller than normal. The smaller spike potentials are propagated at a slower conduction rate than usual.

The spike potential is followed by a *negative afterpotential*, which is of much lower amplitude than the spike potential and typically lasts 5 to 15 milliseconds. During this period the nerve fiber is in a state of heightened excitability and responds to subthreshold stimulation. This period of supernormality is followed by a relatively long (50 to 80 milliseconds) *positive* afterpotential, which is correlated with a period of subnormality. During this time the nerve fiber is less excitable than normal, and conduction velocities are lower.

The *repetition rate of stimuli* influences the excitability of nerve fibers. Rapidly repeated stimuli shorten the negative and increase the positive afterpotentials, prolong the refractory period, and delay the recovery phase. This inhibitory effect was first described by Wedensky, who observed that a fatigued muscle responded only to the first of a series of rapidly repeated stimuli but continued to respond adequately to stimuli presented at a lower repetition rate. The conditions for *Wedensky's inhibition* are met whenever the repetition rate is adjusted so that successive stimuli fall within the relative refractory period of the immediately preceding stimulus.

Transmission of Information Between Neurons

Neurons communicate with one another at axodendritic or axosomatic junctions where the end feet of one cell come into contact with the dendrites or somata (bodies) of other neurons. At these *synaptic junctions*, only a few hundred Angstrom units separate adjacent cells, and transmission of the action potential becomes possible. The electrical disturbance does not simply jump the gap between adjacent cells. Instead, the arrival of an action potential at the end feet of an axon stimulates secretory activity in small vesicles that contain neurohumoral substances in inactive or bound form. When liberated, these chemicals become active and diffuse across the synaptic gap. They subsequently interact with specific receptor sites on the postsynaptic membrane and produce an irritation that leads to a change in the membrane potential of the adjacent cell (see Figure 2–7).

There appear to be many different neural transmitters, and it is generally assumed that different neurohumors may act in different parts of the nervous system. In some instances, the neurohumor depolarizes the postsynaptic membrane by reducing the potential difference between the inside and the outside of the postsynaptic cell membrane. This electrotonic potential is not, itself, propagated, and decays exponentially with distance from the

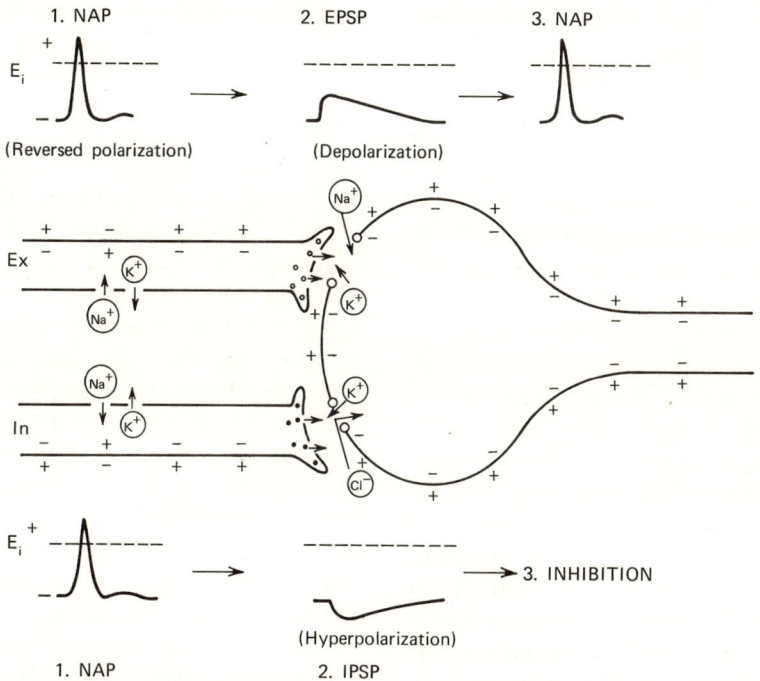

FIG. 2–7. Steps involved in excitatory (Ex) and inhibitory (In) neurohumoral transmission.
1. The nerve action potential (NAP), consisting in a self-propagated reversal of negativity (the internal potential, E_i, goes from a negative value, through zero potential, indicated by the broken line, to a positive value) of the axonal membrane, arrives at the presynaptic terminal and causes release of the excitatory (○) or inhibitory (●) transmitter.
2. Combination of the excitatory transmitter with postsynaptic receptors produces a localized depolarization, the excitatory postsynaptic potential (EPSP), through an increase in permeability to all ions (Na^+ and K^+ chiefly involved). The inhibitory transmitter causes a selective increase in permeability to the smaller ions (K^+ and Cl^- chiefly involved), resulting in a localized hyperpolarization, the inhibitory postsynaptic potential (IPSP).
3. The EPSP initiates a conducted NAP in the postsynaptic neuron; this can, however, be prevented by the hyperpolarization induced by a concurrent IPSP.
  The transmitter is dissipated by enzymatic destruction or by diffusion.

(From Koelle, G. B., "Neurohumoral transmission and the autonomic nervous system." Reprinted with permission of the Macmillan Company from *The pharmacological basis of therapeutics* by L. S. Goodman and A. Gilman, Eds. Copyright © 1970 by The Macmillan Company.)

site of transmitter action. It is called an *excitatory postsynaptic potential* (EPSP). Such EPSP's may (1) involve a sufficiently large area of the postsynaptic membrane to generate a propagated action potential, (2) produce a subthreshold depolarization that decays without further affecting the electrical properties of the postsynaptic membrane, or (3) produce a subthreshold depolarization of the postsynaptic membrane that summates either with adjacent areas of depolarization (due to the action of a transmitter that is released from another end foot) or with previous or subsequent changes in the local portion of the postsynaptic membrane to elicit a propagated action potential.

In other instances a transmitter increases the potential difference across the postsynaptic cell membrane. This induces a state of hyperpolarization and reduces the neuron's excitability. The resulting *inhibitory postsynaptic potentials* (IPSP's) are thought to be the basic mechanism of inhibitory processes in the nervous system.

All postsynaptic potentials are local responses that are not propagated, decay with time, and summate temporally as well as spatially. The size of the postsynaptic potential is related to the intensity of the presynaptic electrical activity. (The intensity of the presynaptic electrical activity is presumed to be related to the quantity of transmitter substance that is released. This, in turn, determines the size of the area of the postsynaptic membrane that becomes hyper- or hypopolarized.)

Some cells exhibit depolarizing as well as hyperpolarizing postsynaptic potentials. Others show either only excitatory or only inhibitory postsynaptic potential changes. Muscle fibers, for instance, develop only depolarizing postsynaptic potentials. Gland cells, on the other hand, always show a hyperpolarization reaction to any form of stimulation. Most neurons in the vertebrate nervous system show both excitatory and inhibitory reactions.

Hyperpolarization and hypo- or depolarization may coexist in different parts of a cell membrane and interact to determine the response of the cell. The transmission of information is thus not completed by the generation of an excitatory postsynaptic potential. The chain of transmission is broken if the excitatory potential cannot exceed the postsynaptic threshold or overcome the inhibition that may be simultaneously generated by other hyperpolarizing inputs to the same cell.

It is important to remember that the hyperpolarizing (inhibitory) postsynaptic potential is itself the end result of synaptic transmission that is initiated by a spike potential. This spike potential represents excitatory activity in the presynaptic cell and requires a depolarizing (excitatory potential) influence to become a propagated electrical disturbance.

The transmission of information across a synaptic junction interposes a delay that may be as long as several milliseconds (typically about 0.3 to 0.4 millisecond). This delay is related to (1) the secretory activity of the presynaptic vesicles, (2) the diffusion of the transmitter substance across the gap that separates the pre- and postsynaptic membrane, (3) the chemical reactions required to bind the transmitter to its receptor site and develop the postsynaptic potential, and (4) the electrogenic reactions necessary to transform the postsynaptic potential into a propagated spike potential.

The identification of specific transmitter substances has been difficult. *Acetylcholine* (ACH) acts as a transmitter at all skeletal neuromuscular junctions and in the parasympathetic nervous system. It is also the transmitter at neural junctions in the ganglia of the sympathetic nervous system. Acetylcholine is present in relatively high concentrations throughout the central nervous system, and there is much evidence to suggest that conduction at many synapses in the brain may be cholinergically mediated.

Norepinephrine acts as a transmitter at most neuromuscular junctions in the sympathetic nervous system. (The sweat glands and some smooth muscles in the walls of blood vessels respond to acetylcholine.) Norepinephrine and closely related substances such as its precursor, dopamine, are nonrandomly distributed in the central nervous system and probably serve transmitter functions at some central synapses.

It is difficult to demonstrate conclusively that any substance acts as a neurohumoral transmitter in the central nervous system because the brain contains many chemical substances that could potentially serve as transmitters of neural impulses. Generally, a transmitter must meet the following criteria: (1) it must mimic the action of neural action potentials; (2) its effectiveness must change as a function of the same chemical or neural manipulations that are known to modify neural excitation; (3) it must occur naturally, preferably in a nonrandom distribution; and (4) a naturally occurring antagonist must inactivate the suspected neurohumor with the rapidity required for the transmission of many discrete neural potentials per second.

In addition to acetylcholine and norepinephrine, the most promising of these suspected transmitters are (1) *dopamine*, a precursor of norepinephrine; (2) *serotonin* (5-hydroxytryptamine) and metabolically related substances that have been found to be selectively active in many parts of the brain; and (3) *GABA* (gamma-amino-butyric acid), which may be an exclusively inhibitory transmitter. (Most neurohumors appear to act as excitatory transmitters at some synapses and as inhibitors at others.) (See Table 1.)

TABLE 1. Some Putative Neurotransmitters and Related Inhibitors or Blocking Agents

Putative Transmitter	Inhibitor or Blocking Agent
Acetylcholine	Atropine (muscarinic); Curare (nicotinic)
N-Epinephrine	Phenoxybenzamine (alpha receptors)
Epinephrine	Dichloroisoproterenol (beta receptors)
Dopamine	Haloperidol
Serotonin	Lysergic acid diethylamide (LSD)
GABA	Picrotoxin

Rather than present largely speculative evidence for the central transmission properties of these suspected substances, it may be more instructive to discuss the properties of the two neurohumors that are known to have transmitter functions in the peripheral nervous system.

When a nerve is stimulated, acetylcholine is released in an active form and is rapidly destroyed by cholinesterase (ChE). This enzyme is in turn inhibited by drugs that protect acetylcholine from hydrolysis and intensify and prolong its excitatory action on neural tissue. The most powerful drugs in this category are *physostigmine* and *diisopropylfluorophosphate* (DFP).

Acetylcholine has two distinct actions at neuroeffector and synaptic junctions. At neuroeffector junctions in the parasympathetic nervous system, the heart, and the endocrine-gland cells, acetylcholine produces effects similar to those of muscarine (a poison derived from certain species of mushrooms). The term *muscarinic* is therefore used to describe these effects. At synaptic junctions in sympathetic ganglia and at skeletal neuroeffector junctions, acetylcholine acts more like nicotine, which first stimulates (depolarizes) and then paralyzes or inhibits (hyperpolarizes) the activity of cells in autonomic ganglia and skeletal muscles. These effects are called *nicotinic*. *Atropine* and related drugs selectively block the muscarinic action of acetylcholine. *Curare* selectively prevents the nicotinic action of the neurohumor.

Structures innervated by cholinergic nerves are stimulated by three types of agents: (1) *choline esters* such as acetylcholine, methacholine, carbachol, and bethanechol; (2) *cholinesterase inhibitors* such as physostigmine, neostigmine, and diisopropylfluorophosphate; and (3) *naturally occurring alkaloids* such as pilocarpine, arecoline, and muscarine.

Epinephrine is the major active principle of the adrenal medulla. Epinephrine acts directly on most smooth muscles, which are innervated by the sympathetic portion of the autonomic nervous system. Denervation of structures that normally receive this innervation greatly increases their sensitivity to circulating epinephrine. Demethylated epinephrine (*norepinephrine*) is released by postganglionic fibers of the sympathetic nervous system and appears to act as the transmitter substance at this neuromuscular junction. (Actually, norepinephrine constitutes only about 80 percent of the compound that is liberated on stimulation of the postganglionic fibers. The other 20 percent is made up largely of epinephrine.) Possible metabolic precursors of norepinephrine are *dihydroxyphenyleserine* and *hydroxytyramine* (*dopamine*). Monoamine oxidase (MAO) and catechol-O-methyltransferase are the two enzymes that are most important for the metabolism of epinephrine and norepinephrine. It is, however, unlikely that these enzymes terminate the transmission of nerve impulses at adrenergic synapses because their action is relatively slow. Instead, it appears that diffusion of the transmitter or its reuptake into cells may serve this important function at adrenergic synapses.

There appear to be two types of neurohumors in this group that act on different receptor sites. Epinephrine acts on both types of receptors. Norepinephrine acts selectively on "alpha" receptors, and compounds such as *isoproterenol* exclusively stimulate "beta" receptors. The alpha and beta components of the adrenergic system can be selectively blocked by drugs such as phenoxybenzamine (which interferes with alpha adrenergic mechanisms) or dichloroisoproterenol (which blocks beta adrenergic functions). Although there are some exceptions, alpha receptors generally mediate excitatory processes and beta receptors are inhibitory.

Activity of Peripheral Nerves

Although nerve fibers are basically alike, they vary in such important parameters as conduction speed, threshold of excitation, and maximal rate of impulse conduction. The electrical activity of a nerve trunk is therefore different from that recorded from a single fiber.

If recording electrodes are placed on the outside of an active nerve trunk, a *compound action potential* is recorded, which represents the sum of neural activity within the nerve trunk. No potential difference is recorded from a nerve trunk in the resting state because its exterior is at the same electrical potential throughout its length. As an action potential approaches, the first electrode becomes negative with respect to the second. As the potential travels further along the nerve fiber, this relationship is reversed, creating a diphasic potential (see Figure 2–8).

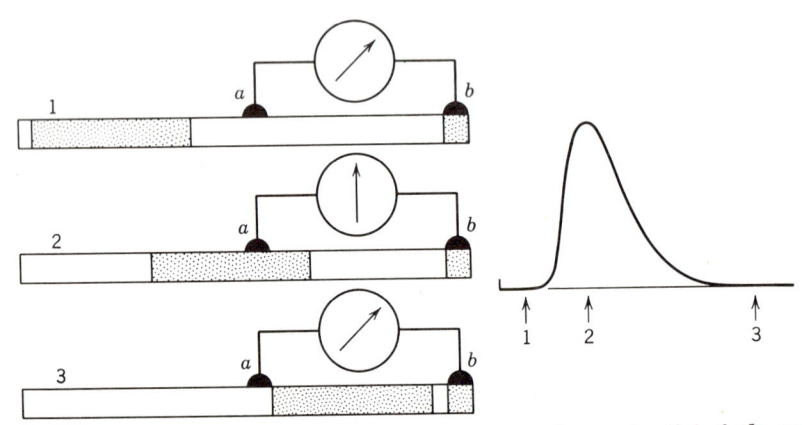

FIG. 2–8. Monophasic recording of the nerve action potential. *Left*, small stippled area under *b* indicates the nerve has been injured at this point. Consequently a steady injury potential is recorded in 1, *b* being negative to *a*. As the action potential (long stippled area) progresses to *a* in 2, *a* and *b* become equipotential. In 3, the action potential progresses beyond *a*, and *b* is once more negative to *a*. *Right*, recorded monophasic action potential; numbered arrows indicate instantaneous potentials recorded at three stages of conduction shown at left.

(From H. D. Patton. Special properties of nerve trunks and tracts. In T. C. Ruch, H. D. Patton, J. W. Woodbury, & A. L. Towe, Eds. *Neurophysiology* (2nd ed.). Saunders, 1965.)

The conduction velocity of individual nerves inside a nerve trunk varies. The action potentials that are transmitted by rapidly conducting fibers may reach the second electrode at the same time that the action potential of more slowly conducting fibers reaches the first. The electrical events at the two electrodes then partially cancel each other, since the recording procedure only permits the recording of potential differences between the two electrodes.

This problem can be circumvented if conduction in the nerve trunk is blocked by crushing, burning, cutting, or anesthetizing the fibers under the second electrode. Since the second electrode is now in contact with a portion of the nerve membrane in which the steady potential has been reduced to zero, an *injury potential* can be recorded at rest between the two electrodes. The arrival of action potentials at the first electrode results in a negative deflection in the injury potential; this is called a *monophasic compound action potential*.

The compound action potential that is monophasically recorded from peripheral nerves usually has an irregular contour that shows several distinct elevations. After a maximal stimulus is applied to a compound nerve (i.e., a stimulus of sufficient intensity to elicit a response from all nerve fibers in the trunk), three major negative deflections occur in the action potential, called *A*, *B*, and *C* waves, respectively.

The first and by far the largest *A* wave consists of a number of distinct portions (see Figure 2–9). The first *alpha* component is so large that the other portions cannot be seen at an amplification that permits visualization of the entire alpha deflection. It is a very rapid and sudden negative deflection that is complete within less than a millisecond. The second *beta* component is much smaller and not quite so brief. The third or *gamma* component consists of a very low-amplitude deflection that is much more prolonged. A fourth *delta* component of the *A* wave can sometimes be seen. The *A* wave is followed by a low-amplitude *B* wave that is not subdivided into distinct components. This is followed, after some delay, by a very small *C* wave of even lower amplitude.

The individual components of this compound action potential are related to the conduction velocity and size of the individual fibers that make up the nerve trunk. Fiber diameters range from less than 1 micron to about 20 microns, and conduction velocity is linearly related to fiber diameter. The large *A* wave reflects the activity of very large, rapidly conducting fibers that typically make up the bulk of most peripheral nerves. The largest and most rapidly conducting fibers of the *A* class give rise to the alpha component. Slightly smaller and slower *A* fibers produce the beta deflection, and still smaller and slower conducting fibers of this group conduct the gamma and delta components of the *A* wave. The *B* and *C* waves are produced by activity in still smaller and more slowly conducting fibers.

The contour of the compound nerve potential is a function of the distribution of fiber sizes in the nerve from which recordings are

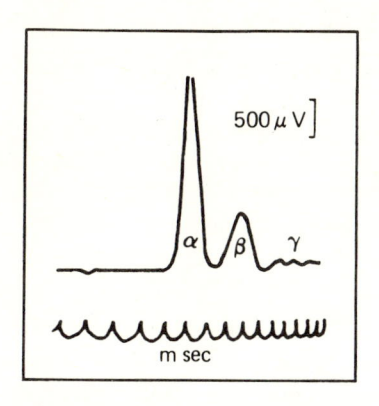

FIG. 2–9. The *A* complex of the compound action potential of a mixed nerve trunk recorded 13.1 cm from the point of stimulation. The full amplitude of the alpha elevation, which is the response of the largest fiber of the *A* group, is outside the limits of the record. The beta and gamma elevations are the responses of the less rapidly conducting fibers of the *A* group.

(From *The Electrical activity of the nervous system* (3rd ed.) by Mary A. B. Brazier. Williams and Wilkins, 1968. After J. Erlanger & H. S. Gasser. *Electrical signs of nervous activity.* Univ. of Pennsylvania Press, 1937.)

obtained. Since there are wide variations among peripheral nerves with respect to the relative distribution of fiber sizes, the shape of compound action potentials varies widely. All nerves contain rapidly conducting *A* fibers, but the individual components of the *A* wave are not always distinguishable because the distribution of *A* fibers within the nerve may not be distinctly multimodal. The *B* and *C* waves are often not seen with submaximal stimuli because the threshold of excitation is also closely related to fiber size (the larger the fiber, the lower its threshold). Moreover, some peripheral nerve trunks do not contain the very small fibers that give rise to the *C* wave or may not contain a sufficient concentration of small fibers of similar diameter to produce a clear and distinct deflection (see Table 2).

Fibers of differing overall diameter vary not only in conduction velocity and threshold but also with respect to the duration and size of the afterpotential that follows the propagation of a spike potential. The distribution of afterpotentials in a nerve trunk results in compound afterpotentials that may change the excitability of the nerve for as long as one second.

TABLE 2. Properties of Mammalian Nerve Fibers[a]

	A	B	s.C	d.r.C
Fiber diameter, microns	1–22	≤3	0.3–1.3	0.4–1.2
Conduction speed, meters/sec	5–120	3–15	0.7–2.3	0.6–2.0
Spike duration, msec	0.4–0.5	1.2	2.0	2.0
Absolutely refractory period, msec	0.4–1.0	1.2	2.0	2.0

[a] The A fibers are myelinated, somatic, afferent and efferent fibers. The B fibers are myelinated, efferent, preganglionic axons found in autonomic nerves. The C fibers are unmyelinated, the s.C group being the efferent postganglionic sympathetic axons, and the d.r.C group the small unmyelinated afferent axons found in peripheral nerves and dorsal roots.

(From H. D. Patton. Special properties of nerve trunks and tracts. In T. C. Ruch, H. D. Patton, J. W. Woodbury, & A. L. Towe, Eds. *Neurophysiology* (2nd ed.). Saunders, 1965.)

Electrical Activity of the Brain

The neurons of the central nervous system are active even in the absence of distinct stimulation to sensory end organs. Individual nerve cells fire spontaneously at regular or irregular intervals. This activity is modulated by the arrival of potentials that reflect the activation of sensory pathways. The compound action potentials of sensory nerves produce complex "*evoked potentials*" in the central nervous system that can be recorded from many parts of the brain because the nerve fibers that transmit these impulses are not insulated as in the periphery but pass directly through conductive tissue.

The spontaneous activity of the brain generates large electrical potentials that are easily recorded from electrodes inside or outside the brain. This spontaneous activity has been studied extensively during the past 50 years, but we still do not know precisely how or where these brain waves originate. One hypothesis holds that the slow potential changes represent a summation of the spike potentials of many nerve cells. According to this hypothesis, the relatively large and slow waves that characterize the brain at rest are composed of action potentials of cells firing in synchrony. The fast, low-amplitude potentials that characterize the brain during arousal are thought to be composed of action potentials of asynchronously firing cells that tend to cancel each other.

Despite extensive research during the past 30 years, it has been impossible to demonstrate very many correlations between overt behavior and specific alterations in the spontaneous activity of the brain. The only clear example of such a correlation is a relationship between an overall state of rest and relaxation and a preponderance of high-voltage, slow (8 to 12 cycles per second) waves in many parts of the brain. This *alpha rhythm* is "blocked" as soon as the organism is aroused by a stimulus. The large, high-amplitude waves are then replaced by fast (30 to 60 cycles per second) low-amplitude wave patterns that are much more irregular than the relatively synchronous alpha waves.

Electroencephalogram (EEG) is the generic term for a graphic recording of the spontaneous activity of the brain. The EEG is typically obtained by connecting recording electrodes to an ink writer via several stages of differential amplification. This magnifies the potential difference between two electrodes in the brain (bipolar recording technique) or between a single electrode in the brain and an "indifferent" electrode located outside the central nervous system (monopolar recording technique). The term *electrocorticogram* is reserved for electroencephalograms obtained from the surface of the cortex (the lateral and dorsal aspect of the brain in man and higher mammals). The electroencephalogram can also be recorded from electrodes that are superficially attached to the skull. This permits the discovery and localization of gross electrical disturbances in man (see Figure 2–10).

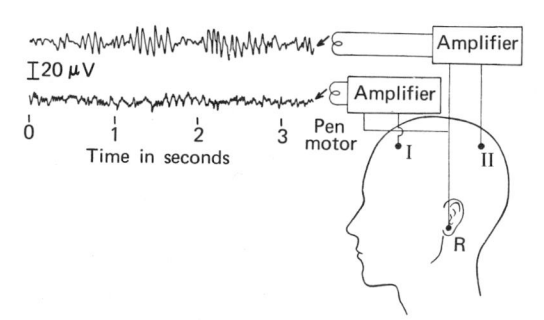

FIG. 2–10. Arrangement for recording EEG. The potential difference between frontal lead (I) and reference lead (R) shows low amplitude, fast activity of waking, relaxed human. Simultaneously, occipital lead (II) shows higher amplitude, slower activity.

(From A. L. Towe. Electrophysiology of the cerebral cortex: Consciousness. In T. C. Ruch, H. D. Patton, J. W. Woodbury, & A. L. Towe, Eds. *Neurophysiology* (2nd ed.). Saunders, 1965.)

The electroencephalogram contains rhythmic waves that recur at different frequencies and at widely differing amplitudes. The normal frequency range is from about 1 cycle per second to about 60 to 80 cycles per second. Amplitudes range from a few microvolts to several hundred microvolts. Computer analyses of the frequency, amplitude, or power spectrum of the EEG show that most frequencies and amplitudes are represented at any point in time and that some "dominant" frequencies occur more often than others.

High-amplitude, slow (8 to 12 cycles per second) *alpha* waves are typical of the relaxed or drowsy organism. Slightly faster high-amplitude activity at about 12 to 15 cycles per second, typically occurring in bursts, is characteristic of sleep. These *spindle waves* alternate during sleep with very slow (1 to 2 cycles per second) *delta* waves. Slightly faster (4 to 7 cycles per second) *theta* waves are commonly recorded from some subcortical parts of the brain. Fast and typically low-amplitude activity (above 20 cycles per second) is generally referred to as *beta* activity. Very fast (above 50 cycles per second) waves are called *gamma* waves (see Figure 2–11).

Repetitive electrical stimulation of some parts of the brain produces biphasic potentials in the electroencephalogram of the cortex. The amplitude of this potential may wax and wane at a frequency that approximates that of the alpha wave (8 to 10 cycles per second). These *recruiting responses* are believed to be similar to spontaneous "burst" activity, which is sometimes seen in the cortical EEG. Evoked responses are potentiated during such bursts of 8 to 10 cycles per second activity.

The Receptor

Basic Receptor Units

Receptor functions may be exercised by the specialized end feet of nerve cells or by specialized cells that act as transducers of particular forms of physical energy into neural impulses. A single receptor may command a "private line" into the central nervous system or may feed information into a neural pathway that is also used by other receptors.

Most higher organisms have receptors specialized to transduce mechanical, thermal, electromagnetic, and chemical energies. Most

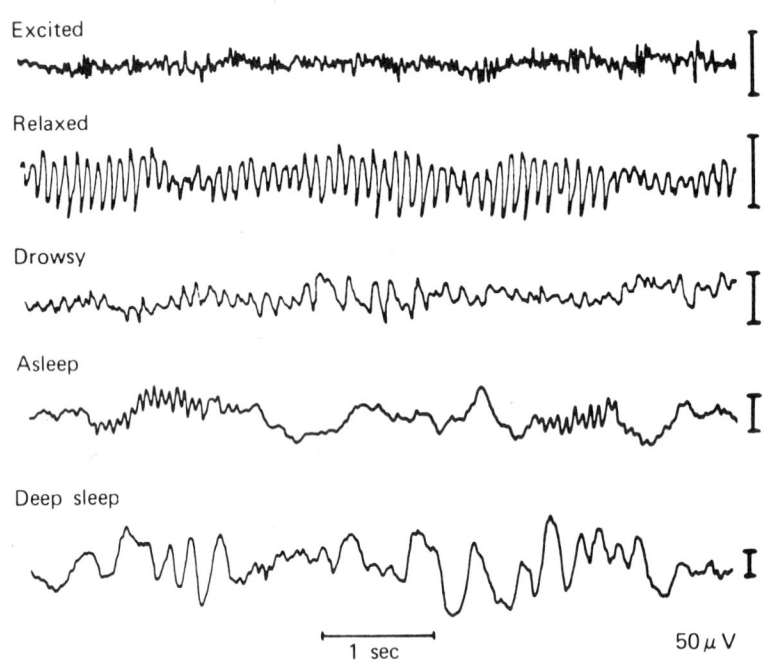

FIG. 2–11. Electroencephalographic records during excitement, relaxation, and varying degrees of sleep. In the fourth strip runs of 14/sec rhythm, superimposed on slow waves, are termed "sleep spindles." Notice that excitement is characterized by a rapid frequency and small amplitude, and that varying degrees of sleep are marked by increasing irregularity and by the appearance of slow waves.

(From H. H. Jasper. Electroencephalography. In W. Penfield & T. C. Erickson. *Epilepsy and cerebral localization.* Thomas, 1941.)

receptors are preferentially sensitive to only one form of energy, although all will respond to intense stimulation in all modalities. In addition, there seem to be receptors that are very insensitive to all types of physical energy and respond only to potentially damaging intensities of stimulation in any modality. The pain receptors fall into the latter category.

A *sensory unit* is defined as those receptors that are part of or connect to a single afferent (i.e., sensory) neuron. Many receptors may contribute information to a single sensory neuron. The receptive fields of some skin receptors, for instance, extend over many square inches. Spatial discrimination within such a field is possible because neighboring receptive fields overlap.

All sensory units represent independent channels of information processing that transmit information about specific changes in the physical and chemical environments of the organism to the central nervous system. The information is coded in terms of spatial and temporal activity patterns in a single unit.

Receptor Potentials

The action of physical energies on nerve endings or specialized receptor cells does not directly induce the electrochemical events responsible for the initiation and propagation of action potentials. Instead, a graded *generator potential* develops, which, in turn, initiates an action potential. Generator potentials that occur in a single receptor are called *receptor potentials.* (A good example of a generator potential that is not a receptor potential is the potential that is recorded from the basilar membrane of the cochlea during the application of a sound wave.)

The magnitude of a receptor potential is a function of stimulus intensity. A certain threshold magnitude of the receptor potential is required before an action potential can be initiated. Once this threshold is crossed, increases in the magnitude of the receptor potential increase the frequency but not the amplitude of action potentials in the associated afferent nerve. The duration of a receptor potential is a direct function of the stimulus duration. A phenomenon similar to summation occurs when the stimulus intensity is increased. True summation of receptor potentials occurs when two brief stimuli are presented in close succession. In this way, a number of subthreshold stimuli can produce additive effects that result in a propagated action potential. This may be responsible for the maximal sensitivity of receptors.

If the repetition rate of successive stimuli is slow, such that the receptor potential generated by the first stimulus has had time to decay completely before the next stimulus arrives, the opposite reaction (i.e., depression) occurs in some receptors. Stimuli arriving within a few milliseconds after the decay of a receptor potential produce generator potentials that are smaller than normal.

Afferent Nerve Activity

In typical receptor cells the propagated action potential is generated in the cell body, whereas the receptor potential develops in the cell's dendritic processes. Specialized receptor cells may show slightly different arrangements, but the basic principle (i.e., the spatial separation of the receptor and action potential) is maintained. The distinction between the receptor and action potentials is maintained when the action of pharmacological agents is considered. Procaine (a local anesthetic), for instance, blocks action potentials in concentrations that do not affect the receptor potential.

Receptors can be classified according to their response to maintained stimulation. *Tonic receptors* signal information to the central nervous system about physical or chemical stimuli that are always present but vary in intensity or concentration. The clearest examples are the kinesthetic receptors in the tendons and joints that relay information about the relative position of limbs. Individual tonic receptors typically respond only to a specific and restricted range of stimulus intensities. Within this range there is an almost perfect relationship between stimulus intensity and impulse frequency. A sudden increase in the intensity of a steady stimulus produces an increase in receptor discharge that greatly exceeds the firing level normally associated with that stimulus intensity. The firing rate declines to normal levels as the receptor adapts to the new stimulus intensity. Conversely, when there is a sudden drop in stimulus intensity, the firing rate decreases to a value much below that appropriate to the stimulus and then the rate gradually recovers.

Phasic sensory receptors operate on somewhat different principles. They do not discharge at a constant and controlled rate that is related to the intensity of some pervasive stimulus. Instead, they respond distinctly to the onset and/or termination of stimuli that are not constantly present in the organism's environment and adapt very rapidly to maintained stimuli.

The most common type of phasic receptor responds to the presentation of a discrete stimulus by initiating a rapid burst of action potentials that gradually diminish when the stimulus is maintained. Some phasic receptors respond only to the onset and/or cessation of a stimulus by initiating a single potential or burst of potentials. Such ON, OFF, or ON–OFF receptors are particularly common in the visual system. The stimulus change in these instances must not always be absolute; ON receptors may fire in response to a sudden increase in stimulus intensity and OFF receptors in response to a sudden decrease.

The basic mechanisms of receptor function are only superficially understood. It is assumed that all receptors generate receptor potentials at portions of the cell membrane that are unable to conduct an action potential. The energy required to initiate and maintain this generator potential does not derive from the physical energy of the stimulus but arises from the receptor cell itself.

Evoked Potentials in the Central Nervous System

Stimulation of a peripheral sensory receptor initiates a generator potential that, in turn, triggers an action potential when the threshold of the cell is exceeded. This potential is then propagated toward the central nervous system by an associated sensory nerve fiber. The body of this fiber is located in the dorsal root (for cutaneous and kinesthetic impulses) or inside the central nervous system; its axon extends some distance into the central nervous system. The action potential is then routed through complex pathways (which will be discussed in the next section) to specific sensory projection areas in the neocortex. If recording electrodes are placed in or near such a primary projection area or in or near the sensory pathway that conducts impulses to this area, a distinct electrical response to peripheral sensory stimulation can be recorded.

Evoked potentials typically consist of an initial, short-latency (8 to 10 millisecond) spike potential followed by a larger and more gradual deflection. The first of these potentials, the *primary evoked potential*, can usually be recorded only from a fairly restricted portion of the brain. This area is assumed to be the exact locus of the sensory representation of the physical stimulus to the related sensory receptor. The slow *secondary evoked potential* can be recorded from most areas of the cortex (see Figure 2–12).

Evoked potentials are often difficult to detect because they are superimposed on the spontaneous (EEG) activity of the brain. Recent technological developments have provided "averaging" devices that summate the evoked response to several hundred stimuli. (The spontaneous electrical activity of the brain is random with respect to the time of stimulation, and repeated averaging of the EEG tends to cancel the spontaneous activity. The evoked potentials always occur within some specific time interval after the application of stimulation; hence, the potentials summate and become more prominent with each repetition.)

Microelectrodes (with a tip diameter of 0.5 to 5 microns) have been used to record the electrical activity of single nerve cells in the brain. The response of single neurons to discrete sensory stimulation may take the form of an increase or decrease in the spontaneous discharge frequency of that neuron or in the

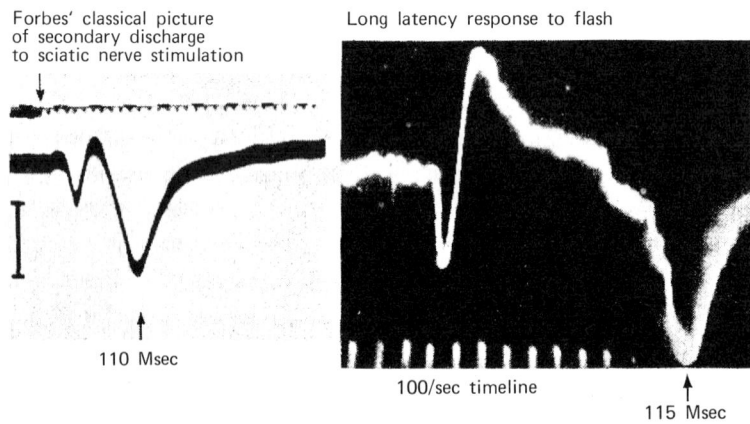

FIG. 2–12. *Left,* response from the contralateral sensory-motor cortex to stimulation (at the arrow) of the sciatic nerve in a cat under pentobarbital anesthesia. The record shows the primary response followed later by the larger secondary response. Vertical calibration mark, 200 μV. The black dots at the top of the illustration represent 0.04-sec intervals. Negativity is recorded upward. *Right,* primary and long-latency response to a flash recorded from the visual cortex of a cat under pentobarbital anesthesia.

(*Left,* from A. Forbes & B. R. Morison. Cortical response to sensory stimulation under deep barbiturate narcosis. *J. Neurophysiol.*, **2**, 1939, 112–128. *Right,* from Mary A. B. Brazier. Studies of evoked responses by flash in man and cat. In *The reticular formation of the brain.* H. H. Jasper, L. D. Proctor, R. S. Knighton, W. C. Noshay, & R. T. Costello, Eds. Little, Brown, 1958.)

elicitation of one or more spike potentials. These are similar to the spike potentials that are recorded from nerve cells in the peripheral nervous system.

The relationship between the evoked potential that is recorded through macroelectrodes (with a tip diameter of 50 to 1000 microns) and the spike response of single units is complex. Recent microelectrode studies have indicated that the contour of the evoked potential that is recorded from a cortical sensory area may be lawfully related to the probability of cellular activity in that region.

The Effector

Basic Effector Units

The *basic effector unit* consists of a single motor neuron, its axon, and a number of muscle fibers that are innervated by the end feet from the axon. The average size of a motor unit varies greatly. In some of the muscles of the eye, which must be capable of very exact and fine adjustments, it is not uncommon to find that one neuron serves only three or four motor fibers. Large muscles that typically react as a whole (such as the biceps), on the other hand, often have innervation ratios of 200:1 or more.

The weakest possible response of a muscle is the contraction of a single motor unit. As stimulation increases, more motor units are activated, and the individual motor units discharge more frequently. If the stimulation is further increased, the frequency of neural discharges reaches *tetanic* limits and the individual twitch responses summate to form a tetanus. Although a single motor unit follows the *all-or-nothing* law of responding, the muscle as a whole does not.

The building blocks of the contractile cells are two proteins, *actin* and *myosin*, consisting of long molecular chains. During contraction, the filaments of actin and myosin slide past each other and produce a shortening of the muscle cell. The energy consumed in the process of muscular contractions derives from a number of chemical reactions. The basic process involves the gradual breakdown of glycogen into lactic acid.

Contraction of a muscle fiber results in either a shortening of the cell or the development of tension, or both. Contracting muscles may shorten and thus produce gross movement. Since weight is carried through space in any movement of a limb, this type of contraction has been called *isotonic* (equal tension). Contractions that cause tension (i.e., a force that opposes other influences such as gravity but does not itself move a limb) are called *isometric* (equal length). This type of contraction is usually employed to prevent movement. A third type of muscular activity, *lengthening*, occurs when the forces opposing an isometric contraction are sufficiently large to stretch or lengthen the muscle while it is actively contracting. This type of muscular activity is typically found whenever muscles operate as antagonistic pairs (see Table 3).

The contraction process is initiated by a depolarization of the muscle cell membrane that occurs as the result of synaptic transmission of an action potential. The latency between membrane depolarization and the mechanical contraction response is of the order of 1 millisecond. The distribution of total muscle response latencies appears to be

TABLE 3. Classes of Muscle Contraction

Type of Contraction	Function	External Force Opposing Muscle	External Work by Muscle	Rate of Energy Supply
Shortening	Acceleration	Less	Positive	Increases
Isometric	Fixation	Same	None	
Lengthening	Deceleration	More	Negative	Decreases

(From J. W. Woodbury, A. M. Gordon, & J. T. Conrad. Muscle. In T. C. Ruch, H. D. Patton, J. W. Woodbury, & A. L. Towe, Eds. *Neurophysiology* (2nd ed.). Saunders, 1965.)

roughly bimodal. Some very fast muscles react within 5 to 10 milliseconds after the arrival of the action potential. Superficial extensors typically fall into the fast-reacting muscle category, having response latencies of about 20 to 35 milliseconds. Deep muscles, on the other hand, particularly those that move a large joint, react slowly; reaction times of over 100 milliseconds are typical. Generally, fast muscles appear pale or almost white. The slower muscles appear red because of a greater concentration of myoglobin. Fast muscles tend to be used for rapid phasic movements of distinct muscle groups, whereas slow muscles typically regulate phasic adjustments such as posture.

Summation or *facilitation* occurs when two maximal stimuli are presented in rapid succession to a muscle or to related neurons. An increase in the intensity of stimulation of a muscle or muscle-related neuron produces a correlated increase in the intensity of contraction up to the point where all fibers of the muscle are activated. Further increases in the intensity of a "maximal" stimulus do not produce a further increase in the muscle response. However, if two maximal stimuli are presented in sufficiently close succession so that the second is presented during the contraction response to the first, a greater response occurs than to a single maximal stimulus. The intensity of this facilitatory effect is a function of the interstimulus interval (the higher the repetition rate, the greater the response) as long as it is longer than the refractory period of the muscle membrane. This *tetanic facilitation* is based on a summation of mechanical events.

If several stimuli are delivered at a very rapid rate, progressive summation occurs; each stimulus then adds a diminishing increment of facilitation until the contraction of the muscle is maintained. This tension is called *tetanus*. Partial or incomplete tetanus occurs when the repetition rate of successive stimuli is too low to maintain the contraction response.

Neuromuscular Transmission

The propagation of an action potential across a neuromuscular junction occurs by means of a neurohumoral transmitter substance. At all skeletal muscle junctions the neurohumor is *acetylcholine*. The sequence of events can be summarized as follows: (1) The arrival of an action potential at the terminal arborization of an axon stimulates the secretion or liberation of stored acetylcholine. The transmitter then diffuses across the small gap between the nerve and the end plate of the muscle. (2) Upon its arrival at the end plate, acetylcholine interacts with a specific receptor complex. This interaction increases the permeability of the end-plate membrane to all ions and decreases the membrane potential toward zero. (3) If this change in the membrane potential is sufficient to produce a suprathreshold depolarization of the end plate, an electrical impulse is propagated from the end plate in all directions. (4) The acetylcholine is rapidly destroyed by acetylcholinesterase, which is stored in high concentrations in the muscle end plate.

Special Properties of Cardiac and Smooth Muscle

Cardiac muscle essentially consists of striated muscle fibers that are not arranged in orderly parallel fashion as in skeletal muscle; the fibers branch and fuse with each other, producing what appears to be a continuous net or *syncytium*. This peculiar anatomical arrangement is thought to be responsible for the simultaneity of action that characterizes the heart muscle.

This spontaneous and synchronous activity of the heart occurs in the absence of direct innervation. The normal stimulus for the contraction of cardiac muscle is a depolarization of the muscle-fiber membrane. This depolarization is brought about by propagated action potentials as in other muscle fibers. However, the action potential is conducted without apparent decrement from one cardiac muscle fiber to another. A stimulus to any portion of a ventricle elicits electrical changes that rapidly spread to all other portions of that segment of the heart.

The typical action potential from cardiac muscle is several hundred milliseconds in duration and roughly equals the duration of the resulting contraction. The duration of the action potential is roughly one half the interval between successive heartbeats.

Stimulation of any portion of the heart can initiate a propagated action potential, but a specialized "pacemaker" region in the sinoatrial node normally determines the rate of cardiac contractions. The membrane potential of cells in this pacemaker region has no stable value but gradually falls toward zero during the diastolic phase of cardiac activity. When this *pacemaker potential* reaches a threshold, an action potential is generated and is propagated to all other portions of the heart. The pacemaker cell membrane then repolarizes until the membrane potential approaches the equilibrium potential for potassium.

There are essentially two varieties of smooth muscles. *Visceral smooth muscles* make up the walls of the gastrointestinal tract and the urogenital tract. They do not show the cross-striations typical of skeletal or cardiac muscle and contract only very slowly. *Multiunit smooth muscle* is found in some very small muscles such as the nictitating membrane of the cat, the intrinsic eye muscles, or the precapillary sphincters. Stimulation of the innervation of a multiunit smooth muscle often sets up a prolonged response resembling incomplete tetanus. This reaction is presumably caused by the release of a transmitter substance (norepinephrine) at the end plate that is not rapidly destroyed and persists for several hundred milliseconds. Slow responses are typical of this type of muscle.

Gland Cells

The *gland cells* are also effectors, although their action and structure differ from those of muscle cells. Secretory cells possess cytoplasmic inclusions called *secretory granules*. Secretion from glandular cells usually results in the liberation of specific substances that are manufactured by the gland cell and are not available from any other source. The secretory process may be initiated by the arrival of neural impulses or by the presence of particular chemical substances (often compounds secreted by other gland cells) at the glandular membrane.

Bibliography

1. Brazier, Mary A. B. Studies of evoked responses by flash in man and cat. In *The Reticular Formation of the Brain*. H. H. Jasper, L. D. Proctor, R. S. Knighton, W. C. Noshay, & R. T. Costello, Eds. Boston: Little, Brown, 1958.
2. Brazier, Mary A. B. *The Electrical Activity of the Nervous System* (3rd ed.). Baltimore: Williams & Wilkins, 1968.
3. Crouch, J. E. & McClintic, J. R. *Human Anatomy and Physiology*. New York: Wiley, 1971.
4. Eccles, J. C. The effects of use and disuse on synaptic function. In *Brain Mechanisms and Learning*. J. F. Delafresnaye, A. Fessard, R. W. Gerard, & J. Konorski, Eds. Oxford: Blackwell Scientific, 1961.
5. Eccles, J. C. *The Physiology of Synapses*. New York: Academic Press, 1964.
6. Erlanger, J., & Gasser, H. S. *Electrical Signs of Nervous Activity*. Philadelphia: Univ. of Pennsylvania Press, 1937.
7. Forbes, A., & Morison, B. R. Cortical responses to sensory stimulation under deep barbiturate narcosis. *J. Neurophysiol.*, 1939, **2**, 112–128.
8. Jasper, H. H. Electroencephalography. In Penfield, W., & Erickson, T. C. *Epilepsy and Cerebral Localization*. Springfield, Ill.: Thomas, 1941.
9. Koelle, G. B. Neurohumoral transmission and the autonomic nervous system. In *The Pharmacological Basis of Therapeutics* (4th ed.). L. S. Goodman & A. Gilman, Eds. New York: Macmillan, 1970.
10. Morgan, C. T., & Stellar, E. *Physiological Psychology*. New York: McGraw-Hill, 1950.
11. Patton, H. D. Special properties of nerve trunks and tracts. In Ruch, T. C., Patton, H. D., Woodbury, J. W., & Towe, A. L., Eds. *Neurophysiology* (2nd ed.). Philadelphia: Saunders, 1965.
12. Peele, T. L. *The Neuroanatomic Basis for Clinical Neurology* (2nd ed.). New York: Blakiston Division, McGraw-Hill, 1961.
13. Towe, A. L., Electrophysiology of the cerebral cortex: consciousness. In Ruch, T. C., Patton, H. D., Woodbury, J. W., & Towe, A. L. Eds. *Neurophysiology* (2nd ed.). Philadelphia: Saunders, 1965.
14. Woodbury, J. W., Gordon, A. M., & Conrad, J. T. Muscle. In Ruch, T. C., Patton, H. D., Woodbury, J. W., & Towe, A. L., Eds. *Neurophysiology* (2nd ed.). Philadelphia: Saunders, 1965.

Chapter 3

ANATOMY OF THE NERVOUS SYSTEM

The Central Nervous System
The Peripheral Nervous System
The Autonomic Nervous System

In the course of embryological development, the nerve cells of the organisms collect in a tubular structure that persists, in modified form, in the adult. The portion of the tube that ends up in the head develops into the *brain* and the remainder forms the *spinal cord*. Together they constitute the *central nervous system* (CNS) (see Figure 3–1).

Information reaches cells in the central nervous system via *afferent* or *sensory* nerves, which project to every portion of the body. The transmission of information from the central nervous system to the peripheral effectors (muscles and glands) occurs via *efferent* or *motor* nerves. *Spinal* nerves (those sensory and motor nerves that enter and originate from the spinal cord) leave the spinal cord at regular intervals. *Cranial* nerves (those sensory and motor nerves that enter and originate from the brain) are irregularly spaced. The cranial and spinal nerves form the *peripheral nervous system* (PNS).

Before we proceed with a more detailed discussion of the nervous system, a few terms should be explained. It is common to discuss the location of parts of the body in relation to three imaginary planes (see Figure 3–2). The *sagittal plane* divides the body into right and left parts. The *median plane* is the sagittal plane that dissects the body into *equal* right and left halves. The *coronal* (or *frontal*) plane divides the body into front and back parts (i.e., the coronal plane runs at right angles to the sagittal plane). The *horizontal* plane divides the body into upper and lower parts.

In man, the front of the body (in the upright position) is considered to be *anterior*, the back *posterior*. *Superior* refers to higher struc-

Anatomy of the Nervous System 37

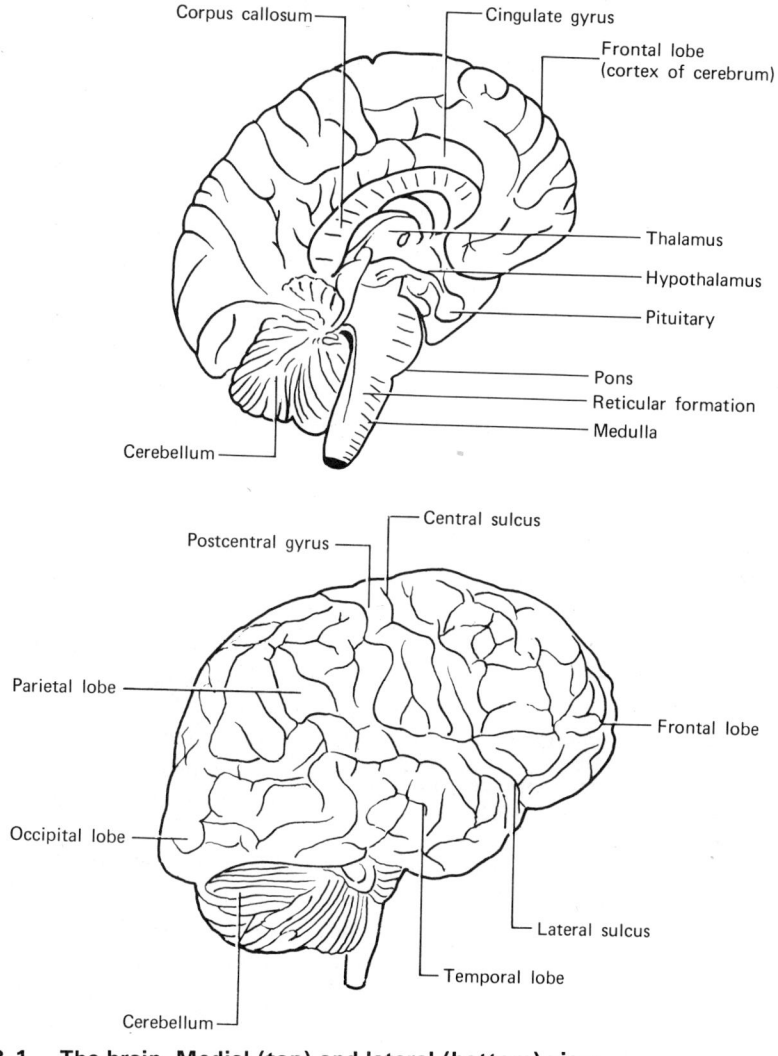

FIG. 3–1. The brain. Medial (top) and lateral (bottom) view.
(After *Human anatomy and physiology* by J. E. Crouch and J. R. McClintic. Copyright © 1971. John Wiley & Sons, Inc.)

tures and *inferior* to lower ones. These terms are usually used only when a reference point is provided. *Cranial* (toward the head) refers to higher structures in a more absolute sense and *caudal* (toward the tail) to lower structures.

In animals, the same terms are used in a slightly different way because the basic orientation of the body is changed. Structures toward the front of the organism are called *ventral* and those located near the back are called *dorsal*. *Cranial* and *anterior* become synonymous, as do *caudal* and *posterior*.

THE CENTRAL NERVOUS SYSTEM

The central nervous system serves two primary functions. (1) It interconnects sensory receptors and motor effectors, which are often located in very different portions of the organism and (2) it permits an integration of the various sensory inputs and resulting motor efferents to assure that the organism is going in only one direction at the same time. In higher organisms this integrative function has become quite complex and includes such

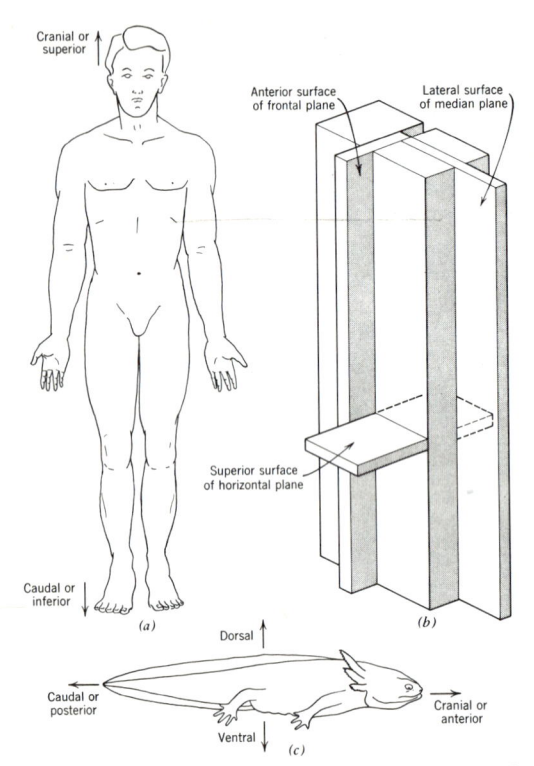

FIG. 3–2. (a) the anatomical position and synonymous terms of direction; (b) a block diagram showing the primary planes and surfaces; (c) an amphibian, illustrating comparative anatomical nomenclature.

(From E. Gardner. *Fundamentals of neurology* (5th ed.). Saunders, 1968.)

refinements as storage mechanisms for sensory information and related mechanisms that permit a comparison of the stored information with present input.

The overall design of the nervous system reflects these basic functions. *Sensory* pathways bring information into the central nervous system and distribute it to its various parts; *motor* pathways bring detailed information from various portions of the brain and spinal cord to the muscles and glands. A complex feltwork of associative neurons performs the many integrative processes.

The Spinal Cord

Gross Anatomy

This organization is most easily seen in the spinal cord. If we transect the spinal cord, two portions can be clearly distinguished. A white outer portion contains the ascending and descending pathways that connect the peripheral nerves with the brain. A butterfly-shaped gray inner section contains motor neurons and interneurons that permit some measure of local integration of sensory and motor functions.

In the simplest case, a sensory neuron enters the spinal cord, sends an axon through the gray matter, and connects directly with a motor neuron near the ventral surface of the spinal gray. This is a *monosynaptic* reflex connection. Sensory neurons may also enter the spinal gray and synapse on short-axon interneurons that communicate with motor neurons within the same segment of the cord. This permits an integration of more complex *segmental* reflexes.

Most of the sensory neurons project directly into the large sensory pathways that ascend toward the brain in the posterior portions of the spinal cord. These axons often give off branches (*collaterals*) that ascend or descend only a short distance before terminating on spinal motor neurons. These *suprasegmental* reflex connections permit an integration of fairly complex motor activities at the spinal level.

The two halves of the spinal cord appear roughly symmetrical. They are joined by a narrow commissure of gray and white matter that contains the *central canal*.

The spinal cord (as well as the brain) is covered by three membranes. These *meninges* separate the delicate neural tissues from the bones that surround the central nervous system. The outermost membrane, the *dura*, is fibrous and tough; the innermost *pia* is soft and pliable. Between them is a thick, flexible *arachnoid* membrane.

At each vertebral segment of the cord, spinal nerves enter and leave. The sensory nerves form distinct bundles (one on either side of the cord) called the *dorsal spinal roots*. Axons from cells in these dorsal roots project into the posterior portions of the cord. Motor nerves leave the spinal cord in a similar pattern and form two *ventral roots* on the anterior surface of the cord. These ventral roots do not contain cell bodies but are made up of axons from motor cells that are located in the anterior and lateral parts of the spinal gray.

Microscopic Anatomy

The butterfly-shaped gray (cellular) portion of the spinal cord is divided into *posterior* and *anterior horns* that are interconnected by *intermediate columns*.

Large motor neurons predominate in the anterior horns. These *lower motor neurons* project axons to the skeletal musculature of the limbs and trunk. The motor cells receive axon terminals from descending motor nerves, interneurons, or peripheral sensory neurons.

The lateral portion of the spinal gray is made up mostly of smaller motor cells that innervate smooth muscles, cardiac muscles, and glands. The axons of these motor neurons form part of the *autonomic nervous system*.

The cells of primary sensory neurons of the peripheral nervous system are located in the dorsal roots. These cells have very long (up to several feet in length) "dendritic" processes that conduct sensory information from sensory receptor structures toward the body of the sensory neuron. From here, long axons project into the posterior spinal cord.

SENSORY COMPONENTS

The dorsal roots contain two classes of fibers: *somatic afferents* from striated muscles, skin, and subcutaneous tissue and *visceral afferents* from smooth muscles, the heart, and the glands.

Two distinct fiber bundles connect each dorsal root with the spinal cord. The *lateral bundle* contains fibers that transmit information about temperature and pain stimuli to the body and viscera. These fibers synapse with neurons that project into the contralateral *lateral spinothalamic tract* or directly to motor neurons for the completion of monosynaptic reflexes (see Figure 3–3).

The lateral spinothalamic tract terminates in the thalamus or in the reticular formation of the brainstem. From the thalamus, pain and temperature impulses are transmitted via the internal capsule to neurons in the parietal lobe of the cerebral cortex.

The second major division of the projection from each dorsal root to the spinal cord, the *medial bundle*, contains fibers from mechanoreceptors in the skin, muscles, and joints. These fibers form two large nerve tracts in the ventral portion of the cord. The *fasciculus gracilis* carries impulses that arise from the lower segments of the body. The *fasciculus cuneatus* carries impulses from upper segments. The individual components of both of these tracts are arranged in a topographic order such that the axons from lower portions of the body run medially and those from the upper portion laterally.

This major pathway for touch and pressure stimuli projects to the nuclei *gracilis* and *cuneatus* in the caudal portion of the brainstem. (Any grouping of nerve cells in the CNS is called a nucleus.) From here, the

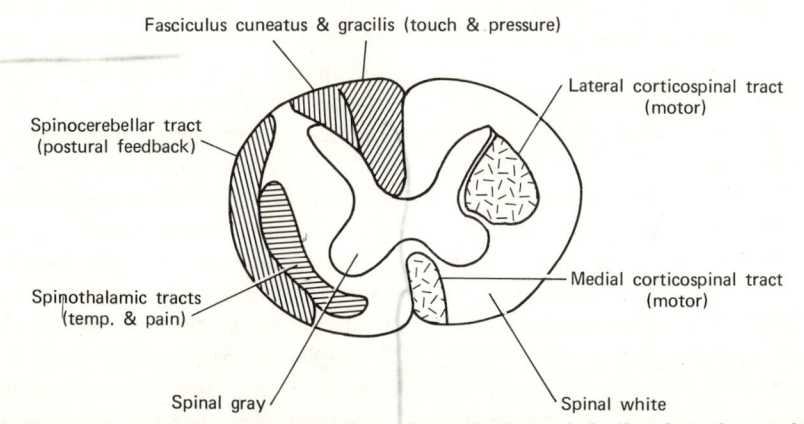

FIG. 3–3. Schematic representation of a spinal cord, indicating the position of the major sensory (left) and motor (right) pathways to and from the brain.

information is transmitted to the thalamus via a large fiber bundle called the *medial lemniscus*. From the thalamus, projections are made to the postcentral gyrus of the parietal lobe.

Destruction of fibers in this important sensory tract impairs the sensation of light pressure and touch as well as important kinesthetic sensations that convey information about the position and movement of the body. *Hypotonia* (a reduction in the resistance of skeletal muscles to passive stretch) then occurs and combines with a loss of feedback from the muscles to produce a condition called *sensory ataxia*, which is characterized by uncoordinated and awkward movements.

Fibers of the medial bundle may also synapse with neurons that project to the other side of the spinal cord and form the *ventral spinothalamic tract*. Axons from the ventral spinothalamic tract join the medial lemniscus in the brainstem and terminate in the thalamus. Their cortical projection is similar to that of the lateral spinothalamic tract.

Some sensory pathways do not reach the cerebral cortex. A *spinotectal tract* terminates in the tectum of the midbrain. A *dorsal spinocerebellar tract* provides connections between sensory endings in muscles or tendons and the motor areas of the cerebellum. A *ventral spinocerebellar tract* makes similar connections.

MOTOR COMPONENTS

The spinal cord and brainstem contain two major motor systems, the *pyramidal* and the *extrapyramidal* pathways.

Large pyramidal cells in the frontal and parietal lobes of the cerebrum project long axons through the internal capsule into the brainstem. Most of these fibers then cross to the other side of the brainstem before descending in the lateral portion of the cord as the *lateral corticospinal tract*. The remaining uncrossed fibers form the *ventral corticospinal tract*. The long axons that make up these major motor pathways may terminate directly on large motor neurons or on interneurons that, in turn, project to the motor cells.

The extrapyramidal motor tracts of the spinal cord arise from various subcortical nuclei that receive afferents from cortical motor areas and related sensory projection areas. A more detailed description of this complex system of interrelated pathways will be presented later.

Summary

The bones of the spine form a hollow tube that is filled with nerve cells and their axons. This spinal cord consists of an inner, gray portion that contains mostly cell bodies and an outer, white portion that contains mostly fibers (i.e., axons). Sensory receptors communicate with the long dendritic processes of cells that are grouped together in small clumps, called dorsal roots, just outside the dorsal surface of the spinal cord. The axons of these cells project into the spinal cord via a medial and a lateral bundle. Some of these axons connect with motor cells that are located in the anterior portion of the spinal gray matter. These connections form pathways for reflexive reactions. Most axons of dorsal root cells project to the brain in anatomically as well as functionally distinct tracts that run in the posterior half of the spinal white matter. The axons that enter the spinal cord via the lateral bundle transmit information from pain and temperature receptors. They form the lateral spinothalamic tract, which terminates in the thalamus, a major relay station for all sensory systems. From here, the signals are relayed to the parietal lobe of the cerebral hemispheres. The axons of the dorsal root cells that enter the spinal cord with the medial bundle carry information from touch and pressure receptors in the skin and in muscle. They form several important tracts in the spinal cord. The fasciculus cuneatus, the fasciculus gracilis, and the ventral spinothalamic tract project to nuclei in the lower brainstem which, in turn, give rise to a major sensory pathway, the medial lemniscus, to the thalamus. From here, information about pressure and touch is relayed to the parietal lobe of the cerebral hemispheres. Some axons from the medial bundle form shorter pathways that relay touch and pressure signals to the midbrain or cerebellum.

The motor components of the spinal cord are collected mainly in its anterior half. Peripheral motor nerves consist of the axons of motor cells in the anterior and lateral portions of the spinal gray. The motor nerves leave the spinal cord in distinct bundles, called ventral roots, which form a pattern symmetrical to that of the dorsal roots. The motor cells of the spinal cord receive some direct inputs from the sensory cells of the dorsal roots, but their principal inputs are two major fiber systems that originate in the brain and descend in the anterior portions of the spinal white matter. The pyramidal motor tracts consist of the very long axons of cells in the frontal lobe of the cerebral hemispheres. The extrapyramidal motor tracts consist of axons of cells that are located in various relay nuclei in the brainstem.

Review Questions

1. Discuss the functional organization of the spinal cord.
2. Describe the principal sensory tracts that ascend in it.
3. Describe the major motor tracts that descend in it.

The Brainstem (see Figure 3–4)

Medulla and Pons

The spinal cord is continuous with the *bulbar* portion of the brainstem via the *foramen magnum*, a large opening in the bone that surrounds the brain. This most caudal portion of the brain is called the *medulla*. The central canal of the spinal cord continues into the medulla and gradually widens to form a canal called the *fourth ventricle*.

The *pontine* portion of the brainstem (or *pons*) is largely hidden from view by the *cerebellum*, a highly convoluted structure that is responsible for an integration of sensory information from muscles and joints. These important afferents are carried by spinocerebellar tracts that enter the cerebellum via two prominent fiber bundles called the *brachium pontis* and the *restiform body*.

The ventral aspects of the pons are covered with a transverse-running fiber bundle, the *brachium conjunctivum*, which interconnects the cerebellum with the motor areas of the cerebrum.

The lower portions of the brainstem that make up the medulla and pons (collectively called the *hindbrain*) are structurally as well as functionally a continuation of the spinal cord. Many of the major sensory and motor pathways give off collaterals in their course through the medulla and pons. These collaterals synapse on cells in the central core of the brainstem that are profusely interconnected and constitute the lower portions of the *reticular formation*.

Midbrain

The rostral aspect of the pons is continuous with the *midbrain* (or *mesencephalon*). This portion of the brainstem is divided into three major sections. The *tectum* takes up the dorsal third, the *tegmentum* the middle, and the *basis pedunculi* the ventral third.

TECTUM

The most prominent aspects of the tectum are four round elevations (two on each side) on the dorsal surface of the brainstem. The lower pair, the *inferior colliculi*, are composed of nuclei that serve as a relay station for the *lateral lemniscus*, which carries auditory signals. These fibers terminate in a distinct pattern such that a topographic distribution of stimulus frequencies occurs. The inferior colliculi project primarily to the medial geniculate

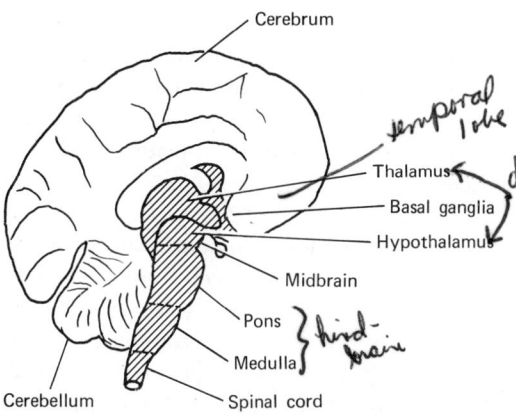

FIG. 3–4. Schematic representation of the brainstem (dark portion of drawing).

(After *Human anatomy and physiology* by J. E. Crouch and J. R. McClintic. Copyright © 1971. John Wiley & Sons, Inc.)

nuclei of the thalamus, which relay auditory signals to the cerebral cortex.

The upper pair of elevations on the tectal brainstem, the *superior colliculi*, are part of the optic system. Terminal fibers from the optic tract terminate only in one portion of the superior colliculi. They maintain a distinct geographic pattern that reflects their origin in the eye. Other parts of the superior colliculi receive afferents from the visual association areas of the cerebral cortex. These connections are part of the complex neural circuit that controls eye movements.

There are no major ascending projections from the superior colliculi because these nuclei act mainly as a relay to lower motor centers that perform reflex adjustments of posture and movement in response to visual stimuli.

TEGMENTUM

The tegmentum consists mainly of a dense feltwork of neurons that are part of the reticular formation. These cells receive afferents from all ascending and descending pathways that course through the brainstem and contribute descending as well as ascending efferents to many of these fiber tracts.

The inner core of the midbrain also contains several nuclei. Some of these innervate the musculature of the eye. Others are part of the vestibular system or contribute to the extrapyramidal motor system.

BASIS PEDUNCULI

The ventral portion of the midbrain consists mainly of fibers that make up the corticospinal and corticobulbar motor system. The major nucleus of this area, the *substantia nigra*, is one of the important relay stations of the extrapyramidal motor system.

Diencephalon

The midbrain is continuous dorsally with the diencephalon, which is commonly divided into the following parts: (1) the *hypothalamus* constitutes the ventral portion, which contains the third ventricle; (2) the *epithalamus* constitutes the dorsal portion; (3) the *subthalamus* represents a continuation of the midbrain tegmentum; and (4) the *thalamus* is a complex mass of nuclei that coordinate most projections between lower portions of the brain and the cerebral hemispheres.

HYPOTHALAMUS

The innermost, *periventricular* zone of the hypothalamus, which surrounds the third ventricle, is essentially an extension of the reticular formation of the midbrain. Except for the *arcuate* or *periventricular* nucleus, this region contains small cells and fibers that are not grouped into distinct nuclei or fiber bundles.

Laterally, a number of distinct nuclei and fiber tracts appear. The *mammillary bodies* make up the posterior portion of this medial zone. These nuclei receive afferents from the hippocampus and project to the thalamus. Anterior to the mammillary bodies, the medial zone contains the *ventromedial* and *dorsomedial nuclei* and, finally, the *anterior hypothalamic area*. The *lateral* zone of the hypothalamus consists largely of an undifferentiated mass of cells and fibers.

The most prominent afferent input to the hypothalamus, the *fornix*, arises in the hippocampus and terminates primarily in the posterior hypothalamus. The anterior and lateral hypothalamus are intimately interconnected with the older "rhinencephalic" portions of the cerebrum via the *medial forebrain bundle*. The anterior hypothalamus also receives projections from the amygdaloid nuclei via the *stria terminalis*.

In addition, the hypothalamus receives anatomically less distinct but functionally important inputs from the brainstem, the frontal lobes of the cerebrum, and the viscera.

The efferent connections of the hypothalamus include the following pathways: (1) The *mammillothalamic tract* projects from the medial mammillary nuclei to the anterior nuclei of the thalamus, which are intimately connected with the cingulate gyrus of the cerebral cortex; (2) the *mammillotegmental tract* collects fibers from many hypothalamic nuclei and projects to the reticular formation of the brainstem; (3) the *periventricular fiber system* has ascending components that terminate in the thalamus and descending components that terminate in the reticular formation of the brainstem or continue into the spinal cord; the descending pathways carry efferents to sympathetic and parasympathetic nuclei and ganglia and form the central portion of the *autonomic motor system;* and (4) the *hypothalamo-hypophyseal* tract arises in the supraoptic and paraventricular nuclei of the hypothalamus and project to the neural lobe of the pituitary (or hypophyseal) gland.

The hypothalamus is the highest center of integration for many visceral functions and contributes importantly to the regulation of many physiological processes that are related to such psychological variables as hunger, thirst, sexual arousal, and emotional behavior.

EPITHALAMUS

The *pineal* gland projects outward from the dorsal surface of the brainstem. It is innervated largely by fibers from the autonomic nervous system and appears to be related to the regulation of biological functions in accordance with changes in the relative amount of daylight.

The *habenular nuclei* are located immediately dorsally to the dorsomedial thalamus. They receive afferents from the hippocampus, amygdala, and hypothalamus and project mainly to the thalamus.

The *posterior commissure* is a large fiber bundle that crosses the brainstem near the boundary between the diencephalon and the midbrain. It contains fibers from cells in many parts of the brain but serves mainly as a diffuse connection between the globus pallidus and the midbrain.

SUBTHALAMUS

The area between the hypothalamus and the thalamus contains a number of discrete nuclei that form part of the extrapyramidal motor system. The most prominent of these are the *zona incerta, nuclei of the fields of Forel,* and *subthalamic nuclei.* Parts of the substantia nigra and red nucleus also project into the subthalamus.

Thalamus

The thalamus takes up the center of the brain, dorsal to the hypothalamus and subthalamus and medial to the internal capsule. In man, each side of the thalamus is divided into an internal and an external segment by a narrow band of fibers. A similar band of fibers separates the thalamus from the *reticular nucleus,* which surrounds the thalamus almost entirely.

The *anterior portion* of the thalamus is made up of three nuclei that receive afferents from the mammillary bodies via the mammillothalamic tract and project to the cingulate gyrus on the medial surface of the cerebral cortex.

Some fibers from all of the major sensory tracts terminate in the small *midline* nuclei that surround the third ventricle. These nuclei project diffusely to all portions of the cerebral cortex. Very little is known about the afferent or efferent connections of the *medial* nuclei that surround the midline nuclei. Most of the *lateral* nuclei are reciprocally interconnected with other thalamic nuclei and project to the parietal lobe of the cerebral cortex. The *ventral* nuclei of the thalamus are important sensory or motor relay stations. Most of the fibers that run in the major sensory pathways terminate in the *posteroventral nucleus.* The efferents from this important sensory relay station project to the parietal cortex. The *lateroventral* nucleus receives afferents from motor nuclei in the brainstem and from the basal ganglia and projects primarily to the motor areas of the cerebral cortex. The *anteroventral nucleus* receives afferents from the frontal cortex and from the globus pallidus and also projects to the cerebral cortex.

The transitional area between the midbrain and the thalamus contains the *medial* and the *lateral geniculate nuclei.* The medial geniculate nuclei receive fibers from the inferior colliculi and lateral lemnisci and project to the primary auditory areas of the cortex. Fibers from the optic tract terminate in the lateral geniculate nuclei, which project to the visual area of the cortex.

The thalamus is essentially enveloped by a thin band of fibers of subthalamic origin, the

Basal Ganglia

The dorsal portion of the brainstem consists of a group of nuclei collectively called *basal ganglia*. The principal components of the basal ganglia are the *globus pallidus*, the *putamen*, the *caudate*, and the *amygdala*. The term *corpus striatum* is applied to the caudate, putamen, and globus pallidus.

The caudate nucleus has two distinct parts, a *head* that is located anterior and lateral to the thalamus, and a thin *tail* that projects along the thalamus and terminates in the amygdaloid complex. The putamen is separated from the head of the caudate by fibers from the *internal capsule* (the major pathway between the brainstem and the cerebrum) and is bordered medially by the globus pallidus. The amygdala is located ventral and lateral to the thalamus in the temporal lobe of the cerebrum.

The striatum receives afferents from three major sources: (1) a *corticostriate* projection that originates mainly in the motor and sensory areas of the cerebral cortex; (2) a *thalamostriate* projection from the thalamus; and (3) a *nigrostriate* projection from the substantia nigra and other lower-brainstem motor centers. The principal direction of conduction within the striatum is from the caudate to the putamen and globus pallidus and from the putamen to the globus pallidus. The striatum projects to motor nuclei of the lower brainstem and to motor cells of the spinal cord.

Functionally, the striatum is part of several complex feedback circuits that constitute the extrapyramidal motor system. Damage to this portion of the brain in man is associated with muscular tremor and a general loss of control over limb movement.

The amygdala lies in the temporal lobe, surrounded by the cortex of the hippocampal gyrus. It is continuous with the hippocampus posteriorly, the tail of the caudate nucleus anteriorly, and the putamen dorsally. The amygdala contains the *corticomedial* and the *basolateral* nuclei. The corticomedial nuclei receive olfactory afferents and project efferents via the *stria medullaris* to the thalamus. The basolateral nuclei are diffusely interconnected with the corticomedial nuclei and with the surrounding cortical tissue of the hippocampal and dentate gyri. This sets up an important pathway between the amygdala and the hypothalamus via the *fornix*, a major fiber bundle that originates, in part, in the hippocampal gyrus.

Summary

The spinal cord widens as it enters the head and forms the brainstem. The distinct geographic separation of cell bodies and fibers that characterizes the spinal cord is gradually lost, although the major fiber tracts continue to run mainly along the surface of the brainstem. The brainstem is conveniently divided into several major subdivisions called medulla, pons, midbrain, diencephalon, and basal ganglia.

The medulla is pretty much a continuation of the upper spinal cord except that it contains more distinct groupings of cells. These nuclei contain cells that form some of the sensory and motor nerves of the head or relay messages along some of the major sensory or motor pathways.

The adjacent pons is largely hidden from view by the cerebellum dorsally and by the three major fiber bundles that connect the brainstem with the cerebellum ventrally. The internal organization of the pons is very similar to that of the medulla.

The upper portion of the pons is continuous with the midbrain. This part of the brainstem is organized in three layers. The dorsal layer, called tectum, contains two sets of nuclei, the colliculi. The superior colliculi are part of the visual system. The inferior colliculi are relay stations for auditory signals. The middle section of the midbrain, called tegmentum, consists mainly of a dense feltwork of closely interconnected neurons. This is the reticular formation. The ventral layer of the midbrain, the basis pedunculi, contains mostly fibers of the pyramidal motor system.

The diencephalon has two major subdivisions, the hypothalamus and the thalamus. The hypothalamus lies directly ahead of the lower portion of the midbrain. It is commonly divided into a medial zone that contains several distinct nuclei (notably the mammillary bodies and the dorsomedial and ventromedial nuclei) and a lateral zone that contains some major fiber bundles as well as some scattered cell bodies. The medial forebrain bundle and the fornix are two of the fiber systems that course through the lateral hypothalamus. The hypothalamus contains cells that contribute to the regulation of feeding, drinking, sexual behavior, and emotional reactions.

Suspended from the ventral surface of the hypothalamus is the pituitary gland, which secretes many hormones that affect behavior and control the secretory activity of other endocrine glands. The secretions of the pituitary gland are controlled by cells in the hypothalamus.

The thalamus is continuous with the dorsal portions of the midbrain. It is made up of a number of discrete nuclei. Many of these nuclei serve as relay stations for the major sensory pathways. The medial geniculate nuclei are part of the auditory system, the lateral geniculate nuclei relay visual information, and the posteroventral nuclei are part of the pathway that carries signals from receptors in the skin and muscles. Other thalamic nuclei serve as relays for the extrapyramidal motor system. Many thalamic nuclei receive inputs from many different sources and project diffusely to all areas of the cerebrum. These nonspecific projection nuclei are related to the reticular formation of the lower brainstem.

The basal ganglia include several nuclei. The caudate, putamen, and globus pallidus form a group, called the corpus striatum, that surrounds the lateral aspects of the thalamus. These nuclei are part of the extrapyramidal motor system. The remaining portion of the basal ganglia consists of several smaller nuclei that are embedded in the cortex of the temporal lobe. They are collectively called amygdala. Two subdivisions, the corticomedial and the basolateral nuclei, are often distinguished. The amygdala receives olfactory inputs but appears to be functionally related most closely to other parts of the brain that integrate emotional or motivational functions.

Review Question

1. List the major subdivisions of the brainstem and their major functions.

The Cerebral Hemispheres

Gross Anatomy (see Figures 3–5 and 3–6)

The cerebral hemispheres have developed so extensively in man and many mammals that

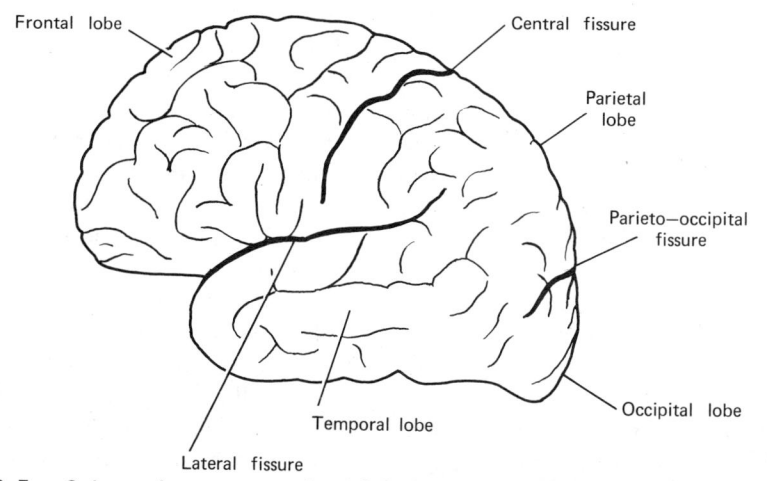

FIG. 3–5. Schematic representation of the human cerebral cortex, lateral view.

Neurophysiology and Neuroanatomy

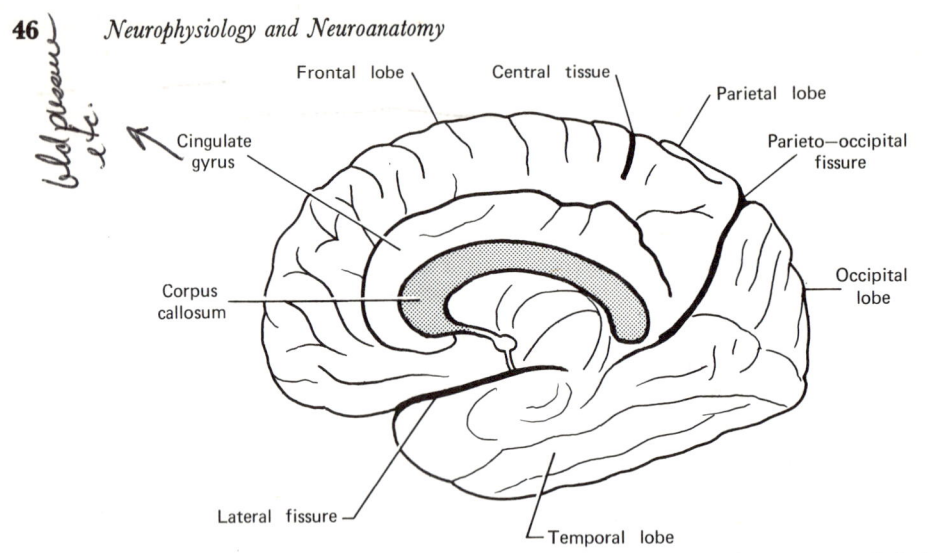

FIG. 3-6. Schematic representation of the human cerebral cortex, medial view.

they obscure much of the brainstem. The surface of the cerebrum of man is convoluted and forms a variable number of ridges (*gyri*) and grooves (*sulci* or *fissures*) that are used as convenient landmarks. The cerebral hemispheres are made up of a thin gray outer shell of cells, the *cortex* (i.e., rind), and a thick, white inner layer of fibers.

The cerebral hemispheres are commonly divided into four *lobes*. The prominent lateral fissure separates the *temporal lobe* (below) from the *frontal* and *parietal lobes* (above). A large area of surface cortex, the *island of Reil*, is buried within the folds of the lateral fissure. The *central fissure* runs at about a 70 degree angle to the lateral fissure, beginning on the medial surface of each hemisphere and continuing over its lateral surface almost into the lateral fissure. The region anterior to the central fissure and above the lateral fissure makes up the frontal lobe. The region posterior to the central fissure and dorsal to the lateral fissure makes up the parietal lobe. A less prominent *parieto-occipital* fissure separates the posterior portions of the parietal lobe from the occipital lobe.

The cortex of each hemisphere continues onto the medial surface of the cerebrum where it surrounds a major fiber bundle, the *corpus callosum*, which interconnects the two hemispheres. The area dorsal to the corpus callosum is called the *cingulate gyrus*. The cingulate gyrus becomes continuous with the hippocampal gyrus posteroventrally, thus forming the *limbic lobe*. The ventral surface of the cerebral hemispheres is constituted of temporal- and frontal-lobe cortex.

The hemispheres contain large *lateral ventricles* that communicate with the third ventricle of the diencephalon. The anterior horns of the lateral ventricles extend into the frontal lobes. The main bodies of the lateral ventricles are located directly beneath the corpus callosum. The posterior horns of the lateral ventricles extend into the occipital lobe. The inferior horns curve into the temporal lobe.

Many of the efferent projections of the cortex are diffuse. Others form discrete fiber bundles or join the major efferent fiber system, the *internal capsule*, which carries most of the pyramidal and extrapyramidal motor fibers. Three major fiber bundles (the *anterior commissure*, the *corpus callosum*, and the *hippocampal commissure*) interconnect the two hemispheres. Neighboring regions of the cerebrum are interconnected profusely and diffusely by short association fibers. Distant regions are typically interconnected by distinct bundles of long association fibers.

The outer cellular layers of the cerebral hemispheres contain in man about 10 to 15 billion cells. Three types of cortical tissue are commonly distinguished. The phylogenetically oldest and structurally simplest (three-layer) cortex is called *allocortex*. The youngest and most complex (six-layer) cortex is called *neocortex*. A transitional type that contains four or five layers is called *juxtallocortex*.

Neocortex

The dorsal and lateral surface of the cerebral hemispheres and much of the ventral surface consist of neocortex. Several types of neocortical tissue can be distinguished. Various maps of the distribution of these tissues have been developed, and one, proposed by Brodmann over 50 years ago, is in general use today.

THE FRONTAL LOBE

The cortex anterior to the central fissure contains the motor areas and a large expanse of cortical matter that has been called "association" area for want of more detailed knowledge of its functions.

The *primary motor area* (area 4 of Brodmann) (see Figure 3–7) takes up the precentral gyrus, immediately anterior to the central fissure. Anteriorly, it is bordered by a *suppressor area* (area 4 s) and by *secondary motor areas* (areas 6 and 8). Cells in all of these areas as well as in some of the "sensory" areas of the parietal lobe contribute fibers to the pyramidal and extrapyramidal motor pathways. Their major afferent inputs are from other regions of the cerebral cortex.

Electrical stimulation of area 4 evokes specific movements. A topographical representation of individual muscles has been demonstrated. Damage to this important motor center typically results in a loss of control over fine movements, particularly of the digits. Stimulation of the adjacent suppressor area produces a general relaxation of muscular tension and interrupts ongoing movements. Stimulation of the secondary motor regions in areas 6 and 8 typically results in gross movements of the limbs or discrete movements of the head or eyes.

The association areas of the prefrontal cortex (areas 9, 10, 11, and 12) make up the rest of the frontal lobe, anterior to the motor areas. This prefrontal cortex is intimately and reciprocally connected with other portions of the cerebrum and with the dorsomedial thalamus and hypothalamus.

The functions of the prefrontal cortex are only poorly understood. Electrical stimulation produces little in the way of distinct behavioral responses. Destruction of large portions of it seems to reduce "emotionality" and the affective response to pain. Other psychological functions, such as short-term memory, may also be modified.

THE PARIETAL LOBE

The area immediately behind the central fissure contains the *primary somatic projection areas* (areas 1, 2, and 3 of Brodmann), and the *somatosensory association areas* (areas 5 and 7). In man, it also includes two *speech areas* (39 and 40). Its posterior border contains part of the *visual motor area* (area 19).

The primary somatic projection areas receive afferents from the posteroventral nucleus of the thalamus, which relays sensory information from all of the skin senses. A distinct topographic pattern of projection is maintained that is similar to the pattern of muscle representation on the precentral gyrus. There is considerable overlap, with respect to sensory as well as motor functions, between the sensory and motor areas of the cortex.

Electrical stimulation of the somatosensory projection and association areas elicits often peculiar sensations such as tingling or itching, burning, or pain in the skin of some portion of the body. Destruction of these areas dulls all skin sensations. They are not completely eliminated because lower somatosensory relay stations, particularly those of the thalamus, can mediate some sensations.

THE OCCIPITAL LOBE

The occipital lobe contains the *primary visual projection area* (area 17) and the *visual association area* (area 18) as well as posterior portions of the *visual motor area* (area 19).

The *striate* cortex of the primary visual projection area receives a topographically organized pattern of inputs from the lateral geniculate nucleus of the thalamus. Projections from the macular portion of the eye terminate most posteriorly. Fibers from more

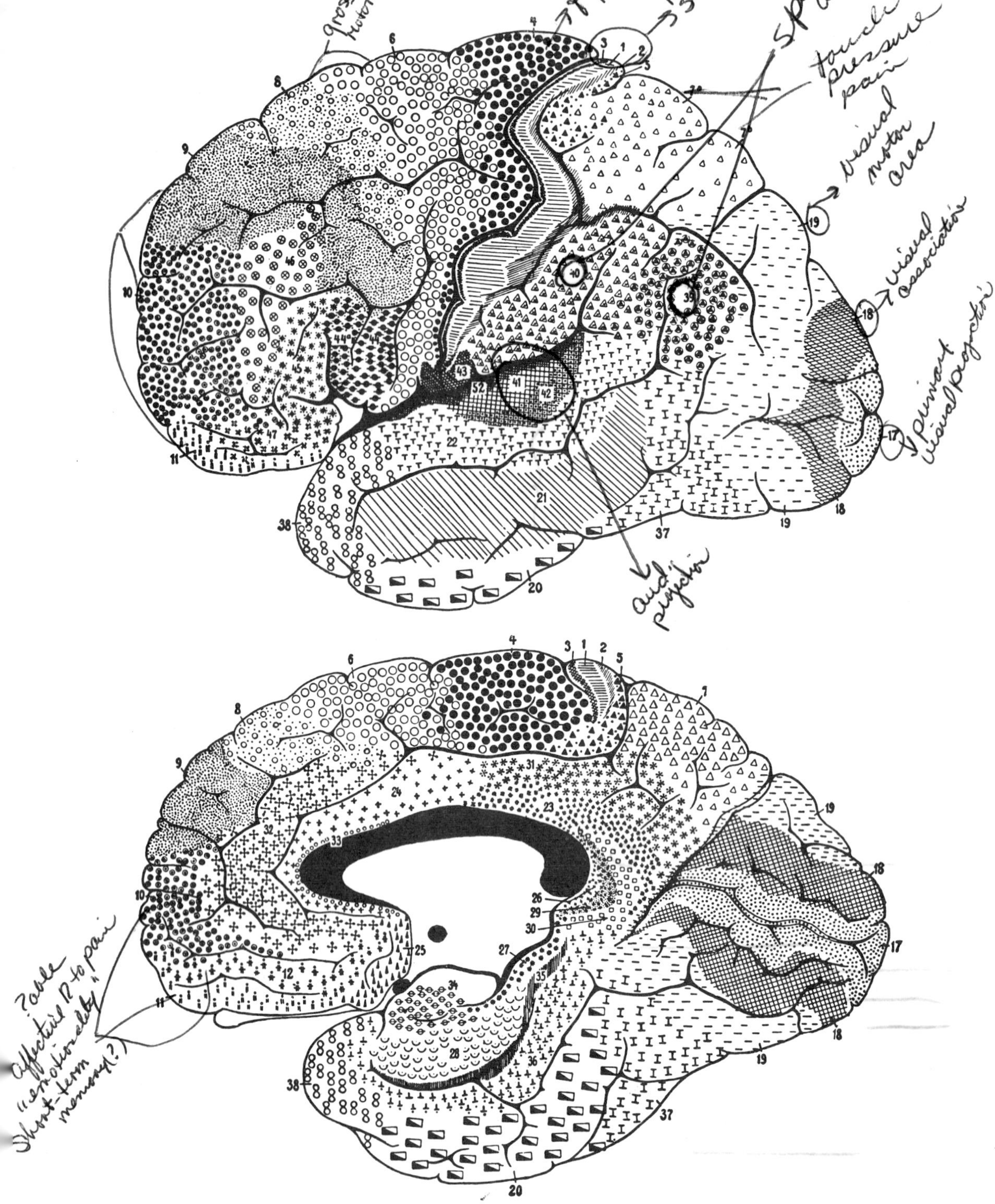

48 *Neurophysiology and Neuroanatomy*

FIG. 3–7. Cytoarchitectural maps of the human cerebral cortex. *Top,* convex surface of the hemisphere; *bottom,* medial surface.

(From *The neuroanatomic basis for clinical neurology* by T. L. Peele. (2nd ed.). McGraw-Hill, 1961. After K. Brodmann. Physiologie des Gehirns. In *Die allgemeine Chirurgie der Gehirnkrankheiten, Neue Deutsche Chirurgie.* Stuttgart: F. Enke, 1914.)

peripheral portions of the eye terminate progressively more anteriorly. Area 17 projects primarily into the adjacent visual association area (area 18). This area does not receive direct projections from the visual system and projects largely to the frontal association areas and to the somatosensory and motor areas that surround the central fissure.

THE TEMPORAL LOBE

Phylogenetically as well as embryologically, the temporal lobe is a relatively late development. Much of it is classified as "association" cortex, largely because we do not yet understand its functions very well.

A notable exception to this is the *primary auditory projection area* (areas 41 and 42). The major part of the auditory projection area (as well as the adjacent auditory association areas) is hidden in the folds of the lateral fissure. Signals from the auditory system are tonotopically projected to several distinct parts of the temporal lobe in many species. Electrical stimulation of the auditory projection areas elicits auditory sensations. Destruction of these areas reduces the ability to perceive sounds but does not eliminate it because subcortical relay stations are capable of mediating basic sensory functions.

The auditory association areas are reciprocally connected with the primary projection areas and with the general association cortex surrounding them. Damage to the auditory association areas in man produces an inability to understand or interpret the meaning of sounds but apparently no primary sensory deficit.

The rest of the temporal lobe is profusely interconnected with the association and sensory projection areas of the frontal, parietal, and occipital lobes. It also projects fibers into the motor pathways and to the thalamus. Damage to the temporal lobe typically results in marked changes in emotional reactivity as well as in "associative" disturbances such as visual or auditory aphasias and agnosias.

THE CINGULATE REGION

The neocortical tissue that surrounds the corpus callosum on the medial surface of the brain is called cingulate gyrus. It receives afferents from the hypothalamus and midbrain via the thalamus and is reciprocally interconnected with all regions of the cerebral hemispheres. It projects efferents also to nuclei of the thalamus, hypothalamus, and striatum.

Electrical stimulation of the cingulate gyrus elicits overt movements and affects such autonomic functions as blood pressure, respiration, cardiovascular responses, pilomotor and sudomotor reactions, and salivation. Lesions in this area typically produce akinesia, indifference to sensory inputs, and general apathy.

Allo- and Juxtallocortex

The older and more primitive cortex develops phylogenetically together with the olfactory system. It is therefore often called *rhinencephalon* (i.e., smell brain), although many parts of it are not directly involved in olfactory functions. It includes the *olfactory nerve, bulb, stalk*, and *nucleus*, the *septal area*, the *diagonal band of Broca*, the *hippocampus*, the *prepyriform cortex* of the temporal lobe, and those portions of the adjacent *hippocampal gyrus* that do not meet the criteria for neocortex. On the basis of functional considerations, the amygdaloid nuclei, the cingulate gyrus, and the hypothalamus are sometimes included.

The *septal area* is located immediately beneath the anterior portion of the cingulate, anterior to the thalamus. It is divided into a medial and a lateral area, which are separated by the lateral ventricles. Both are reciprocally interconnected with the hypothalamus and the hippocampus.

The *hippocampal formation* makes up much of the central portion of each hemisphere. It extends from the septal region over the corpus callosum into the temporal lobe and includes several distinct components. The *hippocampus* proper consists of three-layer cortex. The dorsal portions of the hippocampus become thinner and thinner as they project anteriorly and finally give way to its major efferents, the *fornix fiber system*. The ventral portions of the hippocampus are surrounded by the rudimentary cortex of the *subiculum* and *dentate gyrus*, which are functionally as well as anatomically closely related to the hippocampus.

The principal inputs to the hippocampal formation come from the adjacent temporal-lobe neocortex and from the septal area. Most of its efferents join the fornix, which projects to the septal region, preoptic nuclei, and cingulate gyrus, and to the mammillary bodies and neighboring cells of the hypothalamus.

The rhinencephalon of man and most mammals appears to be concerned primarily with complex integrative processes that may be essential to such psychological events as motivation or memory.

Summary

The cerebral hemispheres of man have distinct lobes. The posterior-most occipital lobe contains the primary visual projections as well as visual association areas. The adjacent parietal lobe, including the cortex dorsal to the lateral fissure and posterior to the central fissure, contains the cortical representations of touch, pressure, and pain sensations as well as some motor functions. The cortex below the lateral fissure makes up the temporal lobe. This area contains the cortical representation of auditory signals as well as auditory association areas. The posterior portions of the frontal lobe contain the origins of the pyramidal motor system as well as cells that contribute to extrapyramidal motor functions. The cortical tissue continues on to the medial surface of each hemisphere. Here, it surrounds the corpus callosum, the big fiber bundle that interconnects the two hemispheres. The cortex of the medial surface is often called the "limbic" lobe. It is functionally related to emotional reactions and other motivational mechanisms. The cortex of the limbic lobe is closely associated with several subcortical areas (notably the hypothalamus) and with the phylogenetically older cortex that makes up the hippocampus. This important structure takes up much of the central area of the hemispheres and partially surrounds the lateral ventricles. The neocortical tissue that makes up most of the dorsal and lateral aspects of the cerebrum subserves mainly sensory and motor functions as well as, perhaps, complex integrative functions. The phylogenetically older cortex of the medial surface of the cerebral hemispheres as well as some aspects of the ventral surface subserve more primitive, motivational functions.

Review Questions

1. List the major subdivisions of the cerebral hemispheres and their major functions.
2. Contrast the functions of the phylogenetically older cortex of the limbic lobe and hippocampus with those of the neocortex.

The Cerebellum (*see Figure 3–8*)

The cerebellum consists of several nuclei that are surrounded by fibers and multilayer cortex. The superior surface of the cerebellum is separated from the occipital lobe of the cerebrum by a double layer of dura. Its ventral surface covers the pontine and upper bulbar portions of the brainstem.

The cerebellum is divided into a wormlike central portion called *vermis*, two *lateral lobes*, and two ventral projections called *flocculi*.

The afferents to the cerebellum terminate on cells in the cerebellar cortex. From here, the information is distributed to the deep nuclei, which are the principal source of efferents from the cerebellum.

Four cerebellar nuclei are buried in the white matter of each lobe. Starting medially, they are called the *fastigial, globose, emboliform,* and *dentate* nuclei. The emboliform and globose nuclei are often collectively called the *interpositus* nucleus.

The cerebellum receives afferents from (1) mechanoreceptors located in muscles and tendons throughout the body; (2) vestibular receptors located in the ear; (3) motor areas of the cerebral cortex; and (4) the visual and auditory system.

The efferent projections of the cerebellum have mainly two targets. (1) The dentate and interpositus nuclei project to the red nucleus and ventral nucleus of the thalamus. This *dentatorubrothalamic* pathway then continues to the motor areas of the cerebral cor-

Anatomy of the Nervous System

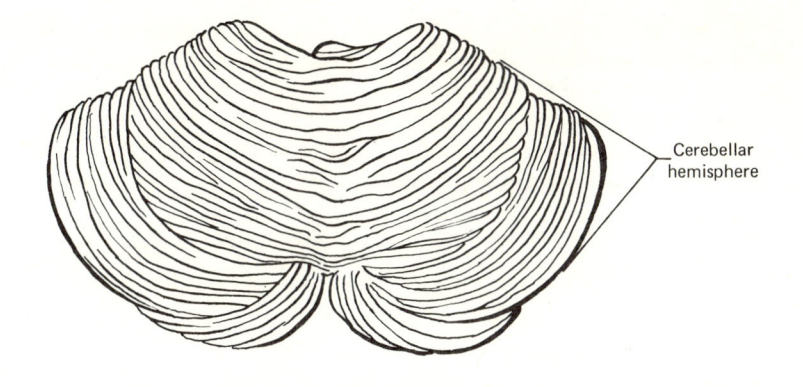

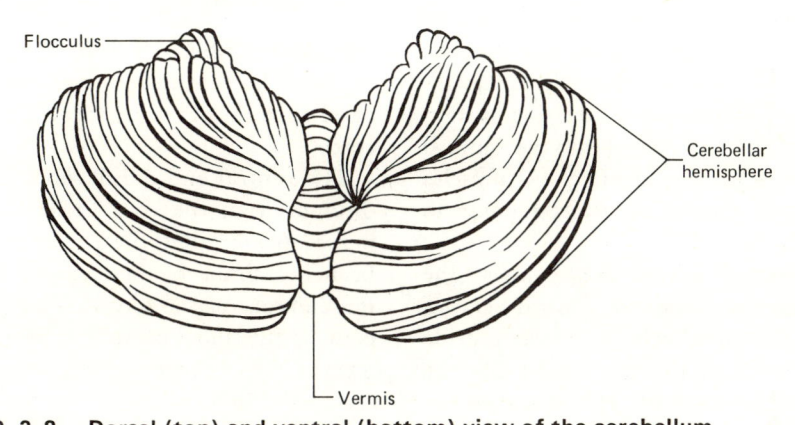

FIG. 3–8. Dorsal (top) and ventral (bottom) view of the cerebellum.
(After *Human anatomy and physiology* by J. E. Crouch and J. R. McClintic. Copyright © 1971. John Wiley & Sons, Inc.)

tex. (2) The fastigial nuclei project to the vestibular nuclei, reticular formation, and cranial-nerve motor nuclei of the brainstem.

The cerebellum serves largely as a coordinating center for reflexive or automatic motor responses. Destruction of all or part of the cerebellum does not abolish any particular motor function. Instead, a general impairment occurs that severely affects the execution of complex movements. The impairment is also reflected in a loss of muscle tonus (*hypotonia*) and a tendency to stumble and fall (*ataxia*). A disturbance of equilibrium, tremor, and sudden "fits" are also frequently seen.

The cerebellum receives extensive projections from all sensory systems, and it has been suggested that it might serve as a primitive sensory projection center. Support for this comes from experiments that have demonstrated detailed, somatotopically organized representations of tactile and proprioceptive sensations as well as discrete visual and auditory "projection areas."

Electrical stimulation of the cerebellum may produce movements or facilitate or inhibit movements elicited by stimulation of the cerebral cortex or by activation of reflex connections.

Summary

The cerebellum consists of four nuclei that are surrounded by highly convoluted cortical tissue. It rides on the dorsal surface of the pons and receives most of its afferent and efferent connections via three big fiber bundles that cover the ventral surface of the pons. The cerebellum receives sensory inputs from most sensory systems but serves mainly to integrate motor functions that are required for the maintenance of postural adjustments.

THE PERIPHERAL NERVOUS SYSTEM

The brain and spinal cord communicate with the organism's environment via nerves that arise or terminate in the central nervous system and project to peripheral sensory receptors and effectors. Sensory receptors are distributed throughout the body. They translate changes in physical energy in the external or internal environment into neural impulses that convey information to the central nervous system. The end product of this integration must, in turn, be transduced into mechanical energy by the peripheral effectors (muscles and glands) to provide an overt reponse to the environment.

The peripheral nerves that connect the receptors and muscles to the central nervous system and to related cellular masses outside the brain and spinal cord make up the peripheral nervous system. It is customary to distinguish *somatosensory*, *somatomotor*, and *autonomic* components. The latter contains both sensory and motor branches.

A distinction is made between the spinal and cranial portions of the peripheral nervous system. Twelve pairs of cranial nerves originate largely from the lower portions of the brainstem, and 31 pairs of segmentally arranged spinal nerves project from the spinal cord. It is customary to group the spinal nerves according to their origin. Beginning at the neck, there are 8 *cervical*, 12 *thoracic*, 5 *lumbar*, 5 *sacral*, and 1 *coccygeal* nerves.

The Spinal Nerves

Each spinal nerve arises from the cord by a *dorsal (afferent) root* and a *ventral (efferent) root* (see Figure 3-9). The dorsal root contains the cells of the afferent fibers. These cells project axons into the spinal cord and receive long

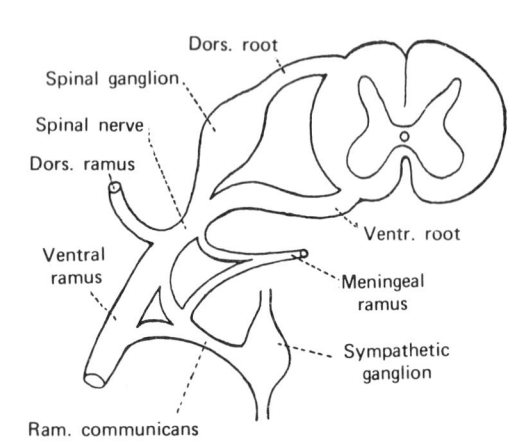

FIG. 3-9. A spinal nerve.
(From *Strong and Elwyn's human neuroanatomy* by R. C. Truex. (4th ed.). Copyright © 1959. The Williams & Wilkins Co., Baltimore.)

"dendritic" processes from peripheral sense organs. The ventral root contains only axons of efferent cells that are located in the spinal cord.

The ventral and dorsal roots unite a short distance from the cord to form a common nerve trunk that forms several distinct branches. Some of these supply the skeletal musculature of the limbs and trunk. Others connect the spinal column to the sympathetic ganglia, which form a chain along the upper sections of the cord.

Peripheral Termination of Sensory Nerves

The afferent components of spinal nerves (i.e., the long "dendritic" process of cells in the dorsal root ganglion) terminate near the external or internal surfaces of the organism and form receptor mechanisms that specialize in the transduction of particular types of physical energy into neural signals. A structural distinction is commonly made between *free nerve endings* and *encapsulated nerve endings*.

Free nerve endings are formed when a poorly myelinated fiber approaches a cutaneous surface. The myelin sheath is then completely lost and the fiber develops terminal arborizations that serve receptor functions. Such receptors are found primarily in the skin and muscles. They appear to be preferentially sensitive to light touch, deep pressure, or pain.

Encapsulated nerve endings are found in many shapes and sizes. All consist essentially of a free nerve ending that invades a capsule of epithelial or muscle tissue. These special receptor structures aid in the transduction of physical energy into the biochemical events that initiate a nerve impulse.

A typical example of an encapsulated receptor is the *Pacinian corpuscle*. It consists of a free nerve ending that is surrounded by a thick, laminated capsule. This pressure receptor is found primarily in ligaments, joint capsules, internal organs, and the wall of the viscera.

Peripheral Termination of Motor Nerves

The motor fibers of spinal nerves are axons from cells in the anterior and medial portion of the spinal cord. Some of these give rise to large (10 to 15 micron diameter) *alpha* fibers which project to skeletal muscle fibers. Others project smaller (4 to 5 micron) fibers to intrafusal muscle fibers of the muscle spindle. These *gamma efferents* represent the efferent link of reflex connections that are responsible for muscle tone and posture.

Motor fibers terminate in grapelike arborizations on distinct elevations (called *end plates*) that develop on the surface of skeletal muscle fibers. The nerve and its coverings are not continuous with the muscle fiber but form a synaptic relationship at the *myoneural junction*. Impulses are transmitted across the gap that separates the neuron from the muscle by means of a chemical transmitter that is liberated from the neuron.

Degeneration and Regeneration of Peripheral Nerves

When a peripheral nerve is sectioned some distance from the cell body, the soma of the cell undergoes a series of changes. The cell eventually regenerates an axonal process that tends to grow in the direction of the organ previously innervated. The severed axon stump distal to the cut degenerates, leaving behind tubules and scar tissue to guide the regenerating axon terminal to the appropriate organ. These regenerative processes have not been demonstrated in the central nervous system.

The Cranial Nerves

The Olfactory System

The primary olfactory receptors are located in the olfactory membrane. A projection from these receptors, the *olfactory rods*, extends to the surface of the olfactory epithelium. The axons of the olfactory receptors join the *olfactory* (first cranial) nerve and enter the olfactory bulb. Here, they synapse with secondary neurons that project axons into the olfactory tracts. Some cells in the olfactory bulb form a feedback loop that acts as an amplification mechanism for olfactory impulses.

The olfactory tracts divide into lateral and medial branches. The medial branch projects to the septal area and the subcallosal gyrus, as well as to the contralateral anterior olfactory nucleus. The lateral branch projects to the prepyriform cortex of the temporal lobe and to the corticomedial nuclei of the amygdala.

The Visual System

The primary visual receptors, the *rods* and *cones*, are located in the *retina* of the eye. The retina has three major layers of cells. The innermost layer, which is farthest from the light, contains the photosensitive elements. It is separated from the inner lining of the eye (the *sclera*) by a densely pigmented *chorioidal* layer.

The two types of visual receptors are nonrandomly distributed in the retina. Cones, which are responsible for the perception of color and fine detail, are densely packed in the central portion of the eye, the *fovea centralis*. Rods, which are responsible for night vision, are not found in this part of the eye. They begin to occur in the perifoveal regions and increase in number and relative density toward the periphery of the retina. The number of cones decreases proportionately.

A human eye contains approximately 6.5 million cones and about 110 to 130 million rods. Groups of rods project to a single bipolar cell. Peripherally located cones may share a bipolar cell or project to bipolar cells that also receive terminal arborizations from rods. The cones in the foveal area establish typically a 1:1 relationship with the second-order elements in the visual pathways.

Bipolar cells communicate with *ganglion cells*, which either continue a private line to the central nervous system or connect with a number of bipolar cells (typically those that have already collected information from several receptor cells). Fibers from these ganglion cells make up the *optic* (second cranial) nerve. The human optic nerve contains roughly one million fibers, which are topographically organized according to their point of origin.

At the optic chiasma a partial decussation of the optic-nerve fibers takes place. Fibers from the temporal half of the retina remain in the ipsilateral optic tract. Those from the nasal half decussate and enter the contralateral optic tract.

In man, approximately 80 percent of the optic fibers terminate in the *lateral geniculate body* of the thalamus in a pattern that reflects their origin in the retina. The remaining 20 percent project to the superior colliculi and serve as the afferent link of the pupillary light reflex and motor adjustments concerned with eye movements.

The cells of the lateral geniculate nucleus project to the ipsilateral primary visual reception area of the occipital cortex. The topographic organization of the visual projections is maintained on the occipital cortex. The visual system thus establishes a point-to-point relationship between specific peripheral receptors and central projection sites. Damage to the visual projections at any stage therefore produces predictable and highly specific losses in visual ability.

The Innervation of the Eye Muscles

The *oculomotor* (third cranial) nerve arises from a V-shaped nucleus in the midbrain. The oculomotor nerve supplies somatic efferents to the ipsilateral *levator* and *superior rectus*, the contralateral *inferior rectus*, both the ipsilateral and the contralateral *internal rectus*, and the *inferior oblique* muscles. Parasympathetic fibers from the Edinger-Westphal nucleus accompany the oculomotor nerve to the *ciliary* ganglion for synapses with cells projecting to the sphincter muscles of the iris.

The *trochlear* (fourth cranial) nerve contains somatic efferent fibers from cells in the ventral portion of the midbrain. The trochlear nerve innervates the contralateral *superior oblique* muscles of the eye.

The *abducens* (sixth cranial) nerve arises from nuclei located below the floor of the fourth ventricle in the caudal third of the pons. It supplies the *external rectus* muscle of the eye.

These oculomotor nerves also contain somatic afferent components that arise from muscle spindles in the ocular muscles. These spindle afferents carry proprioceptive information that is important in the voluntary control of eye movement and position.

The Trigeminal Nerve

The trigeminal nerve supplies somatic afferents and efferents to the skin and mucous membranes of the head. It has three distinct divisions, called the *ophthalmic, maxillary*, and *mandibular* nerves. All three emerge from the *Gasserian* or *semilunar ganglion*.

The ophthalmic nerve contains afferents from the skin of the head and sympathetic fibers from the tear gland. The maxillary division innervates the skin of the face below and lateral to the eyes and nose, the mucous membranes of some sinuses, the nasal cavity, and the upper teeth and gums. The mandibular division supplies afferents to the dura, the anterior two thirds of the tongue, the lower teeth and gums, the skin of the lower face and anterior ear, and the parotid, submaxillary, and sublingual glands. Its motor components supply muscles in the face.

The motor fibers of the trigeminal nerve originate in a nucleus located in the medial third of the pons. The sensory nuclei of the trigeminal nerve extend from the upper spinal cord to upper pontine segments of the brainstem.

The Facial Nerve

The facial nerve contains afferents from taste receptors of some sections of the mouth, cutaneous impulses from portions of the ear, impulses from nasal membranes, and proprioceptive impulses from facial muscles. Its efferent components innervate muscles of the face, scalp, and ear as well as several parasympathetic ganglia that supply the submaxillary, sublingual, and lacrimal glands.

The motor components of the facial nerve arise from a nucleus in the pontine tegmentum. They accompany the *auditory* (eighth cranial) nerve to the internal auditory meatus. The sensory fibers of the facial nerve arise from the *geniculate ganglion*, which lies near the auditory meatus.

The Auditory and Vestibular Systems

THE COCHLEAR DIVISION OF THE EIGHTH CRANIAL NERVE

The primary auditory neurons are located in the *spiral ganglion*. Dendritic processes from these cells terminate on hair cells in the cochlea. Deformation of these hair cells by vibration represents the primary auditory stimulus. Axons from cells in the spiral ganglion form the cochlear division of the auditory nerve. This nerve enters the medulla and terminates in the *ventral* and *dorsal cochlear nuclei*. Secondary fibers from these nuclei ascend in the brainstem in three distinct bundles. These secondary auditory fibers decussate and terminate in (1) the *nucleus of the trapezoid body*, (2) the *superior olivary nucleus*, (3) the *reticular formation*, (4) the *nuclei of the lateral lemniscus*, or (5) the *inferior colliculus*. Tertiary auditory projections from the superior olive and the trapezoid nucleus terminate in the inferior colliculus or pass directly to the *medial geniculate body* of the thalamus. The inferior colliculus relays auditory impulses to the medial geniculate.

The majority of the cells in the medial geniculate project to the primary auditory projection cortex of the temporal lobe. Some degree of tonotopic organization of the auditory projection system is maintained throughout its complex pathways.

THE VESTIBULAR DIVISION OF THE EIGHTH CRANIAL NERVE

The primary neurons of the vestibular branch of the eighth cranial nerve are located in the *ganglion of Scarpa* deep in the internal auditory meatus. Dendritic processes of these bipolar neurons terminate about hair cells in the *maculae sacculi* and *cristae*, complex receptor organs in the inner ear.

Axons from neurons in the vestibular ganglion of Scarpa form the vestibular branch of the auditory nerve. Most fibers of the vestibular nerve terminate in the vestibular nuclei of the brainstem. Some fibers project directly to the cerebellum.

Vestibular impulses are distributed to (1) the spinal cord, (2) the cerebellum, (3) the reticular formation of the brainstem, and (4) the oculomotor nuclei, and more indirectly to (1) some thalamic nuclei, (2) the superior temporal lobe, and (3) the premotor areas of the frontal lobe.

The Glossopharyngeal Nerve

The *sensory components* of the ninth cranial nerve innervate the taste buds on the posterior third of the tongue. These taste fibers synapse centrally with cells in the nucleus of the tractus solitarius, which projects secondary fibers to the posteromedial ventral nucleus of the thalamus. The glossopharyngeal nerve also carries impulses from cutaneous receptors in part of the ear and pain and tactile impulses from the posterior third of the tongue. The motor fibers of the glossopharyngeal nerve arise from the bulbar tegmentum and innervate the pharynx.

The Vagus Nerve

The tenth cranial nerve is a large, mixed nerve that innervates many structures. It gives rise to the following major branches: (1) *laryngeal*, (2) *cardiac*, (3) *bronchial*, (4) *pulmonary*, (5) *esophageal*, (6) *abdominal*, and (7) *pericardiac* nerves.

Its afferent components arise from cells in the lower medulla. Its somatic efferents arise from the tegmentum.

The Spinal Accessory Nerve

The eleventh cranial nerve contains (1) parasympathetic fibers that join the distribution system of the vagus and (2) somatomotor fibers that innervate the pharynx. Spinal components of this nerve innervate the musculature of the neck.

The Hypoglossal Nerve

The hypoglossal nerve is primarily a motor nerve that innervates the tongue. Its fibers arise from the floor of the fourth ventricle. Afferents from proprioceptors in the tongue also use this pathway.

Summary

The peripheral nervous system has two major components, the spinal division and the cranial division. Between each segment of the spine, a sensory nerve enters via two symmetrical dorsal roots and a motor nerve leaves via two symmetrical ventral roots. A short distance from the cord, the sensory and motor nerves of each side of the cord join to form a peripheral nerve. This nerve may divide and subdivide many times but generally innervates only a specific portion of the body. The afferent (i.e., sensory) components of sensory nerves form receptor mechanisms in the skin, the muscles, or in tendons that relay information about temperature, pain, touch, or pressure. The efferent components of peripheral nerves synapse with muscles or glandular tissue.

The cranial division of the peripheral nervous system consists of 12 pairs of cranial nerves, most of which issue from the lower portions of the brainstem. Some of these nerves are pure sensory nerves (i.e., the olfactory, visual, and auditory/vestibular nerves). Others are primarily motor (i.e., the oculomotor, trochlear, and abducens nerves). The majority contain both sensory and motor fibers. The cranial nerves are often associated with very complex and specialized receptor mechanisms that are selectively sensitive to only a few types of stimuli.

THE AUTONOMIC NERVOUS SYSTEM (*see Figure 3-10*)

Those aspects of the peripheral and central nervous system that are concerned with the regulation of visceral functions comprise the *autonomic* nervous system (ANS).

The central representations of the autonomic nervous system are closely intermingled with the somatic aspects of the brain and spinal cord, although some central autonomic pathways and nuclei have been demonstrated. The peripheral components of the autonomic nervous system are anatomically, physiologically, and to some extent pharmacologically distinct from the somatic nervous system.

Gross Anatomy

The peripheral autonomic nervous system consists of a *sympathetic* and a *parasympathetic* division. The primary motor neurons of both branches are located inside the central nervous system and project to peripheral *ganglia*.

Three types of autonomic ganglia have been described. The *vertebral ganglia* form a chain along the ventrolateral surface of the spinal cord. *Collateral ganglia* surround the major visceral arteries. *Terminal ganglia* are widely distributed throughout the viscera, usually within a short distance of the structures that receive the postganglionic efferents.

The preganglionic fibers of the sympathetic nervous system project through the ventral roots of all thoracic and upper two lumbar nerves and reach the vertebral ganglia.

The parasympathetic division contains two anatomically distinct sections. The cranial portion consists of visceral motor fibers from some of the cranial nerves. It projects to autonomic ganglia in the head, heart, lungs, and stomach. The sacral portion contains visceral efferents from lower parts of the spinal cord and projects directly to the pelvic viscera.

Most visceral structures receive both sympathetic and parasympathetic innervation. The two divisions of the autonomic nervous system often act antagonistically, and a delicate balance of opposing sympathetic and parasympathetic influences exists in many visceral functions.

The Sympathetic Division

The preganglionic axons of visceromotor cells from upper portions of the spinal cord project to the vertebral ganglia. The preganglionic fibers may (1) synapse on secondary (post-

Anatomy of the Nervous System 57

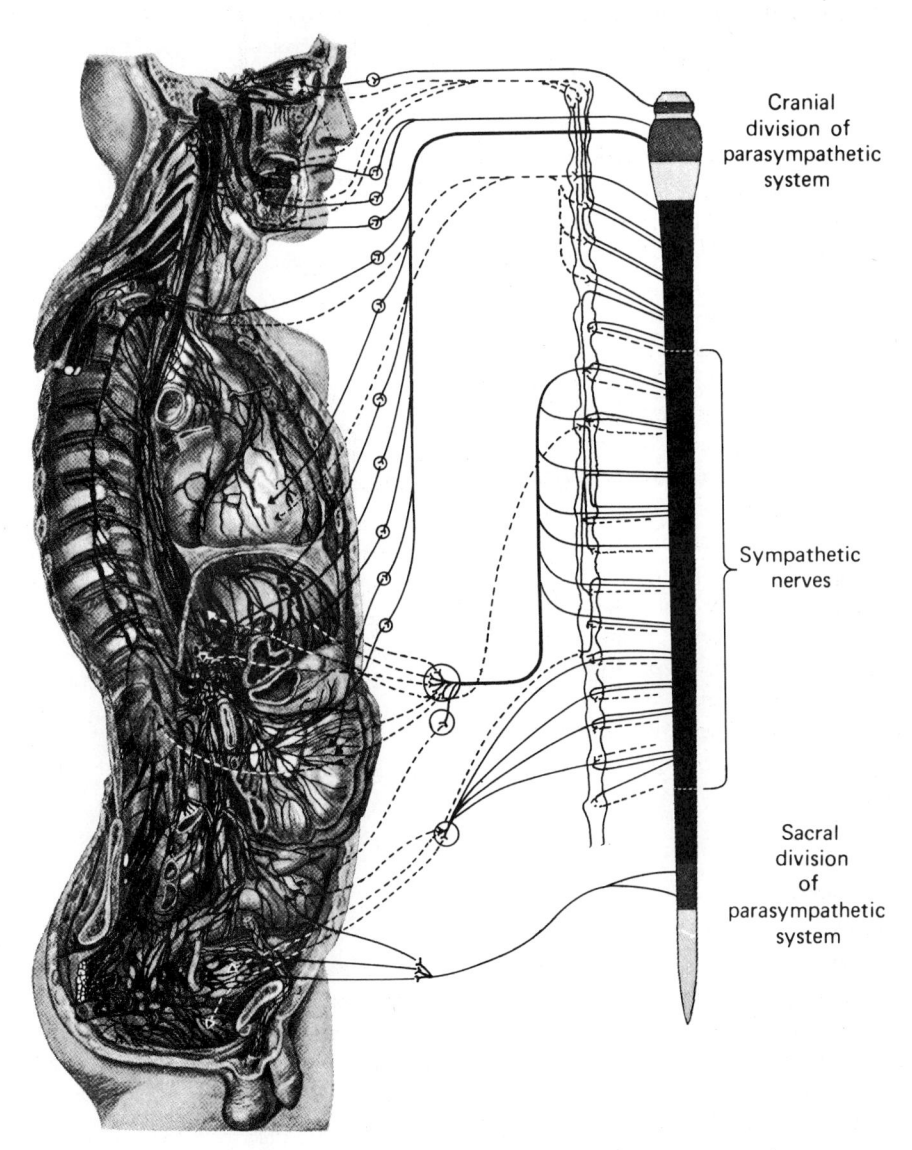

FIG. 3-10. Diagram of the peripheral terminations of the autonomic nervous system.

(After *Atlas of human anatomy. Vol. II* by M. W. Woerdeman. Copyright © 1950. McGraw-Hill Book Company. Used with permission of McGraw-Hill Book Company.)

ganglionic) motor cells either within the ganglion of entry or in higher or lower segments of the chain, or (2) form the splanchnic nerves. The cells of the vertebral ganglia project postganglionic motor fibers to all spinal nerves. These fibers innervate blood vessels and glands of the walls of the viscera.

The synaptic transmission of impulses from preganglionic fibers to postganglionic cells is based on the liberation of the neurohumor *acetylcholine*; the system is thus cholinergic. However, the transmission of impulses at the junction between postganglionic fibers and smooth or cardiac muscle and glands occurs via the release of *norepinephrine* (or *noradrenaline*); that is, the system is *adrenergic*.

The Parasympathetic Divisions

The cells of the craniosacral or parasympathetic division project axons directly to *terminal ganglia* located near the structure to be innervated. Most parasympathetic fibers in the cranial division join the vagus (tenth cranial) nerve and are distributed to ganglia near the pharynx and larynx, the lungs, heart, esophagus, stomach, and the lower intestine. Postganglionic fibers from these relay stations reach terminal ganglia in the heart and bronchial musculature, the walls of the stomach and lower gastrointestinal tract, and the liver, pancreas, and kidney.

The *sacral outflow* of the parasympathetic division consists mainly of preganglionic fibers that leave the lower segments of the spinal cord and form the *pelvic nerve*. They end in terminal ganglia in the colon and rectum. From there, postganglionic fibers project to the accessory generative organs, the bladder, the colon, and the rectum.

The transmission of impulses at the parasympathetic neuroeffector junction as well as at ganglionic synapses occurs via the release of acetylcholine.

Sensory Aspects

The sensory components of the sympathetic nerves originate in the dorsal root ganglia of the thoracic and upper lumbar segments of the cord. These fibers carry signals from pressure and pain receptors in the chest and abdominal viscera.

The vagus contains afferents from cells that carry sensory information from the heart, lungs, and abdominal viscera. The sacral division of the parasympathetic nervous system contains visceral afferents from sensory receptors in the bladder, rectum, and genital organs.

Central Integration

The hypothalamus is considered to be the "head ganglion" of the autonomic nervous system. Stimulation in the anterior hypothalamus and preoptic area tends to excite the parasympathetic division (contraction of the bladder, a fall in blood pressure, pupillary constriction, cardiac slowing or arrest, increased secretion of gastric juices, and increased motility of the stomach and intestine). Stimulation of the posterior hypothalamus generally produces sympathetic reactions (pupillary dilation, increased blood pressure, inhibition of gastric secretion and motility, etc.).

Autonomic responses have also been elicited by stimulation of a number of cortical regions, and evoked potentials have been recorded from many cortical sites following stimulation of interoceptors. These cortical autonomic projections are particularly numerous in some parts of the frontal lobe and in the rhinencephalon. The extensive and diffuse cortical representation of visceral functions in the rhinencephalon has given rise to the term *visceral brain* to describe this part of the cortex.

Autonomic responses are also integrated at lower levels of the brainstem and the cerebellum. Stimulation of the cerebellar nuclei produces such autonomic responses as pupillary dilatation and changes in the muscular tension of intestinal structures. Vasomotor responses appear to be at least partly regulated by "centers" in the lower medulla.

Functional Considerations

The autonomic nervous system permits the organism to adjust to changes in the internal environment. Since these alterations of the *milieu interne* are often the direct result of changes in the external environment, the autonomic nervous system cannot function in isolation.

The following are examples of increased parasympathetic functions: (1) pupillary constriction (myosis) and accommodation of optic muscles; (2) increased secretion of the submaxillary, sublingual, and lacrimal glands; (3) inhibition of cardiac functions and coronary vasoconstriction; (4) constriction of bronchial musculature; (5) increased peristalsis of the digestive tract and increased secretion of hydrochloric acid in the stomach; (6) inhibition of anal and vesicle (urinary) sphincter muscles; and (7) vasodilation of cutaneous vessels.

Excitation of sympathetic functions results in (1) dilatation of the pupils (mydriasis); (2) increase in salivary- and lacrimal-gland secretions; (3) acceleration of cardiac activity and coronary vasodilatation; (4) dilatation of the bronchi; (5) inhibition of peristalsis and vasoconstriction of intestinal blood vessels; (6) contraction of anal and internal (renal) sphincters; and (7) vasoconstriction, excitation of pilomotor muscles, and secretion of sweat glands.

Dysfunctions of the autonomic nervous system are related to many clinical disorders. *Angina pectoris*, a cardiac condition that ranks among the most frequent causes of death in the United States, appears to be intimately related to excessive vasoconstriction of the coronary arteries. *Peptic ulcer*, another common affliction of modern man, is related to an oversecretion of hydrochloric acid and abnormal gastric motility.

Drugs that stimulate, mimic, or enhance the activity of the two divisions of the autonomic nervous system are called *sympathomimetic* or *parasympathomimetic* drugs. Substances that block the transmission of impulses in the autonomic nervous system are called *sympatholytic* (or *adrenolytic*) and *parasympatholytic* (or *cholinolytic*) drugs.

SUMMARY

The viscera are innervated by the autonomic nervous system. In the periphery, two pharmacologically as well as anatomically distinct motor components of the ANS are often distinguished: the sympathetic division arises from upper portions of the spinal cord and synapses in vertebral ganglia. Postganglionic fibers from these ganglia form adrenergic neuroeffector junctions. The parasympathetic division arises from lower portions of the spine and from the brainstem and projects directly to terminal ganglia located near the structure to be innervated. Both the pre- and postganglionic synapses in this system are cholinergic.

Both divisions of the ANS have sensory components that carry pressure and pain sensations from visceral receptors. These sensory fibers reach the spinal cord via somatosensory nerves and continue to travel along the major sensory projections in the CNS. The central representations of the ANS are mainly in the hypothalamus and in portions of the limbic system.

Most viscera receive both sympathetic and parasympathetic innervation. Often the two exert opposing influences and one can consider many visceral functions the result of an equilibration of sympathetic and parasympathetic influences.

Bibliography

1. Brodmann, K. Physiologie des Gehirns. In *Die Allgemeine Chirurgie der Gehirnkrankheiten, Neue Deutsche Chirurgie.* Stuttgart: F. Enke, 1914.
2. Crouch, J. E., & McClintic, J. R. *Human Anatomy and Physiology.* New York: Wiley, 1971.
3. Gardner, E. *Fundamentals of Neurology* (5th ed.). Philadelphia: Saunders, 1968.
4. Gray, H. Peripheral nervous system. In *Anatomy of the Human Body* (27th ed.). C. M. Goss, Ed. Philadelphia: Lea and Febiger, 1959.
5. Peele, T. L. *The Neuroanatomic Basis for Clinical Neurology* (2nd ed.). New York: The Blakiston Division, McGraw-Hill, 1961.
6. Sobotta, J. In *Sobotta-Figge Atlas of Human Anatomy. Vol. III* (8th English ed.). F. H. J. Figge, Ed. New York: Hafner, 1963.
7. Truex, R. C. *Strong and Elwyn's Human Neuroanatomy* (4th ed.). Baltimore: Williams and Wilkins, 1959.
8. Woerdeman, M. W. *Atlas of Human Anatomy. Vol. II.* Philadelphia: Blakiston, 1950.

SECTION 2

The Input and Output Channels of the Organism

To survive in a nonhomogeneous, constantly changing environment, an organism must develop sensors that selectively respond to changes in specific physicochemical aspects of the environment. In higher animals, these sensory mechanisms have become enormously complicated and require integration by several central agencies. We cannot, in the scope of this book, discuss the details of the physical and chemical transformations that are responsible for receptor functions, the exquisite complexity of the coding of the related events, or the resulting perceptual phenomena. It is, however, necessary to acquire an understanding of the principal mechanisms responsible for the transformation of physical energies into corresponding neural signals and of the subsequent processing of sensory information in the central nervous system. The first three chapters of this section of the book describe the input channels of four of the specialized senses that influence man's behavior.

Once the sensory input to the central nervous system has been integrated, related to the activity of motivational mechanisms (see Section 3), and compared with the organism's memory stores (see Section 4), it is often necessary that an overt reaction of the organism be initiated. The remaining chapters of Section 2 describe some of the output channels which mediate these reactions to sensory input.

Chapter 4

VISION

The Visual Stimulus

Transduction of Physical Energy into Physiological Signals

Transfer and Processing of Visual Information in the Central Nervous System

Review

THE VISUAL STIMULUS

All biological organisms respond in some fashion to light. One-celled organisms have light-sensitive spots that permit them to avoid potentially harmful intense light or seek moderate levels of illumination that can be used in the manufacture of energy. More complex, multicellular animals develop specialized photoreceptors. These cells can discriminate between such fine intensity differences that the world becomes an environment of objects; these receptors may also distinguish between the wavelengths of the visible radiations and thus detect what we have come to call color. Many such photoreceptors feed information into complex neural networks that interpret the constantly changing barrage of light stimuli in terms of objects, movements, or color.

Visual perception, whether simple or complex, is the result of an interaction between light and a specialized receptor surface. To understand how visual perceptions come about, we must start by asking: "What is light?" The answer, surprisingly, is far from simple.

Is Light Corpuscular or Continuous?

Light has many properties that suggest that it is composed of individual particles. It also has many properties that are not compatible with such a view and suggest, instead, that light occurs in a continuous, wavelike form. Throughout the history of the physical sciences, this apparent paradox has been the subject of much debate. Strong support for the wave theory of light derived from an experiment that the British physician, Thomas Young, set up many centuries ago. Young argued that two bands of light should interact if they indeed consisted of consecutive and continuous waves. If the light of the two bands was of the same frequency and they met such that the peaks and troughs of their waves coincided, the resulting light should be brighter. If, on the other hand, the two bands of light could be made to meet out of phase, such that the peaks of one wave coincided with the troughs of the other, their effects should cancel and there should be no light. To test this prediction, Young placed a light in front of an opaque screen into which two small slits had been cut. According to his theory, the wave of light from the single source should arrive at the two equidistant slits at exactly the same time. The slits should then split the wave into two new waves that should be perfectly in step with each other. The waves should then spread (i.e., *diffract*) on the other side of the screen and meet at a point exactly halfway between the slits. Here, the two waves should be precisely in phase and thus produce a band of very bright light. On either side of that band, the two waves should be progressively out of phase and tend to cancel. The results should be a pattern of alternating bright and dark bands (now called an *interference pattern*), and that is exactly what Young's experiments demonstrated.

The wave theory of light was further supported when it was discovered that its assumptions could explain the curious behavior of light that is passed through certain crystals. When two crystals with a particular molecular structure are placed end to end, light will pass unimpeded as long as the relationship between the two is optimal. When one of the crystals is rotated slowly, the passage of light decreases until, at one point, it is completely blocked. This *polarization* phenomenon is related to the fact that the molecular structure of the crystals reduces the three-dimensional vibration of light into a two-dimensional pattern. As long as many such horizontal wave patterns are available, this has little effect on the passage of light. However, when the second crystal is placed such that its structure permits passage of only those wave patterns that vibrate perpendicular to those passed by the first crystal, the passage of light is completely obstructed. Intermediate positions of the second crystal reduce the intensity of light by selectively refusing passage to light that vibrates in certain planes. This has made possible the development of glare-reducing "polarizing" sunglasses that selectively filter out the predominantly horizontal waves that are reflected from horizontal surfaces such as snow or water.

The most compelling argument for a corpuscular theory of light derived from the observation that light that strikes a metal surface dislodges discrete particles, called electrons, and thus changes the electrical charge of the metal. This *photoelectric* phenomenon turns out to have some interesting properties that a wave theory of light cannot explain. One of these is the fact that the *number* of electrons ejected per second is proportional to the intensity of the light radiation, but the *energy* of the displaced particles is determined by its wavelength. Around the turn of the century, Albert Einstein suggested that this phenomenon could be explained only if one assumed that light consisted of discrete particles, later called *photons*, whose energy is inversely proportional to wavelength. Complex experiments have since then demonstrated that photons have momentum (and therefore mass) and that many interactions between light and matter can only be explained when one treats them in terms of discrete quanta of light.

Yet, such an interpretation cannot account for various other phenomena such as interference patterns and diffraction, necessitating the assumption that light (as well as other forms of electromagnetic radiation) can be propagated in wave form but is constituted of discrete particles of energy. Some behavior of light is best understood when we consider its periodicity; others make sense only when we consider individual photons.

Some Basic Properties of Light

Photoreceptors are selectively sensitive to radiant energy, which is transmitted in sinusoidal waves. Radiant energy is transmitted by a broad range of frequencies, but the eyes of man and other vertebrates respond only to a very narrow band that extends from roughly 400 to 700 nanometers (nm) and includes only a tiny sliver of the radiant energies that surround us (see Figure 4–1). The amplitude of these waves is related to the intensity of the visual sensation, but the relationship is a complex one, partly because the photoreceptors adapt rapidly to constant illumination. The eyes of man and some other vertebrates contain several types of photoreceptors that are differentially sensitive to particular portions of the visible spectrum of radiant energies. The most ubiquitous of these is sensitive to all frequencies of radiation within the visible spectrum and mediates scotopic (i.e., black/white) visual sensations. Other photoreceptors respond preferentially to narrow bands of frequencies with sensitivity maxima that are typically near 440 nm (blue); 510 nm (green); and 600 nm (yellow-red). These receptors mediate photopic (i.e., color) sensations. The frequency of radiant energy thus becomes the determinant of color.

The philosophers of ancient Greece discovered one of the most important properties of light: it always travels in a straight line and bounces off most surfaces, thereby giving uneven surfaces of three-dimensional objects a peculiar pattern of *reflection*. The pattern of these reflections is predictable because the reflection of light always follows the simple rule that the angle of reflection equals the angle of incidence. This is a most useful fact because it permits identification of familiar objects.

Most surfaces are not perfect reflectors but instead *absorb* a certain amount of the light that strikes them. At the point where light enters a new medium, its speed and direction change. In a vacuum, light travels at about 186,000 miles per second. It is almost as fast in our atmosphere but slows down a great deal when it strikes water or other media such as glass. The extent of the directional change that occurs when light travels from one medium into another (i.e., the degree of bending or *refraction*) is determined by the speed of light in the two media. This "law of refraction" is the basis of many optical instruments that use lenses to direct light toward or away from a particular point.

To act as a stimulus to biological photoreceptors, light must have a minimal duration.

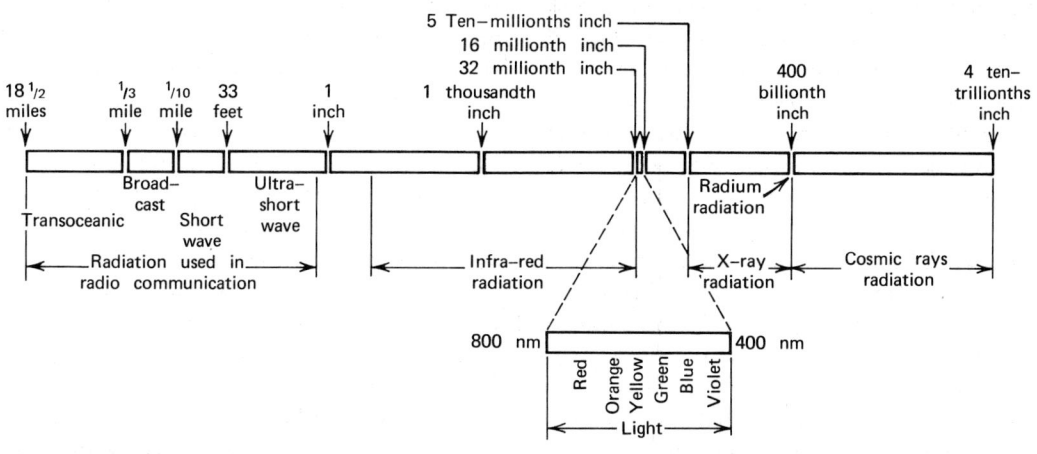

FIG. 4–1. Electromagnetic spectrum, showing the range of wavelengths that stimulate the visual receptors (light).

(From F. L. Dimmick. Color. In *Foundations of psychology*. E. G. Boring, H. S. Langfeld, & H. P. Weld, Eds. Copyright © 1948. John Wiley & Sons, Inc.)

The absolute threshold is usually in the order of milliseconds, but very intense light may be visible even when it is presented only for a few microseconds. Once this threshold is attained, the magnitude of the receptor's response is determined by the intensity of retinal illumination. However, the present state and recent history of the photoreceptor must be considered in this context. All photoreceptors show *adaptation* to the ambient level of illumination and thus change their absolute thresholds. Moreover, photoreceptors are often interrelated such that the effect of a visual stimulus to even a very small portion of the visual field can be influenced by the distribution of radiant energy in adjacent portions of the retinate. This *simultaneous contrast* phenomenon may cause facilitatory (i.e., summation) effects, particularly when approximately equal light sources project to adjacent portions of the retina. It may also produce inhibitory interactions, particularly when a very intense stimulus falls on a portion of the retina that is immediately adjacent to that illuminated by a weak stimulus.

Determinants of Color

Sir Isaac Newton discovered a long time ago that white sunlight is, in fact, composed of a spectrum of colors starting with red and passing through orange, yellow, green, blue, and violet. The simplest way to convince yourself of this surprising fact is to repeat Newton's experiment: if you pass a beam of light through a prism and project the emerging light onto a blank panel, the individual colors will become clearly visible (see Figure 4–2). We have learned, more recently, that the spectrum of light that is visible to man and most mammals covers only a tiny sliver (about 400 to 700 nm) of the broad range of radiant energies that surround us. In man, frequencies near the low end of the visible spectrum (i.e., approximately 400 to 490 nm) give rise to sensations of blue; those in the next higher region (490 to 540 nm), green; those in the next higher region (540 to 600 nm), yellow; and those in the upper segment (600 to 700 nm), red. Wavelengths just

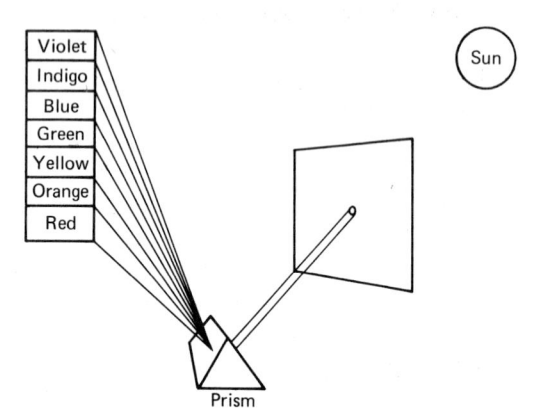

FIG. 4–2. Spectrum, as revealed through use of prism.

below the visible portion of the spectrum are called ultraviolet, those just above it infrared.

Color by Reflection and Diffraction

The only physical stimulus for the perception of color is radiant energy emitted from a primary source or reflected from some surface. Objects do not have color, common sense notwithstanding. They *appear* colorful only because they selectively absorb lights of certain wavelengths and reflect others. A tomato is itself colorless. It appears red because it absorbs all wavelengths below the red portion of the visible spectrum. Pigment molecules in the air, the earth, plants, animals, and all other objects on earth give them their color by selectively absorbing or subtracting certain wavelengths from the spectrum of visible energy. White surfaces reflect all wavelengths about equally and hence appear to be a mixture of all colors. Black surfaces absorb all wavelengths strongly and hence appear to have no color.

But what happens when we mix lights of different wavelengths and project them onto a white surface? Do we see black when we mix a red light of about 700 nm with a green light of 500 nm? The answer, of course, is no. The eye adds the two wavelengths and responds in some fashion to an intermediate value that gives rise to the perception of yellow. In this additive mathematics of colored lights, blue and green add to cyan (blue–green), red and blue to magenta (blue–red), and red and green to yellow. Any three wavelengths from different portions of the spectrum can be mixed to reproduce a variety of colors. Commercial television uses red, green, and blue because combinations of these wavelengths reproduce nearly all colors of the visible spectrum. White, in such an additive system, is the result of concurrent red, green, and blue transmission; black is the result of no transmission at all.

The most colorful objects owe their appearance not so much to their pigment structure but to *diffraction*. Many structures, such as diamonds, differentially slow the passage of certain wavelengths and thus act like a prism. Short violet and blue wavelengths are typically slowed most, the long wavelengths of the red end of the spectrum least. The result is a spreading of the white light into its spectral components and a display of colors. A similar "spreading" can be produced by irregular surfaces that break up a wave into many smaller waves that cross and recross and, by combining or interfering, set up patterns that glow in all colors of the spectrum. Phonograph records, viewed at certain angles, have this property, as does mother-of-pearl.

Color Theories

Just how we respond selectively to radiant energy of different wavelengths is not entirely clear in spite of almost two centuries of heated debate and experimentation. The simplest assumption is that individual receptors respond selectively to particular wavelengths. Such a theory is most unlikely because man can discriminate at least 120 different hues. Even if it were possible to distribute 120 different receptors evenly over the color-sensitive portion of the retina, such an arrangement would not work, since our ability to discriminate detail (i.e., acuity) requires a much finer mosaic of receptors than such a system could provide. These considerations have led to the postulation of theories that, in one way or another, rely on the fact that a mixture of only a few wavelengths can reproduce the entire spectrum of colors.

Thomas Young suggested in 1801 that man might have only three color receptors that are selectively sensitive to the three colors that appear to be "primaries" on a psychological level (i.e., red, yellow, and blue). When it became clear that the laws of light mixtures suggested a different distribution of "primary" wavelengths, Young modified his theory to suggest red, green, and blue (or violet) receptors.

This *trichromatic* theory of color vision was subsequently elaborated by the German physicist and physiologist, von Helmholtz, who proposed that the perception of color could be best explained if one assumed the three color receptors to be sensitive to lights of all wavelengths but preferentially sensitive to one region of the spectrum. This permitted an interpretation of saturation in terms of the relative selectivity of the response of the three receptors. Highly saturated colors were thought to be the result of maximal excitation of only one receptor, accompanied by minimal responses from the other two (hence the saturated appearance of blue, green, and red). Colors of low saturation, such as yellow, owe their pale appearance to submaximal excitation of all three receptors.

The German psychologist, Hering, disagreed with the trichromatic theory of vision because it appeared to contradict common visual experience, which identifies not three but four "primary" colors (blue, green, yellow, and red). Hering also noted that these four colors appeared to be naturally grouped in pairs and consequently seem to complement and oppose each other. Red and green, for instance, do not mix in the same way that green and blue or yellow and red do. A mixture of yellow and blue similarly does not give rise to a simple perception of color, though yellow mixes well with red and blue with green. The same pairing is suggested by an analysis of color afterimages. If one focuses on a patch of colored material and then on a white surface, a negative afterimage of the patch appears that is of the complementary color (a blue patch appears yellow, a red patch green, etc.). A similar phenomenon occurs when one surrounds a gray patch with a green or blue frame. The gray will take on a slightly red appearance if a green frame is used and appear yellow when the frame is blue.

Hering's *opponent-process* theory suggests that we must consider three reactions: red-green, blue-yellow, and black-white. Recent attempts to apply the opponent-process theory rigorously to an explanation of the various phenomena of color vision[47,48] suggest that the eye may contain three or four distinct color receptors that are connected to bipolar and ganglion cells in such a way that pairs are created that oppose each other. Red and green receptors are thought to interact competitively for a common path to the central nervous system, as do yellow and blue (or red-green and blue) receptors.

Color-blind individuals have been examined extensively in the hope that the pattern of their deficits might favor one or the other explanation. People with normal color vision require a mixture of three colors to reproduce all spectral sensations. Color-blind individuals need only one or two. A fair percentage of males cannot differentiate between red and green and are said to be *protanopes* (red blind) or *deuteranopes* (green blind). According to the trichromatic theory, these deficiencies are due to the impairment or absence of red or green receptors—a deceptively simple and elegant explanation until one discovers that the perception of yellow (which should reflect an interaction of the red-green receptors) is entirely normal in many red- or green-blind individuals. The opponent process theory has, of course, no problem explaining this phenomenon since it postulates a separate yellow receptor.

Total color blindness is rare. The few cases on record perceive only white, grey, and black, but show normal spectral luminosity functions. To the extent that differential spectral sensitivity can be assumed to be a characteristic of the black-white system of the opponent-process theory, this presents no trouble for such a theory. The observation is not as easily reconciled with the predictions of a trichromatic theory, which assumes that the perception of white results from the concurrent excitation of all three color receptors. (The objection is not fatal to the theory, since it can be argued that the three receptors are present but incorrectly connected in the monochromat.)

Microelectrode recordings from the visual system generally favor an opponent process interpretation, although the picture is not as clear as one might wish (see below). Slow potentials have been recorded from the retina of some vertebrates that provide support for an opponent-process theory in showing apparently distinct luminosity reactions in addition to red-green and blue-yellow potentials of opposite electrical sign (i.e., B^+Y^-; B^-Y^+; or R^+G^-; R^-G^+). Microelectrode recordings from the ganglion-cell layer of the retina also support the opponent-process theory[86]. Ganglion cells give ON responses selectivity to lights of particular wavelengths and OFF responses to different wavelengths. There is, furthermore, some indication that the OFF responses of the ganglion cells may correspond to the positive component of the graded slow potentials and the ON responses to the negative component. Some cells in the lateral geniculate nucleus of the thalamus increase their activity in response to some wavelengths and decrease it in response to others. In the monkey, these *"spectral opponent"* cells apparently belong to one of four categories: R^+G^-; G^+R^-; Y^+B^-; or B^+Y^-.

Summary and Review Questions

Photoreceptors are sensitive to radiant energies that have a frequency of 400 to 700 nm. The amplitude of these waves is complexly related to the intensity of the visual sensation; their frequency determines the sensation of color in species that have special color receptors.

Many visual phenomena are adequately explained by treating radiant energies as continuous sinusoidal waves. Others require the assumption that these waves are made up of individual quanta of energy that can produce effects on photoreceptors that are independent of the frequency of the radiation.

We can detect objects in our environment by sight because light travels in a straight line and bounces off most surfaces at an angle that is directly proportional to the angle of incidence. This gives each object a unique pattern of reflection that is transmitted to our photoreceptors.

Just as objects do not emit visible radiations but merely reflect them, they also do not have color. They appear colorful only because their pigments selectively absorb radiations of certain frequencies. The object thus differentially reflects some of the energies within the visible spectrum. Precisely how different wavelengths are translated into different color sensations is not yet clear. We almost certainly do not have a specific receptor for each identifiable color. Instead, it appears probable that different color sensations are related to the differential pattern of activation of a few color receptors. The trichromatic theory proposes that all color sensations result from the activation of three color receptors that are maximally sensitive to wavelengths in the blue, green, and red portions of the spectrum. The opponent-process theory suggests that color sensations may be related to competitive interactions within two pairs of color receptors, one maximally sensitive to blue and yellow, the other to red and green.

1. Describe some of the evidence that favors interpretation of light in terms of continuous waves (as opposed to discrete quanta of energy).
2. What happens when radiant energies of the visible spectrum strike an object?
3. What happens when one mixes lights of different colors and projects them onto a white surface?
4. Briefly describe the trichromatic and opponent-process theories of color vision.

TRANSDUCTION OF PHYSICAL ENERGY INTO PHYSIOLOGICAL SIGNALS

The Biological Photoreceptor

The Greek philosophers had the curious notion that man's perception of visual objects was the result of light rays that emerged from his eyes, touched the object, and illuminated it. Aristotle's objection that things should then be equally visible at night was ignored until the 17th century, when a German Jesuit peeled the outer coatings from a freshly slaughtered animal's eye and demonstrated the reflections of the environment on the retina. Since that time, it has become clear that the eye is merely a device that collects reflections from objects and reproduces them, more or less faithfully, on an inner screen that is composed of light-sensitive receptor cells.

A Variety of Eyes

Eyes come in an amazing variety. Some primitive organisms have "*eyespots*" that may be distributed all over the external surface of the animal. Others, such as insects and many marine animals, have developed more complex *compound eyes*, which are made up of many hundreds and sometimes thousands of compartments that are equipped with a fixed lens at the outer end that focuses impinging light rays onto the photoreceptors that are located at the other, inner end of the tube. Since the lenses of compound eyes cannot change focus, sharp images of objects are not possible. Such eyes are, however, efficient movement detectors and are therefore commonly found in predatory animals. Vertebrates, such as fish, birds, and mammals, have still more complicated eyes that contain adjustable lenses and, often, a variety of photoreceptors that selectively respond to particular aspects of radiant energy.

THE HUMAN EYE

The human eye is a complex device (see Figure 4–3). Its outermost, transparent covering, the *cornea*, is a refractive surface and hence part of the focusing apparatus. Behind it is a clear fluid that has similar refractive properties and merely guides the incoming light to an opening in the next structure, the *iris*. The iris governs the amount of light permitted to enter the eye by changing the size of its central circular opening, the *pupil*. After passage through the pupil, light enters a complex lens that changes its characteristics to assure the transmission of a sharply focused image on the retinal layers of the eye.

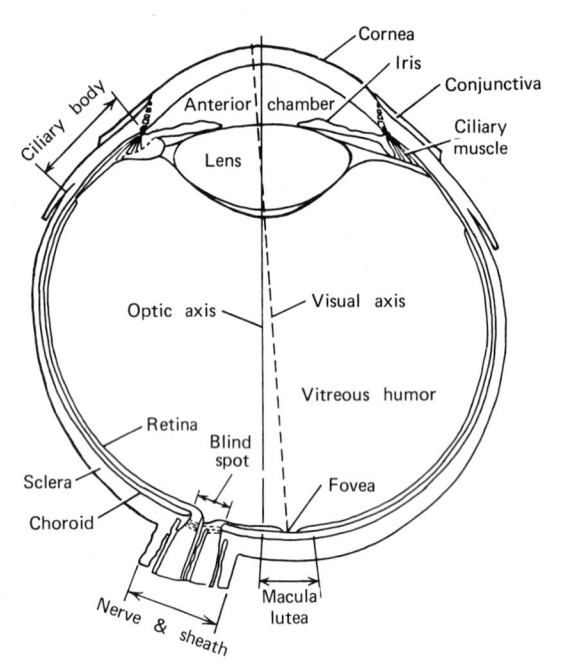

FIG. 4–3. Horizontal section of the right human eye.

(After *The vertebrate eye and its adaptive radiation* by G. L. Walls. Cranbrook Institute of Science, 1942. As modified from M. Salzmann. *The anatomy and physiology of the human eyeball in the normal state.* University of Chicago Press, 1912.)

The percentage of the available light that is admitted to the inner eye is determined entirely by the muscles that control the size of the pupil. In very bright sunlight, the pupillary opening may be no larger than the head of a pin; in the dark it opens to admit as much light as possible and may reach the diameter of a pencil. The size of the pupil is also determined by mechanisms that are concerned with the sharpness of the eye's reproduction of the environment. A reduction in pupillary size increases the sharpness of the retinal image, and any attempt to discern detail in a small picture consequently produces pupillary constriction.

The lens of the human eye is made up of over 2000 fine layers, each of which refracts the light by a minute amount. The lens focuses images on the receptor surface of the retina by changing its overall shape. Objects that are very close to the eye reflect widely divergent light rays, which initiate a reflex to contract the muscles of the eye. This increases the curvature of the lens and produces greater refraction, thereby increasing the concentration of light on the retina. Light from distant sources, on the other hand, produces closely parallel radiations that do not require extensive diffraction to produce a sharp retinal image. Visuomotor reflexes respond to such parallel radiations and flatten the lens, thus reducing its bending power. The muscular reaction that adjusts the lens to light from near and far objects is called *accommodation*.

After an image has been focused by the lens, it passes through the gelatinous substance that makes up most of the inner eye. Since this fluid normally has a refractive index very much like that of the eye's lens, the retinal image is not significantly altered by this process.

The back of the eye is formed by three layers. The outermost *sclera* is a tough, protective layer of cells. The intermediate *choroid* layer contains blood vessels and serves primarily nutritive functions. The innermost *retinal* layer contains the light-sensitive cells that convert the radiant energy that the cornea and lens have mechanically focused on them into biochemical and electrochemical signals that can be transmitted to the brain for further processing.

The human retina contains two types of photoreceptors called *rods* and *cones* because of their physical appearance (see Figure 4–4). There are approximately 130 million rods and cones in the human retina. The cones are concentrated in the central portion of the eye and are used exclusively for daylight vision. They are typically connected to the brain in such a way that a signal from a single cone reaches brain centers for visual integration intact, a feature that permits man to make very fine visual discriminations. Cones also contain pigments that respond selectively to lights of particular wavelengths, thus permitting distinctions of color. As one moves toward the periphery of the retina, the number of cones decreases rapidly and rods begin to dominate. Rods are used in twilight vision. They cannot differentiate between radiations of different wavelengths and are connected to the brain in such a way that several of them

Vision

The Chemistry of Photoreceptor Processes

Radiant energy affects biological photoreceptors by acting on specialized substances called pigments. These pigments undergo catabolic changes in the presence of light and require continual resynthesis if the receptor is to function over extended periods of time. Two such pigments have been isolated in vertebrates—*iodopsin* in the color-sensitive cones and *rhodopsin* in the scotopic rod receptors. Two similar pigments have been found in the retinas of fishes.

Iodopsin and rhodopsin undergo several conversions in the presence of light and eventually dissociate into two substances called *opsin and retinene*. Vitamin A can be oxidized to replenish the supply of retinene and opsin, and these two substances recombine in the dark to form rhodopsin or iodopsin. The chemical reactions that occur during the breakdown and resynthesis of the two known photopigments have recently been elucidated in some detail.[39, 88]

The vital last step in the transduction of radiant energy to physiological signals is, however, still unexplained. We do not yet know how retinene or opsin produce the bioelectric events that are necessary to trigger action potentials that transmit visual information to the central nervous system. We can be fairly certain that retinene, at least in the form that we know it, cannot initiate rapid and explosive neural responses (it is released only very slowly and appears to be quite inert). Opsin, on the other hand, undergoes a number of rapid transformations in response to light and may be responsible for the final step in the photoreceptor conversion.

The specific function of rhodopsin and iodopsin has been well established in experiments that have compared the absorption spectra of these pigments with the spectral sensitivities of rods and cones (see Figure 4–5). In many cases the agreement between spectral sensitivity and absorption spectra is excellent. However, there are instances in which spectral sensitivity cannot be related to the properties of any known pigment, suggest-

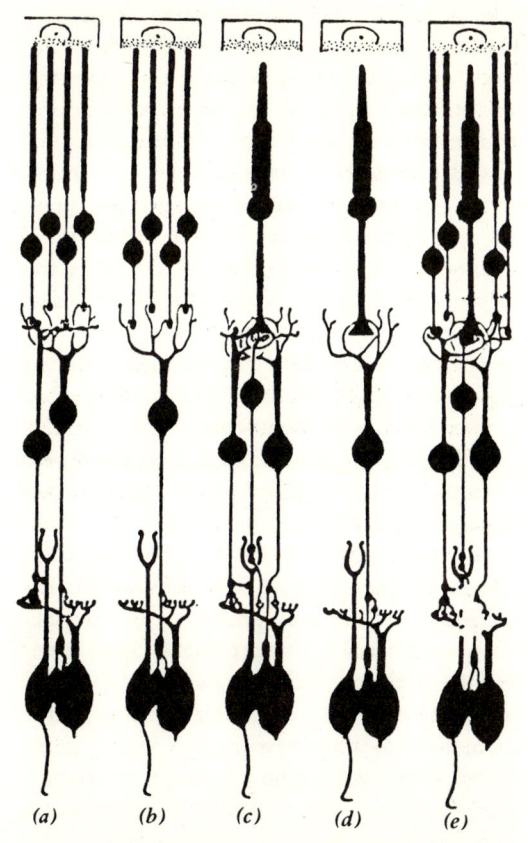

FIG. 4–4. Grouping of primate retinal cells into functional systems. (*a*) and (*b*) are typical rod systems where several receptors relate to one ganglion cell. (*c*) and (*d*) are typical cone systems in which each receptor maintains a "private line" to the brain. (*e*) is a mixed rod and cone system.

(After S. L. Polyak. *The vertebrate visual system.* H. Klüver, Ed. University of Chicago Press, 1957. Copyright 1957 by The University of Chicago. Copyright 1955 under the International Copyright Union.)

use the same lines of communication. This makes fine discriminations impossible and explains why objects appear fuzzy at night.

There is a small area on the retina that does not contain any rods or cones because the optic nerve that communicates with higher portions of the nervous system leaves the eye at this point. The resultant *blind spot* becomes quite noticeable when one places two objects in the visual field and focuses on one of them. If the distance between the eye and these objects is gradually increased, the object that is not in focus will, at some point, disappear totally.

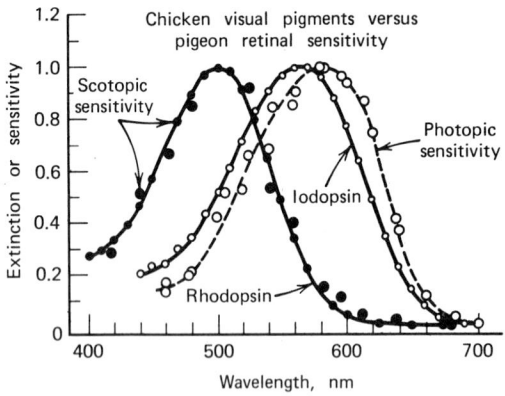

FIG. 4–5. Absorption spectra of rhodopsin and iodopsin, compared with the spectral sensitivities measured electrophysiologically and plotted in terms of the reciprocals of the numbers of incident quanta needed to evoke a constant electrical response.

(After G. Wald, P. K. Brown, & P. H. Smith. Iodopsin. *J. gen. Physiol.*, **38**, 1954–1955, 623–681.)

ing that additional pigments may exist or that the sensitivity of some parts of the visual system may not depend on the activity of a single pigment but rather on an interaction between the neural effects of several photochemical reactions. It has been suggested, in this connection, that spectral sensitivity may, in some instances, be mediated by physiological mechanisms that respond to the *difference* between the light-absorbing properties of two pigments[16] or between the properties of a visual pigment and certain products of its response to light.[17]

It has generally been assumed that the reversible sensitivity changes that occur during prolonged exposure to light are directly related to the bleaching of visual pigments. Rushton and his co-workers[78,79,14] have devised an ingenious technique for estimating this relationship. They measure the bleaching and resynthesis of rhodopsin in the intact eye by comparing the peripheral retinal reflection of blue-green light (which is largely absorbed by rhodopsin) with the retinal reflection of orange (which is only poorly absorbed by the pigment of the rods). These studies show that the rhodopsin content of the rod-containing peripheral retina falls exponentially during exposure to light, reaching an asymptote that is characteristic of the intensity of the stimulus (see Figure 4–6). In the dark, the rhodopsin content rises to roughly normal values within about 30 minutes.

A comparison of Rushton's results with the temporal course of dark and light adaptation suggests that the relationship between sensitivity and visual pigment concentration is not simple. A clear covariance becomes apparent only when the concentration of rhodopsin is compared to the logarithm of visual sensitivity, expressed as the reciprocal of energy. Such a relationship would be expected if the photoreceptor were a compartmentalized structure, each compartment being capable of essentially independent responses to light.

According to this hypothesis, the absorption of a single quantum of radiant energy by such a compartment suffices to discharge most of its visual pigment. This renders the compartment temporarily incapable of further excitation although the remaining pigments continue to absorb light. The rod receptor is

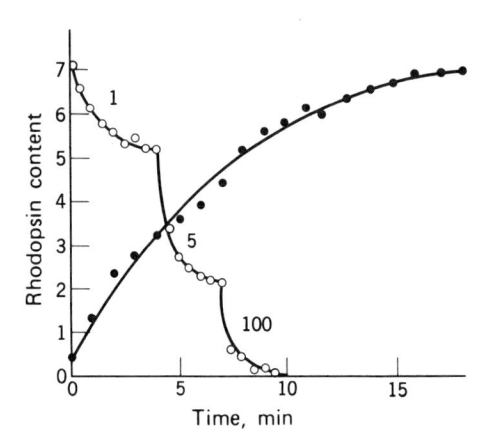

FIG. 4–6. Bleaching and resynthesis of rhodopsin in the human retina. *Open circles*, on exposing the eye successively to lights of increasing brightness, the rhodopsin content falls each time to a new steady-state level at which the rate of bleaching is balanced by the regeneration rate. *Filled circles*, in the dark, rhodopsin regenerates.

(From F. W. Campbell & W. A. H. Rushton. Measurement of the scotopic pigment in the living human eye. *J. Physiol.*, **130**, 1955, 131–147.)

entirely inexcitable only when all compartments have been discharged (i.e., when each compartment has absorbed at least one quantum of light).

The Electrical Activity of the Eye

The photochemical processes that are initiated by the action of radiant energy on photoreceptors must be translated into neural signals that are lawfully related to the intensity and periodicity of the radiation. This is an extraordinarily complex task, and it is not surprising that we do not yet know very much about the mechanisms involved. We have, however, made some progress in recent years, largely by a detailed analysis of the electrical potentials that are generated in the eye and in higher portions of the visual system in response to changes in retinal illumination. The details of these complex observations cannot be reviewed within the scope of this discussion, but a brief look at some of the principal findings may be useful.

The Polarity Potential

The first electrical potential to be recorded from the eye was the resting or polarity potential between the cornea and the back of the eye. It was first described over 100 years ago and was long thought to originate in the photosensitive elements of the retina.[24] More recent observations[34] indicate that it is at least in part due to extraretinal elements, and the *electro-oculogram*, as it is often called, is currently used mainly as a convenient measure of eye movements.[15]

The Electroretinogram (ERG)

A complex electrical potential can be recorded from the eye in response to any significant change in retinal illumination. A record of this response (an *electroretinogram* or ERG) can be obtained by measuring the potential between one electrode on the cornea and another on the forehead. The onset of the ERG response always precedes the appearance of action potentials in the optic nerve, and the frequency and pattern of nerve impulses are lawfully although complexly related to the magnitude, latency, or rise time of some components of the ERG.

When the vertebrate eye is first exposed to a change in illumination, a small negative potential, called a-wave, appears. This is followed by a large positive potential, called b-wave. This compound "on" response is followed by a slow positive potential that gradually rises to some asymptote and remains there during continued stimulation. This c-wave gradually declines following the termination of stimulation and may be followed by a small "off" response called d-wave.

It has been suggested that the components of the ERG may reflect different events in the eye. Granit[30, 31] has proposed that three principal processes may occur (see Figure 4-7). The first of these is thought to arise from the pigment epithelium and to be responsible for the slow positive c-wave. The second is believed to originate in the second-order bipolar neurons of the retina and to give rise to the principal b-wave of the ERG. The third process is thought to be related to chemical reactions in the rod and cone receptors themselves and to give rise to the initial a-wave as well as the d-wave, which often appears at the termination of stimulation.

The b-wave component of the human ERG may reflect primarily scotopic (i.e., rod) functions. Its magnitude is roughly proportional to the logarithm of the intensity of the stimulus (see Figure 4–8), and its spectral sensitivity curve corresponds well to the scotopic luminous efficiency function.[77] The latency of the ERG (i.e., of the initial a-wave) is also proportional to stimulus intensity, but separate scotopic and photopic functions have been reported[32] indicating that wavelength as well as intensity must be considered. Wavelength also affects the shape of many of the components of the ERG,[69] but it has been difficult to interpret this in terms of retinal functions.[83]

Receptor or Generator Potentials

The transformation of radiant energy into physiologically useful signals could be

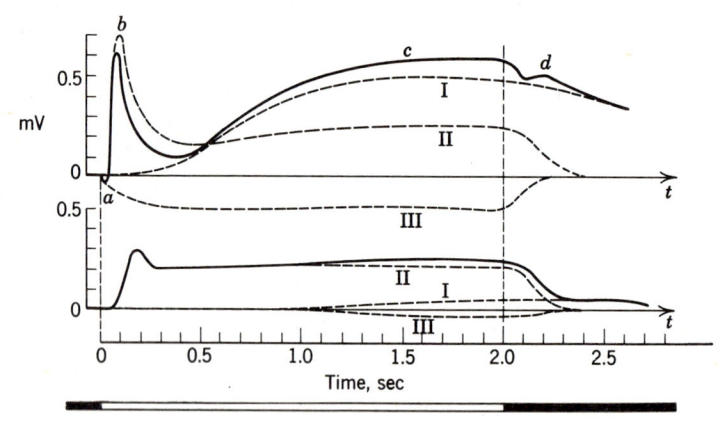

FIG. 4–7. Electroretinogram of the cat. The line below the time scale indicates the presence of the stimulus (white) or its absence (black).

(From *Light, colour and vision* by Y. Le Grand. Chapman & Hall Ltd., 1957. According to data from R. Granit, *J. Physiol.*, **77**, 1933, 207–240.)

achieved, most simply, if the photochemical reaction in the receptor generated an electrical potential that depolarizes related neurons and thus initiates action potentials. Such "generator potentials" have been observed in simple compound eyes (although they may not originate in the receptors themselves)[68] but have not yet been recorded in vertebrates. However, several slow, graded potentials have been observed in the eye of the cat[33, 70, 13] and fishes[81, 62] which may serve similar functions.

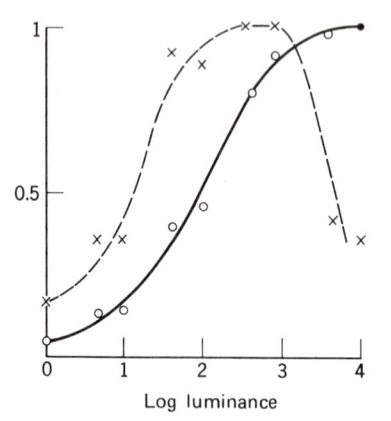

FIG. 4–8. Amplitude of the *b*-wave (———) and and the *c*-wave (– – –) of the dark-adapted eye, as a function of luminance.

(From *Light, colour and vision* by Y. Le Grand. Chapman & Hall Ltd., 1957. According to data from R. Granit, *J. Physiol.*, **77**, 1933, 207–240.)

Three types of slow or *S-potentials* have been found (see Figure 4–9): (a) *luminosity* (L) *potentials*, which appear to be related to scotopic visual processes because they can be recorded from retinas that do not possess color receptors and because their spectral amplitude distribution is not distorted by selective adaptation to lights of selected wavelengths; (b) *yellow-blue* (Y-B) *potentials*; and (c) *red-green* (R-G) *potentials*, which are responses to selected portions of the visible spectrum. The maximum amplitude of the negative portion of the Y-B potential lies near 475 nm (blue). The amplitude then gradually declines to zero near 540 nm and increases again until it reaches a positive maximum near 580 nm (yellow). The red-green potential is similarly biphasic, the negative maximum being near 515 nm (green) and the positive near 600 or 620 nm (red). The R-G and Y-B potentials are subject to selective adaptation—that is, the response to specific wavelengths can be inhibited by prolonged exposure to these wavelengths, and this effect is greatest in the regions of maximum sensitivity. This suggests that four distinct photoreceptors may be responsible for the two biphase responses.

The Activity of Second-Order Neurons

Microelectrodes in the bipolar layer of the

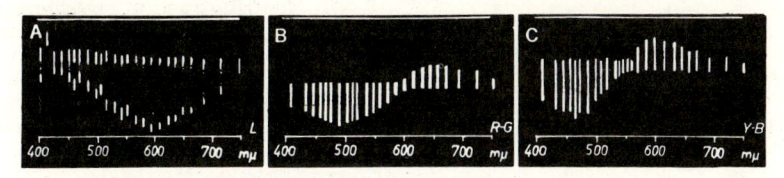

FIG. 4–9. Different types of spectral response curve recordings. A = L response; B = R-G response; C = Y-B response.

(After G. Svaetichin & E. F. MacNichol, Jr. Retinal mechanisms for chromatic and achromatic vision. *Ann. N.Y. Acad. Sci.*, **74**, 1958, 385–399.)

retina have picked up *focal* potentials that have a wave form and time course similar to those of the ERG[84, 85] suggesting that they may be local components of the gross ERG itself.[76] Spike potentials have also been recorded from this region of the retina,[12] although it is not certain that these potentials originate in the bipolar cells.

The Activity of Third-Order Neurons

The third-order neurons of vertebrate eyes are ganglion cells that project axons to the central nervous system via the optic nerve. A burst of action potentials can be recorded from the optic nerve in response to visual stimuli.[1, 2] The frequency of the optic-nerve discharge attains a maximum and then declines to some asymptotic value. Termination of the stimulus causes a sudden increase in the rate of discharge followed by a gradual return to the resting level.

Hartline and associates[35, 36, 37, 38] first isolated individual optic-nerve fibers and demonstrated several distinct components in the compound response of the optic nerve. In the frog, about 20 percent of the fibers (A or ON fibers) responded to the onset of light with a rapid burst of action potentials and continued to respond to maintained stimuli at a lower, steady frequency. About 50 percent of the fibers (B or ON-OFF fibers) responded only to the onset and termination of visual stimuli. The remaining 30 percent (C or OFF fibers) responded only to the cessation of stimulation with a high-frequency burst of impulses that slowed only gradually and outlasted the stimulus by several seconds (see Figure 4–10).

More recent investigations have shown that each optic-tract fiber is related to a large (often 1 mm or more) receptive field on the retina and that ON, OFF, and ON-OFF responses can be recorded from the same nerve fiber, depending on the portion of the receptive field that is stimulated.[57, 58, 3, 4, 30] In the cat, some receptive fields have a central zone from which only ON responses can be elicited, a surrounding region where ON-OFF responses can be obtained, and a fringe area from which only OFF responses can be

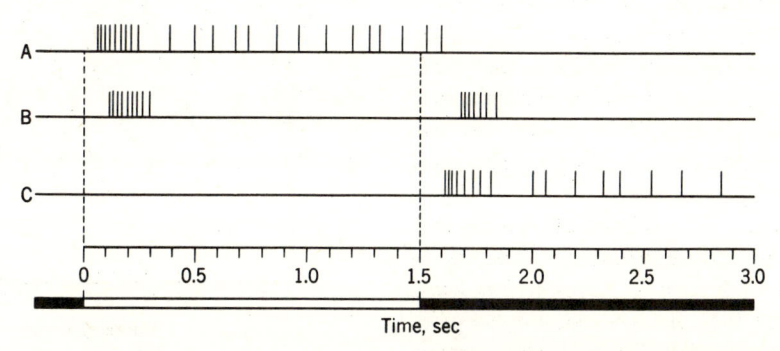

FIG. 4–10. The three kinds of responses of the optic nerve fibers in the frog.

(From *Light, colour and vision* by Y. Le Grand. Chapman & Hall Ltd., 1957. According to H. K. Hartline, *Amer. J. Physiol.*, **130**, 1940, 700–711.)

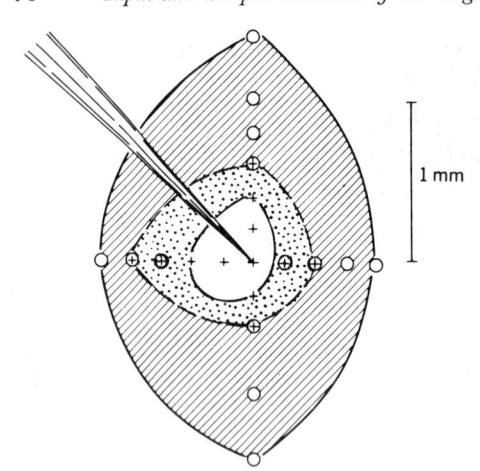

FIG. 4–11. Distribution of discharge patterns within the receptive field of a ganglion cell (located at tip of electrode) of the cat retina. In the central region (crosses) ON discharges were found. In the diagonally hatched part only OFF discharges occurred (circles). In the intermediary zone (stippled area) discharges were ON–OFF. A change in the conditions of illumination (background, etc.) altered the discharge pattern distribution.

(From S. W. Kuffler. Discharge patterns and functional organization of mammalian retina. *J. Neurophysiol.*, **16**, 1953, 37–68

elicited. Other receptive fields show an opposite pattern of organization, the outer fringe being part of the ON system (see Figure 4–11). When two stimuli are simultaneously projected onto the same receptive field such that one stimulates only the ON zone and the other only the OFF zone, the response of the related optic-tract fiber depends on the relative intensity of the stimuli.

When stimuli are presented in such rapid succession that on ON and OFF responses collide, only one of the responses is propagated, essentially unchanged, while the other is completely suppressed. This competitive interaction and related observations led Granit[30, 31] to suggest that the retina may contain two basically antagonistic response systems that compete for the same central connections under some conditions. According to this hypothesis, the ON system responds to threshold stimulation by initiating (a) a series of propagated action potentials and (b) a steady potential that inhibits the OFF system for the duration of the stimulation. The response of the OFF system to the termination of stimulation then represents a release from this inhibition.

The response of individual optic-nerve fibers is significantly influenced by the wavelength of the stimulus in species that have color vision.[29, 30, 87] In the cat, some optic-nerve fibers respond to all wavelengths within the visible spectrum but more readily to some than to others. This response pattern has been called a broad-band *dominator* function, and two somewhat different types have been identified. Some fibers respond with a *scotopic dominator* function that peaks at 500 nm; others respond with a *photopic dominator* function with a maximum near 560 nm.[26, 27, 28, 23] The shape of the scotopic dominator function corresponds quite well to the absorption spectrum of rhodopsin; that of the photopic dominator function agrees well with the absorption spectrum of iodopsin. Some optic-nerve fibers respond only to a narrow band of wavelengths. As many as four different such *modulator* functions have been identified in some eyes with response maxima near wavelengths that correspond to blue, green, yellow, and red (see Figure 4–12). It has been suggested[29, 30] that the scotopic and photopic dominator functions may re-

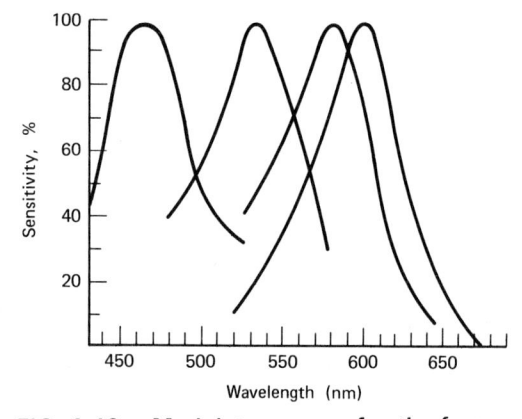

FIG. 4–12. Modulator curves for the frog.

(After R. Granit. A physiological theory of colour perception. *Nature*, **151**, 1943, 11–14.)

flect receptor processes that are responsible for translating brightness differences into neural signals. The organism's response to color is thought to be reflected in the modulator functions, which may reflect more specific photochemical reactions.

It is important to remember that eyes come in a great variety of shapes and that the visual system of different species may perceive light in quite different ways. The frog, for instance, appears to depend on a functional organization of retinal elements that differs significantly from that of the cat. Five types of optic-tract fibers have been described in the frog. Some fibers relate to very small receptive fields and respond maximally to sharp brightness contrasts between adjacent portions of the visual field, thus serving as *boundary detectors*. Others respond even more selectively to boundaries that have curvature and are in motion or are at rest immediately following motion. These fibers have been called *convex boundary detectors*. A third type, called *changing contrast detectors*, responds preferentially to a *change* in contrast between different portions of the visual field. A fourth type, called *dimming detectors*, responds only to a reduction in illumination (similar to the OFF responses seen in the cat), and a fifth type, as yet unclassified, adjusts its discharge frequency in response to changes in illumination such that its frequency is roughly inversely proportional to the intensity of the stimulus. Each of these fiber types may be related to a different type of retinal ganglion cell.[60, 65, 67, 61]

The compound eye of the horseshoe crab shows still a different type of organization.[73, 74, 75] This compound eye consists of units, called *ommatidia*, that contain 10 to 12 receptor cells and one bipolar cell that is the origin of one optic-tract fiber. As far as we know, there are no significant functional differences between different ommatidia and their central projections, but neighboring ommatidia interact in complex ways when more than one is illuminated concurrently. The principal form of interaction is inhibition, the magnitude of the effect varying as a function of the intensity, area, and pattern of illumination. The interaction is not directional (i.e., concurrent illumination of adjacent ommatidia produces mutual inhibition) and appears to be additive (i.e., the concurrent illumination of two ommatidia that are far enough apart not to inhibit each other but close enough to a third to inhibit its activity results in a simple addition of the inhibitory influences from each of them).

Summary and Review Questions

There are many different kinds of photoreceptors and many different ways to organize them into "eyes." Most insects and marine animals have compound eyes containing visual elements that have a fixed lens and thus do not provide a sharp, focused image. Man and other vertebrates have eyes with adjustable lenses and a pupil that permits additional sharpening of the image and limits the light that is admitted to the eye. There are two different kinds of photoreceptors in the human eye–rods that are distributed mainly around the periphery of the retina and cones that are found primarily in the center. Rods respond to radiant energies from all portions of the visible spectrum and serve scotopic (i.e., black/white) sensory functions. Cones respond selectively to frequencies near the blue, green, yellow, or red portions of the spectrum and are responsible for photopic (i.e., color) vision.

Photoreceptors selectively respond to radiant energy because their pigments undergo catabolic changes in the presence of light. In the vertebrate retina, two types of pigments have been isolated. Rhodopsin appears to occur only in the rod receptors that respond to all frequencies of radiation within the visible spectrum and mediate scotopic (i.e., black/white) vision. The second pigment, iodopsin, has an absorption spectrum that is all but identical to the photic sensitivity curve that describes the activation of cone receptors in the human eye. On exposure to light, these pigments dissociate into opsin and retinene, and this process is reversible in the dark. Just how these substances initiate the neural activity that transmits visual information to the central nervous system is as yet unknown.

We have made some progress in this direction in recent years by analyzing the electrical potentials that are generated in the eye. The presentation of a visual stimulus produces a large and complex potential that can be recorded from electrodes outside the eye. This electroretinogram (ERG) consists of a small negative a-wave that appears to be related to the onset of stimulation. It is followed by a relatively large and abrupt positive b-wave that complexly reflects the intensity of stimulation. Next, a large c-wave appears that seems to arise from the pigment epithelium. The offset of stimulation is often followed by a small d-wave.

Several types of potentials have been recorded from microelectrodes in various portions of the retina of cats. Three types of slow S-potentials occur: luminosity potentials that appear to be related to scotopic visual processes and yellow-blue and red-green potentials that have positive and negative response maxima in portions of the visible spectrum that correspond to yellow, blue, green, and red.

Microelectrodes placed onto single optic-nerve fibers of cats have shown that each is related to a relatively large receptive retinal field that typically contains distinct ON, ON-OFF, and OFF regions. The response of such a fiber thus depends not only on the intensity of visual stimulation but also on its distribution within a particular region of the retina. Some optic-nerve fibers respond to all wavelengths within the visible spectrum, but more readily to lights of some wavelengths than to others. Two somewhat different such broad-band dominator functions of spectral sensitivity have been found, a scotopic dominator function that resembles the absorption spectrum of rhodopsin and a photopic dominator function that resembles the absorption spectrum of iodopsin. Other optic-tract fibers respond preferentially to narrow bands of wavelengths. These modulator functions have response maxima near wavelengths that correspond to blue, green, yellow, and red.

It is important to remember that the functional organization of the eye differs markedly between species. For instance, the eye of the frog appears to have response units that are especially sensitive to moving objects and to the direction of their motion. The relatively simple compound eye of the horseshoe crab appears to have only one type of sensory receptor unit, but these units are interconnected to provide an unusually complex pattern of inhibitory interaction.

1. Describe the essential differences between the compound eye of insects and the eye of man.

2. Describe the path of light from the initial incidence on the cornea to the photoreceptor.

3. Describe the photochemical reaction that takes place in the receptor.

4. Describe the effect of retinal illumination on the electroretinogram.

5. Discuss the slow S-potentials that have been recorded from the retinas of cats and fishes. Can they be explained by a trichromatic theory of color vision?

6. Individual optic-nerve fibers appear to be capable of transmitting several different reactions to visual stimuli. How is this possible?

7. Discuss the effects of wavelength on the response of individual optic-nerve fibers. Does this information favor one of the color theories?

TRANSFER AND PROCESSING OF VISUAL INFORMATION IN THE CENTRAL NERVOUS SYSTEM

Strictly speaking, we do not "see" with our eyes. This is dramatically demonstrated by the total blindness that ensues when the connections between the eye and the central nervous system are severed. To be perceived, visual information must be processed and integrated by several brain structures. The advent of microelectrode recording techniques has given us a tool that may help determine what each of these mechanisms accomplishes. At present, we have only some tantalizing pieces of this puzzle.

The Lateral Geniculate Body

One of the principal relay stations of the visual system is the lateral geniculate body of the thalamus. Microelectrode studies[44, 42] have shown that in the cat the retinal receptive fields of individual geniculate cells are composed of discrete concentric ON, OFF, and ON-OFF zones much like the receptive fields of retinal ganglion cells. However, intense stimuli elicit three successive ON responses in the geniculate that arrive after characteristically different latencies of about 30, 140, and 380 milliseconds, as well as two distinct OFF responses that arrive with latencies of about 30 and 170 milliseconds.[5]

The functions of the geniculate body of the primate have been analyzed in considerable detail by DeValois and his associates.[18, 19, 20, 21] Two classes of cells have been described—*opponent* cells, which respond preferentially to the wavelength of the stimulus and appear to transduce information related to the perception of color, and *nonopponent* cells, which respond primarily to the intensity of the stimulus and thus may selectively transduce information related to the perception of brightness (see Figures 4–13 and 4–14).

There are two types of nonopponent cells. The *excitor* cells increase their firing rate in response to any visual stimulus; the *inhibitor* cells decrease their firing rate. Both types of nonopponent cells respond to stimuli from all portions of the visual spectrum and are relatively little affected by changes in their wavelength. Both change their firing rate markedly when the intensity of the stimulus is changed.

Opponent cells have been classified, on the basis of their spectral sensitivity, into four subgroups: (a) R^+G^- cells increase their firing rate in response to stimuli from the red portion of the spectrum and decrease it in response to stimuli from the green region; (b) G^+R^- cells respond in an inverse fashion, increasing their firing rate in response to stimuli from the green portion of the spectrum and decreasing it when red or orange stimuli are presented; (c) Y^+B^- cells are excited by stimuli from the yellow portions of the spectrum and inhibited by stimuli from the blue; (d) B^+Y^- cells respond in an inverse fashion, giving excitatory responses to blue and inhibitory reactions to yellow.

The R^+G^- cells receive excitatory inputs from retinal cones that are maximally sensitive to red stimuli and inhibitory inputs from green cones. The G^+R^- cells receive excitatory inputs from green cones and inhibitory inputs from red-sensitive retinal cells. Although the excitatory and inhibitory processes are not, strictly speaking, identical, it seems that the R^+G^- and G^+R^- cells may carry essentially duplicating information. The response patterns of the R^+G^- and G^+R^- cells are approximate mirror images of each other and the two types of cells discriminate color in similar ways. The B^+Y^- and Y^+B^- cells similarly appear to have common retinal connections (the Y^+B^- cells receive excitatory inputs from red cones and inhibitory inputs from blue-sensitive retinal cells; the B^+Y^- cells have an opposite pattern of connection) and spectral response patterns which approximate mirror images of each other. On the basis of these observations, it has been suggested[19] that the complexity of the visual inputs may be reduced in the geniculate body by the action of a Red-Green and a Yellow-Blue system. Individual cells within these two systems are thought to be capable of fine wavelength discriminations because they receive excitatory and inhibitory inputs from retinal cones which contain different photopigments. Since the absorption spectra of these pigments differ but overlap over most of the visible spectrum, each wavelength produces a unique pattern of facilitatory and inhibitory inputs to the cells of the lateral geniculate.

The fact that the geniculate relay station of the primate visual system seems to transmit information related to the perception of color entirely on the basis of three classes of retinal inputs agrees well with the observation[63] that there appear to be three types of cones in the primate retina that are sensitive to a range of wavelengths surrounding peaks at 440 nm (blue), 535 nm (green), and 570 nm (red). These observations have been interpreted[19]

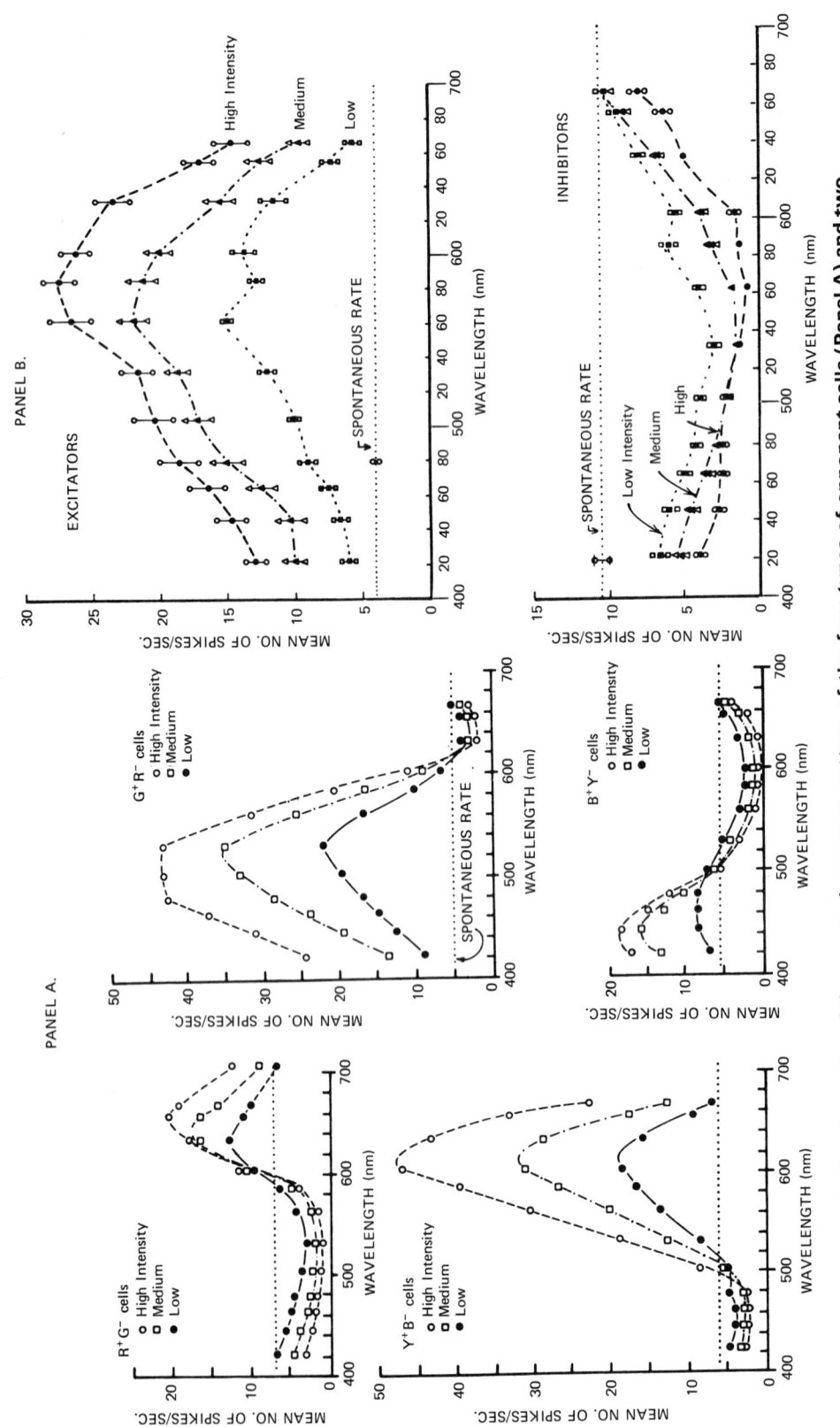

FIG. 4–13. Examples of the spectral response pattern of the four types of opponent cells (Panel A) and two types of nonopponent cells (Panel B) in the primate geniculate body. Changes in the intensity of the stimuli produce relatively small effects on the firing rate of the opponent cells. The nonopponent cells increase or decrease their firing rate to all visual stimuli. They respond relatively little to changes in wavelength but markedly to differences in intensity.

(From R. L. De Valois, I. Abramov, & G. H. Jacobs, Analysis of response patterns of LGN cells. *J. opt. Soc. Amer.*, **56**, 1966, 966–977.)

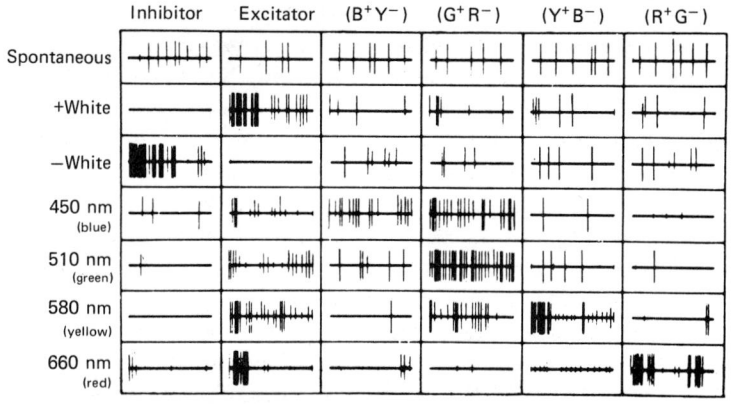

FIG. 4-14. Summary of the response patterns of the six types of cells found in the primate geniculate body (two types of nonopponent cells and four types of opponent cells). (+White indicates an increment in the intensity of white light, -White indicates a decrease.)

(From R. L. De Valois & G. H. Jacobs. Primate color vision. *Science*, **162**, 1 November 1968, 533-540. Copyright 1968 by the American Association for the Advancement of Science.)

to suggest a theory of color vision that relies on the opposing activity of three color receptors. In such a system, the perception of color depends not so much on the intensity of stimulation of any one or two color receptors but on the balance of excitation and inhibition in a system of opposing influences. This notion is in essential agreement with Hering's classical opponent process theory of color vision.

The Superior Colliculi

In the frog, the retina is fully and registrally represented in the superior colliculus.[66, 61] The five types of visual detectors that have been isolated in the frog retina appear to be differentially distributed so that boundary detectors are located in the outer layer of the colliculus and dimming detectors in the deepest layer.

Two novel detector classes appear to be represented in the tectal area that surrounds the colliculi. Neurons called *newness cells* cover the entire visual field with extensively overlapping visual fields of about 30° diameter. These neurons respond only briefly to any sharp change in illumination or movement; the frequency of their discharge is related to the suddenness, speed, and direction of the change. Repeated movements in the same direction produce adaptation.

A second type of tectal neuron appears to have a receptive field that covers most, if not all, of the visual field except for a small "null" region. Stimuli that are projected entirely within the null region do not elicit a response; however, when the same stimulus appears anywhere else in the visual field, a burst of impulses occurs that continues as long as the object moves. If it stops for about 2 minutes, the discharge of this *sameness* neuron dies away and erupts again as soon as the object moves again.

Cortical Mechanisms

It has long been known that the retina projects rather precisely to specific portions of the visual cortex,[11, 64] but the functional organization of the cortical visual representations remained largely a mystery until the recent microelectrode studies of the cortex of the cat by Hubel and Wiesel in this country and Jung and his associates in Germany.

For the purpose of our discussion, the work of Hubel and Wiesel[40, 41, 42, 43, 44, 45, 46] can be summarized as follows. There appear to be distinct cortical representations of the retina in areas 17, 18, and 19. Most cells in area 17 respond to simple visual stimuli, those in corresponding portions of areas 18 and 19 only to "hypercomplex" stimulus configurations (e.g., only to stimuli of a particular length and orientation in space).

Many cells in the visual cortex are spontaneously active in the absence of retinal illumination and often change their discharge frequency even though no corresponding changes in retinal illumination occur. Many cortical cells do not respond to stimuli that cover large portions of the visual field but respond vigorously when only a small region is illuminated (see Figure 4–15). Stimuli that move across the visual field often elicit responses from cells that do not respond to the same stimuli when they are stationary.

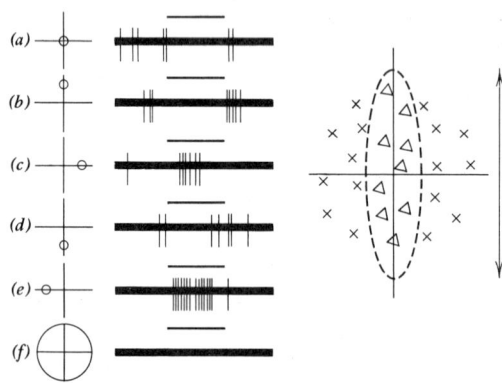

FIG. 4–15. Responses of a cell in the cat's striate cortex to a spot of light. (The complete map of the receptive field is shown at right: X, areas giving excitation; △, areas giving inhibitory effects.) (a) 1° (0.25 mm) spot shone in the center of the field; (b)–(e) 1° spot shone on four points equidistant from center; (f) 5° spot covering the entire field.

(After D. H. Hubel & T. N. Wiesel. Receptive fields of single neurones in the cat's striate cortex. *J. Physiol.*, **148**, 1959, 574–591.)

Most cortical cells respond preferentially to stimulation of a small receptive field on the retina. Their activity is often inhibited by the projection of stimuli to some segments of this receptive retinal field, and the termination of such stimulation induces a burst of activity. The projection of the same stimulus to other portions of the same retinal field gives rise to ON responses. Most of the receptive fields of cells in the visual cortex have distinct excitatory and inhibitory regions, but the relative size and orientation of these antagonistic regions varies greatly. Simultaneous stimulation of the excitatory and inhibitory portions of a receptive field often fails to affect the activity of the related cortical neuron, presumably because of mutual inhibition. Summation effects are seen when two stimuli are projected to different portions of the excitatory or inhibitory regions of the same receptive field.

Almost all receptive fields of cortical neurons are organized so that an oblong central excitatory or inhibitory zone is flanked by thin bands of points that respond in the opposite direction. Receptive fields with horizontal, oblique, or vertical axes can be found in all portions of the visual cortex. The size of the receptive fields of cortical neurons changes as a function of stimulus intensity and background illumination and tends to be much less constant than the size of the receptive fields of retinal or geniculate cells.

When slits of light are moved across the visual field, movement is found to be a much more effective stimulus than any stationary source. The orientation of the stimulus and the direction of the movement determines the magnitude of the cortical response (see Figure 4–16). For example, any horizontal movement of a vertically oriented slit across the receptive field shown in Figure 4–15 produces a marked response. Vertical movements of a horizontally oriented slit of the same dimensions across the same visual field does not produce a reaction (see Figure 4–17). This differential effect is related to the orientation of the slit relative to the axis of the receptive field. If the slit covers the excitatory and inhibitory areas simultaneously, little or no response occurs, but a marked reaction takes place whenever the slit is moved across the antagonistic areas successively. Some of the cortical units respond markedly to movement in one direction but not at all or in a very different fashion to movement of the same stimulus along the same plane in the opposite direction.

Most cortical units respond only to stimulation of one receptive field in either the ipsilateral or the contralateral eye. A few cells respond to receptive fields in comparable portions of the two retinas, and in this case one finds summation as well as competitive

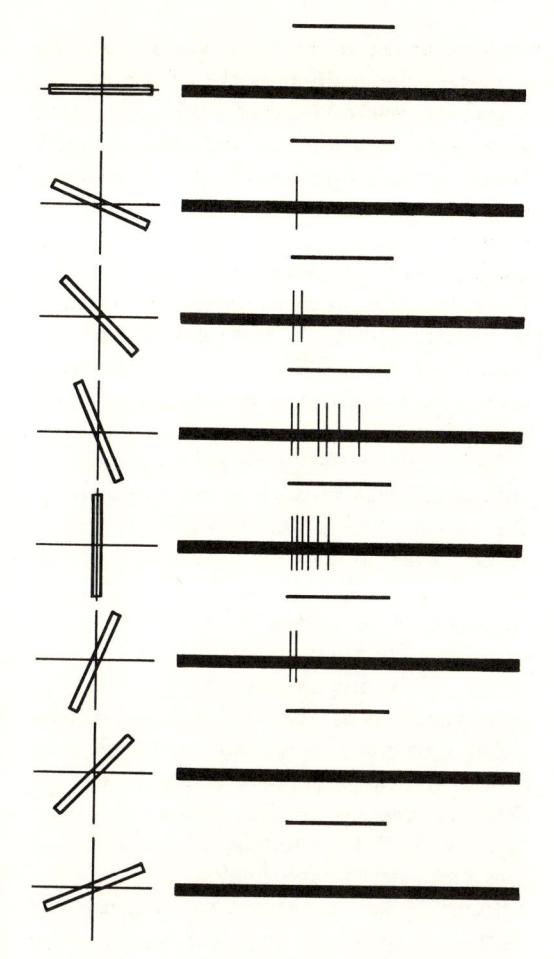

FIG. 4–16. Responses of a cell in the striate cortex to shining a rectangular light spot into the eye such that the center of the slit is superimposed on the center of the receptive field; successive stimuli rotated clockwise.

(After D. H. Hubel & T. N. Wiesel. Receptive fields of single neurones in the cat's striate cortex. *J. Physiol.*, **148**, 1959, 574–591.)

interactions (i.e., simultaneous stimulation of the excitatory or inhibitory portions of the two receptive retinal fields produces additive effects; simultaneous stimulation of the excitatory region of one receptive field in one eye and the inhibitory region in the other may completely block the cells' response).

A group of German workers[6, 7, 10, 8, 9, 49, 50, 53, 55, 54] have analyzed the response of single units in the visual cortex of the cat to diffuse light and simple pattern stimuli. This work is particularly interesting because the observations are related to perceptual phenomena.

Jung and his colleagues have attempted to build a remarkably simple explanation of scotopic vision; their plan reduces its apparent complexity to an interaction between only two basically antagonistic systems that respond selectively to "brightness information" and "darkness information" respectively.

In these studies, the responses of single cells in the occipital cortex to diffuse light, intermittent flashes of light, or a grid of alternating light and dark stripes were recorded. Figure 4–18 shows the five basic response categories that were encountered. Since a particular cortical cell always responded in a characteristic fashion, a corresponding classification of neurons was suggested.

By far the largest category, the *A* neurons, did not respond to diffuse light. Some of these cells reacted to flicker, movement, or contrast between adjacent areas of different brightness. The cells of this category appear to respond to highly specialized visual inputs rather than to gross differences of illumination. Most of the *A*-type neurons were fired or facilitated by thalamic, reticular, or vestibular stimulation, suggesting that these cells might perform stabilizing functions by providing a constant overall level of cortical excitation regardless of gross changes in retinal illumination.

Brightness information per se appeared to be received by *B*-type neurons. These neurons responded promptly and vigorously to the onset of any suprathreshold visual stimulus and maintained an increased level of firing as long as the stimulus was presented. *B*-type neurons constitute about one fourth of the

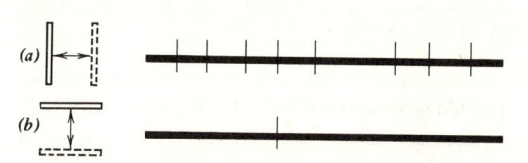

FIG. 4–17. Same unit as in Fig. 4–16. Responses to a slit moved transversely back and forth across the receptive field: (*a*) slit moved horizontally; (*b*) slit moved vertically.

(After D. H. Hubel & T. N. Wiesel. Receptive fields of single neurones in the cat's striate cortex. *J. Physiol.*, **148**, 1959, 574–591.)

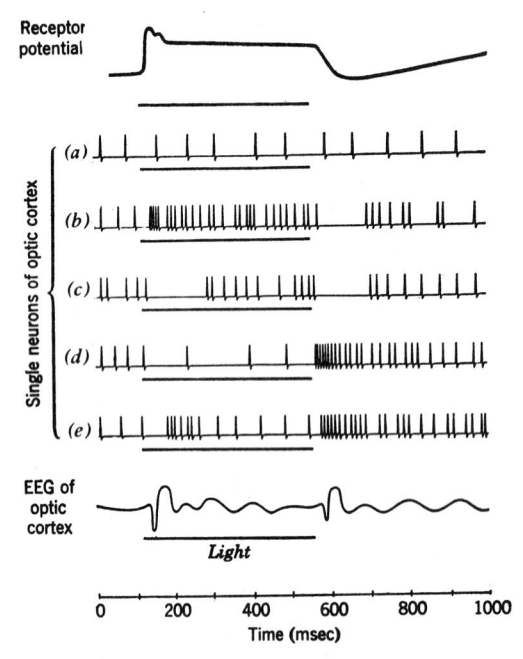

FIG. 4–18. Five types of neuronal responses of the visual cortex to light and dark stimulation and their relation to receptor excitation and to the EEG. The top shows the receptor potential recorded with microelectrode, intracellularly from the cone layer of the retina. The bottom graph shows cortical potentials with the ON and OFF effect from a gross electrode recording on the cortical surface. Graphs (a)–(e) schematic representation of discharges of different neuronal types: (a) neuron, no reaction to light or dark; (b) neuron, activated by light, inhibited by dark with delayed afteractivation (similar to ON element of retina); (c) neuron, inhibitory break for both light and dark; (d) neuron, inhibited by light and activated by dark (reciprocal of (b) neuron, similar to OFF element of retina); (e) neuron, preexcitatory inhibition precedes delayed activation by light, early activation by dark (similar to ON–OFF elements of retina).

(From R. Jung, O. Creutzfeldt, & O. J. Grüsser. Die Mikrophysiologie kortikaler Neurone und ihre Bedeutung fuer die Sinnes- und Hirnfunktionen. *Dtsch. med. Wschr.*, **82**, 1957, 1050–1059.)

population of the striate cortex and appear to be functionally related to the ON elements of the retina and geniculate.

A few neurons, the very rare C-type cells, responded to the onset as well as to the termination of all visual stimuli by a brief but definite period of inhibition of spontaneous activity. A similar inhibition of spontaneous activity occurred in D-type neurons in response to the onset of any visual stimulus. However, the main response of the D-type neurons, a marked burst of activity, occurred after the cessation of the stimulation.[56] Frequently indistinct from the D-type neurons is a class of cells (E-type) that showed inhibitory reactions to light onset as well as marked OFF responses to its cessation but also gave a burst of rapid activity shortly after the stimulus onset (i.e., immediately after the initial period of inhibition). The response of each of the five classes of neurons was reversed in the dark.[8, 9]

Most cells in the visual cortex responded only to afferents from either the ipsilateral or the contralateral retina. Competitive interaction occurred in only 30 percent of the cortical cells. True binocular convergence (equivalence of stimuli to either eye) was found in only about 10 percent of the cells tested. This preponderance of monocular representations at the level of the primary visual projections correlates nicely with the psychophysical observation that each eye develops independent images that may only "secondarily" be fused by associative processes into stereoscopic images.

Jung[51, 52] has attempted to integrate the findings from these single-cell studies with some basic phenomena of visual perception. The subjective sensation of brightness is logarithmically related to the intensity of illumination per unit area, according to the (not entirely adequate) Weber-Fechner law of perception. Jung suggested that the sensation of brightness may find a direct correlate in the activity of the B-type neurons, since their discharge rate also increases roughly as a logarithmic function of stimulus intensity. Differences in brightness (i.e., contrast) may be signaled by the activity of the D-type neurons whose firing rate appears to be inversely related to retinal illumination.

Jung suggested that the scotopic functions of the visual system can be understood in terms of only two antagonistic systems: (1) a *brightness system* that is composed of B-type neurons and (2) a *darkness system* that consists of D-type neurons. The discharge frequency of the B neurons is positively related to the luminance of the stimulus and the perception of brightness; that of the D neurons correlates inversely with brightness. The E units of the visual cortex are thought to correspond to retinal ON-OFF units that are particularly common in peripheral portions of the retina and are believed to function specifically as motion detectors. The response pattern of the E neurons is in most respects so similar to that of the D-type cells that Jung suggested a darkness system that includes E and D units. This theory essentially reduces the scotopic aspects of the visual system to an ON (B-type neurons) and OFF (D- and E-type neurons) mechanism. The C units are so rarely found as to be negligible, and the A neurons, by definition, do not participate in simple visual sensations.

Summary and Review Questions

Our knowledge of the mechanisms that transmit and integrate visual information in the central nervous system is, as yet, quite incomplete. Subcortical relay stations such as the lateral geniculate body of the thalamus and the superior colliculi of the midbrain appear to process information in much the same way as some of the retinal elements themselves. Neurons in the geniculate have been found to have retinal receptive fields that have concentric ON, ON-OFF, and OFF segments much like those of second- or third-order neurons in the visual system. In primates, the geniculate contains two types of neurons: *opponent* cells, which respond preferentially to stimuli from selected portions of the visible spectrum and appear to transmit information about color; and *nonopponent* cells, which respond similarly to stimuli from all portions of the spectrum but are highly sensitive to changes in their intensity. In the frog, neurons have been found in the superior colliculi that show patterns of selective sensitivity to moving objects, sharp contrast boundaries, or changing contrast, which are quite similar to those found in the frog retina. Something new is added in this species at the level of the tectal area that appears to contain cells that respond specifically to "newness" or "sameness."

Recent attempts to analyze the response of individual cells in the visual cortex have indicated that their organization may differ in some respects from that of lower portions of the visual system. Hubel and Wiesel's extensive analysis of units in the cat visual cortex has shown that the receptive fields of cortical cells tend to be oblong rather than round, that movement across such a field is a much more effective stimulus than maintained stimulation, that the direction of movement as well as the shape of the stimulus (i.e., the pattern of retinal illumination) are important determinants of cortical activity, that most cells respond only to stimulation of one eye, and that many cells in the visual cortex are active in the absence of retinal illumination and may change their activity when the level of illumination remains constant. This pattern of activation is not basically different from that seen in lower portions of the visual system but suggests a degree of information processing that is not seen at lower levels.

Jung and his associates have analyzed the response of cortical neurons to diffuse light and to complex stimuli consisting of grids of light and dark areas, and suggested that there may be five types of neurons in the visual cortex. He suggested that three of these may contribute to two antagonistic systems that determine scotopic vision. The brightness system contains only B-type neurons that respond to the onset of all suprathreshold stimuli and maintain an increased level of firing throughout its presentation. The darkness system consists of neurons that inhibit their activity in response to the onset of stimulation but fire when it terminates (D-type); or increase their activity (after a brief period of inhibition) in response to the onset of stimulation and fire again when it terminates (E-type). Jung suggests that the sensation of brightness may be directly related to the activity of B-type neurons and that contrast may be signaled by the activity of the D-type neurons. The E-type neurons are thought to correspond to the ON-OFF cells of the retina and to function as motion detectors. It is difficult to relate the observations of Jung to those of Hubel and Wiesel because they investigated different aspects of the cortical response to light. The two sets of observations are not, however, incompatible, and we can hope that additional data will become available that will enable us to relate them more directly.

1. Contrast the response of neurons in the geniculate and superior colliculus to retinal illumination with that of second- or third-order retinal cells.

2. Describe the pattern of cortical reaction to retinal illumination as reported by Hubel and Wiesel.

3. Describe the five types of cells that Jung and associates found in the visual cortex and relate them to scotopic vision.

Review

The physical stimulus for vision is radiant energy of a frequency between 400 and 700 nm. The amplitude of the radiation is complexly related to the intensity of the sensation and its frequency to the sensation of color (in animals that possess special color receptors). Some properties of visual stimuli are best understood when we consider their wave form and amplitude. Others require an analysis of light in terms of individual quanta of energy.

Man perceives specific objects in his environment because light from the sun, moon, or stars (not to mention the incandescent light bulb) is reflected from them in predictable patterns that are determined by the fact that light always travels in a straight line and is reflected by most objects in a predictable fashion. Color is added to the sensation because pigments differentially absorb lights of some wavelengths.

Photoreceptors react selectively to radiant energy because they contain pigments that break down in the presence of light. Some photoreceptors, called rods, contain a pigment that reacts to light of all wavelengths within the visible spectrum. These receptors serve scotopic (i.e., black/white) vision. Others, called cones, respond more selectively to lights of particular wavelengths and mediate photopic (i.e., color) vision. Just how the many different color sensations that we perceive are produced is still unknown. We almost certainly do not have a special receptor for each color. It is generally accepted that an interaction of three or four different photopic receptors can produce all of the color sensations we are capable of experiencing, but the nature of their interaction is, as yet, in dispute. Trichromatic theories attempt to account for color vision by the interaction of three receptors that are maximally sensitive to wavelengths in the blue, green, and red portions of the spectrum. This theory derives support from the fact that just about all colors can be reproduced by a mixture of blue, green, and red lights. The alternative is an opponent-process theory that suggests, in essence, that color vision is due to competitive interactions within two pairs of receptor mechanisms, one sensitive to blue and yellow, the other to red and green. Electrophysiological recordings from the retina and from subcortical portions of the visual system generally support this type of explanation.

Slow S-potentials have been recorded from the retina of cats that seem to reflect opponent process mechanisms for photopic vision as well as simpler scotopic mechanisms. The latter may be responsible for the luminosity potential, the former for the $blue^+/yellow^-$; and $red^+/green^-$ potentials. In a different species, the monkey, a similar system has been observed in the lateral geniculate body. Some of the neurons of this nucleus respond to all wavelengths in a fashion that suggests their function as brightness detectors. Others give ON responses to stimuli in the red portion of the visible spectrum and OFF responses to green (or vice versa). Another type gives ON responses to stimuli from the short-wave (blue) portion of the spectrum and OFF responses to yellow (or vice versa).

Other electrophysiological observations do not support the opponent-process type of explanation as well. Recordings from the optic-nerve fibers of the cat indicate, for instance, that some of these fibers respond to all wavelengths in the visible spectrum (although they respond more readily to some). A closer analysis of the response of these fibers indicates that there may be two types, one (the scotopic dominator) whose spectral-response curve corresponds closely to the absorption spectrum of rhodopsin, the pigment of the rod receptor, and another (the photopic dominator) whose spectral-response curve resembles that of iodopsin, the pigment of the cone receptors. Other optic-tract fibers (the modulators) respond selectively to narrow bands of wavelengths with response maxima in portions of the spectrum that correspond to blue, green, yellow, and red.

Attempts to analyze the processing of scotopic information at different levels of the visual system have suggested the following organization. Neurons in the ganglion layer of the retina and in subcortical relay stations respond to stimulation of fairly large retinal receptive fields that typically are organized such that a central region of positive (or negative) sign is surrounded by a peripheral zone of opposite sign. For example, stimulation of the central portion of a retinal receptive field may produce pure ON responses in an optic-tract fiber or related geniculate neurons. The region that surrounds this core typically then produces pure OFF responses. ON-OFF responses may be obtained from the transitional region between the core and the adjacent peripheral zone.

An analysis of the cortical response to retinal illumination shows a similar pattern, modified, perhaps, by some additional processing of the visual information. The retinal receptive fields of cortical neurons are typically large and oblong; the neurons often respond preferentially to stimuli that move across this field, and may respond selectively to stimuli of particular sizes and shapes or to the direction of their movement. The response of some cortical cells is proportional to the intensity of retinal illumination. Others respond only briefly to the onset or termination of the stimulus and may be used to code contrast between adjacent portions of the visual field or the movement of stimuli across it.

It is important to remember that these observations have been made in the cat and monkey and that the organization of visual systems may differ significantly in other species. The frog, for instance, appears to have special receptor mechanisms that respond selectively to aspects of the environment (such as contrast or movement) that are useful in the detection of moving objects such as flies and in the prediction of their trajectory across the visual field. Other species such as the horseshoe crab have simple compound eyes that rely on a single visual element but seem to obtain a good deal of information about their environment by a complex pattern of mutually inhibitory interconnections between individual visual elements.

Bibliography

1. Adrian, E. D., & Matthews, R. The action of light on the eye. I: The discharge of impulses in the optic nerve and its relation to the electric change in the retina. *J. Physiol.* (*London*), 1927a, **63**, 378–414.
2. Adrian, E. D., & Matthews, R. The action of light on the eye. II: The processes involved in retinal excitation. *J. Physiol.* (*London*), 1927b, **64**, 279–301.
3. Barlow, H. B. Action potentials from the frog's retina. *J. Physiol.* (*London*), 1953a, **119**, 58–68.
4. Barlow, H. B. Summation and inhibition in the frog's retina. *J. Physiol.* (*London*), 1953b, **119**, 69–88.
5. Bartley, S. H., & Nelson, T. M. Some relations between sensory end results and neural activity in the optic pathway. *J. Psychol.*, 1963, **55**, 121–143.
6. Baumgarten, R. von, & Jung, R. Microelectrode studies on the visual cortex. *Rev. Neurol.*, 1952, **87**, 151–155.
7. Baumgartner, G. Reaktionen einzelner Neurone im optischen Cortex der Katze nach Lichtblitzen. *Pflüg. Arch. Ges. Physiol.*, 1955, **261**, 457–469.
8. Baumgartner, G., & Hakas, P. Reaktionen einzelner Opticusneurone und corticaler Nervenzellen der Katze im Hell-Dunkel-Grenzfeld (Simultankontrast). *Pflüg. Arch. Ges. Physiol.*, 1959, **270**, 29.

9. Baumgartner, G., & Hakas, P. Vergleich der receptiven Felder einzelner on-Neurone des N. opticus, des Corpus geniculatum laterale und des optischen Cortex der Katze. *Zbl. Ges. Neurol. Psychiat.*, 1960, **155**, 243–244.

10. Baumgartner, G., & Jung, R. Hemmungsphaenomene an einzelnen corticalen Neuronen und ihre Bedeutung fuer die Bremsung convulsiever Entladungen. *Arch. Sci. Biol.*, 1955, **39**, 474–486.

11. Brouwer, B., & Zeeman, W. C. P. The projection of the retina in the primary optic neuron in monkeys. *Brain*, 1926, **49**, 1–35.

12. Brown, K. T., & Wiesel, T. N. Analysis of the intraretinal electroretinogram in the intact cat eye. *J. Physiol.*, 1961a, **158**, 229–256.

13. Brown, K. T., & Wiesel, T. N. Localization of origins of electroretinogram components by intraretinal recording in the intact cat eye. *J. Physiol.*, 1961b, **158**, 247–280.

14. Campbell, F. W., & Rushton, W. A. H. Measurement of the scotopic pigment in the living human eye. *J. Physiol. (London)*, 1955, **130**, 131–147.

15. Carmichael, L., & Dearborn, W. F. *Reading and Visual Fatigue*. Boston: Houghton Mifflin, 1947.

16. Dartnall, H. J. A. *The Visual Pigments*. New York: Wiley, 1957.

17. Dartnall, H. J. A. The photobiology of visual processes. In *The Eye. Vol. II. Part II.* H. Davson, Ed. New York: Academic Press, 1962, pp. 321–533.

18. De Valois, R. L. Color vision mechanisms in the monkey. *J. Gen. Physiol.*, 1960, **43**, 115–128.

19. De Valois, R. L. Neural processing of visual information. In *Frontiers in Physiological Psychology*. R. W. Russell, Ed. New York: Academic Press, 1966, pp. 51–91.

20. De Valois, R. L., Jacobs, G. H., & Jones, A. E. Effects of increments and decrements of light on neural discharge rate. *Science*, 1962, **136**, 986–987.

21. De Valois, R. L., Jacobs, G. H., & Jones, A. E. Responses of single cells in primate red-green color vision system. *Optic*, 1963, **20**, 87–98.

22. Dimmick, F. L. Color. In *Foundations of Psychology*. E. G. Boring, H. S. Langfeld, & H. P. Weld, Eds. New York: Wiley, 1948.

23. Donner, K. O., & Granit, R. Scotopic dominator and state of visual purple in the retina. *Acta Physiol. Scand.*, 1949, **17**, 161–169.

24. Du Bois Reymond, E. *Untersuchungen über Thierische Elektrizität*. Berlin: G. Reimer, 1849, Vol. 2, Pt. 1. Cited in Granit, 1955a.

25. Granit, R. The components of the retinal action potential and their relation to the discharge in the optic nerve. *J. Physiol. (London)*, 1933, **77**, 207–240.

26. Granit, R. A physiological theory of color perception. *Nature (London)*, 1943a, **151**, 11–14.

27. Granit, R. "Red" and "green" receptors in the retina of Tropidonotus. *Acta Physiol. Scand.*, 1943b, **5**, 108–115.

28. Granit, R. The spectral properties of the visual receptors of the cat. *Acta Physiol. Scand.*, 1943c, **5**, 219–229.

29. Granit, R. *Sensory Mechanisms of the Retina*. London: Oxford Univ. Press, 1947.

30. Granit, R. *Receptors and sensory perception*. New Haven, Conn.: Yale Univ. Press, 1955.

31. Granit, R. Neural activity in the retina. In *Handbook of Physiology*. Vol. I. J. Field, H. W. Magoun, & V. E. Hall, Eds. Washington, D.C.: Amer. Physiol. Soc., 1959, pp. 693–712.

32. Granit, R., & Wrede, C. M. The electrical responses of light-adapted frog's eyes to monochromatic stimuli. *J. Physiol. (London)*, 1937, **89**, 239–256.

33. Grüsser, O. -J. Rezeptorpotentiale einzelner retinaler Zapfen der Katze. *Naturwissenschaften*, 1957, **44**, 522.

34. Gurian, B., & Riggs, L. A. Electrical potentials within the intact frog retina. *Exp. Neurol.*, 1960, **2**, 191–198.

35. Hartline, H. K. The response of single optic nerve fibers of the vertebrate eye to illumination of the retina. *Amer. J. Physiol.*, 1938, **121**, 400–415.

36. Hartline, H. K. The receptive field of the optic nerve fibers. *Amer. J. Physiol.*, 1940a, **130**, 690–699.

37. Hartline, H. K. The effects of spatial summation in the retina on the excitation of the fibers of the optic nerve. *Amer. J. Physiol.*, 1940b, **130**, 700–711.

38. Hartline, H. K. The nerve messages in the fibers of the visual pathway. *J. Opt. Soc. Amer.*, 1940c, **30**, 239–247.
39. Hubbard, R., & Wald, G. The mechanism of rhodopsin synthesis. *Proc. Nat. Acad. Sci. (U.S.)*, 1951, **37**, 69–79.
40. Hubel, D. H. Single unit activity in striate cortex of unrestrained cats. *J. Physiol. (London)*, 1959, **147**, 226–238.
41. Hubel, D. H. Single unit activity in lateral geniculate body and optic tract of unrestrained cats. *J. Physiol. (London)*, 1960, **150**, 91–104.
42. Hubel, D. H. Integrative processes in ventral visual pathway of the cat. *J. Opt. Soc. Amer.*, 1963, **53**, 58–66.
43. Hubel, D. H., & Wiesel, T. N. Receptive fields of single neurones in the cat's striate cortex. *J. Physiol. (London)*, 1959, **148**, 574–591.
44. Hubel, D. H., & Wiesel, T. N. Integrative action in the cat's lateral geniculate body. *J. Physiol. (London)*, 1961, **155**, 385–398.
45. Hubel, D. H., & Wiesel, T. N. Receptive fields, binocular interaction and functional architecture in the cat's visual cortex. *J. Physiol. (London)*, 1962, **160**, 106–154.
46. Hubel, D. H., & Wiesel, T. N. Receptive fields and functional architecture in two nonstriate visual areas (18 and 19) of the cat. *J. Neurophysiol.*, 1965, **28**, 229–289.
47. Hurvich, L. M., & Jameson, D. Some quantitative aspects of an opponent-colors theory. II. Brightness, saturations, and hue in normal and dichromatic vision. *J. Opt. Soc. Amer.*, 1955, **45**, 602–616.
48. Hurvich, L. M., & Jameson, D. An opponent-process theory of color vision. *Psychol. Rev.*, 1957, **64**, 384–404.
49. Jung, R. Coordination of specific and nonspecific afferent impulses at single neurons of the visual cortex. In *The Reticular Formation of the Brain*. H. H. Jasper, L. D. Proctor, R. S. Knighton, W. C. Noshay, & R. T. Costello, Eds. Boston: Little, Brown, 1958a, pp. 423–434.
50. Jung, R. Excitation, inhibition and coordination of cortical neurons. *Exp. Cell Res.*, 1958b, Suppl. 5, 262–271.
51. Jung, R. Microphysiology of cortical neurons and its significance for psychophysiology. In Festschrift Prof. C. Estable. *An. Facult. Med. Montevideo*, 1959a, **44**, 323–332.
52. Jung, R. Mikrophysiologie des optischen Cortex: Koordination der Neuronenentladungen nach optischen, vestibulaeren und unspezifischen Afferenzen und ihre Bedeutung fuer die Sinnesphysiologie. *Fifteenth General Assembly of the Japanese Medical Congress, Tokyo*, 1959b, **5**, 693–698.
53. Jung, R. Neuronal integration in the visual cortex and its significance for visual information. In *Sensory Communication*. W. A. Rosenblith, Ed. Cambridge, Mass.: M.I.T. Press, 1961, pp. 627–674.
54. Jung, R., & Baumgartner, G. Hemmungsmechanismen und bremsende Stabilisierung an einzelnen Neuronen des optischen Cortex: Ein Beitrag zur Koordination corticaler Erregungsvorgaenge. *Pflüg. Arch. Ges. Physiol.*, 1955, **261**, 434–456.
55. Jung, R., Baumgarten, R. von, & Baumgartner, G. Mikroableitungen von einzelnen Nervenzellen im optischen Cortex: Die lichtaktivierten B-Neurone. *Arch. Psychiat. Nervenkr.*, 1952, **189**, 521–539.
56. Jung, R., Creutzfeldt, O., & Grüsser, O. J. Die Mikrophysiologie kortikaler Neurone und ihre Bedeutung fuer die Sinnes- und Hirnfunktionen. *Dtsch. Med. Wschr.*, 1957, **82**, 1050–1059.
57. Kuffler, S. W. Neurons in the retina: organization, inhibition and excitation problems. *Cold. Spr. Harb. Symp. Quant. Biol.*, 1952, **17**, 281–292.
58. Kuffler, S. W. Discharge patterns and functional organization of mammalian retina. *J. Neurophysiol.*, 1953, **16**, 37–68.
59. Le Grand, Y. *Light, Colour and Vision*. London: Chapman & Hall Ltd., 1957.
60. Lettvin, J. Y., Maturana, H. R., McCulloch, W. S., & Pitts, W. H. What the frog's eye tells the frog's brain. *Proc. Inst. Radio Engr.*, 1959, **47**, 1940–1951.
61. Lettvin, J. Y., Maturana, H. R., Pitts, W. H., & McCulloch, W. S. Two remarks on the visual system of the frog. In *Sensory Communication*. W. A. Rosenblith, Ed. Cambridge, Mass.: M.I.T. Press, 1961, pp. 757–776.
62. MacNichol, E. F., Jr., & Svaetichin, G. Electric responses from the isolated retinas of fishes. *Amer. J. Ophthalmol.*, 1958, **46**, 26–40.

63. Marks, W. B., Dobelle, W. H., & MacNichol, E. F., Jr. Visual pigments of single primate cones. *Science*, 1964, **143**, 1181–1183.

64. Marshall, W. H., & Talbott, S. A. Recovery cycle of the lateral geniculate of the nembutalized cat. *Amer. J. Physiol.*, 1940, **129**, 417–418.

65. Maturana, H. R. Number of fibers in the optic nerve and the number of ganglion cells in the retina of Anurans. *Nature (London)*, 1959, **183**, 1406–1407.

66. Maturana, H. R., Lettvin, J. Y., McCulloch, W. S., & Pitts, W. H. Evidence that cut optic nerve fibers in a frog regenerate to their proper places in the tectum. *Science*, 1959, **130**, 1709–1710.

67. Maturana, H. R., Lettvin, J. Y., Pitts, W. H., & McCulloch, W. S. Physiology and anatomy of vision in the frog. *J. Gen. Physiol.*, 1960, Suppl. 43, 129–175.

68. Miller, W. H., Ratliff, F., & Hartline, H. K. How cells receive stimuli. *Scient. Amer.*, 1961, **205**, 223–238.

69. Motokawa, K., & Mita, T. Über eine einfachere Untersuchungsmethode und Eigenschaften der Aktionsströme der Netzhaut des Menschen. *Tohoku J. Exp. Med.*, 1942, **42**, 114–133.

70. Motokawa, K., Oikawa, T., & Tasaki, K. Receptor potential of vertebrate retina. *J. Neurophysiol.*, 1957, **20**, 186–199.

71. Peele, T. L. *The Neuroanatomic Basis for Clinical Neurology* (2nd ed.). New York: Blakiston Division, McGraw-Hill, 1961.

72. Polyak, S. L. *The Vertebrate Visual System.* H. Klüver, Ed. Chicago: Univ. of Chicago Press, 1957.

73. Ratliff, F. Inhibitory interaction and the detection and enhancement of contours. In *Sensory Communication.* W. A. Rosenblith, Ed. Cambridge, Mass.: M.I.T. Press, 1961, pp. 183–203.

74. Ratliff, F., & Hartline, H. K. The response of Limulus optic nerve fibers to patterns of illumination on the receptor mosaic. *J. Gen. Physiol.*, 1959, **42**, 1241–1255.

75. Ratliff, F., Miller, W. H., & Hartline, H. K. Neural interaction in the eye and the integration of receptor activity. *Ann. N. Y. Acad. Sci.*, 1958, **74**, 210–222.

76. Riggs, L. A. Electrophysiology of vision. In *Vision and Visual Perception.* C. H. Graham, Ed. New York: Wiley, 1965, pp. 81–131.

77. Riggs, L. A., Berry, R. N., & Wayner, M. A. A comparison of electrical and psychophysical determinations of the spectral sensitivity of the human eye. *J. Opt. Soc. Amer.*, 1949, **39**, 427–436.

78. Rushton, W. A. Physical measurement of cone pigment in the living human eye. *Nature (London)*, 1957, **179**, 571–573.

79. Rushton, W. A., Campbell, F. W., Hagins, W. A., & Brindley, G. S. The bleaching and regeneration of rhodopsin in the living eye of the albino rabbit and of man. *Optica Acta*, 1955, **1**, 183–190.

80. Salzmann, M. *The Anatomy and Physiology of the Human Eyeball in the Normal State.* Chicago: Univ. of Chicago Press, 1912.

81. Svaetichin, G. The cone action potential. *Acta Physiol. Scand.*, 1953, **29**, Suppl. 106, 565–600.

82. Svaetichin, G., & MacNichol, E. F., Jr. Retinal mechanisms for chromatic and achromatic vision. *Ann. N. Y. Acad. Sci.*, 1958, **74**, 385–399.

83. Toida, N., & Goto, M. Some mechanisms of color reception found by analyzing the electroretinogram of frog. *Jap. J. Physiol.*, 1954, **4**, 260–267.

84. Tomita, T. Studies on the intraretinal action potential. I. Relation between the localization of micro-pipette in the retina and the shape of the intraretinal action potential. *Jap. J. Physiol.*, 1950, **1**, 110–117.

85. Tomita, T. Electrical activity in the vertebrate retina. *J. Opt. Soc. Amer.*, 1963, **53**, 49–57.

86. Wagner, H. G., MacNichol, E. F., Jr., & Wolbarsht, M. L. The response properties of single ganglion cells in the goldfish retina. *J. Gen. Physiol.*, 1960, **43**, Suppl. 2, 45–62.

87. Wagner, H. G., MacNichol, E. F., Jr. & Wolbarsht, M. L. Functional basis for "on"—center and "off"—center receptive fields in the retina. *J. Opt. Soc. Amer.*, 1963, **53**, 66–70.

88. Wald, G., Brown, P. K., & Smith, P. H, Iodopsin. *J. Gen. Physiol.*, 1954–1955, **38**, 623–681.

89. Walls, G. L. *The Vertebrate Eye and its Adaptive Radiation.* Bloomfield Hills, Mich.: Cranbrook Institute of Science, 1942.

Chapter 5

AUDITION

The Nature of Sound

Transduction of Vibratory Energy into Physiological Signals

Processing of Auditory Information in the Central Nervous System

Review

THE NATURE OF SOUND

Some Basic Properties

Sound results from the vibratory motion of physical objects that are sufficiently elastic to convert energy into motion. These vibrations do not themselves constitute sound, as the British physicist, Boyle, discovered 300 years ago. Boyle placed a bell into a jar and removed all air from the container. No sound could be heard when the bell was rung, demonstrating simply but elegantly that sound is not propagated unless there is a medium (such as air or water) that can be set into vibratory motions that correspond to the vibrations of the object.

Sound travels because the vibrating object displaces molecules in the propagating medium, giving rise to a disturbance that moves rapidly and quite far until it gradually dies down. Sound is propagated at a constant speed in all directions. The disturbance that emanates from an object takes the form of a spherical wave that mirrors every movement of the vibrating source by successive condensation and rarefaction of the air pressure.

When such a sound wave encounters an obstacle in its path, it may scatter around the object (i.e., *diffract*), penetrate it (i.e., be *absorbed*), or *reflect* back from it. If the object is small, the energy of the sound wave is largely diffracted and only a minor disturbance in the sound wave is produced. This property of sound is responsible for the fact that we can hear sounds, particularly those of low frequencies, even though there are many obstacles between our ears and the source of the sound.

If the obstacle is large, some portion of the sound is reflected back at an angle that equals the angle of incidence. This produces echoes and is responsible for many curious properties of sound. Some sound energy is absorbed by objects in its path. Absorption is negligible for very dense objects, such as stone walls and glass, and quite significant for very porous objects, such as curtains, pillows, and carpets —a fact that is used extensively to acoustically engineer homes and concert halls.

The speed of sound has fascinated scientists for many centuries. More than 300 years ago, the French mathematician, Mersenne, computed the time it took echoes to return from an obstacle. He concluded that sound travels in air at about 1038 feet per second. Considering the crudeness of his method, this turns out to be remarkably close to the true value of 1128 feet per second.

Subsequent investigations have shown that the speed of sound in air is significantly affected by temperature. At 32°F the molecules of the air do not move as freely as they do at room temperature, and the speed of sound is only 1087 feet per second. Conversely, when the air is heated to 212°F, sound is propagated at 1266 feet per second. Also, the denser the medium, the faster sound will travel. Its speed reaches about 4800 feet per second in water, 18,000 feet per second in quartz, and nearly 20,000 feet per second in steel. (This explains the curious observation that one can hear an approaching train soonest by applying the ear to the rails.)

Dimensions of Sound Waves

Sound waves vary in four basic dimensions: amplitude, frequency, wave form, and phase. As a sound wave passes an object, the air pressure increases to a peak of compression and then drops below its normal value to a valley of rarefaction. The amplitude of this pressure variation is an exact measure of sound intensity, which, in turn, is complexly related to the psychological variable, *loudness*. Man responds to auditory signals that cover an amazing range of intensities, the annoying sound of a jet liner at takeoff being a million times louder than the barely audible buzz of a mosquito. It has therefore become customary to specify sound intensity in terms of *decibels* (dB), a logarithmic scale that has no absolute zero point. A common reference for the decibel scale is the sound pressure required for an average human listener to hear a 1000 cycle per second (Hertz) tone. This value turns out to be 0.0002 dyne/cm^2 (see Figure 5–1).

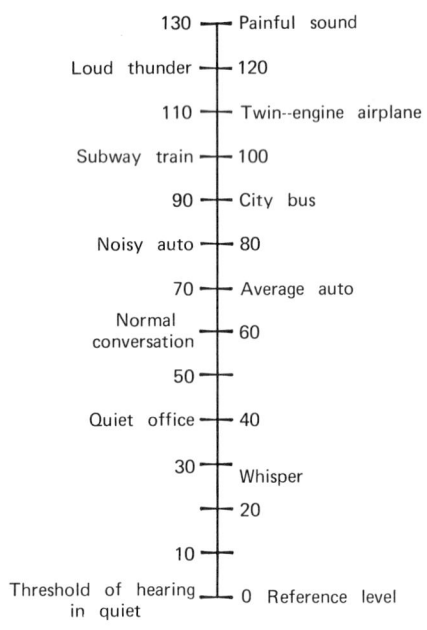

```
130 — Painful sound
Loud thunder — 120
            110 — Twin-engine airplane
Subway train — 100
             90 — City bus
Noisy auto — 80
             70 — Average auto
Normal
conversation — 60
             50
Quiet office — 40
             30
                  Whisper
                  20
             10
Threshold of hearing — 0 Reference level
in quiet
```

FIG. 5–1. Decibel intensities of some common sounds.

(From *Applied experimental psychology* by A. Chapanis, W. R. Garner, & C. T. Morgan. Copyright © 1949. John Wiley & Sons, Inc.)

The frequency of a sound corresponds to the repetition rate of the vibrations (i.e., the distance between successive peaks of condensation and rarefaction of the sound wave), measured in cycles per second or Hertz (Hz). Biological receptors are capable of detecting sounds of a frequency as low as 15 Hz and as high as 150,000 Hz. Man's auditory system does as well as most at the low end of the distribution but is insensitive to sounds above 20,000 Hz. (Since the human ear becomes progressively less sensitive to high frequencies with age, most adults probably should not pay extra for hi-fi components that promise faithful reproduction of frequencies above 16,000 Hz). The psychological variable, *pitch*, is complexly related to the frequency of sound.

The wave form of a sound of a single frequency is perfectly sinusoidal with symmetrical and smoothly curving peaks and valleys. A tuning fork emits such a single frequency and gives rise to the sensation of a pure tone. Nearly all sounds that normally impinge on the human ear are not of a single frequency, largely because most objects vibrate at more than one frequency. When you bow or pick the string of a violin, for instance, the string will vibrate as a whole, by halves, thirds, quarters, and so on. Other strings will also be set into vibration to some extent, and the end product is a complex sound wave that bears little resemblance to the sine wave of single frequency. However, the French mathematician, Fourier, demonstrated in 1801 that even the most complex sounds of a full orchestra can be analyzed in terms of simple sine waves, and that sine waves that make up a musical sound bear a simple relationship to each other—each is a harmonic of the fundamental tone (see Figure 5–2). (The vibration of a body as a whole results in the lowest frequency, called fundamental tone. Vibrations of the same body in parts—halves, thirds, etc.—produce overtones or harmonics. Because the amplitude of vibration is inversely related to frequency, the higher overtones become increasingly inaudible.)

When two sound waves of identical frequencies meet at a point in space, they reinforce or cancel each other, depending on the temporal relationship of the two waves. If the sounds are completely "in phase," i.e., the peaks and valleys of their waves coincide perfectly, the vibrations reinforce each other and increase the amplitude of the composite wave. Conversely, if the two sounds are perfectly "out of phase" such that the peaks of condensation in one coincide with the valleys of rarefaction of the other, they cancel (strange as it may seem, two pure tones that are perfectly out of phase are, indeed, inaudible). Since the amplitudes of the two waves always add, taking sign as well as

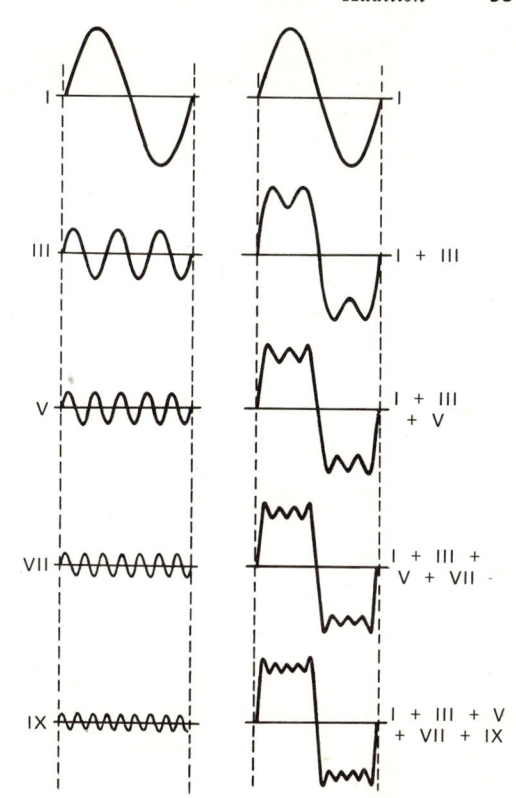

FIG. 5–2. Components of a complex sound wave. As the sine waves shown on the left are added to the fundamental wave at the top, increasingly complex periodic waves shown at the right result.

(From E. B. Newman. Hearing. In *Foundations of psychology*. E. G. Boring, H. S. Langfeld, & H. P. Weld, Eds. Copyright © 1948. John Wiley & Sons, Inc.)

magnitude into account, we can obtain any pattern of interaction between the two extremes of reinforcement and cancellation. When two waves of slightly different frequencies interact, the waves will reinforce each other at certain times and cancel partially or entirely at others.

The Relationship Between Physical Properties and Sensation

Simple "auditory" systems do not transduce sound as we know it but serve as obstacle detectors in environments (such as muddy water) where vision is not adequate. One of the most primitive systems is the lateral line organ of frogs and some fishes, which senses subtle displacements of water currents by unseen obstacles and thus permits rapid and sure movement in murky waters where eyes are all but useless. Bats and porpoises have perfected these sensory abilities to the point where the visual system, though present, adds little to the animals' ability to move among obstacles or locate prey. These *echolocating* animals emit pulsating beeps of sound at frequencies that are beyond the human frequency spectrum (20,000 to 120,000 Hz for the bat, 40,000 to 150,000 Hz for the porpoise). These high-frequency beeps are very intense, guaranteeing discrete echoes from even slightly uneven surfaces. Combined with the echolocating animals' extraordinary sensitivity to these "ultrasonic" sounds (the bat responds to echoes that are one hundred billion times weaker than the sound it emits), this guarantees that the animals can detect even minute objects and identify them as prey to be chased or obstacles to be avoided.

The human auditory system is so exquisitely sensitive that it comes very close to theoretical limits for such a system. It responds to sound waves that displace the eardrum less than one tenth the diameter of a hydrogen molecule and has a frequency range that is barely narrow enough to filter out some annoying sounds. Even a slight improvement in the system's amplification characteristics would expose us to the continual roar of air molecules. Improvements in its frequency characteristics would let us hear the groans of joints and muscles, the rushing of blood through the circulatory system or, at the high-frequency end, the pulsating beeps of bats navigating by echolocation.

The auditory system is, however, far from linear within its remarkable range and consequently does not provide us with sensations that are simply related to the physical characteristics of auditory stimuli. The sensation of pitch is primarily related to the frequency of sound waves, but other factors, such as intensity and duration, often modify this relationship significantly. Loudness similarly is not a simple correlate of stimulus intensity but reflects frequency as well as duration.

The human ear is maximally sensitive to sound waves between 1000 and 3000 Hz, a range that covers most of the sounds that are essential for the identification of speech. Above and below this region of maximal sensitivity, the threshold rises gradually at first but progressively more rapidly towards the extremes of the audible frequency spectrum and reaches absolute limits near 20 and 22,000 Hz (see Figure 5–3). The upper limits

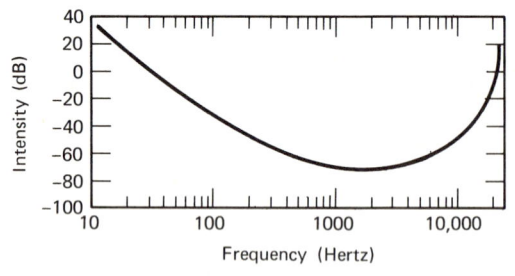

FIG. 5–3. Composite absolute threshold curve for monaural listening, based on the results of five independent studies.

(Adapted from *Hearing: Physiology and psychophysics* by W. Lawrence Gulick. Copyright © 1971 by Oxford University Press, Inc. Reprinted by permission.)

of the frequency spectrum are particularly sensitive to aging. In the very young, frequencies as high as 22,000 Hz may produce distinct auditory sensations. At maturity, this has typically declined to about 16,000 to 18,000 Hz and the aged often do not respond to sounds much above 8000 or 10,000 Hz.[8]

The first attempt to relate loudness to the intensity of the stimulus was made by Fechner. Using Weber's concept of a "just-noticeable difference" or jnd, Fechner arrived at a simple logarithmic rule that states that sensation increases by addition as stimulus intensities are multiplied. Matters have turned out to be more complicated than this simple law suggests, and we now generally use a ratio scale of subjective loudness that is based on magnitude estimations (i.e., subjects are asked to adjust an intensity to be twice as loud or half as loud as a standard).[11, 56] The resulting *sone* scale (from the Latin word for sound) uses an arbitrary zero (1 sone is equal to the loudness of a 1000 Hz tone 40 dB above threshold) and describes the relationship between stimulus intensity and loudness as a power function (i.e., loudness increases only slowly at low intensities but faster and faster towards the top of the loudness function) (see Figure 5–4).

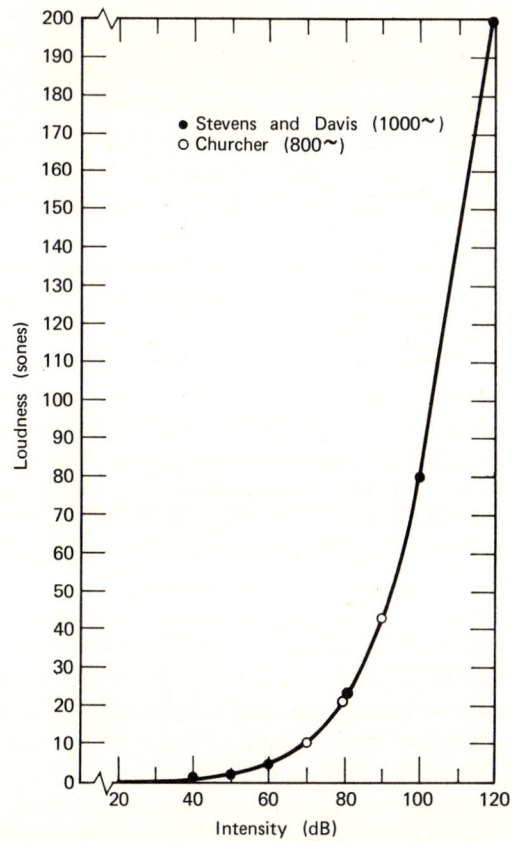

FIG. 5–4. Loudness for tones of 800 and 1000~ as a function of intensity. Data from Stevens and Davis, 1938 (●) and Churcher, 1935 (○).

(Adapted from *Hearing: Physiology and psychophysics* by W. Lawrence Gulick. Copyright © 1971 by Oxford University Press, Inc. Reprinted by permission.)

Instead of scaling the intensity-loudness relationship in terms of equal intervals, we may ask whether the just-noticeable difference (i.e., differential threshold) is indeed constant over frequencies, as Weber's law demands. We find that the size of the jnd is low and relatively constant for frequencies between 1000 and 4000 Hz—the area of lowest absolute threshold in man—but increases rather dramatically for low and high frequencies.[50]

The loudness of a tone is affected by the duration of the stimulus. Up to about 100 or 200 milliseconds, loudness is directly proportional to the product of exposure time and intensity.[42] Beyond about 500 milliseconds duration ceases to be an important variable.[2,3] The sensitivity of the auditory system decreases on prolonged exposure to stimulation.[9,2] Clear "fatigue" effects can be obtained even when the stimulus is only a few decibels above threshold. The amount of fatigue increases with the intensity of the stimulus and the duration of exposure.

Complex tones are louder than pure tones of equal intensity. When the component frequencies of a complex tone are widely separated, its loudness is equal to the sum of the loudnesses of the component tones presented separately. When the component frequencies are similar, the loudness of the complex tone is less than the sum of the compound pure tones, but still greater than the loudness of a pure tone of identical intensity.[31] The loudness of a noise is influenced by the width of its frequency spectrum. If one presents a sound that contains all frequencies between 600 and 1400 Hz, one can define its *bandwidth* (800 Hz) and *center frequency* (1000 Hz). If one maintains the intensity of the sound constant but increases its bandwidth or changes its center frequency, correlated changes in loudness occur. Up to some critical bandwidth, an increase in bandwidth has no effect on loudness. Beyond this critical value, loudness is positively related to bandwidth. The critical bandwidth is narrow at low frequencies (our example center frequency of 1000 Hz has a critical bandwidth of only 160 Hz) but increases sharply for tones of higher frequencies. One fascinating characteristic of critical bandwidths is the fact that their subjective width (i.e., the number of psychological units of pitch that are included) is constant across most of the audible frequency range (the constancy breaks down at the extremes).

The *pitch* of a pure tone is primarily determined by its frequency. However, the two concepts are not identical (e.g., a tone of 25,000 Hz has no pitch for the human observer, and tones of 17,000 and 17,002 Hz have identical pitch even though their frequencies differ). Several variables in addition to frequency influence the pitch of auditory sensations. The intensity of a pure tone influences pitch, particularly towards the extremes of the audible frequency spectrum. An increase in intensity shifts pitch downward in the case of low frequencies but upward in the case of high frequencies. Fortunately for music lovers, intensity shifts do not significantly influence the pitch of the complex tones that constitute music.

The duration of a tone also affects pitch. Very brief tones (less than about 10 milliseconds) are heard as clicks that are devoid of pitch. Slightly longer tones give rise to vague pitch sensations, but a clear and stable discrimination of pitch becomes possible only when the sound is presented for about 250 milliseconds. When the frequency of the tone is taken into consideration, an interesting relationship can be seen. Tones below 1000 Hz must be presented for a critical number of cycles (6 ± 3) to be identified by a distinct pitch. Tones above 1000 Hz must be presented for a critical time interval (about 10 milliseconds).

When a subject is asked to tune an instrument in perceptually equal pitch steps, a scale emerges that bears no simple relationship to the physical properties of the stimulus. To avoid confusion, a new unit called *mel* (from melody) has been created. It is customary, though not necessary, to anchor the mel scale at an arbitrary value such that 1000 mels equal the pitch of a 1000 Hz tone, 40 dB above the threshold. When this is done, a sigmoid function emerges that indicates that lower octaves have fewer mel units than higher octaves (see Figure 5–5).

A related question—does the size of the just noticeable pitch difference (i.e., the difference threshold) change as a function of frequency?—has been asked by psychophysicists.[54] It turns out that the size of the jnd is fairly constant at low frequencies up to about 2000 Hz—a range of approximately six octaves that covers all but the highest octave of a piano. Above 2000 Hz, the size of the jnd increases slowly at first but faster and faster as we approach the upper limits of the frequency spectrum.

The perception of pitch differs remarkably between individuals. Some have such a clearly defined perception that they can unhesitatingly reproduce a tone, such as A above middle C, from memory. Others can reconstruct the tone when given a frame of reference, such as middle C, and still others can not even come close, no matter how much help we give them. We dismiss this as individual differences in "musical ability," but it seems clear that the perception of pitch must differ dramatically between the person with "absolute" pitch and the man who cannot whistle a correct note to save his life.

Sound waves vary only along the dimensions of amplitude and frequency, but even pure tones appear to have characteristics that are not simply related to loudness or pitch. Tones have been classified in terms of volume, brilliance, density, and vocality—to name only a few of the more common attributes that have been used. Psychophysical experiments have suggested that at least some of these characteristics refer to sensations that are significantly different from pitch or loudness. Volume (or size of a sound), for instance, can be reliably differentiated from loudness[49], and high tones appear to have more density than low tones.[7] Volume remains reasonably constant for frequencies between 2000 and 4000 Hz. Lower frequencies have progressively higher volumes, higher frequencies progressively lower volumes. Density is reciprocally related to volume, although it may describe somewhat different aspects of sound.

Complex sounds are also characterized by something called *consonance* or *dissonance*, although the definition of these terms is not always clear. Some investigators have used these terms to rate the pleasantness of sounds;

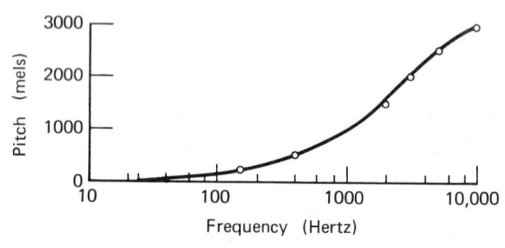

FIG. 5–5. Units of pitch (mels) as a function of stimulus frequency for tones 40 dB SL. A standard 1000∼ tone was assigned arbitrarily a pitch of 1000 mels. Tones of 500 and 2000 mels have pitches half as high and twice as high as the standard even though they correspond to frequencies of 400∼ and 3000∼, rather than 500∼ and 2000∼. Data from Stevens and Volkmann, 1940.

(From *Hearing: Physiology and psychophysics* by W. Lawrence Gulick. Copyright © 1971 by Oxford University Press, Inc. Reprinted by permission.)

others restrict their use to a description of the degree of fusion that exists between the individual components of the sound. The two definitions are not comparable, since a lack of fusion is rated pleasant under some circumstances.

Sounds that reach the human ear almost always consist of several frequencies and amplitudes that interact to give rise to complex auditory perceptions. A violin, flute, piano, and trumpet may be playing the same note at the same absolute intensity and yet their sounds are as different as colors from opposite ends of the visible spectrum. The perception of *timbre* turns out to be related to the fact that different instruments resonate preferentially at particular frequencies and thus give rise to different combinations of *overtones* (vibrations that are multiples of the fundamental or lowest tone).[22, 23]

Summary and Review Questions

Auditory stimuli consist of successive compressions and rarefactions (i.e., vibrations) of the medium, such as air or water, that is in direct contact with the organism's auditory receptors. These vibrations are audible only at some frequencies; man, for instance, responds only to frequencies between about 20 and 20,000 Hz.

Sound waves travel rapidly in air or water and scatter around small objects without being significantly distorted. Large objects absorb some of the impinging sound waves and reflect others back towards their source. Dense objects such as glass reflect most sound waves and absorb only little. Porous objects absorb much and reflect only little. Sounds of a single frequency travel in sinusoidal waves and are perceived as "pure" tones. Complex sounds consist of several such sinusoidal waves that interact and are propagated in a complex wave form that is determined by the fact that sound waves of common phase reinforce each other whereas sound waves of opposite phase cancel when they meet.

The pitch of an auditory sensation is primarily determined by the frequency of the stimulus. However, pitch is also influenced by intensity, particularly at the extremes of the audible spectrum, and by duration (pitch is not a stable attribute of auditory stimuli unless their duration exceeds 250 milliseconds). The loudness of a pure tone is primarily determined by stimulus intensity, but frequency plays an important role below 1000 Hz and above 4000 Hz. Stimulus duration is also important for stimuli shorter than 200 milliseconds. Complex tones are louder than pure tones of identical intensity. This effect is most pronounced when the component frequencies of the complex sound are distributed widely in the audible spectrum. The loudness of noise is related to its center frequency and bandwidth. Up to some critical bandwidth, loudness remains constant. Beyond this value, increases in bandwidth result in increases in loudness. The size of the critical bandwidth increases with the frequency of the center frequency.

1. Describe the stimulus properties that determine (a) loudness; (b) pitch; (c) complexity.

2. Describe the relationship between loudness and the center frequency and bandwidth of a complex auditory stimulus.

3. Describe the interaction of two tones that are out of phase.

4. Why does a given tone such as A above middle C sound different when played on different instruments?

TRANSDUCTION OF VIBRATORY ENERGY INTO PHYSIOLOGICAL SIGNALS

The Anatomy of the Ear

The exquisitely complex structure of the human ear has evolved from simple balance organs of prehistoric animals. Many primitive organisms, such as the jellyfish, are still equipped with similar balancing organs. Others, such as some fishes, frogs, and reptiles, have developed lateral line organs that respond to vibrations in the surrounding water. The ear of man and other vertebrates consists of three major components: the outer, middle, and inner ear (see Figure 5–6).

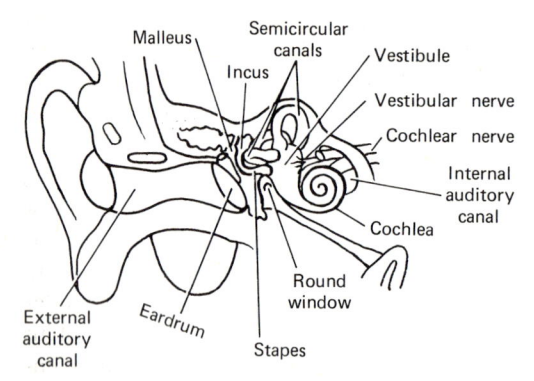

FIG. 5–6. Semidiagrammatic drawing of the ear.

(From H. Davis. Anatomy and physiology of the ear. In *Hearing and deafness*, revised edition, by Hallowell Davis and S. Richard Silverman. Copyright 1947 by Holt, Rinehart and Winston, Inc. Copyright © 1960 by Holt, Rinehart and Winston, Inc. Redrawn by permission of Holt, Rinehart and Winston, Inc.)

The outer ear consists of a trumpet-shaped flap of skin and cartilage called the *pinna* and a short curved tube called the *external auditory meatus*. The meatus is widest at its outer opening and near its inner end, where it is sealed by the ear drum or *tympanic membrane*. The structure of the outer ear canal makes it an excellent resonator that amplifies sound, particularly frequencies between 2000 and 5000 Hz to which man is most sensitive.

The middle ear is encased in the temporal bone. It contains air that is normally maintained at a pressure equal to that of the environment by means of the Eustachian tubes, which communicate with the pharynx.

The principal components of the middle ear are three tiny bones that link the outer and inner ear. Airborne vibrations can travel only to the end of the auditory meatus. Here, they set up mechanical vibrations in the tympanic membrane that are propagated and amplified by the intricate lever system of the middle ear bones. Attached to the center of the eardrum is the *manubrium* of the first of these three bones, the *malleus*. The nature of this attachment is such that the center of the eardrum is drawn inward, giving it the shape of a flat cone. The second little bone, the *incus*, connects the malleus to the third ossicle, the *stapes*, which has its footplate attached to the *oval window* of the cochlea.

Several muscles in the middle ear act as safety devices to protect the delicate inner-ear mechanisms from excessive vibrations. Some stiffen the eardrum while others twist the ossicles of the middle ear so that the stirrup rotates and transmits less force. This safety device is, unfortunately, not up to the demands of modern life, since it can respond only slowly and thus cannot protect the ear against sudden loud noises such as the report of a cannon or the explosive sounds of a jackhammer.

The inner ear lies in a cavity called *labyrinth*, deep in the temporal bone. The labyrinth has three principal divisions: the cochlea, the vestibule, and the semicircular canals.

The cochlea is the only portion of the inner ear that is directly concerned with audition. It consists of a spiral-shaped organ that is longitudinally divided into three tubes (see Figure 5–7). These subdivisions are formed

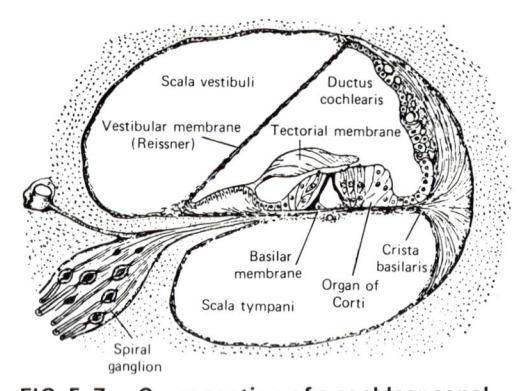

FIG. 5–7. Cross section of a cochlear canal.

(From *Outlines of neuroanatomy* by A. T. Rasmussen. Brown, 1943.)

by two membranes called *Reissner's membrane* and the *basilar membrane*. The two larger tubes, the scala *tympani* and *scala vestibuli*, contain perilymph, similar to cerebrospinal fluid, and communicate with each other through an opening called *helicotrema*. At the basal end of the scala vestibuli is the *oval window*, which is in contact with the stapes. A similar opening in the basal portion of the scala tympani is called the *round window*. The two large scalae enclose a third, smaller tube, the *cochlear duct* or *scala media*. It contains a viscous fluid called endolymph and the *organ of Corti*, which supports the auditory receptor cells.

The mechanical forces that are transmitted by the bones of the middle ear are transformed into hydraulic pressure variations when the stapes strikes the oval window. This sets up movements in the perilymphatic fluids of the scala vestibuli and in the basilar and Reissner's membranes that separate the cochlear duct from the perilymphatic canals. The basilar membrane is light and taut at the basal end of the cochlea and thick and loose near its apex. Vibrations in the perilymphatic fluid induce a propagated wave in the basilar membrane that distributes its maximal displacement in accordance with the frequency of the vibration. High frequencies induce maximal vibrations near its taut basal end, whereas the upper slack part of the membrane responds maximally to low frequencies.

The final transducer of mechanical energy into electrochemical signals that can be interpreted and processed by the nervous system is the organ of Corti. Somehow this tiny (less than one and one-half inches long) organ decodes the hydraulic-pressure changes in its surroundings and derives from them signals that permit discriminations of loudness, pitch, and timbre. Just how this transformation is accomplished is still a mystery, but some of the basic mechanisms are beginning to be understood.

The organ of Corti rests on the basilar membrane and projects into the cochlear duct (see Figure 5–8). Its most prominent component is the *arch of Corti*, which forms a tunnel along the length of the basilar membrane. The medial surface of this tunnel is flanked by a row of *inner hair cells*, its lateral surface by three or four rows of *outer hair cells*. From the upper surfaces of these hair cells, cilia emerge that penetrate the *tectorial* membrane that forms a roof over the organ of Corti. These cilia act as microlevers whenever a movement of the basilar or tectorial membrane produces a shearing motion in them to induce a graded displacement of the cuticular plate from which these hairs arise. This results in the electrochemical event called *generator or trigger potential*, which initiates action potentials in the auditory nerve.

Impedance-Matching Properties of the Ear

Three distinct amplifying mechanisms transduce sound waves into porportional hydraulic pressure changes in the inner ear, which the hair cells of the organ of Corti convert into physiological signals. The resonance of the external auditory canal increases the pressure at the eardrum, the mechanical advantage of the lever system of the middle ear approximately triples the force that is applied to the eardrum, and the size differential between the eardrum and the oval window produces another substantial amplification. This is essential because sound waves traveling in one medium do not readily enter another. The acoustic resistance of a medium depends on its density and elasticity. Contrary to expectation, sound waves in the air do not readily enter water (avid anglers notwithstanding), and the combined amplification of pressure in the outer and middle ear may do little more than match the impedance of the inner ear to that of the air.

The transformation of vibratory energy into mechanical and hydraulic pressure differences unfortunately also results in some distortions of the frequency, phase, and amplitude characteristics of the sound. The

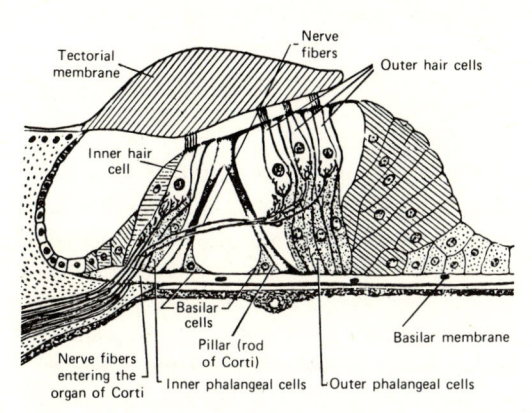

FIG. 5–8. Cross section of the organ of Corti. The outer hair cells are supported by their respective phalangeal cells, which rest in turn on the movable basilar membrane. The phalangeal cells supporting the inner hair cells rest on bone. Motion of the basilar membrane distorts the hair cells.

(From *Outlines of neuroanatomy* by A. T. Rasmussen. Brown, 1943.)

human auditory system responds to a range of roughly 20 to 20,000 Hz but picks up and transmits the middle frequencies much more efficiently than high or low frequencies. This results in a distortion of complex sounds because the intensity relations of their component frequencies are changed. Phase distortions arise in the middle ear because the inertia, stiffness, and friction of its components affect the transmission of vibrations differentially depending on their frequency. This introduces differential delays, and the components of a complex sound wave are therefore displaced in time relative to one another. The ear of the cat, for instance, produces a small advancement of phase for tones below about 800 Hz, a lag for tones of about 2500 Hz, and another small advancement for tones of 3000 Hz. In the very-high-frequency range, the cat shows a marked phase lag.[74, 75] Amplitude distortions become significant only at high intensities. For most of the intensity range that the human ear can handle, the system is surprisingly linear. The range of linearity is, however, not constant across frequencies but becomes narrower as the frequency of the stimulus rises.

Electrical Activity of the Ear

It is generally accepted that the displacement of the cilia of the hair cells that arise from the organ of Corti is an essential step in the transduction of the mechanical energy of sound into neural signals. It is widely believed that this may, in fact, be the crucial last link where mechanical energy is transformed into a graded bioelectric potential that, in turn, triggers action potentials in the primary neurons of the auditory system.

Forty years ago, Wever and Bray[72] recorded an electrical potential from the ear that appeared to reproduce the wave form, frequency, and magnitude of sound exactly (see Figure 5–9). The origin and functions of this potential have been the subject of much debate,[57, 76] but it is now widely accepted[31] that this *cochlear potential* (CP) originates as a result of the bending of the outer hair cells of the organ of Corti in a radial direction[5, 71] and

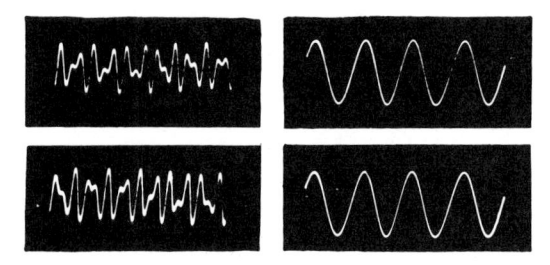

FIG. 5–9. Wave form of the cochlear potentials. The wave at the upper left represents a stimulus tone of 1000~ as recorded with a condenser microphone, and the wave immediately below represents the cochlear potentials recorded in a guinea pig. The wave on the upper right represents a stimulus made up of two tones, 1000 and 1500~ (which form a musical fifth), and the curve below represents the resulting cochlear potentials.

(From *Theory of hearing* by E. G. Wever. Wiley, 1949.)

may serve as a generator or trigger potential that acts as the final transducer of mechanical energy into neural action potentials.[31, 13]

In addition to this cochlear potential, a negative D.C. potential arises in the ear during auditory stimulation. This *summation potential* (SP) is believed to arise from the inner hair cells.[16] Its role in auditory processes is, at present, not clear. Some investigators believe that it may play a role in the generation of action potentials in the auditory nerve[15]; others are convinced that it does not materially contribute to the activation of auditory neurons.[31] We shall concentrate on the properties of the cochlear potential whose role in auditory processes has been more convincingly established.

The cochlear potential (CP) is a graded D.C. potential that has no absolute threshold that is measurable by currently available techniques. Even the slightest sound produces a potential that quite faithfully reproduces the magnitude, wave form and frequency of the stimulus. Unlike neural action potentials, the CP does not show fatigue or habituation in response to repeated presentations of the same stimulus. The origin of the CP along the basilar membrane varies as a function of stimulus frequency (see Figure 5–10). It is strongest near the apex of the cochlea when tones of low frequencies are presented and more prominent near the base of the inner

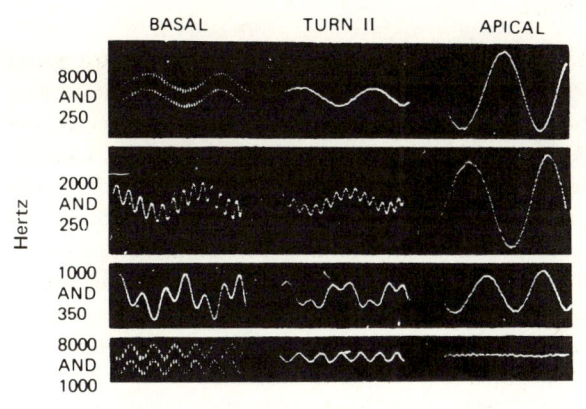

FIG. 5-10. Frequency analysis in the guinea pig. Cochlear potentials from paired electrodes, scalae vestibuli and tympani, in each turn.

(After I. Tasaki, H. Davis, & J.-P. Legouix. The space-time pattern of the cochlear microphonics (guinea pig), as recorded by differential electrodes. *J. acoust. Soc. Amer.*, **24**, 1952, 502-519.)

ear when tones of high frequencies are used. The latency of the cochlear potential is accounted for entirely by the transmission of sound in the ear.

We have already mentioned that the ear is not a perfect transducer of mechanical energy. Although the CP reflects the properties of sound waves quite faithfully, there are several sources of distortion (see Figure 5-11). The phase of the CP often lags behind that of the sound wave, the extent of the lag generally being greater for sounds of higher frequencies.[74, 75] The cochlear response to a complex sound wave is further distorted by the fact

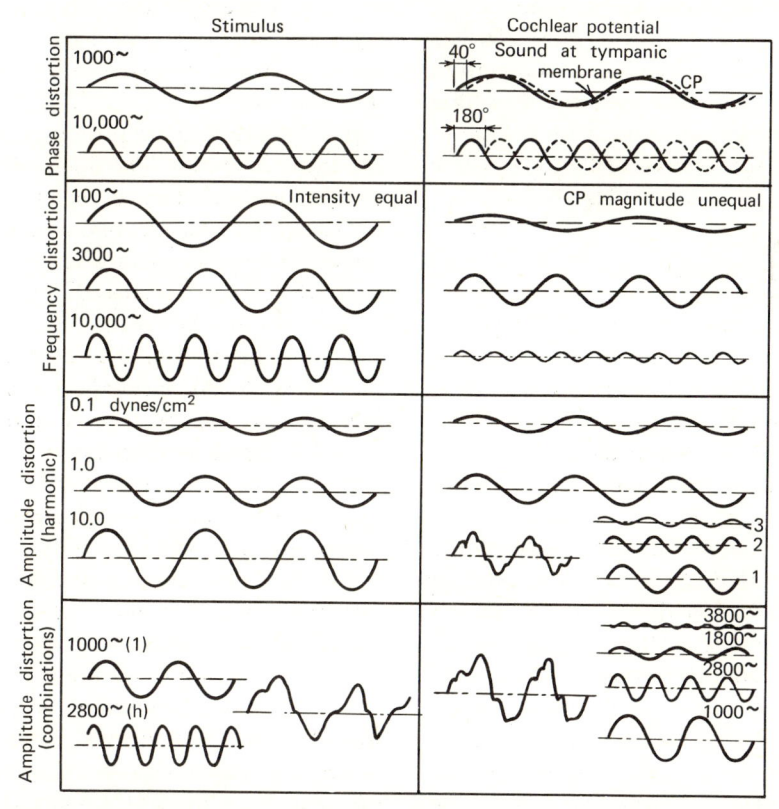

FIG. 5-11. Summary of the kinds of distortion produced by the ear. On the left are the stimuli and on the right are the resultant cochlear potentials.

(From *Hearing: Physiology and psychophysics* by W. Lawrence Gulick. Copyright © 1971 by Oxford University Press, Inc. Reprinted by permission.)

that the ear responds preferentially to frequencies near the middle of the auditory spectrum (i.e., somewhere between 1000 and 4000 Hz). The amplitude of components of the CP that reflect sounds within this range is disproportionately greater than the amplitude of components that reflect higher or lower frequencies.[73] At high sound intensities, further distortions in the CP occur because the linear relationship between stimulus intensity and CP magnitude breaks down. This occurs partly because the ear develops harmonics that are not present in the stimulus[73] and partly because the hair cells themselves bend in response to extreme deformations of the basilar membrane, thus reducing the distortions of their cilia.[76] The concurrent presentation of two tones often produces considerable distortion in the CP's. This "interference" effect is greatest when one records the CP of a tone in the middle frequency range and when the second, interfering tone is of moderate or high intensity. The effect is probably due to the occurrence of summation and difference tones (whenever a tone of 1000 Hz is presented concurrently with a tone of 3000 Hz, a summation tone of 4000 Hz as well as a difference tone of 2000 Hz occurs).

Theories of Hearing

There are two basically different types of theories in this field. "Place" theories suggest that tones of different frequencies selectively activate different portions of the basilar membrane and thus elicit neural activity in unique groups of auditory receptors. The intensity dimension of the resulting sensation is thought to be determined by the amplitude of the stimulation of these receptors and encoded in the frequency of nerve discharge. Competing "frequency" theories of hearing suggest instead that all auditory receptors are sensitive to all frequencies. Each is assumed to transmit impulses at a frequency that is directly proportional to the frequency of the stimulus. The intensity of the sensation is thought to be coded in terms of the number of receptors and neural pathways that are activated. Both of these theories have, as we shall see, several flaws that have forced many modern investigators to suggest some compromise between them.

The first formal version of a place theory of hearing was published by the German physiologist, von Helmholtz,[33] in the latter half of the 19th century. He believed that the basilar membrane consisted of transverse fibers that acted as independently tuned resonators. Sounds of low frequencies were thought to selectively resonate fibers near the apical end of the cochlea and high tones to resonate transverse fibers near the basal end. The intensity of the stimulation was believed to be transmitted by the amplitude of the impulses that are initiated in the nerve fibers that innervate the maximally stimulated portion of the organ of Corti.

The first frequency theory was proposed by Rutherford[53] towards the end of the 19th century. It suggested, in essence, that a single receptor could respond to stimuli of all frequencies and amplitudes and that the resulting rate and pattern of activity in a single nerve fiber could encode all parameters of the stimulus.

Both place and frequency theories have run into difficulties. The fibers of the basilar membrane have turned out to be neither under tension, as the resonance theory assumes, nor independently suspended, as the selective tuning proposed by Helmholtz would require. Moreover, the usefulness of resonator mechanisms has been questioned, since they do not meet the requirements of the auditory system. Resonators that are lightly damped are capable of the requisite degree of frequency discrimination but continue to vibrate after the termination of stimulation and thus make successive discriminations that the ear can clearly make impossible. Heavily damped resonators, on the other hand, cannot transduce the frequency discriminations of which the human ear is clearly capable. Helmholtz' original theory was also contradicted by the demonstration of the all-or-none response of nerve cells, but this is not a crucial problem for place theories in general, since they are free to assume that the frequency of nerve discharge codes the intensity of stimulation.

Rutherford's frequency theory was contradicted by experiments that demonstrated that the recovery cycle of neurons does not permit the transmission of frequencies higher than about 1000 Hz, and that the rate of nerve firing is typically related to stimulus intensity. Rutherford's notion that a neuron could encode all of the properties of sound was further questioned by the demonstration of all-or-none responses in neurons (which indicated that the size of the action potential could not encode stimulus intensity) and by the observation that the shape of the action potential does not mirror the wave pattern of the stimulus, as Rutherford suggested.

Von Békésy[1, 6] has proposed a modern version of the place theory that does not require the assumption of tuned resonators. According to this theory, the pressure changes that are induced in the inner ear by the movement of the stapes produce a traveling wave that progresses longitudinally along the basilar membrane. In accordance with observations made on hydraulic models of the cochlea as well as specimen of the ear itself, the theory proposes that the location of maximum membrane displacement during the passage of this traveling wave varies systematically with the frequency of the stimulus (see Figure 5–12).

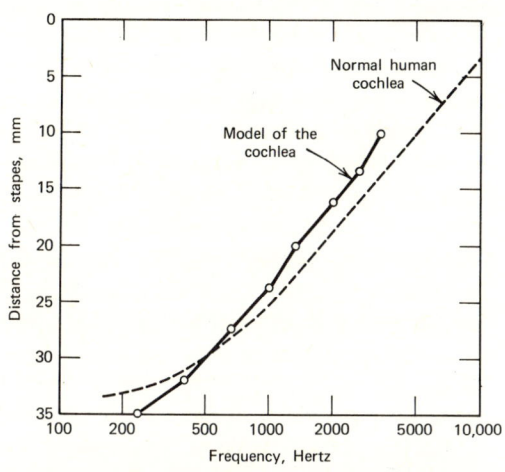

FIG. 5–12. Place of maximum stimulation as a function of frequency in the normal human ear and in a model designed by von Békésy.

(From *Experiments in hearing* by G. von Békésy. Copyright 1960 McGraw-Hill Book Company. Used with permission of McGraw-Hill Book Company.)

The transmission of the traveling wave is thought to be due to passive rather than active properties of the membrane, which is said to act analogous to a rope under tension that is fixed at one end and shaken at the other. The traveling-wave theory has received support from electrophysiological investigations (see below) that have shown that frequency tuned neurons exist at all levels of the central auditory system and that a tonotopic organization of neural elements (i.e., an orderly geographic distribution of frequency representations that reconstructs the distribution of receptors on the basilar membrane) can be found at several cortical as well as subcortical projection sites.

The theory has been questioned mainly on two accounts. A fundamental question has been raised as to whether a differential displacement of the basilar membrane can provide sufficiently selective activation of a sufficient number of discrete "places" to account for man's ability to discriminate frequencies. This problem is particularly bothersome at low frequencies when the displacement is very coarse. Von Békésy has proposed that two mechanisms may operate to increase the selectivity of the system. The auditory receptor may not respond directly to the displacement of the basilar membrane itself but rather to local vortex movements in the cochlear fluids that are strictly limited to the region of maximum membrane displacement. This may be aided by a system of reciprocal lateral inhibition between neural representations of adjacent portions of the basilar membrane.

The second area where the assumptions of the traveling-wave theory have been questioned is in audiology. Aging often produces a progressive loss of sensitivity to high frequencies that is due to calcification of the basal end of the basilar membrane. Although this is the region thought to be specifically activated by high-frequency tones, this observation creates problems for the traveling-wave theory because the calcification of one end of the membrane changes its overall stiffness, and this should produce a shift of the regions that are maximally activated by a given frequency.

Yet, no change in pitch perception occurs. Moreover, when high-tone deafness occurs as a result of damage to the basal portion of the basilar membrane, the effect is typically relative rather than absolute (i.e., high-frequency sounds become audible at high intensities). This is not easily reconciled with the notion that such deafness results from a destruction of regions of the membrane that are necessary for the transduction of high frequencies. Attempts to demonstrate a selective activation of specific portions of the basilar membrane by sounds of different frequencies have typically shown that low tones tend to activate the entire length of the basilar membrane whereas higher frequencies produce an increasingly selective activation of specific aspects of that membrane.[12, 55, 76]

Wever[71] has proposed a compromise place-frequency theory under the name "volley theory" that attempts to combine the best features of both while avoiding most of the major problems that beset the place and frequency theories. Wever proposed, on the basis of extensive phylogenetic studies, that simple auditory systems may use the frequency principle, which is quite capable of encoding frequencies up to several hundred cycles per second. In the course of phylogenetic development, the auditory system is asked to make increasingly finer discriminations among an increasing range of stimulus frequencies, and place of stimulation becomes an additional code for stimulus frequency, specifically for high frequencies, where the frequency principle breaks down.

Wever's theory proposes that low frequencies up to about 400 Hz may be encoded directly in terms of the discharge frequency of individual nerve cells in the auditory system. At these low frequencies, each individual sound wave is thought to produce sufficient displacement of the cilia of the cochlear hair cells to result in the depolarization of associated nerve cells and the propagation of an action potential. The intensity of the stimulus is thought to be represented by the number of receptors and/or neurons that are activated by each wave.

Frequencies between 400 Hz and 4000 or 5000 Hz are thought to be encoded in the frequency of activity not in individual nerve fibers but in the auditory nerve as a whole. This is thought to be possible because of the operation of a *"volley"* principle, which extends the range of frequencies that can be transmitted by a neural system. According to this principle, individual auditory nerve cells are exposed to a generator potential at every cycle of vibration. At low frequencies, the neuron can initiate an action potential every time it is so stimulated and thus follows the frequency of the stimulus perfectly. As the frequency is increased, some peaks of vibration and the resulting generator potential fall into the refractory period of the nerve cell and are thus ignored. The cell has recovered when the next cycle arrives and thus responds to every other cycle of the stimulus (or, more generally, to every nth cycle that falls just outside its refractory period). If another neuron in the auditory system has a slightly different response latency or recovery cycle, it will respond to cycles of vibration that occur while the first neuron is in its refractory period. The gaps in the response pattern of the first neuron are thus filled with the regularly spaced firings of the second. If we assume a random distribution of response latencies among auditory neurons, other fibers will come into action at still other times and thus fill gaps that are wider than a single cycle (see Figure 5–13). If one analyzes the total activity of all auditory fibers, frequencies much in excess of the limits of each individual nerve fiber can be transmitted in this fashion. Theoretically, such a system might be capable of transmitting all of the frequencies that stimulate the human ear and thus permit us to fall back exclusively on the frequency theory of hearing. Recordings obtained from the auditory nerve of several species of animals suggest, however, that this volley principle works only up to frequencies of about 4000 or at most 5000 Hz, perhaps because the limited differences in neural recovery functions do not permit a finer separation of activity patterns.

When volleying occurs, loudness is thought to be coded in terms of the number of nerve fibers that contribute to each discrete action

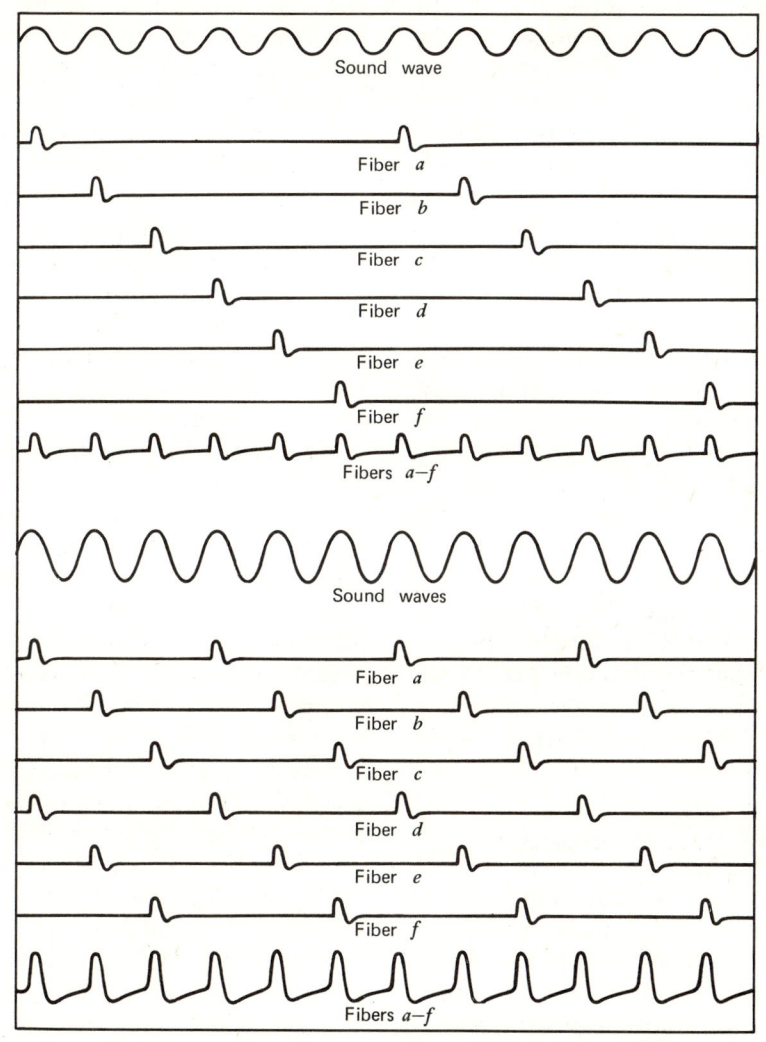

FIG. 5–13. Intensity representation in the volley principle. Above, the pattern of discharge in a group of nerve fibers at one intensity; and below, this pattern at a higher intensity. The frequency is represented in both patterns, but the discharge is larger in magnitude in the second.

(From *Theory of hearing* by E. G. Wever. Wiley, 1949.)

potential in the auditory nerve. An increase in stimulus intensity activates a greater number of fibers and induces previously active fibers to respond sooner in their relative refractory periods so that they can react to more closely spaced generator potentials. These two effects combine to increase the number of impulses per cycle of stimulation.

Beyond 5000 Hz, Wever's theory relies exclusively on the place principle. The location of the receptors that are activated by particular auditory frequencies is thought to play a relatively minor role for low frequencies but to code frequency completely at the upper end of the audible spectrum. At frequencies above 5000 Hz, the rhythmicity of the volleys is lost, but the frequency of nerve discharge per unit time is thought to encode stimulus intensity.

Wever's compromise theory appears to handle all situations nicely, but there are some critical problems. Although recordings obtained from the entire auditory nerve show rather good "following" for frequencies up to 4000 Hz, there is very little evidence that second or higher-order neurons in the auditory system follow even very slow frequencies (see below). Instead, one encounters cells that appear to be frequency-tuned (i.e., responsive only to sounds of particular frequencies), an arrangement that would appear to be more easily predicted by a place theory of hearing. Moreover, some degree of frequency tuning characterizes many of the individual fibers of the auditory nerve itself. The volley principle has been well established in several neural systems, but it is not clear that its operation in the auditory system has the effects proposed by Wever. There are some indications[57] that the amplitude of the compound action potential that is recorded from the auditory nerve changes abruptly at some frequencies, indicating a drop in the number of neural units that contribute to each volley. If such sudden drops are characteristic of the volley mechanism, loudness cannot be encoded in the number of neurons that are active on each burst, as Wever proposes.

Summary and Review Questions

The mechanical energy of sound waves is transduced into neural signals by receptor mechanisms that, in man, are located in the innermost portions of the ear. The human ear is a complex structure that provides several stages of amplification to compensate for the loss of energy that occurs when sound waves in air are transformed into hydraulic pressure waves in the fluids of the inner ear. Part of this amplification occurs because of the resonance of the external auditory meatus; part because of a lever action of the three bones of the middle ear that interconnect the eardrum with the oval window of the cochlea; and part because of an advantage that arises because the area of the tympanic membrane exceeds that of the stapedial footplate by a ratio of 21:1.

A second important transformation occurs in the inner ear. Here, the hydraulic-pressure waves that are initiated by the arrival of sound waves at the eardrum must be translated into proportional bioelectrical signals. The crucial event appears to be the bending of the cilia of hair cells that arise from the organ of Corti. Radial deformation of the outer hair cells in particular gives rise to a graded cochlear potential that may be the last step in the transduction process. This potential reflects the wave form, magnitude, and frequency of the stimulus (although minor distortions of phase, frequency, and amplitude occur) and may act as a trigger or generator potential that directly or indirectly initiates action potentials in the primary neurons of the auditory system.

Two main classes of theories have been developed to account for the transformation of cochlear activity into proportional neural signals. "Place" theories suggest that tones of different frequencies activate different portions of the basilar membrane (and hence different groups of hair cells) and elicit neural activity in unique, spatially organized groups of nerve cells. The intensity of the stimulus is thought to be encoded in the frequency of nerve discharge. "Frequency" theories, on the other hand, propose that all portions of the inner ear respond to sounds of all frequencies and that frequency is encoded in the discharge rate of the neurons of the auditory system. Intensity in such a system is encoded in the number of nerve fibers that are activated by a given stimulus. Both types of explanations have run into conceptual difficulties as well as contradictory experimental evidence.

The original place theories relied on resonator models of the basilar membrane that were found to be inadequate. More recent versions of place theories, notably von Békésy's "traveling-wave" theory, have avoided this problem by suggesting that the hydraulic pressure changes that are set up in the fluids of the inner ear as a consequence of sound stimulation may produce a traveling wave in the basilar membrane even though the latter has no independent resonator properties. There is a fair amount of experimental support for such a theory, but its adequacy has been questioned, partly because it has some difficulties in accounting for man's ability to discriminate low frequencies rather precisely and partly because it cannot readily explain some common clinical dysfunctions of the ear.

A compromise "place-frequency" theory has been proposed by Wever and suggests, in essence, that a pure-frequency mechanism may be operating at low frequencies (below 400 Hz) that are well within the recovery capabilities of neurons; a modified volley-frequency mechanism may operate between 400 and 4000 to 5000 Hz, which encodes stimulus frequency not in the discharge rate of individual nerve fibers but in the firing rate of the entire auditory nerve; and a pure-place mechanism operates for frequencies above 4000 or 5000 Hz, where selective activation of specific portions of the basilar membrane has been shown most convincingly. Wever's compromise theory accounts quite nicely for the observed relationship between sound and cochlear potentials and responses recorded from the auditory nerve (see next section), but it is not supported by microelectrode recordings obtained from higher portions of the auditory system that generally fail to show any evidence of frequency following.

1. Describe the principal anatomical features of the human ear and discuss their functions as transducers and/or amplifiers of sound.

2. Describe the transduction of sound waves into hydraulic pressure waves in the inner ear and their effect on the hair cells of the organ of Corti.

3. Describe the cochlear potential that can be recorded during auditory stimulation and discuss its relationship to the physical properties of the stimulus.

4. Describe the basic assumption of "place" and "frequency" theories of hearing and discuss their major weaknesses.

5. Describe von Békésy's "traveling-wave" theory of hearing. How does it avoid some of the criticisms that have been leveled against other "place" theories? What are its own weaknesses?

6. Describe Wever's volley theory and discuss its weaknesses.

PROCESSING OF AUDITORY INFORMATION IN THE CENTRAL NERVOUS SYSTEM

Action Potentials in the Auditory Nerve

The primary nerve cells of the auditory system that project dendritic processes to the vicinity of the hair cells are located in the *spiral ganglion*. The central projections of these cells are joined by axons from vestibular neurons and form the eighth cranial nerve. The auditory components of this nerve eventually divide into dorsal and ventral branches that terminate in the dorsal and ventral cochlear nuclei of the bulbar brainstem.

The inner hair cells are innervated by two types of neurons. Each fiber from the radial bundle of the auditory nerve projects to a few neighboring inner hair cells and thus establishes very specific connections with the central nervous system. Neurons from the inner spiral bundle of the auditory nerve send collaterals to hair cells along about 1/4 turn of the cochlea, thus establishing a much less specific connection. The outer hair cells are innervated even less specifically by fibers from the outer spiral bundle. Each of these fibers projects collaterals to hair cells along as much as 1/3 of the basilar membrane.

Recordings obtained from the auditory nerve reflect the cochlear potential as well as action potentials from first-order neurons in the auditory system. When pure tones of low frequencies are used, each action potential rides the rising slope of each cochlear potential (see Figure 5–14). This synchrony between auditory nerve discharge and stimulus frequency breaks down at higher frequencies, much to the embarrassment of proponents of frequency theories of hearing.

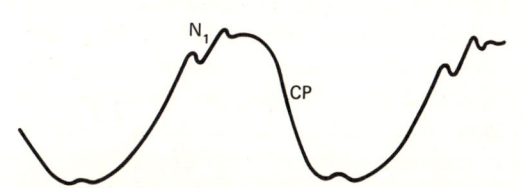

FIG. 5–14. The CP to a pure tone on which N_1 is superimposed near the crest.

(After *Theory of hearing* by E. G. Wever. Wiley, 1949.)

The electrical response of the eighth nerve to auditory stimulation consists of a compound potential that represents the sum of individual nerve action potentials. When fairly intense and discrete stimuli are used, this compound potential contains three distinct components that have been labeled N_1, N_2, and N_3 (see Figure 5–15). Since the time lag between the individual components (1 millisecond) corresponds to the refractory period of neurons, it is generally believed that N_2 and N_3 responses to intense stimuli may represent the repetitive firing of some neurons.

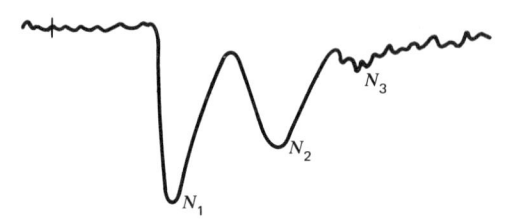

FIG. 5–15. The auditory nerve response to a click (negative down).

(After H. Davis. Excitation of auditory receptors. In *Handbook of physiology. Neurophysiology*. Washington, D.C.: Am. Physiol. Soc., 1959, sec. 1, vol. I, 565–584.)

The amplitude of the compound auditory nerve response is mainly determined by stimulus intensity, the relationship being most adequately described by a power function.[32] Its latency is quite long (0.4 to 1.0 milliseconds), partly because of the response characteristics of the hydraulic mechanisms of the inner ear. About 0.2 to 0.4 milliseconds are not accounted for by this explanation, and it is generally assumed that this relatively long delay may reflect the properties of the generator mechanism that transduces mechanical into neural activity.

The compound action potentials of the auditory nerve reproduce stimulus frequencies up to about 4000 Hz, presumably because different sets of nerve fibers have slightly different thresholds and thus set up volleys of activity.[71] The volley mechanism breaks down above 4000 Hz because the response latencies of individual nerve fibers are not perfectly constant. This variability gradually introduces so much noise into the system that synchronous responses become impossible to detect.

Differential synaptic delay and random variations in the response latency of second- and third-order neurons progressively reduce the auditory system's ability to respond synchronously.

Microelectrode recordings[26, 59, 60, 37] from single fibers of the auditory nerve demonstrate a phenomenon that appears to characterize all central portions of the auditory system. Most cells respond preferentially to a fairly narrow band of frequencies. In the auditory nerve, most fibers respond to a fairly wide range of frequencies below their optimal frequency but show a sharp high-frequency cutoff. The value of this cutoff frequency is related to the origin of the fiber in the cochlea. Fibers that arise from cells that project their dendritic processes to the apical end of the cochlea typically have low-frequency cutoffs. Fibers that relate to the basal end of the cochlea have high-frequency cutoffs. This pattern is, of course, similar to the distribution of cochlear potentials along the basilar membrane and bears a resemblance to the pattern of the traveling wave on the basilar membrane as described by von Békésy.[6]

The bandwidth of frequencies to which individual fibers respond is typically quite narrow for threshold intensities of the stimulus (i.e., the tuning of the cell is quite precise) but broadens markedly at higher intensities (see Figure 5–16). Two types of fibers have been

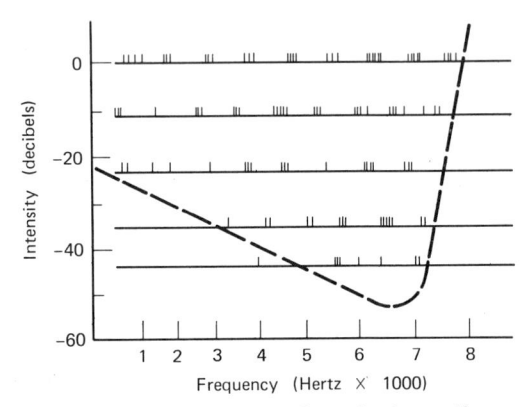

FIG. 5–16. Responses of a single auditory nerve fiber to tone pips of different frequencies and intensities. Dotted line shows boundary of "response area" of this fiber.

(From I. Tasaki. Nerve impulses in individual auditory nerve fibers of guinea pig. *J. Neurophysiol.*, 17, 1954, 97–122.)

found. Type I fibers are tuned to high frequencies and typically have asymmetric response areas around the "best" frequency. Their responsiveness falls off abruptly towards higher frequencies and only gradually towards lower frequencies. Type II fibers are tuned to low frequencies and typically have more symmetrical response areas (see Figure 5–17).

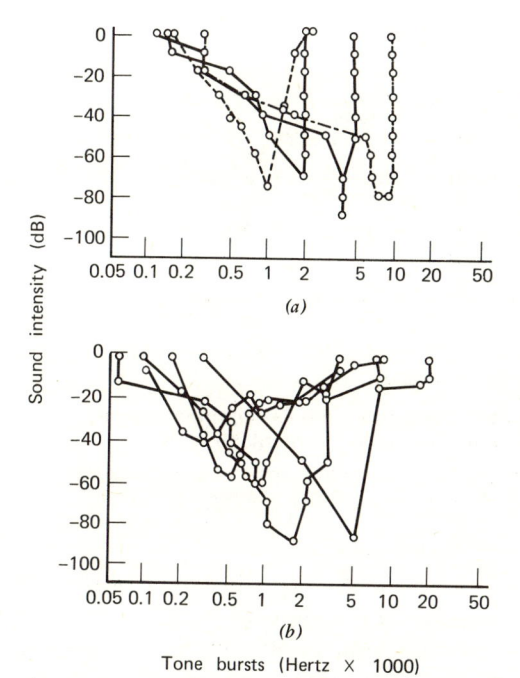

FIG. 5–17. Response areas obtained from primary neurons: (a) usual asymmetrical type; (b) symmetrical type. The ordinate is intensity of sound in decibels; the abscissa, the frequencies of tone bursts.

(From Y. Katsuki. Neural mechanisms of auditory sensation in cats. Reprinted from *Sensory communication* by W. A. Rosenblith (Ed.) by permission of The MIT Press, Cambridge, Massachusetts. Copyright © 1961 by the Massachusetts Institute of Technology.)

Many individual fibers appear to be tuned to the same "best" frequency but begin to respond to it at different threshold intensities, indicating that the activity of individual fibers may code not only frequency but also frequency within a particular intensity range.

Some fibers in the auditory nerve discharge spontaneously. These fibers are often not affected by auditory stimuli. Others do not respond to pure tones but react specifically to broad-spectrum noise or clicks, suggesting a selective sensitivity to complex auditory stimuli.

Activity of Central Auditory Projections

The fibers of the auditory nerve terminate in the dorsal and ventral cochlear nuclei of the medulla in discrete patterns that reflect their origin in the cochlea. Second-order cells in these nuclei project crossed and uncrossed connections to the trapezoid body and superior olive in the pontine portion of the brainstem. From there, some auditory projections are relayed to the cerebellum and the reticular formation. The majority of the tertiary auditory fibers form the lateral lemniscus and project to the inferior colliculi of the midbrain. Some direct projections to the medial geniculate nuclei of the thalamus have also been reported. Collicular cells principally project to the last subcortical relay station, the medial geniculate nuclei. Fifth- or sixth-order projections from the thalamus terminate in the auditory projection areas of the temporal lobe cortex. Electrophysiological observations indicate that an additional, extralemniscal pathway between the brainstem and the auditory cortex exists in some species.[29]

The precise limits of the cortical projections of the auditory system have been difficult to establish. Extensive cortical damage is required before significant degeneration can be demonstrated in the thalamic relay nucleus of the system, and most basic auditory capabilities persist after extensive ablation of the cortical projections. In many species the absolute threshold for pure tones,[38] intensity discriminations,[43] and even frequency discriminations[30] appear unaffected by even massive cortical damage. Pattern discrimination (i.e., temporal frequency discrimination)[30] and sound localization[43] appear to be the only sensory abilities that depend on cortical integration. Even here, we find extensive duplication or "overdetermination," since two or three of the cortical projection areas must be destroyed before a permanent impairment occurs.

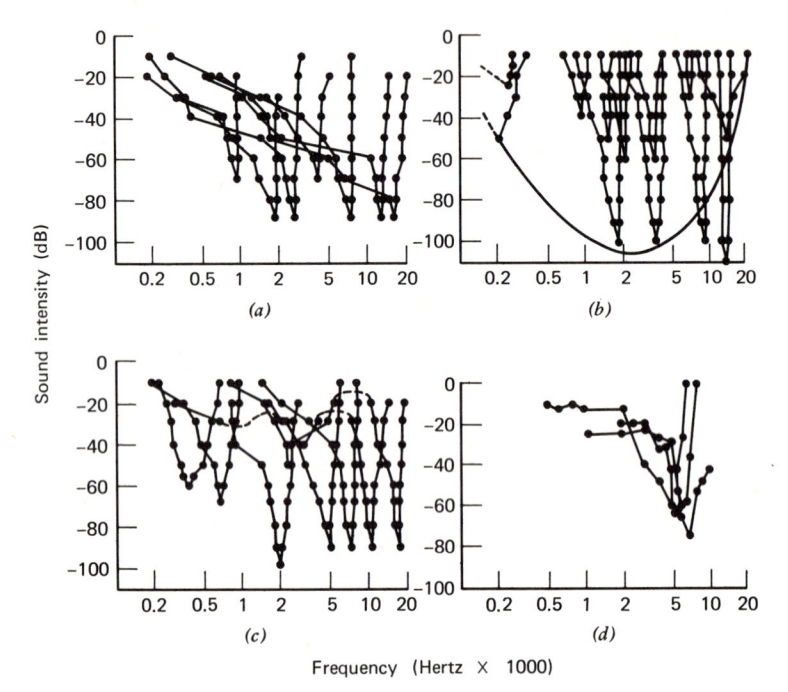

FIG. 5–18. Response areas of single neurons obtained from (*a*) cochlear nerve, (*b*) inferior colliculus, (*c*) trapezoid body, and (*d*) medial geniculate body.

(From Y. Katsuki. Neural mechanisms of auditory sensation in cats. Reprinted from *Sensory communication* by W. A. Rosenblith (Ed.) by permission of The MIT Press, Cambridge, Massachusetts. Copyright © 1961 by the Massachusetts Institute of Technology.)

Subcortical Relay Stations

Microelectrode recordings from second-order neurons in the medulla[26, 27, 61, 37] show frequency tuning similar though more precise than that seen in the auditory nerve (see Figure 5–18). An impressive range of "best" frequencies—extending from about 200 to 50,000 Hz in the cat—has been demonstrated at this level. However, neurons tuned to frequencies below 1000 Hz are quite rare.

Some neurons in the cochlear nucleus have more than one "best-tuned" response area.[41] The absolute thresholds of these cells may differ by as much as 60 dB. The discharge rate of individual cells is proportional within some limits to the intensity of the stimulus (see Figure 5–19). Maximal responses are typically obtained with stimuli about 25 to 30 dB above the threshold of the cell. The discharge rate may reach 400 to 500 pulses per second during the first 100 to 200 milliseconds of an intense stimulus but falls off to one-half or less of this initial rate when stimulation is maintained.

A fair number of cells in the cochlear nucleus discharge at a low rate in the absence of specific auditory stimulation. Many of these cells are inhibited by stimuli of a particular frequency and have clearly defined inhibitory response areas around the "best-tuned" frequency. Inhibitory responses can also be observed in cells that initiate firing in response to a particular stimulus frequency. Often, this positive response is inhibited by the concurrent presentation of a second tone of a particular frequency.[41] This type of interaction may be responsible for the sharpening of the frequency tuning that occurs at this as well as higher levels of the auditory system.

The spatial distribution of frequency tuning in the cochlear nucleus may follow a distinct pattern of tonotopic representation. In the cat, three complete representations of the audible frequency spectrum are found at this level: one in the dorsal cochlear nucleus, another in the posterior portion of the ventral cochlear nucleus, and a third in its anterior region.[51]

The tuning of individual cells becomes progressively more precise as one moves to higher levels of the auditory system. This suggests that inhibitory synaptic interactions may produce a cumulative "sharpening" of frequency discrimination at the cellular level.[37, 52, 35] The response pattern of individual cells also becomes increasingly complex and differentiated. As in the visual system, we find pure ON, OFF, maintained ON, and ON-OFF responses that are often peculiar to

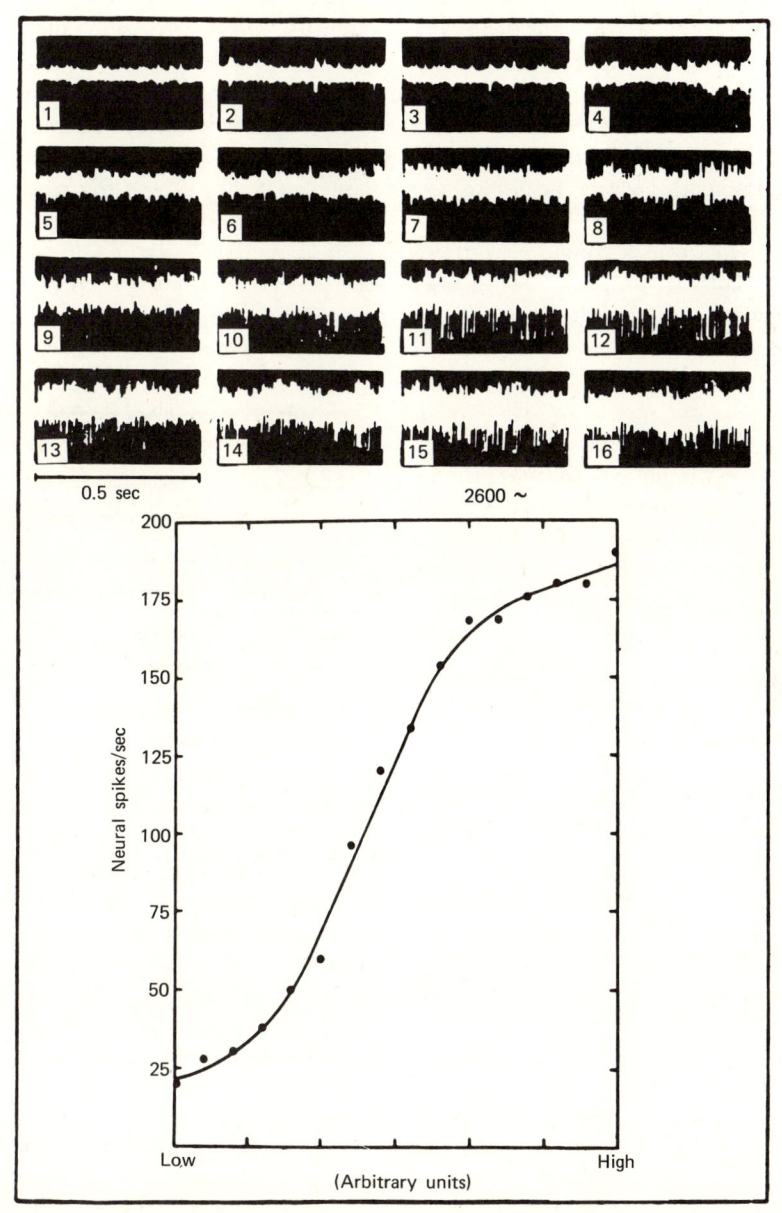

FIG. 5–19. The increase in frequency of discharge in a single auditory neuron with increasing intensity of sound.

(After R. Galambos & H. Davis. The response of single auditory-nerve fibers to acoustic stimulation. *J. Neurophysiol.*, **6**, 1943, 39–57.)

narrow frequency bands. Many neurons in the higher auditory relays give even more complex responses.[52]

Cells in the inferior colliculus tend to show "amplitude tuning" in addition to or instead of frequency tuning. The discharge rate of these cells increases as a function of stimulus intensity until some maximum value is reached. When the intensity is further increased, some cells show a gradual slowing of discharge rate; others stop firing altogether. The latency of the initial responses decreases to some minimal level as the intensity of the stimulus is increased but then remains stable, at the minimum, with further additions to the intensity of the stimulus.[52]

In the cat, two distinct tonotopic representations of the audible frequency range are found at this level: one in the external nucleus of the colliculus and the other, which has an inverted pattern of organization, in the central nucleus.[52]

Some cells in the superior olive and inferior colliculi respond to stimuli to both ears; others discriminate between stimuli presented ipsilaterally, contralaterally, or bilaterally. A variety of interaction patterns can be seen in these cells that suggests that sound localization may be coded even at these relatively low levels of the system.[35, 28]

Auditory Cortex

The organization of the auditory projections to the cortex is complex. Primary evoked potentials are most clearly recorded from the primary auditory area (AI), which occupies much of the middle ectosylvian gyrus in the cat. A distinct map of frequency-specific responses can be obtained that resembles the organization of frequencies on the basilar membrane.[79, 64, 67, 34, 35] This arrangement seems to provide a topographic representation of the frequency tuning of cells in the lower portions of the system. There is also some evidence that, within an area that represents a particular frequency range, there is a topographic representation of intensity that extends at right angles to the frequency continuum.[66] In the cat and dog, the frequency dimension is represented in an anterior-posterior dimension and loudness in a lateral-medial plane.

Microelectrode studies[35] have largely confirmed the picture that has been assembled on the basis of gross evoked potential recordings. They have additionally shown that individual cortical cells tend to respond to rather narrow frequency bands and react to intensity "overloads" much like cells in lower relay stations by complete or partial inhibition. One phenomenon that is rarely seen in low relay stations but characterizes a fair proportion of cortical cells is dual or even triple frequency ranges that cover harmonics of the lowest "best" frequency.

Individual cells in the auditory cortex give ON, sustained ON, ON–OFF, and OFF responses that are quite similar to those seen in the visual system[21] (see Figure 5–20). There

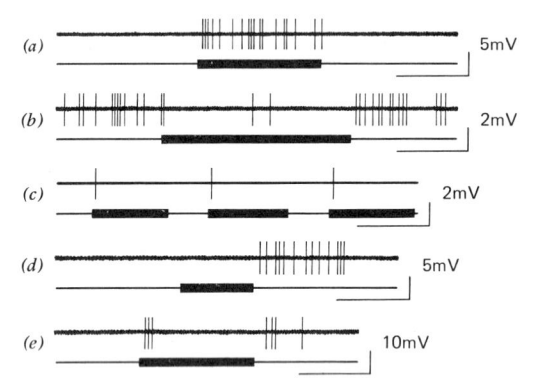

FIG. 5–20. Different types of unit response to tonal stimuli obtained from the unanaesthetized primary auditory cortex of the cat. (a) Sustained excitation; (b) sustained inhibition; (c) ON-response; (d) OFF-response; (e) ON-OFF response. Horizontal time bars = 0.5 sec.

(After E. F. Evans & I. C. Whitfield. Classification of unit responses in the auditory cortex of the unanaesthetized and unrestrained cat. *J. Physiol.*, **171**, 1964, 476–493. From E. F. Evans. Cortical representation. In *Hearing mechanisms in vertebrates*. A. V. S. De Reuck & Julie Knight, Eds. London: J. & A. Churchill, 1968.)

is some evidence that the same cortical cells may give ON responses to some frequencies, sustained ON or ON–OFF responses to higher or lower frequencies, and OFF responses to still other auditory stimuli[20] (see Figure 5–21). Some cortical cells appear to respond only to stimuli of gradually in-

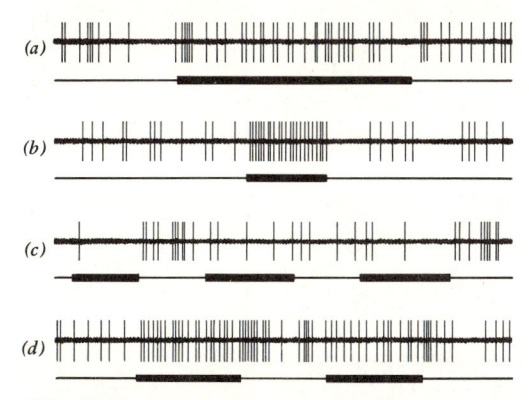

FIG. 5–21. Dependence of nature of responses of a unit in primary auditory cortex on the frequency of the stimulus tone. Tone intensity: 50 dB above threshold. (a) 1.5 kcyc/sec: transient response to onset of tone; (b) 2.5 kcyc/sec: sustained excitatory response; (c) 9 kcyc/sec: inhibitory and OFF responses; (d) 13 kcyc/sec: sustained excitatory and OFF responses. Time bar = 1 sec.

(From E. F. Evans. Cortical representation. In *Hearing mechanisms in vertebrates*. A. V. S. De Reuck & Julie Knight, Eds. London: J. & A. Churchill, 1968.)

creasing frequencies, others only to decreasing or decreasing as well as increasing frequencies[77] (see Figure 5–22). This pattern of selective responding is reminiscent of that described for moving visual stimuli.[36]

A number of additional auditory areas have been described that show topographic distributions of frequency-specific evoked poten-

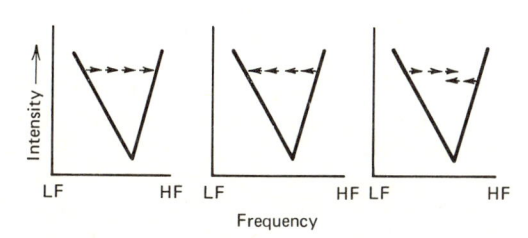

FIG. 5–22. Categories of frequency oriented units; *left*: units responding only to rising tones anywhere within its response area; *center*: units responding only to falling tones anywhere within its response area; *right*: units responding to rising tones in low frequency half of response area and to falling tones in high frequency half.

(From I. C. Whitfield & E. F. Evans. Responses of auditory cortical neurons to stimuli of changing frequency. *J. Neurophysiol.*, 28, 1965, 655–672.)

tial responses similar to that seen in AI (see Figure 5–23). In the cat, all of these areas surround the suprasylvian sulcus. A secondary auditory projection (AII), just ventral to AI, appears to have a topographic organization that is just opposite that of AI. Low frequencies are represented in the posterior portion of AI and the anterior segment of AII, high frequencies in the anterior section of AI and the posterior portion of AII.[79] A third major

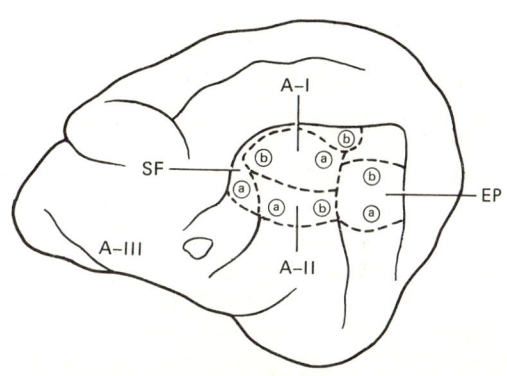

FIG. 5–23. Lateral aspect of the left hemisphere of the cat showing the five auditory areas responsive either to electrical stimulation of first-order neurons within the cochlea or to tonal stimuli. A-I, A-II, EP, and SF are specifically auditory in nature, and each shows selective responsiveness to basal (*b*) and apical (*a*) stimulation. A-III is polysensory.

(From *Hearing: Physiology and psychophysics* by W. Lawrence Gulick. Copyright © 1971 by Oxford University Press, Inc. Reprinted by permission.)

projection has been localized more posteriorly in the posterior ectosylvian gyrus of the cat. Area Ep is organized in a ventral-dorsal fashion with high frequencies represented dorsally. Topographically organized evoked responses have also been recorded from the somatosensory area II;[65] from a portion of insular cortex ventral and anterior to AII;[39, 17] and from the lower bank of the suprasylvian sulcus, an area that has been called the suprasylvian fringe (SF).[78] These observations indicate that each ear is represented in several cortical regions.

Just what purpose these diverse auditory projections serve is not entirely clear. An experiment by Thompson[63] has suggested that very extensive damage to the temporal lobe may interfere with frequency discriminations. However, this is an atypical finding that may reflect a general deficit rather than specific auditory impairment. More generally, it is found that even quite extensive damage to the cortical auditory projections fails to produce permanent impairments in basic auditory functions such as frequency or amplitude discriminations.[43, 30, 19] This suggests that the cortical projections may be necessary only for more complex integrations of auditory information. A number of experimental observations support this interpretation. Conditioned responses, particularly those requiring discriminations of a more complex nature, are lost following auditory cortex damage but can be reacquired,[43, 30] (see also our discussion of cortical lesion effects on learning and memory). Cortical lesions do produce essentially complete stimulus generalization[47] and serious deficits in sound localization.[40, 44]

Centrifugal Influences

The cochlea receives efferents via the olivo-cochlear bundle, which appears to transmit mainly inhibitory influences. Stimulation of the origin of this bundle[25, 18] suppresses the auditory-nerve response to clicks without interfering with the cochlear potential itself (see Figure 5–24). Inhibitory reactions to auditory stimulation of the contralateral ear have been observed in the second-order neurons of the cochlear nucleus.[46] Since these neurons were deprived of direct afferent input in these experiments, this inhibitory reaction also appears to have been mediated by centrifugal influences. It is particularly interesting that this inhibitory effect appears to be frequency specific in a manner that is reminiscent of the positive frequency tuning of auditory neurons. Some of the cells in the cochlear nucleus were maximally inhibited by stimuli of a "best" frequency that was surrounded by an asymmetric "response" area that widened as the intensity of the auditory stimulus to the contralateral ear was increased. Other neurons were inhibited by a broad band of frequencies when the intensity of the stimu-

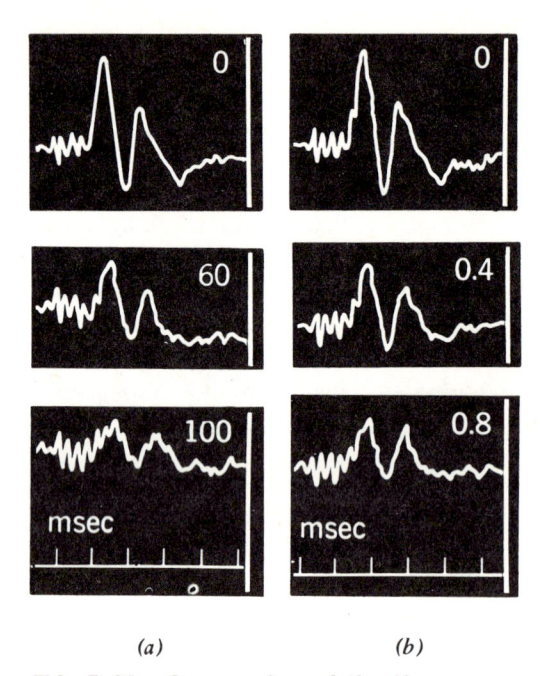

FIG. 5–24. Suppression of the N_1 response in the auditory nerve by electrical stimulation of the olivo-cochlear bundle in the floor of the fourth ventricle. (a) effect of shock frequency, indicated in upper right of each trace, 100/sec is optimal; (b) effect of shock strength at fixed frequency (65/sec). The fast ripple is the cochlear potential.

(From R. Galambos. Suppression of auditory nerve activity by stimulation of efferent fibers to cochlea. *J. Neurophysiol.*, 19, 1956, 424–437.)

lation was low but became increasingly better tuned as the intensity increased.

Summary and Review Questions

The central processing of auditory information appears to rely, at least in part, on two mechanisms: (a) frequency tuning of individual neurons and (b) the maintenance of a spatial organization that reflects the organization of the receptor cells in the cochlea. Frequency following occurs in some first-order auditory nerve fibers as well as in the compound action potential of that nerve but is rarely seen in higher portions of the auditory system. Even first-order auditory neurons commonly respond preferentially to a narrow band of frequencies, the specific nature of the frequency being related to the origin of the fiber in the cochlea. Fibers that arise from the apical portion of the cochlea are typically tuned to best frequencies in the upper portion of the audible spectrum and tend to have asymmetric response areas that are narrow above the best frequency and somewhat broader below it. Fibers that arise from the apical end of the cochlea typically are tuned to frequencies from the lower portion of the audible spectrum and tend to have more nearly symmetric response regions. The width of response regions around a "best" frequency is generally narrow for low stimulus intensities but widens considerably as intensity is increased. Even in the lower links of the auditory system one can find fibers that do not respond to pure tones but react to complex stimuli such as broad-band noise or clicks.

At higher relay stations of the auditory system, one often finds multiple representations of the spatial organization of the basilar membrane, and there is some evidence that some of these representations preferentially code frequency, while others code amplitude. Frequency tuning becomes increasingly precise as one ascends in the auditory system, and various types of amplitude tuning begin to appear. At many subcortical relay stations, a number of cells have similar or identical "best" frequencies and comparable response regions but different absolute thresholds. In many instances, the discharge frequencies of such cells increase as the stimulus intensity increases until some asymptotic value is reached. Further increases in stimulus intensity result in a gradual or abrupt inhibition of the activity of some of these cells. Some neurons in the higher relay stations show ON, ON–OFF, maintained ON, or OFF responses similar to those seen in the visual system, and these responses are often restricted to narrow bands of stimulus frequencies.

The role of the cortical representations of the auditory system has been difficult to investigate because the ear appears to be tonotopically represented in four or five different areas in many species. Even outside these regions one can record primary evoked potentials to some auditory stimuli and find individual cells that appear to respond selectively to sound. Perhaps in part because of this broad distribution of the cortical components of the auditory system, ablation studies have not been able to provide a clear picture of their unique functions. Basic auditory capabilities (such as amplitude and frequency discriminations) are typically reported to remain intact or to recover following even extensive cortical damage.

1. Outline the major relay stations of the auditory system and describe their cortical projections.

2. Can one discern discrete tonotopic patterns of organization in the central relay stations of the auditory system? How are they related to the structure of the ear?

3. Describe the relationship between the amplitude and frequency of the auditory stimulus and the compound action potential in the eighth nerve.

4. Describe the response of single fibers in the auditory nerve to auditory stimuli of different frequencies and compare them with the responses of cells in higher relay stations of the auditory system.

REVIEW

The physical stimulus for an auditory sensation consists of vibrations in an object that are transmitted in the form of successive condensations and rarefactions of the air. When these pressure waves are sinusoidal, we hear pure tones. When they are complex, our auditory sensations are complex. The amplitude of these waves is the principal determinant of loudness; their frequency is primarily responsible for the pitch of the sensation (these relationships are complicated by the nonlinear transduction properties of the ear).

Sound waves are transduced into proportional hydraulic pressure changes by the impedance-matching devices of the outer and inner ear. First, sound waves are amplified by the resonance of the external meatus. They are then transduced into proportional vibrations of the tympanic membrane, which are transmitted to the round window of the inner ear by the three bones of the middle ear. This step involves two stages of amplification needed to compensate for the energy loss that occurs when air-pressure waves are transduced into hydraulic pressures.

Movement of the round window produces hydraulic pressure waves in the fluids of the inner ear that produce a differential movement of some of the membranes of that structure. This, in turn, results in a shearing of the fine cilia that protrude from the hair cells of the organ of Corti, and this is believed to induce the bioelectric events that trigger action potentials in the first-order neurons of the auditory system.

The trigger or generator potential is probably identical or closely related to the cochlear potential, which can be recorded from the ear during auditory stimulation. This graded D.C. potential has no absolute threshold and follows the amplitude, frequency, and wave form of the stimulus faithfully except for distortions that reflect nonlinearity in the mechanics of the ear.

Precisely how the properties of this potential are encoded in the all-or-none action potentials of the central portions of the auditory system is, as yet, not entirely clear. Classically, two types of hypotheses have been suggested. "Place" theories propose that different frequencies selectively activate receptors in different parts of the inner ear and thus initiate activity in different neurons. Stimulus amplitude in such a system is encoded in the frequency of firing in individual neurons. Competing "frequency" theories suggest that all auditory receptors are capable of responding to all frequencies within the audible spectrum and that frequency is coded in the discharge frequency of individual neurons. Amplitude is thought to be coded in terms of the number of units activated. Both explanations have several difficulties. The most persisting problem of modern versions of the "place" theory is a demonstration of sufficiently selective activation of very small segments of the basilar membrane, particularly at low frequencies. The major problem of the "frequency" theories has been the fact that frequency following appears to be limited even in first-order neurons and negligible or absent in higher portions of the auditory system.

Microelectrode recordings of the activity of single neurons in the auditory system have shown that the encoding of auditory signals may rely extensively on frequency tuning and amplitude tuning of individual neurons and on faithful reproductions of geographically organized representation of the frequency-spectrum. Many neurons in the auditory projection system respond preferentially to a "best" frequency and, at threshold intensities, to only a narrow band of similar frequencies. As intensity increases, the width of these response areas increases. Amplitude appears to be further coded by cells that respond to the same best frequency but do so over quite different ranges of stimulus intensities. Both frequency tuning and amplitude tuning appear to become increasingly precise in higher relay stations of the auditory system. At all levels, the auditory cells are typically organized such that one or more tonotopic representations of the frequency spectrum result.

Bibliography

1. Békésy, G. von. Zur Theorie des Hörens; Die Schwingungsform der Basilarmembran. *Physik Zeits.*, 1928, **29**, 793–810.
2. Békésy, G. von. Zur Theorie des Hörens; Über die Bestimmung des einem reinen Tonempfinden entsprechenden Erregungsgebietes der Basilarmembran vermittelst Ermüdungserscheinungen. *Physik. Zeits.*, 1929a, **30**, 115–125 [354–368].
3. Békésy, G. von. Zur Theorie des Hörens; Über die eben merkbare Amplituden-und Frequenzänderung eines Tones; Die Theorie der Schwebungen. *Physik. Zeits.*, 1929b, **30**, 721–745 [207–238].
4. Békésy, G. von. Über die Hörschwelle und Fühlgrenze langsamer sinus-förmiger Luftdruckschwankungen. *Ann. Physik*, 1936, **26**, 554–566.
5. Békésy, G. von. Shearing microphonics produced by vibrations near the inner and outer hair cells. *J. Acoust. Soc. Amer.*, 1953, **25**, 786–790.

6. Békésy, G. von. *Experiments in Hearing*. New York: McGraw–Hill, 1960.

7. Boring, E. G., & Stevens, S. S. The nature of tonal brightness. *Proc. Nat. Acad. Sci., U. S.*, 1936, **22**, 514–521.

8. Bunch, C. C. Age variations in auditory acuity. *Arch. Otolaryng.*, 1929, **9**, 625–636.

9. Caussé, R., & Chavasse, P. Études sur la fatigue auditive. Note Technique No. 1057. Paris: Centre National d'Études des Télécommunications, 10 Dec. 1947, 29ff.

10. Chapanis, A., Garner, W. R., & Morgan, C. T. *Applied Experimental Psychology*. New York: Wiley, 1949.

11. Churcher, B. G. A loudness scale for industrial noise measurements. *J. Acoust. Soc. Amer.*, 1935, **6**, 216–226.

12. Culler, E. A. Symposium: Is there localization in the cochlea for low tones? *Ann. Otol. Rhinol. Laryngol.*, 1935, **44**, 807–813.

13. Davis, H. Excitation of auditory receptors. In *Handbook of Physiology. Vol. I*. J. Field, H. W. Magoun, & V. E. Hall, Eds. Washington, D.C.: Am. Physiol. Soc., 1959, pp. 565–584.

14. Davis, H. Anatomy and physiology of the ear. In *Hearing and deafness* (rev. ed.). H. Davis & S. R. Silverman, Eds. Holt, Rinehart, & Winston, 1960, pp. 61–79.

15. Davis, H. Some principles of sensory receptor action. *Physiol. Rev.*, 1961, **41**, 391–416.

16. Davis, H., Deatherage, B. H., Eldredge, D. H., & Smith, C. A. Summating potentials of the cochlea. *Amer. J. Physiol.*, 1958, **195**, 251–261.

17. Desmedt, J. E. Neurophysiological mechanisms controlling acoustic input. In *Neural Mechanisms of the Auditory and Vestibular Systems*. G. L. Rasmussen & W. F. Windle, Eds. Springfield, Ill.: Thomas, 1960, pp. 152–164.

18. Desmedt, J. E. Auditory-evoked potentials from cochlea to cortex as influenced by activation of the efferent olivo-cochlear bundle. *J. Acoust. Soc. Amer.*, 1962, **34**, 1478–1496.

19. Diamond, I. T., & Neff, W. D. Ablation of temporal cortex and discrimination of auditory patterns. *J. Neurophysiol.*, 1957, **20**, 300–315.

20. Evans, E. F. Cortical representation. In *Hearing Mechanisms in Vertebrates*. A. V. S. De Reuck & Julie Knight, Eds. Boston: Little, Brown, 1968, pp. 272–287.

21. Evans, E. F., & Whitfield, I. C. Classification of unit responses in the auditory cortex of the unanaesthetized and unrestrained cat. *J. Physiol.*, 1964, **171**, 476–493.

22. Fletcher, H. *Speech and Hearing*. Princeton, N. J.: Van Nostrand, 1929.

23. Fletcher, H. Symposium on wire transmission of symphonic music—reports in auditory perspective: basic requirements. *Electr. Engng.*, 1934, **53**, 9.

24. Fletcher, H., & Wegel, R. L. The frequency-sensitivity of normal ears. *Phys. Rev.*, 1922, 2nd series, **19**, 553–565.

25. Galambos, R. Suppression of auditory nerve activity by stimulation of efferent fibers to cochlea. *J. Neurophysiol.*, 1956, **19**, 424–437.

26. Galambos, R., & Davis, H. The response of single auditory-nerve fibers to acoustic stimulation. *J. Neurophysiol.*, 1943, **6**, 39–57.

27. Galambos, R., & Davis, H. Action potentials from single auditory nerve fibers? *Science*, 1948, **108**, 513.

28. Galambos, R., Schwartzkopff, J., & Rupert, A. Microelectrode study of superior olivary nuclei. *Amer. J. Physiol.*, 1959, **197**, 527–536.

29. Galambos, R., Myers, R. E., & Sheatz, G. Extralemniscal activation of auditory cortex in cats. *Amer. J. Physiol.*, 1961, **200**, 23–28.

30. Goldberg, J. M., & Neff, W. D. Frequency discrimination after bilateral ablation of cortical auditory areas. *J. Neurophysiol.*, 1961, **24**, 119–128.

31. Gulick, W. L. *Hearing. Physiology and Psychophysics*. New York: Oxford Univ. Press, 1971.

32. Gulick, W. L., Herrmann, D. J., & Mackey, P. E. The relationship between stimulus intensity and the electrical responses of the cochlea and auditory nerve. *Psychol. Rec.*, 1961, **11**, 57–67.

33. Helmholtz, G. L. F. von. *Die Lehre von den Tonempfindungen als Physiologische Grundlage für die Theorie der Musik*. (First ed.) Braunschweig, Germany: Vieweg Verlag, 1863.

34. Hind, J. E. An electrophysiological determination of tonotopic organization in auditory cortex of cat. *J. Neurophysiol.*, 1953, **16**, 475–489.

35. Hind, J. E., Goldberg, J. M., Greenwood, D. D., & Rose, J. E. Some discharge characteristics of single neurons in the inferior colliculi of the cat. II. Timing of the discharges and observations on behavioral stimulation. *J. Neurophysiol.*, 1963, **26**, 321–341.

36. Hubel, D. H., & Wiesel, T. N. Receptive fields, binocular interactions and functional architecture in the cat's visual cortex. *J. Physiol. (London)*, 1962, **160**, 106–154.

37. Katsuki, Y. Neural mechanisms of auditory sensation in cats. In *Sensory Communication*. W. A. Rosenblith, Ed. Cambridge, Mass.: M.I.T. Press, 1961, pp. 561–583.

38. Kryter, K. D., & Ades, H. W. Studies on the function of the higher acoustic nervous centers in the cat. *Amer. J. Psychol.*, 1943, **56**, 501–536.

39. Loeffler, J. D. An investigation of auditory responses in insular cortex of cat and dog. Ph.D. Dissertation, Univ. of Wisconsin, 1958.

40. Masterton, R. B., & Diamond, I. T. Effects of auditory cortex and ablation on discrimination of small binaural time differences. *J. Neurophysiol.*, 1964, **27**, 15–36.

41. Moushegian, G., Rupert, A., & Galambos, R. Microelectrode study of ventral nuclei of the cat. *J. Neurophysiol.*, 1962, **25**, 515–529.

42. Munson, W. A. The growth of auditory sensation. *J. Acoust. Soc. Amer.*, 1947, **19**, 584–591.

43. Neff, W. D. Neural mechanisms of auditory discrimination. In *Sensory Communication*. W. A. Rosenblith, Ed. Cambridge, Mass.: M.I.T. Press, 1961, pp. 259–278.

44. Neff, W. D., Fisher, J. F., Diamond, I. T., & Yela, M. Role of auditory cortex in discrimination requiring localization of sound in space. *J. Neurophysiol.*, 1956, **19**, 500–512.

45. Newman, E. B. Hearing. In *Foundations of Psychology*. E. G. Boring, H. S. Langfeld, & H. P. Weld, Eds. New York: Wiley, 1948.

46. Pfalz, R. K. J. Centrifugal inhibition of afferent secondary neurons in the cochlear nucleus by sound. *J. Acoust. Soc. Amer.*, 1962, **34**, 1472–1477.

47. Randall, W. L. Generalization after frequency discrimination in cats with central nervous system lesions. In *Stimulus Generalization*. D. I. Motofsky, Ed. Stanford: Univ. of Stanford Press, 1965, pp. 134–153.

48. Rasmussen, A. T. *Outlines of neuroanatomy*. Dubuque, Iowa: Brown, 1943.

49. Rich, G. J. A study of tonal attributes. *Amer. J. Psychol.*, 1919, **30**, 121–164.

50. Riesz, R. R. Differential intensity sensitivity of the ear for pure tones. *Phys. Rev.*, 1928, **31**, 867–875.

51. Rose, J. E., Galambos, R., & Hughes, J. R. Microelectrode studies of the cochlear nuclei of the cat. *Bull. Johns Hopkins Hosp.*, 1959, **104**, 211–251.

52. Rose, J. E., Greenwood, D. D., Goldberg, J. M., & Hind, J. E. Some discharge characteristics of single neurons in the inferior colliculus of the cat. I. Tonotopic organization, relation of spike-counts to tone intensity, and firing patterns of single elements. *J. Neurophysiol.*, 1963, **26**, 294–320.

53. Rutherford, W. The sense of hearing. *J. Anat. Physiol.*, 1886, **21**, 166–168.

54. Shower, E. G., & Biddulph, R. Differential pitch sensitivity of the ear. *J. Acoust. Soc. Amer.*, 1931, **3**, 275–287.

55. Smith, K. R. The problem of stimulation deafness. II. Histological changes in the cochlea as a function of tonal frequency. *J. Exp. Psychol.*, 1947, **37**, 304–317.

56. Stevens, S. S. A scale for the measurement of a psychological magnitude: loudness. *Psychol. Rev.*, 1936, **43**, 405–416.

57. Stevens, S. S., & Davis, H. *Hearing. Its Psychology and Physiology*. New York: Wiley, 1938.

58. Stevens, S. S., & Volkmann, J. The relation of pitch to frequency: a revised scale. *Amer. J. Psychol.*, 1940, **53**, 329–353.

59. Tasaki, I. Nerve impulses in individual auditory nerve fibers of guinea pig. *J. Neurophysiol.*, 1954, **17**, 97–122.

60. Tasaki, I. Hearing. *Ann. Rev. Physiol.*, 1957, **19**, 417–438.

61. Tasaki, I., & Davis, H. Electric responses of individual nerve elements in cochlear nucleus to sound stimulation (guinea pig). *J. Neurophysiol.*, 1955, **18**, 151–158.

62. Tasaki, I., Davis, H., & Legouix, J. P. The space-time pattern of the cochlear microphonics (guinea pig), as recorded by differential electrodes. *J. Acoust. Soc. Amer.*, 1952, **24**, 502–519.
63. Thompson, R. F. Role of cortical association fields in auditory frequency discrimination. *J. Comp. Physiol. Psychol.*, 1964, **57**, 335–339.
64. Tunturi, A. R. Audiofrequency localization in the acoustic cortex of the dog. *Amer. J. Physiol.*, 1944, **141**, 397–403.
65. Tunturi, A. R. Further afferent connections to the acoustic cortex of the dog. *Amer. J. Physiol.*, 1945, **144**, 389–394.
66. Tunturi, A. R. A difference in the representation of auditory signals in the left and right ears in the iso-frequency contours of the right middle ectosylvian auditory cortex of the dog. *Amer. J. Physiol.*, 1952, **168**, 712–727.
67. Tunturi, A. R. Anatomy and physiology of the auditory cortex. In *Neural Mechanisms of the Auditory and Vestibular Systems*. G. L. Rasmussen & W. F. Windle, Eds. Springfield, Ill.: Thomas, 1960, pp. 181–200.
68. Waetzmann, E., & Keibs, L. Hörschwellenbestimmungen mit dem Thermophon und Messungen am Trommelfell. *Ann. Physik*, 1936a, **26**, 141–144.
69. Waetzmann, E., & Keibs, L. Theoretischer und experimenteller Vergleich von Hörschwellenmessungen. *Akust. Zeits.*, 1936b, **1**, 3–12.
70. Wegel, R. L., Riesz, R. R., & Blackman, R. B. Low frequency thresholds of hearing and of feeling in the ear and ear mechanism. *J. Acoust. Soc. Amer.*, 1932, **4**, 6.
71. Wever, E. G. *Theory of Hearing*. New York: Wiley, 1949.
72. Wever, E. G., & Bray, C. W. The nature of acoustic responses: the relation between sound frequency and frequency of impulses in the auditory nerve. *J. Exp. Psychol.*, 1930, **13**, 373–387.
73. Wever, E. G., & Bray, C. W. Distortion in the ear as shown by the electrical responses of the cochlea. *J. Acoust. Soc. Amer.*, 1938, **9**, 227–233.
74. Wever, E. G., & Lawrence, M. The transmission properties of the middle ear. *Ann. Otol. Rhinol. Laryngol.*, 1950a, **59**, 5–18.
75. Wever, E. G., & Lawrence, M. The transmission properties of the stapes. *Ann. Otol. Rhinol. Laryngol.*, 1950b, **59**, 322–330.
76. Wever, E. G., & Lawrence, M. *Physiological Acoustics*. Princeton, N. J.: Princeton Univ. Press, 1954.
77. Whitfield, I. C., & Evans, E. F. Responses of auditory cortical neurons to stimuli of changing frequency. *J. Neurophysiol.*, 1965, **28**, 655–672.
78. Woolsey, C. N. Organization of cortical auditory system. In *Sensory Communication*. W. A. Rosenblith, Ed. Cambridge, Mass.: M.I.T. Press, 1961, pp. 235–257.
79. Woolsey, C. N., & Walzl, E. M. Topical projection of nerve fibers from local regions of the cochlea to the cerebral cortex of the cat. *Bull. Johns Hopkins Hosp.*, 1942, **71**, 315–344.

Chapter 6

THE CHEMICAL SENSES

Olfactory and Gustatory Stimuli

Transduction of Odor and Taste Stimuli into Physiological Signals

Processing of Olfactory and Gustatory Information in the Central Nervous System

Review

OLFACTORY AND GUSTATORY STIMULI

The chemical senses are of great importance to the survival of many species, but man relies much more extensively on visual and auditory information. We consequently do not have as extensive and detailed observations on olfaction and taste and have, as yet, found little that would distinguish these modalities in any fundamental way from vision and audition. It seems, moreover, that the mechanisms responsible for receptor activation and information coding may be similar in the two chemical senses of man, and it may be appropriate to concentrate our attention on one of them. In this chapter, we shall discuss olfactory processes in some detail and only note briefly whenever the related gustatory mechanisms seem to depart significantly from the pattern set by olfaction.

The sense of smell has not received as much systematic attention as vision or audition, partly because it is not a very important aspect of man's sensorium. It is nice to be able to smell food or the intoxicating perfume of a flower garden in bloom, but we can survive quite well when a severe cold makes us almost totally *anosmic* (unable to detect odors). The scientific neglect of olfactory processes has still other reasons. Although many objects in our environment give off distinct odors, it has been exceedingly difficult to define the physical properties that are responsible for specific odors. In part, this is due to the fact that the olfactory receptors are inaccessible (only a small patch of skin at the very top of the nose serves olfactory functions), in part to the curious inability of man to decide how many different odors there are.

Our difficulties begin when we attempt to define the general properties of olfactory stimuli. It was long believed that olfaction, like audition, was the result of vibrations in the air. The alternative to this wave theory of olfaction is a theory that holds that particles of the odorous substance must come into direct contact with the olfactory receptor before its odor can be perceived. We are not accustomed to thinking that the objects that surround us emit continual streams of particles, and it is easy to understand why scientists have been reluctant to abandon the wave theory of olfaction. It is nevertheless clear today that most matter does give off a steady stream of molecules and that the relatively small number of molecules needed to coat the olfactory receptor surface can be emitted by an object for a million years before a measurable weight loss occurs.[83] Some form of the corpuscular theory is therefore generally accepted today, and the current theoretical battles are fought over the nature of the interaction between odorous particles and the olfactory receptor.

If matter emits molecules and it is the contact between molecules and the olfactory receptor that gives rise to olfactory sensations, why do not all objects give off an odor? Or, for that matter, why do different substances emit unique odors? What property of molecules determines specific odors? We do not yet have entirely satisfactory answers to any of these questions.

The seemingly infinite variety of "taste" sensations that enrich our lives is largely due to the stimulation of olfactory receptors. If we close the nose, apples and onions become all but indistinguishable, fine wines take on the slightly sour taste of vinegar, and the delicate "flavor" of fruits is lost almost entirely. If we analyze the sensations that remain after the influence of olfactory inputs has been removed, taste turns out to be reduceable to a few seemingly simple sensations.

Some Basic Properties of Olfactory and Gustatory Stimuli

A recent review of the many theories that have been advanced to account for the odorous or taste properties of substances[83] concluded that all probably contain some of the truth but none all of it. It may therefore be useful to forego a review of the individual theories and, instead, briefly discuss the principal factors that have been proposed.

Volatility

Modern theories agree that a substance must be volatile (i.e., continually emit a steady stream of molecules to the atmosphere) in order to serve as an olfactory or taste stimulus. Volatility is a function of temperature, and many substances, such as metals, cotton, and nylon, are completely nonvolatile and nonodorous at some temperatures but not at others. Temperature thus becomes an important property.

Solubility

Some investigators[83] consider solubility to be a rather unimportant factor, largely because historic experiments[13,128] have shown that the application of solutions of odorants directly to the olfactory mucosa does not help but hinders olfactory perception. Solubility in water as well as lipoids nonetheless appears to be a common property of olfactory and taste stimuli, and most theories include this factor in their list of important characteristics.

Adsorbability

Adsorption plays a central role in many modern olfactory theories. It is used, for instance, to explain why even minute concentrations of some odor molecules initiate activity in the olfactory system (in adsorption, a substance becomes concentrated from a three-dimensional to a two-dimensional system), and why the interaction of receptor and odor molecules results in electrochemical reactions that may give rise to action potentials (adsorption of a gas on a solid surface provides energy). All substances that are easily adsorbed are odorous (the reason for the single exception to this—water—is presumably the fact that water is always present at the olfactory receptor). Adsorbability may, of course, also play an important role in gustation.

That adsorption is indeed a critical step in olfaction was demonstrated in a series of ingenious experiments, performed on the head of a freshly killed sheep.[82] All openings except the nostrils were sealed. Air containing various odorants was then blown into one of the nostrils and examined as it returned through the other. It was found that the air that emerged from the second nostril was quite inodorous, even when rather intense odors were injected at the first. A state of saturation was reached after some seconds, and the air emerging from the sheep's nostril became odorous. The physical rather than chemical nature of the adsorption process was demonstrated by its reversibility.

Reactivity

It is generally assumed that the degree of saturation is an important determinant of the effectiveness of olfactory stimuli because unsaturated substances typically emit stronger odors than do saturated ones.

Molecular Vibrations

Many of the modern attempts to account for the selective activation of chemical receptors suggest that the excitation of olfactory and perhaps gustatory receptors depends directly or indirectly on intermolecular vibrations in the stimulus. These vibrations are believed to affect chemical receptors because they resonate or interfere with the vibrations of the receptor mechanisms. The vibrations of specific substances can be assessed by their *Raman shift*. (When monochromatic light shines through chemically pure substances, the light scatters into longer and shorter wavelengths. This scattering is called Raman shift. The extent and pattern of scattering is a unique characteristic of each pure substance.)

Some of the earlier vibration theories[45] assumed that only substances with a Raman shift in the infrared region could affect chemical receptors. More recent versions[131] have emphasized Raman shifts of longer wavelengths because the short wavelengths are not active at body temperatures. Some impressive correlations between the Raman frequencies of substances and their odors have been published. Substances with similar odors tend to have similar Raman frequencies and substances with dissimilar odors generally have dissimilar Raman frequencies, even when they are mirror images of each other structurally.[131,132] Odorless substances, such as hydrogen, carbon monoxide, and methane have Raman frequencies beyond the limits believed to be important in olfaction.[60] However, some exceptions have been noted,[30] and it is clear that our understanding of vibrational phenomena in olfaction is incomplete.

Properties of Specific Odor and Taste Stimuli

It seems rather certain that a substance that has most or all of the properties discussed above is an *odorivector* (i.e., a substance that emits particles that elicit olfactory sensations when in contact with an olfactory receptor). But what determines the specific nature of the sensation? A number of factors have been proposed, and there is some measure of empirical support for every one of them. The crucial experiment that would help us select the *essential* properties of specific odorivectors is, however, still missing.

Most of the mechanisms that we shall discuss may describe not only the interaction of olfactory stimuli and related receptors but, more generally, the action of chemicals on chemical receptors or the action of certain types of chemicals on gustatory receptors. All of them have, at one time or another, been considered as an explanation for the selective activation of gustatory receptors. Most of the scanty evidence for them comes, however, from observations of olfactory stimuli, and we shall therefore emphasize this aspect of the story.

Differential Adsorbability

Some theories[83] assume that selective adsorption by chemical receptors may be one of the means of attaining specific activity in the olfactory and gustatory systems. Such an interpretation is suggested by the observation that different adsorbents react differently to particular odors and that substances that have similar smells typically show similar adsorption characteristics.[81] However, the correlations between odor and adsorption characteristics are not perfect (some rather different odorivectors have very similar adsorption properties), and there is, as yet, no direct evidence that olfactory receptors do indeed differ with respect to their adsorbent properties.

Special Chemical Groups

Some of the earlier theories of olfaction assumed that specific odors were characterized by the presence of particular chemical groupings.[139] Each "basic" odor was believed to be related to a unique group, and complex odors were thought to be the result of several such groupings acting in concert. Each group was thought to stimulate only a particular type of olfactory receptor.

Extensive experimental investigations of the correlation between odor quality and the chemical constituents of related odorivectors have shown that we cannot always predict the odor of a substance on the basis of its chemical composition alone. It is generally true that structurally similar chemicals give rise to similar odors, but there are important exceptions. Some structurally similar compounds, even stereoisomers which are mirror images of each other, have very different odors, and structurally quite different substances can smell alike.

An interesting observation in this connection is the fact that some of the naturally occurring elements are odorous in their normal, atomic state. Seven elements give rise to olfactory sensations in their polyatomic state, but only two odors—garlic and chlorine—are produced. (Arsenic, phosphorus, and ozone smell like garlic; the halogens—fluorine, chlorine, bromine, and iodine—like chlorine.) It appears from this that simple molecules cannot give rise to some of the olfactory sensations that have been described as "simple" or "basic" on the basis of psychological experience.

If we arrange the elements in an electrochemical series according to the potential difference that exists between the element and a solution of its salts, odorivectors take up the lowest six positions. The top nine positions are olfactory-negative (i.e., they suppress odors when combined with other odorivectors). The implications of this intriguing relationship are as yet not clear.

Stereochemical Factors

An interesting variation of the earlier structural hypotheses has been advanced by Amoore.[4] Though extensively modified over the years,[5, 6, 7, 10] the basic proposition remains the same. This *stereochemical* theory suggests, in essence, that the quality of odors is determined by the size and shape of the molecules of the olfactory stimulus. Older versions of this theory suggested that olfactory receptors may have receptor sites that correspond in size and shape to those of the molecules of the particular odorivectors, thus explaining the specificity of olfactory stimulation. Recent experimental findings suggest that there may be seven basic odors (ethereal, camphoraceous, musky, floral, fruity, pungent, and putrid), of which only five are specified entirely by their stereochemical properties (see Figure 6–1). The remaining two (pungent and putrid) are thought to be related to the electrical properties of their molecular structure.

The importance of stereochemical characteristics was demonstrated in experiments[8, 9, 10] in which observers were asked to rate 106 odors in terms of their similarity to five standards selected to represent the five stereochemically determined basic odor categories. The results of these experiments show that there is a highly significant (though far from perfect) correlation between odor quality and molecular size and shape. The

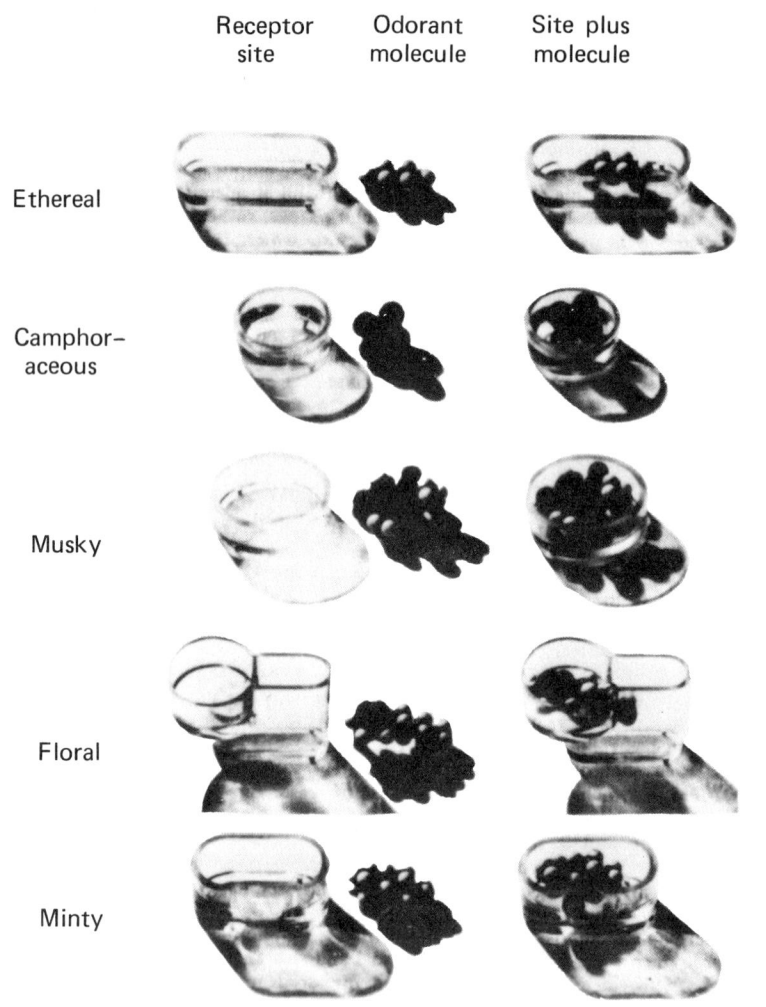

FIG. 6–1. Models of olfactory receptor sites and molecules that "fit" them in the stereochemical theory of odor.

(From J. E. Amoore. Current status of the steric theory of odor. *Ann. N.Y. Acad. Sci.*, **116**, 1964, 457–476.)

correlation coefficients ranged from 0.52 to 0.66, suggesting that the stereochemical properties of molecules determine some but perhaps not all of the characteristics of olfactory stimuli.

Molecular Vibrations

Implicit in the vibrational theories of chemical stimulation is the assumption that odors or tastes may be characterized by the frequency of intermolecular vibrations.[45, 131, 132] Specific receptors are thought to respond preferentially to particular frequency bands such that compound stimuli that contain a particular pattern of molecules from different sources give rise to a unique pattern of neural activity. These molecular vibrations can be measured by the frequency of the Raman shift and are expected to have wavelengths that correspond to the lengths of the hairs that protrude from the receptor cells. Direct experimental support for the molecular-vibration theory is, however, still lacking.

Infrared Absorption

A theory that is related in many ways to the molecular vibration theories has been proposed by Beck and Miles.[18] The infrared absorption theory suggests that the olfactory receptors may be a source of infrared radiation and that individual receptors may, by virtue of their size and shape, radiate particular wavelengths. Odorous particles that are suspended in the air are thought to absorb particular infrared wavelengths and thus induce a selective cooling and resultant energy loss in some receptors. Different groups of receptors could be tuned to wavelengths corresponding to each of the basic odors, and the overall pattern of receptor activity could be a signal for complex odor combinations.

In its simplest form, this theory cannot account for the fact that some optical isomers have the same absorption spectra but quite different odors[135] or the observation that a few odorous substances, such as paraffin, do not absorb infrared light at all. Beck[17] has attempted to show that these objections can be answered by the consideration of infrared scattering and such general properties of odorivectors as solubility and particle size. The experimental support for the infrared absorption theory is, however, weak and, to some extent, controversial.[67]

Selective Enzyme Inhibition

Enzymes are proteins that act as catalysts for the chemical reactions that take place in all living cells. A number of investigators have suggested that olfactory sensations may be the result of an inhibitory effect on specific enzyme reactions that, in turn, interfere with normally occurring reactions in the receptor cell.[71] Different enzymes are believed to be related to each of the basic odors. Quantitative differences in odors are thought to be reflected by the intensity of the enzyme inhibition.

Histochemical investigations have shown that certain enzymes are present only in olfactory but not in adjacent nonolfactory tissues[28] and that one of these enzymes (phosphatase) appears to be selectively inhibited by a particular odorivector (vanillin).[47] There is also some evidence that different enzymes have different locations on the olfactory mucosa.[48] We do not yet understand enzyme reactions in sufficient detail to judge the appropriateness of this mechanism in sensory systems but should keep the possibility in mind.

Relationship Between Physical Properties and Sensation

One of the principal difficulties that faces the investigator of olfactory sensations has been man's inability to decide how many different odors there are and how they should be identified and classified. One of the unique problems of olfaction is the fact that most individuals insist on including their likes and dislikes in any classification of odors. Few scientists would dream of dividing visual or auditory stimuli on the basis of their degree of pleasantness, but classifications of odors as "repulsive," "putrid," "fragrant," and the like are not at all uncommon.

The influence of affective reactions on our reaction to taste stimuli is so marked that one leading investigator[103] has suggested that all gustatory sensations can be reduced to two behavioral classifications—acceptance and rejection. Such a classification cuts across the more traditional stimulus groupings, since some substances give rise to pleasant tastes at low concentrations and to distinctly unpleasant sensations at higher concentrations. Since there is no detectable change in the response of taste receptors or associated neural pathways during a shift in preference (other than that which is due to the required change in stimulus intensity), the influence of affective reactions must be assumed to be a central influence on taste sensations.[105]

One of the most influential odor classifications is Zwaardemaker's[138,139] system, which contains nine basic odor classes (ethereal, aromatic, balsamic, ambrosial, alliaceous, burned, caprilic, repulsive, and nauseating), which are in turn subdivided into two or three subdivisions. It is often suggested that these nine categories represent truly "basic" odors and that there may be nine corresponding olfactory receptors that are uniquely or preferentially sensitive to these substances. There is, however, little or no evidence for these speculations except some historical experiments by Zwaardemaker[140] and others[91] showing that the perception of odors of a particular category is more severely inhibited when the nose is exposed for some time to another member of the same category than when odors of other categories are used as adapting stimuli (see Figure 6-2). These selective-adaptation experiments do suggest some receptor specificity,

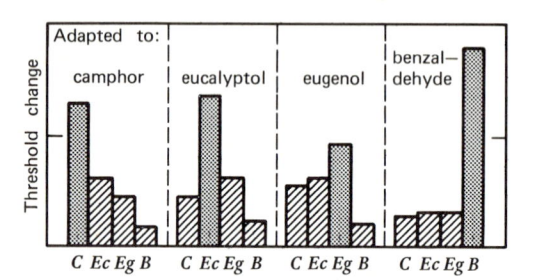

FIG. 6–2. Effects of adaptation on olfactory thresholds. Four substances are used (C, camphor; Ec, Eucalyptol; Eg, Eugenol; B, Benzaldehyde). The stippled bars indicate the changes that occur after adaptation to the substance tested. The diagonally-hatched bars indicate the changes in the thresholds of substances other than that used for adaptation (i.e., cross-adaptation). Notice that adaptation to benzaldehyde markedly raised the threshold for the same odor but had little effect on the threshold of other odors. Camphor, Eucalyptol, and Eugenol, on the other hand, show a significant amount of reciprocal adaptation but little interaction with Benzaldehyde.

(After C. Pfaffmann. Taste and smell. In *Handbook of experimental psychology*. S. S. Stevens, Ed. Copyright © 1951. John Wiley & Sons, Inc.)

but much more extensive and controlled observations are needed before we can hope to interpret their often complex findings in terms of specific receptor classifications.

Henning[61, 62] revised Zwaardemaker's system on the basis of extensive psychophysical experimentation and arrived at a classification of odors that contained six "primary" odors (fragrant, ethereal, resinous, spicy, putrid, and burned). Henning believed that the odors of each of the six classes could be identified by their chemical constitution and that all odors could be represented by various combinations of the basic elements. The relationship between the six primary odors was thought to be represented by a prism, each primary odor forming one of its corners. Henning suggested that the boundaries between the primary-odor classifications merged gradually in such a way that the corners of the prism represented not so much elementary odors as turning points on a quality continuum.

The simplest and most widely used odor classification was published by Crocker and Henderson.[37] Their system consists of four basic components (fragrant, acid, burned, and caprylic), which can be present in any one of eight intensities. Any odor can thus be characterized by a number from 0000 to 8888—a coding system that is widely used by the perfume industry. The smell of a rose, for instance, has been assigned the value 6423, indicating that the average observer believes its odor to contain 6 units of the "fragrant" odor classification, 4 of the "acid," 2 of the "burned," and 3 of the "caprylic." Although it all sounds a bit complicated, a number of investigators[27, 36, 110] have come to the conclusion that even untrained observers can use the system with a good degree of consistency. We must be careful, however, not to extrapolate from this practical success of the system. There is no evidence whatsoever that these four odor classes correspond to "basic" odors in any physiological sense or that corresponding receptors can be found in the olfactory mucosa.

Amoore's[4, 7, 8, 9] stereochemical classification system assumes that there are seven basic odors, of which five are categorized purely on the basis of the shape and size of their molecules and the remaining two by their electrical properties. The relationship between odor and molecular shape or size has been the object of speculation for many centuries (Lucretius, for instance, suggested that pleasant odors might be composed of round particles whereas pungent smells might have hooked or barbed components), but there is, as yet, little empirical evidence to support Amoore's system of classification. It was originally thought that specific olfactory-receptor sites might correspond to each of his classifications (or at least the five stereochemical groups), but this aspect of the theory has been withdrawn.[8,9] It is nonetheless surprising that a classification system that is based largely on molecular structure should arrive at categories (ethereal, camphoraceous, musky, floral, minty, pungent, and putrid) that are quite similar to those developed purely on psychophysical grounds, and the relationship between molecular structure and odor may be a lead that should be followed in future investigations.

Man is not nearly as confounded by taste as by olfactory stimuli. Although there is no overwhelming chemical or physical evidence for such a grouping, most human subjects quite readily agree that there are four primary tastes—bitter, sweet, salty, and sour—and that almost all taste sensations can be attributed to combinations of these basic tastes. (There are some peculiar "hydroxyl" and some "metallic" tastes that do not fit into this classification, but these are rare and typically disregarded.)

Moreover, in the case of two of these tastes, there is relatively good agreement as to their physical basis. All sour stimuli contain hydrogen ions, and the higher the concentration of this cation, the more intense the sour taste. All salty stimuli consist of solute salts that often give rise to taste sensations that include bitter, sour, or sweet, but are primarily salty. The free anion appears to determine the character of the sensation, the cation the intensity of the taste. Adaptation to one acid reduces the sensitivity of the system to all other acids, suggesting that there may be only one receptor mechanism for sour tastes. Salt, on the other hand, produces adaptation only for the specific salt used, indicating that there may be as many unique receptor mechanisms for salty tastes as there are distinguishable salts.

We know, as yet, very much less about the determinants of sweetness. It is typically associated with low molecular weight and the presence of certain chemical groups that have been called "glucophores" and "auxoglucs," but this is not an adequate description of the physical basis of sweet taste since some intensely sweet substances, such as saccharin, do not have either characteristic. The sensation of bitter is similarly not associated with a single class of chemical substances or easily identifiable physical characteristics. It is generally associated with high molecular weight and high concentrations, but there are important exceptions to this rule. There is some evidence to suggest that there may be several receptor mechanisms for sweet and bitter. Adaptation to some sweet and bitter substances does not reduce the system's sensitivity to some others, and some people are "tasteblind" with respect to certain bitter substances but quite normal with respect to others.

It is difficult to obtain a measure of the limits of olfactory sensitivity because the olfactory system adapts rapidly to odors that are presented for more than a few seconds at a time. This adaptation is not restricted to the odor that causes it but affects thresholds for similar odors. The taste receptors do not adapt as rapidly or completely as does the olfactory system, and adaptation rarely affects taste stimuli from other categories. Adaptation often fails to generalize even within some of the four taste categories (complete generalization occurs only for sour stimuli). To say anything about olfactory thresholds that has any claim to general validity is all but impossible because the threshold varies enormously for different odors. Musk, for instance, can be detected in concentrations of 0.00004 milligrams per liter of air, whereas ethyl ether requires 5.83 milligrams per liter of air. The exquisite sensitivity of the olfactory system to some odors is demonstrated by the fact that some chemical substances (notably musk or vanillin) can be detected in concentrations that are at least one million times lower than those needed for detection by chemical assay.

In the case of the gustatory system, stable thresholds are difficult to obtain because the receptor mechanisms continually break down (because of the strains of mastication) and regenerate. It is nonetheless generally agreed that man, as well as most other vertebrates, is most sensitive to bitter substances and that sensitivity typically falls off in the order of sweet, sour, and salty (sweet would be last if we included only organic sugars).

It is one of the peculiarities of the olfactory system that we have no simple scale of odor intensities and cannot always judge the intensity of an odor by its absolute threshold, as one might naively expect. Musk, for instance, has one of the lowest absolute thresholds and is quite persistent and pervasive. However, even at very high concentrations, musk is rarely rated as a very intense odor. A number of attempts have therefore been made to arrive at magnitude estimations that are more or less independent of the absolute threshold of an odor. Some of these[19] have asked observers to rate the intensity of various odors in reference to a single standard. These cross-odor comparisons are difficult to make and the procedure has not been very successful. Apparently more feasible are intensity judgments in reference to a standard intensity of the same odor[68] or assessments of the threshold change that is produced by exposure to the undiluted odorant.[83] When this procedure is used to rank the intensity of solutions of increasing concentration of the same odorant, a peculiar relationship between apparent intensity and concentration becomes apparent. Increasing concentrations of an odorant give rise to more and more intense odors only up to a certain limit, which for some substances is reached at very low concentrations. Further increases in the concentration of the odorant do not produce any increment in the subjective sensation of intensity, suggesting that all available receptor sites may be taken up at even fairly low concentrations.[83]

In gustation, the jnd remains remarkably stable over a wide range of intensities as long as one considers only one taste stimulus. However, when one attempts to compare the sweetness of two substances that are an equal number of jnd's above threshold, it becomes apparent that here, as in other modalities, summed jnd's do not produce useful scales.

Adaptation to a continuously presented stimulus is one of the most remarkable properties of the olfactory system. We are unaware of any odor only minutes after entering a room filled with cigarette smoke, kitchen odors, or the penetrating stench of human sweat. The rapidity of adaptation is a direct function of the vapor pressure (and hence molecular concentration) of the odor.[130] Certain odors even undergo qualitative changes during the adaptation process (the odor of nitrobenzol, for instance, changes from bitter almond to tar or pitch), suggesting that some olfactory receptors may be more rapidly affected by adaptation than others.[117] Adaptation to one substance may also modify the quality of the odor of other substances[44] or selectively reduce the sensitivity to other odors. Since these cross-adaptation effects are typically selective (i.e., adaptation to one odor raises the threshold of some odors drastically but has little or no effect on others), they suggest that certain classes of odors may be mediated by common receptors that can be selectively adapted or fatigued. If this were true, it should be possible to categorize odors in "natural" classes, based on common physiological mechanisms. So far, this has not proven to be a fruitful approach, partly, perhaps, because of the enormous numbers of comparisons required. Attempts to validate existing classifications of odors by this technique have also not been very successful.[44]

In gustation, we find often marked adaptation to similar stimuli within a particular category (salt being the exception), but there is no evidence for cross-quality adaptation. On the contrary, the sensitivity to all other taste stimuli is enhanced following adaptation to sweet or salty stimuli, and adaptation to quinine improves the sensitivity to sour and salty stimuli.[38, 80]

Summary and Review Questions

Molecules of olfactory and taste stimuli must come into direct contact with the chemical receptor. Olfactory stimuli must be volatile (i.e., emit a steady stream of their molecules), and both olfactory and gustatory stimuli must be soluble in water or fat and be easily adsorbed. It is helpful though apparently not essential that they be unsaturated.

Just how the molecules of olfactory and taste stimuli interact with chemical receptors and what properties of the stimulus are responsible for the activation of specific receptors is as yet not clear. Some theories hold that chemical receptors are activated by intermolecular vibrations and that specific receptors respond preferentially to selected frequency bands. This might occur because the length of the hairs that protrude from the receptor cells corresponds to the frequency of the molecular vibrations of the stimulus. It has also been suggested that chemical receptors may emit radiations in the infrared spectrum that could be selectively absorbed by particular molecules. This, in turn, might produce a selective cooling in some classes of receptors. Other hypotheses suggest that olfactory and taste stimuli may be characterized by their chemical composition, by their stereochemical properties (i.e., the size and shape of their molecules), or by their selective effects on enzymatic reactions in the receptor cell. There is considerable evidence for each of these notions but also, in each case, some contradictory observations that indicate that other factors or a combination of factors may have to be considered.

Investigations of olfactory functions have been complicated by man's curious inability to decide how many different odors there are and how they should be classified. Various numbers and types of "basic" odors have been proposed that are thought to reflect the activation of specific classes of receptors. The currently most widely used system relies on only four classes of odors (fragrant, acid, burnt, caprylic) and describes each specific odor as a mixture of these.

It has similarly been difficult to establish the absolute and differential sensitivity of the olfactory system. The system shows rapid and nearly complete adaptation to even intense odors, and this effect generalizes to a variety of "similar" odors, often in an unpredictable fashion. Matters are further complicated by the fact that the olfactory system is exquisitely sensitive with respect to some odors but hardly responds to others. Moreover, once activated, the system's capacity is quite small for some odors (i.e., increases in odor concentration produce correlated changes in sensation only across a narrow range of stimulus intensities).

Man has found it less difficult to classify gustatory stimuli into four seemingly "basic" categories (bitter, sweet, sour, and salty), although there is some evidence that the simplicity of this system may be misleading. Sourness appears to be determined primarily by the concentration of hydrogen ions in acids. Since adaptation to one acid reduces the sensitivity of the gustatory receptor to all other acids, it appears probable that there may, indeed, be one sour receptor mechanism. Salty taste sensations also appear to be simply determined by the concentration of the free anion in solute salts, but there is no evidence of cross-adaptation, indicating that there may be unique receptor mechanisms for each one of them. Sweetness is typically associated with low molecular weight and the presence of certain chemical groups, but substances that do not meet these criteria may be sweet. There is evidence of limited cross-adaptation between some sweet substances, indicating a limited number of "sweet receptors." Bitter tastes are typically associated with high molecular weights and high concentrations, but there are, once again, some bitter-tasting substances that do not satisfy these rules. As in the case of sweet tastes, there is evidence for limited cross-adaptation between some but not all types of bitter-tasting substances.

1. Some objects give off odors; others do not. How do they differ?

2. Describe, in a few sentences, the principal hypotheses that have been offered to explain why objects emit specific odors or specific taste sensations.

3. Man has found it difficult to decide how many basic odors there are and precisely how they smell. Discuss some of the principal reasons for this and present some odor classifications that have been proposed.

4. Why is it difficult to discuss the limits of olfactory sensitivity?

5. Describe the properties of gustatory stimuli that correlate with their classification into four "basic" categories.

6. Compare the effects of adaptation in the olfactory and gustatory systems.

TRANSDUCTION OF ODOR AND TASTE STIMULI INTO PHYSIOLOGICAL SIGNALS

Anatomy of the Nose and Olfactory Receptors

The nose serves primarily as an air conditioner that removes dirt and dust from the air and preheats it to a temperature that does not damage the ultrafine structure of the lungs. Olfactory functions are, at least in man, secondary, and the olfactory receptors take up only a small fraction of the nasal surface.

The interior of the nose is arranged in horizontal folds that expose inhaled air to a large surface of warm and moist skin and thus achieve the necessary warming and cleaning. Above and somewhat behind all of these folds is a small area, called the *olfactory cleft*, which contains the olfactory receptors. This region is recessed from the main airstream and only about 2 percent of odor molecules in the air reach them during normal breathing.[118] It is only when we sniff that eddy currents are set up in the convoluted pathways of the nose, which bring a significant number of odor molecules into the olfactory cleft.

The olfactory epithelium contains olfactory receptors as well as supporting cells. Both are equipped with hairlike processes that project into the mucous. Each supporting cell has about 1000 very short hairs, called *microvilli*.

Each olfactory receptor has from 1 to 20 longer hairs or *cilia*.[34, 42] The supporting cells may play an important role in olfactory-receptor function, but the nature of their contribution is, as yet, not clear. The large number of long and short "hairs" that project from the receptor and supporting cells enormously increase the surface area of the small patch of olfactory epithelium so that it may exceed that of the rest of the body. The olfactory cilia are believed to contain the actual receptor sites for odor molecules, since they arise from the only portion of the receptor that is not carefully insulated by a thick sheath.[43]

The olfactory receptor is a bipolar neuron that gives rise to a very thin axon that links it directly to the brain (see Figure 6–3). These fibers form small bundles that penetrate the *cribriform plate* (part of the ethmoid bone) and enter the olfactory bulb. Here they enter *glomeruli* and terminate on *mitral* or *tufted* cells.

The axons of the second-order mitral cells course through the *lateral olfactory tract* and terminate primarily in the ipsilateral *prepyriform* cortex, which acts as the cortical projection area for olfaction. A few axons from these mitral cells terminate in neighboring structures, such as the corticomedial portion of the amygdala and the anterior olfactory nucleus.

The axons of the second-order tufted cells project primarily through the anterior commissure to *granule* cells in the opposite olfactory bulb.[75] Microelectrode recordings

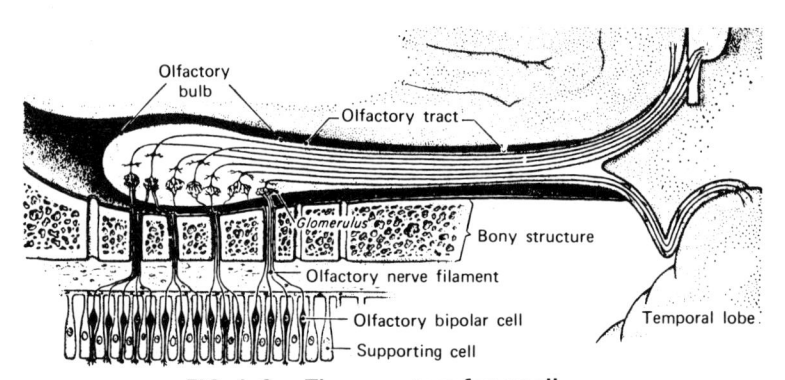

FIG. 6–3. The receptors for smell.
(After D. Krech & R. S. Crutchfield. *Elements of psychology*. Knopf, 1959.)

from these projections[31] suggest that most of these crossed connections serve inhibitory functions. This interpretation is supported by the observation that removal of this tonic inhibitory influence by unilateral bulb destruction markedly increases the spontaneous and induced activity of the cells in the remaining bulb.

Primary thalamic and neocortical projections have been identified for all sensory systems except olfaction. The primary as well as secondary projections of the olfactory system are paleocortical. Some portions of the nonspecific thalamic nuclei have indirect anatomical connections with the olfactory bulb,[50] but no direct projections have been demonstrated. Thalamic stimulation produces recruiting responses and slow potential changes in the olfactory bulb,[33] and thalamic responses to olfactory-bulb stimulation have been recorded.[24] The extremely long latencies of these responses suggests, however, that these connections cannot be part of the primary olfactory system.

Anatomy of Gustatory Receptors and Their Central Projections

Several taste receptors typically cluster in goblet-shaped taste "buds" that occur in or on some of the circular or oblong elevations, called *papillae*, on the dorsal surface of the tongue (see Figure 6–4). Taste buds cover the surface of *fungiform* (mushroom-shaped) papillae, which are scattered over the anterior and posterior surface of the tongue, or fill the circular trenches of the *circumvallate* papillae, which form chevronlike rows near the base of the tongue. The most common papillae do not contain taste receptors.

Taste buds contain two types of cells: spindle-shaped receptor cells that project a fine hair through a pore into the mouth, and thicker hairless cells. The latter were long thought to serve only supporting functions but are now believed to represent a developmental stage of the hair cell itself.[73, 103] The hair cells are subject to extraordinary mechanical forces during mastication, and rarely live longer than 10 to 12 days. In the

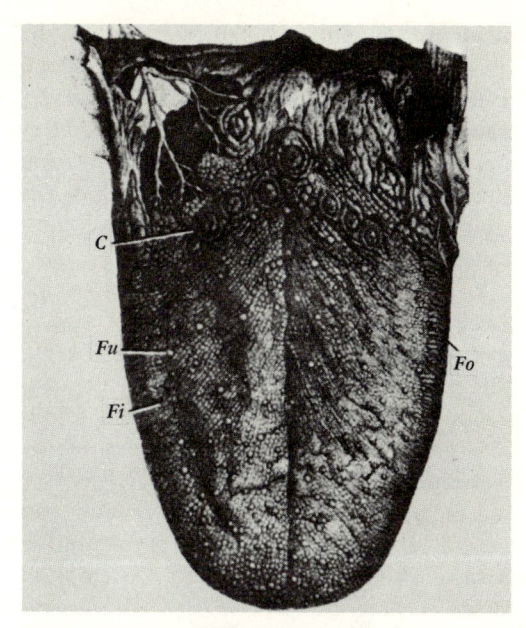

FIG. 6–4. Dorsal surface of the tongue partially dissected to show the nerves to the posterior part. The circumvallate (*C*), fungiform (*Fu*), and filiform (*Fi*) papillae are shown. The foliate papillae (*Fo*) are not clearly visible in this view since they are on the lateral surface of the tongue. Taste buds occur in *C*, *Fo*, and not in *Fi*.

(From H. C. Warren & L. Carmichael. *Elements of human psychology*. Houghton Mifflin, 1930.)

young, they are continually replaced so that the population of receptors remains stable. After age 45 or 50, this regeneration process slows down and the number of taste receptors and gustatory sensitivity decline markedly.[3, 109]

The nerve fibers that subserve taste sensations do not form a single cranial nerve. Fibers arising from the anterior part of the tongue form the *chorda tympani* branch of the *lingual* (seventh cranial) nerve. Receptors on the posterior part of the tongue are innervated by fibers that travel with the *glossopharyngeal* (ninth cranial) nerve. A few taste fibers join the *vagus* (tenth cranial) nerve. These anatomical divisions are of interest because the different taste sensations are not randomly represented on the tongue (the back of the tongue is most sensitive to bitter, the tip to sweet and salty, and the medial edges to sour). The response patterns that are recorded from either the seventh or ninth nerve are therefore not representative of the response capabilities of the gustatory system, a fact that is often forgotten. However, transection of either nerve alone produces little effect on taste preference-aversion functions in animals, suggesting that the topographic organization may not be as complete as is commonly assumed.[100]

In the medulla, all taste fibers join the *tractus solitarius* and terminate in the rostral portion or the nucleus of that tract. From here, the taste projections ascend in the contralateral *medial lemniscus*. These fibers terminate on cells in the *arcuate* nucleus of the thalamus, which project to the facial-sensory and facial-motor regions of the frontal and parietal lobes.[29, 23] The cortical representation of taste also includes insular and temporal cortex in some species.[14]

Theoretical Models of Receptor Activation

We do not, as yet, understand how odor molecules interact with the olfactory receptor surface to initiate a disturbance in the receptor membrane and thus give rise to action potentials. Some of the olfactory theories that we have reviewed in our discussion of the olfactory stimulus contain speculations about this important step, but supporting data have been hard to come by.

The infrared absorption theory of Beck and Miles,[18] for instance, suggests that odor molecules selectively absorb certain infrared wavelengths and thus produce a cooling and energy loss in some olfactory receptors. To the extent that individual receptors could, by virtue of their unique size and shape, emit unique frequencies of infrared radiation, this energy loss could produce selective membrane disturbances that give rise to action potentials. The evidence for selective infrared absorption is, however, so weak that this does not seem to be a very promising lead.

The enzyme theories[71] suggest that odor molecules somehow inhibit one or more enzymes that are essential to normal cellular reactions. Such a disturbance could conceivably produce a momentary breakdown of the resting membrane potential and give rise to action potentials. However, a large number of enzymes with rather unusual properties would have to be discovered in the olfactory receptor to make this system work.

There are, finally, some theories that are specifically designed to explain the receptor process itself and have little or nothing to say about the properties of the stimulus. Perhaps the best known of these is Davies' puncturing theory.[40, 41, 39] It suggests that odor molecules are adsorbed into the lipid membrane of the receptor cell. When it is then desorbed (i.e., removed), the molecule is thought to leave a puncture in the membrane that remains open for a fraction of a second until the cell can repair the damage. During this time, an exchange of ions occurs (potassium flows out of the hole, sodium into it), and this initiates a propagated membrane disturbance in accordance with the general neurophysiological model that we have described in the second chapter. The beauty of this theory rests in its simplicity and in its promise of relatively easy quantification of the stimulus-receptor interaction. Some correlational support for the theory is available but direct evidence is unfortunately lacking.

Adaptations of any of the theories that have been proposed to explain the selective activation of olfactory receptors can be used to account for specificity in the gustatory system, although we have typically less evidence for a particular mechanism than in the case of olfaction.[107, 46, 76, 83] A possible exception to this is the enzyme-inhibition theory. A nonrandom distribution of enzymes in the papillae of the tongue[28] as well as differential acceleration or inhibition of specific enzyme reactions by specific taste stimuli[47, 48] have been reported. This theory unfortunately requires some rather unlikely assumptions about enzymatic functions here as well as in the case of the olfactory receptor.

Electrophysiology of Chemical Receptors

The Electro-olfactogram

The presentation of an olfactory stimulus results in a slow negative potential called

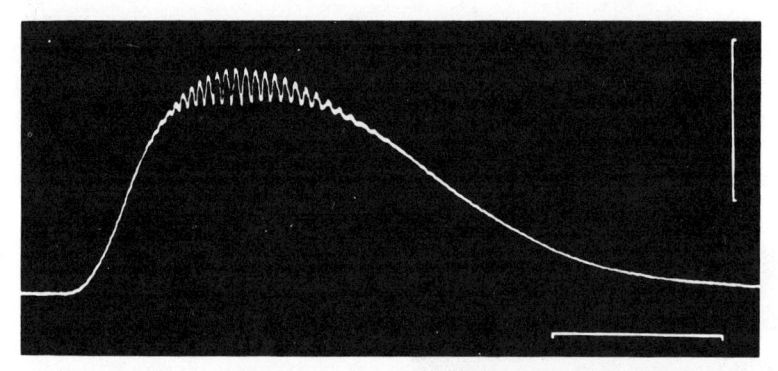

FIG. 6–5. The electro-olfactogram (EOG) depicts the slow negative potential which is recorded from the olfactory mucosa during the presentation of odors. The amplitude of this potential is, within limits, proportional to the logarithm of the stimulus intensity. Rhythmic waves are typically superimposed on the slow potential.

(From D. Ottoson. Analysis of the electrical activity of the olfactory epithelium. *Acta physiol. scand.*, 35, 1956, Suppl. 122, 1–83.)

electro-olfactogram (EOG) in the olfactory epithelium[94, 95] (see Figure 6–5). Some species also give an EOG response to the cessation of olfactory stimulation,[122, 123, 124, 112, 113] which has been likened to the OFF response of other sensory systems. A third, positive potential (hyperpolarization) has been recorded, particularly in response to odorous substances that are not soluble in water.[52, 125]

The shape and ionic mechanisms of the negative EOG response are similar to those of generator potentials in other sensory modalities, and it is widely assumed that the EOG may perform similar functions in the olfactory receptor. The shape and ionic mechanism of the positive potential resemble those of the inhibitory potentials that can be recorded from spinal motor neurons and neuromuscular junctions, suggesting that inhibitory mechanisms may operate even at the receptor level in the olfactory system.

It is believed that the negative EOG potentials may give rise to ON responses of the olfactory nerve and that the positive receptor potential may elicit OFF responses. It has been suggested that an interaction between these two slow potentials may result in graded facilitatory or inhibitory influences.[121, 120] There is some evidence suggesting that the negative EOG response may reflect a summation of olfactory-receptor activity and that the amplitude of the EOG is proportional, within some limits, to stimulus intensity[87, 126, 127] (see Figures 6–6 and 6–7).

Some observations suggest, however, that the EOG potential may not originate in the olfactory receptor and may not represent functional events that are essential to the processing of olfactory information.[120] Under some conditions it is possible to inhibit EOG responses without producing a noticeable difference in the olfactory-nerve response to odors, questioning the hypothesis that the potential normally acts as a generator potential for olfactory receptors.[111] A close inspection of the temporal relationship between the EOG response and olfactory-nerve reaction to odors further questions this relationship in showing that the EOG does not, in all instances, precede the neural response. It is possible that these inconsistencies reflect only the inadequacy of our recording procedures, which may not be capable of distinguishing true EOG potentials from various artifacts, but the question of generator potentials in the olfactory system must be considered unsettled at this moment.

Single-Cell Activity

Microelectrode recordings from the olfactory mucosa or from single fibers of the olfactory nerve have shown that olfactory receptors fire "spontaneously" (i.e., in the absence of specific olfactory stimulation). However, since it is essentially impossible to obtain a truly odorless environment for these tests, it is possible that this spontaneous activity is not, in fact, independent of odor.

The presentation of an olfactory stimulus increases or decreases receptor activity.

A variety of response patterns have been recorded that suggest that olfactory receptors may be arranged along quantitative as well as

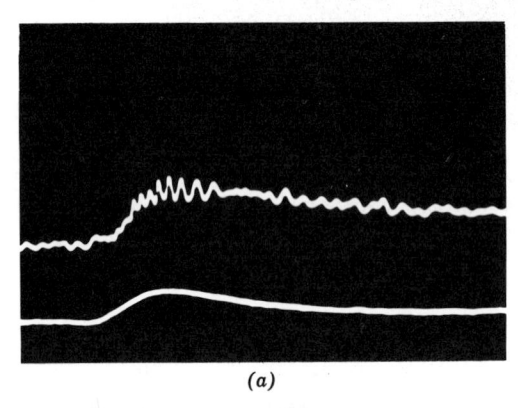

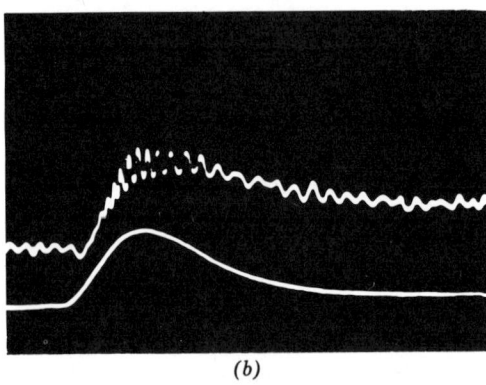

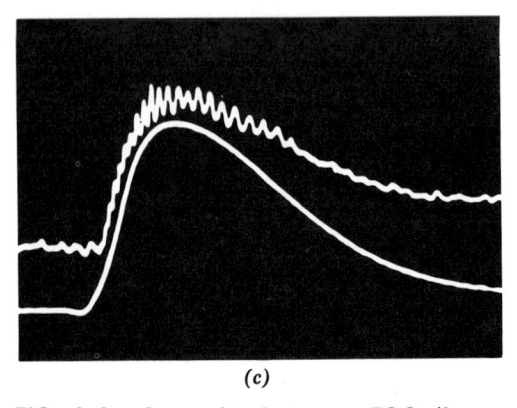

FIG. 6–6. Congruity between EOG (lower trace) and slow bulbar potential (upper trace). Recordings of responses to stimulation with butanol at increasing concentration (a)–(c).

(From D. Ottoson. Comparison of slow potentials evoked in the frog's nasal mucosa and olfactory bulb by natural stimulation. *Acta physiol. scand.*, **47**, 1959, 149–159.)

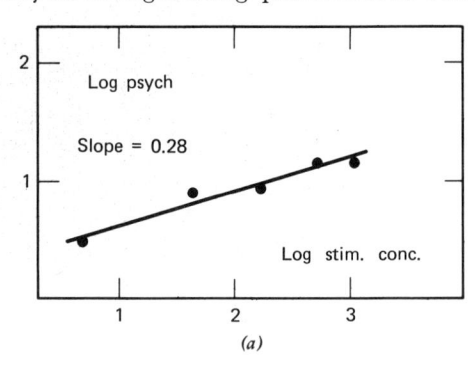

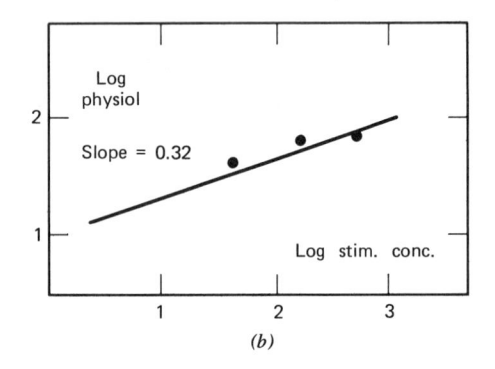

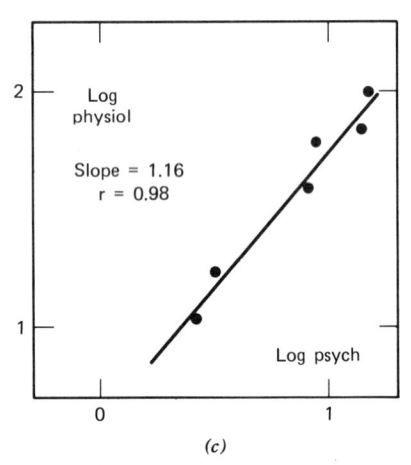

FIG. 6–7. Psychophysical and electrophysiological measurements of odor intensities for different concentrations of methyl benzoate. (a) data from psychophysical measurements; (b) measurements of EOG; (c) correlation diagram between psychophysical and electrophysiological data.

(From E. von Sydow. Comparison between psychophysical and electrophysiological data for some odor substances. In *Theories of odor and odor measurement*. N. N. Tanyolac, Ed. London: Unwin, 1968.)

qualitative continua. Some cells respond only to particular types of odors; others react exclusively to the intensity dimension of olfactory stimulation. Still others, probably the majority, respond to both qualitative and quantitative aspects of stimulation.[114, 25, 26] Individual receptors are capable of a repertoire of response that extends from maximum excitation to maximum inhibition and includes every conceivable intermediate state.[77] However, each cell appears to "order" olfactory stimuli in a unique fashion along this response continuum and may thus respond to a particular combination of odor quantity and quality in a unique fashion.[53] It seems probable, however, that the perception of a specific odor may depend on the decoding of the total pattern of activity in the olfactory nerve or some segment thereof rather than the activity of a single receptor cell.[114]

Microelectrode recordings of the responses of single taste receptors[70] have demonstrated an extraordinarily wide range of sensitivities. Some taste receptors begin to fire in response to threshold concentrations of several different taste stimuli and increase their firing rate as a function of increasing concentration. Others respond preferentially although apparently never uniquely to stimuli of particular taste categories. Recordings from single fibers in the glossopharyngeal or chorda tympani nerves similarly suggest that the taste receptors do not simply fall into four "basic" categories.[102, 137] Instead, it seems that each receptor may have a number of different receptor sites that are selectively sensitive to chemicals of particular categories. Some cells have many receptor sites for a particular substance and only relatively few for others and hence respond preferentially, although not exclusively, to a single type of stimulus. Other receptors appear to have more nearly equal populations of two or more different receptor sites and are therefore less selective in their reaction to gustatory stimuli[104] (see Figure 6–8).

Pharmacological data support the notion that four distinct receptor mechanisms may

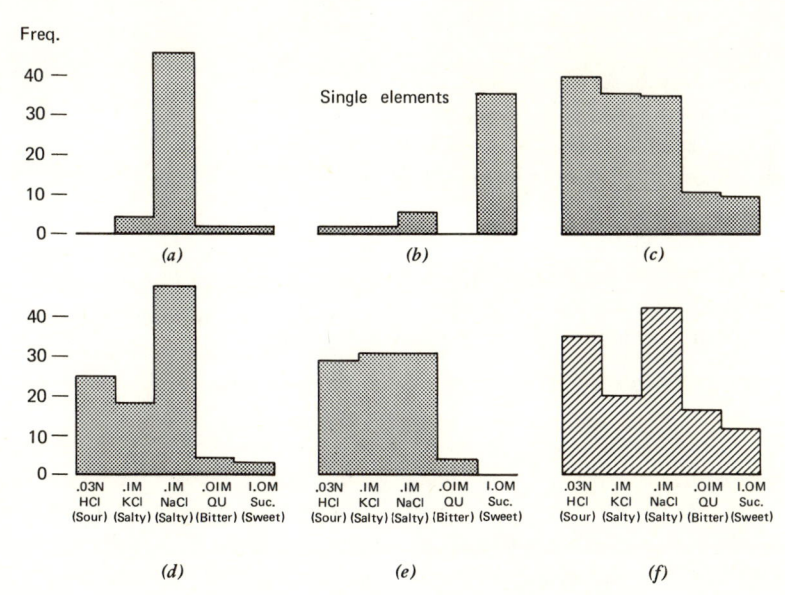

FIG. 6–8. Examples of response patterns of individual fibers of the rat chorda tympani to taste stimuli to the tongue (stippled bars). Notice that some fibers respond preferentially to one type of stimulus (a) and (b), whereas others respond to stimuli of two (c) or three (d) and (e) classes. Some individual fibers respond selectively to stimuli within a class of taste qualities (a) and (d). When the activity of all chorda tympani fibers is summed and integrated, an overall response pattern appears (diagonally-hatched bars), which is different from that of most individual fibers.

(After C. Pfaffmann. Gustatory nerve impulses in rat, cat, and rabbit. *J. Neurophysiol.*, **18**, 1955, 429–440.)

exist.[117] Most common anesthetics reduce or prevent bitter sensations at concentrations that do not affect other tastes. Increasing concentrations of these drugs reduce salt and sour but leave sweet relatively intact. Some drugs (such as stovaine or Gymnemic acid) abolish sweet and bitter but leave sour and salty tastes entirely intact (see Figure 6-9).

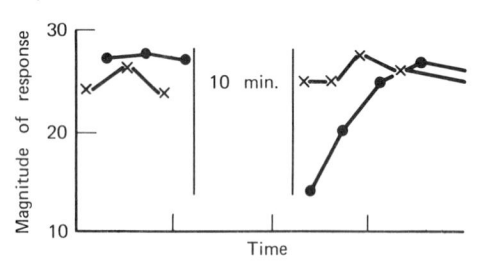

FIG. 6-9. Differential suppression of the response of the chorda tympani to sucrose (●——●) and sodium chloride (×——×) by gymnemic acid.

(After E. C. Hagstrom. Nature of taste stimulation by sugar. Ph.D. dissertation, Brown Univ., 1957.)

Moreover, if one uses high concentrations of some anesthetics to abolish all taste sensations, an orderly sequence of recovery occurs, sweet sensations returning first, salty and sour next, and bitter last. These observations are, of course, not in conflict with the electrophysiological data, since it is quite possible that drugs may affect some receptor sites on a given receptor differentially. They do, however, suggest that our taste categories may correspond in some way to gustatory receptor mechanisms even though we may not have directly corresponding receptor types.

Summated Potentials

Because the olfactory receptors and their axons are extraordinarily small, it has been very difficult to record the activity of single units. A common solution to this problem has been the recording of multiple-unit activity from small fascicles of the olfactory nerve. Running averages of this activity are often recorded by simple integration.[20]

It has been demonstrated with this technique that small nerve fascicles, 10 to 40 microns in diameter, project to discrete regions of the olfactory mucosa that are typically oval and less than one millimeter long.[126] A comparison of the activity of several fascicles suggests that different regions of the olfactory mucosa may selectively respond to particular odors, either because of a topographic distribution of specific receptor types or because of a nonrandom distribution of odor molecules on the mucosa. Our understanding of these relationships is still quite imperfect, but the few available data suggest that the spatiotemporal patterning of receptor activity may contribute to the coding of odor information.[88]

If the multiple-unit activity of an olfactory nerve fascicle is recorded with a D.C. amplifier, a slow potential appears in response to olfactory stimulation. This potential is similar in many ways to the EOG of the olfactory mucosa[96, 97] but may represent a different aspect of the receptor process.[127]

The transfer impedance of the olfactory mucosa undergoes marked changes in response to olfactory stimulation.[53] These impedance changes are believed to reflect average receptor activity, since their shape and magnitude tend to be the same for homologous chemicals anywhere on the mucosa.

Summary and Review Questions

Odors act on receptor cells that are located in the uppermost portion of the nose. It is believed that odors activate these receptors by acting on the hairlike cilia that protrude from them, but the nature of this interaction is as yet unknown. Some theories suggest that odor molecules selectively absorb radiant energy of certain wavelengths that are emitted by olfactory receptors. This is thought to cool the receptor and thereby initiate a generator potential. Others propose that odor molecules may momentarily reverse the membrane potential of the receptor either by inhibiting some of the enzymes that are essential for its maintenance or by puncturing the membrane in the process of desorption.

Attempts to record the electrophysiological events that accompany the transduction of odors into correlated neural signals have produced evidence of several slow graded potentials that may serve as generator potentials in the olfactory system. Most prominent of these are a positive (inhibitory) and negative (excitatory) potential that make up the electro-olfactogram. The amplitude of these potentials generally correlates well with the intensity of olfactory stimulation, but there are some disturbing instances in which the correlation between stimulus and EOG breaks down, and it is not certain, at this time, whether these potentials do, indeed, trigger the neural response to olfactory stimuli. Recordings from single olfactory-nerve fibers have shown complex response patterns. Some cells respond only to particular types of odors; others react exclusively to the intensity dimension of all odors. The majority of the olfactory receptors appear capable of responding within some limits to qualitative as well as quantitative aspects of the stimulus. Recordings obtained from small fascicles of olfactory-nerve fibers suggest that there may be "receptive fields" on the olfactory mucosa that are selectively sensitive to certain odors.

The gustatory receptors are hair cells that form small colonies in some of the "buds" or papillae that cover the tongue. Receptors on the posterior portion of the tongue are innervated by the glossopharyngeal nerve, those on the anterior part by the chorda tympani. These nerves ascend in the medial lemniscus and relay in the arcuate nucleus of the thalamus on their way to the pre- and post-central gyri of the cerebral cortex.

Just how this system transduces taste stimuli into neural signals is, as yet, not clear. It appears that each taste receptor may have a number of different receptor sites that are differentially sensitive to different types of chemicals. Depending on the relative concentration of different receptor sites, each individual receptor is thus more sensitive to one or more classes of chemicals than to others. Electrophysiological observations have not succeeded in proving that special receptors exist for each of the four seemingly basic taste categories, but there are some pharmacological observations to support such a classification. How the system attains whatever selective activation may exist is still unknown. Most theories in this area rely on selective adsorption, enzyme inhibition, molecular size or shape, intermolecular vibrations, and the like, in a more or less direct analogy to the receptor mechanisms that have been hypothesized to explain the activation of olfactory receptor mechanisms.

1. Describe the organization of the olfactory system.

2. Discuss the nature of the interaction between odor molecules and olfactory receptors.

3. Describe the electrophysiological responses of the olfactory receptor and the olfactory nerve.

4. Describe the anatomy of the gustatory system.

5. Discuss the physiological and pharmacological evidence that supports or fails to support the classification of taste sensations into four basic categories.

6. Briefly list some of the theories that attempt to explain how different substances selectively activate specific classes of gustatory receptors.

PROCESSING OF OLFACTORY AND GUSTATORY INFORMATION IN THE CENTRAL NERVOUS SYSTEM

Olfactory-Bulb Activity

Slow Potentials

Olfactory stimulation gives rise to slow potentials in the olfactory bulb that are similar in appearance to the EOG potentials of the olfactory mucosa. However, the bulb potentials do not show the marked adaptation to repeated stimulation that characterizes the EOG potential and can otherwise be dissociated from it.[96, 97] The bulb potentials follow the EOG potential by about 50 milliseconds but precede activation of bulbar neurons.

Electrical stimulation of the olfactory nerve gives rise to a complex bulb response that contains four distinct components.[92, 134] An analysis of the time course and interrelationship of these components suggests that they may represent distinct aspects of olfactory activity.[93] The first component is believed to to be related to the action potential of olfactory-nerve fibers, the second to presynaptic activity in the glomeruli, the third to dendritic postsynaptic activity of mitral cells, and the fourth to the activity of granule cells.

Electroencephalographic Recordings

Macroelectrode recordings from the olfactory bulb show large rhythmic oscillations during each inspiration of an odor. Between inspirations, these *induced waves* are replaced by smaller, irregular *intrinsic* waves[2] (see Figure 6–10). Destruction of the olfactory mucosa eliminates the induced waves, suggesting that they may be related to olfactory processes.

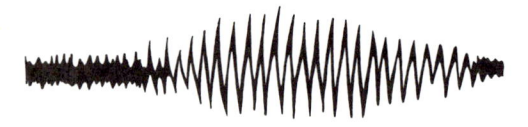

FIG. 6–10. Induced waves recorded from the olfactory bulb of a rabbit after olfactory stimulation.
(After E. D. Adrian. The electrical activity of the mammalian olfactory bulb. *EEG clin. Neurophysiol.*, **2**, 1950, 377–388.)

Amplitude and/or frequency analyses of these induced waves suggest that each burst may contain two or three distinct phases[84] and that specific odors may induce characteristic discharge patterns.[63] The presentation of an odor typically synchronizes the spontaneous activity and markedly increases its amplitude in one or more frequency bands. However, pure inhibitory reactions (a decrease in the amplitudes of particular frequencies) have been observed,[64,65] and some odors give rise to "mixed" responses (i.e., the amplitude of some frequencies increases while that of others decreases).[63] Some noxious odors produce a nearly complete flattening of the olfactory-bulb activity, but this may merely reflect a complete absence of respiratory activity.[51]

There is some evidence[63] that the frequency of olfactory-bulb activity may be related to the stereochemical properties of the olfactory stimulus. Stereochemically similar stimuli typically produce peak amplitude in the same narrow EEG frequency band. Compounds of high molecular weight, such as the "floral" substances in Amoore's system, typically produce peak amplitudes at frequencies between 35 and 75 Hz. Compounds of low molecular weight, such as the "camphoraceous" odors of Amoore's system, typically produce peak amplitudes between 75 and 125 Hz. The olfactory-bulb EEG suggests some topographic organization, since the frequency of the peak reactions to an odor differs, often quite considerably, between electrode sites.

Single- and Multiple-Unit Activity

Recordings of multiple-unit activity[84,85] show some "spontaneous" activity in the olfactory bulb in the absence of specific olfactory stimulation. The presentation of odors typically results in a burst of increased activity that is repeated with each inspiration. A closer analysis of this response shows that the pattern of activity that is induced by a particular odor may be unique to that odor and electrode site. Some recording sites do not respond at all to some odors but show abrupt or gradual changes in unit activity in response to others. The unique features of these reactions are difficult to predict but tend to be constant for a particular odor from trial to trial and from day to day.[84,86]

Microelectrode recordings from single mitral cells in the olfactory bulb have shown giant spike potentials in the absence of specific olfactory stimulation.[106] Granule and tufted cells also discharge spontaneously, the granule cell discharge always being out of phase with that of the mitral and tufted cells.[16] This intrinsic activity persists when the olfactory mucosa and central olfactory projections are destroyed.

Olfactory stimulation may increase or decrease the discharge frequency of particular olfactory-bulb neurons.[134] As many as six different response patterns have been distinguished, including ON, ON-OFF, and OFF responses. Some investigators have interpreted these response patterns to suggest corresponding receptor types.[2,115] However, this hypothesis cannot account for the observation[79] that different odors may elicit very different, even opposite response patterns from the same cell in the olfactory bulb.

Cortical Projections of the Olfactory System

Olfactory stimulation produces evoked potentials that can be recorded from the prepyriform cortex, periamygdaloid area, olfactory tubercle, septal area, and hippocampus.[1, 78] The latency of the prepyriform potential is short, suggesting monosynaptic connections. The latency of responses in all other areas is long, and these areas are consequently assumed to be only secondarily related to olfactory processes.

Electrical stimulation of the olfactory bulb produces evoked potentials in the prepyriform cortex that have very short latencies ipsilaterally and rather long latencies contralaterally. Many cells are facilitated by olfactory-bulb stimulation, but a fair number show a reduction in firing rate (see Figure 6–11). The olfactory bulb seems to exert tonic inhibitory influences on the prepyriform cortex, since removal of one olfactory bulb significantly lowers the response threshold in both ipsilateral and contralateral prepyriform regions.[31]

The presentation of olfactory stimuli to the nasal mucosa of only one nostril influences the activity of cells in both olfactory bulbs and cortical projections. The response of cells ipsilateral to the stimulation is typically excitatory, that of cells contralateral to the stimulation inhibitory.[79, 31]

Electrical as well as chemical stimulation of the prepyriform cortex reduces the spontaneous activity of olfactory-bulb neurons and inhibits their response to olfactory stimulation.[69, 12] These effects appear to be mediated by cells in the prepyriform cortex that project axons through the anterior commissure. Prepyriform lesions or transection of the anterior commissure increase the amplitude of spontaneous and induced activity in the olfactory bulb.[69, 32] Most of these centrifugal fibers terminate on granule cells or in the glomeruli of mitral cells.[35]

Activity of the Chorda Tympani and Glossopharyngeal Nerves

The activity of the whole chorda tympani nerve, which supplies the fungiform papillae

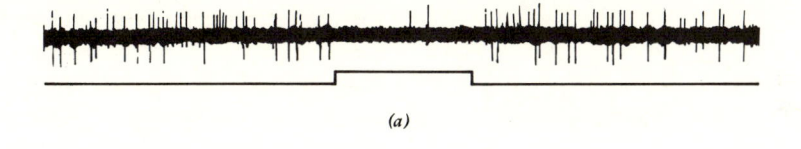

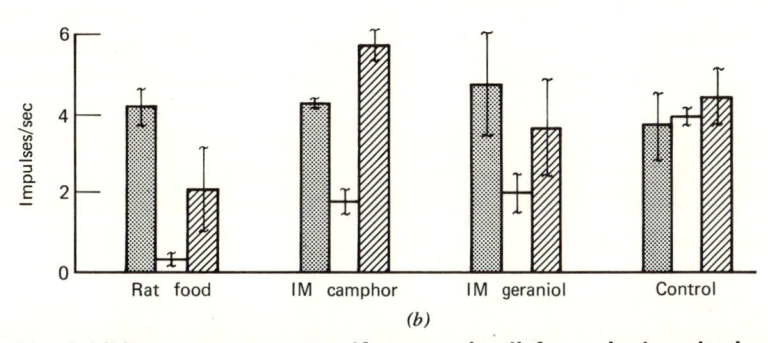

FIG. 6–11. Inhibitory responses to olfactory stimuli from single units in the prepyriform cortex of rat. (a) Sample record period of olfactory stimulation shown in lower trace. (b) Comparison of responses of same unit to three odors and pure air control. Stippled bars indicate resting firing rates immediately preceding stimuli; open bars, firing rates during stimuli; diagonally-hatched bars, firing rates immediately following stimuli.

(From L. B. Haberly. Single unit responses to odor in the prepyriform cortex of the rat. *Brain Res.*, **12**, 1969, 481–484.)

of the anterior tongue, is determined by the quality as well as the quantity of taste stimuli[136, 54] (see Figure 6–12). As one might expect on the basis of their absolute behavioral thresholds, bitter stimuli such as quinine are most effective; sour, salt, and sweet are less so, in that order. For a given taste quality, the magnitude of the chorda tympani response becomes a direct function of concentration. This relationship tends to be linear except at its extremes.[101, 102] Analyses of single-fiber activity in the chorda tympani[102, 49] show much the same pattern of activity as is seen in single olfactory receptors. Chorda tympani fibers typically respond to two or more classes of taste stimuli and react more intensely to one of the categories than to any other. An example[103, 104] may help to illustrate how such a coding system might work. At the simplest, two-fiber level, we may find that both respond to salts and sugars, but one (A) responds

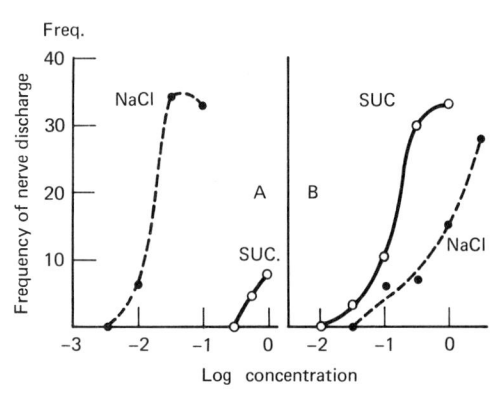

FIG. 6–13. Comparison of the response pattern of two individual chorda tympani fibers in the rat to sweet and salty taste stimuli.

(From C. Pfaffmann. Gustatory nerve impulses in rat, cat, and rabbit. *J. Neurophysiol.*, **18**, 1955, 429–440.)

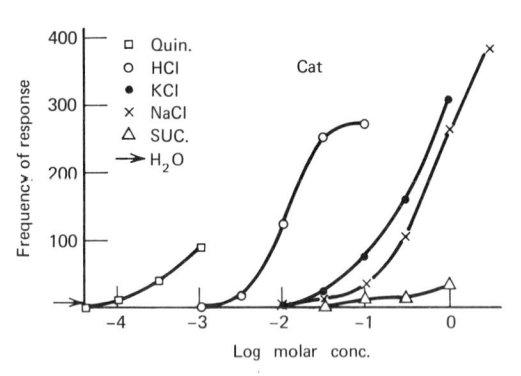

FIG. 6–12. Summated chorda tympani response (arbitrary units) to increasing concentrations of different taste stimuli.

(From C. Pfaffmann. Gustatory nerve impulses in rat, cat, and rabbit. *J. Neurophysiol.*, **18**, 1955, 429–440.)

preferentially to sugars and the other (B) to salt (see Figure 6–13). The system signals "salt" when the activity of B is greater than A and "sugar" when the activity of A is greater than B. When we add more fibers to this system, each preferentially sensitive to some class or taste stimuli, a complex coding mechanism evolves. Activity in any particular fiber may be part of such a system's response to several stimuli, and only the overall pattern of activity in all channels may be unique to a given sensation. We do not yet have suffi- ciently detailed knowledge about the nature of interactions in the taste system, but it seems certain that the complexities of sensory phenomena here as in other sensory systems cannot depend entirely on a simple one-to-one relationship between stimulus properties and single receptor or nerve activity.

The lingual branch of the glossopharyngeal nerve innervates taste buds in the papillae in the posterior third of the tongue. Since these receptors are preferentially sensitive to bitter and sour stimuli, it is not surprising to find that the glossopharyngeal nerve of a variety of species shows marked selective activation in response to stimuli of these categories.[136, 98, 133] However, intense salty and sweet stimuli also elicit glossopharyngeal-nerve activity in many species, indicating that the differential sensitivity of this part of the system is not absolute. In some species, there is also a marked "water" response in the glossopharyngeal nerve.[105, 11, 15]

Since the chorda tympani, as well as the glossopharyngeal nerve, seems to be capable of carrying information about all varieties of taste stimuli, we might wonder whether the two channels simply duplicate information. This does not seem to be true. The nature of the interaction differs somewhat between species, but it is clear that certain divisions of labor exist. If we restrict our discussion to the rat, about which we have the most complete information, the following conclusions can be drawn.

Bitter stimuli, such as quinine, affect the glossopharyngeal at lower concentrations and result in greater activity at all concentrations.[21,23] The quinine threshold of the glossopharyngeal nerve is comparable to the behavioral detection threshold in rats.[23]

Sour stimuli also elicit glossopharyngeal responses at concentrations that are below the threshold of the chorda tympani, but the magnitude of the response to suprathreshold concentrations is about equal in the two nerves. The threshold of both nerves is below the aversion and absolute detection threshold for hydrochloric acid.[22,72]

Sucrose preference and detection thresholds[109,72] are comparable to the chorda tympani threshold for sweet substances.[58] The threshold of the glossopharyngeal nerve is somewhat higher.[105]

In some species the response to salty stimuli is quite different in the two nerves. The chorda tympani of the rat does not carry responses to pure water and responds proportionally to the concentration of sodium chloride. The glossopharyngeal nerve, on the other hand, responds less to low NaCl concentration than to pure water and thus gives a biphasic response to salt solutions (an apparent inhibition at low concentrations and a facilitation at concentrations above 0.1 M). The preference and detection thresholds[108,72] for sodium chloride coincide with that of the chorda tympani. The threshold of the glossopharyngeal nerve is considerably higher.[105]

The taste buds of mammals degenerate when the associated nerve fibers are cut and are formed again from the epithelium of the tongue when the nerve regenerates.[55,90] If one cuts both major taste nerves and reconnects them so that the central stump of the chorda tympani is connected to the peripheral segment of the glossopharyngeal nerve and vice versa, one can empirically determine whether the quality of sensation is the result of receptor specificity or of its central projections.

When this is done[89] we find that the chorda tympani, which regrows to form taste buds in the posterior portion of the tongue, shows a response pattern to taste stimuli that is similar to that normally carried in the glossopharyngeal nerve. Similarly, glossopharyngeal fibers, forced to innervate taste buds in the anterior segment of the tongue, respond like normal chorda tympani fibers. It thus seems that the properties of the taste receptors are determined by the tissue from which they are formed rather than by their central connections.

The central projections of the gustatory system appear to be topographically organized to some extent. Multiple-unit activity in the nucleus of the fasciculus solitarius,[59] for instance, shows that neurons that respond maximally to sucrose are found in the ventral portion of that nucleus and that bitter stimuli, such as quinine, elicit maximal activity from more dorsal points.

Observations of taste-induced activity in the thalamic relay[66] similarly show a topographic organization. Some regions of the nucleus ventralis posteromedialis (VPM) respond selectively to only one class of taste stimuli. The majority of neurons are sensitive to two or more stimulus categories as in the periphery, but it appears that there may be some "sharpening" (increased specificity) as well as topographic organization in the higher representations of the gustatory system.

Summary and Review Questions

Macroelectrode recordings from the olfactory bulb have shown that the presentation of olfactory stimuli elicits (1) slow potentials similar to the EOG and (2) "induced waves" in the EEG. The slow potentials of the olfactory bulb typically follow the EOG potential and precede the activation of neurons in the olfactory bulb. The frequency-amplitude pattern of the induced waves appears to differ systematically for different odors, and there is some evidence that the nature of the response may be related to the stereochemical properties of the stimulus.

Multiple-unit recordings from the olfactory bulb have suggested that specific types of odors may selectively activate or inhibit specific portions of the olfactory bulb. Microelectrode recordings obtained from single cells in the olfactory bulb have shown as many as six types of responses to different odors, including ON, maintained ON, ON-OFF, and OFF responses. It has been difficult to relate these response patterns to transduction mechanisms for particular types of odors in view of the observation that individual cells often respond to more than one odor.

Primary evoked responses to odors are recorded from the prepyriform cortex of the temporal lobe. Evoked responses are also seen in other structures, but their long latencies suggest that these are not primary projections. An analysis of the single-unit activity in the prepyriform cortex indicates that the direct projections from the olfactory bulb to the ipsilateral prepyriform cortex are mainly excitatory whereas the indirect projections to the contralateral cortical projections are mainly inhibitory.

Gustatory information is processed by two anatomically as well as functionally distinct central pathways. The glossopharyngeal nerve innervates the posterior segments of the tongue, which are most sensitive to bitter and sour stimuli. This nerve responds, as a whole, more readily to threshold concentrations of these substances than does the chorda tympani, which innervates the anterior portions of the tongue. The glossopharyngeal nerve responds somewhat less readily to sweet substances than the chorda tympani, and its response to salty stimuli is often biphasic because low concentrations of salt inhibit water receptors, which are represented in the glossopharyngeal nerve of many species.

An analysis of the response of single gustatory nerve fibers indicates that the selective responses that characterize the whole glossopharyngeal and chorda tympani nerves may reflect relative rather than absolute sensitivity differences in individual receptors. Individual chorda tympani fibers typically respond to two or more classes of gustatory stimuli, although they often respond preferentially to stimuli of one of the four categories. It has been suggested that gustatory sensations may be coded not by the response pattern of a single receptor or nerve fiber but by the pattern of activation in several related fibers that have somewhat different sensitivity patterns.

1. Describe the relationship between the EOG and slow potentials in the olfactory bulb.

2. Describe the relationship between the nature of the olfactory stimulus and the pattern of amplitude and frequency changes in the induced waves that can be recorded from the olfactory bulb.

3. Describe the responses of olfactory-bulb cells to particular odors.

4. Describe the cortical projections of the olfactory system and their response to odors.

5. Describe the functional differences between the two main central channels of the gustatory system.

6. Compare the response of individual fibers in the gustatory nerves to the response of gustatory receptors.

REVIEW

The olfactory system has been difficult to study. For openers, we have man's curious inability to decide just how many different odors there are and whether any of them might be "primary" or "basic." Directly related to this problem is the fact that we do not yet know for sure what properties of a substance make it an odorivector, and we know even less about the qualities responsible for its emission of specific odors. It seems clear that most odors arise from substances that are volatile, soluble, and adsorbable, but we do not know whether these attributes are essential or sufficient for olfactory stimulation.

Gustatory sensations are more readily classified into four "basic" categories (bitter, sweet, sour, and salty), although it is not clear that these distinctions adequately reflect the physical properties of gustatory stimuli or specific receptor types. Salty tastes appear to be related to the free anion of solute salts, but cross-stimulus adaptation studies suggest that there may be as many receptor mechanisms as there are salts. Sour tastes appear to be related to the concentration of hydrogen ions in acids, suggesting a single receptor mechanism. Sweet and bitter are more complexly related to the physical properties of the stimulus. Sweetness appears to be related to low molecular weight and the presence of certain chemical groupings, but there are notable exceptions that do not fit this rule. Bitter tastes are common to substances with high molecular weight, but there are, once again, exceptions. Cross-stimulus adaptation studies indicate that there may be several sweet and bitter receptor mechanisms.

Many theories have been suggested to account for different olfactory or taste sensations, but there is, as yet, none that can satisfactorily predict all phenomena. There are (a) enzyme theories, which propose that different molecules may inhibit different enzymes and thus produce membrane potentials in specific cells; (b) infrared-absorption theories, which suggest that specific classes of chemical receptors may emit radiant energies in the infrared portion of the spectrum and that different molecules may absorb radiations of particular wavelengths and thus differentially cool some receptor sites; (c) stereochemical theories, which propose that chemical receptors may be equipped with special receptor sites corresponding in size, shape, or electrochemical properties to those of different types of molecules; (d) molecular vibration theories, which suggest that the frequency of intermolecular vibrations of odor or taste stimuli may selectively activate special receptor types; and (e) other hypotheses, which rely on such factors as selective adsorption or special chemical groupings to account or selective receptor activation.

The study of olfactory processes has been further complicated by some of the properties of the olfactory system itself. Its anatomy makes it very difficult to control the intensity of stimulation or its distribution on the receptor surface at any point in time. The remarkably swift and complete adaptation of olfactory receptors to specific stimuli and the often unpredictable pattern of interaction of this effect with the system's response to different odors has further complicated the situation. If one adds to this the fact that the human nose is extremely sensitive to some odors, and all but insensitive to closely related substances, and that it responds to very different ranges of intensities for different stimuli, one can begin to appreciate some of the difficulties that have beset investigators in this field.

It is thus not surprising that we do not yet know how specific chemical signals are transduced into proportional tastes or smells. There is some evidence that olfactory stimuli produce slow potentials in the vicinity of the olfactory receptor, and it has been suggested that some of these, particularly the EOG potentials, may serve the function of generator or trigger potentials. Such an interpretation is, however, contradicted by some experimental findings. An analysis of the activity of individual cells in the olfactory mucosa or of individual fibers in the olfactory nerve indicates that most olfactory receptors may respond to limited intensities of a limited variety of olfactory stimuli. However, some receptors respond selectively to specific odors and still others respond to changes in the intensity of apparently all odors. Small fascicles of the olfactory nerve may innervate discrete "receptive fields" on the olfactory mucosa, and different receptive fields may respond selectively to specific odors, suggesting a spatial organization of the different types of olfactory receptors.

Gustatory receptors appear to have several types of receptor mechanisms that respond differentially to stimuli of different taste categories. A receptor may have a large number of receptor sites for a particular type of chemical and only few for others, and thus respond preferentially to a single class of stimuli. Other receptors appear to have more nearly equal populations of two or more different receptor sites and respond less selectively. Pharmacological observations indicate that some receptor sites may be differentially sensitive to certain local anesthetics.

The processing of olfactory information in the central nervous system has been studied extensively in recent years, but the relationship between specific odors, related receptor potentials, and olfactory-bulb or prepyriform-cortex activity is still only poorly understood. Olfactory stimuli elicit slow graded potentials in the olfactory bulb that are similar but apparently not identical to the EOG potentials of the olfactory mucosa. In addition, one can observe "induced waves" in the EEG of the olfactory bulb that show amplitude changes at selected frequencies that appear to be related lawfully to the intensity or quality of the stimulus.

Multiple-unit recordings from the olfactory bulb have suggested a spatial organization that may reflect the receptive fields seen in the olfactory mucosa. An analysis of the response of individual cells in the olfactory bulb demonstrates ON, ON-OFF, and OFF response patterns that are similar to those seen in other modalities. The central projections of the olfactory bulb appear to be organized such that projections to the prepyriform cortex of the same hemisphere produce excitatory effects and projections to the contralateral hemisphere have inhibitory consequences.

We know even less about the central processing of gustatory information. Receptors on the posterior portion of the tongue are innervated by the glossopharyngeal nerve, which, as a whole, responds more readily to bitter and sour and less readily to sweet stimuli than does the chorda tympani, which innervates anterior parts of the tongue. In some species, the glossopharyngeal nerve gives a biphasic response to salty stimuli because it carries fibers that relate to water receptors on the tongue. Individual fibers in the glossopharyngeal or chorda tympani nerves typically respond to two or more types of gustatory stimuli, although a preferential sensitivity to particular stimuli is not uncommon. The higher central projections of the gustatory system are, to some extent, topographically organized in a pattern that reflects the bitter-sweet-sour-salty classification of gustatory stimuli.

Bibliography

1. Adrian, E. D. Olfactory reactions in the brain of the hedgehog. *J. Physiol.*, 1942, **100**, 459–473.
2. Adrian, E. D. The electrical activity of the mammalian olfactory bulb. *EEG Clin. Neurophysiol.*, 1950, **2**, 377–388.
3. Allara, E. Ricerche sull'organo del gusto dell' nomo. I: La struttura delle papille gustative nelle varie eta della vita. *Arch. Ital. Anat. Embr.*, 1939, **42**, 506–564.
4. Amoore, J. E. The stereochemical specificities of human olfactory receptors. *Perfum. Ess. Oil Rec.*, 1952, **43**, 321–323, 330.
5. Amoore, J. E. The stereochemical theory of olfaction. 1. Identification of the seven primary odours. *Proc. Sci. Sect. Toilet Goods Assoc.*, Supplement to No. 37, 1962a, 1–12.
6. Amoore, J. E. The stereochemical theory of olfaction. 2. Elucidation of the stereochemical properties of the olfactory receptor sites. *Proc. Sci. Sect. Toilet Goods Assoc.*, Supplement to No. 37, 1962b, 13–23.
7. Amoore, J. E. Current status of the steric theory of odor. *Ann. N. Y. Acad. Sci.*, 1964, **116**, 457–476.
8. Amoore, J. E. Psychophysics of odor. *Cold Spr. Harb. Symp. Quant. Biol.*, 1965, **30**, 623–637.
9. Amoore, J. E. Stereochemical theory of olfaction. In *Symposium on Foods: the Chemistry and Physiology of Flavours*. H. W. Schultz, E. A. Day, & L. M. Libbey, Eds. Westport, Conn.: Avi Publishing Co., 1967, pp. 119–147.
10. Amoore, J. E., & Venstrom, D. Correlations between stereochemical assessments and organoleptic analysis of odorous compounds. In *Olfaction and Taste. II.* T. Hayashi, Ed. Oxford: Pergamon Press, 1967, pp. 3–17.
11. Appelberg, B. Species differences in the taste qualities mediated through the glossopharyngeal nerve. *Acta Physiol. Scand.*, 1958, **44**, 129–137.
12. Angeleri, F., & Carreras, M. Problemi di fisiologia dell' olfatto. I: Studio elettrofisiologico delle vie centrifughe di origine paleocorticale. *Riv. Neurobiol.*, 1956, **2**, 255–274.

13. Aronsohn, E. Cited in Moncrieff, R. W. *The Chemical Senses.* London: Leonard Hill, 1967.
14. Bagshaw, M. H., & Pribram, K. H. Cortical organization in gustation (Macaca mulatta). *J. Neurophysiol.*, 1953, **16**, 499–508.
15. Baldwin, B. A., Bell, F. R., & Kitchell, R. L. Gustatory nerve impulses in ruminant ungulates. *J. Physiol. (London)*, 1959, **146**, 14–15.
16. Baumgarten, R. von, Green, J. D., & Mancia, M. Slow waves in the olfactory bulb and their relation to unitary discharges. *EEG Clin. Neurophysiol.*, 1962, **14**, 621–634.
17. Beck, L. H. Osmics: theory and problems related to the initial events in olfaction. In *Medical Physics. Vol. II.* O. Glasser, Ed. Chicago: Year Book Publishers, 1950, pp. 658–664.
18. Beck, L. H., & Miles, W. R. Some theoretical and experimental relationships between infrared absorption and olfaction. *Science*, 1947, **106**, 511.
19. Beck, L. H., Kruger, L., & Calabresi, P. Observations on olfactory intensity. I. Training procedures, methods, and data for two aliphatic homologous series. *Ann. N. Y. Acad. Sci.*, 1954, **58**, 225–238.
20. Beidler, L. M., & Tucker, D. Response of nasal epithelium to odor stimulation. *Science*, 1955, **122**, 76.
21. Beidler, L. M., Fishman, I. Y., & Hardiman, C. W. Species differences in taste responses. *Amer. J. Physiol.*, 1955, **181**, 239.
22. Benjamin, R. M. Cerebral mechanisms in gustatory discrimination. Unpublished Ph. D. dissertation. Brown University, 1953, 140 pp.
23. Benjamin, R. M., & Pfaffmann, C. Cortical localization of taste in albino rat. *J. Neurophysiol.*, 1955, **18**, 56–64.
24. Berry, C. M., Hagamen, W. D., & Hinsey, J. C. Distribution of potentials following stimulation of the olfactory bulb in cat. *J. Neurophysiol.*, 1952, **15**, 139–148.
25. Boeckh, J. Peripheral inhibition as a code in insect olfaction. Abstracts of papers presented at XXIII International Congress of Physiological Sciences, 1965, 379.
26. Boeckh, J. Inhibition and excitation of single insect olfactory receptors, and their role as a primary sensory code. In *Olfaction and Taste. II.* T. Hayashi, Ed. Oxford: Pergamon Press, 1967, pp. 721–735.
27. Boring, E. G. A new system for the classification of odor. *Amer. J. Psychol.*, 1928, **40**, 345–349.
28. Bourne, G. H. Alkaline phosphatase in taste buds and nasal mucosa. *Nature*, 1948, **161**, 445–446.
29. Bremer, F. Centre cortical du goût chez le Lapin. *C. R. Soc. Biol.*, 1923, **89**, 432–433.
30. Buijs, K., Schutte, C. J. H., & Verster, F. Absence of correlation between odour and molecular vibration. *Nature*, 1961, **192**, 751–752.
31. Callens, M. *Peripheral and Central Regulatory Mechanisms of the Excitability in the Olfactory System.* Brussels: Academic Press, 1967.
32. Carreras, M., & Angeleri, F. Problemi di fisiologia dell' olfatto. II. Una ipotesi sulla regolazione centrale dell' attività afferente nel sistema olfattico. *Riv. Neurobiol.*, 1956, **2**, 275–297.
33. Carreras, M., Mancia, D., & Mancia, M. Slow potential changes induced in the olfactory bulb by central and peripheral stimuli. In *Olfaction and Taste. II.* T. Hayashi, Ed. Oxford: Pergamon Press, 1967, pp. 181–191.
34. Clark, W. E. le Gros. Observation on the structure and organization of the olfactory receptors of the rabbit. *Yale J. Biol. Med.*, 1956, **29**, 83–95.
35. Cragg, B. G. Centrifugal fibers to the retina and olfactory bulb and composition of the supraoptic commissure in the rabbit. *Exp. Neurol.*, 1962, **5**, 406–427.
36. Crocker, E. C. *Flavor.* New York: McGraw-Hill, 1948.
37. Crocker, E. C., & Henderson, L. F. Analysis and classification of odors. *Amer. Perfum. Ess. Oil Rev.*, 1927, **22**, 325–356.
38. Dallenbach, J. W., & Dallenbach, K. M. The effects of bitter-adaptation on sensitivity to the other taste qualities. *Amer. J. Psychol.*, 1943, **56**, 21–31.
39. Davies, J. T. A theory of the quality of odours. *J. Theoret. Biol.*, 1965, **8**, 1–7.
40. Davies, J. T., & Taylor, F. H. A model system for the olfactory membrane. *Nature*, 1954, **174**, 693–694.

41. Davies, J. T., & Taylor, F. H. The role of adsorption and molecular morphology in olfaction: the calculation of olfactory thresholds. *Biol. Bull.*, 1959, **117**, 222–238.
42. De Lorenzo, A. J. Electron microscopic observations of the olfactory mucosa and olfactory nerve. *J. Biophys. Biochem. Cytol.*, 1957, **3**, 839–850.
43. De Lorenzo, A. J. Studies on the ultrastructure and histophysiology of cell membranes, nerve fibers and synaptic junctions in chemoreceptors. In *Olfaction and Taste. I.* Y. Zotterman, Ed. Oxford: Pergamon Press, 1963, pp. 5–17.
44. Duncan, D. R., & Bean, C. M. Perception and measurement of odour. *Nature*, 1950, **165**, 394–395.
45. Dyson, G. M. The scientific basis of odour. *Chem. Ind. (London)*, 1938, **57**, 647–651.
46. Ehrensvärd, G. C. H., & Cheesman, D. F. The specific adsorption of alcohols at the salicylaldehyde/water intersurface. *Science*, 1941, **94**, 23–25.
47. El-Baradi, A. F., & Bourne, G. H. Localization of gustatory and olfactory enzymes in the rabbit and the problems of taste and smell. *Nature*, 1951a, **168**, 977–979.
48. El-Baradi, A. F., & Bourne, G. H. Theory of tastes and odors. *Science*, 1951b, **113**, 660–661.
49. Fishman, I. Y. Single fiber gustatory impulses in rat hamster. *J. Cell. Comp. Physiol.*, 1957, **49**, 319–334.
50. Gastaut, R., & Lammers, H. J. *Anatomie du Rhinencéphale.* Paris: Masson et Cie, VIII, 1961, 166 pp.
51. Gault, F. P., & Leaton, R. N. Electrical activity of the olfactory system. *EEG Clin. Neurophysiol.*, 1963, **15**, 299–304.
52. Gesteland, R. C. Initial events of the electro-olfactogram. *Ann. N. Y. Acad. Sci.*, 1964, **116**, 440–447.
53. Gesteland, R. C. Differential impedance changes of the olfactory mucosa with odorous stimulation. In *Olfaction and Taste. II.* T. Hayashi, Ed. Oxford: Pergamon Press, 1967, pp. 821–831.
54. Gordon, G., Kitchell, R., Ström, L., & Zotterman, Y. The response pattern of taste fibers in the chorda tympani of the monkey. *Acta Physiol. Scand.*, 1959, **46**, 119–132.
55. Guth, L. Taste buds on the cat's circumvallate papilla after reinnervation by glossopharyngeal, vagus, and hypoglossal nerves. *Anat. Rec.*, 1958, **130**, 25–37.
56. Haberly, L. B., Single unit responses to odor in the prepyriform cortex of the rat. *Brain Res. (Amsterdam)*, 1969, **12**, 481–484.
57. Hagstrom, E. C. Nature of taste stimulation by sugar. Unpublished Ph.D. dissertation, Brown Univ., 1957, 55pp.
58. Hagstrom, E. C., & Pfaffmann, C. The relative taste effectiveness of different sugars for the rat. *J. Comp. Physiol. Psychol.*, 1959, **52**, 259–262.
59. Halpern, B. P. Chemotropic coding for sucrose and quinine hydrochloride in the nucleus of the fasciculus solitarious. In *Olfaction and Taste. II.* T. Hayashi, Ed. Oxford: Pergamon Press, 1967, pp. 549–562.
60. Hands, A. R. Do smells have frequencies? *New Scientist*, 1961, **11**, 175.
61. Henning, H. *Der Geruch.* Leipzig: Barth, 1916.
62. Henning, H. *Der Geruch* (2nd ed.). Leipzig: Barth, 1924.
63. Hughes, J. R., & Hendrix, D. E. The frequency component hypothesis in relation to the coding mechanism in the olfactory bulb. In *Olfaction and Taste. II.* T. Hayashi, Ed. Oxford: Pergamon Press, 1967, pp. 51–87.
64. Hughes, J. R., & Mazurowski, J. A. Studies on the supracallosal mesial cortex of unanesthetized, conscious mammals. II. Monkey B. Responses from the olfactory bulb. *EEG Clin. Neurophysiol.*, 1962a, **14**, 635–645.
65. Hughes, J. R., & Mazurowski, J. A. Studies on the supracallosal mesial cortex of unanesthetized conscious mammals. II. Monkey C. Frequency analysis of responses from the olfactory bulb. *EEG Clin. Neurophysiol.*, 1962b, **14**, 646–653.
66. Ishiko, N., Amatsu, M., & Sato, Y. Thalamic representation of taste qualities and temperature change in the cat. In *Olfaction and Taste. II.* T. Hayashi, Ed. Oxford: Pergamon, 1967, pp. 563–572.
67. Johnston, J. W., Jr. Infrared loss theory of olfaction untenable. *Physiol. Zool.*, 1953, **26**, 266–273.

68. Jones, F. N. Scales of subjective intensity for odors of diverse chemical nature. *Amer. J. Physiol.*, 1958, **71**, 305–310.
69. Kerr, D. I. B., & Hagbarth, K. E. An investigation of olfactory centrifugal fiber system. *J. Neurophysiol.*, 1955, **18**, 362–374.
70. Kimura, K., & Beidler, L. M. Microelectrode study of taste bud of the rat. *Amer. J. Physiol.*, 1956, **187**, 610–611.
71. Kistiakowsky, G. B. On the theory of odor. *Science*, 1950, **112**, 154–155.
72. Koh, S. D., & Teitelbaum, P. Absolute behavioral taste thresholds in the rat. *J. Comp. Physiol. Psychol.*, 1961, **54**, 223–229.
73. Kolmer, W. Über das Vorkommen von Geschmacksknospen im Ductus nasopalatinus der Ratte. *Anat. Anz.*, 1927, **63**, 248–251.
74. Krech, R., & Crutchfield, R. S. *Elements of Psychology*. New York: Knopf, 1959.
75. Lammers, H. J. Quoted by Gastaut, H., & Lammers, H. J. *Anatomie du Rhinencéphale*. Paris: Masson et Cie, VII, 1959, 166 pp.
76. Lasareff, P. Untersuchungen über die Ionentheorie der Reizung. III. Ionentheorie der geschmacksreizung. *Pflüg. Arch. Ges. Physiol.*, 1922, **194**, 293–297.
77. Lettvin, J. Y., & Gesteland, R. C. Speculations on smell. *Cold Spr. Harb. Symp. Quant. Biol.*, 1965, **30**, 217–225.
78. MacLean, P. D., Horwitz, N. H., & Robinson, F. Olfactorylike responses in piriform area to non-olfactory stimulation. *Yale J. Biol. Med.*, 1952, **25**, 159–175.
79. Mancia, M., Baumgarten, R. von., & Green, J. D. Response patterns of olfactory bulb neurons. *Arch. Ital. Biol.*, 1962, **100**, 449–462.
80. Mayer, B. Messende Untersuchungen über die Umstimmung des Geschmackswerkzeugs (Quantitative studies of the adaptation of the sense of taste). *Zeits. Sinnesphysiologie*, 1927, **58**, 133–152.
81. Moncrieff, R. W. The odorants. Basic odor research correlation. *Ann. N. Y. Acad. Sci.*, 1954, **58**, 73–82.
82. Moncrieff, R. W. The sorptive properties of the olfactory membrane. *J. Physiol.*, 1955, **130**, 543–558.
83. Moncrieff, R. W. *The Chemical Senses*. London: Leonard Hill, 1967.
84. Moulton, D. G. Electrical activity in the olfactory system of rabbits with indwelling electrodes. In *Olfaction and Taste. I.* Y. Zotterman, Ed. Oxford: Pergamon Press, 1963, pp. 71–84.
85. Moulton, D. G. Differential sensitivity to odors. In *Sensory Receptors. Cold Spr. Harb. Symp. Quant. Biol.*, 1965, **30**, 201–206.
86. Moulton, D. G. Spatio-temporal patterning of response in the olfactory system. In *Olfaction and Taste. II.* T. Hayashi, Ed. Oxford: Pergamon Press, 1967, pp. 109–116.
87. Mozell, M. M. Olfactory and neural responses in the frog. *Amer. J. Physiol.*, 1962, **203**, 353–358.
88. Mozell, M. M. The effect of concentration upon the spatiotemporal coding of odorants. In *Olfaction and Taste. II.* T. Hayashi, Ed. Oxford: Pergamon Press, 1967, pp, 117–124.
89. Oakley, B. Altered taste responses from cross-regenerated taste nerves in the rat. In *Olfaction and Taste. II.* T. Hayashi, Ed. Oxford: Pergamon Press, 1967, pp. 535–547.
90. Oakley, B., & Benjamin, R. M. Neural mechanisms of taste. *Physiol. Rev.*, 1966, **46**, 173–211.
91. Ohma, S. La classification des odeurs aromatiques en sous-classes. *Arch. Néerl. Physiol.*, 1922, **6**, 567–591.
92. Orrego, F. The reptilian forebrain. I. The olfactory pathways and cortical areas in the turtle. *Arch. Ital. Biol.*, 1961a, **99**, 425–445.
93. Orrego, F. The reptilian forebrain. II. Electrical activity in the olfactory bulb. *Arch. Ital. Biol.*, 1961b, **99**, 446–465.
94. Ottoson, D. Sustained potentials evoked by olfactory stimulation. *Acta Physiol. Scand.*, 1954, **32**, 384–386.
95. Ottoson, D. Analysis of the electrical activity of the olfactory epithelium. *Acta Physiol. Scand.*, 1956, **35**, Suppl. 122, 1–83.
96. Ottoson, D. Studies on slow potentials in the rabbit's olfactory bulb and nasal mucosa. *Acta Physiol. Scand.*, 1959a, **47**, 136–148.
97. Ottoson, D. Comparison of slow potentials evoked in the frog's nasal mucosa and olfactory bulb by natural stimulation. *Acta Physiol. Scand.*, 1959b, **47**, 149–159.

98. Pfaffmann, C. Gustatory afferent impulses. *J. Cell. Comp. Physiol.*, 1941, **17**, 243–258.

99. Pfaffmann, C. Taste and smell. In *Handbook of Experimental Psychology.* S. S. Stevens, Ed. New York: Wiley, 1951, pp. 1143–1171.

100. Pfaffmann, C. Taste preference and aversion following lingual denervation. *J. Comp. Physiol. Psychol.*, 1952, **45**, 393–400.

101. Pfaffmann, C. Species differences in taste sensitivity. *Science*, 1953, **117**, 470.

102. Pfaffmann, C. Gustatory nerve impulses in rat, cat, and rabbit. *J. Neurophysiol.*, 1955, **18**, 429–440.

103. Pfaffmann, C. The sense of taste. In *Handbook of Physiology. Vol. I.* J. Field, H. W. Magoun, & V. E. Hall, Eds. Washington, D.C.: Am. Physiol. Soc., 1959a, pp. 507–533.

104. Pfaffmann, C. The afferent code for sensory qualities. *Amer. Psychologist*, 1959b, **14**, 226–232.

105. Pfaffmann, C., Fisher, G. L., & Frank, M. K. The sensory and behavioral factors in taste preferences. In *Olfaction and Taste. II.* T. Hayashi, Ed. Oxford: Pergamon Press, 1967, pp. 361–381.

106. Phillips, C. G., Powell, P. T. S., & Shepherd, G. M. Responses of mitral cells to stimulation of the lateral olfactory tract in the rabbit. *J. Physiol.*, 1963, **168**, 65–88.

107. Renqvist, Y. Über den Geschmack. *Skand. Arch. Physiol.*, 1919, **38**, 97–201.

108. Richter, C. P. Salt taste thresholds of normal and adrenalectomized rats. *Endocrinology*, 1939, **24**, 367–371.

109. Richter, C. P., & Campbell, K. H. Sucrose taste thresholds of rats and humans. *Amer. J. Physiol.*, 1940, **128**, 291–297.

110. Ross, S., & Harriman, A. E. A preliminary study of the Crocker-Henderson odor classification system. *Amer. J. Psychol.*, 1949, **62**, 399–404.

111. Shibuya, T. Dissociation of olfactory neural response and mucosal potential. *Science*, 1964, **143**, 1338–1340.

112. Shibuya, T., & Takagi, F. S. Electrical response and growth of olfactory cilia of the olfactory epithelium of the newt in water and on land. *J. Gen. Physiol.*, 1963a, **47**, 71–82.

113. Shibuya, T., & Takagi, F. S. Olfactory epithelium: unitary responses in the turtoise. *Science*, 1963b, **140**, 495–496.

114. Shibuya, T., & Tucker, D. Single unit responses of olfactory receptors in vultures. In *Olfaction and Taste. II.* T. Hayashi, Ed. Oxford: Pergamon Press, 1967, pp. 219–233.

115. Shibuya, T., Ai, N., & Takagi, S. Response types of single cells in the olfactory bulb. *Proc. Japan. Acad.*, 1962, **38**, 231–233.

116. Skramlik, E. von. *Handbuch der Physiologie der niederen Sinne. I. Die Physiologie des Geruchs und Geschmackssinnes.* Leipzig: Georg Thieme, 1922, 346–520.

117. Skramlik, E. von. *Handbuch der Physiologie der niederen Sinne. Bd. 1. Die Physiologie des Geruchs und Geschmackssinnes.* Leipzig: Thieme, 1926.

118. Stuiver, M. Biophysics of the sense of smell. Ph.D. dissertation. Groningen, Holland: Univ. of Groningen, 1958.

119. Sydow, E. von. Comparison between psychophysical and electrophysiological data for some odor substances. In *Theories of odor and odor measurement.* N. N. Tanyolac, Ed. London: Unwin, 1968, pp. 297–301.

120. Takagi, S. F. Are EOG's generator potentials? In *Olfaction and Taste. II.* T. Hayashi, Ed. Oxford: Pergamon Press, 1967, pp. 167–179.

121. Takagi, S. F., & Omura, K. Responses of the olfactory receptor cells to odours. *Proc. Jap. Acad.*, 1963, **39**, 253–255.

122. Takagi, S. F., & Shibuya, T. The "on" and "off" responses observed in the lower olfactory pathway. *Jap. J. Physiol.*, 1960a, **10**, 99–105.

123. Takagi, S. F., & Shibuya, T. The electrical activity of the olfactory epithelium studied with micro- and macro-electrodes. *Jap. J. Physiol.*, 1960b, **10**, 385–395.

124. Takagi, S. F., & Shibuya, T. Electrical activity of lower olfactory nervous system of toad. In *Electrical Activity of Single Cells.* Y. Katsuki, Ed. Bunkyo-ku, Tokyo, Igaku-Shoin, 1960c.

125. Takagi, S. F., Wyse, G. A., & Yajima, T. Anion permeability of the olfactory receptive membrane. *J. Gen. Physiol.*, 1966, **50**, 473–489.

126. Tucker, D. Olfactory, vomeronasal and trigeminal receptor responses to odorants. In *Olfaction and Taste. I.* Y. Zotterman, Ed. Oxford: Pergamon Press, 1963a, pp. 45–69.

127. Tucker, D. Physical variables in the olfactory stimulation process. *J. Gen. Physiol.*, 1963b, **46**, 453–489.

128. Veress, E. Über die Reizung des Riechorgans durch directe Einwirkung riechender Flüssigkeiten. *Arch. Ges. Physiol.*, Bd., 1903, **95**, 368–408.

129. Warren, H. C., & Carmichael, L. *Elements of Human Psychology*. Boston: Houghton Mifflin, 1930.

130. Woodrow, H., & Karpman, B. A new olfactometric technique and some results. *J. Exp. Psychol.*, 1917, **2**, 431–447.

131. Wright, R. H. Odour and molecular vibration. I. Quantum and thermodynamic considerations. *J. Appl. Chem.*, 1954, **4**, 611–615.

132. Wright, R. H. *The Sense of Smell*. London: George Allen & Unwin, 1964.

133. Yamada, K. The glossopharyngeal nerve response to taste and thermal stimuli in the rat, rabbit and cat. *Kumamoto Med. J.*, 1965, **18**, 106–108.

134. Yamamoto, C. Olfactory bulb potentials to electrical stimulation of the olfactory mucosa. *Japan. J. Physiol.*, 1961, **11**, 545–554.

135. Young, C. W., Fletcher, D. F., & Wright, N. On olfaction and infra-red radiation theories. *Science*, 1948, **108**, 411–412.

136. Zotterman, Y. Action potentials in the glossopharyngeal nerve and in the chorda tympani. *Skand. Arch. Physiol.*, 1935, **72**, 73–77.

137. Zotterman, Y. Elektrophysiologie der Geschmacksrezeptoren. *Berl. Med.*, 1956, **7**, 205–208.

138. Zwaardemaker, H. *Die Physiologie des Geruchs*. Leipzig: W. Engelmann, 1895.

139. Zwaardemaker, H. Methoden der untersuchung des geschmackes und der geschmackstoffe. *Handbuch der Biologischen Arbeitsmethoden*, 1921, **5**, 437–454.

140. Zwaardemaker, H. Odeur et chimisme. *Arch. néerl. Physiol.*, 1922, **6**, 336–354.

Chapter 7

THE MOTOR SYSTEM

Structure and Innervation of Muscle

Reflex Mechanisms

Central Pathways and Centers of Integration

Posture, Locomotion, and Complex Voluntary Movements

The Endocrine System

STRUCTURE AND INNERVATION OF MUSCLE

There are two types of effectors. Muscles respond to stimulation by chemical reactions that change their overall configuration. Glands secrete chemical substances, called hormones, into the bloodstream or the body cavities.

There are two types of muscles. Primitive *smooth* muscles are found mainly in the viscera. They are under the control of the autonomic nervous system and exert their influence by varying the pressure on the contents of the visceral structures. Only a few smooth muscles are under voluntary control. More complex *striated* muscles are usually attached to tendons and bones. They are controlled by somatic efferents and provide postural support and initiate movement by changes in their configuration. Most striated muscles can be brought under voluntary control.

Muscles rarely achieve a state of complete relaxation. Even at rest, most muscles maintain a *tonic* level of contraction. When stimulated, all contract, but this simple response may produce a variety of effects. Some muscles, called *extensors*, are connected across the larger angle of a joint in such a way that the contraction response causes a straightening or extension of the limb. These muscles are opposed by *flexors*, which are connected across the smaller angle of the joint in such a way that a contraction response produces a bending or flexion of the limb. Still others control the lateral movement of a limb. Joints typically have several types of muscles that maintain a certain degree of tonic tension and thus provide support for basic posture. Muscles that act in concert are called *synergists*; muscles that provide opposing forces are called *antagonists*.

When two sets of antagonistic muscles are stimulated equally, the resulting contraction of the individual muscle fibers increases the tension of the muscle without significantly changing its length. These *isometric* contractions do not result in movement of the limb but are essential to postural adjustments. When the stimulation of synergistic muscles is strong enough to overcome the tension of opposing antagonists, the synergists will produce an overall shortening of the muscle. Such *isotonic* muscle contractions are the basis of movement.

Muscle tissue consists of two types of fibers. The principal work of the muscle is performed by *extrafusal* muscle fibers, which are innervated by large, fast-conducting *alpha* motor neurons. Each extrafusal fiber is composed of many fine filaments that consist of two proteins, *actin* and *myosin*. In response to stimulation, the relationship between these basic components changes in an as yet poorly understood fashion to produce an overall shortening of the extrafusal muscle fiber. Even in the longest muscle, individual extrafusal fibers rarely exceed a total length of 10 to 12 cm. They interconnect with other extrafusal fibers until the total muscle is long enough to span the required distance.

The second type of muscle fiber, called *intrafusal* fiber, serves sensory rather than motor functions. The intrafusal fiber contains sensory receptors that signal the state of contraction of the extrafusal muscle fibers as well as any momentary change in their tension. The intrafusal muscle fibers receive a motor innervation from *gamma* motor neurons, which adjust the tension of the intrafusal fiber and thus bias the sensitivity of the sensory endings. Several extrafusal and intrafusal muscle fibers intermingle within a bag of connective tissue to form a muscle.

The skeletal musculature is innervated by alpha motor neurons in the ventral horn of the spinal cord. Sherrington[85,86] called these neurons the *final common path* of the motor system because very complex central processes interact to determine the activity of each alpha neuron.

Visceral muscles receive afferents from cells in ganglia outside the central nervous system. These *postganglionic* motor cells, in turn, are innervated by cells in the ventrolateral portion of the spinal cord or in the motor nuclei of the brainstem.

The axons of motor neurons divide into small fibrils before synapsing with muscle tissue. Individual muscle fibers typically receive only one such fibril. Each motor neuron consequently controls a number of muscle fibers. The size of such a *motor unit* varies with the functional requirements of the innervated tissue. Muscles used to perform delicate movements may have an innervation ratio of only three muscle fibers per neuron. Larger muscles that maintain posture and effect gross limb movements may have an innervation ratio of 150:1.

Summary and Review Questions

There are two types of muscles—smooth muscles, which are found mainly in the viscera and striated muscles, which make up the skeletal musculature. The principal work of a muscle is performed by the extrafusal muscle fiber, which is innervated by alpha motor neurons. The second component of each muscle, the intrafusal muscle fiber, serves primarily sensory rather than motor functions. It receives motor innervation from gamma motor neurons and contains spindle receptors that relate information about the state of tension in the muscle to the central nervous system.

1. Describe the innervation of a muscle.
2. Describe the basic structure of a muscle.
3. Discuss how the same muscular reaction (contraction) can account for all types of limb movements.

REFLEX MECHANISMS

The simplest mechanism for the mediation of a response is a monosynaptic reflex arc. A cell in the dorsal horn of the spinal gray matter receives sensory inputs from a peripheral receptor ending and relays this information directly to a ventral horn motor cell, which initiates a muscular response to it. Monosynaptic connections at all levels of the spinal cord are responsible for the *stretch* reflexes that determine the degree of tension in all muscles. We are rarely aware of these primitive reflexes which are the basis for postural control and locomotion because the stimuli that elicit them do not, typically, give rise to a conscious sensation.[57] Before we can discuss more complex, integrated reactions of the motor system, a closer look at this servomechanism may be useful.

Basic Feedback Mechanisms

In order to accomplish the myriad adjustments in muscle tension that are continually required to achieve postural stability, particularly during walking or the execution of other complex movements, the nervous system monitors the state of tension of each and every muscle in the body. The complexities of this multiple-channel feedback system are staggering, and it is not surprising that the physiological machinery that serves these functions is so intricate that we are only beginning to understand some of the peripheral components of the system. We can only guess, at present, how infinitely more complex the associated central mechanisms must be.

Tendon Organs

The simplest and crudest branch of this feedback system is built around a mechanoreceptor, called a *Golgi tendon organ*, in the tendon that joins muscles to bone[67] (see Figure 7–1). The tendon organs are in series with the muscle and thus stretch when the muscle contracts as well as when the muscle is stretched by the action of an antagonist. At rest, tendon organs have a slow steady-state discharge. When stretched, this gives way to a brief burst of activity followed by a rapid return to the steady-state frequency.[25] This receptor therefore signals a change in muscle tension, not its terminal position.

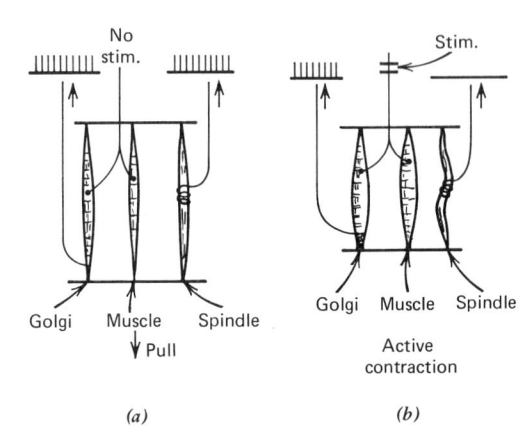

FIG. 7–1. Golgi spindle receptors have a series relationship to the muscle fibers. Spindles are in parallel. (*a*) Pull on the muscle increases the rate of firing of both receptors. (*b*) Active contraction of the muscles will cause an increase in discharge of the Golgi tendon organ and a decrease in rate of discharge from the spindle.

(From *Elements of neurophysiology* by S. Ochs. Copyright © 1965. John Wiley & Sons, Inc.)

The Golgi tendon organs initiate activity in large, rapidly conducting fibers. These type I afferents are multisynaptically related to spinal motor neurons that innervate muscles that are attached to the tendon of origin as well as to muscles that act in an antagonistic fashion. An increase in tendon-organ activity inhibits the motor neurons that control the directly related muscles and facilitates the motor neurons that control antagonistic muscles. This *negative feedback* system is an essential component of the finely tuned system that controls postural adjustments, as we shall see in a moment.

Spindle Receptors

More complex information about the state of a muscle comes from receptors in the intrafusal muscle spindles (see Figure 7–2). The muscle spindles are interspersed with the extrafusal muscle fibers and are arranged in parallel to them. There are two types of sensory endings in the muscle spindles.[57] The *annulo-spiral* endings derive from the very large and most rapidly conducting type I fibers and are often called type I or primary sensory endings. The second type of sensory ending, called *flower-spray* ending, derives from slower conducting sensory fibers and is therefore called a type II or secondary ending.

Because the muscle spindles are arranged in parallel to the extrafusal motor fibers, they stretch (and the sensory endings are stimulated) when the muscle stretches and contract (producing a reduction of activity in the sensory endings) when the muscle contracts.[42] Both types of spindle receptors are characterized by a steady-state discharge. The frequency of this discharge is a function of muscle tension. The type I or annulospiral endings signal not only the length of the muscle but also the velocity at which it is being stretched. The type II or flower-spray endings are less sensitive to dynamic changes and signal mainly instantaneous stretch.[42] The two types of endings thus respond similarly when the muscle is at rest but differ in their response to a change in muscular tension.

The type I annulo-spiral afferents are monosynaptically related to alpha motor neurons that innervate related extrafusal muscle fibers. An increase in type I receptor activity thus sets up a *positive feedback* system.

The positive feedback system of the type I spindle receptors balances the negative feedback mechanism, which responds to information from the Golgi tendon organs. The type II or flower-spray afferents affect the balance between these two opposing influences in a complex fashion. Typically, the type II afferents facilitate flexor muscles and inhibit extensor muscles, regardless of their own location. This tends to give the positive feedback system an edge with respect to flexion responses. The negative feedback system is strengthened with respect to extensor muscles —a biasing system that is reflected in many reflex responses.

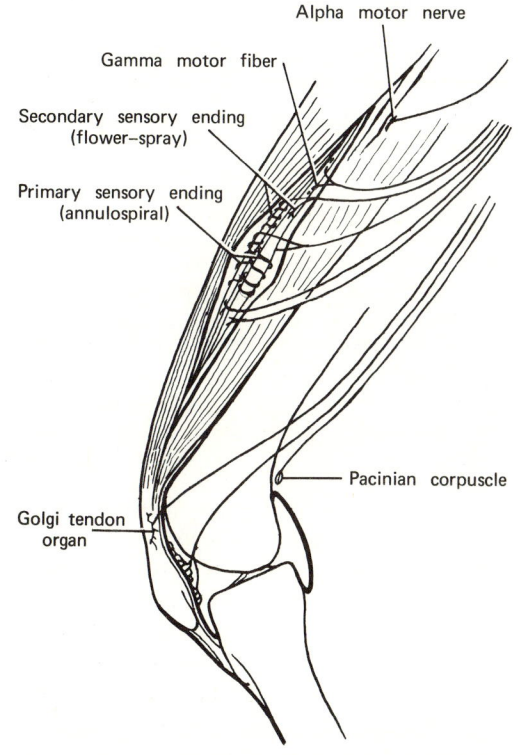

FIG. 7–2. Nerve endings in voluntary muscles, tendons, and joints. The neuromuscular spindle, which is disproportionately enlarged, is illustrated, with only two intrafusal muscle fibers. The neuromuscular spindles and the neurotendinous endings of Golgi subserve roles in reflex activity. The Pacinian corpuscles subserve pressure and vibratory sensations. The nerve endings associated with the neuromuscular spindle include the primary sensory (annulospiral) endings and secondary sensory (flower spray) endings. The primary sensory endings are innervated by group IA nerve fibers; the secondary sensory fibers, by group II nerve fibers.

(After *The human nervous system* by C. R. Noback & R. J. Demarest. Copyright 1967 McGraw-Hill Book Co. Used with permission of McGraw-Hill Book Company.)

Gamma Efferents

The feedback control of muscular tension is modified by the activity of gamma motor fibers, which innervate the intrafusal muscle spindles (see Figure 7–3). Activation of gamma motor neurons produces a contraction of the intrafusal fiber and thus a stretching and activation of the spindle receptors. This activates the positive feedback system of the type I afferents as well as the biasing influence of the type II fibers. In turn, this causes a change in the tension of the associated extrafusal fibers and, finally, an activation of the compensatory influences of the negative feedback system of the Golgi tendon organs.

This complex series of events is triggered primarily by stimulation of cutaneous touch and pain receptors. The components of the system are interconnected in such a way that stimulation of cutaneous receptors in one limb increases the activity of the gamma efferents to flexor muscles in that limb and inhibits the activity of gamma efferents that relate to opposing tensor muscles. Because of the resultant changes in gamma afferent activity, the system is thus biased so that a flexion response of the stimulated limb and a compensating extension response of the contralateral limb are facilitated.

The gamma motor system is affected by a variety of central influences. Electrical stimulation of essentially all aspects of the pyramidal and extrapyramidal motor systems can modify the activity of gamma motor neurons. The direction of the effect of stimulation at a particular site on the gamma innervation of a particular muscle may change from excitation to inhibition as the intensity or frequency of the stimulation is changed, suggesting that the central influences are extraordinarily complex.

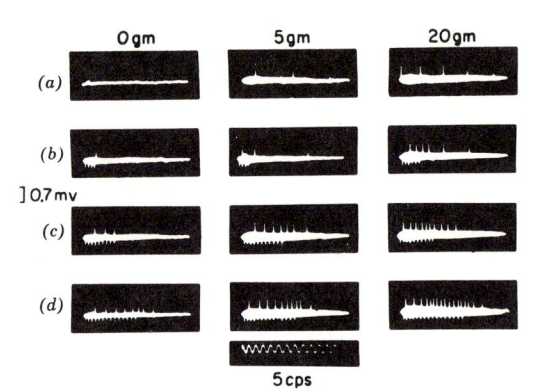

FIG. 7–3b. Afferent discharge in single dorsal root fiber shown in the three columns at muscle loads of 0, 5, and 20 gms. Without gamma stimulation (*a*), there is an increase in the rate of discharge with increased stretch; 4 to 6 stimulations of the gamma motor neurons leading to the spindles (*b*) increased the sensory discharge to stretch; 9 to 11 stimulations increased the rate of response to stretch still further (*c*). With 14 to 16 stimulations (*d*) the discharge rate was still further enhanced.

(From S. W. Kuffler, C. C. Hunt, & J. P. Quilliam. Function of medullated small-nerve fibers in mammalian ventral roots: efferent muscle spindle innervation. *J. Neurophysiol.*, **14**, 1951, 29–54.)

Multisynaptic Reflexes

Many of the simplest reflex connections are completed within one segment of the spinal cord. They are called *segmental reflexes*. More complex reflexes involve many segments of the spinal cord. Such *intersegmental reflexes* may interact to produce complex reactions to compound stimuli. Complex motor patterns such as locomotion depend on the simultaneous or successive activation of several cooperative or competitive reflex connections.

The simplest multisynaptic connection between sensory receptors and muscle fibers is a disynaptic reflex arc that links the Golgi tendon organ via a single interneuron with motor neurons that innervate related motor fibers. This simple reflex is antagonistic to the monosynaptic stretch reflex. Stretching a muscle initially produces afferents in the spindle receptors that are part of the stretch reflex. If the stretch continues, the Golgi tendon organ is stimulated and this gives rise to inhibitory influences. These are conducted

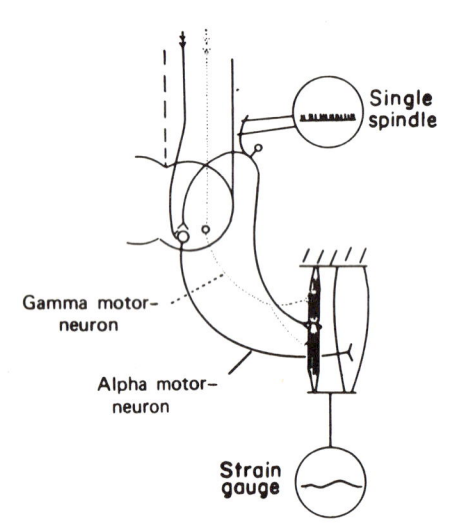

FIG. 7–3a. Discharges recorded from a single spindle fiber in the dorsal root. The dotted line shows gamma motor neuron axons terminating on the spindle; the solid line, alpha motor neurons terminating on muscle fibers. Upper CNS influences on these motor neurons are also indicated.

(From R. Granit. *Receptors and sensory perception*. Yale Univ. Press, 1955.)

over the disynaptic reflex arc and eventually override the excitatory influence of the monosynaptic reflex.

A good example of a more complex, multisynaptic reflex connection is the *flexion* reflex. It consists of a contraction of the flexor muscles ipsilateral to painful cutaneous stimulation. A reciprocal connection provides concurrent inhibitory influences to antagonistic extensor muscles. This produces a relaxation of the extensor muscles and permits movement of the stimulated limb away from the source of stimulation. The flexion reflex is generally accompanied by a *crossed extensor* reflex that consists of a contraction of the extensor muscles and a relaxation of the flexor muscles in the corresponding contralateral limb.

The reflex connections that we have discussed so far are complete within the spinal cord. They are normally under inhibitory as well as excitatory control of many central mechanisms,[26] but they can function in the absence of these influences. However, the organization of several segmental and intersegmental reflexes into postural and locomotor reactions requires the activation of motor centers in the brainstem, cerebellum, and cerebral cortex. The resulting suprasegmental reflexes depend on sensory feedback from muscle spindles, tendon organs, cutaneous receptors, vestibular sources, and visual signals. In response to this complex sensory feedback, the suprasegmental reflexes automatically (i.e., without conscious effort) and continually adjust the tension of the skeletal musculature to maintain posture under changing environmental conditions.

Summary and Review Questions

The simplest mechanism for the mediation of a response is a reflex. Even complex postural adjustments are based on an integration of many different reflexes, which may involve many levels of the spinal cord. The system basically relies on a negative feedback system that responds to afferents from tendon organs and on an opposing positive feedback system that responds to afferents from annulo-spiral endings (see Figure 7–4). An additional biasing influence that favors the negative feedback system with respect to extensor muscles relies on information from flower-spray endings. The basic feedback system is further modified by the activity of gamma motor efferents, which bias the feedback loops by stimulating contraction responses of the intrafusal muscle spindles. These gamma efferents are influenced by inputs from skin receptors as well as by many central motor centers.

1. Describe the relationship between muscular tension and activity in the three principal sensory components of a muscle, the tendon organ, annulo-spiral ending, and flower-spray ending.

2. How is a change in the sensory feedback from each of the three sensory components of a muscle translated into muscular activity?

3. Discuss the biasing influence of the gamma motor system.

4. Illustrate the operating of these feedback and biasing mechanisms by describing the stretch reflex.

CENTRAL PATHWAYS AND CENTERS OF INTEGRATION

Some of the motor neurons of the spinal cord and brainstem establish direct, monosynaptic connections with cells in the motor areas of the cerebral cortex. Others relate to interneurons, which, in turn, are directly or indirectly connected to cortical neurons or to cells in a variety of subcortical motor centers.

Pyramidal Motor System

Some cortical cells project long axons directly to spinal cord motor neurons or related interneurons. These fibers course through a distinct elevation in the lower brainstem called the pyramids and are therefore labelled pyramidal fibers. Most pyramidal fibers cross to the opposite side of the body before descending in the spinal cord and terminate on interneurons. In primates 10 to 20 percent terminate directly on alpha motor neurons and thus provide a direct path for the precise activation of individual muscles.[74]

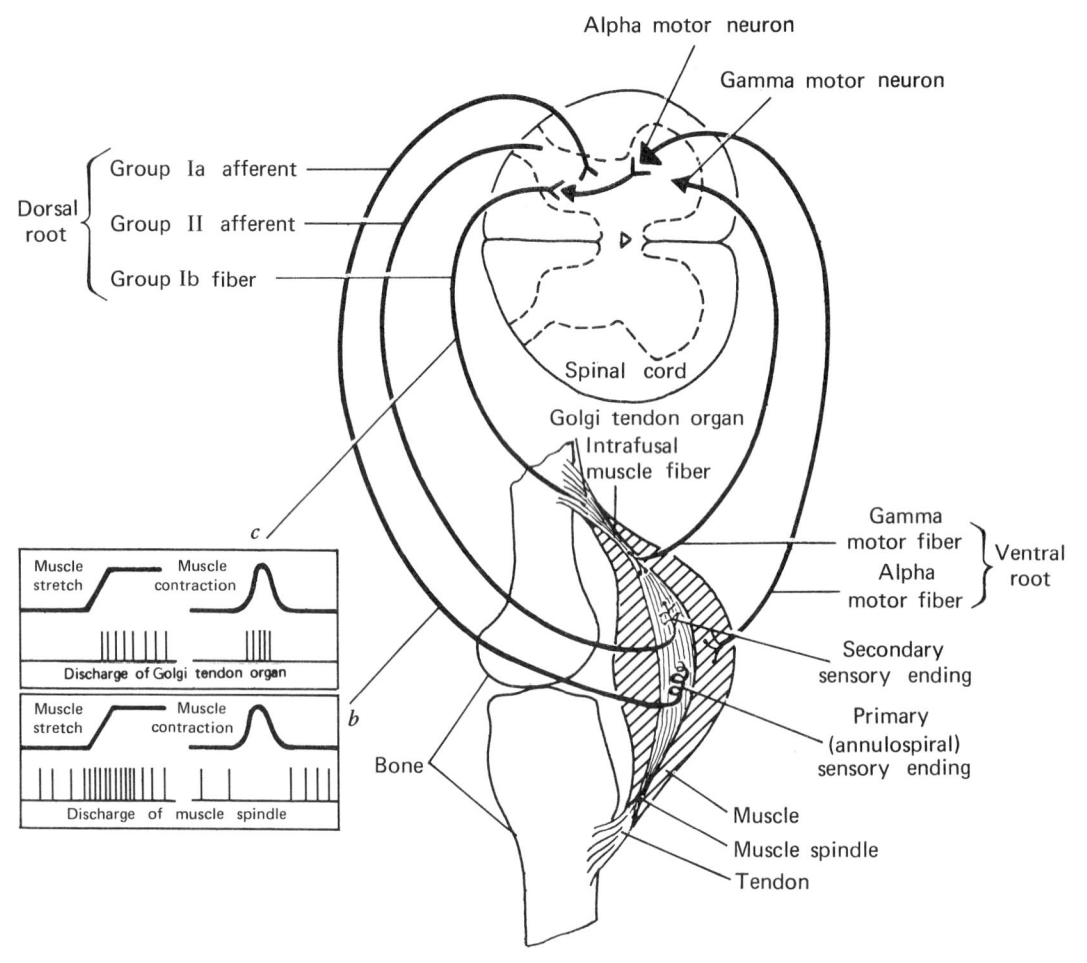

FIG. 7–4. The motor and sensory supply of a skeletal muscle. The upper part of the diagram shows a section of the spinal cord, the lower part, a joint and the muscle that controls it. The records on the left (*b*, *c*) show the types of discharge recorded from a Golgi tendon organ and a muscle spindle before and during muscle contraction.

(From *Experimental neurology* by P. Glees. Oxford: Clarendon Press, 1961. Adapted from G. Rushworth, *Cerebral Palsy Bull.*, **7**, 1959, 3–7.)

Transection of the pyramidal tracts produces a nearly complete loss of control over precise movements that are essential for skilled patterns of motor coordination. The severity of this effect is greater in man and subhuman primates than in lower species.[1, 96] Some voluntary movements can usually be performed but tend to be clumsy, poorly coordinated with postural adjustments, and often ineffectual because of poor aim.

Electrical stimulation of the pyramidal tract elicits muscular contractions[6] or even complex patterns of movements such as walking or scratching.[49, 50]

Decortication results in total degeneration of the pyramidal tracts.[59] An analysis of the effects of more *selective lesions* indicates that only about 30 to 40 percent of the pyramidal fibers originate in the primary motor cortex. Many arise from the adjacent sensory projections of the parietal cortex. Even the occipital and temporal lobes contribute a significant number of pyramidal motor fibers.[52, 103]

Electrical stimulation of the cortex can produce precise movements, and a mapping of these reactions[72] has shown a fairly precise representation of the skeletal musculature on the primary motor cortex of the precentral gyrus (area 6) and the adjacent premotor area (area 4) (see Figure 7-5). Organized movements rather than individual muscle contractions are usually elicited, but this may be an artifact of our crude stimulation procedures. The particular movement that is elicited by stimulation of a given site in the motor cortex may depend on the position of the limb at the onset or termination of stimulation.[105] A second, supplementary motor area has been found on the medial wall of the hemisphere, just above the primary motor region.[108,109] Stimulation of this region can produce integrated movements even after the primary motor areas have been destroyed. A third, topographic representation of the skeletal musculature has been localized in the somatosensory cortex of the post-central region.[46] This region also continues to function after the primary and secondary motor regions are destroyed.[110]

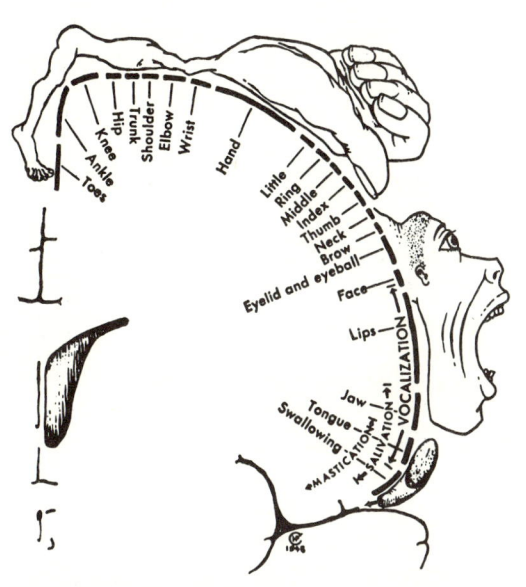

FIG. 7-5. The localization pattern on the human motor cortex.

(Reprinted with permission of The Macmillan Company from *The cerebral cortex of man* by W. Penfield & T. Rasmussen. Copyright 1950 by The Macmillan Company.)

Microelectrode recordings from spinal motor neurons[54] have shown that electrical stimulation of the motor cortex may facilitate inhibitory as well as excitatory reflex connections in the cord. These effects are mediated by the pyramidal tracts. The facilitation of excitatory reflexes is typically accomplished by a direct action on alpha neurons. The inhibitory reactions seem to be due mostly to stimulation of spinal interneurons, which, in turn, exert inhibitory influences on alpha motor neurons.[12]

The pyramidal motor system is a relatively late development phylogenetically, and its importance varies considerably from species to species. Even in primates, it is possible to elicit discrete movements by electrical stimulation of any of the cortical motor regions even after the pyramidal tract is transected, emphasizing the importance of the diffuse, extrapyramidal system to be considered next.

Extrapyramidal Motor System

The extrapyramidal system consists of several interacting components: (a) cortical neurons in all parts of the cerebral hemispheres; (b) the basal ganglia; (c) some diencephalic nuclei; (d) some mesencephalic nuclei; (e) reticular components and cranial nerve nuclei in the lower brainstem; and (f) the cerebellum. There are few anatomically distinct connections between these structures, but every postural adjustment and movement requires an extensive interaction between them.

Cortical Mechanisms

The origin of the *cortical component* of the extrapyramidal system is so widespread and apparently diffuse that it has been impossible to isolate functionally distinct areas. The extensive subcortical integration of the cortical extrapyramidal influences suggests that many of the cortical connections may be used mainly to provide detailed sensory input to the subcortical motor centers.

Basal Ganglia

The nuclei of the *striatum* and *pallidum* are

158 *Input and Output Channels of the Organism*

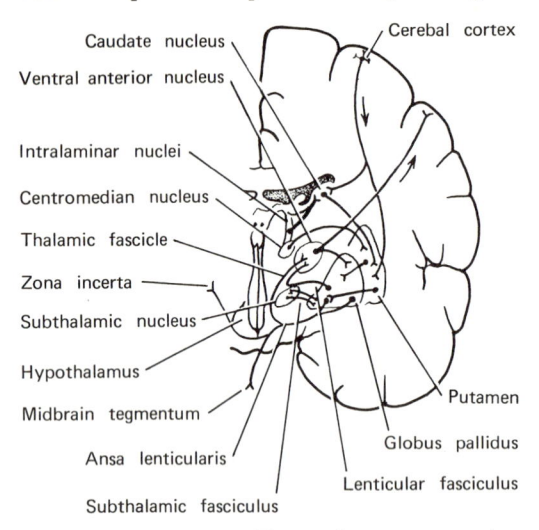

FIG. 7–6. Diagram illustrating some major interconnections of the basal ganglia, thalamus, and cerebral cortex. A core circuit is suggested: cerebral cortex to caudate nucleus and putamen; caudate nucleus to putamen; putamen to globus pallidus; globus pallidus to ventral anterior nucleus of thalamus; ventral anterior nucleus to cerebral cortex. Fibers from the globus pallidus (pallidofugal fibers) project to the ventral anterior nucleus of the thalamus. A few pallidofugal fibers project to the ventral medial nucleus of the hypothalamus, zona incerta, and midbrain tegmentum. The subthalamic nucleus and the globus pallidus are reciprocally connected by the subthalamic fasciculus, which passes through the internal capsule. The centromedian nucleus projects to the putamen, and other intralaminar thalamic nuclei project to the caudate nucleus.

(After *The human nervous system* by C. R. Noback & R. J. Demarest. Copyright 1967 McGraw-Hill Book Co. Used with permission of McGraw-Hill Book Company.)

major integrative centers for the extrapyramidal motor system (see Figure 7–6). The striatum exerts inhibitory influences on cortical neurons that are involved in the execution of voluntary movements. This ascending inhibitory influence is essential for the performance of skilled movements. Extensive bilateral damage to the pallidum produces catalepsy.[60] (The skeletal musculature is flaccid in catalepsy, and there is a general loss of control over the limbs' musculature. Very unusual postures can be assumed that are then maintained for minutes or even hours.) Smaller pallidal lesions are sometimes used clinically to control Parkinson's disease (characterized by an increase in muscle tone, tremor, and impairment of voluntary activity). Electrical stimulation of the anterior pallidum inhibits the activity of cortical motor neurons.[38] Stimulation of the posterior pallidum may produce opposite, facilitatory effects.[68]

Bilateral destruction of the striatum of cats and monkeys produces a syndrome of obstinate progression.[55] Extensive damage to the striatum of man produces rapid involuntary movements, hypotonia, poor coordination, and lack of postural support. Discrete movements can be elicited by electrical stimulation of some portions of the striatum, and there is evidence of a topographic organization of the body's musculature at this level.[22] However, the primary influence of the striatum appears to be inhibitory. A general inhibition of cortically induced movement[39] as well as "motor sleep" (lack of spontaneous activity and inhibition of motor responses to sensory inputs)[34] have been reported during stimulation of some parts of the striatum.

Low-frequency stimulation of some parts of the striatum elicits slow, rhythmic EEG changes in the motor cortex as well as sleep or behavioral arrest. High-frequency stimulation of the same points produces cortical desynchronization and behavioral arousal.[7,8,9,37] These findings suggest that there may be two opposing systems. One, activated by low-frequency stimulation, inhibits cortical processes. The other, activated by high-frequency stimulation, exerts facilitatory influences.

The electrical activity of the caudate and striatum appears to be closely linked to that of the cortex, hippocampus, and thalamus. The low-voltage activity that normally characterizes the striatum is replaced by high-voltage slow waves as soon as the connections to the cortex are severed. Microelectrode studies have shown that about 60 percent of the neurons of the striatum respond to stimulation of skin and muscle receptors,[84] suggesting an interesting sensory-motor interaction at this point in the extrapyramidal system.

Diencephalic Nuclei

Lesions in the *subthalamic nucleus* produce violent involuntary movements that begin in proximal muscles and gradually spread to the extremities.[41] Electrical stimulation of the subthalamic nuclei elicits rhythmic locomotor responses,[104] and it has been suggested[43] that this portion of the extrapyramidal system may be specifically responsible for rhythmic limb movements.

The *medial thalamus* receives inputs from all sensory modalities as well as from cerebellar and reticular sources. It projects to the striatum and thereby influences the excitability of cortical motor neurons. Animals with medial-thalamic lesions do not show gross motor disturbances but appear to have difficulties initiating voluntary responses to specific stimuli.[99] Low-frequency stimulatiou of this region induces electrophysiological as well as behavioral sleep[33] and a depression of reflex activity.[35,36] High-frequency stimulation produces cortical recruiting responses and behavioral as well as electrophysiological arousal,[28] a pattern of effects which is similar to the effects of stimulation of some aspects of the striatum.

The *ventrolateral (VL) and anteroventral (VA) nuclei of the thalamus* receive most of the efferent projections from the pallidum. Electrical stimulation of these nuclei produces discrete movements. Lesions result in contralateral ataxia and poor postural control.

Mesencephalic Components

One of the most important way stations of the extrapyramidal system is the *substantia nigra*. It seems to provide essential "starter" impulses which bias postural reflex adjustments. This results in postural adjustments that are essential for phasic motor response and primes the musculature involved in the phasic contractions so that exact movements can be organized by a subsequent alpha motor neuron discharge. Lesions in the substantia nigra are responsible for most symptoms of Parkinson's disease. The hypertonicity and the commonly associated inability to initiate movements are thought to be due to a loss of central control over some aspects of the gamma efferent system. Lesions in the substantia nigra also produce a loss of automatic movements and general motor stiffness.

Electrical stimulation in the substantia nigra does not elicit distinct movements but increases the extensor tonus of anterior limbs.[58]

The *red nucleus* appears to bias the activity of cerebral and cerebellar motor neurons. Bilateral destruction of this region produces extensor rigidity and increased resistance to passive movement as well as involuntary movements of the extremities.[48] Two distinct syndromes have been observed in human patients. Damage to the upper portion of the red nucleus produces a loss of control over voluntary movements and tremor.[15] Lesions in the lower half of the nucleus produce rhythmic contractions of the muscles of the extremities. The only effect of electrical stimulation in this region of the midbrain is an upward motion of the head.[31]

Reticular and Vestibular Mechanisms

The reticular formation of the brainstem exerts important regulatory influences on spinal motor neurons via the gamma efferent system. Electrical stimulation of the inhibitory portions of this system reduces spinal reflexes, motor responses caused by cortical stimulation, and decerebrate rigidity.[56,79] Stimulation of the facilitatory regions of the reticular formation reinforces excitatory impulses to the spinal motor neurons and facilitates reflex activity.[80] Although the reticular mechanisms are commonly labeled positive and negative, their influence is not always uniform. Stimulation of the "inhibitory" regions inhibits flexion responses but elicits or facilitates extensor reflexes.[93]

The vestibular nuclei of the lower brainstem exert facilitatory influences on tonic reflex connections in the spinal cord. These vestibular influences are essential for the maintenance of equilibrium and orientation in space.

Cerebellum

The cerebellum is a major integrative center for postural adjustments, locomotion, and other reflexes (see Figure 7–7). Posture depends on the tonic discharge of spinal cord motor neurons, and the cerebellum affects this

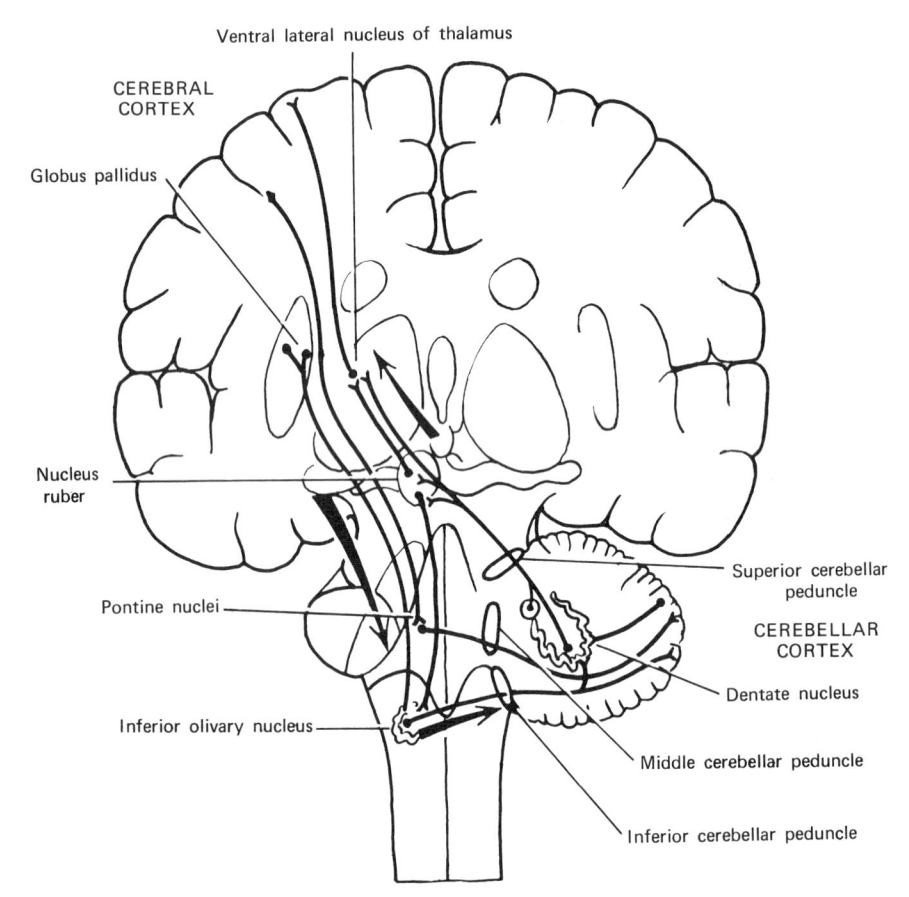

FIG. 7–7. Cerebellar connections with the cerebral cortex, thalamus, basal ganglia, and some brain stem nuclei.
(After *The human nervous system* by C. R. Noback & R. J. Demarest. Copyright 1967 McGraw-Hill Book Co. Used with permission of McGraw-Hill Book Company.)

tonic activity in a number of ways. It exerts inhibitory influences on the vestibulospinal pathways,[19] modulates the reticulospinal control of the gamma efferent system,[25] and facilitates the motor functions of the cerebral cortex.[5] The anterior lobe of the cerebellum primarily influences the lower portion of the extrapyramidal system via descending pathways to the brainstem and spinal cord. The posterior lobe acts primarily on ascending components of the system.

Total destruction of the cerebellum produces uncontrollable movements of the hindlimbs, rigid extension of the forelimbs, and excessive tendon and other postural reflexes. Animals gradually compensate for the excessive facilitation of spinal motor neurons that is caused by the removal of cerebellar inhibition. Locomotion of a lumbering and unsure nature can be relearned, but a basic lack of control over phasic muscle contraction remains.

Electrical stimulation of the vermian portion of the *anterior lobe* facilitates or inhibits the activity of spinal motor neurons. A topographic representation of the musculature of the body on the anterior vermis has been described.[89,27] The anterior cerebellum appears to have both excitatory and inhibitory components that are characterized by slightly different responses to particular frequencies[62] and/or amplitudes of electrical stimulation.[75,76] Ablation of the anterior lobe results in extensor rigidity of the extremities and in some ataxia and tremor of trunk and head muscles.[13, 14]

The threshold of motor cells in the cerebral cortex is lowered during stimulation of the *posterior cerebellum*.[20] The elicitation of overt movements by electrical stimulation of the cerebral motor cortex may be facilitated or inhibited by concurrent stimulation of the posterior cerebellum.[90, 88] Electrical or chemical stimulation of the posterior vermis produces electrophysiological arousal.[16, 61]

Destruction of the posterior vermis produces exaggerated postural tonus and disturbances of voluntary movement that are similar to those seen after damage to the anterior vermis. Posterior lobe damage produces tremor, ataxia, hypotonia, and poorly organized reflex responses.[4, 23]

The *fastigial nuclei* of the cerebellum receive afferents from the anterior lobe. Complete destruction of these nuclei produces spasticity.[92] The *interpositus and dentate nuclei* receive afferents from the posterior cerebellum. Destruction of the interpositus nuclei produces tremor, ataxia, and loss of placing reactions.[13, 14] Lesions of the dentate nuclei produce only minor impairments of reflex activity.

Summary and Review Questions

In addition to the primary reflex connections of the spinal cord, the central nervous system contains two major motor pathways. Some spinal motor neurons that control small muscles in the extremities receive a direct innervation from cortical motor cells via the pyramidal motor system. These connections are particularly important for the control of precise movements. This pathway assumes special importance in primates that require fine control over the digits of the hands and feet. The cortical components of the pyramidal motor system are topographically organized in three major motor regions (one in the precentral portion of the frontal lobe, the second on the postcentral portion of the parietal lobe, and a third on the medial surface of the cerebral hemisphere, just above the precentral region). Other portions of the cerebral cortex also contribute fibers to the pyramidal tracts.

The phylogenetically older extrapyramidal motor system involves all portions of the cerebral cortex; the basal ganglia (the striatum and pallidum); the subthalamic nucleus and the medial, ventrolateral, and anteroventral nuclei of the thalamus; the substantia nigra, red nucleus, and reticular formation of the lower brainstem; and the cerebellum. This system is diffusely but extensively interconnected and forms several feedback loops that may be responsible for different levels of integration. Functionally, the extrapyramidal system is concerned with postural adjustments (in part via the gamma efferent system) as well as coarse voluntary movements.

1. Describe the loss of motor function that is seen in primates after destruction of the pyramidal tracts.

2. Describe some of the typical disabilities seen after damage to various components of the extrapyramidal motor system.

POSTURE, LOCOMOTION, AND COMPLEX VOLUNTARY MOVEMENTS

Postural Adjustments

Posture refers to the complex muscular adjustments that resist the displacement of the body or any of its parts by gravity. Man's upright posture requires the continual integration of afferent information from tens of thousands of receptors that monitor the body's position in relation to the environment. The principal sources of information are (1) muscle spindle receptors and tendon organs that signal the relative state of tension of individual muscles; (2) tendon organs that are sensitive to flexor and extensor movements or rotation of joints; and (3) specialized vestibular receptors of the inner ear that respond to the position of the head in relation to the basic planes of space. Additional important information may arise from slowly adapting mechanoreceptors in the skin and in the walls of the viscera. Distance receptors such as the eye and ear provide information about the position of the body in relation to its environment.

Basic adjustments for minute deviations of individual limbs or the entire body from a voluntarily selected posture occur automatically and continually throughout every minute of life. *Resistive* mechanisms such as the simple stretch reflex oppose the movement of a limb and initiate its return to the basic position. *Compensatory* mechanisms initiate active movements to restore the status quo after a disturbance can no longer be corrected by the resistive mechanisms.

The details of the neural and muscular cooperation that make these complex adjustments possible are only poorly understood. There is some experimental evidence for distinct tonic and phasic motor systems. In mammals a distinction can be made between "red" muscles, which are concerned primarily with sustained postural contractions, and "white" muscles, which respond more rapidly and discretely as part of phasic muscular responses.[63] Some single muscle units are preferentially activated in the course of voluntary movements; others react more promptly to signals for postural adjustments.[18] The motor neurons that innervate "tonic" muscles are typically smaller than those related to the "phasic" muscle fibers[17] and tend to fire at low uniform rates.[21] Motor neurons that innervate muscles that are used in "phasic" contractions typically alternate bursts of rapid discharges with longer periods of silence. Their axons tend to be large and conduction rates consequently high.[44, 45]

The principal postural reflexes are integrated by spinal mechanisms and can be elicited from spinal animals after some recuperation from spinal shock. However, central facilitatory and inhibitory influences normally modify these simple reflexes and integrate them into more complex response patterns.

Locomotion

Locomotion is essentially a problem of high-order postural adjustments. All basic reflex mechanisms that contribute to the organism's ability to stand or to adjust its position in relation to the environment are involved. The simple stretch reflex, for instance, is essential for restraining antagonists in alternating contractions and for limiting the excursions of limbs in motion. The positive supporting reaction is the primary standing reflex. It is also basic to the static phase of movement. More complex postural reflexes maintain or restore the equilibrium of the body during and after movement.

Some reflex adjustments are peculiar to locomotion. *Negative supporting reactions* permit the organism to lift a leg off the ground and swing it forward, largely because the movement is unopposed by gravitational forces. These reactions alternate with *extensor thrust reflexes*, which are positive supporting responses to changes in the tension around the toe pads. The basic postural reflexes are aided by kinetic *progression reflexes* based on sensory feedback from the vestibular system.

Although the total pattern of muscular adjustments required to complete coordinated movements is complex, the basic reflexes that contribute the motion itself are simple. Reflex flexion of one hindleg initiates a reflex extension of the opposite hindleg and a flexor extension of the diagonal forelimb.[85] The apparently complex sequence of reflexes that constitute locomotion may occur purely reflexly.

Complex Voluntary Movements

Survey of Neural and Muscular Mechanisms

Complex skilled movements are the end product of the selective activation and/or inhibition of a large number of specific muscles. The pattern of excitation must be coordinated so that the combined action of all units results in an organized spatiotemporal sequence of motor responses. These complex motions are poorly described in terms of the specific action of each of the muscles that contributes to them. A particular complex movement is specified primarily by its consequences and may never be precisely duplicated in terms of the specific pattern of activation or inhibition of individual muscle groups.

The execution of skilled patterns of movement depends primarily on cortical influences that are transmitted to the primary motor neurons via the pyramidal motor system.[95, 97] Two types of pyramidal motor mechanisms exist. Some areas of the cortex (notably the precentral gyrus) contain discrete topographic representations of individual muscles. Others harbor cells that are more diffusely related to muscle groups that cooperate in complex movements.[10, 73] The few (3 to 4 percent) pyramidal-tract fibers that originate from giant Betz cells in the precentral gyrus are thought to establish direct, monosynaptic connections with spinal cord motor neurons and may thus play a special role in the control of skilled movements.[66, 3]

Clinical studies of motor disorders and their relationship to damage in restricted portions of the brain[72, 71] indicate that the motor cortex is intimately related to all cortical and many subcortical regions. Some investigators[66] therefore speak of the motor cortex as "a funnel of convergence" for the stream of impulses that produce voluntary movements.

Circumcision of cortical areas or transection of transcortical pathways has little or no effect on motor functions,[69, 91] suggesting that different areas of the cortex are interconnected via subcortical relay stations. Penfield[70, 71] has suggested that the subcortical coordination of this corticocortical flow of information may be achieved by a "centrencephalic" system of centers and pathways. Although Penfield did not specify the anatomical structures involved in this integrative mechanism, we may assume, on the basis of its functional assignment, that the mesencephalic reticular formation and nonspecific thalamic projection system most closely fit the suggested pattern of action.

The details of this subcortical, integrative process and its anatomical representation remain to be specified, but the general concept of such a coordinating system is all but inescapable. The hypothesized system originates the impulses that selectively facilitate or inhibit specific cortical motor functions. It thus represents, in some sense, the "highest" controlling mechanism in the brain.

Role of Servomechanisms in Movement

The importance of sensory information in the control and coordination of skilled voluntary movements is intuitively obvious and has been demonstrated in many clinical and experimental situations. It is clear that visually guided movements cannot be exercised when the visual feedback is eliminated, but less conspicuous sensory inputs are equally essential. For instance, deafferentation of a limb produces motor deficits that are difficult to distinguish from those produced by major insult to the motor system itself. Not only is sensory feedback essential for the control of skilled movements, but the selective sensitivity of particular muscle groups and the postural adjustments that are important prerequisites for the initiation and successful completion of any movement are also directly determined by sensory feedback from the muscles themselves.

The coordination and adjustment of muscle tonus and phasic contractions of individual muscle groups in response to a kaleidoscope of ever-changing sensory input are best analyzed in terms of interlocking servomechanisms (see Figure 7–8). The individual components of such a system are interconnected so that any discrepancy between the current state of a muscle and the intended outcome of the movement results in automatic, corrective action. Such a multiple-feedback system continues to operate, essentially automatically and without supervision from higher centers, until the intended action is completed. Once the integrative mechanisms of the brain have arrived at a master plan for the movement and initiate its inception, individual motor adjustments may essentially take care of themselves.

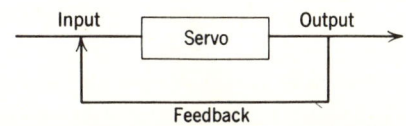

FIG. 7–8. The principle of organization of a servomechanism unit.

(After T. C. Ruch. Motor systems. In *Handbook of experimental psychology*. S. S. Stevens, Ed. Copyright © 1951. John Wiley & Sons, Inc.)

Some of these servomechanisms are directly related to receptors in the muscle to be controlled and have therefore been called "output-informed" feedback circuits. Others interconnect integrative mechanisms in the central nervous system and receive only secondary (i.e., processed) information. These systems have been called "input-informed" circuits (see Figure 7–9).

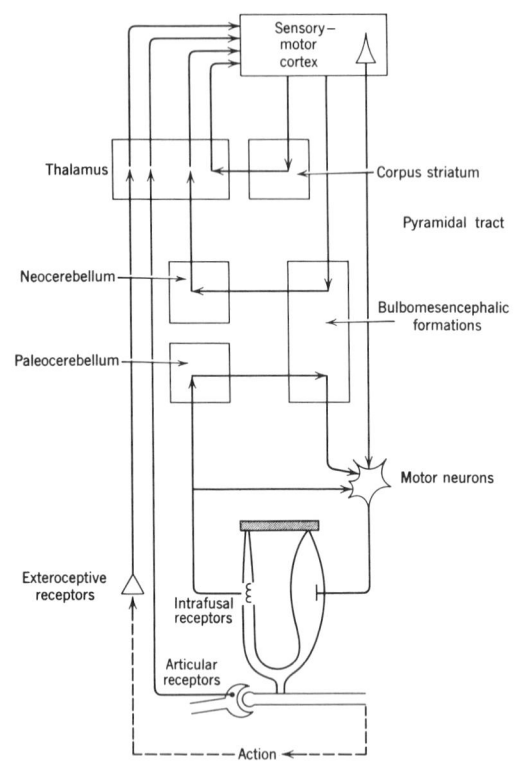

FIG. 7–9. Examples of output- and input-informed circuits which play a part in the control of motor command.

(From J. Paillard. The patterning of skilled movements. In *Handbook of physiology. Neurophysiology.* Washington, D.C.: Am. Physiol. Soc., 1960, sec. 1, vol. III, 1679–1708.)

Many postural adjustments depend on output-informed feedback systems that respond automatically to sensory feedback from muscles, tendons, joints, and cutaneous receptors. The central reticulospinal and vestibulospinal control over the gamma efferents that bias the sensitivity of the spindle receptors is an excellent example of the influence of higher-order feedback mechanisms on the lower systems. The gamma afferents return information to the cerebellum and other central integrative centers; they thus establish higher-order feedback connections that interact to permit the precise control of individual muscles. The corticocerebellocortical system is a still higher level of feedback integration of the input-informed variety,[81] which may serve to amplify and extend in time the motor influences that arise from the cortex. In this circuit the cerebellum may "compare" the commands issued from the cerebral cortex with feedback from muscle spindles and may arrive at compromise instructions that result in a modification of the cortical output and corrective action in peripheral muscles.

Acquisition of Skilled Movements

This type of analysis has some interesting implications for the development of skilled motor movements. The organism's repertoire of complex movements is very small at birth. Control over many individual muscles is largely missing, and most of the specific motor acts (such as standing or walking) that characterize the adult have yet to be acquired. The individual muscular contractions that make up a skilled movement are functional at birth or soon thereafter. However, the spatiotemporal pattern of muscular activity that is peculiar to a skilled voluntary motion has to be learned. This requires a series of progressive adjustments in the feedback systems just discussed.

A sequence of successive approximations can usually be discerned in the course of motor learning. The process starts with unnecessarily massive and effortful motions usually involving much if not all of the body, progresses through a number of stages of increasing refinement (these characterize the commonly observed plateaux of skilled motor performance), and eventually reaches a level of integration that is characterized by minimal effort and highly specialized responses from specific muscle groups.

The most difficult aspect of this process is the disruption or inactivation of existing patterns of sensory-motor integration that previously satisfied the requirements of the organism but now interfere with the establishment of the novel feedback systems. This interference is smallest in the infant, who is therefore capable of acquiring remarkably complex patterns of motor coordination with relative ease. In the mature individual, many well-established sensory-motor patterns exist, and it is quite difficult to "teach an old dog new tricks" (as anyone will testify who ever attempted to learn to ride a bicycle after the age of 25).

During the initial stage of acquiring a complex, skilled movement, man and most animals rely heavily on feedback from the optic system. Corrections are made primarily as a result of visually perceived deviations of the limb or extremity from the target. During this stage skilled movements are effortful and require great "concentration." As learning progresses, more and more of the control is relegated to feedback circuits; these circuits rely on proprioceptive information from the muscles that are used in the act itself or support related postural responses. Each segment of the movement or muscle contraction thus becomes a signal for the next, initiating a sequence of events that can proceed essentially automatically (i.e., on the basis of local feedback systems rather than "higher" control) once the movement is initiated. Eventually information from the eye is used only to initiate the sequence, and the response itself is guided by local circuits. This partial automation undoubtedly accounts for the resistance of some overlearned response patterns (such as feeding and drinking) to central nervous system damage.

The acquisition of skilled movements can thus be discussed in terms of three basic processes: (1) the initial establishment of novel spatiotemporal combinations of reflexive, innate, or previously learned movements; (2) the inhibition or disruption of other innate or learned sensory-motor feedback systems that interfere with the performance of the novel response pattern; and (3) the transfer of feedback control to kinetic sensory mechanisms and progressively lower levels of integration.

Summary and Review Questions

Even simple acts such as standing or sitting require an integration of sensory feedback from literally tens of thousands of sources and finely tuned adjustments in an equally large number of intrafusal and extrafusal muscle fibers. The principal sources of sensory inputs to this incredibly complex system are the muscle-spindle receptors and tendon organs, which are sensitive to the state of tension in individual muscles; the specialized vestibular receptors in the inner ear, which signal the position of the head; and feedback from skin and distance receptors, which signal the relative position of the body with respect to other objects in the environment. Locomotion requires additional feedback from complex multisegmental reflex connections as well as an activation of cortical mechanisms that integrate voluntary influences on muscular activity. Complex voluntary movements require all of these adjustments in addition to an activation of the pyramidal motor system that controls small muscles in the arms, legs, and digits. In man, only some of the primitive reflex connections are functional at birth and one can observe the gradual development of increasingly precise control over fine movements as the child matures.

1. Discuss the feedback systems that are activated by the requirements of postural adjustments, locomotion, and complex movements.

2. Describe some of the complex reflexes that are activated during locomotion.

3. Discuss the organization of cortical components of the motor system and its role in motor functions.

4. Describe the acquisition of skilled movements.

THE ENDOCRINE SYSTEM

Complex organisms respond to changes in the environment not only by initiating or inhibiting muscular activity but also by secreting a variety of chemical substances. These *hormones* are essential, rate-limiting factors in many metabolic processes. Their influence on

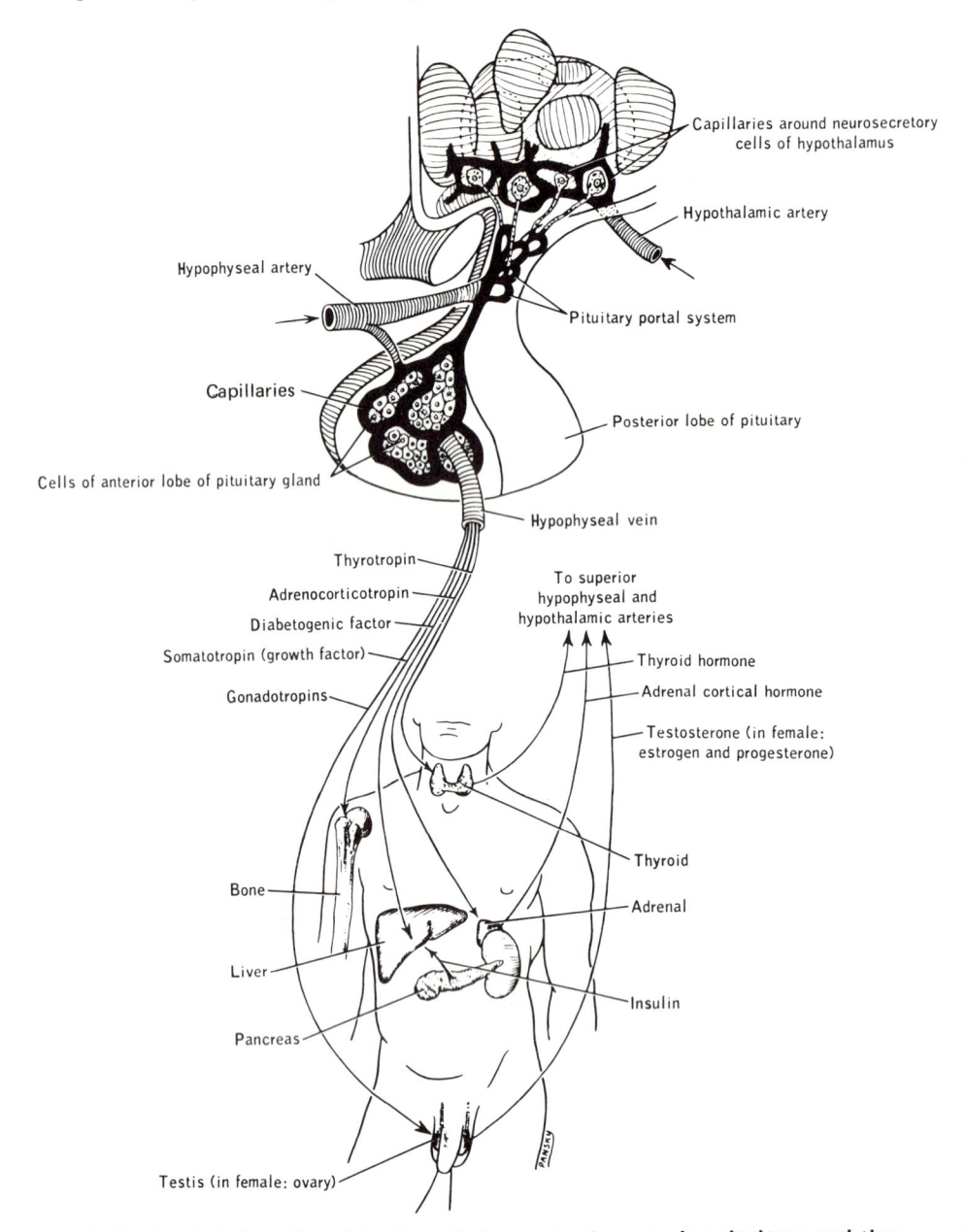

FIG. 7–10. Relationship of the hypothalamus to the anterior pituitary and thus to the other endocrines, the liver, and the bone marrow.

(After E. L. House & B. Pansky. *A functional approach to neuroanatomy.* After Netter CIBA Clinical Symposium. Copyright 1960 McGraw-Hill Book Company. Used with permission of McGraw-Hill Book Company.)

behavior is clearest, perhaps, for the hormones that determine the sexual responsiveness of the organism. However, many subtler hormonal influences affect other motivational mechanisms and determine directly or indirectly the organism's response to its environment. Closer attention to such nonneural factors will contribute significantly to our understanding of psychophysiological relationships.

Hormones are chemical substances secreted by endocrine glands. These glands form a reciprocating system that regulates many metabolic processes as well as the development and function of many tissues. The activity of the endocrine system is closely linked functionally and developmentally to the nervous system. Endocrine glands can act independently of neural influences but are normally activated by neural mechanisms and may be considered nonspecific extensions of the nervous system.

Hormones regulate the *rates* of chemical processes (without contributing energy or matter to the tissues on which they act) by inhibiting or exciting enzyme systems. This means that hormones cannot initiate new processes but merely modulate existing functions—a distinction that tends to be forgotten.

The production and secretion of hormones are affected by other hormones and neural influences as well as by general nutritional and metabolic conditions in the organism. A change in the secretory activity of an endocrine gland affects the activity of other glands of the system. This interaction complicates the interpretation of experimental or clinical observations of the effects of artificial or pathologic increases or decreases of a specific hormone.

Hypophysis

The hypophysis (or *pituitary* gland) has been called the master gland of the organism because it secretes a variety of hormones that significantly influence the activity of other glands of the endocrine system (see Figures 7–10 and 7–11). In most species the gland rests in a depression of the sphenoid bone, beneath the ventral surface of the diencephalon.

The hypophysis is conveniently divided into a posterior lobe (*neurohypophysis*) and an anterior lobe (*adenohypophysis*). The glandular (anterior) lobe and the neural (posterior) lobe of the hypophysis are, in effect, two independent organs. No functional relationship between the two aspects of the gland have yet been established, and we shall treat them separately in our discussion.[32, 29]

Adenohypophysis

The secretory action of the anterior lobe is under neural (hypothalamic) control, which is exercised by chemical rather than neural means. The connecting link between the gland and the nervous system is the portal blood supply. The blood in these vessels

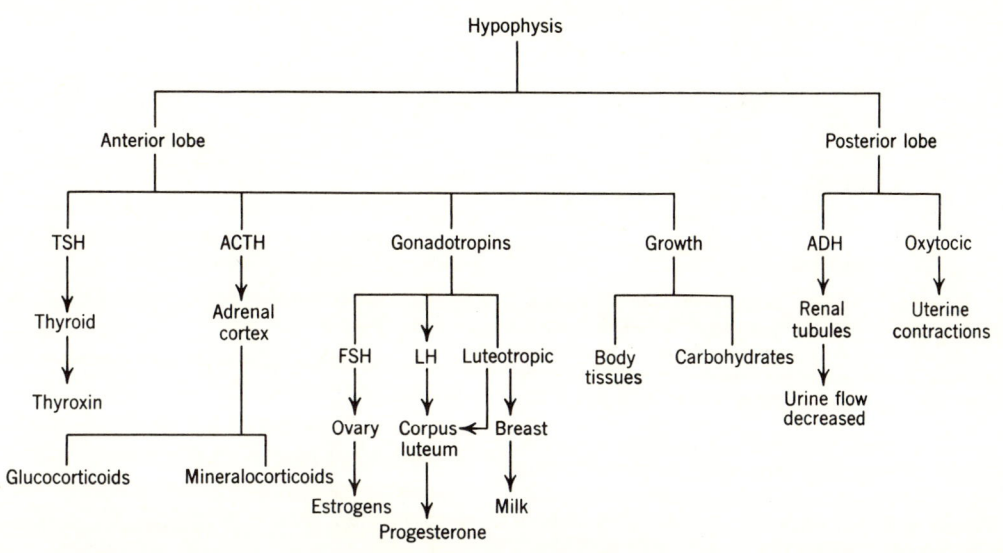

FIG. 7–11. The functions of the hypophyseal hormones.

(From *The physiology of man* by L. L. Langley & E. Cheraskin. Copyright 1958 McGraw-Hill Book Co. Used with permission of McGraw-Hill Book Company.)

flows from the medial hypothalamus to the anterior lobe of the pituitary gland. Neurons in the hypothalamus produce a variety of neurohumoral substances, called *releasing factors*, and secrete them into the portal blood supply in order to stimulate the release of specific hormones from the pituitary gland (see Figure 7-12). The hypothalamus has been divided into several discrete zones that secrete different releasing factors that stimulate or inhibit the release of particular hormones from the pituitary. Just how these factors act on the glandular tissue to produce their effects is, as yet, a mystery.[11]

The anterior lobe releases six major hormonal substances. Four of these, the two *gonadotrophins*, *adrenocorticotrophin* (ACTH), and *thyrotrophin*, control the activity of other endocrine glands. The remaining two hormones, the *lactogenic hormone* and the *growth hormone*, act primarily on metabolic processes, although they, too, affect other glands. The trophic hormones are also essential to the morphological development and normal functioning of their respective target glands (see Sawyer[83] for a review).

The gonadotrophins act directly on the gonads and influence sexual behavior.[111,102,101] The *follicle-stimulating hormone* (FSH) induces the development of ovarian follicles in the female and stimulates the growth of the seminiferous tubules and the maintenance of spermatogenesis in the male. The second gonadotrophin is called *luteinizing hormone* (LH) in the female and *interstitial-cell stimulating hormone* (ICSH) in the male. In the female, this hormone acts synergistically with the follicle-stimulating hormone to regulate the final stages of follicular development, ovulation, and *estrogen* secretion. It also induces luteinization and the secretion of the gonadal hormone *progesterone*. In the male, ICSH stimulates the development of the interstitial tissues of the testes and the secretion of *androgen*, the male gonadal hormone.

Thyrotrophin and *adrenocorticotrophin* (ACTH) are essential for the normal growth and secretory function of the thyroid and adrenal glands, respectively.

The *lactogenic hormone* (*prolactin*) is responsible for the initiation and maintenance of lactation by mammary glands that have been primed for action by the previous secretion of ovarian hormones.[53] The lactogenic hormone also affects the ovaries by aiding in the maintenance of the corpora lutea; it has also been called *luteotrophin*.

The *growth hormone* (*somatotrophin*) accelerates the growth of bones and tissues in both young and adult organisms. Chronic treatment with this hormone produces giantism. Following hypophysectomy, the organism fails to develop properly, and a condition of hypophyseal dwarfism appears.[87]

In addition to these specific hormonal effects, a variety of general metabolic processes depend on anterior pituitary secretions.

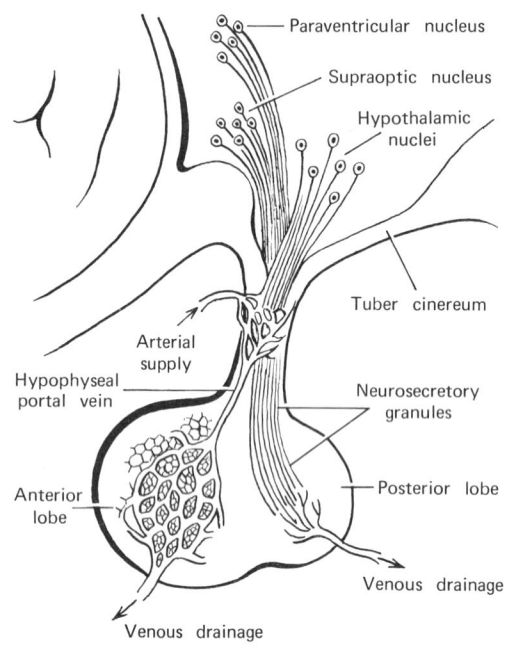

FIG. 7-12. The hypothalamohypophyseal tract and the hypophyseal portal vein. Neurosecretions are transported via nerve fibers of the hypothalamohypophyseal tract from the supraoptic and paraventricular nuclei to the posterior lobe of the hypophysis; they are conveyed from this lobe via the bloodstream. Other neurosecretions, elaborated in other hypothalamic nuclei, are conveyed via the hypophyseal portal vein to the anterior lobe of the hypophysis.

(After *The human nervous system* by C. R. Noback & R. J. Demarest. Copyright 1967 McGraw-Hill Book Co. Used with permission of McGraw-Hill Book Company.)

Among the more important symptoms of anterior pituitary damage are a disturbance of the carbohydrate metabolism (hypoglycemia) and an increased utilization of carbohydrates and fats. Some of the metabolic reactions may be caused by indirect effects on the adrenal cortex. The metabolic effects of pituitary hormones have a direction of action that is typically opposite to that of insulin.

Neurohypophysis

The posterior lobe of the pituitary gland, in contrast to the anterior portion, is richly innervated, primarily by the *supraopticohypophyseal tract*, which originates from the paraventricular and supraoptic nuclei of the hypothalamus. If this tract is transected, the neurohypophysis shows pronounced atrophic changes and becomes largely nonfunctional.

The hormones of the posterior pituitary appear to be manufactured by cells in the supraoptic and paraventricular nuclei of the hypothalamus. The hormones are then transported down the axons of the hypothalamic neurons and are *stored* in the neurohypophysis. They are liberated into the blood system upon the arrival of *neural* impulses that travel along the same axons that are responsible for the transport of the hormonal substances from the hypothalamus to the pituitary. According to this view, the fibers of the supraopticohypophyseal tract serve the dual function of neural secretomotor innervation and neurosecretory transport system (see Harris[30] for further details of this mechanism).

Three types of hormonal factors of neurohypophyseal origin have been isolated. *Antidiuretic hormone* (ADH) acts on the renal tubules to regulate the concentration of urine and thus contributes to the regulation of the organism's fluid balance. Removal of the posterior lobe results in the constant secretion of very dilute urine, a condition called *polyuria*. The secretion of ADH is under the control of hypothalamic neurons, which appear to be selectively sensitive to the osmolarity of the hypothalamic blood supply. As the osmotic pressure rises, more ADH is secreted, and the dilution of the urine is decreased so that as much water is retained in the body as is commensurate with the excretory needs of the organism. When the fluid balance of the body becomes positive and the osmotic pressure of the blood drops, less ADH is secreted and urinary dilution increases.[94]

The second neurohypophyseal hormone, *oxytocin*, acts primarily on the lactating breast and the uterus. The release of oxytocin is elicited by stimulation of the female reproductive organs and the nipples of the breast. This hormone is responsible for the expulsion of milk from the mammary glands and plays an important role in parturition and sperm transport in the uterus.[2]

The third and least understood component of neurohypophyseal origin is *vasopressin*, a hormone that affects peripheral vasomotor activity. Injections of this hormone produce arteriolar and capillary constriction and thus elevate blood pressure.

Adrenals

The adrenal glands, like the pituitary, are functionally and morphologically two distinct organs. The larger glandular portion (the adrenal *cortex*) surrounds the neural portion (the adrenal *medulla*) in the adult mammal. The secretory functions of the *adrenal cortex* are under the exclusive control of the adrenocorticotrophic hormone (ACTH), which is liberated by the adenohypophysis.

Secretions from the adrenal cortex are essential to a variety of metabolic processes. Complete removal of the adrenal glands leads to death within 5 to 15 days unless substitution therapy is instituted. The principal symptoms are lack of appetite, nausea, diarrhea, asthenia, hypoglycemia, hemoconcentration, and renal failure. In man, a similar syndrome of adrenal insufficiency is called *Addison's disease*.

Adrenalectomized animals are unable to draw on stored body proteins and cannot maintain a normal carbohydrate metabolism. This inability is responsible for a precipitous drop in blood sugar during fasting.

These divergent effects are not caused by the secretion of a single hormone. A variety of hormonal substances have been isolated from the adrenal cortex, and more may be discovered as chemical techniques improve. So far, 28 different steroids that appear to have specific hormonal functions have been isolated. Even when all of these have been extracted from adrenal-cortex extract, an *amorphous* fraction that contains one or more additional active substances of unknown chemical structure remains. Among the active steroids that have been isolated are several *androgenic* substances that affect sexual behavior.[107]

The *adrenal medulla* is made up of modified sympathetic ganglion cells that secrete epinephrine (adrenalin) and norepinephrine (noradrenalin). The secretory organs are connected with preganglionic fibers of the sympathetic nervous system. Their activity is controlled completely by these neural pathways.

The level of epinephrine secretion varies as a function of the general level of stimulation of the nervous system. Very little or none is secreted under basal conditions (sleep), but even relatively mild activity (such as walking) produces a marked secretory activity. Strong stimuli, particularly if prolonged, painful, or "emotional," flood the entire organism with epinephrine and norepinephrine.[100]

Norepinephrine acts as the transmitter agent for postganglionic sympathetic impulses. Circulating epinephrine therefore produces effects that are identical to neural activity in the sympathetic nervous system.

Epinephrine generally has a vasoconstrictor action, although moderate doses may produce dilation of the vessels in skeletal and cardiac muscles. It has a powerful stimulating effect on heart muscles, increasing both the frequency and force of contractions. As a direct result of its vasomotor and cardiomuscular effects, epinephrine tends to raise blood pressure, pulse rate, and cardiac output. It produces variable effects on smooth muscles (usually in the direction of contraction) and increases the rate of glycogenolysis in liver and muscle, producing hyperglycemia. Epinephrine also stimulates the secretion of adrenocorticotrophin, thyrotrophin, and gonadotrophin by the adenohypophysis, thereby indirectly extending its effects to other metabolic processes.

Pancreas

The pancreas secretes a single hormonal substance called *insulin*. A lack of this pancreatic secretion produces polyuria, glycosuria, ketonuria, marked wasting of the body, and death in a comatose state. These are also the symptoms of *diabetes mellitus*, a rather common disorder caused by pancreatic hypofunction. This condition was almost invariably fatal until the pancreatic hormone was synthesized.

Insulin-deficient organisms show severe hyperglycemia and glycosuria. There is a decrease in the organism's ability to utilize carbohydrates for oxidative purposes, fat formation, and glycogen storage. Fats and proteins are used in greater quantities to supply the needed energy, severely depleting the fat and protein stores.[106] The normal rate of insulin secretion varies as a function of carbohydrate intake and is regulated by the concentration of glucose in the blood.

Thyroid

In most species the thyroid gland consists of two lobes located on either side of the trachea. The gland contains an extraordinarily high concentration of iodine, which is normally stored in organic combination with *thyroglobulin*. Most of the iodine occurs in the form of *diiototyrosine*, which has little, if any, hormonal action. Roughly 25 percent of the available iodine is found in the form of *thyroxin*, the major hormone of the gland.[78]

The presence of thyroid tissue is not essential to survival, but severe metabolic disturbances result from thyroxin deficiency. In young organisms, a partial inhibition of growth and development is observed. In man, this leads to a condition known as *cretinism*, characterized by dwarfism and severe mental deficiency. In the adult organism, thyroxin deficiency produces a marked slowing of the basal metabolic rate, a reduction of pulse rate, cardiac output, and circulation, as well as a general hyporeactivity to external stimulation. Clinically more prevalent is a hyperthyroid condition that is characterized by an elevated metabolic rate, diuresis, depletion of liver glycogens, and a marked hypersensitivity of the autonomic nervous system that is reflected in nervousness and emotional hyperreactivity.

The activity of the thyroid gland is almost entirely determined by the secretion of thyrotrophic hormone by the anterior pituitary gland. Both the formation and secretion of thyroxin are affected by this hormone.

Parathyroid

A variable number (commonly two pairs) of small glands are usually found in the vicinity of the thyroid glands. The "parathyroid hormone" has not yet been chemically identified, but an extract can be prepared from parathyroid tissue that counteracts apparently all symptoms of hypoparathyroid function. It is commonly assumed that there is only one active parathyroid hormone because the principal action of the parathyroid extract concerns only the very closely related metabolism of calcium and phosphorus.

When the parathyroid hormone is absent, the serum-calcium concentration falls, with a consequent rise in serum-phosphate levels. The low calcium level produces an extreme hyperirritability of the nervous system and leads to tetany, convulsions, and death. An acute overdosage of the hormone, on the other hand, produces a shocklike state and death from circulatory collapse caused, at least in part, by the ensuing phosphaturia.

The secretory activity of the parathyroid glands is governed by the calcium concentration of the blood, but no intermediary mechanism has yet been discovered. Neither direct neural control nor pituitary trophins have been established to date.[77]

Summary and Review Questions

Many important activities of the organism are regulated by hormones secreted by endocrine glands. These glands receive direct neural innervation, but their secretory activity is controlled to a large extent by humoral mechanisms. Neurons in the hypothalamus secrete a variety of releasing factors or neurohumors that act on the pituitary gland (hypophysis) to stimulate or inhibit the release of hormones that, in turn, influence the secretory activity of other endocrine glands.

The pituitary has two principal and functionally independent components. The anterior pituitary or adenohypophysis responds to releasing factors of hypothalamic origin by secreting six major hormones: two gonadotrophins, which control the secretions of the gonads; adrenocorticotrophic hormone (ACTH), which controls the activity of the adrenal cortex; thyrotrophin, which regulates the release of thyroxin from the thyroid gland; and two additional hormones called lactogenic and growth hormone, which act primarily on metabolic processes. The posterior pituitary or neurohypophysis stores hormones that are manufactured in the hypothalamus and transported to the pituitary along the axons of cells that also initiate their release from the pituitary. The principal hormones of the neurohypophysis are antidiuretic hormone (ADH) which regulates renal functions; oxytocin, which acts on the breast and uterus; and vasopressin, which controls the diameter of blood vessels throughout the body.

The adrenal gland also consists of two components: the adrenal cortex, which secretes a variety of hormones in response to the release of ACTH by the pituitary, and the adrenal medulla, which secretes epinephrine and norepinephrine in response to direct neural influences on the gland. The secretions of the adrenal cortex are essential for survival, but we do not yet understand exactly how their actions are mediated. Norepinephrine is the neurotransmitter at sympathetic neuroeffector junctions and thus acts on smooth muscle in much the same way as activation of the sympathetic nervous system itself.

The gonads secrete male (androgens) and female (estrogens) sex hormones in response to the pituitary release of the two gonadotrophic hormones, follicle-stimulating hormone (FSH) and luteinizing (LH) (or interstitial cell stimulating hormone) (ICSH). These are essential for sexual receptivity and functioning of the reproductive apparatus.

The thyroid gland secretes thyroxin (which is essential for normal growth and many metabolic functions in adulthood) in response to the pituitary release of thyrotrophic hormone.

The pancreas secretes a single hormone, insulin, which is essential to carbohydrate metabolism. The parathyroid glands secrete an as yet unidentified hormone that is important to the metabolism of calcium and phosphorus.

1. Describe the hypothalamic control of the secretions of the anterior and posterior pituitary.

2. List the hormones (and their targets) that are secreted by the anterior and posterior pituitary.

3. Describe the principal hormones of the endocrine system and the nature of their action.

Bibliography

1. Barron, D. H. The results of unilateral pyramidal section in the rat. *J. Comp. Neurol.*, 1934, **60**, 45–56.

2. Berde, B. *Recent Progress in Oxytocin Research.* Sprinfield, Ill.: Thomas, 1961.

3. Bernhard, C. G., & Bohm, E. Cortical representation of the cortico-motoneuronal system in monkeys. *Experientia*, 1954, **10**, 312–315.

4. Bremer, F. *Traité de Physiologie Normale et Pathologique.* R. LeCervelet, G. H. Roger, & L. Binet, Eds. Paris: Masson, 1935.

5. Bremer, F. Activité électrique du cortex cérébral dans les états de sommeil et de veille chez le chat. *C. R. Soc. Biol. (Paris)*, 1936, **122**, 464–467.

6. Brookhart, J. M. Study of cortico-spinal activation of motor neurons. *Res. Publ., Ass. Res. Nerv. Ment. Dis.*, 1952, **30**, 157–173.

7. Buchwald, N. A., Wyers, E. J., Okuma, T., & Heuser, G. The "caudate–spindle." I: Electrophysiological properties. *EEG Clin. Neurophysiol.*, 1961a, **13**, 509–513.

8. Buchwald, N. A., Heuser, G., Wyers, E. J., & Lauprecht, C. W. The "caudate-spindle." III: Inhibition by high frequency stimulation of subcortical structures. *EEG Clin. Neurophysiol.*, 1961b, **13**, 525–530.

9. Buchwald, N. A., Wyers, E. J., Lauprecht, C. W., & Heuser, G. The "caudate-spindle." IV: A behavioral index of caudate-induced inhibition. *EEG Clin. Neurophysiol.*, 1961c, **13**, 531–537.

10. Bucy, P. C. *The Precentral Motor Cortex* (2nd ed.). Urbana: Univ. of Illinois Press, 1949.

11. Campbell, H. J. Control of hormone secretion. In *The Biological Basis of Medicine. Vol. II.* E. E. Bittar, & N. Bittar, Eds. London: Academic Press, 1968, pp. 47–100.

12. Carpenter, D., Lundberg, A., & Norrsell, U. Primary afferent depolarization evoked from the sensori-motor cortex. *Acta Physiol. Scand.*, 1963, **59**, 126–142.

13. Chambers, W. W., & Sprague, J. M. Functional localization in cerebellum. *A.M.A. Arch. Neurol. Psychiat.*, 1955a, **74**, 653–680.

14. Chambers, W. W., & Sprague, J. M. Functional localization in the cerebellum. *J. Comp. Neurol.*, 1955b, **103**, 105–129.

15. Chiray, E., Foix, C., & Nicolesco, J. Hémitremblement du type de la sclérose en plaques, par lésion rubrothalamo sous-thalamique. Syndrome de la région supéro-externe du noyan rouge, avec attiente silencieuse ou non du thalamus. *Rev. Neurol.*, 1923, **39**, 305–310.

16. Crepax, P., & Fadiga, E. La stimolazione chimica della corteccia cerebrale di gatto. *Arch. Sci. Biol.*, 1956, **40**, 66–80.

17. Denny-Brown, D. E. The histological features of striped muscle in relation to its functional activity. *Proc. Roy. Soc. (London), B*, 1929, **104**, 371–411.

18. Denny-Brown, D. E. Interpretation of the electromyogram. *A.M.A. Arch. Neurol. Psychiat.*, 1949, **61**, 99–128.

19. DeVito, R. V., Brusa, A., & Arduini, A. Cerebellar and vestibular influences on Deitersian units. *J. Neurophysiol.*, 1956, **19**, 241–253.

20. Dusser de Barenne, J. *Handbuch der Neurologie.* O. Bumke & O. Foerster, Eds. Berlin: Springer, 1937.

21. Eccles, J. C., Eccles, M., & Lundberg, A. The convergence of monosynaptic excitatory afferents onto many different species of alpha motoneurones. *J. Physiol. (London)*, 1957, **137**, 22–50.
22. Forman, D., & Ward, J. W. Responses to electrical stimulation of caudate nucleus in cats in chronic experiments. *J. Neurophysiol.*, 1957, **20**, 230–244.
23. Fulton, J. F., & Dow, R. S. Cerebellum: summary of functional localization. *Yale J. Biol. Med.*, 1937, **10**, 89–119.
24. Glees, P. *Experimental Neurology*. Oxford: Clarendon Press, 1961.
25. Granit, R. *Receptors and Sensory Perception*. New Haven, Conn.: Yale Univ. Press, 1955.
26. Granit, R., & Kaada, B. Influence of stimulation of central nervous structures on muscle spindles in cat. *Acta Physiol. Scand.*, 1952, **27**, 130–160.
27. Hampson, J. L., Harrison, C. R., & Woolsey, C. N. Cerebrocerebellar projections and somatotopic localization of motor function in cerebellum. *Res. Publ., Ass. Res. Nerv. Ment. Dis.*, 1952, **30**, 299–316.
28. Hanbery, J., & Jasper, H. H. Independence of diffuse thalamocortical projection system shown by specific nuclear destructions. *J. Neurophysiol.*, 1953, **16**, 252–271.
27. Harris, G. W. *Neural Control of the Pituitary Gland*. London: Edward Arnold, 1955.
30. Harris, G. W. Central control of pituitary secretion. In *Handbook of Physiology. Vol. II.* J. Field, H. W. Magoun, & V. E. Hall, Eds. Washington, D.C.: Am. Physiol. Soc. 1960, pp. 1007–1038.
31. Hassler, R. Die extrapyramidalen Rindensysteme und die zentrale Regelung der Motorik. *Dtsch. Z. Nervenheilk.*, 1956, **175**, 233–258.
32. Heller, H. *The Neurohypophysis*. New York: Academic Press, 1957.
33. Hess, R., Jr., Koella, W. P., & Akert, K. Cortical and subcortical recordings in natural and artificially induced sleep in cats. *EEG clin. Neurophysiol.*, 1953, **5**, 75–90.
34. Hess, W. R. Zwischenhirn und Motorik. *Helv. Physiol. Pharmacol. Acta*, 1948, Suppl. 5 (entire issue).
35. Hess, W. R. *Das Zwischenhirn* (2nd ed.). Basel: Schwabe, 1954a.
36. Hess, W. R. *Diencephalon, Autonomic and Extrapyramidal Functions*. New York: Grune and Stratton, 1954b.
37. Heuser, G., Buchwald, N. A., & Wyers, E. J. The "caudate-spindle." II: Facilitatory and inhibitory caudate-cortical pathways. *EEG Clin. Neurophysiol.*, 1961, **13**, 519–524.
38. Hodes, R. S., Peacock, S. M., & Heath, R. G. Influence of the forebrain on somatomotor activity. *J. Comp. Neurol.*, 1951, **94**, 381–408.
39. Hodes, R. S., Heath, R. G., & Hendley, C. D. Cortical and subcortical electrical activity in sleep. *Trans. Amer. Neurol. Ass.*, 1952, **77**, 201–203.
40. House, E. L., & Pansky, B. *A Functional Approach to Neuroanatomy*. New York: McGraw-Hill, Blakiston Div., 1960.
41. Jakob, A. *Die Extrapyramidalen Erkrankungen*. Berlin: Springer, 1923.
42. Jansen, J. K. S., & Matthews, P. B. C. The effects of fusimotor activity on the static responsiveness of primary and sensory endings of muscle spindles in the decerebrate cat. *Acta Physiol. Scand.*, 1962, **55**, 376–386.
43. Jung, R., & Hassler, R. The extrapyramidal motor system. In *Handbook of Physiology. Vol. II.* J. Field, H. W. Magoun, & V. E. Hall, Eds. Washington, D.C.: Am. Physiol. Soc., 1960, pp. 863–927.
44. Kawakami, M. Electro-myographic investigation on the functional differentiation of the hand and foot muscles. *Jap. J. Physiol.*, 1954a, **4**, 1–6.
45. Kawakami, M. Electro-myographic investigation on the human external sphincter muscle of anus. *Jap. J. Physiol.*, 1954b, **4**, 196–204.
46. Kennard, Margaret, A., & McCulloch, W. S. Motor response to stimulation of cerebral cortex in absence of areas 4 and 6 (Macaca mulatta). *J. Neurophysiol.*, 1943, **6**, 181–189.
47. Kuffler, S. W., Hunt, C. C., & Quilliam, J. P. Function of medullated small-nerve fibers in mammalian ventral roots: efferent muscle spindle innervation. *J. Neurophysiol.*, 1951, **14**, 29–54.
48. Lafora, G. R. Myoclonus: physiological and pathological considerations. *Excerpta Med. Sect. 8. Neurol. Psychiat.*, 1955, **8**, 769–770.

49. Landau, W. M. Patterns of movement elicited by medullary pyramidal stimulation in the cat. *EEG Clin. Neurophysiol.*, 1952, **4**, 527–546.
50. Landau, W. M. Autonomic responses mediated via the corticospinal tract. *J. Neurophysiol.*, 1953, **16**, 299–311.
51. Langley, L. L., & Cheraskin, E. *The Physiology of Man.* (2nd ed.). New York: McGraw-Hill, 1958.
52. Lassek, A. M. The pyramidal tract. *J. Nerv. Ment. Dis.*, 1942, **95**, 721–729.
53. Linzell, J. L. Physiology of the mammary glands. *Physiol. Rev.*, 1959, **39**, 534–576.
54. Lundberg, A., & Voorhoeve, P. E. Effects from the pyramidal tract on spinal reflex arcs. *Acta Physiol. Scand.*, 1962, **56**, 201–219.
55. Magendie, F. *Leçons sur les Fonctions et les Maladies du système Nerveux.* Paris: Steinheil, 1841.
56. Magoun, H. W., & Rhines, Ruth. An inhibitory mechanism in the bulbar reticular formation. *J. Neurophysiol.*, 1946, **9**, 165–171.
57. Matthews, P. B. C. Muscle spindles and their motor control. *Physiol. Rev.*, 1964, **44**, 219–288.
58. Mettler, F. A. Extensive unilateral cerebral removals in primate: physiological effects and resultant degeneration. *J. Comp. Neurol.*, 1943, **79**, 185–245.
59. Mettler, F. A. On the origin of the fibers in the pyramid of the primate brain. *Proc. Soc. Exp. Biol. Med.*, 1944, **57**, 111–113.
60. Mettler, F. A. Fiber connections of the corpus striatum of the monkey and baboon. *J. Comp. Neurol.*, 1954, **82**, 169–204.
61. Mollica, A., Moruzzi, G., & Naquet, R. Décharges réticulaires induites par la polarisation du cervelet: leurs rapports avec le tonus postural et la réaction d'éveil. *EEG Clin. Neurophysiol.*, 1953, **5**, 571–584.
62. Moruzzi, G. Effects at different frequencies of cerebellar stimulation upon postural tonus and myotatic reflexes. *EEG Clin. Neurophysiol.*, 1950, **2**, 463–469.
63. Needham, D. M. Red and white muscle. *Physiol. Rev.*, 1926, **6**, 1–28.
64. Noback, C. R., & Demarest, R. J. *The Human Nervous System.* New York: McGraw-Hill, Blakiston Division, 1967.
65. Ochs, S. *Elements of Neurophysiology.* New York: Wiley, 1965.
66. Paillard, J. The patterning of skilled movements. In *Handbook of Physiology. Vol. III.* J. Field, H. W. Magoun, & V. E. Hall, Eds. Washington, D.C.: Am. Physiol. Soc., 1960, pp. 1679–1708.
67. Patton, H. D. Reflex regulation of posture and movement. In *Medical Physiology and Biophysics.* T. C. Ruch & J. F. Fulton, Eds. Philadelphia: Saunders, 1960, pp. 167–198.
68. Peacock, S. M., & Hodes, R. S. Influence of the forebrain on somato-motor activity. *J. Comp. Neurol.*, 1951, **94**, 409–428.
69. Penfield, W. L'écorce cérébrale chez l'homme. *Année Psychol.*, 1940, **39**, 1–32.
70. Penfield, W. Mechanisms of voluntary movement. *Brain*, 1954, **77**, 1–17.
71. Penfield, W., & Jasper, H. H. *Epilepsy and the Functional Anatomy of the Human Brain.* Boston: Little, Brown, 1954.
72. Penfield, W., & Rasmussen, T. *The Cerebral Cortex of Man. A Clinical Study of Localization of Function.* New York: Macmillan, 1950.
73. Phillips, C. G. Cortical motor threshold and the thresholds and distribution of excited Betz cells in the cat. *Quart. J. Exp. Physiol.*, 1956, **41**, 70–84.
74. Phillips, C. G., & Porter, R. The pyramidal projection to motoneurons of some muscle groups of the baboon's forearm. In J. C. Eccles, & J. P. Schadé, Eds. *Progress in Brain Research. Vol. 12. Physiology of Spinal Neurons.* Amsterdam: Elsevier, 1964.
75. Pompeiano, O. Sulle rispaste crociate degli arti a stimolazione della corteccia vermania de lobus anterior nel gatto decerebrato. *Boll. Soc. Ital. Biol. Sper.*, 1955, **31**, 808–816.
76. Pompeiano, O. Sul meccanismo delle risposte posturali crociate alla stimolazione di an emiverme de *lobus anterior* nel Gatto decerebrato. *Arch. Sci. Biol.*, 1956, **40**, 513–522.
77. Rasmussen, H. Parathyroid hormone. *Amer. J. Med.*, 1961, **30**, 112–128.
78. Rawson, R. W. Modern concepts of thyroid physiology (symposium). *Ann. N.Y. Acad. Sci.*, 1960, **86**, 311–676.

79. Rhines, Ruth, & Magoun, H. W. Brainstem facilitation of cortical motor responses. *J. Neurophysiol.*, 1946, **9**, 219–229.
80. Rhines, Ruth, & Magoun, H. W. *Spasticity and the Extrapyramidal System.* Springfield, Ill.: Thomas, 1947.
81. Ruch, T. C. Motor systems. In *Handbook of Experimental Psychology.* S. S. Stevens, Ed. New York: Wiley, 1951, pp. 154–208.
82. Rushworth, G. The nature of the functional disorder in the hypertonic states. *Cerebral Palsy Bull.*, 1959, **7**, 3–7.
83. Sawyer, W. H. Neurohypophysial hormones. *Pharmacol. Rev.*, 1961, **13**, 225–277.
84. Segundo, J. P., & Machne, X. Unitary responses to afferent volleys in lenticular nucleus and claustrum. *J. Neurophysiol.*, 1956, **19**, 325–339.
85. Sherrington, C. S. Decerebrate rigidity, and reflex coordination of movements. *J. Physiol. (London)*, 1898a, **22**, 319–332.
86. Sherrington, C. S. Experiments in examination of the peripheral distribution of the fibers of the posterior roots of some spinal nerves. *Phil. Trans. Roy. Soc. London, B.* 1898b, **90**, 49–186.
87. Smith, R. W., Jr., Graebler, O., & Long, C. N. H. *The Hypophysial Growth Hormone, Nature and Actions.* New York: McGraw-Hill, 1955.
88. Snider, R. S., & Magoun, H. W. Facilitation produced by cerebellar stimulation. *J. Neurophysiol.*, 1949, **12**, 335–345.
89. Snider, R. S., McCulloch, W. S., & Magoun, H. W. A cerebello-bulbo-reticular pathway for suppression. *J. Neurophysiol.*, 1949, **12**, 325–334.
90. Snider, R. S., Magoun, H. W., & McCulloch, W. S. A suppressor cerebello-bulbo-reticular pathway from anterior lobe and paramedian lobules. *Fed. Proc.*, 1947, **6**, 207.
91. Sperry, R. W. Cerebral regulation of motor coordination in monkeys following multiple transection of sensorimotor cortex. *J. Neurophysiol.*, 1947, **10**, 275–294.
92. Sprague, J. M., & Chambers, W. W. Regulation of posture in intact and decerebrate cat. I: Cerebellum, reticular formation, vestibular nuclei. *J. Neurophysiol.*, 1953, **16**, 451–463.
93. Sprague, J. M., & Chambers, W. W. Control of posture by reticular formation and cerebellum in the intact, anesthetized and unanesthetized and in the decerebrated cat. *Amer. J. Physiol.*, 1954, **176**, 52–64.
94. Thorn, N. A. Mammalian anti-diuretic hormone. *Physiol. Rev.*, 1958, **38**, 169–195.
95. Tower, S. S. Pyramidal lesion in the monkey. *Brain*, 1940, **63**, 36–90.
96. Tower, S. S. The production of spasticity in monkeys by lesions in the pons. *Anat. Rec.*, 1942, Suppl. 82, 450–451.
97. Tower, S. S. The pyramidal tract. In *The Precentral Motor Cortex* (2nd ed.). P. C. Bucy, Ed. Urbana: Univ. of Illinois Press, 1949, pp. 149–172.
98. Umbach, W. The role of the nucleus caudatus in subcortico-cortical relationships. *EEG Clin. Neurophysiol.*, 1955, **7**, 665.
99. Vanderwolf, C. H. Limbic-diencephalic mechanisms of voluntary movement. *Psychol. Rev.*, 1971, **78**, 83–113.
100. Vane, J. R., Wolstenholme, G. E. W., & O'Connor, M. *Adrenergic Mechanisms.* Ciba Foundation Symposium. Boston: Little, Brown, 1960.
101. Velardo, J. T. *Endocrinology of Reproduction.* New York: Oxford Univ. Press, 1958.
102. Villee, C. A. *Control of Ovulation.* New York: Pergamon Press, 1961.
103. Walberg, F., & Brodal, A. Pyramidal tract fibres from temporal and occipital lobes: experimental study in cat. *Brain*, 1953, **76**, 491–508.
104. Waller, W. H. Progression movements elicited by subthalamic stimulation. *J. Neurophysiol.*, 1940, **3**, 300–307.
105. Ward, J. W. Motor phenomena elicited in the unanesthetized animal by electrical stimulation of the cerebral cortex. *Proc. Ass. Res. Nerv. Dis.*, 1950, **30**, 223–237.
106. Williams, R. H. *Diabetes.* New York: Paul Hoeber, 1960.
107. Wolstenholme, G. E. W., & O'Connor, M. *Metabolic Effects of Adrenal Hormones.* Ciba Foundation Study Group 6. Boston: Little, Brown, 1960.

108. Woolsey, C. N., Settlage, P. H., Meyer, D. R., Sencer, W., Hamuy, T. P., & Travis, A. M. Patterns of localization in precentral and "supplementary" motor areas and their relation to the concept of a premotor area. *Ass. Res. Nerv. Dis. Proc.*, 1950a, **30**, 238–264.

109. Woolsey, C. N., Settlage, P. H., Meyer, D. R., Sencer, W., Hamuy, T. P., & Travis, A. M. Somatotopic organization of "supplementary motor area" of the monkey. *Amer. J. Physiol.*, 1950b, **163**, 763.

110. Woolsey, C. N., Travis, A. M., Barnard, J. W., & Ostenso, R. S. Motor representation in the postcentral gyrus after chronic ablation of precentral and supplementary motor areas. *Fed. Proc.*, 1953, **12**, 160.

111. Young, W. C. *Sex and Internal Secretions.* Baltimore: Williams and Wilkins, 1961.

Chapter 8

THE RETICULAR FORMATION AND NONSPECIFIC THALAMIC PROJECTION SYSTEM

The Reticular Formation of the Brainstem

The Nonspecific Thalamic Projection System

THE RETICULAR FORMATION OF THE BRAINSTEM

Basic Structural and Functional Considerations

The simplest neural mechanism for the mediation of the organism's response to environmental change is a direct connection between a sensory receptor and a motor neuron. Such monosynaptic reflex connections are common in primitive organisms. As the need for more complex response capabilities arises in the course of phylogenetic development, a system of interneurons develops that provides more flexible connections between the sensory and motor systems. Out of this undifferentiated mass of short-axon neurons develop functionally as well as structurally distinct nuclei and pathways that constitute much of the central nervous system of the most highly developed vertebrates. Vestiges of the undifferentiated system of interneurons persist in the brainstem and upper spinal cord. Because the microscopic structure of this network of neurons resembles a fishnet or reticulum, it has been called the reticular formation.

In man and other highly developed mammals, the reticular formation is no longer an entirely undifferentiated system of short-axon neurons. Several systems of long-axon projections have been identified,[36] and as many as 98 anatomically distinct cellular groupings or nuclei have been described.[40] Corresponding functional distinctions have been made in only a few instances, but this is probably due to our ignorance rather than an inherent lack of functional organization.

Anatomical Boundaries. The reticular formation extends from the lower border of the medulla to the diencephalon. The vestiges of the phylogenetically prominent spinal reticular formation are generally considered to be a separate, though functionally related, system of interneurons. The upper boundary of the reticular formation is poorly defined. Much of the hypothalamus, subthalamus, septal area, and even portions of the thalamus are developmentally as well as functionally related to the reticular formation. These regions are nevertheless often not included (so that the border between the midbrain and hypothalamus becomes the upper limit of the reticular formation) because their clear anatomical and functional subdivisions do not fit the classic picture of an undifferentiated reticulum.

Throughout its course in the brainstem, the reticular formation is surrounded by the pathways and nuclei of the sensory and motor systems.

Microscopic Structure. The cells of the central core of the brainstem reticular formation are characterized by extensive and profusely branching dendritic fields that permit the channeling of impulses from divergent sources to a single neuron. Physiologically, such channeling results in a convergence of afferents from many different sources on a single reticular neuron and permits the integrative activity ascribed to the system as a whole. It is not uncommon, for instance, to find single cells in the midbrain reticular formation that respond to stimulation of receptors in more than one sensory modality as well as inputs from cerebellar or cortical sources.[49]

The central core of the reticular formation is characterized by cells that have diffusely branching dendritic fields and short axons. The reticular cells of the lateral areas of the brainstem project bifurcating axons into the medial portion, one leg typically taking an ascending course, the other a descending one.

Afferent and Efferent Connections. The functional organization of the reticular formation follows the same basic plan throughout its extent. Its central core gives rise to efferent projections to the spinal cord as well as cortical and subcortical regions. This central output system is surrounded by cells that receive afferent inputs from all sensory systems as well as cerebellar, cortical, and subcortical sources. Many of these afferent and efferent connections of the reticular formation are diffuse and multisynaptic. However, two long-axon ascending fiber systems have been described[36] that project to the thalamus, subthalamus, septal area, basal ganglia, and hypothalamus. Rapidly conducting spinal pathways that terminate on spinal interneurons have also been isolated.[28]

Cortical influences on the reticular formation originate in the motor cortex,[23] the sensory-motor cortex,[23] the temporal lobe,[31] the orbitofrontal cortex,[56] and various rhinencephalic areas.[1] Some of these corticoreticular fibers course through the internal capsule and upper brainstem in the company of the pyramidal tract,[46] but most corticoreticular connections are diffuse.

The reticular formation of the lower brainstem projects to the cortex either directly via diffuse extrathalamic projections that course through the ventrolateral diencephalon[36,48] or indirectly via the midline and intralaminar nuclei of the thalamus.[57] The intralaminar and midline nuclei of the thalamus are so intimately related functionally and anatomically to the reticular formation of the lower brainstem that many authors consider them to be part of a general reticular system.

The reticular formation receives important extrapyramidal inputs from the basal ganglia, indirectly via the thalamic nuclei[44] and directly from the cerebellum.[55,26] Cells in the bulbar portion of the reticular formation project extensively to the cerebellum.

Reticular Influences on Sensory Mechanisms

The relationship between perception and the physical energies that impinge on the sensorium is not adequately described by a simple law of proportionality. The sensory pathways conduct impulses that are directly related to the environment only under anesthesia. In the awake organism, the sensory input is distorted by influences that arise from a variety of central sources and seem to be integrated by the midbrain reticular formation.

Sensory input must be integrated with information from other concurrently active sensory systems as well as from association areas and memory-storage mechanisms in the central nervous system. The end-product of this interaction rather than the primary sensory input is thought to give rise to the subjective perception of the environment.[22]

On the basis of information that may originate in almost any part of the central or peripheral nervous system, the reticular formation maintains a constantly fluctuating state of excitation that biases the sensitivity of sensory receptors and relay stations. The net effect of this biasing influence may be facilitatory or inhibitory, although the basic mechanism appears to be one of selective disinhibition. (The reticular formation maintains a tonic inhibitory influence on all sensory mechanisms. Facilitatory effects are achieved by a decrease in this inhibition rather than an active facilitation.)

The inhibitory influence of the reticular formation is typically smallest when the sensory signal is novel, unexpected, or intense, or when it assumes special significance as a cue for stimuli that are associated with pain or the maintenance of homeostasis. It is largest when the sensory input duplicates information classed as "unimportant" and already stored in the memory banks of the brain.

Reticular influences may modify sensory information at the receptor level[12] and at each synaptic relay along the pathways to the cortical projection areas.[13] A good deal of information is lost or distorted by these reticular influences that reflect the organism's previous experience with similar sensory signals, its current state of attention, other concurrent sensory input as well as the organism's current state of general reactivity. It is thus no longer possible to think of a perception as the end-product of a relatively simple transducer process at the receptor level, followed by undistorted transmission of impulses to primary cortical projection areas that initiate neural activity that is directly proportional to the physical stimulus. At least four neural systems interact to determine our perceptions: (1) the classical lemniscal pathways and direct projections from the receptors of the special senses; (2) the extralemniscal pathways, which offer an alternate, multisynaptic pathway to higher centers of integration; (3) the reticular formation, which provides the pathways for many of the interactions between the different systems; and (4) the extrapyramidal motor system, which exercises a significant control over receptor activity.

Reticular Influences on Motor Functions

The reticular formation of the brainstem transmits many of the influences that modulate the basic pattern of spinal reflexes in accordance with postural requirements or motor "commands" from cortical centers of integration. Stimulation of the reticular formation may elicit distinct movements[51] or result in novel postural adjustments.[54] More typically, such stimulation facilitates or inhibits spinal motor mechanisms and thus modifies rather than elicits tonic or phasic movements. Early investigations of the descending influences of the reticular formation[29, 30] emphasized the existence of distinct facilitatory and inhibitory "centers" in the brainstem. More recent observations suggest that the anatomical distinction between facilitatory and inhibitory areas is not absolute.[3,53,54]

Inhibitory influences on reflexly or cortically elicited movements can be elicited by electrical stimulation of many parts of the brainstem reticular formation as well as from related nuclei in the thalamus and septal area.[16, 3] All spinal reflexes are susceptible to reticular inhibition, but the simple monosynaptic stretch reflex (which begins to look rather complex) appears to be particularly sensitive.[11]

Spinal reflexes as well as cortically evoked movements may also be facilitated by stimulation of portions of the reticular formation, particularly in the midbrain and pons and related midline and intralaminar nuclei of the thalamus.[41, 29, 30] These facilitatory effects travel over spinal pathways that are distinct from those carrying inhibitory influences.[38] Multisynaptic reflexes appear to be particularly susceptible to reticular facilitation.[11]

Ascending Reticular Influences on Cortical Functions (see Figure 8–1)

The brainstem reticular formation has received a great deal of experimental as well as speculative attention in the past 20 years because its ascending influences appear to participate in the control of the organism's general state of arousal or reactivity to sensory input. It has been known for some time that a transection of the mesencephalic brainstem results in behavioral coma. The electroencephalographic record of the brain rostral to this transection no longer shows the cyclical changes that characterize an intact brain but only the slow, high-amplitude activity that is normally seen in sleep. Stimulation of the two sensory systems that are still connected to their cortical projections in this *cerveaux isolé* preparation (vision and olfaction) does not result in an activation of the cortical EEG record. When the transection is made lower in the brainstem, near the junction between the spinal cord and medulla, a much more normal cortical EEG obtains. Such an *encephal isolé* preparation shows largely normal cycles of cortical activity and responds, though in an obviously limited fashion, to stimuli presented to receptors of the head.

When these observations were first reported,[6] it was thought that the cortex of the *cerveaux isolé* could not maintain a state of wakefulness and reactivity because a large percentage of the sensory afferents could not reach it. The *encephal isolé* was thought to be capable of maintaining a normal cycle of cortical activity because its sensorium included all of the cranial nerves. Sleep and cortical arousal were believed to be a function of sensory input to the cortex.

This interpretation was challenged when Moruzzi and Magoun[35] demonstrated in 1949 that electrical stimulation of the reticular formation of an anesthetized *encephal isolé* could induce long-lasting cortical "arousal" (high-frequency, low-amplitude EEG activity). The resulting concept of an "ascending reticular activating system" (ARAS) gained support when it was found that lesions restricted to the midbrain reticular formation reproduced the *cerveaux isolé* syndrome (behavioral coma and cortical slow wave activity), whereas transection of the classical sensory pathways to the cortex did not.[20, 21]

Subsequent investigations have suggested that this arousal function may be exercised only by a small aspect of the reticular formation. Brainstem transections at the midpontine level, just ahead of the root of the trigeminal nerve, reproduce the *cerveaux isolé* syndrome.[47] Transections of the brainstem just behind this region do not. Since it has been possible in some experiments to obtain normal cortical activity patterns even when the transection was slightly anterior to the root of the trigeminal nerve,[4] this sensory influx does not appear to account for the difference between the pre- and post-trigemi-

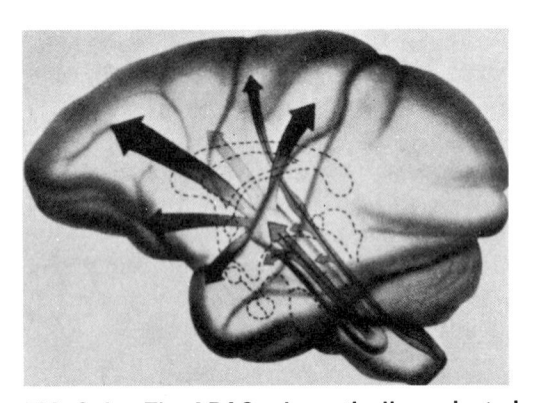

FIG. 8–1. The ARAS schematically projected on the brain of the monkey. The reticular formation, consisting of the multineuronal, multisynaptic central core of the region from medulla to hypothalamus, receives collaterals from classical sensory pathways and projects diffusely upon the cortex. Impulses via specific sensory pathways are brief, discrete, direct and of short latency in contrast to those via the unspecific ARAS which are persistent, diffuse, and of long latency.

(From D. B. Lindsley. Attention, consciousness, sleep and wakefulness. In *Handbook of physiology. Neurophysiology.* Washington, D.C.: Am. Physiol. Soc., 1960, sec. 1, vol. III, 1553–1593.)

nal transection. Moruzzi[34] has suggested that the *nucleus reticularis pontalis oralis*, which takes up much of the reticular formation at this level, may contain the essential arousal mechanism.

The isolation of this function may explain some hitherto puzzling observations. For instance, the activity of many neurons in the brainstem reticular formation does not correlate in any simple fashion with the cortical EEG activity.[32, 27] Also, fairly extensive damage to the reticular formation of the brainstem does not always produce behavioral coma and cortical depression. This is particularly true when care is taken to avoid surgical trauma by multistage lesions.[8,9] A more extensive discussion of behavioral and electrophysiological arousal will be presented in a later chapter.

Central Influences on Reticular Functions (*see Figure 8-2*)

Cerebral Cortex. Emphasis on the "arousal" functions of the reticular formation has tended to obscure the importance of corticoreticular influences. Essentially all parts of the cerebral cortex project to the brainstem reticular formation.[43] Stimulation of almost any cortical region gives rise to facilitatory or inhibitory influences on reticular neurons, the direction of the effect depending on the parameters of stimulation as well as the current state of the organism. It is not uncommon to find that cells in the reticular formation increase their firing rate during and following cortical stimulation under some circumstances and decrease it in response to the same stimulation at other times, presumably because other inputs to the cortical or reticular cells influence their interaction.[5] Some areas of the cortex, notably the "suppressor areas," give rise to predominantly inhibitory influences on reticular cells.[23]

Cerebellum. Facilitatory as well as inhibitory influences on reticular functions also arise from the cerebellum. Some of the cells that exert this influence respond to sensory inputs from the spindle receptors, thus completing a feedback loop. Facilitatory and inhibitory effects can be elicited by stimulation of the same cerebellar site. The direction of the effect depends on stimulus parameters and the state of the organism.[52, 33]

Cerebellar influences on reticular functions are represented in a topographic pattern. Electrical stimulation may facilitate or inhibit specific muscles or even individual muscle fibers.[39] Beyond that, a gross functional distinction can be made. The vermis of the cerebellum mediates postural adjustments and appears to be nonspecifically related to the central core of the reticular formation. The cerebellar cortex, on the other hand, influences specific muscular activity and projects more selectively to cells in the lateral parts of the reticular formation.[7]

Basal Ganglia. Some aspects of the brainstem reticular formation are sometimes considered part of the extrapyramidal motor system. Such an interpretation is tempting because (1) no direct pathways can be demonstrated between the basal ganglia or cerebellum and the spinal motor neuron; (2) at least some of the important relay nuclei of the extrapyramidal motor system (such as the red

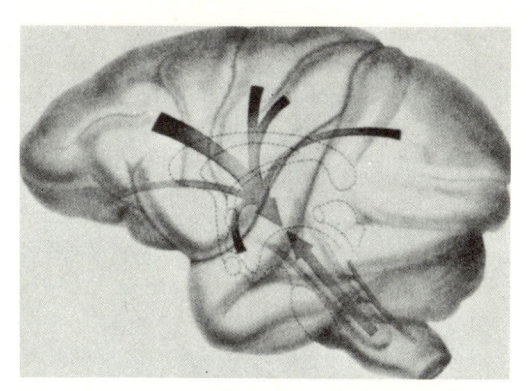

FIG. 8-2. Corticofugal pathways and collaterals of classical afferent pathways converging on the reticular formation of the lower brainstem. Stimulation of widespread cortical areas gives rise to electric potentials in the reticular formation. Afferent impulses from all sources and impulses originating in the cortex are capable of exciting the ascending reticular activating system (ARAS), which in turn maintains the cortex and behavior in a state of arousal and alertness.

(From J. D. French, R. Hernández-Peón, & R. B. Livingston. Projections from cortex to cephalic brainstem (reticular formation) in monkey. *J. Neurophysiol.*, **18**, 1955, 74.)

nucleus and substantia nigra of the midbrain) are developmentally part of the reticular formation; (3) many of the basal ganglia project or receive afferents from thalamic nuclei that are part of the nonspecific projection system; and (4) stimulation of the striatum does not typically elicit movements but facilitates or inhibits motions that are reflexly or cortically evoked in much the same fashion as stimulation of the brainstem reticular formation.

THE NONSPECIFIC THALAMIC PROJECTION SYSTEM

The nonspecific thalamic projections represent the rostral continuation of the brainstem reticular formation. They consist of the intralaminar and midline nuclei of the thalamus and the reticular nuclei of subthalamic origin. This "nonspecific" thalamic system projects to all regions of the cortex, and a fairly precise topographic organization of these projections has been observed.[14]

The anatomical pathways for this important influence on cortical functions have not yet been unequivocally established. Some of the impulses that originate in the midline and intralaminar nuclei may be relayed to the cortex via the reticular nucleus—the only part of the system that has direct cortical projections.[45,15] Connections between the midline and intralaminar nuclei and the caudate nucleus[37,2] and putamen[24,25] have been described, suggesting additional thalamocortical projections via the striatum. The nonspecific thalamic nuclei also project to the sensory and relay nuclei of the thalamus but do not seem to make use of the associated pathways to the cortex.[14]

Electrical stimulation of the nonspecific thalamic nuclei produces distinct "spindling" (see Figure 8–3) in the cortical EEG, and this unusual pattern has been used to define the anatomical limits of the system and its primary connections. These spindling or "recruiting" responses appear first in the frontal lobes and somewhat later in the posterior association areas. Cortical cells that respond to stimulation of the sensory nuclei of the thalamus are not typically fired by stimulation of the nonspecific nuclei. However,

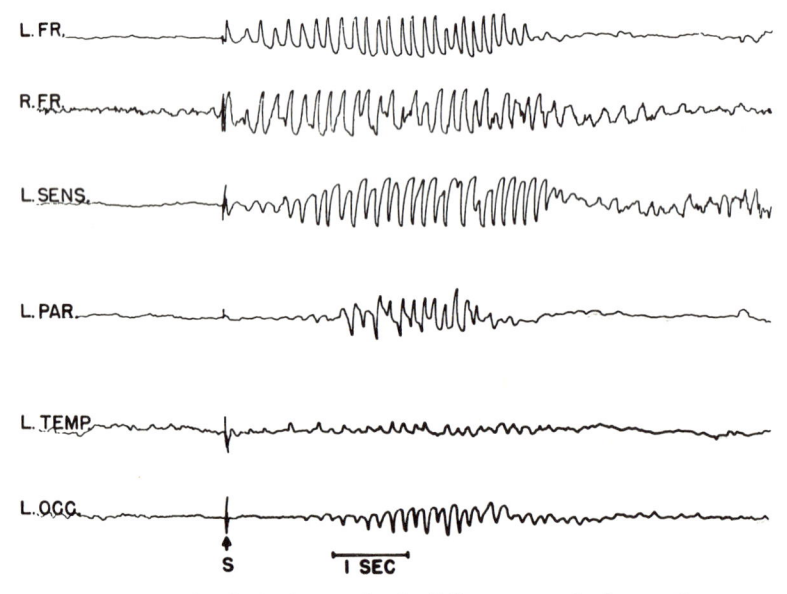

FIG. 8–3. Tripping of spindle bursts in six different cortical areas in response to a single shock in the nucleus centralis medialis of the thalamus of the cat under pentobarbital anesthesia.

(From H. H. Jasper. Unspecific thalamocortical relations. In *Handbook of physiology. Neurophysiology.* Washington, D.C.: Am. Physiol. Soc., 1960, sec. 1, vol. II, 1307–1321.)

their threshold to subsequent stimulation may be significantly affected. Some cortical cells respond to stimulation of the nonspecific thalamic nuclei by adjusting their firing rate upward or downward so that pools of neighboring neurons fire in synchrony with the thalamic stimulation. A similar timing or synchronizing influence on the discharge of neurons in the specific thalamic nuclei has also been described.[42]

Functional Considerations. The nonspecific thalamic nuclei are intimately related to the lemniscal and extralemniscal sensory systems via direct collaterals, reciprocal intrathalamic connections, and afferents from the brainstem reticular formation.

The most important connections of the nonspecific thalamic system relate to its function as the dorsal extension of the midbrain reticular formation. Electrophysiological and behavioral activation can be obtained from stimulation of the nonspecific nuclei, and large lesions in the anterior portions of the system produce behavioral coma and electrophysiological sleep much like stimulation or ablation of portions of the midbrain reticular formation. The effects of thalamic stimulation and ablation are, however, rarely as severe or prolonged, presumably because extrathalamic reticulocortical pathways can maintain some influence on the cortex.[20, 21]

Sharpless and Jasper[50] have observed two different types of cortical activation patterns and suggest that one may be mediated by the thalamic portion of the reticular system. The prolonged "tonic" activation that differentiates general wakefulness from sleep is thought to originate in the brainstem reticular formation and to be mediated by extrathalamic projections to the cortex. A brief "phasic" activation that may direct momentary "attention" to particular sensory inputs is thought to be mediated by the nonspecific thalamic system.

There are other differences between the thalamic and midbrain portions of the system. Stimulation of the thalamic nuclei often produces sleep or behavioral inhibition, whereas brainstem stimulation almost always produces excitatory effects on cortical functions and behavioral arousal.[17] The thalamic and midbrain portions of the reticular formation may also differ with respect to the specificity of their action. The "nonspecific" thalamic nuclei are quite specifically related to particular portions of the cortex, whereas the lower reticular formation exerts general activating influences on all cortical areas regardless of the modality of the arousing stimulus. This general influence may provide an essential background of excitation against which the specific activation of cortical areas by the thalamic mechanisms can occur.

Bibliography

1. Adey, W. R., Merrillees, C. R., & Sunderland, S. The entorhinal area: behavioural, evoked potential, and histological studies of its interrelationship with brain-stem regions. *Brain*, 1956, **79**, 414–439.
2. Akimoto, H., Yamaguchi, N., Okabe, K., Nakagawa, T., Nakamura, I., Abe, K., Torii, H., & Masahashi, K. On the sleep induced through electrical stimulation on dog thalamus. *Folia Psychiat. Neurol. Jap.*, 1956, **10**, 117–146.
3. Austin, G. M. Suprabulbar mechanisms of facilitation and inhibition of cord reflexes. *Res. Publ., Ass. Res. Nerv. Ment. Dis.*, 1952, **30**, 196–222.
4. Batini, C., Moruzzi, G., Palestini, M., Rossi, G. F., & Zanchetti, A. Effects of complete pontine transections on the sleep-wakefulness rhythm: the midpontine pretrigeminal preparation. *Arch. Ital. Biol.*, 1959, **97**, 1–12.
5. Baumgarten, R. von, & Mollica, A. Der Einfluss sensibler Reizung auf die Entladungsfrequenz Kleinhirnabhängiger Reticulariszellen. *Arch. Ges. Physiol.*, 1954, **259**, 79–96.
6. Bremer, F. Cerveau isolé et physiologie du sommeil. *C. R. Soc. Biol.*, 1935, **118**, 1235–1241.
7. Chambers, W. W., & Sprague, J. W. Functional localization in the cerebellum. I: Organization in longitudinal cortico-nuclear zones and their contribution to the control of posture, both extrapyramidal and pyramidal. *J. Comp. Neurol.*, 1955, **103**, 105–129.

8. Doty, R. W., Beck, E. C., & Kooi, K. A. Effect of brainstem lesions on conditioned responses of cats. *Exp. Neurol.*, 1959, **1**, 360–385.
9. Feldman, S. M., & Waller, H. J. Dissociation of electrocortical activation and behavioral arousal. *Nature*, 1962, **196**, 1320–1322.
10. French, J. D., Hernández-Peón, R., & Livingston, R. B. Projections from cortex to cephalic brainstem (reticular formation) in monkey. *J. Neurophysiol.*, 1955, **18**, 74–95.
11. Gernandt, B. E., & Thulin, C. A. Reciprocal effects upon spinal motoneurons from stimulation of bulbar reticular formation. *J. Neurophysiol.*, 1955, **18**, 113–129.
12. Granit, R., & Kaada, B. R. Influence of stimulation in central nervous structures on muscle spindles in cat. *Acta Physiol. Scand.*, 1952, **27**, 130–150.
13. Hagbarth, K. E., & Kerr, D. I. B. Central influences on spinal afferent conduction. *J. Neurophysiol.*, 1954, **17**, 295–307.
14. Hanbery, J., & Jasper, H. H. Independence of diffuse thalamo-cortical projection system shown by specific nuclear destructions. *J. Neurophysiol.*, 1953, **16**, 252–271.
15. Hanbery, J., Ajmone-Marsan, C., & Dilworth, Margaret. Pathways of non-specific thalamo-cortical projection system. *EEG Clin. Neurophysiol.*, 1954, **6**, 103–118.
16. Hodes, R., Peacock, S. M., & Heath, R. G. Influence of the fore-brain on somato-motor activity. *J. Comp. Neurol.*, 1951, **94**, 381–408.
17. Hunter, J., & Jasper, H. H. Effect of thalamic stimulation in unanesthetised animals. *EEG Clin. Neurophysiol.*, 1949, **1**, 305–324.
18. Jasper, H. H. Unspecific thalamocortical relations. In *Handbook of Physiology. Vol. II.* J. Field, H. W. Magoun, & V. E. Hall, Eds. Washington, D.C.: Am. Physiol. Soc. 1960, pp. 1307–1321.
19. Lindsley, D. B. Attention, consciousness, sleep and wakefulness. In *Handbook of Physiology. Vol. III.* J. Field, H. W. Magoun, & V. E. Hall, Eds. Washington, D.C.: Am. Physiol. Soc., 1960, pp. 1553–1593.
20. Lindsley, D. B., Bowden, J. W., & Magoun, H. W. Effect upon the EEG of acute injury to the brain stem activating system. *EEG Clin. Neurophysiol.*, 1949, **1**, 475–486.
21. Lindsley, D. B., Schreiner, L. H., Knowles, W. B., & Magoun, H. W. Behavioral and EEG changes following chronic brainstem lesions in the cat. *EEG Clin. Neurophysiol.*, 1950, **2**, 483–498.
22. Livingston, R. B. Central control of receptors and sensory transmission systems. In *Handbook of Physiology. Vol. I.* J. Field, H. W. Magoun, & V. E. Hall, Eds. Washington, D.C.: Am. Physiol. Soc., 1959, pp. 741–760.
23. McCulloch, W. S., Graf, G., & Magoun, H. W. A cortico-bulbo-reticular pathway from area 4-s. *J. Neurophysiol.*, 1946, **9**, 127–132.
24. McLardy, T. Projection of the centromedian nucleus of the human thalamus. *Brain*, 1948, **71**, 290–303.
25. McLardy, T. Diffuse thalamic projection to cortex: an anatomical critique. *EEG Clin. Neurophysiol.*, 1951, **3**, 183–188.
26. McMasters, R. E. Efferent projections of the deep nuclei of the cerebellum of the cat. *Anat. Rec.*, 1957, **127**, 331–332.
27. Machne, X., Calma, I., & Magoun, H. W. Unit activity of central cephalic brainstem in EEG arousal. *J. Neurophysiol.*, 1955, **18**, 547–558.
28. Magoun, H. W. Caudal and cephalic influences of brainstem reticular formation. *Physiol. Rev.*, 1950, **30**, 459–474.
29. Magoun, H. W., & Rhines, Ruth. An inhibitory mechanism in the bulbar reticular formation. *J. Neurophysiol.*, 1946, **9**, 165–171.
30. Magoun, H. W., & Rhines, Ruth. *Spasticity: the Stretch Reflex and Extrapyramidal Systems.* Springfield, Ill.: Thomas, 1947.
31. Mettler, F. A. Corticifugal fiber connections of cortex of *Macaca mulatta*: temporal region. *J. Comp. Neurol.*, 1935, **63**, 25.
32. Mollica, A., Moruzzi, G., & Naquet, R. Décharges réticulaires induites par la polarisation du cervelet: leurs rapports avec le tonus postural et la réaction d'éveil. *EEG Clin. Neurophysiol.*, 1953, **5**, 571–584.
33. Moruzzi, G. *Problems in Cerebellar Physiology.* Springfield, Ill.: Thomas, 1950.
34. Moruzzi, G. Reticular influences on the EEG. *EEG Clin. Neurophysiol.*, 1964, **16**, 2–17.
35. Moruzzi, G., & Magoun, H. W. Brainstem reticular formation and activation of the EEG. *EEG Clin. Neurophysiol.*, 1949, **1**, 455.

36. Nauta, W. J. H., & Kuypers, H. G. J. M. Some ascending pathways in the brain stem reticular formation. In *The Reticular Formation of the Brain*. H. H. Jasper, L. D. Proctor, R. S. Knighton, W. C. Noshay, & R. T. Costello, Eds. Boston: Little, Brown, 1958, pp. 3–30.

37. Nauta, W. J. H., & Whitlock, D. G. An anatomical analysis of the non-specific thalamic projection system. In *Brain Mechanisms and Consciousness*. E. D. Adrian, F. Bremer, H. H. Jasper, & J. F. Delafresnaye, Eds. Springfield, Ill.: Thomas, 1954, pp. 81–116.

38. Niemer, W. T., & Magoun, H. W. Reticulospinal tracts influencing motor activity. *J. Comp. Neurol.*, 1947, **87**, 367–379.

39. Nulsen, F. E., Black, S. P. W., & Drake, C. G. Inhibition and facilitation of motor activity by the anterior cerebellum. *Fed. Proc.*, 1948, **7**, 86–87.

40. Olszewski, J. The cytoarchitecture of the human reticular formation. In *Brain Mechanisms and Consciousness*. E. D. Adrian, F. Bremer, H. H. Jasper, & J. F. Delafresnaye, Eds. Springfield, Ill.: Thomas, 1954, pp. 54–80.

41. Peacock, S. M., & Hodes, R. Influence of the forebrain on somato-motor activity. *J. Comp. Neurol.*, 1951, **94**, 409–426.

42. Purpura, D. P., & Shofer, R. J. Intracellular recording from thalamic neurons during reticulo-cortical activation. *J. Neurophysiol.*, 1963, **26**, 494–505.

43. Ramón y Cajal, S. *Histologie du Système Nerveux de l'Homme et des Vertébrés* (reprinted from original, 1909–1911). Madrid: Consejo Superior de Investigaciones Cientificas, 1952–1955.

44. Ranson, S. W., & Ranson, S. W., Jr. Efferent fibers of corpus striatum. *Res. Publ., Ass. Res. Nerv. Ment. Dis.*, 1942, **21**, 69–76.

45. Rose, J. E. Cortical connections of reticular complex of thalamus. *Res. Publ., Ass. Res. Nerv. Ment. Dis.*, 1952, **30**, 454–479.

46. Rossi, G. F., & Brodal, A. Corticofugal fibres to the brain-stem reticular formation: an experimental study in the cat. *J. Anat.*, 1956, **90**, 42–62.

47. Rossi, G. F., & Zirondoli, A. On the mechanism of the cortical desynchronization elicited by volatile anesthetics. *EEG Clin. Neurophysiol.*, 1955, **7**, 383–390.

48. Scheibel, M. E., & Scheibel, A. B. Structural substrates for integrative patterns in the brainstem reticular core. In *The Reticular Formation of the Brain*. H. H. Jasper, L. D. Proctor, R. S. Knighton, W. C. Noshay, & R. T. Costello, Eds. Boston: Little, Brown, 1958, pp. 31–55.

49. Scheibel, M. E., Scheibel, A. B., Mollica, A., & Moruzzi, G. Convergence and the interaction of afferent impulses on single units of reticular formation. *J. Neurophysiol.*, 1955, **18**, 309–331.

50. Sharpless, S., & Jasper, H. H. Habituation of the arousal reaction. *Brain*, 1956, **79**, 655–680.

51. Snider, R. S., & Stowell, A. Receiving areas of the tactile, auditory, and visual systems in the cerebellum. *J. Neurophysiol.*, 1944, **7**, 331–357.

52. Snider, R. S., McCulloch, W. S., & Magoun, H. W. A cerebello-bulbo-reticular pathway for suppression. *J. Neurophysiol.*, 1949, **12**, 325–334.

53. Sprague, J. M. Stimulation of reticular formation in intact, unanesthetized and in decerebrated cats. *Fed. Proc.*, 1953, **12**, 137.

54. Sprague, J. M., & Chambers, W. W. Control of posture by reticular formation and cerebellum in the intact, anesthetized and unanesthetized and in the decerebrated cat. *Amer. J. Physiol.*, 1954, **176**, 52–64.

55. Sprague, J. M., Cohen, D., & Chambers, W. W. Efferent cerebellar pathways to brainstem. *Anat. Rec.*, 1957, **127**, 372.

56. Wall, P. D., Glees, P., & Fulton, J. F. Corticofugal connexions of posterior orbital surface in rhesus monkey. *Brain*, 1951, **74**, 66–71.

57. Whitlock, D. G., & Schreiner, L. H. Some connections of the midline region and centre median nucleus of the thalamus of the cat. *Anat. Rec.*, 1954, **118**, 368.

SECTION 3

Biological Bases of Motivation

A species cannot survive unless the behavior of its members is predictable. Indeed, we become quite disturbed whenever our predictions of the behavior of others turn out to be incorrect, and we remove from society those individuals who repeatedly behave in unpredictable ways. Behavioral scientists from all persuasions and disciplines therefore share a basic interest in the laws that govern behavior and thus make it predictable.

In very simple organisms, behavior is predictable because it is reflexive—that is, the system is largely prewired and hence invariant. As organisms become increasingly complex, they develop capabilities for adapting to changing environmental conditions, and prewiring becomes increasingly inefficient and ineffective. A complex nervous system is then developed that can continuously monitor the state of innumerable physiological and biochemical processes that are essential to life and the relationship of complex sensory inputs to each of them. To survive, complex biological organisms must regulate their energy and fluid balances, obtain adequate but not excessive quantities of certain chemicals, prevent damage to their structure, and finally, assure procreation to permit survival of the species.

Since most biological organisms have little control over the expenditures of energy and fluids, much of their behavior is controlled by the need to obtain nutrients and fluids in amounts appropriate to changing demands. Man's behavior is not, typically, directly controlled by these contingencies because food and water are in relatively abundant supply. However, man's more complex acquisitive behavior can be considered an analogue of appetitive behavior in more primitive organisms. The laws that have been found to govern such behavior have not, as far as we can tell, changed appreciably.

Similarly, we are rarely faced with the need to avoid physical damage, except in times of war, but have devised complex behaviors to escape or avoid situations that are potentially harmful or detrimental to our well-being in more devious ways. Again, it seems that the basic laws that govern the organism's response to noxious stimulation may apply, regardless of the complexity of the situation.

The laws that govern sexual behavior do seem to have changed in emphasis if not in basic content in the course of evolution, apparently at least in part because the sensations that accompany copulatory behavior become increasingly rewarding as the sensory capabilities of the organism increase. Copulation seems to serve purely procreative purposes in species below primates, and sexual behavior is determined to a large extent by hormonal factors. In man, and to some extent in apes and some monkeys, copulation serves social and affective purposes as well and the importance of reflexive, hormonal mechanisms decreases.

Section 3 considers some of the mechanisms that mammals have developed in the course of evolution to deal effectively with some of these basic problems. We will discuss mainly such apparently simple matters as hunger and thirst, affective and behavioral reactions to pain, and the hormonal and situational determinants of sexual behavior. However, the basic laws that we hope to discover in the process may apply to many more complex behaviors.

Chapter 9

HUNGER AND THE REGULATION OF FOOD INTAKE

Introduction

Peripheral Influences

Central Regulatory Mechanisms

The Correlation Between Hunger and Energy Needs

Review and Summary

INTRODUCTION

In the most general terms, we would like to know why all biological organisms ingest enough nutrients to survive and how, under varying environmental conditions, they manage to consume an amount of food that is almost exactly commensurate with their current energy expenditure. This problem has special significance for the psychologist who has traditionally used hunger as the prototype of "primary" or "biological" motivation and has freely generalized his observations of the effects of food deprivation to other drive states.

The first thing we notice when we consider the organism's logistics with respect to food intake is the fact that food deprivation, the typical operational definition of hunger, is not always the principal, and in some instances, not even an important determinant of food intake and hunger.

When we eat and just how much per meal is determined to a significant degree by how good the food is, how cold (or warm) it happens to be at the moment, and how much exercise we have had recently. Many other factors become important under special circumstances. Food intake may be zero in spite of prolonged deprivation if the food is encountered in a novel environment that holds unknown dangers or when temporarily more "important" stimuli (such as cues previously associated with pain) vie for one's attention. Similarly, food intake may be low in spite of extensive deprivation because one is ill or distracted.

The causation of feeding behavior is, then, not quite as simple as the traditional operational definition of hunger in terms of time of deprivation suggests. Instead, we must consider a variety of influences that we have, for the sake of convenience, divided into those that (a) primarily affect "peripheral" neural or hormonal mechanisms and those that (b) act more directly on central functions. You may find this distinction at times arbitrary, but it helps to organize our discussion.

Let us try to get an overview of the problem. Hunger reflects the activity of regulatory mechanisms that are represented in a number of subcortical and perhaps also cortical pathways in the brain that react to neural as well as chemical signals. The inputs to these regulatory mechanisms reflect the constantly changing energy household of the organism. Every second the body uses energy, which must be obtained from foods. The quantity of energy used per unit time varies as the organism's activity and other energy demands (such as environmental temperature) change. Walking, for instance, requires 10 to 20 times more energy than sitting, and running may use up to 5 to 10 times more than walking. The organism must be capable of metering the changing energy expenditure to assure an adequate but not excessive compensatory intake of food. Moreover, foods vary widely with respect to their energy content (or "calories"), and the organism must somehow monitor the energy equivalent of the ingested foods to prevent an imbalance in its energy household.

These requirements add up to a pretty tall order, and one may wonder how successful such a regulation can be. It turns out that even the not-overly-intelligent laboratory rat manages to achieve a surprisingly accurate energy balance, even when we try to fool it in a number of ways. Forced to run on a treadmill, rats compensate for this energy loss by a directly proportional increase in food intake. Within some limits, this adjustment is perfect and the animals maintain a stable body weight. Only when prolonged periods of forced exercise (over five hours) are scheduled daily does the compensatory intake fall off and the animals lose weight.[103] Rats also adjust their intake when their diet is diluted with up to 75 percent nonnutrient roughage[82] or when they are shifted from a low-calorie, high-carbohydrate diet to a high-calorie, high-fat diet.[91] Caloric adjustments also occur in response to changes in environmental temperatures, food intake rising in the cold and declining in the heat.[49]

A closer look at the pattern of food intake under changing energy requirements suggests the operation of two cooperating influences. One is concerned with short-term, meal-to-meal and day-to-day constancies. The second adjusts the often substantial errors that creep into the short-term regulation. Between the two, our laboratory rats do a fine job of maintaining a constant energy balance.

You may wonder why the lowly rat achieves, apparently without much effort, a feat that many millions of overweight dieters seem incapable of. The answer is simple. On the one hand, man has mechanized his environment and controlled its temperature to the point where energy expenditure is minimal (even a rat will eventually get fat when restrained in a small cage that prevents locomotor activity). On the other hand, man has provided himself with a plethora of exquisite foods (as well as such high-calorie beverages as alcohol) and eats, in many instances, not in response to hunger cues but to satisfy his desire for particular taste sensations. In many overweight persons, this basic problem is further complicated by social pressures (i.e., the constant nibbling at parties) or emotional problems that seem to drive as many people to eat as they do to drink.

Review Questions

1. Is the operational definition of hunger in terms of hours of food deprivation adequate? What other factors would you consider? Why?

2. Do biological organisms achieve a perfect energy balance? What types of experimental paradigms have been used to investigate this matter?

PERIPHERAL INFLUENCES

Historical Perspectives

Hunger and appetite have been favorite topics of literary essays throughout the history of man. Even the Greek philosophers of the pre-Christian era speculated about the origin of man's motivation to seek nourishment periodically. The first scientific treatises on the subject date back to some of the natural scientists of the 18th and 19th centuries.

Implicit in all of the early physiological theories of hunger is the assumption that gastric mechanisms autonomously regulate food intake on the basis of information from the stomach and that neural or chemical changes elsewhere in the body are essentially irrelevant. Haller,[69] for instance, proposed that hunger seemed to be a sensation of exclusively peripheral origin, which he believed to arise as a direct consequence of the stimulation of nerves in the stomach. He believed that specific "hunger nerves" might be excited by the grinding of the walls of the empty stomach. Erasmus Darwin[32] also believed that hunger arose directly from the stomach but thought that it reflected the absence of motility, which normally attended digestive processes. A more chemically oriented hypothesis was supported by Soemmering[138] and others who believed, in agreement with many of today's laymen, that the sensation of hunger might be due to an action of gastric juices (which are neutralized in the process of digestion) on the innervation of an empty stomach. Perhaps the last unequivocal statement of a purely gastric interpretation of hunger is Carlson's[29] suggestion that "the gastric hunger mechanism is primarily automatic and independent of blood changes as well as central nervous influences."

It must have been clear even to these pioneering physiologists that variations in food intake do not affect only the digestive tract, but they made little or no provision for neural or chemical feedback mechanisms that must correlate gastric activity with the needs of the organism. Cannon's[27] more recent "local" theory of hunger and appetite holds that deprivation may influence the activity of some parts of the brain but suggests that this does not directly lead to drive stimulation. The perception of the motivational state is instead thought to depend on a consequent stimulation of receptors in the stomach. Such an interpretation receives a good deal of support from our daily experience of "hunger pangs" (most of us are willing to swear that we respond to sensations of gastric origin when we go to lunch or dinner), but extensive experimental study of gastric factors has so far failed to support our intuition. Peripheral oral or gastric influences may contribute signals that are commonly used to regulate intake, but they clearly are not essential.

Cannon's theory of hunger is analogous to the James-Lange theory of emotion, which similarly has retained a good deal of popular appeal because of its apparent agreement with our daily experience. Thus, James suggested that an emotion arises in response to sensations that are brought about by motor reactions to the emotion-inducing stimulus. Cannon similarly held that we are hungry because we experience stomach contractions (in contrast to more "centrally" oriented theories, which would suggest that we may have stomach contractions because we are hungry).

Signals Arising from the Mouth and Gastrointestinal (GI) Tract

Taste sensations are an important determinant of food intake in our affluent society but play only a small role in basic regulatory functions. Almost all animals respond to taste stimuli, though often in ways which differ from our own. Most have clear taste preferences and select some dietary components over other equally nutritious ones on this basis. In most instances it is even possible, though often difficult, to induce prolonged overeating and obesity by offering highly preferred foods. All species also have pronounced aversions to some taste sensations and will starve to death rather than accept nutritious diets that induce such sensations. However, between these extremes, most species accept an often surprisingly wide range of diets and balance their energy equation regardless of taste or texture.

That oral factors are, indeed, not essential to energy regulation has been shown in experiments that demonstrate that rats are capable of regulating intake although no food passes through their mouths. In these studies, rats are trained to press a lever for rewards consisting of intragastric injections of small quantities of a liquid diet.[40] The animals learn to obtain their total daily food ration in this fashion and to adjust their daily work output in response to changes in the caloric content of the diet. Similar precise adjustments are made when the size of each injection is doubled or halved or when the ratio of rewards to lever presses is changed.

Most of the early investigations of hunger were concerned with the stomach, since it seemed to be the source of hunger as well as satiety signals. Well before the turn of the century, many of the great physiological laboratories of Europe[131, 43] attempted to demonstrate the role of gastric factors by cutting the sensory or motor innervation of the stomach. The results of the many studies agreed in demonstrating that even complete denervation of the stomach in man as well as a variety of other mammals did not significantly affect food intake or the sensations of hunger or satiety.

Because it is difficult to make sure that all of the nerve branches to the stomach were removed in these early experiments, they were more recently replicated by better equipped investigators.[14, 111] Their results agree with the early reports in showing that complete vagotomy (which eliminates stomach contractions) and splanchnectomy (which eliminates sensory signals from the stomach) do not significantly affect the organism's ability to regulate food intake. Denervation also does not change the pattern or size of individual meals, suggesting that satiety as well as hunger signals are intact. This is confirmed by clinical reports of patients who have undergone similar surgical interventions.[55, 54]

These observations demonstrate that the neural feedback from the stomach cannot be an essential component of hunger and satiety. That chemical signals from the upper part of the GI tract are similarly dispensable is suggested by clinical reports of individuals who survive quite well after their stomach is entirely removed. These people report normal sensations of hunger and satiety and are perfectly capable of regulating their food intake within normal limits (they do have to eat more often because only small quantities of food can be stored in the upper intestine).[156, 92] Rats whose stomachs have been surgically removed have been shown to (1) learn a maze that leads to food reward as well and as rapidly as normal controls, (2) obtain normal scores in an obstruction-box experiment when the reinforcement for crossing an electrified grid is food, and (3) show as much activity in connection with the accustomed time of feeding as do control animals.[153]

These experiments demonstrate that the stomach cannot be a source of essential signals but tell us nothing about its role in the intact organism. Do we, under normal circumstances, eat when the stomach churns and emits sensations that we have come to call "hunger pangs?" Do we cease to eat, at least in part, because of distress signals from an extended stomach?

Many experiments have demonstrated that periods of gastric motility correlate well with reports of hunger sensations in man. The first of these experiments was reported by Cannon and Washburn in 1912[28] and forms the basis of Cannon's theory of motivation (see Figure 9–1). In these experiments, stomach motility was monitored before, during, and after the usual time of eating by means of X-ray observations as well as pneumographic recordings from a balloon swallowed into the stomach. The contractions of the empty stomach were found to coincide with hunger sensations, and each separate contraction appeared to be synchronous with a single "hunger pang."

In later studies, these contractions have been extensively investigated, and there is little doubt concerning their periodicity and

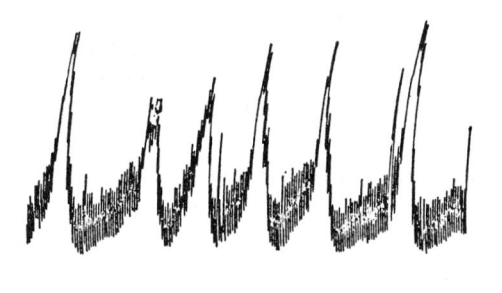

FIG. 9–1. The top record represents intragastric pressure (the small oscillations due to respiration, the large to contractions of the stomach); the second record is time in minutes (10 min.); the third record is the report of hunger pangs.

(From W. B. Cannon & A. L. Washburn. An explanation of hunger. *Amer. J. Physiol.*, 29, 1912, 441–454.)

correlation with hunger sensations.[104] There is, however, some question about their origin. Contractions have been recorded from all parts of the stomach,[29, 151] but the pacemaker for this activity may reside somewhere below the stomach. Contractions of the duodenum always precede each stomach contraction,[78] and there are instances where the duodenum contracts but the stomach remains inactive. When this occurs, human subjects report hunger sensations in the absence of stomach contractions.[119] Moreover, the placement of foods directly into the stomach fails to reduce its activity whereas injections of nutrients into lower portions of the GI tract inhibit all gastric motility.[104] These observations are important because the many experiments that demonstrate that denervation or removal of the stomach fails to interfere with hunger do not rule out possibly essential neural or chemical influences from the lower intestine. This problem has received little experimental attention because it is difficult to keep an organism alive and functioning normally after removal or complete denervation of the lower tract.

Some experiments have suggested that the motility of the stomach and lower GI tract may be under hormonal rather than neural control. If one fashions a pouch from stomach tissue and implants it almost anywhere in the body cavity, the pouch will contract rhythmically in synchrony with the stomach even though it has no innervation. Moreover, the pouch motility is affected by fasting and food intake as well as by the injection of nutrients into the upper intestine.[126] These observations are important in suggesting that at least some aspects of satiety may be mediated chemically rather than neurally. We will return to the question of hormonal mediation at a later point in our discussion.

For the moment, let us briefly turn to another aspect of satiety—stomach distention. Most of us have had the distressing experience of overeating in the course of a Thanksgiving dinner and can testify to the fact that at some upper limit the stomach sends out SOS signals that override all other considerations. For most of us, this remains a relatively rare experience, and the question arises whether less intense signals contribute to satiety when stomach distention is within normal limits.

The stomach is particularly well equipped to monitor its contents because its walls contain very sensitive stretch receptors that influence neural activity in brain structures that are thought to be specifically related to satiety.[133]

The possible contribution of stomach distention to satiety has been studied in two experimental paradigms. One approach has been the addition of nonnutritive but filling materials such as cellulose to the diet. It is typically found in these experiments that animals maintain a relatively constant caloric intake (i.e., continue to eat in spite of an unusual degree of stomach distention) when the percentage of the nonnutritive bulk is small. When it is high, the animals compromise, eating greater quantities than normal but not enough to maintain a positive energy balance.[2] These findings suggest that stomach distention may be a factor only at the extremes of the organism's capabilities.

Such a conclusion is supported by the results of the second group of experiments, which have shown that food injected directly into the stomach shortly before mealtime does not affect subsequent intake unless more than about 20 percent of the normal daily ration is injected.[80] Somewhat more indirect support comes from related experiments that demonstrate that food injected directly into the stomach is rewarding to hungry animals whereas similar injections of nonnutritive bulk are not, and mechanical distention of the stomach brought about by inflation of a balloon is aversive.[109, 84]

Conclusions and Review Questions

The experimental and clinical literature shows rather unequivocally that none of the oral or gastric influences that have been investigated in the past century are essential to the regulation of food intake and the sensation of hunger and satiety. This does not necessarily imply that some or all of these influences may not be important signals under normal conditions or that some as yet undiscovered peripheral signals (such as secretions from the lower GI tract) may not turn out to be essential mediators in the complex feedback system that regulates the organism's energy balance. Even if it turns out to be true that food intake and hunger are controlled directly by regulatory "centers" in the brain, as many current researchers think, this "master control" must somehow be appraised of the state of the organism's energy equation, the current rate of energy loss, and the energy equivalent of the ingested foodstuffs. Many of the related neural or chemical signals undoubtedly arise from peripheral sources, and their identification and study is an important aspect of this field.

1. Historically, what has been the most popular explanation of hunger and satiety?
2. How does Cannon's theory differ from this view?
3. What is the most convincing evidence that one does not need to taste food in order to regulate intake in accordance with the body's energy requirements?
4. It is widely held that the sensation of hunger directly reflects stomach contractions. Can you refute this belief? (You should be able to cite several different lines of evidence).
5. Is there any evidence to rule out an essential role of hormonal influences from the stomach?
6. Is the activity of the stomach and lower GI tract under neural or hormonal control?
7. How does stomach distention affect food intake?
8. How would you summarize the role of oral and gastric influences on hunger and satiety (in no more than three to four sentences)?

CENTRAL REGULATORY MECHANISMS

Historical Perspectives

Some of the pioneering physiologists of the 19th century proposed that food intake must be regulated by control centers in the brain. Magendie,[95] for instance, postulated a neural center somewhere in the brain, which he believed to give rise to periodic hunger sensations quite irrespective of the activity of the stomach or, for that matter, of the organism's energy balance. Subsequent theoreticians[13] improved on the early models by suggesting that the activity of the brain centers might be affected by deprivation-related changes in the composition of the blood as well as by neural influences from the GI tract. The core of this theory—that some changes take place in the blood of deprived animals that directly or indirectly affect a "hunger center" somewhere in the brain—was subsequently accepted by many physiologists and psychologists and continues to play an important role in our thinking today.

Early clinical observations of excessive food intake (hyperphagia) and obesity[45, 42] correlated these symptons with damage to the diencephalic aspects of the base of the brain. This suggested that the postulated "hunger center" might be located in the hypothalamus, and this possibility has given rise to an extensive investigation of its role in hunger and satiety.

Many of the early investigators thought that hypothalamic obesity might be due to a disturbance of pituitary functions. It was not until the development of stereotaxic procedures made it possible to determine the location of lesions precisely that the area responsible for hyperphagia and obesity became localized in the ventromedial hypothalamus anterior to the pituitary gland itself. As we shall see in a moment, remnants of the old controversy remain even today, and an endocrine influence on the hypothalamic obesity seems to be likely after all.

Other areas of the brain have been related to hunger and food intake by some of the early clinical and experimental investigations, but the significance of these observations has only recently been appreciated. For instance, Brown and Schaefer[24] reported 80 years ago that large temporal-lobe lesions produced overeating and obesity in monkeys, but only within the last decade has this interesting finding been further investigated. Similarly, many of the early studies of the functions of the frontal lobe reported that lesions here increased food intake in monkeys by as much as 300 percent,[48] but this source of apparently major influences on food intake is even today not well understood.

In more recent years, a number of "limbic" structures have been related to hunger and the regulation of food intake, but we have not yet learned how the different regions interact. Because we know a good deal more about the hypothalamic "centers," it will be convenient to divide our discussion into hypothalamic and extrahypothalamic influences and to give perhaps unfair weight to the areas where we are most knowledgeable.

Most contemporary theories of hunger follow a model that was first explicitly stated by Eliot Stellar.[141] According to this view, food intake is regulated by two interacting hypothalamic "centers": an excitatory feeding center that is thought to be represented in the lateral hypothalamus, and an inhibitory satiety center believed to be located in the ventromedial hypothalamus (see Figure 9–2). Hormonal as well as neural influences from peripheral as well as central sources are thought to influence hunger and food intake by acting on these hypothalamic centers. The satiety center, for reasons that we will discuss later, is thought to influence hunger indirectly by inhibiting the lateral feeding center. Hunger, according to this hypothesis, is directly proportional to the amount of activity in the lateral hypothalamic feeding center. There is a good deal of experimental support for this appealingly parsimonious hypothalamic theory of hunger, as we shall see in a moment. Recent experiments have raised some problems with this interpretation and suggest that other central mechanisms may play a more important role than the emphasis on hypothalamic centers suggests, but this does not detract from its usefulness as a working model.

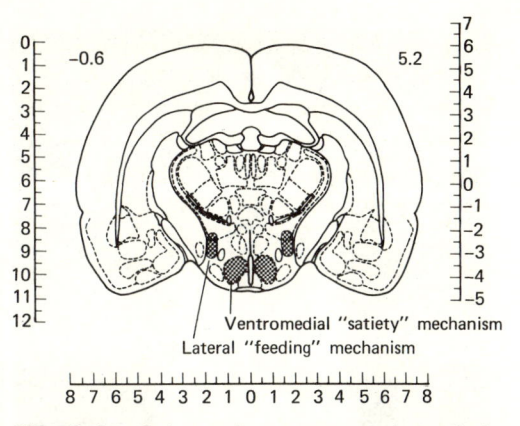

FIG. 9–2. Schematic representation of the lateral excitatory and ventromedial inhibitory aspects of the hypothalamic feeding system.

(After *A stereotaxic atlas of the rat brain.* Louis J. Pellegrino and Anna J. Cushman. Copyright © 1967 Meredith Corporation. By permission of Appleton-Century-Crofts, Educational Division, Meredith Corporation.)

The Hypothalamic Satiety Center

The postulation of a diencephalic satiety center rests primarily on the observation that bilateral lesions in or near the ventromedial nuclei of the hypothalamus produce hyperphagia (overeating) and obesity.[73] The animals eat excessively for a "dynamic" period of 4 to 12 weeks and then return to near normal intake (the so-called "static" phase), which maintains the abnormal body weight but does not add to it (see Figure 9–3). If the intake of an animal in the static phase is limited until its weight drops to prelesion levels, another dynamic period of overeating and rapid weight gain occurs as soon as food is made freely available, suggesting that the lesion-induced disturbance is permanent.[23] Unilateral damage to the ventromedial

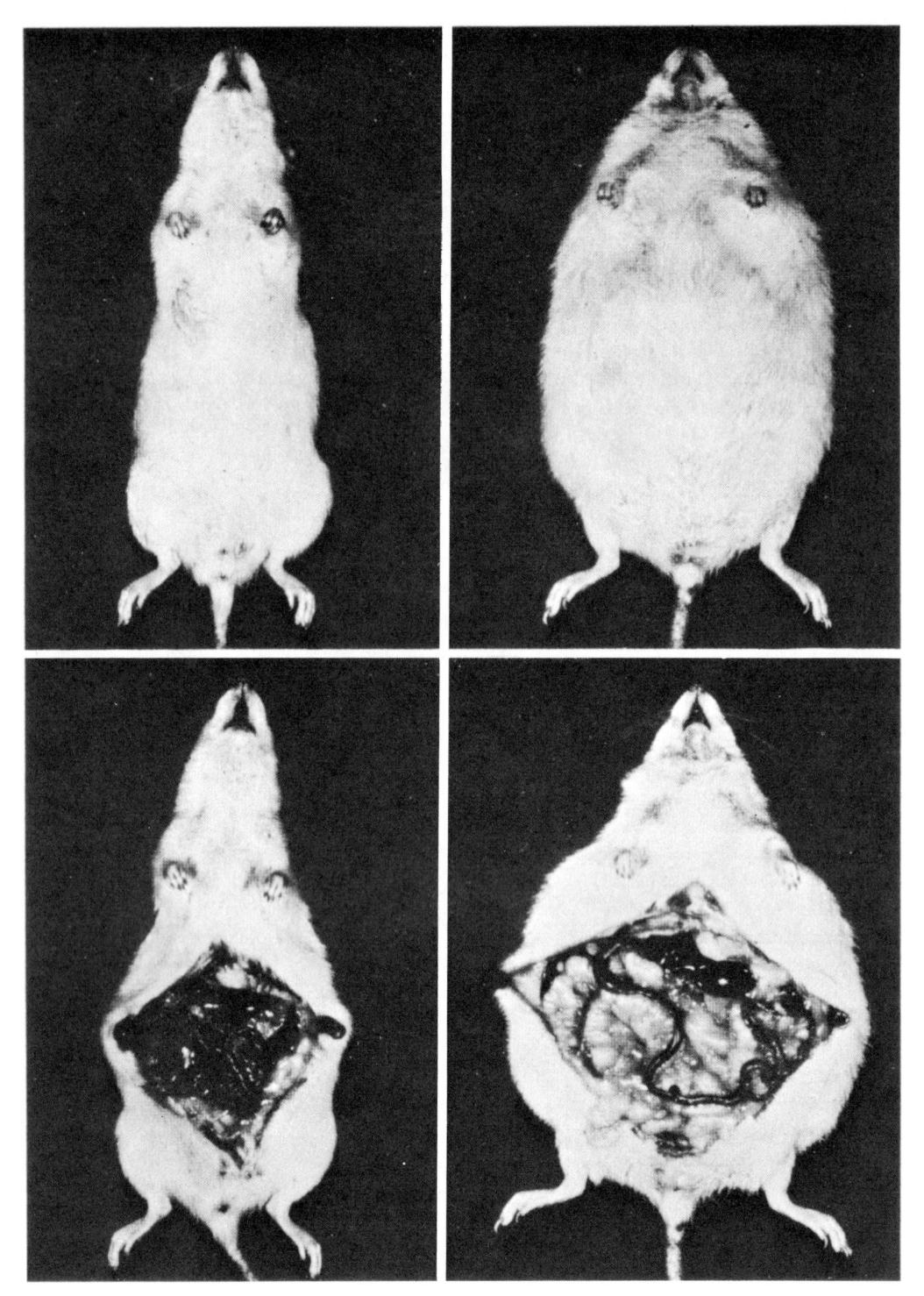

FIG. 9–3. Comparison of one hypothalamic obese rat and one control rat at autopsy, 19 weeks after operation.

(From G. C. Kennedy. The hypothalamic control of food intake in rats. *Proc. Roy. Soc.* (*London*), B, **137**, 1950, 535–548.)

area produces similar but less spectacular and less prolonged changes in food intake.[101]

Since lesions posterior and lateral to the ventromedial nuclei also produce hyperphagia and obesity, it has been suggested that the effects of ventromedial damage may be due to the destruction of cells that project posteriorly to the mesencephalic brainstem.[20] Strong support for this interpretation has recently been obtained.[64] Marked and prolonged hyperphagia, hyperdipsia, and obesity were observed after the posterior fiber connections of the ventromedial hypothalamus were severed by surgical procedures that produced no damage to the cellular components of that region (see Figure 9–4). The lateral connections of the ventromedial region also appear to be directly related to the typical effects of lesions in this area. This was shown

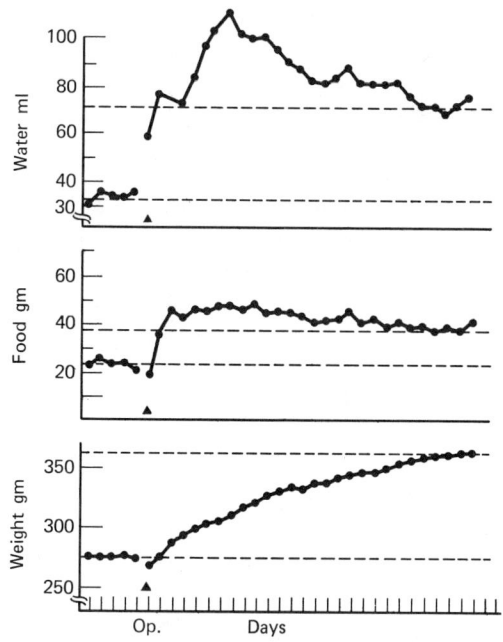

FIG. 9–4. Food and water intake and body weight of 10 animals with transverse knife cuts through the posterior hypothalamus just behind the ventromedial nuclei. (The cuts destroyed all posterior connections except those running in the fornix or in the ventrolateral hypothalamus. The dashed lines indicate the preoperative base line and the terminal level achieved after surgery.)

(From S. P. Grossman. Changes in food and water intake associated with an interruption of the anterior or posterior fiber connections of the hypothalamus. *J. comp. physiol. Psychol.*, **75**, 1971, 23–31. Copyright 1971 by the American Psychological Association, and reproduced by permission.)

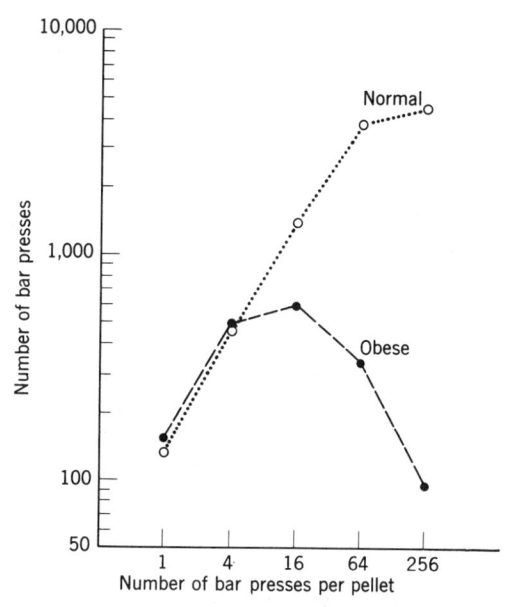

FIG. 9–5. Mean number of bar presses (per 12-hr period) of normal and obese hyperphagic animals as a function of the number of bar presses required to obtain each pellet.

(After P. Teitelbaum. Random and food-directed activity in hyperphagic and normal rats. *J. comp. physiol. Psychol.*, **50**, 1957, 486–490. Copyright 1957 by the American Psychological Association, and reproduced by permission.)

in recent experiments that demonstrated that knife cuts lateral to the ventromedial area that separate it from the lateral feeding center also produce hyperphagia and obesity. No damage to the posterior projections occurred in these experiments.[132]

One peculiar characteristic of animals with ventromedial hypothalamic lesions (or knife cuts lateral or posterior to it) is that they overeat only if a palatable diet is available. These animals are *hypophagic* (i.e., they eat less than normals) when the available food is stale and starve to death in the midst of plenty when the texture or taste of the diet is unpleasant. When required to work for their daily ration, these animals also do not work as hard as normals, even when the rewards are palatable. They do not work at all when the reinforcements are presented only infrequently, on schedules that produce very high rates of responding in normal rats[110, 143] (see Figure 9–5).

The peculiar overreaction to the sensory qualities of the diet or "finickiness" suggests that the animals with ventromedial lesions are not simply more hungry or less sated than normals, as one might expect if the damaged area served exclusively as a satiety center. It has been suggested[149] that in the absence of normal satiety cues, the taste and texture of the diet may become more important. This explanation may not, however, be the whole story because recent experiments[61] have shown that a blockade of ventromedial functions also reduces the animals' willingness to work for water rewards although the daily water intake is unchanged.

A closer look suggests that lesions in the ventromedial area produce changes in a bewildering variety of physiological functions, which may contribute to the observed disturbances of the animals' energy balance. At least some animals with ventromedial lesions become grossly obese without overeating,[117] suggesting that metabolic disturbances must be part of the lesion syndrome. Abnormalities in fat-[15, 16] as well as carbohydrate-[152] metabolism (which, in turn, upset the functions of many glands) have also been described. Most of these changes are probably secondary to the abnormal food intake and cannot be the cause of it, but their possible contribution to obesity is less clear.

Ventromedial lesions also often sharply reduce locomotor activity, and it has been suggested that this reduction in energy expenditure may be one of the principal reasons for the hypothalamic obesity.[72] However, inactivity cannot by itself account for the obesity because in some instances hyperphagia and obesity can be observed in lesioned animals with entirely normal activity levels. Moreover, some animals with grossly abnormal activity levels fail to become obese.[74]

Ventromedial lesions interfere with still another aspect of the body's energy equation. Shortly after surgery, heat production falls precipitously and recovers only gradually to levels that are commensurate with the increasing size of the obese animal.[20] The energy that is normally dissipated in the form of heat is stored as excess fat in these animals and this contributes to the obesity. The magnitude of this influence is, however, typically small, and the time course of the temperature disturbance is considerably shorter than the dynamic phase of the obesity.

Many of the early clinical investigators of hypothalamic obesity thought that a disturbance of pituitary functions and the consequent disruption of the endocrine system might be responsible for the adiposity. Hetherington's pioneering stereotaxic research[72, 75] demonstrated that obesity and hyperphagia can occur in the absence of gross pituitary malfunction. Endocrine influences were consequently ignored until recent experiments[155] demonstrated that female rats show a more marked degree of obesity following ventromedial damage than males with comparable lesions and that the endocrine system of the female rat with ventromedial lesions is grossly abnormal.

It seems, however, that none of the metabolic or endocrine disturbances that are typically seen in the rat after ventromedial hypothalamic lesions can, by itself, be a necessary condition for obesity. Although most ventromedial lesions disturb most or all of these functions, there are instances on record in which each one individually has been spared. This suggests that each of these functions is at least to some extent anatomically distinct and only accidentally part of the "ventromedial syndrome."

Lesions in the ventromedial hypothalamus often increase stomach acidity and induce ulceration of the stomach linings.[44] This is of interest in the context of our discussion because clinical studies of ulcer patients show that the pain associated with gastrointestinal erosion is alleviated by frequent food intake.[50] Although an increase in the size of each meal rather than more frequent meals appears to be the main cause of obesity in animals with ventromedial lesions,[146] part of their abnormal intake may be due to gastric irritation rather than increased hunger.

None of these factors accounts satisfactorily for the paradoxical effects of ventromedial lesions on food intake. Several hypotheses have been advanced but none is entirely satisfying. Teitelbaum[144] has suggested that the amount of body fat may, itself, be regulated and that the ventromedial hypothalamus may contain receptors for some metabolites that signal the current state of the organism's fat deposits. Lesions in this area would then not interfere with food intake or hunger per se but rather with the restraining influence that is normally exercised by excessive deposits. Although this interpretation accounts for a good deal of the experimental literature, it does not explain (a) why food intake should be greatest immediately after surgery when the fat deposits are smallest and (b) why the animals should be finicky and unwilling to work for food rewards.

Miller,[107] on the other hand, suggests that the food motivation of animals with ventromedial lesions might be actually lower than normal and that overeating may be the result of an interference with satiety mechanisms that normally inhibit the feeding center. This is perhaps the most widely accepted interpretation, but it glosses over some aspects of the problem. It does not, for instance, explain how the drop in hunger motivation comes about (unless the feeding center is much more extensive than is currently believed, accidental damage to it can be ruled out as a possible explanation of the hypothesized decrease in hunger) or why the typical pattern of finickiness is seen.

Reynolds[124] has suggested that the ventromedial hypothalamus may have nothing at all to do with food intake or hunger. He explains the overeating and obesity of the animal with ventromedial lesions by suggesting that the lesion may irritate and, in effect, stimulate the adjacent feeding center. This hypothesis is based on the observation that ventromedial lesions that are made with special techniques that minimize the irritative reactions in surrounding tissue do not, in some instances, produce hyperphagia and obesity.[123, 122] This would seem to be an appealingly simple explanation were it not for the fact that some of the nonirritative lesions do produce hyperphagia.[77, 132] Just why some of these lesions do not is one of the more intriguing mysteries of this field.

Some years ago, a quite different possibility occurred to me[61] while I was thinking about the experimental literature that shows that animals with lesions in the ventromedial nucleus are extraordinarily nasty and difficult to handle.[158] It is, of course, possible that diverse functions may be regulated by neural pathways that overlap at some point in the brain, but the effects of ventromedial lesions on food intake are sufficiently peculiar that I decided to investigate the possibility that the change in feeding behavior might be secondary to a general change in "affect." This hypothesis suggests that the lesioned animals may overeat because of a disinhibited reaction to the positive aspects of a palatable diet and undereat because of a similarly disinhibited reaction to the negative aspects of an adulterated food. Their poor performance on intermittently rewarded instrumental tasks could be due to an excessive reaction to nonrewards.

I tested this scheme by observing the animals in a situation in which they worked (pressed a lever) for water as well as food rewards and found that their performance was poor regardless of the nature of the drive or reinforcement. That the animals also overreact to stimuli of other modalities was shown in a subsequent escape-avoidance test in which the lesioned animals learned faster than normals to avoid a very mild shock. I have subsequently found that animals with ventromedial lesions also overreact to the taste properties of water (i.e., they drink more than normals of a nonnutritive sweet solution and less of a slightly bitter solution) and fight more, at least in some circumstances, and I continue to find an interpretation of the hypothalamic hyperphagia in terms of a general disinhibition an attractive alternative.

The hypothesis is supported by the results of earlier experiments that attempted to modify food intake by electrical stimulation of the ventromedial area. Stimulation of this area reduces or inhibits food intake as a satiety-center hypothesis predicts[148] but also inhibits water intake and appears to be aversive as shown by the fact that animals learn to press a lever to avoid it.[85]

The disinhibition hypothesis has some difficulties with reports of electrophysiological studies that suggest that the EEG,[134, 6] as well as the activity of individual cells,[9] of the ventromedial area appear to react to gastric distention and changes in blood sugar. However, aside from the somewhat dubious reliability of some of these electrophysiological observations, it seems quite possible that excessive stomach distention (normal stomach motility did not produce the observed changes) or extreme hyper- or hypoglycemia may themselves be noxious events that affect the suggested affect-related mechanism.

The Lateral Hypothalamic Feeding Center

Animals with bilateral lesions in the lateral hypothalamus at the level of the ventromedial nuclei are aphagic (i.e., do not eat) as well as adipsic (i.e., do not drink).[3, 150] The animals typically do not cooperate in attempts to force-feed and water them, and they die unless food and water are provided by intragastric injection. If the animals with lateral lesions are kept alive by this technique, a gradual recovery of food (but not water) intake regulation occurs.[144] The recovery seems to be partly mediated by tissue surrounding the lesion, since an enlargement of the damaged area in recovered animals produces another period of aphagia. Cortical influences also appear to affect the recovery process, since a brief depression of cortical activity produces a complete and prolonged relapse in the recovered lateral animal.[147]

The pattern of recovery from lateral hypothalamic damage seems to proceed in four distinct phases[148] (see Figure 9–6). During the first stage, the animals refuse foods and water entirely and spit out any food that is placed into their mouths. The duration of this phase is variable but is typically long enough that the animals die of starvation and dehydration unless artificial feeding is instituted. The duration of this first stage of absolute aphagia and adipsia does not seem to correlate well with lesion site within the lateral hypothalamus or the size of the lesion. In the second state, wet and particularly palatable foods such as chocolate or eggnog are accepted in small quantities, but supplementary intragastric feeding is necessary to maintain life. Dry food and water are still absolutely refused, suggesting

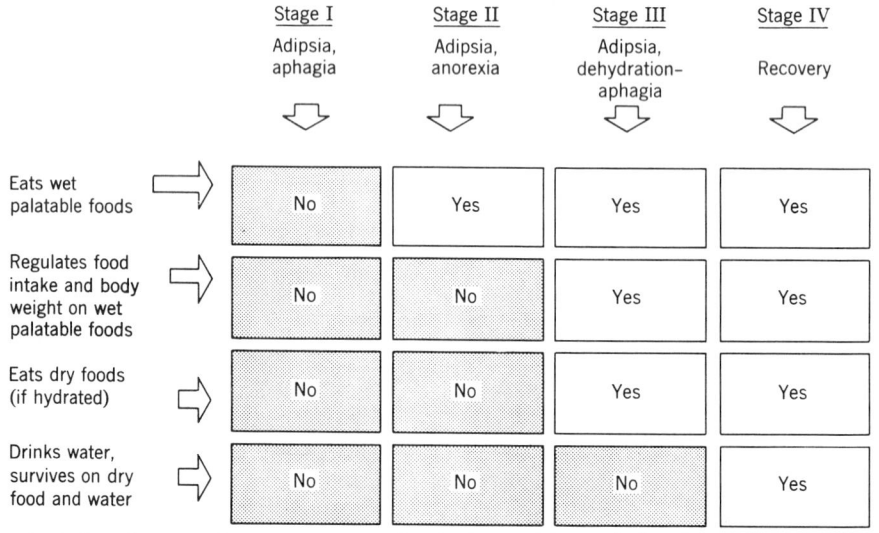

	Stage I Adipsia, aphagia	Stage II Adipsia, anorexia	Stage III Adipsia, dehydration- aphagia	Stage IV Recovery
Eats wet palatable foods	No	Yes	Yes	Yes
Regulates food intake and body weight on wet palatable foods	No	No	Yes	Yes
Eats dry foods (if hydrated)	No	No	Yes	Yes
Drinks water, survives on dry food and water	No	No	No	Yes

FIG. 9–6. Stages of recovery seen in the lateral hypothalamic syndrome. The critical behavioral events are listed on the left.

(From P. Teitelbaum & A. N. Epstein. The lateral hypothalamic syndrome: recovery of feeding and drinking after lateral hypothalamic lesions. *Psychol. Rev.*, **69**, 1962, 74–90. Copyright 1962 by the American Psychological Association, and reproduced by permission.)

that taste rather than hunger motivates the ingestion of the palatable diets.

During the third and perhaps most interesting phase, the animals regulate their caloric intake when wet and palatable foods are available but still refuse dry food and water and die when placed on a standard laboratory diet. These animals work (i.e., press a bar) to obtain liquid food that is injected directly into their stomach,[40] suggesting that taste is no longer essential for the elicitation of feeding behavior. At this stage, adipsia seems to be the primary cause of the remaining disturbance in food intake. If the liquid diet is replaced by dry food, the animals continue to eat for several days but completely refuse water. They eventually become completely dehydrated and cease feeding. This is in marked contrast to the first two stages, in which adequate hydration does not prevent the aphagia. It is interesting that during this third stage of aphagia and adipsia, the animals can be made "hyperphagic" with respect to palatable foods by additional ventromedial lesions.[160]

In the fourth and final recovery stage, rats with lateral hypothalamic lesions maintain a normal regulation of caloric intake and body weight even on a dry-food diet. The "recovered" laterals eventually respond appropriately to dilution of their diet and to a lowering of ambient temperature but do not increase their intake in response to insulin. This suggests that the lateral hypothalamus may contain an essential part of the system that is responsible for reactions to low levels of blood sugar.[41] A permanent deficit in the ability to regulate water intake also remains in "recovered" laterals.[144] We shall discuss this matter in more detail in the next chapter. Fully recovered lateral animals also, somewhat surprisingly, are finicky eaters and die of starvation rather than accept a slightly bitter diet.

It has recently been suggested that the aphagia seen in rats with lateral hypothalamic lesions might not reflect a basic breakdown of neural control over feeding per se but merely a lowering of the set point for weight regulation. This suggestion is based on the surprising finding that the duration of the aphagia and hypophagia can be reduced, often quite dramatically, by starving the animal (and thereby reducing its body weight) prior to lesioning the lateral hypothalamus.[118] These observations may require some revision of our thinking about the hypothalamic influences on feeding behavior, but it seems quite probable that the hypothalamus contains mechanisms concerned not only with weight regulation but, more specifically, with food intake.

Lateral hypothalamic lesions unquestionably produce long-term inhibitory effects on food intake. What is not so clear is whether these effects are due to the destruction of cells that constitute a feeding center rather than the interruption of pathways that interconnect other regions of the brain and happen to course through the hypothalamus. Transection of the medial forebrain bundle (MFB), the major fiber bundle that pervades the lateral hypothalamus, anterior or posterior to the level of the lateral hypothalamic feeding center, does not produce primary effects on food or water intake.[113] However, lesions in the feeding center do produce degeneration in the pallidofugal fiber system,[112] as well as a marked depletion of the neurohumor dopamine in the globus pallidus,[17] and lesions in the globus pallidus, the origin of these fibers, also produce long-lasting aphagia and adipsia.

Recent investigations of the role of pallidofugal connections support the conclusion that the effects of hypothalamic and pallidal lesions on food and water intake are due to an interference with a common system. The principal finding is that surgical knife cuts along the lateral border of the hypothalamus (which do not produce significant direct damage to the cellular components of the hypothalamus or the globus pallidus but interrupt all connections between them) produced prolonged aphagia and adipsia as well as signs of finickiness[66] (see Figure 9–7 and Table 1).

Damage to the midbrain tegmentum, which contains the caudal projections of the pallidofugal fiber system, also produces long-term aphagia and adipsia.[30] Moreover, the

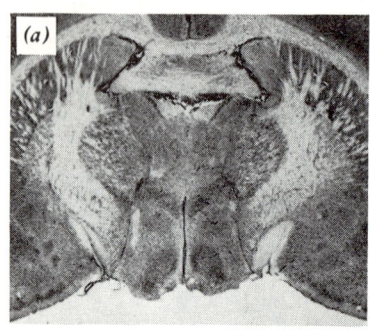

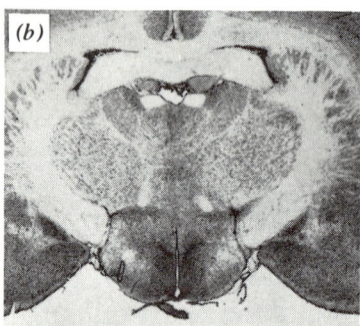

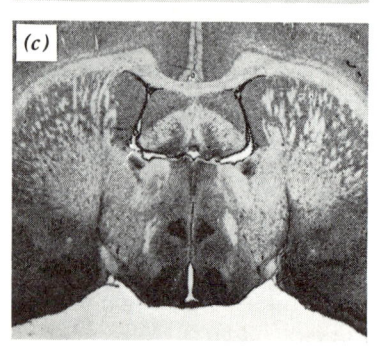

FIG. 9–7. Examples of the histological data from animals with parasagittal knife cuts (*a*) through the medial quadrant of the lateral hypothalamus; (*b*) along the lateral border of the hypothalamus; and (*c*) lateral to the lateral border of the hypothalamus.

(From S. P. Grossman & Lore Grossman. Food and water intake in rats with parasagittal knife-cuts medial or lateral to the lateral hypothalamus. *J. comp. physiol. Psychol.*, **74**, 1971, 148–156. Copyright 1971 by the American Psychological Association, and reproduced by permission.)

mild and temporary disturbances in food and water intake that are seen after a unilateral lateral hypothalamic lesion can be converted into long-term aphagia and adipsia by the addition of a contralateral lesion in the midbrain tegmentum[51] or globus pallidus.[145] It has been suggested in this connection[52] that lateral hypothalamic lesions may not produce long-term effects on food and water intake unless they damage aspects of the internal capsule that carry corticofugal as well as some pallidofugal fibers to the midbrain tegmentum.

Electrical stimulation studies have not helped, so far, to decide between the alternative interpretations of these observations. Some of the earlier studies reported large increments in food intake following electrical stimulation of sites in the lateral hypothalamus, but the effects were often delayed by as much as 24 hours.[25,34] More recently, stimulus-bound feeding (i.e., eating that starts and stops within seconds after the onset and termination of the stimulation) has been observed.[86,106] In some instances, eating begins soon after the onset of stimulation but continues for 10 to 20 minutes after its termination.[137] Stimulation at the same site

TABLE 1. Recovery Pattern of Food and Water Intake in Rats with Parasagittal Knife Cuts in the Medial Third of the Lateral Hypothalamus (Medial Cuts), Along the Lateral Border of the Hypothalamus (Lateral Cuts), and Approximately 0.5–1.0 Mm. Lateral to the Hypothalamus (Far-Lateral Cuts)

Number of Days Before:	Medial Cuts	Lateral Cuts	Far-Lateral Cuts
Acceptance of			
Liquid diet	2–15	14–30	2–6
Pellets	4–8	26–80+	4–13
Powdered food	5–20	40–80+	8–80+
Caloric regulation of			
Liquid diet	4–18	15–80+	3–10
Pellets	80+ [a]	26–80+	4–14
Powdered food	10–80+	80+	8–80+
Regulation of water intake			
With food	10–21 [a]	26–80+	6–14
Without food	14–80+	80+	8–80+

[a] These animals overate on pellets and adjusted water intake accordingly. *Source:*

(From S. P. Grossman & Lore Grossman. Food and water intake in rats with parasagittal knife-cuts medial or lateral to the lateral hypothalamus. *J. comp. physiol. Psychol.*, **74**, 1971, 148–156. Copyright 1971 by the American Psychological Association, and reproduced by permission.)

may elicit feeding when the animal is surrounded by food, and drinking when it happens to be in the vicinity of water. Moreover, prolonged repetition of the stimulation often suffices to change the nature of the response from eating to drinking or vice versa.[154] These observations emphasize how closely interwoven the feeding and drinking systems are in the hypothalamus (as well as in other regions of the brain). They unfortunately do not tell us whether the electrical stimulation may be activating fiber tracts or cells. Moreover, the distribution of stimulation-positive sites appears to be much broader than the traditional limits of the lateral hypothalamic feeding center, suggesting that we may be dealing with projections to or from the feeding center, if such there be.

Morgane[113] has discussed the possibility that the lateral hypothalamus may contain two different pathways that influence hunger motivation in somewhat different ways. He distinguishes (a) a far-lateral region where lesions produce long-term aphagia and adipsia, and stimulation not only elicits food intake but also motivates instrumental behavior such as crossing an electrified grid to gain access to a lever that is programmed to produce food rewards of various reinforcement schedules and (b) a midlateral region, closer to the ventromedial nuclei, where lesions produce only a temporary inhibition of food and water intake, and stimulation elicits food ingestion but not food-rewarded instrumental behavior. The far-lateral region is thought to carry out primary metabolic functions via the pallidofugal fiber system, whereas the midlateral region is believed to exercise motivational influences via the medial forebrain bundle. This distinction is based largely on the observation that lesions in the medial forebrain bundle anterior or posterior to the feeding regions do not interfere with feeding responses to electrical stimulation of either region but do abolish the instrumental behavior previously elicited by stimulation of the far-lateral region.

Chemical stimulation studies[57, 58] support the view that the lateral hypothalamus contains cell bodies that are related to feeding behavior. They also suggest, in agreement with the results of electrical stimulation studies, that the distribution of these cells is not confined to the area that is traditionally defined as the feeding center. In a series of experiments that were designed to demonstrate the functional independence of the hunger and thirst centers (lesions as well as electrical stimulation of the lateral hypothalamus almost invariably affect food and water intake concurrently), I observed that microinjections of an adrenergic neurohumor (norepinephrine), which may act as a transmitter in the central nervous system, into many hypothalamic sites elicited feeding in sated rats. The effect was prolonged (up to 40 minutes) and the animals sometimes consumed as much as half their normal daily intake during the poststimulation period. Norepinephrine injections into the lateral hypothalamus also produced a rise in blood sugar as well as a fall in body temperature, suggesting that the injections may have activated a general mechanism for the correction of nutritional deficits.[108] Injections of a different, cholinergic neurohumor (acetylcholine), which acts as a transmitter in the parasympathetic nervous system, into many of the same hypothalamic sites elicits drinking (see Figure 9–8).

Of particular importance in the context of our discussion is the observation[58] that the injection of drugs that specifically interfere with the action of adrenergic neurohumors inhibited food intake in deprived animals and prevented feeding responses to norepinephrine injections. The administration of agents that specifically interfere with cholinergic transmission inhibited the drinking response to acetylcholine. Since these drugs are thought to act at synaptic junctions, these data suggest that the hypothalamus may indeed contain cells that are related to feeding. However, a mapping of the injection sites showed many positive points outside the lateral hypothalamus, and more recent experiments[18, 31] show that many can be found outside the hypothalamus itself, suggesting that these cells may be the terminal projections of a diffuse fiber system.

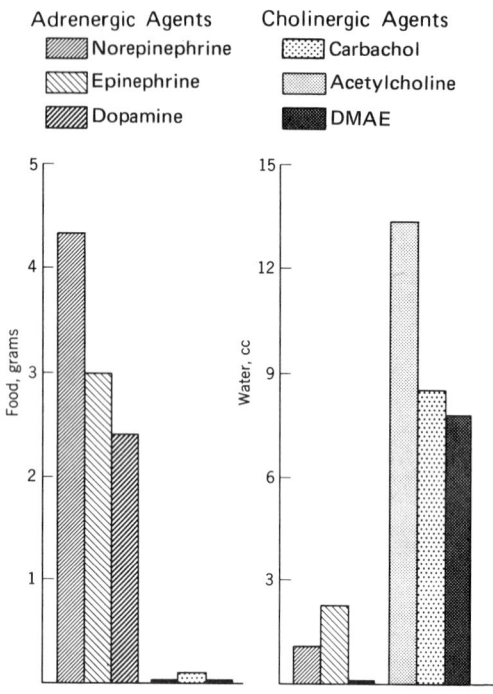

FIG. 9-8. Effects of adrenergic and cholinergic stimulation of the hypothalamus on food and water intake of sated animals during a 1-hr poststimulation period.

(From S. P. Grossman. Behavioral effects of direct chemical stimulation of central nervous system structures. *Int. J. Neuropharmacol.*, 3, 1964, 45-58. Permission granted for Pergamon Press copyright.)

Recent extensions of this work have indicated that both the medial and the lateral components of the hypothalamic feeding system may be adrenergically mediated in the rat. Some peripheral neurons are selectively sensitive to different types of adrenergic neurohumors, and it has been hypothesized that there may be two quite different varieties for which some cells may develop specific receptor sites. The two varieties have been called alpha- and beta-adrenergic substances. The recent elegant work of Leibowitz[87, 88] suggests that the lateral hypothalamus may contain neurons that normally inhibit eating and that these cells are selectively sensitive to beta-adrenergic agents, whereas the medial hypothalamus contains neurons that normally stimulate eating and are selectively sensitive to alpha-adrenergic agents (see Table 2). Microinjections of beta-adrenergic agents into the lateral hypothalamus suppress eating, presumably by inhibiting cells in the lateral excitatory portion of the feeding system. Injections of alpha-adrenergic agents into the medial hypothalamus elicit feeding by inhibiting inhibitory or "satiety" influences. The system is internally consistent. Chemicals that selectively interfere with the action of alpha-adrenergic agonists reduce feeding, and drugs that block the action of beta-adrenergic agonists elicit eating. The observed pattern of results suggests that the medial and lateral portions of the hypothalamic feeding system may be reciprocally interconnected in such a way that activation of the ventromedial region results in the excitation of beta-adrenergic receptors in the lateral hypothalamus that inhibit cells that normally exert facilitatory influences on feeding. Stimulation of the lateral region, conversely, results in the activation of alpha-adrenergic receptors in the medial hypothalamus that inhibit cells that normally exert inhibitory "satiety" influences.

The results of the chemical stimulation experiments are particularly interesting because subsequent investigations (see below) have suggested that the pharmacological "coding" that permits selective activation of the hypothalamic mechanisms may also characterize many extrahypothalamic pathways that are related to feeding or drinking behavior. It is, however, not clear to what extent these observations can be generalized to species other than the rat. Some experiments suggest that both feeding and drinking may be cholinergically mediated in the rabbit[139] and adrenergically mediated in the monkey.[135]

There is at this moment no question that food as well as water intake are affected by damage as well as electrical or chemical stimulation of the hypothalamus. However, questions have been raised concerning the possibility that these effects may be related to sensory or motor rather than motivational factors. More specifically, one can ask whether an animal with lateral hypothalamic lesions may experience normal hunger and thirst but find it impossible to chew or swallow—or, conversely, whether animals eat or drink following electrical or chemical stimulation not because they are hungry or

TABLE 2. Localization of the Alpha-adrenergic "Feeding" Receptors and the Beta-adrenergic "Satiety" Receptors Within the Hypothalamus

Category of adrenergic drug	Site of hypothalamic injection		
	Medial ⟵⟶ Lateral		
	VMA	PA	LA
1. Alpha agonist: Stimulates alpha "feeding" receptors	↑	↑	O
2. Alpha antagonist: Blocks alpha "feeding" receptors	↓	↓	O
3. Beta agonist: Stimulates beta "satiety" receptors	O	↓	↓
4. Beta antagonist: Blocks beta "satiety" receptors	O	↑	↑

Conclusions:

a. Alpha and beta receptors are *inhibitory*
b. Alpha receptors inhibit medial "satiety" cells ⟶ *increase* eating
   Beta receptors inhibit lateral "feeding" cells ⟶ *decrease* eating

Summary of the localization results showing the effects on food intake (increase ↑; decrease ↓; no effect O) of adrenergic and adrenolytic drugs injected directly into one of these three hypothalamic sites: the ventromedial area (VMA), the medio-lateral perifornical area (PA), and the lateral area (LA).

(From Sarah F. Leibowitz. Central adrenergic receptors and the regulation of hunger and thirst. *Res. Publ., Ass. Res. nerv. ment. Dis.*, 1972, in press.)

thirsty but because we elicit chewing and swallowing motions and the animals eat or drink perhaps because of conditioned associations. These questions are not as far-fetched as they may seem. Many motor pathways course through the lateral hypothalamus (the pallidofugal fiber system is itself part of the extrapyramidal motor system), and lateral hypothalamic lesions markedly change the chemistry of cells in extrapyramidal relay stations such as the caudate nucleus. Catatonia (a motor disturbance that is characterized by the assumption and maintenance of abnormal postures) is also typically seen after such lesions.

The literature nonetheless suggests that we may be dealing with primarily motivation effects. Electrical as well as chemical stimulation elicits previously learned instrumental responses and motivates the acquisition of novel food-rewarded conditioned responses.[161,57] Furthermore, there appears to be a negative correlation between the efficacy of hypothalamic lesions in producing aphagia and catatonia, the more anterior lesions producing the most prolonged aphagia whereas more posterior lesions produce the most pronounced catatonia.[12] Furthermore, animals that have learned to feed themselves intragastrically by pressing a lever show complete aphagia and adipsia following lateral lesions although no chewing or swallowing motions are required.[128] Recent investigations of the effects of surgical interruption of the lateral connections of the hypothalamus observed marked motor deficits, but these disappeared long before any recovery of food or water intake occurred.[66] It would thus seem that lateral hypothalamic lesions may produce primary motivational effects on food intake, although possible contributions of specific deficits in ingestive behaviors such as swallowing and chewing cannot be completely dismissed.

Extrahypothalamic Influences

Early clinical interest in hypothalamic obesity for many decades focused the research as well as theory in this field on the regulatory functions of the hypothalamus. This trend was strengthened when the lateral feeding "center" was discovered, and the emphasis on hypothalamic mechanisms continues to some extent today. Lesions as well as electrical or chemical stimulation of a number of extrahypothalamic structures do, however, affect food intake, often quite dramatically, and it is becoming increasingly apparent that food intake and hunger are regulated by a complex system of interrelated "centers" and pathways. Since the extrahypothalamic components of this system have not been investigated very thoroughly, we can do little more at this point than describe the effects of lesions and stimulation in some of the apparently more important structures.

Globus Pallidus and Midbrain Tegmentum

We have already discussed the experiments that relate two extrahypothalamic areas, the globus pallidus and its projection in the midbrain tegmentum, to feeding behavior. Lesions in both of these areas produce inhibitory effects on feeding as well as drinking behavior that appear to be as complete and prolonged as those seen after lateral hypothalamic damage.[30, 112] Recent investigations have, moreover, suggested that the same pathways may be involved, since a unilateral lesion in the midbrain[51] or globus pallidus[145] appears to complement a contralateral lateral hypothalamic lesion in such a way that these asymmetrical combinations reproduce the prolonged effects of bilateral hypothalamic damage. Whether the lateral hypothalamus contains a feeding center or merely pathways that interconnect the globus pallidus and midbrain tegmentum is not certain at the moment.

Temporal Lobe and Amygdala

One of the first investigations of temporal-lobe functions[24] reported 80 years ago that damage to this area of the brain produced hyperphagia in monkeys. Often large, although typically temporary, increases in food intake have more recently been reported in many species, including man.[47, 46]

In the last decade much research has attempted to localize the feeding-related aspects of the temporal lobe more precisely, and there is now some agreement that they are probably concentrated in the amygdala and, perhaps, the pyriform cortex immediately adjacent to it. Excitatory as well as inhibitory influences appear to be diffusely represented in this complex of nuclei, and there is as yet little consensus with respect to their precise localization. Aphagia or hypophagia have been reported primarily following damage to anterior portions of the amygdala.[53] More posterior lesions tend to produce opposite, facilitatory effects, but the resulting hyperphagia often persists only for a few weeks.[4, 65]

Electrical stimulation of the posterior amygdala depresses both food and water intake in deprived animals. A smaller depression of food (but not water) intake occurs during

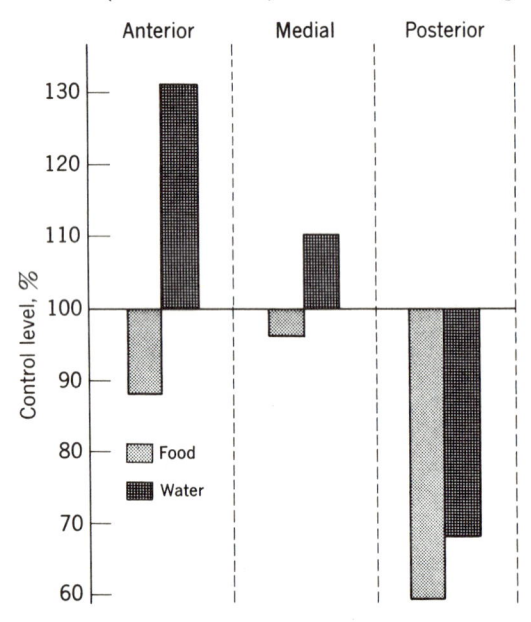

FIG. 9–9. Food and water intake of deprived animals during 1 hr of electrical stimulation of the ventral amygdala. Data are expressed as a percentage of the average intake on control tests without the electrical stimulation.

(From S. P. Grossman & Lore Grossman. Food and water intake following lesions or electrical stimulation of the amygdala. *Amer. J. Physiol.*, **205**, 1963, 761–765.)

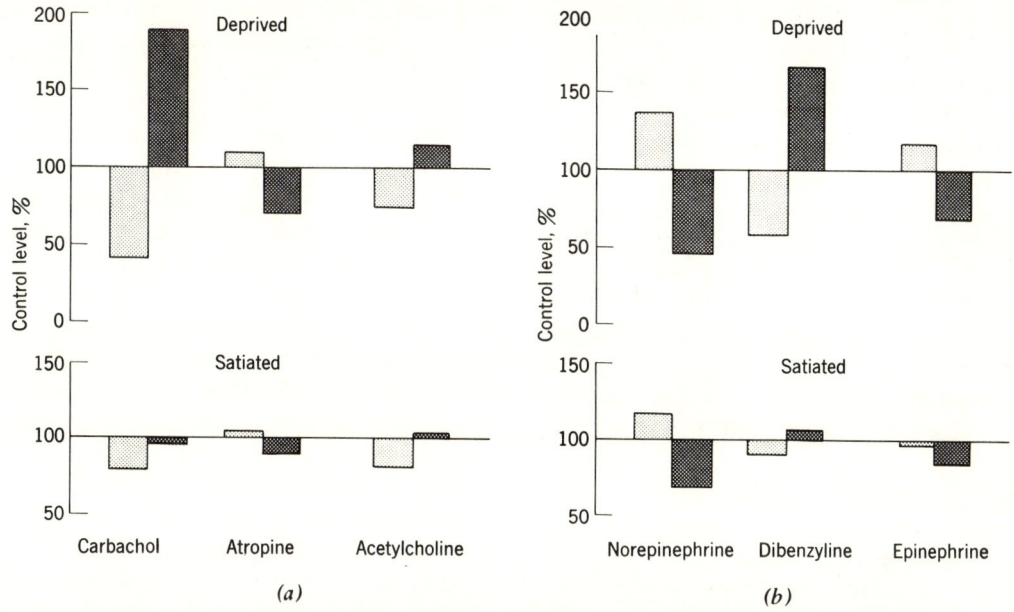

FIG. 9–10. (a) Average bar-pressing performance for food (gray) and water (black) after cholinergic stimulation (carbachol, acetylcholine) or blockade (atropine) of the ventral amygdala. The data are expressed as a percentage of the average pre- and poststimulation control level. (b) After adrenergic stimulation (norepinephrine, epinephrine) or blockade (dibenzyline).

(From S. P. Grossman. Behavioral effects of chemical stimulation of the ventral amygdala. *J. comp. physiol. Psychol.*, **57**, 1964, 29–36. Copyright 1964 by the American Psychological Association, and reproduced by permission.)

anterior stimulation[65] (see Figure 9–9). This inhibitory effect on food (but not water) intake disappears following lesions in the ventromedial hypothalamus.[159]

Chemical stimulation of the amygdala[59] does not elicit food or water intake in sated rats but potentiates feeding and drinking in deprived animals. The same neurohumor (norepinephrine) that elicits feeding when injected into the lateral hypothalamus facilitates feeding as well as food-rewarded instrumental behavior when applied to the amygdaloid complex. The cholinergic neurohumor (acetylcholine) that elicits drinking when applied to the hypothalamus potentiates drinking and water-rewarded instrumental behavior when applied to the amygdala (see Figure 9–10).

Hippocampal Formation

Damage to the hippocampus often produces hyperphagia as well as hyperdipsia, but the effects are typically transitory and not very large.[46,37] A number of experiments have reported apparently more permanent facilitatory effects on food-rewarded instrumental behavior.[37,116] Hippocampal seizure activity, on the other hand, does not seem to interfere with food-rewarded discrimination learning.[67] It is difficult to judge at the moment to what extent the results of these experiments may be specifically related to hunger because hippocampal lesions also typically induce hyperactivity, hyperreactivity, perseverative tendencies, and memory deficits, which may affect behavior in all of the instrumental test situations. (See our discussion of the role of the hippocampus in emotional behavior and in learning and memory.)

Frontal Cortex

Frontal lobotomy produces overeating in man[83] as well as other mammals.[157] Even relatively small lesions in many aspects of the frontal lobe produce hyperphagia and polyphagia (the ingestion of inedible substances).[125] In some instances, these effects are only temporary. The hyperphagia does not always produce obesity because many frontal-cortex lesions produce a sharp increase in locomotor activity, and this rise in energy expenditure cancels the excessive food intake.[129] That some portions of the frontal lobe may also exert facilitatory influences on food intake is suggested by the observation that small lesions occasionally produce aphagia.[5] Electrical as well as chemical stimulation of the frontal cortex elicits sniffing, licking, chewing, and sometimes, eating.[94]

Thalamus

Lesions in the medial thalamus interfere with taste sensations and, paradoxically, produce hyperphagia. The two effects appear to be independent, since slightly higher lesions do not produce the hyperphagia, although taste sensations appear to be lost completely.[130] Electrical stimulation of some anterior thalamic nuclei elicits feeding in sated animals. Sometimes such stimulation produces local seizure activity, which is followed by ravenous eating.[96]

Pharmacologically Defined Pathways

We have already mentioned that the distribution of norepinephrine-sensitive "feeding" points is not restricted to the lateral hypothalamic feeding center as defined on the basis of lesion studies. The initial reports of the phenomenon[56, 57] demonstrated that positive placements extended from the perifornical area ventrolaterally to the zona incerta dorsomedially. In more recent experiments a broader distribution of positive points, which includes a number of extrahypothalamic areas, has been demonstrated. Just how extensive this adrenergic feeding system is is still the subject of debate. Some investigators[31] have observed small feeding responses to adrenergic stimulation of most components of the limbic system, including the hypothalamus, preoptic area, medial thalamus, medial septal area, cingulate gyrus, and hippocampus. Others[18] report more substantial feeding responses to stimulation of a more restricted list of structures, including the anterior hypothalamus, zona incerta, ventral thalamus, and lateral septal area.

Perhaps as interesting as the distribution of positive placements are some of the negative sites. Microinjections of adrenergic or cholinergic drugs into the midbrain tegmentum, where lesions produce long-term aphagia and adipsia, do not elicit food or water intake in sated animals or modify feeding or drinking in deprived animals. Their performance of food-rewarded instrumental behaviors is typically affected by both types of drugs, but this reaction appears to be related to a shift in general reactivity or arousal rather than hunger motivation per se.[62]

Conclusions

The classic view of the central regulation of hunger and food intake postulates an excitatory lateral hypothalamic feeding center and an inhibitory ventromedial satiety center. Both receive hormonal as well as neural signals from peripheral as well as other central sources. The satiety center affects food intake and hunger by a direct braking action on the lateral feeding center, and hunger motivation is therefore directly proportional to the activity of this center.

What, then, are the problems that we have encountered in our discussion of the research literature? First, there is some doubt about the specificity of the inhibitory ventromedial influence. Damage to this region seems to influence behavior in a variety of situations, and it appears possible that the hyperphagia that is often seen after ventromedial lesions may at least in part be due to disturbances not specifically related to satiety. Second, the lateral hypothalamic feeding center may consist not of a grouping of cells but of fibers that interconnect the globus pallidus and midbrain tegmentum.

Recent reports of the effects of chemical stimulation suggest the need for further modifications of the model. Microinjections of alpha-adrenergic agonists into the medial hypothalamus of rats elicit feeding in sated rats and increase the intake of deprived animals, whereas similar injections of beta-adrenergic agonists into the lateral hypothalamus inhibit food intake specifically. The pattern of drug effects suggests that the medial and lateral portions of the hypothalamic feeding system may be reciprocally related in such a way that stimulation of the lateral region results in the activation of alpha-adrenergic receptors in the medial hypothalamus and thus inhibits cells that normally exert inhibitory or "satiety" influences on feeding. Stimulation of the medial region conversely results in activation of beta-adrenergic receptors in the lateral hypothalamus and thereby inhibits cells that normally exert facilitatory effects on feeding.

The extensive distribution of sites that respond positively to chemical stimulation has prompted renewed interest in the literature, which indicates that feeding behavior is often modified by lesions in many extrahypothalamic structures. A study that used "roving" electrodes to investigate the effects of electrical stimulation at over 6000 brain sites[127] shows a similarly broad distribution of the feeding system and suggests that the concept of feeding or satiety "centers" may not be very useful. Feeding or feeding-related behaviors were elicited from almost all portions of the limbic system in this experiment, and a stochastic analysis of the distribution of positive points failed to demonstrate significant clustering (i.e., the probability of obtaining a feeding response from any area never reached one or zero, and fully 85 percent of the positive sites were outside the lateral hypothalamus). These observations suggest that we may have to trade the appealingly simple notion of autonomous hypothalamic "centers" for a more complex concept that includes neural pathways that appear to be diffusely represented in many subcortical as well as some cortical areas.

Review Questions

1. State Stellar's hypothalamic theory of hunger.

2. Summarize the principal evidence for a ventromedial satiety "center."

3. Describe the feeding behavior of animals with bilateral lesions in the ventromedial hypothalamus.

4. What are some possible explanations of their apparently paradoxical behavior?

5. Why do animals with ventromedial lesions become obese?

6. What are the effects of electrical stimulation of the ventromedial hypothalamus?

7. Describe the electrophysiological changes that can be recorded from the ventromedial hypothalamus that may be related to hunger or satiety.

8. Describe the feeding behavior of animals with lateral hypothalamic lesions. (Include a description of the recovery process.)

9. What parts of the brain seem to be responsible for the recovery from lateral lesions?

10. Describe the effects of electrical stimulation in the lateral hypothalamus.

11. Describe Morgane's proposal of distinct metabolic and motivational feeding systems in the lateral hypothalamus.

12. Describe the effects of chemical stimulation and inhibition in the hypothalamus on food intake.

13. What evidence can you cite to support the contention that the effects of lesions or stimulation in the lateral hypothalamus affect motivational rather than motor functions?

14. List four extrahypothalamic sites where lesions produce hyperphagia.

15. List four extrahypothalamic sites where lesions produce aphagia.

16. Describe the effects of electrical and chemical stimulation of some of the extrahypothalamic sites where lesions modify food intake.

17. Discuss the effects of chemical stimulation of the amygdala.

THE CORRELATION BETWEEN HUNGER AND ENERGY NEEDS

Some of the early central theories of hunger proposed that the activity of some "hunger center" in the brain might have a built-in periodicity such that every n number of hours we experience hunger. This would permit a crude regulation of intake, provided food was always freely available every time the hunger center became active and no unusual energy demands were made between meals. We have seen that the energy balance of man as well as most lower organisms must be regulated by much more sophisticated mechanisms because food intake varies systematically, not only as a function of time since the last meal, but also with the quantity and quality of that meal, physical activity during the interim, environmental temperature, and the like. These observations suggest that the central "hunger center" or "centers" must somehow monitor energy expenditure as well as energy-, rather than simply food-intake. Perhaps the most interesting question in the area of hunger research concerns the mechanisms by which the central regulatory centers are appraised of the current state of the organism's energy balance.

We have already discussed one potential messenger system—the neural feedback from the mouth and stomach. This system undoubtedly contributes information to the central regulatory centers, at least under some circumstances. It cannot, as we have seen, be an essential cog in the machinery because food intake is regulated quite adequately when this neural feedback is eliminated. The possible contribution of lower portions of the digestive tract have not yet been adequately studied, but it seems improbable that the energy equivalent of the diet or the energy expenditure of the organism could be metered here. Nonetheless, further study of these influences is needed before we can entirely dismiss neural feedback from the GI tract.

These considerations suggest that the essential messenger system may be chemical rather than neural—that is, the central regulatory mechanisms may respond directly to the concentration of nutrients or some of their metabolites in the bloodstream. That this might be true was suggested by the results of some early experiments, which demonstrated that the transfusion of blood from a starving dog induced stomach contractions in a sated animal[90] as well as by more recent experiments that show that blood transfusions from a sated rat decrease the intake of a deprived animal.[33] What we do not as yet know is what constituent of the blood is responsible for these results.

One look at the requirements such a messenger must meet rules out many potential prospects. The periodicity of hunger and food intake in most species is quite short, and regulatory compensations for unusual energy losses seem to occur almost instantaneously. The chemical messenger must thus show rapid fluctuations that are proportional to energy expenditure and intake. The metabolism of fats and proteins is too slow to meet these requirements. Most investigators have therefore concentrated their attention on the carbohydrate metabolism, which is relatively rapid and operates with minimal reserves (an essential requirement if energy losses are to show up rapidly). The body's carbohydrate stores are rapidly depleted during fasting or increased energy expenditure. Since the availability of carbohydrates determines the rate of glycogen synthesis from body proteins as well as fat utilization, prompt adjustments of the carbohydrate levels is essential to survival. Moreover, brain cells use glucose almost exclusively and deteriorate rapidly when the blood-glucose level falls below some minimal level. These considerations suggest that the carbohydrate metabolism, particularly blood sugar, may be one of the essential messengers that keep the brain informed about the current status of the body's energy balance. A large and not always entirely consistent literature concerning this possibility exists.

Glucostatic Mechanisms

A formal glucostatic theory of hunger was first proposed by Jean Mayer. The original version of this theory suggested that some regulatory center(s) in the brain might contain glucoreceptors that are sensitive to the level of sugar in the blood and initiate feeding whenever its absolute level falls below some minimal value. It soon became apparent that this theory could not account for the fact that food intake and hunger are high under some unusual circumstances even though the concentration of sugar in the blood is high. Many diabetic patients, for instance, overeat in spite of abnormally high blood-sugar levels. Food intake also often continues after a prolonged period of fasting even when blood sugar has risen to very high levels.

These considerations led Mayer[99, 100] to suggest that the absolute level of sugar in the blood might not always adequately reflect its availability to the glucoreceptors because glucose must cross the cell membrane before it can be used and metered. This transmembrane transport requires a series of chemical reactions that may, under some conditions, be retarded so that the glucoreceptor takes a low reading even though glucose levels are high. This led to a modification of the glucostatic theory, which now states that hunger and food intake are proportional to the glucose *utilization* by the central glucoreceptors. Under most conditions the rate of utilization is, in turn, directly proportional to the availability (i.e., absolute concentration) of sugar in the blood and thus reflects the organism's requirements. Under some pathological conditions, this proportionality breaks down and food-intake regulation is disrupted. Mayer further proposed that the difference between the concentration of sugar in the arteries that supply the brain and the concentration in the venous return from the brain (A-V difference) might be a good measure of central glucose utilization (although it is not specifically a measure of glucose utilization by the postulated glucoreceptors).

The glucostatic theory of hunger very elegantly solves some problems that beset other theoretical schemes. Energy expenditure, whether due to physical activity, low environmental temperatures, or simply fasting, is reflected promptly in the body's sugar reserves. Similarly, all forms of nutritious and digestible foods restore the sugar reserves. Thus, one relatively simple mechanism seems to take care of what appeared to be a very difficult problem. The theory has consequently enjoyed a good deal of interest and support although the experimental evidence for it is not entirely satisfying, as we shall see in a moment. Before we survey some of the relevant findings, I would like to point out that the elegance of the proposed feedback system is potentially misleading. Many species, including cats, dogs, and under some circumstances man, eat an entire meal in a period of time that is much too short to permit any significant absorption of nutrients from the gastrointestinal tract. Food intake stops and satiety occurs long before the blood sugar begins to increase. It is possible to circumvent this problem by postulating conditioned responses to stimuli that are normally associated with eating, but this introduces requirements that are not met by the glucostatic theory itself. Satiety presents a problem for all existing theories of hunger because the known chemical mechanisms are too slow, and it is difficult to understand how the neural mechanisms, quite aside from being apparently dispensable, could meter the caloric value of the diet. Let us turn, then, to some experiments that have investigated the role of blood sugar in hunger itself.

Intravenous injections of glucose decrease gastric motility. The administration of insulin (a hormone that lowers blood sugar) increases stomach as well as duodenal contractions (see Figure 9–11) and produces sensations of hunger in man.[26, 121] However, hypoglycemia (i.e., a low blood-sugar level) is under some circumstances associated with a decrease in stomach motility,[120] and the normal activity of the gastrointestinal tract does not correlate very well with the level of blood sugar,[114] suggesting that glucose does not regulate food intake primarily by a direct action of peripheral gastric mechanisms.

The glucostatic theory is quite handsomely supported by clinical as well as experimental observations of the effects of insulin on food intake and hunger. When this hormone is administered in compounds that prevent its rapid absorption, food intake increases markedly, sometimes to more than twice the normal level. This effect seems to be directly related to the insulin effect on blood sugar, since other procedures for the induction of hypoglycemia are also effective in raising

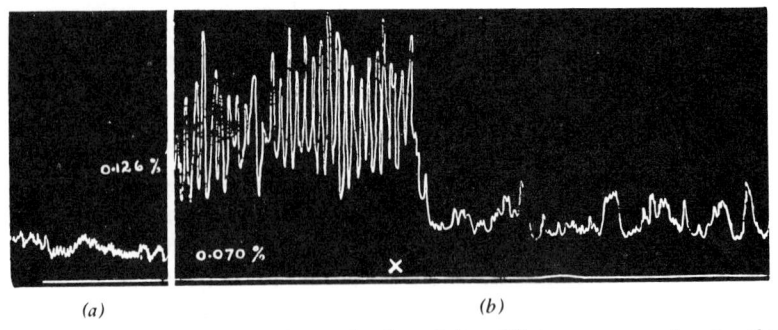

FIG. 9–11. Records of gastrointestinal activity. Water manometer tracing of gastric "hunger contractions." (a) Before insulin injections, blood sugar 0.126. (b) 90 min after injection of 40 units of insulin, blood sugar 0.070. x, intravenous injection of 10 grams glucose.

(From E. Bulatão & A. J. Carlson. Contribution to the physiology of the stomach. Influence of experimental changes in blood sugar level on gastric hunger contractions. *Amer. J. Physiol.*, **69**, 1924, 107–115.)

food intake.[93] The insulin effect is seen after stomach denervation, suggesting, once more, that changes in glucose concentration do not affect food intake because of peripheral effects.[55]

Specific support for Mayer's hypothesis that feeding may be related to glucose utilization rather than simply glucose availability was obtained in some recent experiments that demonstrated that a glucose analogue that decreases intracellular glucose utilization in the brain increased feeding in the rat as well as the monkey.[136]

If Mayer's hypothesis is correct, a rise in blood sugar (hyperglycemia) produced by intravenous injections of glucose should induce satiety and stop food intake. A number of investigators have reported a reduction in food intake following glucose injections, but the magnitude of the effect has been disappointingly small.[79, 102]

More substantial support for a glucostatic theory of hunger can be derived from the clinical observation that calorically adequate diets produce large arteriovenous (A-V) glucose differences, which presumably indicate high levels of central glucose utilization and satiety, whereas low calorie diets produce only small A-V differences.[98]

Support for the suggestion that glucoreceptors may be present in the hypothalamic feeding or satiety centers can be adduced from a variety of observations. The first of these concerns the fact that the administration of a combination of gold (which is very poisonous) and glucose, called gold-thioglucose (GTG), produces damage to the central nervous system that appears to be most severe in the area of the ventromedial hypothalamus. Most species do not survive such injections but one, the mouse, does and becomes markedly obese.[97] Since other gold compounds do not show this selective affinity for the ventromedial hypothalamus, it would seem that the GTG concentrates there because glucose is preferentially attracted to this site. It has recently been shown that fiber connections between the medial and lateral hypothalamus degenerate following gold-thioglucose injections, further supporting Mayer's hypothesis.[11] A special affinity of glucose for the ventromedial hypothalamus has also been shown in experiments that demonstrate that radioactively labeled glucose concentrates in this region.[8]

The glucostatic theory is supported, to some extent, by electrophysiological investigations that have shown that experimentally induced hyperglycemia increases the EEG activity of the ventromedial hypothalamus and slightly decreases the activity of the lateral hypothalamic region. Hypoglycemia produces opposite although much smaller and more variable effects.[6, 7] Recordings of the activity of single cells in these areas also show a correlation between glucose utilization and unit activity. The correlation is typically positive for neurons in the ventromedial area and negative for units in the lateral region[36] (see Figure 9-12).

Given this apparently impressive array of experimental support for a glucostatic theory of hunger, why do we persist in searching for other, perhaps complementary, mechanisms? Aside from the nagging problem of satiety, there are some soft spots in the experimental evidence that supports this theory in general. Most disturbing, perhaps, is the fact that glucose injections that raise the blood sugar to rather high levels produce only small effects on food intake. Furthermore, the correlations between hunger and measures of central glucose utilization, although positive, are far from perfect. Even the apparently strong support that the insulin experiments provide is not unequivocal, since insulin does not increase general glucose utilization in the brain.[76] Epinephrine, which produces hyperglycemia and reduces appetite, similarly does not affect the level of overall glucose utilization in the brain. Mayer[100] has countered these observations by suggesting that the central glucoreceptors of the feeding system may not act like other brain cells with respect to these drugs. There is, however, no independent experimental support for this suggestion, and alternatives (such as the metering of metabolites other than sugar) may have to be considered.

It should be clear in this connection that the other sources of support for the glucostatic theory are also open to question. Goldthioglucose destroys many different regions of the brain, suggesting not only that glucoreceptors are not unique to the hypothalamic feeding centers, but also that the drug's effects on feeding and fat deposition may not be as unique as one might wish. Similarly, none of the electrophysiological investigations have shown that the recorded EEG or single-cell responses to blood-sugar changes are peculiar to the hypothalamus or in any way directly related to hunger or food intake. Alternative interpretations (such as the possibility that hypoglycemia may have a general debilitating effect and hyperglycemia a general excitatory action) have not yet been adequately ruled out.

The finding that is perhaps most difficult to explain within the framework of a glucostatic theory is the observation that glucose injections into the hypothalamus do not reduce or inhibit food intake.[38,63] Intraventricular injections of glucose have been reported to suppress feeding,[71] but this does not seem to be related to a direct action on hypothalamic glucoreceptors. The fact that the presence of high concentrations of glucose in the immediate environment of the hypothalamic cells that are thought to act as glucoreceptors is not a sufficient condition for satiety is a restriction of the glucostatic theory that appears to seriously limit its usefulness. There is, finally, some evidence that lesions in the ventromedial hypothalamus that result in hyperphagia and obesity do not significantly interfere with the animal's response to insulin,

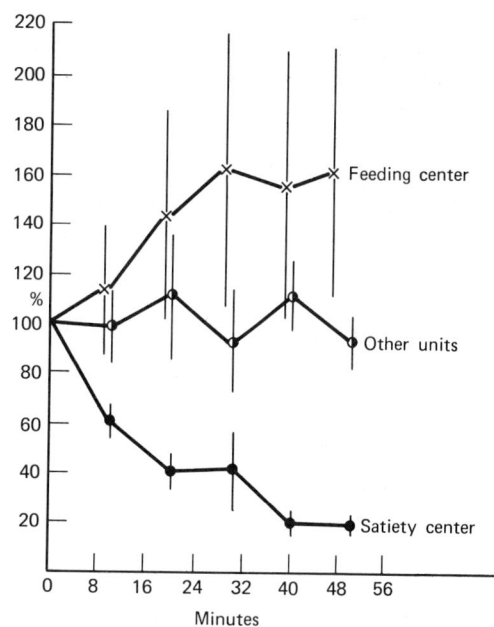

FIG. 9-12. Mean spike frequencies (with standard deviations) of neurons of the feeding center, satiety center, and other hypothalamic areas (6 units each) following the intracarotid infusions of 2-deoxy-d-glucose (a drug which inhibits central glucose utilization). Values are percentages of control values obtained for respective units before administration of 2-deoxy-d-glucose.

(From T. Desiraju, M. G. Banerjee, & B. K. Anand. Activity of single neurons in the hypothalamic feeding centers: effect of 2-deoxy-d-glucose. *Physiol. & Behav.*, **3**, 1968, 757-760. Permission granted for Pergamon Press copyright.)

suggesting that this region cannot be an essential aspect of the neural system that stimulates feeding in response to hypoglycemia.[41]

The Thermoregulatory Theory

The only currently available alternative or addition to the glucostatic theory of food intake for which there is significant experimental support is Brobeck's[21,22] thermoregulatory theory. Brobeck proposed, in essence, that the organism's energy equation may be balanced primarily by temperature-regulating mechanisms and that food intake may be controlled by the same mechanisms. Early statements of this theory suggested that "animals eat to keep warm and stop eating to prevent hyperthermia." More recent versions have proposed that the interaction of body temperature and food intake may not require a conscious appreciation of temperature sensations but a direct "central heating" of the hypothalamic mechanisms that regulate body temperature.

The thermoregulatory theory has stimulated a good deal of research and is supported by a variety of experimental findings. Man and other homeothermic animals eat more in cold environments than when it is hot.[81,21] Moreover, the body's heat production increases during the metabolism of foodstuffs, and the magnitude of this heating effect varies for the different components of the diet. The thermoregulatory theory predicts that the satiety value of a particular food should be determined by the magnitude of its effect on heat production, and several studies support such an interpretation. Thus, rats modify the amount of food intake in such a way that a constant effect on heat production, rather than a constant energy intake, obtains.[142] A correlation between the thermal effects of a diet and rate of weight gain on it has also been reported.[105]

Booth and Strang[19] first suggested that this increased heat production might be a signal for satiety on the basis of their observation that eating resulted in a rise in skin temperature. This observation has been replicated by recent investigators, but an interpretation of satiety purely in terms of a sensation of warmth has not found much favor because even large increments in skin temperature do not always reduce hunger or food intake.

Brobeck[22] consequently suggested that the feeding-related increase in heat production might affect hunger by acting directly on cells of the anterior hypothalamus and preoptic area that are known to regulate body temperature, at least in part, in accordance with the temperature of their immediate environment. More specifically, the thermoregulatory theory now suggests that the temperature of the hypothalamus should covary, under normal circumstances, with hunger and satiety, and that a rise in hypothalamic temperature should produce satiety. A number of investigators have reported a rise in the temperature of the anterior hypothalamus during feeding,[70,1] but feeding-unrelated motor activities such as standing up, walking, or motions of the arm apparently produce similar temperature changes.[35] Local heating of the preoptic area of goats has been reported to inhibit feeding and induce drinking, whereas cooling produced opposite effects.[10] However, the temperature changes needed to produce these effects were much larger than any normally seen in the brain, and recent attempts to replicate the experiments in rats, using more moderate temperature changes, have produced directly opposite effects.[140]

Some years ago, I[68] investigated the relationship of food intake to hypothalamic temperature and came to the conclusion that a direct heating of the body's thermostat cannot be a major primary influence on food intake. Here are some of the observations that led to this conclusion (see Figures 9–13 and 9–14). Feeding did produce a rise in brain temperature in rats as well as cats, but the cessation of feeding did not always coincide with the attainment of maximal temperatures in the anterior hypothalamus. That satiety cannot be related to particular hypothalamic temperatures was suggested by the observation that meal size was independent of the level of hypothalamic temperature at the beginning

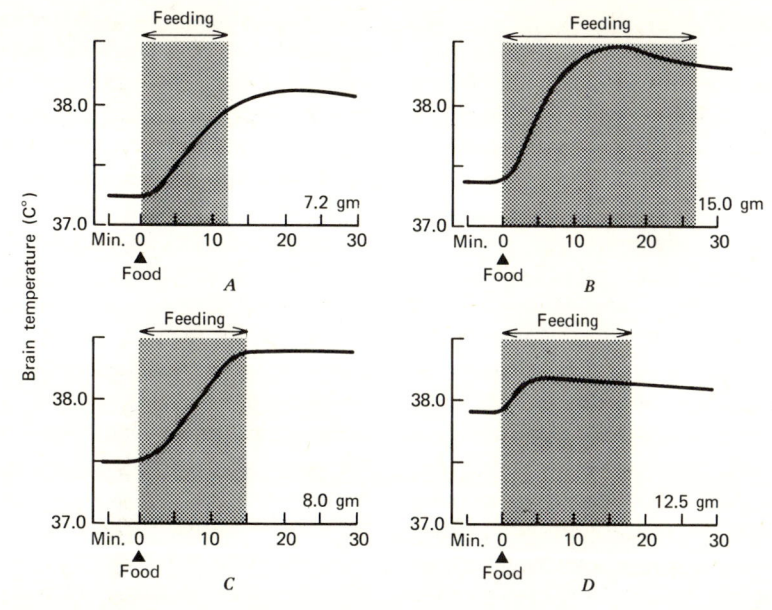

FIG. 9-13. Patterns of preoptic temperature changes commonly seen during feeding in the rat. The same animals may show different response patterns at different times.

(From S. P. Grossman & A. Rechtschaffen. Variations in brain temperature in relation to food intake. *Physiol. & Behav.*, **2**, 1967, 379–383. Permission granted for Pergamon Press copyright.)

or end of the meal. Another set of experiments showed that a rapid change in hypothalamic temperature also cannot be the cause of satiety. After some habituation, cats ate normal quantities of very cold or very hot food although their hypothalamic temperatures rose or fell rapidly by as much as 5°C, presumably because of a direct heat radiation through the roof of the mouth. These results indicate that a hypothalamic temperature change is neither a sufficient nor a necessary condition for satiety. A follow-up study suggested further that the onset of feeding behavior is also independent of hypothalamic temperature within normal limits. Long-term recordings of brain temperatures failed to show consistent correlations between food deprivation (up to 72 hours) and brain temperature in several cats.

Food intake does, without question, vary when environmental or body temperatures are raised or lowered beyond a normal range, but the relatively small temperature changes that occur in the brain as well as peripherally as a consequence of eating do not seem to be a major determinant of satiety under normal conditions. Body and brain temperature similarly do not seem to vary as a function of food deprivation and thus cannot be a primary determinant of hunger.

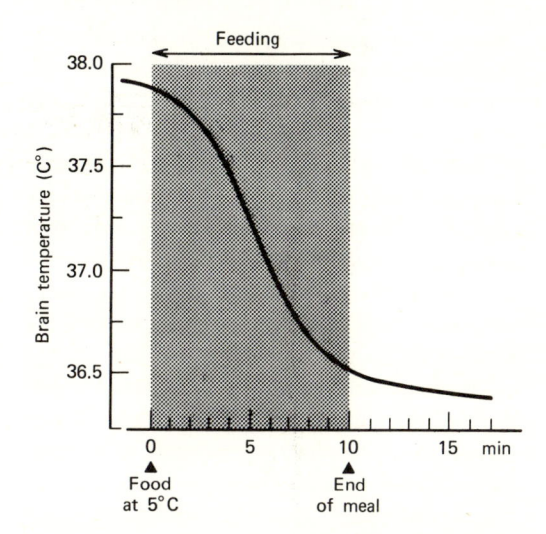

FIG. 9-14. Drop in preoptic temperature of one cat during ingestion of cold (5°C) meat.

(From S. P. Grossman & A. Rechtschaffen. Variations in brain temperature in relation to food intake. *Physiol. & Behav.*, **2**, 1967, 379–383. Permission granted for Pergamon Press copyright.)

Conclusions

It is clear that the central mechanisms that regulate food intake and hunger must be appraised of the status of the organism's energy balance as well as the energy equivalent of foods that have just been ingested. Many stomach-denervation and -removal experiments suggest that this feedback is probably not neural, and the effects of blood transfusions confirm the suspicion that at least some of the relevant information is carried by chemical messengers. A consideration of the rapidity of the adjustment to changes in energy expenditure or energy intake suggests that the fat- and protein-metabolisms are too slow to provide useful metabolites. Much of the search has consequently concentrated on the carbohydrate metabolism. Following Jean Mayer's proposal that the needs of the organism might be reflected most directly in the level of sugar in the blood and that glucoreceptors in the central hunger mechanisms might respond directly to this information, much attention has been focused on glucostatic mechanisms. Mayer's theory is supported by such observations as the following: (a) insulin-induced hypoglycemia produces stomach contractions, hunger sensation, and food intake, whereas glucose-induced hyperglycemia results in opposite although small effects; (b) calorically adequate diets are associated with high levels of central glucose utilization, whereas calorically inadequate diets are not; and (c) changes in blood sugar produce changes in gross EEG as well as single-cell activity in the central satiety and hunger centers. There are some soft spots in this seemingly impressive array of experimental support for the theory, but its main problem is the observation that glucose injections directly into the hypothalamic centers that are thought to contain the glucoreceptors do not reduce food intake.

The only adjunct or alternative to the glucostatic theory for which there is a significant amount of experimental support is Brobeck's thermoregulatory theory, which suggests that the organism's food intake is controlled as an integral part of its temperature regulation. This interpretation is supported by the observation that abnormally high or low environmental temperatures modify food intake; that eating produces a rise in temperature both peripherally and in the brain; and that the satiety value of a diet seems to be correlated with the magnitude of its effect on body temperature. Early versions of the thermoregulatory theory, which suggested that a conscious appreciation of the post-ingestion increase in skin temperature might be an essential satiety signal, have been abandoned because not all changes in skin temperature affect food intake. More recent versions of the theory assume that the temperature of the anterior hypothalamic thermostat is, itself, the principal signal for food ingestion or satiety. Recent experiments suggest, however, that this cannot be a major determinant of food intake under normal conditions because changes in hypothalamic temperature do not correlate well with deprivation or satiety.

Review Questions

1. State Jean Mayer's current glucostatic theory of hunger. How does it differ from the first version?

2. How does this theory account for satiety? Comment on the adequacy of this explanation.

3. Discuss the relationship between gastric motility and blood sugar.

4. Discuss the effects of experimentally induced hypo- or hyperglycemia on food intake.

5. Discuss the experimental evidence that suggests that feeding-related glucoreceptors may be concentrated in the hypothalamic feeding and satiety centers.

6. Discuss the major "soft spots" in the experimental support for the glucostatic theory.

7. State Brobeck's thermoregulatory theory of food intake.

8. Summarize the experimental support for such a theory.

9. Discuss the experimental observations that suggest that feeding may not, under normal conditions, be regulated by thermoregulatory mechanisms.

REVIEW AND SUMMARY

Historically, hunger was thought to be a sensation of purely peripheral origin. We are sated when our stomach is full and become hungry as it empties. This very sensible explanation cannot, unfortunately, be correct because feelings of hunger and satiety persist after denervation or removal of the stomach. The contractions of the intact stomach do seem to correlate with sensations of hunger and excessive stomach distention with satiety, but neither is essential to the regulation of food intake.

Another historical explanation—that a hunger center somewhere in the brain initiates feeding behavior periodically, regardless of the activity of the stomach or the organism's current energy needs—also has turned out to be inadequate, though perhaps a little closer to the truth.

It is currently believed that hunger and satiety may be regulated by a complex neural pathway that includes (a) a ventromedial hypothalamic inhibitory mechanism, (b) a lateral hypothalamic excitatory mechanism, and (c) a variety of excitatory and inhibitory extrahypothalamic influences of cortical (frontal lobe, hippocampus) as well as subcortical (amygdala, thalamus, globus pallidus, midbrain tegmentum) origin.

Damage to the excitatory aspects of the feeding system produces hypo- or aphagia usually accompanied by hypo- or adipsia. The course of this effect has been studied most extensively after lateral hypothalamic damage. The results of these investigations suggest that hunger and caloric regulation of intake (but not hypoglycemic control) recover after some weeks or months of complete or partial aphagia and that the recovery process follows a predictable and orderly pattern. It is assumed that the recovery is due to the remaining excitatory influences in the system.

Damage to the inhibitory aspects of the feeding system produces an apparently permanent hyperphagia. This has again been studied most carefully and extensively following hypothalamic damage. These studies have shown that ventromedial lesions may upset the organism's energy balance by reducing locomotor activity, interfering with pituitary functions, temporarily upsetting temperature regulation, and disturbing various metabolic processes. Lesioned animals overeat and become very obese when a palatable diet is available. After a "dynamic" period of excessive intake and weight gain, the animals stabilize intake and body weight at relatively constant although elevated levels (the "static" phase of the lesion effect). Whether this overeating can be attributed to an increase in hunger or a decrease in satiety is, however, questionable because the lesioned animals eat less than normals when the diet is not very palatable and starve to death rather than accept a bitter or otherwise unpleasant diet. They also do not work as hard as normals for food- (as well as water-) rewards and show abnormal reactions to aversive stimulation, suggesting that more than a simple disturbance of satiety influences may be involved in the lesion syndrome. It is not yet clear whether the complexity of the lesion effect reflects the nature of a unitary function of the ventromedial region or merely our inability to affect individual functions in areas of geographic overlap. We also do not yet know whether the same complications apply to the hyperphagia that is produced by damage to other inhibitory aspects of the feeding system. There is some evidence to suggest that the inhibitory aspects of the central feeding system may rely on alpha-adrenergic transmitters (which exert inhibitory influences on it), whereas the excitatory pathways may rely on beta-adrenergic neurohumors (which, in turn, inhibit this aspect of the feeding system).

Perhaps the most interesting question in the area is how the central regulatory mechanisms may be appraised of (a) the current status of the organism's energy balance and (b) the caloric value of recently ingested foods. Two hypotheses, which are not contradictory or mutually exclusive, have dominated in recent years.

Mayer's glucostatic theory holds that the state of the organism's energy balance is directly reflected in the level of sugar in the blood and that special cells in the central regulatory centers meter this concentration by sensing their own rate of glucose uptake and utilization. This theory is supported by a variety of experimental observations. Injections of insulin, which produce a fall in blood sugar, also elicit stomach contractions, sensations of hunger, and increased food intake. Conversely, injections of glucose, which raise the level of sugar in the blood, decrease food intake, although the effect is typically small. The hypothalamic localization of the glucoreceptors is suggested by experiments that demonstrate that glucose tends to concentrate in the ventromedial hypothalamus and that changes in blood sugar modify the EEG as well as single-cell activity of this area. The glucostatic theory has several problems, including the disappointingly small effects of glucose injections, rather imperfect correlations between food intake and measures of central glucose utilization, and the fact that insulin, which does affect food intake significantly, probably does not affect central glucose utilization. Furthermore, the theory predicts that an increase in the glucose concentration of the environment of the hypothalamic glucoreceptors should produce satiety. A number of studies have, however, shown that glucose injections into the hypothalamus do not reduce food intake.

The only serious current alternative or addition to the glucostatic theory is Brobeck's thermoregulatory theory, which holds that "animals eat to keep warm and stop eating to prevent hyperthermia." The original version of this theory, which suggested that satiety might be signaled by a conscious appreciation of feeding-related increases in skin temperature, has been discarded because satiety does not always occur when skin temperature is increased. Instead, Brobeck has suggested that eating may produce a "central heating" effect, that is, it may directly raise the temperature of the hypothalamic thermostat that is believed to regulate body temperature as well as food intake on the basis of its own temperature. This appealing theory is supported by the observation that eating produces a rise in hypothalamic temperature and that excessive heating or cooling of the central thermostat interferes with normal food-intake regulation and presumably hunger. The theory does not, however, appear to describe a mechanism that controls food intake under normal circumstances, since food intake and satiety do not depend on either the absolute temperature of the hypothalamus or a temperature change in this region as long as these temperatures are within the normal range of body temperature.

Bibliography

1. Abrams, R. M., & Hammel, H. T. Hypothalamic temperature in unanesthetized albino rats during feeding and sleeping. *Amer. J. Physiol.*, 1964, **206**, 641–646.

2. Adolph, E. F. Urges to eat and drink in rats. *Amer. J. Physiol.*, 1947, **151**, 110–125.

3. Anand, B. K., & Brobeck, J. R. Localization of a feeding center in the hypothalamus of the rat. *Proc. Soc. Exp. Biol. Med.*, 1951, **77**, 323–324.

4. Anand, B. K., & Brobeck, J. R. Food intake and spontaneous activity of rats with lesions in the amygdaloid nuclei. *J. Neurophysiol.*, 1952, **15**, 421–431.

5. Anand, B. K., Dua, S., & Chhina, G. S. Higher nervous control over food intake. *Ind. J. Med. Res.*, 1958, **46**, 277–287.

6. Anand, B. K., Dua, S., & Singh, B. Electrical activity of the hypothalamic "feeding centres" under the effect of changes in blood chemistry. *EEG Clin. Neurophysiol.*, 1961a, **13**, 54–59.

7. Anand, B. K., Subberwal, U., Manchanda, S. K., & Singh, B. Glucoreceptor mechanism in the hypothalamic feeding centres. *Ind. J. Med. Res.*, 1961b, **49**, 717–724.

8. Anand, B. K., Talwar, G. P., Dua, S., & Mhatre, R. M. Glucose and oxygen consumption of hypothalamic feeding centers. *Ind. J. Med. Res.*, 1961c, **49**, 725–732.

9. Anand, B. K., Chhina, G. S., Sharma, K. N., Dua, S., & Singh, B. Activity of single neurons in the hypothalamic feeding centers: effect of glucose. *Amer. J. Physiol.*, 1964, **207**, 1146–1154.

10. Andersson, B., & Larsson, B. Influence of local temperature changes in the preoptic area and rostral hypothalamus on the regulation of food and water intake. *Acta Physiol. Scand.*, 1961, **52**, 75–89.

11. Arees, E. A., & Mayer, J. Anatomical connections between medial and lateral regions of the hypothalamus concerned with food intake. *Science*, 1967, **157**, 1574–1575.

12. Balagura, S., Wilcox, R. H., & Coscina, D. V. The effect of diencephalic lesions on food intake and motor activity. *Physiol. & Behav.*, 1969, **4**, 629–633.

13. Bardier, E. *Les Fonctions Digestives*. Paris: O. Doin, 1911.

14. Bash, K. W. An investigation into a possible organic basis for the hunger drive. *J. Comp. Psychol.*, 1939, **28**, 109–134.

15. Bates, M. W., Nauss, S. F., Hagman, N. C., & Mayer, J. Fat metabolism in three forms of experimental obesity: body composition. *Amer. J. Physiol.*, 1955a, **180**, 301–309.

16. Bates, M. W., Mayer, J., & Nauss, S. F. Fat metabolism in three forms of experimental obesity: fatty acid turnover. *Amer. J. Physiol.*, 1955b, **180**, 309–311.

17. Bédard, P., Larochelle, L., Parent, A., & Poirier, L. J. The nigrostriatal pathway: a correlative study based on neuroanatomical and neurochemical criteria in the cat and the monkey. *Exptl. Neurol.*, 1969, **25**, 365–377.

18. Booth, D. A. Localization of the adrenergic feeding system in the rat diencephalon. *Science*, 1967, **158**, 515–517.

19. Booth, G., & Strang, J. M. Changes in temperature of the skin following the ingestion of food. *Arch. Intern. Med.*, 1936, **57**, 533–543.

20. Brobeck, J. R. Mechanisms of the development of obesity in animals with hypothalamic lesions. *Physiol. Rev.*, 1946, **26**, 541–559.

21. Brobeck, J. R. Food intake as a mechanism of temperature regulation. *Yale J. Biol. Med.*, 1947–1948, **20**, 545–552.

22. Brobeck, J. R. Regulation of feeding and drinking. In *Handbook of Physiology. Vol. II.* J. Field, H. W. Magoun, & V. E. Hall, Eds. Washington, D.C.: Am. Physiol. Soc. 1960, pp. 1197–1206.

23. Brobeck, J. R., Tepperman, J., & Long, C. N. H. Experimental hypothalamic hyperphagia in the albino rat. *Yale J. Biol. Med.*, 1943, **15**, 831–853.

24. Brown, S., & Schaefer, E. A. An investigation into the functions of the occipital and temporal lobes of the monkey's brain. *Phil. Trans. Roy. Soc. London*, 1888, **179**, 303–327.

25. Brügger, M. Fresstrieb als hypothalmisches Symptom. *Helv. Physiol. Pharmacol. Acta*, 1943, **1**, 183–198.

26. Bulatão, E., & Carlson, A. J. Contribution to the physiology of the stomach. Influence of experimental changes in blood sugar level on gastric hunger contractions. *Amer. J. Physiol.*, 1924, **69**, 107–115.

27. Cannon, W. B. Hunger and thirst. In *Handbook of General Experimental Psychology.* C. Murchison, Ed. Worcester, Mass.: Clark Univ. Press, 1934, pp. 247–263.

28. Cannon, W. B., & Washburn, A. L. An explanation of hunger. *Amer. J. Physiol.*, 1912, **29**, 441–454.

29. Carlson, A. J. *The Control of Hunger in Health and Diseases*. Chicago: Univ. of Chicago Press, 1916.

30. Collins, E. Localization of an experimental hypothalamic and midbrain syndrome simulating sleep. *J. Comp. Neurol.*, 1954, **100**, 661–697.

31. Coury, J. N. Neural correlates of food and water intake in the rat. *Science*, 1967, **156**, 1763–1765.

32. Darwin, E. *Zoonomia (London)*, 1801, **3**, 322.

33. Davis, J. D., Gallagher, R. J., Ladove, R. F., & Turausky, A. J. Inhibition of food intake by a humoral factor. *J. Comp. Physiol. Psychol.*, 1969, **67**, 407–414.

34. Delgado, J. M. R., & Anand, B. K. Increased food intake induced by electrical stimulation of the lateral hypothalamus. *Amer. J. Physiol.*, 1953, **172**, 162–168.
35. Delgado, J. M. R., & Hanai, T. Intracerebral temperatures in free-moving cats. *Amer. J. Physiol.*, 1966, **211**, 755–769.
36. Desiraju, T., Banerjee, M. G., & Anand, B. K. Activity of single neurons in the hypothalamic feeding centers: effect of 2-deoxy-d-glucose. *Physiol. & Behav.*, 1968, **3**, 757–760.
37. Ehrlich, A. Effects of tegmental lesions on motivated behavior in rats. *J. Comp. Physiol. Psychol.*, 1963, **56**, 390–396.
38. Epstein, A. N. Reciprocal changes in feeding behavior produced by intrahypothalamic chemical injections. *Amer. J. Physiol.*, 1960a, **199**, 969–974.
39. Epstein, A. N. Water intake without the act of drinking. *Science*, 1960b, **131**, 497–498.
40. Epstein, A. N., & Teitelbaum, P. Regulation of food intake in the absence of taste, smell, and other oropharyngeal sensations. *J. Comp. Physiol. Psychol.*, 1962, **55**, 753–759.
41. Epstein, A. N., & Teitelbaum, P. Specific loss of the hypoglycemic control of feeding in recovered lateral rats. *Amer. J. Physiol.*, 1967, **213**, 1159–1167.
42. Erdheim, J. Über Hypophysenganggeschwülste und Hirncholesteatome. *S.-B. Akad. Wiss. Wien.*, 1904, **113**, Abt. III, 537–726.
43. Ewald, J. R. *Klinik der Verdauungskrankheiten.* Cologne: Bergmann, 1893.
44. Feldman, S. E., Behar, A. J., & Birnbaum, D. Gastric lesions following hypothalamic stimulation. *Arch. Neurol. (Chicago)*, 1961, **4**, 308–317.
45. Fröhlich, A. Dr. Alfred Fröhlich stellt einen Fall von Tumor der Hypophyse ohne Akromegalie vor. *Wien. Klin. Rdsch.*, 1902, **15**, 883.
46. Fuller, J. L., Rosvold, H. E., & Pribram, K. H. The effects on affective and cognitive behavior in the dog of lesions of the pyriform amygdala-hippocampal complex. *J. Comp. Physiol. Psychol.*, 1957, **50**, 89–96.
47. Fulton, J. F. *Frontal Lobotomy and Affective Behavior.* New York: Norton, 1951, pp. 78–82.
48. Fulton, J. F., Jacobsen, C. F., & Kennard, Margaret A. A note concerning the relation of the frontal lobes to posture and forced grasping in monkeys. *Brain*, 1932, **55**, 524–536.
49. Gasnier, A., & Mayer, A. Récherches sur la regulation de la nutrition. I: Analités et côtés des mécanismes régulateurs. *Ann. Physiol. Physicochim. Biol.*, 1939, **15**, 145–156.
50. Gilmour, J. Clinical aspects of carcinoma of stomach in diagnosis. *Brit. Med. J.*, 1958, **5073**, 745–748.
51. Gold, R. M. Aphagia and adipsia following unilateral and bilaterally asymmetrical lesions in rats. *Physiol. & Behav.*, 1967, **2**, 211–220.
52. Gold, R. M. Diencephalic feeding mechanisms: chemical implant studies. Paper presented at the Symposium on Approaches to Neural Control of Hunger. *Second Annual Winter Conference on Brain Research*, Snowmass at Aspen, Colorado, 1969.
53. Green, J. D., Clemente, C. D., & de Groot, J. Rhinencephalic lesions and behavior in cats. *J. Comp. Neurol.*, 1957, **108**, 505–546.
54. Grossman, M. I., & Stein, I. F. The effect of vagotomy on the hunger-producing action of insulin in man. *J. Appl. Physiol.*, 1948, **1**, 263.
55. Grossman, M. I., Cummins, G. M., & Ivy, A. C. The effect of insulin on food intake after vagotomy and sympathectomy. *Amer. J. Physiol.*, 1947, **149**, 100.
56. Grossman, S. P. Eating or drinking elicited by direct adrenergic or cholinergic stimulation of hypothalamus. *Science*, 1960, **132**, 301–302.
57. Grossman, S. P. Direct adrenergic and cholinergic stimulation of hypothalamic mechanisms. *Amer. J. Physiol.*, 1962a, **202**, 872–882.
58. Grossman, S. P. Effects of adrenergic and cholinergic blocking agents on hypothalamic mechanisms. *Amer. J. Physiol.*, 1962b, **202**, 1230–1236.
59. Grossman, S. P. Behavioral effects of chemical stimulation of the ventral amygdala. *J. Comp. Physiol. Psychol.*, 1964a, **57**, 29–36.
60. Grossman, S. P. Behavioral effects of direct chemical stimulation of central nervous system structures. *Int. J. Neuropharmacol.*, 1964b, **3**, 45–58.

61. Grossman, S. P. The VMH: a center for affective reactions, satiety, or both? *Physiol. & Behav.*, 1966, **1**, 1–10.
62. Grossman, S. P. Behavioral and electroencephalographic effects of microinjections of neurohumors into the midbrain reticular formation. *Physiol. & Behav.*, 1968a, **3**, 777–787.
63. Grossman, S. P. Hypothalamic and limbic influences on food intake. *Fed. Proc.*, 1968b, **27**, 1349–1360.
64. Grossman, S. P. Changes in food and water intake associated with an interruption of the anterior or posterior fiber connections of the hypothalamus. *J. Comp. Physiol. Psychol.*, 1971, **75**, 23–31.
65. Grossman, S. P., & Grossman, Lore. Food and water intake following lesions or electrical stimulation of the amygdala. *Amer. J. Physiol.*, 1963, **205**, 761–765.
66. Grossman, S. P., & Grossman, Lore. Food and water intake in rats with parasagittal knife-cuts medial or lateral to the lateral hypothalamus. *J. Comp. Physiol. Psychol.*, 1971, **74**, 148–156.
67. Grossman, S. P., & Mountford, Helen. Effects of chemical stimulation of the dorsal hippocampus on learning and performance. *Amer. J. Physiol.*, 1964, **207**, 1387–1393.
68. Grossman, S. P., & Rechtschaffen, A. Variations in brain temperature in relation to food intake. *Physiol. & Behav.*, 1967, **2**, 379–383.
69. Haller, A. Fames et sitis. *Elementa Physiol.*, 1776, **6**, 185.
70. Hamilton, C. L. Interactions of food intake and temperature regulation in the rat. *J. Comp. Physiol. Psychol.*, 1963, **56**, 476–488.
71. Herberg, L. J. Hunger reduction produced by injecting glucose into the lateral ventricle of the rat. *Nature (London)*, 1960, **187**, 245–246.
72. Hetherington, A. W. The relation of various hypothalamic lesions to other phenomena in the rat. *Amer. J. Physiol.*, 1941, **133**, 326–327.
73. Hetherington, A. W., & Ranson, S. W. Hypothalamic lesions and adiposity in the rat. *Anat. Rec.*, 1940, **78**, 149.
74. Hetherington, A. W., & Ranson, S. W. The spontaneous activity and food intake of rats with hypothalamic lesions. *Amer. J. Physiol.*, 1942a, **136**, 609–617.
75. Hetherington, A. W., & Ranson, S. W. Effect of early hypophysectomy on hypothalamic obesity. *Endocrinology*, 1942b, **31**, 30–34.
76. Himwich, H. E., Bowman, K. M., Daly, C., Fazekas, J. F., Wortis, J., & Goldfarb, W. Cerebral blood flow and brain metabolism during insulin hypoglycemia. *Amer. J. Physiol.*, 1941, **132**, 640–647.
77. Hoebel, B. G. Hypothalamic lesions by electrocauterization: disinhibition of feeding and self-stimulation. *Science*, 1965, **149**, 452–453.
78. Ivy, A. C., Vloedman, D. A., & Keane, J. The small intestine in hunger. *Amer. J. Physiol.*, 1925, **72**, 99.
79. Janowitz, H. D., & Grossman, M. I. Effect of intravenously administered glucose on food intake in the dog. *Am r. J. Physiol.*, 1949a, **156**, 87.
80. Janowitz, H. D., & Grossman, M. I. Effect of variations in nutritive density on intake of food in dogs and cats. *Amer. J. Physiol.*, 1949b, **158**, 184–193.
81. Johnson, R. E., & Kark, R. M. Environment and food intake in man. *Science*, 1947, **105**, 378–379.
82. Kennedy, G. C. The hypothalamic control of food intake in rats. *Proc. Roy. Soc. (London), B*, 1950, **137**, 535–548.
83. Kirschbaum, W. R. Excessive hunger as a symptom of cerebral origin. *J. Nerv. Ment. Dis.*, 1951, **113**, 95.
84. Kohn, M. Satiation of hunger from food injected directly into the stomach versus food ingested by mouth. *J. Comp. Physiol. Psychol.*, 1951, **44**, 412–422.
85. Krasne, F. B. General disruption resulting from electrical stimulation of ventromedial hypothalamus. *Science*, 1962, **138**, 822–823.
86. Larsson, S. On the hypothalamic organization of the nervous mechanisms regulating food intake. *Acta Physiol. Scand.*, 1955, **32**, 1–40.
87. Leibowitz, Sarah F. Reciprocal hunger-regulating circuits involving alpha-and beta-adrenergic receptors located, respectively, in the ventromedial and lateral hypothalamus. *Proc. Nat. Acad. Sci. U.S.*, 1970, **67**, 1063–1070.

88. Leibowitz, Sarah F. Hypothalamic alpha- and beta-adrenergic systems regulate both hunger and thirst in the rat. *Proc. Nat. Acad. Sci. U.S.*, 1971, **68**, 332–334.

89. Leibowitz, Sarah F. Central adrenergic receptors and the regulation of hunger and thirst. *Res. Publ., Ass. Res. Nerv. Ment. Dis.*, 1972 (in press).

90. Luckhardt, A. B., & Carlson, A. J. Contributions to the physiology of the stomach. XVII: On the chemical control of the gastric hunger mechanism. *Amer. J. Physiol.*, 1915, **36**, 37.

91. Lundbaek, K., & Stevenson, J. A. F. Reduced carbohydrate intake after fat feeding in normal rats and rats with hypothalamic hyperphagia. *Amer. J. Physiol.*, 1947, **151**, 530–537.

92. MacDonald, R. M., Ingelfinger, F. J., & Belding, H. W. Late effects of total gastrostomy in man. *New Engl. J. Med.*, 1947, **237**, 887.

93. Mackay, E. M., Calloway, J. W., & Barnes, R. H. Hyperalimentation in normal animals produced by protamine-insulin. *J. Nutr.*, 1940, **20**, 59.

94. MacLean, P. D., & Delgado, J. M. R. Electrical and chemical stimulation of fronto-temporal portion of limbic system in waking animal. *EEG Clin. Neurophysiol.*, 1953, **5**, 91–100.

95. Magendie, F. *Lehrbuch der Physiologie.* Tübingen: Ostrander, 1826.

96. Maire, F. W. Eating and drinking responses elicited by diencephalic stimulation in unanesthetized rats. *Fed. Proc.*, 1956, **15**, 124.

97. Marshall, N. B., Barnett, R. J., & Mayer, J. Hypothalamic lesions in goldthioglucose injected mice. *Proc. Soc. Exp. Biol. Med.*, 1955, **90**, 240.

98. Mayer, J. The glucostatic theory of regulation of food intake and the problem of obesity. *Bull. New Engl. Med. Cent.*, 1952, **14**, 43.

99. Mayer, J. Glucostatic mechanisms of regulation of food intake. *New Engl. J. Med.*, 1953, **249**, 13–16.

100. Mayer, J. Regulation of energy intake and the body weight. The glucostatic theory and the lipostatic hypothesis. *Ann. N. Y. Acad. Sci.*, 1955, **63**, 15–43.

101. Mayer, J., & Barnett, R. J. Obesity following unilateral hypothalamic lesions in rats. *Science*, 1955, **121**, 599.

102. Mayer, J., & Bates, M. W. Blood glucose and food intake in normal and hypophysectomized alloxan-treated rats. *Amer. J. Physiol.*, 1952, **168**, 812–819.

103. Mayer, J., Marshall, N. B., Vitale, J. J., Christensen, J. H., Mashayekhi, M. B., & Stare, F. J. Exercise, food intake and body weight in normal rats and genetically obese adult mice. *Amer. J. Physiol.*, 1954, **177**, 544–547.

104. Meschan, I., & Quigley, J. P. Spontaneous motility of the pyloric sphincter and adjacent regions of the gut in the unanesthetized dog. *Amer. J. Physiol.*, 1938, **121**, 350.

105. Mickelsen, O. S., Takahashi, S., & Craig, C. Experimental obesity. I: Production of obesity in rats by feeding high-fat diets. *J. Nutr.*, 1955, **57**, 541.

106. Miller, N. E. Motivational effects of brain stimulation and drugs. *Fed. Proc.*, 1960, **19**, 846–853.

107. Miller, N. E. Some psychophysiological studies of motivation and of the behavioral effects of illness. *Bull. Brit. Psychol. Soc.*, 1964, **17**, 55.

108. Miller, N. E. Chemical coding of behavior in the brain. *Science*, 1965, **148**, 328–338.

109. Miller, N. E., & Kessen, M. L. Reward effects of food via stomach fistula compared with those of food via mouth. *J. Comp. Physiol. Psychol.*, 1952, **45**, 555–564.

110. Miller, N. E., Bailey, C. J., & Stevenson, J. A. F. "Decreased hunger" but increased food intake resulting from hypothalamic lesions. *Science*, 1950, **112**, 256–259.

111. Morgan, C. T., & Morgan, J. D. Studies in hunger. II. The relation of gastric denervation and dietary sugar to the effect of insulin upon food intake in the rat. *J. Gen. Psychol.*, 1940, **57**, 153–163.

112. Morgane, P. J. Electrophysiological studies of feeding and satiety centers in the rat. *Amer. J. Physiol.*, 1961a, **201**, 838–844.

113. Morgane, P. J. Medial forebrain bundle and "feeding centers" of the hypothalamus. *J. Comp. Neurol.*, 1961b, **117**, 1–26.

114. Mulinos, M. G. The gastric hunger mechanism. IV. The influence of experimental alterations in blood sugar concentration on the gastric hunger contractions. *Amer. J. Physiol.*, 1933, **104**, 371.
115. Pellegrino, L. J., & Cushman, Anna J. *A Stereotaxic Atlas of the Rat Brain*. New York: Appleton-Century-Crofts, 1967.
116. Peretz, E. The effect of hippocampal ablation on the strength of food-obtained responses. *Amer. Psychologist*, 1963, **18**, 464.
117. Poirier, L. J., Mouren-Mathieu, Anne-Marie, & Richer, Claude-Lise. Obesity in the absence of absolute hyperphagia in monkeys with hypothalamic lesions. *Rev. Canad. Biol.*, 1962, **21**, 127–134.
118. Powley, T. L., & Keesey, R. E. Relationship of body weight to the lateral hypothalamic feeding syndrome. *J. Comp. Physiol. Psychol.*, 1970, **70**, 25–36.
119. Quigley, J. P. The role of the digestive tract in regulating the ingestion of food. *Ann. N. Y. Acad. Sci.*, 1955, **63**, 6–14.
120. Quigley, J. P., & Lindquist, J. L. Action of phlorizine on hunger contractions in the normal and vagotomized dog. *Amer. J. Physiol.*, 1930, **92**, 690.
121. Quigley, J. P., Johnson, V., & Solomon, E. I. Action of insulin on the motility of the gastro-intestinal tract. I. Action on the stomach of normal fasting man. *Amer. J. Physiol.*, 1929, **90**, 89.
122. Rabin, B. M., & Smith, C. J. Behavioral comparison of the effectiveness of irritative and non-irritative lesions in producing hypothalamic hyperphagia. *Physiol. & Behav.*, 1968, **3**, 417–420.
123. Reynolds, R. W. Ventromedial hypothalamic lesions without hyperphagia. *Amer. J. Physiol.*, 1963, **204**, 60–62.
124. Reynolds, R. W. An irritative hypothesis concerning the hypothalamic regulation of food intake. *Psych. Rev.*, 1965, **72**, 105–116.
125. Richter, C. P., & Hawkes, C. D. Increased spontaneous activity and food intake produced in rats by removal of the frontal poles of the brain. *J. Neurol. Psychiat.*, 1939, **2**, 231.
126. Robins, R. B., & Boyd, T. E. The fundamental rhythm of the Heidenhain pouch movements and their reflex modifications. *Amer. J. Physiol.*, 1923, **67**, 166.
127. Robinson, B. W. Forebrain alimentary responses: some organizational principles. In *Thirst, First International Symposium on Thirst in the Regulation of Body Water*. M. J. Wayner, Ed. New York: Pergamon Press, 1964, pp. 411–424.
128. Rodgers, W. L., Epstein, A. N., & Teitelbaum, P. Lateral hypothalamic aphagia: motor failure or motivational deficit? *Amer. J. Physiol.*, 1965, **208**, 334–342.
129. Ruch, T. C., & Shenkin, H. A. The relation of area 13 on orbital surface of frontal lobes to hyperactivity and hyperphagia in monkeys. *J. Neurophysiol.*, 1943, **6**, 349–360.
130. Ruch, T. C., Patton, H. D., & Brobeck, J. R. Hyperphagia and adiposity in relation to disturbances of taste. *Fed. Proc.*, 1942, **1**, 76.
131. Schiff, M. *Physiologie de la Digestion*. Florence: 1867; Berlin: Hirschwald, 1868.
132. Sclafani, A., & Grossman, S. P. Hyperphagia produced by knife cuts between the medial and lateral hypothalamus in the rat. *Physiol. & Behav.*, 1969, **4**, 533–538.
133. Sharma, K. N. Receptor mechanisms in the alimentary tract: their excitation and functions. In *Handbook of Physiology*. Vol. I. C. Code, Ed. Washington, D.C.: Am. Physiol. Soc., 1967, pp. 225–237.
134. Sharma, K. N., Anand, B. K., Dua, S., & Singh, B. Role of stomach in regulation of activities of hypothalamic feeding centers. *Amer. J. Physiol.*, 1961, **201**, 593–598.
135. Sharpe, L. G., & Myers, R. D. Feeding and drinking following stimulation of the diencephalon of the monkey with amines and other substances. *Exp. Brain Res.*, 1969, **8**, 295–310.
136. Smith, G. P., & Epstein, A. N. Increased feeding in response to decreased glucose utilization in the rat and monkey. *Amer. J. Physiol.*, 1969, **217**, 1083–1087.
137. Smith, O. A., Jr. Food intake and hypothalamic stimulation. In *Electrical Stimulation of the Brain*. D. E. Sheer, Ed. Austin: Univ. of Texas Press, 1961, pp. 367–370.
138. Sömmerring, S. T. *De Corporis Humani Fabrica*. 1794, **6**, 237.
139. Sommer, Sally R., Novin, D., & LeVine, M. Food and water intake after intrahypothalamic injections of carbachol in the rabbit. *Science*, 1967, **156**, 983–984.

140. Spector, N. H., Brobeck, J. R., & Hamilton, C. L. Feeding and core temperature in albino rats: changes induced by preoptic heating and cooling. *Science*, 1968, **161**, 286–288.

141. Stellar, E. The physiology of motivation. *Psychol. Rev.*, 1954, **61**, 522.

142. Strominger, J. L., & Brobeck, J. R. A mechanism of regulation of food intake. *Yale J. Biol. Med.*, 1953, **25**, 383.

143. Teitelbaum, P. Random and food-directed activity in hyperphagic and normal rats. *J. Comp. Physiol. Psychol.*, 1957, **50**, 486–490.

144. Teitelbaum, P. Disturbances in feeding and drinking behavior after hypothalamic lesions. In *Nebraska Symposium on Motivation*. M. R. Jones, Ed. Lincoln: Univ. of Nebraska Press, 1961, pp. 39–69.

145. Teitelbaum, P. Motivation and control of food intake. In *Handbook of Physiology. Vol. I*. C. Code, Ed. Washington, D.C.: Am. Physiol. Soc., 1967, pp. 319–335.

146. Teitelbaum, P., & Campbell, B. A. Ingestion patterns in hyperphagic and normal rats. *J. Comp. Physiol. Psychol.*, 1958, **51**, 135–141.

147. Teitelbaum, P., & Cytawa, J. Spreading depression and recovery from lateral hypothalamic damage. *Science*, 1965, **147**, 61–63.

148. Teitelbaum, P., & Epstein, A. N. The lateral hypothalamic syndrome: recovery of feeding and drinking after lateral hypothalamic lesions. *Psychol. Rev.*, 1962, **69**, 74–90.

149. Teitelbaum, P., & Epstein, A. N. The role of taste and smell in the regulation of food and water intake. In *Olfaction and taste. I*. Y. Zotterman, Ed. Oxford: Pergamon Press, 1963, pp. 347–360.

150. Teitelbaum, P., & Stellar, E. Recovery from the failure to eat, produced by hypothalamic lesions. *Science*, 1954, **120**, 894–895.

151. Templeton, R. D., & Quigley, J. P. Action of insulin on motility of gastro-intestinal tract: action on Heidenhain pouch. *Amer. J. Physiol.*, 1930, **91**, 467–474.

152. Tepperman, J., Brobeck, J. R., & Long, C. N. H. The effects of hypothalamic hyperphagia and of alterations in feeding habits on the metabolism of the albino rat. *Yale J. Biol. Med.*, 1943, **15**, 855–879.

153. Tsang, Y. C. Hunger motivation in gastrectomized rats. *J. Comp. Psychol.*, 1938, **26**, 1–17.

154. Valenstein, E. S., Cox, V. C., & Kakolewski, J. W. Modification of motivated behavior by electrical stimulation of the hypothalamus. *Science*, 1968, **159**, 1119–1121.

155. Valenstein, E. S., Cox, V. C., & Kakolewski, J. W. Sex differences in hyperphagia and body weight following hypothalamic damage. *Ann. N. Y. Acad. Sci.*, 1969, **157**, 1030–1048.

156. Wangenstein, O. H., & Carlson, A. J. Hunger sensations in a patient after total gastrectomy. *Proc. Soc. Exp. Biol. Med.*, 1931, **28**, 545–547.

157. Watts, J. W., & Fulton, J. F. Intussusception—the relation of the cerebral cortex to intestinal motility in the monkey. *New Engl. J. Med.*, 1934, **210**, 883–896.

158. Wheatley, M. D. The hypothalamus and affective behavior in cats. *Arch. Neurol. Psychiat. (Chicago)*, 1944, **52**, 296–316.

159. White, N. M., & Fisher, A. E. Relationship between amygdala and hypothalamus in the control of eating behavior. *Physiol. & Behav.*, 1969, **4**, 199–206.

160. Williams, D. R., & Teitelbaum, P. Some observations on the starvation resulting from lateral hypothalamic lesions. *J. Comp. Physiol. Psychol.*, 1959, **4**, 458–465.

161. Wyrwicka, Wanda, Dobrzecka, C., & Tarnecki, R. The effect of electrical stimulation of the hypothalamic feeding center in satiated goats on alimentary conditioned reflexes, type II. *Acta Biol. Exp. (Warsaw)*, 1960, **20**, 121–136.

Chapter 10

THIRST AND THE REGULATION OF WATER INTAKE

Introduction

Peripheral Influences

Central Regulatory Mechanisms

The Correlation Between Thirst and Water Needs

Review and Summary

INTRODUCTION

Life evolved in the sea, and all biological organisms still consist primarily of water. Since all life processes in some way or another require water, there must be a constant supply to assure survival. As long as the organism is surrounded by water, this presents no problem. As it ventures onto dry land, mechanisms must be evolved to maintain an internal environment that is essentially similar to the sea in an external milieu that is often almost totally devoid of water. This is not a simple problem because water is continually lost due to (a) evaporation from the lungs and body surface; (b) secretion by sweat glands, which play an essential role in cooling the body; and (c) excretion of waste products by urination and defecation (see Table 1). The rate of water loss is determined by a variety of influences such as activity, ambient and body

TABLE 1. Water Balance in the Body

Input		Output	
Source	Amount/Day (ml)	Source	Amount/Day (ml)
Ingestion of food and drink	2300	Lungs	300
		Skin	500
		Urine	1500
Metabolic water	200	Feces and mouth	200
Total	2500	Total	2500

(From *Human anatomy and physiology* by J. E. Crouch and J. R. McClintic. Copyright © 1971. John Wiley & Sons, Inc.)

225

temperature, and the concentration of indigestible and potentially harmful matter in the food and water supply. Since most organisms cannot store very large quantities of water, the regulation of its intake is a critical matter for survival. How this regulation is achieved is the subject of this chapter.

Man as well as most other mammals consist of about 70 to 75 percent water and maintain their total water content within about ± 0.2 percent of body weight—a surprisingly narrow range. Under normal conditions, thirst develops as the organism's water balance becomes negative and this assures corrective action, provided water is available in the environment (see Figure 10–1). Conversely, when excess water intake or retention raises the body's fluid balance above the upper limits of its tolerance level, corrective action in the form of urinary excretion occurs.

We cannot, unfortunately, define thirst exclusively in terms of the body's water balance. Not only would this be a somewhat impractical definition because the body's water content is not easily metered or even estimated, but it would also, under some circumstances, be inaccurate. At times, we become intensely thirsty although our water balance is positive. Eating spicy foods, for instance, can induce thirst sensations that are entirely unrelated to the state of our fluid balance. Conversely, there are some circumstances in which even a large fluid deficit does not induce thirst.

The simplest solution to the problem would seem to be a definition of thirst in terms of the sensations from the mouth and throat that appear to be the immediate stimuli for drinking. Unfortunately, these local sensations do not seem to be essential for the regulation of water intake and thirst, as we shall see in a moment. The signals from the mouth and throat undoubtedly contribute to the experience of thirst under normal circumstances, and we shall spend some time discussing their role. However, there is no simple relationship between these sensations and water need or water intake, and we shall have to consider other factors that may influence the organism's water balance more directly.

It is currently believed that thirst may reflect the activity of regulatory mechanisms that are represented in several subcortical structures and respond to changes in the absolute volume of water in the body as well as changes in the quantity of water relative to the quantity of some salts (i.e., the tonicity of the body fluids).

PERIPHERAL INFLUENCES

Historical Perspectives

Prescientific attempts to account for the urge to drink assumed that water intake and thirst were directly related to sensations of peripheral origin. Aristotle, for instance, suggested that thirst sensations might arise directly from the stomach. Galen, the famous medical authority of the pre-Christian era, thought it might arise from the heart and lungs. The most persistent and popular theory of thirst is credited to Hippocrates. According to his views, thirst refers to the sensations that arise from the mouth and throat when they become dry and parched because of a loss of body fluids. This "dry-mouth" theory of thirst was revived in

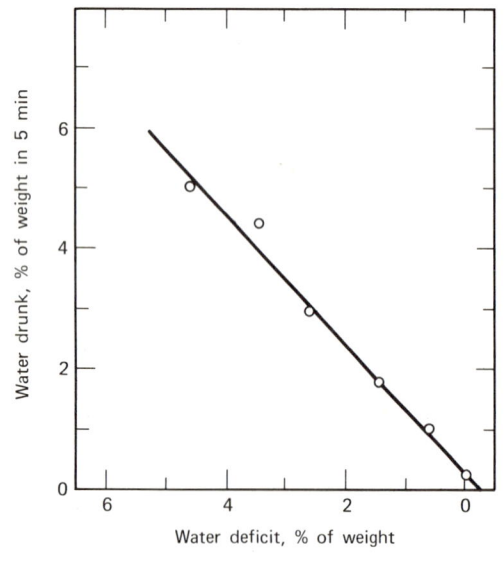

FIG. 10–1. Water drunk in the first 5 min after water was allowed to dogs initially dehydrated to various extents.

(After E. F. Adolph. Measurements of water and drinking in dogs. *Amer. J. Physiol.*, **125**, 1939, 75–86.)

the 18th century by Haller[57] and has continued to enjoy great popularity since then because it seems to confirm what we all "know"; we drink not because we become conscious of a need for water but because the throat becomes dry.

Scientific interest in the regulation of water intake and thirst dates back several hundred years to the physiological research centers that began to flourish at European universities during the 18th and 19th centuries. As early as 1821, an extensive summary of research and theory relevant to the "urge to drink" was published in France.[85] It contained such a bewildering variety of observations and theoretical interpretations that Magendie,[73] one of the great pioneers of French physiology, suggested that thirst should be considered an "instinctive sentiment which does not admit of any explanation." Fortunately, his views did not prevail and theoretical as well as experimental interest in thirst continued unabated.

Much of the early research was concerned with the dry-mouth theory, and an impressive body of evidence against such an interpretation was available well over 100 years ago. The most famous of the early experiments is Claude Bernard's[18] demonstration that wetting the mouth and throat does not alleviate thirst. Bernard cut the esophagus of a horse and brought the cut ends to the surface of the throat. When the animal became thirsty and began to drink, the water wetted the mouth and throat but gushed out of the cut esophagus without reaching the stomach. The animal drank incessantly and swallowed huge quantities of water before stopping, apparently only when exhausted. When the cut ends of the esophagus were reconnected so that water could enter the stomach, drinking stopped after the animal had consumed a normal quantity. Bernard repeated this experiment in dogs and concluded that a dry-mouth theory could not account for thirst or satiety. Others reached similar conclusions following the demonstration that rinsing the mouth with water produced little or no effect on thirst sensations in man[86] or that transection of the glossopharyngeal and lingual nerves (which carry sensory information from the mouth and throat) did not reduce water intake in dogs.[70]

In spite of these unequivocal findings, most of the early investigators were loath to admit that the sensations that introspectively are so obviously the stimuli for drinking might not be essential determinants of thirst. Many clung desperately to a few apparently positive findings, such as the observation that the application of local anesthetics to the mouth and throat seemed to alleviate thirst sensations temporarily.[67]

The dry-mouth theory was restated in slightly modified form by W. B. Cannon as recently as 1934 and retains its popularity in psychological circles even today. According to Cannon's[22] revision, thirst is a sensation that arises from receptors in the mouth and throat that are sensitive to the moisture content of the surrounding mucosa. As the body loses water, the viscosity of the blood is maintained by the withdrawal of water from the tissues, much of the water coming from the salivary glands (saliva is 97 percent water). After a time, these glands can no longer secrete enough saliva to maintain the normal moisture of the mouth and throat. The resulting dryness irritates the thirst receptors and gives rise to a burning sensation that we recognize as thirst.

Signals Arising from the Mouth and Throat

Cannon's[22] version of the dry-mouth theory takes into account many experimental findings that suggest that water moves from the cells of the body into the extracellular spaces during deprivation (see below) and provides a plausible explanation of the relationship between water-deprivation and oral sensations under normal conditions. It cannot account for many experimental findings that show conclusively that these sensations are not essential to a regulation of water intake in accordance with the organism's needs. Since this regulation is, by definition, based on what we have called thirst, a dry-mouth theory is not adequate for our purposes. Sensations from the mouth and throat do, under normal circumstances, correlate with water loss and are undoubtedly one of the signals to which we respond when we look for water. Many of us find it, in fact, difficult to believe that we could be thirsty without these sensations. Let us therefore take a close look at the experimental literature.

Cannon's dry-mouth theory is nicely supported by the observation[4] that the rate of salivary flow in man is a nearly linear function of the fluid content of the body. Salivation drops sharply before the body's water loss reaches the point where corrective action is required and stops completely when a fluid deficit of about 8 percent of body weight occurs. The correlation between water loss and rate of salivation is good enough (-0.74 in one study) to suggest to some experimenters that salivation might be a good objective measure of thirst.[4] That this correlation does not reflect causal relationships is suggested by the observation that drugs that elicit profuse salivation do not alleviate thirst or reduce water intake,[4] and that the complete surgical removal of the salivary glands fails to affect water intake under normal circumstances.[80] Human subjects who congenitally lack these glands also report normal thirst sensations and regulate their intake in accordance with body needs, although they drink somewhat more frequently than normal to alleviate the dryness of the mouth.[91]

Further evidence against a dry-mouth theory comes from recent replications of some of the pioneering research of the French physiologists of the 19th century. Extensive denervation of the mouth and throat (transection of the trigeminal, glossopharyngeal, and chorda tympani nerves) does not interfere with the regulation of water intake in dogs;[17] the ingestion of water that is permitted to wet the mouth and throat but not to enter the stomach does not alleviate thirst in dogs;[16] and anesthetization of the mouth and throat produces little or no effect on thirst sensations or water intake in man as well as lower animals.[68,5]

Some investigators have apparently succeeded in dissociating thirst from the sensation of dryness of the mouth. For instance, intravenous injections of fairly concentrated salt solutions produce a dry throat long before a desire for water is noticed. Moreover, the dryness disappears almost instantaneously following the intravenous injections of glucose, whereas the desire for water persists for some time afterwards.[109]

If the sensations from the mouth and throat are as dispensable as these findings suggest, why then do we experience such intense thirst sensations after overstimulating oral receptors by eating very spicy or very salty foods? An ingenious explanation of this apparently paradoxical observation has been suggested by Wolf.[110] His hypothesis suggests that receptors in the mouth and the brain cells that meter the state of the organism's water balance may undergo similar changes when the fluid balance becomes negative. The resultant changes in the activity of the thirst-related brain cells serve as unconditioned stimuli for thirst. The concurrent sensations from the mouth and throat might become conditioned stimuli because of their frequent association with thirst. Although we have, as yet, been unable to test this interesting hypothesis experimentally, it is an appealing adjunct to current theories of thirst, which uniformly find it difficult to explain why a wet anchovy should induce thirst in an organism in perfect water balance.

The receptors of the mouth and throat probably do not give rise to signals that are an *essential* component of thirst. They may, however, originate signals that contribute importantly to satiety. Some evidence for an oral "metering" of fluid intake comes from experiments[104] that have studied the effects of intragastric injections of water on the sham-drinking of dogs with interrupted and externalized esophagi. In agreement with earlier reports, these experiments show that water that does not reach the stomach does not alleviate thirst, but they also show that the amount of water sham-drunk, although excessive, is proportional to the body's deficit. The mechanism for this oral metering of fluid intake is as yet unknown. Some interesting possibilities are suggested by the observation that some species are equipped with oral receptors that selectively respond to distilled water. Others have receptors that appear to be specifically inhibited by water and, to a lesser extent, by weak salt solutions. These receptors are activated by salt solutions that are more concentrated than the body fluids.[112] The possible role of these receptors in satiety has not yet been investigated, but it seems plausible that their activity might contribute relevant information.

It has also been suggested[110] that the stimulation of cold receptors in the mouth may, at least temporarily, alleviate thirst. Rats have been found to lick a tube from which a puff of cold air emanates every time the animals touch the opening of the tube. This "air-drinking" is seen only in thirsty animals and reduces subsequent water intake in spite of the fact that the air puffs evaporate saliva and thus further decrease the body's water stores.[59]

Signals Arising from the Stomach

Since the metering of fluid intake in animals with interrupted and externalized esophagi is poor, satiety must depend on signals from lower portions of the GI tract. Some species of animals, notably dogs, replenish a moderate water deficit in one very brief period of uninterrupted drinking and stop long before any of the ingested water could possibly be absorbed into the general circulation (see Figure 10–2). This indicates that satiety cannot depend on a reversal of the conditions that are believed to give rise to thirst sensations (see below) and suggests that an independent satiety mechanism may exist. The rapidity of the inhibition (some species stop drinking immediately after the intragastric injection of water)[3] suggests further that the principal signal may be neural and may arise directly from the stretch receptors of the walls of the stomach.

This possibility has been investigated by a number of investigators. The results of these studies suggest that stomach distention may operate as a limiting factor that comes into play sooner in some species than in others. Neural feedback from the stomach may also

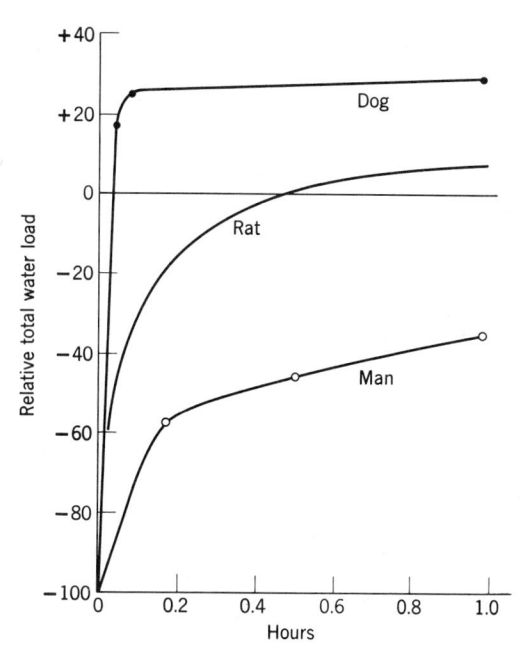

FIG. 10–2. Water intakes during the first hour of drinking in three species.

(From *Physiological regulations* by E. F. Adolph. Copyright 1943, The Ronald Press Company, New York.)

provide satiety signals under normal circumstances, but does not seem to be essential. Inflating a balloon that is inserted into the stomach inhibits deprivation-induced drinking in animals with externalized esophagi[105] (see Figure 10–3). It also reduces the thirst that is normally elicited by injections of concentrated salt solutions.[79] However, the inflation of stomach balloons is aversive,[75] perhaps because it induces pain and nausea, and the observed inhibition of drinking may not be specifically related to thirst. That this may be true is suggested by the observation that denervation of the stomach eliminates the inhibitory influences of balloon inflation[105] but does not reduce water intake in response to salt injections[62] or water deprivation.[29]

Conclusions

Sensory feedback from the mouth and throat is a prominent aspect of the stimulus complex to which we respond when we search for water. It nonetheless does not appear to be an essential component of thirst, since man as well as

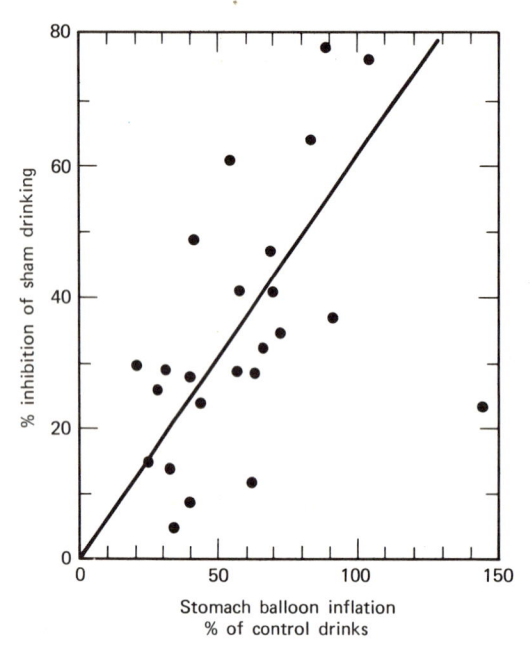

FIG. 10–3. Inhibition of sham drinking by inflation of stomach balloon.

(After E. J. Towbin. Gastric distention as a factor in the satiation of thirst in esophagostomized dogs. *Amer. J. Physiol.*, **159**, 1949, 533–541.)

lower organisms can maintain control over the body's fluid balance when these signals are partially or completely eliminated. Stimulation of these receptors may, under some circumstances, induce thirst sensations, but the elimination of signals from these receptors does not reduce thirst in the presence of a negative water balance.

Salivary flow is positively correlated with general tissue dehydration and water need and may be an objective, if somewhat impractical, measure of thirst under normal conditions. However, thirst can occur when salivary flow is adequate. Drugs that increase salivary flow do not reduce thirst significantly, and continual wetting of the mouth and throat provides little or no respite for the thirsty. Conversely, the congenital absence or surgical removal of the salivary glands does not interfere with the normal regulation of water intake. Anesthetization of the mouth and throat produces only minor and temporary effects on thirst and water intake, and deafferentation does not seem to interfere at all.

These observations suggest that, as a comprehensive explanation of thirst, Cannon's dry-mouth theory is not adequate. More is involved in the regulation of the organism's fluid balance than sensory feedback from the mouth and throat.

Review Questions

1. State Cannon's theory of thirst. How does it differ from earlier versions of the dry-mouth theory?

2. Can we define thirst in terms of the body's fluid balance? In terms of oral sensations?

3. Why do we become thirsty after eating spicy and salty foods?

4. Summarize the evidence against a dry-mouth theory of thirst that was available 100 years ago.

5. What additional negative evidence has accumulated in the last 100 years?

6. Discuss the correlation between salivary flow and thirst. Can it describe a causal relationship?

7. Discuss the evidence that suggests that some oral "metering" of fluid intake may occur.

8. What evidence do we have for a gastric "metering" of fluid intake?

9. Summarize, in a few sentences, the role of oral and gastric factors in thirst and satiety for water.

CENTRAL REGULATORY MECHANISMS

Historical Perspectives

Nearly all of the prescientific attempts to account for man's urge to drink attributed it to the sensation of dryness of the mouth and throat. The physiologists of the 18th and 19th centuries generally accepted this interpretation even though conflicting experimental evidence rapidly accumulated. A few voices in the wilderness suggested in the first half of the 19th century that the brain might exercise some regulatory control over water intake,[30] but this view was not very influential. Central theories of thirst became more fashionable during the first decades of our century although there was, as yet, little experimental or clinical support for such an explanation. Some theorists suggested that dehydration might increase the concentration of solids in the blood and result in thirst because these solids might irritate the cortex;[68] others thought that some "vegetative center" might translate sensory signals from the mouth and throat into thirst sensations.[21] A German physiologist[84] even proposed that increased salt concentrations in the blood might excite receptors in the mouth and throat that transmit signals to a diencephalic thirst center—a surprisingly close approximation to current views, considering the fact that it was formulated before relevant experimental observations became available.

Experimental evidence for a diencephalic thirst center became available only later when diabetes insipidus (a disease characterized by an inability to retain water and a consequent excessive intake) was traced to tumor growth and damage to the hypothalamus.[16] Clinical studies demonstrated 30 years ago that mechanical stimulation of the floor of the third ventricle elicited thirst sensations in patients undergoing brain surgery. The experimental study of the role of the hypothalamic mechanisms in thirst and water intake regulation did not proceed, however, until the 1950's.

Hypothalamic Thirst Mechanisms

Bilateral lesions in the lateral hypothalamus of rats produce adipsia (a refusal to ingest water),[6] which is almost always accompanied by aphagia (a refusal to eat).[103] As we have seen in the preceding discussion of hunger, the lesioned animals gradually recover and eventually maintain normal body weight on a standard laboratory diet of dry food and water. Although the "recovered" lateral animal does not respond appropriately to hypoglycemia, its regulation of food intake appears to be normal under normal circumstances. The same appears to be true for water intake until one examines the animals' drinking behavior more closely. It then becomes clear that at least some of the "recovered" lateral animals (presumably those with the most complete damage to the thirst mechanism) have not recovered at all. Their water intake turns out to be related exclusively to the ingestion of dry food. These animals do not drink in response to even prolonged periods of water deprivation when food is not available and cannot adjust to maintenance schedules that make water available only during restricted periods of the day. They have been called "prandial" drinkers because they drink only to wash down dry food.[102] Unilateral lesions in the lateral hypothalamus have been reported[47] to result in a less prolonged and severe adipsia (and aphagia) that appears to be completely reversible.

Nearly all animals with lateral hypothalamic lesions show disturbances of food- as well as water-intake regulation. However, occasionally one is found to be deficient only with respect to thirst. These animals eat normal quantities of food as long as water is provided by intragastric injections.[78] A few cases of pure aphagia have also been reported,[88] indicating that the lateral hypothalamic feeding and drinking mechanisms are, indeed, independent.

The exact location of the hypothalamic thirst mechanism differs somewhat between species. (For instance, it appears to be located more anteriorly and medially in the dog and goat than in the rat.) Its general functions, however, seem to be very similar in all species. Lesions in the hypothalamic thirst system always produce adipsia and, in most species, a concurrent aphagia.

Electrical stimulation of the lateral hypothalamus of sated rats elicits water or food intake.[75] At some electrode placements, threshold intensities of stimulation reliably elicit drinking, and higher intensities are needed to elicit feeding, suggesting that selective excitement of the drinking mechanism is possible. However, recent experiments[106] suggest that frequent repetition of such stimulation in the absence of water may reverse the order of preference in such a way that threshold intensities of stimulation come to elicit feeding.

Electrical stimulation of the hypothalamic thirst mechanism in goats elicits "compulsive" drinking. Stimulated animals not only consume very large quantities of water[12] but also drink such highly aversive fluids as concentrated salt solution or urine.[8] At some electrode sites, this is accompanied by a reduction of urine flow, which suggests that the stimulation increased the pituitary secretion of antidiuretic hormone (ADH).

Some of the earlier stimulation experiments[9] reported that stimulation-elicited thirst could not be conditioned to a previously neutral stimulus and concluded that the effects of electrical stimulation might not be quite like normal deprivation-induced thirst. This is probably not a justified conclusion because normal thirst also cannot be conditioned. More recent experiments[14] have put the question to a fairer test and demonstrated that animals will perform instrumental responses that were learned while they were thirsty when electrical stimulation is presented.

Chemical stimulation of the lateral hypothalamus of sated rats[48,49] elicits food or water intake, depending on the nature of the chemical injected. Microinjections of a cholinergic neurohumor (acetylcholine) elicit drinking (and inhibit feeding); similar injections of an adrenergic neurohumor (norepinephrine) elicit feeding (and inhibit drinking). Injections of drugs that selectively interfere with neural transmission at cholinergic synapses prevent the drinking response to cholinergic stimulation and reduce water intake in deprived animals.[50] That cholinergic stimulation of the lateral hypothalamus elicits a motivational state similar to thirst is suggested by the observation that sated rats, trained to operate one lever for food rewards and a second lever for water, work only on the water-rewarded lever following cholinergic stimulation.[49]

Recent extensions of this work by Leibowitz[65] suggest that the observed inhibition of drinking by norepinephrine may be due to the activation of an inhibitory component of the thirst system, which, in turn, is opposed by a beta-adrenergic excitatory component. These investigations replicated the observation that alpha-adrenergic agents such as norepinephrine inhibit drinking in deprived animals and further found that intrahypothalamic injections of beta-adrenergic substances such as isoproterenol elicit drinking in sated animals. The pharmacological specificity of these effects was demonstrated in experiments showing an inhibition of water intake following the central administration of beta-adrenergic blocking agents and the facilitation of drinking by alpha-adrenergic blockers (see Table 2). Although an indirect action of some of these compounds on peripheral components of the thirst system has not yet been ruled out, it has been suggested[66] that the hypothalamic thirst system may be intimately related to the adrenergic components of the feeding system. The beta-adrenergic system may provide a mechanism for concurrent thirst stimulation and hunger suppression. The alpha-adrenergic system may operate in a reciprocal fashion

TABLE 2. Effects of Hypothalamically-injected Drugs upon Hunger and Thirst

DRUGS	HUNGER	THIRST
α-ADRENERGIC AGONIST	↑	↓
α-ADRENERGIC BLOCKER	↓	↑
β-ADRENERGIC AGONIST	↓	↑
β-ADRENERGIC BLOCKER	↑	↓
CHOLINERGIC AGONIST	↓	↑

Changes in hunger and thirst (increase ↑; decrease ↓) resulting from hypothalamic injections of adrenergic, adrenolytic, and cholinergic drugs. In each of the five drug categories, the behavioral changes are found to be antagonistic.

(From Sarah F. Leibowitz. Central adrenergic receptors and the regulation of hunger and thirst. *Res. Publ., Ass. Res. nerv. ment. Dis.*, 1972, in press.)

to stimulate hunger and inhibit thirst. The cholinergic components of the thirst system appear to oppose the alpha-adrenergic components of both the hunger and thirst systems but act synergistically with their beta-adrenergic components.

Cholinergic stimulation of the lateral hypothalamus also reduces the volume of urine and increases its concentration.[76] This reaction is presumably related to the release of antidiuretic hormone by the pituitary gland and suggests that stimulation of the lateral hypothalamic thirst mechanism not only induces thirst but also activates mechanisms that conserve water in times of need. This stimulation-induced retention of fluids also indicates that the drinking response to cholinergic stimulation is not secondary to urinary water loss—an important point in view of the hypothalamic origin of diabetes insipidus.

The hypothalamic thirst mechanism also appears to be selectively sensitive to salt solutions of a higher concentration than that of normal body fluids. Microinjections of such salt solutions into the hypothalamus of goats[11] as well as rats[32] elicit copious drinking. These findings are of theoretical significance because water deprivation increases the concentration of salts in the blood. The fact that the cells of the hypothalamic thirst mechanism may be selectively sensitive to high salt concentrations provides an important clue as to how thirst may be related to the body's water needs. We shall comment further on this point when we discuss this correlation in detail.

It has recently been shown[33] that thirst can also be elicited by microinjections of angiotensin (a vasoconstrictor agent that is closely related to the enzyme renin that is formed by the kidney) into many hypothalamic, preoptic, and septal sites (see Figure 10–4). These observations are of particular interest because a direct action of angiotensin on portions of the central thirst system may explain the results of recent experiments (see below) that have suggested that the kidney may itself play an important role in the regulation of thirst.

The evidence for a hypothalamic "satiety" influence on thirst is, as yet, weak. The

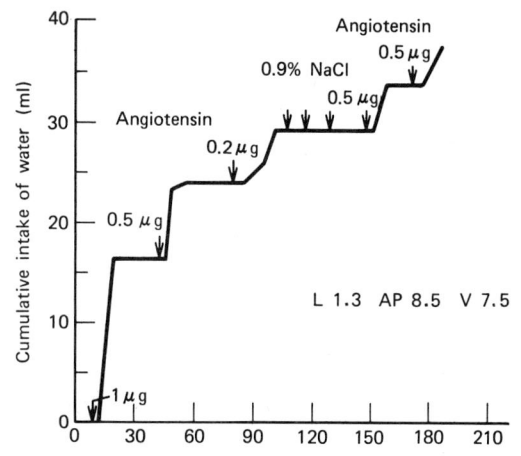

FIG. 10–4. The cumulative amounts of water drunk by a rat given intracranial injections of angiotensin, and 0.9% saline. The stereotaxic coordinates used in implanting the cannulae are on the right of the figure. L, mm lateral to the center of the sagittal sinus; AP, mm anterior to the ear bars; V, mm depth from the dural surface.

(From A. N. Epstein, J. T. Fitzsimons, & Barbara J. Simons. Drinking caused by the intracranial injection of angiotensin into the rat. *J. Physiol.*, **200**, 1968, 98–100.)

strongest indication that such a mechanism may exist comes from the recent chemical stimulation experiments that we have just discussed. Lesions in the hypothalamus do not, typically, increase water intake except in cases in which an involvement of the hypothalamo-hypophyseal system produces a primary disturbance in urine flow[92] or when exaggerated dry-food intake increases prandial water needs.[87] These observations indicate that the pathways that may mediate inhibitory influences on water intake may be very diffusely represented in the hypothalamus. Recent investigations[54] have shown that transection of the posterior fiber connections of the medial hypothalamus result in hyperdipsia that far exceeds the prandial requirements of the accompanying hyperphagia (see Figure 10–5). It is not yet clear whether a secondary involvement of pituitary secretions can be ruled out in these experiments.

Extrahypothalamic Influences

Largely on the basis of the observation that complete and prolonged adipsia can be produced by relatively small hypothalamic

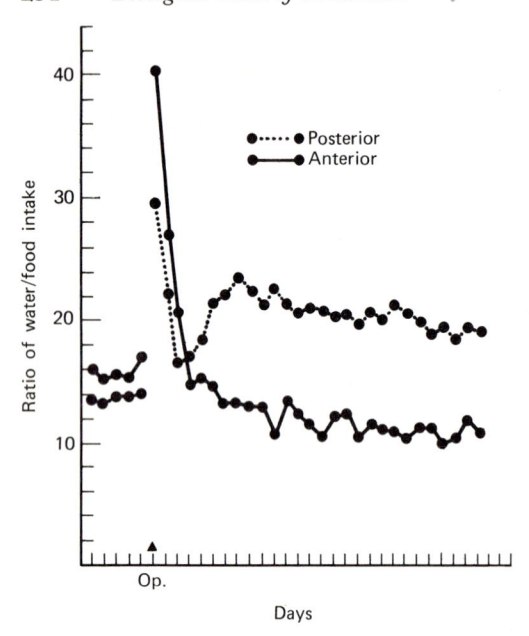

FIG. 10–5. The relationship between food and water intake of 10 animals with transverse knife cuts through the posterior hypothalamus and of 9 animals with similar cuts through the anterior hypothalamus.

(From S. P. Grossman. Changes in food and water intake associated with an interruption of the anterior or posterior fiber connections of the hypothalamus. *J. comp. physiol. Psychol.*, 75, 1971, 23–31. Copyright 1971 by the American Psychological Association, and reproduced by permission.)

lesions, it has been generally assumed that thirst may be regulated by an autonomous "thirst center" in this portion of the brain.

This interpretation was first questioned by the observation[43] that lesions in the brainstem of a rat that destroy the subcommissural organ (SCO) also produce adipsia and that electrical stimulation of this region increases water intake. The posterior hypothalamus and the area of the subcommissural organ are closely interconnected by several major pathways, and it has been suggested[45] that the two regions may exercise complementary regulatory influences on thirst and water intake. This possibility is particularly intriguing in view of the fact that lesions in the general area of the subcommissural organ reduce the secretion of the adrenal salt-retaining hormone aldosterone.[100]

A number of additional extrahypothalamic influences have been discovered in recent years. Lesions in the globus pallidus[81] produce effects on water (as well as food) intake that are essentially indistinguishable from those seen after lateral hypothalamic lesions. That these lesions may interfere with a common pathway is indicated by several observations. Mild and temporary inhibitory effects of a unilateral lateral hypothalamic lesion can be converted into complete and long-term adipsia and aphagia by the addition of a contralateral lesion in the globus pallidus.[101] Interruption of the fiber connections between the globus pallidus and the lateral hypothalamus by surgical knife cuts that produce no direct cellular damage in either structure also result in prolonged adipsia.[56]

Facilitatory as well as inhibitory influences on water intake have been localized in the amygdaloid complex.[55] Electrical stimulation of the anterior amygdala increases water intake but inhibits feeding in deprived animals. Stimulation of more posterior sites inhibits both food and water intake. Small lesions in the posterior amygdala produce hyperdipsia as well as hyperphagia (a pattern that is quite different from that seen after ventromedial hypothalamic damage). Lesions at the anterior stimulation sites decrease water (but not food) intake.

Recent experiments[58, 71] have added still another structure, the medial septal area, to the growing list of regions that seem to contain thirst-related pathways. Lesions in the posterior aspect of the medial septal area produce diuresis and a consistent and sometimes marked facilitatory effect on thirst, which is reflected in a rise in ad libitum intake (see Figure 10–6)[71, 20] as well as an enhancement of water-rewarded instrumental behavior.[58] This appears to be due to a primary hyperdipsia that is not secondary to prandial drinking, excessive urine flow, or changes in the composition of the blood.[20] It is interesting to note that only those septal lesions that result in a significant depletion of brain acetylcholine produce hyperdipsia.[89] In the goat, destruction of the preoptic region results in complete adipsia but does not affect food intake.[10]

The results of chemical stimulation studies indicate an even broader distribution of the

Thirst and the Regulation of Water Intake **235**

instrumental responding in deprived animals[51] (see Figure 10–7).

The chemical stimulation experiments, as well as the results of recent lesion studies, suggest that the neural substrate of thirst and water-intake regulation may be much more extensive and diffuse than we had anticipated only a few years ago. We do not yet know much about the nature of the contribution that individual components of this complex system of pathways may make and cannot suggest a comprehensive hypothesis concerning their interaction in determining thirst until further experimental data become available.

Conclusions

Although speculations about a thirst center were published almost 150 years ago, experi-

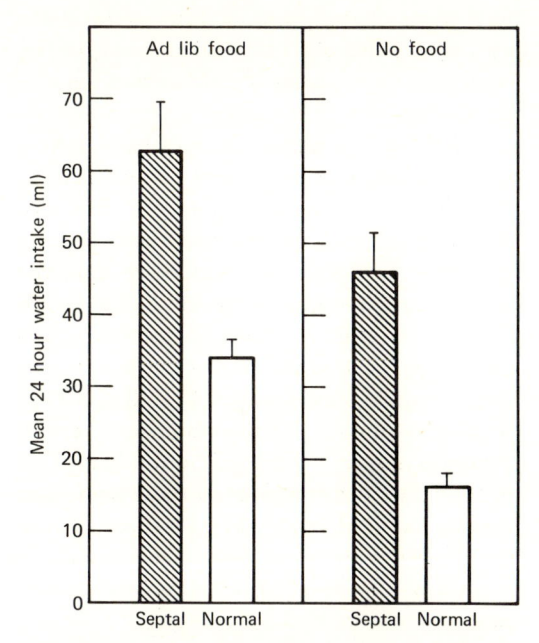

FIG. 10–6. Mean 24-hr water intake (ml) of rats with septal lesions (shaded columns) and normal rats when food was available continuously (left panel) and when food was absent.

(From E. M. Blass & D. G. Hanson. Primary hyperdipsia in the rat following septal lesions. *J. comp. physiol. Psychol.*, **70**, 1970, 87–93. Copyright 1970 by the American Psychological Association, and reproduced by permission.)

thirst circuit. Microinjections of cholinergic substances into portions of the hypothalamus, ventral thalamus, preoptic region, medial septal area, hippocampus, and cingulate region have been shown to elicit drinking in sated rats. The responses are similar and sometimes even more intense than those obtained by chemical stimulation of the lateral hypothalamic component of the thirst system.[49,52,35] The drinking response to chemical stimulation at all sites can be prevented or inhibited by injections of cholinergic "blockers" (drugs that interfere with the action of cholinergic transmitters) either into the site of cholinergic stimulation[50] or into other positive sites in the pharmacologically defined circuit.[69]

Cholinergic stimulation sometimes produces complex effects on water intake. For instance, microinjections of cholinergic substances into the amygdaloid complex do not elicit water intake in sated rats but greatly augment drinking as well as water-rewarded

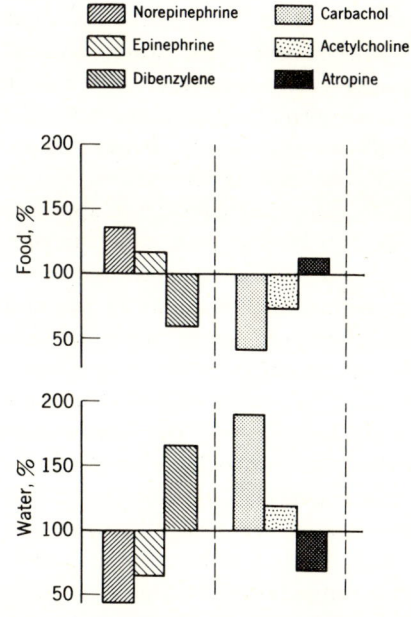

FIG. 10–7. Effects of adrenergic (norepinephrine, epinephrine) and cholinergic (carbachol, acetylcholine) stimulation or adrenergic (dibenzylene) and cholinergic (atropine) blockade of the ventral amygdala on food- and water-rewarded instrumental responses of deprived rats. The results are expressed as a percentage of the average performance on pre- and postdrug control tests.

(After S. P. Grossman. Behavioral effects of direct chemical stimulation of central nervous system structures. *Int. J. Neuropharmacol.*, **3**, 1964, 45–58. Permission granted for Pergamon Press copyright.)

mental evidence for a central regulatory influence has become available only during the past two or three decades. The initial clues for the localization of this regulatory mechanism came from clinical observations of diabetes insipidus following damage to the hypothalamus of man.

Initial experimental interest consequently concentrated on this region of the brain and rapidly produced evidence for a hypothalamic thirst "center" that overlaps extensively, at least in some species, with the lateral hypothalamic feeding "center". Damage to this area produces complete adipsia, which appears to be permanent in some instances. Most animals with such lesions eventually accept water and maintain normal intake on a dry-food and water diet, but their drinking turns out to be related to their desire to ingest dry food rather than to thirst itself. Electrical as well as chemical stimulation of the hypothalamic thirst mechanism elicits water intake. The effects of such stimulation are sufficiently similar to normal, deprivation-induced thirst to motivate previously learned water-rewarded instrumental behaviors. The hypothalamic thirst mechanism also appears to be selectively sensitive to concentrated salt solutions—a very important clue as to how the hypothalamic cells may be appraised of the state of the organism's fluid balance.

No hypothalamic satiety center has as yet been identified for thirst. Ventromedial hypothalamic lesions upset the food/water ratio and thus the fluid balance of the organism, but this is entirely due to an increased food intake without compensatory adjustments in drinking. Animals with such lesions also work less for water (as well as food) rewards, but this may not be specifically related to a change in hunger or thirst motivation. Lesions in the posterior hypothalamus produce extreme hyperdipsia, but this is not related to a primary disturbance of thirst motivation. These lesions upset pituitary functions and lead to the continual loss of water by urination (diabetes insipidus). The animals must ingest huge quantities of water to prevent dehydration (and are, in fact, responding entirely appropriately to the organism's needs). Interruption of the posterior fiber connections of the region of the ventromedial nuclei results in hyperdipsia but this effect may be temporary.

Chemical stimulation studies have shown that drinking can be elicited or modified by drug injections into a number of extrahypothalamic sites, suggesting that the thirst circuit may be much more extensive than the early ablation studies suggested. That this is indeed the case is indicated by recent experiments, which have shown that damage to the (a) globus pallidus, (b) midbrain tegmentum, and (c) subcommissural organ produces adipsia, the magnitude and duration of the effect being similar to those seen after hypothalamic damage. Less dramatic hypodipsic reactions have been seen following anterior amygdaloid lesions. Damage to more posterior portions of the amygdala or to the medial septal area results in mild hyperdipsia (see Figure 10–8).

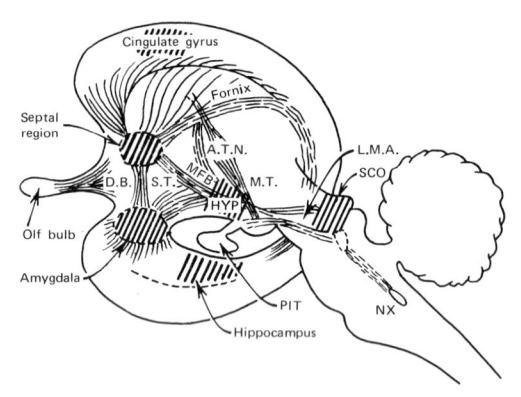

FIG. 10–8. Distribution of neural pathways related to thirst (diagonally hatched areas).
(After P. D. MacLean. The limbic system with respect to self-preservation and the preservation of the species. *J. nerv. ment. Dis.*, **127**, 1958, 1–11. Copyright 1958. The Williams & Wilkins Co., Baltimore.)

Review Questions

1. The investigation of what disease led to the discovery of the hypothalamic thirst mechanisms? Describe its principal symptoms. Are they due to a primary disturbance of thirst?

2. Describe the drinking behavior of rats with bilateral damage to the lateral hypothalamus.

3. Stimulation of the lateral hypothalamus elicits drinking in sated rats. Discuss the question of whether this is due to the elicitation of thirst.

4. Discuss the evidence that suggests that the central regulation of thirst may involve an extensive network of pathways outside the hypothalamus.

5. Is there any evidence for a central satiety mechanism for thirst?

THE CORRELATION BETWEEN THIRST AND WATER NEEDS

The Organism's Fluid Compartments

To serve its biological function, thirst must correlate rather precisely with the organism's water needs. The classical dry-mouth theory of thirst accounted for this correlation quite easily by assuming that a loss of body water would automatically reduce the availability of saliva and thus stimulate thirst receptors. We have seen that this attractively simple explanation cannot, in fact, account for thirst in various experimental situations and must now look for alternatives. If water intake and thirst are regulated by a central mechanism, as the research literature indicates, how is this mechanism appraised of a depletion of the body's water reserves or their replenishment by the ingestion of fluids? To investigate this question, we must learn how and where the body stores its water and what effects deprivation or drinking have on these stores.

The body fluids are stored in two major compartments (see Table 3). The *intracellular* compartment refers to the water found inside the cells of the body. It is separated by a semipermeable membrane, the cell wall, from the *extracellular* compartment, which includes the fluids that surround all of the cells of the body, as well as the fluids found in the blood vessels. There is a constant exchange of fluids as well as solids between these two compartments because the extracellular fluids provide the nutrients for and remove the waste products of all cellular activity.

Both fluid compartments contain substances other than water, and some of these, having large molecules, cannot pass through the semipermeable membrane that separates the two compartments. This is important to our discussion because the presence of solutions of unequal concentrations on opposite sides of a semipermeable membrane produces an *osmotic pressure* gradient (i.e., water will move from the region of lower concentration to the region of higher concentration until an equilibrium of the two solutions is established). To visualize this situation, imagine a chamber that is divided into two compartments by a wall that allows water to pass freely but does not permit the passage of some larger molecules. If we place pure water into one compartment and the same amount of water plus some sodium chloride salt into the other, water will flow into the compartment that contains the salt. In the body, both the intracellular and extracellular compartments contain some salts at all times, but their concentrations often differ. When this is true, water moves either into or out of the cells to reestablish the equilibrum of the two solutions (see Figure 10–9).

It is possible to measure the *absolute osmotic pressure* (i.e., the pressure that a given solution

TABLE 3. Major Subdivisions of the Body Water

Compartment	Approximate Percent of Body Weight	Approximate Percent of Body Fluid	Amount in a 70-kg Man (liters)
Extracellular fluid	25	35	17
Plasma	5	7	3
Interstitial fluid	20	28	14
Intracellular fluid	40	65	29
Total Body water	65	100	46

(From *Human anatomy and physiology* by J. E. Crouch and J. R. McClintic. Copyright © 1971. John Wiley & Sons, Inc.)

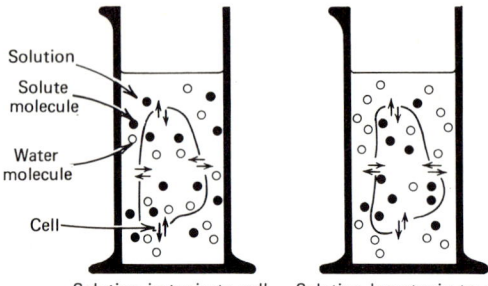

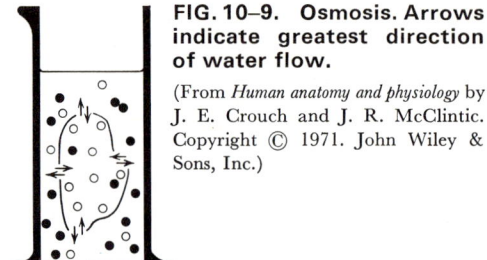

FIG. 10–9. Osmosis. Arrows indicate greatest direction of water flow.

(From *Human anatomy and physiology* by J. E. Crouch and J. R. McClintic. Copyright © 1971. John Wiley & Sons, Inc.)

would exert against pure water) in a variety of ways, and this measure is an often useful index of the concentration of salts. More often, we want to know what the *relative osmotic pressure* is (i.e., the pressure that exists between two solutions that are separated by a semipermeable membrane).

What happens to the body's water stores during water deprivation? We continue to urinate, sweat, and evaporate water from the lungs and body surfaces. Although sweat and urine contain a fair amount of salt, their concentration is normally quite a bit lower than that of the body's fluids. Deprivation therefore increases the concentration of salt in the extracellular fluid compartment (i.e., increases its absolute osmotic pressure). This, in turn, sets up relative pressure gradients between the two compartments that force water out of the cells. Notice that the absolute osmotic pressure of both compartments is increased as a result of water deprivation. When deprivation continues for prolonged periods of time, the cells become increasingly unable to give up water to the extracellular compartment because water is an essential medium for all cellular reactions. The absolute osmotic pressure of the extracellular compartment then rises sharply, and a relative pressure gradient between the two compartments is maintained.

When water is ingested, the absolute osmotic pressure of the extracellular fluids falls. The relative osmotic pressure gradient between the two compartments remains until enough water has moved into the cell to reestablish an equilibrium between the salt concentrations in the extra- and intracellular fluid compartments. At this point, the body's fluid balance is reestablished. The big question is: How does the organism regulate this important process?

Metering the body's total fluid level, though perhaps an essential component of the regulatory process under some circumstances, is not an adequate assessment of the organism's needs under others. For instance, when we ingest very salty foods, a serious depletion of the cellular water stores may occur although the total fluid content of the body is high. Conversely, we continually lose salts by sweating and urinary excretion and must replenish the supply to prevent severe disturbances of the organism's water household regardless of the total fluid content of the body. (As we continue to lose salts from the extracellular fluids, a relative osmotic pressure gradient develops that forces more and more water into the cells, producing overhydration and, eventually, damage to the cell.)

These observations suggest that the organism must meter not only the absolute level of its fluid stores but also the concentration of salts in them. As we shall see, much research has been concerned with the intriguing question of just how the body achieves this regulation and whether it regulates the absolute or relative osmotic pressure of the fluids in its two major storage compartments.

Before we turn to a discussion of this research, a few terms must be identified. When the body is in water balance (i.e., when the absolute osmotic pressure of the intracellular and extracellular compartments are identical), its fluids under normal circumstances contain about 0.9 percent sodium chloride salt. Solutions that contain the same ratio of solutes (such as NaCl) to solvent (such as water) as the body fluid are said to be *isotonic* to it, provided that the solute cannot cross the cellular membranes. Given the same restriction, solutions of higher concentration are called *hypertonic* and those of lower concentrations, *hypotonic*.

Osmometric Influences

Some of the earlier theories of thirst[27, 30] suggested that water deprivation might increase the viscosity of the blood. This, in turn, was thought to stimulate receptors in the mouth and throat and thus give rise to the sensation of thirst. Around the turn of the century, Mayer[74] demonstrated experimentally that water deprivation did indeed increase the absolute osmotic pressure of the blood. He suggested that the hypertonicity of the blood might irritate receptors in the walls of the blood vessels that reflexly induce dilation of these vessels. This, in turn, was thought to produce the oral sensations that initiate drinking. Only a year later, another French physiologist named Wettendorff[108] replicated Mayer's experiment and reported that the absolute osmotic pressure of the blood increased significantly only after 24 hours of water deprivation. Since the body loses a good deal of water during the first 24 hours of deprivation, Wettendorff suggested that early in deprivation, relative pressure gradients develop that force water out of the cells and thus maintain the absolute pressure of the extracellular fluid at relatively low levels. He thought that thirst could not be due to a metering of the absolute osmotic pressure of the extracellular fluid because this pressure did not change fast enough. Instead, he proposed that thirst might be related to the movement of water out of the cell. Cells might be sensitive to the consequent change in cell size or membrane tension and signal this information to some coordinating center in the brain, which then gives rise to thirst sensations.

With some modifications, this notion continues to play an important role today. As we shall see, we are not yet entirely sure whether cell size, the movement of water through the cell wall, or a relative osmotic pressure gradient per se may be the essential stimulus for thirst. What is fairly clear is that the "osmoreceptor" functions are probably not shared by all cells (otherwise a reduction of sensory feedback from the body should interfere with thirst), as Wettendorff suggested, but may instead be a unique property of some brain cells that are specifically concerned with the regulation of thirst.

The osmometric theory of thirst is handsomely supported by the observation that the ingestion or intravenous injection of hypertonic salt solutions induces intense thirst in man[15] and water intake in experimental animals[61] (see Figure 10–10). That relative rather than absolute osmotic pressures are monitored is indicated by the observation that injections of substances such as urea that increase the absolute osmotic pressure of the extracellular fluid but fail to set up relative pressure gradients (because they pass readily through the cell membrane) do not induce thirst and water intake.[46] (Actually, these substances do produce a small temporary effect

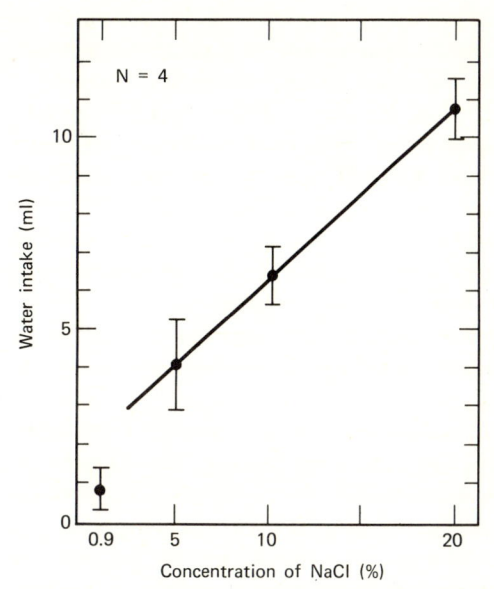

FIG. 10–10. Mean (± SD) water intake of four rats in response to intravenous injections of 1 ml of NaCl solutions of varying concentrations.

(From J. D. Corbit. Effect of intravenous sodium chloride on drinking in the rat. *J. comp. physiol. Psychol.*, **60**, 1965, 397–406. Copyright 1965 by the American Psychological Association, and reproduced by permission.)

on thirst and water intake because of the transient pressure differences that exist until the concentration of urea molecules inside and outside the cell has equilibrated.) An alternative interpretation of this finding—that thirst might be related specifically to the absolute concentration of sodium chloride in the blood—has been disproven in experiments that demonstrate that intravenous injections of hypertonic solutions of sorbital (which does not cross the cell membrane and consequently sets up relative osmotic pressure gradients but actually reduces the absolute concentration of sodium and chloride in the blood) induces intense thirst.[63]

The osmometric theory of thirst is also supported by the discovery of cells in the hypothalamus that appear to be selectively activated by hypertonic solutions. Some of the hypothalamic osmoreceptors seem to control fluid intake; others regulate water loss by urinary excretion. That this might be one of the mechanisms by which the body regulates its fluid balance was first suggested by the observation[107] that injections of hypertonic saline into the diencephalic blood supply increase the secretion of antidiuretic hormone (ADH) and decrease urinary water loss. Further investigations of this relationship[7] demonstrated that microinjections of hypertonic sodium chloride solutions into the posterior hypothalamus increase ADH secretion but do not evoke drinking, whereas similar injections into the anterior lateral hypothalamus induce drinking without affecting renal functions. In some species, such as the goat, the thirst-related osmoreceptors are located in the thirst "center" as defined by the results of lesions or electrical stimulation. In these species, damage to the anterior aspects of the lateral hypothalamus results in complete adipsia.[12, 13] In other species, such as the rat, the osmoreceptors are similarly located in the anterior hypothalamus or preoptic region but the thirst "center" has moved backwards. In these species, lesions in the lateral hypothalamus back at the level of the ventromedial nuclei result in complete adipsia. Lesions in the anterior osmoreceptor zone selectively abolish the drinking which is normally evoked by hypertonicity of the extracellular fluids.[19]

When we look at the experimental evidence that more specifically supports a cellular dehydration theory of thirst, the picture is not quite as consistent. Strictly speaking, such a theory[28] suggests that thirst is related to the movement of water out of the cell and the resultant shrinkage in cell size, and that satiety is related to a movement of water into the cell. Several investigators have attempted to test this hypothesis by withdrawing salts from the extracellular fluids, thus causing an influx of water into the cell. (If thirst is due to the presence of a relative osmotic pressure gradient or the actual movement of water through the cell membrane, this should produce thirst. If, on the other hand, thirst is related to cell shrinkage, the withdrawal of salts from the extracellular spaces and the resulting overhydration of the cell should instead produce sensations of satiety.) The results of these experiments favor the cellular-dehydration theory in showing that drinking does not occur.[26] An acute depletion of sodium chloride from the extracellular fluid has, in fact, been shown to produce a long-lasting depression of fluid intake,[64] as the dehydration theory suggests (see Figure 10–11).

On the other hand, there are numerous clinical[31, 93] as well as experimental[60] reports of intense thirst and excessive water intake in animals and man maintained chronically on salt-deficient diets that undoubtedly produced cellular overhydration and expansion. This thirst is not alleviated by the ingestion of water (which only aggravates the situation) but by the consumption of hypertonic salt solutions. These observations present some difficulties for the cellular-dehydration theory of thirst and suggest that the osmoreceptors may be sensitive not only to a decrease in cellular size but perhaps to any significant change in cellular size above as well as below some normal range.[109]

There is, at this time, no question that all conditions that cause a movement of water out of the cellular compartment and a consequent shrinkage of the cell result in thirst. However, satiety may not simply reflect a

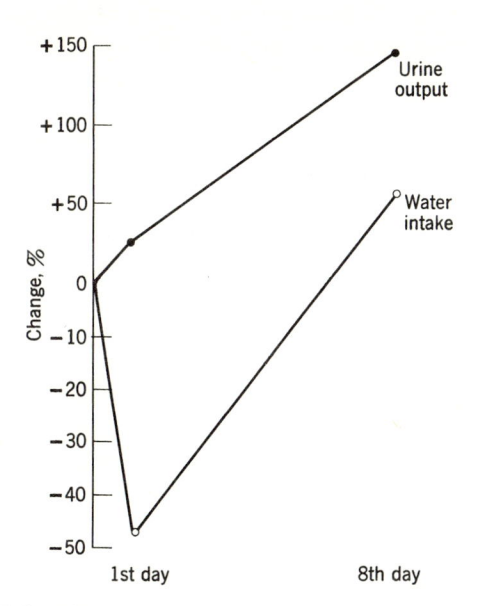

FIG. 10–11. Effects of acute depletion of sodium chloride from extracellular fluid on water intake and urine output.

(After K. C. Huang. Effect of salt depletion and fasting on water exchange in the rabbit. *Amer. J. Physiol.*, **181**, 1955, 609–615.)

a 10 to 15 percent decrease in blood plasma volume always produces thirst[36,94] (see Figure 10–12). A number of different techniques have been used to produce this state of *hypovolemia*.[83,34,97] Since each produces somewhat different effects on the distribution of the body's fluid stores and their osmotic pressures, we can be fairly certain at this time that the effective stimulus for thirst in all of these studies is a decrease in blood plasma[95] rather than a decrease in the total extracellular fluid, as some investigators proposed a few years ago.[36]

The loss of blood plasma not only depletes the body's water stores but also causes a significant reduction in total salt content.[99] Water ingestion does little to repair plasma-fluid deficits because the low salt concentration of the blood causes much of the ingested reversal of this movement of water (for one thing, drinking usually stops long before the equilibrium between the extracellular and intracellular fluids is reestablished). We are also not yet certain that an excessive influx of water may not also produce thirst.

Volumetric Influences

It has been known for some time that a substantial loss of blood produces thirst. The osmometric or cellular-dehydration theories of thirst cannot readily account for this phenomenon because blood is part of the body's extracellular fluid and its depletion does not produce any change in the osmotic pressure gradients between the body's fluid compartments. Since an osmometric theory also cannot explain the extreme thirst of patients on a salt-deficient diet, several investigators have recently examined the possibility that the osmometric system might be supplemented by a volumetric mechanism that responds to changes in the quantity of extracellular fluid.

This experimental analysis has shown that

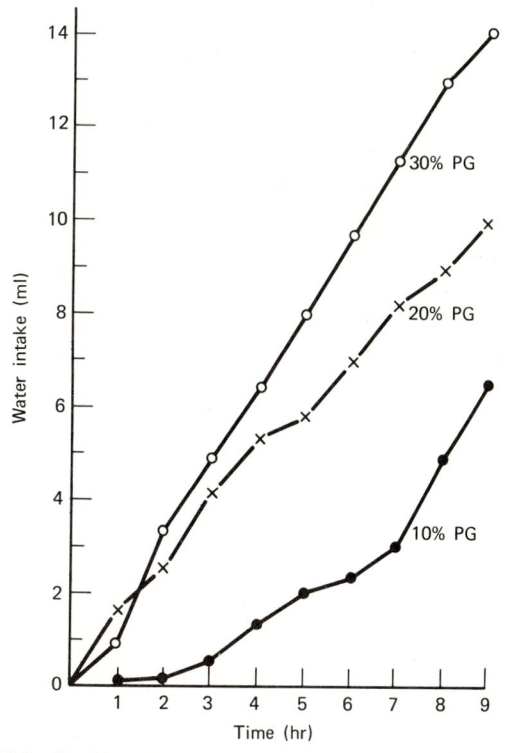

FIG. 10–12. Water intake in rats given subcutaneous injections of polyethylene glycol (PG) in various concentrations. This treatment reduces blood-plasma volume and elicits drinking.

(From E. M. Stricker. Some physiological and motivational properties of the hypovolemic stimulus for thirst. *Physiol. & Behav.*, **3**, 1968, 379–385. Permission granted for Pergamon Press copyright.)

water to osmose into the interstitial portion of the extracellular fluid compartment and eventually into the cells themselves. It is thus not surprising to find that stomach loads of hypertonic salt solution reduce hypovolemic thirst much more effectively than comparable quantities of water.[97] Moreover, blood plasma loss elicits not only thirst but also a somewhat delayed specific hunger for salt,[111] which insures the ingestion of the needed salts. The effects of hypovolemia and cellular dehydration appear to be additive,[83, 40] but an increase in blood volume (i.e., a state of hypervolemia) does not inhibit drinking in water-deprived animals, suggesting that the osmometric and volumetric mechanisms operate essentially independently.[24]

Volume receptors that are specifically related to the hypovolemic thirst have not yet been demonstrated. Rats that have "recovered" from lateral hypothalamic damage do not drink in response to blood plasma losses (or in response to cellular dehydration)[98] (see Figure 10–13), but it is not clear that this is related to a loss of the volumetric receptor system itself, particularly in view of the fact that compensatory increases in total daily intake have been observed in these animals.[96] It has been suggested that plasma volume might be metered directly by pressure receptors in the blood vessels[42] or volume receptors in the subcommissural organ,[44] but there is as yet little experimental evidence for these hypotheses.

It has been suggested[94] that this volumetric mechanism may be responsible for drinking in salt-depleted patients and that cellular overhydration and expansion may be associated with thirst only because the movement of water into the cell decreases the volume of extracellular fluid. This hypothesis receives some experimental support[94] from the observation that hyperhydration produced by stomach loading (which should induce cellular overhydration without depleting the blood plasma) does not elicit drinking, whereas other procedures (which induce cellular overhydration at the expense of blood plasma) do.

The Role of the Kidney

The kidney is the primary channel for water and waste loss and thus contributes importantly to the organism's water balance. When there is too much water in the body, the kidney begins to secrete a large volume of very dilute urine until a normal water balance is achieved. Conversely, in times of water deprivation, the kidney conserves water by excreting smaller and smaller volumes of increasingly concentrated urine.

A number of recent observations have, however, suggested that the kidney may influence the organism's water balance not only by controlling a major route of water loss but also by initiating thirst and water intake. Various surgical procedures that lower arterial blood pressure in the kidney (such as ligation of the inferior vena cava or constriction of the abdominal aorta) induce drinking in sated animals.[37, 39] Since kidney extracts also induce

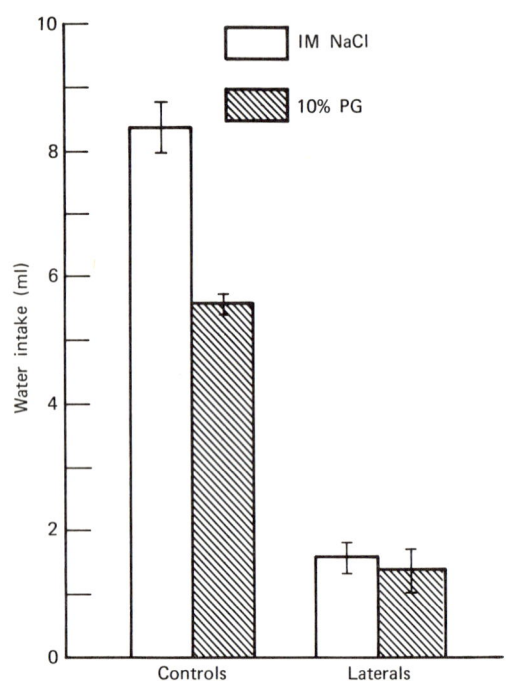

FIG. 10–13. Water intake of normal (control) rats and rats with lateral hypothalamic lesions in response to treatments which produce hyperosmolarity (1 molar NaCl) or hypovolemia (10% PG).

(From E. M. Stricker & G. Wolf. Behavioral control of intravascular fluid volume: Thirst and sodium appetite. *Ann. N.Y. Acad. Sci.*, **157**, 1969, 553–568. Data from E.M. Stricker & G. Wolf. *Proc. Soc. exp. Biol. Med.*, **124**, 1967, 816–820.)

drinking,[82] it has been suggested that these effects may be due to the release of a "thirst factor" that is thought to be renin. This enzyme is released from the kidney and becomes a potent vasopressor, called angiotensin, after some reactions with substances in the blood. This hypothesis is supported by the observation that intravenous injections of angiotensin also induce drinking in rats in normal water balance[38] (see Figure 10–14). A possible mechanism for this interesting action of the kidney on thirst has been suggested by the finding that microinjections of very small quantities of angiotensin into the hypothalamus, preoptic region, and septal area also elicit water ingestion in sated rats.[33]

Thermoregulatory Influences

Man's water balance is to a significant degree affected by environmental temperatures. In the heat, large quantities of sweat must be secreted in order to prevent overheating. (Animals that do not possess sweat glands attempt to achieve similar results by panting or spreading saliva over their body surface.) When first exposed to heat, man excretes a highly concentrated sweat. Although the fluid loss may be considerable, little thirst results because the absolute osmotic pressure of the extracellular fluids remains largely unaffected. As we become acclimated, the salt concentration of the sweat decreases and sweating consequently increases the concentration of the extracellular salts. This causes a compensatory influx of water from the cells into the extracellular compartment and produces thirst. A direct interaction between the temperature-regulating mechanisms of the brain and thirst is suggested by the observations[10] that heating the preoptic area induces drinking in sated goats and inhibits feeding in hungry animals, whereas local cooling of this region inhibits drinking in thirsty animals but elicits feeding in sated goats (see Figure 10–15). These results suggest that water as well as food intake may be influenced by the activity of temperature-sensitive elements of the preoptic area. This interpretation is supported by the finding that destruction of the preoptic heat-loss center produces complete adipsia in the goat.[10] However, this direct central interaction between thirst and temperature regulation may operate only at extreme temperatures, since very large preoptic temperature changes are required to produce the effects on food and water intake in the goat. Recent attempts to replicate the findings in the rat[90] have observed opposite effects on food and water intake, suggesting that the nature of the thirst-temperature interaction may be different in different species.

Conclusions

The organism's fluid reserves are stored in two major compartments separated by a semipermeable membrane. The absolute quantity of certain salts in the intracellular compartment remains constant because these salts cannot, under normal circumstances, cross the cell membrane. A loss of fluids from the extracellular compartment, due to sweating, evaporation, or urinary excretion, consequently sets up an osmotic pressure gradient between

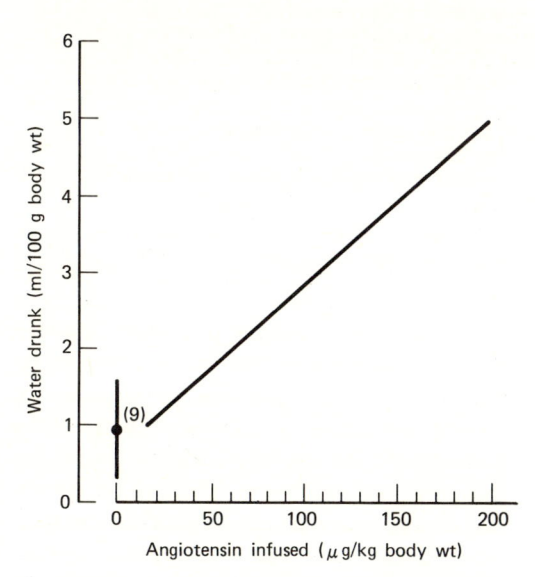

FIG. 10–14. Water drunk by nephrectomized rats in 6 hours in response to infusions of angiotensin. The mean value ± SD for the control rats is given on the left with the number of observations in parentheses.

(After J. T. Fitzsimons, & Barbara J. Simons. The effect on drinking in the rat of intravenous infusion of angiotensin, given alone or in combination with other stimuli of thirst. *J. Physiol.*, **203**, 1969, 45–57.)

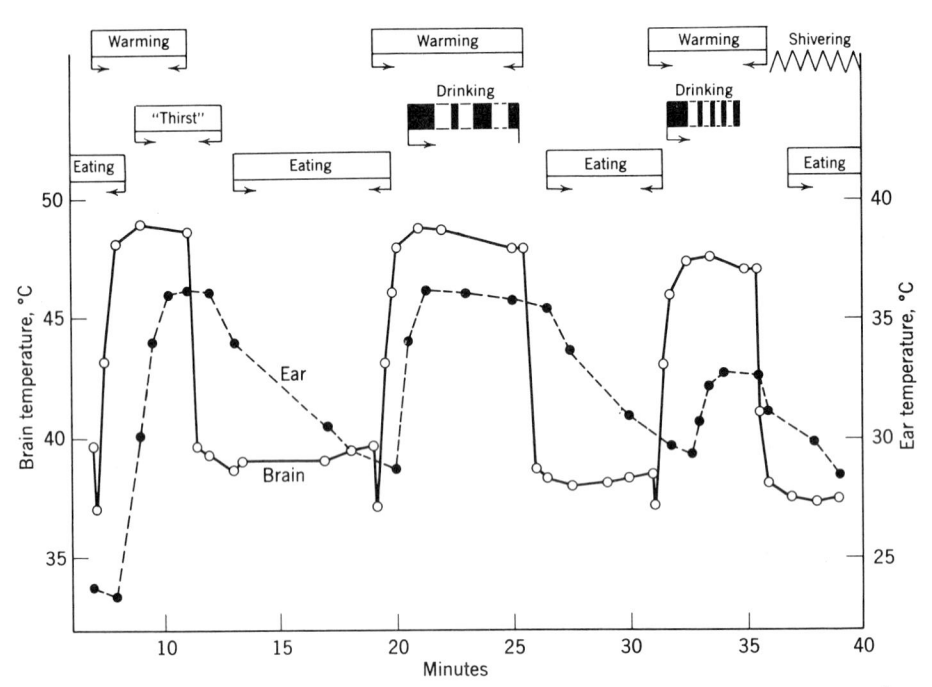

FIG. 10–15. Results of warming the preoptic area and rostral hypothalamus in the previously hungry goat. Brain temperature was recorded close to the surface of the thermode. The goat was fed hay at the beginning of the experiment and had free access to water except during the first period of central warming. During the periods of warming, eating stopped simultaneously to the onset of peripheral vasodilatation (rise of ear temperature) and started again when ear surface temperature had begun to fall after discontinuation of central warming. The perfusion of the thermode with warm water induced a strong urge to drink. During the first period of central warming, when the water container was temporarily removed, this urge was evidenced by the animal's licking the drops of water coming from the outlet tubing of the thermode ("thirst") and later on by repeated drinking of large amounts of water during the periods of central warming.

(From B. Andersson & S. Larsson. The influence of local temperature changes in the preoptic areas and rostral hypothalamus on regulation of food and water intake. Acta. Physiol. Scand., 52, 1961, 75–89.)

the intracellular and extracellular compartments and forces water out of the cells. A loss (or inadequate resupply) of salts from the extracellular fluids sets up opposite pressure gradients that force water into the cells.

If thirst is to adequately reflect water need, it must reflect not only the total fluid content of the body (which at times does not signal major disturbances in the body's fluid stores) but also the concentration of salts in these fluids. That the body does just that is indicated by the fact that the ingestion or intravenous injection of hypertonic salt solutions induces thirst and water intake even though the total quantity of body fluids is increased.

We even have some pretty good ideas about how the organism meters the salt concentration of its fluids. Injections of solutions that increase the absolute osmotic pressure of the body fluids but do not cause a significant movement of water out of the cells do not elicit thirst. Conversely, injections of solutions that decrease the extracellular concentration of sodium and chloride but cause water to leave the cell do induce thirst. This suggests that thirst may be specifically related to cellular dehydration and the consequent shrinkage of cell size. However, cellular overhydration, due to a chronic reduction of the extracellular salt concentrations, also produces thirst, suggesting that any significant change in cell size may elicit thirst.

Cells that appear to act specifically as osmoreceptors have been localized in the hypothalamic thirst "centers" of the goat and rat. When tiny quantities of a hypertonic solution are injected into this area, drinking occurs. Osmoreceptors in more anterior portions of the hypothalamus seem to regulate water loss by controlling the release of ADH by the pituitary gland.

Recently, additional volumetric mechanisms have been discovered that appear to influence thirst under some conditions. The operation of volumetric influences is suggested by the fact that thirst and water intake occur when a significant portion of the body fluids are lost even though the osmotic pressure of the extra- and intracellular fluids remains constant. It seems, however, that this mechanism comes into play only after fairly large amounts of fluid have been lost, suggesting that it may not regulate normal day-to-day fluid intake.

Thirst is also influenced by environmental temperatures because water loss through sweating or evaporation is an important aspect of the body's temperature regulation. There is some evidence that extreme changes in the ambient temperature of the central thermostat may affect water as well as food intake, but we do not yet have sufficient information on this mechanism to speculate about its possible role in thirst regulation under normal circumstances.

Review Questions

1. Describe the organism's fluid compartments.

2. Explain the difference between absolute and relative osmotic pressure.

3. Discuss the changes in the body's water stores that occur as a result of water deprivation and the subsequent ingestion of water.

4. Discuss the evidence for a cellular-dehydration theory of thirst. Is there any evidence it cannot readily explain?

5. Discuss thermal influences on thirst.

6. Could thirst be regulated adequately only by a metering of the body's total fluid content? Only by a metering of osmotic pressure relationships?

7. Explain the functions of the hypothalamic osmoreceptors.

8. Why do people on a restricted-salt diet often become very thirsty? Can you explain why their thirst does not seem to disappear even after large quantities of water are ingested?

REVIEW AND SUMMARY

Most prescientific as well as early scientific theories of thirst suggested that water intake may be regulated quite simply by oral sensations. As the body's water stores are depleted, the mouth and throat dry out and this irritates special "thirst receptors." When we ingest water, these receptors are inhibited and thirst disappears. This appealingly simple dry-mouth theory of thirst was restated by W. B. Cannon as recently as 1934 and continues to be popular in psychological textbooks today.

It is not, unfortunately, an adequate explanation of thirst because thirst sensations persist even after the mouth and throat are bathed in water or saliva as long as water is prevented from entering the stomach. Conversely, thirst disappears promptly when water is injected directly into the stomach in spite of the fact that the mouth and throat remain dry for quite some time. Because oral sensations appear to be such an important component of the stimulus for drinking, a variety of experiments have been devised to study their role further. All agree that an interference with such sensations does not significantly modify thirst or the regulation of water intake in accordance with the body's requirements. Thirst appears normal after most of the sensory nerves to the mouth and throat have been cut or the sensory receptors inactivated by the topical application of a local anesthetic. Surgical removal or congenital absence of salivary glands increases the frequency of drinking somewhat but does not upset the regulation of fluid intake or increase total daily consumption. Salivary flow and the dryness of the mouth correlate quite well with the organism's water needs under most normal circumstances and may indeed provide an objective measure of thirst. They do not, however, represent essential signals for thirst.

There is some evidence that water intake may be metered to some extent by oral factors, but this influence permits only a very crude assessment. Stomach distention also appears to play a role in satiety, primarily by setting an upper limit to the amount that can be consumed at one sitting. It may also contribute a second, very crude metering of intake but cannot, by itself, account for the adjustment of intake to need.

If sensory signals from peripheral sources do not accurately reflect thirst or satiety, how then is the essential correlation between water intake and loss achieved? It is currently believed that thirst, as well as the rate of water loss, is controlled by central regulatory mechanisms located in the hypothalamus as well as several extrahypothalamic regions.

Damage to the lateral hypothalamus, globus pallidus, midbrain tegmentum, or subcommissural organ produces complete and in some instances permanent adipsia. This is usually accompanied by aphagia. Food and water intake gradually return, but many of the recovered animals drink only in order to be able to eat dry food. Complete adipsia returns as soon as the food is removed. Less dramatic hypodipsic reactions have been reported following anterior amygdaloid lesions. Damage to the posterior aspect of the amygdala or to the medial septal region produces opposite facilitatory effects on water intake as well as on water-rewarded instrumental behavior.

Electrical as well as chemical stimulation of the hypothalamus elicits water intake in sated animals. Chemical stimulation of a number of extrahypothalamic regions, including the preoptic area, ventral thalamus, medial septal region, cingulate gyrus, and dorsal hippocampus, also elicits drinking in sated rats, suggesting that the distribution of thirst-related pathways may be even more extensive than the lesion studies suggest.

Chemical stimulation experiments have suggested that the hypothalamus may contain a beta-adrenergic neural system responsible for concurrent thirst stimulation and hunger suppression as well as an alpha-adrenergic component that operates in a reciprocal fashion to stimulate hunger and inhibit thirst. The widespread cholinergic components of the thirst system appear to act synergistically with the beta-adrenergic component but oppose the alpha-adrenergic aspects of the system.

Lesions in the hypothalamus do not, typically, result in a primary hyperdipsia, suggesting that the inhibitory components of the thirst system may be very diffusely represented in this portion of the brain.

Currently available data indicate that the central regulatory mechanisms correlate thirst with the organism's water needs mainly by relying on information from specialized cells, called osmoreceptors, that react specifically to the reduction in cell size that accompanies cellular dehydration. Osmoreceptors in the hypothalamic component of the thirst circuit have been shown to give rise to thirst and copious water ingestion in response to microinjections of a hypertonic salt solution into their immediate environment. Similar cells in the posterior hypothalamus control the pituitary release of antidiuretic hormone in accordance with the tonicity of their environment and thus regulate urinary water loss.

Volumetric and thermal influences on thirst as well as a renal "thirst factor" have been demonstrated, but the mechanism that determines thirst under most normal circumstances appears to rely on information about the concentration of salts in the body fluids. When the body is in perfect water balance, the extracellular and intracellular concentrations of salts are equal. During water deprivation, the extracellular fluids are depleted of water and the osmotic pressure of the remaining fluid increases. This sets up a relative pressure gradient between the extracellular and intracellular fluids and forces water out of the cells. This dehydration, or the resultant shrinkage of the cell, appears to be the essential stimulus for thirst.

When we drink, the absolute osmotic pressure of the extracellular fluid falls and water moves back into the cells. Unfortunately, satiety seems to occur in most species long before the equilibrium between the extra- and intracellular fluids can be reestablished. Since the body can easily rid itself of excess fluid via urinary excretion, a precise regulation of intake is not as important as it is in the case of food. It nonetheless seems that the known oral and gastric satiety influences are too crude to account for the degree of regulation commonly seen in most species. We are, as yet, at a loss to explain the apparent metering of intake.

Bibliography

1. Adolph, E. F. Measurements of water drinking in dogs. *Amer. J. Physiol.*, 1939, **125**, 75–86.

2. Adolph, E. F. *Physiological Regulations*. Copyright 1943, The Ronald Press Co., New York.

3. Adolph, E. F. Thirst and its inhibition in the stomach. *Amer. J. Physiol.*, 1950, **161**, 374–386.

4. Adolph, E. F. and associates. *Physiology of Man in the Desert*. New York: Interscience, 1947.

5. Adolph, E. F., Barker, J. P., & Hoy, P. A. Multiple factors in thirst. *Amer. J. Physiol.*, 1954, **178**, 538–562.

6. Anand, B. K., & Brobeck, J. R. Hypothalamic control of food intake in rats and cats. *Yale J. Biol. Med.*, 1951, **24**, 123–140.

7. Andersson, B. The effect of injections of hypertonic NaCl-solutions into different parts of the hypothalamus of goats. *Acta Physiol. Scand.*, 1953, **28**, 188–201.

8. Andersson, B. Observations on the water and electrolyte metabolism in the goat. *Acta Physiol. Scand.*, 1955, **33**, 50–65.

9. Andersson, B., & Larsson, S. An attempt to condition hypothalamic polydipsia. *Acta Physiol. Scand.*, 1956, **36**, 377–382.

10. Andersson, B., & Larsson, S. The influence of local temperature changes in the preoptic area and rostral hypothalamus on regulation of food and water intake. *Acta Physiol. Scand.*, 1961, **52**, 75–89.

11. Andersson, B., & McCann, S. M. A further study of polydipsia evoked by hypothalamic stimulation in the goat. *Acta Physiol. Scand.*, 1955a, **33**, 333–346.

12. Andersson, B., & McCann, S. M. Drinking, antidiuresis and milk ejection from electrical stimulation within the hypothalamus of the goat. *Acta Physiol. Scand.*, 1955b, **35**, 191–201.

13. Andersson, B., & McCann, S. M. The effect of hypothalamic lesions on the water intake of the dog. *Acta Physiol. Scand.*, 1956, **35**, 312–320.

14. Andersson, B., & Wyrwicka, Wanda. Elicitation of a drinking motor conditioned reaction by electrical stimulation of the hypothalamic "drinking area" in the goat. *Acta Physiol. Scand.*, 1957, **41**, 194.

15. Arden, F. Experimental observations upon thirst and on potassium overdosage. *Aust. J. Exp. Biol. Med. Sci.*, 1934, **12**, 121–122.

16. Bellows, R. T., & Van Wagenen, W. P. The relationship of polydipsia and polyuria in diabetes insipidus. A study of experimental diabetes insipidus in dogs with and without esophageal fistulae. *J. Nerv. Ment. Dis.*, 1938, **88**, 417–473.

17. Bellows, R. T., & Van Wagenen, W. P. The effect of resection of the olfactory, gustatory and trigeminal nerves on water drinking in dogs without and with diabetes insipidus. *Amer. J. Physiol.*, 1939, **126**, 13–19.

18. Bernard, C. Leçons de physiologie expérimentale appliquée à la médecine. *Cours du Semestre d'Été, 1855. Vol. II.* Paris: Baillière, 1856, pp. 49–52.

19. Blass, E. M., & Epstein, A. N. A lateral preoptic osmosensitive zone for thirst in the rat. *J. Comp. Physiol. Psychol.*, 1971, **76**, 378–394.

20. Blass, E. M., & Hanson, D. G. Primary hyperdipsia in the rat following septal lesions. *J. Comp. Physiol. Psychol.*, 1970, **70**, 87–93.

21. Brunn, F. The sensation of thirst. *J. Amer. Med. Ass.*, 1925, **85**, 234–235.

22. Cannon, W. B. Hunger and thirst. In *A Handbook of General Experimental Psychology*. Carl Murchison, Ed. Worcester, Mass.: Clark Univ. Press, 1934, pp. 247–263.

23. Corbit, J. D. Effect of intravenous sodium chloride on drinking in the rat. *J. Comp. Physiol. Psychol.*, 1965, **60**, 397–406.

24. Corbit, J. D. Effect of hypervolemia on drinking in the rat. *J. Comp. Physiol. Psychol.*, 1967, **64**, 250–255.

25. Crouch, J. E., & McClintic, J. R. *Human Anatomy and Physiology*. New York: Wiley, 1971.

26. Darrow, D. C., & Yannet, H. The changes in distribution of body water accompanying increase and decrease in extracellular electrolyte. *J. Clin. Invest.*, 1935, **14**, 266–275.

27. Darwin, E. *Zoonomia, or, the Laws of Organic Life*. London: Johnson, 1801.

28. Dill, D. B. *Life, Heat and Altitude*. Cambridge, Mass.: Harvard Univ. Press, 1938.

29. Di Salvo, N. A. Factors which alter drinking responses of dogs to intravenous injections of hypertonic sodium chloride solutions. *Amer. J. Physiol.*, 1955, **180**, 139–145.

30. Dumas, C. L. *Principes de physiologie*. Vol. *IV*. Paris: Déterville, 1803.

31. Elkinton, J. R., & Squires, R. D. The distribution of body fluids in congestive heart failure. I: Theoretic considerations. *Circulation*, 1951, **4**, 679–696.

32. Epstein, A. N. Reciprocal changes in feeding behavior caused by intrahypothalamic chemical injections. *Amer. J. Physiol.*, 1960, **199**, 969.

33. Epstein, A. N., Fitzsimons, J. T., & Simons, Barbara J. Drinking caused by the intracranial injection of angiotensin into the rat. *J. Physiol.*, 1968, **200**, 98–100.

34. Falk, J. L. Water intake and NaCl appetite in sodium depletion. *Psychol. Rep.*, 1965, **16**, 315–325.

35. Fisher, A. E., & Coury, J. N. Cholinergic tracing of a central neural circuit underlying the thirst drive. *Science*, 1962, **138**, 691–693.

36. Fitzsimons, J. T. Drinking by rats depleted of body fluid without increase in osmotic pressure. *J. Physiol.*, 1961, **159**, 297–309.

37. Fitzsimons, J. T. Drinking caused by constriction of the inferior vena cava in the rat. *Nature (London)*, 1964, **204**, 479–480.

38. Fitzsimons, J. T. Hypovolaemic drinking and renin. *J. Physiol.*, 1966, **186**, 130–131.

39. Fitzsimons, J. T. The kidney as a thirst receptor. *J. Physiol.*, 1967, **191**, 128–129.

40. Fitzsimons, J. T., & Oatley, K. Additivity of stimuli for drinking in rats. *J. Comp. Physiol. Psychol.*, 1968, **66**, 450–455.

41. Fitzsimons, J. T., & Simons, Barbara J. The effect on drinking in the rat of intravenous infusion of angiotensin, given alone or in combination with other stimuli of thirst. *J. Physiol.*, 1969, **203**, 45–57.

42. Gauer, O. H., & Henry, J. P. Circulatory basis of fluid volume control. *Physiol. Rev.*, 1963, **43**, 423–481.

43. Gilbert, G. J. The subcommissural organ. *Anat. Rec.*, 1956, **126**, 253–265.

44. Gilbert, G. J. The subcommissural organ: a regulator of thirst. *Amer. J. Physiol.*, 1957, **191**, 243–247.

45. Gilbert, G. J. The subcommissural organ. *Neurology*, 1960, **10**, 138.

46. Gilman, A. The relation between blood osmotic pressure, fluid distribution and voluntary water intake. *Amer. J. Physiol.*, 1937, **120**, 323–328.

47. Gold, R. M. Aphagia and adipsia produced by unilateral hypothalamic lesions in rats. *Amer. J. Physiol.*, 1966, **211**, 1274–1276.

48. Grossman, S. P. Eating or drinking elicited by direct adrenergic or cholinergic stimulation of hypothalamus. *Science*, 1960, **132**, 301–302.

49. Grossman, S. P. Direct adrenergic and cholinergic stimulation of hypothalamic mechanisms. *Amer. J. Physiol.*, 1962a, **202**, 872–882.

50. Grossman, S. P. Effects of adrenergic and cholinergic blocking agents on hypothalamic mechanisms. *Amer. J. Physiol.*, 1962b, **202**, 1230–1236.

51. Grossman, S. P. Behavioral effects of chemical stimulation of the ventral amygdala. *J. Comp. Physiol. Psychol.*, 1964a, **57**, 29–36.

52. Grossman, S. P. Effects of chemical stimulation of the septal area on motivation. *J. Comp. Physiol. Psychol.*, 1964b, **58**, 194–200.

53. Grossman, S. P. Behavioural effects of direct chemical stimulation of central nervous system structures. *Int. J. Neuropharmacol.*, 1964c, **3**, 45–58.

54. Grossman, S. P. Changes in food and water intake associated with an interruption of the anterior or posterior fiber connections of the hypothalamus. *J. Comp. Physiol. Psychol.*, 1971, **75**, 23–31.

55. Grossman, S. P., & Grossman, Lore. Food and water intake following lesions or electrical stimulation of the amygdala. *Amer. J. Physiol.*, 1963, **205**, 761–765.

56. Grossman, S. P., & Grossman, Lore. Food and water intake in rats with parasagittal knife-cuts medial or lateral to the lateral hypothalamus. *J. Comp. Physiol. Psychol.*, 1971, **74**, 148–156.

57. Haller, A. Fames et sitis. *Elementa Physiol.*, 1776, **6**, 185.

58. Harvey, J. A., Lints, C. E., Jacobson, L. E., & Hunt, H. F. Effects of lesions in the septal area on conditioned fear and discriminated instrumental punishment in the albino rat. *J. Comp. Physiol. Psychol.*, 1965, **59**, 37–48.

59. Hendry, D. P., & Rasche, R. H. Analysis of a new non-nutritive positive reinforcer based on thirst. *J. Comp. Physiol. Psychol.*, 1961, **54**, 477–483.

60. Holmes, J. H., & Cizek, L. J. Observations on sodium chloride depletion in the dog. *Amer. J. Physiol.*, 1951, **164**, 407–414.

61. Holmes, J. H., & Gregersen, M. I. Relation of the salivary flow to the thirst produced in man by intravenous injection of hypotonic salt solution. *Amer. J. Physiol.*, 1947, **151**, 252–257.

62. Holmes, J. H., & Gregersen, M. I. Observations on drinking induced by hypertonic solutions. *Amer. J. Physiol.*, 1950a, **162**, 326–337.

63. Holmes, J. H., & Gregersen, M. I. Role of sodium and chloride in thirst. *Amer. J. Physiol.*, 1950b, **162**, 338–347.

64. Huang, K. C. Effect of salt depletion and fasting on water exchange in the rabbit. *Amer. J. Physiol.*, 1955, **181**, 609–615.

65. Leibowitz, Sarah F. Hypothalamic alpha- and beta-adrenergic systems regulate both thirst and hunger in the rat. *Proc. Nat. Acad. Sci. U.S.*, 1971, **68**, 332–334.

66. Leibowitz, Sarah F. Central adrenergic receptors and the regulation of hunger and thirst. *Res. Publ., Assn. Res. Nerv. Ment. Dis.*, 1972, in press.

67. Lepidi-Chioti, G., & Fubini, A. Influenza delle penellazioni faringee di cloridrato di cocaina nella sensazione della sete e nella secrezione della saliva parotidea umana. *G. Accad. Med. Torino*, 1885, **33**, 905–906.

68. Leschke, E. Über die Durstempfindung. *Arch. Psychiat.*, 1918, **59**, 773–781.

69. Levitt, R. A., & Fisher, A. E. Anticholinergic blockade of centrally induced thirst. *Science*, 1966, **154**, 520–521.

70. Longet, F. A. *Traité de Physiologie. Vol. I.* Paris: Baillière, 1868, pp. 21–38.

71. Lubar, J. F., Schaeffer, C. F., & Wells, D. G. The role of the septal area in the regulation of water intake and associated motivational behavior. *Ann. N. Y. Acad. Sci.*, 1969, **157**, 875–893.

72. MacLean, P. D. The limbic system with respect to self-preservation and the preservation of the species. *J. Nerv. Ment. Dis.*, 1958, **127**, 1–11.

73. Magendie, F. *A Summary of Physiology.* John Revere, Trans. Baltimore: Coale, 1822.

74. Mayer, A. Variations de la tension osmotique de sang chez les animaux privés de liquides. *C. R. Soc. Biol. (Paris)*, 1900, **52**, 153–155.

75. Miller, N. E. Experiments on motivation. Studies combining psychological, physiological, and pharmacological techniques. *Science*, 1957, **126**, 1271–1278.

76. Miller, N. E. Chemical coding of behavior in the brain. *Science*, 1965, **148**, 328–338.

77. Miller, N. E., Samlinger, R. I., & Woodrow, P. Thirst–reducing effects of water by stomach fistula vs. water by mouth measured by both a consummatory and an instrumental response. *J. Comp. Physiol. Psychol.*, 1957, **50**, 1–5.

78. Montemurro, D. G., & Stevenson, J. A. F. Adipsia produced by hypothalamic lesions. *Canad. J. Biochem.*, 1957, **35**, 31–37.

79. Montgomery, A. V., & Holmes, J. H. Gastric inhibition of the drinking response. *Amer. J. Physiol.*, 1955, **182**, 227–231.

80. Montgomery, M. F. The role of the salivary glands in the thirst mechanism. *Amer. J. Physiol.*, 1931, **96**, 221–227.

81. Morgane, P. J. Medial forebrain bundle and "feeding centers" of the hypothalamus. *J. Comp. Neurol.*, 1961, **117**, 1–26.

82. Nairn, R. C., Masson, G. M. C., & Corcoran, A. C. The production of serous effusions in nephrectomized animals by the administration of renal extracts and renin. *J. Path. Bact.*, 1956, **71**, 155–163.

83. Oatley, K. Changes of blood volume and osmotic pressure in the production of thirst. *Nature (London)*, 1964, **202**, 1341–1342.

84. Oehme, C. Die Entstehung der Durstempfindung und die Regulation der Wasserzufuhr. *Dtsch. Med. Wschr.*, 1922, **48**, 277.

85. Rullier, J. Soif. *Dict. Sci. Méd. (Paris)*, 1821, **51**, 448–490.

86. Schiff, M. *Leçons sur la Physiologie de la Digestion, Faites au Muséum d'Histoire Naturelle de Florence. Vol. I.* Emile Levier, Ed. Florence and Turin: Loescher, 1867, pp. 41–42.

87. Sclafani, A., & Grossman, S. P. Reactivity of hyperphagic and normal rats to quinine and electric shock. *J. Comp. Physiol. Psychol.*, 1971, **74**, 157–166.

88. Smith, R. W., & McCann, S. M. Alterations in food and water intake after hypothalamic lesions in the rat. *Amer. J. Physiol.*, 1962, **203**, 366–370.

89. Sorensen, J. P., & Harvey, J. A. Decreased brain acetylcholine after septal lesions in rats: correlation with thirst. *Physiol. & Behav.*, 1971, **6**, 723–726.

90. Spector, N. H., Brobeck, J. R., & Hamilton, C. L. Feeding and core temperature in albino rats: changes induced by preoptic heating and cooling. *Science*, 1968, **161**, 286–288.

91. Steggerda, F. R. Observations on the water intake in an adult man with dysfunctioning salivary glands. *Amer. J. Physiol.*, 1941, **132**, 517–521.

92. Stevenson, J. A. F. Neural control of food and water intake. In *The Hypothalamus*. W. Haymaker, Evelyn Anderson, & W. J. H. Nauta, Eds. Springfield, Ill.: Thomas, 1969, pp. 524–621.

93. Strauss, M. B. *Body Water in Man, the Acquisition and Maintenance of the Body Fluids.* Boston: Little, Brown, 1957.

94. Stricker, E. M. Extracellular fluid volume and thirst. *Amer. J. Physiol.*, 1966, **211**, 232–238.

95. Stricker, E. M. Some physiological and motivational properties of the hypovolemic stimulus for thirst. *Physiol. & Behav.*, 1968, **3**, 379–385.

96. Stricker, E. M. Personal communication, 1971.

97. Stricker, E. M., & Wolf, G. Hypovolemic thirst in comparison with thirst produced by hyperosmolarity. *Physiol. & Behav.*, 1967a, **2**, 33–37.

98. Stricker, E. M., & Wolf, G. The effects of hypovolemia on drinking in rats with lateral hypothalamic damage. *Proc. Soc. Exp. Biol. Med.*, 1967b, **124**, 816–820.

99. Stricker, E. M., & Wolf, G. Behavioral control of intravascular fluid volume: thirst and sodium appetite. *Ann. N. Y. Acad. Sci.*, 1969, **157**, 553–568.

100. Taylor, Anna N., & Farrell, G. Effects of brain stem lesions on aldosterone and cortisol secretion. *Endocrinology*, 1962, **70**, 556–566.

101. Teitelbaum, P. Motivation and control of food intake. In *Handbook of Physiology. Vol. I.* C. F. Code, Ed. Washington, D.C.: Am. Physiol. Soc., 1967, pp. 319–335.

102. Teitelbaum, P., & Epstein, A. The lateral hypothalamic syndrome: recovery of feeding and drinking after lateral hypothalamic lesions. *Psychol. Rev.*, 1962, **69**, 74–90.

103. Teitelbaum, P., & Stellar, E. Recovery from the failure to eat, produced by hypothalamic lesions. *Science*, 1954, **120**, 894–895.

104. Towbin, E. J. Gastric distention as a factor in the satiation of thirst in esophagostomized dogs. *Amer. J. Physiol.*, 1949, **159**, 533–541.

105. Towbin, E. J. The role of the gastrointestinal tract in the regulation of water intake. In *Thirst, First International Symposium on Thirst in the Regulation of Body Water*. M. J. Wayner, Ed. New York: Pergamon Press, 1964, pp. 79–92.

106. Valenstein, E. S., Cox, V. C., & Kakolewski, J. W. Modification of motivated behavior by electrical stimulation of the hypothalamus. *Science*, 1968, **159**, 1119–1121.

107. Verney, E. B. The antidiuretic hormone and the factors which determine its release. *Proc. Roy. Soc. (London)*, B, 1947, **135**, 25–106.

108. Wettendorff, H. Modifications du sang sous l'influence de la privation d'eau. Contribution à l'étude de la soif. Travaux du laboratoire de physiologie. *Instituts Solvay*, 1901, **4**, 353–384.

109. Wolf, A. V. Osmometric analysis of thirst in man and dog. *Amer. J. Physiol.*, 1950, **161**, 75–86.

110. Wolf, A. V. *Thirst: Physiology of the Urge to Drink and Problems of Water Lack*. Springfield, Ill.: Thomas, 1958.

111. Wolf, G., & Stricker, E. M. Sodium appetite elicited by hypovolemia in adrenalectomized rats: re-evaluation of the "reservoir" hypothesis. *J. Comp. Physiol. Psychol.*, 1967, **63**, 252–257.

112. Zotterman, Y. Species differences in the water taste. *Acta Physiol. Scand.*, 1956, **37**, 60–70.

Chapter 11

THE HORMONAL AND NEURAL BASIS OF SEXUAL BEHAVIOR

Introduction

Measures and Definitions of Sexual Behavior

The Role of Environmental Stimuli

The Hormonal Basis of Sexual Behavior

Neural Influences

Review and Summary

INTRODUCTION

Sexual behavior occurs primarily in social situations, and it is often difficult to distinguish social actions that are sexually motivated from those that are not. Dancing may be part of sexually motivated courtship behavior but may also reflect rather different social motives. Similarly, the sniffing, nosing, and biting often seen in dogs, cats, and rats may or may not be sexually motivated.

Sexual motivation, unlike hunger or thirst, is not based on a periodically recurrent biological need that must be satisfied to permit survival. Gratification of the sex drive may be psychologically desirable but is not physiologically essential or even important. The arousal of sexual motivation depends, in part, on environmental cues such as the presence of a partner, shelter, or a familiar environment. It is also influenced by hormonal mechanisms that determine whether a response to potentially arousing environmental cues can occur and by neural influences that integrate sex-related sensory inputs and hormonal signals.

Unlike hunger and thirst, sexual motivation may be learned, at least in part. When monkeys are reared without mothers or age-mates, sexual behaviors may be completely absent in adulthood. When paired, these monkeys live together like brothers and sisters. When a male of this group is paired with a sexually receptive and experienced normal female, only fighting occurs. Similarly, when an isolation-reared female is paired with an experienced normal male, the female rebuffs all advances and cowers in a corner. The uncooperative behavior of the isolation-reared monkeys persists in spite of social contacts in adulthood.[76] Social isolation during infancy also has some detrimental effects on sexual behavior in guinea pigs,[125] but exposure to the other sex during rearing is not essential for the development of successful mating behavior in the rat.[24]

MEASURES AND DEFINITIONS OF SEXUAL BEHAVIOR

It has been difficult to study sexual behavior experimentally. Man considers sexual motivation and behavior a very private matter that he is reluctant to discuss or submit to experimental study. Animal experiments have been difficult to conduct because it is next to impossible to maintain experimental control over the level of sexual motivation or even to measure it adequately. Our old standby, the operational definition, is not very useful in this instance. Time of deprivation is an almost meaningless variable, and even a long list of conditions, such as "female in heat, sexually experienced adult male, both deprived and adapted to the experimental situation," does not guarantee that mating will take place. Some female dogs, for instance, seem to have more sex appeal than others, and what looks very attractive to one male may not appeal to another. Females, of course, have their own preferences[29] and it is consequently difficult to study sexual behavior in the traditional paradigms that have been used to obtain objective measures of other drives.

Many experimental studies of sexual behavior have consequently relied on observational records of such obvious sexual reactions as intromission or ejaculation. The results of these studies are unambiguous but often not very enlightening. Much important information is lost, and the nature of the measure makes it difficult to assess the intensity of the drive or the magnitude of the incentive or reward properties of the sexual act itself. Several attempts have been made to improve the observational procedures by classifying potentially sexual social behaviors that precede copulation. The intensity of the arousal of the female rat, for instance, has been measured by recording the presence and extent of the body posture that the rat assumes to facilitate access to her genitalia (see Figure 11–1). Female rats in anestrus do not show this *lordosis* response and fight off any advances from a male. As the female comes into heat, she may respond to the advances of a sexually experienced and aggressive male, and the degree of receptivity is reflected in the completeness of the lordosis response. It becomes

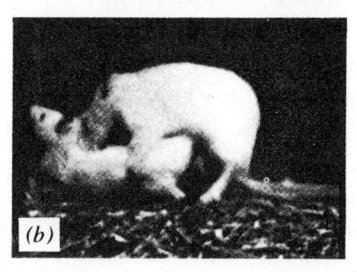

FIG. 11–1. Stages of sexual arousal in the female rat. (a) No heat. The female defends herself against the male with one of her hindlegs. (b) Heat. Pronounced lordosis during mounting.
(From A. M. Hemmingsen. Studies on the oestrous-producing hormone (oestrin). *Skand. Arch. Physiol.*, 65, 1933, 97–250.)

more and more pronounced as the female is sexually aroused. Under optimal conditions, the female may assume the lordosis response even before the male has made any advances. Several experiments have used rating scales of the intensity of the lordosis response, and as many as twelve different stages have been discriminated.[81] A variation of this technique consists of the recording of the minimal stimulus needed to elicit a lordosis response. When maximally receptive, female rats may assume the lordosis posture even in response to manual stimulation. At increasingly lower levels of arousal, she responds to another female, an immature male, a sexually "sluggish" male and, finally, only to an experienced aggressive male.

Attempts to obtain more sensitive measures of sexual motivation in the male have relied on observations of the frequency or latency of such potentially sex-related activities as ear twitching, nuzzling, sniffing, licking, mounting, and intromission.[72] The frequency of sexual responses to inappropriate objects such as animals of another species[18, 19] or wax models of a female[124] has also been used.

Many investigators are not satisfied with the reliability of these rating techniques. Some have tried to use copulation-rewarded instrumental response measures, such as running speed in an alley,[28] latency of hurdle jumping,[114] or the frequency of wheel-turning.[39] The success of these studies has been limited because the experimenter has little control over the drive state or the magnitude of the incentive motivation. Other investigators have tried to measure the strength of sexual motivation indirectly by recording the maximal intensity of noxious stimulation an animal will tolerate in order to gain access to a sexual partner. Typically, these experimenters have used some variation of the Columbia Obstruction Box, which consists of a goal compartment (containing a female "reward"), a start compartment (containing the male suitor), and, in between, an electrified grid floor. The intensity of the electric shock that the male will cross or even attempt to cross is used as a measure of sexual drive.[99] Although this measure correlates tolerably well with other indices of sexual motivation,[121] it is not a very good index because the reaction to footshock itself varies enormously from animal to animal and may, indeed, be influenced by the general activation that occurs during sexual arousal.

Summary and Review Questions

The study of sexual motivation has been complicated by the fact that it is difficult to control or even measure the intensity of the sex drive or the incentive or reward value of copulation. What may be a sexually motivated response in one situation may reflect completely different social motives in another.

Attempts to use observational measures of sexual behavior have led to the development of rating scales of various behaviors that precede copulation or of the quality of the stimulus required to elicit sexual responses. The success of these measures has been marginal. Attempts to use copulation-rewarded instrumental responses similarly have not produced entirely satisfactory results because the incentive value of a given male or female is unpredictable and may vary widely for different partners. In spite of these problems, quite a bit is known about the neural and hormonal basis of sexual motivation as well as the nature of the environmental stimuli that contribute to its arousal.

1. Describe the major differences between sexual motivation and such drives as hunger or thirst.

2. Discuss the disadvantages of observational measures of sexual behavior.

3. Why are measures of copulation-rewarded instrumental behavior difficult to use?

4. What alternative measures of sexual motivation have been used? What difficulties have been encountered with these measures?

THE ROLE OF ENVIRONMENTAL STIMULI

Unlike hunger and thirst, which depend exclusively on signals arising within the organism, sexual motivation is at least to some extent dependent on environmental stimuli. The most essential source of environmental stimuli is the sexual partner itself, but many more subtle influences exist. Beach[23] has classified these sex-related stimuli as follows.

1. *Stimuli that do not elicit sexual arousal or sexual behavior but are essential for the development of the necessary physiological conditions.* Environmental temperatures and illumination are examples of such stimuli. Many seasonal breeders (i.e., animals that come into heat only once or twice per year) are incapable of sexual arousal during the cold season. As it becomes warm, hormonal and anatomical changes occur that set the stage for sexual arousal and

copulation.[128] An increase in the amount of daylight during the spring and early summer serves as a signal for hormonal development in other species.[94]

2. *Stimuli that do not elicit sexual behavior but predispose the organism to respond to a potential mate.* For instance, the males of many species stake out a sexual territory and will not mate outside its boundaries.[98] Others mate only when natural shelter or nesting materials are available.[100] Some species of aquatic birds and some reptiles will not engage in sexual behavior unless a body of water is in the immediate vicinity.

3. *Stimuli that derive from an animal of the opposite sex.* These stimuli are essential to the elicitation of sexual arousal under most normal circumstances. Particularly in lower species, specific sensory cues are often uniquely able to elicit sexual behavior. Many insects, for instance, respond only to the odor that emanates from scent glands but ignore the female from whom they were removed.[82] Many species of fish respond exclusively to very specific visual stimuli and will try to mate with the shadow of a female[31] or with a crude model that has the bloated midsection of receptive females[124] (see Figure 11-2). As we ascend the phylogenetic scale, more and more stimuli come into play. For instance, in some species of frogs, the detection of a potential partner is based entirely on visual cues, but mating behavior itself is determined by auditory and tactual cues. Sexually unresponsive females and males are slim and utter a warning croak when approached by a male. The male indiscriminately clasps any other frog but attempts copulation only with fat frogs that do not croak.[102] Birds locate a potential partner primarily by auditory cues, hence much of their "singing," but distinguish a receptive female from other males exclusively on the basis of often very specific markings. For instance, male flickers are characterized by a black "moustache." If such coloring is added to a female, she no longer elicits sexual responses from males.[101]

In the more highly developed animals, the importance of specific stimuli disappears, and it becomes difficult to demonstrate that any particular sensory modality is important to sexual arousal and mating behavior. Perhaps most surprising is the finding that sensory information from the genitalia does not seem to play an essential role in sexual arousal. Female rabbits, for instance, continue to mate and appear unaffected by anesthetization[46] or deafferentation[33] of the vagina. In female rats, mating similarly is little changed by complete removal of the vagina and uterus. Male cats also show normal sexual arousal, although often marginally successful copulatory behavior, following deafferentation of the penis.[10]

Extensive study of the sexual behavior of animals deprived of visual, olfactory, auditory, and tactile sensations[33, 18, 9] have led to the following conclusions. As long as the presence of a potential mate can be detected, sexual arousal and attempts at copulation occur. Whether this information is carried by visual, auditory, olfactory, or tactile stimuli appears not to matter. The sexual behavior of the male of the species is typically more severely affected by a reduction in sensory input, but this may be due to the fact that the male has a more active role in mating behavior, which requires complex sensory-motor integrations. There is no evidence to suggest that sexual arousal itself is more sensitive to sensory deprivation in the male.

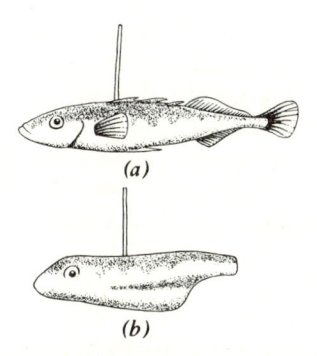

FIG. 11-2. Two models of a female fish. (*a*) Model offering many characteristics, except the swollen abdomen. (*b*) Model which has extremely swollen abdomen but lacks most other characteristics.

(From N. Tinbergen. An objectivistic study of the innate behaviour of animals. *Bibl. biotheor.*, **1**, 1942, 39-98. Reprinted with permission of E. J. Brill, Leiden.)

Summary and Review Questions

Sexual arousal is, in part, determined by the presence of specific environmental stimuli. Some of these stimuli, such as warm temperatures and plenty of daylight, are essential in some seasonal breeders for the development of hormonal conditions that are a prerequisite for sexual arousal. Others, such as the presence of sufficient water, shelter, or nesting material, are necessary for the development of psychological conditions that are conducive to sexual arousal. The third and most important group of stimuli are those that identify a potential mate. In lower organisms, sexual arousal often depends on specific stimuli, such as the odor that emanates from the scent glands of an insect or the coloring of a bird's face. As we ascend the phylogenetic scale, this dependence on specific cues disappears and sexual behavior occurs as long as sufficient sensory information is available to detect the potential mate and to perform the sensory-motor integrations that are necessary for the achievement of successful copulatory movements. Since the male typically plays a more active role in mating behavior than the female, a reduction in sensory input tends to affect the female less severely.

1. List the three categories of sexual stimuli that we have discussed.
2. Give at least two examples for each of these categories.
3. Discuss the importance of specific sensory cues to sexual arousal, including relevant phylogenetic and sex differences.

THE HORMONAL BASIS OF SEXUAL BEHAVIOR

Sexual arousal occurs only in environments that provide appropriate eliciting stimuli such as a receptive partner, shelter, and the like. However, in almost all species, no amount of stimulation will arouse sexual motivation and behavior unless the organism is physiologically ready to mate. The physiological basis for responses to sexual stimuli is provided, in part, by hormonal events that affect the anatomy and functions of the gonads as well as the neural centers that control sexual motivation.

Basic Endocrine Mechanisms

The sexual receptivity of the female of all infrahuman species waxes and wanes as a function of cyclic hormonal changes. The sexual motivation of the male, in contrast, remains essentially stable after puberty because the hormone balance of the male does not undergo these fluctuations. The principal sex hormones (*estrogen* and *progesterone* in the female; *testosterone* and *androstene dione* in the male) are produced in the gonads (called *ovaries* in the female and *testes* in the male). The secretory activity of the gonads is controlled by two *gonadotrophic* hormones, which are released by the anterior pituitary gland. The secretory activity of the pituitary is, in turn, under the control of neural mechanisms in the hypothalamus that are sensitive to the hormones of the gonads.

In the female, the pituitary gonadotrophic hormones are called *follicle stimulating hormone* (*FSH*) and *luteinizing hormone* (*LH*). The interaction between the gonadal and gonadotrophic hormones is as follows. The pituitary secretes FSH and this stimulates the growth of secretory cells, called follicles, in the ovaries. The follicles then begin to secrete estrogen, which acts on hypothalamic mechanisms to stimulate the secretion of certain neurohumors, called *releasing factors*, into the portal system that supplies blood to the anterior pituitary (see Figure 11–3). This, in turn, causes the release of LH from the pituitary, and the presence of LH further stimulates follicular development and increased secretion of estrogen. Eventually, the hypothalamus releases a substance that induces ovulation (i.e., the rupture of the follicles and subsequent release of an egg or ovum, ready for fertilization). Ovulation occurs independently of copulation in many species; in others, it is triggered by the act of copulation. The ruptured follicle then develops into a complex structure, called the *corpus luteum*, which begins to secrete the second major ovarian hormone, progesterone, as well as some estrogen. The concerted action of estrogen and

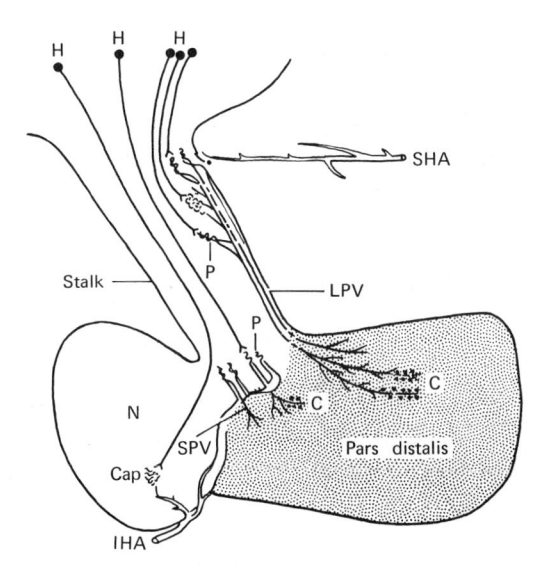

FIG. 11–3. Diagram showing the suggested pathways by which individual nerve cells in the hypothalamus (H) transmit neurohumors via their axons into loops of the primary capillary bed (P), and thence through the long (LPV) and short (SPV) portal vessels, to control the output of hormone from cells (C) in a given area of pars distalis. Cap, capillary bed of the infundibular process (N), which is also innervated by nerve cells in the hypothalamus. SHA, superior hypophysal artery; IHA, inferior hypophysal artery.

(From J. H. Adams, P. M. Daniel, & Marjorie M. L. Prichard. Observations on the portal circulation of the pituitary gland. *Neuroendocrinology*, **1**, 193–213, 1965/1966, Figure 5.)

progesterone modifies the tissues of the uterus in such a way that a fertilized egg can be implanted. If fertilization does not occur within a few days or weeks, the corpus luteum regresses, and the secretion of progesterone and estrogen consequently decreases. This, in turn, induces the secretion of releasing factors from the hypothalamus that stimulate the release of FSH from the pituitary, and a new cycle begins.

In the human female, the degeneration of the corpus luteum eventually leads to the discarding of the lining of the uterus and menstrual bleeding, which typically continues for about 4 to 5 days. It is followed by a preovulatory stage that lasts for about 7 to 10 days and is terminated by ovulation. Unless fertilization occurs, the cycle closes with a progestational period of 12 to 14 days. The ovum is available for fertilization only during the first few days of this stage.

In all subprimate species, sexual receptivity is almost entirely restricted to the period just before and after ovulation. This period is called *estrus* or heat. Nonhuman primates tend to concentrate their sexual activities in the period of estrus, but the female often receives an aggressive male even when not in heat. In man, the relationship between the hormonal cycle and sexual receptivity breaks down. The human female does not, typically, show cyclic variations in sexual arousal.

In the male, the sex-hormone balance and sexual receptivity are not subject to cyclic fluctuations, apparently because the male sex hormones suppress the hypothalamic mechanisms that are responsible for the cyclic release of gonadotrophins in the female. Instead, there is an apparently quite steady secretion of releasing factors from the hypothalamus that induce the pituitary release of FSH and the second gonadotrophin (called *interstitial cell stimulation hormone* or ICSH in the male). The release of FSH stimulates the development of special cells in the testes that produce spermatozoa. The presence of ICSH, on the other hand, encourages the maturation of secretory cells that liberate the male sex hormones (collectively called *androgens*).

Hormones and Sexual Arousal

Sexual receptivity in the female is highest when estrogen production is at its peak and the follicles are ready to release the ovum. The female of most species does not permit copulation at any other time. In primates, this strict relationship no longer holds, apparently in part because other social considerations become more important. Rhesus monkeys, for instance, are most receptive just before and after ovulation but can be induced to copulate at any time at the insistence of an aggressive partner.[8] Female chimps also receive the male at any point of the menstrual cycle, although most sexual interactions occur during the ovulatory period.[3] In the human female, the relationship between sexual receptivity and hormonal influences is completely obscured. The human female does not show increased sexual arousal when the ovum is ready for fertilization and may actually be especially receptive just before and after menstruation when the hormone levels are low.[68] This may be related in part to a desire to avoid a pregnancy rather than to primary changes in sexual motivation.

That hormonal conditions and sexual arousal are indeed causally related in subprimate species has been shown by the fact that seasonal breeders, such as mares, as well as cyclic breeders, such as rats, can be brought into heat during anestrus by the administration of gonadotrophins[74, 53] or estrogens.[75] Gonadal hormones also influence sexual development during adolescence. For instance, daily estrogen treatments significantly advance the age of puberty (i.e., first mating) in female[19, 21] as well as male[120] rats.

The gradual decline of sexual motivation with age also appears to be related to hormonal influences. Menopause in the human female occurs as a consequence of the depletion of gonadal secretory cells and consequent disturbances of pituitary secretions. In the male, menopause does not occur, but the secretions of the gonads and sexual motivation do decrease in later years. Many experiments have shown that the sexual vigor of aging bulls, stallions, dogs, and rats can be restored by the implantation of gonads from young animals[108] or the injection of gonadal hormones.[119] Clinical observations indicate that old men also show increased sexual interest following gonadal hormone treatments.[95]

Effects of Castration in the Male

The findings that we have so far reviewed indicate that gonadal and gonadotrophic hormones play an important role in sexual behavior. The next two sections of this chapter will ask, more specifically, whether these hormones are indeed essential.

Castration in the male (i.e., removal of the testes) does not make it impossible for the male to engage in copulatory behavior. However, the resultant hormonal deficiencies typically produce an inhibition of sexual behavior. There are marked species as well as individual differences with respect to the severity of the effects of castration in the male. Some species, such as fish, typically show little or no effect.[35] Others, such as rats and man, show a wide spectrum extending from little or no effect to complete inhibition. In many species, including man, prepubertal castration produces more severe effects than postpubertal removal of the testes,[41, 47] but this is not true for other species such as rats.[27]

That the behavioral effects of castration in the male are due to the resultant lack of sex hormones rather than anatomical changes is indicated by the effectiveness of androgen therapy. Testicular implants or injections of testosterone restore sexual motivation to normal levels even in prepubertally castrated males.[116, 115] Some copulatory behaviors appear almost immediately after the injection of androgenic hormones,[97] suggesting a direct action of the hormone on drive-related neural mechanisms, but in most species, prolonged hormone treatments are needed before ejaculation becomes possible. In man, sexual motivation returns rapidly following androgen injections, but the ability to ejaculate often fails to recover.[96] That sex hormones do, indeed, act on the brain and affect sexual receptivity directly is suggested by the observation[88] that implants of estradiol into the preoptic area stimulate female sexual behavior without affecting pituitary release of LH or FSH.

Effects of Castration in the Female

Castration in the female of all infrahuman species results in a complete cessation of all sexual activity due to an apparently total lack of sexual motivation. In contrast to the male, which often continues to display sexual behavior for months after castration, the ovariectomized female almost immediately ceases to be receptive and vigorously resists any sexual advances. The age at castration is not a factor, since castration even late in life completely abolishes sexual behavior.[5, 99] Castration also interferes with the activity cycle typical of the female of many species.

Immediately after ovariectomy, activity drops sharply and the cyclical variations disappear.[106]

The only exception to the rule is the human female. Although castration produces many of the anatomical and physiological changes normally seen during menopause, sexual motivation is often not at all impaired.[48] A review of the clinical literature suggests that removal of the ovaries can produce a wide spectrum of effects on the human female, ranging from complete loss of libido to an essentially unchanged sexual life.

Injections of gonadal hormones restore the estrous cycle and mating behavior (as well as the activity cycle) in the female of all species.[9, 107] Estrogen alone sustains some sexual motivation in the rat and guinea pig, but the level of receptivity is typically low. When combined injections of estrogen and progesterone are administered, the sexual behavior of the castrated female can no longer be differentiated qualitatively or quantitatively from that of normals.[20, 30] This progesterone potentiation is, however, not universal. Progesterone injections decrease sexual receptivity in normal as well as estrogen-primed ovariectomized females of some species.[93, 7] In man, estrogen treatments stimulate sexual motivation in castrated females, but much of the effect may be attributable to suggestion.[80] Progesterone produces primarily inhibitory effects in castrated as well as normal women.[69]

Hormone-Induced Reversal of Sexual Behavior

The importance of hormonal influences on sexual behavior is also illustrated by the results of gonadal transplants (see Figure 11-4). Female sexual behavior is increased following the implantation of ovaries in castrated male rats and guinea pigs.[118] Hemicastrated animals that retain one gonad and receive one from the opposite sex are often bisexual. They display male mating responses to a normal female and female lordosis reactions to the advances of a normal male.[117]

It is commonly found that androgen-treated normal females exhibit male mating behavior in response to a receptive female but female sexual reactions to the advances of a normal male. Normal males given high and sustained doses of estrogen typically show similar bisexual interests.[6, 17] In man, estrogen treatments have been reported to lower sexual motivation in the male but increase it in the female.[65, 52] Androgen treatments have little effect on normal human males. In females their effect is variable.[1, 70] It is commonly assumed that the nature of the response to androgen treatments depends on the level of endogenous androgens in the female, but direct experimental support for this explanation is lacking.

Bisexual behavior is not uncommon in normal males and females in man as well as many infrahuman species. In most lower mammals, the female frequently displays male mating behavior in response to immature males as well as other females. The male occasionally, but less frequently, exhibits female sexual behaviors.[15]

The prevalence of bisexual behavior in animals treated with hormones of the opposite sex has led to the suggestion that bisexual and homosexual behavior in man may be caused by a hormone imbalance.[58] In support of this hypothesis, it has been reported that the androgen-estrogen ratio is lower in male homosexuals than in normal males.[56] Also, several clinical studies have reported a reduction in homosexual tendencies following prolonged androgen treatment.[89] It is, however, clear that hormonal factors are merely predisposing influences in homosexuality in man and that environmental factors contribute importantly to the development of homosexual tendencies.[22]

Endocrine Effects on the Development of Sex-Related Hypothalamic Mechanisms

The most exciting recent development in this field are experimental observations that suggest that gonadal hormones may influence the development of some portions of the brain. When a single dose of a synthetic male sex hormone (testosterone propionate) is given to

FIG. 11–4. Effect of transplantation of testes or ovaries on secondary sex characteristics of fowl.

(From *A textbook of physiological psychology* by S. P. Grossman. Copyright © 1967. John Wiley & Sons, Inc.)

guinea pigs between the 30th and 35th day of pregnancy, their genetically female offspring have external genitalia that are indistinguishable from those of normal males (their internal sexual organs are those of the female). Smaller doses of this hormone have no effect on the external genitalia, but the animals do not come into behavioral heat in adulthood (in spite of the fact that the genital apparatus is in a state of permanent estrus) and respond poorly or not at all to injections of estrogen and/or progesterone that bring normal anestrus females into heat.[104, 63] In the mouse and rat (which have much shorter gestation periods), the "critical period" for this developmental effect of the male sex hormone is somewhere between birth and about 10 days of age.[62, 29]

Female rats that receive testosterone during the critical neonatal period display more male mating behaviors in adulthood than do normal females.[104, 79, 55] This "masculinization" effect may, however, be peculiar to some types of male sexual responses and may not extend to mounting behavior itself.[129, 130] These observations suggest that the presence of the male sex hormone at a critical time in development somehow "defeminizes" the genetic female.

Removal of the male sex hormones by castration has been shown to produce opposite "feminizing" effects on the male rat. Male rats that are subjected to castration one or five days after birth show female sexual behaviors (i.e., lordosis) when estrogen and progesterone are administered in adulthood. Males castrated later in life rarely display this typically female behavior even in response to mounting attempts by normal males.[64] Injections of estrogen during the critical period do not facilitate the development of female sexual behavior in castrated males. On the contrary, males that are castrated in infancy and receive estrogen injections at the same time do not respond to estrogen and progesterone in adulthood (i.e., act like females that received testosterone during the critical period).[45]

On balance, these observations suggest that the mechanisms that control sexual behavior are basically female. The action of the male sex hormones during development defeminizes and, perhaps, masculinizes the system in the genetic male as well as in the genetic female that is treated with testosterone during the critical period in development.

It is commonly assumed that this effect of the male sex hormone is related to a direct disabling or suppressing effect of the hormone on hypothalamic mechanisms that are responsible for the cyclic release of gonadotrophins that induce ovulation in the normal female (see Figure 11–5). This assumption is not yet proven but is supported by the following observations: (a) lesions in the suprachiasmatic/preoptic region produce effects that are similar to those of testosterone injections during the critical period;[51, 13] and (b) electrical stimulation of this region induces ovulation even in "testosterone-sterilized" animals.[12, 60]

There are, however, a few observations that suggest that we may need to proceed cautiously in interpreting the effects of prepubertal testosterone treatments. Very small doses of testosterone reproduce the hormonal effects of larger doses (i.e., permanent estrus and lack

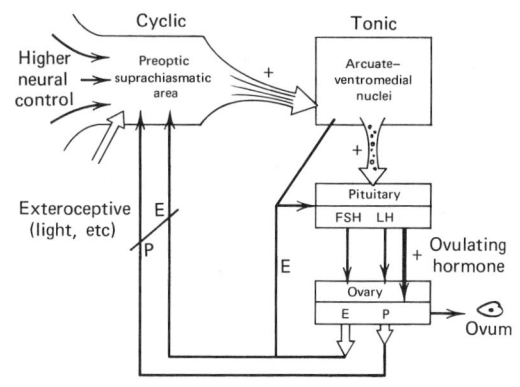

FIG. 11–5. Hypothalamic events which occur after prepubertal treatment of female rats with androgen, or destruction of the anterior preoptic area. In the absence of the cyclic control for the ovulatory discharge of gonadotropin, only tonic hypothalamic influences on adenohypophyseal function can be manifested. While sufficient FSH and LH are released to cause follicular development and estrogen secretion, ovulation does not occur and the persistent estrus syndrome ensues. In the male this control is adequate for maintenance of spermatogenesis and androgen production. E, estrogen; OV. H., ovulating hormone; T, testosterone.

(From C. A. Barraclough. Modifications in reproductive function after exposure to hormones during the prenatal and early postnatal period. In *Neuroendocrinology. Vol. II.* L. Martini & W. F. Ganong, Eds. Academic Press, 1967.)

of ovulation) but do not result in the markedly reduced or absent sexual receptivity. Indeed, there are reports of apparently greater sexual receptivity in such animals.[11] Matters are further complicated by the fact that injections of female sex hormones during the critical period also produce the hormonal dysfunctions that characterize the testosterone-treated female, but the estrogen-treated animals show normal mating behavior.[73, 59]

Summary and Review Questions

Gonadal hormones are important determinants of sexual motivation. Their influence is greatest in lower species and affects the female more than the male. In the female, the interaction between pituitary gonadotrophins and gonadal secretions produces cyclic fluctuations in the level of sex hormones and this is reflected in sexual receptivity. The female of most subprimate species permits copulation only during a small portion of this cycle, called estrus, when the level of estrogen is highest and eggs are available for fertilization. Castration (i.e., ovariectomy) produces an immediate and complete cessation of all sexual activity in all infrahuman species. That this is due to the resultant change in hormone levels is shown by the observation that the implantation of sex glands or the administration of female sex hormones reinstates sexual motivation promptly and completely.

In primates and man, this close relationship disappears. Monkeys and apes prefer to mate during estrus but will receive the male at other times. The human female shows no increased sex drive during ovulation and may even be most receptive just before and after menstruation when the hormone levels are lowest. Castration often results in little or no decrease in sexual motivation in the human female.

The male hormone household is not subject to the cyclic fluctuations that characterize the female, and sexual motivation in the male consequently remains constant during much of the life cycle. Castration does not inhibit sexual behavior in several infrahuman species as well as man, and results in only a gradual disappearance of sexual activity in others.

The influence of gonadal hormones on sexual motivation is also demonstrated by the results of gonadal transplants or hormone therapy in castrates. Injections of estrogen or, in some species, estrogen plus progesterone, completely restore sexual receptivity in castrated females. Implantation of ovaries produces similar effects. Androgen treatments or testicular implants restore sexual motivation in male castrates. Female castrates given testicular implants or prolonged androgen treatments gradually develop male mating behavior. Castrated males given ovarian transplants or prolonged estrogen treatments similarly begin to act like females. Hemicastrates, given a transplant of one sex gland from the opposite sex, are often bisexual.

Recent observations indicate that the male sex hormones may also have an important developmental function. When testosterone injections are given to females of several species during a critical period in their development, they do not come into heat in adulthood, fail to respond to exogenous female sex hormones, and display more male sexual behaviors than normal females. These observations suggest that the mechanisms that regulate mating behavior may be basically female and may, in the male, be modified by the action of testosterone on neural mechanisms that normally produce the cyclic release of gonadotrophins.

1. Describe the influence of hormones on the sexual behavior of the female.

2. How is the sexual behavior of the male affected by hormonal mechanisms?

3. Discuss the effects of hormones on the development of neural mechanisms related to sexual behavior.

4. Discuss the effects of castration in the male and female. Are there species differences?

5. How do hormone replacement therapy or gonadal transplants affect the castrated male or female?

6. What are the effects of sex hormones or gonadal transplants from the opposite sex on castrated males and females?

7. How do hemicastrated males and females respond to such implants or hormone treatments?

NEURAL INFLUENCES

Hypothalamic Mechanisms

Sexual motivation appears to be controlled primarily by hypothalamic mechanisms. Part of this influence is indirect and involves regulation of the secretory activity of the anterior pituitary gland. Lesions in and just behind the ventromedial nuclei of the hypothalamus produce a state of complete and permanent anestrus.[109] The ovaries and testes begin to degenerate because FSH and LH are no longer secreted. The secretion of gonadal hormones consequently stops and the animals completely lose interest in the opposite sex. That this deficit is related directly and exclusively to the lesion-induced disruption of gonadal hormones is shown by the observation that sexual motivation is temporarily restored when sex hormones are administered systemically.[112]

A second regulatory influence on sexual motivation is exercised by a hypothalamic mechanism that, in most species, is located in the anterior hypothalamus or adjacent portions of the preoptic area. Lesions near the supraoptic nuclei of the hypothalamus of female cats,[50] guinea pigs,[32] and rats[57] completely eliminate all sexual responses. The lesion-induced deficit in sexual behavior cannot be reversed by hormone treatments.[110] In some species, such as the rabbit, this second hypothalamic mechanism is probably located in the premammillary region of the posterior hypothalamus.[109] The precise localization of the two hypothalamic "sex centers" in man has not yet been described, but it is clear that both exist because damage to the hypothalamus often reduces or eliminates sexual motivation. This may or may not be accompanied by hormonal disturbances.[14]

There is also some evidence for the presence of an inhibitory hypothalamic influence in some species. Some lesions in the medial hypothalamus bring anestrous and even spayed female rats into behavioral heat without changing the animals' hormone balance or ovarian structure.[85, 61] An increase in the copulatory activity of male rats following such lesions has also been reported.[87] It is, however, not yet clear whether these facilitatory effects may not be due to an irritative (i.e., stimulating) effect of lesions near facilitatory mechanisms.

Electrical stimulation of the medial hypothalamus results in the secretion of releasing factors that stimulate the release of gonadotrophic hormones by the pituitary. Stimulation of the gland itself does not[77] (see also Campbell[34]). Isolated components of mating behavior, such as penile erection, have been elicited by hypothalamic stimulation in many species. More coordinated copulatory reactions have been seen only in the rat.[126]

Electrophysiological studies of the hypothalamus have shown that vaginal stimulation[105] or sexual arousal due to precoital "love play"[66] produces significant changes in the EEG recorded from the anterior hypothalamus of cats and rabbits. A more generalized EEG reaction to vaginal stimulation can be recorded from many subcortical and even some cortical leads, and this reaction can be elicited by electrical stimulation of the ventromedial nuclei of the hypothalamus.[111]

That the hypothalamic "sex centers" may contain neurons that are selectively sensitive to the level of sex hormones in the blood is suggested by several observations. Individual cells in the hypothalamus have been shown to alter their firing rate in response to systemic or direct applications of sex hormones.[84, 86, 103] Moreover, estrogen has been shown to enter the brain and concentrate in cells of the preoptic region and ventromedial and arcuate nuclei (as well as some portions of the amygdala).[122, 4] That the hypothalamus may control sexual arousal in accordance with information from these hormone receptors is suggested by the fact that the implantation of very small quantities of female sex hormone into the anterior hypothalamus and preoptic area of female rats[88] and cats[78] or the posterior hypothalamus of rabbits[38] induces behavioral heat. Similar implants of female sex hormones into the ventromedial region inhibit the release of gonadotrophins from the pituitary.[37] Injections of the male hormone testosterone into the lateral preoptic region of male rats have been reported to produce indiscriminate copulatory behavior.[49]

It has been suggested[11] (see Figure 11-6) that sexual behavior may be regulated by two hypothalamic mechanisms. One, located in the ventromedial region of most species, appears to be responsible for the tonic secretion of releasing factors that stimulate the steady release of gonadotrophins from the pituitary. This steady release of hormones is sufficient to maintain estrogen production and the acyclic sexual receptivity of the male, but cannot initiate the surge of gonadotrophin required to produce ovulation in the female. A second mechanism that is isolated in the preoptic region of many species normally responds to the release of progesterone, which occurs at some stage of the estrous cycle (as well as, perhaps, in response to exteroceptive

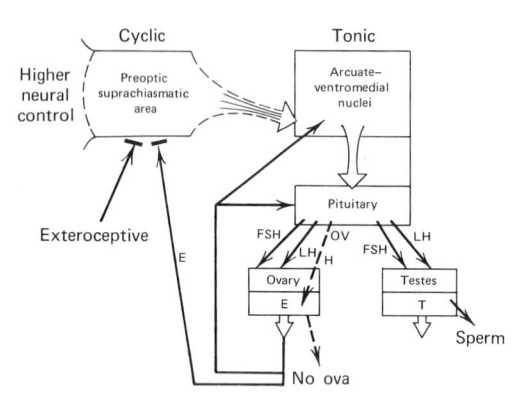

FIG. 11-6. Diagrammatic representation of the events that may occur at the hypothalamic, pituitary, and gonadal level to result in steroid secretion and ovulation. When proper estrogen (E) to progesterone (P) ratios are reached, the preoptic area becomes responsive to exteroceptive and interoceptive influences, is activated, and in turn it activates the arcuate-ventromedial nuclear area. Sufficient LRF is released to cause the ovulatory discharge of gonadotropin and ovulation.

(From C. A. Barraclough. Modifications in reproductive function after exposure to hormones during the prenatal and early postnatal period. In *Neuroendocrinology*. Vol. II. L. Martini & W. F. Ganong, Eds. Academic Press, 1967.)

and interoceptive stimuli), by initiating the burst of gonadotrophin release that is required to achieve ovulation. It is thought that the preoptic "cycling" mechanism acts on the pituitary only indirectly by stimulating the ventromedial region. In the male, this preoptic cycling mechanism is inactivated by the action of testosterone during some stage of neural development. The ventromedial region functions normally and thus produces the acyclic sexual receptivity typical of the male. The fact that the preoptic area may be the site of progesterone action is suggested by the observation that progesterone treatments restore normal cyclic sexual behavior in animals that are spontaneously acyclic[42] but do not do so in animals that are made acyclic by lesions in the preoptic region or by prepubertal testosterone treatments.[13]

Limbic Influences

The sexual behavior of the female appears to be controlled entirely by hypothalamic influences. Female cats,[9] rats,[23] and rabbits[33] maintain normal estrous cycles, mating behavior, and pregnancies after complete decortication. The sexual behavior of the male of these species, on the other hand, is severely impaired or abolished by decortication[33] as well as by less complete cortical damage.[16] However, no specific portion of the cortex seems to be particularly related to sexual behavior, and a closer look at the behavior pattern of the lesioned animals suggests that these deficits may be due to an impairment of sensory and motor functions rather than effects on sexual motivation per se.[57] This impairment is not equally reflected in the behavior of females because the female is typically passive and requires little sensory feedback or precise motor coordination.

Numerous observations suggest that the amygdaloid complex may play a more direct role in the regulation of mating behavior, but the nature of this influence is the subject of much debate. Many investigators have reported that lesions in the temporal lobe, particularly in the pyriform cortex adjacent to the amygdala and in the amygdala itself, produce hypersexuality in man,[123] male monkeys,[83] and male cats[67] (see Figure 11-7). Unfortunately, these observations have not been related to a preoperative base line of sexual activity, and the observed hypersexuality is merely one of many behavioral changes. Many authorities in the field are consequently not convinced that the lesions produce specific disinhibitory or facilitatory effects on sexual behavior.[25]

There are more convincing indications that the amygdala influences the secretory activity of the pituitary via its projections to the hypothalamus[40,127] and that lesions in the amygdala in young rats produce precocious puberty.[36] These observations are particularly interesting when viewed in conjunction with the observation that the only extrahypothalamic region in the brain that concentrates sex hormones is the amygdala.[122,131]

It has been suggested[90] that the entire limbic system and related subcortical projections

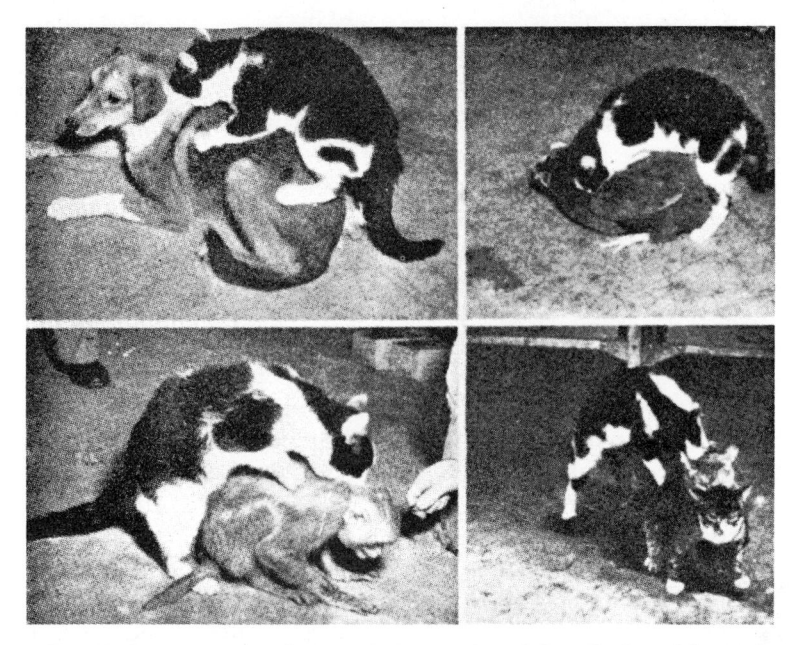

FIG. 11-7. Various phases of abnormal sexual activity displayed by male cats with lesions in the amygdala and pyriform cortex. The lower right photograph illustrates attempts at "tandem copulation" among four male preparations.

(From L. H. Schreiner & A. Kling. Behavioral changes following rhinencephalic injury in cat. *J. Neurophysiol.*, **16**, 1953, 643.)

that seem to contribute to the regulation of appetitive as well as emotional behaviors may also influence sexual arousal. The evidence for such a contribution is, as yet, slim. It consists essentially of the following observations. Isolated components of male mating behavior, such as penile erection or ejaculation, have been elicited by electrical stimulation of several structures in this circuit, but coordinated sexual behavior has never been reported.[91, 92] Lesions in some of the same areas have been reported to produce a state of heat in anestrous cats, although the hormonal balance was unaffected.[54] Intramuscular injections of gonadal or gonadotrophic hormones produce EEG changes in some portions of the limbic circuit.[43, 44]

Summary and Review Questions

The neural integration of sexual behavior appears to take place primarily in the hypothalamus and to rely on hormonal mechanisms for at least some of its influence. The rate of secretion of gonadotrophic hormones by the pituitary is primarily determined by the secretion of specific releasing factors by cells in the ventromedial hypothalamus. Damage to this important regulatory center produces ovarian and testicular atrophy and complete asexuality. The primary hormonal basis of this effect is demonstrated by the fact that injections of gonadal or gonadotrophic hormones can induce heat and mating behavior in animals with lesions in this portion of the brain.

A second regulatory center appears to be located in the preoptic region. This mechanism appears to respond to the sudden surge of progesterone that occurs at some stage in the estrous cycle of the female by stimulating the release of large quantities of gonadotrophic hormones needed to effect ovulation. This effect may be mediated by the releasing system of the ventromedial hypothalamus. Damage to this important cyclic mechanism leaves the female in a state of permanent vaginal estrus but sexually unresponsive and unable to ovulate. In the male, this cyclic influence appears to be inactivated by the presence of the male sex hormone, testosterone, at a critical time in neural development. The sexual receptivity of the male is consequently determined primarily by the tonic release of gonadotrophic hormones, which is under the control of the ventromedial hypothalamus.

Many observations suggest that the amygdaloid complex may also play an important role in the regulation of hormonal mechanisms and sexual behavior, perhaps via its intimate connections with the hypothalamus. There is good evidence for a direct regulatory action on the appearance of puberty, but the amygdaloid influence on adult sexual behavior is a matter of controversy.

1. Describe the nature of the hypothalamic influences on pituitary function and mating behavior.

2. Discuss the effects of temporal lobe damage on sexual behavior.

3. How do hormonal influences on sexual behavior interact with neural mechanisms?

REVIEW AND SUMMARY

Sexual behavior has many unique characteristics. Although it is determined to a large extent by hormonal mechanisms, the sex drive does not reflect a biological need, and its satisfaction is not essential or even important to the survival of the individual. Sexual behavior may be at least partially learned and cannot develop in the absence of specific eliciting stimuli in the environment.

Three categories of environmental influences have been described. Some, such as ambient temperature and the presence of sufficient daylight, trigger hormonal secretions that are essential for sexual arousal. Others, such as the presence of nesting material or shelter, predispose a physiologically ready animal to respond to a potential mate. The third and most important source of stimuli is the sexual partner itself. In lower species, sexual arousal often occurs only in response to very specific eliciting stimuli, such as the odor or bloated abdomen of a receptive female. In more highly developed species, this dependence on particular triggers disappears, and sexual arousal occurs as long as sufficient sensory information for the identification of a receptive partner is available. Sensory deprivation severely interferes with male mating behavior, but this may be largely due to a loss of sensory-motor integration needed for copulatory behavior rather than to an impairment of sexual motivation per se.

In all species except man, sexual motivation is a direct reflection of hormonal influences. This is most evident in the female because her receptivity varies directly as a function of cyclic fluctuations in the sex hormone level. These fluctuations are absent in the male, and sexual motivation consequently remains nearly stable after puberty. The female of subprimate species can be sexually aroused only during a brief period called heat or estrus, when the level of estrogen is high and a mature ovum is available for fertilization. In primates this strict relationship breaks down, and the female accepts an insistent male during any portion of the estrous cycle. The receptivity of the human female appears to be entirely independent of the cyclic fluctuations in her sex hormone balance.

Castration of the female of all infrahuman species produces a complete and immediate cessation of all sexual responses due, apparently, to a complete loss of sexual motivation. The hormonal nature of this impairment is demonstrated by a return of sexual receptivity following ovarian transplants or sex-hormone injections. Castration of the male does not affect sexual behavior in some individuals of some species; in others, sexual motivation disappears, but the decline is often very gradual. Hormone replacement therapy or testicular transplants restore the sexual activity of the male castrate to precastration levels.

The importance of gonadal hormones is also demonstrated by the effects of gonadal transplants or hormones from the opposite sex. Castrated females display male mating behavior following the implantation of testes or injections of androgens. Male castrates similarly display female mating behavior following ovarian transplants or injections of estrogen. Hemicastrated animals often display bisexual behavior following the implantation of a gonad from the opposite sex.

The neural control of sexual motivation is exercised primarily by hypothalamic mechanisms. Neurons in the ventromedial hypothalamus influence sexual motivation by the secretion of releasing factors that, in turn, stimulate the release of gonadotrophic hormones by the anterior pituitary. A second regulatory mechanism is located in the anterior hypothalamus or preoptic region of most species (in some it is found in the posterior hypothalamus). This second mechanism appears to be responsible for the cyclicity of female sexual receptivity and to achieve this important influence by instigating a sudden release of gonadotrophic hormones from the pituitary when they are needed for ovulation. In the male, this cyclic mechanism appears to be suppressed by the action of the male sex hormone during a critical period of neural development. The implantation of sex hormones into the anterior hypothalamus brings anestrous animals into behavioral heat. This suggests that hormonal influences on sexual motivation may be mediated by hormone receptors in the hypothalamus that meter the level of hormones in the blood.

There is also some evidence that the amygdaloid complex may modify the release of gonadotrophic hormones from the pituitary and thus sexual receptivity, but the nature of this influence is as yet poorly understood.

Bibliography

1. Abel, S. Androgenic therapy in malignant disease of the female genitalia. *Amer. J. Obstet. Gynec.*, 1945, **49**, 327–342.
2. Adams, J. H., Daniel, P. M., & Prichard, Marjorie M. L. Observations on the portal circulation of the pituitary gland. *Neuroendocrinology*, 1965/1966, **1**, 193–213.
3. Allen, E., Diddle, A. W., Burford, T. H., & Elder, J. H. Analysis of urine of the chimpanzee for estrogenic content during various stages of the menstrual cycle. *Endocrinology*, 1936, **20**, 546–549.
4. Anderson, C. H., & Greenwald, G. S. Autoradiographic analysis of estradiol uptake in the brain and pituitary of the female rat. *Endocrinology. Vol. II*, 1969, **85**, 1160–1165.
5. Ball, J. Sexual responsiveness in female monkeys after castration and subsequent estrin administration. *Psychol. Bull.*, 1936, **33**, 811.
6. Ball, J. The effect of male hormone on the sex behavior of female rats. *Psychol. Bull.*, 1937, **34**, 725.
7. Ball, J. Effect of progesterone upon sexual excitability in the female monkey. *Psychol. Bull.*, 1941, **38**, 533.
8. Ball, J., & Hartman, C. G. Sexual excitability as related to the menstrual cycle in the monkey. *Amer. J. Obstet. Gynec.*, 1935, **29**, 117–119.
9. Bard, P. Oestrual behavior in surviving decorticate cats. *Amer. J. Physiol.*, 1936, **116**, 4–5.
10. Bard, P. *The Hypothalamus and Central Levels of Autonomic Function*. Baltimore: Williams and Wilkins, 1940.
11. Barraclough, C. A. Modifications in reproductive function after exposure to hormones during the prenatal and early postnatal period. In *Neuroendocrinology, Vol. II*. L. Martini & W. F. Ganong, Eds. New York: Academic Press, 1967, pp. 61–99.
12. Barraclough, C. A., & Gorski, R. A. Evidence that the hypothalamus is responsible for androgen-induced sterility in the female rat. *Endocrinology*, 1961, **68**, 68–79.
13. Barraclough, C. A., Yrarrazaval, S., & Hatton, R. A possible hypothalamic site of action of progesterone in the facilitation of ovulation in the rat. *Endocrinology*, 1964, **75**, 838–845.
14. Bauer, D. Endocrine and other clinical manifestations of hypothalamic disease. *J. Clin. Endocrinol.*, 1954, **14**, 13.
15. Beach, F. A. Sex reversals in the mating pattern of the rat. *J. Genet. Psychol.*, 1938, **53**, 329–334.
16. Beach, F. A. Effects of cortical lesions upon the copulatory behavior of male rats. *J. Comp. Psychol.*, 1940, **29**, 193–239.
17. Beach, F. A. Female mating behavior shown by male rats after administration of testosterone propionate. *Endocrinology*, 1941, **29**, 409–412.

18. Beach, F. A. Analysis of the stimuli adequate to elicit mating behavior in the sexually inexperienced male rat. *J. Comp. Psychol.*, 1942a, **33**, 163–207.
19. Beach, F. A. Copulatory behavior in prepuberally castrated male rats and its modifications by estrogen administration. *Endocrinology*, 1942b, **31**, 679–683.
20. Beach, F. A. Effects of testosterone propionate upon the copulatory behavior of sexually inexperienced male rats. *J. Comp. Psychol.*, 1942c, **33**, 227–247.
21. Beach, F. A. Importance of progesterone to induction of sexual receptivity in spayed female rats. *Proc. Soc. Exp. Biol. Med.*, 1942d, **51**, 369–371.
22. Beach, F. A. *Hormones and Behavior.* New York and London: Paul Hoeber, 1948.
23. Beach, F. A. Instinctive behavior: reproductive activities. In *Handbook of Experimental Psychology.* S. S. Stevens, Ed. New York: Wiley, 1951, pp. 387–434.
24. Beach, F. A. Normal sexual behavior in male rats isolated at fourteen days of age. *J. Comp. Physiol. Psychol.*, 1958, **51**, 37–38.
25. Beach, F. A. Cerebral and hormonal control of reflexive mechanisms involved in copulatory behavior. *Physiol. Rev.*, 1967, **47**, 289–316.
26. Beach, F. A. Locks and beagles. *Amer. Psychol.*, 1969, **24**, 971–989.
27. Beach, F. A., & Holz-Tucker, A. M. Mating behavior in male rats castrated at various ages and injected with androgen. *J. Exp. Zool.*, 1946, **101**, 91–142.
28. Beach, F. A., & Jordan, L. Effects of sexual reinforcement upon the performance of male rats in a straight runway. *J. Comp. Physiol. Psychol.*, 1956, **49**, 105–110.
29. Beach, F. A., Noble, R. G., & Orndoff, R. K. Effects of perinatal androgen treatment on responses of male rats to gonadal hormones in adulthood. *J. Comp. Physiol. Psychol.*, 1969, **68**, 490–497.
30. Boling, J. L., & Blandau, R. J. The estrogen-progesterone induction of mating responses in the spayed female rat. *Endocrinology*, 1939, **25**, 359–371.
31. Breder, C. M., & Coates, C. W. Sex recognition in the guppy, *Lebistes reticulatus* (Peters). *Zoologica*, 1935, **19**, 187–207.
32. Brookhart, J. M., Dey, F. L., & Ranson, S. W. The abolition of mating behavior by hypothalamic lesions in guinea pigs. *Endocrinology*, 1941, **28**, 561–565.
33. Brooks, C. McC. The role of the cerebral cortex and of various sense organs in the excitation and execution of mating activity in the rabbit. *Amer. J. Physiol.*, 1937, **120**, 544–553.
34. Campbell, H. J. Control of hormone secretion. In *The Biological Basis of Medicine. Vol. II.* E. E. Bittar & N. Bittar, Eds. London: Academic Press, 1968, pp. 48–100.
35. Clark, G. Prepubertal castration in the male chimpanzee, with some effects of replacement therapy. *Growth*, 1945, **9**, 327–339.
36. Critchlow, V., & Bar-Sela, Mildred E. Control of the onset of puberty. In *Neuroendocrinology, Vol. II.* L. Martini & W. F. Ganong, Eds. New York: Academic Press, 1967, pp. 101–162.
37. Davidson, J. M. Feedback control of gonadotropin secretion. In *Frontiers in Neuroendocrinology.* W. F. Ganong & L. Martini, Eds. London: Oxford Univ. Press, 1969, pp. 343–388.
38. Davidson, J. M., & Sawyer, C. H. Effects of localized intracerebral implantation of oestrogen on reproductive function in the female rabbit. *Acta Endocrinol.*, 1961, **37**, 385–393.
39. Denniston, R. H. Qualification and comparison of sex drive under various conditions in terms of a learned response. *J. Comp. Physiol. Psychol.*, 1954, **47**, 437–440.
40. Eleftheriou, B. E., & Pattison, M. L. Effect of amygdaloid lesions on hypothalamic follicle-stimulating hormone-releasing factor in the female deermouse. *J. Neuroendocrin.*, 1967, **39**, 613–614.
41. Engle, E. T. The testis and hormones. In *Problems of Ageing* (2nd ed.). E. V. Cowdry, Ed. Baltimore: Williams and Wilkins, 1942.
42. Everett, J. W. The restoration of ovulatory cycles and corpus luteum formation in persistent estrous rats by progesterone. *Endocrinology*, 1940, **27**, 681–686.
43. Fauré, J. De certains aspects du comportement en rapport avec des variations hormonales provoquées chez l'animal. *J. Physiol. (Paris)*, 1956, **48**, 529–531.

44. Fauré, J., & Gruner, J. Sur les modifications de l'activité bioélectrique du rhinencéphale et du thalamus recueillies sous l'influences des oestrogènes et des androgènes chez l'animal. *Rev. neurol.*, 1956, **94**, 161–168.

45. Feder, H. H., & Whalen, R. E. Feminine behavior in neonatally castrated and estrogen-treated male rats. *Science*, 1965, **147**, 306–307.

46. Fee, A. R., & Parks, A. S. Studies on ovulation: effect of vaginal anesthesia on ovulation in rabbit. *J. Physiol. (London)*, 1930, **70**, 385–388.

47. Feiner, L., & Rothman, T. Study of a male castrate. *J. Amer. Med. Ass.*, 1939, **113**, 2144–2146.

48. Filler, W., & Drezner, N. Results of surgical castration in women over forty. *Amer. J. Obstet. Gynec.*, 1944, **47**, 122–124.

49. Fisher, A. E. Maternal and sexual behavior induced by intracranial chemical stimulation. *Science*, 1956, **124**, 228.

50. Fisher, C., Ingram, W. R., & Ranson, S. W. *Diabetes Insipidus and the Neurohumoral Control of Water Balance*. Ann Arbor, Mich.: Edward, 1938.

51. Flerkó, B., & Bardós, V. Zwei verschiedene effekte experimenteller läsion des hypothalmus auf die gonaden. *Acta Neuroveget. (Vienna)*, 1959, **20**, 248–262.

52. Foote, R. M. Diethylstilbestrol in the management of psychopathological states in males. *J. Nerv. Ment. Dis.*, 1944, **99**, 928–935.

53. Friedgood, H. B. Induction of estrous behavior in anestrous cats with the follicle-stimulating and luteinizing hormones of the anterior pituitary gland. *Amer. J. Physiol.*, 1939, **126**, 229–233.

54. Gastaut, H. Corrélations entre le système nerveux végétatif et les systèmes de la vie de relation dans le rhinencéphale. *J. Physiol. Path. Gén.*, 1952, **44**, 431–470.

55. Gerall, A. A., & Ward, I. L. Effects of prenatal exogenous androgen on the sexual behavior of the female albino rat. *J. Comp. Physiol. Psychol.*, 1966, **62**, 370–375.

56. Glass, S. J., Deuel, H. J., & Wright, C. A. Sex hormone studies in male homosexuality. *Endocrinology*, 1940, **26**, 590–594.

57. Goldstein, A. C. *Hormones, Brain Function, and Behavior*. H. H. Hoagland, Ed. New York: Academic Press, 1957.

58. Gordon, M. B. Endocrine consideration of genito-urinary conditions in children. *Urol. Cutan. Rev.*, 1941, **45**, 3–7.

59. Gorski, R. A. Modification of ovulatory mechanisms by postnatal administration of estrogen to the rat. *Amer. J. Physiol.*, 1963, **205**, 842–844.

60. Gorski, R. A., & Barraclough, C. A. Effects of low dosages of androgen on the differentiation of hypothalamic regulatory control of ovulation in the rat. *Endocrinology*, 1963, **73**, 210–216.

61. Goy, R. W., & Phoenix, C. H. Hypothalamic regulation of female sexual behavior: establishment of behavioral oestrus in spayed guinea pigs following hypothalamic lesions. *J. Reproduct. Fertil.*, 1963, **5**, 23–40.

62. Goy, R. W., Phoenix, C. H., & Young, W. C. A critical period for the suppression of behavioral receptivity in adult female rats by early treatment with androgen. *Anat. Rec.*, 1962, **142**, 307.

63. Goy, R. W., Bridson, W. E., & Young, W. C. Period of maximum susceptibility of the prenatal female guinea pig to the masculinizing actions of testosterone propionate. *J. Comp. Physiol. Psychol.*, 1964, **57**, 166–174.

64. Grady, K. L., Phoenix, C. H., & Young, W. C. Role of the developing rat testis in differentiation of the neural tissues mediating mating behavior. *J. Comp. Physiol. Psychol.*, 1965, **59**, 176–182.

65. Graller, D. L., Felson, H., & Schiff, L. Use of stilbestrol in males. *The Association for the Study of Internal Secretions. Program.* 25th annual meeting, 1941, p. 27.

66. Green, J. D. Electrical activity in the hypothalamus and hippocampus of conscious rabbits. *Anat. Rec.*, 1954, **118**, 304.

67. Green, J. D., Clemente, C. D., & de Groot, J. Rhinencephalic lesions and behavior in cats. *J. Comp. Neurol.*, 1957, **108**, 505–545.

68. Greenblatt, R. B. Hormonal factors in libido. *J. Clin. Endocrinol.*, 1943, **3**, 305–306.

69. Greenblatt, R. B. *Office Endocrinology* (2nd ed.). Baltimore: Thomas, 1944.

70. Greenblatt, R. B., Mortara, F., & Torpin, R. Sexual libido in the female. *Amer. J. Obstet. Gynec.*, 1942, **44**, 658–663.
71. Grossman, S. P. *A Textbook of Physiological Psychology.* New York: Wiley, 1967.
72. Grunt, J. A., & Young, W. C. Differential reactivity of individuals and the response of the male guinea pig to testosterone propionate. *Endocrinology,* 1952, **51**, 237–248.
73. Hale, H. B. Functional and morphological alterations of the reproductive system of the female rat following prepuberal treatment with estrogens. *Endocrinology,* 1944, **35**, 499–506.
74. Hammond, J. Recent scientific research on horse breeding problems. *Yorkshire Agric. Soc. J.,* 1938, 2–16.
75. Hammond, J. Control of ovulation in farm animals. *Nature (London),* 1944, **153**, 702.
76. Harlow, H. F. The heterosexual affectional system in monkeys. *Amer. Psychol.,* 1962, **1**, 1–9.
77. Harris, G. W. Electrical stimulation of hypothalamus and mechanism of neural control of adenohypophysis. *J. Physiol. (London),* 1948, **107**, 418–429.
78. Harris, G. W. The reticular formation, stress, and endocrine activity. In *The Reticular Formation of the Brain.* H. H. Jasper, L. D. Proctor, R. S. Knighton, W. C. Noshay, & R. T. Costello, Eds. Boston: Little, Brown, 1958, pp. 207–221.
79. Harris, G. W., & Levine, S. Sexual differentiation of the brain and its experimental control. *J. Physiol. (London),* 1962, **163**, 42P (Abstract).
80. Heller, C. G., Farney, J. P., & Myers, G. B. Development and correlation of menopausal symptoms, vaginal smear and urinary gonadotrophin changes following castration in 27 women. *J. Clin. Endocrinol.,* 1944, **4**, 101–108.
81. Hemmingsen, A. M. Studies on the oestrous-producing hormone (oestrin). *Skand. Arch. Physiol.,* 1933, **65**, 97–250.
82. Kellogg, V. Some silkworm moth reflexes. *Biol. Bull. Woods Hole,* 1907, **12**, 152–154.
83. Klüver, H., & Bucy, P. C. Preliminary analysis of functions of the temporal lobes in monkeys. *Arch. Neurol. Psychiat. (Chicago),* 1939, **42**, 979–1000.
84. Komisaruk, B. R., McDonald, P. G., Whitmoyer, D. I., & Sawyer, C. H. Effects of progesterone and sensory stimulation of EEG and neuronal activity in the rat. *Exper. Neurol.,* 1967, **19**, 494–507.
85. Law, T., & Meagher, W. Hypothalamic lesions and sexual behavior in the female rat. *Science,* 1958, **128**, 1626–1627.
86. Lincoln, D., & Cross, B. Effect of oestrogen on the responsiveness of neurones in the hypothalamus, septum, and preoptic area of rats with light-induced persistent oestrus. *J. Endocrinol.,* 1967, **37**, 191–203.
87. Lisk, R. D. Inhibitory centers in sexual behavior in the male rat. *Science,* 1966, **152**, 669–670.
88. Lisk, R. D. Sexual behavior: hormonal control. In *Neuroendocrinology. Vol. II.* L. Martini & W. F. Ganong, Eds. New York: Academic Press, 1967, pp. 49–98.
89. Lurie, L. A. The endocrine factor in homosexuality. Report of treatment of 4 cases with androgen hormone. *Amer. J. Med. Sci.,* 1944, **208**, 176–184.
90. MacLean, P. D. The limbic system in relation to central grey and reticulum of the brainstem. *Psychosom. Med.,* 1955, **17**, 355.
91. MacLean, P. D., & Ploog, D. W. Cerebral representation of penile erection. *J. Neurophysiol.,* 1962, **25**, 30–55.
92. MacLean, P. D., Denniston, R. H., & Dua, S. Further studies on cerebral representation of penile erection: caudal thalamus, midbrain, and pons. *J. Neurophysiol.,* 1963, **26**, 273–293.
93. Makepeace, A. W., Weinstein, G. L., & Friedman, M. H. The effect of progestin and progesterone on ovulation in the rabbit. *Amer. J. Physiol.,* 1937, **119**, 512–516.
94. Marshall, F. H. A. Exteroceptive factors in sexual periodicity. *Biol. Rev.,* 1942, **17**, 68–90.
95. Miller, N. E. Old minds rejuvenated by sex hormone. *Sci. News Letter,* Sept. 1938, **24**, 201.
96. Moehlig, R. C. Castration in the male. Notes on the hypothalamico-pituitary gonadal system. *Endocrinology,* 1940, **27**, 743–748.

97. Moore, C. R., & Price, D. Some effects of testosterone and testosterone propionate in the rat. *Anat. Rec.*, 1938, **71**, 59–78.

98. Nice, M. M. The role of territory in bird life. *Amer. Midl. Nat.*, 1941, **26**, 441–487.

99. Nissen, H. W. The effects of gonadectomy, vasotomy, and injections of placental and orchic extracts on the sex behavior of the white rat. *Genet. Psychol. Monogr.*, 1929, **5**, 451–547.

100. Noble, G. K. *The Biology of the Amphibia.* New York: McGraw-Hill, 1931.

101. Noble, G. K. Courtship and sexual selection of the flicker (*Colaptes auratus luteus*). *Auk*, 1936, **53**, 269–282.

102. Noble, G. K., & Aronson, L. R. The sexual behavior of Anura. I. The normal mating pattern of *Rana pipiens*. *Bull. Amer. Mus. Nat. Hist.*, 1942, **80**, 127–142.

103. Pfaff, D. W., & Pfaffmann, C. Olfactory and hormonal influences on the basal forebrain of the male rat. *Brain Res.*, 1969, **15**, 137–156.

104. Phoenix, C. H., Goy, R. W., Gerall, A. A., & Young, W. C. Organizing action of prenatally administered testosterone propionate on the tissues mediating mating behavior in the female guinea pig. *Endocrinology*, 1959, **65**, 369–382.

105. Porter, R. W., Cavanaugh, E. G., Critchlow, B. V., & Sawyer, C. H. Localized changes in electrical activity of the hypothalamus in estrous cats following vaginal stimulation. *Amer. J. Physiol.*, 1957, **189**, 145–151.

106. Richter, C. P. Animal behavior and internal drives. *Quart. Rev. Biol.*, 1927, **2**, 307–343.

107. Richter, C. P. The effect of early gonadectomy on the gross body activity of rats. *Endocrinology*, 1933, **17**, 445–450.

108. Runge, S. Testicular grafting in domestic animals. *Vet. J.*, 1943, **99**, 231–236 and *Biol. Abstr.*, 1944, **18**, 4482.

109. Sawyer, C. H. Effects of central nervous system lesions on ovulation in the rabbit. *Anat. Rec.*, 1956, **124**, 358.

110. Sawyer, C. H. Triggering of the pituitary by the central nervous system. In *Physiological Triggers.* T. H. Bullock, Ed. Washington, D. C.: American Physiological Society, 1957, pp. 164–174.

111. Sawyer, C. H. Reproductive behavior. In *Handbook of Physiology. Vol. II.* J. Field, H. W. Magoun, & V. E. Hall, Eds. Washington, D.C.: Am. Physiol. Soc., 1960, pp. 1225–1240.

112. Sawyer, C. H., & Robinson, B. Separate hypothalamic areas controlling pituitary gonadotropic function and mating behavior in female cats and rabbits. *J. Clin. Endocrinol.*, 1956, **16**, 914.

113. Schreiner, L. H., & Kling, A. Behavioral changes follwing rhinencephalic injury in cat. *J. Neurophysiol.*, 1953, **16**, 643–659.

114. Seward, J. P., & Seward, G. H. Studies on the reproductive activities of the guinea pig. I. Factors in maternal behavior. *J. Comp. Psychol.*, 1940, **29**, 1–24.

115. Shapiro, H. A. Effect of testosterone propionate upon mating. *Nature (London)*, 1937, **139**, 588–589.

116. Steinach, E. Umstimmung des geschlechtcharacters bei Saeugetieren durch Austausch der Pubertaetsdruesen. *Zbl. Physiol.*, 1911, **25**, 723–735.

117. Steinach, E. Pubertaetsdruesen und Zwitterbildung. *Arch. Entwickl.-Mech. Org.*, 1916, **42**, 307.

118. Steinach, E. *Sex and Life.* New York: Viking, 1940.

119. Steinach, E., & Kun, H. Die Wirkungen des maennlichen Sexualhormons auf die psychischen und somatischen Geschlechtsmerkmale. *Akad. Anz. Ada. Wiss. (Wien)*, 1933, No. 18.

120. Stone, C. P. Precocious copulatory activity induced in male rats by subcutaneous injections of testosterone propionate. *Endocrinology*, 1940, **26**, 511–515.

121. Stone, C. P., Barker, R. G., & Tomlin, M. I. Sexual drive in potent and impotent male rats as measured by the Columbia obstruction apparatus. *J. Gen. Psychol.*, 1935, **47**, 33–48.

122. Stumpf, W. E. Estradiol-concentrating neurons: Topography in the hypothalamus by dry mount autoradiography. *Science*, 1968, **162**, 1001–1003.

123. Terzian, H., & Dalle Ore, G. Syndrome of Klüver and Bucy reproduced in man by bilateral removal of the temporal lobes. *Neurology*, 1955, **5**, 373–380.

124. Tinbergen, N. An objectivistic study of the innate behaviour of animals. *Bibl. Biotheor.*, 1942, **1**, 39–98.
125. Valenstein, E. S., Riss, W., & Young, W. C. Experiential and genetic factors in the organization of sexual behavior in male guinea pigs. *J. Comp. Physiol. Psychol.*, 1955, **48**, 397–403.
126. Vaughn, E., & Fisher, A. E. Male sexual behavior induced by intracranial electrical stimulation. *Science*, 1962, **137**, 758–760.
127. Velasco, M. E., & Taleisnik, S. Release of gonadotropins induced by amygdaloid stimulation in the rat. *Endocrinology*, 1969, **84**, 132–139.
128. Wells, L. J. Seasonal sexual rhythm and its experimental modification in the male of the thirteen-lined ground squirrel (*Citellus tridecemlineatus*). *Anat. Rec.*, 1935, **62**, 409–444.
129. Whalen, R. E., & Edwards, D. A. Hormonal determinants of the development of masculine and feminine behavior in male and female rats. *Anat. Rec.*, 1967, **157**, 173–180.
130. Whalen, R. E., Edwards, D. A., Luttge, W. G., & Robertson, R. T. Early androgen treatment and male sexual behavior in female rats. *Physiol. & Behav.*, 1969, **4**, 33–40.
131. Zigmond, R. E., & McEwen, B. S. Selective retention of oestradiol by cell nuclei in specific brain regions of the ovariectomized rat. *J. Neurochem.*, 1970, **17**, 889–899.

Chapter **12**

AFFECTIVE BEHAVIOR

Introduction

Peripheral Components of Emotional Reactions

Brainstem Influences on Emotional Behavior

Conclusions

INTRODUCTION

Experimental study of the motivational basis of emotional behavior has been hampered by the fact that we cannot yet define precisely what we mean when we talk about an "emotion". All of us unhesitatingly describe some reactions as "emotional" and distinguish them without difficulty from other "rational" matters but cannot give a very satisfactory answer when asked to describe the reason for this distinction. Individually, each of us is willing to acknowledge being motivated by fear, anger, frustration, pleasure, or love and to assign these diverse experiences to a common class of "emotional" reactions. Indeed, we do not question the universality of the emotional experience and freely interpret the behavior of others, including our pets, as being motivated by emotional experiences similar to our own. The success of our interaction with others shows that the capacity for emotional reactions similar to our own must indeed be present in all of us. What complicates our interactions as well as the experimental study of the emotions is the fact that the relationship between particular stimuli and emotions is not constant. There are, to be sure, a few stimuli that seem to elicit fear universally, at least with respect to all members of a species. Man, for instance, seems to be innately afraid of the dark, monkeys dislike snakes, and man as well as monkeys fears perceptual incongruity such as a head without a body. By and large, however, we learn to fear, love, or hate particular people or objects and cannot assume that others, particularly the animals on which we experiment, share the same learning experiences.

Matters are further complicated by the fact that different emotions interact not only with each other but also with quite different motivational influences. This makes it difficult and sometimes impossible to infer the presence of a particular emotion on the basis of an overt behavioral reaction. Thus, a soldier in battle may attack an enemy not because the predominant emotional reaction is anger or aggressiveness but because he is afraid of being killed unless he kills first. Similarly, the research literature abounds with descriptions of "rage" that are typically based on the observation that an animal strenuously objected to handling. A closer look at these animals often suggests that their behavior may have been motivated by fear rather than aggression as is often inferred.

These considerations indicate that we must distinguish between the experience and the expression of an emotion in the research that we shall discuss in this chapter. Since there is, as yet, no reliable measure of emotional experience in man or the animals on whom we experiment, we must remember to be cautious when we try to interpret behavioral reactions in terms of emotional experiences. In order to minimize this problem, most of the research on the determinants of emotional behavior has been concerned with reactions to pain or the threat of pain. The response to noxious stimulation is as universal a reaction as one can find, and we can be confident that the related emotional experiences fall within a fairly narrow and well-defined category that includes fear as well as aggression.

PERIPHERAL COMPONENTS OF EMOTIONAL REACTIONS

Peripheral-Origin Theories of Emotion

Emotional reactions are accompanied by changes in the autonomic nervous system and in the activity of certain endocrine glands. This produces sensations such as the dry throat, sweaty hands, and butterflies in the stomach that we experience during exposure to stress. Historically, these sensations were themselves thought to be the emotions. This peripheral-origin theory was formally stated almost 100 years ago by William James[74] and Carl Lange[92] and continues to influence the thinking of many psychologists of our generation in spite of the fact that it is almost certainly not correct. According to this theory (see Figure 12–1), environmental stimuli impinge on distance receptors and elicit activity in the sensory areas of the cortex. This reflexly produces excitation in somatic as well as autonomic motor pathways and consequent changes in muscle tension, blood pressure, heart rate, sweat secretion, and the like. This, in turn, stimulates interoceptors and initiates impulses that return to cortical receiving areas that monitor autonomic and skeletal motor functions. This gives rise to perceptions that add the emotional quality to the original perception of the environmental stimulus.

Few serious investigators of emotional behavior today accept the proposition that the perception of visceral and somatic motor

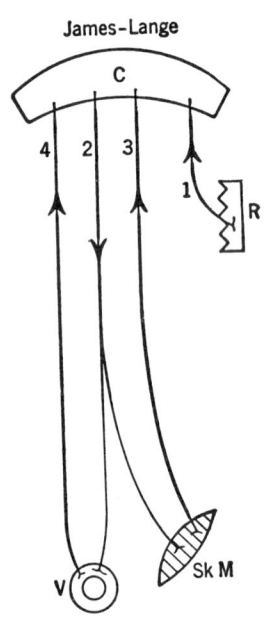

FIG. 12–1. Diagram of the James-Lange theory of emotion. R, receptor; C, cerebral cortex; V, viscera; Sk M, skeletal muscle; Th, thalamus. The connecting lines represent nerve paths; direction of impulses is indicated by arrows.

(From W. B. Cannon. Again the James-Lange and the thalamic theories of emotion. *Psychol. Rev.*, **38**, 1931, 281–295.)

reactions constitutes the emotion. However, a good many do believe that the pattern of these reactions may differ for different emotions and that the perception of the peripheral changes may contribute to the perception of the emotion if only because their frequent association may have produced conditioned responses. If true, emotional reactions should be somehow impaired and incomplete when the feedback from the peripheral musculature is reduced or abolished. Let us see what experimental investigation of that subject has demonstrated.

Shortly after the publication of the initial versions of the peripheral-origin theory, a number of experiments demonstrated that stimuli that normally elicited fear, rage, and attack behavior in dogs and cats continue to do so after the spinal cord is cut or the sympathetic nervous system destroyed.[154, 20] Neither procedure completely eliminates all sensory feedback from the body because several cranial nerves collect afferents from the autonomic nervous system. It is nonetheless damaging to the peripheral-origin theory that one should be able to eliminate much of the sensory feedback without affecting emotional behavior in the slightest. We do not, of course, know that the emotional behavior seen in these experiments is accompanied by emotional experience and that it is an unconditioned rather than a conditioned reaction. There are, however, some clinical obervations that seem to rule out this possibility. The most interesting case history is that of a woman who broke her neck in a fall from a horse. She reported emotions of grief, joy, affection, and displeasure that seemed unchanged although much of the sensory feedback from her body (as well as the control over the body musculature) was lost. It is possible to argue that even this does not represent conclusive evidence against a peripheral-origin theory since the experience of emotion, although originally dependent on feedback from the viscera and skeletal musculature, might itself become conditioned (i.e., the presentation of stimuli that, in the past, were associated with grief or affection might elicit a conditioned emotional reaction quite independent of peripheral feedback). Although logically correct, this argument effectively removes the peripheral-origin theory from the realm of science, since it is no longer experimentally testable. By the time an infant has learned to communicate his emotional reactions, the presumably much more primitive process of emotional conditioning has undoubtedly taken place.

A number of additional objections to the James-Lange theory have been raised without succeeding in discrediting it entirely. The great physiologist, W. B. Cannon,[20] firmly believed in peripheral-origin theories of hunger and thirst but opposed a corresponding interpretation of emotional behavior. He argued that peripheral responses could not be the basis for emotional experience because (1) the visceral responses are too slow; (2) similar reactions occur in quite different emotions as well as some nonemotional circumstances; (3) the viscera are not sensitive enough; and (4) the artificial elicitation of visceral reactions fails to induce emotional experiences.

These objections are well taken but do not provide conclusive evidence against the James-Lange theory. Visceral reactions are indeed slow, but several experiments suggest that a complete emotional reaction also develops only several seconds after the presentation of the emotion-inducing stimulus.[125] Similarly, individual physiological functions such as heart rate or respiration do show comparable reactions in different emotional and nonemotional situations, but the total pattern of sensory feedback from the viscera and somatic musculature undoubtedly differs as the theory demands. It is also true that the viscera are not very sensitive, but we nonetheless become aware of sudden changes in heart rate, vasomotor activity (flushing), or sweating and less specific concomitants of emotional reactions such as a lump in the throat or butterflies in the stomach. Finally, all attempts to mimic the visceral reactions to emotional stimuli have relied on injections of the adrenal hormone, epinephrine, which produce many of the sympathetic reactions normally seen in fear. They do not, however, affect the parasympathetic nervous system or the skeletal musculature and do not therefore reproduce the total pattern of sensations produced by fear-inducing stimuli. Moreover, epinephrine injections do elicit reports of sensations akin to fear in situations totally devoid of relevant environmental stimuli[20] and seem to potentiate normal emotional reactions.[155, 146]

Where, then, do we stand with respect to a peripheral-origin theory of emotion? The experimental evidence indicates that sensory feedback from the body is not an essential component of emotional behavior and emotional experience in the adult. The fact that the survival of emotional experience may be due to the development of conditioned emotional reactions in childhood cannot, however, be excluded. However, a closer look at the mechanisms that such a theory proposes suggests that it is not logically tenable. As it stands, the James-Lange theory predicts that every stimulus should produce visceral and somatic motor reactions and give rise to an emotion. This is clearly not the case. We must add a screening mechanism that determines whether a particular stimulus should give rise to a specific pattern of autonomic and somatic motor reactions. Since the emotional reaction to almost all stimuli is learned, this screening device cannot rely on simple innate anatomical connections but must be capable of comparing the sensory input with the organism's memory to determine the appropriate emotional reaction. When such a screening mechanism is added to the James-Lange theory, it becomes quite clear that the causation of emotions is not to be found in the pattern of feedback from the somatic and autonomic musculature but rather in the activity of the screening device itself that determines the nature of the muscular reaction.

Physiological Correlates of Emotion

Changes in heart rate, respiration, or sweating are probably not the basis of the emotions but seem to be secondary to them. However, each emotion may give rise to a unique pattern of peripheral physiological reactions, and we might be able to objectively measure the nature and intensity of emotional experience by recording these response patterns. Many investigators have worked on this problem in the last 50 years, and we now know that matters are not as simple as one might have hoped. Many early investigators reported that autonomic measures such as changes in skin resistance could be used to identify specific emotional reactions—a liar could be found out because his breathing changed just before telling a lie. When these claims were investigated more carefully, it turned out that all measures of autonomic functions respond, to a greater or lesser extent, to emotion-inducing stimuli and react more promptly or more strongly the more intense the emotional reaction. However, these measures respond to all sudden, novel, or intense stimuli and reflect the general level of arousal or activation rather than specific emotions.

Stimuli that have special meaning may elicit intense and immediate reactions even though they are not very intense, sudden, or novel, but one cannot tell whether the emotional experience is pleasant or unpleasant. Your heart may beat faster in response to your girl friend's name but also when you are watching an automobile accident or a football game. The selective reaction to stimuli that have acquired special meaning is nonetheless useful. Since a particular stimulus may have special meaning only to you, the mere fact that you respond to it whereas others do not tells us something about your emotional experiences. It is this feature that, more than anything else, has contributed to the continued use and popularity of various measures of autonomic function. It is often helpful to the clinical observer to know that his patient responds abnormally to such words as "mother," "father," "sister," or to pictures of nude males or females. Even though the nature of the emotion is not revealed by the physiological response, the fact that an unusual reaction occurred may be significant. Many courts admit into evidence the results of "lie detector" tests that consist of two or three physiological measures. These tests work because to the bank robber who shot and killed a teller to make his getaway, the

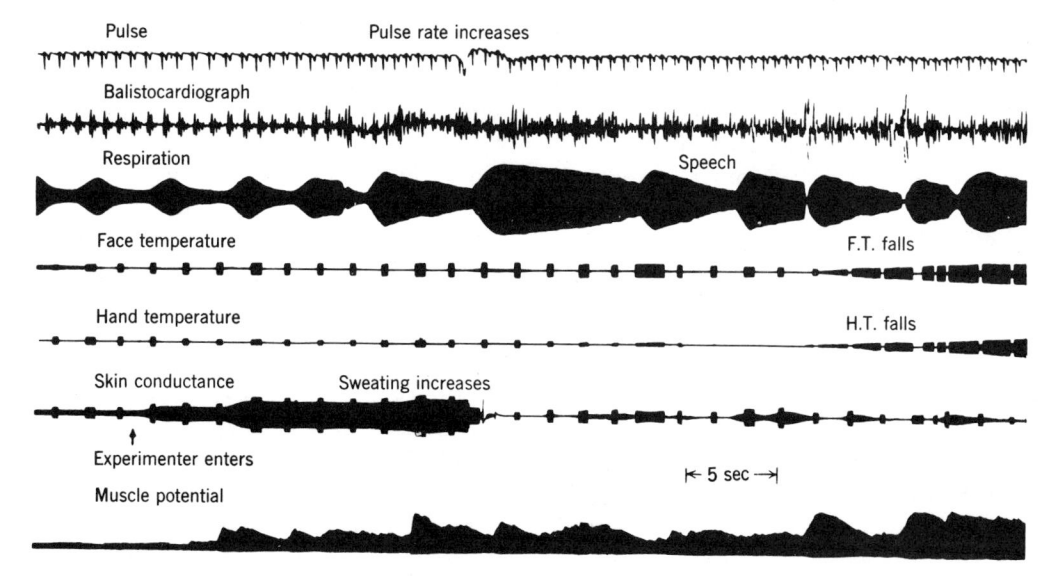

FIG. 12–2. Polygraph record of common autonomic measures of arousal.
(From A. F. Ax. The physiological differentiations of fear and anger in humans. *Psychosom. Med.*, 15 1953, 433–442.)

words "bank," "teller," or "murder" have acquired special meaning. The lie-detector tests also often work in less dramatic circumstances simply because most of us feel guilty when we tell an outright lie even though it may be inconsequential. The resulting increase in arousal may be reflected in the sweatiness of our hands or the frequency of our heartbeats. So, if you cut classes to go to the beach and tell your teacher the next day that you could not attend because you were terribly ill, be sure you are not hooked up to an autonomic response recorder (see Figure 12–2).

Beyond this practical usefulness, there is still hope that each emotion might, after all, be uniquely related to a particular *pattern* of physiological responses. Even though all emotions seem to affect all of the measures that we have developed to date, not all of them respond in exactly the same fashion to all emotional experiences. Some respond differently to stimuli that elicit fear than to stimuli that evoke anger and aggression. Others appear to differentiate between positive and negative affect. Still others respond in qualitatively similar ways to all emotion-inducing stimuli but give larger responses to some. We have not yet come up with the magic combination of measures that permits certain identification of specific emotional experiences but have not entirely given up hope. It is clear that such a battery of tests will have to include many different measures and that some of the current favorites may not be the most sensitive or selective contributors. Technological progress is continually adding to our armament of recording techniques as well as our capabilities for analyzing data. A computer analysis of a profile of autonomic and somatic motor responses to a carefully selected list of stimuli may be able to arrive at a standard that can be used to obtain an objective picture of emotional experience. A unique set of standards will undoubtedly be needed for each individual because our experiences with emotional stimuli vary so widely. Many of the currently used measures may not be sufficiently selective to be included in such a battery, but it might be interesting to briefly discuss some of them.

The most popular of the many measures of autonomic activity that have been used in the past 50 years are recordings of the electrical potentials of the skin. The relationship between emotional phenomena and changes in skin resistance or its reciprocal, skin conductance (also called psychogalvanic reflex or galvanic skin response) has intrigued psychologists for nearly a century. The absolute level of skin conductance, called base-line conductance, serves as a measure of general reactivity. The transitory change in skin conductance that occurs upon the presentation of many stimuli is thought to reflect the intensity of the arousal response to the stimulus, without identifying the nature of the emotional reaction that may have occurred. Skin conductance is measured either by recording the very small voltage that always exists between any two points on the skin or by recording the current that flows in response to the application of a known small voltage to the skin.

Changes in skin conductance occur one to two seconds after the presentation of a stimulus. The magnitude of the response, but not its latency, are a function of stimulus intensity. The magnitude of the response is also influenced by the base-line conductance, and it is therefore customary to report a percentage change from base line. Repeated presentations of the same stimulus produce habituation, and this effect transfers to other stimuli within as well as across sensory modalities.[24]

Skin-conductance changes occur in response to all sudden, intense, or novel stimuli and probably reflect general arousal. Conductance changes have been recorded in situations in which subjective emotional experience could not be reported. Conversely, verbal reports of emotions are not always accompanied by skin-conductance changes. Moreover, very pleasant and very unpleasant stimuli often produce similar changes in skin conductance,[31] indicating that this measure cannot discriminate the direction of the affective response.

Various measures of cardiovascular activity are also widely used. Perhaps the most popular is heart rate itself. The pumping action of the heart can be monitored by amplifying the sound it generates. Your physician's stethoscope operates on this principle. Several integrating devices are available that give a direct reading of heart rate per minute. A more sophisticated record of the activity of the heart, the electrocardiogram, is obtained by recording the electrical potentials that are generated by the heart muscle when it contracts.

Another measure of cardiovascular activity is the diameter of blood vessels. When a part of the body becomes very active, the blood vessels dilate to permit an increased flow of blood. Recordings of the volume of a finger or arm or of temperature changes that result from dilation or constriction of the blood vessels in it are the most popular indices of vascular change.

Blood pressure is a combined measure of cardiovascular activity. As blood is forced through the blood vessels, pressure gradients develop that reflect the amount of blood pumped by the heart as well as the diameter of the vessels through which it must pass. Your physician records blood pressure by listening to the sound of blood gushing through a partially occluded artery. This is done most easily by applying a stethoscope (a small microphone) to an artery just below a pressure cuff. As the pressure in the cuff is increased, the movement of the blood becomes audible because it passes the point of occlusion only periodically during the period of maximum heart-muscle contraction. The pressure read just before the pulse becomes audible is used as an index of diastolic (i.e., minimum) blood pressure. As the artery is further occluded, blood stops flowing and the sound disappears. The pressure read just before this happens is taken as a measure of systolic (i.e., maximum) blood pressure.

Stressful stimulation increases heart rate and produces vasoconstriction, thereby increasing blood pressure. The magnitude of this reaction varies between individuals, and there is little evidence for a unique relationship between specific emotions and a particular pattern of cardiovascular activity.[14] Clinical investigations have suggested that fear reactions may produce vascular reactions in the upper intestine that are different from those seen during anger (hence the prevalence of ulcers in chronically fearful patients), but this hardly provides a practical measure of emotionality.[172]

Gastric motility itself has been used as a measure of emotionality in some unusual clinical situations. Fear reactions seem to inhibit stomach activity completely, but this inhibition is not unique to fear. Any painful or unpleasant stimulus produces partial or complete inhibition of gastric motility, and many emotional reactions are not accompanied by a change in stomach motility.[17] The measure has not been widely used because the procedures used to obtain adequate records are rather forbidding.

In addition to these involuntary, autonomic responses, a variety of somatomotor reactions have been recorded. When we talk about the tensions of a trying day, we refer largely to an abnormally high level of general muscle tonus. This can be recorded by amplifying the electrical potentials that are generated in a muscle during contraction. Such *electromyographic* recordings are typically obtained from muscles in the neck or shoulders that are particularly prone to tension-induced increases in tonic activity. Muscle tonus provides a satisfactory measure of general alertness,[83] and an abnormally high tonus is a common symptom in chronic anxiety. However, muscle tonus is also increased by exercise and various nonemotional stimuli.

One of the most popular physiological measures of activation or arousal is the rate of respiration. Breathing is partially under voluntary control, but sudden or intense stimuli elicit largely involuntary reactions. The respiratory reactions are most easily recorded by stretching a gas- or air-filled tube tightly around the chest and abdomen and connecting it to a strain gauge that records the changes in the pressure of the gas or air in the tube. Another simple technique relies on the fact that the exhaled air is several degrees warmer than the inhaled air. A temperature-sensitive thermistor, taped to one nostril, can record these temperature changes easily.

The respiratory cycle consists of three fairly distinct cycles (inhalation, exhalation, and the pause in between) that can vary independently. It is common to report either the ratio of the duration of the inhalation and exhalation phases (the I/E ratio) or to divide the duration of the inhalation phase by the duration of the entire cycle.[173] Many of the early investigators of respiratory activity reported near perfect correlations between the magnitude of the I/E ratio and lying[10] or specific emotional reactions.[40] More recent investigations have typically shown that respiratory changes accompany most emotional reactions as well as a good many nonemotional ones. There is some evidence for a differential reaction to pleasant and unpleasant stimuli,[144] but a correlation with specific emotions is not typically found.

Considerable success in distinguishing between positive and negative affect has recently been achieved by photographic recordings of pupil size. Emotionally positive stimuli appear to increase the diameter of the pupil, whereas emotionally negative stimuli decrease it.[67] Pupillary dilation and constriction can occur over a fairly wide range and it is possible that the magnitude of response may provide a reliable index of the intensity of the emotional response.

There is also some evidence that a biochemical analysis of the blood or urine may provide some measure of the nature or intensity of affective responses. Interest in these measures dates back to Cannon's[22] "*emergency theory of emotion,*" which holds that emotional stimuli activate the entire sympathetic nervous system and elicit the release of epinephrine and norepinephrine from the adrenal medulla. This was thought to be essential for a mobilization of bodily resources and to prepare the body for vigorous reactions. Sympathetic activation and adrenal activation unquestionably accompany emotional arousal, but there is much doubt whether this in any significant way facilitates the body's reaction to emotional stimuli. There is, however, some evidence that gross changes in emotional reactivity may be reflected in the level of adrenal medullary hormone secretion.[159] Moreover, several investigators have suggested that emotional states such as fear and anger may be characterized by unique patterns of epinephrine and norepinephrine secretion.[4, 138]

More recently, attempts have been made to relate emotional reactions to the pituitary secretion of adrenocorticotrophic hormone (ACTH), which regulates the release of steroid hormones from the adrenal cortex.[69] Destruction of the anterior portion of the pituitary gland prevents the release of ACTH and interferes with the acquisition of avoidance behavior in rats.[29] Injections of ACTH facilitate the acquisition of passive avoidance responses[94] and retard extinction of active avoidance responses.[123] These effects are not related to adrenal reactions to ACTH since they occur in adrenalectomized animals.[118] The secretion of steroid hormones by the adrenal cortex nevertheless varies as a function of environmental stress[43] and is elevated in avoidance situations.[112] Moreover, the proficiency of avoidance behavior appears to correlate well with the level of steroid secretion before and during training.[12, 169] It is clear that ACTH release occurs during emotional arousal in man, but it is too early to tell whether the relatively complicated analysis of ACTH secretion can add anything of importance to a routine analysis of emotional reactions.

Last, but not least, we shall turn our attention to the electroencephalographic (EEG) recordings that can be obtained from human subjects by amplifying the electrical potentials picked up by electrodes on the skull. The behavioral state of relaxation is characterized by regular large waves that oscillate at a frequency of about 8 to 10 cycles per second. Any sudden, novel, or intense stimulus blocks this *alpha* EEG pattern and replaces it by a low-amplitude, high-frequency *arousal* pattern. Frequently repeated stimuli lose their ability to block the alpha rhythm unless they are intense or have acquired special meaning. Electrical stimulation of the reticular formation of the brainstem blocks the alpha rhythm. Lesions in this region abolish behavioral and EEG arousal completely.[122, 97]

These observations led Lindsley[96] to propose an *activation theory* that attempts to account for emotions in terms of variations in cortical arousal. The theory suggests, in essence, that somatic as well as autonomic sensory inputs converge on the reticular formation, which, in turn, controls the level of cortical arousal in accordance with the intensity of these afferents. When the input to the reticular formation is low, the organism is relaxed and the electrical activity of the brain is in synchrony. As the input to the reticular formation increases, the organism alerts and orients towards the source of stimulation. The EEG activity of the cortex then becomes desynchronized and the low-amplitude fast activity that characterizes arousal appears (see Figure 12–3). Emotion-inducing stimuli are thought to have a peculiar capacity to activate the reticular formation and thus produce intense cortical arousal. The theory does not, unfortunately, explain why this should be so.

The EEG is not a very useful practical measure of arousal, since even intensely emotional stimuli have little or no effect on the cortical EEG record once it has shifted to the low-amplitude high-frequency pattern characteristic of alertness. There is no evidence that different emotional reactions might produce peculiar patterns of EEG reactions or that one can measure the intensity of the emotional response by an analysis of the EEG record. Cortical arousal may indeed be a prerequisite for emotional behavior, but it does not account for the variety of emotional experience.

Darrow[26] has suggested a different relationship between the EEG and emotional behavior. He proposed that stimuli that elicit fear or anxiety might randomly activate many neurons in the brain. The summation of this random activity would tend to cancel most of the potential differences and thus give rise to the fast low-amplitude EEG pattern that characterizes arousal. All stimuli that do not induce fear are thought to activate only small pools of neurons in a nonrandom fashion. Summation of this rhythmic activity would give rise to the high-amplitude, low-frequency EEG patterns seen during relaxation. All

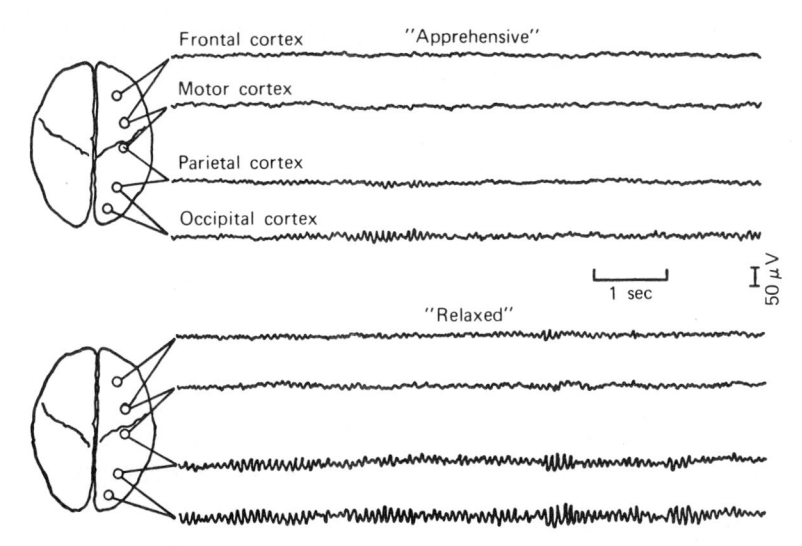

FIG. 12–3. Electroencephalograms from a normal subject during an apprehensive period and a relaxed period. Notice the reduction or suppression of alpha rhythm during apprehension.

(From D. B. Lindsley. Emotions and the electroencephalogram. In *Feelings and emotions*. M. L. Reymert, Ed. McGraw-Hill, 1950.)

emotions other than fear thus would be characterized by the slow-wave alpha rhythm. (According to this theory, we always see low-amplitude, fast activity in awake animals and human subjects because the test situation induces fear.)

Summary and Review Questions

Emotional reactions include autonomic, somatic, and endocrine responses. Historically, our perception of these peripheral physiological reactions was thought to constitute the emotional experience itself. The peripheral-origin theories have some difficulty explaining why the removal of sensory feedback from most of the body does not seem to impair emotional behavior in animals or emotional experience in man. Their major shortcoming, however, is the fact that they cannot explain why some stimuli elicit emotional reactions and others do not.

Physiological reactions do, nevertheless, accompany all emotional responses and may indeed provide at least some of the cues we use in distinguishing different emotions. Many investigators have attempted to correlate specific physiological reactions with particular emotions in the hope that each emotion might give rise to a unique pattern of physiological change. Measures of sweat secretion, heart rate, vasoconstriction or dilatation, blood pressure, respiration, pupil size, endocrine activity, and cortical EEG have been extensively studied. All currently available measures reflect emotional experience and provide an adequate record of general arousal but are not sufficiently selective to serve as an index of the intensity of a particular emotion. Some do appear capable of distinguishing the direction or the intensity of affect, and it is possible that a computer analysis of a large number of such tests may some day provide a measure that can distinguish categories of emotional experience and provide some index of their intensity.

1. State the James-Lange theory.

2. Can it account for emotional experience?

3. What experimental evidence can you cite in support of it?

4. Are there experimental or clinical observations that this theory finds difficult to explain?

5. How does it account for them?

6. If you were asked to select three physiological correlates of emotional behavior, which would you choose and why?

7. Describe the endocrine responses to stress that have been investigated as a possible measure of emotionality.

8. Describe Lindsley's activation theory.

9. Describe Cannon's emergency theory.

BRAINSTEM INFLUENCES ON EMOTIONAL BEHAVIOR

The Hypothalamus and Lower Brainstem

Emotional reactions can be elicited in cats and dogs after the brainstem has been completely severed just behind the posterior hypothalamus.[48, 174] The behavior of these animals has been called "pseudoaffective" because it is poorly coordinated, often not directed towards the source of noxious stimulation, and entirely stimulus-bound (i.e., the reaction stops abruptly when the stimulus is terminated).[104] These observations indicate that many of the peripheral physiological responses that normally accompany emotional reactions to noxious stimulation may be integrated by the lower brainstem. The immediate disappearance of these reactions following the cessation of stimulation suggests that they may be reflexly elicited and may not be accompanied by emotional experience.

Other experimental observations demonstrate that the midbrain interacts with higher integrative mechanisms in the intact animal. Small bilateral lesions in the central grey of the midbrain markedly reduce emotional reactivity to noxious stimulation and abolish the rage reactions that are normally elicited by electrical stimulation of the hypothalamus and amygdala. Electrical stimulation of the central grey elicits rage responses even after some of the higher integrative mechanisms have been destroyed.[41]

Emotional behavior is to some extent integrated by hypothalamic mechanisms. Decorticated animals are hypersensitive and display poorly directed and poorly coordinated "rage" reactions to many previously neutral stimuli. This hyperexcitability persists when the thalamus and basal ganglia are also removed but disappears abruptly when the hypothalamus is destroyed or disconnected from the lower brainstem.[6]

Lesions in the ventromedial hypothalamus produce a sharp and apparently permanent increase in emotional reactivity. Previously neutral stimuli, such as normal handling, elicit vicious and well-directed attack behavior.[170] The animals overreact to painful stimulation and learn and perform simple escape and avoidance responses in a shuttle box better than normals[52, 56] (see Figure 12–4). Passive-avoidance behavior (i.e., refraining from previously rewarded behavior that is now punished) is impaired by this lesion. This disinhibitory effect may, in part, reflect an increase in appetitive motivation,[152] but this does not appear to be the whole story. In some instances, the animals tolerate severe punishment to obtain food rewards but then refuse to consume them.[116] The effects of ventromedial hypothalamic lesions on active as well as passive avoidance behavior are duplicated by a selective blockade of the cholinergic components of this region.[111, 115]

The area's influence on affective behavior also becomes apparent when one considers aggressive behaviors. Rats with ventromedial hypothalamic lesions fight more readily and more viciously when confronted with painful stimulation[33, 56] (see Figure 12–5), but become submissive and appear less willing to engage in combat in a food-competition situation. Interspecies aggressive reactions do not appear to be affected.[56] The lesion effects on aggressive behaviors are not duplicated by a local blockade of cholinergic components of the area,[55] suggesting that different neural systems may subserve escape/avoidance and aggressive reactions in this region of the brain. Indeed, we have been unable to influence aggressive reactions by local applications of any of a number of possible neurohumors and related blocking agents. It thus appears possible that the lesion-produced effects on aggressive reactions may be due to the interruption of a fiber system that courses through the ventromedial hypothalamus but does not synapse there.

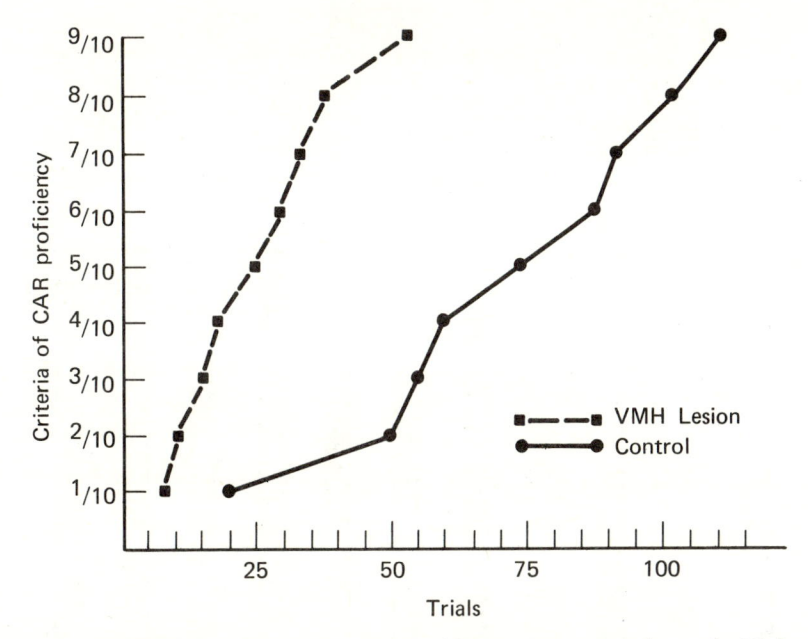

FIG. 12–4. Acquisition of conditioned avoidance responses in a shuttlebox. Data expressed in terms of the number of trials (abscissa) required to reach increasingly stringent criteria of avoidance performance (ordinate).

(From S. P. Grossman. Aggression, avoidance, and reaction to novel environments in female rats with ventromedial hypothalamic lesions. *J. comp. physiol. Psychol.*, **78**, 1972, 274–283. Copyright 1972 by the American Psychological Association, and reproduced by permission.)

An analysis of the pathways that may be responsible for the observed effects of ventromedial lesions[54, 57] has suggested that some of the lateral and posterior connections of the medial hypothalamus may be specifically related to avoidance behavior but not to aggressive reactions, whereas some of the region's anterior connections appear to be related specifically to aggressive behavior but not to avoidance reactions. Somewhat surprisingly, an interruption of the lateral connections of the hypothalamus (a procedure that interrupts a good many of its connections with the amygdala) did not significantly affect aggressive or avoidance behaviors. These observations are potentially important because they indicate that aggressive and avoidance responses may not, in a simple way, represent alternative responses to noxious stimulation.

Damage to several other hypothalamic regions seems to reduce emotional reactivity, but the animals are typically drowsy, inactive, and somnolent, and it is not clear that the reduction in reactivity is in any way specifically related to a disturbance of emotional functions.[71, 137]

Electrical or chemical stimulation of many hypothalamic sites elicits attack, defense, or flight reactions, accompanied by many of the autonomic responses that characterize normal emotional behavior.[168, 109] The response to such stimulation is often well-directed and properly executed and cannot be distinguished from normal reactions to noxious stimulation.[68]

Electrical stimulation of the medial hypothalamus often results in "affective attack" responses—the animals hiss and growl, show typical sympathetic signs of arousal, and attack members of the same as well as other species. Stimulation of more lateral regions typically induces "stalking attack" responses that appear to be related more specifically to predation and feeding.[168, 71] In many instances, this stimulation-elicited attack behavior results in death. Rats[89] have been induced to kill mice; cats[168] and opposum[142] kill rats. Microinjections of cholinergic agents

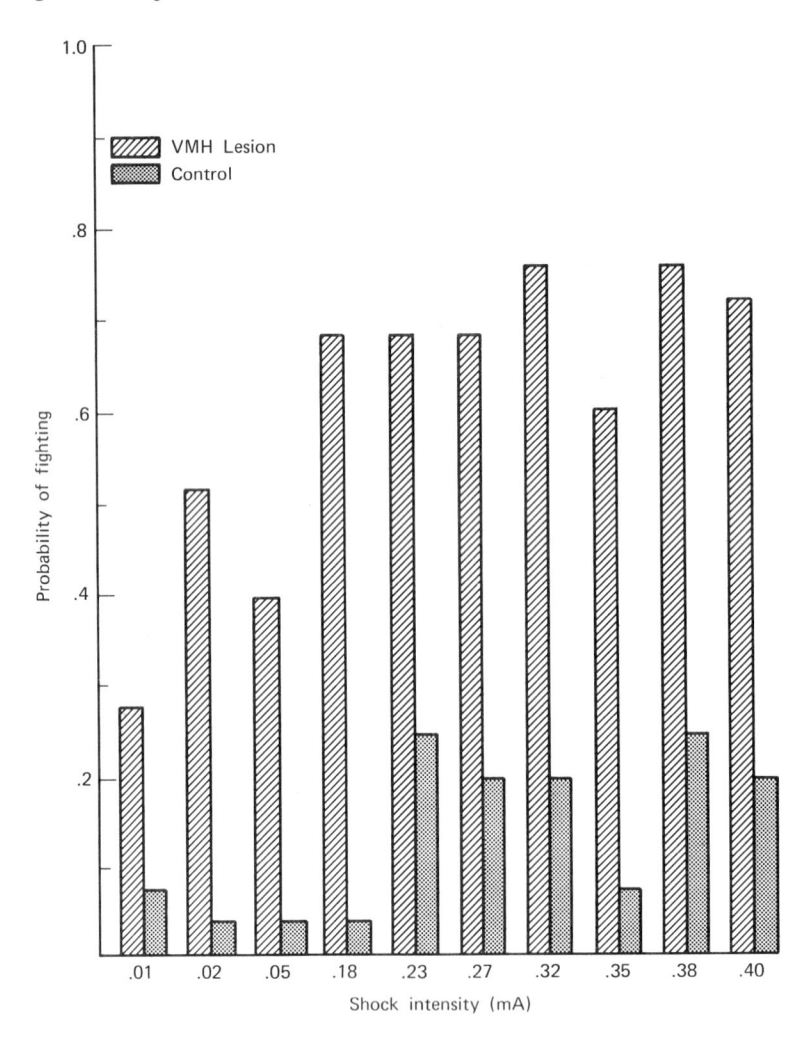

FIG. 12–5. Probability of fighting between normals or between rats with ventromedial hypothalamic lesions in response to footshock of various intensities.

(From S. P. Grossman. Aggression, avoidance, and reaction to novel environments in female rats with ventromedial hypothalamic lesions. *J. comp. physiol. Psychol.*, **78**, 1972, 274–283. Copyright 1972 by the American Psychological Association, and reproduced by permission.)

produce similar effects in rats,[156] suggesting that at least some of the lateral hypothalamic pathways that mediate aggressive reactions may be cholinergic. It is interesting to note that during hypothalamic stimulation cats will perform instrumental responses in order to obtain access to a rat they can attack.[141]

Stimulation that elicits these affective reactions is aversive. Animals learn and perform instrumental responses such as lever pressing or wheel turning to escape from it.[117, 89] At some sites the stimulation appears to produce both positive and negative affective reactions, since animals perform one response to turn such stimulation on and then quickly perform another to terminate it.[140] At other sites, the effects of the stimulation appear to be entirely negative, since animals learn and perform instrumental responses not only to escape from the stimulation but also to avoid it.[117] Lateral hypothalamic stimulation also interferes with avoidance behavior.[23]

At some hypothalamic sites, electrical stimulation elicits rage or attack behavior that does not seem to be accompanied by affective reactions. During such stimulation, cats may snarl, hiss, spit, or claw but attempt to continue such activities as drinking, grooming, or even purring as long as the "rage" reaction does not interfere with the ongoing behavior.[113] These relatively rare observations are significant because they have given rise to the theoretically important suggestion that the hypothalamus may contain the efferent "motor" control center for emotional reactions but may not itself contribute directly to emotional experience.

In spite of the overwhelming evidence for the importance of hypothalamic mechanisms in the integration of affective and aggressive behavior, some observations suggest that at least one species—the cat—can display apparently normal aggressive and affective reactions when the hypothalamus is surgically isolated from the rest of the brain.[39] It is difficult to be sure that all connections of the hypothalamus are severed in these experiments, but it is clear and somewhat surprising that affective attack behavior persists when its major afferent and efferent connections are interrupted.

Thalamic Influences

Anatomically, the thalamus is ideally suited for an integration and analysis of sensory inputs because the afferent pathways of all sensory modalities except olfaction relay in it. Moreover, some "nonspecific" thalamic nuclei collect sensory inputs from all modalities either directly via projections from the sensory relay nuclei or indirectly via connections with the reticular formation. The nonspecific nuclei, in turn, project to all areas of the cerebral cortex and are thus in a unique position to affect behavioral reactions to environmental stimuli.

A possible role of the thalamus in emotional experience was first suggested by clinical reports of patients with tumors or vascular damage in this area. Many of these patients react excessively to potentially emotion-inducing stimuli.[64] Others show apparently uncontrollable fits of laughter or weeping without being able to report a corresponding subjective experience.[25]

These observations led to the formulation of the *thalamic theory of emotion*, first presented about 50 years ago by W. B. Cannon[20] and subsequently extended by Bard[5] (see Figure 12–6). This theory suggests that the thalamus is the "seat" of the emotions and that it is normally inhibited by cortical influences. Very intense, unconditioned stimuli override this cortical inhibition and directly activate the thalamus. Stimuli that elicit learned emotional reactions first travel to the cortex. Here, they are recognized on the basis of memory, and the inhibition of the thalamic mechanism is released. When the thalamus is thus activated, impulses are sent to (a) peripheral somatic and autonomic effectors to initiate the overt expression of the emotion and (b) cortical mechanisms to evoke the conscious experience of the emotion.

The Cannon-Bard theory has received wide acceptance in psychology. The notion

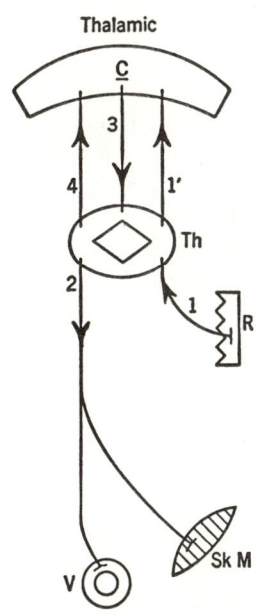

FIG. 12–6. Diagram of the thalamic theory of emotion. R, receptor; C, cerebral cortex; V, viscera; Sk M, skeletal muscle; Th, thalamus. The connecting lines represent nerve paths; the directions of impulses are indicated by arrows. Corticothalamic path 3 is inhibitory in function.

(From W. B. Cannon. Again the James-Lange and the thalamic theories of emotion. *Psychol. Rev.*, **38**, 1931, 281–295.)

of a primitive subcortical seat of the emotions that is held in check by "rational" cortical influences fits nicely with many clinical speculations. Because of this apparent face validity, the theory has retained its influence in spite of some serious objections. For instance, the principal experimental support for the concept of cortical inhibition of thalamic mechanisms is the hyperemotionality of decorticated animals. This hyperreactivity persists, however, after the thalamus has been destroyed and disappears only after *hypothalamic* influences are eliminated. The hypothalamus, on the other hand, does not have the extensive sensory afferents and cortical projections that the thalamic theory requires. The theory also would seem to predict that all stimuli should elicit emotional reactions once the inhibitory influences of the cortex are removed. This is not the case even though many previously neutral stimuli elicit "rage" reactions in the decorticated animal.

This is not to say that the thalamus may not contribute to the control of emotional reactions. Lesions in the anterior thalamic nuclei reduce the irritability that is seen in some mental patients and decrease emotional reactivity to noxious stimuli in experimental animals.[158] Other thalamic lesions increase emotional reactivity,[148] although neurotic tendencies may be reduced or eliminated.[130] Electrical stimulation of many posterior thalamic sites has been reported to elicit attack or defensive reactions in cats and monkeys.[28]

The Limbic System: Theoretical Views

The cerebral cortex contains three distinct types of tissues. Phylogenetically the youngest and structurally most complex portion is called the *neocortex*. When you look at the top or side of the cerebral hemispheres, almost everything you see is neocortex. Most somatic sensory and motor functions as well as some "associative" functions are carried out by the neocortex. Although undoubtedly involved in every emotional reaction, these functions are not peculiar to emotions and will not concern us here.

The *juxtallocortex* is phylogenetically older and structurally simpler than the neocortex. When you cut the brain in half lengthwise, most of the cortex surrounding the corpus callosum and the underlying thalamus is made up of juxtallocortex. Particularly important for our discussion are the cingulate gyrus and the frontotemporal juxtallocortex.

The oldest and most primitive cortex is called *allocortex*. It makes up the hippocampal formation, the cortical portion of the septal area, and much of the lower temporal lobe that surrounds the amygdaloid complex and ventral hippocampus.

The term *limbic system* is not always applied consistently and may include all or part of the allo- and juxtallocortex as well as several functionally related subcortical and even neocortical regions. It will be convenient for our purpose to define it as all of the allo- and juxtallocortex plus (1) the amygdaloid nuclei of the temporal lobe; (2) all of the septal area (which contains some subcortical nuclei in many species); and (3) the granular cortex of the frontal lobe. (The amygdala, subcortical septal components, and portions of the frontal cortex are included because of their intimate anatomical and functional connection with other "limbic" structures that are the focus of our discussion.) (See Figure 12–7.)

The original classification of the limbic system, also called *rhinencephalon* or "smell-brain," was based on the observation that all of its components receive primary or secondary projections from the olfactory bulb. However, most of the rhinencephalon does not serve primary olfactory functions in higher animals but seems to be concerned with motivational and, perhaps, associative functions. Electrophysiological studies have shown that many components of the limbic system receive sensory inputs from all sensory modalities.[108] Electrical or chemical stimulation often elicits diffuse autonomic reactions[77] in addition to such motivated or affective behaviors as feeding, drinking, attacking, and fleeing. Damage to portions of the limbic system almost always affects aggressive and avoidance behaviors, as we shall see in a

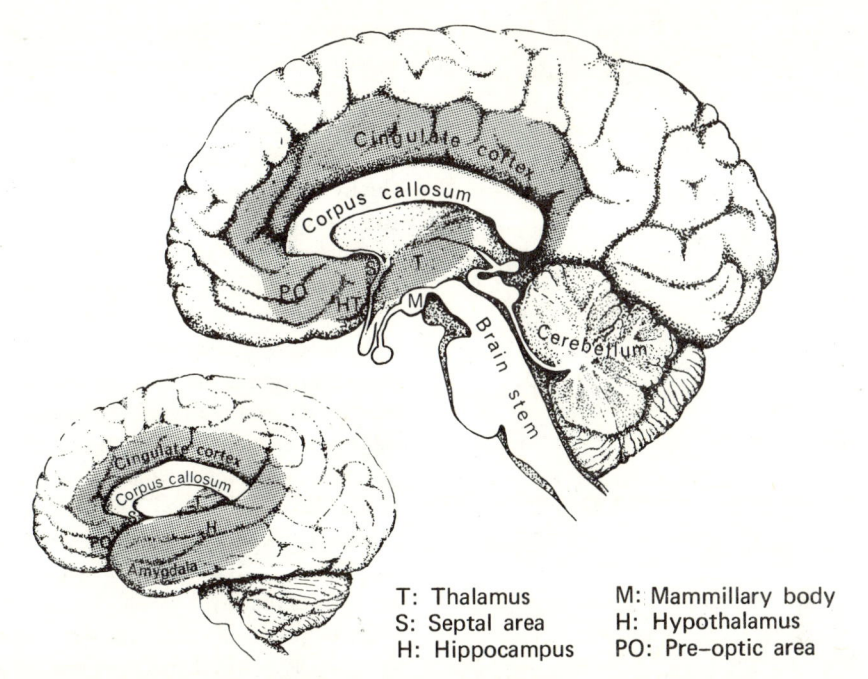

T: Thalamus   M: Mammillary body
S: Septal area   H: Hypothalamus
H: Hippocampus   PO: Pre-optic area

FIG. 12–7. Medial view of the human brain. The large drawing shows a true medial view with the temporal lobe obscured by the brain stem and cerebellum. In the smaller drawing the temporal lobe is superimposed to show the complete neural circuit (lightly stippled) which regulates not only emotional behavior but also the basic motivational processes such as hunger and thirst.

(From S. P. Grossman. Exploring the brain with chemicals. *Discovery*, **27**, 1966, 19–23.)

moment. Olfactory discriminations are not affected unless the olfactory bulb itself is involved.[160, 161]

The limbic system's role in behavior was first suggested by investigators who were convinced that the expression of the emotions was mediated by hypothalamic mechanisms, but who were unwilling to assign the experiential component of the emotional reaction to subcortical structures. Their attention was drawn to the limbic system because of its intimate anatomical connection with the hypothalamus.

The first formal statement of a "limbic" theory of emotions was published about 40 years ago by Papez[128, 129] (see Figure 12–8). This theory proposed that the cingulate gyrus might function as a cortical "receiving area" for "emotional" signals from the hypothalamus in much the same way that the striate cortex of the occipital lobe functions with respect to visual stimuli. The experience of emotion, according to Papez, depends on the projection of impulses from the cingulate gyrus to neocortical areas that are also activated by the emotion-inducing stimulus. More specifically, Papez proposed that emotion-provoking stimuli might somehow be "recognized" by primitive sensory centers in the subthalamic region. These signals would then be shunted to the anterior and medial hypothalamus, which Papez believed to be responsible for the integration of appropriate overt emotional reactions. In turn, these mechanisms were thought to initiate activity in the mammillary bodies of the posterior hypothalamus, which also receive inputs from the cortex to allow memory or "imagination" to influence the emotions. From the mammillary bodies, signals were thought to travel to (1) peripheral autonomic and somatic effectors to produce overt emotional reactions and (2) the cingulate gyrus to permit the experience of emotion.

At the time of its formulation, there was little experimental or clinical evidence for

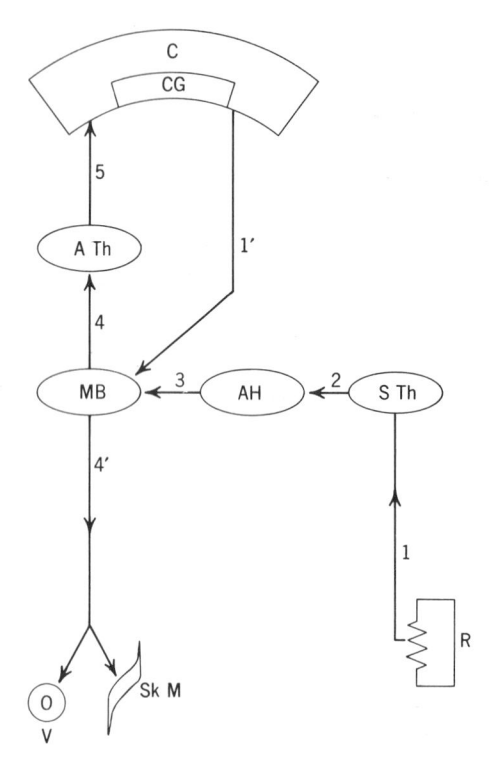

FIG. 12–8. Diagram of the Papez cortical theory of emotion. R, sensory receptor; S Th, subthalamic sensory receiving centers; AH, anterior and medial hypothalamus; MB, mammillary bodies; A Th, anterior nuclei of thalamus; CG, cingulate gyrus; C, cortex; V, viscera; Sk M, skeletal muscles.

(From *A textbook of physiological psychology* by S. P. Grossman. Copyright © 1967. John Wiley & Sons, Inc.)

any of the proposed pathways or functions. We now know that the details of Papez' theory are almost certainly wrong. It nevertheless rendered an invaluable service in stirring up experimental interest and theoretical controversy concerning the role of limbic mechanisms in emotional behavior and is indirectly responsible for much of the progress of recent years.

MacLean[105] reexamined Papez' theory in the light of the experimental findings that were published during the first decade after its publication and suggested some important revisions. He agreed with Papez' basic premise that the hypothalamus served as a "motor center" for the emotions and that only a cortical mechanism could appreciate the complex sensations that compose an emotional experience. MacLean also concurred in the assumption that the integration of emotional experience must take place in the limbic system or rhinencephalon, not only because of its intimate anatomical connections with the hypothalamus but also because it contains the cortical representations of the visceral functions that are affected by emotional reactions and of the olfactory inputs that MacLean believed to be essential to emotional experiences. (Olfactory inputs seemed to be particularly relevant to emotional and, indeed, all motivational influences because olfactory cues are used to detect food, sexual partners, enemies, and so on.)

MacLean departed from Papez' theory primarily in deemphasizing the role of the cingulate gyrus. Its place of central importance was assumed by the hippocampus and related parts of the temporal lobe. More specifically, MacLean proposed that the hippocampal gyrus (which takes up part of the side and bottom of the temporal lobe) may function as an "affectoceptor" area. It projects primarily to the hippocampus, which MacLean thought to function as the "affectomotor" cortex that is directly responsible for the emotional reaction. The cingulate gyrus assumes the role of a visceromotor region that is responsible for the autonomic aspects of the emotional reaction. The "affectoceptor" cortex of the hippocampal gyrus is thought to be closely related to the amygdaloid complex, which MacLean believed to be involved in other motivational functions such as feeding and sleep.

MacLean's revision lacks the simplicity and completeness of Papez' theory. No attempt is made to follow the course of events from the reception of a stimulus to the consequent experience and expression of an emotion nor to explain why some stimuli evoke a particular emotion and others do not. It nonetheless served an important function in further drawing attention to the limbic system and has generated much fruitful research.

The research of the two decades since MacLean published his theory has shown that the integration of emotional reactions may be much more complex than the early theories proposed. Essentially all aspects of the limbic system (as well as thalamic, hypothalamic, and midbrain mechanisms) appear to contribute in some way or another to emotional reactions. Apparently similar, if not identical, changes in affective behavior can be produced by stimulation or damage in different parts of the limbic system, and no single component of it appears to be uniquely responsible for a particular class of emotional reactions such as fear, rage, or aggressiveness. The hippocampus, hippocampal gyrus, and amygdala are almost certainly involved in the integration of emotional reactions, but their role does not appear to be as essential as MacLean's theory proposes. The same holds for the cingulate gyrus that played such an important role in Papez' theory as well as for other parts of the limbic circuit.

We do not, at present, have a satisfactory theory to relate limbic functions to affective behavior. The past decades have produced a cornucopia of relevant experimental observations, but we have as yet been unable to interpret them in any consistent fashion. Lesions as well as electrical or chemical stimulation and inhibition of portions of the limbic system produce a bewildering variety of effects on appetitive drive states as well as the organism's reaction to noxious stimulation and nonreward. Most current investigators do not even attempt to interpret the results of their investigations in terms of general changes in affective reactions, but discuss them in purely descriptive terms, such as an inability to inhibit previously rewarded responses or previously appropriate sets of attitudes, or a change in incentive motivation. The current aversion to such concepts as "affect" or "emotion" reflects, in part, a healthy development toward more objective approaches to research in this field. However, it also seems to stifle potentially constructive thought about the central integration of emotional reactions and may obscure recognition of potentially relevant observations. Here, as in other areas of research, it pays best to keep an open mind and to retain the ability to consider all possible explanations of an experimental finding without the constraints of bias.

The Limbic System: Experimental Findings

The Frontal Lobe

Complete removal of the neocortex produces tameness and placidity in many species, suggesting that the limbic system may receive excitatory inputs from some aspects of the neocortex.[7] That the unresponsiveness of the neodecorticated animal is not merely the result of its sensory and motor impairments is demonstrated by a sharp increase in reactivity following additional damage to the amygdala, cingulate gyrus, or hippocampus.[6,43]

A number of observations suggest that the placidity of the neodecorticated animal may result from a removal of excitatory influences that originate in the frontal lobe. Tameness and docility following damage to the frontal lobe of monkeys was described almost 100 years ago.[42] It has subsequently been reported that the angry reactions to the frustration of nonreward (extinction), which are typically seen in normal chimpanzees, disappeared following frontal lobe lesions.[47] The animals seemed unusually friendly and cooperative following surgery and appeared to forget quickly any reason for anger or disappointment.[45] Recent experimental analyses of this phenomenon[18] have shown that animals with frontal lesions also continue to respond to previously rewarded stimuli in spite of punishment. This "perseveration" is characteristic of animals with lesions in other parts of the limbic system, as we shall see in a moment, and may reflect a basic disturbance in the affective response to noxious stimuli.

A Brazilian neurophysiologist named Moniz[120] argued that the behavioral changes seen after frontal lobe lesions in the monkey were precisely those needed to alleviate many mental diseases that are characterized by anxiety, irrational fears, and emotional hyperexcitability. He damaged the frontal lobes of 20 patients and published an enthusiastic report of his findings. This rapidly led to the acceptance of the surgical procedure, and more than 20,000 patients were subjected to frontal "lobotomies" or "leucotomies" (see Figure 12-9) of varying extent during the next

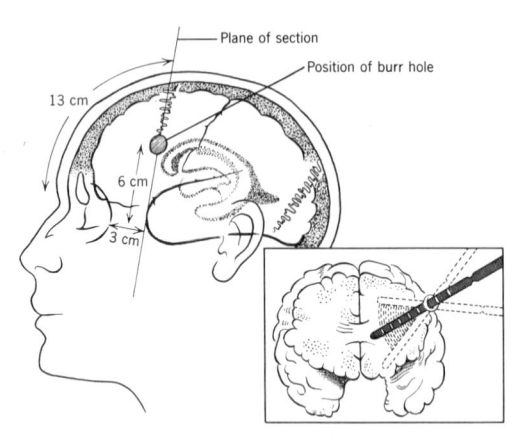

FIG. 12–9. Technique of leucotomy as performed by Freeman and Watts. (A leucotomy is a frontal lobotomy which is guided by bone rather than by cerebral landmarks.).

(From H. Elliott, S. Albert, & W. Bremner. A program for prefrontal lobotomy with report of effect on intractable pain. *D.V.A. Treatment Serv. Bull.*, **3**, 1948, 26–35.)

15 years. During this period, much valuable information about the long-term effects of frontal lobe damage became available. It soon became apparent that the glowing reports of Moniz and others were misleading. About half of the patients did, indeed, seem to benefit with respect to their irrational anxiety symptoms or uncontrollable emotional outbursts. However, many of them also showed intellectual deficits that were often worse than the original problem.[145] Many investigators have attempted to produce more selective effects by damaging only specific parts of the frontal lobe[114] or by cutting only some of its connections to the hypothalamus or cingulate gyrus.[153] Others investigated whether lesions in specific portions of the frontal lobe might be differentially effective for certain types of mental patients.[139] Some success has been reported with this more limited approach,[32] but the possibility of potentially severe "side effects" has not been eliminated.[27]

The clinical use of frontal lobe lesions disappeared almost entirely when tranquilizing drugs became available which relieve fears, anxieties, and depressions, and calm the most excitable patient without significantly affecting other mental functions. There has been a related decline of interest in the functional organization of the frontal lobe. A review of the available case histories and experimental data shows that the frontal neocortex undoubtedly participates in the integration of emotional reactions, but the precise nature of this influence is as yet unclear. Many investigators assume that the frontal lobe may be important primarily as a link between the rest of the neocortex and the hypothalamic or limbic mechanisms that are specifically related to emotional reactions.

Before we consider some of the allo- and juxtallocortical components of the limbic system, it should be pointed out that not all frontal lesions lower emotional reactivity. Vicious rage reactions to previously neutral stimuli have been seen after small lesions in some parts of the frontal lobe of cats,[13] monkeys,[82] and dogs.[3] It is, unfortunately, not certain that this paradoxical increase in affective reactivity may not be a result of irritative effects of the lesion on surrounding tissue.

Temporal Lobe and Amygdala

One of the classic investigations of the role of the limbic system in emotional reactions was performed over 30 years ago by Klüver and Bucy.[90] These investigators removed most or all of the temporal lobes (including the amygdala and part of the hippocampus) and found that previously aggressive and intractable rhesus monkeys became tame and friendly. The animals appeared to have lost the ability to experience fear or anger and even touched such innately fear-inducing objects as a hissing snake. The lesioned animals also were hyperactive and constantly mouthed everything in sight, including such objects as nails, feces, or a burning match. They also masturbated frequently and attempted copulation with members of other species—abnormal sexual behavior that is rarely seen in normal monkeys. Klüver and Bucy suggested that their animals behaved as if the consequences of their actions no longer mattered.

Subsequent investigators have attempted to study the role of more discrete temporal lobe mechanisms by observing the effects of smaller lesions in it. The results of these experiments suggest that many aspects of the temporal lobe appear to be related to affective behavior. The precise nature of the many different mechanisms that have been implicated by this research is, however, still poorly understood. Lesions in many parts of the temporal lobe, including the frontotemporal cortex, the amygdala, the cortex surrounding the amygdala, and the ventral hippocampus, lower emotional reactivity and result in tameness and docility in monkeys,[119, 135] dogs,[44] cats,[147] and rats.[150] The animals also typically lose social status,[44] presumably because their threshold for attack behavior is raised. The changes in emotional reactivity are often accompanied by other components of the "temporal lobe syndrome" described by Klüver and Bucy. Amygdala lesions also reduce the hyperirritability that results from damage to the septal area[150] or to the ventromedial hypothalamus[1] of rats and inhibit mouse-killing in wild rats.[78] Electrical stimulation of this region often elicits rage and aggressive reactions.[1]

Some investigators[158, 7] have reported that amygdaloid lesions in cats may produce an increase in emotional reactivity, but recent experiments indicate that these findings may be a consequence of the irritative (i.e., stimulating) effects of the lesion on surrounding tissue.

A single injection of a small amount of acetylcholine into the amygdaloid complex establishes a seizure focus in cats[49] and rats.[9] In cats, this seizure activity persists for weeks and even months and is accompanied by pronounced "personality" changes. The animals are vicious and extremely hypersensitive to all stimuli (see Figure 12–10). They attack, at the slightest provocation, man as well as other cats without regard to personal safety. In albino rats, only temporary EEG and behavioral seizures occur in response to such injections. The animals' emotional reactivity nonetheless appears to be permanently altered. Weeks after the disappearance of the seizure focus, these animals do not learn some simple avoidance responses, although they have no difficulty in acquiring more complex conditioned appetitive reactions. The deficit seems to be related to a stimulating action on amygdaloid influences since small lesions at the injection site facilitate the acquisition of the avoidance response.

Larger lesions in the amygdaloid complex have been reported to interfere with the acquisition and performance of "active" as well as "passive" avoidance responses in rats[70, 131] and cats.[165] Animals with such lesions also do not acquire conditioned emotional reactions as readily as normals[79] and fail to respond appropriately to changes in positive reinforcement contingencies in a variety of situations.[149] They are capable of learning even complex appetitively reinforced discriminations,[131] but their performance often breaks down when the experiment is changed to a "go"–"no go" paradigm, which requires the withholding of responses on "no go" trials.[19]

A disinhibition of punished behavior can also be produced by microinjections of norepinephrine into the amygdaloid complex, suggesting that the passive avoidance deficit that is commonly seen after amygdaloid lesions may be due to the removal of an adrenergic inhibitory influence.[110] The total pattern of behavior of the amygdalectomized animal suggests that it may be less reactive not only to noxious stimulation and punishment but also to positive reinforcement. It has been suggested[110] that the amygdaloid complex may be one of the sites where the neural pathways that mediate the effects of reward and punishment can interact.

Hippocampus

Electrical as well as chemical stimulation of the hippocampus facilitates or elicits emotional reactions. Although an enhancement of "pleasure" reactions has been reported,[106] the more typical reaction to hippocampal stimulation involves rage and attack behavior.[107, 124] The effects of hippocampal lesions are less clear-cut. Increments[127] as well as decrements[44] in emotional reactivity have been reported and in many species, such as the rat, it is difficult to detect any gross change in emotionality.

Behavioral changes become readily apparent in many appetitive as well as aversive

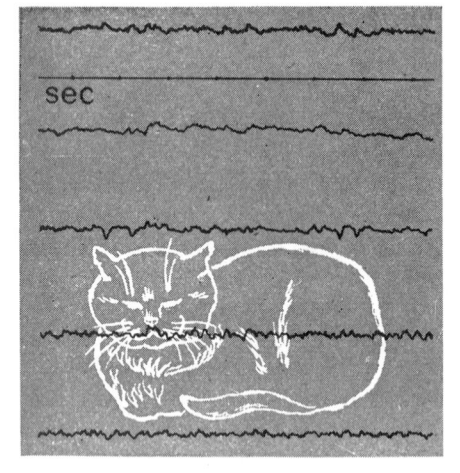

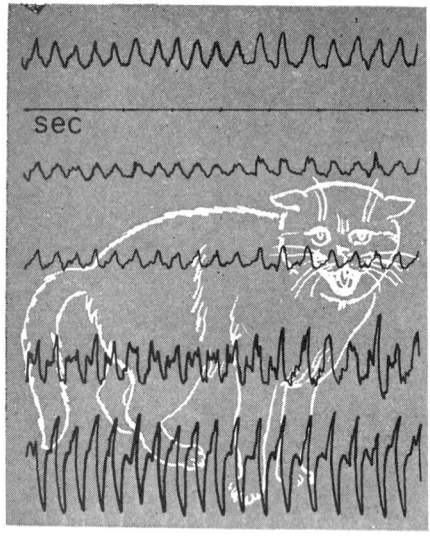

FIG. 12–10. Changes in the emotional makeup of a cat after acetylcholine has been injected into the temporal lobe of its brain. (*a*) is a record of brainwaves just before the injection, (*b*) immediately afterwards, when the cat became vicious, and (*c*) several hours after the stimulation during an epileptic-like seizure.

(From S. P. Grossman. Exploring the brain with chemicals. *Discovery*, **27**, 1966, 19–23.)

test situations, but the variety of the deficits has made it difficult to arrive at a meaningful interpretation. In man, hippocampal lesions often result in a severe memory deficit.[153] Infrahuman species do not show a clear-cut inability to remember,[84] but react abnormally in so many test situations that selective memory deficits often cannot be ruled out. Animals with hippocampal lesions learn simple discriminations perfectly well,[86] but learn poorly in some complex mazes.[75] Preoperatively acquired "active" avoidance responses are often lost following hippocampal damage,[134, 2] but the acquisition of the same responses is typically not affected[2] or even facilitated.[73]

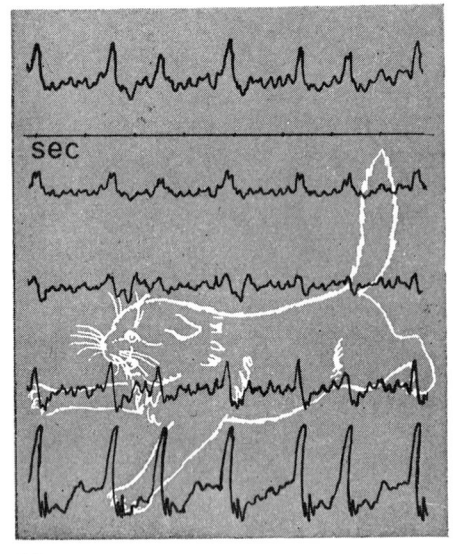

It has been suggested that at least part of the deficit seen in animals with hippocampal lesions may result from an inability to inhibit previously rewarded behaviors and to adapt to changing reward contingencies.[85] This interpretation is supported by experiments demonstrating (1) greater resistance to extinction in both appetitive[76] and aversive[73] instrumental learning situations; (2) a deficient reaction to changes in reward contingencies;[36] (3) an impairment of reversal learning;[93, 86] (4) a lack of reaction to novel stimuli;[66] and (5) poor performance in "passive" avoidance situations.

Rats with hippocampal lesions also do not show the tendency to spontaneously alternate responses in a two-choice situation, which characterizes normal members of this species,[30] and are deficient in learning to alternate.[136] These observations have led to the suggestion that animals with hippocampal lesions may persevere in unlearned as well as learned response tendencies, but there is some evidence to the contrary.[87, 171]

Cingulate Gyrus

Lesions in the cingulate gyrus sharply, though sometimes only temporarily, lower the emotional reactivity of normally aggressive monkeys.[157, 133] Shortly after surgery, these animals appear to lose all affective capacities and treat man as well as other monkeys as if they were inanimate subjects. Ward[167] has described this unusual behavior as follows: "Such an animal shows no grooming behavior or acts of affection toward its companions. In fact, it treats them as it treats all inanimate objects and will walk on them, bump into them if they happen to be in the way and will even sit on them. It will openly eat food in the hand of a companion without being prepared to do battle and appears surprised when it is rebuffed. Such an animal never fights or tries to escape when removed from a cage."

Monkeys with cingulate lesions show no detectable intellectual deficits and learn or perform instrumental discrimination responses as well as normals. A lack of affect is reflected only in their response to nonreward. When a normal monkey makes a correct discrimination and his reward is snatched from under his nose, he throws a temper tantrum and refuses to work in the experimental situation for at least a day. Monkeys with cingulate lesions react little, if at all, to this indignity and willingly return to the problem.[45]

Because the effects of cingulate lesions seem to be more clearly restricted to affective behaviors than those of frontal or temporal lobe lesions, cingulectomies have been used widely in the treatment of anxiety neuroses and obsessions.[45] Although this operation has benefited a large proportion of patients, its use has declined in recent years because of the availability of tranquilizer drugs that achieve similar behavioral effects without incurring the risk of major brain surgery. Experimental interest in the functions of the cingulate cortex showed a correlated decline until a detailed analysis of the behavior of rats and cats with cingulate lesions suggested that this area may originate important facilitatory influences that potentially affect all behavior. The story is as yet incomplete, partly, no doubt, because we are not sure exactly what we are looking for.

Lesions in the cingulate gyrus,[101] some of its afferent pathways,[162] or the tissues underneath it,[100] impair the acquisition of some types of "active" avoidance responses. The effect is most clearly seen in a shuttle box where the animals are in continual approach-avoidance conflict because they are required to avoid or escape painful stimulation by jumping into the compartment where they were last shocked or threatened. The deficit is marginal[132] or absent[99] in "one-way" avoidance situations that avoid this conflict. The same lesions improve performance in "passive" avoidance situations where the animals are punished unless they withhold previously rewarded responses.[101]

Septal Area

Lesions in the septal area produce a pattern of behavioral changes that is in many respects opposite that seen after cingulectomy. An increase in emotional reactivity, viciousness, and exaggerated "rage" responses to normal handling have been observed in monkeys,[46] cats,[170] and rats.[15] However, the effect is not seen in all lesioned animals and appears to be more common in some species, such as the rat,[88] than others, such as the cat.[121] The postsurgical hyperirritability diminishes with continued handling[16] (see Figure 12–11).

The lesioned animals do not show simple intellectual deficits, but their reactions to punishment or nonreward are grossly abnormal. A number of investigators[101, 102, 151] have attempted to account for the septal lesion syndrome in terms of an increase in "perseverative" tendencies. This is a perfectly valid description of what animals with septal

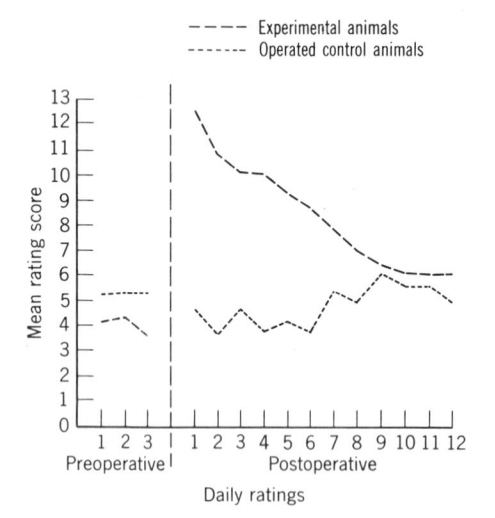

FIG. 12–11. Changes in emotional reactivity following septal lesions.

(After J. V. Brady & W. J. H. Nauta. Subcortical mechanisms in emotional behavior: affective changes following septal forebrain lesions in the albino rat. *J. comp. physiol. Psychol.*, **46**, 1953, 339–346. Copyright 1953 by the American Psychological Association, and reproduced by permission.)

lesions seem to do in many test situations, but tells us little about the functions of the septum that are responsible for the behavioral changes.

More and more data are becoming available[60, 61, 59] which suggest that the septal area may contain a number of different functions. Just as we have learned not to speak of the functions of the hypothalamus or thalamus, but to distinguish between often very small areas within these major subdivisions of the brain, it is becoming increasingly clear that destruction of the septal area (which often includes damage to surrounding tissue) may not affect a single function or even closely related functions. What is needed, at this time, is a much more detailed analysis of the effects of small lesions within the septal region or of other procedures which affect functionally instead of purely anatomically defined pathways to and from this area. An analysis of the vast literature on the effects of gross septal lesions should give us some idea of what to expect.

Rats with large septal lesions learn and perform conditioned emotional responses (CER) only poorly. Normal animals rapidly learn to "freeze" and stop all ongoing activity when a stimulus is presented that signals unavoidable painful shock. Rats with septal lesions do not learn this simple "fear" reaction very well[62] and fail to display a preoperatively learned CER.[15] They continue to lever-press even when each response is punished by a painful shock[63] and show a similar disregard for punishment in traditional "passive" avoidance situations where the response of eating or drinking is itself punished.[101]

The behavior of rats and cats with septal lesions in "active" avoidance situations is more difficult to predict. In the shuttle box (which presents an approach-avoidance conflict because the animals must jump into the compartment where they were last shocked or threatened), septal animals typically learn faster than normals.[88, 91] The performance of preoperatively acquired avoidance responses, on the other hand, is often impaired.[121, 103] Selective excitation of cholinergic synapses in the septal area inhibits the acquisition of shuttle-box avoidance responses,[50] and a pharmacological blockade of these neurons replicates the facilitatory effects of septal lesions on shuttle-box avoidance behavior.[61, 80]

In other "active" avoidance situations, which avoid the complications of an approach-avoidance conflict, septal lesions typically interfere with the acquisition of avoidance behavior in rats[166, 126] as well as cats.[175, 58] A selective blockade of the cholinergic components of the septal area duplicates these inhibitory effects on active avoidance learning (as well as the facilitatory effects seen in the shuttle-box apparatus), but fails to produce passive avoidance deficits.[59, 55] These observations are of theoretical importance because they suggest that different mechanisms may be responsible for the lesion effects on active and passive avoidance behavior. All types of active avoidance responses appear to be influenced by a common cholinergic pathway that synapses in the septal area. Passive avoidance (i.e., the response to punishment), on the other hand, appears to be mediated by a different pathway that is either not mediated cholinergically or does not synapse in the septal area.

Septal lesions also produce marked changes in intra- as well as interspecies aggressive behaviors. Intraspecies fighting that is elicited by painful stimulation (i.e., shock-induced fighting) is facilitated,[11,116] but fighting that is related to food competition or territorial defense is markedly decreased[116]—an apparently paradoxical pattern of effects that is remarkably similar to that seen in animals with ventromedial hypothalamic lesions. It is particularly interesting that a selective blockade of the cholinergic components of the septum (or of the ventromedial hypothalamus) does not modify aggressive reactions.[115] The effects of septal and hypothalamic lesions on aggressive reactions do, however, differ in two important respects. Septal lesions do, in all instances, elicit mouse killing in tame laboratory rats whereas hypothalamic lesions do not, and all of the septal lesion effects on aggressive reactions are temporary, showing a time-course that is remarkably similar to that described for the overt display of "rage" behavior.[116]

The performance of animals with septal lesions is impaired in many appetitive situations because the animals fail to adjust to changes in the reward contingencies. When reinforcements are programmed such that only responses are rewarded that occur a fixed time after the last reward (a "fixed-interval" schedule), normal animals do not respond at all for some time after a reward has been presented and respond more and more rapidly as time elapses and the next reward becomes more and more probable. Rats with septal lesions do not adjust to these contingencies and respond equally throughout the period between rewards.[34,35] Nor do they learn to maximize rewards in similar situations where responses that occur before the end of a waiting period are punished because each premature response resets the clock that determines the period of nonreinforcement. Normal animals adjust to such a DRL (differential reinforcement of low rates of responding) schedule quite rapidly and withhold responses until the end of the nonreinforcement period. Rats with septal lesions never do.[37] Recent experiments[81] have shown that this deficit is not simply because of an increased tendency to perseverate. Even when a cue is provided that signals a period of nonreinforcement in a lever-pressing situation, septal rats continue to respond as if the reinforcement contingencies had not changed.[151]

A similar tendency to ignore changes in the probability of reward is seen in simple position habit reversals. Cats with septal lesions learn this task very well, particularly when their first choice (i.e., innate preference) is selected for reward. However, these animals have a very difficult time when the reward conditions are reversed after they attain some criterion of perfection.[176] These observations once again suggest a lack of response to the reward contingencies.

There are, moreover, some observations that suggest quite specifically that the animals with septal lesions overreact in some fashion to positive as well as to negative stimuli. For instance, rats with septal lesions appear to be more reactive to unavoidable shock,[98] bright lights,[150] novel stimuli,[163] and sweet as well as bitter-tasting rewards.[8]

Summary and Review Questions

The integration of emotional reactions appears to involve many subcortical and cortical mechanisms. Some autonomic responses to emotion-inducing noxious stimuli are reflexly controlled by mechanisms in the lower brainstem. A more complete integration of emotional responses seems to occur within the hypothalamus. Lesions in the ventromedial hypothalamus remove inhibitory influences that normally hold aggressive reactions to noxious stimulation in check. Lesioned animals are vicious and overreact to any form of stimulation. They learn and perform active avoidance responses better than normals, but they do not inhibit punished or nonrewarded behaviors. Shock-induced fighting is elicited more easily, but the lesioned animals become submissive in other situations. Electrical or chemical stimulation of many medial hypothalamic sites elicits flight-, defense-, or attack-reactions that are often well directed and indistinguishable from normal affective responses to noxious stimulation. Stimulation of these regions is aversive.

Damage or stimulation of several thalamic nuclei, particularly those of the anterior and dorsal regions, modifies affective reactivity. However, a thalamic theory of emotion, as suggested by Cannon and Bard, does not seem to be supported by the empirical evidence. Such a theory proposes in essence that the thalamus initiates both overt emotional behavior and emotional experience when released from cortical inhibition. However, the hyperemotionality of decorticated animals does not disappear when the thalamus is destroyed, suggesting that its role cannot be as central as the theory suggests.

Most of the research of recent years has attempted to elucidate the relationship between affective reactions and the "limbic" system or related neocortical and subcortical structures. This is due, at least in part, to Papez' formulation of a theory of emotional behavior, which suggested that the limbic system, particularly the cingulate gyrus, might be the "affectoceptor" cortex that gives rise to emotional experiences. This theory was modified by MacLean, who suggested that the hippocampal gyrus of the temporal lobe might be the receiving area for emotional stimuli and that emotional experience might require processing of this information by the "affectomotor" cortex of the hippocampus proper.

The research that these theories encouraged has shown that the integration of emotional reactions appears to be a more complex matter than the early theories suggested. Complete removal of the neocortex produces tameness and docility. This may be caused by the removal of excitatory influences that originate in the frontal lobe since frontal lobe lesions produce similar effects on affective reactivity.

Many aspects of the temporal lobe, including the frontotemporal cortex, the amygdala, the cortex surrounding the amygdala, and the hippocampus, appear to contribute additional excitatory influences on affective reactions. Removal of the temporal lobe as well as discrete lesions in many of its parts reduce emotional reactivity and seem to interfere with an appreciation of the consequences of behavior. Animals with temporal lobe lesions typically learn active as well as passive avoidance responses poorly and fail to react appropriately to changes in positive reward contingencies. Electrical stimulation of many points in the amygdala elicits rage or attack behavior.

Hippocampal lesions produce little or no change in affective reactivity but interfere with the performance of active as well as passive avoidance responses. The lesions also produce what appears to be an inability to respond to changes in positive as well as negative reward contingencies.

Lesions in the cingulate gyrus lower emotional reactivity. Cingulectomized monkeys rarely fight and respond little if at all to frustration or nonreward. They learn conflictful shuttle-box avoidance responses poorly but have little difficulty with one-way avoidance problems. Passive avoidance behavior, which requires the withholding of previously rewarded responses, is improved.

Damage to the septal area produces a pattern of behavioral effects that is in many ways opposite that seen after cingulate lesions. Animals with septal lesions appear to be hyperreactive and are temporarily vicious and difficult to handle. Such animals do not learn or perform conditioned emotional reactions as well as normals. They learn active avoidance responses better than their controls in the conflictful shuttle-box situation, but are typically impaired on other active as well as passive avoidance problems. A selective blockade of the cholinergic components of the septum reproduces the lesion effects on active but not on passive avoidance behavior.

1. The hypothalamus is often discussed as a "motor center" for affective reactions. What are the principal experimental findings that support this suggestion?

2. What is the role of lower brainstem mechanisms in emotional behavior?

3. State the Cannon-Bard theory of emotions and discuss the experimental evidence for it.

4. Contrast the "limbic" theories of Papez and MacLean. What new evidence can you bring to bear in support of them?

5. Describe the behavior of animals with frontal lobe lesions and compare it with the behavior of animals with lesions in the temporal lobe.

6. Contrast the behavioral effects of septal and cingulate cortex lesions.

7. Many lesions in the limbic system seem to interfere with the ability to adjust to changes in the reinforcement contingencies. Give some specific examples of the resultant behavioral deficits.

8. This abnormal tendency to perseverate in previously rewarded responses is often accompanied by changes in avoidance behavior. Discuss the possibility that both effects may be caused by a common functional impairment.

CONCLUSIONS

Only a narrow range of emotional reactions—those occurring in response to noxious stimulation or the withholding of positive reward—has been experimentally studied. Strictly speaking, our conclusions must be limited to this type of reaction. However, we may hope that the pattern of organization of peripheral and central influences on these negative emotional reactions may be at least similar to that of the mechanisms that subserve positive affect. What, then, have we learned in the past 50 years of experimental and theoretical interest in the physiological substrate of emotional reactions?

Clinical as well as experimental observations have suggested that a "peripheral-origin" theory, here as in the case of the basic appetitive drives, does not provide an adequate explanation of behavior. Peripheral autonomic and somatic motor responses accompany most emotional reactions, and our perception of these physiological changes may become a classically conditioned component of emotional experience. However, they do not seem to be the primary and essential basis of emotional experience, as William James suggested 100 years ago.

Changes in such physiological functions as heart rate, sweating, or respiration do not seem to be the basis for emotional experience, but they do accompany emotional reactions. A good deal of research has been devoted to the possibility that different emotions might give rise to different patterns of physiological reactions. If this were true, a battery of relatively easily obtainable measures could provide objective measures of the quality and quantity of emotional experience—an invaluable tool for therapy as well as research in this field. We do not yet have any test that even comes close to this ideal. Some individual measures appear to be capable of distinguishing positive from negative affect; others have some success in separating fear from anger; and many can serve as an index of the intensity of emotional experience. Batteries of tests are commonly used to detect the emotional reactions that in most of us accompany lying, but we are, as yet, far from our goal. The increasing availability of computers may make it possible in the not too distant future to analyze each individual's reactions in terms of a set of norms which are unique for that person.

The integration of emotional reactions seems to involve many subcortical mechanisms as well as much of the primitive cortex that makes up the base and medial surface of the cerebral hemispheres. Individual autonomic reactions that normally accompany emotional reactions seem to be reflexly controlled by mechanisms in the lower brainstem. More complete "rage" or "attack" reactions can be elicited by stimulation of the central grey of the brainstem. Similar stimulation of many hypothalamic sites elicits flight-, defense-, or attack-reactions that are often indistinguishable from normal reactions to noxious stimulation. Many investigators have assumed, therefore, that overt emotional responses are integrated by these hypothalamic mechanisms.

There has been a general tendency to search for cortical mechanisms that might, in turn, mediate the subjective experience of emotion that accompanies the overt reactions. Largely on the basis of intimate anatomical connections, it was suggested 30 years ago that some components of the limbic system might play this role. Extensive experimental study of this possibility has indicated that the entire limbic cortex as well as the neocortex of the frontal lobe and several subcortical nuclei seem to be in some way related to affective reactions. We do not yet know whether some or all parts of this complex circuit, which also seems to play an important role in appetitive drives, act as a unit or what the contributions of individual components may be.

Lesions in many aspects of the limbic system produce apparently similar effects on aggressive behaviors, escape-avoidance behavior, and reactivity to frustration and nonreward. Emotional reactivity appears to be decreased following lesions in the frontal neocortex, the limbic cortex of the cingulate gyrus and temporal lobe, and in some subcortical nuclei of the amygdaloid complex. Normally aggressive animals become tame and friendly and display little anger when frustrated or deprived of earned rewards following such lesions. These animals typically do not learn avoidance responses as rapidly as normals and are unable to withhold previously rewarded responses when the rewards are omitted, or even when the responses are punished. They also perform poorly in situations where high-response rates are not rewarded or even punished. Although there are significant variations between the individual areas with respect to the magnitude of each of these effects, the overall picture is quite consistent. However, a similar inability to respond appropriately to changes in positive as well as negative reward contingencies characterizes animals with lesions that have little or no effect on overt emotionality or even produce hyperirritability. Damage to the hippocampus, for instance, does not seem to produce overt changes in emotional reactivity unless seizure foci develop in the tissue surrounding the lesion. Animals with such lesions also acquire (although not always remember) active avoidance responses quite well, but seem to be unable to inhibit previously learned responses. Lesions in the septal area produce an apparently similar perseverative tendency, but also interfere with active avoidance learning (except in the shuttle box where it seems to be facilitated) and increase affective reactivity temporarily.

It appears likely that the components of the limbic system, which we have treated as units, do not, in fact, subserve unitary functions and that the behavioral effects of large lesions that have been used in most research may reflect an impairment in many distinct and perhaps not always related functions. Moreover, the pattern of behavioral change may reflect the relative extent of destruction of some functions and may thus differ with the size and precise location of the lesion. Current research is tending more and more towards the use of small lesions or pharmacological techniques for the selective inactivation or excitation of more distinct pathways, and it is to be hoped that the next decade will provide more detailed analyses of limbic functions.

Bibliography

1. Anand, B. K., & Brobeck, J. R. Hypothalamic control of food intake in rats and cats. *Yale J. Biol. Med.*, 1951, **24**, 123–140.
2. Andy, O. J., Peeler, D. F., Jr., & Foshee, D. P. Avoidance and discrimination learning following hippocampal ablation in the cat. *J. Comp. Physiol. Psychol.*, 1967, **64**, 516–519.
3. Auleytner, B., & Brutkowski, S. Effects of bilateral prefrontal lobectomy on the classical (type I) defense conditioned reflexes and some other responses related to defensive behavior in dogs. *Acta Biol. exp. (Warsaw)*, 1960, **20**, 243–262.
4. Ax, A. F. The physiological differentiation of fear and anger in humans. *Psychosom. Med.*, 1953, **15**, 433–442.
5. Bard, P. On emotional expression after decortication with some remarks on certain theoretical views, parts I and II. *Psychol. Rev.*, 1934, **41**, 309–329, 424–449.

6. Bard, P. Central nervous mechanisms for the expression of anger in animals. In *Feelings and emotions*. M. L. Reymert, Ed. New York: McGraw-Hill, 1950, pp. 211–237.
7. Bard, P., & Mountcastle, V. B. Some forebrain mechanisms involved in expression of rage with special reference to suppression of angry behavior. *Res. Publ. Ass. Res. nerv. ment. Dis.*, 1948, **27**, 362–404.
8. Beatty, W. W., & Schwartzbaum, J. S. Enhanced reactivity to quinine and saccharine solutions following septal lesions in the rat. *Psychon. Sci.*, 1967, **8**, 483–484.
9. Belluzzi, J., & Grossman, S. P. Avoidance learning: Long-lasting deficits after temporal lobe seizure. *Science*, 1969, **166**, 1435–1437.
10. Benussi, V. Die Atmungsymptome der Luege. *Arch. ges. Psychol.*, 1914, **31**, 244–273.
11. Blanchard, R. J., & Blanchard, D. C. Limbic lesions and reflexive fighting. *J. comp. physiol. Psychol.*, 1968, **66**, 603–605.
12. Bohus, B., Endroczi, E., & Lissak, K. Correlations between avoiding conditioned reflex activity and pituitary adrenocortical function in the rat. *Acta physiol. hung.*, 1964, **24**, 79–83.
13. Bond, D. D., Randt, C. T., Bidder, T. G., & Rowland, V. Posterior septal fornical and anterior thalamic lesions in the cat. *Arch. Neurol. Psychiat. (Chicago)*, 1957, **78**, 143–162.
14. Boshes, B. Emotions, hypothalamus and the cardiovascular system. *Amer. J. Cardiol.*, 1958, **1**, 212–223.
15. Brady, J. V., & Nauta, W. J. H. Subcortical mechanisms in emotional behavior: affective changes following septal forebrain lesions in the albino rat. *J. comp. physiol. Psychol.*, 1953, **46**, 339–346.
16. Brady, J. V., & Nauta, W. J. H. Subcortical mechanisms in emotional behavior: The duration of affective changes following septal and habenular lesions in the albino rat. *J. comp. physiol. Psychol.*, 1955, **48**, 412–420.
17. Brunswick, D. The effect of emotional stimuli on the gastro-intestinal tone. *J. comp. Psychol.*, 1924, **4**, 19–79.
18. Brutkowski, S. Prefrontal cortex and drive inhibition. In *The frontal granular cortex and behavior*. J. M. Warren & K. Akert, Eds. New York: McGraw-Hill, 1964, pp. 242–270.
19. Brutkowski, S., Fonberg, Elzbieta, & Mempel, E. Elementary type II (instrumental) conditioned reflexes in amygdala dogs. *Acta Biol. exp. (Warsaw)*, 1960, **20**, 263–271.
20. Cannon, W. B. The James-Lange theory of emotions: A critical examination and an alternative. *Amer. J. Psychol.*, 1927, **39**, 106–124.
21. Cannon, W. B. Again the James-Lange and the thalamic theories of emotion. *Psychol. Rev.*, 1931, **38**, 281–295.
22. Cannon, W. B. *The wisdom of the body* (2nd ed.). New York: Norton, 1939.
23. Carder, B. Lateral hypothalamic stimulation and avoidance in rats. *J. comp. physiol. Psychol.*, 1970, **71**, 325–333.
24. Coombs, C. H. Adaptation of the galvanic response to auditory stimuli. *J. exp. Psychol.*, 1938, **22**, 244–268.
25. Dana, C. L. The anatomic seat of the emotions: A discussion of the James-Lange theory. *Arch. Neurol. Psychiat. (Chicago)*, 1921, **6**, 634–639.
26. Darrow, C. W. A new frontier: neurophysiological effect of emotion on the brain. In *Feelings and emotions*. M. L. Reymert, Ed. New York: McGraw-Hill, 1950, pp. 247–260.
27. Dax, E., Cunningham, F., Reitman, B., & Radley-Smith, E. J. Prefrontal leucotomy: 1. Investigations into clinical problems. 2. Vertical and horizontal incisions of the frontal lobes. 3. Physiological aspects. Summary of three papers presented at the International Congress of Psychosurgery, Lisbon, 1948. *Dig. Neurol. Psychiat.*, 1948, **16**, 533.
28. Delgado, J. M. R. Cerebral structures involved in transmission and elaboration of noxious stimulation. *J. Neurophysiol.*, 1955, **18**, 261–275.
29. DeWied, D. Influence of anterior pituitary on avoidance learning and escape behavior. *Amer. J. Physiol.*, 1964, **207**, 255–259.
30. Douglas, R. J., & Isaacson, R. L. Hippocampal lesions and activity. *Psychonom. Sci.*, 1964, **1**, 187–188.
31. Dysinger, D. W. A comparative study of affective responses by means of the impressive and expressive methods. *Psychol. Monogr.*, 1931, **187** (monograph).

32. Egan, G. Results of isolation of the orbital lobes in leucotomy. *J. ment. Sci.*, 1949, **95,** 115–123.

33. Eichelman, B. S., Jr. Effect of subcortical lesions on shock-induced aggression in the rat. *J. comp. physiol. Psychol.*, 1971, **74**, 331–339.

34. Ellen, P., & Powell, E. W. Temporal discrimination in rats with rhinencephalic lesions. *Exp. Neurol.*, 1962a, **6**, 538–547.

35. Ellen, P., & Powell, E. W. Effects of septal lesions on behavior generated by positive reinforcement. *Exp. Neurol.*, 1962b, **6**, 1–11.

36. Ellen, P., & Wilson, A. S. Perseveration in the rat following hippocampal lesions. *Exp. Neurol.*, 1963, **8**, 310–317.

37. Ellen, P., Wilson, A. S., & Powell, E. W. Septal inhibition and timing behavior in the rat. *Exp. Neurol.*, 1964, **10**, 120–132.

38. Elliott, H., Albert, S., & Bremner, W. A program for prefrontal lobotomy with report of effect on intractable pain. *D.V.A. Treatment Serv. Bull.*, 1948, **3**, 26–35.

39. Ellison, G. D., & Flynn, J. P. Organized aggressive behavior in cats after surgical isolation of the hypothalamus. *Arch. ital. Biol.*, 1968, **106**, 1–20.

40. Feleky, A. M. The influence of emotions on respiration. *J. exp. Psychol.*, 1916, **1**, 218–241.

41. Fernandez de Molina, A., & Hunsperger, R. W. Organization of the subcortical system governing defense and flight reactions in the cat. *J. Physiol. (London)*, 1962, **160**, 200–213.

42. Ferrier, D. The Croonian Lecture. Experiments on the brain of monkeys (second series). *Phil. Trans.*, 1875, **165**, 433–488.

43. Friedman, S. B., Ader, R., Grota, L. J., & Larson, Truus. Plasma corticosterone response to parameters of electric shock stimulation in the rat. *Psychosom. Med.*, 1967, **29**, 323–328.

44. Fuller, J. L., Rosvold, H. E., & Pribram, K. H. The effect on affective and cognitive behavior in the dog of lesions of the pyriform–amygdala hippocampal complex. *J. comp. physiol. Psychol.*, 1957, **50**, 89–96.

45. Fulton, J. F. *Frontal lobotomy and affective behavior. A neurophysiological analysis.* New York: Norton, 1951.

46. Fulton, J. F., & Ingraham, F. D. Emotional disturbances following experimental lesions of the base of the brain. *J. Physiol. (London)*, 1929, **67**, 27–28.

47. Fulton, J. F., & Jacobsen, C. F. The functions of the frontal lobes, a comparative study in monkeys, chimpanzees and man. *Advanc. mod. Biol. (Moscow)*, 1935, **4**, 113–123. Abstract from the second international neurological congress, London, 1935, pp. 70–71.

48. Goltz, F. Der Hund ohne Grosshirn. *Pflüg. Arch. ges. Physiol.*, 1892, **51**, 570–614.

49. Grossman, S. P. Chemically induced epileptiform seizures in the cat. *Science*, 1963, **142**, 409–411.

50. Grossman, S. P. Effect of chemical stimulation of the septal area on motivation. *J. comp. physiol. Psychol.*, 1964, **58**, 194–200.

51. Grossman, S. P. Exploring the brain with chemicals. *Discovery*, 1966a, **27**, 19–23.

52. Grossman, S. P. The VMH: A center for affective reaction, satiety, or both? *Physiol. & Behav.*, 1966b, **1**, 1–10.

53. Grossman, S. P. *A textbook of physiological psychology.* New York: Wiley, 1967.

54. Grossman, S. P. Avoidance behavior and aggression in rats with transections of the lateral connections of the medial or lateral hypothalamus. *Physiol. & Behav.*, 1970, **5**, 1103–1108.

55. Grossman, S. P. Unpublished observations, University of Chicago, 1971.

56. Grossman, S. P. Aggression, avoidance, and reaction to novel environments in female rats with ventromedial hypothalamic lesions. *J. comp. physiol. Psychol.*, 1972, **78**, 274–283.

57. Grossman, S. P., & Grossman, Lore. Surgical interruption of the anterior or posterior connections of the hypothalamus: Effects on aggressive and avoidance behavior. *Physiol. & Behav.*, 1970, **5**, 1313–1317.

58. Hamilton, L. W. Active avoidance impairment following septal lesions in cats. *J. comp. physiol. Psychol.*, 1969, **69**, 420–431.

59. Hamilton, L. W., & Grossman, S. P. Behavioral changes following disruption of central cholinergic pathways. *J. comp. physiol. Psychol.*, 1969, **69**, 76–82.

60. Hamilton, L. W., McCleary, R., & Grossman, S. P. Behavioral effects of cholinergic septal blockade in the cat. *J. comp. physiol. Psychol.*, 1968, **66**, 563–568.
61. Hamilton, L. W., Kelsey, J. E., & Grossman, S. P. Variations in behavioral inhibition following different septal lesions in rats. *J. comp. physiol. Psychol.*, 1970, **1**, 79–86.
62. Harvey, J. A., Jacobson, L. E., & Hunt, H. F. Long-term effects of lesions in the septal forebrain on acquisition and retention of conditioned fear. *Amer. Psychologist*, 1961, **16**, 449.
63. Harvey, J. A., Lints, C. E., Jacobson, L. E., & Hunt, H. F. Effects of lesions in the septal area on conditioned fear and discriminated instrumental punishment in the albino rat. *J. comp. physiol. Psychol.*, 1965, **59**, 37–48.
64. Head, H. *Studies in neurology.* London: Oxford Univ. Press, 1920.
65. Hebb, D. O. *Organization of behavior: A neuropsychological theory.* New York: Wiley, 1949.
66. Hendrickson, C., & Kimble, D. P. Hippocampal lesions and the orienting response. Paper presented at the 47th annual meeting of the Western Psychological Association, San Francisco, May, 1967.
67. Hess, E. H. Attitude and pupil size. *Sci. Amer.*, 1965, **212**, 46–54.
68. Hess, W. R., & Akert, K. Experimental data on role of hypothalamus in mechanism of emotional behavior. *A. M. A. Arch. Neurol. Psychiat.*, 1955, **73**, 127–129.
69. Hoagland, H. Some endocrine stress responses in man. In *The physiology of emotions.* A. Simon, Ed. Springfield, Ill.: Thomas, 1961.
70. Horvath, F. E. Effects of basolateral amygdalectomy on three types of avoidance behavior. *J. comp. physiol. Psychol.*, 1963, **56**, 380–389.
71. Hutchinson, R. R., & Renfrew, J. W. Stalking-attack and eating behaviors elicited from the same sites in the hypothalamus. *J. comp. physiol. Psychol.*, 1966, **61**, 360–367.
72. Ingram, W. R., Barris, R. W., & Ranson, S. W. Catalepsy: An experimental study. *Arch. Neurol. Psychiat. (Chicago)*, 1936, **35**, 1175–1197.

73. Isaacson, R. L., Douglas, R. J., & Moore, R. Y. The effect of radical hippocampal ablation on acquisition of avoidance responses. *J. comp. physiol. Psychol.*, 1961, **54**, 625–628.
74. James, W. What is emotion? *Mind*, 1884, **9**, 188–205.
75. Jarrard, L. E., & Lewis, T. C. Effects of hippocampal ablation and intertrial interval on complex maze acquisition and extinction. *Amer. J. Psychol.*, 1967, **80**, 66–72.
76. Jarrard, L. E., Isaacson, R. L., & Wickelgren, W. O. Effects of hippocampal ablation and intertrial interval on runway acquisition and extinction. *J. comp. physiol. Psychol.*, 1964, **57**, 442–444.
77. Kaada, B. R. Somato-motor, autonomic and electrocorticographic responses to electrical stimulation of "rhinencephalic" and other forebrain structures in primates, cat and dog. *Acta physiol. scand.*, 1951, **24**, Suppl. 83, 1–285.
78. Karli, P. The Norway rat's killing response to the white mouse. An experimental analysis. *Behaviour*, 1956, **10**, 81–103.
79. Kellicutt, M. H., & Schwartzbaum, J. S. Formation of a conditioned emotional response (CER) following lesions of the amygdaloid complex in rats. *Psychol. Rep.*, 1963, **12**, 351–358.
80. Kelsey, J. E., & Grossman, S. P. Cholinergic blockade and lesions in the ventro-medial septum of the rat. *Physiol. & Behav.*, 1969, **4**, 837–845.
81. Kelsey, J. E., & Grossman, S. P. Non-perseverative disruption of behavioral inhibition following septal lesions in rats. *J. comp. physiol. Psychol.*, 1971, **75**, 302–311.
82. Kennard, Margaret A. Effect of bilateral ablation of cingulate area on behavior of cats. *J. Neurophysiol.*, 1955, **18**, 159–169.
83. Kennedy, J. L., & Travis, R. C. Prediction and control of alertness. II: Continuous tracking. *J. comp. physiol. Psychol.*, 1948, **41**, 203–210.
84. Kimble, D. P. The effects of bilateral hippocampal lesions in rats. *J. comp. physiol. Psychol.*, 1963, **56**, 273–283.
85. Kimble, D. P. Hippocampus and internal inhibition. *Psychol. Bull.*, 1968, **70**, 285–295.

86. Kimble, D. P., & Kimble, R. J. Hippocampectomy and response perseveration in the rat. *J. comp. physiol. Psychol.*, 1965, **3**, 474–476.

87. Kimble, D. P., Kirkby, R. J., & Stein, D. G. Response perseveration interpretation of passive avoidance deficits in hippocampectomized rats. *J. comp. physiol. Psychol.*, 1966, **61**, 141–143.

88. King, F. A. Effects of septal and amygdaloid lesions on emotional behavior and conditioned avoidance responses in the rat. *J. nerv. ment. Dis.*, 1958, **126**, 57–63.

89. King, M. B., & Hoebel, B. G. Killing elicited by brain stimulation in rats. *Comm. Behav. Biol.*, 1968, Part A, **2**, 173–177.

90. Klüver, H., & Bucy, P. C. "Psychic blindness" and other symptoms following bilateral temporal lobectomy in rhesus monkeys. *Amer. J. Physiol.*, 1937, **119**, 352–353.

91. Krieckhaus, E. E., Simmons, H. J., Thomas, G. J., & Kenyon, J. Septal lesions enhance shock avoidance behavior in the rat. *Exp. Neurol.*, 1964, **9**, 107–113.

92. Lange, C. G. *Om Sindsbevaegelser. et psyko. fysiolog. studie.* Copenhagen: Krønar, 1885.

93. Lash, L. Response discriminability and the hippocampus. *J. comp. physiol. Psychol.*, 1964, **57**, 251–256.

94. Levine, S., & Jones, Lucy E. Adrenocorticotropic hormone (ACTH) and passive avoidance learning. *J. comp. physiol. Psychol.*, 1965, **59**, 357–360.

95. Lindsley, D. B. Emotions and the electroencephalogram. In *Feelings and emotions.* M. L. Reymert, Ed. New York: McGraw-Hill, 1950, pp. 238–246.

96. Lindsley, D. B. Emotion. In *Handbook of experimental psychology.* S. S. Stevens, Ed. New York: Wiley, 1951, pp. 473–516.

97. Lindsley, D. B., Bowden, J. W., & Magoun, H. W. Effect upon the EEG of acute injury to the brain stem activating system. *EEG clin. Neurophysiol.*, 1949, **1**, 475–486.

98. Lints, C. E., & Harvey, J. A. Altered sensitivity to footshock and decreased brain content of serotonin following brain lesions in the rat. *J. comp. physiol. Psychol.*, 1969, **67**, 23–31.

99. Lubar, J. F. Effects of medial cortical lesions on the avoidance behavior of the cat. *J. comp. physiol. Psychol.*, 1964, **58**, 38–46.

100. Lubar, J. F., Perachio, A. A., & Kavanagh, A. J. Deficits in active avoidance behavior following lesions of the lateral and posterolateral gyrus of the cat. *J. comp. physiol. Psychol.*, 1966, **62**, 263–269.

101. McCleary, R. A. Response specificity in the behavioral effects of limbic system lesions in the cat. *J. comp. physiol. Psychol.*, 1961, **54**, 605–613.

102. McCleary, R. A. Response-modulating functions of the limbic system: Initiation and suppression. In *Progress in physiological psychology.* Vol. I. E. Stellar & J. M. Sprague, Eds. New York: Academic Press, 1966, pp. 209–272.

103. McCleary, R. A., Jones, C., & Ursin, H. Avoidance and retention deficits in septal cats. *Psychonom. Sci.*, 1965, **2**, 85–86.

104. Macht, M. B., & Bard, P. Studies on decerebrate cats in the chronic state. *Fed. Proc.*, 1942, **1**, 55–56.

105. MacLean, P. D. Psychosomatic disease and the "visceral brain." *Psychosom. Med.*, 1949, **11**, 338–353.

106. MacLean, P. D. The limbic system and its hippocampal formation: Studies in animals and their possible application to man. *J. Neurosurg.*, 1954, **11**, 29–44.

107. MacLean, P. D., & Delgado, J. M. R. Electrical and chemical stimulation of frontotemporal portion of limbic system in the waking animal. *EEG clin. Neurophysiol.*, 1953, **5**, 91–100.

108. MacLean, P. D., Horwitz, N. H., & Robinson, F. Olfactory-like responses in pyriform area to non-olfactory stimulation. *Yale J. Biol. Med.*, 1952, **25**, 159.

109. MacPhail, E. M., & Miller, N. E. Cholinergic brain stimulation in cats: failure to obtain sleep. *J. comp. physiol. Psychol.*, 1968, **65**, 499–503.

110. Margules, D. L. Noradrenergic basis of inhibition between reward and punishment in amygdala. *J. comp. physiol. Psychol.*, 1968, **66**, 329–334.

111. Margules, D. L., & Stein, L. Cholinergic synapses in the ventromedial hypothalamus for the suppression of operant behavior by punishment and satiety. *J. comp. physiol. Psychol.*, 1969, **67**, 327–335.

112. Mason, J. W., Brady, J. V., & Sidman, M. Plasma 17-hydroxycorticosteroid levels and conditioned behavior in the rhesus monkey. *Endocrinology*, 1957, **60**, 741–752.

113. Masserman, J. H. Is the hypothalamus a center of emotion? *Psychosom. Med.*, 1941, **3**, 3–25.

114. Mettler, F. A., Ed. (The Columbia-Greystone Associates). *Selective partial ablation of the frontal cortex. A correlative study of its effects on human psychotic subjects.* New York: Paul Hoeber, 1949, Chapter 14.

115. Miczek, K., & Grossman, S. P. Unpublished observations, University of Chicago, 1971.

116. Miczek, K., & Grossman, S. P. Effects of septal lesions on inter- and intra- species aggression in rats. *J. comp. physiol. Psychol.*, 1972, in press.

117. Miller, N. E. Learning and performance motivated by direct stimulation of the brain. In *Electrical stimulation of the brain*. D. E. Sheer, Ed. Austin: Univ. of Texas Press, 1961, pp. 387–396.

118. Miller, R. E., & Ogawa, N. The effect of adrenocorticotrophic hormone (ACTH) on avoidance conditioning in adrenalectomized rats. *J. comp. physiol. Psychol.*, 1962, **55**, 211–213.

119. Mishkin, W. Visual discrimination performance following partial ablations of the temporal lobe. II: Ventral surface vs. hippocampus. *J. comp. physiol. Psychol.*, 1954, **47**, 187–193.

120. Moniz, E. *Tentatives opératoires dans le traitement de certaines psychoses.* Paris: Masson, 1936.

121. Moore, R. Y. Effects of some rhinencephalic lesions on retention of conditioned avoidance behavior in cats. *J. comp. physiol. Psychol.*, 1964, **57**, 65–71.

122. Moruzzi, G., & Magoun, H. W. Brain stem reticular formation and activation of the EEG. *EEG clin. Neurophysiol.*, 1949, **1**, 455–473.

123. Murphy, J. V., & Miller, R. E. The effect of adrenocorticotrophic hormone (ACTH) on avoidance conditioning in the rat. *J. comp. physiol. Psychol.*, 1955, **48**, 47–49.

124. Naquet, R. Effects of stimulation of the rhinencephalon in the waking cat. *EEG clin. Neurophysiol.*, 1954, **6**, 711–712.

125. Newman, E. B., Perkins, F. T., & Wheeler, R. H. Cannon's theory of emotion: A critique. *Psychol. Rev.*, 1930, **37**, 305–326.

126. Nielson, H. C., McIver, A. H., & Boswell, R. S. Effect of septal lesions on learning, emotionality, activity and exploratory behavior in rats. *Exp. Neurol.*, 1965, **11**, 147–157.

127. Orbach, J., Milner, B., & Rasmussen, T. Learning and retention in monkeys after amygdalahippocampal resection. *Arch. Neurol. (Chicago)*, 1960, **3**, 230–251.

128. Papez, J. W. A proposed mechanism of emotion. *Arch. Neurol. Psychiat. (Chicago)*, 1937, **38**, 725–743.

129. Papez, J. W. Cerebral mechanisms. *J. nerv. ment. Dis.*, 1939, **89**, 145–159.

130. Pechtel, C., Masserman, J. H., Schreiner, L., & Levitt, M. Differential effects of lesions of the medio-dorsal nuclei of the thalamus on normal and neurotic behavior in the cat. *J. nerv. ment. Dis.*, 1955, **121**, 26–33.

131. Pellegrino, L. Amygdaloid lesions and behavioral inhibition in the rat. *J. comp. physiol. Psychol.*, 1968, **65**, 483–491.

132. Peretz, E. The effects of lesions of the anterior cingulate cortex on the behavior of the rat. *J. comp. physiol. Psychol.*, 1960, **53**, 540–548.

133. Pribram, K. H., & Fulton, J. F. An experimental critique of the effects of anterior cingulate ablations in monkey. *Brain.* 1954, **77**, 34–44.

134. Pribram, K. H., & Weiskrantz, L. A comparison of the effects of medial and lateral cerebral resections on conditioned avoidance behavior of monkeys. *J. comp. physiol. Psychol.*, 1957, **50**, 74–80.

135. Pribram, K. H., Mishkin, M., Rosvold, H. E., & Kaplan, S. J. Effects on delayed-response performance of lesions of dorsolateral and ventromedial frontal cortex of baboons. *J. comp. physiol. Psychol.*, 1952, **45**, 565–575.

136. Racine, R. J., & Kimble, D. P. Hippocampal lesions and delayed alternation in the rat. *Psychonom. Sci.*, 1965, **3**, 285–286.

137. Ranson, S. W. Somnolence caused by hypothalamic lesions in the monkey. *Arch. Neurol. Psychiat. (Chicago)*, 1939, **41**, 1–23.

138. Regan, P. F., & Reilly, J. Circulating epinephrine and norepinephrine in changing emotional states. *J. nerv. ment. Dis.*, 1958, **127**, 12–16.

139. Reitman, F. Orbital cortex syndrome following leucotomy. *Amer. J. Psychiat.*, 1946, **103**, 238–241.

140. Roberts, W. W. Both rewarding and punishing effects from stimulation of posterior hypothalamus of cat with same electrode at same intensity. *J. comp. physiol. Psychol.*, 1958, **61**, 400–407.

141. Roberts, W. W., & Kiess, H. O. Motivational properties of hypothalamic aggression in cats. *J. comp. physiol. Psychol.*, 1964, **58**, 187–193.

142. Roberts, W. W., Steinberg, M. L., & Means, L. W. Hypothalamic mechanisms for sexual, aggressive, and other motivational behaviors in the opossum, *Didilphis Virgiana*. *J. comp. physiol. Psychol.*, 1967, **64**, 1–15.

143. Rothfield, L., & Harman, P. On the relation of the hippocampal-fornix system to the control of rate responses in cats. *J. comp Neurol.*, 1954, **101**, 265–282.

144. Ruckmick, C. A. *The psychology of feeling and emotion.* New York: McGraw-Hill, 1936.

145. Rylander, G. Personality analysis before and after frontal lobotomy. *Res. Publ., Ass. Res. nerv. ment. Dis.*, 1948, **27**, 691–705.

146. Schachter, S., & Wheeler, L. Epinephrine, chlorpromazine, and amusement. *J. abnorm. soc. Psychol.*, 1962, **65**, 121–128.

147. Schreiner, L. H., & Kling, A. Behavioral changes following rhinencephalic injury in cat. *J. Neurophysiol.*, 1953, **16**, 643–659.

148. Schreiner, L. H., Rioch, D. McK., Pechtel, C., & Masserman, J. H. Behavioral changes following thalamic injury in the cat. *J. Neurophysiol.*, 1953, **16**, 254.

149. Schwartzbaum, J. S. Changes in reinforcing properties of stimuli following ablation of the amygdaloid complex in monkeys. *J. comp. physiol. Psychol.*, 1960, **53**, 388–395.

150. Schwartzbaum, J. S., & Gay, Patricia E. Interacting effects of septal and amygdaloid lesions in the rat. *J. comp. physiol. Psychol.*, 1966, **61**, 59–65.

151. Schwartzbaum, J. S., Thompson, J. B., & Kellicutt, M. H. Auditory frequency discrimination and generalization following lesions of the amygdaloid area in rats. *J. comp. physiol. Psychol.*, 1964, **57**, 257–266.

152. Sclafani, A., & Grossman, S. P. Reactivity of hyperphagic and normal rats to quinine and electric shock. *J. comp. physiol. Psychol.*, 1971, **74**, 157–166.

153. Scoville, W. B. The limbic lobe in man. *J. Neurosurg.*, 1954, **11**, 64–66.

154. Sherrington, C. S. Experiments on the value of vascular and visceral factors in the genesis of emotion. *Proc. roy. Soc. (London), B*, 1900, **66**, 390–403.

155. Singer, J. E. The effects of epinephrine, chlorpromazine, and dibenzyline upon the fright response of rats under stress and non-stress conditions. Ph.D. Dissertation, Univ. of Minnesota, 1961.

156. Smith, D. E., King, M. B., & Hoebel, B. G. Lateral hypothalamic control of killing: evidence for a cholinoceptive mechanism. *Science*, 1970, **167**, 900–901.

157. Smith, W. K. The results of ablation of the cingular region of the cerebral cortex. *Fed. Proc.*, 1944, **3**, 42–43.

158. Spiegel, E. A., Miller, H. R., & Oppenheimer, M. J. Forebrain and rage reactions. *J. Neurophysiol.*, 1940, **3**, 538–548.

159. Ström-Olsen, R., & Weil-Malherbe, H. Humoral changes in manic depressive psychosis with particular reference to the excretion of catecholamines in urine. *J. ment. Sci.*, 1958, **104**, 696–704.

160. Swann, H. G. The function of the brain in olfaction. II: The results of destruction of olfactory and other nervous structures upon the discrimination of odors. *J. comp. Neurol.*, 1934, **59**, 175.

161. Swann, H. G. The function of the brain in olfaction. III: Effects of large cortical lesions on olfactory discrimination. *Amer. J. Physiol.*, 1935, **111**, 257.

162. Thomas, G. J., & Slotnick, B. Effects of lesions in the cingulum on maze learning and avoidance conditioning in the rat. *J. comp. physiol. Psychol.*, 1962, **55**, 1085–1091.

163. Thomas, G. J., Moore, R. Y., Harvey, J. A., & Hunt, H. F. Relation between the behavioral syndrome produced by lesions in the septal region of the forebrain and maze learning of the rat. *J. comp. physiol. Psychol.*, 1959, **52**, 527–532.

164. Ursin, H. The temporal lobe substrate of fear and anger. *Acta psychiat. neurol. scand., Kbh.*, 1960, **35**, 378–396.

165. Ursin, H. Effect of amygdaloid lesions on avoidance behavior and visual discrimination in cats. *Exp. Neurol.*, 1965, **11**, 298–317.
166. Vanderwolf, C. H. Effect of combined medial thalamic and septal lesions on active-avoidance behavior. *J. comp. physiol. Psychol.*, 1964, **58**, 31–37.
167. Ward, A. A., Jr. The anterior cingular gyrus and personality. *Res. Publ., Ass. Res. nerv. ment. Dis.*, 1948, **27**, 438–445.
168. Wasman, M., & Flynn, J. P. Directed attack elicited from hypothalamus. *Arch. Neurol.*, 1962, **6**, 220–227.
169. Wertheim, G. A., Conner, R. L., & Levine, S. Avoidance conditioning and adrenocortical function in the rat. *Physiol. & Behav.*, 1969, **4**, 41–44.
170. Wheatley, M. D. The hypothalamus and affective behavior in cats: A study of the effects of experimental lesions, with anatomic correlations. *Arch. Neurol. Psychiat. (Chicago)*, 1944, **52**, 296–316.
171. Winocur, G., & Mills, J. A. Hippocampus and septum in response inhibition. *J. comp. physiol. Psychol.*, 1969, **67**, 352–357.
172. Wolf, S., & Wolff, H. G. *Human gastric function.* New York: Oxford Univ. Press, 1943.
173. Woodworth, R. S., & Schlosberg, H. *Experimental psychology.* New York: Henry Holt, 1954.
174. Woodworth, R. S., & Sherrington, C. S. A pseudoaffective reflex and its spinal path. *J. Physiol. (London)*, 1904, **31**, 234–243.
175. Zucker, I. Effect of lesions of the septal-limbic area on the behavior of cats. *J. comp. physiol. Psychol.*, 1965, **60**, 344–352.
176. Zucker, I., & McCleary, R. A. Perseveration in septal cats. *Psychonom. Sci.*, 1964, **1**, 387–388.

Chapter 13

REWARD AND PUNISHMENT

Introduction

The Anatomy of Reward and Punishment

Anomalous Effects of Brain Stimulation

Relationship to Primary Drives

Conclusions and Review

INTRODUCTION

Man as well as members of other species behave in all circumstances so as to maximize positive experiences or "pleasure" and to minimize pain or other "unpleasant" stimulation. This hedonistic principle is at the heart of modern psychological theories of behavior even though subjective terms such as pleasure are typically avoided. Modern theories generally assume that the behavior of organisms is directed toward minimizing stimulation[38] or toward maintaining the total level of sensory input within some "normal" limits.[21] These theories attempt to provide objective definitions for the condition that we call "pleasure" or "displeasure," but they do not deny that behavior is controlled by an anticipation of reward or the escape or avoidance of punishment. The concept of "reinforcement" is critical not only to theories of motivation that attempt to explain why the organism behaves at all but also, as we shall see later, to theories of learning that attempt to account for the acquisition of particular behaviors.

In spite of the importance of the concept of "reward" we knew only little about the physiological mechanisms that mediate the influence of positive and negative reinforcement until 1954, when Olds and Milner[57] observed, quite accidentally, that some rats seemed to enjoy electrical stimulation of certain parts of the brain. The animals learned their way through mazes and could be taught to press levers to obtain such stimulation. At about the same time, Neal Miller and his associates[41] discovered that hypothalamic stimulation, which elicited apparently emotional responses such as flight or attack behavior, seemed to be aversive. Rats as well as cats learned to press a lever to terminate such stimulation and developed conditioned emotional reactions to stimuli that were frequently associated with the brain stimulation.

These observations indicated that electrical stimulation of certain areas of the brain could serve as positive as well as negative reinforcement and suggested that anatomically distinct substrates of reward and punishment might be demonstrable. The exciting implications of this possibility have been studied by many investigators and we now have a large and not always entirely consistent literature on the subject. Aside from the anatomical distribution of the pathways that mediate the rewarding or punishing effects of brain stimulation, much of the experimental interest has been devoted to determining whether the stimulation-induced reward or punishment effects are independent of the elicitation or reduction of specific drive states and to what extent they are comparable to conventional reinforcement. Before we explore these issues, it may be worthwhile to describe the basic experimental situation.

Small wire electrodes that are insulated except at the tip are implanted into the brain. After some days of recuperation, these electrodes are connected to a source of electric current. The experimenter first delivers brief (usually 0.1 to 0.5 sec.) bursts of alternating current to the brain to determine the threshold for an overt reaction to the stimulation (such as orienting responses and head-turning). He then repeats the stimulation to ascertain whether it has positive or negative reward properties. If the stimulation produces positive effects, the animals become active, explore their environment, and rapidly learn to initiate bursts of stimulation when a manipulandum such as a lever or wheel is provided. If the stimulation effect is negative, the animals learn to stay away from a manipulandum which produces it or to operate a lever or wheel to terminate or avoid it. These effects have been observed in man,[74] as well as many infrahuman species, and there is little reason to doubt the universality of the phenomenon.

Once established, the reinforcing properties of the brain stimulation are remarkably stable (see Figure 13-1). In one experiment, rats worked on a lever that provided stimulation rewards almost without pause for 20 days, averaging 29.2 responses per minute.[93] In another, monkeys worked until completely exhausted before settling down to a daily schedule of 16 hours of work for brain-stimulation rewards alternating with 8 hours of sleep.[31] When animals are tested only infrequently, no change in the reward effect is seen even when the experiments are continued for many months.[77, 28]

An increase in the intensity of the stimulating current does not always enhance its positive or negative reinforcing properties. This is true because the effect of an electric current on a given neuron remains constant once the cell's threshold has been exceeded. More intense stimulation cannot increase the response of a previously activated cell. It does excite previously inactive cells that are farther from the electrode. If these cells are part of the reward mechanism, this enhances the effect of the stimulation. If these cells are motivationally neutral, no change in the reward effect occurs. The reward effect may indeed be reduced or abolished if these cells are part of the pathways that mediate punishment.[53] In the lateral hypothalamus, the response to threshold intensities of stimulation is typically positive and an increase in current intensity often increases its desirability. At electrode sites in the medial hypothalamus, on the other hand, the initial response to threshold intensities is often negative or only mildly positive. An increase in current intensity often produces a fall in response rate, indicating that the positive reward properties of the stimulation have been decreased. At some stimulation sites, a small increase in intensity may decrease responding, indicating a current spread to elements of the punishment system, but further increases in stimulation intensity may once again facilitate responding, suggesting that the reward and punishment systems are, at some points, very

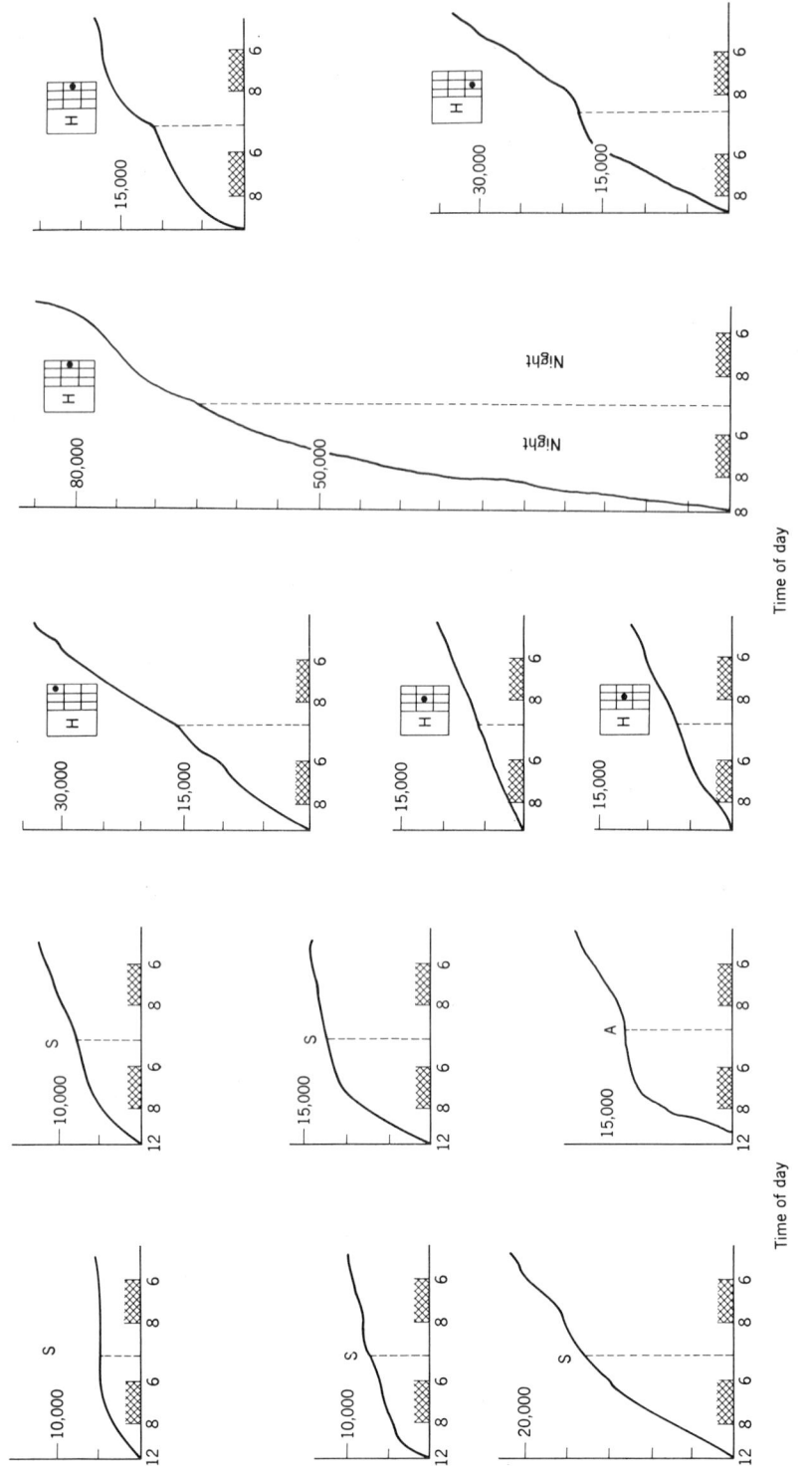

FIG. 13–1. Self-stimulation response rates of animals with electrodes implanted in the forebrain and hypothalamic areas in a continuous 48-hr test period. S, septal region; A, amygdala; H, hypothalamus. The boxes marked H indicate the electrode positions in the hypothalamus as medial to lateral (left to right) and anterior posterior (top to bottom). The dotted lines represent the end of the first 24-hr period. The shaded areas on the abscissa represent the period of darkness from 8 p.m. to 6 a.m. The animals with hypothalamic electrodes produced self-stimulation rates in the same order of magnitude on the second day as on the first, which was not true of most of the animals with electrodes in the forebrain.

(From J. Olds. Self-stimulation of the brain. *Science*, **127**, 14 February 1958, 315–324.)

closely intertwined.[88] In addition to stimulus intensity, the magnitude of the reward or punishment effect is determined by the shape, frequency, and duration of the electric pulses[91, 27] as well as the interpulse interval.[17] Microinjections of very small quantities (3 mμl) of chemicals which chelate calcium into various brain structures also have been shown to be rewarding (i.e., animals press a lever repeatedly to obtain such injections).[100]

Summary and Review Questions

Behavior is controlled by its consequences. We act in all circumstances in order to gain maximum pleasure and to minimize pain or punishment. Just what constitutes or defines pleasure, reward, or punishment is the subject of much debate, but there is no question that our brain is constructed in such a fashion that responses which are followed by positive consequences are strengthened whereas others which produce negative consequences disappear. How this might be achieved was largely a mystery until 1954 when the work of Olds and Milner and of Neal Miller suggested that there might be specific pathways in the brain for reward and punishment and that these pathways could be selectively activated by electrical stimulation of discrete areas of the brain.

Since then we have learned that this seems to be true for all species and that the magnitude of the reward or punishment is determined not only by the location of the stimulation but also, not always monotonically, by its intensity, duration, and spatiotemporal pattern.

1. Discuss the concept of "reward magnitude" in relation to the intensity or duration of brain stimulation.
2. What other factors influence the reward properties of brain stimulation?

THE ANATOMY OF REWARD AND PUNISHMENT

The Reward System

Following the initial demonstration of the reinforcing properties of brain stimulation, Olds[54, 60] as well as others have mapped the distribution of positive and negative reward sites and attempted to relate the motivational effects to specific neural pathways. A large part of the brain, notably most of the neocortex of the cerebral hemispheres and much of the thalamus, appears to be motivationally neutral.[55] Positive reward effects can be obtained from stimulation sites in the ventral tegmentum of the midbrain and in much of the hypothalamus and the limbic system as we have previously defined that elusive term (including such subcortical regions as the amygdala and septal area and all of the primitive cortex of the hippocampus, cingulate gyrus and basal temporal lobe as well as some neocortex of the frontal and temporal lobes). By far, the highest response rates are obtained from electrodes in the posterior and lateral hypothalamus, which contain the densest concentration of fibers from the medial forebrain bundle (MFB) and from some midbrain regions that are the origin or termination of the MFB fibers. Since this massive fiber bundle interconnects the "limbic midbrain"[48] with the hypothalamus, preoptic region, and the remainder of the limbic system, some investigators have suggested that some or even all of the reward effect of brain stimulation might be related to the MFB (see Figure 13-2). There is some experimental support for this hypothesis. Lesions in the MFB decrease the rate of responding for brain stimulation rewards.[46] The effect is greater for stimulation sites anterior to the site of the lesion,[58] suggesting that the reward-related impulses travel downward in the MFB. An additional role of ascending MFB fibers, which are thought to be adrenergic, is suggested by the observation that rewarding brain stimulation causes the release of the adrenergic neurohumor norepinephrine in the hypothalamus and amygdala whereas neutral stimulation, even of the MFB itself, does not.[85]

Central adrenergic mechanisms have been further implicated in the reward phenomenon by the observation that intraventricular injections of a drug that selectively destroys aminergic nerve terminals inhibit lever pressing for brain stimulation rewards[86] (see

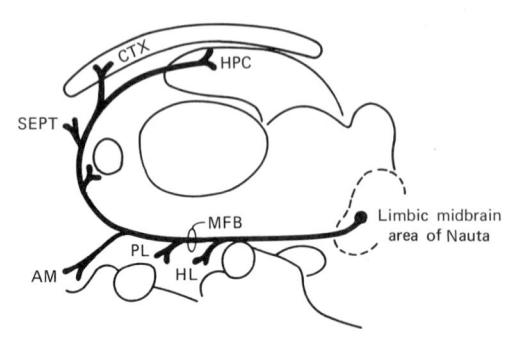

FIG. 13–2. Ascending adrenergic pathway of reward mechanism of self-stimulation system. Norepinephrine-containing neurons originating in Nauta's limbic midbrain area ascend in the medial forebrain bundle (MFB) and terminate in hypothalamus (HL), preoptic area (PL), amygdala (AM), septum (SEPT), hippocampus (HPC), and neocortex (CTX).

(From L. Stein. Psychopharmacological substrates of mental depression. In *Antidepressant drugs*. S. Garattini & M. N. G. Dukes, Eds. Amsterdam: Excerpta Medica Foundation, 1967. International Congress Series #122. Copyright 1966 Excerpta Medica Foundation.)

Figure 13–3). Moreover, systemic injections of drugs that release norepinephrine in the brain enhance the reinforcing property of brain stimulation, and drugs that block adrenergic transmission inhibit it[81, 67] (see Figure 13–4). However, these effects are not seen at all reward sites,[66] suggesting that reward may not be a purely adrenergic phenomenon.

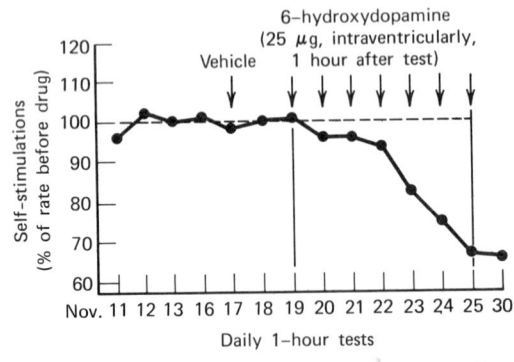

FIG. 13–3. Suppression of self-stimulation by repeated doses of 6-hydroxydopamine (averaged data of three rats).

(From L. Stein & C. D. Wise. Possible etiology of schizophrenia: progressive damage to the noradrenergic reward system by 6-hydroxydopamine. *Science*, **171**, 12 March 1971, 1032–1036. Copyright 1971 by the American Association for the Advancement of Science.)

That the anatomical substrate of the reward system may also involve pathways outside the MFB is suggested by a number of studies[94, 32] that have shown that even large MFB lesions produce little or no effect on the rewarding properties of stimulation at some electrode sites. Since lesions in the septal area,[95] amygdala,[96] hippocampal formation,[98] or preoptic area[59] also do not inhibit brain stimulation-rewarded behavior, it seems likely that the central pathways that mediate positive reward may be diffuse and characterized by redundancy and plasticity.[92, 4]

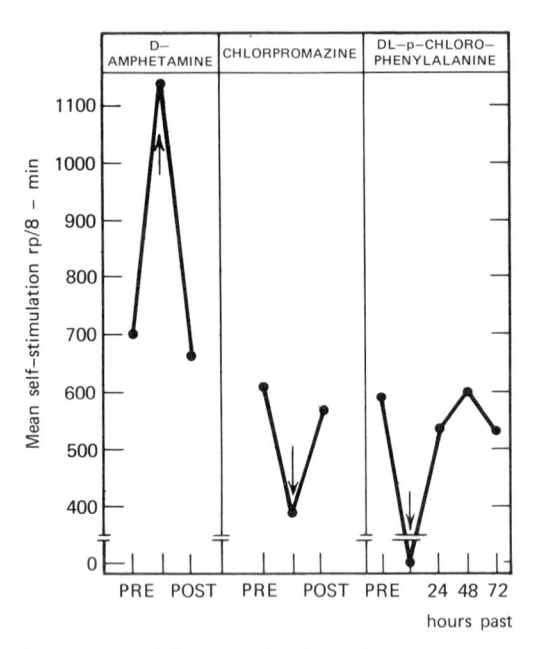

FIG. 13–4. Mean self-stimulation responses per 8 min on the days before, during, and after systemic administration of various drugs.

(From D. L. Margules. Noradrenergic rather than serotonergic basis of reward in the dorsal tegmentum. *J. comp. physiol. Psychol.*, **67**, 1969, 32–35. Copyright 1969 by the American Psychological Association, and reproduced by permission.)

The Punishment System

The anatomical substrate of negative reinforcement, or punishment, is even less well defined at the moment. Electrical stimulation of diffusely scattered points in the amygdala, hippocampus, thalamus, lateral and medial hypothalamus, dorsal tegmentum, and periventricular grey of the midbrain have been shown to be aversive,[61, 99] the aversive points often being very closely adjacent to positive sites. The distribution of the aversive sites does not correspond to the location of the classical pain pathways, suggesting that the negative effects of the stimulation may be independent of pain itself.

The punishment pathway does overlap extensively with the distribution of sites from which emotional reactions such as flight, defense, or attack reactions can be evoked,[22] and some specific correlations between the intensity of the aversive reaction and the nature of the emotional response have been described. Stimulation of hypothalamic and midbrain sites that elicit "alarm" reactions in cats is sufficiently aversive to serve as the unconditioned stimulus in a variety of situations. Cats learn to turn a wheel to avoid or escape such stimulation and acquire a conditioned emotional reaction (CER) which itself motivates escape responses to the apparatus in which they have been repeatedly stimulated. The animals also rapidly acquire a passive avoidance reaction when stimulated only while feeding in a particular place. On the other hand, stimulation of sites in the posterior hypothalamus that elicit "flight" reactions motivates the acquisition of escape responses, but the animals do not learn active or passive avoidance reactions or a conditioned emotional reaction.[39,40]

The reason for this becomes clear when the animals are permitted to initiate as well as terminate the brain stimulation. Cats with electrodes at "alarm" points learn promptly to terminate the stimulation and carefully avoid performing a second response that initiates it. Animals with electrodes at "flight" points, on the other hand, learn to press one lever to initiate such stimulation and another to terminate it.[70,71] After some training, these animals shuttle back and forth between the two manipulanda, alternately turning the stimulation on and off,[3] suggesting that the stimulation may have an initial positive component that is superceded by concurrent or delayed negative effects.

It has been suggested[82] that the aversive effects of brain stimulation may be related to the cholinergic periventricular fiber system (PVS) that parallels the MFB along much of its route. The PVS fibers ascend from the central grey of the midbrain to the medial hypothalamus and thalamus. Interconnecting fibers descend from the amygdala and the frontal cortex.[49] The distribution field to the PVS includes much of the area in which aversive stimulation sites have been found, and its close relationship with the MFB[47,49] could provide essential pathways for an interaction between the positive and negative reward systems (see Figure 13–5).

Some observations suggest that cholinergic components of the medial hypothalamus[36] as well as some adrenergic components of the amygdaloid complex[33] may participate in the organism's response to punishment. There is as yet no direct evidence that these effects or the aversive effects of brain stimulation are directly related to the periventricular fiber system.

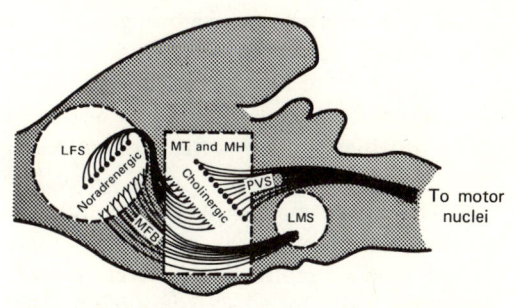

FIG. 13–5. Diagram representing hypothetical relationships between reward and punishment mechanisms inferred from chemical stimulation experiments of Margules and Stein (1967), Margules (1968), and Stein et al. (1968). A rewarding stimulus releases behavior from periventricular system (PVS) suppression by the following sequence of events: (1) Activation of medial forebrain bundle (MFB) by stimuli previously associated with reward (or the avoidance of punishment) causes release of norepinephrine into amygdala and other forebrain suppressor areas (LFS). (2) Inhibitory action of norepinephrine suppresses activity of the LFS, thus reducing its cholinergically mediated excitation of medial thalamus and hypothalamus (MT & MH). (3) Decreased cholinergic transmission at synapses in MT and MH lessens the activity in the periventricular system, thereby reducing its inhibitory influence on motor nuclei of the brain stem.

(From L. Stein. Chemistry of purposive behavior. In *Reinforcement and behavior*. J. T. Tapp, Ed. Academic Press, 1969.)

Summary and Review Questions

Rewarding effects of brain stimulation can be obtained from the ventral tegmentum of the midbrain, the posterior and lateral hypothalamus, the preoptic area, the septal region, hippocampus, cingulate gyrus, amygdala, some limbic cortex of the temporal lobe, and some frontal neocortex. It has been suggested that the medial forebrain bundle, which interconnects many of these areas, may mediate the stimulation-induced reward effects and that the self-stimulation phenomenon may depend on central adrenergic pathways. The reward properties of stimulation at some sites are, however, unaffected by MFB lesions or by a pharmacological blockade of central adrenergic functions, suggesting that other pathways may contribute to the reward effect.

Negative reinforcement or punishment has been obtained from the amygdala, hippocampus, thalamus, medial hypothalamus, dorsal tegmentum, and central grey of the midbrain. It has been suggested that the aversive effects of brain stimulation may be predominantly cholinergic and may be related to the distribution field of the periventricular fiber system (PVS), which runs parallel to the MFB along much of its course and connects to it at many points.

The aversive motivational effects are obtained from all sites where stimulation elicits such emotional behavior as flight, defense, or attack responses, and there is some evidence to suggest that the aversiveness of the stimulation may correlate with the nature of the emotion that is elicited. Stimulation of "alarm" points in the hypothalamus, for instance, is sufficiently aversive to motivate active as well as passive avoidance, as well as conditioned emotional responses. Stimulation of closely adjacent "flight" points, on the other hand, appears to have a positive component. Animals learn to escape from such stimulation but do not avoid it actively or passively and may even work to turn it on when another response is available to terminate it.

1. Describe the pathway that seems to be related to the rewarding effects of brain stimulation.

2. What evidence suggests that central adrenergic mechanisms may be especially relevant to self-stimulation behavior?

3. Describe the pathway that seems to be related to the punishing or aversive effects of brain stimulation.

4. What evidence suggests that the positive and negative reinforcement pathways may sometimes be concurrently activated?

ANOMALOUS EFFECTS OF BRAIN STIMULATION

Many hundreds of experiments have been designed to determine whether the effects of rewarding brain stimulation are, in all respects, identical to those of conventional reinforcers. The first description of the stimulation-reward effect evoked the criticism that the stimulation might simply produce perseverative motor responses devoid of any motivational or "intentional" components and that the nature of the test situation assured the recurrence of the response that the experimenter defined as "instrumental". We now know that this simplistic explanation cannot be true. Animals have been trained to run mazes,[51] learn brightness discriminations,[29] alternate between two manipulanda to regulate the intensity of stimulation[84] or to control the duration of the stimulation,[3] and perform appropriately on reinforcement schedules that do not reward simple repetitive responding.[65, 89]

There is also no question about the magnitude of the stimulation reward. The earlier investigations[51] demonstrated that animals learned and performed instrumental responses as well or better for brain-stimulation rewards than for food rewards when 24 hours food deprived. Recent studies have shown that animals, given a choice to work for food[78] or water[19] rewards on one lever and for brain-stimulation rewards on another, prefer to work for brain stimulation even when 24- or 48-hours deprived. Man[2] as well as rats[73] disregard palatable foods when given an opportunity to work for brain-stimulation rewards even when quite hungry.

Nonetheless, the rewarding effects of brain stimulation are not, in all instances, identical to those of conventional reinforcers. Rats, cats, and monkeys learn to work for brain-stimulation rewards that are presented on various aperiodic reinforcement schedules and emit response patterns that are characteristic for each particular schedule.[77,6] However, some animals work less hard for brain stimulation when the reward density is decreased and do not work at all on poor reward schedules that maintain high levels of responding for food or water rewards.[11] However, this is not characteristic of all reward sites. Some animals work on fixed-ratio schedules that reinforce only every 150th response[11] or on variable-interval schedules that reinforce only responses which occur 2 minutes on the average after the last reinforcement.[8] The exceptions may nonetheless be significant because they contradict the many observations which suggest that brain-stimulation rewards appear to be more desirable than conventional reinforcers.

It is also apparently difficult and in some instances impossible to transfer the reinforcing properties of brain stimulation to previously neutral stimuli in a conditioning experiment. Some investigators[79] have reported that secondary reinforcing properties can be acquired in a classical conditioning paradigm by stimuli that are frequently associated with brain stimulation. However, others[75,42] have been unable to replicate this finding at other stimulation sites.

Less difficult to explain on the basis of the apparent superiority of brain-stimulation rewards are the results of studies[5,7] which show that some animals do not acquire or display a previously acquired conditioned emotional reaction (CER) while working for brain-stimulation rewards. In these experiments, rats were trained to lever press for water or brain-stimulation rewards. When a stable performance level was reached, a CS was introduced that signaled brief but painful grid shock. The animals showed the classic suppression of lever pressing (the CER) when working for water rewards but not when working for brain stimulation. Even when the reward contingencies were alternated repeatedly, the rats continued to suppress responding while working for water but not while working for brain stimulation[5] (see Figure 13–6). This apparent inability or unwillingness to display conditioned emotional reactions while working for brain stimulation again does not characterize all animals, and the intensity of the stimulation may in some instances determine whether the CER occurs.[6]

The unwillingness of animals to suppress responding during a signal for unavoidable shock may be caused by their unwillingness to miss out on brain-stimulation rewards. Their behavior on reinforcement schedules that reward slow response rates, although less adaptive, may be similarly explained. Normal monkeys learn quite rapidly to maximize rewards on a schedule that reinforces only responses that are separated by 20 seconds or more (a DRL or "differential reward of low rates of responding" schedule). When shifted to brain-stimulation rewards after learning to work successfully on such a

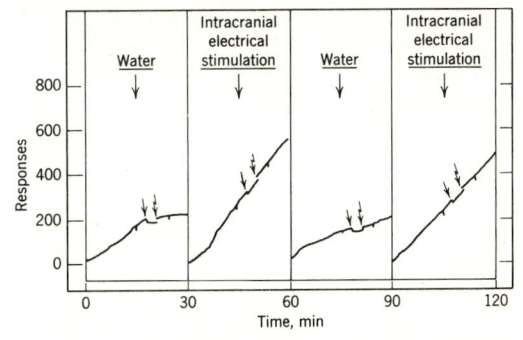

FIG. 13–6. Cumulative response curves showing the differential effect of the conditioned-anxiety procedure during a 2-hr experimental session with alternate 30-min periods of a variable-interval (mean of 16 sec) water and intracranial electrical stimulation reward. The oblique unbroken arrows indicate the onset of the conditioned auditory stimulus; the oblique broken arrows indicate the termination of the CS contiguously with the brief unconditioned grid shock stimulus to the feet during each of the alternate 30-min periods.

(From J. V. Brady. A comparative approach to the experimental analysis of emotional behavior. In *Experimental psychopathology*. P. H. Hoch & J. Zubin, Eds. Grune & Stratton, 1957. Reproduced by permission.)

schedule for food rewards, the animals appear unable or unwilling to inhibit responding and consequently decrease their chance of earning rewards.[6] Because it takes a long time to stabilize behavior on such a reward schedule, this experiment has not been repeated sufficiently often to be sure whether this unwillingness to withhold responses is indeed characteristic of all brain-stimulation sites.

Some animals also behave quite abnormally in extinction situations when working for brain-stimulation rewards. Stimulation-rewarded animals extinguish rapidly[75] even when the manipulandum is withdrawn, so that nonrewarded responses are prevented.[26] This tendency to extinguish may also be responsible for the observation that some animals require a "priming" stimulation (i.e., a free reward) at the beginning of each test session,[28] and that massed practice and short intertrial intervals often produce more superior learning and performance than the spaced practice and longer intertrial intervals, which work much better when conventional reinforcers are used.[76]

These observations gave rise to the notion[15,16] that rewarding brain stimulation might not only reinforce the response that produces it, but may also provide the rapidly decaying motivation to obtain more of the same. This speculation has aroused a good deal of interest and controversy. Many experimenters have shown that the anomalous reactions to brain-stimulation rewards can be avoided by special training procedures[64,89] or modifications in the delivery procedure of the conventional and brain-stimulation rewards,[20] suggesting that the differences between the effects of brain stimulation and conventional rewards might be caused by procedural matters. Moreover, not all animals show the anomalous effects of brain-stimulation rewards,[30,28] and a series of experiments[28] has suggested an explanation that does not require the assumption of a concurrent activation of drive and reward mechanisms. In these experiments it was shown that rats with electrodes entirely within the medial forebrain bundle did not show anomalous effects in several test situations, whereas rats with electrodes in surrounding tissues did. A comparison of the behavior of the two groups of animals suggested further that the animals that showed the anomalous reward effects might be in an approach-avoidance conflict. This interpretation was supported by the demonstration that painful tailshock, given every time an animal pressed a lever for rewarding brain stimulation, produced anomalous reactions in animals with MFB electrodes (see Figure 13–7).

This suggests that electrical brain stimulation may not always produce purely rewarding effects and that the apparently anomalous effects of some stimulation-rewards may be because of the resultant approach-avoidance conflict. This hypothesis accounts for many of the observed differences between conventional and brain-stimulation rewards and explains why some observers have been more impressed by the differences than others. It is nonetheless possible that brain stimulation may, in some instances, produce sensory or motor effects that could interact in a different fashion with the reward properties of the stimulation and produce unpredictable behavioral reactions.

Trowill and associates[90] have proposed a quite different explanation for the anomalous

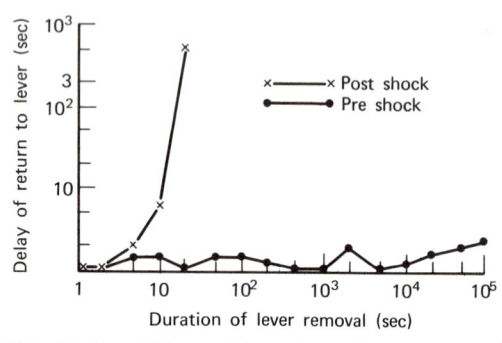

FIG. 13–7. Effect of duration of lever removal on time taken to resume responding by nonprimers before and after 10 daily sessions in which tailshock was administered concurrently with brain stimulation. (Curves represent group means.)

(From E. Kent & S. P. Grossman. Evidence for a conflict interpretation of anomalous effects of rewarding brain stimulation. *J. comp. physiol. Psychol.*, **69**, 1969, 381–390. Copyright 1969 by the American Psychological Association, and reproduced by permission.)

behavior that some animals display when working for brain-stimulation rewards. It was observed[62, 63] that fully sated rats work quite hard for vary palatable rewards such as a large shot of chocolate milk and that these animals extinguish more rapidly and show less spontaneous recovery than food-deprived animals. The nondeprived rats also showed the peculiar extinction-without-responding effect previously seen only in animals working for brain-stimulation rewards and could be induced to work once again by the delivery of a free "priming" reward. These observations suggest that in some instances rats may work for brain-stimulation rewards not because they are "driven" to do so, but merely because the incentive value of the reward is very large. This interesting interpretation does not account for the brain-stimulation phenomenon itself since many animals do not display the anomalous behavior apparently characteristic of "nondriven" animals and because there appears to be an intimate relationship between specific drives and the rewarding properties of brain stimulation in many instances (see below). It is possible that two functionally quite distinct neural systems may exist which are responsible for the rewarding effects of brain stimulation. Routtenberg,[72] for instance, has suggested that a "motivational" system may originate in the dorsal tegmentum of the midbrain which sustains low to moderate rates of self-stimulation and that an independent "incentive" system may originate in the ventral tegmentum which is responsible for the very high rates of self-stimulation (and perhaps the anomalous behaviors) which are occasionally seen.

Summary and Review Questions

Brain stimulation has been shown to be pleasurable in man as well as reinforcing in various test situations in many infrahuman species. It has been reported that some animals rewarded with brain stimulation (1) do not work well on "poor" reinforcement schedules; (2) do not inhibit responses on DRL reward schedules that punish high response rates; (3) perform better when trials are massed and intertrial intervals are very short; and (4) extinguish rapidly even when the rewarded response is prevented. These observations have given rise to the hypothesis that brain stimulation may not only reinforce the response that produces it, but also motivate the following response, both effects decaying rapidly.

However, it has recently been shown that anomalous reactions are not typical of all stimulation sites. A closer look at the behavior of the animals that do show the unusual responses to stimulation reward suggests further that the animals may not experience "pure" reward effects, but find themselves in an approach-avoidance conflict. If we assume that the positive effects of the stimulation have a somewhat shorter temporal as well as spatial decay function than its negative consequences, a conflict interpretation accounts nicely for all of the anomalous reactions. It has recently been shown that nondeprived rats working for very palatable conventional reinforcers show many of the anomalous behaviors seen in some rats working for brain stimulation. This suggests that animals may work for brain stimulation in some instances in the absence of relevant drive stimulation merely because of the very high incentive value of the reward.

1. List as many of the "anomalous" effects of rewarding brain stimulation as you can.

2. Explain in some detail how the "conflict" hypothesis accounts for these effects.

3. Are there some apparently anomalous effects that are not readily explained by the conflict hypothesis? What other explanations can you give?

RELATIONSHIP TO PRIMARY DRIVES

Granted that animals learn and perform instrumental responses to stimulate some areas of the brain or to avoid stimulation of other areas—why do they do it? Having the power to stimulate or avoid stimulation of some part of the brain is not something Mother Nature normally provides, and we cannot explain "self-stimulation" behavior on the basis of innate drives. Or can we? Is it possible that activation of the reward system reduces or satisfies normally occurring drives such as hunger or thirst and perhaps does so much more promptly and completely than consummatory behavior? Might a thirsty animal learn to self-stimulate because the stimulation produces instant and complete relief of thirst? Does he continue to stimulate, without any sign of satiation, because the relief is temporary and thirst continues to increase in spite of the stimulation? Should we assume that this relationship is unique or could it be that the neural pathways that mediate the effects of reward are connected to all drive-related mechanisms in the brain such that excitation of the reward system might reduce or satisfy any drive that happens to be activated at the moment? Many investigators have asked these and related questions.

At a given electrode site, the rate of self-stimulation is often directly and uniquely related to the intensity of a particular drive state. The rewarding properties of stimulation of the lateral hypothalamus, for instance, vary directly as a function of food deprivation.[52, 18] Moreover, stimulation of the ventromedial hypothalamic "satiety center" or excessive food intake inhibits self-stimulation in the lateral hypothalamus as well as eating. Ventromedial lesions produce opposite facilitatory effects on self-stimulation as well as eating.[24, 25] Marked changes in the rate of lever pressing for lateral hypothalamic stimulation have also been seen following the injection of hormones such as glucagon or insulin, which modify food intake,[1] and after intragastric injections of glucose and saline.[24] The reinforcing properties of stimulation at some medial and posterior hypothalamic sites, on the other hand, are reduced or abolished by castration and reinstated by hormone treatments.[52] The onset of estrus increases the rate of self-stimulation at these

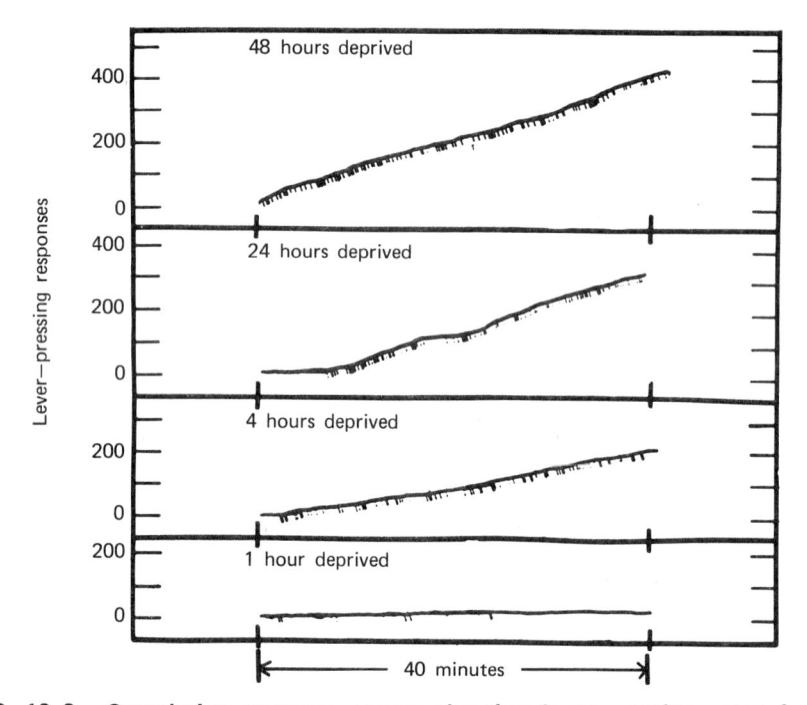

FIG. 13–8. Cumulative response curves showing lever-pressing rates for a variable-interval (mean of 16 sec) intracranial electrical stimulation reward during four separate 40-min experimental sessions following 1, 4, 24, and 48 hrs of deprivation, respectively. Oblique "pips" indicate reinforcements.

(From J. V. Brady, J. J. Boren, D. G. Conrad, & M. Sidman. The effect of food and water deprivation upon intracranial self-stimulation. *J. comp. physiol. Psychol.*, **50**, 1957, 134–137. Copyright 1957 by the American Psychological Association, and reproduced by permission.)

sites.[68] Stimulation at these electrode sites elicits copulatory behavior in male rats as well as instrumental responses that are rewarded by access to a receptive female.[12] At some electrode sites, the rewarding properties of stimulation vary as a function of water deprivation[9, 7] (see Figure 13–8). At some of these sites, the rewarding stimulation elicits drinking and is more rewarding when water is present.[44, 37] The rate of self-stimulation in the anterior hypothalamic thermoregulatory region similarly varies as a function of environmental temperature.[10]

These results leave no doubt that the rewarding properties of stimulation at many sites vary as a function of specific drive states and this relationship appears, in all instances, to be a unique one. When the rate of self-stimulation at a given site varies as a function of food deprivation, it does not, typically, react to castration or water deprivation or vice versa.[52, 97] What we unfortunately do not yet know is whether the relationship between the rewarding effects of brain stimulation and specific drive states describes a causal interaction that is essential to all self-stimulation behavior. A number of investigators have failed to observe a consistent relationship between stimulation at some sites and food deprivation,[69] estrus,[23] or castration.[50] It is possible that the electrodes just were not in the part of the brain that shows a correlation with the drive state that was investigated in each of these studies, but there is one recent report that seems to have excluded this possibility.[44]

In the many instances where a clear relationship between the rewarding properties of brain stimulation and a specific drive state exists, the nature of that relationship has turned out to be puzzling. A priori, one expects that the stimulation would be rewarding because it reduces or satisfies the related drive state. However, several studies have shown that the converse appears to be true. Rewarding lateral or posterior hypothalamic stimulation *elicits* eating,[35, 13] drinking,[45] or copulation,[12] leaving one with the apparent paradox that the elicitation of a drive rather than its reduction seems to be reinforcing (see Figure 13–9).

How can we account for this observation? Several explanations have been suggested. Perhaps the simplest is the "it feels so good when you stop" hypothesis, which suggests that the stimulation per se has nothing to do with reward or reinforcement but simply elicits a very high drive level. The animal then experiences an abnormally rapid and large drive reduction when the stimulation stops and this, itself, might be the rewarding event. Stimulating an already activated drive mechanism might be easier than arousing a dormant one, thus explaining the relationship between self-stimulation and natural drive states. Although logically plausible, particularly because the brain-stimulation rewards typically consist of very short bursts of stimulation, this explanation has difficulties explaining why some animals select fairly long trains of stimulation when given an opportunity to do so.[27]

Another interpretation[56] suggests that it may be unpleasant to be completely sated and that the elicitation of some appetite or sexual arousal might indeed be rewarding, particularly when a relevant reward is readily

FIG. 13–9. Copulation during brain stimulation. Electrical stimulation in a posterior hypothalamic self-stimulation site elicits immediate sexual behavior which persists even after ejaculation. Each ON period lasts 3 minutes.

(From A. R. Caggiula & B. G. Hoebel. "Copulation reward site" in the posterior hypothalamus. *Science*, **153**, 9 September 1966, 1284–1285. Copyright 1966 by the American Association for the Advancement of Science.)

accessible. Such an explanation is supported by the observation that the rate of self-stimulation does indeed increase when an appropriate conventional reward is available,[37] but it is difficult to see why a stimulation-induced increase in hunger should be more rewarding in an animal that is already starving.

If the reward properties of brain stimulation are, in fact, determined entirely by specific drives, as so much of the literature suggests, another hypothesis becomes plausible. Self-stimulation then occurs by definition only when a drive mechanism is active (although perhaps not sufficiently so as to induce consummatory behaviors). Stimulation of the related reward mechanism may then produce drive-reduction and the animal continues to stimulate in order to experience this drive reduction. When a conventional reinforcer is also available, the rewarding experience of the drive reduction may draw the animal's attention to it and elicit consummatory behavior. This hypothesis accounts for much of the research literature but has some problems explaining why apparently sated animals can be induced by brain stimulation to eat[87] or drink[43] quantities that are clearly in excess of any required to produce complete satiation.

On the basis of experimental observations which suggest that some brain-stimulation rewards may not, in all instances, act like normal reinforcers, Deutsch[15,16] has suggested that rewarding brain stimulation may not only reinforce the response that produced it but also provide the drive for the next response. Assuming that the motivational effects of the stimulation persist somewhat longer than the reward effects, this hypothesis explains why a completely sated animal works for brain stimulation. Increased levels of natural drive would presumably summate with the stimulation effects and make a drive reduction more and more rewarding. The anomalous effects of brain stimulation that gave rise to this explanation do not seem to be characteristic of all rewarding stimulation and explanations other than drive-decay have been advanced to account for them when they do occur.[28] These explanations obviate the need for the somewhat awkward postulation of a direct relationship between the self-stimulation reward and drive induction and leave an option that accounts for the concurrently available literature in a simpler way.

The pathways that mediate reward may indeed be intimately related geographically to motivational mechanisms and it may consequently be all but impossible to stimulate reward neurons without concurrent activation of motivation-related cells. However, the drive state that is elicited by this stimulation may not motivate the next response, as Deutsch suggests. Rewarding brain stimulation may be reinforcing because it reduces the drive it elicits. This explanation differs from the "it feels so good when you stop" hypothesis in suggesting that the reward effect occurs instantaneously upon the onset of stimulation even though its magnitude may be enhanced by the effect of the stimulation on motivational pathways. It differs from Deutsch's explanation by suggesting that drive induction and drive reduction are instantaneous and that the motivation for self-stimulation is not related to the decaying effects of the previous stimulation. Animals self-stimulate because they learn that this provides an experience of a "natural" drive, which is instantaneously reduced. Electrical stimulation of reward sites may, in other words, at the same time activate reward pathways and provide the reason why that should be pleasurable. No wonder that human patients who apparently enjoy such stimulation immensely and prefer it to food or drink seem unable to explain the sensations that are elicited except in such vague terms as "It feels so very good."[14,2]

Summary and Review Questions

The reinforcing properties of brain stimulation have been shown in many instances to be directly related to the state of activation of specific drive states such as hunger, thirst, or sexual arousal. The interaction appears to be specific (i.e., at a given electrode site, the rewarding properties of the stimulation vary only as a function of one particular drive), but it is not yet clear whether it describes a causal relationship that is essential for all self-stimulation behavior. Nor is the nature of the interaction presently well understood. A priori, one would expect that rewarding brain stimulation should reduce the related drive state. Apparently, that is not what happens or at least not all that happens. Rewarding brain stimulation often seems to *elicit* primary drives such as hunger, thirst, or sexual arousal. Just why we should find it pleasurable to do so is the subject of many speculations.

Some believe that complete satiation is, indeed, aversive and that the elicitation of appetitive or sexual arousal might itself be rewarding. Others propose that it might be worthwhile eliciting a drive state because of the relief that one can produce at will by terminating the stimulation. A more complex explanation suggests that self-stimulation occurs only when a drive mechanism is activated and that the experience of stimulation induced drive reduction may draw attention to relevant natural rewards and thus elicit consummatory behavior.

It seems more plausible that the reward and motivation systems may be so intimately related anatomically that the stimulation of reward neurons always activates motivation-related mechanisms. There are currently two theories to account for the apparent paradox that results.

One suggests that the reward and motivation systems have different physiological properties such that stimulation reinforces the response that produced it and motivates the *next* response. This hypothesis accounts nicely for some of the anomalous effects of brain stimulation but cannot explain why the reinforcement should at times seem quite normal. I have suggested an alternative explanation which proposes that stimulation may *concurrently* activate both reward and motivational mechanisms and that the reward effect may be directly related to the reduction of the stimulation-induced drive state. The motivation for self-stimulation, according to this interpretation, is not related in a direct fashion to the immediately preceding stimulation but to the learned appreciation of the control over drive induction and its immediate reduction.

1. Describe the empirical evidence that suggests a relationship between the rewarding effects of brain stimulation and specific drives.

2. Describe two explanations of self-stimulation behavior which assume that the brain stimulation does not, per se, activate reward or pleasure mechanisms. What experimental observations do these theories find difficult to explain?

3. Describe two explanations of self-stimulation behavior which assume that the stimulation elicits both rewarding and motivational effects. What is the essential difference between the two?

4. Can you think of an experimental observation that is not explained by any of these hypotheses?

CONCLUSIONS AND REVIEW

The most basic question one can ask about behavior is: "Why does it occur?" In the preceding chapters, we have sought specific answers to this question such as "because we are hungry, thirsty, sexually aroused, or experience an emotional reaction such as fear or rage." In the current discussion, we have looked at the question of causality in a more general framework.

Man as well as members of other species seem to behave so as to maximize pleasure and minimize punishment regardless of whether the positive or negative affect is related to food or water deprivation, sexual arousal, or some emotional experience. Psychologists have traditionally tried to avoid such subjective terms as "pleasure" but devise theories, such as the pervasive "law of effect," that do, in fact, assume that behavior is controlled directly by its positive or negative consequences. Much of the resistance to the concept of positive or negative affect as determinants of behavior derives from the fact that it has been difficult to study these phenomena experimentally.

About 20 years ago, it was reported that electrical stimulation of certain areas of the brain appeared to produce rewarding or punishing effects that could be used to direct and maintain behavior. Much of the initial interest in these observations derived from the hope that brain stimulation might activate general reward or punishment mechanisms which might be the anatomical substrate of the hedonistic pleasure-pain principle. Extensive study of the effects of rewarding or aversive brain stimulation has shown that this is probably not true. Instead, it seems that rewarding brain stimulation concurrently elicits or intensifies specific drive states such as hunger and results in the experience of immediate reward or drive reduction. Punishing stimulation appears to elicit specific emotional reactions without providing simultaneous relief or drive reduction.

In some instances, the rewarding effects of stimulation appear anomalous. Stimulation rewards do not always maintain behavior on "poor" reward schedules or on schedules that punish high rates of responding. Stimulation rewarded behavior also often extinguishes rapidly and sometimes disappears even merely as a function of time. One explanation of these effects is that brain stimulation not only rewards the response that produces it but also provides the rapidly decaying motivation for the next response that produces it again. Another interpretation which takes into account the recent observation that the anomalous effects are not seen at all stimulation sites suggests instead that rewarding stimulation concurrently elicits and reduces a specific drive. The motivation for self-stimulation, according to this hypothesis, is provided by the experience of drive induction, accompanied by immediate drive reduction, and is thus a learned consequence of repeated stimulation. The motivation for self-stimulation does not depend directly on the immediately preceding stimulation and thus does not decay simply as a function of time. This hypothesis accounts for the occurrence of anomalous effects by postulating concurrent activation of the reward and punishment systems and a resultant approach-avoidance conflict. The anomalous schedule and extinction effects are thought to be caused by slightly different temporal and spatial decay functions for the positive and negative effects of the stimulation. The conflict hypothesis is supported by anatomical observations which suggest that the reward and punishment systems are very closely related at many levels of the brain and by experiments which have shown that animals often work hard to obtain stimulation of a particular part of the brain and equally hard to turn it off after a few seconds.

The anatomical substrate of the reward and punishment system is, as yet, only partially understood. Positive effects have been obtained from the ventral tegmentum, lateral and posterior hypothalamus, septal area, hippocampus, cingulate gyrus, amygdala, temporal lobe limbic cortex, and some of the neocortex of the frontal lobe. Transection of the medial forebrain bundle or an interference with central adrenergic transmission have been shown to inhibit self-stimulation behavior at many electrode sites. However, the rewarding effects of stimulation at other sites do not appear to be affected by these manipulations, suggesting that other pathways also contribute to the reward phenomenon.

Negative effects of stimulation can be obtained from many closely associated areas, notably the dorsal tegmentum, medial and anterior hypothalamus, medial thalamus, hippocampus, and amygdala. It has been suggested that the aversive effects may be related to an activation of cholinergic components of the periventricular fiber system (PVS), which parallels the course of the MFB along much of its route. The distribution of aversive effects does not follow the classical pain pathways, suggesting that direct sensory effects are not responsible for the punishment. Stimulation is always aversive when it elicits specific emotional reactions such as flight or defense reactions, and there is some evidence to suggest that the intensity of the punishment effect may correlate with the nature of the emotion which is produced.

Much remains to be learned about the effects of positive and negative reinforcement, but the work of the past two decades has gone a long way toward clarifying some of the issues for us. It now seems reasonable that each motivational mechanism may have a component that mediates the influence of reward, be it positive or negative, and that the nature of the reward influence, though not the mechanism for it, may be identical regardless of the drive state involved. The observations of brain-stimulation reward and punishment, far from forcing acceptance of a general pleasure principle, may end up providing important confirmation of the nature of drive reduction as an essential basis of reward.

Bibliography

1. Balagura, S., & Hoebel, B. G. Self-stimulation of the lateral hypothalamus modified by insulin and glucagon. *Physiol. & Behav.*, 1967, **2**, 337–340.
2. Bishop, M. P., Elder, S. T., & Heath, R. G. Intracranial self-stimulation in man. *Science*, 1963, **140**, 394–395.
3. Bower, G. H., & Miller, N. E. Rewarding and punishing effects from stimulating the same place in the rat's brain. *J. comp. physiol. Psychol.*, 1958, **51**, 669–678.
4. Boyd, E. S., & Gardner, L. C. Effect of some brain lesions on intracranial self-stimulation in the rat. *Amer. J. Physiol.*, 1967, **213**, 1044–1052.
5. Brady, J. V. A comparative approach to the experimental analysis of emotional behavior. In *Experimental psychopathology*. P. H. Hoch & J. Zubin, Eds. New York: Grune and Stratton, 1957.
6. Brady, J. V. Temporal and emotional factors related to electrical self-stimulation of the limbic system. In *The reticular formation of the brain*. H. H. Jasper, L. D. Proctor, R. S. Knighton, W. C. Noshay, & R. T. Costello, Eds. Boston: Little, Brown, 1958, pp. 689–703.
7. Brady, J. V. Motivational-emotional factors and intracranial self-stimulation. In *Electrical stimulation of the brain*. D. E. Sheer, Ed. Austin: Univ. of Texas Press, 1961, pp. 413–430.
8. Brady, J. V., & Conrad, D. G. Some effects of limbic system self-stimulation upon conditioned emotional behavior. *J. comp. physiol. Psychol.*, 1960, **53**, 128–137.
9. Brady, J. V., Boren, J. J., Conrad, D. G., & Sidman, M. The effect of food and water deprivation upon intracranial self-stimulation. *J. comp. physiol. Psychol.*, 1957, **50**, 134–137.
10. Briese, E., Echeverría, Yolanda, & de Quijada, Mary G. Ambient temperature and self-stimulation. *Acta physiol. lat.-amer.*, 1966, **16**, 209–215.
11. Brodie, D., Moreno, O. M., Malis, J. L., & Boren, J. J. Nonreversibility of the appetitive characteristics of intracranial stimulation. *Amer. J. Physiol.*, 1960, **199**, 707–709.
12. Caggiula, A. R., & Hoebel, B. G. "Copulation-reward site" in the posterior hypothalamus. *Science*, 9 September 1966, **153**, 1284–1285.
13. Coons, E. E., & Cruce, J. A. F. Lateral hypothalamus: Food and current intensity in maintaining self-stimulation of hunger. *Science*, 1968, **159**, 1117–1119.
14. Delgado, J. M. R., & Hamlin, H. Spontaneous and evoked electrical seizures in animals and in humans. In *Electrical studies on the unanesthetized brain*. E. R. Ramey & D. S. O'Doherty, Eds. New York: Paul Hoeber, 1960, pp. 133–152.
15. Deutsch, J. A. *The structural basis of behavior*. Chicago: Univ. of Chicago Press, 1960.
16. Deutsch, J. A. Learning and electrical self-stimulation of the brain. *J. theoret. Biol.*, 1963, **4**, 193–214.
17. Deutsch, J. A. Behavioral measurement of the neural refractory period and its application to intracranial self-stimulation. *J. comp. physiol. Psychol.*, 1964, **58**, 1–9.
18. Elder, S. T., Montgomery, N. P., & Rye, M. M. Effects of food deprivation and methamphetamine on fixed-ratio schedules of intra-cranial self-stimulation. *Psych. Rep.*, 1965, **16**, 1225–1233.
19. Falk, J. Septal stimulation as a reinforcer of and an alternative to consummatory behavior. *J. exp. Anal. Behav.*, 1961, **4**, 213–215.
20. Gibson, W. E., Reid, L. D., Sokai, M., & Porter, P. B. Intracranial reinforcement compared with sugar-water reinforcement. *Science*, 1965, **148**, 1357–1358.

21. Grossman, S. P. The physiological basis of specific and non-specific motivational processes. In *Nebraska symposium on motivation: 1969.* W. J. Arnold, Ed. Lincoln: Univ. of Nebraska Press, 1969, pp. 1–46.
22. Hess, W. R. *Das Zwischenhirn: Syndrome, Lokalisationen, Funktionen* (2nd ed.). Basel: Schwabe, 1954.
23. Hodos, W., & Valenstein, E. S. Motivational variables affecting the rate of behavior maintained by intracranial stimulation. *J. comp. physiol. Psychol.*, 1960, **53**, 502–508.
24. Hoebel, B. G. Inhibition and disinhibition of self-stimulation and feeding: Hypothalamic control and postingestional factors. *J. comp physiol. Psychol.*, 1968, **66**, 89–100.
25. Hoebel, B. G., & Teitelbaum, P. Hypothalamic control of feeding and self-stimulation. *Science*, 1962, **135**, 375–377.
26. Howarth, C. I., & Deutsch, J. A. Drive decay: The cause of fast "extinction" of habits learned for brain stimulation. *Science*, 1962, **137**, 35–36.
27. Keesey, R. E. Duration of stimulation and the reward properties of hypothalamic stimulation. *J. comp. physiol. Psychol.*, 1964, **58**, 201–207.
28. Kent, E., & Grossman, S. P. Evidence for a conflict interpretation of anomalous effects of rewarding brain stimulation. *J. comp. physiol. Psychol.*, 1969, **69**, 381–390.
29. Kling, J. W., & Matsumiya, Y. Relative reinforcement values of food and intracranial stimulation. *Science*, 1962, **135**, 668–670.
30. Kornblith, C., & Olds, J. T-maze learning with one trial per day using brain stimulation reinforcement. *J. comp. physiol. Psychol.*, 1968, **66**, 488–491.
31. Lilly, J. C. Learning motivated by subcortical stimulation: The start and stop patterns of behavior. In *The reticular formation of the brain.* H. H. Jasper, L. D. Proctor, R. S. Knighton, W. C. Noshay, & R. T. Costello, Eds. Boston: Little, Brown, 1958, pp. 705–721.
32. Lorens, S. A. Effect of lesions in the central nervous system on lateral hypothalamic self-stimulation in the rat. *J. comp. physiol. Psychol.*, 1966, **62**, 256–262.
33. Margules, D. L. Noradrenergic basis of inhibition between reward and punishment in amygdala. *J. comp. physiol. Psychol.*, 1968, **66**, 329–334.
34. Margules, D. L. Noradrenergic rather than serotonergic basis of reward in the dorsal tegmentum. *J. comp. physiol. Psychol.*, 1969, **67**, 32–35.
35. Margules, D. L., & Olds, J. Identical "feeding" and "rewarding" systems in the lateral hypothalamus of rats. *Science*, 1962, **135**, 374–375.
36. Margules, D. L., & Stein, L. Neuroleptics vs. tranquilizers: Evidence from animal behavior studies of mode and site of action. In *Neuro-psychopharmacology.* H. Brill, J. O. Cole, P. Deniker, H. Hippius, & P. B. Bradley, Eds. Amsterdam: Excerpta Medica Foundation, 1967, pp. 108–120.
37. Mendelson, J. Lateral hypothalamic stimulation in satiated rats: The rewarding effects of self-induced drinking. *Science*, 1967, **157**, 1077–1079.
38. Miller, N. E. Liberalization of basic S-R concepts: Extensions to conflict behavior, motivation, and social learning. In *Psychology: A study of a science. Vol. II.* S. Koch, Ed. New York: McGraw-Hill, 1959, pp. 196–292.
39. Miller, N. E. Implications for theories of reinforcement. In *Electrical stimulation of the brain.* D. E. Sheer, Ed. Austin: Univ. of Texas Press, 1961a, pp. 575–581.
40. Miller, N. E. Learning and performance motivated by direct stimulation of the brain. In *Electrical stimulation of the brain.* D. E. Sheer, Ed. Austin: Univ. of Texas Press, 1961b, pp. 387–396.
41. Miller, N. E., Roberts, W. W., & Delgado, J. M. R. *Learning motivated by electrical stimulation of the brain.* Motion picture shown at the experimental division of the American Psychological Association, Sept. 1953, and the International Congress of Psychology, Montreal, June, 1954.
42. Mogenson, G. J. An attempt to establish secondary reinforcement with rewarding brain self-stimulation. *Psychol. Rep.*, 1965, **16**, 163–167.
43. Mogenson, G. J. General and specific reinforcement systems for drinking behavior. *Ann. N. Y. Acad. Sci.*, 1969a, **157**, 779–797.
44. Mogenson, G. J. Water deprivation and excessive water intake during self-stimulation. *Physiol. & Behav.*, 1969b, **4**, 393–397.

45. Mogenson, G. J., & Stevenson, J. A. F. Drinking and self-stimulation with electrical stimulation of the lateral hypothalamus. *Physiol. & Behav.*, 1966, **1**, 151–154.
46. Morgane, P. J. Limbic-hypothalamic-midbrain interaction in thirst and thirst motivated behavior. In *Thirst*. M. J. Wayner, Ed. Oxford: Pergamon, 1964, pp. 429–453.
47. Nauta, W. J. H. Hippocampal projections and related neural pathways to the midbrain in the cat. *Brain*, 1958, **81**, 319–340.
48. Nauta, W. J. H. Some neural pathways related to the limbic system. In *Electrical studies on the unanesthetized brain*. E. R. Ramey & D. S. O'Doherty, Eds. New York: Paul Hoeber, 1960, pp. 1–16.
49. Nauta, W. J. H. Central nervous organization and the endocrine motor system. In *Advances in neuroendocrinology*. A. V. Nalbandov, Ed. Urbana: Univ. of Illinois Press, 1963, pp. 5–21.
50. Newman, B. L. Behavioral effects of self-stimulation of the septal area and related structures. *J. comp. physiol. Psychol.*, 1961, **54**, 340–345.
51. Olds, J. Run-way and maze behavior controlled by basomedial forebrain stimulation in the rat. *J. comp. physiol. Psychol.*, 1956, **49**, 507–512.
52. Olds, J. Effects of hunger and male sex hormones on self-stimulation of the brain. *J. comp. physiol. Psychol.*, 1958a, **51**, 320–324.
53. Olds, J. Self-stimulation of the brain. *Science*, 14 February 1958b, **127**, 315–324.
54. Olds, J. Differentiation of reward systems in the brain by self-stimulation technics. In *Electrical studies on the unanesthetized brain*. E. R. Ramey & D. S. O'Doherty, Eds. New York: Paul Hoeber, 1960, pp. 17–49.
55. Olds, J. Differential effects of drive and drugs on self-stimulation at different brain sites. In *Electrical stimulation of the brain*. D. E. Sheer, Ed. Austin: Univ. of Texas Press, 1961, pp. 350–366.
56. Olds, J. The central nervous system and the reinforcement of behavior. *Amer. Psychol.*, 1969, **24**, 114–132.
57. Olds, J., & Milner, P. Positive reinforcement produced by electrical stimulation of the septal area and other regions of the rat brain. *J. comp. physiol. Psychol.*, 1954, **47**, 419–427.
58. Olds, J., & Olds, M. E. The mechanisms of voluntary behavior. In *The role of pleasure in behavior*. R. G. Heath, Ed. New York: Harper & Row, 1964, pp. 23–54.
59. Olds, M. E., & Hogberg, D. Subcortical lesions and mass retention in the rat. *Exp. Neurol.*, 1964, **10**, 296–304.
60. Olds, M. E., & Olds, J. Approach-escape interaction in rat brain. *Amer. J. Physiol.*, 1962, **203**, 803–810.
61. Olds, M. E., & Olds, J. Approach-avoidance analysis of rat diencephalon. *J. comp. Neurol.*, 1963, **120**, 259–295.
62. Panksepp, J., & Trowill, J. A. Intraoral self injection: I. Effects of delay of reinforcement on resistance to extinction and implications for self-stimulation. *Psychonom. Sci.*, 1967a, **9**, 405–406.
63. Panksepp, J., & Trowill, J. A. Intraoral self injection: II. The simulation of self-stimulation phenomenon with a conventional reward. *Psychonom. Sci.*, 1967b, **9**, 407–408.
64. Pliskoff, S. S., & Hawkins, T. D. Test of Deutsch's drive-decay theory of rewarding self-stimulation of the brain. *Science*, 1963, **141**, 823–824.
65. Pliskoff, S. S., Wright, J. E., & Hawkins, D. T. Brain stimulation as a reinforcer: intermittent schedules. *J. exp. Anal. Behav.*, 1965, **8**, 75–88.
66. Poschel, B. P. H. Mapping of rat brain for self-stimulation under monoamine oxidase blockade. *Physiol. & Behav.*, 1969, **4**, 325–331.
67. Poschel, B. P. H., & Ninteman, F. W. Excitatory (anti-depressant?) effects of monoamine oxidase inhibitors on the reward system of the brain. *Life Sci.*, 1964, **3**, 903–910.
68. Prescott, R. G. W. Estrous cycle in the rat: Effects on self-stimulation behavior. *Science*, 1966, **152**, 796–797.
69. Reynolds, R. W. The relationship between stimulation voltage and hypothalamic self-stimulation in the rat. *J. comp. physiol. Psychol.*, 1958, **51**, 193–198.
70. Roberts, W. W. Rapid escape learning without avoidance learning motivated by hypothalamic stimulation in cats. *J. comp. physiol. Psychol.*, 1958a, **51**, 391–399.

71. Roberts, W. W. Both rewarding and punishing effects from stimulation of posterior hypothalamus of cat with same electrode at same intensity. *J. comp. physiol. Psychol.*, 1958b, **51**, 400–407.
72. Routtenberg, A. The two arousal hypotheses: Reticular formation and limbic system. *Psychol. Rev.*, 1968, **75**, 51–80.
73. Routtenberg, A., & Lindy, J. Effects of the availability of rewarding septal and hypothalamic stimulation on barpressing for food under conditions of deprivation. *J. comp. physiol. Psychol.*, 1965, **60**, 158–161.
74. Sem Jacobsen, C. W. Effects of electrical stimulation on the human brain. *EEG clin. Neurophysiol.*, 1959, **11**, 379.
75. Seward, J. P., Uyeda, A. A., & Olds, J. Resistance to extinction following cranial self-stimulation. *J. comp. physiol. Psychol.*, 1959, **52**, 294–299.
76. Seward, J. P., Uyeda, A. A., & Olds, J. Reinforcing effect of brain stimulation on run-way performance as a function of interval between trials. *J. comp. physiol. Psychol.*, 1960, **53**, 224–227.
77. Sidman, M., Brady, J. V., Conrad, D. G., & Schulman, A. Reward schedules and behavior maintained by intracranial self-stimulation. *Science*, 1955, **122**, 830–831.
78. Spies, G. Food versus intacranial self-stimulation reinforcement in food-deprived rats. *J. comp. physiol. Psychol.*, 1965, **60**, 153–157.
79. Stein, L. Secondary reinforcement established with subcortical stimulation. *Science*, 1958, **127**, 466–467.
80. Stein, L. Psychopharmacological substrates of mental depression. In *Anti-depressant drugs*. S. Garattini & M. N. G. Dukes, Eds. Amsterdam: Excerpta Medica Foundation, 1967a, pp. 130–140.
81. Stein, L. Noradrenergic substrates of positive reinforcement: site of motivational action of amphetamine and chlorpromazine. In *Neuropsycho-pharmacology* (Proc., Fifth Intern. Congress, CINP). H. Brill, J. O. Cole, P. Deniker, H. Hippius, & P. B. Bradley, Eds. Amsterdam: Excerpta Medica Foundation, 1967b, p. 765.
82. Stein, L. Chemistry of reward and punishment. In *Psychopharmacology: A review of progress, 1957–1967*. D. H. Efron, Ed. Washington, D. C.: U. S. Govt. Printing Office, 1968, pp. 105–123.
83. Stein, L. Chemistry of purposive behavior. In *Reinforcement and behavior*. J. T. Tapp, Ed. New York: Academic Press, 1969.
84. Stein, L., & Ray, O. S. Self-regulation of brain stimulating current intensity in the rat. *Science*, 1959, **130**, 570–572.
85. Stein, L., & Wise, C. D. Release of norepinephrine from hypothalamus and amygdala by rewarding medial forebrain bundle stimulation and amphetamine. *J. comp. physiol. Psychol.*, 1969, **67**, 189–198.
86. Stein, L., & Wise, C. D. Possible etiology of schizophrenia: progressive damage to the noradrenergic reward system by 6-hydroxydopamine. *Science*, 12 March 1971, **171**, 1032–1036.
87. Steinbaum, E. A., & Miller, N. E. Obesity from eating elicited by daily stimulation of the hypothalamus. *Amer. J. Physiol.*, 1965, **208**, 1–5.
88. Steiner, S. S., & D'Amato, M. R. Rewarding and aversive effects of amygdaloid self-stimulation as a function of current intensity. *Psychonom. Sci.*, 1964, **1**, 27–28.
89. Stutz, R. M., Lewin, I., & Rocklin, K. W. Generality of "drive-decay" as an explanatory concept. *Psychonom. Sci.*, 1965, **2**, 127–128.
90. Trowill, J. A., Panksepp, J., & Gandelman, R. An incentive model of rewarding brain stimulation. *Psych. Rev.*, 1969, **76**, 264–281.
91. Uyeda, A., & Gengerelli, J. Influence of rectangular pulses and sine waves of varying frequency on brain self-stimulation in the rat. *Psychol. Rep.*, 1959, **5**, 641–647.
92. Valenstein, E. S. The anatomical locus of reinforcement. In *Progress in physiological psychology*. E. Stellar & J. M. Sprague, Eds. New York: Academic Press, 1966, pp. 149–190.
93. Valenstein, E. S., & Beer, B. Continuous opportunity for reinforcing brain stimulation. *J. exp. Anal. Behav.*, 1964, **7**, 183–184.
94. Valenstein, E. S., & Campbell, J. F. Medial forebrain bundle-lateral hypothalamic area and reinforcing brain stimulation. *Amer. J. Physiol.*, 1966, **210**, 270–274.
95. Ward, H. P. Basal tegmental self-stimulation after septal ablation. *A. M. A. Arch. Neurol.*, 1960, **3**, 158–162.

96. Ward, H. P. Tegmental self-stimulation after amygdaloid ablation. *A. M. A. Arch. Neurol.*, 1961, **4**, 657–659.

97. Wilkinson, H. A., & Peele, T. L. Modification of intracranial self-stimulation by hunger satiety. *Amer. J. Physiol.*, 1962, **203**, 537–541.

98. Wilkinson, H. A., & Peele, T. L. Intracranial self-stimulation in cats. *J. comp. Neurol.*, 1963, **121**, 425–440.

99. Wurtz, R. H., & Olds, J. Amygdaloid stimulation and operant reinforcement in the rat. *J. comp. physiol. Psychol.*, 1963, **56**, 941–949.

100. Olds, J., Yuwiler, A., Olds, M. E., & Yun, C. Neurohumors in hypothalamic substrates of reward. *Amer. J. Physiol.*, 1964, **207**, 242–254.

Chapter 14

SLEEP, AROUSAL, ATTENTION, AND HABITUATION

Sleep

Arousal, Attention and Habituation

SLEEP

Introduction

A good third of our lives is spent in a state of reduced activity that we call sleep. Many animals sleep off and on throughout the day and night and may spend as much as 75 percent of their lives in this state. Others, including man, develop circadian (i.e., about 24 hours) rhythms of sleep and wakefulness. The internal clock that determines the sleep-wakefulness cycle is remarkably accurate even in the absence of external cues. Rats[153] as well as man[125] go to sleep and arise at the same time of day even though isolated from the day-night light cycle and other information about the passage of time. (Sometimes these biological clocks are a little fast or a little slow. The amount of sleep remains constant, but the person goes to sleep a few minutes earlier or later each day.)

We identify the state of sleep with rest and recuperation and indeed seem to develop a "need" for it. Prolonged sleep-deprivation does not typically lead to death (although some instances have been reported)[173] but may induce hallucinations, loss of memory[131] and various other pathological behavior changes which suggest that the nervous system is not functioning properly.[14] This conclusion is supported by the presence of reversible degenerative changes in many parts of the brains of sleep-deprived animals.[109,110]

Yet, sleep is not a state of generally reduced function. Voluntary movements are suspended, and the response threshold to most stimuli is elevated, but many of the body's activities go on unaltered or even at an increased rate. Perhaps most surprising is the fact that the brain itself is not inactive during sleep. There are subtle changes in the activity level of some brain cells and even gross changes in the total pattern of electrical (EEG) activity of the brain, but these are signs of altered activity instead of inactivity.

Nor are we, in normal sleep, as unresponsive to environmental stimuli as is commonly assumed. Repetitive stimuli whose significance or rather lack thereof has been well established do not elicit overt responses, and the threshold of almost all stimuli is somewhat elevated, but this does not seem to be caused by a general lack of reactivity. A mother awakens promptly at the faint sounds of an infant's discomfort, a cat arouses immediately when the odor of fresh fish or meat is in the air, and all of us respond to our name even though it is spoken in a whisper.

A closer look at sensory functions reveals that afferent signals are, in fact, processed during sleep even when there is no overt response to them. The transmission properties of the classical sensory pathways and relay stations may be changed in subtle ways, but there is no indication of a general inhibition. Depending on the nature of the stimulus and the locus of the recording electrode, the evoked potentials that reflect summated responses to afferent signals are sometimes larger[42] and sometimes smaller[36] during sleep. The same stimulus may produce a reduced response during one sleep phase and an increased reaction during another.[45] The reaction of many individual cortical cells is larger during sleep than during wakefulness (although the signal-to-noise ratio tends to be smaller because the level of background activity is also elevated).[39] The response of many other cells in the cortical sensory areas is unchanged during sleep.[135]

Many "vegetative" functions such as heart rate,[94] pulse rate,[15] blood pressure,[167] body temperature,[136] and respiration[155] are reduced during sleep. However, others such as the contraction of the sphincter muscles of the eye, rectum, and urinary canal are markedly increased.[81]

The activity of the skeletal musculature is generally decreased during sleep. This seems to be the result of reduced activity of the central components of the motor system rather than a reduced reactivity to sensory input because the threshold for the elicitation of movements by electrical stimulation of the motor cortex is itself increased.[83] Spinal reflexes are also reduced and sometimes absent during sleep.[54] This widespread reduction in somatomotor function is not, however, without exception. Particular sleep postures, such as perching on one leg, often require special muscular effort during sleep.

Sleep is thus not as basically different from wakefulness as it subjectively appears and turns out to be difficult to define, particularly with respect to other species. Strange as it may seem, we must rely on gross behavioral and electrophysiological changes that are not, strictly speaking, unique to the sleep state. Behaviorally, we include in our definition of sleep a "typical" posture, reduction in general muscle tonus, eyelid closure, and a general reduction in reactivity to stimulation. Some or all of these behavioral changes also occur during the resting phase of wakefulness, during illness, and during anesthesia or coma. Electrophysiologically, we rely on EEG patterns that are typical but not entirely unique to sleep. Some drugs, such as atropine, induce a sleeplike EEG pattern in awake and responsive subjects;[49] others, such as reserpine, induce an "aroused" EEG pattern in subjects who are quite unresponsive to the environment,[103] suggesting that the EEG "correlates" of sleep may not always reflect changes in brain function that are causally related to sleep.

Summary and Review Questions

Most species display cyclic variation in responsiveness to the environment along a continuum that extends from alert arousal to deep sleep. Although we can identify a periodic "need" for sleep, man as well as members of other species can go without sleep for an astounding number of hours before serious sensory and motor impairments become noticeable, and some species, such as the bullfrog, do not seem to sleep at all.[82]

Biological Bases of Motivation

Subjectively, sleep is very different from waking, but a closer look at the state of the organism indicates that sleep may not be quite as unique as it sometimes seems. Afferent signals appear to be processed by sensory pathways, some aspects of the autonomic as well as skeletal musculature are activated, and the brain itself appears to be processing information.

1. Discuss the pattern of activity in the brain during sleep and wakefulness.

2. Discuss the processing of sensory stimuli during sleep.

3. Give a few examples of skeletal and autonomic motor functions that are increased during sleep.

4. Does the sleep-wakefulness cycle depend on the day-night cycle?

Electrophysiology of Sleep

Much of our knowledge of sleep comes from recent experiments that were made possible by the fact that the gross EEG, which is such a disappointingly poor index of brain function during the waking state, shows marked and reliable changes when the organism goes to sleep (see Figures 14-1 and 14-2). About 30 years ago, Loomis and his associates[117, 118] demonstrated that the human EEG record shows a series of successive changes with the onset of sleep. First, the 8 to 10 Hz "alpha" waves, which characterize the resting stage of wakefulness, begin to drop out. Irregular low voltage activity appears instead; it may include bursts of "spindle" activity at about 14 Hz and, finally, large, very slow "delta" waves.

About 20 years later, it was recognized that not all sleep was characterized by slow waves. Periodically, the EEG of man as well as many infrahuman species changes abruptly to a low-amplitude, high-frequency pattern that is essentially indistinguishable from the EEG of an awake and attentive organism. This "paradoxical" sleep state appears to be related to dreaming[32, 33] (see Figure 14-3). Rapid eye movements typically occur during this state and many investigators identify it as rapid-eye-movement or REM sleep. The paradoxical sleep state is further characterized by complete loss of tonus in some skeletal muscle groups and by the appearance of spike activity in many portions of the pons, the lateral geniculate nucleus of the thalamus, and in the occipital lobe of the neocortex. Because of their distribution, these spikes are sometimes called ponto-geniculo-occipital or PGO spikes.[101, 21] Since it has not yet been possible to reliably identify any of the transi-

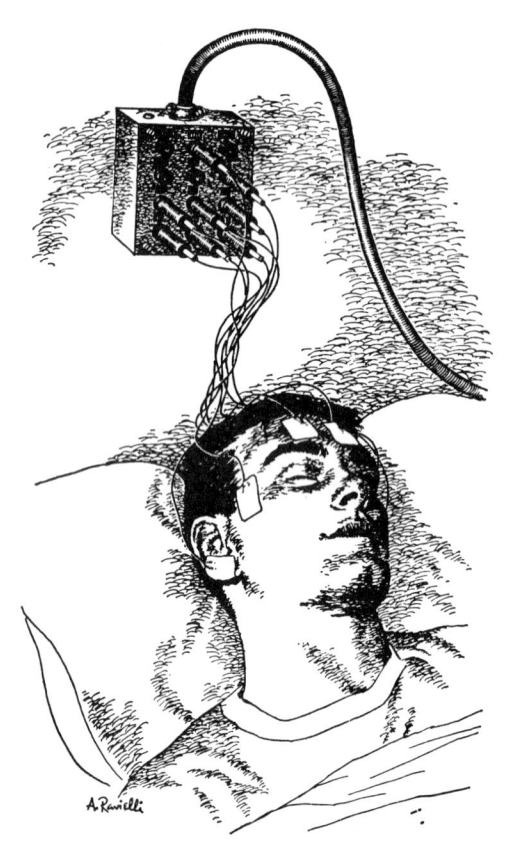

FIG. 14-1. A subject in a sleep experiment. Electrodes are tiny metal discs which lie flat over various areas of the face and scalp and which are held in place either by elastic bandages or by collodion-impregnated gauze pads. Wires lead from each electrode disc to a receptacle in a "terminal box" at the head of the subject's bed. From this box a cable runs to an adjacent room where the electroencephalograph produces a "write-out" of the subject's brain waves and eye movements.

(Reprinted by permission of Charles Scribner's Sons from THE PSYCHOLOGY OF SLEEP, page 15, by David Foulkes. Copyright © 1966 David Foulkes.)

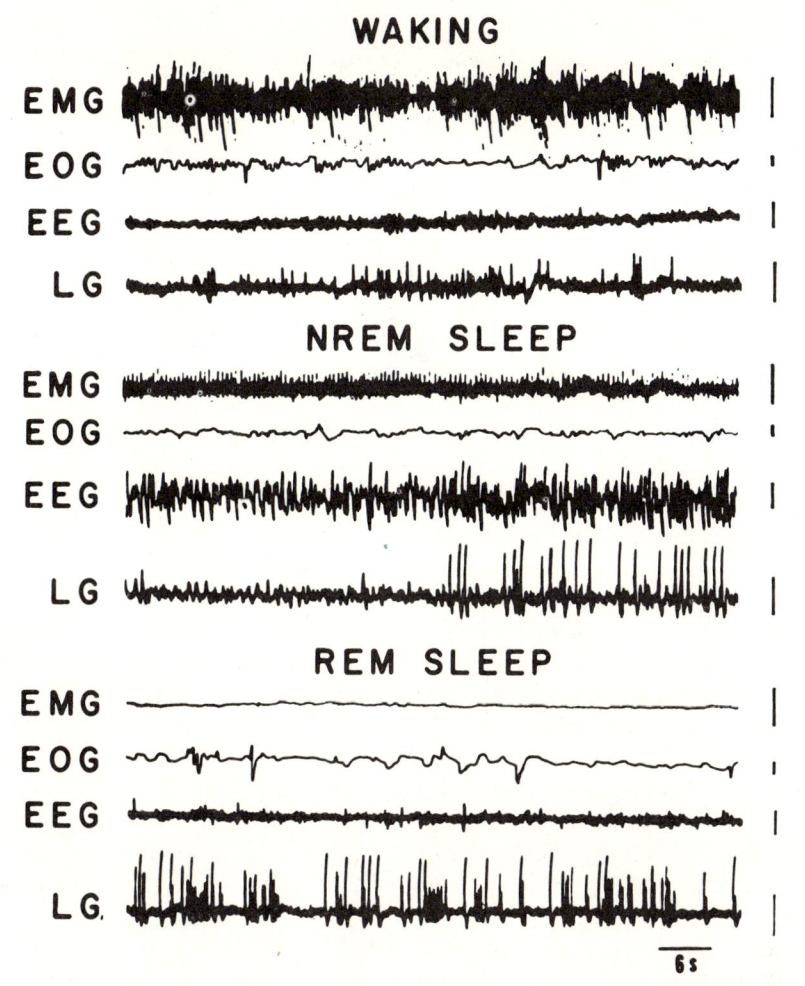

FIG. 14–2. The three main polygraphic aspects of waking and sleep in the cat. In the waking state there is a high level of electroencephalographic activity and eye movements followed by pontine-geniculate-occipital (PGO) spikes. In NREM sleep, muscle tonus is slightly decreased; there are no eye movements and few PGO spikes. During REM sleep, the electromyographic activity is abolished; the electroencephalographic pattern is low voltage, mixed frequency. In this tracing, the eye movements are preceded by lateral geniculate spikes.

(Adapted from M. Jouvet. Biogenic amines and the states of sleep. *Science*, **163**, 3 January 1969, 32–41. Copyright 1969 by the American Association for the Advancement of Science.)

tional stages of slow-wave sleep with major physiological or psychological changes, we shall distinguish only slow-wave and paradoxical sleep in our discussion.

The relationship between the two principal sleep states has been extensively studied in recent years. Paradoxical sleep interrupts slow-wave sleep at fairly regular intervals. On the average, paradoxical sleep makes up only about 20 percent of the total sleep time, the duration of individual episodes of paradoxical sleep being very brief early in the sleep period and increasing, as much as tenfold, toward morning. The duration of the slow-wave sleep periods tends to remain constant during the night. The percentage of paradoxical sleep decreases, and the duration of the slow-wave sleep periods increases from infancy to adulthood.[104]

More "refined" electrophysiological measures have been less successful than the gross EEG in reliably differentiating sleep from

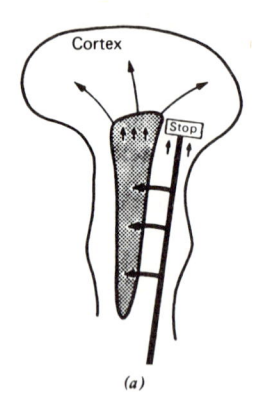

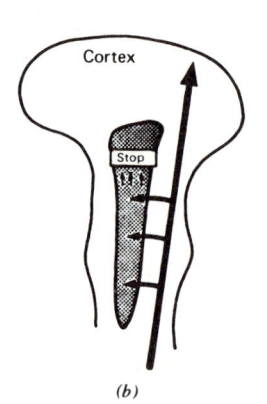

FIG. 14–3. (*a*) The state of cat (*a*) of Fig. 14–4. (*b*) The state of cat (*b*) of Fig. 14–4.

(From *Sleeping and waking: physiology and psychology* by I. Oswald. Elsevier, 1962.)

wakefulness. A number of investigators[24, 183, 102] have reported changes in the "steady" DC potentials of the cortex during the transition from wakefulness to sleep and vice versa, but the magnitude and even direction of these changes has differed from experiment to experiment, perhaps because of methodological factors. Attempts to record changes in the activity of single cells cortically or subcortically have not been much more successful. Many investigators have found that during sleep the background activity of many brain cells tends to become periodic instead of random and that neighboring cells that perhaps share a common functional assignment often show a similar periodicity.[112, 27] Others have reported that although the discharge frequency of any given cell may increase, decrease, or remain unaffected during the transition from wakefulness to sleep, the average discharge frequency of a large sample of cells may decrease reliably.[135, 160] Still others have noted that the direction of the change in single cell activity often depends on the characteristic firing pattern of the cell. Cells that discharge only infrequently during sleep tend to increase their firing rate during wakefulness.[43] Other relationships between the size or firing pattern of individual cells and their reaction to sleep have been reported,[41, 88] and this information may someday help us to understand sleep and its functions better. At present, it is an exercise in futility to attempt to interpret the implications of the often apparently conflicting reports.

Summary and Review Questions

The transition from wakefulness to sleep is accompanied by reliable EEG changes that include: (1) the gradual decline of 8 to 10 Hz "alpha" waves, (2) the appearance of sleep "spindles", and (3) the appearance of very slow (0.5 to 2.0 Hz) "delta" waves. After this "slow wave sleep" has continued for some time, the EEG record abruptly changes to the low-voltage, high-frequency pattern that characterizes alertness. During this "paradoxical" sleep stage, some muscles completely relax and rapid eye movements occur. When human subjects are awakened from paradoxical sleep they almost always report having dreamed. Throughout the night, slow-wave sleep alternates with paradoxical sleep, the duration of the latter steadily increasing toward morning.

Individual neurons in the brain behave in unpredictable ways during the transition from sleep to wakefulness and vice versa. Some show no reaction at all; others may increase or decrease their firing rate or modify the pattern but not the overall rate of discharge.

1. Describe the sequence of EEG changes that accompany the transition from wakefulness to sleep.

2. Define paradoxical sleep. How is it different from slow-wave sleep?

3. Describe the pattern of slow-wave sleep and paradoxical sleep during the night.

4. Does the activity of individual brain cells show predictable changes during the transition from wakefulness to sleep or from one sleep stage to another?

The Neuroanatomical Substrate

Sleep can be viewed from two quite different theoretical points of view. The classical theory of sleep assumes that it is an entirely passive phenomenon (i.e., that it reflects the absence of influences from neural mechanisms which maintain the organism in a state of wakefulness). Sleep, according to this view, is the natural state of the organism, and wakefulness rather than sleep requires explanation. The Nobel-prize winning research of W. R. Hess[81] first suggested about 50 years ago that sleep may, instead, be an active phenomenon that requires the activation of particular neural "sleep centers." Both views, as we shall see, can muster a good deal of experimental support.

Sleep as a Passive Phenomenon

Early theories of sleep assumed that it resulted from a reduction of sensory input. This view appeared to be handsomely supported by Bremer's[19] classical observation that a complete transection of the brainstem at the midbrain level, which cuts off all except visual and olfactory sensory inputs to the cortex, produced a permanently "sleeping" animal behaviorally as well as electrophysiologically. The theory seemed further supported by the observation that transections of the brainstem just above the spinal cord, which leave all sensory feedback from the head intact, did not affect the basic sleep-wakefulness cycle.

About 15 years later, Magoun and his associates made a series of discoveries that indicated that wakefulness might depend not directly on sensory input to the cortex but on the level of activity in what came to be called the "ascending reticular arousal system" or ARAS of the brainstem. It was found that

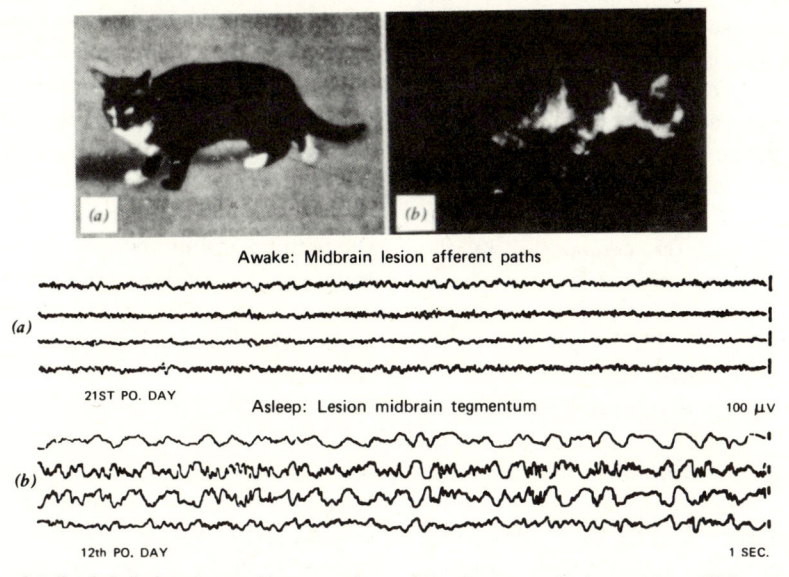

FIG. 14–4. (*a*) Animal standing awake, with characteristic waking EEG pattern (*a*), has interruption of long ascending sensory tracts but an intact reticular formation. (*b*) Animal lying persistently asleep, with sleeping EEG pattern (*b*), has intact sensory tracts but damage to midbrain reticular formation. Information from sense organs still reaches the cortex but cannot be handled efficiently by the latter without the diffuse facilitation from the reticular formation.

(From D. B. Lindsley, L. H. Schreiner, W. B. Knowles, & H. W. Magoun. Behavioral and EEG changes following chronic brainstem lesions in the cat. *EEG clin. Neurophysiol.*, **2**, 1950, 483–498.)

electrical stimulation of the brainstem reticular formation produces EEG arousal even in anesthetized animals[133] and that lesions in the reticular formation resulted in apparently permanent stupor accompanied by slow-wave cortical EEG patterns, whereas destruction of the classical sensory pathways in the brainstem did not alter the sleep-wakefulness cycle[115, 116] (see Figure 14–4). These observations gave rise to the hypothesis that wakefulness depends directly on a tonic flow of impulses from the reticular formation to the cortex and that sleep represents the absence or reduction of this ascending arousal influence.

The research of the past 20 years has suggested that this appealingly simple view may not tell the entire story. When brainstem lesions are made in several stages[1] or when special provisions are made for postoperative care,[35] large segments of the reticular formation can be removed without permanently affecting the sleep-wakefulness cycle. Studies of the effects of transections of the brainstem at various levels[12,156] (see Figure 14–5) have suggested that only a very small portion of the brainstem reticular formation, which has been identified as the *n. reticularis pontis oralis*,[132] may be essential to arousal. The role of even this influence in sleep has been questioned by the demonstration that cortical "arousal"—that is, low-voltage, high-frequency EEG activity—occurs during sleep[32, 33] and that behavioral wakefulness can occur in the absence of EEG activation.[16]

Sleep as an Active Phenomenon

W. R. Hess[81] discovered almost 50 years ago that low-frequency electrical stimulation of the medial thalamus induced behavioral sleep that appeared similar in all respects to natural sleep. Soon after the onset of stimulation, the animals looked for a convenient place to sleep, curled up, and soon appeared to be soundly asleep. They continued to sleep when the stimulation was terminated, but could be awakened by sensory stimuli of moderate intensities. High-frequency stimulation of the same area aroused a sleeping animal, suggesting that the medial thalamus does not function in a simple way only as a "sleep center." This has been underscored by more recent observations which have shown that damage to the medial thalamus produces stupor and somnolence.[47]

More recent stimulation studies have shown that low-frequency stimulation of essentially all nonspecific projection nuclei of the thalamus induce cortical synchronization or "spindling" similar to the EEG pattern seen in the early phases of slow-wave sleep. The spindle activity that is induced by thalamic stimulation has been called "recruiting response" because it gets larger and larger with continued stimulation.[127] Many investigators further report that prolonged or repeated stimulation in the nonspecific projection nuclei of the thalamus induces sleep.[7, 8, 94]

Moruzzi[132] has incorporated these observations in a theory of sleep and wakefulness that suggests in essence that the brainstem reticular formation may contain a "waking center," which is responsible for maintaining a state of cortical arousal and behavioral wakefulness, and that the nonspecific thalamic projection system may contain an inhibitory "sleep center," which synchronizes cortical activity and induces sleep. However, sleep is influenced by a number of other areas, and it appears likely that a complex of interrelated pathways instead of a single center may regulate its occurrence.

Electrical stimulation of some portions of the pontine and midbrain reticular formation induces behavioral as well as EEG sleep.[95, 44] Small lesions, restricted to the raphé nucleus of the brainstem, abolish both slow-wave and paradoxical sleep, whereas more lateral lesions in the *locus coeruleus* of the *n. pontis caudalis* selectively abolish paradoxical sleep. The presence of additional active sleep "centers" in lower portions of the brainstem is suggested by the fact that transection of the brainstem in the midpontine region produces insomnia[11] (see Figure 14–5).

Another "waking center" has been described in the anterior hypothalamus. Damage to adjacent portions of the preoptic area have been reported to have more selective inhibitory effects on paradoxical sleep.[120] Lesions in this area produce insomnia.[139]

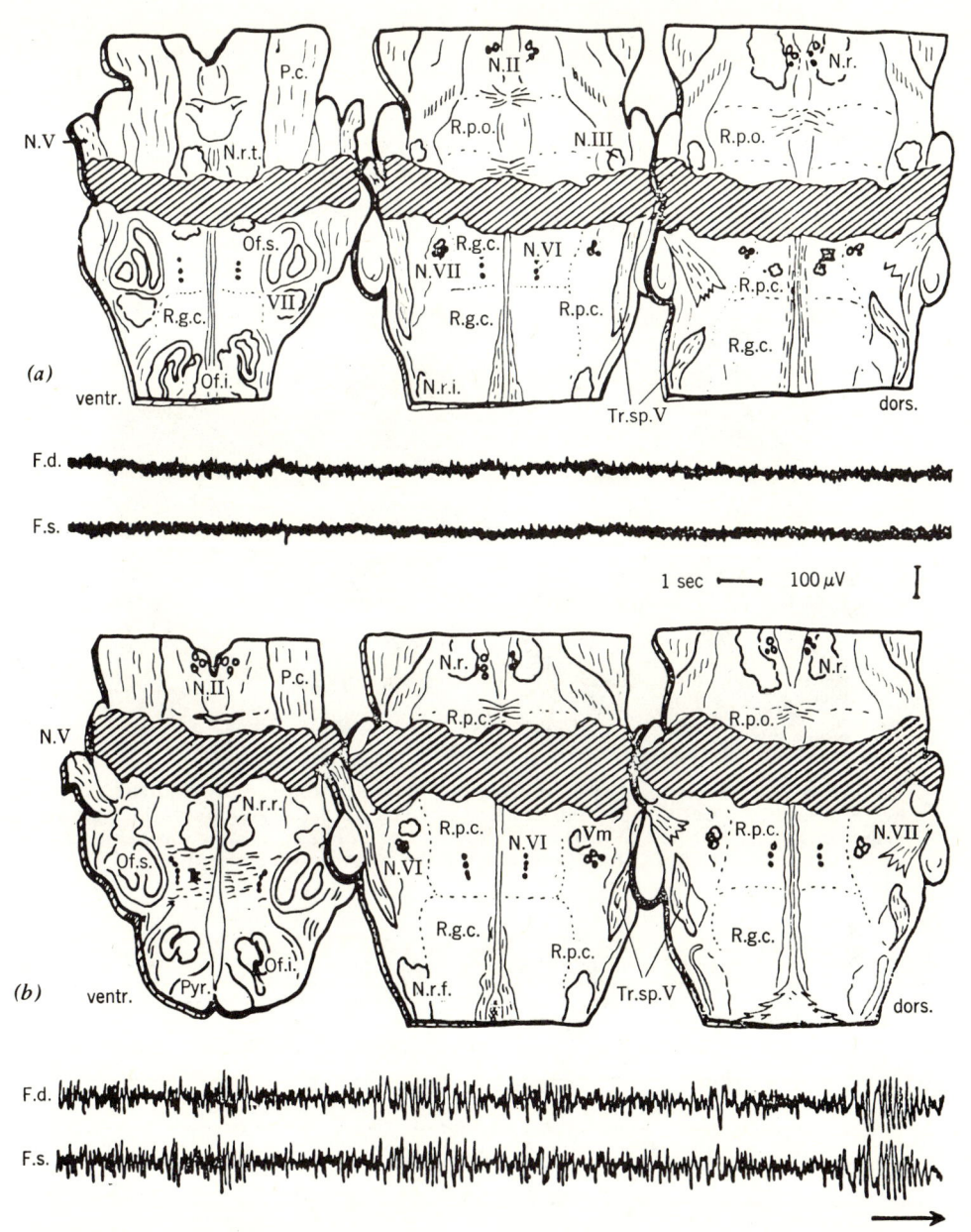

FIG. 14–5. EEG pattern from right (F.d.) and left (F.s.) frontal cortex following (a) midpontine and (b) rostropontine transection.

(From C. Batini, G. Moruzzi, M. Palestini, G. F. Rossi, & A. Zanchetti. Effects of complete pontine transections on the sleep-wakefulness rhythm: The midpontine pretrigeminal preparation. *Arch. ital. Biol.*, **97**, 1959, 1–12.)

Electrical stimulation of this region as well as the preoptic area and still more anterior portions of the basal forebrain induce behavioral and EEG sleep[171, 172] (see Figure 14–6). It has been suggested that these effects may result from damage or stimulation of a "hypnogenic" pathway that interconnects the orbitofrontal cortex with the brainstem and thalamus,[140] and mediates inhibitory influences that are essential to sleep. Microinjections of the synaptic transmitter substance, acetylcholine, into many sites along the trajectory of this pathway have been reported to induce sleep in some experiments,[70] supporting this hypothesis.

Summary and Review Questions

Sleep can be viewed as the natural state of biological organisms to which they revert whenever the neural mechanisms that sustain alertness tire or become inactive. It was long thought that alertness directly reflected the level of sensory inputs to the cortex and that sleep occurred automatically whenever the total level of sensory stimulation fell below some minimum.

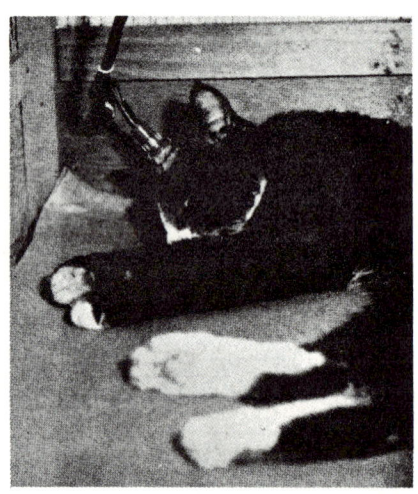

FIG. 14–6. (*a*) Behavioral response to electrical stimulation of the basal forebrain area in the cat. In this alert but unaroused animal (left) the induction of sleep was accomplished in approximately 20 seconds and was accompanied by an equally rapid shift in the EEG to a pattern of slow-wave activity.

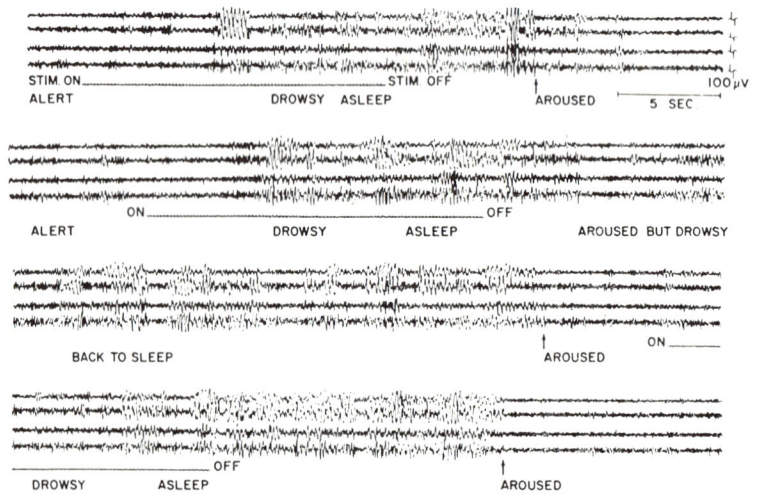

(*b*) Electroencephalographic patterns of sleep induced by basal forebrain stimulation in a behaving cat. The behavioral state of the animal was consistent with the electrical patterns recorded diffusely from various cortical areas. Stim = stimulation.

(From M. B. Sterman & C. D. Clemente. Forebrain inhibitory mechanisms: Sleep patterns induced by basal forebrain stimulation in the behaving cat. *Exp. Neurol.*, **6**, 1962, 103–117.

FIG. 14–7. (*a*) Dots indicate sites at which low frequency stimulation induces EEG or behavioral NREM sleep; large dots represent the most effective locations. (*b*) Results of cerebral lesion on sleep. The oblique line indicates the plane of the mediopontine transection that produces an increase in arousal. This occurs probably because the ascending reticular activating system (in dots) is left intact in front of the section, whereas most of the sleep-inducing structures (raphé nuclei in black) are located behind the section. Decortication (in shaded area) suppresses slow cerebral activity during behavioral sleep.

(From M. Jouvet. Neurophysiological and biochemical mechanisms of sleep. In *Sleep: Physiology and pathology*. A. Kales, Ed. Philadelphia: Lippincott, 1969.)

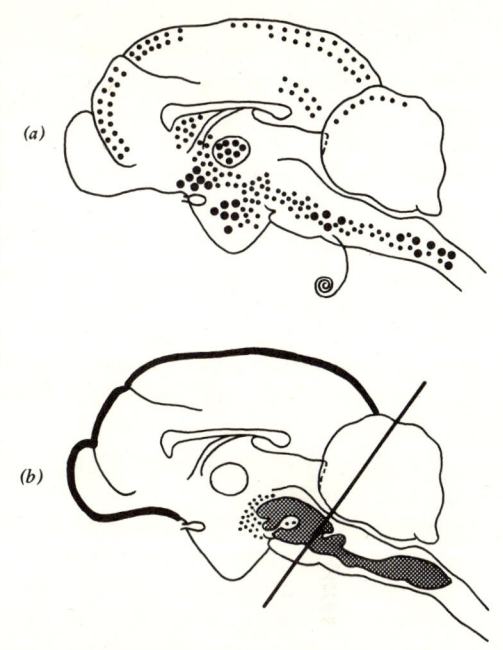

The work of Magoun and associates suggests instead that arousal might require tonic influences from an "arousal system" in the reticular formation of the brainstem. Sleep, according to this view, occurs whenever the reticular formation becomes inactive from fatigue or habituation.

A quite different concept of sleep, first proposed by W. R. Hess, suggests that sleep may instead be an active state that requires the activation of a "sleep center." Hess discovered that low-frequency stimulation of the medial thalamus induced behavioral sleep and suggested that this might be the location of the sleep center. Subsequent investigators have shown that stimulation of several regions in the basal forebrain as well as in the pontine reticular formation can induce sleep and that lesions in these areas induce insomnia. These observations suggest that sleep may require activation of a complex inhibitory pathway which may include the orbitofrontal cortex, basal forebrain, thalamus, and some aspects of the brainstem reticular formation. This inhibitory influence may affect cortical functions directly via the nonspecific thalamic projections or indirectly by exerting inhibitory or synchronizing effects on components of the brainstem reticular formation that are concerned with the initiation and maintenance of wakefulness (see Figure 14–7).

1. Discuss the evidence which suggests that alertness requires inputs from the reticular formation of the brainstem to the cortex and that sleep may be a result of a reduction of this input.

2. The concept of an ascending reticular activating system in the brainstem may require modification in view of some recent experimental findings. Discuss this issue, citing some relevant observations.

3. It has been suggested that some aspects of the nonspecific thalamic projection system may function as a "sleep center" that inhibits or synchronizes cortical functions directly. Discuss, citing relevant experiments.

4. What evidence can you cite to support the alternative hypothesis that a complex inhibitory pathway may induce sleep by acting directly on components of the reticular activating system?

The Chemistry of Sleep

Since ancient times it has been thought that sleep "detires" and somehow removes the waste products that accumulate as a result of heightened bodily activity during wakefulness. Some of the early investigators of sleep demonstrated that intracerebral injections of cerebrospinal fluid from fatigued dogs produced drowsiness and sleep in nonfatigued dogs.[151, 162] These experiments have been replicated in other species[149] and extended by showing that similar effects can be obtained by using the cerebrospinal fluid of hibernating or anesthetized animals.[108] It is, however, difficult to evaluate the implications of these findings because the exchange of cerebrospinal fluid produces fever and other physiological abnormalities.

A more convincing demonstration of humoral sleep-inducing factors has been made in cross-perfusion experiments. In these studies, the circulatory systems of two animals are interconnected such that most of the blood passes through both animals. Several investigators have reported that electrical stimulation of the medial thalamus of one member of such a pair often induces sleep in both of them.[107, 128] Blood transfusions from sleeping[127] or hibernating[31] animals also have been reported to induce sleep. Unfortunately, sleep is often very loosely defined in these experiments, and it is not clear that one can generalize from the often quite abnormal experimental situations to sleep under normal conditions. This is particularly true in view of the fact that Siamese twins who have a common blood circulation are known to sleep quite independently. Experimental as well as theoretical interest in a "hypnotoxin" or "hypnogen" nonetheless continues.

At a different level of analysis, there has been much recent interest in the possibility that the neural pathways that mediate sleep may be characterized by unique neurohumoral properties, particularly by a selective sensitivity to monoamines such as serotonin or norepinephrine. Jouvet[96, 99] has presented a formal monoaminergic theory of sleep that is integrated to some extent with anatomical and physiological data. According to this theory, cyclical biochemical changes occur in the brain that are related to the sleep-wakefulness rhythm. Wakefulness is thought to depend on the activation of the ascending reticular formation by an unknown neurohumor. The transition to slow-wave sleep occurs, according to Jouvet, because of the activation of cells in the raphé nuclei of the brainstem, which contain serotonin. The transition to paradoxical sleep is believed to occur when norepinephrine-containing cells in the locus coeruleus of the brainstem are activated. The evidence for this interesting hypothesis is, as yet, incomplete and not entirely consistent.

Serotonin is a possible synaptic transmitter substance that is found primarily in the lower brainstem, hypothalamus, and pineal gland.[111] Given systemically, the drug does not cross the blood-brain barrier, but it is possible to manipulate its concentration in the brain by the administration of its precursors or substances that interfere with its metabolism.

Many investigators have reported that an increase in brain serotonin modifies sleep, but the nature of the effect appears to be complex and possibly obscured by species differences. Very high doses of a serotonin precursor have been reported to induce slow-wave sleep and completely block paradoxical sleep in cats.[97] Lower doses have been reported to increase the frequency and/or duration of paradoxical sleep in rats and man.[145, 67] Direct injections of small quantities of a serotonin precursor into the brainstem reticular formation, preoptic region, or medial thalamus have been reported to induce slow-wave sleep in cats.[184, 185]

Jouvet's interesting speculation that serotonin may be particularly important for slow-wave sleep is based mainly on an ingenious experiment[97] which demonstrated in cats that large doses of reserpine (which almost completely deplete both serotonin and norepinephrine stores in the brain) suppressed both slow-wave and paradoxical sleep for about 12 hours but induced the PGO spikes that are normally seen only during paradoxical sleep. When a serotonin precursor was injected shortly after the reserpine treatment, these spikes were suppressed and slow-wave sleep was initiated. A precursor of norepinephrine, on the other hand, increased the frequency of the PGO spikes and induced paradoxical as well as slow-wave sleep. More recently, Jouvet[100] has reported that a drug which selectively interferes with the synthesis of serotonin in the brain produces prolonged insomnia in cats. Relatively low doses of this drug have been reported to selectively block slow-wave sleep in the monkey, leaving paradoxical sleep essentially normal[180, 28] (see Figure 14–8).

That the effects of drugs which modify the serotonin content of the brain may specifically result from their action on cells of the raphé nucleus is suggested by the observation[98, 99] that lesions in this nucleus decrease the brain content of serotonin and produce insomnia, the magnitude of both effects being well correlated with the size of the lesion. We cannot, unfortunately, rule out alternative explanations of these findings, since longitudinal lesions in the brainstem that spare the raphé nuclei also result in a loss of sleep.[122]

There are numerous other results which suggest that serotonin may be in some way related to sleep, but it is not clear that Jouvet's appealingly simple model tells the whole story. Electrical stimulation of the raphé nucleus which releases serotonin in the forebrain fails to induce any sign of sleep.[6, 5]

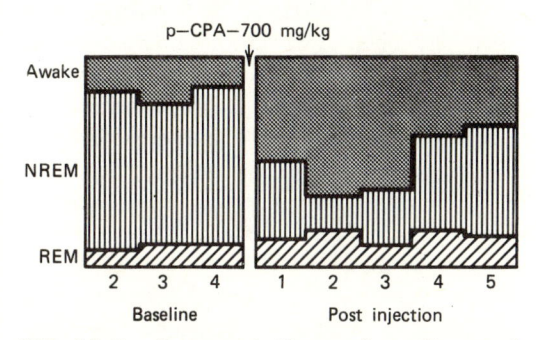

FIG. 14–8. Bar graph illustrating effects of p-chlorophenylalanine (a drug that selectively interferes with the synthesis of serotonin in the brain) on sleep-waking behavior of a monkey. There is a marked decrease in NREM sleep and of total sleep, while REM sleep is essentially unchanged. The abscissa represents consecutive 8-hr periods of sleep (10 P.M.–6. A.M.); the ordinate, percentage of total time.

(From E. D. Weitzman. Biogenic amines and sleep stage activity. In *Sleep: Physiology and pathology.* A. Kales, Ed. Philadelphia: Lippincott, 1969.)

Even more disturbing is the observation that drug treatments which interfere with the synthesis of serotonin produce only relatively brief suppressive effects on sleep. Normal sleep patterns return often long before brain serotonin returns to normal levels.

Norepinephrine is a synaptic transmitter in the sympathetic nervous system and is present at synaptic junctions throughout most of the brainstem.[29] Peripheral injections of this drug produce arousal and alerting,[157] but there is good reason to believe that this may not be because of a direct central action since norepinephrine does not cross the blood-brain barrier except at some "weak" points.

When norepinephrine is given intracisternally, intraventricularly, or systemically in animals with an immature blood-brain barrier, sleep or sedation is almost always reported.[123] Injections of norepinephrine directly into the brain tissue may result in arousal[25, 26] or sleep,[184, 185] depending on the site of the injection.

The most reliable support for an involvement of norepinephrine in sleep and particularly in paradoxical sleep comes from experiments showing that drugs which selectively deplete the brain content of norepinephrine cause a marked and selective depression in paradoxical sleep in monkeys[179, 28] (see Figure 14–9). That these effects may be caused by a depletion of norepinephrine in the locus coeruleus is suggested by the observation that lesions in this area produce similar selective inhibitory effects on paradoxical sleep. The picture, unfortunately, may once again be complicated by species differences. Several investigators have been unable to observe changes in sleep-wakefulness patterns in the rat after drug treatments that deplete norepinephrine from the brain,[124, 18] and an increase in paradoxical sleep has been reported in man.[66]

Although there is substantial evidence for an involvement of serotonergic and noradrenergic pathways in sleep, we clearly cannot assume that all sleep-related neurons are aminergic. Many investigators have reported sleep-induction or arousal from deep sleep following microinjections of cholinergic

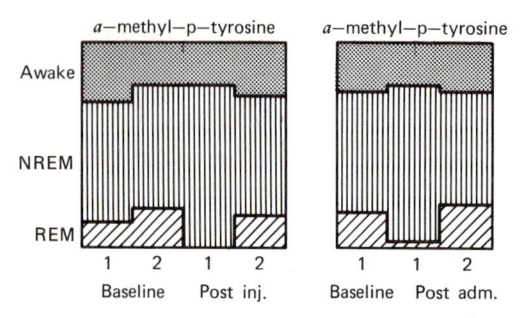

FIG. 14–9. Effects of α-methyl-p-tyrosine (a drug that depletes brain norepinephrine) on sleep-waking behavior of a monkey. The abscissa represents consecutive 8-hr night sleep periods (10 A.M.–6 P.M.); the ordinate, percentage of total time. There is a marked decrease in REM sleep and the time spent awake. A marked increase in NREM sleep accompanies these changes.

(From E. D. Weitzman. Biogenic amines and sleep stage activity. In *Sleep: Physiology and pathology*. A. Kales, Ed. Philadelphia: Lippincott, 1969.)

substances such as acetylcholine or carbachol into the thalamus,[80] preoptic area,[185] or brainstem,[25] and it has been suggested[70] that the "hypnogenic" pathway that interconnects the orbitofrontal cortex and thalamus with the midbrain may be entirely cholinergic.

Summary and Review Questions

Most early theories of sleep assumed that sleep might rid the body of waste products and proposed that a "hypnotoxin" might accumulate in the blood during wakefulness. There is some experimental evidence that the blood of sleeping or hibernating animals may contain a factor that can induce sleep in awake animals, but these findings are hard to square with the common observation that Siamese twins can sleep quite independently.

There is much current interest in the possibility that the brainstem pathways that regulate sleep may use possibly unique neurohumoral mechanisms. Considerable evidence suggests that changes in the brainstem concentration of serotonin or of noradrenaline, or both, modify the sleep-wakefulness cycle, but the exact nature of the coding system, if such there be, is not yet understood.

Jouvet has proposed an aminergic theory of sleep that suggests in essence that slow-wave sleep requires the activation of serotonergic neurons in the raphé nucleus of the brainstem and that paradoxical sleep results from the activation of adrenergic cells in the locus coeruleus. This hypothesis accounts for a good deal of the pharmacological evidence in this area, but it is contradicted by a few observations.

There is little doubt that an increase in brain serotonin modifies sleep, at least in some species, but it takes extraordinarily high doses of precursors to actually induce slow-wave sleep and prevent paradoxical sleep, as Jouvet's theory predicts, and as he, indeed, observed. Drugs that reduce the brain concentration of serotonin have been reported to block slow-wave sleep or induce total insomnia, but the time course of the behavioral and biochemical effects is quite different.

It is similarly clear that the level of noradrenaline in the brain affects sleep and wakefulness, but the mechanism of its action is as yet unknown. Systemic injections of this drug increase alertness, but this may be because of peripheral effects of the drug that affect the reticular activating system only indirectly. When the drug is given such that it bypasses the blood-brain barrier, sleep or coma are almost always seen. When it is injected directly into brain tissue, both arousal and sleep have been reported, the direction of the effect possibly being determined by the locus of the injection. A specific relationship between noradrenaline and paradoxical sleep is indicated by the observation that drugs which selectively deplete the brain stores of this drug selectively interfere with paradoxical sleep in the cat.

Unfortunately, we cannot be certain that the relationship between biogenic amines and sleep-wakefulness that have been observed in the cat and monkey also hold true in man and other species. Moreover, there are some curious inconsistencies which suggest that even in the cat and monkey matters may be more complicated than the results of the initial experiments in this very young field suggest.

1. Discuss the experimental support for the suggestion that sleep may be induced by a blood-born hypnotoxin.

2. Describe the principal evidence for a serotonergic influence on sleep.

3. Describe the principal evidence for a noradrenergic influence on sleep.

4. Present Jouvet's aminergic theory of sleep.

AROUSAL, ATTENTION, AND HABITUATION

The first time a novel stimulus is presented or the intensity of a continuously present stimulus is changed, we "pay attention," orient toward the source of stimulation, and may approach it to investigate its nature. The ubiquity of this orienting response intrigued the Russian physiologist, Ivan Pavlov,[150] because it seemed to be an essential component of every conditioning experiment, and he investigated it in some detail.

Hans Berger,[13] who first investigated the human EEG in 1929, observed that the behavioral-orienting response is accompanied by a marked change in the electrical activity of the brain. When we are resting or inattentive, the cortical EEG record is characterized by fairly regular large "alpha" waves at 8 to 10 Hertz. As soon as a novel stimulus is presented, this alpha rhythm is blocked and replaced by asynchronous, fast, low-amplitude "beta" activity. Many investigations of the role of autonomic reactions in emotional behavior (see Chapter 12) have shown that the orienting response is also accompanied by often marked changes in heart rate, respiration, sweating, and so on (see Figure 14–10).

Orienting responses are elicited by stimuli of all sensory modalities. Even weak novel stimuli initially elicit alerting behavior. More intense stimuli generally elicit more pronounced orienting reactions and continue to do so longer. All orienting responses gradually disappear unless the environmental change turns out to have motivational "significance." There are marked individual differences with respect to the intensity and completeness of the orienting response. Some subjects respond maximally to nearly all novel or sudden stimuli and continue to do so for a long time after the stimulus has been identified as "insignificant." Others show only brief and partial

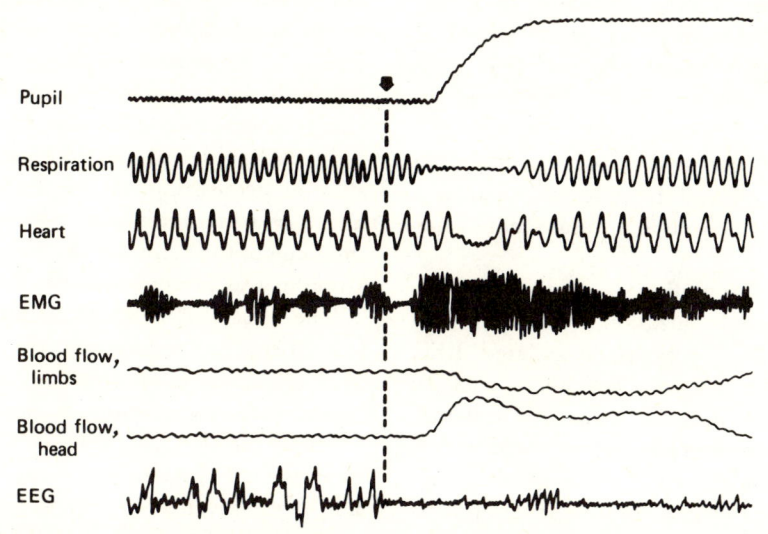

FIG. 14–10. The orienting reflex. When a sudden, novel, or significant stimulus is presented to a human subject (arrow), the pupil dilates, respiration is temporarily arrested, the heartbeat slows temporarily, muscle tone (EMG) increases, blood flow in the limbs decreases but blood flow in the head increases, the EEG shifts to a low-voltage fast aroused pattern, and the subject turns his head toward the source of stimulation.

(From *Psychology* by H. F. Harlow, J. L. McGaugh, & R. F. Thompson. Copyright 1971 Albion Publishing Company. Used with permission of Albion Publishing Company.)

reactions (usually a brief alpha block and behavioral attention but little or no autonomic response), which disappear after only a few trials. The most persistent sign of alerting reactions to stimulation is the modification of the electrical activity of the brain, and many investigators have studied these changes in some detail.

Electrophysiological Reactions to Novel Stimuli

Cortical Desynchronization

EEG desynchronization appears after about half the latency of the behavioral orienting reaction and does not terminate with the cessation of stimulation.[3,154] Stimuli of all modalities are capable of producing cortical desynchronization, but stimuli of modalities that are particularly important in a given species do so more easily and persistently. Man, for instance, depends heavily on visual information and shows most marked and prolonged cortical desynchronization in response to visual stimuli.[91,154] Cats, on the other hand, respond preferentially to sounds, and rats are most easily aroused by olfactory stimuli.[90] Even more important than the modality of the stimulus is its potential significance. An unexpected soft light produces more prolonged desynchronization than a bright but expected light;[154] a subject's name evokes more pronounced reactions than neutral words;[10] and the squeal of a mouse is by far the most effective arousal stimulus for a cat.[175]

The first presentation of a novel stimulus produces desynchronization in all neocortical areas as well as presumably related EEG changes in the midbrain reticular formation and nonspecific thalamic projection system.[2,177] With repeated presentations of the stimulus, this "generalized" alpha block disappears and only the relevant sensory projection area continues to show desynchronization reactions. As we continue to habituate to the stimulus, even this "localized" alpha block shortens and may eventually disappear.[55,159] Stimuli in such "primary" modalities as vision in man and audition in the cat often continue to elicit localized desynchronization responses for many thousands of trials and may never completely habituate.[130,177]

The rapidity and completeness of habituation is a function of the complexity of the stimulus. In one experiment, it was shown that the EEG response to single clicks disappeared after only six trials; about 40 were needed to habituate the reaction to pure tones; and many more to habituate the generalized alpha block to a series of rapidly alternating tones.[164]

The effects of habituation are remarkably specific,[92,57] but some generalization occurs. Cats habituated to a 500 Hz tone do not show desynchronization reactions to a 600 cycles per second tone, but do respond to tones of 100 or 1000 Hz (see Figure 14–11). The extent of the generalization becomes apparent when one compares the rapidity of the habituation process to similar stimuli. Cats initially respond to a sound although they are habituated to a tone of a similar frequency, but their response to the second tone habituates much faster.[9] In man, habituation may involve complex dimensions. In one experiment, subjects were habituated to words of similar meaning but dissimilar sounds. When similar sounding words that had different meanings were subsequently presented, all subjects responded promptly. Habituation did, however, generalize to other words of similar meaning.[158,159] Subjects habituated to a complex compound stimulus consisting of tactile, visual, and auditory stimuli responded promptly when only one of the components of the compound stimulus was presented alone.[177]

The effects of habituation are often prolonged but not permanent. Within hours or at most a few days after the last nonreinforced stimulus presentation, localized alpha blocking usually reappears. Generalized cortical desynchronization, autonomic reactions, and overt behavioral responses typically reappear a few days later. The effects of habituation also disappear when the habituated stimulus is preceded by a novel stimulus,[73,74,75] when it is presented during barbiturate anesthesia,[76,77] or after lesions[78] or complete transection of the brainstem.[146] These obser-

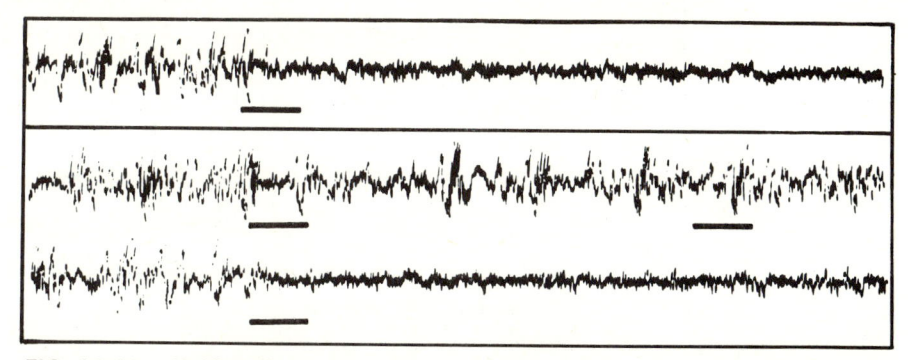

FIG. 14–11. Habituation of the EEG arousal reaction. The top trace shows a marked and prolonged desynchronization response to the first presentation of a novel 500 Hz tone (solid bar under EEG record). The second line shows the very brief response elicited by the 36th presentation of the same tone (first solid bar) and the complete absence of a reaction to the 37th presentation (second solid bar). The third tracing shows the response of the same animal to a novel tone of a different frequency (100 Hz), presented only a minute after the 37th presentation of the first tone.

(After S. Sharpless & H. H. Jasper. Habituation of the arousal reaction. *Brain,* **79**, 1956, 655–680.)

vations suggest that we must be careful in accepting habituation as a simple model of learning, as some investigators suggest. It should, perhaps, be compared more directly to extinction, which also shows some of the instabilities characteristic of habituation.

Other EEG Correlates

Neocortical desynchronization is often accompanied by high amplitude slow waves in the hippocampus. These hippocampal "theta" waves typically disappear, and the hippocampal activity becomes desynchronized, when the neocortical EEG shifts back to "alpha" activity. Since most other limbic and subcortical structures do not show a consistent EEG response to novel stimulation, the inverse relationship between the hippocampal and neocortical EEG activity suggests that the hippocampus may play a special role in the orienting or arousal response. Just what that role may be has been the subject of considerable controversy.

The initial investigators of the hippocampal reaction to novel stimuli[62] suggested that the slow theta waves might represent a special type of arousal response typical of the simple cortex that makes up the hippocampus. This interpretation requires the assumption that the same electrophysiological response pattern (high amplitude slow waves) represents inhibition in one portion of the brain (the neocortex shows slow waves during sleep) but excitation or arousal in another. This is not entirely impossible, but many investigators prefer an alternative interpretation based on the observation that the correlation of neocortical desynchronization and hippocampal slow waves is not as invariant as was initially thought (see Figure 14–12). In conditioning experiments, a previously habituated stimulus rapidly comes to elicit the localized alpha block reaction when it is paired with an unconditioned stimulus, but hippocampal theta waves seem to appear only when the first behavioral orienting reactions to the CS begin to be made. Often, the hippocampal "arousal" reaction can be seen throughout training but begins to diminish and eventually disappears when the conditioned response is firmly established and the CS no longer elicits overt orienting reactions.[61]

In delayed response situations, where behavioral orienting to the baited goal compartment continues to be important, the

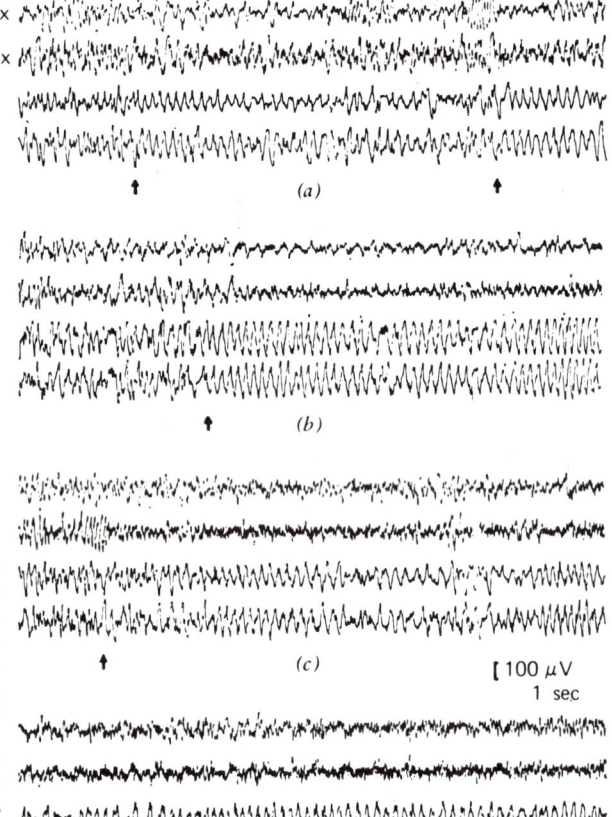

FIG. 14–12. Variations in the relationship between hippocampal theta and cortical desynchronization. All stimuli (indicated by arrows) were tones. In (a) a tone produces hippocampal theta activity but not cortical desynchronization. A second, louder tone intensifies the theta activity and results in cortical arousal. In (b) hippocampal theta precedes cortical arousal. In (c) the reverse pattern occurs. In (d) hippocampal theta is elicited in an animal which shows marked cortical desynchronization.

(From J. D. Green & A. Arduini. Hippocampal electrical activity in arousal. *J. Neurophysiol.*, 17, 1954, 533–557.)

hippocampal theta has been reported to persist even after prolonged training.[84] These observations have been interpreted[59, 60] to suggest that the hippocampus may normally inhibit orienting responses to insignificant stimuli and that this inhibitory influence may be suppressed by novel stimuli or during the early stages of conditioning when a previously neutral and habituated stimulus takes on special significance. After the nature of this significance and the required response are well established, gross orienting responses as well as hippocampal theta once again become unnecessary and drop out. This interpretation is supported by the observation[59] that electrical stimulation of the hippocampus interferes with all ongoing activity and induces orienting reactions to moving objects that were previously ignored. Moreover, destruction of the septal area, which appears to be a source of inhibitory influences,[119] abolishes hippocampal theta activity.[62]

Vanderwolf[176] has recently suggested an interesting alternative explanation of hippocampal slow waves. On the basis of extensive examinations of the behavior of animals before, during, and after the appearance of theta activity in the hippocampus, Vanderwolf proposes that the EEG pattern may not be specifically related to either attention or conditioning but accompanies all voluntary movements (which, of course, occur during orienting as well as during conditioning). According to this hypothesis, behavioral inhibition as well as autonomic or involuntary behaviors are associated with high-voltage irregular slow waves, voluntary movement with the high-voltage regular waves typical of theta rhythm, and low-amplitude irregular activity with the abrupt cessation of voluntary movement. The amplitude of the theta rhythm is thought to be directly related to the amplitude of the voluntary movement (a relationship that might explain the gradual disappearance of theta activity in some situations). This hypothesis has obvious difficulties with the observation that theta activity occurs during paradoxical sleep when the somatic motor system appears to be in a state of relaxation,[181] as well as during periods of obvious quiescence in the waking state.[22] To account for these observations, Vanderwolf proposes that low frequency theta (less than 8 Hz in the rat) may be related to an "intent to move" instead of to movement itself, whereas actual movements occur only after the theta rhythm has shifted to 8 to 10 Hz. Shifts in theta frequency have been observed by several investigators in the course of conditioning experiments,[38,181] but it is not yet clear whether the suggested interpretation can account for this phenomenon in all instances. Vanderwolf's hypothesis is an intriguing one, particularly in view of recent reports that theta is not observed in conditioning situations even during the time of maximal attention to the discriminanda unless overt movements occur.[30,187]

We might be able to interpret the functional significance of the hippocampal theta rhythm more easily if the pathways that exercise important influences on it were known. It is clear that lesions in the medial septum[62] and medial thalamus[37] abolish hippocampal theta and that stimulation of several sites in the medial hypothalamus and preoptic region elicit it.[186] These influences do not tie the hippocampal rhythm very closely to any portion of the motor system. However, it is possible that the hippocampus may relate cortical motor functions to currently active drive mechanisms via these connections, as Vanderwolf[176] suggests.

Single Cell Responses

It is generally assumed that the desynchronized low-voltage EEG, which characterizes arousal and attention, reflects an increase in cortical activity and a lowering of the response threshold of cortical neurons, whereas the slow waves commonly seen during sleep reflect inhibitory influences. A closer look at the activity of individual cortical cells suggests that this may not always be a warranted assumption. We have already seen that the transition from wakefulness to sleep or vice versa does not produce general changes in the activity of cortical neurons.[40,135] Studies of the change in unit activity during the transition from rest to alertness suggest a similar lack of general correlation. The firing rate of individual cortical cells may increase, decrease, or remain stable during cortical EEG desynchronization.[152] Attempts to correlate the nature of the change in unit activity with the resting activity of individual cells[121] suggest that cells which are active during rest and relaxation tend to stop firing when a novel stimulus is presented; cells which are silent during the resting state often start to fire, and some cells which are active during the resting state stop briefly and then increase their activity level. Attempts to measure the threshold of individual cortical neurons before and during EEG desynchronization suggest that many cells in the primary sensory receiving area of the arousal stimulus show a decreased threshold during the EEG desynchronization. However, other cortical regions show a marked threshold increase in spite of the fact that the gross EEG activation pattern seems in these areas to be identical.[105] In the sensory areas of the cortex, cells have been found that do not respond to appropriate peripheral stimulation unless the organism pays attention to it.[86] Unfortunately, it is not yet clear at what level of the sensory pathway this inhibitory influence occurs. An understanding of the effects of novelty on the activity of single cortical neurons is essential if we are to understand the nature of the orienting reaction, but it is clear that we do not as yet have enough information to interpret the isolated and sometimes conflicting observations available today.

Evoked Potentials

Whenever a novel stimulus is presented, an evoked potential can be recorded from the cortical projection area of its sensory modality.

Smaller evoked responses can be recorded from other portions of the brain, but we shall be concerned mainly with the primary potentials that appear in the classical sensory pathways and related cortical projection areas. Up to some limit, the amplitude of the evoked potential is proportional to the intensity of the stimulus, but such factors as novelty, significance, or attention appear to modify this relationship. If one records auditory evoked responses from the cortex of a cat and suddenly presents a mouse, the auditory potentials disappear. The potentials reappear as soon as the distracting stimulus is removed[74] (see Figure 14–13). This influence of "attention" is seen in all sensory modalities[148, 23] and may involve more complex interactions. For instance, cortical potentials that are evoked by brief light flashes are reduced or absent in human subjects when they are asked to perform arithmetic problems during the experiment[72] and are larger than usual when the subjects are asked to pay attention to the light flashes.[53, 169]

Many investigators attribute this inhibition or enhancement of the cortical evoked potential to a selective facilitation of sensory pathways to which one "pays attention" and a correlated inhibition of other sensory modalities.[74, 64, 34] Others[137, 138] feel that the interaction between attention and the magnitude of the evoked potentials is due in part to artifact (e.g., the cat's orienting response toward the mouse changes the position of its ears with respect to the source of the sound) and partly to a nonspecific facilitatory or inhibitory influence of the reticular formation on cortical activity. Nonspecific effects are suggested by the following kinds of observations. Attention to visual stimuli not only enhances the related evoked potential but also the response to sound-evoked potentials;[137] "irrelevant" stimuli produce potentials of similar magnitude as "relevant" stimuli in a conditioning situation;[137, 138] the sudden presentation of a mouse not only inhibits auditory potentials but has similar effects on cortical potentials that are evoked

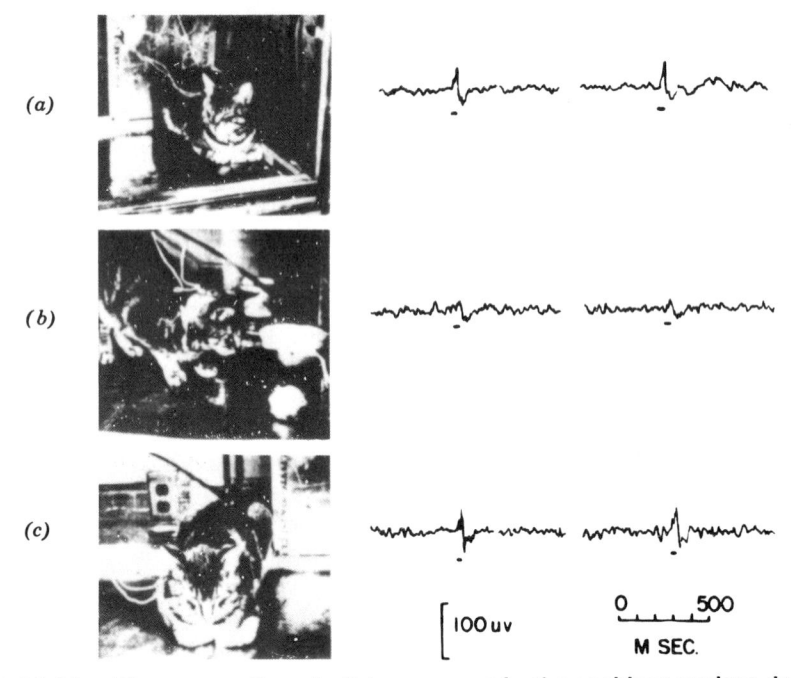

FIG. 14–13. Direct recording of click responses in the cochlear nucleus during three periods; the photographs were taken simultaneously. Top and bottom, cat is relaxed; the click responses are large. Middle, while the cat is visually attentive to the mice in the jar, the click responses are diminished in amplitude.

(From R. Hernández-Peón, H. Scherrer, & M. Jouvet. Modification of electric activity in cochlear nucleus during "attention" in unanesthetized cats. *Science*, **123**, 24 February 1956, 331–332.)

by other visual stimuli;[85] similar intramodality inhibitory effects have been observed in other sensory modalities.[166, 174] These observations clearly indicate that nonspecific interactions occur, but it is not as certain, at the moment, that more selective influences may not also contribute to the observed effects of attention.

The amplitude of evoked potentials gradually decreases unless the stimulus that elicits them is very intense or acquires significance as a conditioned signal. First to disappear is the generalized potential that can initially be recorded from almost all parts of the cortex. Additional, unreinforced stimulus presentations reduce the magnitude of the evoked potential in the sensory projection area as well as in lower parts of the classical sensory pathways. However, the evoked potentials of the sensory cortex or of the association areas do not diminish with repeated stimulus presentations under some circumstances.[182, 165, 174]

Summary and Review Questions

Novel, sudden, or intense stimuli of all sensory modalities elicit a complex reaction that has behavioral, autonomic, and electrophysiological components. Behaviorally, we orient toward the source of stimulation and may approach it if we find it novel. This is accompanied by changes in heart rate, perspiration, respiration, and so on, which suggest a nonspecific alerting reaction that may be an essential prerequisite for subsequent specific responses. When the stimulus is repeatedly presented and turns out to have no motivational significance, these orienting or alerting reactions gradually disappear in a process called habituation. Habituation occurs even with widely spaced trials and must be distinguished from adaptation or neural "fatigue." Even after the overt behavioral and autonomic reactions have disappeared, complex electrophysiological responses remain, and these persisting indices of arousal have received much experimental attention.

Novel or intense stimuli of all modalities block the "alpha" rhythm that characterizes the waking brain at rest and induce low-voltage, high-frequency discharges. This desynchronization initially occurs in all areas of the cortex, but it comes to be localized in the sensory projection area of the stimulus after some habituation trials. Even this localized EEG reaction may eventually disappear under some conditions, but it takes many thousands of trials (behavioral orienting reactions typically disappear after only 10 to 20 trials).

The neocortical desynchronization reaction is often accompanied by high-amplitude slow waves in the hippocampus. These "theta" waves seem to be associated with behavioral orienting instead of neocortical desynchronization per se, suggesting that the hippocampus may inhibit orienting responses to stimuli of established insignificance and thus contribute to the process of habituation. Alternatively, the theta rhythms may be related to voluntary movements or the intent to move.

Attempts to relate the activity of single cells in the cortex or reticular formation to arousal or habituation have not, as yet, demonstrated generally applicable principles. However, it seems certain that arousal and attention are not simply caused by an increase in cellular activity in any major subdivision of the brain, just as sleep cannot be said to be related to a general decrease in brain function.

The processing of sensory information, as reflected in the gross evoked potentials that are recorded with macroelectrodes, seems to vary as a function of arousal or attention. In the course of habituation, the amplitude of evoked potentials decreases. This inhibition is first seen cortically but may eventually involve even lower segments of the sensory pathways. The magnitude of evoked potentials is also suddenly decreased when distracting stimuli are presented, suggesting that something like "attention" may be involved in the habituation phenomenon.

1. Discuss some of the factors that determine the intensity of the arousal and orienting response and the rapidity of its habituation.

2. Describe the EEG responses to novel stimuli and the process of their gradual disappearance during habituation.

346 Biological Bases of Motivation

3. Discuss the activity of single cells in the cortex in relation to EEG arousal.
4. Discuss the habituation of evoked potentials.

Neuroanatomical Mechanisms

Arousal

The classical explanation of arousal or alerting attributes it to the arrival of sensory stimuli at the cortex. The discoveries of Magoun and associates[133, 115, 116] suggested 20 years ago that arousal might instead be caused by the activation of an "ascending reticular activating system" or "ARAS" which was believed to respond to stimuli of all sensory modalities and to produce cortical activation proportional to the significance of the sensory input. The ascending reticular activating system was thought to be opposed by some components of the nonspecific thalamic projection system that exert synchronizing, inhibiting effects on cortical activity. The results of some more recent experiments suggest that we may have to modify this appealingly simple explanation. However, a closer look at the overall picture indicates that many of the basic notions may turn out to be correct. Here, then, are the outlines of the system and some relevant experimental observations.

Large lesions in the midbrain reticular formation produce behavioral coma and abolish all signs of EEG arousal, whereas similar lesions in the classical sensory pathways of the brainstem do not.[115, 116] Electrical stimulation rostral to a lesion in the brainstem reticular formation produces cortical desynchronization.[116] Stimulation of the reticular formation of intact animals results in behavioral as well as electroencephalographic arousal from sleep,[113, 163] and there is no evidence for specific connections between subdivisions of the brainstem and particular regions of cortex.[48] Stimulation of the brainstem reticular formation may also enhance the response of the classical sensory pathways to environmental stimulation[142] and facilitate perception.[50] Electrodes in the brainstem reticular formation can pick up evoked potentials in response to stimuli of most, if not all, sensory modalities[48, 170] and even single brainstem neurons often respond to stimuli of several modalities.[161, 147]

Damage to the nonspecific thalamic projection system (the nuclei of the midline, the intralaminar nuclei, and the reticular nucleus that surrounds most of the thalamus) produces behavioral coma and abolishes all cortical synchronization or "spindling" activity.[47] Low-frequency electrical stimulation of these nuclei induces EEG spindles that appear similar to those seen in some sleep stages[129] and may result in behavioral sleep.[81] The distribution of these spindles seems to be determined by the locus of stimulation within the nonspecific projection system, suggesting that its connections may be quite specific in spite of its name.[89] Animals with a high brainstem transection that effectively excludes all influences from the brainstem reticular formation show continual EEG synchronization.

Given this internally consistent literature, it is easy to see how the hypothesis developed that the midbrain reticular formation provided the stimuli responsible for arousal, whereas the nonspecific thalamic projection system was responsible for opposite, inhibitory influences and sleep. The research of the last 15 years has raised some disquieting questions without producing much in the way of alternative suggestions.

For instance, the brainstem reticular formation is neither anatomically nor functionally "diffuse," as the ARAS concept originally proposed.[143, 20] Nor is it quite true that all primary sensory pathways converge on the reticular formation. Some, notably the pain pathways of the spinothalamic system, actually synapse in it and become part of it. Others, such as the visual system, project only indirectly to the reticular formation, and still others, such as the primary somatosensory pathways, do not seem to connect with it at all.[20, 141] Some neurons of the reticular formation do indeed respond to stimuli of several sensory modalities (see Figure 14–14), but the large majority of them respond specifically to inputs from only one sensory system

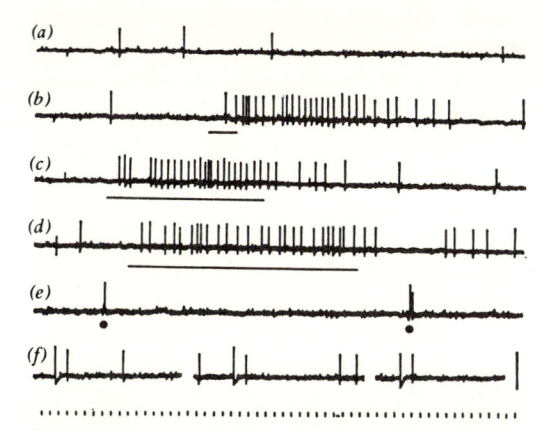

FIG. 14–14. Convergence of tactile, acoustic, and cortical stimuli on a neuron in the pontine reticular formation. (*a*) Spontaneous discharge. (*b*) Tapping the ipsilateral forelimb. (*c*) Rubbing the back. (*d*) Touching whiskers. (*e*) Hand claps. (*f*) Shocks to the sensorimotor cortex (indicated by the stimulus artifact).

(From M. Palestini, G. F. Rossi, & A. Zanchetti. An electrophysiological analysis of pontine reticular regions showing different anatomical organization. *Arch. ital. Biol.*, **95**, 1957, 97–109.)

and many do not react to any sensory signals at all.[161] Moreover, the activity of most of the cells in the reticular formation is not in any simple way correlated with cortical arousal.[121, 147] Indeed, the majority of cells in the reticular formation decrease their spontaneous activity during the transition from sleep to wakefulness,[88] and those cells that do show an increase in firing rate during arousal return to low base-line levels long before the cortical EEG arousal response subsides.[126]

Perhaps most damaging to the notion of a diffuse reticular arousal system is the well documented fact[35, 1] that major segments of the brainstem reticular formation can be destroyed without producing significant permanent effects on cortical EEG or behavioral arousal if the lesions are gradually enlarged or special nursing care maintains the animals during the initial period of impaired reactivity that follows large single-stage lesions. Recent experiments suggest, in fact, that only a very small region of the pons, called the *nucleus reticularis pontis oralis*, may be specifically related to cortical arousal.[132] Whether even this small region is indeed essential to behavioral arousal is not certain, since the relationship between cortical desynchronization and behavioral alertness has turned out to be not as invariable as early investigators believed. During the deepest sleep the cortical EEG shows a desynchronized low-amplitude pattern normally seen only during arousal and attention.[32, 33] Conversely, moderate doses of the cholinergic blocking agent atropine induce cortical slow waves indistinguishable from those seen in slow-wave sleep without reducing general alertness or interfering with the organism's ability to learn and perform novel appetitively as well as aversively reinforced instrumental behaviors.[17]

The discovery of arousal-related EEG changes in the hippocampus[62] suggests, moreover, that the arousal function may not be entirely and uniquely organized in the brainstem reticular formation. The exact nature of the hippocampal influence is not yet clear, but it seems possible that some aspect of the reticular formation may mediate arousal reactions to stimulation of exteroceptors, whereas the hippocampus may be responsible for arousal reactions to internal "drive" stimulation.

The role of the nonspecific thalamic projection system as a pacemaker for slow, high-amplitude cortical activity and a source of general inhibitory influences has not been seriously questioned, but some aspects of the system have been shown to have arousing instead of inhibitory functions regarding cortical activities.[8, 89] Moreover, many recent experiments have suggested that the inhibitory influence may not be unique to the thalamus. An extensive system of centers and pathways, including the orbitofrontal cortex, thalamus, septal area, preoptic region, anterior hypothalamus, and midbrain reticular formation, seems to exercise inhibitory influences on wakefulness and alertness.[139, 171, 172, 80]

Attention and Habituation

Attention is difficult to define experimentally and even more difficult to measure. Therefore, few investigators have tried to describe the neuroanatomical basis of this elusive process. Lindsley[114] has suggested that some aspects of the nonspecific thalamic projection system may serve a selective orienting function and direct attention to specific features of the environment. Logically, this is a plausible hypothesis because the nonspecific projection system has very specific connections with all portions of the cortex and would be in an ideal position to facilitate one cortical function selectively while inhibiting others. However, there is as yet little experimental evidence to support this interpretation.

Evoked potentials that are recorded from various subcortical relay stations in decorticated cats seem to be inhibited by the presentation of other, novel stimuli,[69] suggesting that attention, as defined in these experiments, may reflect subcortical influences. However, we do not have more specific information that might permit a more precise localization.

Habituation, in a purely phenomenological sense, involves the gradual disappearance of arousal reactions, and it is tempting to look on this process as an active or perhaps passive inhibition of whatever pathways mediate arousal. Indeed, there is some evidence that habituation may occur not only cortically but also in lower portions of the sensory pathways, and that some aspects of the brainstem reticular formation influence the habituation process. The specificity of the habituation process as well as the complexity of the determining factors in some experiments suggest, however, that cortical mechanisms may also be involved.

Many investigators have reported that evoked potentials to stimuli of all sensory modalities disappear from the cortex long before any changes are seen in the lower portions of the classical sensory pathways,[73, 113, 56] suggesting that habituation may not be primarily caused by a decreased efficiency of the sensory pathways (see Figure 14–15). However, the evoked potentials do eventually diminish even in lower levels of the sensory systems, indicating that habituation may at least in part be related to neural mechanisms that are capable of affecting the transmission properties of the lower sensory pathways. A primary candidate for such a function is the brainstem reticular formation.

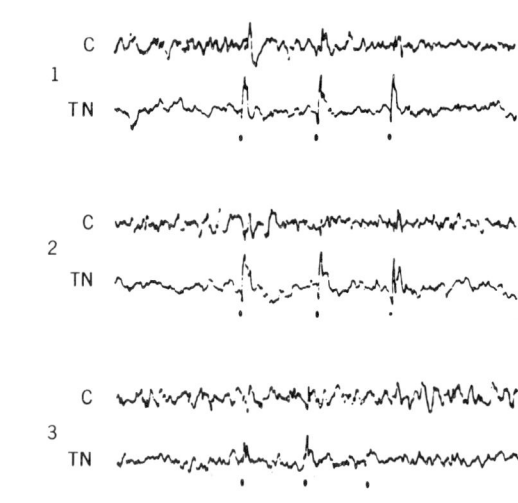

FIG. 14–15. Potentials evoked by tactile stimuli applied to the face of a cat. Simultaneous records from the sensory-motor cortex (C) and from the spinal fifth sensory nucleus (TN). The cortical potentials (1) disappeared earlier (2) than the bulbar potentials (3).

(From R. Hernández-Peón. Neurophysiological correlates of habituation and other manifestations of plastic inhibition (internal inhibition). In *The Moscow colloquium on electroencephalography of higher nervous activity*. H. H. Jasper & G. D. Smirnov, Eds. *EEG clin. Neurophysiol.*, 1960, Suppl. 13, 101–114.)

Electrical stimulation of the reticular formation reduces or inhibits evoked potentials throughout the somatosensory,[63] visual,[58] and auditory[52] pathways. There is some evidence that this inhibition may be partly mediated by motor mechanisms such as changes in the aperture of the eye[4] or the tension of the inner ear muscles,[87] but part of it appears to be a result of direct inhibition of neural transmission at the first or second synapse.[134]

Lesions in the brainstem reticular formation often have opposite, facilitatory effects. Previously habituated responses reappear following relatively small brainstem lesions[78] and this "dishabituation" effect is often modality specific (i.e., different lesions are required to dishabituate responses to stimuli of different modalities).[79]

It has been reported that habituation of evoked potentials can be observed even after the brainstem has been transected just above the spinal cord,[71] suggesting that the spinal cord components of the reticular formation may, at least under some circumstances, be capable of mediating habituation. However, the habituation of gross arousal reactions cannot be obtained after neodecortication[93] and is markedly retarded after smaller neocortical damage, particularly in the frontal lobe.[106, 93] This suggests neocortical influences that may be especially important when habituation requires fine discrimination.

Summary and Review Questions

Electrophysiological arousal and behavioral alerting may be related to activating influences on cortical functions that arise in some portions of the brainstem reticular formation, particularly the nucleus reticularis pontis oralis. Complementary inhibitory influences that result in cortical synchrony arise from some components of the nonspecific thalamic projection system and, possibly, from associated pathways that involve the basal forebrain and some portions of the midbrain reticular formation. The nonspecific thalamic projection system also appears to be the source of selective activating or arousal influences on specific areas of the cortex and thus, in conjunction with its widespread inhibitory influence, may be a determining factor in selective attention.

1. Discuss the concept of an "ascending reticular arousal system" in light of recent experimental evidence. Can we retain the basic notion? What modifications would you suggest?

2. Describe the role of the nonspecific thalamic projection system in arousal and habituation, citing some supporting evidence for your conclusions.

3. Describe the hippocampal arousal response and discuss the role of the hippocampus in arousal and in orienting.

Conclusions

At any moment in time, literally thousands of stimuli impinge on our sensorium. We clearly cannot respond to all of them but must retain the ability to do so should one of them turn out to have or acquire special significance as a signal for food, water, a sexual partner, or enemy. To satisfy this seemingly impossible condition, we have developed complex neural mechanisms that modulate our reactivity to sensory input in accordance with the organism's history and current requirements.

The very first time a stimulus is presented, we immediately attend to it, and our entire nervous system alerts in anticipation of a possibly necessary reaction. If the stimulus turns out to have no immediate significance for us, we gradually habituate and respond less and less whenever it is presented. First, the overt orienting reaction and associated autonomic responses disappear. Next, the general arousal reaction of the brain diminishes, leaving only a barely perceptible desynchronization reaction in the cortical projection area of the stimulus. Even the processing of the stimulus itself gradually becomes less and less effective, and the magnitude of the summated potential that it evokes diminishes. The effects of this habituation are prolonged but fortunately (because the stimulus may some day acquire important signal value) not permanent. When a stimulus is not presented for a few days or weeks, it once again elicits an arousal reaction. Habituation is also reversed, almost immediately, when the stimulus is associated with motivationally significant events or with other novel stimuli that might be significant for survival.

We are rarely aware of the interplay of neural influences that determine whether we respond to any aspect of the environment. This monumental evaluation process nonetheless continues without respite day and night throughout our lives. The basic process is modified by cyclical variations in overt responsiveness, which we identify with sleep and wakefulness. During some portion of each day our general level of reactivity decreases and we become totally "unaware" of the many background stimuli that do not require overt reactions. Even significant stimuli may have to be more intense to evoke an overt reaction during this period. Although most motor functions are decreased or even suspended, others continue without modification or may even be facilitated. Sensory signals do not elicit overt responses but appear to be processed within the nervous system. Most importantly, there is no indication of a generally lowered activity in any region of the brain.

How the nervous system accomplishes the amazingly complex task of determining the significance of literally billions of stimuli each day with the lightning speed that makes it possible to respond appropriately to some of them is without doubt one of the most intriguing mysteries of our lives. Not surprisingly, we have as yet only some glimpses of the mechanisms that may be involved and can only speculate about the nature of their interaction. Our best guess at the moment is that the organism's overall level of reactivity as well as its responsiveness to specific stimuli may be determined by an interplay of excitatory and inhibitory influences that arise in some parts of the brainstem reticular formation, in the nonspecific thalamic projection system, in the basal forebrain, and in the hippocampus.

Specific aspects of the brainstem reticular formation, notably the region of the nucleus reticularis pontis oralis, seem to be the source of activating or desynchronizing influences that increase cortical reactivity and arousal. A more specific alerting function regarding selected areas of the neocortex appears to be exercised by components of the nonspecific thalamic projection system. These facilitatory influences are opposed by inhibitory components of the brainstem reticular formation as well as by a complex system of centers and pathways, which includes some parts of the nonspecific thalamic projection system, the orbitofrontal cortex, the preoptic region and anterior hypothalamus, and several discrete portions of the midbrain and pontine reticular formation. The hippocampus may be specifically concerned with behavioral alerting and orienting behavior and, perhaps, with the initiation of appropriate voluntary responses.

The locus coeruleus of the pons appears to be specifically related to "paradoxical" sleep, and it has been suggested that its neurons may be selectively sensitive to the neurohumor adrenaline. Serotonergic cells in the more medially located raphé nucleus may be responsible, at least in part, for slow-wave sleep. Other aspects of the brainstem reticular formation that have not yet been as specifically identified neuroanatomically or pharmacologically appear to be related to the habituation of arousal reactions to stimuli of particular sensory modalities.

The inhibitory influences of the nonspecific thalamic projection system may play an important role in the initiation of sleep and in the maintenance of slow-wave sleep. More specifically, the thalamus may act directly on the cortex to induce synchrony and inhibition, and indirectly, via the basal forebrain, to activate the sleep "centers" of the midbrain reticular formation.

Just how these opposing forces interact to produce a smoothly functioning organism is not yet clear. It has been suggested that the excitatory components of the brainstem reticular formation may respond to sensory input by attempting to maintain a state of cortical desynchronization and arousal. This influence is opposed by inhibitory components of the reticular formation if a comparison with memory stores indicates that the sensory input has in the past been without significance for survival. Stimuli that do succeed in passing this hurdle may selectively arouse relevant aspects of the cortex because of the interplay between general inhibitory and selective excitatory influences within the nonspecific thalamic projections and associated pathways. The resulting overt orienting response may further require disinhibition of the hippocampus.

Bibliography

1. Adametz, J. H. Rate of recovery of functioning in cats with rostral reticular lesions. *J. Neurosurg.*, 1959, **16**, 85–97.

2. Adey, W. R., Dunlop, C. W., & Hendrix, C. E. Hippocampal slow waves. *Arch. Neurol. (Chicago)*, 1960, **3**, 74–90.

3. Adrian, E. D., & Matthews, B. H. C. The Berger rhythm: Potential changes from the occipital lobes of man. *Brain*, 1934, **57**, 355–384.

4. Affani, J., Mancia, M., & Marchiafava, P. L. Role of the pupil in changes in evoked responses along the visual pathways. *Arch. ital. Biol.*, 1962, **100**, 287–296.

5. Aghajanian, G. K., & Sheard, M. H. Behavioral effects of mid-brain raphé stimulation—dependence upon serotonin. *Comm. Behav. Biol.*, 1968, **1A**, 37–41.

6. Aghajanian, G. K., Rosecrans, J. A., & Sheard, M. H. Serotonin: Release in the forebrain by stimulation of midbrain raphé. *Science*, 1967, **156**, 402–403.

7. Akert, K., Koella, W. P., & Hess, R., Jr. Sleep produced by electrical stimulation of the thalamus. *Amer. J. Physiol.*, 1952, **168**, 260–267.

8. Akimoto, H., Yamaguchi, N., Okabe, K., Nakagawa, T., Nakamura, I., Abe, K., Torii, H., & Masahashi, K. On the sleep induced through electrical stimulation on dog thalamus. *Folia Psychiat. Neurol. Jap.*, 1956, **10**, 117–146.

9. Apelbaum, J., Silva, E. E., Frick, O., & Segundo, J. P. Specificity and biasing of arousal reaction habituation. *EEG clin. Neurophysiol.*, 1960, **12**, 829–840.

10. Bagchi, B. K. The adaptation and variability of response of the human brain rhythm. *J. Psychol.*, 1937, **3**, 463–485.

11. Batini, C., Moruzzi, G., Palestini, M., Rossi, G. F., & Zanchetti, A. Persistent patterns of wakefulness in the pretrigeminal midpontine preparation. *Science*, 1958, **128**, 30–32.

12. Batini, C., Moruzzi, G., Palestini, M., Rossi, G. F., & Zanchetti, A. Effects of complete pontine transections on the sleep-wakefulness rhythm: The midpontine pretrigeminal preparation. *Arch. ital. Biol.*, 1959, **97**, 1–12.

13. Berger, H. Über das Elektrenkephalogramm des Menschen. *Arch. Psychiat.*, 1929, **87**, 527–570.

14. Bliss, E. L., Clark, L. D., & West, C. D. Studies of sleep deprivation—relationship to schizophrenia. *Arch. Neurol. Psychiat.*, 1959, **81**, 348–359.

15. Boas, E. P., & Goldschmidt, E. F. *The heart rate*. Springfield, Ill.: Thomas, 1932, 162 pp.

16. Bradley, P. B. The central action of certain drugs in relation to the reticular formation of the brain. In *The reticular formation of the brain*. H. H. Jasper, L. D. Proctor, R. S. Knighton, W. C. Noshay, & R. T. Costello, Eds. Boston: Little, Brown, 1958, pp. 123–149.

17. Bradley, P. B. Intermediation between administered drugs and behavioral effects: The electrophysiological approach. In *Ciba foundation symposium on animal behaviour and drug action*. H. Steinberg, A. V. S. de Reuck & Julie Knight, Eds. Boston: Little, Brown, 1964, pp. 338–344.

18. Branchey, M., & Kissin, B. The effect of alpha-methyl-para-tyrosine on sleep and arousal in the rat. *Psychonom. Sci.*, 1970, **19**, 281–282.

19. Bremer, F. Cerveau "isolé" et physiologie du sommeil. *C. R. Soc. Biol.*, 1935, **118**, 1235–1241.

20. Brodal, A. *The reticular formation of the brain stem, anatomical aspects and functional correlations*. London: Oliver and Boyd, 1957.

21. Brooks, D. C., & Bizzi, E. Brain stem electrical activity during deep sleep. *Arch ital. Biol.*, 1963, **101**, 648–665.

22. Brown, B. B. Frequency and phase of hippocampal theta activity in the spontaneously behaving cat. *EEG clin. Neurophysiol.*, 1968, **24**, 53–62.

23. Brust-Carmona, H., & Hernández-Peón, R. Sensory transmission in the spinal cord during attention and tactile habituation. Proceedings of the 21st international congress of physiology, Buenos Aires, 1959.

24. Caspers, H. Shifts of the cortical steady potential during various stages of sleep. *Editions du Centre National de la Recherche Scientifique*, 1965, **127**, 213–229.

25. Cordeau, J. P., Moreau, A., & Beaulnes, A. EEG and behavioral effects of microinjections of drugs in the brain stem of cats. Proc. 5th Internat. Congr., *EEG clin. Neurophysiol.*, Excerpta Med., Int. Congr., Series 37, 1961.

26. Cordeau, J. P., Moreau, A., Beaulnes, A., & Laurin, C. EEG and behavioral effects of microinjection of drugs in the brain stem of cats. *Proc. XXII Internat. Congr. Physiol. Sci., Excerpta Med., Int. Congr.*, Series 48, 1962.

27. Creutzfeldt, O., & Jung, R. Neuronal discharge in the cat's motor cortex during sleep and arousal. In *Ciba foundation symposium on the nature of sleep*. G. E. W. Wolstenholme & M. O'Connor, Eds. Boston: Little, Brown, 1961, pp. 131–170.

28. Crowley, T. J., Smith, E., & Lewis, O. F. The biogenic amines and sleep in the monkey—a preliminary report. Paper presented before A.P.S.S., Denver, 1968.

29. Dahlström, A., & Fuxe, K. Evidence for the existence of monoamine neurons in the central nervous system. IV. Distribution of monoamine nerve terminals in the central nervous system. *Acta physiol. scand.*, 1965, **64**, Suppl. 247.

30. Dalton, A., & Black, A. H. Hippocampal electrical activity during the operant conditioning of movement and refraining from movement. *Comm. Behav. Biol.*, 1968, **2**, 267–273.

31. Dawe, A. R., & Spurrier, W. A. Hibernation induced in ground squirrels by blood transfusion. *Science*, 1969, **163**, 298–299.

32. Dement, W., & Kleitman, N. The relation of eye movements during sleep to dream activity: An objective method for the study of dreaming. *J. exp. Psychol.*, 1957a, **53**, 339–346.

33. Dement, W., & Kleitman, N. Cyclic variations in EEG during sleep and their relation to eye movements, body motility, and dreaming. *EEG clin. Neurophysiol.*, 1957b, **9**, 673–690.

34. Donchin, E., & Cohen, L. Averaged evoked potentials and intramodality selective attention. *EEG clin. Neurophysiol.*, 1967, **22**, 537–546.

35. Doty, R. W., Beck, E. C., & Kooi, K. A. Effect of brain stem lesions on conditioned responses of cats. *Exp. Neurol.*, 1959, **1**, 360–385.

36. Dumont, S., & Dell, P. Facilitation réticulaire des mécanismes visuels corticaux. *EEG clin. Neurophysiol.*, 1960, **12**, 769–796.

37. Eidelberg, E., White, J. C., & Brazier, Mary A. B. The hippocampal arousal pattern in rabbits. *Exp. Neurol.*, 1959, **1**, 483–490.

38. Elazar, Z., & Adey, W. R. Spectral analysis of low frequency components in the electrical activity of the hippocampus during learning. *EEG clin. Neurophysiol.*, 1967, **23**, 225–240.

39. Evarts, E. V. Effects of sleep and waking on spontaneous and evoked discharges of single units in visual cortex. *Fed. Proc.*, 1960, **19**, 828–837.

40. Evarts, E. V. Effects of sleep and waking on activity of single units in the unrestrained cat. In *Ciba foundation symposium on the nature of sleep*. G. E. W. Wolstenholme & M. O'Connor, Eds. Boston: Little, Brown, 1961, pp. 171–187.

41. Evarts, E. V. Temporal patterns of discharge of pyramidal tract neurons during sleep and waking in the monkey. *J. Neurophysiol.*, 1964, **27**, 152–171.

42. Evarts, E. V., Fleming, T. C., & Huttenlocher, P. R. Recovery cycle of visual cortex of the awake and sleeping cat. *Amer. J. Physiol.*, 1960, **199**, 373–376.

43. Evarts, E. V., Bental, E., Bihari, B., & Huttenlocher, P. R. Spontaneous discharges of single neurons during sleep and waking. *Science*, 1962, **135**, 726–728.

44. Favale, E., Loeb, C., Rossi, G. F., & Sacco, G. EEG synchronization and behavioral signs of sleep following low frequency stimulation of the brainstem reticular formation. *Arch. ital. Biol.*, 1961, **99** 1–22.

45. Favale, E., Loeb, C., & Manfredi, M. Cortical responses evoked by stimulation of the optic pathways during natural sleep and during arousal. *Arch. int. Physiol.*, 1964, **72**, 221–228.

46. Foulkes, D. *The psychology of sleep*. New York: Scribner's, 1966.

47. French, J. D. Brain lesions associated with prolonged unconsciousness. *A.M.A. Arch. Neurol. Psychiat.*, 1952, **68**, 727–740.

48. French, J. D., Amerongen, F. K., & Magoun, H. W. An activating system in brainstem of monkey. *A.M.A. Arch. Neurol. Psychiat.*, 1952, **68**, 577–590.

49. Funderbunk, W. H., & Case, T. J. The effect of atropine on cortical potentials. *EEG clin. Neurophysiol.*, 1951, **3**, 213–223.

50. Fuster, J. M. Effects of stimulation of brain stem on tachistoscopic perception. *Science*, 1958, **127**, 150.
51. Galambos, R. Suppression of auditory nerve activity by stimulation of efferent fibers to the cochlea. *J. Neurophysiol.*, 1956, **19**, 424–437.
52. Galambos, R., Sheatz, G., & Vernier, V. G. Electrophysiological correlates of a conditioned response in cats. *Science*, 1956, **123**, 376–377.
53. García-Austt, E., Bogacz, J., & Vanzulli, A. Significance of the photic stimulus on the evoked responses in man. In *Brain mechanisms and learning*. J. F. Delafresnaye, A. Fessard, R. W. Gerard, & J. Konorski, Eds. Oxford: Blackwell Scientific, 1961, pp. 603–623.
54. Gassel, M. M., Marchiafava, P. L., & Pompeiano, O. Tonic and phasic inhibition of spinal reflexes during deep, desynchronized sleep in unrestrained cats. *Arch. ital. Biol.*, 1964, **102**, 471–499.
55. Gastaut, H., Jus, A., Jus, C., Morrell, F., Storm Van Leeuwen, W., Dongier, S., Naquet, R., Regis, H., Roger, A., Bekkering, D., Kamp, A., & Werre, J. Etude topographique des réactions électro-encéphalographiques conditionées chez l'homme. *EEG clin. Neurophysiol.*, 1957, **9**, 1–34.
56. Gershuni, G. V., Kozhevnikov, V. A., Maruseva, A. M., Avakyan, R. V., Radionova, E. A., Altoman, J. A., & Soroko, V. I. Modifications in electrical responses of the auditory system in different states of the higher nervous activity. In *The Moscow colloquium on electroencephalography of higher nervous activity*. H. H. Jasper & G. D. Smirnov, Eds. *EEG clin. Neurophysiol.*, 1960, Suppl. 13, 115–123.
57. Glickman, S. E., & Feldman, S. M. Habituation to direct stimulation of the reticular formation. *Fed. Proc.*, 1960, **19**, 288.
58. Granit, R. Centrifugal and antidromic effects on ganglion cells of retina. *J. Neurophysiol.*, 1955, **18**, 388–411.
59. Grastyán, E. The hippocampus and higher nervous activity. In *The central nervous system and behavior*. (Second Conference). Mary A. B. Brazier, Ed. New York: Josiah Macy, Jr., Foundation, 1959, pp. 119–205.
60. Grastyán, E. The significance of the earliest manifestations of conditioning in the mechanism of learning. In *Brain mechanisms and learning*. J. F. Delafresnaye, A. Fessard, R. W. Gerard, & J. Konorski, Eds. Oxford: Blackwell Scientific, 1961, pp. 243–263.
61. Grastyán, E., Lissak, K., Madarasz, I., & Donhoffer, H. Hippocampal electrical activity during the development of conditioned reflexes. *EEG clin. Neurophysiol.*, 1959, **11**, 409–430.
62. Green, J. D., & Arduini, A. Hippocampal electrical activity in arousal. *J. Neurophysiol.*, 1954, **17**, 533–557.
63. Hagbarth, K. E., & Kerr, D. I. B. Central influences on spinal afferent conduction. *J. Neurophysiol.*, 1954, **18**, 388–411.
64. Haider, M. Vigilance, attention, expectancy and cortical evoked potentials. *Acta Psychol.*, 1967, **27**, 246–252.
65. Harlow, H. F., McGaugh, J. L., & Thompson, R. F. *Psychology*. San Francisco: Albion Publishing Co., 1971.
66. Hartmann, E. Reserpine: Its effect on the sleep-dream cycle in man. *Psychopharmacologia*, 1966, **9**, 242–247.
67. Hartmann, E. The effect of l-tryptophane on the sleep-dream cycle in man. *Psychonom. Sci.*, 1967, **8**, 479–480.
68. Hernández-Peón, R. Neurophysiological correlates of habituation and other manifestations of plastic inhibition (internal inhibition). In *The Moscow colloquium on electroencephalography of higher nervous activity*. H. H. Jasper & G. D. Smirnov, Eds. *EEG clin. Neurophysiol.*, 1960, Suppl. 13, 101–114.
69. Hernández-Peón, R. Reticular mechanisms of sensory control. In *Sensory communication*. W. A. Rosenblith, Ed. Cambridge, Mass.: M.I.T. Press, 1961, pp. 497–520.
70. Hernández-Peón, R. Central neuro-humoral transmission in sleep and wakefulness. In *Progress in Brain Research. Vol. 18. Sleep mechanisms*. K. Akert, C. Bally, & J. P. Schadé, Eds. Amsterdam: Elsevier, 1965, pp. 96–117.
71. Hernández-Peón, R., & Brust-Carmona, H. Functional role of subcortical structures in habituation and conditioning. In *Brain mechanisms and learning*. J. F. Delafresnaye, A. Fessard, R. W. Gerard, & J. Konorski, Eds. Oxford: Blackwell Scientific, 1961, pp. 393–412.

72. Hernández-Peón, R., & Donoso, M. Influence of attention and suggestion upon subcortical evoked electrical activity in the human brain. *Proceedings of the first international congress of neurological sciences*, Brussels, 1957. Vol. III. *EEG clin. Neurophysiol.* London: Pergamon Press, 1959.

73. Hernández-Peón, R., Guzmán-Flores, C., Alcaraz, M., & Fernández-Guardiola, A. Photic potentials in the visual pathway during attention and photic habituation. *Fed. Proc.*, 1956a, **15**, 91–92.

74. Hernández-Peón, R., Scherrer, H., & Jouvet, M. Modification of electric activity in cochlear nucleus during "attention" in unanesthetized cats. *Science*, 24 February 1956b, **123**, 331–332.

75. Hernández-Peón, R., Scherrer, H., & Valasco, M. Central influences on afferent conduction in the somatic and visual pathways. *Acta neurol. lat.-amer.*, 1956c, **2**, 8–22.

76. Hernández-Peón, R., Alcocer-Cuarón, C., Lavin, A., & Santibañez, G. Regulación centifuga de la actividad eléctrica del bulbo olfatoria. *I Reun. Cient. Cienc. Fisiol. Montevideo*, 1957a, 192–193.

77. Hernández-Peón, R., Guzmán-Flores, C., Alcaraz, M., & Fernández-Guardiola, A. Sensory transmission in visual pathway during "attention" in unanesthetized cats. *Acta neurol. lat.-amer.*, 1957b, **3**, 1–8.

78. Hernández-Peón, R., Jouvet, M., & Scherrer, H. Auditory potentials at the cochlear nucleus during acoustical habituation. *Acta neurol. lat.-amer.*, 1957c, **3**, 144–156.

79. Hernández-Peón, R., Guzmán-Flores, C., Alcaraz, M., & Fernández-Guardiola, A. Habituation in the visual pathway. *Acta neurol. lat.-amer.*, 1958, **4**, 121–129.

80. Hernández-Peón, R., Chávez-Ibarra, G., Morgane, P., & Timo-Iaria, C. Limbic cholinergic pathways involved in sleep and emotional activity. *Exp. Neurol.*, 1963, **8**, 93–111.

81. Hess, W. R. Über die Wechselbeziehungen zwischen psychischen und vegetativen Funktionen. *Schweiz. Arch. Neurol. Psychiat.*, 1925, **16**, 36–55, 285–306.

82. Hobson, J. A. Electrographic correlates of behavior in the frog with special reference to sleep. *EEG clin. Neurophysiol.*, 1967, **22**, 113–121.

83. Hodes, R., & Suzuki, J.-I. Comparative thresholds of cortex, vestibular system and reticular formation in wakefulness, sleep and rapid eye movement periods. *EEG clin. Neurophysiol.*, 1965, **18**, 239–248.

84. Holmes, J. E., & Adey, W. R. Electrical activity of the entorhinal cortex during conditioned behavior. *Amer. J. Physiol.*, 1960, **199**, 741–744.

85. Horn, G. Electrical activity of the cerebral cortex of the unanesthetized cat during attentive behavior. *Brain*, 1960, **83**, 57–76.

86. Hubel, D. H., Henson, C. D., Rupert, A., & Galambos, R. Attention units in the auditory cortex. *Science*, 1959, **129**, 1279–1280.

87. Hugelin, A., Dumont, S., & Paillas, N. Formation réticulaire et transmission des informations auditives au niveau de l'oreille moyenne et des voies acoustiques centrales. *EEG clin. Neurophysiol.*, 1960, **12**, 797–818.

88. Huttenlocher, P. R. Evoked and spontaneous activity in single units of medial brain stem during natural sleep and waking. *J. Neurophysiol.*, 1961, **24**, 451–468.

89. Jasper, H. H. Unspecific thalamo-cortical relations. In *Handbook of physiology*. Vol. II. J. Field, H. W. Magoun, & V. E. Hall, Eds. Washington, D.C.: Am. Physiol. Soc., 1960, pp. 1307–1322.

90. Jasper, H. H., & Cruikshank, Ruth M. Electroencephalography. II: Visual stimulation and the after image as affecting the occipital alpha rhythm. *J. gen. Psychol.*, 1937, **17**, 29–48.

91. Jasper, H. H., Cruikshank, Ruth M., & Howard, Helen. Action currents from the occipital region of the brain in man as affected by variables of attention and external stimulation. *Psychol. Bull.*, 1935, **32**, 565.

92. John, E. R., & Killam, K. F. Studies of electrical activity of brain during differential conditioning in cats. In *Recent advances in biological psychiatry*. Vol. II. J. Wortis, Ed. New York: Grune and Stratton, 1960, pp. 138–148.

93. Jouvet, M. Recherches sur les mécanismes neurophysiologiques du sommeil et de l'apprentissage négatif. In *Brain mechanisms and learning*. J. F. Delafresnaye, A. Fessard, R. W. Gerard, & J. Konorski, Eds. Oxford: Blackwell Scientific, 1961, pp. 445–479.

94. Jouvet, M. Recherches sur les structures nerveuses et les mécanismes responsables des différentes phases du sommeil physiologique. *Arch. ital. Biol.*, 1962, **100**, 125–206.

95. Jouvet, M. The rhombencephalic phase of sleep. In *Progress in Brain Research. Vol. 1. Brain mechanisms.* G. Moruzzi, A. Fessard, & H. H. Jasper. Eds. Amsterdam: Elsevier, 1963, pp. 406–424.

96. Jouvet, M. Étude de la dualité des états de sommeil et des mécanismes de la phase paradoxale. *Editions du Centre National de la Recherche Scientifique*, 1965, **127**, 397–449.

97. Jouvet, M. Mechanisms of paradoxical sleep: A neuropharmacological approach. *Res. Publ. Ass. Res. nerv. ment. Dis.*, 1967, **45**, 86–126.

98. Jouvet, M. Insomnia and decrease of cerebral 5-hydroxytryptamine after destruction of the raphé system in the cat. *Adv. Pharmacol.*, 1968, **6**(B), 265–279.

99. Jouvet, M. Biogenic amines and the states of sleep. *Science*, 3 January 1969a, **163**, 32–41.

100. Jouvet, M. Neurophysiological and biochemical mechanisms of sleep. In *Sleep: Physiology and pathology.* A. Kales, Ed. Philadelphia: Lippincott, 1969b, pp. 89–100.

101. Jouvet, M., Vimont, P., & Delorme, F. Supression élective du sommeil paradoxal chez le Chat par les inhibiteurs de la monoamineoxydase. *C. R. Soc. Biol.* (Paris), 1965, **159**, 1595–1599.

102. Kawamura, H., & Sawyer, C. H. D-C potential changes in rabbit brain during slow-wave and paradoxical sleep. *Amer. J. Physiol.*, 1964, **207**, 1379–1386.

103. Killam, E. K., Killam, K. F., & Shaw, T. The effect of psychotherapeutic compounds on central afferent and limbic pathways. *Ann. N. Y. Acad. Sci.*, 1957, **66**, 784–805.

104. Kleitman, N. Phylogenetic, ontogenetic and environmental determinants in the evolution of sleep-wakefulness cycles. In *Sleep and altered states of consciousness. Res. Publ. Ass. Res. nerv. ment. Dis., Vol. 45.* S. S. Kety, E. V. Evarts, & H. L. Williams, Eds. Baltimore: Williams and Wilkins, 1967, pp. 30–38.

105. Kogan, A. B. The manifestations of processes of higher nervous activity in the electrical potentials of the cortex during free behavior of animals. In *The Moscow colloquium on electroencephalography of higher nervous activity.* H. H. Jasper & G. D. Smirnov, Eds. *EEG clin. Neurophysiol.*, 1960, Suppl. 13, 51–64.

106. Konorski, J. On the influence of the frontal lobes of the cerebral hemispheres on higher nervous activity. In *Problems of the modern physiology of the nervous and muscle system.* Georgian S. S. R. Tbilisi Acad. Sci., 1956.

107. Kornmüller, A. E., Lux, H. D., Winkle, K., & Klee, M. Neurohumoral ausgelöste Schlafzustände an Tieren mit gekreuztem Kreislauf unter der Kontrolle von EEG-Ableitungen. *Naturwissenschaften*, 1961, **48**, 503–505.

108. Kroll, F. W. Über das Vorkommen von übertragbaren schlaferzeugenden Stoffen im Hirn schlafender Tiere. *Z. ges. Neurol. Psychiat.*, 1933, **146**, 208–218.

109. Legendre, R., & Piéron, H. Les rapports entre les conditions physiologiques et les modifications histologiques des cellules cérébrales dans l'insomnie expérimentale. *C. R. Soc. Biol.*, 1907a, **62**, 312–314.

110. Legendre, R., & Piéron, H. Retour à l'état normal des cellules nerveuses après les modifications provoquées par l'insomnie expérimental. *C. R. Soc. Biol.*, 1907b, **62**, 1007–1008.

111. Lewis, G. P. (Ed.) *5-Hydroxytryptamine.* London: Pergamon, 1958.

112. Li, C. L. Synchronization of unit activity in the cerebral cortex. *Science*, 1959, **129**, 783–784.

113. Lifschitz, W. Auditory evoked potentials in the central nervous system during acoustic habituation. Reported in Hernández-Peón, R. Neurophysiological correlates of habituation and other manifestations of plastic inhibition (internal inhibition). In *The Moscow colloquium on electroencephalography of higher nervous activity.* H. H. Jasper & G. D. Smirnov, Eds. *EEG clin. Neurophysiol.*, 1960, Suppl. 13, 101–114.

114. Lindsley, D. B. Psychophysiology and motivation. In *Nebraska symposium on motivation.* M. R. Jones, Ed. Lincoln, Neb.: Univ. of Nebraska Press, 1957, pp. 44–105.

115. Lindsley, D. B., Bowden, J. W., & Magoun, H. W. Effect upon the EEG of acute injury to the brainstem activating system. *EEG clin. Neurophysiol.*, 1949, **1**, 475–486.
116. Lindsley, D. B., Schreiner, L. H., Knowles, W. B., & Magoun, H. W. Behavioral and EEG changes following chronic brainstem lesions in the cat. *EEG clin. Neurophysiol.*, 1950, **2**, 483–498.
117. Loomis, A. L., Harvey, E. N., & Hobart, G. A. Cerebral states during sleep, as studied by human brain potentials. *J. Exp. Psychol.*, 1937, **21**, 127–144.
118. Loomis, A. L., Harvey, E. N., & Hobart, G. A. Distribution of disturbance-patterns in the human electroencephalogram, with special reference to sleep. *J. Neurophysiol.*, 1938, **1**, 413–430.
119. McCleary, R. A. Response-modulating functions of the limbic system: initiation and suppression. In *Progress in physiological psychology. Vol. I.* E. Stellar & J. M. Sprague, Eds. New York: Academic Press, 1966, pp. 210–272.
120. McGinty, D. J., & Sterman, M. B. Sleep suppression after basal forebrain lesions in the cat. *Science*, 1968, **160**, 1253–1255.
121. Machne, X., Calma, I., & Magoun, H. W. Unit activity of central cephalic brainstem in EEG arousal. *J. Neurophysiol.*, 1955, **18**, 547–558.
122. Mancia, M. Electrophysiological and behavioural changes owing to splitting of the brain-stem in cats. *EEG clin. Neurophysiol.*, 1969, **27**, 487–502.
123. Mandell, A., & Spooner, C. E. Psychochemical research studies in man. *Science*, 1968, **162**, 1442–1453.
124. Marantz, R., & Rechtschaffen, A. The effect of alpha-methyl-tyrosine on sleep in the rat. *Perceptual & Motor Skills*, 1967, **25**, 805–808.
125. Mills, J. N. Circadian rhythms during and after three months in solitude underground. *J. Physiol.*, 1964, **174**, 217–231.
126. Mollica, A., Moruzzi, G., & Naquet, R. Décharges réticulaires induites par la polarisation du cervelet: leurs rapports avec le tonus postural et la réaction d'éveil. *EEG clin. Neurophysiol.*, 1953, **5**, 571–584.
127. Monnier, M., & Hösli, L. Dialysis of sleep and waking factors in blood of the rabbit. *Science*, 1964, **146**, 796–798.
128. Monnier, M., Koller, Th., & Graber, S. Humoral influences of induced sleep and arousal upon electrical brain activity of animals with crossed circulation. *Exp. Neurol.*, 1963, **8**, 264–277.
129. Morison, R. S., & Dempsey, E. W. A. A study of thalamo-cortical relations. *Amer. J. Physiol.*, 1942, **135**, 280–292.
130. Morrell, F. Some electrical events involved in the formation of temporary connections. In *The reticular formation of the brain.* H. H. Jasper, L. D. Proctor, R. S. Knighton, W. C. Noshay, & R. T. Costello, Eds. Boston: Little, Brown, 1958, pp. 545–560.
131. Morris, G. O., & Singer, M. T. Sleep deprivation. Transactional and subjective observations. *Arch. gen. Psychiat.*, 1961, **5**, 453–461.
132. Moruzzi, G. The historical development of the deafferentation hypothesis of sleep. *Proc. Amer. Philos. Soc.*, 1964, **108**, 19–28.
133. Moruzzi, G., & Magoun, H. W. Brain stem reticular formation and activation of the EEG. *EEG clin. Neurophysiol.*, 1949, **1**, 455–473.
134. Moushegian, G., Rupert, A., Marsh, J. T., & Galambos, R. Evoked cortical potentials in absence of middle ear muscles. *Science*, 1961, **133**, 582–583.
135. Murata, K., & Kameda, K. The activity of single cortical neurons of unrestrained cats during sleep and wakefulness. *Arch. ital. Biol.*, 1963, **101**, 306–331.
136. Murray, E. J., Williams, H. L., & Lubin, A. Body temperature and psychological ratings during sleep deprivation. *J. exp. Psychol.*, 1958, **56**, 271–273.
137. Näätänen, R. Selective attention and evoked potentials. *Annales Academiae Scientiarum Fennicae B* 151, **1**, 1–226, 1967. Helsinki: Suomalaisen Kirjallisuuden Kirjapaino Oy.
138. Näätänen, R. Evoked potential, EEG, and slow potential correlates of selective attention. *Acta Psychologica* 33. *Attention and performance. III.* A. F. Sanders, Ed. Amsterdam: North-Holland Publ. Co., 1970, 178–192.
139. Nauta, W. J. H. Hypothalamic regulation of sleep in rats. An experimental study. *J. Neurophysiol.*, 1946, **9**, 285–316.

140. Nauta, W. J. H. Some efferent connections of the prefrontal cortex in the monkey. In *The frontal granular cortex and behavior*. J. M. Warren & K. Akert, Eds. New York: McGraw-Hill, 1964, pp. 397–409.

141. Nauta, W. J. H., & Kuypers, H. G. J. M. Some ascending pathways in the brainstem reticular formation. In *The reticular formation of the brain*. H. H. Jasper, L. D. Proctor, R. S. Knighton, W. C. Noshay, & R. T. Costello, Eds. Boston: Little, Brown, 1958, pp. 3–30.

142. Ogawa, T. Midbrain reticular influences upon single neurons in lateral geniculate nucleus. *Science*, 1963, **139**, 343–344.

143. Olzewski, J., & Baxter, D. *Cytoarchitecture of the human brain stem*. Philadelphia: Lippincott, 1954.

144. Oswald, I. *Sleeping and waking: Physiology and psychology*. Amsterdam: Elsevier, 1962.

145. Oswald, I. Drugs and sleep. *Pharm. Rev.*, 1968, **20**, 273–304.

146. Palestini, M., & Lifschitz, W. Functions of bulbo-pontine reticular formation and plastic phenomena in the central nervous system. In *Brain mechanisms and learning*. J. F. Delafresnaye, A. Fessard, R. W. Gerard, & J. Konorski, Eds. Oxford: Blackwell Scientific, 1961, pp. 413–431.

147. Palestini, M., Rossi, G. F., & Zanchetti, A. An electrophysiological analysis of pontine reticular regions showing different anatomical organization. *Arch. ital. Biol.*, 1957, **95**, 97–109.

148. Palestini, M., Davidovich, A., & Hernández-Peón, R. Functional significance of centrifugal influences upon the retina. *Acta neurol. lat.-amer.*, 1959, **5**, 113–131.

149. Pappenheimer, J. R., Miller, T. B., & Goodrich, C. A. Sleep promoting effect of cerebrospinal fluid from sleep deprived goats. *Proc. Nat. Acad. Sci. U.S.*, 1967, **58**, 513–517.

150. Pavlov, I. *Conditioned reflexes. An investigation of the physiological activity of the cerebral cortex*. New York: Oxford Univ. Press, 1927.

151. Piéron, H. *Le problème physiologique du sommeil*. Paris: Masson, 1913, 520 pp.

152. Ricci, G. F., Doane, B., & Jasper, H. H. Microelectrode studies of conditioning: technique and preliminary results. *Proceedings of the first international congress of neurological sciences*, Brussels, 1957, 401–415.

153. Richter, C. P. Sleep and activity: their relation to the 24-hour clock. In *Sleep and altered states of consciousness. Res. Publ., Ass. Res. nerv. ment. Dis.* S. S. Kety, E. V. Evarts, & H. L. Williams, Eds. Baltimore: Williams and Wilkins, 1967, pp. 8–29.

154. Rheinberger, M. B., & Jasper, H. H. Electrical activity of the cerebral cortex in the unanesthetized cat. *Amer. J. Physiol.*, 1937, **119**, 186–196.

155. Robin, E. D., Whaley, R. D., Crump, C. H., & Gravis, D. M. Alveolar gas tensions, pulmonary ventilation and blood pH during physiologic sleep in normal subjects. *J. clin. Invest.*, 1958, **37**, 981–989.

156. Roger, A., Rossi, G. F., & Zirondoli, A. Rôle des afférences des nerfs crâniens dans le maintien de l'état vigile de la préparation "encéphale isolé." *EEG clin. Neurophysiol.*, 1956, **8**, 1–13.

157. Rothballer, A. B. The effects of catecholamines on the central nervous system. *Pharm. Rev.*, 1959, **11**, 494–547.

158. Rusinov, V. S., & Smirnov, G. D. Electroencephalographic investigation of conditioned reflexes in man. *Proceedings of the fourth international congress on EEG and clinical neurophysiology*. Brussels, 1957a.

159. Rusinov, V. S., & Smirnov, G. D. Quelque données sur l'étude électroencéphalographique de l'activité nerveuse supérieure. *EEG clin. Neurophysiol.*, 1957b, Suppl. 6, 9–23.

160. Saito, Y., Maekawa, K., Takenaka, S., & Kasmatsu, A. Single cortical unit activity during EEG arousal. *EEG clin. Neurophysiol.*, 1957, Suppl. 9, 95–98.

161. Scheibel, M. E., Scheibel, A. B., Mollica, A., & Moruzzi, G. Convergence and interaction of afferent impulses on single units of reticular formation. *J. Neurophysiol.*, 1955, **18**, 309–331.

162. Schnedorf, J. G., & Ivy, A. C. An examination of the hypnotoxin theory of sleep. *Amer. J. Physiol.*, 1939, **125**, 491–505.

163. Segundo, J. P., Naquet, R., & Buser, P. Effects of cortical stimulation on electrocortical activity in monkeys. *J. Neurophysiol.*, 1955, **18**, 236–245.

164. Sharpless, S., & Jasper, H. H. Habituation of the arousal reaction. *Brain*, 1956, **79**, 655–680.

165. Shaw, J. A., & Thompson, R. F. Dependence of evoked cortical association responses on behavioral variables. *Psychonom. Sci.*, 1964a, **1**, 153–154.

166. Shaw, J. A., & Thompson, R. F. Inverse relation between evoked cortical association responses and behavioral orienting to repeated auditory stimuli. *Psychonom. Sci.*, 1964b, **1**, 399–400.

167. Snyder, F., Hobson, J. A., & Goldfrank, F. Blood pressure changes during human sleep. *Science*, 1963, **142**, 1313–1314.

168. Sokolov, E. N. Higher nervous functions: The orienting reflex. *Ann. Rev. Physiol.*, 1963, **25**, 545–580.

169. Spong, P., Haider, M., & Lindsley, D. B. Selective attentiveness and cortical evoked responses to visual and auditory stimuli. *Science*, 1965, **148**, 395–397.

170. Starzl, T. E., Taylor, C. W., & Magoun, H. W. Collateral afferent excitation of reticular formation of brain stem. *J. Neurophysiol.*, 1951, **14**, 479–496.

171. Sterman, M. B., & Clemente, C. D. Forebrain inhibitory mechanisms: Cortical synchronization induced by basal forebrain stimulation. *Exp. Neurol.*, 1962a, **6**, 91–102.

172. Sterman, M. B., & Clemente, C. D. Forebrain inhibitory mechanisms: Sleep patterns induced by basal forebrain stimulation in the behaving cat. *Exp. Neurol.*, 1962b, **6**, 103–117.

173. Tarozzi, G. Sull' influenza dell' insonnio sperimentale sul ricambio materiale. *Riv. Pat. Nerv. Ment.*, 1899, **4**, 1–23.

174. Thompson, R. F., & Shaw, J. A. Behavioral correlates of evoked activity recorded from association areas of the cerebral cortex. *J. comp. physiol. Psychol.*, 1965, **60**, 329–339.

175. Travis, L. E., & Milisen, R. L. Brain potentials from the rat. *J. gen. Psychol.*, 1936, **49**, 405–409.

176. Vanderwolf, C. H. Limbic-diencephalic mechanisms of voluntary movement. *Psychol. Rev.*, 1971, **78**, 83–113.

177. Voronin, L. G., & Sokolov, E. N. Cortical mechanisms of the orienting reflex and its relation to the conditioned reflex. In *The Moscow colloquium on electroencephalography of higher nervous activity*. H. H. Jasper & G. D. Smirnov, Eds. *EEG clin. Neurophysiol.*, 1960, Suppl. 13, 335–346.

178. Weitzman, E. D. Biogenic amines and sleep stage activity. In *Sleep: Physiology and pathology*. A. Kales, Ed. Philadelphia: Lippincott, 1969, pp. 232–244.

179. Weitzman, E. D., McGregor, P., Moore, C., & Jacoby, J. The effect of alpha-methyl-para-tyrosine on sleep patterns of the monkey: A preliminary report. *Psychophysiology*, 1968a, **5**, 210.

180. Weitzman, E. D., Rapport, M. M., McGregor, P., & Jacoby, J. Sleep patterns of the monkey and brain serotonin concentration: effect of p-chloro-phenylalanine. *Science*, 1968b, **160**, 1361–1363.

181. Whishaw, I. Q., & Vanderwolf, C. H. Hippocampal correlates of movement. *Proceedings of the Canad. Fed. Biol. Soc.*, 1970, **13**, 48.

182. Worden, F. G., & Marsh, J. T. Amplitude changes of auditory potentials evoked at cochlear nucleus during acoustic habituation. *EEG clin. Neurophysiol.*, 1963, **15**, 886–881.

183. Wurtz, R. H., Goldring, S., & O'Leary, J. L. Cortical D.C. potentials accompanying paradoxical and slow wave sleep in the cat. *Fed. Proc.*, 1964, **23**, 209.

184. Yamaguchi, N., Marczynski, T. J., & Ling, G. M. The effects of electrical and chemical stimulation of the preoptic region and some non-specific thalamic nuclei in unrestrained, waking animals. *EEG. clin. Neurophysiol.*, 1963, **15**, 154.

185. Yamaguchi, N., Ling, G. M., & Marczynski, T. J. The effects of chemical stimulation of the preoptic region, nucleus centralis medialis, or brain stem reticular formation with regard to sleep and wakefulness. *Recent. Adv. Biol. Psychiat.*, 1964, **6**, 9–20.

186. Yokota, T., & Fujimori, B. Effects of brainstem stimulation upon hippocampal electrical activity, somato-motor reflexes and autonomic functions. *EEG clin. Neurophysiol.*, 1964, **16**, 375–383.

187. Young, G. A., & Black, A. H. The relationships between electrical activity of the hippocampus and overt skeletal behavior in the dog and rat. Paper presented at the meeting of the Eastern Psychological Association, Atlantic City, N. J., April, 1970.

Chapter 15

THEORIES OF MOTIVATION

Introduction
Drive Stimulation Theories
Activation or Arousal
A Contemporary Hypothesis
Conclusions and Review

INTRODUCTION

In the past chapters we have discussed the physiological bases for some "simple" biological drive states and some mechanisms that may mediate the aversive and rewarding effects of drive induction and reduction. Now that we have this information, can we integrate it into a theoretical framework that could be used to account in a more general sense for all biological drive states? Are the mechanisms that regulate hunger sufficiently similar to those that control thirst to permit us to discern a master plan for all appetitive drives? What about sexual arousal or emotional reactions? Theoretical synthesis is never an easy task and becomes especially difficult in areas of research where most of the relevant empirical information is only a few years old. We do not yet have a very elegant theoretical scheme to describe the physiological basis of motivational influences, but it seems important to see just how far we can go before we run out of information.

The most basic concern of any living organism is to avoid damaging stimuli. All species develop withdrawal reflexes as a first line of protection against such stimulation. In more complex species, these reflexes do not suffice to assure survival, and the organisms develop a special sensory modality—pain—which uniquely reacts to excessive or damaging stimulation. Strong stimuli of all modalities elicit pain sensations and many species develop special pain receptors to protect the outer and inner surfaces of the body that are only sparsely populated by receptors of other modalities. Since each painful stimulation produces damage, complex organisms cannot survive simply by escaping from such stimulation. They therefore develop the ability to store information and thus acquire the ability to avoid repeated exposure to a particular pain stimulus. A process of generalization then occurs which permits the organism to recognize novel potentially painful stimuli because they are in some way similar to others that have damaged the organism in the past.

All surviving species learn to avoid painful and potentially damaging stimulation and this provides the basis for the most fundamental motivational influences on behavior. It is tempting to propose that all biological drives may reflect this innate need to prevent or escape intense stimulation, and such "drive-stimulation" theories of motivation have been around since the time of the Greek philosophers.

There can be no question that man as well as members of other surviving species behave in all instances so as to escape, avoid, or minimize pain and that the drive-stimulation explanation is an appropriate description of a good deal of behavior. It is only when we ask whether specific drive stimulation can account for all types of behaviors that difficulties arise. Do we, in addition to minimizing pain, also behave so as to maximize pleasure, as the hedonists proposed many hundreds of years ago? If so, just what constitutes "pleasure" and is it indeed more than the absence of pain? We have seen in the last chapter that the stimulation of certain brain areas appears to be "pleasurable," but also that this effect seems to be closely related to specific biological drives. Do we eat or drink to remove painful hunger or thirst sensations or even in anticipation of such sensations? Do we copulate to reduce the storm of sensory stimuli that a potential mate can elicit? The answers to these questions are far from simple, as we have seen. Although it seems intuitively obvious that we drink because the mouth and throat dry out, and eat because our stomach complains, it has not been possible to demonstrate that these signals are in any way essential for the regulation of food or water intake or the experience of hunger or thirst. Similarly, the removal of all types of stimuli that contribute to sexual arousal does not seem to have the inhibitory effects one would expect if specific drive stimulation in its simplest form provided the motivational basis for sexual behavior. These observations do not rule out more complex conceptualizations of the drive stimulation hypothesis because none of the experiments have, so far, succeeded in eliminating all of the relevant sensory feedback or, for that matter, identified all possibly important mechanisms of stimulation. However, they have hastened the evolution of theoretical thought from the simple "local theories" of motivation, which were still popular only 30 years ago, to the much more complex, centrally oriented theories of today.

Even today's drive-stimulation theories find it difficult to accommodate the rapidly growing literature which demonstrates that man as well as members of many infrahuman species do not always find a reduction in sensory input rewarding and sometimes exert considerable effort to produce a change or increment in stimulation. Rats cross electrified grids to reach a novel, complex environment;[22] monkeys learn difficult problems when the reward consists only of a peek at an interesting environment;[5] and man as well as members of other species find it excruciatingly difficult to live for any length of time in environments that minimize all stimulation.[3] Moreover, man as well as many animals voluntarily engage in actions that are potentially dangerous and increase the overall level of stimulation.[2,9] Drive-stimulation hypotheses of motivation account for these observations by postulating a "boredom drive" (i.e., the absence or monotony of stimulation itself may give rise to drive stimulation), but the mechanisms for this drive state are not sufficiently similar to those of other drives to make this a very satisfying answer.

Many current theories of motivation instead suggest that all biological organisms require a minimal level of sensory input to sustain a degree of "arousal" or "activation" of the brain that is essential for its function. According to these theories, an organism adapts to a range of sensory inputs from internal as well as external sources and becomes motivated by either a decrease or an increase in sensory input which threatens to disrupt the activity of the central nervous system. On closer inspection, this explanation does not turn out to be so different from the drive stimulation explanation (it merely adds a mechanism that accounts for the boredom drive), and we shall suggest a marriage of the two concepts in the closing paragraphs of our discussion. To lay the foundation for this synthesis, we shall first briefly review the evolution of the drive-stimulation and arousal theories.

Summary and Review Questions

All surviving species develop mechanisms to escape or avoid potentially damaging stimulation of any part of the body. In primitive organisms, these protective mechanisms are largely reflexively organized. As they evolve in more complex biological systems, these reflexes are no longer adequate and anticipatory responses that may involve complex behavioral reactions take their place. The mechanisms that integrate these avoidance responses are the source of the most primitive motivational influences.

It has been tempting to suggest that all biological drive states derive from this primitive need and that all drives are related to intense and potentially damaging stimulation. This negative explanation of motivation has had many supporters, but it has been difficult to demonstrate the drive-inducing role of specific stimuli. Drive-stimulation theories have, moreover, had serious difficulty explaining the recently documented propensity of man as well as lower animals to seek novelty and variety of sensory input.

An alternative explanation is based on the proposition that all motivation can be reduced to the organism's need to maintain a minimal level and variety of sensory input to support normal brain function and to avoid intense and disruptive stimulation. This "activation" theory of motivation accounts nicely for man's propensity to seek novelty and provides a physiological basis for the energizing aspects of motivation[4] but fails to explain why we eat when hungry and do not attempt to reduce other stimulation.

1. State the basic "drive stimulation" hypothesis.
2. State the basic "arousal" hypothesis.
3. Are they logically mutually exclusive?

DRIVE-STIMULATION THEORIES

Most of the psychological theories of motivation until quite recently reflected "local" physiological theories, such as Cannon's[7] theory of hunger and thirst. One of the most influential examples of this approach in experimental psychology is Hull's[13] suggestion that the survival of the individual requires the maintenance of optimal environmental conditions and that specific drive stimulation arises whenever a deviation from these optimal conditions produces a "need." Such a need was thought to stimulate specific sensory receptors and thus elicit neural impulses which travel to "central ganglia" that control the muscles or glands whose action is required to reduce the need. Satiation in this theoretical framework depends directly and exclusively on the reduction of the need state and the consequent cessation of drive stimulation.

The simplicity of this theory is appealing but the experimental evidence suggests, as we have seen, that the notion of specific drive stimulation, taken literally, is probably an oversimplification. Removal of sensory feedback from the mouth, throat, stomach, or genitalia does little to diminish thirst, hunger, or sexual arousal, and the artificial induction of specific stimuli that could function as drive stimulation does not seem to elicit anything resembling the drive state itself. It is, of course, possible that in each instance we have simply failed to isolate the essential source of drive stimulation, but it seems more probable that no single sensory input may be essential or sufficient for the instigation of drive states.

Drive stimulation may instead refer to a complex pattern of sensory as well as chemical changes, and it is questionable whether all of these inputs result in the experience of a specific sensation, as the local theories imply.

These difficulties were first discussed by Karl Lashley[15] who proposed over 30 years ago that motivation, far from representing a simple sensory response to specific drive stimuli, must be the end product of a complex integration of neural and humoral influences that reflect various physiological processes and act on regulatory centers in the brain. He did not have sufficient experimental data to suggest a neuroanatomical substrate for these regulatory centers or to specify individual physiological processes that might contribute to their activation, but his careful description of the general properties of the interaction between peripheral and central mechanisms has significantly influenced all later theories.

Beach's[1] work on the physiological basis of sexual behavior supported Lashley's multifactor approach in showing that sexual arousal appeared to be determined by the total amount of sensory input, interacting with hormonal mechanisms and memory, and that no single sensory modality appeared to be essential for the arousal or gratification of the sex drive. Others[24] have more recently demonstrated that all of these influences appear to be integrated by a single regulatory "center," as Lashley's hypothesis suggested.

Although the outlines of a centrally oriented theory of motivation were discernible in these early writings, the first formal statement of such a theory appeared in Morgan's[19] textbook, *Physiological Psychology*. Morgan's "central theory of drive" has been amended over the years,[20] but its major postulates have remained essentially unchanged. The theory proposes that a drive should be regarded as a state of neural activity in a system of centers and pathways in the brain. Each system was thought to be concerned only with one drive although some overlap and interaction between individual systems could occur. A *central motive state* or CMS was thought to be aroused by sensory inputs from extero- as well as interoceptors and by chemical changes in the blood and in the interstitial fluids that surround all cells. Once such a CMS was elicited, it was thought to persist without additional inputs because of reverberatory activity or tonic influences from other neural centers.

According to Morgan, a central motive state "predisposes the organism to react in certain ways to particular stimuli and not to react to others." It primes the organism to approach or withdraw from stimuli that have certain characteristics or, as Morgan puts it: "The CMS functions as a selective valve or switch for certain S-R relationships and not others." He further suggested that a CMS could also emit random behavior such as locomotor activity, which often must precede or accompany responses that are more specifically related to the prevailing drive. The satisfaction or reduction of a central motive state may occur in several ways, according to this theory. The elimination of the peripheral or humoral drive stimuli that originally aroused the CMS reduces it. Alternatively, some humoral messenger, different from the humoral factors that evoked the CMS, may reduce it. Also, "stimulation in the course of drive-instigated behavior" or such behavior itself may account for the reduction of a CMS.

In more recent writings, Morgan[20] has suggested that the reverberating activity of the reticular formation of the brainstem may be the most general kind of central motive state and that this general drive determines the predisposition of the organism to react to the environment and to develop more specific motive states. He also proposed that a lack of sensory input may itself set up a CMS but did not elaborate on the mechanisms for this particular one. Morgan's description of the anatomical substrate of the central motive state has remained fairly vague. Motives are said to be complexly regulated by "elaborate mechanisms, involving much of the forebrain and the brainstem." The hypothalamic centers that have been shown to contribute to the regulation of biological drives are thought to act as "volume controls" for these complex neural mechanisms.

Stellar[25, 26] has developed a multifactor theory of motivation that provides a more specific anatomical substrate for the central motive state. His "hypothalamic" theory of motivation has generated a great deal of interest and research in the last 15 years. The central hypothesis is best stated in Stellar's own words.

> The amount of motivated behavior is a direct function of the amount of activity in certain excitatory centers of the hypothalamus. . . . The activity of these centers, in turn, is determined by a large number of factors which can be grouped in four general classes: (a) *inhibitory centers* which serve only to depress the activity of the excitatory centers, (b) *sensory stimuli* which control hypothalamic activity through the afferent impulses they can set up, (c) the *internal environment* which can influence the hypothalamus through its rich vascular supply and the cerebrospinal fluid, and (d) *cortical and thalamic centers* which can exert excitatory and inhibitory influences on the hypothalamus[25] (see Figure 15–1).

The aspect of this theory that has aroused most controversy and stimulated most research is the unequivocal selection of hypothalamic "centers" as the substrate of motivational activity in the brain. The hypothalamic centers were selected because damage to restricted parts of the hypothalamus was known to produce changes in specific drive states that seemed to be larger and more permanent than the effects of lesions anywhere else in the brain. The exclusive emphasis on hypothalamic mechanisms was undoubtedly a carefully considered risk because even 15 years ago it was clear that many aspects of the limbic system contribute importantly to motivational states. We now know that lesions outside the hypothalamus can have as pronounced and permanent effects on sleep, hunger, thirst, and emotional reactions as damage to the hypothalamic centers and are increasingly tempted to question whether the parsimony of the hypothalamic theory may not be misleading. There are, however, drive states, such as sexual arousal in the female, that do seem to depend exclusively on a hypothalamic center, and some recent observations[27] suggest that at least some of the extrahypothalamic mechanisms may influence motivational processes indirectly via the hypothalamus, as Stellar suggested. Further study of the relationship between limbic and hypothalamic functions is needed before we can place them into proper perspective.

One of the unique aspects of Stellar's theory is the postulation of inhibitory centers that modify drive states indirectly by inhibiting the excitatory centers. The inhibitory centers are thought to be the origin of satiation, which thus becomes subject to independent central regulation. The postulation of a separate satiety mechanism is logically desirable in view of the experimental evidence that the physiological processes which are thought to give rise to a drive state are not affected by the corrective action within the often brief period required for satiation. However, the experimental evidence for separate satiety centers is still meager in spite of intense study. There is some evidence for inhibitory influences on feeding and emotional behavior but little for any other drive state. Moreover, the inhibitory effects on food intake may be secondary to a disinhibition of affective reactions, leaving possibly only one hypothalamic inhibitory center. The uniqueness of even

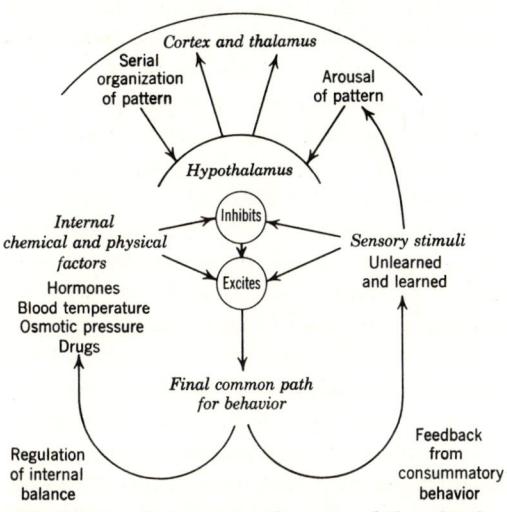

FIG. 15–1. Schematic diagram of the physiological factors contributing to the control of motivated behavior.
(From E. Stellar. The physiology of motivation. *Psychol. Rev.*, **61**, 1954, 5–22. Copyright 1954 by the American Psychological Association, and reproduced by permission.)

this influence is questionable, since similar disinhibitory effects on emotional reactivity are seen after damage to a number of extrahypothalamic sites.

Stellar's theory proposes, in agreement with many experimental observations, that no single sensory input to the motivational centers may be indispensable. The activity of these centers is instead believed to be determined by the sum total of afferent impulses to the hypothalamus from receptors that monitor stimuli in the internal as well as external environment. Some of the sensory input to the hypothalamus may, however, stimulate the postulated inhibitory centers and thus reduce the activity of the excitation centers. Sensory inputs are thought to be carried to the hypothalamus by direct collaterals from the primary sensory pathways, an arrangement which suggests a direct influence which does not require conscious perception of drive stimuli. This, in turn, implies that the perception of hunger, thirst, or sexual arousal may not be an essential correlate of drive stimulation and that motivational states can exist without conscious appreciation of the related sensations.

The internal environment is thought to exert important influences on the hypothalamic drive centers, primarily via chemical changes in the blood. Stellar summarized the contribution of the internal environment as follows:

> A variety of kinds of changes in the internal environment can play a role in the regulation of motivation: variations in the concentration of certain chemicals, especially hormones, changes in osmotic pressure, and changes in blood temperature. The best hypothesis at present is that these internal changes operate by contributing to the activity of the excitatory hypothalamic centers controlling motivation. An equally important, but less well-supported hypothesis is that internal changes, normally produced by consummatory behavior operate in the production of satiation by depressing excitatory centers or arousing inhibitory centers of the hypothalamus.[25]

The research of recent years has supported this interpretation of the role of chemical signals from the internal environment although we have not come much closer to identifying specific humoral factors. The meager data on the effects of osmotic stimuli and sex hormones suggest, however, that chemical changes in the blood or tissue fluids may trigger motivational reactions even in the absence of other inputs.

Perhaps the weakest aspect of the hypothalamic theory is the treatment of extrahypothalamic influences that are assigned to unspecified "cortical and thalamic centers." The research of the past decade has shown that a variety of subcortical mechanisms such as the midbrain tegmentum, globus pallidus, septal area and amygdala, as well as much or all of the primitive cortex of the midline and base of the brain and even some neocortex of the frontal and temporal lobes influence motivational reactions. Indeed, it is often not clear that the hypothalamic centers are more important than some of the extrahypothalamic mechanisms or that they do indeed represent "centers" instead of pathways that interconnect other structures. It is this aspect of Stellar's theory that we shall attempt to modify in agreement with the current research literature in a later section of our discussion.

Summary and Review Questions

The simplest drive stimulation explanation of motivation is the "local" theory, which has been popular since ancient Greece. According to this interpretation, deviations in vital physiological functions stimulate specific receptors and give rise to unique, unpleasant sensations that one learns to associate with behavior which reduces or removes these sensations. Although supported by a lot of "common sense" observations, it has been impossible to demonstrate that any specific sensory modality is essential for any of the basic biological drives or that particular stimuli do, in fact, elicit them. More recent drive stimulation hypotheses have consequently assumed that drives reflect multiple sensory and hormonal inputs to an integrative center in the brain. Morgan's "central motive state" and Stellar's equation of motivation and hypothalamic activity are examples of this evolution.

Morgan's theory of motivation suggests that drive stimuli from various neural or chemical sources stimulate neural activity in a complex system of centers and pathways in the forebrain and brainstem and that this sets up a central motive state or CMS. Once established, the CMS persists until corrective action has restored the physiological imbalance that gave rise to the drive stimulation. Recent versions of this theory suggest that activation of the reticular formation may produce a basic general drive and that the absence of stimulation can itself set up a CMS.

Stellar's hypothalamic theory suggests that biological drives directly reflect the activity of specific hypothalamic drive centers which are influenced by: (a) inhibitory centers; (b) sensory input; (c) chemical signals from the internal environment; and (d) cortical and thalamic centers. Drives are reduced, according to this theory, because the consequences of motivated behavior increase the activity of the inhibitory centers. The influence of sensory input is thought to be direct, permitting drive-induction without conscious appreciation of related sensations. No single modality is thought to be essential.

1. State the basic propositions of "local" theories of motivation.

2. Cite some experimental support for such an interpretation.

3. Discuss the evidence which suggests that "local" theories do not adequately account for motivated behavior.

4. Describe the basic outlines of Morgan's theory.

5. What are its major shortcomings?

6. Describe Stellar's hypothalamic theory.

7. Comment on its adequacy.

ACTIVATION OR AROUSAL

The concept of "arousal" or "generalized drive" has been around for some time. Cannon's[6] "generalized energy" and Pavlov's[23] "orienting reflex" are two of the more famous examples of this notion in physiology. The concept was introduced to psychology by Duffy[8] to explain variations in responsiveness to stimulation that were not related to changes in specific drive states and forms the basis of Hull's[13] conceptualization of non-specific drive (D).

Interest in arousal or activation as a determinant of behavior was rekindled when Magoun and his associates demonstrated that the midbrain reticular formation seemed to control cortical activation and thus determined the organism's responsiveness to the environment.[21, 17, 18] Subsequent investigations have shown that the reticular formation also exerts some control over the primary sensory[11] and motor[17] pathways and seems to determine such arousal-related influences as habituation.[12]

Largely on the basis of this information, Lindsley[16] proposed an "activation" theory of motivation that differed in its basic orientation from the drive stimulation theories of Stellar, Morgan, and others. Lindsley proposed that the problem of motivation could be reduced to a tendency to maintain a level of sensory input to the brain that is sufficiently high to evoke and support some minimal level of neural activity but not intense enough to be disruptive. When the level of stimulation of internal as well as external receptors falls below this optimal range, the organism is believed to become active and seek a change or increment in sensory input. When the level of stimulation exceeds the upper limit of the optimal range, behaviors are activated that reduce stimulation. Food or water deprivation and sexual arousal eventually lead to consummatory behavior simply because the drive stimulation exceeds the optimal range of inputs to the brain.

More specifically, Lindsley proposed that motivational events may have two distinct aspects: (1) a state of general arousal or activation that gives rise to attention and originates in the midbrain reticular formation, and (2) a specific alerting response to stimuli that are directly related to the sensory inputs that give rise to the arousal. This function is thought to be exercised by the nonspecific thalamic projection system.

The arousal theory explains rather nicely why man as well as members of other species should abhor sensory isolation, and work, often quite hard, to obtain novel or complex sensory inputs. It does not by itself predict why some weak stimuli produce a great deal of activation whereas others do not. Presumably, a feedback mechanism could be added that endows certain stimuli with special arousing properties because, in the past, they have been associated with emotional reactions. A more significant shortcoming of the arousal theory is the fact that it does not explain why the organism, once aroused, decides on a specific course of action (i.e., why the stimuli associated with food deprivation give rise to an arousal state that cannot be reduced by a decrease in visual, auditory, olfactory, or somatic stimuli). Moreover, we have seen that the physiological conditions that are presumed to be responsible for hunger-related drive stimulation are not immediately affected by food intake. It would seem that the ingestion of food, particularly in species that hunt a living prey, would produce a rather enormous increase in arousal instead of the predicted decrease. Even civilized man undoubtedly experiences a great deal of added arousal during copulation, and it would seem that simply avoiding or escaping from the presence of a potential mate would be a more practical way to reduce general arousal if that were all one wanted out of life.

Lindsley's theory has nevertheless served an important function in drawing attention to nonspecific motivational influences that tend to be forgotten by drive stimulation theorists and by suggesting a physiological basis for some drive states (such as the apparent need for novel stimulation), which are also not adequately explained on the basis of simple drive stimulation.

More recent arousal theories[10, 14] suggest that the motivational properties of stimuli are determined not by their absolute intensity but by their relationship to the background level of stimulation to which the organism is adapted. A little discrepancy or incongruity is thought to produce a small increment in arousal from an essentially zero base line and this is assumed to be innately pleasurable. Too much of a deviation from the adaptation level or from "expectation," on the other hand, is thought to produce a large increment in arousal, and this is believed to be innately aversive. Closer inspection of these theories shows that they do, in fact, deny the role of specific drive stimulation but simply add the provision that the absence of sensory input can itself activate such stimulation.

Summary and Review Questions

"Nonspecific drive" or "general arousal" are concepts that have been used widely in psychology as well as physiology. The discovery of the role of the reticular formation in cortical arousal as well as sensory and motor functions renewed interest in the influence of nonspecific arousal mechanisms and led to the formation of Lindsley's "activation" theory of motivation. This theory reduces all motivation to the organism's innate tendency to maintain a level of sensory input that is intense and varied enough to support normal neural activity but not sufficiently intense to disrupt brain functions. The organism's state of general reactivity or arousal is thought to be determined by the ascending components of the brainstem reticular formation. A second, more selective orienting reaction is thought to be related to the activity of the nonspecific thalamic projection system. The activation theory of motivation explains the pervasive influence of the organism's general state of reactivity and solves the riddle why man as well as many animals would seek novelty. However, it does not explain why a particular drive stimulation evokes only those responses that reduce it.

1. State Lindsley's activation theory.
2. What is its anatomical substrate?
3. Discuss its success in predicting behavior.

A CONTEMPORARY HYPOTHESIS

In our brief review of psychophysiological theories of motivation, we have found that neither the specific stimulation models of Stellar and Morgan nor the activation theory of Lindsley accounts in an entirely satisfactory fashion for the complexities of behavior and that the two approaches seem to be in many ways complementary. It therefore seems worthwhile to try to arrive at a new hypothesis by modifying some of the earlier interpretations in accordance with the current research literature.

Let us start with the not very novel or controversial assumption that members of all surviving species must be endowed with regulatory mechanisms that insure corrective action whenever a vital physiological function deviates from a normal range of operation. In some instances, this regulation is entirely automatic. The adjustments of heart rate, vasomotor functions, and pulse pressure to changing energy demands is one example of such a mechanism. In other instances, the regulation requires changes in overt behavior and this, in turn, requires what we call motivational influences.

The proposed model applies directly to such drive states as hunger and thirst, which reflect the deviation of a vital physiological function such as the osmolarity or volume of the body fluids or the availability of energy reserves. Reactions of an emotional nature presumably reflect anticipatory responses to stimuli which in the past have exceeded the normal range of function of some sensory system and gave rise to physical damage and pain. The hypothesis accounts for our need for sensory input by suggesting that the brain, like other physiological systems, functions well only within a limited range of conditions that include sensory feedback from the environment. Many experiments have proven that this is indeed the case. Man's apparent need for novelty can be explained in this connection because sensory receptors adapt to frequently repeated stimuli, and sensory pathways and relay stations habituate (that is, gradually cease responding to even infrequently repeated stimuli that do not have biological significance). The combined effect of habituation and adaptation may explain why we get bored unless we maintain a complex and constantly changing environment. "Boredom" may be a learned, anticipatory response similar to the fear or anxiety reactions that play such an important role in our daily lives.

Granted that drive states reflect the organism's need to maintain various physiological functions within some specified limits by corrective action, how are these regulatory influences organized and how do they affect behavior? Let us assume that the deviation of each physiological function that requires such regulation gives rise to distinct neural or chemical signals that affect regulatory centers in the brain. In the case of thirst, we know that the osmolarity and volume of the bodily fluids provide such signals. In the case of hunger, the level of blood sugar or some other metabolite may serve similar functions. We do not, as yet, know what signals other physiological functions may use. In the case of tissue damage and pain, the primary escape reaction may be reflexly organized and anticipatory avoidance responses subsequently acquired by conditioning. The need for a variety of sensory feedback from the environment may depend on a complex interchange of neural signals between the reticular formation, which may act as a sensory receptor in this connection, and the cerebral cortex.

The various signals may affect motivational processes directly by acting on regulatory centers in the brain or indirectly by stimulating peripheral or central sensory receptors that, in turn, modulate the activity of the central regulatory centers. Some of these signals may influence the activity of several regulatory centers. Most of the vital physiological functions may use several, essentially duplicating signal systems such that the elimination or artificial excitation of any one system does not significantly interfere with the activity of the regulatory center.

Behavioral as well as physiological evidence suggests that the organism's reaction to these signals may be determined by an interaction between the resulting specific drive states and nonspecific motivational influences that reflect the organism's general level of arousal or reactivity.

Specific drive states are believed to be organized by a system of centers and pathways, which includes the midbrain tegmentum, hypothalamus, preoptic and septal areas, hippocampus, cingulate gyrus, amygdala, the primitive cortex of the temporal lobe, and some of the neocortex of the frontal lobe. Some of the components of this system may serve as primary or secondary receptors for specific neural or chemical signals. Others integrate the total feedback from a particular physiological function to determine when corrective action becomes necessary. Still more complex integrative mechanisms within this circuit compare the state of activation of each of the individual regulatory systems to determine which one most urgently requires access to the organism's attention and motor facilities.

The nonspecific motivational influences are believed to arise from aspects of the midbrain reticular formation and the nonspecific thalamic projection system. These general drive mechanisms respond to: (1) all sensory inputs to the organism; (2) neural and chemichal changes or consequent neural signals that reflect deviations in vital physiological functions; and (3) feedback from the specific regulatory centers as well as cortical sources concerned with memory. The activity of the nonspecific motivational mechanisms does not merely reflect the sum total of their afferent inputs but, because of such influences as adaptation and habituation, the biological significance of the input. The nonspecific circuits do not initiate specific behavioral reactions but modulate the threshold of cortical as well as subcortical neurons and thus provide what psychologists have called the "energizing" aspect of motivation. Some components of the nonspecific drive circuit may respond specifically to inputs from the regulatory centers for specific drives and selectively process sensory information relevant to the dominant drive state (a mechanism for selective attention). Related efferent components of the reticular formation may react to inputs from the dominant specific drive centers by facilitating related effector systems.

Behavioral reactions that return a particular physiological function to optimal levels of operation are terminated when the activity of a specific regulatory center falls below that of another pathway, which thus gains access to the attention and motor facilities of the organism. Initially this requires either a reduction in the "drive stimulation" that signals the physiological imbalance, or a sudden increment in some other specific drive. This relationship is, however, modified by experience, and we may stop eating long before the blood sugar levels have returned to normal levels because we have learned that a certain amount of food will do so eventually.

This theory of motivation is more complex than earlier versions, in accordance with the experimental findings of recent years. It accounts adequately for appetitive drives such as hunger and thirst, aversive drives such as fear, and the need for a variety of sensory inputs to the brain. The suggested anatomical substrate for specific and nonspecific drive states is undoubtedly involved in motivational functions. The specific role of individual components of the suggested systems or the nature of their interaction is as yet largely unknown and hence unspecified in our hypothesis. The reseach of the next decade should help to fill in some of these blanks. The proposed satiety mechanism (i.e., drive stimulation reduction supported by learning) is the simplest form of satiation. It may turn out that the behavior which will eventually reduce drive stimulation may initially activate independent neural or chemical signal systems that inhibit the central drive mechanisms. There is, as yet, little experimental evidence for such a separate satiety mechanism and no compelling reason to complicate our model by postulating something about which we know little or nothing.

Summary and Review Questions

A closer look at the drive stimulation and activation theories indicates that neither can easily account for all forms of behavior and that they are complementary with respect to their areas of strength and weakness. We have therefore tried to combine the best features of both approaches to develop a motivational theory in accord with the current research literature. This theory proposes, in essence, that: (1) All biological drives are based on a deviation of vital physiological functions from an optimal range of operation. (2) Using a multiple-channel system of essentially duplicating neural and chemical signals, each physiological function which is thus regulated determines the activity of a specific regulatory mechanism in the brain and modulates the activity of a common nonspecific motivational mechanism. (3) The specific regulatory mechanisms include aspects of the limbic system and anatomically related subcortical and neocortical structures and exercise three principal functions. They act as receptors for various neural and chemical signals, integrate the total input, and correlate their activity with that of other, concurrently active regulatory mechanisms. (4) The nonspecific motivational mechanism is thought to involve ascending as well as descending components of the reticular formation and the nonspecific projection system of the thalamus. This mechanism responds to all sensory stimuli, chemical and neural signals from the internal environment, and feedback from the specific regulatory centers as well as memory stores. It functions, primarily, to adjust the organism's overall level of reactivity in accordance with specific drive stimulation and to selectively process sensory and motor signals related to the dominant drive state.

1. State the basic outline of the compromise theory of motivation that has been suggested.

2. In your opinion, does it account adequately for all types of behavior?

3. What improvements (deletions, additions, or alterations) could you suggest to make it more useful?

CONCLUSIONS AND REVIEW

We have attempted to abstract from the empirical evidence of the past chapters and the theoretical models of recent years a framework of a general physiological theory of motivation. Even a cursory glance at the problem suggests that all surviving species are endowed with protective mechanisms that maintain all vital physiological functions within a range of optimal activity. In simple species this regulation depends largely on reflex integration. In more complex organisms that are not as easily maintained in a constantly changing environment, complex behavioral reactions are required which involve the entire organism. This behavior must be initiated and sustained by what psychologists have called drives or motives. Perhaps the most basic question we must ask in this context is whether this tendency to maintain various physiological functions within some normal range of activity could be the basis of all biological drives and whether the mechanisms for this regulation might be the same for different drive states. Two somewhat different mechanisms of regulation have been suggested.

Proponents of specific drive stimulation interpretations have argued that each physiological function is related to a specific regulatory center in the brain and initiates a drive by signaling via several neural and chemical pathways any deviation from its optimal range of activity to this center. The oldest and simplest version of such a theory is Cannon's "local" theory of hunger and thirst, which suggests that we eat because our stomach growls and drink because the throat becomes parched. It has been impossible to demonstrate experimentally that any specific sensory signal is essential for any biological drive. More recent versions of the drive stimulation theory have therefore proposed that a variety of sensory and chemical signals may influence a given drive by acting directly or indirectly on some regulatory center in the brain. There is little quarrel with this basic model. The principal question has become: "Where are these regulatory centers?" Are they neatly localized in the hypothalamus, as Stellar's model proposes, or are they complexly and diffusely represented in much of the limbic cortex and associated subcortical and neocortical structures, as recent research as well as Morgan's somewhat cryptic description suggests? There is no question about the involvement of many extrahypothalamic mechanisms in motivation, but we do not yet know how these seemingly diverse influences interact. Recent studies have shown major motivational effects of lesions outside the hypothalamus, removing the principal reason for the emphasis on hypothalamic centers.

"Arousal" or "activation" interpretations of motivation have been vigorous competitors of the specific drive stimulation theories since the discovery of a distinct anatomical substrate for apparently related physiological processes in the brainstem. Arousal theories generally hold that the problem of motivation can be reduced to an innate tendency to maintain a minimum level of sensory stimulation which permits normal neural activity in the brain and to avoid or escape excessive stimulation which disrupts neural activity. Specific drives such as hunger or thirst motivate corrective behavior, according to this interpretation, simply because the intensity of drive-related stimulation threatens to exceed the normal capacity of the brain or some part of it. Such an interpretation accounts for the observation that man as well as many animals seek varied sensory inputs and expend effort to increase or alter the level of stimulation. It also describes a physiological and anatomical basis for what psychologists such as Brown[4] have called the "energizing" function of motivation but does not, by itself, have a ready answer as to why a hungry person should seek food and not attempt to reduce the level of stimulation in other ways. What is missing is what Brown called the "cue" or "directive" function of motivation, which is such a prominent aspect of the specific drive-stimulation hypothesis.

I have therefore suggested an alternative representing a marriage between the two types of explanations. According to this interpretation, all biological motivational states, including the need for varied sensory input, are thought to activate (1) specific regulatory mechanisms that are represented in the limbic system and associated subcortical and neocortical structures and (2) nonspecific motivational mechanisms in the midbrain reticular formation and nonspecific thalamic projections. It is the function of the nonspecific motivational mechanism in this system to determine the organism's overall level of reactivity and to selectively process sensory and motor signals which are related to the momentarily dominant specific drive state. The specific regulatory mechanisms collect and integrate information about specific physiological functions and determine the class of behavioral reactions, such as food seeking or mating, which is needed to reduce the momentarily dominant drive state. The selection of specific responses within such a class of behavior is made on the basis of experience. Satiation, according to this model, occurs when the physiological function that initiated the drive stimulation returns to normal levels, but this mechanism is very slow and must be modified by conditioning.

Bibliography

1. Beach, F. A. A review of physiological and psychological studies of sexual behavior in mammals. *Physiol. Rev.*, 1947, **27**, 240–307.
2. Berlyne, D. E. Novelty and curiosity as determinants of exploratory behavior. *Brit. J. Psychol.*, 1950, **41**, 68–80.
3. Bexton, W. H., Heron, W., & Scott, T. H. Effects of increased variation in the sensory environment. *Canad. J. Psychol.*, 1954, **8**, 70–76.
4. Brown, J. S. *The motivation of behavior.* New York: McGraw-Hill, 1961.
5. Butler, R. A. Discrimination learning by rhesus monkeys to visual exploration motivation. *J. comp. physiol. Psychol.*, 1953, **46**, 95–98.
6. Cannon, W. B. *Bodily changes in pain, hunger, fear and rage.* (Rev. ed.) New York: Appleton, 1929. Originally published in 1915.
7. Cannon, W. B. Hunger and thirst. In *Handbook of general experimental psychology.* C. Murchison, Ed. Worcester, Mass.: Clark Univ. Press, 1934, pp. 247–263.
8. Duffy, E. Emotion: An example of the need for reorientation in psychology. *Psychol. Rev.*, 1934, **41**, 184–198.

9. Hebb, D. O. Drives and the C.N.S. (conceptual nervous system). *Psychol. Rev.*, 1955, **62**, 243–254.

10. Helson, H. *Adaptation-level theory*. New York: Harper & Row, 1964.

11. Hernández-Peón, R. Reticular mechanisms of sensory control. In *Sensory communication*. W. A. Rosenblith, Ed. Cambridge, Mass.: M.I.T. Press, 1961, pp. 497–520.

12. Hernández-Peón, R., & Brust-Carmona, H. Functional role of subcortical structures in habituation and conditioning. In *Brain mechanisms and learning*. J. F. Delafresnaye, A. Fessard, R. W. Gerard, & J. Konorski, Eds. Oxford: Blackwell Scientific, 1961, pp. 393–412.

13. Hull, C. L. *Principles of behavior*. New York: Appleton-Century, 1943.

14. Hunt, J. McV. Intrinsic motivation and its role in psychological development. In *Nebraska symposium on motivation: 1965*. D. Levine, Ed. Lincoln: Univ. of Nebraska Press, 1965, pp. 189–282.

15. Lashley, K. S. Experimental analysis of instinctive behavior. *Psychol. Rev.*, 1938, **45**, 445–471.

16. Lindsley, D. B. Psychophysiology and motivation. In *Nebraska symposium on motivation: 1957*. M. R. Jones, Ed. Lincoln: Univ. of Nebraska Press, 1957, pp. 44–105.

17. Lindsley, D. B., Bowden, J., & Magoun, H. W. Effect upon the EEG of acute injury to the brain stem activating system. *EEG clin. Neurophysiol.*, 1949, **1**, 475–486.

18. Lindsley, D. B., Schreiner, L. H., Knowles, W. B., & Magoun, H. W. Behavioral and EEG changes following chronic brainstem lesions in the cat. *EEG clin. Neurophysiol.*, 1950, **2**, 483–498.

19. Morgan, C. T. *Physiological psychology*. New York: McGraw-Hill, 1943.

20. Morgan, C. T. Physiological mechanisms of motivation. In *Nebraska symposium on motivation: 1957*. M. R. Jones, Ed. Lincoln: Univ. of Nebraska Press, 1957, pp. 1–35.

21. Moruzzi, G., & Magoun, H. W. Brainstem reticular formation and activation of the EEG. *EEG clin. Neurophysiol.*, 1949, **1**, 455–473.

22. Nissen, H. W. A study of exploratory behavior in the white rat by means of the obstruction method. *J. genet. Psychol.*, 1930, **37**, 361–376.

23. Pavlov, I. *Conditioned reflexes. An investigation of the physiological activity of the cerebral cortex*. New York: Oxford Univ. Press, 1927.

24. Sawyer, C. H., & Robinson, B. Separate hypothalamic areas controlling pituitary gonadotropic function and mating behavior in female cats and rabbits. *J. clin. Endocrinol.*, 1956, **16**, 914–915.

25. Stellar, E. The physiology of motivation. *Psychol. Rev.*, 1954, **61**, 5–22.

26. Stellar, E. Drive and motivation. In *Handbook of physiology*. Vol. III. J. Field, H. W. Magoun, & V. E. Hall, Eds. Washington, D.C.: Am. Physiol. Soc., 1960, pp. 1501–1527.

27. White, N. M., & Fisher, A. E. Relationship between amygdala and hypothalamus in the control of eating behavior. *Physiol. & Behav.*, 1969, **4**, 199–205.

SECTION 4

Biological Bases of Learning and Memory

In the preceding section of this book, we discussed some of the basic motivational influences that energize and direct responses to changes in the internal or external environment. Being hungry, thirsty, or sexually aroused rarely suffices, however, to produce appropriate actions. Most organisms are endowed with a repertoire of unconditioned reflexes that are functional soon after birth, but this limited spectrum of behaviors cannot sustain life except in some very primitive species. Complex organisms develop increasingly complicated mechanisms to maintain stable physiological conditions under a wide range of environmental influences, and a stereotyped genetic coding of reactions to specific stimuli becomes impractical. The behavior repertoire therefore becomes increasingly plastic. This development reaches a point in higher mammals where the organism is unable to survive unless tutored for a significant portion of its life. Man and other complex organisms would long ago have become extinct were it not for the fact that new adaptive response patterns are continually learned and substituted for old ones that are no longer adequate. It is, indeed, difficult to demonstrate more than a handful of unconditioned behaviors in man because of the pervasive influence of learning on all aspects of our lives.

What, then, is the physiological basis for the plasticity of man's behavior? What happens when we learn to modify our reactions to specific environmental stimuli or when we attempt to recall a previously learned behavior pattern? More specifically, we would like to know the nature of the physicochemical changes that take place in certain neurons and to understand these events well enough to learn why they seem to occur only under certain circumstances.

In the last section of this book, you will find discussions of the results of some of the experiments that have been addressed to these problems in recent years. We have not, as yet, progressed very far toward our goals, but the recent advances in our understanding of the genetic mechanisms that transmit "memories" from one generation to the next permit us to hope that significant progress may be just around the corner.

Chapter 16

THE NATURE OF LEARNING

Some Behavioral Considerations
Basic Issues
Consolidation of Memory Traces
Review

SOME BEHAVIORAL CONSIDERATIONS

Conceptual Issues

Just how learning takes place and what its physiological basis might be has intrigued scientists for centuries. Within recent decades, we have made some progress in understanding the environmental conditions that promote learning and we have developed theories to describe the interaction of some of the relevant variables. In spite of this advance, some fundamental questions have remained unanswered, and it is important to keep these questions in mind throughout our discussion.

The first question one might ask about learning is whether all modifications of behavior that occur as a function of experience involve a common "learning" process regardless of the environmental or physiological conditions that initiate it. More specifically, one can ask whether classical conditioning, which results in the transfer of an innate reflex to a previously neutral stimulus, reflects the same basic process as instrumental conditioning, which requires the reorganization of previously acquired behaviors into novel response sequences. Or, whether the acquisition of a concept such as "vacuum" represents the same basic process as salivary conditioning. Or, more perplexing yet, whether learning not to respond to some stimulus because it has no significance (habituation) or has lost its significance (extinction) is identical or even similar to learning that mediates the acquisition of reinforced responses.

Most investigators in this field tacitly assume that there is a common learning process and that the different experimental paradigms reflect quantitatively instead of qualitatively different events. This convenient fiction is not, however, based on very sound evidence, and there are many experimental observations which suggest that there may be basically different types of learning processes.

The role of reinforcement raises another fundamental and still controversial issue. Is reinforcement necessary for learning itself or merely for the performance of a learned response? Can we learn a novel response without ever performing it implicitly or explicitly (see Figure 16–1)? We cannot, at this time, review the many experiments that have attempted to deal with these questions. A survey of this literature indicates, however, that the answers to these questions are not simple. Unreinforced or "sensory-sensory" learning may take place in some unusual circumstances, although it is always difficult to discount the possibility of inadvertent reward in experiments that seem to demonstrate such learning. However, there is no doubt that unreinforced learning does not take place in many situations and is, at best, slow and inefficient. In the laboratory, it is easy to show that the pairing of two entirely neutral stimuli rarely produces an association between them even though they are presented on literally hundreds or thousands of trials. Our daily experience suggests a similar conclusion. Few people can describe the appearance of the houses in the next block even though they have passed them thousands of times on their way to work, or describe the arrangement of books in their own bookshelves.

Very much more precise answers are badly needed before we can expect to understand the physiological changes that are responsible for altered reactions to the environment. It is certainly not clear that we can disregard motivational influences and account for learning on the basis of concurrent or sequential activation of neural pathways which results in the "use" of previously nonfunctional connections, as all current physiological and biochemical theories of learning attempt to do.

The attractively simple explanation that learning occurs as a direct consequence of the "use" of previously nonfunctional connections because of concurrent activation of related pathways is beset by another problem which is often disregarded. There is a large and generally consistent literature showing that simultaneous presentations of the conditioned and unconditioned stimuli produce poor if any learning and that little or no conditioning occurs when the UCS precedes the CS. The ideal condition for learning exists only when the CS precedes the UCS by some period of time, the duration of this interval varying substantially for different experimental paradigms. It is difficult to account for these observations in terms of differential neural conduction delays for the CS and UCS signals because the pairing of two unconditioned stimuli produces very good learning provided one precedes the other by an appropriate time.

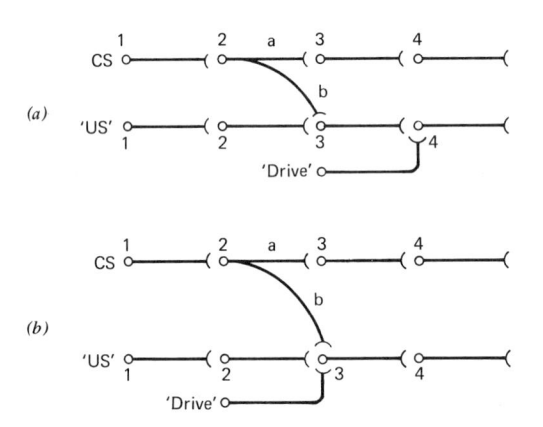

FIG. 16–1. Two models for the influence of motivation on conditioned responses. In (a), conditioning proceeds independent of drive influences. Motivation in this model is essential only for the activation of the last (motor) link in the circuit. In (b), the input from the drive-related neuron is an essential part of the learning process itself. Unless there is concurrent input to "US"–3 from the drive neuron, CS–2b cannot cross the synapse even when "US"–2 is concurrently active. (The terms CS and US are used to facilitate comparison of this scheme with Figures 16–3 and 16–4. There is no US in the strict sense of the term in this situation).

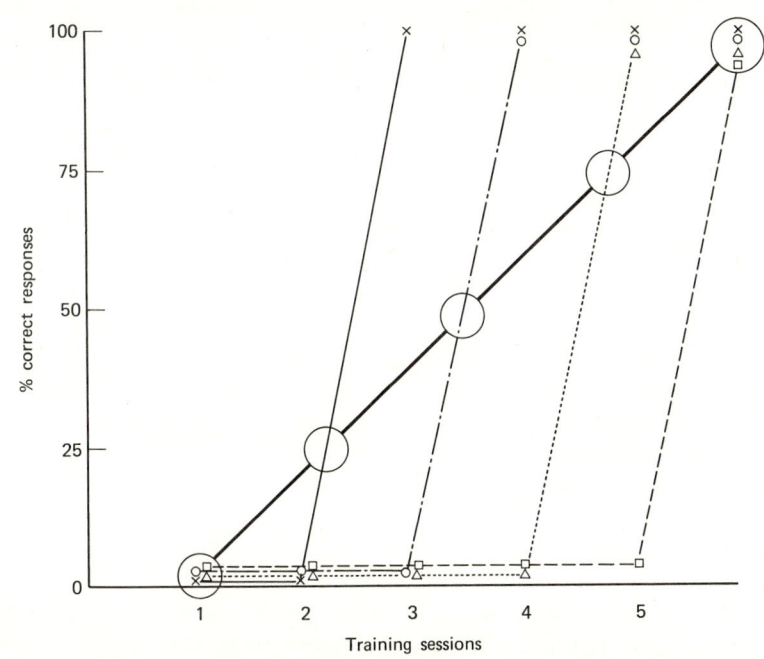

FIG. 16-2. Four animals (×, ○, △, □) learn the same problem. Each one learns the correct response instantaneously, but each of the animals does so at a different time. When the learning curve of the group is graphed (large circles), a potentially misleading picture emerges which suggests that the learning process may require gradual, incremental facilitation.

Explanations of learning in terms of a gradual and incremental facilitation of previously nonfunctional connections may, in still another sense, fail to reflect the behavioral literature adequately. They are based on behavioral theories of learning such as those of Hull and Spence, which postulate that a memory trace develops gradually. This is an adequate description of the *average* learning curve of a population of subjects, particularly in learning situations that require the elaboration and sequencing of many individual memories. However, even in such complex situations, individual animals often perform learned responses perfectly soon after they have made the first "correct" response (provided correct responses cannot occur accidentally, as in many discrimination problems) (see Figure 16-2), and a closer look at the few incorrect responses which are subsequently made suggests that the animal may be exploring alternate solutions instead of simply failing to remember the correct one.

There is, in any case, excellent evidence that some quite permanent memories can be acquired in a single trial and that "repeated use," as postulated by nearly all physiological and biochemical theories of learning, is not an essential condition for learning.

Practical Problems

Experimental investigations of the physiological, anatomical, or biochemical bases of learning are complicated by the fact that we can, as yet, measure learning or its end product, memory, only in terms of overt behavioral reactions. The presence or absence of a behavioral response depends, however, on the appropriate activation of intact motivational, sensory, and motor mechanisms as well as memory traces, and it is often difficult to distinguish these nonassociative influences. Regardless of how well a memory is established, it can be reflected in overt behavior only if appropriate motivational mechanisms are activated, the conditions of the experiment provide relevant incentives, other "distracting" stimuli are eliminated, and the organism's sensory and motor functions are unimpaired. A priori, these conditions seem to be obvious, but a look at the research literature in this field shows how difficult it is to make sure that all of them are satisfied. For instance, if we find that an animal with a particular brain lesion no longer performs a preoperatively learned response, we have no reason to assume that memory itself is affected. Particularly if we find that the animal also cannot relearn the problem (as one might expect if memories are indeed specifically localized, as the initial experiment assumed), many difficult control experiments are needed to demonstrate that the operation did not make it impossible to perform some aspect of the required response; that the animal was capable of perceiving and concentrating on the relevant aspects of the environment; and that the motivational state which determines the incentive value of the available rewards remained unchanged. Even if the animal turns out to be capable of relearning, it is possible that it does so on the basis of very different cues than were originally used and that the apparent loss of memory might be caused by simple sensory impairments, or that it must compensate for the loss of a previously used motor adjustment and learn to perform the conditioned response in a different way.

Electrophysiological investigations have similar problems. How do we interpret a change in the amplitude or frequency of the EEG, shape or amplitude of the evoked potential, or firing pattern of single neurons during conditioning? Does the organism pay attention to a previously ignored part of the environment? Does it anticipate reward? Does the consumption of the reward require a different integration of posture and movement? Or, are we indeed observing a functional change in pathways related to learning, consolidation, or memory retrieval? What about the biochemical mechanisms that have attracted so much attention in recent years? Changes in the biochemistry of a particular region of the brain are, a priori, no more likely to reflect events that are uniquely related to learning than any of the electrophysiological measures. These considerations do not make it impossible to investigate the physical basis of learning and memory, but they do suggest that we must be extremely cautious in interpreting the results of experiments.

Summary and Review Questions

Difficult conceptual problems arise when we consider the physical consequences of learning. It is not clear, for instance, that (1) we should expect to find similar anatomical, physiological, or biochemical changes in different types of learning situations; (2) concurrent "use" of two neural pathways is a *sufficient* condition for learning (e.g., the consequences of reinforcement may be an essential aspect of the learning process); (3) concurrent "use" of two neural pathways is an *essential* condition for learning (the most advantageous temporal arrangement of CS and UCS would seem to preclude this); (4) learning is, indeed, an incremental process as far as a single neural junction is concerned.

These problems are compounded by the fact that we cannot, as yet, observe and record the process of learning or its end product—the memory trace. Instead, we rely on measures of behavioral, electrophysiological, anatomical, or biochemical events, which may reflect sensory, motor, and motivational processes to an unknown degree. Behaviorally, we cannot be certain that the appearance of a "correct" response indicates that learning has taken place or that a memory trace has been established. Almost all experimental paradigms permit the occurrence of spurious "correct" responses and cannot prevent the withholding of conditioned responses after learning has been completed (the subject may have learned that behavior X leads to reward but may perform behavior Y to test the hypothesis that it, too, may be reinforced). If we could identify the electrophysiological or biochemical consequences of learning and differentiate them reliably from other processes, our problems would be largely solved. Unfortunately, we do not as yet know what to look for and may not have the technology required to observe the undoubtedly subtle changes in neural activity that occur as a result of learning.

1. Discuss the adequacy of the widely held notion that concurrent "use" of two neural pathways is a sufficient and necessary condition for learning.

2. Design an experiment such that the probability is maximized that (a) correct responses do not occur by accident and (b) conditioned responses occur as soon as learning has been completed.

BASIC ISSUES

Modern theories of memory agree that learning requires a persisting modification of neural functions and that this most probably involves facilitation of impulse transmission at selected synapses. Just where these synapses are and what the physical cause of the altered functional relation between two neurons might be are the principal issues that divide the field.

Some theories suggest that learning may uniquely involve neurons in anatomically identifiable centers or pathways and that the end product of learning, that is, memory, is stored in geographically discrete neural structures. This expectation is basic to the thousands of experiments that have attempted to investigate learning-related functions by destroying or stimulating parts of the brain or by recording changes in the electrical or chemical activity of single cells or groups of cells. Others take the view that the complex neural events that underly learning, attention, perception, recognition, and the like may represent a modulation of ongoing activity throughout the brain. In between these extremes are hypotheses suggesting that learning may involve the activation of specific and relatively simple pathways which are, however, diffusely represented in the brain or may be "overdetermined" or redundant so that the elimination or artificial stimulation of any one of its aspects would not affect memory functions.

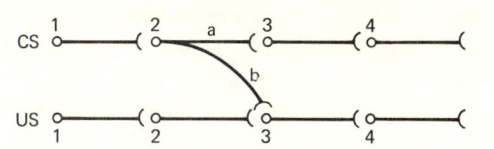

FIG. 16–3. A simple interconnection between the pathways of the CS and US which can result in conditioning. CS–2b does not, initially, fire US–3. When CS–2b and US–2 are concurrently activated, CS–2b can fire US–3 or participate in its depolarization, and this produces a measure of "facilitation" which persists so that subsequent impulses along CS–2b can again fire US–3.

We find no more agreement when it comes to a description of the nature of the physical change which is responsible for the altered function in any of the proposed circuits. Most contemporary theorists believe that learning results in the facilitation of transmission at previously nonfunctional or high-resistance synapses (see Figure 16–3), but there is no agreement on the cause of the facilitation. It is often suggested that repeated "use" of neural junctions activates feedback circuits and thus induces "reverberatory" activity which outlasts the stimulation (see Figure 16–4). Some investigators believe that this continued activation and reactivation may itself be the event responsible for synaptic facilitation. Others hold that reverberatory activity can only account for short-term memories and that permanent changes in

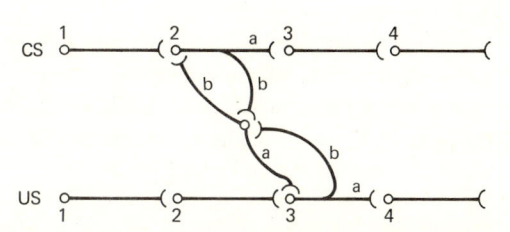

FIG. 16–4. A more complex model of the connections between the CS and US pathways includes feedback loops that could induce "reverberatory" activity and thus initiate processes responsible for persisting facilitation. CS–2b cannot initially fire the interneuron which connects CS and US pathways. It does so when US–3b is concurrently activated. Once the interneuron is activated, it reactivates CS–2 as well as US–3 and thus sets up reverberatory activity. This activity would presumably continue until fatigue or slight differences in the refractory periods of the neurons in the feedback circuit intervene.

synaptic efficiency require secondary anatomical and/or biochemical changes. An enlargement of the presynaptic end feet or a proliferation of the neurotransmitter-containing presynaptic vesicles are some of the mechanisms that have been suggested in this connection. The recent discovery that genetic information is coded in the structure of single deoxyribonucleic acid (DNA) molecules has given rise to the speculation that learning may somehow alter the biochemical makeup of the postsynaptic cell membrane to make it selectively sensitive to the pattern of impulses that produced the initial "use" of the synapse.

Memories vary considerably with respect to their temporal stability. We may, for instance, look up a telephone number and remember it just long enough to dial it. On the other hand, some equally brief encounters with unusual events in our childhood may be vividly remembered even decades later, and there is some evidence that at least some memories may be permanently established even though we may lose access to them. These observations suggest that there may be fundamentally different types of memory traces or that a memory may undergo several transformations. Just how many different memories or memory stages there are and what their duration and properties might be have been questions of much contemporary argument and experimentation.

Before we take a close look at some specific theoretical points of view and the evidence that can be cited to support them, it might be interesting to trace the historical development of some of the principal issues.

Historical Perspectives

Man has been intrigued with the influence personal history plays in determining his behavior since the dawn of civilization. Many of the writings of the philosophers of ancient Greece contain speculations about the nature of memory. The concept of a memory "trace" that is somehow engraved on our mind was first proposed by Plato, long before the functions of the brain were understood. Very little progress was made until the 18th century, partly at least because many religions discouraged scientific inquiry into the functions of the human body. In the early 18th century, the dam broke, and an avalanche of scientific speculation raised most of the basic issues that continue to concern us today.

That learning may produce incremental facilitation of neural pathways as a result of repeated use was first proposed by Charles Bonnet.[5] (More specifically, he suggested that active neurons vibrate and that vibration at a particular frequency might be more easily achieved following repeated presentation of the same stimulation.) The location of the memory trace became one of the most heatedly debated scientific issues of the early 19th century. At one end of the continuum were phrenologists such as Gall and Spurzheim[16] who believed that each memory or class of memories was stored in specific parts of the brain and that these "active" brain areas increased in size and could consequently be identified by "bumps" on the skull. Many contemporary anatomists[11] rejected the theory that "bumps" on the skull could be used to locate specific functions but believed that memories could indeed be found in geographically identifiable structures in the brain. Others[24] thought that memories might be found anywhere in the brain or even[21] that the ability to learn and remember might be an attribute of all living tissue.

William James[32] proposed an explanation of learning remarkably similar to Pavlov's later theories, which continue to be popular today. He suggested that concurrent activation of two neural centers might cause the formation of connections between them, the direction of the "energy flow" being determined by the temporal sequence of activation.

In the latter part of the 19th century, physiologists began to experiment on animals, concentrating their attention on the easily accessible cortical portion of the brain. It was soon established that simple memories survived destruction of any cortical region, and the law of "equipotentiality," which subsequently influenced the research and writing of Lashley and other physiological psychologists, became generally accepted.[19,15]

The most profound change in our thinking about the physical basis of learning occurred because of Waldeyer's[55] demonstration that the brain is not a continuous gelatinous mass but instead consists of many billions of structurally independent cells. Waldeyer suggested that the individual cells might communicate with one another via junction points (later called synapses), and the basic problem for the learning theorist became one of explaining how the synaptic resistance between neural pathways or centers might be reduced during learning and how this facilitation could be retained.

Contemporary Approaches

The recent history of research in the area of learning and memory is characterized by fundamental changes in the nature of the questions asked as well as the techniques employed.

Almost all of the investigations prior to 1950 were concerned with the discovery of the gross anatomical substrate of memory. They depended almost exclusively on descriptions of the behavioral deficits seen after brain damage in man as well as various species of experimental animals. By 1950, it was clear that the organism's general ability to learn and remember was not discretely and exclusively localized in any specific part of the brain. This epoch of research culminated with the publication of Lashley's famous article entitled, "In Search of the Engram,"[36] which concluded, on the basis of a lifetime of research, that the size rather than the location of cortical lesions determined the nature and severity of the learning or memory deficit (see Figure 16–5). Lashley suggested, on the basis of these findings, that all parts of the brain might be "equipotential" with respect to the ability to store memory traces. We have since then learned that the brain is not as devoid of organization as Lashley's pessimistic conclusions suggested (his results were influenced by a lack of adequate mapping of sensory and motor functions in the rat as well as by the use of behavioral tests that could be mastered on the basis of information from two or more sensory modalities). Clinical observations as

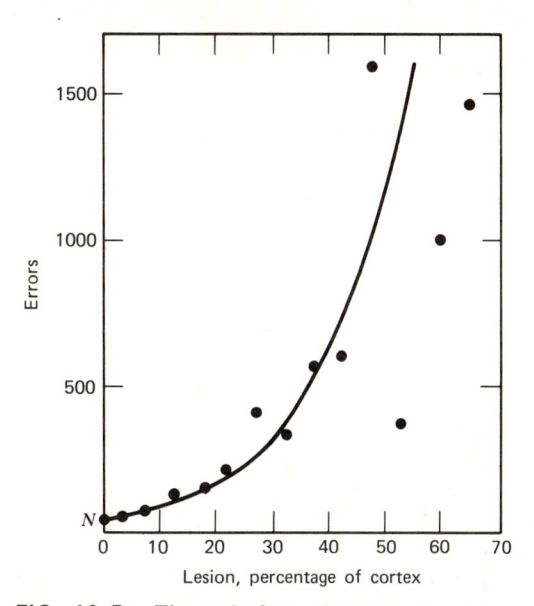

FIG. 16–5. The relation of errors in maze learning to extent of cerebral damage in the rat. The extent of brain injury is expressed as the percentage of the surface area of the isocortex destroyed. Data from 60 normal and 127 brain-operated animals are averaged by class intervals of 5 percent destruction. The curve is the best fitting one of logarithmic form.

(From K. S. Lashley. In search of the engram. *Soc. Exp. Biology, Animal Behaviour*, 1950, Symposium IV, 454–482.)

well as animal research have implicated the hippocampus and related aspects of the temporal lobe in short-term memory. Recent neuroanatomical as well as neurophysiological investigations have suggested that the somatosensory "association" areas may also play an important role in the formation, storage, and/or retrieval of memories. It is nonetheless clear that the ability to form simple memories is not confined to any particular portion of the brain and may, indeed, be a property of all neural tissue.

The apparent lack of a specific anatomical localization of mechanisms uniquely related to learning or memory, combined with the development of technological advances in the field of electronics, led to a reorientation of research in the early 1950s. Many investigators reasoned that it might be possible to describe the apparently diffuse neural pathways that are activated during acquisition and/or recall by recording the electrical activity of many brain structures concurrently. Most of the initial studies recorded the endogenous electroencephalographic (EEG) activity or evoked potentials (E.P.) to the conditioned or unconditioned stimuli. Some investigators have used repetitive "tracer" stimuli in attempts to impose an easily observable rhythm on the EEG activity of responsive brain structures. More recently, sophisticated techniques have been used to record the activity of single cells or direct current (D.C.) potentials. The electrophysiological approach has generated thousands of experimental reports and a good deal of information about such learning-related processes as "attention," "orienting," and "habituation." It has not, so far, captured a good likeness of the elusive memory trace. None of the measures have succeeded in demonstrating local changes that are unique to learning or recall even though sophisticated computer analyses of the data have been used in recent years. Interest in the electrophysiological "correlates" of learning or recall persists in many laboratories, but other approaches have become fashionable in the 1960s.

Much of the research of the past ten years has been devoted to investigations of the nature of memory instead of its location in the brain. Throughout the history of this area, theorists speculated about the nature of the physiological and/or anatomical changes that occur when a memory trace is established. Little or no empirical research was devoted to this important question until recently because microscopic or molecular techniques were not as yet available. Interest in this approach blossomed when molecular biologists demonstrated that DNA appeared to be the means by which very complex sets of genetic instructions were passed on. As the mechanisms for this genetic code became better understood, it seemed that the memories established through learning might involve the same or similar intracellular biochemical processes, notably the manufacture of specific proteins. This expectation has generated an enormous amount of research which has done little more, so far, than demonstrate that we do not yet know how to ask the right questions. However, the prospects of success are still tantalizing, and we can expect continued activity in this field in the 1970s.

A related recent line of inquiry has made use of various techiques for producing gross temporary disturbances of neural activity to ask whether the formation of a memory trace can be understood best as a series of related time-dependent processes. Electroconvulsive shock as well as various drug treatments have been used in this research, and a very large if not always internally consistent literature has developed in the past decade. It is clear that memories are more susceptible to interference shortly after training than later on, but it is not obvious whether one or several processes are implicated by these observations or just what importance one should attach to the often quite different temporal relationships described in different experiments.

Summary

The principal questions in this area evolve around the following theoretical issues: (1) Does learning result in unique electrophysiological, anatomical, or biochemical events in geographically unspecified regions of the brain or in nonspecific changes in the relationship of specific "memory cells" in selected subdivisions of the brain? (2) Do all memory traces involve similar electrophysiological, anatomical, or biochemical changes or must we look for different types of memories, depending on the nature of the task or the age of the memories?

Technological advances have to a large degree determined the direction of research in this field. Prior to 1950, most investigators attempted to demonstrate the gross geographic location of memory traces by observing the effects of lesions in discrete cortical and subcortical portions of the brain. The results of these studies suggested that learning per se may not require participation of any individual subdivision of the brain. This gave rise to the hypothesis that learning might result instead in a modification of the activity of widely and diffusely represented neural pathways. About 1950, electronic devices became available which permitted the concurrent monitoring of the electrical activity of many regions of the brain, and a generation of investigators devoted their lives to the study of the electrophysiological correlates or consequences of learning. More recently, attention has been attracted by the possibility that the establishment of memory traces might involve biochemical mechanisms similar to those recently shown to be responsible for the storage and transmission of genetic information.

1. Describe the major issues that are of current concern for most investigators of the physiological bases of learning and/or memory.

2. Can one discern distinct "periods" in the history of this field?

CONSOLIDATION OF MEMORY TRACES

We have previously questioned the assumption that learning in such diverse paradigms as classical conditioning and concept formation results in basically similar memory traces. We must now ask the even more fundamental question whether, within a particular learning situation, more than one type of memory trace may be established.

We all have had the experience of looking up a telephone number in the directory, dialing it, and getting a "busy" signal. Unless the number is familiar, we must look it up again when we want to try it once more only a few seconds later. Clearly, a memory trace was established that lasted just long enough for dialing. Yet, we can easily establish a more permanent memory of a telephone number when it is that of a friend whom we intend to call frequently. Even such a memory may not be really permanent, since we often cannot recall the telephone number of a friend we haven't called for many years. Yet, some vivid memories of unusual events seem to be available for recall even after decades.

Around the turn of the century, investigators of verbal learning[45] first suggested that short-term and long-term memories might have different properties. They further proposed that a memory may undergo a period of "consolidation" before it becomes part of one's long-term memory stores. Clinical investigations of the deleterious effects of accidental brain damage on memory (see Chapter 18) also indicate that two or more types of memories may exist. It is common, for instance, to find that an adult patient may remember even very difficult materials (such as calculus or biochemistry) that were learned long before the brain injury occurred but may be entirely incapable of recalling the seemingly obvious fact that he had been introduced to Dr. X only a few minutes ago. The temporal characteristics of "long-" and "short"-term memory differ in this instance from those used in the verbal learning experiments (where "short" refers to seconds and "long" refers to a few minutes), but the basic notion—that there is more than one type of memory—is the same. Distinctions between short- and long-term memories have also been made on the basis of the common clinical observation that a blow to the head often results in the victim's inability to remember who struck the blow and the circumstances leading up to it. This "retrograde amnesia" typically extends for a period of hours or days before the accident, thus giving still another definition of long-term memory traces that are apparently exempt from the effects of accidental damage and short-term memories that are not.

Experimental investigations of simple avoidance responses in mice and rats have suggested still different temporal characteristics for long- and short-term memories. In one of these studies,[41] mice were given a single training trial in a passive avoidance situation (i.e., the animals were required to withhold a prepotent response). The animals showed little or no recall when tested 5 or 30 seconds after the training trial but performed well when tested 1 or 24 hours later. These observations suggest that the animals may not have had access to short-term memory traces similar to those used by man in the

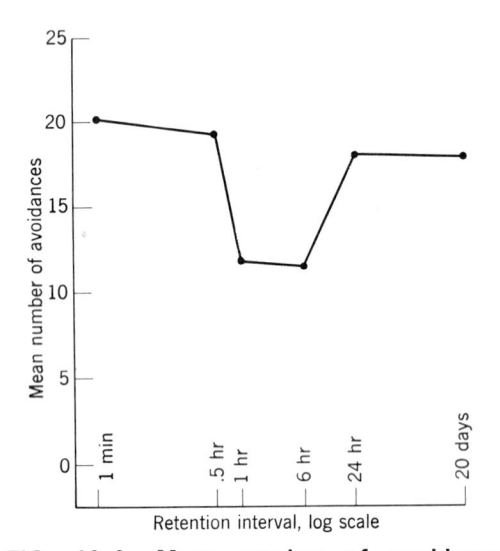

FIG. 16–6. Mean number of avoidance responses as a function of retention interval.

(After L. J. Kamin. Retention of an incompletely learned avoidance response: Some further analysis. *J. comp. physiol. Psychol.*, **56**, 1963, 713–718. Copyright 1963 by the American Psychological Association, and reproduced by permission.)

dialing of a telephone number but did "consolidate" a long-term memory during the first few seconds or minutes after training. Slightly different values have been obtained when rats were given a few training trials in an active, shuttle-box avoidance situation[33] (see Figure 16–6). Although incompletely trained, these animals remembered well when tested 1 or 30 minutes or 1 or 20 days after training but not when tested after 1 or 6 hours. The temporal aspects of this period of "unavailability" are different from those of the preceding experiments (perhaps because repeated training trials were given), but both sets of observations suggest that long-term memories can be developed at a time when recall is not possible.

The notion of a dual or multiple memory trace has been incorporated into many physiological, anatomical, and biochemical theories of learning and memory. Most contemporary theories propose that learning must result in a temporary change in synaptic function which, in turn, leads to a sequence of anatomical and/or biochemical changes that eventually result in more permanent memory traces. Short-term memories are thought to depend on reverberatory electrical activity in feedback circuits, a temporary swelling of end feet, or an interaction of neurohumors and related enzymes. Long-term memories, on the other hand, are thought to be based on permanent growth of axonal tissue, permanent changes in protein synthesis, or even on modifications of the genetic code of the cells involved (see Figure 16–7).

It is common usage to discuss the literature in this field in terms of "memory consolidation" and to assume that long-term memories are based on the transient functional changes responsible for short-term recall. It should be clear, however, that more than one independent memory process may be involved. Many experiments have shown that memories are particularly vulnerable shortly after acquisition and may, indeed, be temporarily unavailable for recall. This is com-

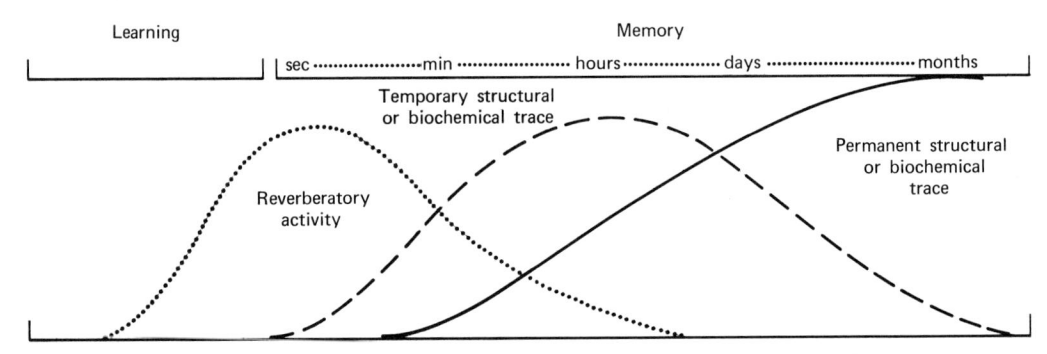

FIG. 16–7. The temporal relationships between different types of memory traces which have been proposed. The different memory processes may be independent (i.e., the development of temporary or permanent structural changes may take place even when the reverberatory activity—and short-term memory—are blocked) or they may be interdependent.

patible with the consolidation hypothesis but does not exclude the possibility that learning may result in two or more independent memory traces that have different incubation and decay constants. It is also possible that treatments which impair or eliminate recall may not at all block the formation of a permanent memory trace but interfere with access to it. This would, of course, produce the same apparent "memory deficits" on our behavioral measures even though processes related to memory retrieval rather than consolidation or learning are involved. Our experimental procedures are, unfortunately, not yet sufficiently sophisticated to permit a discrimination between these alternatives in most instances.

Effects of Electroconvulsive Shock (ECS)

The first experimental investigations of memory consolidation were undertaken about 30 years ago when it became apparent that electroconvulsive shock (ECS) treatments often induced a selective retrograde amnesia for events that immediately preceded the treatment. Very brief, very intense electric shocks applied to electrodes on opposite sides of the head induce EEG seizures as well as brief periods of unconsciousness and convulsion. Such electroconvulsive shock treatments became widely used in the treatment of psychiatric patients about 30 years ago, and are still used in cases of extreme withdrawal and general unresponsiveness to psychotherapy. The rationale for this treatment is that ECS may disrupt ongoing brain functions which are obviously not conducive to treatment and permit the appearance of new and perhaps more useful patterns of brain activity in the subsequent period of reorganization. ECS treatments were widely used until it became apparent that the patients were disorganized with respect to time and space for some time after each treatment and often seemed to experience amnesia for the events which led up to the convulsive experience. Long-term memories, as well as the patient's ability to learn after the ECS treatment, did not seem to be affected. Drugs such as Metrazol or insulin, which induce convulsive reactions similar to those of ECS, were also found to interfere with the recall of recent experiences.

The potential usefulness of these techniques for experimental investigations of the temporal characteristics of memory traces was soon discovered. Drugs as well as ECS treatments have been widely used in recent years to study time-dependent memory processes. The effects of various drugs are discussed in detail in Chapter 19. We shall concentrate here on the effects of ECS. There is no doubt that ECS treatments, given shortly after training, impair performance on subsequent tests of recall. What is not clear, even after years of investigation, is whether the observed impairment is caused by an interference with processes essential for the "consolidation" of long-term memories. Several alternative interpretations have been offered, and there is some evidence that not everything that looks like a loss of recent memory is indeed due to a disruption of consolidation.

Several different experimental paradigms have been used to investigate the effects of ECS on memory or, more specifically, on recall. The initial investigations[13,14] relied on standard appetitive instrumental learning paradigms and multiple (one per trial) ECS

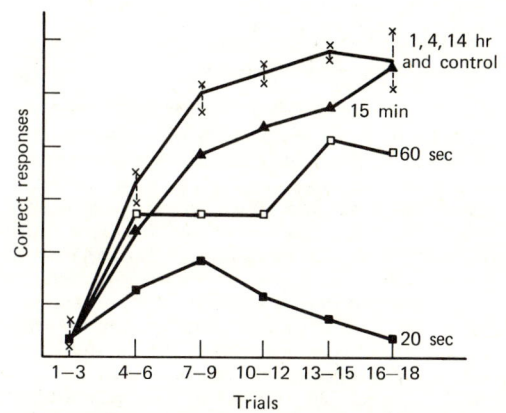

FIG. 16–8. Effect of ECS on acquisition. ECS was given 20 sec, 1 min, 15 min, or 1, 4, and 14 hr after each learning trial.

(After C. P. Duncan. The retroactive effect of electroshock on learning. *J. comp. physiol. Psychol.*, 42, 1949, 32–44. Copyright 1949 by the American Psychological Association, and reproduced by permission.)

treatments. In such situations, learning is significantly retarded by ECS treatments given up to 30 to 60 minutes after each training trial (see Figure 16–8). Although painful foot shock, given in place of the ECS treatment, was shown to be effective only when given within a few seconds after each trial,[14] it soon became clear that repeated ECS treatments are noxious to man[17] as well as rats.[25] This suggests that at least some of the deficits which were observed in these paradigms may be a result of punishment of correct responses.

Subsequent experiments consequently have used simple instrumental training situations where significant learning can occur in only a few training trials.[54] Most recent investigations have used passive avoidance paradigms, which involve only a single trial and only one ECS[47, 22] (see Figure 16–9).

A third paradigm has been used by investigators interested specifically in the clinically important possibility that ECS treatments may selectively interfere with the recall of emotional reactions.[27] In these experiments, rats are trained to lever press for food rewards that are available on some intermittent reinforcement schedule. They are then exposed to a classical conditioning procedure where a tone (or light) is repeatedly associated with painful, unavoidable, and inescapable foot shock. On subsequent trials, the CS for foot shock is presented while the animals are lever pressing for food rewards, and a complete cessation of operant responding is typically observed. This "conditioned emotional response" (CER) is stable over repeated tests but disappears after repeated ECS treatments[29] (see Figure 16–10).

TABLE 1. Comparison of the ECS Effects on Performance on Recall Tests in Several Experimental Paradigms. (Note particularly the marked differences between the CER paradigm and the passive avoidance and multiple-trial maze learning paradigms.)

	Multiple-ECS Multiple-Trial Paradigm	Single-ECS Single-Trial Paradigm	Single- or Multiple-ECS CER Paradigm
Effective Training-Treatment Interval	15–60 min.	10 sec. to several hours	weeks or months
Spontaneous Recovery?	No	No	Yes
Overt Convulsions Necessary?	No	No	Yes

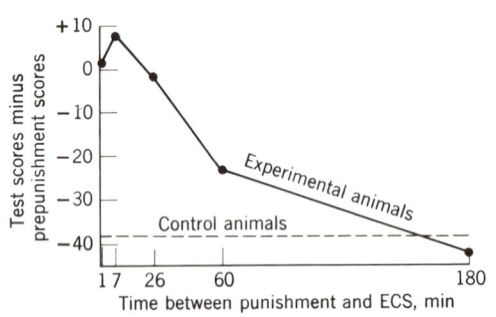

FIG. 16–9. Effects of ECS on retention as a function of the time interval between learning and ECS. Rats were trained to lever-press for food rewards and then given one painful shock through the lever. ECS was administered 1, 7, 26, 60, or 180 min after the punishment. On a subsequent retention test, all experimental animals except those receiving ECS 180 min after the punishment returned to the lever faster than the controls, indicating a loss of memory. The animals that received ECS 1, 7, or 26 min after the punishment returned to the lever as fast or faster than before the punishment.

(From J. T. Heriot & P. D. Coleman. The effect of electroconvulsive shock on retention of a modified "one-trial" conditioned avoidance. *J. comp. physiol. Psychol.*, **55**, 1962, 1082–1084. Copyright 1962 by the American Psychological Association, and reproduced by permission.)

Several features of these experiments (see Table 1) deserve additional comment:

1. In contrast to the effects of ECS in other experimental situations, the CER response is significantly impaired even when the ECS treatments are given days or even weeks after the classical conditioning that established the CER. In one experiment[7] repeated ECS treatments were effective even when given 30 days after the CER training, and some effects were seen as late as 90 days afterwards.

2. ECS treatments, given a few days after the establishment of the CER, interfere with the conditioned emotional response on tests given 30 days but not 90 days afterwards.[6]

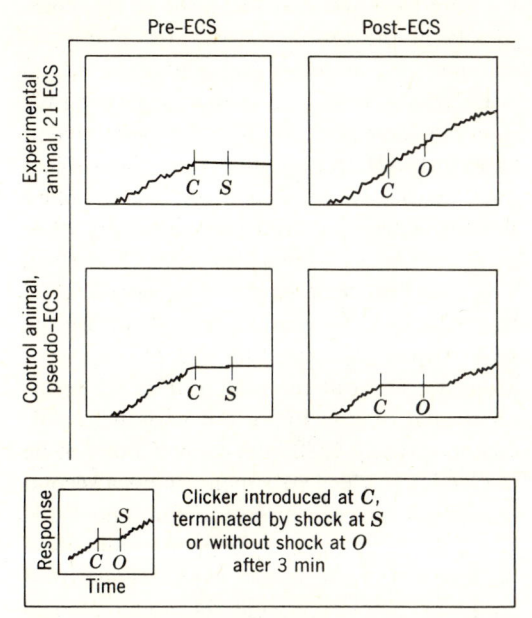

FIG. 16–10. Effect of ECS on CER. Typical cumulative curves for two rats.

(From H. F. Hunt & J. V. Brady. Some effects of electroconvulsive shock on a conditioned emotional response ("anxiety"). *J. comp. physiol. Psychol.*, **44**, 1951, 88–98. Copyright 1951 by the American Psychological Association, and reproduced by permission.)

This spontaneous recovery can be prevented by the administration of ECS on alternate days during the training-testing period.[9] The reappearance of a CER several months after it was inhibited by ECS indicates that the treatment does not prevent consolidation in this instance but may somehow block access to the established memory. This interpretation is supported by the observation[30] that extinction trials, given during the post-ECS time while the CER could not be elicited, were effective in preventing CER responses on subsequent test trials when the ECS effect on the CER would normally have disappeared.

3. Repeated ECS treatments block the CER if given 24 hours apart but not if given only minutes or seconds apart.[10]

4. The effects of ECS given several days after training appear to be specific to the CER. The more complex lever-pressing response (which is inhibited by the intact CER) is entirely unaffected by ECS treatments regardless of whether the CER training is given before or after the establishment of the operant lever-pressing response.[18, 8]

5. The ECS-induced blockade of the conditioned emotional response occurs only when the ECS treatment induces overt clonic convulsions. Drugs which prevent the convulsions obliterate the effect.[31, 28]

The pattern of ECS effects on conditioned emotional responses suggests that it is not the result of an interference with memory consolidation. Instead, access to the classically conditioned "fear" responses seems to be temporarily blocked by ECS treatments. This blocking effect does not appear to be related to possibly occurring punishing effects of the ECS treatments, since repeated painful foot shocks, given on a similar schedule, do not duplicate the ECS effect.[4] The temporal parameters of the ECS effect on conditioned emotional reactions, their instability, and their apparent specificity indicate that processes different from those reflected in other training situations may be responsible for them. We shall therefore concentrate on the effects of ECS in other experimental paradigms.

Most recent investigations of the effects of electroconvulsive shock on recall have attempted to describe (a) the maximal effective training/ECS interval, (b) the permanence of the ECS-induced inhibition of recall, and (c) the possibility that ECS may affect performance on recall tests without disrupting memory traces.

The Duration of the Training/ECS Interval

With the exception of the CER experiments discussed above, all experimental investigations of ECS effects on memory agree that the treatment must be administered very shortly after training. Just what "very shortly" means has, however, been the object of controversy. Some investigators have reported significant amnesic effects of ECS treatments given one or even several hours after the completion of training.[34, 41] (Even longer effective training/ECS intervals have been reported [see Chapter 19] when convulsions are induced by drugs.) Other investigators report little or

388 *Biological Bases of Learning and Memory*

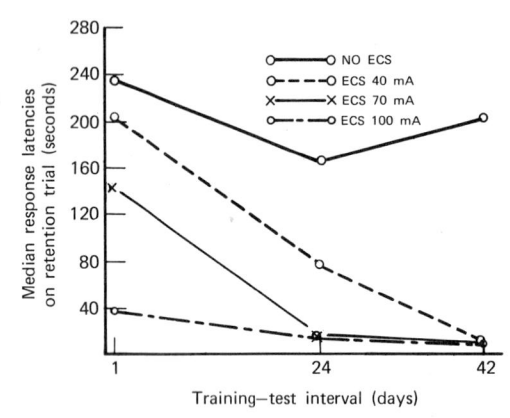

FIG. 16–11. Median response latencies as a function of ECS intensity and the training-test interval. The animals were trained in a one-trial passive-avoidance situation to refrain from entering one compartment of the apparatus. Long latencies thus indicate good retention.

(From R. A. Hughes, R. J. Barrett, & O. S. Ray. Retrograde amnesia in rats increases as a function of ECS-test interval and ECS intensity. *Physiol. & Behav.*, **5**, 1970, 27–30.)

no amnesia when more than 20 or 30 seconds elapse between training and the ECS treatment.[48] Longer[3] as well as more intense[49] ECS treatments apparently produce more prolonged effects than shorter and less intense currents (see Figure 16–11). The magnitude of the disruption that a single ECS treatment produces also seems to be related to the intensity of the reward or punishment involved in the original training,[50] and there are indications[43, 41] that the duration of the effective training/ECS interval increases as the complexity of the problem and, presumably, of the memory, increases (see Figure 16–12).

Even very brief (0.5 second) training/ECS intervals have been found to be ineffective in experiments[39] that familiarized the subject with the passive avoidance apparatus before the single training trial was given. In other experiments,[52] a 6-hour training/ECS interval was found to be effective if a second UCS (foot shock) was given 0.5 seconds before the ECS treatment, suggesting that the degree of arousal present at the time of the ECS treatment might be an important variable. A 30-second training/ECS interval was found to be ineffective in this experiment unless a second foot shock was given just before the ECS. Even 24-hour training/ECS intervals have been reported effective in experiments[44] that gave the ECS treatment 24 hours after a single passive avoidance trial but preceded the ECS by a second presentation of the CS.

The Permanence of the ECS-Induced Inhibition of Recall

It is generally assumed that ECS treatments, given shortly after training, inhibit memory consolidation and thus exert permanent effects on recall. Experiments specifically designed to demonstrate the longevity of the ECS effect have produced somewhat discordant results. Some investigators[12, 49] have reported undiminished ECS effects after one

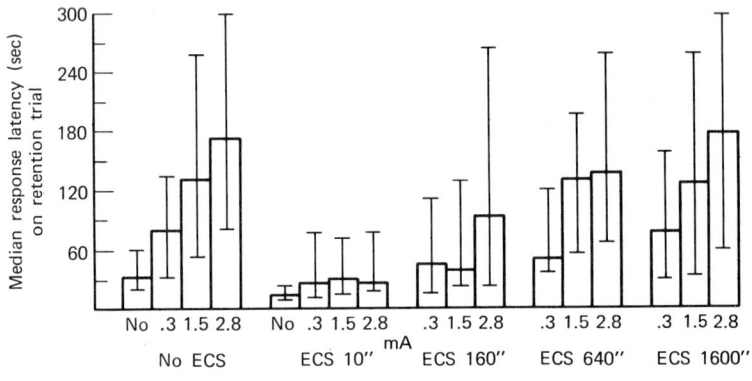

FIG. 16–12. Effect of foot-shock intensity and training-ECS interval on acquisition of a passive-avoidance response by mice.

(From O. S. Ray & L. W. Bivens. Reinforcement magnitude as a determinant of performance decrement after electroconvulsive shock. *Science*, **160**, 19 April 1968, 330–332. Copyright 1968 by the American Association for the Advancement of Science.)

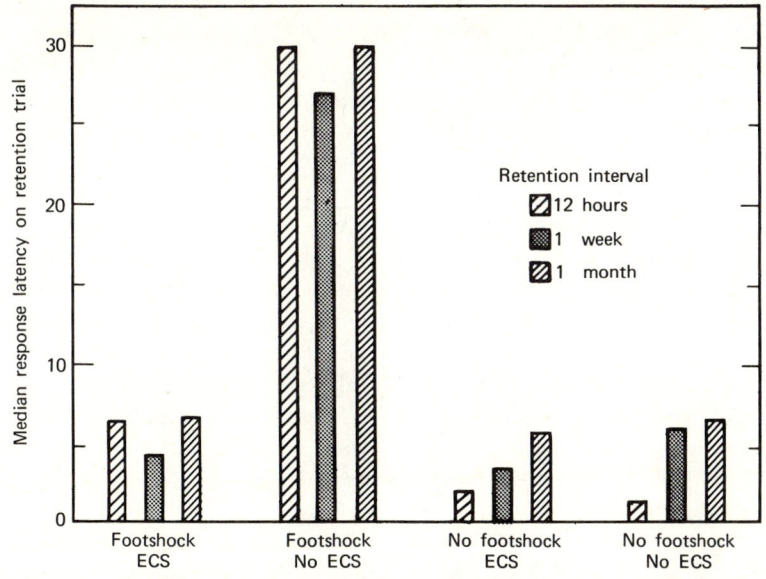

FIG. 16–13. Permanence of ECS-induced retrograde amnesia. Mice were given a single trial in a step-through inhibitory avoidance task and treated with footshock and ECS as indicated. Independent groups were given retention tests 12 hours, 1 week, or 1 month later.

(From M. W. Luttges & J. L. McGaugh. Permanence of retrograde amnesia produced by electroconvulsive shock. *Science*, **156**, 21 April 1967, 408–410. Copyright 1967 by the American Association for the Advancement of Science.)

month or more even when repeated tests were administered[40] (see Figure 16–13). Others have reported that repeated tests can reverse the inhibitory influence of a single ECS treatment.[56, 23] There is some indication that more intense ECS treatments may produce more prolonged effects on recall and that long-term effects may require ECS intensities that produce overt convulsions.[46] Shorter training/ECS intervals may also be more effective than longer ones.

ECS Effects on Performance

Electroconvulsive shocks as well as drug treatments that induce convulsions, given shortly after training, unquestionably interfere with the performance of learned responses on subsequent tests of recall. Why this occurs is not yet clear. The initial ECS experiments were undertaken in the expectation that a brief scrambling of the electrical activity of the brain might selectively disrupt short-term memories, which are thought to depend on such labile functional memory traces as reverberatory activity in recently organized pathways. Most contemporary investigators of the effects of ECS and convulsive drugs share this expectation, although it is clear that convulsive treatments also produce a broad spectrum of effects that are not directly related to short-term memory but may affect performance on tests of recall. Unfortunately, it is often difficult to judge to what extent such "side effects" may influence the outcome of a particular experiment.

The most elusive problem in this area arises from the fact that ECS treatments seem to be aversive. Patients are often upset after an ECS experience and quite commonly develop a profound aversion to the treatment, partly at least because they do not recall the circumstances leading up to it.[17] It has been suggested that the ECS experience, although not subject to recall, may induce anxiety or fear, which becomes conditioned to the treatment situation. In the typical animal learning experiment, such a conditioned emotional reaction to the test situation would interfere with performance, and this inhibition could easily be mistaken for a memory deficit. Many experimenters have examined this problem. The most conservative conclusion one can draw from this literature is that ECS probably induces both amnesic and aversive effects and that the conditions of individual experiments determine the extent to which behavior is influenced by one or the other effect.[25]

Rats learn to avoid the arm of a T-maze where they repeatedly receive ECS treatments[42] and inhibit unconditioned responses (such as stepping down from a small platform) which are repeatedly followed by ECS.[25] These observations indicate not only that repeated ECS treatments are aversive but also that animals are capable of remembering the consequences of a response that is followed by ECS. On the other hand, a single ECS treatment, given shortly after a single learning trial that involves punishment of a learned or unlearned behavior, seems to interfere with recall. On subsequent tests, the ECS-treated animals perform the punished responses more often than controls instead of less frequently, as one would predict if the memory of the second punishment were intact. In this instance, the ECS effect on memory appears to outweigh its aversive properties. We cannot, of course, conclude that a single ECS treatment therefore does not produce any aversive effects and we do not know to what extent the outcome of single ECS experiments may be influenced by this factor.

Attempts have been made to separate the aversive and amnesic effects by administering ECS in the home cage instead of in the training apparatus. This reduces the conditioned association of the aversive effects of the treatment with the correct response and should reduce or eliminate the influence of the aversive effects of ECS. When a fairly long time is allowed to elapse between the end of training and ECS in the home cage, the treatment seems to be ineffective.[1,2] However, with shorter training/ECS intervals, a performance deficit occurs that seems to be independent of the location of the ECS treatment.[38,48]

It is generally assumed that ECS disrupts functional memory traces without permanently damaging neural pathways essential for learning, memory, or recall. The relatively few experiments that have tried to demonstrate the adequacy of this assumption have not done so unambiguously. ECS treatments interfere with acquisition, at least in some circumstances. They do so particularly when administered shortly before training or when given repeatedly,[35] and seem to affect complex problems more readily than simple ones.[51] Such "proactive" inhibitory effects have not been observed in all training situations,[57,53] and it is not clear that mechanisms specifically related to learning are responsible for them. A conditioned emotional response, for instance, could interfere with acquisition as well as performance.

The results of some experiments have indicated that ECS treatments may interfere with recall even when given long after the end of training, provided the CS or UCS are presented shortly before the ECS.[44,52] This suggests that ECS may not, or may not only, interfere with the formation of a memory trace but somehow may block access to it.

Summary and Review Questions

Clinical as well as experimental evidence suggests that we may have several different kinds of memories. Some types of brain lesions selectively interfere with short-term recall. Temporary disturbances of general brain function caused by accidental injury often produce a similar impairment. Memories sometimes seem to be unavailable for recall a few seconds or minutes after training even when there is no interference with normal brain activity. These observations are compatible with the widely held notion that a memory must undergo "consolidation" before it becomes part of the organism's long-term memory stores. They do not, however, rule out alternative possibilities that learning may result in several different types of memories which have different incubation and decay constants, or that a loss of recall may reflect a failure to gain access to a perfectly intact permanent memory trace.

Experimental investigations in this field have typically used electroconvulsive shock

(ECS) to study the effects of a brief scrambling of the electrical activity of the brain on recall. Three questions have attracted most attention: (1) Are the amnesic effects of ECS permanent? (2) How long after training are ECS treatments effective? (3) Is the observed inhibition of performance on recall tests caused by amnesia?

If the amnesic reaction to ECS is because of an interference with memory consolidation, as many investigators in this field believe, the effect should be permanent. Many experimenters have shown long-lasting ECS effects on recall in passive avoidance situations, but there is some evidence that repeated testing may reverse the amnesia. The inhibitory effects of ECS on conditioned emotional reactions show spontaneous recovery after 60 to 90 days, and delays of this magnitude have not yet been used in other experimental paradigms. There is, moreover, some clinical evidence that the retrograde amnesia which results from general trauma may be reversible to a large extent. It is unfortunately difficult to judge to what extent this may occur spontaneously (i.e., without prompting by friends and relatives).

In appetitive learning situations that involve multiple ECS treatments, recall is significantly impaired when the ECS treatments are given within 30 to 60 minutes after each trial. Similar learning/ECS delays have been found effective in passive avoidance experiments that involve only a single learning trial and a single ECS treatment. There is some evidence, however, to suggest that the true amnesic effects of ECS may require much shorter training/ECS delays.

Electroconvulsive shock may selectively block access to memories of aversive events. Repeated treatments have been shown to block conditioned emotional responses even when the treatment/ECS delay amounted to several weeks or months. This effect is not permanent and can thus not be caused by an interference with memory consolidation.

An interpretation of the theoretical implications of the ECS effects on recall is complicated by the fact that the treatment appears to be aversive. When ECS is given repeatedly, its aversive properties appear to overcome whatever amnesic effects it may have, and animals as well as humans learn to avoid situations which have, in the past, been associated with ECS. The amnesic effects seem to dominate in experiments involving only a single ECS treatment, but it is not clear to what extent behavior may nonetheless be influenced by aversive reactions.

1. Describe the clinical and experimental evidence which suggests that there may be different kinds of short- and long-term memory traces.

2. Summarize the effects of ECS on recall in (a) single-trial passive avoidance situations and (b) experiments involving conditioned emotional reactions superimposed on an operant response such as lever pressing.

3. Describe the temporal gradient of ECS effects on recall performance. Are there any proactive effects? How long is the effective training/ECS interval? Are ECS effects permanent?

4. It is generally assumed that the effects of ECS on recall are caused by an interference with memory consolidation. Discuss alternative interpretations such as a blockade of access to intact memories or a performance deficit due to aversive properties of ECS.

REVIEW

A theoretical and experimental analysis of the physical basis of learning and of its end product, memory, is hampered by many conceptual as well as practical problems that we must keep in mind throughout our discussion of this field. It is not clear whether we are, indeed, dealing with a single learning process in all situations; whether different kinds of learning paradigms give rise to different kinds of memories; or even whether the same paradigm may produce several fundamentally different types of memories that may or may not be interdependent. The voluminous literature on the effects of disruptive treatments such as electroconvulsive shock shows clearly that traumatic events which occur shortly after learning interfere with recall and do so in proportion to their temporal proximity to the learning experience. However, it is not clear to what extent these effects are caused by a selective effect on memory consolidation. Some experiments suggest that these treatments may merely block access to well-established memories; others indicate that the aversive properties of the treatments induce emotional reactions that may interfere with performance instead of recall itself.

Matters are further complicated by the fact that we have, as yet, only vague ideas about the nature of the functional and structural changes that learning produces in the nervous system or where to look for them. Most probably, learning requires a facilitation of synaptic transmission in selected parts of the brain, but how or where this facilitation may occur is still a mystery. It is widely assumed that learning initially produces temporary functional changes (such as reverberatory activity in feedback circuits), which in turn initiate more permanent structural and/or biochemical traces (such as growth or enlargement of synaptic end feet, induction of neurotransmitter production, or the manufacture of specific novel proteins), but nobody has ever observed such events in vivo. Our failure may be partly because memory traces do not appear to be neatly localized in any given anatomical subdivision of the central nervous system.

These conceptual problems are compounded by the practical problems that arise because we cannot, as yet, observe or record learning or its end product, memory, directly. Instead, we must rely on (1) changes in overt behavior that reflect sensory, motor, or motivational processes in addition to the results of learning; or (2) electrophysiological or biochemical events in the central nervous system which have not yet been shown to be exclusively related to associative processes (or any other, for that matter). It is surprising, perhaps, that we know as much as we do about this complex subject.

Bibliography

1. Adams, H. E., & Lewis, D. J. Electroconvulsive shock, retrograde amnesia, and competing responses. *J. comp. physiol. Psychol.*, 1962a, **55**, 299–301.

2. Adams, H. E., & Lewis, D. J. Retrograde amnesia and competing responses. *J. comp. physiol. Psychol.*, 1962b, **55**, 302–305.

3. Alpern, H. P., & McGaugh, J. L. Retrograde amnesia as a function of duration of electroshock stimulation. *J. comp. physiol. Psychol.*, 1968, **65**, 265–269.

4. Beckwith, W. C., & Hunt, H. F. The effects of electro-convulsive shock and severe pain upon the retention of a discrimination based on punishment. *Amer. Psychologist*, 1955, **10**, 555.

5. Bonnet, C. *Essai de psychologie.* Paris: Sorbonne, 1754.

6. Brady, J. V. The effects of electro-convulsive shock on a conditioned emotional response: the permanence of the effect. *J. comp. physiol. Psychol.*, 1951, **44**, 507–511.

7. Brady, J. V. The effect of electro-convulsive shock on a conditioned emotional response: The significance of the interval between the emotional conditioning and the electroconvulsive shock. *J. comp. physiol. Psychol.*, 1952, **45**, 9–13.

8. Brady, J. V., & Hunt, H. F. A further demonstration of the effects of electroconvulsive shock on a conditioned emotional response. *J. comp. physiol. Psychol.*, 1951, **44**, 204–209.

9. Brady, J. V., Stebbins, W. C., & Galambos, R. The effect of audiogenic convulsions on a conditioned emotional response. *J. comp. physiol. Psychol.*, 1953, **46**, 363–367.

10. Brady, J. V., Hunt, H. F., & Geller, I. The effect of electro-convulsive shock on a conditioned emotional response as a function of the temporal distribution of treatments. *J. comp. physiol. Psychol.*, 1954, **47**, 454–457.

11. Broca, P. Remarques sur le siège de la faculté du langage articulé, suivies d'une observation d'aphémie. *Bull. Soc. Anat. (Paris)*, 1861, **6**, 330–357.

12. Chevalier, J. A. Permanence of amnesia after a single post-trial electroconvulsive seizure. *J. comp. physiol. Psychol.*, 1965, **59**, 125–127.

13. Duncan, C. P. The effect of electroshock convulsions on the maze habit in the white rat. *J. exp. Psychol.*, 1945, **35**, 267–278.
14. Duncan, C. P. The retroactive effect of electroshock on learning. *J. comp. physiol. Psychol.*, 1949, **42**, 32–44.
15. Ferrier, D. *The Functions of the brain.* London: Smith, Elder, 1886.
16. Gall, F. J., & Spurzheim, J. G. Anatomie et physiologie du système nerveux en général et du cerveau en particulier, avec des observations sur la possibilité de reconnoître plusieurs dispositions intellectuelles et morales de l'homme et des animaux par la configuration de leurs têtes. Paris: Sorbonne, 1810–1819. (4 cols.)
17. Gallinek, A. Fear and anxiety in the course of electroshock therapy. *Amer. J. Psychiat.*, 1956, **113**, 428–434.
18. Geller, I., Sidman, M., & Brady, J. V. The effect of electro-convulsive shock on a conditioned emotional response: A control for acquisition recency. *J. comp. physiol. Psychol.*, 1955, **48**, 130–131.
19. Goltz, F. Über die Verrichtungen des Grosshirns. *Arch. ges. Physiol.*, 1881, **26**, 1–49.
20. Harlow, H. F., McGaugh, J. L., & Thompson, R. F. *Psychology.* San Francisco: Albion, 1971.
21. Hering, E. Über das Gedächtniss als eine allgemeine Funktion der organisierten Materie. *Almanach Kaiserl. Akad. Wiss. (Wien)*, 1870, **20**, 253–278.
22. Heriot, J. T., & Coleman, P. D. The effect of electro-convulsive shock on retention of a modified "one-trial" conditioned avoidance. *J. comp. physiol. Psychol.*, 1962, **55**, 1082–1084.
23. Herz, M. J., & Peeke, H. V. S. ECS-produced retrograde amnesia. Permanence vs. recovery over repeated testing. *Physiol. & Behav.*, 1968, **3**, 517–521.
24. Hitzig, E. *Untersuchungen über das Gehirn.* Berlin: Hirschwald, 1874.
25. Hudspeth, W. J., McGaugh, J. L., & Thompson, C. W. Aversive and amnesic effects of electroconvulsive shock. *J. comp. physiol. Psychol.*, 1964, **57**, 61–64.
26. Hughes, R. A., Barrett, R. J., & Ray, O. S. Retrograde amnesia in rats increases as a function of ECS-test interval and ECS intensity. *Physiol. & Behav.*, 1970, **5**, 27–30.
27. Hunt, H. F. Electro-convulsive shock and learning. *Trans. N. Y. Acad. Sci.*, 1965, Ser. II, **27**, 923–945.
28. Hunt, H. F., & Beckwith, W. C. The effect of electro-convulsive shock under phenurone, dilantin, or amphetamine medication on a conditioned emotional response. *Amer. Psychologist*, 1956, **11**, 442.
29. Hunt, H. F., & Brady, J. V. Some effects of electro-convulsive shock on a conditioned emotional response ("anxiety"). *J. comp. physiol. Psychol.*, 1951, **44**, 88–98.
30. Hunt, H. F., Jernberg, P., & Brady, J. V. The effect of electro-convulsive shock on a conditioned emotional response: The effect of post-ECS extinction on the reappearance of the response. *J. comp. physiol. Psychol.*, 1952, **45**, 589–599.
31. Hunt, H. F., Jernberg, P., & Otis, L. S. The effect of carbon disulphide convulsions on a conditioned emotional response. *J. comp. physiol. Psychol.*, 1953, **46**, 465–469.
32. James, W. *Principles of psychology.* New York: Henry Holt, 1890.
33. Kamin, L. J. Retention of an incompletely learned avoidance response: Some further analysis. *J. comp. physiol. Psychol.*, 1963, **56**, 713–718.
34. Kopp, R., Bohdanecky, Z., & Jarvik, M. E. Long temporal gradient of retrograde amnesia for a well-discriminated stimulus. *Science*, 1966, **153**, 1547–1549.
35. Kopp, R., Bohdanecky, Z., & Jarvik, M. E. Proactive effect of a single electro-convulsive shock (ECS) on one-trial learning in mice. *J. comp. physiol. Psychol.*, 1968, **65**, 514–517.
36. Lashley, K. S. In search of the engram. *Soc. exp. Biol.*, 1950, Symposium **4**, (Animal Behaviour), 454–482.
37. Lashley, K. S., & Wiley, L. E. Studies of cerebral function in learning: IX. Mass action in relation to the number of elements in the problem to be learned. *J. comp. Neurol.*, 1933, **57**, 3–55.
38. Leonard, D. J., & Zavala, A. Electroconvulsive shock, retroactive amnesia, and the single-shock method. *Science*, 1964, **146**, 1073–1074.
39. Lewis, D. J., Miller, R. R., & Misanin, J. R. Selective amnesia in rats produced by electro-convulsive shock. *J. comp. physiol. Psychol.*, 1969, **69**, 136–140.

40. Luttges, M. W., & McGaugh, J. L. Permanence of retrograde amnesia produced by electroconvulsive shock. *Science*, 21 April 1967, **156**, 408–410.

41. McGaugh, J. L. Time-dependent processes in memory storage. *Science*, 1966, **153**, 1351–1358.

42. McGaugh, J. L., & Madsen, M. C. Amnesic and punishing effects of electroconvulsive shock. *Science*, 1964, **144**, 182–183.

43. McGaugh, J. L., & Petrinovich, L. F. Effects of drugs on learning and memory. *Intern. Rev. Neurobiology*, 1965, **8**, 139–196.

44. Misanin, J. R., Miller, R. R., & Lewis, D. J. Retrograde amnesia produced by electroconvulsive shock after reactivation of a consolidated memory trace. *Science*, 1968, **160**, 554–555.

45. Müller, G. E., & Pilzecker, A. Experimentelle Beiträge zur Lehre vom Gedächtnis. *Z. Psychol.*, 1900, Suppl. 1.

46. Pagano, R. R., Bush, D. F., Martin, G., & Hunt, E. B. Duration of retrograde amnesia as a function of electroconvulsive shock intensity. *Physiol. & Behav.*, 1969, **4**, 19–21.

47. Pearlman, C. A., Jr., Sharpless, S. K., & Jarvik, M. E. Retrograde amnesia produced by anesthetic and convulsant agents. *J. comp. physiol. Psychol.*, 1961, **54**, 109–112.

48. Quartermain, D., Paolino, R. M., & Miller, N. E. A brief temporal gradient of retrograde amnesia independent of situational change. *Science*, 1965, **149**, 1116–1118.

49. Ray, O. S., & Barrett, R. J. Disruptive effects of electro-convulsive shock as a function of current levels and mode of delivery. *J. comp. physiol. Psychol.*, 1969, **67**, 110–116.

50. Ray, O. S., & Bivens, L. W. Reinforcement magnitude as a determinant of performance decrement after electroconvulsive shock. *Science*, 19 April 1968, **160**, 330–332.

51. Russell, R. W. Effects of electroshock convulsions on learning and retention in rats as functions of difficulty of the task. *J. comp. physiol. Psychol.*, 1949, **42**, 137–142.

52. Schneider, A. M., & Sherman, W. Amnesia: a function of the temporal relation of footshock to electroconvulsive shock. *Science*, 1968, **159**, 219–221.

53. Siegel, P. S. The effect of electroshock convulsions on the acquisition of a simple running response in the rat. *J. comp. Psychol.*, 1943, **36**, 61–65.

54. Thompson, R., & Dean, W. A further study on the retroactive effect of ECS. *J. comp. physiol. Psychol.*, 1955, **48**, 488–491.

55. Waldeyer, W. von. Über einige neuere Forschungen im Gebiete der Anatomie des Zentralnervensystems. *Berl. klin. Wschr.*, 1891, **28**, 691.

56. Zinkin, Sheila, & Miller, A. J. Recovery of memory after amnesia induced by electroconvulsive shock. *Science*, 1967, **155**, 102–104.

57. Zubin, J., & Barrera, S. E. Effect of convulsive therapy on memory. *Proc. Soc. exp. Biol. Med.*, 1941, **48**, 596–597.

Chapter 17

ANATOMICAL SUBSTRATE OF LEARNING AND MEMORY

Introduction

Neocortical Influences

The Hippocampus and its Diencephalic Projections

Other Portions of the CNS

Pathways that Mediate the Conditioned and Unconditioned Stimuli

Minimal Anatomical Substrates for Learning

General Summary

INTRODUCTION

Learning produces its effects on behavior by initiating physicochemical changes in the central nervous system. Conceptually the simplest and most direct approach to the study of this phenomenon is to search for the location of these changes. Investigations of the anatomical substrate of the memory trace or "engram" were initiated as soon as the gross organization of the mammalian brain became known and continued to be the principal avenue of attack on the problem until sophisticated electrophysiological and biochemical techniques became available 25 or 30 years ago. The search continues today in many laboratories, and we are far, indeed, from the answers that appeared so obvious when it began nearly 50 years ago.

Literally thousands of investigators have attempted to localize the memory trace by observing the behavioral effects of damage to more or less restricted portions of the brain. Some have made lesions prior to behavioral experiments that require the acquisition of novel behaviors and asked whether the experimental animals are as capable of learning as their normal controls. Others have placed the lesion after the animals had mastered the tasks and asked whether memory or mechanisms essential for retrieval could be demonstrated in particular portions of the brain. These two approaches possibly ask quite different questions, since we cannot be sure that the neural processes which are responsible for the initial formation of a memory trace occur in the same parts of the brain that are responsible for its permanent storage and/or recall.

Both approaches assume implicitly that the physicochemical changes which take place during learning, consolidation, or retrieval occur preferentially in some portions of the brain. In the simple case of classical conditioning, for example, it is widely assumed that the process of conditioning consists essentially of synaptic facilitation in pathways which interconnect the representation of the CS and UCS. In more complex situations, it is typically assumed that the sequential association of many different sensory inputs produces a pattern of facilitation in regions of the brain that are specifically concerned with "associative" processes or memory storage. This type of interpretation is supported mainly, as we shall see, by clinical observations of the effects of neurosurgical interventions in man. (Electrical stimulation of discrete points of the human brain sometimes elicits complex and apparently long-forgotten memories, and damage to some portions of the human brain appears to specifically interfere with the recall or formation of memories.) Research on infrahuman species has generally failed to demonstrate a similarly discrete organization of memories and related processes. This has given rise to the speculation that all neural tissue (and perhaps even nonneural glial tissue) may be capable of modified activity as a function of experience in learning situations and that memories may be diffusely represented throughout much of the brain. We shall examine these proposals in a later segment of our discussion.

In this, as in other areas of research, many controversies exist, not so much with respect to the experimental observations themselves (although sometimes baffling discrepancies occur because of seemingly slight differences in procedure) but primarily with respect to their interpretation. Before we discuss some examples of the literature in this field, some general caveats may be useful.

If we fail to observe an impairment in the performance of learned responses following destruction of a particular part of the brain, it is not logically correct to assume that this region does not participate in learning or recall. The pathways mediating learning or recall may be redundant, and destruction of some portion of them may therefore not produce a significant loss of function. Moreover, our crude behavioral tests may not reveal some of the functional deficits that may, in fact, occur.

If we do observe an impairment in learned behavior, it is equally inappropriate to conclude that the engram has been localized. Until we understand the nature of the physicochemical events that occur as a result of learning well enough to monitor them directly, we can only record the behavioral consequences of learning. These overt manifestations of altered brain function are, however, dependent on many neural processes not specifically related to learning. Failure to perform previously learned behaviors or to acquire them may be caused by an interference with sensory signals (i.e., the animal may be unable to discriminate the conditioned stimulus); motor functions (i.e., the animal may be unable to perform the conditioned response); or motivational processes (i.e., the animal may not be interested in obtaining the reward or avoiding the punishment scheduled to reinforce correct responses). Behavioral deficits may also result from an interference with neural pathways related to such psychological processes as attention or inhibition. Much experimental evidence suggests, for instance, that damage to cortical as well as some subcortical regions makes it difficult for an animal to "concentrate" on the problem at hand or to refrain from responding to stimuli that are irrelevant, punished, or no longer rewarded. The resultant behavioral deficits can easily be misinterpreted in terms of an interference with mechanisms related to memory.

A further complication is introduced by our ignorance of functional neuroanatomy. Since we do not yet understand the functional organization of most parts of the brain except in gross outline, it is essentially impossible to limit a lesion (or the effects of stimulation) to areas that subserve a single function. There is, in fact, a good deal of evidence to suggest that most, if not all, psychological functions may be diffusely represented and that any geographically defined region of the brain may contain more than a single function. This, unfortunately, implies that even small lesions (or low amplitude stimulation) simultaneously modify several functionally unrelated neural processes and that the resultant behavioral change may be complexly determined. In some instances, this may hide the fact that pathways related to learning or recall were involved in the lesion. In other experiments, behavioral deficits which appear to be related to learning ability or memory may in fact reflect a combination of effects on unrelated neural processes.

Electrical or chemical stimulation experiments present unique conceptual problems. If a neural pathway is normally active in the course of learning or recall, it is difficult to see how nonspecific stimulation could do anything but interfere in much the same way as a lesion. Indeed, facilitatory effects of stimulation are probably more appropriately interpreted as caused by an activation of processes (such as motivation and attention) that are not specifically related to the acquisition, storage, or recall of memory. However, matters are complicated by the possibility of subthreshold facilitation (as opposed to outright stimulation). Particularly chemical "stimulation" may make the propagation of an impulse at a synapse more likely without triggering neural activity. To what extent such effects occur in the course of electrical stimulation is difficult to guess, but the current flow around a stimulating electrode declines gradually and subthreshold facilitatory effects on more distant neural elements cannot be disregarded.

In view of these difficulties, it is perhaps not surprising that many thousands of investigations using ablation or stimulation techniques have not yet succeeded in localizing the memory trace. Indeed, one might be surprised that these experiments have produced as much useful information about the functional organization of the brain as they have.

Summary

Many experiments have been designed to localize the events that occur during learning or during the consolidation of the resultant memory trace or "engram." Destruction of some parts of the brain makes it difficult or impossible for man to form new memory traces but not to recall previously established memories. These areas appear to be active in the consolidation of memory traces but not in their permanent storage. No single subdivision of the brain appears to be essential for simple forms of learning or the recall of simple conditioned responses in animals.

The relationship between specific portions of the brain and learning or memory is difficult to study because we cannot, as yet, measure a memory trace itself. Instead, we are restricted to recording the behavioral consequences of learning, and these are influenced by many variables. Lesions or stimulation of the brain may make it impossible to learn a particular conditioned response because the CS cannot be perceived or because the response itself is no longer under voluntary control. Alternatively, the animal may no longer care to avoid the punishment or receive the reward intended to reinforce the learned behavior.

NEOCORTICAL INFLUENCES

Learning and Recall in Neodecorticated Animals

Learning occurs in fish that do not have cortical tissue[110] as well as in invertebrates that do not really have a brain at all.[74] However, the phylogenetic development of complex and readily modifiable responses to changes in the environment correlates well with the development of neocortical tissue and, more specifically, with the development of cortical tissue not directly concerned with sensory or motor functions. Many investigators have suggested that these correlations may reflect causal relationships and that learning and memory storage may be uniquely dependent on cortical processes in higher species.

This interpretation appeared to be supported by early Russian investigators who reported that a dog could not be conditioned after the neocortex had been removed. These and related observations led to the formulation of Pavlov's theory of cortical "analyzers," which proposes, in effect, that conditioning consists simply of a facilitation of direct pathways between the cortical representations of the conditioned and unconditioned stimuli. This theory continues to be influential even though replications of the early experiments demonstrated many years ago that neodecortication does not obliterate all memories and that neodecorticated dogs can establish even fairly complex conditioned responses when special care is taken to avoid emotional reactions during training or testing.[95, 11] The behavioral repertoire of neodecorticated animals is, of course, severely limited because of sensory and motor impairments, but there is no evidence that their basic ability to learn or remember is specifically reduced (see Figure 17–1).

Amnesia Caused by Spreading Depression

The role of neocortical mechanisms in learning has more recently been investigated by observing the effects of a temporary and reversible depression of cortical function. Mechanical or chemical stimuli applied directly to the surface of the cortex produce a high amplitude DC potential, accompanied by a depression of cortical activity, which spreads from the point of stimulation to the nearest deep fissure. In animals (such as rats and rabbits) with essentially smooth cortices, the depression spreads over the surface of the entire cerebral hemisphere.[70] Several investigators have analysed the behavioral consequences of such "spreading depressions."

Spreading depression produces more severe behavioral impairments than complete removal of the cortex, presumably because the animals are tested a few minutes after the loss of cortical function and have not had time to compensate for it. Simple postural reflexes are only little affected but more complex motor behavior and locomotor activity are depressed. Many regulatory functions of presumed subcortical origin (such as water metabolism, thermoregulation, and sleep-wakefulness) are disturbed, but this does not adequately account for the profound impairments seen in recently learned behavior.[14, 15] Rats trained to rear up on signal for food rewards or jump onto the wire-mesh wall of their cage to avoid painful foot shock fail to do so when spreading depression is produced in both cortical hemispheres (see Figure 17–2). The animals appear to be capable of perceiving the CS and UCS and perform the jumping response when the shock UCS itself is presented. Sensory and motor deficits undoubtedly influence the behavior of these animals, but it appears unlikely that the complete absence of simple learned responses can be explained in this fashion.

Even unilateral spreading depression interferes with the formation of memory traces.

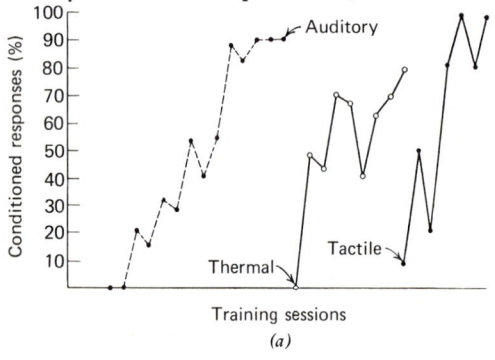

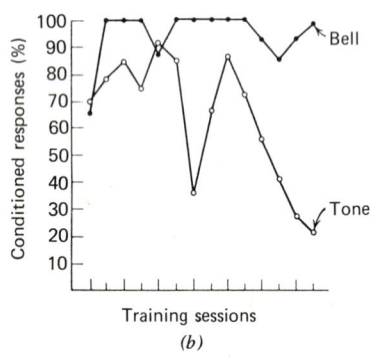

FIG. 17–1. (a) Rate of conditioning to acoustic, thermal, and tactile stimuli following complete decortication. (b) Auditory discrimination following complete decortication. Response to the bell was always reinforced with shock. The CR to the tone was extinguished by the omission of shock.

(After E. Girden, F. A. Mettler, G. Finch, & E. Culler. Conditioned responses in a decorticate dog to acoustic, thermal, and tactile stimulation. *J. comp. Psychol.*, **21**, 1936, 367–385.)

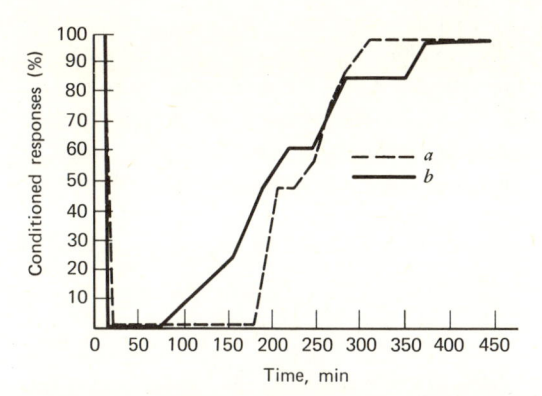

FIG. 17–2. Effect of spreading depression from application of 25% KCl to the occipital region of both hemispheres. Ordinate, percent of (a) alimentary and (b) defensive conditioned responses. Abscissa, time from the moment of KCl application in minutes.

(After J. Bureš & O. Burešova. The use of Leão's spreading cortical depression in research on conditioned reflexes. In *The Moscow colloquium on electroencephalography of higher nervous activity*. H. H. Jasper & G. D. Smirnov, Eds. *EEG clin. Neurophysiol.*, 1960, Suppl. 13, 359–376.)

In one experiment, rats were trained to select the right (or left) of two paths to escape from painful shock. They were subsequently exposed to reversed reinforcement conditions with one of the cerebral hemispheres depressed. On retest, these animals selected the originally correct path (i.e., ignored the intervening reversal learning) when spreading depression was set up in the hemisphere that was normal during the reversal learning. They selected the most recently correct response (i.e., ignored the initial training) when spreading depression was established in the hemisphere that was depressed during reversal learning. These experiments show quite elegantly that a memory that is established when the neocortical mantle of one hemisphere is functioning normally is not available for recall when the activity of that hemisphere is subsequently depressed, even though other parts of the brain are presumably functioning nearly normally at the time of the attempted recall. However, only a few trials appear to be necessary to transfer the memory trace from one hemisphere to another. When the animals were trained under unilateral spreading depression and given only a few test trials with both hemispheres intact, training proceeded rapidly even when the previously trained hemisphere was depressed.

Ablation of Sensory Cortex

The specific contribution of the sensory areas of the cortex to learning and/or recall has been difficult to study. The exact boundaries of the primary sensory projection areas are not clearly drawn in many species, and the total amount of sensory cortex, including "association" cortex, is often not well established. This has resulted in the publication of reports of remarkably little behavioral impairment following "complete" destruction of the cortical projection areas of the conditioned stimulus. Other investigators have probably overestimated the severity of learning or memory related deficits because animals with extensive cortical damage have complex sensory losses, which may make it difficult for the subject to perceive and attend to the stimulus used in the test situation. Many experiments have shown that prolonged periods of recuperation, patient handling, and special training or test procedures (such as punishment of incorrect responses in addition to reward of correct ones) often succeed in demonstrating unsuspected abilities in animals with cortical damage.

If one reviews the extensive literature in this field with these considerations in mind, two principles seem to emerge: (1) "Destruction of the visual, auditory, or somesthetic sensory areas of the cortex does not make it impossible to acquire conditioned responses." Rats, cats, and dogs have been shown capable of learning even some fairly complex conditioned responses (such as lifting the right leg to stimulus A and the left to stimulus B) after apparently complete destruction of the primary sensory projections and most, if not all, of the related "association" areas. For instance, dogs without area 17 learn to lift a leg to avoid painful shock or to obtain food rewards when the CS is a slight shift in the intensity of a visual stimulus.[138, 139] Dogs and cats also acquire auditory intensity and frequency discriminations after extensive damage to the auditory cortex,[103, 16] and roughness and form discriminations can be learned after damage to the somatosensory cortex.[140, 65]

Whereas learning ability appears to be little impaired by damage to the cortical sensory projections or related association areas, there is consistent evidence that preoperatively acquired conditioned responses are severely impaired. In fact, many experimenters have concluded that preoperatively learned responses are completely lost following destruction of the primary sensory areas and that subsequent retraining shows no evidence of any savings. That this conclusion may be influenced in many instances by inadequate testing and handling procedures is suggested by the demonstrated persistence of conditioned responses in neodecorticated animals (see above) as well as reports from many laboratories that some conditioned responses do, in fact, survive complete destruction of the sensory projections of the CS. Simple avoidance responses or classically conditioned eye-blink responses to light have been demonstrated postoperatively.[77, 138] Preoperatively learned conditioned responses to tactile stimuli[3] and even fairly complex auditory discriminations have also been demonstrated in some experiments.[79, 20]

It is nonetheless clear that we can formulate our second principle as follows: (2) "Destruction of the sensory projection areas, particularly when accompanied by destruction of the related 'association' areas, produces severe adverse effects on preoperatively learned conditioned responses." Since relearning of these responses is generally possible and occurs in about the same number of trials required for the initial conditioning, it has been suggested that simple sensory deficits cannot be responsible for these impairments. (It is, however, possible that the animal must postsurgically learn to respond to aspects of the stimulus to which it preoperatively had not attended.)

The extensive impairment of preoperatively acquired behavior and the apparently normal pattern of reacquisition indicates that the sensory areas of the cortex may not be essential to learning but may participate in learning or recall when functional. According to this hypothesis, even simple learning may involve the sensory cortex when it is present. Access to memories that were established when the sensory areas were intact may be difficult when the same cortical functions cannot be activated. When the sensory areas of the cortex are removed prior to training, simple learning can occur, presumably via subcortical components of the sensory projection systems.

We have so far considered only very simple forms of learning in order to specifically illuminate the role of the cortical sensory mechanisms in learning and recall. When one looks at discrimination learning, problem solving, or other complex forms of learning, a picture emerges which is complicated by questions about the sensory capacities of the animal. In spite of the similarity that characterizes the spatial organization of peripheral sensory receptors and their cortical projection, it seems that rats, cats, and monkeys can perform even complex discriminations when only a small percentage of the primary sensory cortex is intact. Moreover, it does not seem to matter which part of the cortical projection is spared. This "equipotentiality" was first demonstrated in the visual system of the rat by the extensive work of Karl Lashley[67] and has more recently been confirmed in other species and other modalities.[2, 20]

Complete destruction of the primary visual cortex (area 17) prevents recall as well as reacquisition of color or form discriminations, presumably because of sensory deficits. Brightness discriminations are typically "lost" following destruction of area 17 but can be reacquired, although often only laboriously and slowly.[66, 63] In the case of the auditory projections, it is difficult to distinguish between primary sensory cortex and related association cortex. Partial destruction of the auditory cortex typically produces little or no impairment in either acquisition or recall. More extensive damage often causes a "loss" of preoperatively learned discriminations, but relearning, involving about as many trials as the initial training, is possible. Even complex frequency discriminations can be relearned under some conditions.[16] Only pattern discriminations and problems requiring the spatial localization of sounds appear to be lost permanently by complete destruction of the cortical auditory projections.[20,89] This suggests that the auditory cortex may be specifically related to the perception of temporal relationships between auditory stimuli but not to the perception of sound frequency or intensity.

Ablation of "Association" Cortex

The neocortex of relatively simple mammalian brains such as that of the rat is almost entirely devoted to sensory and motor functions. In more complex brains, increasingly large portions of the neocortex are not related to sensory or motor functions. It is widely believed that these "association" areas are the anatomical substrate for "higher" mental processes because their phylogenetic development parallels the appearance of complex learned behavior.

The "association" areas are defined largely on the basis of the observations that: (1) electrical stimulation fails to elicit skeletal or autonomic motor responses, and (2) sensory stimuli of all modalities elicit evoked potentials that differ in shape as well as amplitude from the primary potentials that are recorded from the sensory areas. (Most individual cells in the association areas respond to stimuli of more than one modality and many respond to stimuli of all modalities.)

The location of association cortex varies from species to species. In primates, one can distinguish (1) a large anterior association region that comprises a large portion of the frontal lobe anterior to the motor cortex, (2) a smaller posterior association region that includes the cortex surrounding the junction of the parietal, occipital, and temporal lobe, and (3) a diffuse and small temporal association region that includes portions of the anterior and ventral temporal lobe.

Although the term "association" cortex implies that learning might be a function of these regions, there is little evidence to support this conclusion. Lesions in the association areas produce marked behavioral changes, which become more noticeable in complex behavioral tests, but an interference with basic abilities to learn and/or remember does not seem to be responsible for the observed impairments.

Extensive damage to the frontal association cortex does not impair the ability to acquire or recall simple conditioned responses. Deficits become apparent primarily when the subjects are required to (1) select a response on the basis of information not presented at the time of testing or (2) alter the basic strategy of selecting correct responses (see Figure 17–3). The first type of task is exemplified by

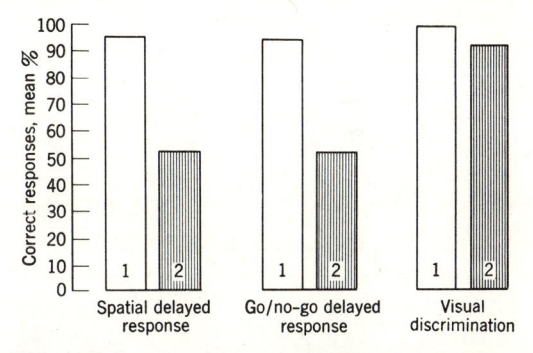

FIG. 17–3. Average performance of four chimpanzees on spatial and go/no-go delayed responses and on a visual pattern discrimination. The first column in each set represents the average performance during the week preceding frontal lobotomy and the second column represents the performance during the third week after the operation.

(After H. E. Rosvold, M. K. Szwarcbart, A. F. Mirsky, & M. Mishkin. The effect of frontal-lobe damage on delayed response performance in chimpanzees. *J. comp. physiol. Psychol.*, **54**, 1961, 368–374. Copyright 1961 by the American Psychological Association, and reproduced by permission.)

delayed-response problems. In the simplest case, the subject is shown two or more objects and a reward is hidden under one of them. An opaque screen is then lowered so that the subject cannot keep his eyes on the baited object. After some delay, the screen is removed and the subject is permitted one choice. Variations of this procedure include delayed alternation where a subject is simply asked to alternate between two objects or to select the same object twice before switching to the other. The second type of task is exemplified by passive avoidance or extinction paradigms where the subject is punished or not rewarded for performing a previously correct response. More complex behavioral tests have been designed to examine a subject's reluctance to switch strategies. A few examples will be discussed below.

Normal monkeys learn delayed response problems easily even when several minutes intervene between the baiting of the correct object and the response to it. Monkeys with frontal lobe lesions do very poorly on these tasks, particularly when long delays are used. Since the same animals perform normally when tested on seemingly more complex simultaneous visual or auditory discrimination problems, the discoverers of the delayed-response deficit[53] believed that it reflected a specific interference with short-term memory.

The principal results of these early experiments have been replicated in many laboratories, but it now seems probable that an interference with mechanisms not specifically related to learning or memory may be responsible for the observed deficit in delayed responding. Animals with frontal lobe lesions can master such problems quite well when distractions are minimized. It seems that monkeys with frontal lobe damage cannot "concentrate" on the problem at hand. They have no difficulty remembering the correct choice if their attention can be captured by the relevant stimuli and distractions are avoided during the delay interval. For instance, frontal monkeys learn delayed response problems quite well when their attention is drawn to the correct object by permitting them to obtain a reward before (as well as after) the delay period;[29] when the lights are turned off during the delay period;[75] when trained under the influence of a sedative;[131] or when the relevance of the discriminanda is emphasized by prolonged training on various learning problems.[18]

Monkeys with frontal lobe lesions are often hyperactive, and this may contribute to the delayed response deficit, since it makes it difficult to maintain postural mnemonics (such as orienting towards the side of the apparatus where the baited object is located). However, hyperactivity is not a sufficient condition for the delayed-response deficit,[97] and there is no clear correlation between the severity of the locomotor disinhibition and the extent of the delayed response problem.

The initial investigations of the behavioral effects of frontal lobe lesions suggested that visual and auditory discriminations were not affected. Subsequent experiments, using more sophisticated learning tasks, have shown that many frontal lobe lesions do, in fact, produce

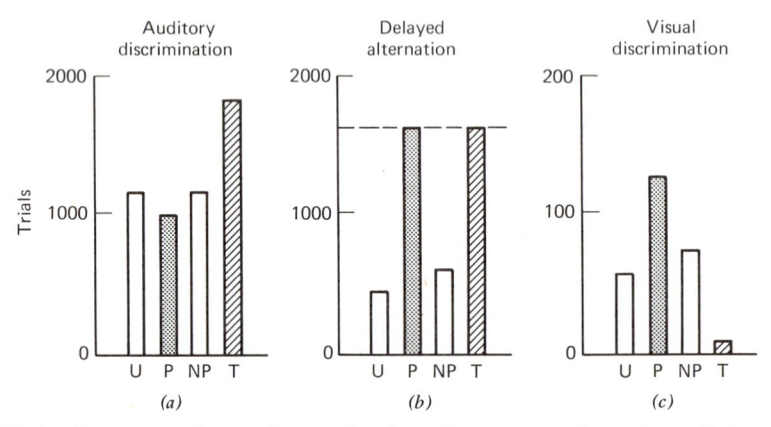

FIG. 17–4. Postoperative trials to criterion of unoperated monkeys (U) and of animals with lesions in the frontal lobe which (P) involved the regions of the sulcus principalis, (NP) spared this region, or (T) involved all frontal cortex on acquisition of (a) go/no-go auditory discrimination (white noise versus 1000-Hz tone); (b) 3-sec delayed alternation; and (c) go/no-go object discrimination.

(After C. G. Gross & L. Weiskrantz. Some changes in behavior produced by lateral lesions in the macaque. In *The frontal granular cortex and behavior.* J. M. Warren & K. Akert, Eds. Copyright 1964 McGraw-Hill Book Company. Used with permission of McGraw-Hill Book Company.)

impairments that are often modality specific. Mechanisms that affect behavior in situations involving visual discriminations, auditory discriminations, or delayed-response problems may be represented in different parts of the frontal lobe[136, 106, 38] (see Figure 17–4). These discrimination deficits may in some instances contribute to the delayed response deficit, but they do not appear to be a sufficient or necessary condition for producing it.[98, 38]

Early investigators of frontal lobe functions noted that monkeys with frontal lobe lesions tended to persevere in previously rewarded behaviors when the conditions of the experiment were changed.[46] Subsequent investigations of the visual and auditory discrimination deficits often seen in these animals demonstrated that the impairment was most marked when the problem was of the "go/no-go" variety and that most errors occurred on "no-go" trials when the monkey must withhold a response that is rewarded on the "go" trials.[99, 136] The perseverative tendencies of the frontal monkey have been specifically studied in several complex experiments. Evidence for perseverative responding has been obtained in experiments requiring the reversal of previously learned object- or spatial-preferences,[82] extinction of search strategies,[101] or responses to objects that were not baited on the preceding trial.[82] However, the frontal monkeys also have an exaggerated tendency to respond to novelty and consequently tend to switch to novel cues.[12, 101]

This leaves us with the apparent paradox that monkeys with frontal lesions perseverate in situations where responses to a particular cue have been repeatedly rewarded but switch to novel stimuli faster than normals when a response to novelty is as likely to be rewarded as a response to familiar objects. It has been suggested[98] that monkeys with frontal lobe lesions may simply be more sensitive to the reward conditions of the experiment (and hence persevere in previously rewarded behavior but select novel cues in preference to familiar ones that have not previously been associated with reward). This explanation accounts nicely for many of the behavioral deficits of the frontal monkey but alternative hypotheses, such as response perseveration or perseveration of central mediating processes[82] cannot be rejected.

The effects of frontal lobe lesions have been studied most extensively in monkeys because they have a good deal more frontal association cortex than other laboratory animals. Similar deficits, particularly of delayed responding, have been seen in dogs[68, 69] and cats,[133] but the severity of the impairment appears to be less pronounced in these species.

The effects of frontal lobe lesions have been extensively studied in man, but an interpretation of these clinical observations is complicated by the fact that lesions are made only in patients with emotional disorders. Frontal lesions often reduce aggressiveness and exaggerated reactions to frustration in man[84] as well as monkeys,[31] and frontal lobotomies have been made in thousands of patients before the advent of tranquilizers. Intellectual deficits have been reported by many neurosurgeons following even small frontal lobe lesions, and some have suggested that these deficits might specifically result from an interference with short-term memory.[104, 32] Others report impairments in "abstract thinking" but no effects on short-term memory per se,[109] and most investigators have concluded that frontal lobe damage in man does not modify the ability to learn or recall per se.[47, 76]

Electrical stimulation of the frontal lobes of monkeys has produced conflicting results. The acquisition of delayed alternation responses has been reported to be impaired,[137] whereas the performance of previously acquired delayed alternation responses[105] or the acquisition of auditory discriminations[137] appeared to be normal. Low-amplitude stimulation of the frontal cortex has been reported to facilitate the acquisition of delayed alternation behavior as well as the reversal of a position habit.[119]

The posterior association cortex and temporal lobe cortex have not received as much experimental attention as the frontal lobe. Complex auditory and visual discrimination tasks typically reflect an impairment following damage to the posterior association cortex or anterior temporal lobe.[83] Modality-specific impairments are produced by lesions in different portions of the posterior association area of the primate.[9, 4, 96, 83] Delayed response tasks do not show an impairment,[45] but complex learning problems which require the formation of learning sets,[78, 12] "detour" learning,[134] sensory-sensory preconditioning,[128] or the association of stimuli of different modalities[28, 127] typically do (see Figure 17–5).

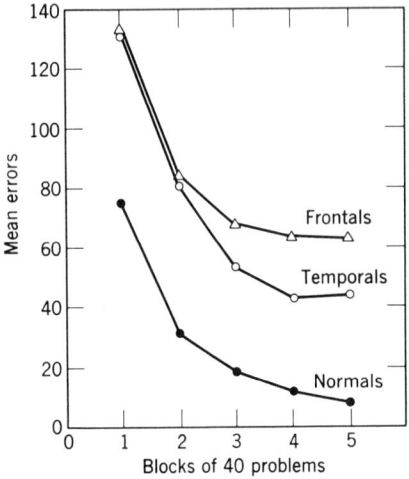

FIG. 17–5. Mean errors on learning set. Each block represents 40 problems or 400 trials. Each group consisted of four animals.
(After M. Mishkin. Perseveration of central sets after frontal lesions in monkeys. In *The frontal granular cortex and behavior*. J. M. Warren & K. Akert, Eds. Copyright 1964 McGraw-Hill Book Company. Used with permission of McGraw-Hill Book Company. Data from E. S. Brush, M. Mishkin, & H. E. Rosvold. *J. comp. physiol. Psychol.*, 54, 1961, 319–325).

Summary and Review Questions

Dogs can learn and recall simple conditioned responses after complete removal of the neocortex. This indicates that neocortical influences are not essential to the formation, storage, or retrieval of simple memories, but it does not tell us whether cortical mechanisms may participate in these functions when present or whether they may even be essential to the acquisition or recall of more complex memories that cannot be examined in the neodecorticated animal because of sensory or motor limitations.

Destruction of the sensory regions of the cortex does not eliminate simple learned behaviors. Such lesions do make it impossible to acquire or recall complex discriminations involving such stimulus attributes as color or pattern. It is generally assumed that this impairment is because of sensory deficits, but this point turns out to be difficult to prove since the demonstration of sensory abilities in animals relies on conditioning procedures. Less complex learned responses are often lost following destruction of the relevant sensory areas, but retraining, involving roughly the same number of trials as the initial learning, is possible. This pattern of results suggests that the sensory cortex may not be essential to either acquisition, storage, or recall, but may contribute to these functions when present and functional.

Lesions in the frontal "association" cortex produce behavioral deficits that become most noticeable in two types of test situations. Frontal animals find it difficult (1) to respond to cues that are not available at the moment of responding (e.g., delayed responding) or (2) to alter the strategy of responding when the reinforcement conditions are changed (as during extinction or the introduction of punishment). Frontal animals also have difficulties with visual and auditory discriminations and are often hyperactive. These deficits may contribute to the animals' difficulties in many test situations but do not appear to be essential or sufficient to produce the deficits seen in delayed responding or response inhibition.

It is often suggested that the delayed-response deficit of frontal animals might be related to an interference with short-term memory. However, frontal animals perform delayed response problems well when the potential for distraction is minimized. It therefore appears more appropriate to consider the frontal animal deficient in its ability to concentrate or pay attention to relevant aspects of the environment.

Intellectual deficits are sometimes reported in human patients with frontal lobe lesions, but most neurosurgeons agree that mechanisms specifically related to learning or memory are probably not responsible for the manifold behavioral effects of the lesions.

We have much less information about the functions of the posterior association cortex. Animals with lesions in these areas do not show a delayed-response deficit or specific difficulties in adjusting to changes in reinforcement conditions but show often modality-specific deficits in complex discrimination experiments.

1. Review the evidence which indicates that neocortical influences are not essential to learning or recall.

2. What observations suggest that neocortical mechanisms may participate in learning or recall when functional? What areas of the cerebral hemispheres have been implicated in these functions?

3. Animals with frontal lobe damage are typically deficient in delayed response situations that require a response to cues not present at the time of responding. Is this a result of short-term memory deficit?

4. Animals with frontal lobe lesions persevere in previously correct but now unrewarded or punished behaviors. Could this be related to a general change in their response to reinforcement?

5. Frontal lobe lesions produce a variety of behavioral effects. Can these be the causes of the observed deficits in delayed response or perseverative responding?

THE HIPPOCAMPUS AND ITS DIENCEPHALIC PROJECTIONS

Clinical Observations in Man

Clinical observations of patients with tumors in the temporal lobe first drew attention to the possibility that this portion of the brain might be involved in memory functions. Patients with large bilateral tumors appear to have lost all memories of recent events and cannot form new memories. However, they are often capable of recalling detailed events which happened in their youth.[36]

Neurosurgeons have made temporal lobe lesions for the relief of epileptiform seizures and various personality disorders. This has provided a wealth of information on the effects of specific types of lesions. Since only a minority of these cases have come to autopsy, the precise extent of the damage is often not known but the correlation between the surgeon's intentions and the histological data which have become available is typically good.

Essentially complete bilateral removal of the temporal lobe, including much of the hippocampus, all of the amygdala, and a good deal of temporal lobe cortex (see Figure 17–6) produces severe adverse effects on all

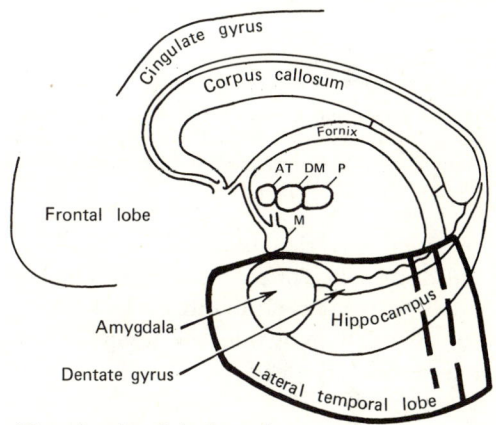

AT = Anterior thalamic nucleus
DM = Dorsal-medial thalamic nucleus
M = Mammillary body
P = Pulvinar thalamic nucleus

FIG. 17–6. Schematic diagram of damage to the entire temporal lobe which produces severe memory deficits in man.

(After R. G. Ojemann. Correlations between specific human brain lesions and memory changes. A critical survey of the literature. *Neurosciences Res. Prog. Bull.*, **4**, (Suppl.), 1966, 1–70.)

types of memories. In one case,[121] such a lesion produced an apparently complete loss of memory. The patient did not remember anything about the past, did not understand questions about himself or his family, did not recognize close friends, and appeared disoriented with respect to his surroundings. Only little memory impairment is seen when this type of lesion is made unilaterally.[93] Patients with unilateral temporal lobe damage often have some difficulties with visually

406 *Biological Bases of Learning and Memory*

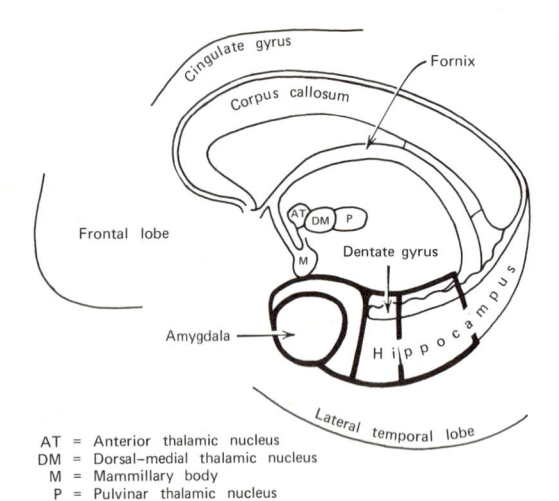

FIG. 17–7. Schematic diagram of lesions in the medial temporal lobe which result in severe memory deficits in man.

(After R. G. Ojemann. Correlations between specific human brain lesions and memory changes. A critical survey of the literature. *Neurosciences Res. Prog. Bull.*, **4**, (Suppl.), 1966, 1–70.)

AT = Anterior thalamic nucleus
DM = Dorsal–medial thalamic nucleus
M = Mammillary body
P = Pulvinar thalamic nucleus

presented or verbal materials as well as a mild disturbance of recent memory, but the impairments are typically mild.

Smaller lesions within the temporal lobe produce marked effects on memory only when the medial portion, containing the hippocampus, is involved (see Figure 17–7). Damage to the amygdaloid complex alone does not result in memory deficits.[86] Bilateral destruction of the lateral portion of the temporal lobe (which spares the hippocampus) sometimes produces difficulties with visually presented materials but no general memory deficit.[5,1] On the other hand, lesions which involve a significant portion of the hippocampus invariably produce recent memory deficits and an apparently complete and permanent inability to acquire new memories. Such patients have a more or less complete amnesia for all events since the lesion was made. The deficits often also include a period of several months or even years before surgery, but recall of memories established earlier in life is typically intact. Such patients may have perfect recall of their academic training and function well in their profession as long as interruptions that require short-term recall of where the chain of activity was interrupted can be prevented.[115, 80] Unilateral destruction of the hippocampus typically does not produce marked changes in memory or learning ability unless electrical seizures or other functional disturbances occur on the contralateral side of the brain.[81]

The major connection between the hippocampus and subcortical and limbic structures is the fornix which interconnects the mammillary region, hypothalamus, and septum with the hippocampus (see Figure 17–8). Since the mammillary bodies themselves have been implicated in memory storage and retrieval (see below), it would seem plausible to expect memory deficits following transection of the fornix. Some neurosurgeons have reported such deficits, but most descriptions of patients who have undergone bilateral fornicotomy fail to report any change in memory or learning ability.[21, 17] A person found to be congenitally devoid of the fornix and fimbria has been reported to have an entirely normal memory.[87]

The principal targets of the fornix, the

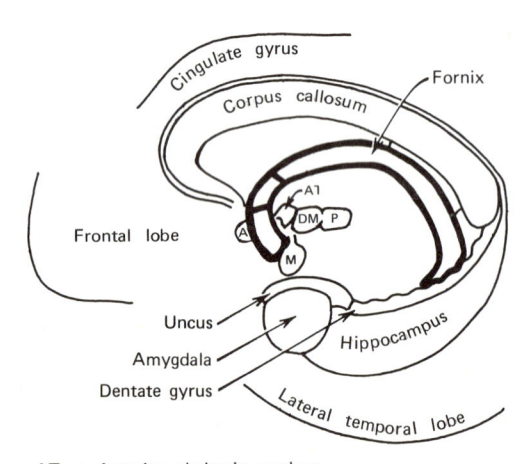

FIG. 17–8. Schematic diagram of lesions in the fornix which do not typically affect memory in man.

(After R. G. Ojemann. Correlations between specific human brain lesions and memory changes. A critical survey of the literature. *Neurosciences Res. Progr. Bull.*, **4**, (Suppl.), 1966, 1–70.)

AT = Anterior thalamic nucleus
DM = Dorsal–medial thalamic nucleus
M = Mammillary body
P = Pulvinar thalamic nucleus

mammillary bodies of the posterior hypothalamus, have been implicated in memory because they, as well as portions of the medial thalamus (but not the hippocampus) are destroyed in patients with Korsakoff's psychosis.[6] This disease is characterized by a partial retrograde amnesia and an often total inability to record new memories. There is some evidence that the mammillary bodies as well as the thalamic nuclei may be responsible for the memory deficit. Bilateral destruction of the mammillary bodies has been reported to result in a complete inability to form new memories.[54] Less severe deficits in acquisition as well as retention of previously learned materials have been reported following lesions in the dorsal medial nuclei of the thalamus.[118]

These observations suggest that in man the hippocampus and perhaps the mammillary region and medial thalamus may form a pathway essential to the storage of new memories without itself being necessary for recall of well-established memories. The hippocampus and directly associated structures thus do not appear to be the site of memory storage itself.

Experimental Studies in Infrahuman Subjects

Experimental investigations of the role of the hippocampus and its projections in the diencephalon have supported the hypothesis that it plays a role in learning or memory storage but also indicate that this pathway may play a less critical role in infrahuman species. Even massive destruction of the hippocampus does not interfere with the acquisition or recall of simple conditioned responses or sensory discriminations.[126, 56, 60] Such lesions do interfere with acquisition and recall in more complex situations such as multiunit mazes or conditional problems.[60] The acquisition or performance of tasks specifically requiring short-term memory on each trial, such as alternation[100] or delayed responding,[56] are most severely impaired. These lesion effects are, however, less severe than those seen in man (there is little evidence of a general retrograde amnesia and most animals do eventually master even complex problems requiring short-term memory).

Hippocampal lesions produce effects on active avoidance behavior that are not easily explainable on the basis of our hypothesis that the hippocampus may be essential for the formation of short-term memories but not for long-term storage or recall. In the same species (the rat), the acquisition or recall of active avoidance responses has been reported to be impaired,[122] normal,[51] or facilitated[52] following hippocampal damage. Passive avoidance responses, on the other hand, are learned poorly if at all by rats with hippocampal lesions.[61] It is tempting to consider this as further evidence for a short-term memory deficit. However, the animals' often normal performance in other simple learning situations as well as their inability to withhold punished unconditioned behaviors[120] suggest that hippocampal lesions may specifically interfere with the animals' ability to inhibit responding.

Evidence for a selective effect of hippocampal lesions on short-term memory has recently been obtained in experiments which investigated the effects of surgical interruptions of the major afferent and efferent connections of the hippocampus. When combined entorhinal and fornix lesions were made 3 hours after the completion of training, cats performed poorly on a recall test given 3 to 4 weeks after surgery. The same lesions, made 8 days after the completion of training, had no effect on performance on the recall test. Neither fornix nor entorhinal lesion alone produced reliable effects in these experiments, suggesting that the disruptive effects of the combined lesions may have been due to the extensive isolation of the hippocampus shortly after training (see Figure 17–9).[130, 57]

Microinjections of pentylenetetrazol (a drug that facilitates synaptic transmission) into the dorsal hippocampus of rats either immediately before or after each daily training session in a maze have been reported to facilitate acquisition.[41] Similar injections of potassium chloride, a drug which disrupts hippocampal functions, did not interfere with acquisition in the same situation.[43] This pattern of results suggests that hippocampal

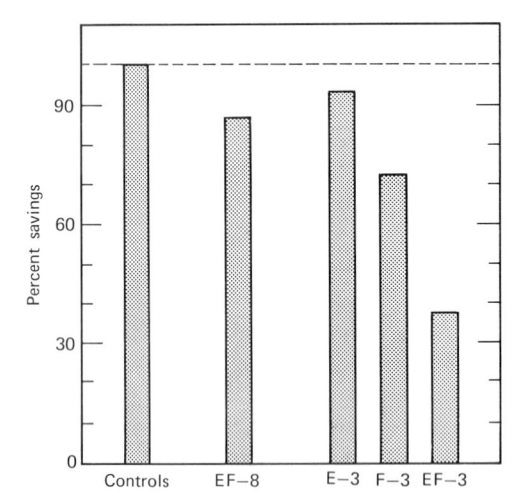

FIG. 17-9. Percentage savings during postoperative retraining for all groups. (EF, combined lesion of both fornix and entorhinal area; E and F, either lesion alone. The designation 3 or 8 indicates whether the group was lesioned 3 hr or 8 days after reaching criterion preoperatively.)

(From E. Uretsky & R. A. McCleary. Effect of hippocampal isolation on retention. *J. comp. physiol. Psychol.*, **68**, 1969, 1-8. Copyright 1969 by the American Psychological Association, and reproduced by permission.)

functions may be activated during the process of memory consolidation even in subprimate species but also supports the impression, gained from the results of hippocampal lesions, that learning can proceed essentially normally in the rat when the hippocampus is not functional.

The mammillary region and related aspects of the thalamus of the rat similarly seem to be involved but not as critically as in man in learning or memory storage. Lesions just lateral to the mammillary bodies have been reported to retard the acquisition of a brightness discrimination and impair the retention of avoidance responses, but the effects have typically been small.[126, 125] An interruption of the mammillothalamic tracts, which relate this region to the medial thalamus, also interferes to some extent with the retention of avoidance responses and retards reacquisition.[123, 124] Lesions in the dorsomedial thalamus have been reported to impair the performance of preoperatively learned behaviors in a variety of appetitive as well as aversive test situations.[111, 92, 19] The amnesic effect of such lesions is severe and prolonged in some instances,[19] but small and temporary in others.[94] Unfortunately, these lesions typically produce marked hyperirritability, and it is often not clear to what extent the observed effects on recall or learning may be influenced by concomitant changes in emotionality.

Summary and Review Questions

Bilateral damage to the temporal lobe produces marked adverse effects on learning and recall in man. The severity of the effect appears to be directly proportional to the amount of destruction in the hippocampus. Patients with extensive bilateral damage to the hippocampi appear capable of learning new associations but cannot transfer them into storage. They consequently do not remember events that occurred only a few minutes ago and are incapable of recalling even dramatic changes in their lives that occurred any time after surgery. This amnesia often extends to events which occurred some weeks or months before the operation, but memories which were established long before are available in surprising clarity and detail.

Research with infrahuman species has generally shown a similar picture. However, the hippocampus does not appear to play as critical a role in species other than man because simple conditioned responses can be acquired and recalled without difficulty even after extensive hippocampal damage. Deficits become apparent only when complex learned responses are examined, particularly when they require reactions to cues not present at the time of testing.

The hippocampus is intimately connected via the fornix with the mammillary bodies of the hypothalamus and these, in turn, project to the medial thalamus. Both of these areas (but not the hippocampus) are destroyed in Korsakoff's psychosis, a disease characterized by pronounced memory deficits. Damage to these regions also produces behavioral deficits in infrahuman species, which may reflect an interference with mechanisms related to learning or recall. However, these deficits are not as severe as those seen in man and are complicated by changes in emotional reactivity.

1. Describe the effects of hippocampal lesions on man's ability to learn or recall.

2. Describe the behavior of infrahuman species after hippocampal lesions.

3. Compare your answers to questions 1 and 2.

4. Can all of the effects of hippocampal lesions on the behavior of infrahuman species be explained in terms of a memory deficit? What alternative hypothesis can be suggested?

OTHER PORTIONS OF THE CNS

There is little clinical or experimental evidence to suggest that any other portion of the central nervous system might be specifically related to learning, memory storage, or recall.

Damage to some of the amygdaloid nuclei modifies reactions to reward and punishment and appears to interfere with the ability to generalize previously learned strategies of responding to novel situations, but there is no evidence of a simple memory deficit or inability to acquire novel behaviors.[112, 113, 114]

The acquisition of active avoidance responses is typically retarded in amygdalectomized animals,[10, 135] but this may be caused by incidental damage to the surrounding piriform cortex. Lesions restricted to the cortical, central, or basal nuclei of the amygdala have marked facilitatory effects on active avoidance behavior.[42] In view of the marked changes in "emotional" reactivity resulting from some of these lesions, it appears likely that an interference with motivational instead of associative mechanisms may be responsible for the observed changes in avoidance behavior.

These comments also apply to some of the behavioral deficits that are seen after septal lesions. The acquisition of active avoidance behavior may be facilitated or depressed, depending on the nature of the task.[44] The performance of preoperatively acquired active avoidance responses, on the other hand, is typically impaired.[85] Perseverative responding is seen in various passive avoidance or punishment situations as well as during extinction.[73] When required to work on reinforcement schedules (such as FI or DRL), which reward infrequent responding, rats with septal lesions overrespond.[27, 59] Septal lesions thus may influence behavior in many

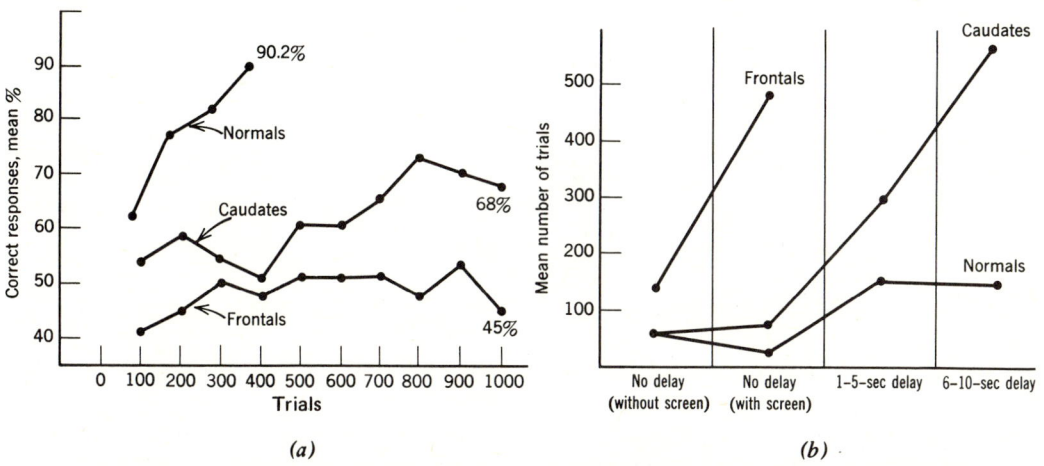

FIG. 17-10. Effects of caudate nucleus and frontal cortex lesions on (*a*) a single delayed alternation in the Wisconsin General Test Apparatus (average learning curves); (*b*) a delayed response in the WGTA (number of trials to learn including criterion).

(After K. Bättig, H. E. Rosvold, & M. Mishkin. Comparison of the effects of frontal and caudate lesions on delayed response and alternations in monkeys. *J. comp. physiol. Psychol.*, **53**, 1960, 400–404. Copyright 1960 by the American Psychological Association, and reproduced by permission.)

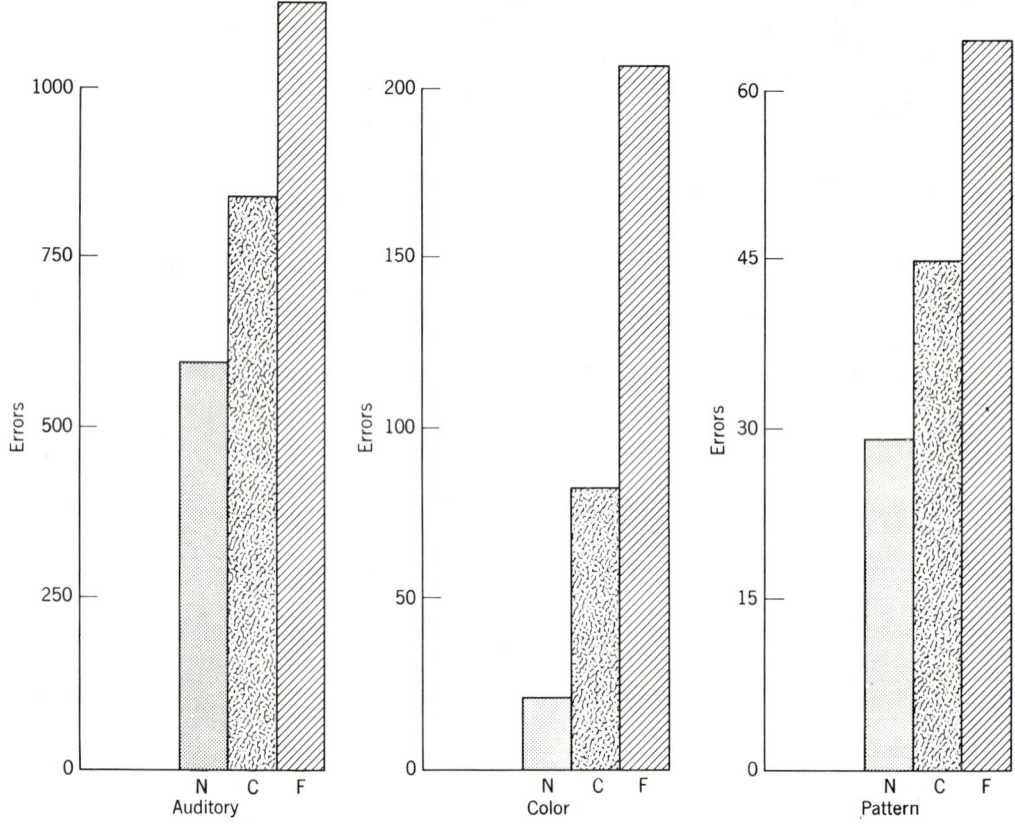

FIG. 17-11. Effects of caudate nucleus and frontal cortex lesions on visual (color and pattern) and auditory discrimination learning. The ordinates of the three graphs are drawn to different scales to emphasize the similarity of the relative differences among the groups. N, normals; C, caudate lesions; F, frontal lesions.

(After K. Bättig, H. E. Rosvold, & M. Mishkin. Comparison of the effects of frontal and caudate lesions on discrimination learning in monkeys. *J. comp. physiol. Psychol.*, **55**, 1962, 458–463. Copyright 1962 by the American Psychological Association, and reproduced by permission.)

learning situations, but their effect does not seem to be specifically related to mechanisms involved in acquisition, storage, or recall.

The caudate nucleus is intimately related to the frontal cortex, and a number of investigators have compared the effects of lesions in the two structures. It is typically reported that delayed responses are difficult to learn following both caudate and frontal lesions (see Figure 17–10) and that visual and auditory discriminations that are immune to the effects of cortical lesions are also unaffected by caudate nucleus damage.[105, 107] More complex visual and auditory discriminations that are impaired by frontal lesions are also adversely affected by damage to the caudate nucleus (see Figure 17–11).[7] These similarities suggest that the effects of caudatal as well as frontal lesions may be caused by an interference with a common mechanism. A review of the extensive literature on the effects of frontal lesions suggests that a primary interference with memory storage or recall is probably not involved in these deficits. Small lesions in the caudate nucleus of the rat markedly interfere with the acquisition of simple active[90] as well as passive[62] avoidance behaviors. These effects can probably not be attributed to a general change in affective reactivity since rats with caudate lesions respond apparently normally to noxious stimulation. It appears unlikely, however, that mechanisms specifically related to learning or memory should be responsible for the observed deficits, since caudate lesions do not interfere with the acquisition or recall of more complex appetitive behavior. Electrical[13] as well as chemical[50] stimulation of the caudate nucleus generally interfere with recently acquired behavior, but these effects appear to be due to an activation of general inhibitory mechanisms instead of functions specifically related to learning or recall (see Figure 17–12).

It is often suggested that the diffuse connections of the reticular formation of the brainstem with primary as well as secondary sensory and motor pathways make it an ideal site for the establishment of novel interconnections which are thought to be responsible for learning. A few experimenters have reported retention deficits for simple conditioned responses[48] following brainstem lesions and facilitation of acquisition following stimulation.[37,33] These results have been interpreted to suggest a role of reticular mechanisms at least in some types of learning, but alternative explanations in terms of an interference with sensory mechanisms, nonspecific arousal, or motivational processes have not been ruled out. As we have seen in previous chapters, portions of the reticular formation are importantly related to tonic as well as phasic arousal. Lesions in the brainstem almost always interfere with these processes, and several investigators have shown that animals who have recovered from these effects can be trained or retrained to perform conditioned responses.[24, 64]

Summary and Review Questions

There is no compelling experimental or clinical evidence that regions of the central nervous system other than some aspects of the neocortex and the hippocampus and its projections participate in learning or recall.

Many portions of the limbic system, including the amygdala, septal area, hypothalamus, and thalamus seem to be involved in the acquisition of conditioned emotional reactions, avoidance behavior, or reactions to nonreward or punishment. However, the organism's ability to form, store, or recall memories does not depend on the integrity of these influences.

The diffuse connections of the reticular formation of the brainstem and thalamus provide an ideal anatomical substrate for the kinds of interneural processes most theorists in this area believe to be responsible for learning. There is, however, little evidence to support this appealing hypothesis. Animals often learn or perform learned responses poorly after extensive damage to the brainstem, but it is not obvious that these deficits can be attributed to an interference with learning or recall.

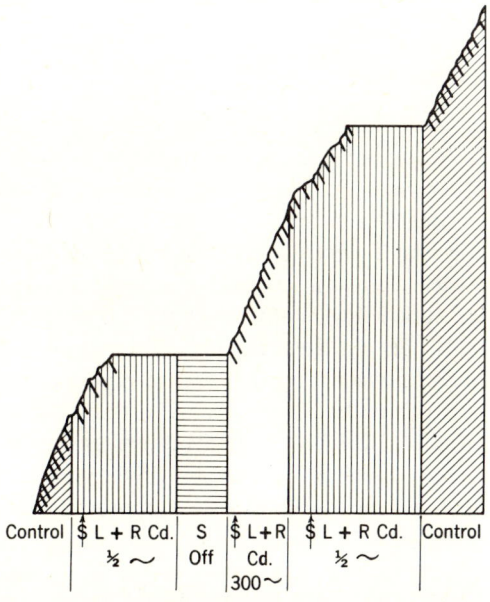

FIG. 17–12. Effect of high- and low-frequency stimulation of the caudate nucleus on rate of bar pressing for a food reward. Slope of the curve is proportional to the rate of response. Control: responses for food reward before caudate stimulation. SL+R Cd(½∼): bilateral stimulation of the caudate nuclei at a rate of 1 p/2 sec first slows and then stops pressing. Off: caudate stimulation is stopped; the cat still does not respond. SL+R Cd(300∼): bilateral high-frequency stimulation of the caudate nuclei (300 p/sec) causes immediate return to the control rate of bar pressing.

(From N. A. Buchwald, E. J. Wyers, C. W. Lauprecht, & G. Heuser. The "caudate-spindle." IV: A behavioral index of caudate-induced inhibition. *EEG clin. Neurophysiol.*, **13**, 1961, 531–537.)

1. What evidence can you marshal in support of the suggestion that subcortical mechanisms are important for learning and recall?

Pathways that Mediate the Conditioned and Unconditioned Stimuli

We have seen that simple conditioned responses can be acquired and recalled following complete neodecortication. Older portions of the cortex, such as the hippocampus and associated temporal lobe tissue, although related to memory storage, also do not appear to be essential to the formation or recall of simple memories, at least in infrahuman species. These observations suggest that simple forms of learning, such as classical conditioning, may involve a subcortical interaction between the pathways that mediate the CS and UCS—a notion many theorists in this field have found appealing. There are, however, some experimental findings which indicate that the subcortical pathways of either the CS or UCS are not essential to conditioning. It has long been known that electrical stimulation of sensory as well as nonsensory portions of the cortex can serve as the conditioned stimulus in classical conditioning experiments.[71] More recently, it has been shown that a leg flexion response elicited by electrical stimulation of the motor cortex (the UCS) can be conditioned to electrical stimuli applied directly to the sensory cortex of cats, dogs, and monkeys,[23] a procedure that bypasses the primary sensory pathways to the cortex. Conditioning can be established in such a paradigm in animals with complete transections of the corpus callosum (which interconnects the two hemispheres) even when the CS and UCS are applied to opposite hemispheres.[35] This suggests that subcortical connections are responsible for the conditioning seen in these experiments, but it seems unlikely that antidromic activation of primary sensory pathways could be responsible.

These experiments may have important implications for our understanding of learning in addition to apparently ruling out an essential role for the direct interconnections between the subcortical pathways of the CS and UCS. Since the unconditioned response was elicited by direct stimulation of motor pathways and care was taken to avoid excitation of pain pathways, it has been suggested that the success of these experiments demonstrates that motivational influences are not essential for conditioning.[22] This may not be an entirely warranted conclusion since there is evidence that the elicitation of involuntary movements may itself provide a motivational component for the execution of a voluntary response to a CS,[132] but it is clear that the role of motivational mechanisms and reinforcement in these experiments requires future research.

Summary

Conditioning has been achieved when the CS consists of electrical stimulation of sensory or nonsensory cortex, and an unconditioned leg flexion response is elicited by a UCS that consists of electrical stimulation of the motor cortex. This procedure effectively bypasses the subcortical pathways of the CS and UCS and rules out the formation of direct connections between them. It is not equally clear that this conditioning occurs in the complete absence of motivational influences, as has been suggested, because the involuntary leg flexion may itself provide a motive for the acquisition of the CS.

MINIMAL ANATOMICAL SUBSTRATES FOR LEARNING

The experimental evidence discussed in preceding sections of this chapter indicates that no single geographically defined portion of the brain may be essential for learning, retention, or recall, at least in infrahuman species. This suggests that all neural tissue and perhaps associated glial cells may be capable of altering their functions as a consequence of the particular type of activation that occurs in situations which we call learning or conditioning paradigms. If this is true, it should be possible to demonstrate learning in small portions of the nervous system which are isolated from the rest of the brain.

In the complexly organized mammal this is difficult to do because of the specialization of sensory and motor systems. The closest we can come to a simplified nervous system that could possibly show learning is to ask whether the isolated spinal cord or components of it can learn. The answer seems to be a qualified "yes." Reasonably consistent classical conditioning has been reported in dogs in experiments where foot shock is used as the UCS, manual pressure of the animal's tail as the CS, and contraction of an individual leg muscle (rather than leg flexion) is considered a conditioned response.[116, 117] Attempts to replicate these findings in more traditional paradigms where only the flexion of the entire leg is recorded have been largely unsuccessful, possibly because the spinal animal does not have sufficient control over antagonistic muscles to perform the response.[58] Conditioned leg flexion responses have been observed in the isolated spinal cord of very young kittens and a puppy[25] (see Figure 17-13), suggesting that the functional organization of the immature spinal cord may be more easily modifiable than that of adult animals. Classical conditioning of scratching reflexes has also been observed in adult spinal frogs,[30] possibly because lower portions of the central nervous system may be more autonomous in less highly developed species.

Habituation, which many investigators in this field consider a special form of learning because it involves a selective change in neural function due to repeated "use," has been demonstrated in spinal mammals. If periodic shocks are given to the hindleg of a rat with a high spinal transection, the unconditioned leg flexion response gradually disappears. When the foot shocks are stopped for 5 or 10 minutes, the flexions are again elicited, demonstrating that the response decrement was not caused by permanent damage.[102] Variables (such as stimulus frequency, stimulus intensity, and prior experience with habituation) that affect the habituation of leg flexion responses in intact animals also do so in similar ways in the spinal animal.[129] This suggests that the habituation of the leg flexion response may involve only spinal neurons even when higher connections are available.

A different way of asking how complex a nervous system may be necessary for learning is to see whether animals with very rudimentary neural connections can display the phenomenon. A great deal of controversy has been generated by the question whether primitive planaria can learn. This species has recently been used in many investigations of the biochemical basis of learning (see Chapter 19), and it has become important to discriminate between conditioning and phenomena

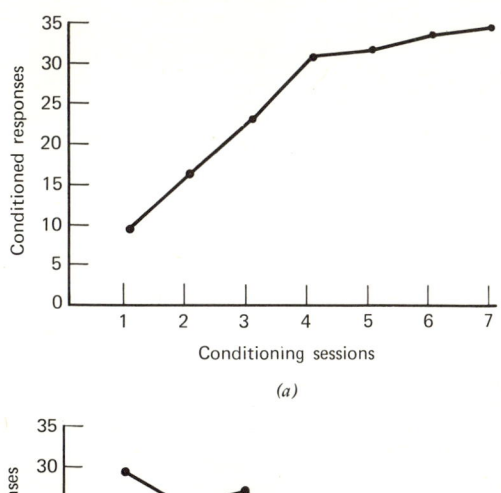

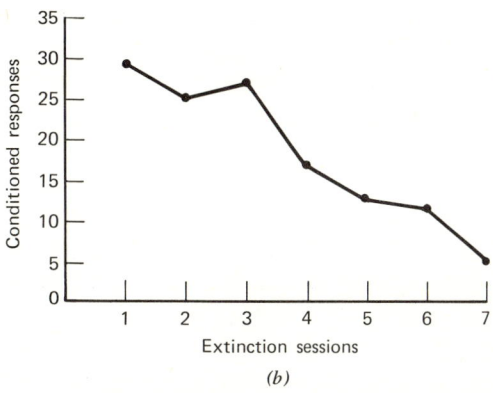

FIG. 17–13. Conditioned leg flexion responses in spinal kittens. (*a*) Mean number of conditioned responses in 7 consecutive conditioning sessions of 40 trials each. (*b*) Mean number of conditioned responses in 7 consecutive extinction sessions of 40 trials each.

(After R. A. Dykman & P. S. Shurrager. Successive and maintained conditioning in spinal carnivores. *J. comp. physiol. Psychol.*, **49**, 1956, 27–35. Copyright 1956 by the American Psychological Association, and reproduced by permission.)

such as sensitization, which can produce similar behavioral effects. Strictly speaking, it appears that planaria may not display classical conditioning as defined in mammals.[55] However, they do modify their behavior in a somewhat less specific fashion whenever intense and potentially harmful stimuli are presented (i.e., show sensitization), and this may itself be a learning analogue in primitive animals. Sensitization requires a modification of neural activity, which persists for some time after the stimulus that is responsible for it is terminated. The fact that this response may not be unique to a particular conditioned stimulus may not be terribly important in a simple organism with a very limited sensory system.

Less controversial are some experiments that have shown remarkably adaptive learned responses in the cockroach.[72] Intact cockroaches clean their antennae by pulling them down to the mouth with one of the anterior legs. If one cuts these legs off, no antennae cleaning occurs for several days. Eventually, however, the roach learns to balance on three legs, placed so that the body is centered on this tripod, and to use the remaining fourth leg to bring the antennae to its mouth.

Conditioned avoidance responses have even been demonstrated in the headless cockroach.[49] In these experiments, the leg of a headless roach is suspended over a dish of water such that every time the animal extends the leg it comes into contact with the water and completes an electric circuit which delivers a shock to the leg (see Figure 17–14). After some time, the headless roach will maintain a flexed leg position nearly all of the time and thus avoid the shock. Paired controls which receive the same number of shocks regardless of the position of their leg do not show this adaptive reaction, suggesting that we may indeed be dealing with conditioned responses. Most surprisingly, this "learning" persists even after all neural tissue above the leg itself is removed.[26]

Summary and Review Questions

Animals with very simple nervous systems can learn and remember. Complex interconnections and special storage mechanisms are apparently not essential for the basic modifications in the nervous system that occur when we say that an organism has "learned." Even in complex mammals, the relatively simple organization of the spinal cord appears to be sufficient to permit conditioning in the absence of higher influences.

1. Why is it important to know whether animals with simple nervous systems learn?

2. Would it surprise you to hear that single-celled organisms can learn?

REVIEW

Animals with relatively rudimentary nervous systems are capable of modifying their behavior in response to changing environmental requirements. It is thus clear that the ability to learn or remember does not require the complexities of the mammalian brain. However, as the complexity of the central nervous system increases in the course of phylogenetic development, so does specialization. Discrete parts of the brain increasingly assume specific

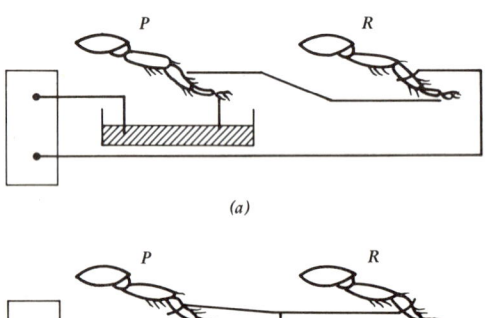

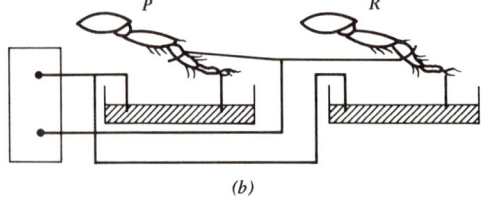

FIG. 17–14. Conditioning in the cockroach leg. (a) Training phase. The P leg is shocked whenever it touches the water and the R leg is shocked whenever the P leg is shocked. (b) Testing phase. Each leg is now shocked when it touches the water independently of the other.

(From G. A. Horridge. Learning of leg position by the ventral nerve cord in headless insects. *Proc. Roy. Soc.* (*London*), Series B, **157**, 1962, 33–62.)

responsibility for sensory, motor, or motivational functions, and one may ask whether processes related to learning, memory storage, or recall follow this general trend.

Since the phylogenetic development of behavioral complexity or plasticity parallels closely the development of neocortical tissue, we first inquired into the role of the cerebral hemispheres. The answers were complex, but several conclusions appear warranted. (1) No portion of the neocortex appears to be essential for the formation, storage, or retrieval of simple memories. (2) The sensory areas, including the adjacent sensory association areas, may be involved in learning or memory storage under normal circumstances, and access to memories that are formed when they are intact is often difficult when they are not functional. (3) The association cortex of the frontal lobe appears to be important for the integration of attentional processes as well as the organism's response to reinforcement or nonreinforcement. Lesions in the frontal lobe consequently result in deficits in most complex learning or recall situations, but mechanisms specifically related to learning or memory do not appear to be responsible for them.

Damage to the hippocampus produces an apparent inability to consolidate memories in man. Patients with hippocampal lesions do not remember events that occurred only minutes ago and have no recall of events that happened any time after the surgery was performed. There is also often some retrograde amnesia for events that preceded surgery by a few weeks or months, but recall of older memories is typically intact. Damage to the hippocampi of infrahuman species produces behavioral deficits, which may be caused by a similar difficulty in establishing memory traces. Animals with hippocampal lesions are, however, capable of learning many problems quite well, suggesting that this structure is not as critical as it appears to be in man.

When we inquire about the possible contribution of subcortical structures, the following picture emerges. The mammillary bodies and medial thalamus have been implicated in learning and memory by the fact that patients with Korsakoff's syndrome (which involves a loss of memory and apparent inability to learn) have lesions in these areas. Selective destruction of these regions in infrahuman species produces behavioral deficits that may be related to an impairment of memory functions, but the effects are not as severe or specific as one might have suspected on the basis of the clinical data.

Most if not all portions of the limbic system, including associated subcortical structures, appear to be involved in the integration of the organism's reaction to noxious stimulation (including nonreward of previously reinforced behavior). Lesions in the limbic system produce marked effects on acquisition and performance in situations that involve aversive reinforcement or punishment, but these may not be caused by a selective interference with learning or memory per se.

Lesions in the brainstem generally impair the animals' reactions to conditioned stimuli more than they affect innate responses, but this probably reflects a general lability that characterizes recently learned behaviors. There is not compelling evidence to suggest that the behavioral deficits seen after brainstem lesions may not be due to sensory or motor deficits or to a general reduction in arousal, reactivity, or related processes.

When we inquire about experimental support for the widely held belief that simple conditioning may involve a direct interaction between the pathways of the CS and UCS, the answer is negative unless we assume that subcortical and cortical components of the sensory systems can act interchangeably. Elimination of the cortical sensory areas does not preclude the formation of conditioned responses. The subcortical sensory pathways also do not appear to be essential since conditioning can occur when the CS as well as the UCS are applied directly to the cortex. This effectively bypasses the sensory pathways, although the larger question of motivation for the conditioned response may not be as easily answered.

Bibliography

1. Adams, R. D., Collins, G. H., & Victor, M. Troubles de la mémoire et de l'apprentissage chez l'homme. Leurs relations avec des lésions des lobes temporaux et du diencephale. In *Physiologie de L'Hippocampe*. (Colloques Internationaux du Centre National de la Recherche Scientifique No. 107) Paris: C.N.R.S., 1961, 273–295.
2. Allen, W. F. Effects of destroying three localized cerebral cortical areas for sound on correct conditioned differential responses of the dog's foreleg. *Amer. J. Physiol.*, 1945, **144**, 415–428.
3. Allen, W. F. Effect of bilateral destruction of three lateral cerebral cortical areas on correct conditioned differential responses from general cutaneous stimulation. *Amer. J. Physiol.*, 1946, **147**, 454–461.
4. Bagshaw, M. H., & Pribram, K. H. Cortical organization in gustation (Macaca mulatta). *J. Neurophysiol.*, 1953, **16**, 499–508.
5. Baily, P., Green, J. R., Amador, L., & Gibbs, F. A. Treatment of psychomotor states by anterior temporal lobectomy. A report of progress. *Res. Publ., Ass. Nerv. Ment. Dis.*, 1953, **31**, 341–346.
6. Barbizet, J. Defect of memorizing of hippocampal-mammillary origin: A review. *J. Neurol. Neurosurg. Psychiat.*, 1963, **26**, 127–135.
7. Bättig, K., Rosvold, H. E., & Mishkin, M. Comparison of the effects of frontal and caudate lesions on delayed response and alternations in monkeys. *J. comp. physiol. Psychol.*, 1960, **53**, 400–404.
8. Bättig, K., Rosvold, H. E., & Mishkin, M. Comparison of the effects of frontal and caudate lesions on discrimination learning in monkeys. *J. comp. physiol. Psychol.*, 1962, **55**, 458–463.
9. Blum, J. S., Chow, K. L., & Pribram, K. H. A behavioral analysis of the organization of the parieto-temporo-preoccipital cortex. *J. comp. Neurol.*, 1950, **93**, 53–100.
10. Brady, J. V., Schreiner, L., Geller, I., & Kling, A. Subcortical mechanisms in emotional behavior: The effect of rhinencephalic injury upon the acquisition and retention of a conditioned avoidance response in cats. *J. comp. physiol. Psychol.*, 1954, **49**, 179–186.
11. Bromiley, R. B. Conditioned response in a dog after removal of neocortex. *J. comp. physiol. Psychol.*, 1948, **41**, 102–110.
12. Brush, E. S., Mishkin, M., & Rosvold, H. E. Effects of object preferences and aversions on discrimination learning in monkeys with frontal lesions. *J. comp. physiol. Psychol.*, 1961, **54**, 319–325.
13. Buchwald, N. A., Wyers, E. J., Lauprecht, C. W., & Heuser, G. The "caudate-spindle." IV: A behavioral index of caudate-induced inhibition. *EEG clin. Neurophysiol.*, 1961, **13**, 531–537.
14. Bureš, J., & Burešova, O. The use of Leão's spreading cortical depression in research on conditioned reflexes. In *The Moscow colloquium on electroencephalography of higher nervous activity*. H. H. Jasper & G. D. Smirnov, Eds. *EEG clin. Neurophysiol.*, 1960a, Suppl. 13, 359–376.
15. Bureš, J., & Burešova, O. The use of Leão's spreading depression in the study of inter-hemispheric transfer of memory traces. *J. comp. physiol. Psychol.*, 1960b, **53**, 558–565.
16. Butler, R. A., Diamond, I. T., & Neff, W. D. Role of auditory cortex in discrimination of changes in frequency. *J. Neurophysiol.*, 1957, **20**, 108–120.
17. Cairns, H., & Mosberg, W. H., Jr. Colloid cyst of the third ventricle. *Surg. Gynec. Obstet.*, 1951, **92**, 545–570.
18. Campbell, R. J., & Harlow, H. F. Problem solution by monkeys following bilateral removal of the prefrontal areas. V: Spatial delayed reactions. *J. exp. Psychol.*, 1945, **35**, 110–126.
19. Cardo, B. Action de lésions thalamiques et hypothalamiques sur le conditionnement de fuite et la différenciation tonale chez le rat. *J. Physiol. (Paris)*, 1960, **52**, 537–553.
20. Diamond, I. T., & Neff, W. D. Ablation of temporal cortex and discrimination of auditory patterns. *J. Neurophysiol.*, 1957, **20**, 300–315.
21. Dott, N. M. Surgical aspects of the hypothalamus. In *The hypothalamus: morphological, functional, clinical and surgical aspects*. W. E. LeGros Clark, J. Beattie, G. Riddoch, & N. M. Dott, Eds. Edinburgh: Oliver and Boyd, 1938, pp. 131–185.

22. Doty, R. W. Conditioned reflexes formed and evoked by brain stimulation. In *Electrical stimulation of the brain*. D. E. Sheer, Ed. Austin: Univ. of Texas Press, 1961, pp. 397–412.
23. Doty, R. W., & Giurgea, C. Conditioned reflexes established by coupling electrical excitations of two cortical areas. In *Brain mechanisms and learning*. J. L. Delafresnaye, A. Fessard, R. W. Gerard, and J. Konorski, Eds. Oxford: Blackwell Scientific, 1961, pp. 133–151.
24. Doty, R. W., Beck, E. C., & Kooi, K. A. Effect of brain-stem lesions on conditioned responses of cats. *Exp. Neurol.*, 1959, **1**, 360–385.
25. Dykman, R. A., & Shurrager, P. S. Successive and maintained conditioning in spinal carnivores. *J. comp. physiol. Psychol.*, 1956, **49**, 27–35.
26. Eisenstein, E. M., & Cohen, M. J. Learning in an isolated prothoracic insect ganglion. *Anim. Behav.*, 1965, **13** (Suppl. 1), 104–108.
27. Ellen, P., & Powell, E. W. Effects of septal lesions on behavior generated by positive reinforcement. *Exptl. Neurol.*, 1962, **6**, 1–11.
28. Evarts, E. V. Effect of ablation of prestriate cortex on auditory-visual association in monkey. *J. Neurophysiol.*, 1952, **15**, 191–200.
29. Finan, J. L. Delayed response with pre-delay reinforcement in monkeys after the removal of the frontal lobe. *Amer. J. Psychol.*, 1942, **55**, 202–214.
30. Franzisket, L. Characteristics of instinctive behavior and learning in reflex activity of the frog. *Anim. Behav.*, 1963, **11**, 318–324.
31. Fulton, J. F. *Physiology of the nervous system*. New York: Oxford Univ. Press, 1949.
32. Fulton, J. F. *Frontal lobotomy and affective behavior. A neurophysiological analysis*. New York: Norton, 1951.
33. Fuster, J. M. Tachistoscopic perception in monkeys. *Fed. Proc.*, 1957, **16**, 43.
34. Girden, E., Mettler, F. A., Finch, G., & Culler, E. Conditioned responses in a decorticate dog to acoustic, thermal, and tactile stimulation. *J. comp. Psychol.*, 1936, **21**, 367–385.
35. Giurgea, C., & Raiciulescu, N. Nai date asupra reflexului conditionat prin ercitarea directa a cortexului cerebral. *Rev. Fiziol. norm. Pat.*, 1957, **4**, 218–225.
36. Glees, P., & Griffith, H. B. Bilateral destruction of the hippocampus (cornu Ammonis) in a case of dementia. *Mschr. Psychiat. Neurol.*, 1952, **129**, 193–204.
37. Grastyán, E., Lissak, K., & Kikesi, F. Facilitation and inhibition of conditioned alimentary and defensive reflexes by stimulation of the hypothalamus and the reticular formation. *Acta physiol. Acad. Sci. hung.*, 1956, **9**, 133–151.
38. Gross, C. G., & Weiskrantz, L. Evidence for dissociation between impairment on auditory discrimination and delayed response in frontal monkeys. *Exp. Neurol.*, 1962, **5**, 453–476.
39. Gross, C. G., & Weiskrantz, L. Some changes in behavior produced by lateral lesions in the macaque. In *The frontal granular cortex and behavior*. J. M. Warren & K. Akert, Eds. New York: McGraw-Hill, 1964, pp. 74–101.
40. Grossman, S. P. *A textbook of physiological psychology*. New York: Wiley, 1967.
41. Grossman, S. P. Facilitation of learning following intracranial injections of pentylenetetrazol. *Physiol. & Behav.*, 1969, **4**, 625–628.
42. Grossman, S. P. The role of the amygdala in escape-avoidance behaviors. In *The neurobiology of the amygdala*. B. Eleftheriou, Ed. New York: Plenum Press, 1972 (in press).
43. Grossman, S. P., & Mountford, Helen. Learning and extinction during chemically induced disturbance of hippocampal functions. *Amer. J. Physiol.*, 1964, **207**, 1387–1393.
44. Hamilton, L. W. Active avoidance impairment following septal lesions in cats. *J. comp. physiol. Psychol.*, 1969, **69**, 420–431.
45. Harlow, H. F. The development of learning in the rhesus monkey. *Amer. Scientist*, 1959, **47**, 459–479.
46. Harlow, H. F., & Dagnon, J. Problem solution by monkeys following bilateral removal of the prefrontal areas. I: The discrimination and discrimination-reversal problems. *J. exp. Psychol.*, 1943, **32**, 351–356.
47. Hebb, D. O. Man's frontal lobes. A critical review. *Arch. Neurol. Psychiat.*, 1945, **54**, 10–24.

48. Hernández-Peón, R., Brust-Carmona, H., Eckhaus, E., Lopez-Mendoza, E., & Alcocer-Cuarón, C. Functional role of brainstem reticular systems in a salivary conditioned response. *Fed. Proc.*, 1956, **15**, 91.

49. Horridge, G. A. Learning leg position by the ventral nerve cord in headless insects. *Proc. Roy. Soc. (London)*, 1962, Series B, **157**, 33–52.

50. Hull, C. D., Buchwald, N. A., & Ling, G. Effects of direct cholinergic stimulation of forebrain structures. *Brain Res.*, 1967, **6**, 22–35.

51. Hunt, H. F., & Diamond, I. T. Some effects of hippocampal lesions on conditioned avoidance behavior in the cat. In *Proceedings of the fifteenth international congress of psychology*. Brussels, 1957, 203–204.

52. Isaacson, R. L., Douglas, R. J., & Moore, R. Y. The effect of radical hippocampal ablation on acquisition of avoidance responses. *J. comp. physiol. Psychol.*, 1961, **54**, 625–628.

53. Jacobsen, C. F., Wolfe, J. B., & Jackson, T. A. An experimental analysis of the functions of the frontal association area in primates. *J. nerv. ment. Dis.*, 1935, **82**, 1–14.

54. Jasper, H. H. Cited in W. J. H. Nauta. Some brain structures and functions related to memory. *Neurosciences Res. Prog. Bull.*, 1964, **2**, 14.

55. Jensen, D. Paramecia, planaria, and pseudo-learning. *Animal Behav.*, 1965, **13** (Suppl. 1), 9–20.

56. Karmos, G., & Grastyán, E. Influence of hippocampal lesions on simple and delayed conditional reflexes. *Acta physiol. Acad. Sci. hung.*, 1962, **21**, 215–224.

57. Kaufmann, P. The effect of hippocampal isolation on short-term memory for an appetitively reinforced task. Ph.D. dissertation, University of Chicago, 1971.

58. Kellogg, W. N. Is "spinal conditioning" conditioning? *J. exp. Psychol.*, 1947, **37**, 263–265.

59. Kelsey, J. E., & Grossman, S. P. Non-perseverative disruption of behavioral inhibition following septal lesions in rats. *J. comp. physiol. Psychol.*, 1971, **75**, 302–311.

60. Kimble, D. P. The effects of bilateral hippocampal lesions in rats. *J. comp. physiol. Psychol.*, 1963, **56**, 273–283.

61. Kimura, D. Effects of selective hippocampal damage on avoidance behavior in the rat. *Canad. J. Psychol.*, 1958, **12**, 213–218.

62. Kirkby, R. J., & Kimble, D. P. Avoidance and escape behavior following striatal lesions in the rat. *Exp. Neurol.*, 1968, **20**, 215–227.

63. Klüver, H. An analysis of the effects of the removal of the occipital lobes in monkeys. *J. Psychol.*, 1936, **2**, 49–61.

64. Kreindler, A., Ungher, I., & Volanskii, D. Effect of a circumscribed lesion of the reticular formation in the brain stem on the higher nervous activity of dogs. *Sechenov physiol. J., U.S.S.R.*, 1959, **45**, 247–256.

65. Kruger, L., & Porter, P. B. A behavioral study of the functions of the rolandic cortex in the monkey. *J. comp. Neurol.*, 1958, **109**, 439–467.

66. Lashley, K. S. *Brain mechanisms and intelligence*. Chicago: Univ. of Chicago Press, 1929.

67. Lashley, K. S. In search of the engram. *Soc. exp. Biol.*, 1950, Symposium 4, 454–482.

68. Lawicka, W., & Konorski, J. The physiological mechanism of delayed reactions. III: The effect of prefrontal ablations on delayed reactions in dogs. *Acta Biol. exp. (Warsaw)*, 1959, **19**, 221–231.

69. Lawicka, W., & Konorski, J. The effects of prefrontal lobectomies on the delayed responses in cats. *Acta Biol. exp. (Warsaw)*, 1961, **21**, 141–156.

70. Leão, A. A. P. Spreading depression of activity in the cerebral cortex. *J. Neurophysiol.*, 1944, **7**, 359–390.

71. Loucks, R. B. Studies of neural structures essential for learning. II: The conditioning of salivary and striped muscle responses to faradization of cortical sensory elements and action of sleep upon such mechanisms. *J. comp. Psychol.*, 1938, **25**, 315–332.

72. Luco, J. V. Plasticity of neural function in learning and retention. In *Brain function. Vol. II: RNA and brain function: Memory and learning*. Mary A. B. Brazier, Ed. Los Angeles: Univ. of California Press, 1964, pp. 135–159.

73. McCleary, R. A. Response-modulating functions of the limbic system: Initiation and suppression. In *Progress in physiological psychology*. Vol. I. E. Stellar & J. M. Sprague, Eds. New York: Academic Press, 1966, pp. 210–272.

74. Maier, N. R. F., & Schneirla, T. C. *Principles of psychology*. New York: McGraw-Hill, 1935.

75. Malmo, R. B. Interference factors in delayed response in monkeys after removal of frontal lobes. *J. Neurophysiol.*, 1942, **5**, 295–308.

76. Malmo, R. B. Psychological aspects of frontal gyrectomy and frontal lobotomy in mental patients. In *The frontal lobes*. J. F. Fulton, C. D. Aring, & S. B. Wortis, Eds. Baltimore: Williams and Wilkins, 1948, pp. 537–564.

77. Marquis, D. G., & Hilgard, E. R. Conditioned lid responses to light in dogs after removal of the visual cortex. *J. comp. Psychol.*, 1936, **22**, 157–178.

78. Meyer, D. R. Some psychological determinants of sparing and loss following damage to the brain. In *Biological and biochemical bases of behavior*. H. F. Harlow & C. N. Woolsey, Eds. Madison: Univ. of Wisconsin Press, 1958, pp. 173–192.

79. Meyer, D. R., & Woolsey, C. N. Effects of localized cortical destruction on auditory discriminative conditioning in cat. *J. Neurophysiol.*, 1952, **15**, 149–162.

80. Milner, B. The memory defect in bilateral hippocampal lesions. *NLM Psychiat. Res. Rep.*, 1959, **11**, 43–52.

81. Milner, B., & Penfield, W. The effect of hippocampal lesions on recent memory. *Trans. Amer. Neurol. Ass.*, 1955, **80**, 42–48.

82. Mishkin, M. Perseveration of central sets after frontal lesions in monkeys. In *The frontal granular cortex and behavior*. J. M. Warren & K. Akert, Eds. New York: McGraw-Hill, 1964, pp. 219–241.

83. Mishkin, M., & Weiskrantz, L. Effects of delaying reward on visual-discrimination performance in monkeys with frontal lesions. *J. comp. physiol. Psychol.*, 1958, **51**, 276–281.

84. Moniz, E. *Tentative opératoires dans le traitement de certaines psychoses*. Paris: Masson, 1936.

85. Moore, R. Y. Effects of some rhinencephalic lesions on retention of conditioned avoidance behavior in cats. *J. comp. physiol. Psychol.*, 1964, **57**, 65–71.

86. Narabayashi, H., Nagao, T., Saito, Y., Yoshida, M., & Nagahata, M. Stereotaxic amygdalectomy for behavior disorders. *Arch. Neurol.*, 1963, **9**, 11–26.

87. Nathan, P. W., & Smith, M. C. Normal mentality associated with a maldeveloped "rhinencephalon." *J. Neurol. Neurosurg. Psychiat.*, 1950, **13**, 191–197.

88. Nauta, W. J. H. Some brain structures and functions related to memory. *Neurosciences Res. Prog. Bull.*, 1964, **2**, 14–15.

89. Neff, W. D., & Diamond, I. T. The neural basis of auditory discrimination. In *Biological and biochemical bases of behavior*. H. F. Harlow & C. N. Woolsey, Eds. Madison: Univ. of Wisconsin Press, 1958, pp. 101–126.

90. Neill, D., & Grossman, S. P. Behavioral effects of lesions or cholinergic blockade in the dorsal or ventral caudate. *J. comp. physiol. Psychol.*, 1970, **71**, 311–317.

91. Ojemann, R. G. Correlations between specific human brain lesions and memory changes. A critical survey of the literature. *Neurosciences Res. Prog. Bull.*, 1966, **4** (Suppl.), 1–70.

92. Pechtel, C., Masserman, J. H., Schreiner, L., & Levitt, M. Differential effects of lesions of mediodorsal nuclei of thalamus on normal and neurotic behavior in cat. *J. nerv. ment. Dis.*, 1955, **121**, 26–33.

93. Penfield, W., & Milner, B. Memory deficit produced by bilateral lesions in the hippocampal zone. *A.M.A. Arch. Neurol. Psychiat.*, 1958, **79**, 475–497.

94. Peters, R. H., Rosvold, H. E., & Mirsky, A. F. The effect of thalamic lesions upon delayed response-type test in the rhesus monkey. *J. comp. physiol. Psychol.*, 1956, **49**, 111–116.

95. Poltyrew, S. S., & Zeliony, G. P. Grosshirnrinde und Assoziations-funktion. *Z. Biol.*, 1930, **90**, 157–160.

96. Pribram, Helen B., & Barry, J. Further behavioral analysis of parieto-temporo-preoccipital cortex. *J. Neurophysiol.*, 1956, **19**, 99–106.

97. Pribram, K. H. Some physical and pharmacological factors affecting delayed response performance of baboons following frontal lobotomy. *J. Neurophysiol.*, 1950, **13**, 373–382.
98. Pribram, K. H. A further experimental analysis of the behavioral deficit that follows injury to the primate frontal cortex. *Exp. Neurol.*, 1961, **3**, 432–466.
99. Pribram, K. H., & Mishkin, M. Analysis of the effects of frontal lesions in monkey. III: Object alternation. *J. comp. physiol. Psychol.*, 1956, **49**, 41–45.
100. Pribram, K. H., Wilson, W. A., Jr., & Connors, J. Effects of lesions of the medial forebrain on alternation behavior of rhesus monkeys. *Exp. Neurol.*, 1962, **6**, 36–47.
101. Pribram, K. H., Ahumada, A., Hartog, J., & Ross, L. A progress report on the neurological processes disturbed by frontal lesions in primates. In *The frontal granular cortex and behavior*. J. M. Warren & K. Akert, Eds. New York: McGraw-Hill, 1964, pp. 28–55.
102. Prosser, C. L., & Hunter, W. S. The extinction of startle responses and spinal reflexes in the white rat. *Amer. J. Physiol.*, 1936, **117**, 609–618.
103. Raab, D. H., & Ades, H. W. Cortical and midbrain mediation of a conditioned discrimination of acoustic intensities. *Amer. J. Psychol.*, 1946, **59**, 59–83.
104. Reitman, F. Orbital cortex syndrome following leucotomy. *Amer. J. Psychiat.*, 1946, **103**, 238–241.
105. Rosvold, H. E., & Delgado, J. M. R. The effect on delayed-alternation test performance of stimulating or destroying electrically structures within the frontal lobes of the monkey's brain. *J. comp. physiol. Psychol.*, 1956, **49**, 365–372.
106. Rosvold, H. E., & Mishkin, M. Non-sensory effects of frontal lesions on discrimination learning and performance. In *Brain mechanisms and learning*. J. F. Delafresnaye, A. Fessard, R. W. Gerard, & J. Konorski, Eds. Oxford: Blackwell Scientific, 1961, pp. 555–576.
107. Rosvold, H. E., Mishkin, M., & Szwarcbart, M. K. Effects of subcortical lesions in monkeys on visual-discrimination and single-alternation performance. *J. comp. physiol. Psychol.*, 1958, **51**, 437–444.
108. Rosvold, H. E., Szwarcbart, M. K., Mirsky, A. F., & Mishkin, M. The effect of frontal-lobe damage on delayed response performance in chimpanzees. *J. comp. physiol. Psychol.*, 1961, **54**, 368–374.
109. Rylander, G. Personality changes after operations on the frontal lobes. Clinical study of 32 cases. *Acta Psychiat. Neurol.*, 1939, Suppl. 20, 269–274.
110. Schiller, P. H. Delayed response in the minnow. *J. comp. physiol. Psychol.*, 1948, **41**, 233–238.
111. Schreiner, L. H., Rioch, D. McK., Pechtel, C., & Masserman, J. H. Behavioral chgesan following thalamic injury in cat. *J. Neurophysiol.*, 1953, **16**, 234–246.
112. Schwartzbaum, J. S. Changes in reinforcing properties of stimuli following ablation of the amygdaloid complex in monkeys. *J. comp. physiol. Psychol.*, 1960a, **53**, 388–395.
113. Schwartzbaum, J. S. Response to changes in reinforcing conditions of bar pressing after ablation of the amygdaloid complex in monkeys. *Psychol. Rep.*, 1960b, **6**, 215–221.
114. Schwartzbaum, J. S., & Pribram, K. H. The effects of amygdalectomy in monkeys on transposition along a brightness continuum. *J. comp. physiol. Psychol.*, 1960, **53**, 396–399.
115. Scoville, W. B., & Milner, B. Loss of recent memory after bilateral hippocampal lesions. *J. Neurol. Neurosurg. Psychiat.*, 1957, **20**, 11–21.
116. Shurrager, P. S., & Culler, E. A. Phenomena allied to conditioning in the spinal dog. *Amer. J. Physiol.*, 1938, **123**, 186–187.
117. Shurrager, P. S., & Culler, E. A. Conditioned extinction of a reflex in a spinal dog. *J. exp. Psychol.*, 1941, **28**, 287–303.
118. Spiegel, A., Wycis, H. T., Orchinik, C. W., & Freed, H. The thalamic and temporal orientation. *Science*, 1955, **121**, 771–772.
119. Stamm, J. S. Retardation and facilitation in learning by stimulation of frontal cortex in monkeys. In *The frontal granular cortex and behavior*. J. M. Warren & K. Akert, Eds. New York: McGraw-Hill, 1964, pp. 102–125.
120. Teitelbaum, H., & Milner, P. Activity changes following partial hippocampal lesions in rats. *J. comp. physiol. Psychol.*, 1963, **56**, 284–289.

121. Terzian, H., & Dalle Ore, G. Syndrome of Klüver and Bucy. Reproduced in man by bilateral removal of the temporal lobes. *Neurology*, 1955, **5**, 373–380.

122. Thomas, G. J., & Otis, L. S. Effects of rhinencephalic lesions on conditioning of avoidance responses in the rat. *J. comp. Physiol.*, 1958, **51**, 130–134.

123. Thomas, G. J., Fry, F. J., Fry, W. J., & Slotnick, B. Behavioral alterations in cats following mammillothalamic tractomy. *Physiologist*, 1959a, **2**, 114–115.

124. Thomas, G. J., Moore, R. Y., Harvey, J. A., & Hunt, H. F. Relation between the behavioral syndrome produced by lesions in the septal region of the forebrain and maze learning of the rat. *J. comp. physiol. Psychol.*, 1959b, **52**, 527–532.

125. Thompson, R., & Hawkins, W. F. Memory unaffected by mamillary body lesions in the rat. *Exp. Neurol.*, 1961, **3**, 189–196.

126. Thompson, R., & Massopust, L. C., Jr. The effect of subcortical lesions on retention of a brightness discrimination in rats. *J. comp. physiol. Psychol.*, 1960, **53**, 488–496.

127. Thompson, R. F., & Johnson, R. H. Role of association areas of the cerebral cortex in auditory-visual conditional learning in the cat. *XVIII Int. Cong. Psychol.*, 1966, **1**, 319.

128. Thompson, R. F., & Kramer, R. F. Role of association cortex in sensory preconditioning. *J. comp. physiol. Psychol.*, 1965, **60**, 186–191.

129. Thompson, R. F., & Spencer, W. A. Habituation: a model phenomenon for the study of neuronal substrates of behavior. *Psychol. Rev.*, 1966, **73**, 16–43.

130. Uretsky, Ella, & McCleary, R. A. Effect of hippocampal isolation on retention. *J. comp. physiol. Psychol.*, 1969, **68**, 1–8.

131. Wade, Marjorie. The effect of sedatives upon delayed responses in monkeys following removal of the prefrontal lobes. *J. Neurophysiol.*, 1947, **10**, 57–61.

132. Wagner, A. R., Thomas, E., & Norton, T. Conditioning with electrical stimulation of motor cortex: evidence of a possible source of motivation. *J. comp. physiol. Psychol.*, 1967, **64**, 191–199.

133. Warren, J. M. The behavior of carnivores and primates with lesions in the prefrontal cortex. In *The frontal granular cortex and behavior*. J. M. Warren & K. Akert, Eds. New York: McGraw-Hill, 1964, pp. 168–191.

134. Warren, J. M., Warren, H. B., & Akert, K. *Umweg* learning by cats with lesions in the prestriate cortex. *J. comp. physiol. Psychol.*, 1961, **54**, 629–632.

135. Weiskrantz, L. Behavioral changes associated with ablation of the amygdaloid complex in monkeys. *J. comp. physiol. Psychol.*, 1956, **49**, 381–391.

136. Weiskrantz, L., & Mishkin, M. Effects of temporal and frontal cortical lesions on auditory discrimination in monkeys. *Brain*, 1958, **81**, 406–414.

137. Weiskrantz, L., Mihailovic, L., & Gross, C. G. Stimulation of frontal cortex and delayed alternation performance. *Science*, 1960, **131**, 1443–1444.

138. Wing, K. G. The role of the optic cortex of the dog in the retention of learned responses to light: Conditioning with light and shock. *Amer. J. Psychol.*, 1946, **59**, 583–612.

139. Wing, K. G. The role of the optic cortex of the dog in the retention of learned responses to light: Conditioning with light and food. *Amer. J. Psychol.*, 1947, **60**, 30–67.

140. Zubeck, J. P. Studies in somesthesis. I: Role of the somesthetic cortex in roughness discrimination in the rat. *J. comp. physiol. Psychol.*, 1951, **44**, 339–353.

Chapter 18

ELECTROPHYSIOLOGY OF LEARNING

Introduction

Electroencephalographic (EEG) Correlates of Conditioning

Evoked Potentials

Responses of Single Cells

DC Potentials

Review

INTRODUCTION

Ablation experiments have made it clear that the organism's ability to learn and to remember is not a unique function of any one geographical subdivision of the brain. It may nevertheless be possible, given adequate means of recording and analysis, to observe the development of a memory trace and identify the pathways involved in its formation by concurrently monitoring the electrical activity of many diverse aspects of the brain. Moreover, it should be possible to investigate with electrophysiological techniques the nature of the changes occurring as a result of learning, consolidation, or recall.

Berger's[3] discovery that the brain spontaneously generates rhythmic electrical potentials that are influenced by the organism's state of reactivity to the environment provided the first tool for the study of changes in neural activity which might occur as a result of learning. Supplemented by stereotaxic procedures which permit the accurate placement of recording electrodes in subcortical structures, the electroencephalogram (EEG) has been used by many investigators. Its usefulness is, unfortunately, curtailed by the fact that after several decades of extensive investigation, we still do not know exactly how it is generated or what it represents. Most investigators who use the EEG as a measure of local neural activity assume that it represents a summation of the bioelectric activity of a population of neurons surrounding the tip of the recording electrode. There is, however, some evidence that the EEG may represent electrical fields that involve very large

Electrophysiology of Learning **423**

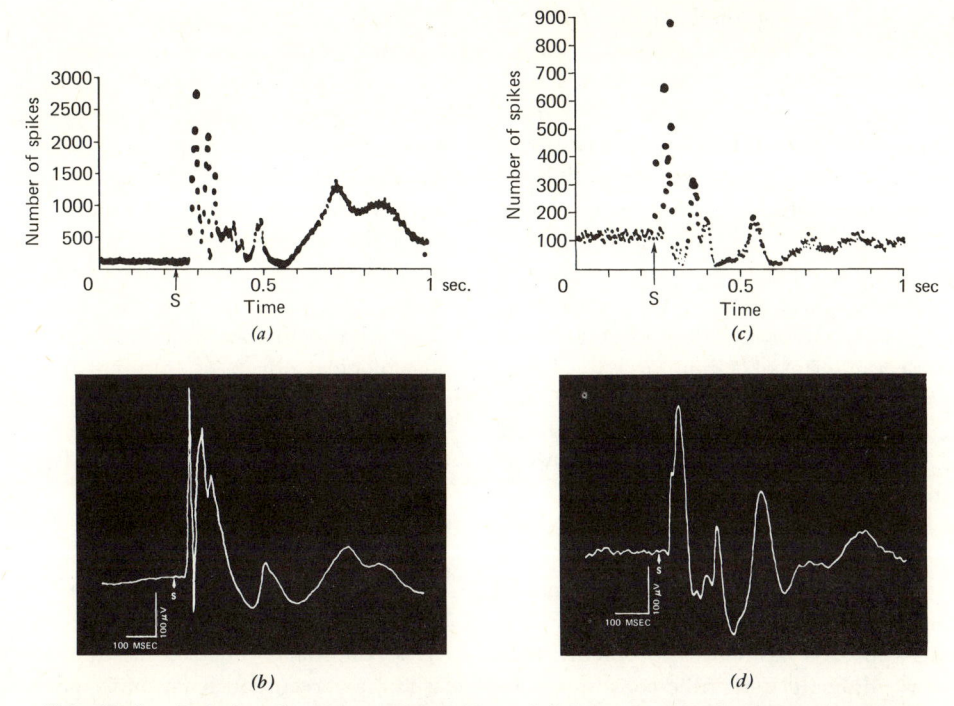

FIG. 18–1. Relation between probability of firing of a single cell and evoked potential waveform. (*a* & *c*) Frequency distribution of spikes from a single cell in the visual cortex of a cat after stimulation with 4918 or 3150 flashes, respectively; (*b* & *d*) averaged evoked potential recorded from the same microelectrode. Ordinate (for unit distributions): number of times the cell fired in response to light flash. Abscissa (for unit distributions): time, in 100-msec divisions.

(From S. S. Fox & J. H. O'Brien. Duplication of evoked potential waveform by curves of probability of firing by a single cell. *Science,* **147,** 19 February 1965, 888–890. Copyright 1965 by the American Association for the Advancement of Science.)

populations of cells and that changes in the activity of a few hundred or even thousands of cells do not produce a significant alteration in the EEG record. Some investigators have applied very sophisticated computer analyses to EEG data in an attempt to demonstrate subtle changes in the power spectrum, frequency-distribution, or phase-relation of EEG potentials. Even these elegant statistical procedures have not, by and large, shown an unambiguous relationship between the EEG and functional changes in specific portions of the brain except during gross changes in alertness.

The EEG is nonetheless still used by many investigators in this field. Others have turned to alternative measures of neural activity as they became available through recent advances in electronic technology. Some have used the gross potential which is evoked by the presentation of any novel, sudden, or intense sensory stimulus in most regions of the brain. We once again are not entirely certain how this evoked potential (E.P.) is generated and precisely what it represents in terms of the activity of individual neurons. There is, however, some evidence[18] that it is lawfully related to the probability of firing of cells in the vicinity of the recording electrode (see Figure 18–1). Evoked potentials, as the name implies, are always elicited by environmental stimuli and thus do not reflect changes in the ongoing activity of a particular portion of the brain. They may nonetheless be a useful measure of the effects of conditioning procedures, since learning may specifically involve a change in the processing of sensory information.

Other investigators have analyzed slow

shifts in the base line of the EEG. Modern EEG amplifiers filter out these "direct current" (DC) shifts and treat them as unwanted interference. A number of investigators have suggested, however, that these DC shifts may reflect changes in the activity of cells near the recording electrode more faithfully than the EEG itself and have reported some impressive correlations with behavioral events. Once again, we do not yet know how these DC shifts are produced or what precisely they reflect in terms of cellular activity. However, any measure that purports to reliably reflect correlations between physiological and behavioral activity must receive attention in this still uncharted field.

In recent years it has become increasingly popular to record the activity of individual cells. We are, in this instance, reasonably certain that we know what is being measured, but this approach has its own problems. It is still very difficult and time-consuming to obtain records of the activity of single cells for any length of time because, contrary to popular misconception, most cells are not very active spontaneously and because the brain and hence each individual cell moves with respect to the rest of the body ever so slightly. Even a little bit of movement changes the distance between the recording electrode and the cell, and this affects the amplitude of the potential which is recorded from it. Often a cell moves entirely out of range of the recording electrode just at the time one is ready to record important information. At other times, the cell may move only slightly, but the resultant change in the recorded potential makes it impossible to differentiate it from the response of other cells. These problems are most acute in relatively long-term experiments that require the observation of responses to conditioned stimuli before and after they have been repeatedly associated with an unconditioned stimulus. To obtain data from even 10 or 20 cells often takes months. This results in a sampling problem, since one cannot assume that all cells in a geographically defined subdivision of the brain subserve the same function.

None of the electrophysiological measures currently available provide an unambiguous measure of the activity of functionally or even geographically defined populations of neurons. It is thus not surprising that the many investigations that have attempted to use these measures to demonstrate specific, learning-related changes in the activity of particular aspects of the brain have not, as yet, been very successful. Some of these studies have, however, obtained interesting correlations between the behavioral and electrophysiological effects of training and a brief look at some of these data may be useful.

ELECTROENCEPHALOGRAPHIC (EEG) CORRELATES OF CONDITIONING

Conditioned Alpha Blocking

When an organism is resting, regular, large EEG potentials, which occur at about 8 to 12 Hz, are recorded from many parts of the

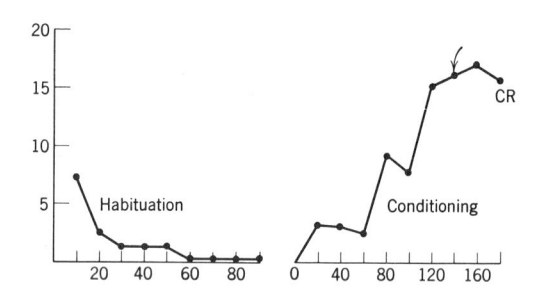

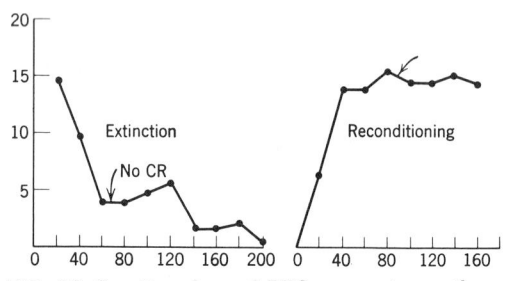

FIG. 18–2. Number of EEG arousal reactions (ordinate) to a tonal CS per block of 10 or 20 presentations (abscissa) for a cat. The first appearance of a flexion CR in the course of training and retraining, and its full disappearance during extinction, is noted by the arrows.

(From R. W. Doty. Discussion of Gastaut's paper. In *The reticular formation of the brain*. H. H. Jasper, L. D. Proctor, R. S. Knighton, W. C. Noshay, & R. T. Costello, Eds. Little, Brown, 1958.)

cortex. These "alpha waves" are displaced by irregular, fast, and very small potentials as soon as any sudden, novel, or intense stimulus is presented that attracts the organism's attention. It is generally assumed that this "alpha block" or "arousal" response reflects an increase in cellular activity.

The EEG arousal response gradually disappears from most parts of the cortex when repeated presentations of a stimulus demonstrate that it does not require a reaction. When such a stimulus is then used as the CS in a conditioning experiment, the alpha block reappears once again, but its distribution may be different than before and may, in fact, change as the organism acquires the conditioned response. The "conditioned" alpha block appears typically before conditioned motor responses are made and extinguishes less rapidly than the overt CR when the reinforcement is withheld[64, 65] (see Figure 18-2). Initially, the CS elicits conditioned alpha blocking in all portions of the cortex. On later trials, the response becomes localized in the motor cortex and in the sensory projection areas of the CS and UCS.[74] These EEG patterns may reflect changes in the processing of information about the conditioned stimulus, but the EEG response to the CS is not, itself, an essential aspect of conditioning. Learning can take place, apparently unimpaired, after the alpha block has been inhibited by drugs.[44]

After a few presentations most stimuli produce alpha blocking only in the sensory projection area of the modality of the stimulus. If one repeatedly pairs an auditory or somatic stimulus that does not produce alpha blocking in the visual cortex with a visual stimulus that does affect the EEG of the visual area, something like sensory-sensory conditioning takes place. After some pairings, the auditory or somatic CS elicits an alpha block specifically in the visual cortex[22] (see Figure 18-3). This conditioned EEG response is not very strong or stable,[45] but it has been observed in a variety of classical conditioning paradigms such as cyclic, delayed, trace, differential, and even backward conditioning.[32] More extensive and stable conditioned EEG desynchronization has been obtained when a painful shock was used as the UCS. The conditioned desynchronization in these experiments could even be obtained without arousing a sleeping cat.[31]

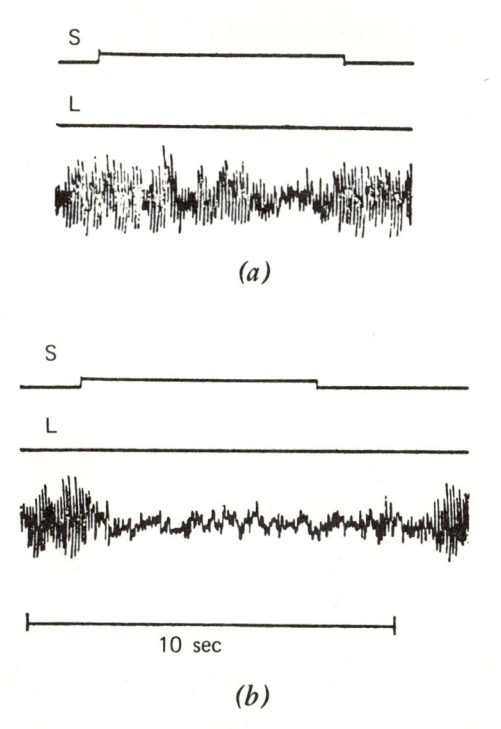

FIG. 18-3. Simple CR. Control shows that sound (S) without light (L) had no effect on alpha waves. Trial 9 shows blocking of alpha rhythm as the CR to sound.

(From H. H. Jasper & C. Shagass. Conditioning the occipital alpha rhythm in man. *J. exp. Psych.*, **28**, 1941, 373–388.)

Slow-Wave Activity

During long CS-UCS intervals, very large slow waves often appear in the cortical EEG.[58] The CS initially produces an alpha block that persists until the UCS has been presented. As conditioning proceeds, the alpha block to the CS shortens and large slow waves appear, followed by a second alpha block just prior to the onset of the UCS. It has been suggested[22] that these slow waves may reflect inhibitory processes analogous to Pavlov's[73] "internal inhibition" because (1) the CS elicits only slow waves at some stages

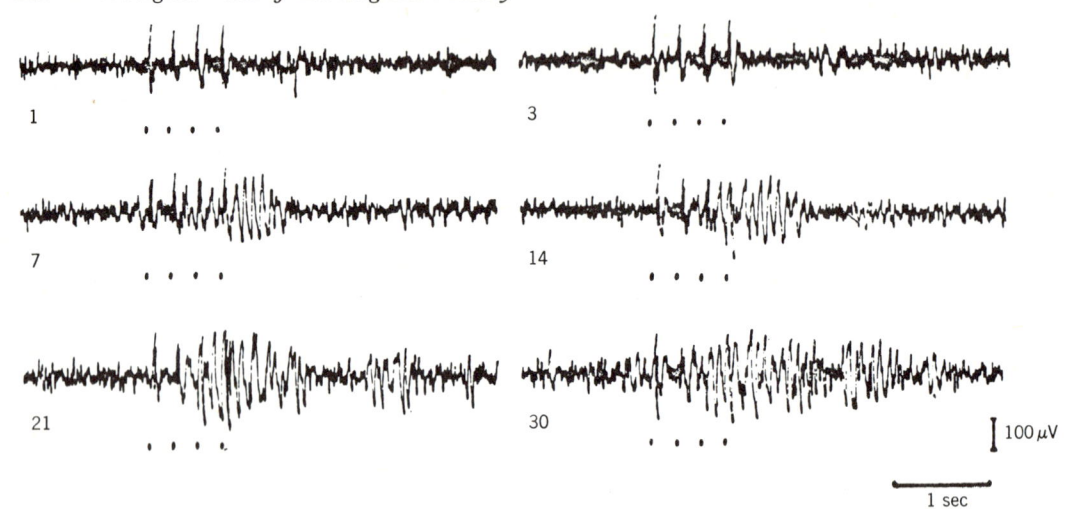

FIG. 18–4. Electrical activity from the visual cortex of a cat previously conditioned to flashes of light (four flashes at a rate of 1/sec) associated with an electric shock delivered to a leg. The numbers correspond to trials without reinforcement. Notice the shift from frequency-specific responding to slow waves in the course of extinction.

(From R. Hernández-Péon. Neurophysiological correlates of habituation and other manifestations of plastic inhibition (internal inhibition). In *The Moscow colloquium on electroencephalography of higher nervous activity.* H. H. Jasper & G. D. Smirnov, Eds. *EEG clin. Neurophysiol.*, 1960, Suppl. 13, 101–114.)

of extinction (see Figure 18–4) and (2) differential stimuli that signal the absence of the UCS elicit slow waves under some circumstances.[46] The relationship between slow-wave activity and behavioral manifestations of inhibition is, however, far from perfect. In one recent experiment, synchronous slow waves appeared on only about 70 percent of the trials on which behavioral inhibition was evident.[88]

Cortical slow-wave activity (and behavioral sleep) can be induced by electrical stimulation of the basal forebrain. When such stimulation is paired with an auditory CS, the latter soon comes to elicit slow waves (though rarely sleep itself).[89]

Large slow waves appear in the hippocampus and associated subcortical structures during behavioral alerting and arousal.[26] The frequency as well as amplitude of these "theta" waves undergo apparently lawful changes during classical[4] as well as instrumental conditioning.[1] Hippocampal theta activity typically does not accompany the initial alerting reactions to the CS but begins to appear as the first behavioral CR's are made. The hippocampal slow waves generally become more prominent during acquisition but eventually subside as the conditioned responses become well established.[25]

There is some evidence that theta activity may be modified in a lawful fashion within each successful (i.e., correct) trial. In one series of experiments,[15] most of the theta activity occurred at frequencies near 4 Hz during the presentation of a signal which indicated that a trial was about to start. The theta frequency abruptly switched to 5 Hz when the visual discriminanda were shown and increased to 6 Hz when the approach response to the correct stimulus was initiated. The theta frequency returned to a base-line of about 4 Hz in this experiment as soon as the goal, containing the food reinforcement, was reached. No lawful changes in theta frequency occurred when the animals made incorrect responses. In these as well as other studies,[91] a desynchronization of hippocampal activity was observed just before or after the animals obtained the reward. This desynchronization reaction has been attributed to general activation.[91]

Recent investigations of the behavior of animals during the occurrence of theta activity in the hippocampus[84] indicate that this slow-wave pattern may generally accompany voluntary movements. The amplitude of the theta waves appears to be related to the magnitude of the voluntary movement (a relationship that might explain the waxing and waning of theta activity in habituation and conditioning experiments), and to be unrelated to attentional processes unless they lead to movement.[12, 92] Theta waves can be recorded from perfectly motionless animals,[5] but it can be argued that this occurs only when an "intent to move" is present.[84] The observed relationship of theta activity to motion does not discredit the hypothesis that these slow waves may, in some way, be related to conditioning. Theta activity does not accompany all movements but appears to be unique to voluntary (i.e., learned) responses to specific environmental cues. It is thus possible that the theta activity may be a correlate of the transfer process responsible for the integration of conditioned responses.

Theta rhythms and even slower (1 to 3 Hz) synchronous waves have also been observed in EEG records obtained from amygdala and other subcortical structures during the performance of learned responses.[16] These slow potentials may reflect neural activity which is in some way related to learning or memory storage, but it is clear that they are not essential to the learning process since septal lesions or drug treatments which abolish slow wave activity do not generally impair learning or recall.[26, 50]

High-Frequency Rhythms

A good deal of attention has been devoted in recent years to the possibility that learning or memory consolidation may result in the generation of particular EEG frequencies in some parts of the brain. Particularly, the appearance of relatively large potentials at approximately 40 Hz at some stages of learning has seemed promising to many investigators. Bursts of EEG potentials near this frequency have been observed in many portions of the limbic system during alerting as well as during various phases of learning. The rhythm is particularly prominent during classical conditioning experiments involving unavoidable shocks[20, 76] as well as during instrumental avoidance learning,[51] and a specific relationship with emotional reactions has been proposed.[52] Forty Hertz activity has also been seen in appetitive instrumental learning situations and the term "consolidation rhythm" has been applied to it.[82] However, it seems likely that the 40 Hz activity may be associated with exploratory reactions to novel stimuli instead of conditioning per se, since interruption of nasal airflow or destruction of the olfactory bulb (which make sniffing but not learning impossible) abolish these rhythms.[72]

EEG Responses to Repetitive "Tracer" Stimuli

Several investigators have attempted to identify the structures that may be preferentially active during conditioning by recording frequency-specific responses to so-called "tracer" stimuli. All discrete sensory stimuli produce evoked potentials that are superimposed on the cortical EEG. Stimuli that have a low-frequency periodicity tend to "drive" the EEG at the same frequency. This frequency-specific EEG response is more prominent and may involve areas of the brain that do not normally show "driving" when the stimulus is used as a CS in classical or instrumental conditioning experiments.[35]

"Tracer" stimuli have been used in many experiments. One of the most ambitious attempts to demonstrate their usefulness was reported a decade ago by John and Killam.[37, 38, 39] In the first of these experiments, a 10 Hz flickering light was used as the CS in a shuttle-box avoidance experiment. Before the beginning of training, all frequency specific responses to the CS were habituated. During the initial CS-UCS pairings, frequency-specific (10 Hz) EEG activity reappeared throughout the brain. The magnitude of the 10 Hz rhythm increased or decreased in specific parts of the brain during training.

After the animals had mastered the task, differential conditioning (i.e., the presentation of a nonreinforced, 7 Hz flickering light) was begun. Initially, the differential stimulus (DS) elicited avoidance responses as well as 10 Hz "driving" of the cortical EEG. The behavioral reactions gradually extinguished and the "inappropriate" 10 Hz EEG rhythms disappeared.

In an extension of these studies, cats were trained to lever press for milk rewards in response to a light that flickered at 10 Hz and to make an avoidance response whenever the light flickered at 6 Hz. Both stimuli were then presented in the lever-pressing situation. Whenever the animals lever pressed in response to the 6 Hz avoidance signal, most regions of the brain showed "driving" at 10 Hz—the stimulus for lever pressing. Similarly, whenever lever pressing was inhibited by a 10 Hz stimulus, most areas of the brain showed driving at or near 6 Hz—the frequency of the stimulus previously used in the avoidance experiment. The investigators concluded from these observations that "tracer" stimuli may establish "reference standards" in some parts of the brain and that conditioned responses to these stimuli may require a comparison of the pattern of incoming sensory information with this standard.

An increase in "frequency-specific" activity of the EEG (the term is often used loosely to include "similar" frequencies, harmonics, or subharmonics of the training stimulus) has been observed by many investigators, particularly when a stimulus assumes special significance for an organism. However, the suggestion that the rhythm of the EEG may itself carry information has as yet been unsubstantiated. Indeed, the presence of "frequency-specific" EEG activity does not seem to correlate well with the occurrence of correct responses[53] and may be more pronounced during the first training trials (when the animal is maximally aroused but not yet conditioned) than after the significance of the CS has been established.[56] A similarly transient pattern of frequency-specific activity has been seen in experiments where the frequency of the stimulus is a cue to the solution of a discrimination problem without, itself, being the stimulus that must be compared to a standard reference on each individual trial.[10]

Summary and Review Questions

Many investigators have attempted to correlate learning with changes in the amplitude or frequency of the EEG. We have discussed four types of EEG responses.

1. *Alpha block.* Habituated EEG "arousal" responses reappear when a stimulus is used as a CS. The "conditioned" alpha block may appear only in the motor cortex and in the sensory projection area of the UCS at some stages of training. The alpha block can be inhibited by drugs that do not significantly impair learning, indicating that it is not an essential part of the conditioning process, although its appearance or disappearance may provide important clues to information processing in the brain.

2. *Slow Waves.* Large, rhythmic slow waves occur cortically as well as subcortically at some stages of training. The cortical slow waves have been related to behavioral inhibition, but the correlation is not perfect. The magnitude and frequency of slow waves recorded from the hippocampus change during conditioning, but it is not clear whether processes specifically related to conditioning instead of "attention," "inhibition," or "expectation" are responsible for these effects. Lawful changes in the frequency of the hippocampal "theta" rhythm have also been seen during individual learning trials. Hippocampal slow waves have recently been related to voluntary (i.e., conditioned) movements or the intent to move and may in some way reflect the transfer process that intervenes between the retrieval of a memory and the execution of a learned response. The slow waves do not appear to be essential to conditioning since they are abolished by lesions and drug treatments that do not generally impair acquisition or recall.

3. *High-Frequency Rhythms.* Many attempts have been made to relate specific EEG frequencies to learning or recall. Large 40 Hz synchronous potentials have been recorded from the amygdala and related subcortical regions during acquisition, particularly in situations involving negative reinforcement. It has been suggested that this activity may be specifically related to consolidation or to emotional reactions, but the observation that the 40 Hz rhythms are abolished by obstruction of nasal air flow indicates that they may be specifically related to exploratory behavior.

4. *EEG "Driving."* Stimuli that have a low-frequency periodicity tend to induce "frequency-specific" EEG activity in some parts of the brain. This is particularly prominent and may involve regions of the brain that do not normally show frequency specific activity during conditioning. Stimuli that do not elicit EEG driving come to do so when repeatedly paired with stimuli that elicit frequency-specific EEG activity. This appearance of EEG driving may reflect learning-related changes in the processing of sensory information, but several observations suggest that this may be related to attentional instead of associative processes.

1. Describe the evidence which suggests that the EEG alpha block may serve as an index of learning-related changes in neural activity.

2. Relate neocortical and hippocampal slow waves to behavior in learning situations.

3. What evidence do you have that specific EEG frequencies may be related to conditioning?

4. How are DC potentials related to behavior?

5. Discuss in general terms the usefulness of EEG recordings in experiments designed to elucidate the nature of the learning process.

Evoked Potentials

The amplitude of the evoked response to sensory stimuli depends not only on the in-

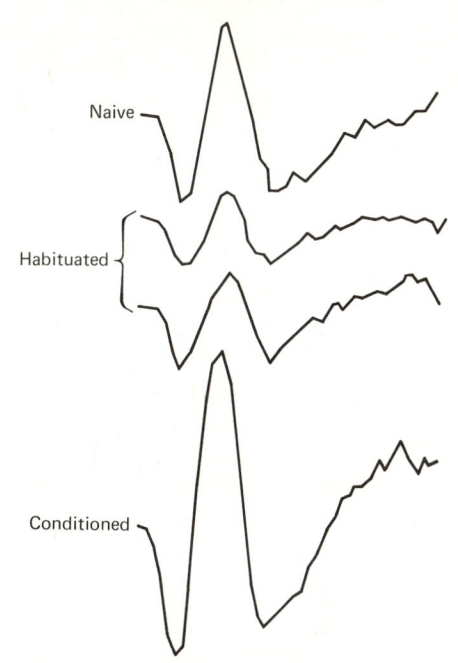

FIG. 18–5. Click-evoked responses, averaged by computer, recorded bipolarly from the cortex of the superior temporal gyrus in the monkey.

(After R. Galambos & G. S. Sheatz. An electroencephalograph study of classical conditioning. *Amer. J. Physiol.*, **203**, 1962, 173–184.)

tensity of the eliciting stimulus but also on its novelty or "significance." Evoked potentials may never habituate completely but their amplitude decreases during repeated, nonreinforced presentations of a stimulus and increases again when it is used as a CS (see Figure 18–5). Some investigators[2] have suggested that the evoked response to a CS may be maximal at the stage of training where the first behavioral CR occurs. Others[41] have reported that the evoked potential may first appear in the motor cortex at this time. Recent computer analyses of averaged evoked responses[35] indicate that the most prominent early phases of the EP may show only quantitative changes during conditioning. The late phases of the EP, however, appear to undergo important qualitative changes, and there is reason to believe that these may be related to learning although the nature of this relationship is, as yet, not clear. Among the findings which support this interpretation are: (1) disruption of the late (but not of the early) phases of the EP disrupts performance severely;[34] (2) the contour of the late components of the evoked potential are different on correct and incorrect trials;[36] and (3) the late components of the EP are "appropriate" to the behavioral response (i.e., when an ambiguous stimulus elicits a CR, the EP resembles that normally elicited by the CS).[40] On the basis of these and related observations, it has been suggested that the early components of the evoked potential may reflect the action of the eliciting stimulus directly whereas the late components may reflect the response of some neural mechanisms to that input, possibly on the basis of a readout of stored information.

Computer analyses have shown that the evoked potentials recorded concurrently from different parts of the brain[35] become increasingly similar during the process of learning. This similarity is most apparent on trials when the animal performs a correct response. Similar evoked potentials are typically seen in the thalamic and mesencephalic reticular formation, the primary sensory projection areas of the cortex, and the hippocampus. It is interesting, in this context, that cats[19] as well as human subjects[75] can be trained in a simple instrumental conditioning paradigm to change the amplitude of a late component of the evoked response.

Summary

The magnitude of evoked potentials changes in the course of conditioning, and there is some evidence that they may appear during training in portions of the brain where they are not normally recorded. Particularly the late components of the EP may be selectively affected by conditioning procedures. It has been suggested that these late components may reflect the organism's response to the stimulus (which may involve a retrieval of relevant memories) instead of the direct action of the stimulus on sensory mechanisms alone.

RESPONSES OF SINGLE CELLS

Macropotentials such as the EEG, evoked potential, or DC shift reflect the activity of an unknown population of individual neurons. Since the organization of the brain does not, in most instances, place functionally related neurons into the same geographically defined location, many investigators have despaired of ever finding meaningful correlations between the summated potentials of large regions of the brain

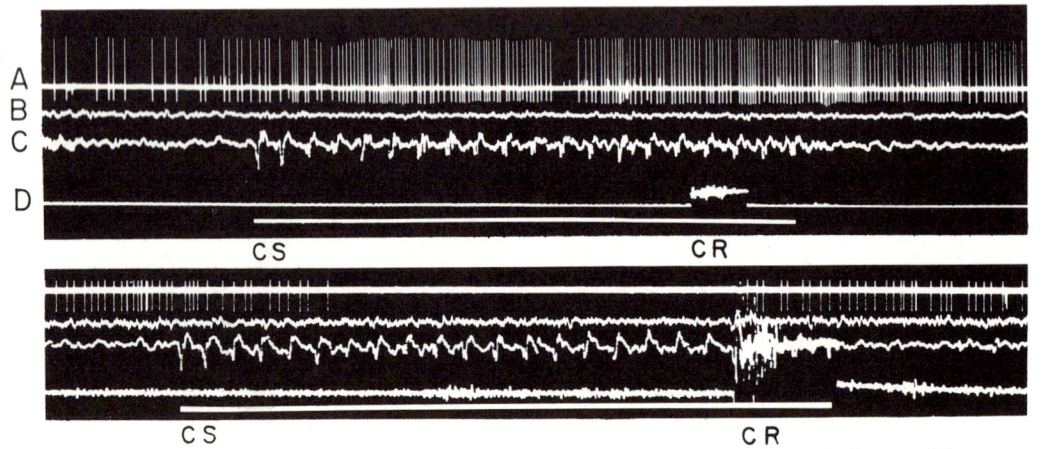

FIG. 18–6. Two patterns of unit activity in the motor cortex during a CS presentation. *Top*, increased firing during CS and response. *Bottom*, inhibition of unit during CS. A, microelectrode in motor cortex; B, EEG record from motor area; C, EEG record from occipital area; D, EMG.

(From H. H. Jasper, G. F. Ricci, & B. Doane. Patterns of cortical neuronal discharge during conditioned responses in monkeys. In *Neurological basis of behaviour*. G. E. W. Wolstenholme & Cecilia M. O'Connor, Eds. London: J. & A. Churchill, 1958.)

and specific behavioral changes. Technological advances have made it increasingly possible to monitor the activity of single cells, even in unanesthetized and unrestrained animals, and this technique is beginning to be applied to experiments that are relevant to the subject of learning. Two somewhat different approaches have been used. The more common experimental paradigm involves the recording of the spike activity of single cells before, during, and after conditioning. The second consists of attempts to reinforce changes in the activity of particular brain cells in conditioning paradigms.

A number of experimenters have reported changes in cellular activity in various regions of the brain during conditioning. However, there is little consistency in the pattern of the observed effects (see Figure 18–6). A fairly common finding is that cells in the reticular formation of the brainstem or thalamus, in the hippocampus, and in the sensory projection areas of the CS or UCS which do not originally respond to the to-be-conditioned stimulus come to do so during learning.[90, 6] There is also some indication that different aspects of the brain (notably the reticular formation, thalamus, hippocampus, and relevant sensory areas) may be selectively activated by the CS during trials on which learning (as opposed to habituation or overtraining) takes place.[59] In some experiments, the CS comes to elicit a response pattern in some single nerve cells that is quite different from that seen when the CS or UCS are presented alone prior to training, but similar to that evoked by the CS-UCS combination.[63] An interaction between conditioned and unconditioned stimuli has even been observed in situations where the UCS by itself does not affect the firing rate of a particular neuron. For instance, some cells in the subcortical relays of the visual system are unaffected by the overall level of illumination of the visual field. Some of these cells can be trained to respond differently to a visual stimulus when it is presented against a background of high or low illumination.[55]

It is, unfortunately, not clear whether these changes in cellular activity represent processes specifically related to learning or memory itself. One group of studies has consistently shown changes in the firing rate of individual cells in the dorsal hippocampus or midbrain reticular formation which appear to be related to "expectancy," motivation, or reward[69] (see Figure 18–7). The firing rate of these cells increased just before a reward for a conditioned instrumental response was presented and was higher the greater the animal's motivation for that particular reward. Especially in the hippocampus, cells were often found that responded whenever the delivery of a specific reward (such as a food pellet) was promised but not when a signal for another reward (such as a drop of water) was given. These observations emphasize that we must be

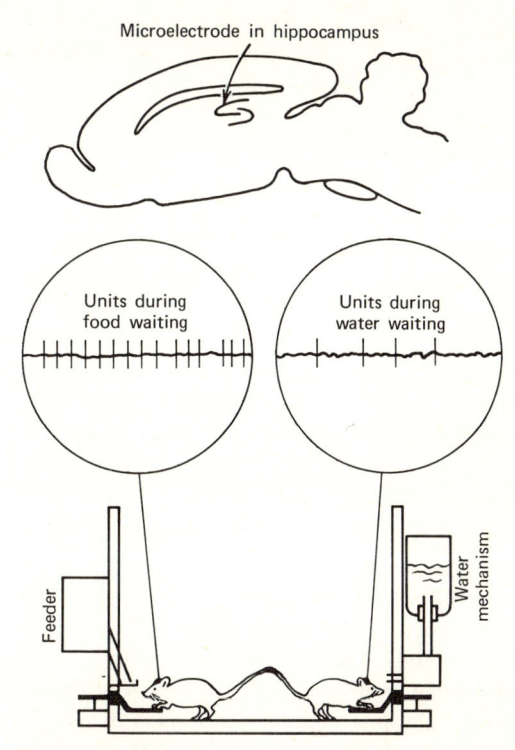

FIG. 18–7. A unit in hippocampus that fired rapidly during food waiting but at control levels during water waiting.

(From J. Olds. The central nervous system and the reinforcement of behavior. *Amer. Psychologist,* **24,** 1969, 114–132. Copyright 1969 by the American Psychological Association, and reproduced by permission. Data from J. Olds, W. D. Mink, & P. J. Best. Single unit patterns during anticipatory behavior. *EEG clin. Neurophysiol.,* **26,** 1969, 144–158.)

cautious in interpreting changes in neural firing rate which occur during conditioning. As an animal learns, many things, including the probability of reinforcement or frustration, change.

Successful "conditioning" of single cells was first reported in 1961.[70] In these pioneering experiments, a cell was located that was spontaneously active under the conditions of the experiment. Rewarding brain stimulation, which did not, by itself, affect the firing rate of the cell, was then used to reinforce an increase or a decrease in its activity level. Most neocortical cells responded little, if at all, to this operant conditioning procedure, but many subcortical cells, and cells in the hippocampus, did. After as few as 10 or 20 reinforcements, some cells that previously fired only once or twice per second responded continuously at discharge rates of up to 30 per second. These experiments have been replicated and extended[67,68] and more conventional reinforcers such as food pellets have been used to augment the activity of single brain cells.[17] There is, however, no compelling reason to assume that the activity of the neurons under study was specifically conditioned in these experiments. It seems logically more plausible, in fact, that the "conditioned" cell may be part of a neural network related, directly or indirectly, to an overt or covert reaction to the CS and that the conditioning procedure modifies the activity of many a neuron. It is nevertheless instructive that we can monitor these changes at one point in the nervous system, and future applications of this technique may enhance our understanding of the events that occur as a result of learning.

There is some evidence from studies of simple nervous systems that the activity of a single neuron can, indeed, be altered in a conditioning paradigm, even in situations where the influence of other cells may be ruled out. In one of these studies,[42,43] two separate afferent pathways to a single neuron in the abdominal ganglion of a sea slug were identified. These pathways were then electrically stimulated such that stimulation of pathway A produced only a marginal response from the ganglionic neuron, whereas stimulation of pathway B resulted in a burst of activity. Stimulation of A was then used as a CS for stimulation of B in a classical conditioning paradigm. After several pairings, stimulation of A alone produced a burst of activity similar to that previously seen only in response to stimulation of pathway B. Repeated stimulation of B alone (i.e., sensitization) did not produce this effect. In view of the simplicity of the neural connections involved in this experiment, it seems possible that its results may directly reflect changes in synaptic efficacy as a result of conditioning.

Summary and Review Questions

Individual cells in the reticular formation of the brainstem and thalamus, in the hippocampus, and in the sensory projection areas of the cortex may respond differently to a stimulus after it has acquired significance as a CS. These changes in unit activity appear to be peculiar to learning situations. However, several observations indicate that changes in "expectancy," "motivation," or "reinforcement" rather than associative processes may be important determinants of cellular activity in many of these instances.

The activity level of individual nerve cells can be brought under operant control using brain stimulation as well as conventional reinforcers. It appears probable, however, that this may reflect the development of conditioned motor responses instead of the selective conditioning of activity in single neurons.

Describe the evidence which suggests that the activity of single neurons may serve as a useful measure of learning-related changes in brain function. Discuss the limitations of this technique.

DC POTENTIALS

When one amplifies the potential between two scalp electrodes or between two electrodes inside the brain, a steady direct current (DC) potential can be recorded on which the rhythmic variations of the EEG are superimposed. Most EEG amplifiers are designed to filter out the slow shifts in this base line potential that occur over time. We do not yet know how this DC potential is generated, but it seems probable that the activity of glial cells as well as neurons contributes to it.[49, 71] The DC potential varies over time but does not, in most circumstances, show periodic rhythmicity.[66]

The functional significance of this DC potential has attracted a good deal of experimental interest as well as speculation in recent years because it increases or decreases in response to environmental stimuli in an apparently systematic fashion. The nature of the reaction has suggested to some investigators that it may reflect cortical processes specifically related to "expectancy," "attention," or "reaction potential."

All novel stimuli elicit a DC shift.[47, 27] Typically, a discrete, stimulus-bound shift towards increased negativity occurs in the cortical sensory projection area of the stimulus, accompanied by a more diffuse and prolonged change in the DC potential of other areas of the brain.[54] Both gradually disappear unless the eliciting stimulus has biological significance or signals other events that do. The time course of this habituation process is similar to the disappearance of the alpha block, but on individual trials the DC shift may be entirely dissociated from the EEG, indicating that it may reflect independent functional changes.[78]

Recent experimental interest in the DC shift derives from the observation that stimuli which elicit an overt or covert reaction that produces positive reward or avoids punishment continue to produce large DC shifts.[59, 78] These persisting reactions have been studied in man as well as rats, cats, and monkeys. Quite dissimilar experimental paradigms have been used, and it is not clear that the responses which have been observed in all of them reflect the same basic processes. In man, as many as three different DC components have been described even within a single experiment,[13] and very different interpretations for them have been offered.

Rowland and associates[79, 80] have shown in cats that the magnitude of the DC response is determined by (1) the intensity of the drive which is related to the eliciting

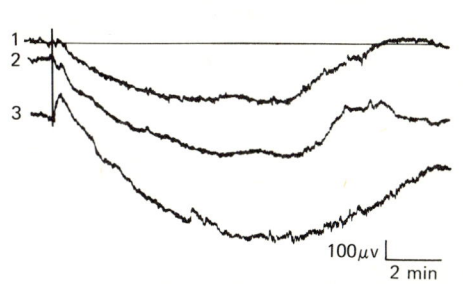

FIG. 18–8. Sustained cortical slow potential accompanying lapping of high-incentive evaporated milk–fish–meal homogenate by cat deprived of food and water for 24 hours.

(After V. Rowland. Steady potential phenomena of cortex. In *The Neurosciences, A study program.* G. C. Quarton, T. Melnechuk, & F. O. Schmitt, Eds. The Rockefeller University Press, 1967.)

stimulus (i.e., only hungry animals show a large DC shift to food or food-related stimuli) (see Figure 18–8) and (2) the degree of association between the eliciting stimulus and some positive or negative reinforcement. This indicates that the magnitude of the DC response as well as its probability increase during conditioning. Rowland[78] has pointed out that these two variables (drive and habit strength) are the factors that determine *reaction potential* in Hull's[29] theory of behavior and suggested that the probability and/or magnitude of the DC reaction may be a direct measure of this elusive variable.

Walter and associates[85, 86, 11] have described a DC shift in man that occurs in the interval between a signal and the subject's response to it. This so-called "contingent negative variation" or C.N.V. (also called "readiness potential" or "expectancy wave") is recorded only when overt or covert responses to the eliciting stimulus are required.[48, 24] Like the DC shift seen in animals, the C.N.V. appears to be largest during the acquisition of a conditioned response [57, 9] and is influenced by motivational factors.[7, 30] A DC shift is also seen during alerting reactions[8] and appears to be suppressed by distracting stimuli.[83] These observations suggest that it may, in part, reflect central processes related to "attention."

Several investigators have attempted to distinguish several components of the DC response. Some believe that a motor potential or "intention wave" related specifically to movement can be isolated.[87] Others distinguish between a "premotion potential" and a "motor potential."[13] An interpretation of these data is, however, complicated by the fact that eye movements produce DC potentials that are easily confounded with the cortical DC shifts.

The functional importance of the DC response is not yet clear. It has been suggested[78] that the DC potential may reflect an integration of transient neural responses which occurs either in dendritic fields or in glial cells. Several different roles for this integrated activity have been suggested. It may "prime" specific groups of neurons for action[86] or translate evanescent neural activity into "retained experience."[78] A specific role of the DC reaction in learning is suggested by experiments which have shown that processes similar to learning appear to be facilitated when DC shifts are experimentally produced in some parts of the brain.[81] For instance, when a DC shift is produced in portions of the motor cortex that control leg flexion, the presentation of a tone or light will elicit this motor reaction. It continues to be evoked for 10 to 15 minutes after the termination of the DC current, suggesting that a degree of facilitation is retained. Microelectrode recordings show that cells in the area to which the DC current is applied which do not normally respond to auditory stimuli do so after DC shift has been introduced.[60,61] The application of anodal current (which produces a negative DC shift) facilitates conditioned responses, whereas the application of cathodal DC current (which produces a positive DC shift) interferes with conditioning.[62]

Summary and Review Questions

The direct current (DC) potential that exists between portions of the brain and the rest of the organism changes in a lawful fashion when a novel, sudden, or "meaningful" stimulus is presented. The magnitude of this DC response appears to be a function of motivational as well as associative variables, and it has been suggested that it may reflect neural events related to "reaction potential" as defined by Hull. Direct current shifts are particularly prominent just before an overt response to a stimulus occurs, and the DC response has consequently been related to "expectancy," "intention," or even plain motor activity. The experimental induction of DC shifts in some parts of the cortex seems to facilitate or, depending on the direction of the shift, inhibit learning or learning-related neural processes.

Describe the experimental evidence which suggests that shifts in the DC potential between some areas of the brain may reflect neural events related to learning.

REVIEW

If, as many investigators believe, learning involves not one but many diverse areas of the central nervous system, only concurrent recordings of the activity of many brain regions can provide a sufficiently complete picture of learning-related changes in neural activity to permit a glimpse at the development of a memory trace. We do not, unfortunately, have unambiguous measures of neural activity in functionally related populations of cells and cannot adequately specify the size of the geographically defined populations that contribute to the summated potentials (EEG, EP, and DC) which we record. Analyses of the activity of individual cells are still sufficiently difficult to make a survey of statistically adequate samples impossible. In spite of these methodological difficulties, we have some interesting correlations between behavioral and electrophysiological measures that may be relevant to learning.

The EEG record changes significantly in the course of learning. Previously habituated alpha-block responses to the CS reappear and may, at some stages of training, appear in areas of the brain that did not show selective blocking prior to training. Slow waves occur in many parts of the neocortex, particularly during periods of behavioral inhibition. Similar slow-wave activity is seen in the hippocampus and associated subcortical areas at many stages of training, and there is some evidence that the frequency of this "theta" activity may change during a correct trial. However, it is not clear to what extent inhibitory or attentional processes may be responsible for these changes. Large 40 Hz rhythms have been recorded from the amygdala and related subcortical structures during training, but these rhythms may be related to exploratory behavior instead of learning per se. Attempts to follow the development of memory traces by the use of intermittent stimuli which induce "frequency-specific" EEG activity have shown that EEG "driving" appears and disappears from specific portions of the brain during training.

Other electrophysiological responses that have been correlated with learning include: (1) the magnitude of the evoked potential to the CS in selected portions of the brain or the contour of its late components: (2) the similarity between evoked potentials in different portions of the brain; (3) changes in the firing pattern of individual neurons, particularly in the brainstem reticular formation, thalamus, hippocampus, and cortical sensory projection areas; and (4) shifts in the DC potential in response to conditioned stimuli.

In some instances, the observed electrophysiological changes appear to be unique to learning situations and even to specific stages of training. It is not, however, clear that this coincidence requires the assumption that the observed changes reflect neural events specifically related to learning. There is considerable evidence that changes in "attention," "expectancy," "frustration," or "reward" that occur during learning may be responsible for at least some of the observed electrophysiological reactions.

Bibliography

1. Adey, W. R., Dunlop, C. W., & Hendrix, C. E. Hippocampal slow waves: Distribution and phase relations in the course of approach learning. *Arch. Neurol. (Chicago)*, 1960, **3**, 74–90.
2. Artemyev, V. V., & Bozladnova, N. I. Electrical reaction of the auditory area of the cortex of the cerebral hemispheres during the formation of a conditioned defense reflex. *Tr. Inst. Fiziol. (Moskow)*, 1952, **1**, 228.
3. Berger, H. Über das Elektrenkephalogramm des Menschen. I. *Arch. Psychiat. Nervenkr.*, 1929, **87**, 527–570.
4. Bremner, F. J. Hippocampal electrical activity during classical conditioning. *J. comp. physiol. Psychol.*, 1968, **66**, 35–39.
5. Brown, B. B. Frequency and phase of hippocampal theta activity in the spontaneously behaving cat. *EEG clin. Neurophysiol.*, 1968, **24**, 53–62.
6. Bureš, J. Discussion. In *Anatomy of memory*. D. P. Kimble, Ed. Palo Alto: Science and Behavior Books, Inc., 1965, pp. 49–51.
7. Cant, B. R., & Bickford, R. G. The effect of motivation on the contingent negative variation (CNV). *EEG clin. Neurophysiol.* 1967, **23**, 594.
8. Caspers, H. Changes in cortical D. C. potentials in the sleep-wakefulness cycle. In *Ciba foundation symposium on the nature of sleep*. G. E. W. Wolstenholme & M. O'Connor, Eds. Boston: Little, Brown, 1960, pp. 237–259.
9. Chiorini, J. R. Slow potential changes from cat cortex during classical aversive conditioning. Ph.D. Dissertation, University of Iowa, 1966.
10. Chow, K. L. Brain waves and visual discrimination learning in monkey. In *Recent advances in biological psychiatry. Vol. II.* J. Wortis, Ed. New York: Grune and Stratton, 1960, pp. 149–157.
11. Cohen, J., & Walter, W. G. The interaction of responses in the brain to semantic stimuli. *Psychophysiol.*, 1966, **2**, 187–196.
12. Dalton, A., & Black, A. H. Hippocampal electrical activity during the operant conditioning of movement and refraining from movement. *Comm. Behav. Biol.*, 1968, **2**, 267–273.
13. Deecke, L., Scheid, P., & Kornhuber, H. H. Distribution of readiness potential, premotion positivity, and motor potential of the human cerebral cortex preceding

voluntary finger movements. *Exp. Brain Res.*, 1969, **7**, 158–168.

14. Doty, R. W. Discussion of Gastaut's paper. In *The reticular formation of the brain*. H. H. Jasper, L. D. Proctor, R. S. Knighton, W. C. Noshay, & R. T. Costello, Eds. Boston: Little, Brown, 1958, pp. 580–589.

15. Elazar, Z., & Adey, W. R. Spectral analysis of low frequency components in the electrical activity of the hippocampus during learning. *EEG clin. Neurophysiol.*, 1967a, **23**, 225–240.

16. Elazar, Z., & Adey, W. R. Electroencephalographic correlates of learning in subcortical and cortical structures. *EEG clin. Neurophysiol.*, 1967b, **23**, 306–319.

17. Fetz, E. E. Operant conditioning of cortical unit activity. *Science*, 1969, **163**, 955–958.

18. Fox, S. S., & O'Brien, J. H. Duplication of evoked potential waveform by curve of probability of firing of a single cell. *Science*, 19 February 1965, **147**, 888–890.

19. Fox, S. S., & Rudell, A. P. Operant controlled neural event: Formal and systematic approach to electrical coding of behavior in brain. *Science*, 1968, **162**, 1299–1302.

20. Galambos, R. Electrical correlates of conditioned learning. In *The central nervous system and behavior (first conference)*. Mary A. B. Brazier, Ed. New York: Josiah Macy, Jr. Foundation, 1959, 375–415.

21. Galambos, R., & Sheatz, G. S. An electroencephalograph study of classical conditioning. *Amer. J. Physiol.*, 1962, **203**, 173–184.

22. Gastaut, H. Etat actuel des connaissances sur l'électroencéphalographie du conditionnement. Colloque de Marseille. *EEG clin. Neurophysiol.*, 1957, Suppl. 6, 133–160.

23. Gastaut, H., Jus, A., Jus, C., Morrell, F., Storm Van Leeuwen, W., Dongier, S., Naquet, R., Regis, H., Roger, A., Bekkering, D., Kamp, A., & Werre, J. Etude topographique des réactions électroencéphalographiques conditionées chez l'homme. *EEG clin. Neurophysiol.*, 1957, **9**, 1–34.

24. Gilden, L., Vaughn, H. G., Jr., & Costa, L. D. Summated human EEG potentials with voluntary movements. *EEG clin. Neurophysiol.*, 1966, **20**, 433–438.

25. Grastyán, E., Lissak, K., Madarasz, I., & Donhoffer, H. Hippocampal electrical activity during the development of conditioned reflexes. *EEG clin. Neurophysiol.*, 1959, **11**, 409–430.

26. Green, J. D., & Arduini, A. Hippocampal electrical activity in arousal. *J. Neurophysiol.*, 1954, **17**, 533–557.

27. Gumnit, R. The distribution of direct current responses evoked by sounds in the auditory cortex of the cat. *EEG clin. Neurophysiol.*, 1961, **13**, 889–895.

28. Hernández-Peón, R. Neurophysiological correlates of habituation and other manifestations of plastic inhibition (internal inhibition). In *The Moscow colloquium on electroencephalography of higher nervous activity*. H. H. Jasper & G. D. Smirnov, Eds. *EEG clin. Neurophysiol.*, 1960, Suppl. 13, 101–114.

29. Hull, C. L. *Essentials of behavior*. New Haven, Conn.: Yale Univ. Press, 1951.

30. Irwin, D. A., Rebert, C. S., McAdam, D. W., & Knott, J. R. Slow potential changes (CNV) in the human EEG as a function of motivational variables. *EEG clin. Neurophysiol.*, 1966, **21**, 412–413.

31. Izquierdo, I., Wyrwicka, Wanda, Sierra, G., & Segundo, J. P. Etablissement d'un reflexe de trace pendant le sommeil naturel chez le chat. *Actualités Neurophysiol.*, 1965, **6**, 277–296.

32. Jasper, H. H., & Shagass, C. Conditioning the occipital alpha rhythm in man. *J. exp. Psychol.*, 1941, **28**, 373–388.

33. Jasper, H. H., Ricci, G. F., & Doane, B. Patterns of cortical neuronal discharge during conditioned responses in monkeys. In *Ciba Foundation symposium on the neurological basis of behaviour*. G. E. W. Wolstenholme & Cecilia M. O'Connor, Eds. Boston: Little, Brown, 1958, pp. 277–294.

34. John, E. R. Neural mechanisms of decision making. In *Information storage and neural control*. W. S. Fields & W. Abbott, Eds. Springfield, Ill.: Thomas, 1963, pp. 243–282.

35. John, E. R. *Mechanisms of memory*. New York: Academic Press, 1967.

36. John, E. R., & Ahn, H. Unpublished observations, 1966. Cited in John, E. R. *Mechanisms of memory*. New York: Academic Press, 1967.

37. John, E. R., & Killam, K. F. Electrophysiological correlates of avoidance conditioning in the cat. *J. Pharmacol. exp. Therap.*, 1959, **125**, 252–274.

38. John, E. R., & Killam, K. F. Studies of electrical activity of brain during differential conditioning in cats. In *Recent advances in biological psychiatry*. Vol. II. J. Wortis, Ed. New York: Grune & Stratton, 1960a.
39. John, E. R., & Killam, K. F. Electrophysiological correlates of differential approach-avoidance conditioning in cats. *J. nerv. ment. Dis.*, 1960b, **136**, 183–201.
40. John, E. R., Shimokochi, M., & Bartlett, F. Neural readout from memory during generalization. *Science*, 1969, **164**, 1519–1521.
41. Jouvet, M., & Hernández-Peón, R. The neurophysiological mechanisms concerning habituation, attention and conditioning. *EEG clin. Neurophysiol.*, 1957, Suppl. 6, 39–49.
42. Kandel, E. R., & Tauc, L. Augmentation prolongée de l'efficacité d'une voie afférente d'un ganglion isolé après l'activation couplée d'une voie plus efficace. *J. Physiol. (Paris)*, 1963, **55**, 271–272.
43. Kandel, E. R., & Tauc, L. Mechanisms of prolonged heterosynaptic facilitation in a giant ganglion cell of aplysia depilans. *Nature*, 1964, **202**, 145–147.
44. Key, B. J., & Bradley, P. B. The effect of drugs on conditioned arousal responses. *EEG clin. Neurophysiol.*, 1959, **11**, 841.
45. Knott, J. R., & Henry, C. E. The conditioning of the blocking of the alpha rhythm of the human electroencephalogram. *J. exp. Psychol.*, 1941, **28**, 134–144.
46. Kogan, A. B. The manifestation of processes of higher nervous activity in the electrical potentials of the cortex during free behavior of animals. In *The Moscow colloquium on electroencephalography of higher nervous activity*. H. H. Jasper & G. D. Smirnov, Eds. *EEG clin. Neurophysiol.*, 1960, Suppl. 13, 51–64.
47. Köhler, W., & Wegener, J. Currents of the human auditory cortex. *J. cell. comp. Physiol.*, 1955, **45** (Suppl. 1), 25–54.
48. Kornhuber, H. H., & Deecke, L. Hirnpotentialänderungen bei Willkürbewegungen und passiven Bewegungen des Menschen: Bereitschafts Potential und reafferente Potentiale. *Pflüg. Arch. ges. Physiol.*, 1965, **284**, 1–17.
49. Kuffler, S. W., Nicholls, J. G., & Orkand, R. V. Physiological properties of glial cells in the central nervous system of amphibia. *J. Neurophysiol.*, 1966, **29**, 768–787.
50. Leaton, R. N. Effects of scopolamine on exploratory motivated behavior. *J. comp. physiol. Psychol.*, 1968, **66**, 524–527.
51. Lesse, H. Electrographic recordings of amygdaloid activity during a conditioned response. *Fed. Proc.*, 1957, **16**, 79.
52. Lesse, H. Rhinencephalic electrophysiological activity during "emotional behavior" in cats. *Psychiat. Res. Rep. Amer. psychiat. Ass.*, 1960, **12**, 224–237.
53. Liberson, W. T., & Ellen, P. Conditioning of the driven brain wave rhythm in the cortex and the hippocampus of the rat. In *Recent advances in biological psychiatry*. Vol. II. J. Wortis, Ed. New York: Grune and Stratton, 1960, pp. 158–171.
54. Lickey, M. E., & Fox, S. S. Localization and habituation of sensory evoked D. C. responses in cat cortex. *Exp. Neurol.*, 1966, **15**, 437–454.
55. Lindsley, D. F., Chow, K. L., & Gollender, M. Dichoptic interactions of lateral geniculate neurons of cats to contralateral and ipsilateral eye stimulation. *J. Neurophysiol.*, 1967, **30**, 628–644.
56. McAdam, D., Snodgrass, L., Knott, J. R., & Ingram, W. R. Some preliminary observations of electrical changes in deep brain structures during acquisition of a classical conditioned response. *EEG clin. Neurophysiol.*, 1961, **13**, 146.
57. McAdam, D. W., Irwin, D. A., Rebert, C. S., & Knott, J. R. Conative control of the contingent negative variation. *EEG clin. Neurophysiol.*, 1966, **13**, 1553–1593.
58. Morrell, F. Electroencephalographic studies of conditioned learning. In *The central nervous system and behavior (first conference)*. Mary A. B. Brazier, Ed. New York: Josiah Macy, Jr. Foundation, 1959, pp. 307–374.
59. Morrell, F. Microelectrode and steady potential studies suggesting a dendritic locus of closure. In *The Moscow colloquium on electroencephalography of higher nervous activity*. H. H. Jasper & G. D. Smirnov, Eds. *EEG clin. Neurophysiol.*, 1960, Suppl. 13, 65–80.
60. Morrell, F. Effect of anodal polarization on the firing pattern of single cortical cells. *Ann. N. Y. Acad. Sci.*, 1961, **92**, 860–876.
61. Morrell, F. Information storage in nerve cells.

In *Information storage and neural control*. W. S. Fields & W. Abbott, Eds. Springfield, Ill.: Thomas, 1963, pp. 189–229.

62. Morrell, F., & Naitoh, P. Effect of cortical polarization on a conditioned avoidance response. *Exp. Neurol.* 1962, **6**, 507–523.

63. Morrell, F., Engle, J., & Bouris, W. Unpublished observations, 1966. Cited in John, E. R. *Mechanisms of memory*. New York: Academic Press, 1967.

64. Motokawa, K. Electroencephalograms of man in the generalization and differentiation of conditioned reflexes. *Tohoku J. exp. Med.*, 1949, **50**, 225–234.

65. Motokawa, K., & Huzimori, B. Electroencephalograms and conditioned reflexes. *Tohoku J. exp. Med.*, 1949, **50**, 215–223.

66. Norton, S., & Jewett, R. E. Frequencies of slow potential oscillations in the cortex of cat. *EEG clin. Neurophysiol.*, 1965, **19**, 377–386.

67. Olds, J. Operant conditioning of single unit responses. *Proc. XXIII Intern. Conf. Physiol. Sci., Tokyo*, 1965a, IV, 372–380.

68. Olds, J. Operant control of tegmental neuron patterns. *Fed. Proc.*, 1965b, **24**, 522.

69. Olds, J. The central nervous system and the reinforcement of behavior. *Amer. Psychologist*, 1969, **24**, 114–132.

70. Olds, J., & Olds, Marianne E. Interference and learning in palaeocortical systems. In *Brain mechanisms and learning*. J. F. Delafresnaye, A. Fessard, R. W. Gerard, & J. Konorski, Eds. Oxford: Blackwell Scientific, 1961, pp. 153–187.

71. Orkand, R. K., Nicholls, J. G., & Kuffler, S. W. The effect of nerve impulses on the membrane potential of glial cells in the central nervous system of amphibia. *J. Neurophysiol.*, 1966, **29**, 788–806.

72. Pagano, R. R., & Gault, F. P. Amygdala activity: A central measure of arousal. *EEG clin. Neurophysiol.*, 1964, **17**, 255–260.

73. Pavlov, I. *Conditioned reflexes. An investigation of the physiological activity of the cerebral cortex.* New York: Oxford Univ. Press, 1927.

74. Rabinovich, M. Ia. The electrical activity in different layers of the cortex of the motor and acoustic analysers during the elaboration of conditional defensive reflexes. *Pavlov J. Higher Nerv. Activ.*, 1958, **8**, 507–519.

75. Rosenfeld, J. P., Rudell, A. P., & Fox, S. S. Operant control of neural events in humans. *Science*, 1969, **165**, 821–823.

76. Rowland, V. Conditioning and brain waves. *Scient. Amer.*, 1959, **201**, 89–96.

77. Rowland, V. Steady potential phenomena of cortex. In *The neurosciences, A Study Program*. G. C. Quarton, T. Melnechuk, & F. O. Schmitt, Eds. New York: Rockefeller Univ. Press, 1967.

78. Rowland, V. Cortical steady potential (direct current potential) in reinforcement and learning. In *Progress in physiological psychology. Vol. II.* E. Stellar & J. M. Sprague, Eds. New York: Academic Press, 1968, pp. 1–77.

79. Rowland, V., & Goldstone, M. Appetitively conditioned and drive-related bioelectric baseline shift in cat cortex. *EEG clin. Neurophysiol.*, 1963, **15**, 474–485.

80. Rowland, V., Bradley, H., School, P., & Deutschman, D. Cortical steady-potential shifts in conditioning. *Conditional Reflex*, 1967, **2**, 3–22.

81. Rusinov, V. S. An electrophysiological analysis of the connecting function in the cerebral cortex in the presence of a dominant area. *Intern. Congr. Physiol.*, 19th, Montreal, 1953, Abstr., 719.

82. Sheer, D. E. Electrophysiological correlates of memory consolidation. In *Molecular mechanisms in memory and learning*. G. Ungar, Ed. New York: Plenum Press, 1970, pp. 177–211.

83. Tecce, J. J., & Scheff, N. M. Attention reduction and suppressed direct-current potentials in the human brain. *Science*, 1969, **164**, 331–333.

84. Vanderwolf, C. H. Limbic-diencephalic mechanisms of voluntary movement. *Psychol. Rev.*, 1971, **78**, 83–113.

85. Walter, W. G. The contingent negative variation. An electrical sign of significant association in the human brain. *Science*, 1964a, **146**, 434.

86. Walter, W. G. The convergence and interaction of visual, auditory and tactile responses in human nonspecific cortex. *Ann. N. Y. Acad. Sci.*, 1964b, **112**, 320–361.

87. Walter, W. G. Slow potential changes in the human brain associated with expectancy, decision and intention. *EEG clin. Neurophysiol.*, 1967, Suppl. 26, 123–130.

88. Weinberger, N. M., Velasco, M., & Lindsley, D. B. The relationship between cortical synchrony and behavioral inhibition. *EEG clin. Neurophysiol.*, 1967, **23**, 297–305.

89. Wyrwicka, Wanda, Sterman, M. B., & Clemente, C. D. Conditioning of induced electroencephalographic sleep patterns in the cat. *Science*, 1962, **137**, 616–618.

90. Yoshii, N., & Ogura, H. Studies on the unit discharge of brainstem reticular formation in the cat. I. Changes of reticular unit discharge following conditioning procedure. *Med. J. Osaka Univ.*, 1960, **11**, 1–17.

91. Yoshii, N., Shimokochi, M., Miyamoto, K., & Ito, M. Studies on the neural basis of behavior by continuous frequency analysis of EEG. In *Progress in brain research. Vol. 21a. Correlative neurosciences: fundamental mechanisms.* T. Tokizane & J. P. Schadé, Eds. Amsterdam: Elsevier, 1966, pp. 217–250.

92. Young, G. A., & Black, A. H. The relationships between electrical activity of the hippocampus and overt skeletal behavior in the dog and rat. Paper presented at the meeting of the Eastern Psychological Association, Atlantic City, N. J., April, 1970.

Chapter 19

BIOCHEMISTRY AND NEUROPHARMACOLOGY OF LEARNING AND MEMORY

Effects Learning on Brain Chemistry

Transfer of Training by Brain Extracts

Effects of Drugs on Acquisition

Effects of Drugs on Recall

State-Dependent Learning

Review

EFFECTS OF LEARNING ON BRAIN CHEMISTRY

Introduction

Techniques for the examination of the chemical composition of small samples of brain tissue have been developed in recent years. It has thus become possible to ask whether learning can be shown to result in transient or permanent changes in some chemical reaction and, more specifically, whether such changes might be unique to some areas of the brain. This approach has produced some provocative observations, but we must exercise caution in their interpretation. The search for localized biochemical results of learning or consolidation not only assumes that learning produces unique changes in geographically specified gross subdivisions of the brain but requires that the changes which are produced by a relatively brief exposure to a learning situation are sufficiently large to be detectable by our still very crude assay techniques. Since no portion of the brain appears to be essential for learning, at least in the infrahuman species used in this research, and since there is little electrophysiological evidence for a selective activation of any particular area during learning or recall, the first assumption must be questioned. If one considers the literally millions of learning experiences to which an animal is exposed during infancy, childhood, and adulthood, the second assumption becomes similarly open to criticism.

One may counter both arguments by pointing to the literature which, as we shall see in a moment, seems to show that quite massive changes in RNA-, protein-, or transmitter-metabolism do take place in specific portions of the brain in the course of learning. The apparent success of the biochemical assay techniques makes it important for us to discuss some of these findings. It does not, however, provide sufficient assurance that the observed biochemical changes are specifically related to learning or memory. Simple activation of neural pathways produces similar biochemical changes,[122, 146] and it has, as yet, been impossible to isolate learning-related changes from these general indicators of activity.

Hydén[88] has suggested that activation of neural pathways may produce quantitative changes in RNA or protein synthesis, whereas only learning-related activity results in the formation of novel RNA or protein molecules. Changes in the composition of RNA molecules have been observed in experiments involving the presentation of novel sensory stimuli rather than learning as we normally define it,[142] but it is possible to argue that the perception of any novel object may give rise to a memory trace that permits recognition of the object when it is presented again. Broadening the definition of learning in this fashion unfortunately complicates the investigation of "learning"-related phenomena enormously because the temporal contiguity of the CS and UCS may represent a novel compound stimulus in all learning situations.

The early experiments in this field were executed in laboratories that were not optimally equipped for behavioral research. These studies often failed to provide even some of the more rudimentary behavioral controls, and one is left to wonder whether the reported changes in biochemical processes might be caused by an activation of sensory, motor, motivational or, indeed, associative mechanisms. Behavioral controls are increasingly being included in contemporary research in this field, and recent studies seem to provide good evidence that biochemical changes can be observed in trained animals but not in animals that receive very similar treatments. The crux of the matter lies in the word "similar." One can be very clever in making the treatments of a trained animal and its "yoked control" very similar, but it is impossible to duplicate the conditions of the learning experiment exactly. The very fact that a specific response is rewarded may not only selectively activate specific segments of the sensory and motor systems but also produce changes in neural pathways related to reinforcement itself.

In spite of these many difficulties, much excitement is currently being generated by the apparent correlation of biochemical events and learning. We can expect significant advances in this area as refinements of biochemical assay techniques become available, particularly if sophisticated behavioral techniques can increasingly be incorporated into this research.

Content and Composition of RNA

Hydén's hypothesis that learning might involve the formation of novel RNA molecules (see Chapter 20) has received some experimental support from studies which demonstrate changes in the composition, quantity, or concentration of RNA in some parts of the brain. Hydén[89, 90] trained rats to walk up a thin long wire that was set at an angle of 45 degrees to the horizontal. The composition of RNA extracted from neurons of the vestibular nucleus of the brainstem was altered temporarily by this training but not by control procedures which were intended to produce activation of vestibular mechanisms without permitting learning (see Figure 19–1). Hydén suggested that this change in RNA composition might be unique to the vestibular nucleus (i.e., to the sensory system involved in the learning experience) since tissue taken from the midbrain reticular formation of trained rats did not show qualitative changes. The RNA composition of the vestibular neurons returned to normal 24 hours after the completion of training, suggesting that the synthesis of novel RNA molecules cannot, in this experiment, be essential to the maintenance of a memory trace. (The observed changes in RNA

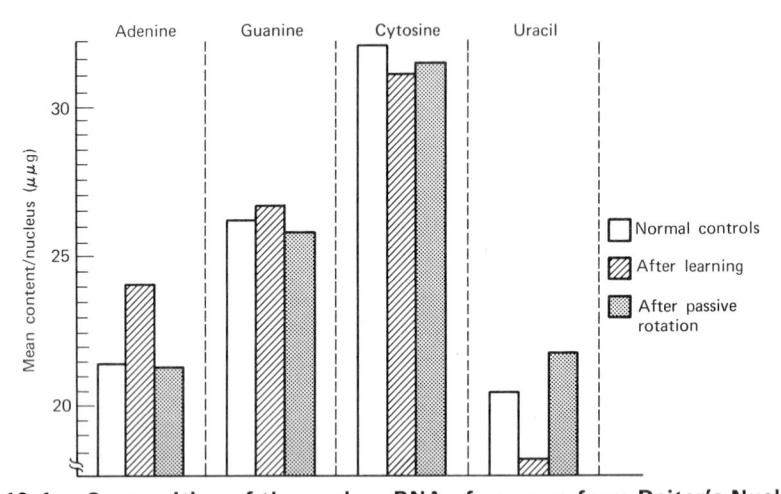

FIG. 19–1. Composition of the nuclear RNA of neurons from Deiter's Nucleus.
(Data from H. Hydén & E. Egyházi. Nuclear RNA changes of nerve cells during a learning experiment in rats. *Proc. Nat. Acad. Sci. U.S.*, **48**, 1962, 1366–1373.)

composition might nonetheless be important in the chain of events which leads to the consolidation of a permanent memory trace.) It is, unfortunately, not clear that learning rather than differential activation of some components of the vestibular system is responsible for the temporary production of novel RNA molecules. The control procedures undoubtedly resulted in an activation of some vestibular functions but probably involved different aspects of this complex system than the balancing learned by the experimental animals.

More recently, Hydén[91] has trained rats to reach into a tube to obtain bits of food. Rats, like people, have distinct "handedness" preferences and use consistently either the right or the left front paw in this test. Hydén permitted some rats to use the preferred paw and trained others to switch to the non-preferred one. He then examined the RNA extracted from tissue of the motor cortex involved in the movement of the front paws. He found that the RNA composition and concentration of tissue from the hemisphere which is contralateral to the non-preferred paw differed from that taken from the hemisphere ipsilateral to the non-preferred paw in animals which were trained to use it. No difference was seen in animals which were allowed to use their preferred paw. In spite of the neatness of the experiment, it is unfortunately not clear that the observed changes in RNA metabolism are caused by learning instead of the massive activation of previously inactive portions of the motor system or associated sensory feedback.

Several recent studies have attempted to study the role of RNA in learning by observing the uptake of precursors of RNA in selected regions of the brain. In several species and very different training situations, large increases in precursor uptake, which indicate a rise in RNA synthesis by as much as 50 percent, have been seen (see Figure 19–2). In one avoidance experiment, this change appeared to be limited to the diencephalon and other limbic structures.[173] One might be tempted to conclude that a reaction to the shock or threat of shock might be responsible for the observed RNA changes, but they were not seen in the brains of mice required to perform the avoidance response after some overtraining or in "yoked" control mice which received the same number of CS-UCS presentations as the trained animals but had no opportunity to make escape or avoidance responses.[1] These important control experiments suggest that the increased RNA synthesis that was observed in these experiments may indeed be specifically related to learning.

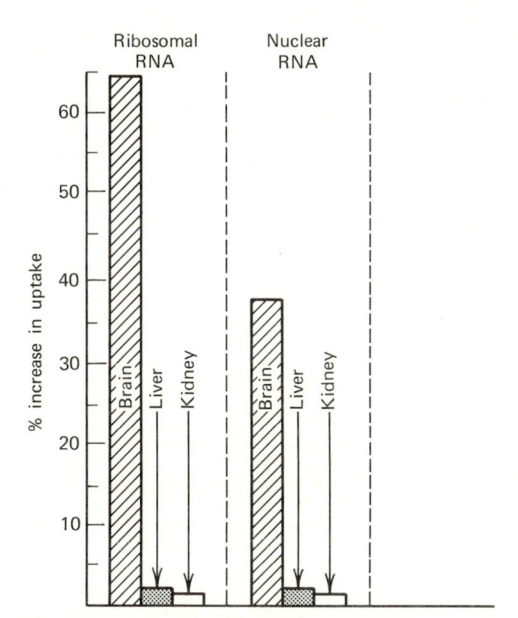

FIG. 19–2. Average percentage increase in the uptake of radioactivity labelled RNA precursors consequent to learning.
(Data from J. W. Zemp, J. E. Wilson, K. Schlesinger, W. O. Boggan, & E. Glassman. Brain function and macromolecules. I. Incorporation of uridine into RNA of mouse brain during short-term training experience. *Proc. Nat. Acad. Sci. U.S.*, **55**, 1966, 1422–1431.)

A somewhat different localization of learning-related changes in RNA synthesis has been reported in experiments using appetitive learning tasks. An analysis of the uptake of an RNA precursor into the brains of rats given prolonged training in a maze which involved repeated reversals of a position habit showed a significant increase in RNA synthesis only in the hippocampus and pyriform cortex.[22] The observed RNA changes may be related to learning since control animals trained to perform the same response but not given the reversal training did not show them. Unfortunately, the task requires response inhibition, and animals with hippocampal lesions are known to be deficient on all such tasks although they perform quite well in other more complicated situations.

In goldfish, it has been shown that training increases the incorporation of an intracranially injected RNA precursor in the entire brain. This effect (as well as memory) is blocked by injections of the protein-synthesis inhibitor, puromycin, suggesting that increased RNA synthesis may depend on the continued synthesis of new proteins.[151]

Some investigators have recently attempted to demonstrate the formation of novel RNA molecules during learning in hybridization experiments.[117, 118, 119] Under some conditions, RNA molecules attach themselves to the part of the gene that is responsible for their synthesis. Thus, if one adds RNA extracted from a particular part of the brain to a solution containing DNA from this region, the RNA will bind to the DNA and eventually saturate the related binding sites on the gene. If one then adds more of the *same* RNA to the solution, no uptake of it occurs. However, if one adds different RNA molecules, they find vacant binding sites on the gene and uptake occurs. If learning involves the formation of novel RNA molecules, extracts from "trained" brains should produce RNA uptake in solutions that are saturated with the RNA of "untrained" brains. This complex experiment has been attempted, and the preliminary results suggest that training in an avoidance situation may result in the formation of novel RNA molecules in rat brains.

Changes in RNA composition[93] or metabolism[41] have also been seen in planaria. These animals contract when shocked and can be trained to produce this response to a warning signal. Whether this is due to learning as we customarily define this term or to some form of sensitization is not clear. However, the response to the CS does reflect a change in the nervous system of the animal that occurs as a function of repeated exposure to the shock, and it is interesting that the acquisition of this reaction is correlated with RNA changes similar to those seen in trained mammals. Even more interesting, perhaps, is the observation that an enzyme which destroys RNA seems to interfere with the retention of the flexion response to the CS under some conditions. This has been shown in experiments[42] which take advantage of the fact that planaria regenerate when cut in half. The two halves of a "trained" planarian show evidence of "retention" after regeneration is completed. However, when the two halves are placed into a solution which contains an RNA-destroying enzyme, only the worm which is formed by regeneration of the tail seems to remember. The worms which must regenerate a head (and nearly all of the primitive nervous system of these animals) do not.

Protein Synthesis

Several investigators have attempted to demonstrate an effect of learning on protein synthesis in particular regions of the brain irrespective of the mechanisms responsible for these events. It has been reported that protein synthesis is selectively increased in some portions of the hippocampus[92] and the motor cortex[112] when rats are trained to reach for food with a previously "nonpreferred" paw (see discussion above). Training in a simple one-way avoidance situation has been reported to increase protein synthesis in the pyriform cortex and decrease it in sensory motor areas of the cortex. However,

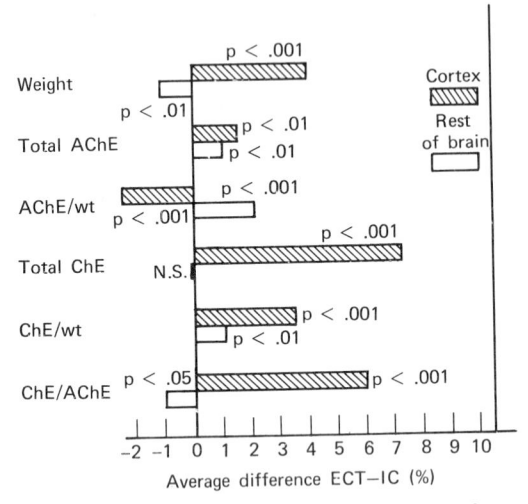

FIG. 19-4. Differences in brain weight, acetylcholinesterase (AChE), and less-specific cholinesterase (ChE), in the cortex and rest of brain of rats reared in a complex environment and exposed to behavioral training (ECT) and rats reared in impoverished conditions (IC).

(Data from M. R. Rosenzweig, E. L. Bennett, & M. C. Diamond. Chemical and anatomical plasticity of brain: Replications and extensions. In *Macromolecules and behavior* (2nd ed.). J. Gaito, Ed. New York: Appleton-Century-Crofts, 1972.)

the recorded changes were small and not always statistically significant.[63] Increases in specific types of proteins have been observed in the brains of pigeons trained to peck one of two keys for food rewards[19] (see Figure 19-3).

Acetylcholine and Acetylcholinesterase

Small but consistent differences in the content or concentration of acetylcholine or acetylcholinesterase have been observed when strains of rats that were genetically selected on the basis of their ancestors' superior or poor performance in a maze learning situation were compared.[149] Rats reared in "enriched complex environments" (i.e., large cages complete with toys and playmates) that are thought to offer optimal conditions for learning have also been reported to have somewhat different concentrations of ACh and AChE in the brain than rats reared in "impoverished conditions" (i.e., small cages isolated from environmental stimulation) (see Figure 19-4). The effects observed in

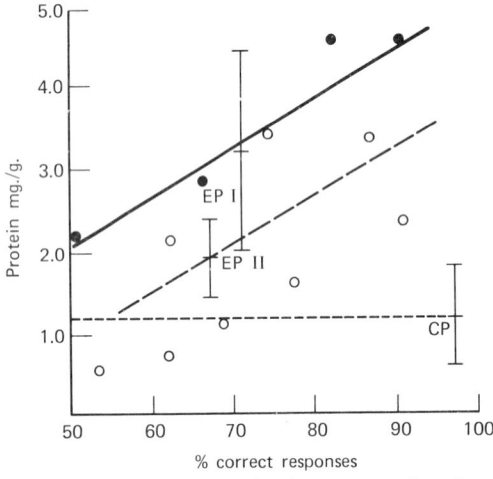

FIG. 19-3. Relationship between the frequency of correct responses and the presence of a particular protein (fraction 11A) in the brain of pigeons. EP-I (filled circles) and EP-II (open circles) are two groups of experimental animals. The dashed line labeled CP represents the average amount of this protein in the brains of untrained pigeons.

(From *The Biochemistry of Memory* by Samuel Bogoch. Copyright © 1968 by Oxford University Press, Inc. Reprinted by permission.)

these experiments appear to be consistent and replicable, but their implication for our understanding of learning-related functions is not clear. Although statistically reliable, the observed changes in ACh or AChE are very small, and their interpretation is complicated by concurrent changes in brain weight and nonspecific cholinesterase (ChE). Moreover, regional differences occur which complicate the picture further. For instance, rats that are reared in complex environments have significantly lower concentrations of AChE in all cortical areas than rats reared in "impoverished environments," but the rest of the brain shows a seemingly paradoxical concurrent increase in AChE concentration.

Summary and Review Questions

Learning which results in a change in behavior must produce modifications in neural functions and these, in turn, are based on subtle changes in some biochemical reactions. Some molecular biologists believe that recent technological advances in biochemistry may provide the tools needed to analyze the chemical events which occur in selected parts of the brain during learning. An interpretation of the findings in this very young field is complicated by the fact that any cellular reaction involves biochemical changes. We do not yet know how the biochemical reactions that may uniquely occur during learning differ from the many others that are responsible for other activities of the brain. Some possibly important changes in brain chemistry have recently been observed during or following learning, and increasingly elegant control experiments are being designed to demonstrate the specificity of these effects.

Hydén has suggested that learning might directly or indirectly involve a change in the composition of RNA molecules. This is supported by experiments which have shown qualitative changes in RNA synthesis in portions of the sensory or motor pathways that are activated during learning. Control experiments suggest that similar activation in the absence of training may produce only quantitative changes in RNA synthesis.

Quantitative changes in RNA and protein synthesis have also been seen in the hippocampus and associated temporal lobe structures following exposure to appetitively reinforced learning problems, and it has been suggested that a change in the normal activity of these structures (as reflected in an increase in RNA or protein-synthesis) may be the important event during learning. Similar changes in RNA synthesis have been seen in the diencephalon and associated limbic system structures during avoidance learning, again suggesting that an increased RNA or protein-synthesis may be a valid indicator of the participation of particular structures in learning or related processes.

The distribution of the transmitter acetylcholine or of an enzyme that destroys it in the brain seems to be affected by environmental complexity and early experience. It has not, however, been possible to relate the distribution of these substances to learning per se.

1. Discuss some of the difficulties encountered in the interpretation of the changes in brain chemistry that seem to occur during learning.

2. Describe the evidence which suggests that quantitative or qualitative changes in RNA and protein synthesis may occur in specific parts of the brain.

TRANSFER OF TRAINING BY BRAIN EXTRACTS

A great deal of interest and controversy has been aroused by recent reports of experiments purporting to demonstrate that memories can be "transferred" from one organism to another by injections of extracts from "trained" brains into naive animals. If true, this observation is of enormous significance because it would unequivocally show that memories are stored in biochemical form and that unique biochemical changes occur whenever an organism learns anything. Indeed, a transfer of the effects of training demands not only that very specific biochemical changes occur as a result of learning but also that these biochemical events are sufficiently specified in terms of the cells that produce them to affect only analogous cells in untrained animals.

When reports of successful transfer of training experiments first appeared, many investigators felt that the phenomenon was logically improbable and contradicted by well-established experimental evidence. The enormity of the implications of a transfer of the effects of training nonetheless goaded many into attempts to replicate and/or extend the initial findings. The results of these experiments have, unfortunately, been mixed. Many competent experimenters have been unable to produce any evidence for transfer of training in a variety of experimental situations.[29] Others have reported successful experiments, but the effects have been disappointingly small and often not statistically reliable.[147] A few investigators have produced consistent and significant transfer of training effects and have proceeded to refine the relevant biochemical and behavioral techniques. Some of the environmental variables that appear to be conducive to transfer of training have been described, and increasingly sophisticated assays of the components of the brain extracts that might be responsible for it have become available.[159, 147]

There are by now many reports of apparently successful transfer of training experiments, and it appears unlikely that the observed effects could be caused entirely by statistical or procedural artifact. It is entirely possible that what is transferred in these experiments is not a memory of a specific conditioned response but a more or less specific sensitization or desensitization of sensory or "attentional" processes. Attempts to eliminate this possibility by the demonstration of intramodality discriminations have not, so far, been successful. Even the transfer of a modality specific sensitization or desensitization due to experience would seem to be potentially important for our understanding of biochemical processes that might also be involved in learning. Moreover, a transfer of events more specifically related to learning, although not proven, has also not been ruled out.

That the effects of training might be "transferred" from one organism to another was first suggested by experiments on planaria. This little worm contracts when shocked and can be trained to contract in response to previously ineffective stimuli when the latter are repeatedly paired with shock. Whether this is a result of conditioning instead of sensitization or related phenomena has been the subject of much heated debate.[96, 110] The matter is a philosophical one since the nature of the answer depends on one's definition of learning. Whatever happens in this training situation to the primitive nervous system of the planarian does seem to transfer to another worm under some conditions. This was first shown in experiments where trained worms were chopped into little pieces and fed to untrained ones. The cannibals subsequently learned the same conditioned response faster than their controls.[109] Similar effects have been obtained with injections of RNA- and protein-rich extracts from trained "donors."[171]

Transfer of training has also been observed in more complex maze-learning situations. Here, the specificity of the learned response (selecting one of the two arms of the maze on the basis of brightness cues) is more obvious. The specificity of the transfer effect, unfortunately, is not. Planaria trained to select the same brightness cues as the cannibalized "donor" learn faster than normals but so do planaria trained to select the brightness that was incorrect for the cannibalized "donor."[111] It is clear that something transferred but not what.

It has also been reported that planaria learn a shock-reinforced contraction response to light more rapidly than normals after feeding previously shocked (but not trained) "donors."[164] Planaria fed donors which were previously trained not to respond to light also habituate significantly faster than normals.[168] These observations indicate that effects of training which are not traditionally called "learning" may transfer under some conditions. This raises questions about the possible influence of such variables on the transfer of apparently more specific conditioned responses. However, the fact that sensitization or desensitization can seemingly be transferred by cannibalization in the planarian does not rule out the possibility that the effects of learning may do so, too.

Subsequent experiments have attempted to demonstrate transfer of training in mammals in which conditioned responses of varying complexity are more easily established and identified. In 1965, four laboratories in different parts of the world (Czechoslovakia, Denmark, Texas, and California) independently reported that transfer of training could be obtained in the laboratory rat. The behavioral tasks included habituation of a startle response;[160] approaching a food cup;[5] pushing a panel in response to a compound CS;[143] or selecting one of the arms of a maze on the basis of brightness cues.[56] All of these effects were obtained by intraperitoneal injections of extracts from the brains of trained "donors" into naive animals before subjecting them to similar training.

Since these initial reports were published, transfer of training has been observed in many different training situations. However, many investigators have been unable to obtain such effects, and it is clear that the phenomenon is difficult to demonstrate. Just what environmental or biochemical variables determine the outcome of transfer of training experiments has been the subject of many recent studies.

One of the simplest paradigms—habituation—has consistently produced positive effects in at least one laboratory and seems to provide evidence for a transfer of modality-specific changes in reactivity.[159] Significant repeatable transfer effects have also been seen in simple passive avoidance situations where rats must inhibit an innate tendency to enter dark places or to step down from a confining platform[159] (see Figure 19-5). Other seemingly simple classical conditioning paradigms have not permitted the demonstration of transfer effects,[104] and simplicity per se does not appear to be an important variable. The apparently simple paradigms used by some of the investigators who first reported positive effects[5] have not allowed

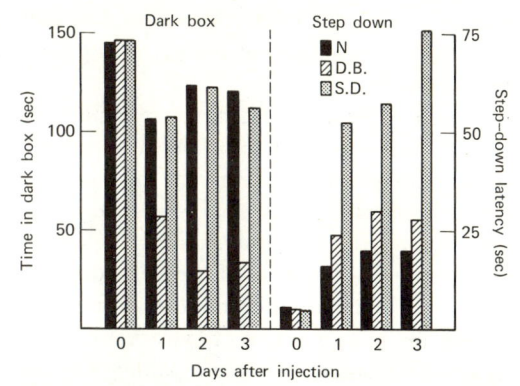

FIG. 19-5. Transfer of training in two passive-avoidance situations. Half of the "donors" were trained to avoid a dark box, the other half to avoid stepping down from a small platform. The data shown at left represent the average time in the dark box (TDB) on subsequent tests given to naive animals injected with brain extracts from untrained animals (solid bars); or with brain extracts from animals trained to avoid the dark box (cross-hatched bars) or with brain extracts from animals trained to avoid stepping down from a small platform (stippled bars).

The data shown on the right represent the average latency to stepping down from a platform of naive animals injected with brain extracts from untrained animals (solid bars), or with brain extracts from animals trained to avoid the dark box (cross-hatched bars) or with brain extracts from animals trained to avoid stepping down from the same platform (stippled bars). Note (1) there is evidence of significant "transfer" in both situations, and (2) the effect appears to be specific to the training situations (i.e., recipients of brains from dark-box avoiders don't do better in the step-down test and recipients of brains from step-down avoiders don't do better in the dark-avoidance situation.

(From G. Ungar. Role of proteins and peptides in learning and memory. In *Molecular mechanisms in memory and learning.* G. Ungar, Ed. Plenum Press, 1970.)

replication by others.[29] On the other hand, more complex behavioral training paradigms have been reported to be well suited to the demonstration of such effects.[147] There is some indication that transfer of training effects are more easily obtained when animals are trained to make a distinct response (such as turning left) in response to a distinct cue (such as the presence or absence of illumination), but this alone is no guarantee for success. The duration of training also seems to be a factor in these experiments, only relatively recent but well established memories seemingly being able to transfer.[147]

Several investigators have reported so-called "inversion" effects. In these experiments, rats which are given injections of brain extracts from a donor trained to go left or towards the light show a preference for right or dark choices. There is, moreover, some evidence that different doses of the same extract or the same dose of extracts obtained at different stages of training may produce positive or negative transfer effects.[147] Such findings emphasize that we must be cautious in interpreting any transfer of training in terms of its implications for learning or memory.

Much research has been devoted to the nature of the active ingredient of brain extracts which do permit whatever transfer of training occurs. A variety of different extraction procedures have been used. It is probable that few, if any, laboratories employ precisely the same extracts because many of the variables that seem to affect their potency and consistency are only gradually becoming known.[147, 159]

All extracts contain RNA, proteins, peptides, and some sugars in varying concentrations. Most of the experimenters in this field initially believed, in accordance with the then dominant biochemical explanation of learning, that the active ingredient might be RNA. However, it has been shown that the large RNA molecules probably do not cross the blood-brain barrier in significant quantities[108] and that procedures which tend to inactivate RNA or eliminate it from the extract do not interfere with the transfer effect. Most contemporary investigators consequently hold that the active substance must be a small molecule which is most probably a peptide.[159, 147]

Summary and Review Questions

One of the exciting, if still controversial, developments in this field has been the possibility that some of the biochemical changes that occur during learning may be transferable to another organism. It is not yet clear that whatever transfers represents memory traces instead of the results of sensitization or desensitization of certain sensory or motor functions, but the chemical transfer of even such changes seems to be of significance. The transfer phenomenon is unfortunately very elusive, perhaps because we do not yet know how to set up optimal environmental conditions for it or precisely how to treat the brain extract to make sure that the active ingredient stays viable. There are, however, over 100 reports of positive effects, and it seems unlikely that statistical or procedural gremlins can be blamed for all of them.

Transfer of some effects of training has been observed in habituation experiments as well as in more complex experiments requiring discriminated responses to specific stimuli. The transfer of training effect occurs apparently more easily when the subjects are required to make (or inhibit) very distinct responses to intense sensory stimuli in situations involving positive instead of negative reinforcement.

The composition of the molecules which are responsible for whatever transfer there may be is not yet known. Macromolecules such as RNA are, however, unlikely candidates because they do not cross the blood-brain barrier in significant quantities.

1. Describe a typical "transfer of training" experiment.

2. Describe the environmental conditions which appear to be conducive to the demonstration of transfer of training.

3. Discuss the implications of an experiment which *proves* that transfer of training occurs. Would it be important if explanations of the effect in terms of modality-specific sensitization or desensitization could not be ruled out?

EFFECTS OF DRUGS ON ACQUISITION

Cholinergic Mechanisms

Several investigators[24, 46] have suggested that an increase in the availability and/or release of a neurohumoral transmitter may be responsible for the synaptic facilitation which is believed to occur as a consequence of learning. We do not, as yet, know enough about the many potential transmitters in the central nervous system to evaluate this possibility in general. However, we do know a good deal about one transmitter—acetylcholine (ACh)—and can use it as a model to see what kind of experimental evidence there is for these hypotheses.

The possibility that pathways specifically related to learning, consolidation, or recall may be cholinergically mediated has been investigated in recent experiments that have tested the prediction that (1) learning should increase the total amount of ACh liberated in the brain; (2) drugs which protect ACh from destruction (such as diisopropyl fluorophosphate [DFP]) should improve acquisition or memory retrieval; and (3) drugs which interfere with or block the action of ACh (such as atropine or scopolamine) should interfere with acquisition, consolidation, or retrieval. There is experimental evidence in support of some of these predictions, and we shall presently look at some examples from this literature. A few words of caution may first be in order.

Many central cholinergic pathways are not in any way related to learning or memory storage but subserve sensory, motor, or motivational functions. Moreover, all skeletal motor functions are mediated cholinergically, and systemic injections of drugs which modify cholinergic transmission undoubtedly produce gross motor deficits. These "side effects" make it difficult to interpret any behavioral changes seen after systemic or central injections of drugs that modify transmission at cholinergic synapses. Indeed, many investigators have discussed the behavioral effects of cholinergic drugs and related blockers in terms of attention or inhibitory functions instead of learning (see below). Since attention and response inhibition are integral components of all learning situations, it has been difficult to rule out these alternative interpretations.

Systemic or Central Injections of Cholinergics or Acetylcholinesterase Inhibitors

Systemic injections of diisopropyl fluorophosphate (DFP) inhibit central as well as peripheral acetylcholinesterase (AChE). Within some limits, this should facilitate cholinergically mediated pathways because a reduced AChE level permits a more prolonged action of a given quantity of ACh. However, at some point this facilitation turns into inhibition because prolonged depolarization of a postsynaptic membrane prevents the transient electrochemical events which are the source of propagated action potentials.

Several investigators have used chronic systemic injections of DFP to study the role of cholinergically mediated pathways in learning and/or recall.[150, 144, 6] The results are consistently negative. A chronic reduction of AChE activity up to 75 percent of normal does not facilitate or impair acquisition of conditioned avoidance food-rewarded responses. Even smaller chronic reductions in AChE level produce perseverative responding during extinction in aversive as well as appetitive test situations, but these effects do not appear to be caused by a change in learning ability and may not even have been the result of a change in the central level of AChE activity.[67]

Systemic injections of drugs that stimulate or facilitate transmission at cholinergic synapses have been reported to facilitate acquisition when administered in low doses but to interfere when given in high doses (presumably because very high concentrations of the transmitter produce prolonged postsynaptic depolarization, which does not permit the conduction of discrete action potentials). The best example of this biphasic effect is nicotine. Single low doses of nicotine facilitate avoidance[20] as well as appetitively reinforced maze learning[145] (see Figure 19-6), and even repeated "fuming" with tobacco smoke has been reported to have beneficial effects on maze learning.[136] Larger doses of nicotine or prolonged exposure to tobacco smoke have been reported to

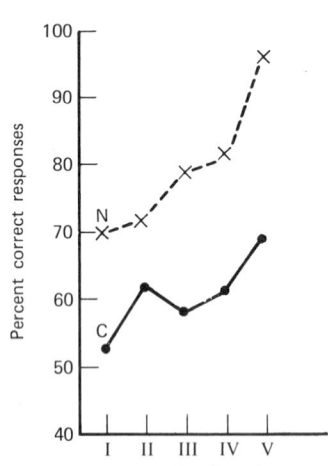

FIG. 19-6. Effects of nicotine on visual discrimination learning. Discrimination between the patterns ▲ as positive and △ as negative using a two-choice Thompson-Bryant apparatus. Each point represents the mean of 10 rats during 20 consecutive trials. C, control group; N, nicotine treated animals (0.2 mg/kg s.c. 15 minutes before each daily test).

(From F. Bovet-Nitti. Facilitation of simultaneous visual discrimination by nicotine in the rat. *Psychopharmacologia*, **10**, 1966, 59–66. Berlin-Heidelberg-New York: Springer.)

impair avoidance[51] learning as well as maze learning.[136]

Microinjections of cholinergic substances directly into various portions of the brain have resulted in a variety of behavioral effects suggesting that cholinergic synapses are represented at all levels of the central nervous system and contribute to a wide variety of functions. Injections of cholinergic drugs such as carbachol into the midline or reticular nuclei of the thalamus interfere with the acquisition of avoidance responses (see Figure 19-7) as well as recently acquired food or water rewarded instrumental behaviors.[77] The same injections do not interfere with "unlearned" behavior such as escape, feeding, or drinking, suggesting a drug effect on pathways that are somehow related to acquisition or recall. Microinjections of cholinergics into the midbrain reticular formation facilitate the acquisition of avoidance responses[71, 72] but interfere with the acquisition of food-reinforced brightness discriminations in a maze.[74] Although a modification of associative functions cannot be ruled out in these experiments, it appears likely that these effects result from a change in the organism's level of general reactivity.

Carbachol injections into the septal area completely prevent the acquisition of avoidance responses[69] and reduce the rate of lever pressing for food as well as water rewards, although food intake is not modified and water intake actually increased by the injection.[126] It is, once again, difficult to rule out drug effects on pathways that may be directly or indirectly related to learning or memory, but the overall pattern of effects as well as the results of lesions in this portion of the brain suggest that the observed behavioral changes may instead be caused by a facilitation of inhibitory processes and, perhaps, a modification of the organism's reaction to punishment.

Carbachol injections into the amygdaloid complex result in long-persisting deficits in avoidance learning,[15, 68] but the acquisition of food-rewarded discrimination responses appears to be normal.[14] A careful examination

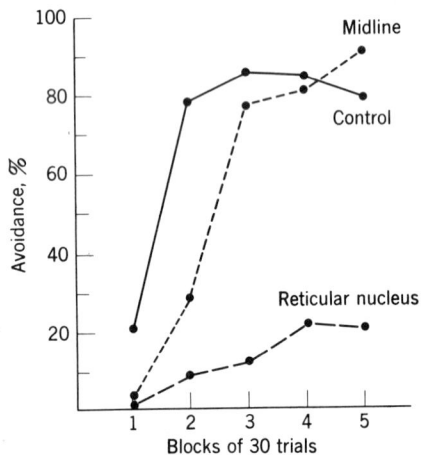

FIG. 19-7. Avoidance learning in a shuttle box following cholinergic stimulation of the midline thalamus (·----·); or reticular nucleus (·——·).

(From S. P. Grossman, R. H. Peters, P. E. Freedman, & H. I. Willer. Behavioral effects of cholinergic stimulation of the thalamic reticular formation. *J. comp. physiol. Psychol.*, **59**, 1965, 57–65. Copyright 1965 by the American Psychological Association, and reproduced by permission.)

of these effects indicates that the observed impairment in avoidance learning appears to be related to a change in affective reactivity instead of an inhibition of associative processes.[14]

Effects of Systemic or Central Injections of Anticholinergics

Systemic injections of drugs such as scopolamine, which block transmission at central as well as peripheral cholinergic synapses, typically result in perseveration in previously correct but no longer rewarded or even punished behaviors and thus interfere with the acquisition of passive avoidance behavior, reversal learning, alternation responses, and habituation.[31, 80] A disinhibition of unrewarded behavior may also account for the observation that such drugs enhance the rate of performance of many intermittently reinforced conditioned responses.[94, 64, 18] Not so easily explained in these terms is the finding that these drugs also facilitate the acquisition of discrete trial avoidance behavior,[103, 80] but it is not clear that this effect should be attributed to mechanisms specifically related to associative functions.

Attempts to study the site of scopolamine action in the brain have shown that scopolamine injections into the ventromedial hypothalamus[70, 120] and medial septal area[69, 97, 80] produce effects on active as well as passive avoidance behavior that are essentially identical to those seen after systemic administration of this drug. Atropine injections into midline thalamic nuclei[76] or amygdaloid nuclei[15] also enhance the acquisition of active avoidance behavior, but the general behavioral reaction to these injections suggests that mechanisms not specifically related to acquisition or recall may be involved.

Adrenergic Mechanisms

Many investigators have studied the effects of epinephrine and related drugs such as norepinephrine and amphetamine on learning and the performance of learned behaviors because (1) the adrenal secretion of epinephrine is an important aspect of the organism's reaction to stress and (2) epinephrine acts as a synaptic transmitter at some peripheral synapses and norepinephrine appears to perform similar functions in many parts of the brain.

Somewhat suprisingly, the removal of the adrenal cortex (which abolishes the release of epinephrine in response to stress) produces little or no effect on the acquisition of avoidance behaviors.[125, 106] The administration of epinephrine similarly fails to affect the acquisition of avoidance responses,[156] although some exceptions to this rule have been reported.[152, 102] Changes in avoidance learning have been reported following microinjections of norepinephrine into the midbrain reticular formation, but this effect seems to be related to a general change in arousal instead of an action on pathways mediating learning.[72]

Amphetamine is not itself a neurotransmitter, but it modifies neural activity in many portions of the brain, presumably by its effects on synaptic mechanisms that release or are activated by norepinephrine and related neurohumors. Systemic injections of amphetamine significantly facilitate the acquisition as well as the performance of avoidance behavior in a wide variety of test situations (see Figure 19–8).[161, 81] Food and

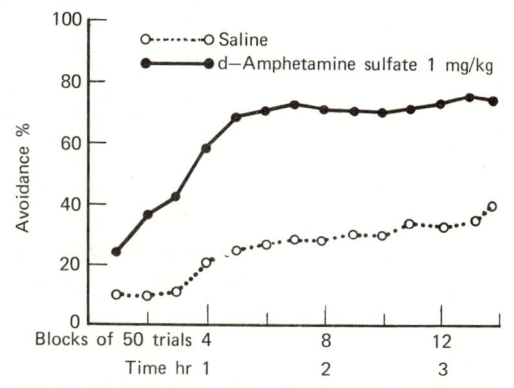

FIG. 19–8. Enhancement of avoidance learning by d-amphetamine. The drug was injected i.p. 30 min prior to the beginning of the session. Each point represents an average of 12 animals.

(From A. S. Kulkarni. Facilitation of instrumental avoidance learning by amphetamine: an analysis. *Psychopharmacologia*, **13**, 1968, 418–425. Berlin-Heidelberg-New York: Springer.)

water rewarded responding is typically increased (although ad libitum intake is depressed) when the reward contingencies generate low rates of behavior, but it is depressed when they generate high rates of responding.[33] It is unlikely that these effects are due to a drug effect on mechanisms specifically related to learning, consolidation, or recall.

Other Drugs

Systemic injections of CNS depressants such as barbiturates typically impair acquisition, but the cause of the deficit is as yet poorly understood. Impairments have been seen when these drugs are given after each daily learning trial[170] or when repeated injections are given as much as 40 days before the beginning of training.[121] Even a single dose of pentobarbital, given to rat mothers 19 1/2 days after conception, has been reported to result in significant learning deficits when the offspring were tested in adulthood.[4] Depressants given immediately before training also retard acquisition, but it is not clear that this impairment is specifically related to an interference with memory storage, consolidation, or retrieval. Several investigators[148, 124] have reported that low doses of pentobarbital retard acquisition but do not interfere with performance of a previously learned response, but this may demonstrate only the well known fact that behavior is particularly easily disrupted during acquisition.

Reports that a particular drug might facilitate learning or recall typically generate a good deal of attention, not only because they promise to contribute to our understanding of the mechanisms involved in learning but also because of the obvious practical implications of such a discovery. Many false alarms have been sounded because drugs can enhance acquisition, or more correctly, performance during acquisition, by modifying nonassociative processes such as general attention, alertness, and reactivity to shock or positive reward. It may be worthwhile to mention some of the more celebrated cases since the literature is often slow in correcting inappropriate impressions.

One of the historically famous cases dates back to a report, published nearly 30 years ago, that glutamic acid, one of the non-essential amino acids, might facilitate learning.[174] Interest in this drug remained high for many years because some investigators subsequently seemed to obtain positive effects, particularly in dull animals.[85, 86] Unfortunately, most attempts to replicate these findings have not been successful.[155, 87]

More recently, a good deal of excitement was generated by the suggestion that pre- as well as post-training injections of magnesium pemoline, a drug which may affect brain RNA metabolism,[66] seemed to facilitate acquisition and recall of avoidance behaviors.[138, 139, 52] Subsequent experiments[62, 140] have indicated that whatever effects magnesium pemoline may have are probably related to a general stimulant effect instead of a specific action on pathways concerned with learning or memory.

Summary and Review Questions

Many drugs affect behavior during learning, but these effects are usually not specifically related to a change in the organism's ability to learn. Our brief review concentrated on drugs that inhibit or facilitate neurohumoral transmission in the brain because it is often suggested that the synaptic facilitation that is widely thought to occur during learning might be caused by an increase in the availability of a transmitter.

There is very little evidence that drugs which facilitate or inhibit the transmission of signals at central cholinergic synapses facilitate or interfere with acquisition per se. This conclusion must be tempered by the fact that we often do not know how complete an inhibition a particular treatment produces or how much facilitation of synaptic mechanisms may indeed result in a blockade instead of an enhancement of neural transmission. Cholinergic drugs and related blocking agents do affect behavior in predictable ways in many learning situations, but this appears to be mainly because of a drug action on neural mechanisms related to inhibition, attentional processes, or the organism's reaction to nonreward or punishment. The apparent failure of these drugs to basically modify the course of acquisition is surprising since there is some evidence (see below) that the process of consolidation can be significantly affected by cholinergic drugs and related blockers.

Drugs that modify transmission at adrenergic synapses also modify behavior in various appetitive and aversive test situations, but it is again clear that this is not caused by a drug action on pathways specifically related to learning or recall.

Barbiturates seem to interfere with learning and/or recall under many situations, but the specificity of this effect has not yet been established.

1. Review the evidence for the suggestion that drugs which facilitate (or inhibit) transmission at cholinergic synapses in the brain facilitate (or inhibit) learning.

2. Describe the behavioral effects of drugs that facilitate or initiate transmission at adrenergic synapses.

EFFECTS OF DRUGS ON RECALL

Inhibitors of Protein Synthesis

It is generally assumed that the alterations in neural tissue which occur as a result of learning must involve a change in protein synthesis. Logically, this conclusion seems all but inescapable because any form of cellular activity requires protein synthesis. Definitive experimental proof of this relationship is, however, hard to come by. Several investigators have endeavored to demonstrate the essential role of protein synthesis in learning by observing the effects of drugs that are known to inhibit it. Two substances, puromycin and acetoxycycloheximide (ACHM) or the closely related cycloheximide (CHM), have been used in most of the related studies.

Systemic injections of puromycin[57] or intracranial injections aimed at the ventricular system or frontal lobes[58] do not produce significant effects on the recall of a simple Y-maze avoidance response. Bilateral puromycin injections into the temporal lobe, on the other hand, produce nearly complete amnesia on recall tests given 3 to 6 days after the completion of training. These injections were effective when given up to 48 hours or more after the last training trial, a training-treatment delay which is significantly greater than any found to be effective for other drugs or ECS (electroconvulsive shock) treatments. When puromycin injections were given bilaterally into the ventricular spaces, frontal lobe, and temporal lobe, amnesia was produced even when the drug was given as much as 60 days after the completion of training.

The differential effects of puromycin injections into the temporal lobe on relatively recent memories were further demonstrated in experiments which involved two stages of training. First, mice were trained to go right (or left) in a maze. After this habit was well established, three weeks of rest were allowed, followed by reversal training which required extinction of the previously learned response and acquisition of the previously incorrect alternative. Puromycin was injected one day after the animals reached a stiff performance criterion on the reversal task. On a recall test, given 3 to 4 days later, the puromycin-treated animals were found to revert to the originally learned habit, presumably because the drug interfered selectively with the more recent memory of the reversal training.

Intracranial injections of puromycin produce toxicity symptoms (such as lethargy and weight loss) which persist for several days. It has nevertheless been reported that mice given such injections 5 hours before the beginning of avoidance training in a Y-maze learn as well as normals in spite of the fact that protein synthesis is maximally inhibited at the time of training. These animals performed the conditioned avoidance response well on a recall test given 15 minutes after the completion of training but seemed to have forgotten everything 3 hours later. When they were retrained, these animals required as many training trials as naive mice.[8]

There is some evidence that the ability of puromycin to block access to well-established memories may not hold true for all species. Only one other species, the goldfish, has been investigated so far, and this animal shows puromycin effects which have a time course reminiscent of ECS or other drug treatments. Recall is blocked when puromycin is given immediately before or after training, but this effect diminishes as the training-injection interval is lengthened and seems to be completely gone when an hour or more intervenes.[2, 45]

It was long thought that the amnesic effects of puromycin might be caused by an interference with consolidation processes that required protein synthesis. A number of recent observations suggest, however, that the drug's effects on recall may be neither caused by an interference with the formation of memory traces nor directly related to its effects on protein metabolism. The first conclusion is suggested by the observation[60] that the amnesic effects of puromycin can be reversed by intracranial saline injections given as long as 60 days after the puromycin. The second conclusion appears warranted because other drugs, such as acetoxycycloheximide (ACHM) or its relative, cyclohexi-mide (CHM), which inhibit protein synthesis at least as thoroughly as puromycin, have very different effects on memory.

In the training paradigm where puromycin blocks recall even days or weeks after training, ACHM has no detectable effect. Indeed, the disruptive effects of puromycin can be blocked by the addition of ACHM or CHM to the injections.[59, 9] ACHM injections given several hours before training have no effect on acquisition even though protein synthesis in the brain is reduced by 95 percent. Recall is also normal on tests given several hours later. An effect on recall becomes apparent only when the training is incomplete (i.e., when the criterion for the completion of training is 3 avoidances in 4 trials instead of the more commonly used 9 out of 10). In this case, an impairment is seen on recall tests given more than 3 hours after the completion of training (see Figure 19–9). Recall appears entirely normal on earlier tests, suggesting that ACHM may specifically interfere with the consolidation of "short-term" memory into more permanent memory traces.[10]

When more difficult tasks are employed,

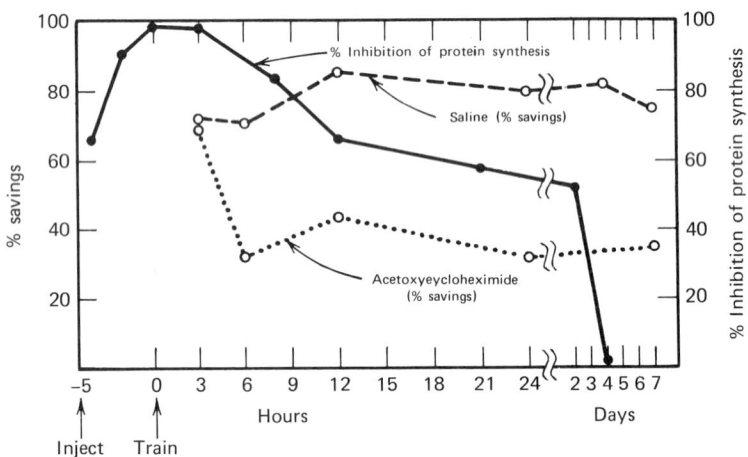

FIG. 19–9. Effect of intracerebral acetoxycycloheximide on cerebral protein synthesis and recall. Mice were injected in both temporal regions of the brain with NaCl with or without acetoxycycloheximide. Five hours later they were trained to escape shock by choosing the correct limb of a maze to a criterion of 3 out of 4 consecutive correct responses. Retention was determined at the indicated times. There was no significant difference in the savings of the two groups 3 hours after training but thereafter acetoxycycloheximide-injected mice had significantly poorer savings (P < 0.5, or less) than saline-injected mice.

(After S. H. Barondes & H. D. Cohen. Delayed and sustained effect of acetoxycycloheximide on memory in mice. *Proc. Nat. Acad. Sci. U.S.*, **58**, 1967, 157–164.)

ACHM produces similar deficits on delayed recall tests even when the animals are trained to a criterion of 9 correct responses in 10 trials. However, further overtraining once again protects the memory.[36,37] In these tests, ACHM produces some effects on later recall when given after the training is completed, but much larger effects are obtained when the drug is given before training. Since intracranial injections of ACHM do not produce a significant inhibition of protein synthesis in the brain for some hours, the effectiveness of post-training injections is especially important because it indicates that the drug may act on mechanisms related to consolidation instead of learning, as the pretrial injection results suggest. This is supported by the observation that post-trial systemic injections of ACHM also produce a delayed blocking effect on memory[11] (see Figure 19–10). The delayed effects of ACHM have also been seen in goldfish where memory is reported to be normal a few hours after training but severely impaired on a test given three days after training.[44]

It is difficult, at this time, to evaluate the incomplete picture presented by these results. It is clear that essentially normal learning can occur when the brain's ability to synthesize proteins is inhibited by as much as 90 to 95 percent. Moreover, when sufficient overtraining is provided during the time of maximum inhibition of protein synthesis, subsequent recall is also normal, suggesting that a stable memory can be formed. That protein synthesis may nevertheless be a factor in learning or consolidation is suggested by the delayed amnesic effects of ACHM given several hours before training. The fact that ACHM treated animals perform normally during acquisition suggests that neural tissue can function adequately when protein synthesis is severely curtailed, and it may not be surprising that consolidation can also occur.

What is, as yet, a mystery is why puromycin produces such powerful effects on recall even days or weeks after training. It has been reported that intracranial injections of puromycin produce hippocampal seizures, which persist for several hours and are followed by a severe flattening of the EEG record, and it is possible that this may be responsible for the apparent blocking of access to well-established memories.[38,35] Rats with hippocampal seizures can, however, learn a more complex visual discrimination in a T-maze when hippocampal seizures are produced prior to each daily training session,[75] and it is not clear by what mechanism the saline injections could counteract such seizures. It has been suggested that the differential effects of ACHM and puromycin may occur because ACHM (but not puromycin) may inhibit protein degradation as well as synthesis (thus protecting whatever proteins are synthesized) or that ACHM (but not puromycin) may protect RNA from degradation and thus preserve templates for the

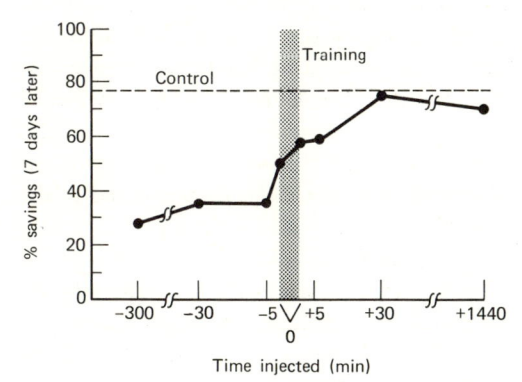

FIG. 19–10. Effect of subcutaneous administration of acetoxycycloheximide at various times before or after training on recall. Mice were trained to escape shock by choosing the lighted limb of a T-maze to a criterion of 5 out of 6 correct responses. Approximately 90% of cerebral protein synthesis was inhibited within 10–15 minutes of subcutaneous injection of acetoxycycloheximide. All mice were tested for retention 7 days after training, long after they had recovered from the drug. The mice injected before or within 5 minutes after training all had significantly less savings ($P < 0.5$ or less, Mann-Whitney U test) than saline controls. The mice injected 5 or more minutes before training had significantly less savings than those injected immediately after training. Injections 30 minutes or more after training had no effect on recall.

(After S. H. Barondes & H. D. Cohen. Memory impairment after subcutaneous injection of acetoxycycloheximide. *Science*, **160**, 3 May 1968, 556–557. Copyright 1968 by the American Association for the Advancement of Science.)

synthesis of proteins.[61] Experimental tests of these interesting hypotheses have not yet been described.

RNA and RNA Inhibitors

Much of the early support for Hydén's hypothesis that learning might involve changes in the configuration of RNA molecules came from clinical and experimental studies of the effects of RNA or RNA inhibitors. Much interest was generated by clinical reports[30] that the oral administration of yeast RNA improved short-term memory by as much as 100 percent in senile patients. Animal experiments have reported much smaller but significant facilitatory effects on learning and resistance to extinction when RNA was administered daily for several weeks before training as well as during it[40] (see Figures 19–11 and 19–12). However, this effect is apparently seen only in learning situations where general activation and increased locomotor activity are conducive to the acquisition of conditioned responses, and it appears unlikely that mechanisms specifically related to learning or recall are responsible for it.[163, 43] A general stimulant effect of RNA given systemically or intracranially may also account for reports of improved performance in lever-pressing situations.[25, 154]

Pretraining injections of tricyanoaminopropene (TCAP), a drug which increases the RNA content of nerve cells, have also been

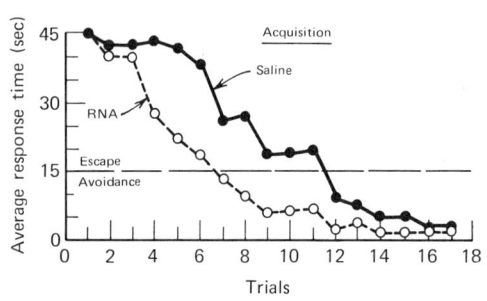

FIG. 19–11. Acquisition of avoidance responses after ten days of daily injections of yeast RNA.

(From L. Cook & A. B. Davidson. Effects of yeast RNA and other pharmacological agents on acquisition, retention and performance in animals. In *Psychopharmacology: a review of progress, 1957–1967.* D. H. Efron, Ed. U.S. Govt. Printing Office, 1968.)

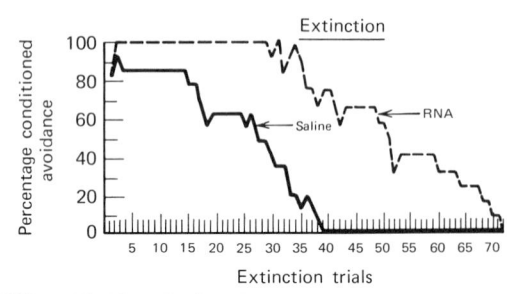

FIG. 19–12. Extinction of a conditioned avoidance response. The animals were trained to a criterion of 5 consecutive avoidance responses and then given 35 days of daily injections of yeast RNA or saline before the beginning of extinction.

(From L. Cook & A. B. Davidson. Effects of yeast RNA and other pharmacological agents on acquisition, retention and performance in animals. In *Psychopharmacology: a review of progress, 1957–1967.* D. H. Efron, Ed. U.S. Govt. Printing Office, 1968.)

reported to be without significant effect on acquisition[26] but to enhance performance on retention tests given 1 or 2 days after the completion of training[32] and to increase rate of responding in a lever-pressing situation.[153] Facilitatory effects on acquisition have also been reported,[53, 107] but these appear to be caused by general activating properties of the drug.[79]

Drugs such as Actinomycin-D, which interfere with RNA synthesis, typically do not produce significant effects on learning or recall,[13, 34] even when cerebral RNA synthesis is inhibited by 90 to 95 percent. There are, however, some indications that the long-term stability of memories may be decreased by these drugs.[3]

CNS Stimulants or Depressants

Inhibitory Effects

Large doses of many CNS stimulants such as strychnine or pentylenetetrazol (Metrazol) produce electrical seizures throughout the brain and overt convulsions. These treatments produce amnesic effects similar but probably not identical to those seen after electroconvulsive shock (ECS). Metrazol, for instance, has been reported to produce virtually complete retrograde amnesia when given as late as eight hours after acquisition[135] in training situations where ECS is ineffective as soon as one hour after the completion of training.[165] However, even high doses of the drug do not produce a more complete amnesic effect than ECS when the treatments are given five minutes after acquisition,[165] suggesting that Metrazol may produce effects on memory that are qualitatively instead of quantitatively different from those of ECS.

Overt convulsions are not, apparently, an essential determinant of the amnesic effect of some drugs. Small amnesic effects with a short time course that resembles that of ECS have been seen after systemic injections of various CNS stimulants (such as amphetamine, caffeine, and picrotoxin), which do not induce seizure activity.[166] Subconvulsive doses of Metrazol do not produce retrograde amnesia,[165, 132] but amnesic effects are seen with higher doses in animals which are protected from seizures.[54]

Nor is the disruptive effect of drugs limited to CNS stimulants. Clinical observations indicate that anesthetics such as thiopental[95] or barbiturates[123] produce amnesic effects in man. Similar effects have been seen after ether[55] or carbon dioxide anesthesia [141] in rats. The time course of these effects is short (in the order of minutes) and resembles that of ECS instead of that of convulsive doses of Metrazol.

Facilitatory Effects

Large doses of many CNS stimulants produce retrograde amnesia when administered within minutes or hours after the completion of training.[166] Smaller doses of these drugs have long been known to facilitate acquisition,[101] and recent work by McGaugh and associates [114] indicates that a similar facilitatory effect on recall can be demonstrated when these drugs are administered within 15 minutes of the completion of training. Since the direct effects of the drugs can be assumed to have dissipated before the test trial, these observations appear to rule out various interpretations of the observed facilitation in terms of increased general activation, alertness, motivation, and so on. Facilitatory effects of post-trial injections of strychnine have been observed in mazes, one-trial passive avoidance situations, avoidance situations involving visual discriminations or oddity problems, as well as delayed alternation tasks (see Figure 19–13).[115, 83, 137] Structurally dissimilar compounds which

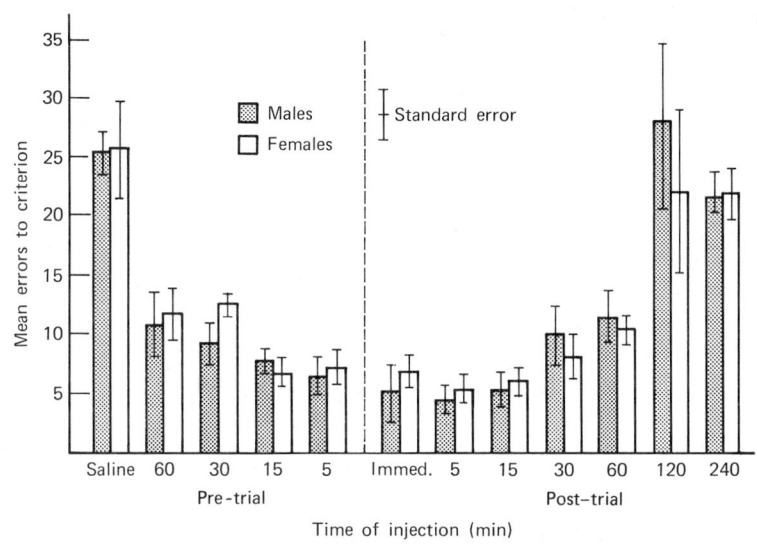

FIG. 19–13. **Effects of 1.0 mg/kg strychnine sulphate on a black-white discrimination task. Twelve mice (6 males and 6 females) per group.**

(From J. L. McGaugh & J. A. Krivanek. Strychnine effects on discrimination learning in mice: effects of dose and time of administration. *Physiol. & Behav.*, **5**, 1970, 1437–1442.)

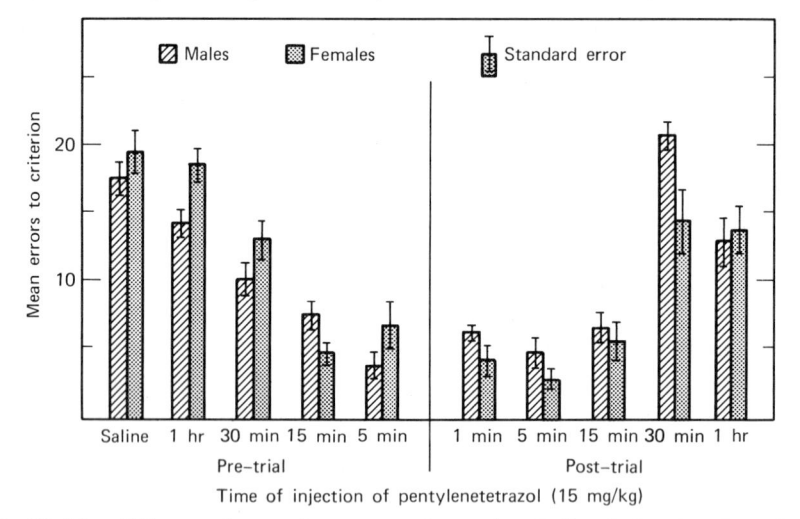

FIG. 19–14. Effects of pentylenetetrazol on visual discrimination learning in mice. Each mean based on 6 animals.

(From J. Krivanek & J. L. McGaugh. Effects of pentylenetetrazol on memory storage in mice. *Psychopharmacologia*, **12**, 1968, 303–321. Berlin-Heidelberg-New York: Springer.)

appear to produce strychnine-like central effects have been shown to produce similar facilitatory effects on recall.[116, 84, 167]

Other CNS stimulants such as picrotoxin,[23] Metrazol,[98] caffeine,[133] physostigmine,[158] and nicotine[127] have been reported to facilitate recall when given a few minutes after the initial training (see Figure 19-14). We do not, as yet, have sufficient data to permit a detailed analysis of the temporal parameters involved. It seems certain, however, that these drugs must be administered within a few minutes after training to produce the facilitatory effect on later recall, suggesting that mechanisms similar to those affected by ECS may be involved.

Attempts to demonstrate a specific locus of action of these facilitatory effects on recall[73] have shown that microinjections of small quantities of pentylenetetrazol into the dorsal hippocampus of rats either immediately before or after each daily training session in a maze facilitated acquisition, the effect of post-trial injections being reliably greater (see Figure 19–15).

Cholinergics and Anticholinergics

Although cholinergic and anticholinergic drugs do not seem to affect acquisition selectively, some observations suggest that cholinergic pathways may play a role in consolidation. When injected into previously trained animals, anticholinergic drugs such

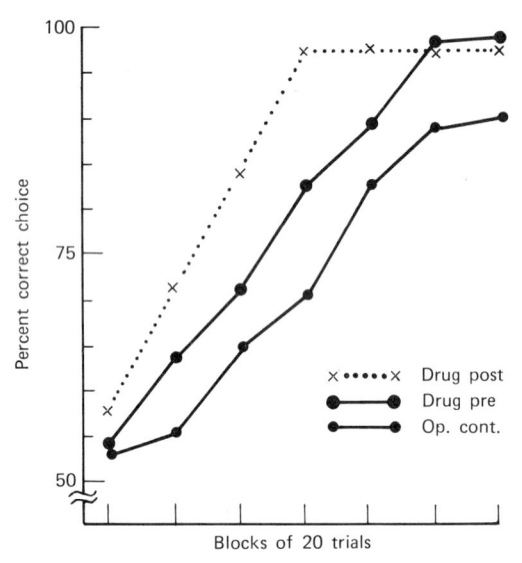

FIG. 19–15. Acquisition of a brightness discrimination in a T-maze. The performance of animals which received bilateral injections of 5–10 μg of pentylenetetrazol into the hippocampus 5 min before or immediately after each daily training session is compared with that of sham-injected controls.

(From S. P. Grossman. Facilitation of learning following intracranial injections of pentylenetetrazol. *Physiol. & Behav.*, **4**, 1969, 625–628. Permission granted for Pergamon Press copyright.)

as scopolamine or atropine produce "amnesic" effects that seem to be independent of the nature of the training situation (i.e., such effects have been observed in active and passive avoidance situations as well as in more complex test situations involving appetitive reinforcements).[82, 162, 28, 134] Systemic injections of reversible AChE inhibitors such as physostigmine have also been reported to interfere with recall when administered 30 minutes or as long as 7 days after training.[158, 50, 27]

Scopolamine injections into the brain have been reported to produce amnesia when given 1 and 3 days after training but not when administered after 4 or 7 days.[49, 169] These observations are particularly intriguing in view of reports from the same laboratory that intracranial injections of large doses of DFP which produced a significant inhibition of AChE in most of the brain also produced amnesia for previously learned approach and avoidance responses. However, these effects were seen when the drug treatments were given 30 minutes or 4 to 7 days after training (when scopolamine injections were not effective) but not when administered 3 days after training (when scopolamine injections did produce amnesic effects)[46, 169] (see Figure 19–16). To confuse matters even further, DFP was found to facilitate performance when given 21 or 28 days after training when normal controls performed poorly presumably because of forgetting.[48, 169] Poorly learned habits were facilitated by DFP even at training-testing intervals which resulted in amnesic drug effects when the same habit was well established.[105]

Deutsch[47] has interpreted these observations to suggest that DFP may facilitate central pathways related to consolidation when the normal activity in these pathways is low due to forgetting, but interfere with memory because of prolonged depolarization of postsynaptic membranes when the normal activity of these pathways is high during the consolidation process. Scopolamine, on the other hand, is thought to produce its major inhibitory effects when the normal conductance in these pathways is low and to be

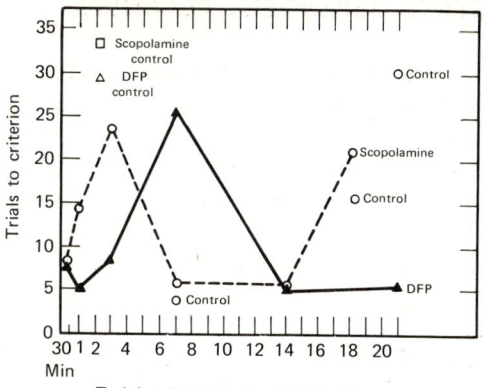

FIG. 19–16. Effects of intracerebral injections of DFP or scopolamine on recall of a water-rewarded brightness discrimination. The drugs were injected at various intervals (shown on the abscissa) after the completion of training. The ordinate indicates the number of trials required to attain a criterion of 10 consecutive correct responses on a recall test given 21 hours after the drug injections. The control points shown in the top left of the illustration represent the performance of animals which did not receive the original training but learned the problem for the first time 21 hours after the injections. The remaining three control points indicate the performance of control animals which did receive the initial training and were retrained 21 hours after control injections. In this experiment scopolamine produced a marked inhibitory effect when given 3 days after training but not when given earlier or later. DFP produced marked inhibitory effects when given 7 days after training but appeared to facilitate recall 21 days after training when the recall of the control animals was poor.
(From N. I. Wiener & J. A. Deutsch. Temporal aspects of anticholinergic- and anticholinesterase-induced amnesia for an appetitive habit. *J. comp. physiol. Psychol.*, 66, 1968, 613–617. Copyright 1968 by the American Psychological Association, and reproduced by permission.)

relatively ineffective when the amount of ACh released because of endogenous activity is high. This explanation accounts neatly for the observed pattern of results but requires some rather unorthodox assumptions. An interpretation of Deutsch's data is further complicated by several facts: (1) all injections were made while the animals were under anesthesia, and this itself is known to produce amnesic effects; (2) the amnesic effects of at least some of the drugs are not seen when spaced instead of massed trials are used during testing.

STATE-DEPENDENT LEARNING

An interpretation of the inhibitory effects of pretrial injections of some drugs on recall is complicated by the possibility that learning may be "state-dependent." Indeed, it is common to find that animals who are trained under the influence of a drug which affects CNS functions perform well when subsequently tested in the drugged state but poorly when tested without the drug (the latter is, of course, the paradigm used in many of the drug studies concerned with memory consolidation). A change from undrugged to drugged conditions often produces similar though typically smaller impairments.[131]

The failure to generalize from the drugged to the nondrugged state and vice versa may reflect the fact that drugs such as alcohol, tranquilizers, CNS stimulants and depressants, or muscle relaxants produce such marked effects on the subject's perception of the training or testing situation that he does not recognize it when the drug is withdrawn. Drugs undoubtedly can produce effects which can serve as conditioned stimuli,[130] and one would expect a generalization decrement when they are removed or added to a test situation.

However, this may not be an adequate explanation of state-dependent learning, at least under some circumstances. In some instances there is a complete dissociation between the drugged and nondrugged state which seems difficult to explain in terms of a simple generalization decrement[129] (see Figure 19–17). In many others, there is a pronounced decrement when the animals are trained with a drug and tested without it, but little or no effect when the animals are trained without the drug and tested with it.[7] Since in some of these instances acquisition is in fact facilitated by the drug, it is difficult to understand how the generalization decrement explanation could account for this asymmetry. Moreover, in some instances an asymmetrical dissociation occurs between two drug states (i.e., animals trained under the influence of drug A do not perform well under drug B, but

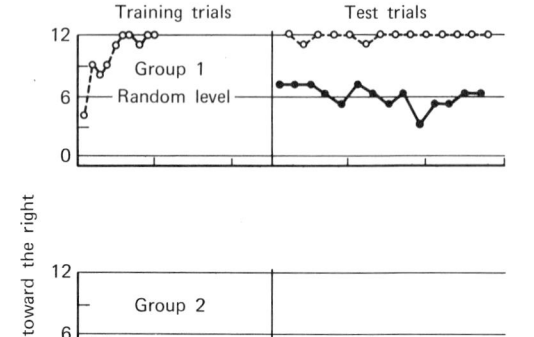

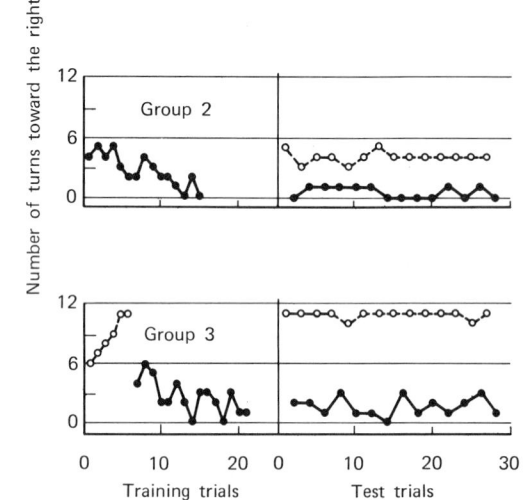

FIG. 19–17. Three examples of "state-dependent" learning. The animals were trained to avoid shock by turning right (or left) in a shuttle box and subsequently tested when drugged by a large dose of a common anesthetic (solid lines, filled circles) or when "sober" (dashed lines, open circles). The drugged and sober tests were alternated, 1/day. Group 1 was trained to go right while sober, and continued to perform well when tested in the same condition. When tested under the influence of the drug, performance fell to chance levels. That this is not merely due to the debilitating effects of the drug is indicated by the performance of group 2 which was trained to go left under the influence of the drug and continued to perform this response well on subsequent drug tests but reverted to near chance levels when tested sober. The animals of group 3 were first trained to go right while sober and then trained to go left while under the influence of the drug. Their consistent performance on subsequent tests indicates that conflicting memories can be established under drugged and sober conditions.

(After D. A. Overton. State-dependent or "dissociated" learning produced with pentobarbital. *J. comp. physiol. Psychol.*, **57**, 1964, 3–12. Copyright 1964 by the American Psychological Association, and reproduced by permission.)

animals trained with drug B appear normal when tested with drug A), even though there is a similar dissociation between both drugs and the nondrugged state.[17] State-dependent learning has also been observed in human subjects who learned verbal materials under the influence of small doses of alcohol, amphetamine, or amobarbital,[157] an observation which is also not easily explained by the stimulus-change hypothesis.

A number of investigators[65,17] have suggested an alternative explanation, which may account for at least some instances of state-dependent acquisition. According to this hypothesis, centrally acting drugs may selectively affect some aspects of the nervous system. Under the influence of such drugs, learning might involve neural pathways which are not involved in the undrugged state, and the memories that are thus acquired might not be accessible when the drug wears off.

The simplest specific version of this hypothesis was suggested many years ago to account for the puzzling observations that (1) simple conditioned responses which were established in curarized animals could not be elicited after the drug wore off, and (2) conditioned responses which were established in the noncurarized state could not be evoked under curare.[65] In a close analogy to the effects of cortical lesions (memory is often lost but retraining possible), it was suggested that curare might selectively suppress cortical functions. Responses learned in the functionally "decorticated" state, presumably by subcortical mechanisms, would then not be available when the cortex once again functioned normally. Access to responses learned cortically would similarly be lost under the influence of such a drug.

Recent models have been less explicit in assigning selective drug effects to specific portions of the nervous system but retain the basic notion that more than one neural substrate for conditioning may exist and that drugs may selectively block the normally "dominant" substrate and force the organism to fall back on mechanisms with different chemical affinities.[17]

Summary and Review Questions

It is generally assumed that learning involves quantitative if not qualitative changes in protein synthesis. If this is indeed the case, the brain must work with an enormous safety margin since drugs such as acetoxycycloheximide (ACHM), which inhibit central protein synthesis by as much as 95 percent, do not interfere with learning. It is, of course, possible that the pathways involved in learning may be somehow protected against substances that interfere with protein synthesis, but mechanisms for such a selective protection have not been demonstrated to date.

Some inhibitors of protein synthesis, such as puromycin, have very pronounced inhibitory effects on recall even when administered many days or weeks after learning. However, this effect may not be caused by an interference with protein synthesis per se (because other protein inhibitors do not produce this effect) and may instead reflect a blocking of access to an intact memory rather than an interference with its formation (because the drug effects can be reversed by intracranial injections of saline).

Other protein synthesis inhibitors, such as ACHM, produce a marked inhibition of protein synthesis in the brain but only relatively small and delayed inhibitory effects on recall when given up to 5 hours before or immediately after training. These results may be caused by an interference with mechanisms concerned specifically with consolidation.

Drugs which facilitate the synthesis of RNA in the brain have been reported to facilitate recall, but there is reason to believe that these effects may be due to a general stimulant effect of these treatments. Drugs that interfere with RNA synthesis apparently do not modify either learning or recall.

Drugs that nonspecifically facilitate neural activity have been reported to facilitate learning and recall when given in small doses. These effects are seen when the treatments are given shortly after (as well as before) training, suggesting that a facilitation of mechanisms related to consolidation may be responsible for them. Large doses of the same CNS stimulants produce overt or covert seizures and result in amnesic effects similar, in most instances, to those seen after electroconvulsive shock.

Drugs which selectively modify transmission at central cholinergic synapses have been reported to result in time-dependent facilitatory or inhibitory effects on recall. The very complicated pattern of results suggests that a facilitation of central cholinergic pathways may produce beneficial effects on recall at a time when the activity of memory-related pathways is low but interfere with recall at a time when these mechanisms are active in the consolidation of memory traces.

An interpretation of the effects of drugs on recall is complicated by the fact that many drugs produce "state-dependent" learning. Recall is often good when the subjects are tested under the same (drug or placebo) conditions that prevailed during training. When the conditions of training and testing differ (the typical paradigm for tests of drug effect on recall), memory often appears unavailable for recall. To some extent, this dissociation may simply occur because the organism's reaction to a drug becomes part of the stimulus situation. However, there are instances of "asymmetrical" dissociations that are not readily explained in these terms. Alternative hypotheses have been suggested proposing that some drugs may selectively act on neural pathways normally used for learning or recall. When these are blocked, the organism may fall back on other pathways that are not affected by the drug. The memories which are thus established in a "secondary" system may then not be available for recall after the primary mechanisms have once again become functional.

1. Contrast the effects of inhibitors of protein synthesis on learning and recall.

2. Contrast the effects of puromycin and acetoxycycloheximide on recall.

3. Describe the behavioral effects of drugs which enhance or inhibit RNA synthesis in the brain.

4. Describe the effects of CNS stimulants (such as Metrazol) on recall.

5. Describe the effects of cholinergics or anticholinergics on recall.

6. Describe state-dependent learning. Why does it occur?

REVIEW

It has been clear for some time that any change in neural function must involve alterations in biochemical processes, but specific evidence for learning-related changes in brain chemistry has been available for only about ten years. The field is so young that in most instances we do not yet have conclusive evidence for particular mechanisms or adequate controls for alternative explanations. It is, nonetheless, the most active and exciting aspect of learning-related research today.

Stable genetic information is transmitted by deoxyribonucleic acid or DNA. These instructions are implemented by ribonucleic (RNA) molecules, which are formed on DNA templates and, in turn, act as models for the synthesis of proteins. Since the DNA molecules must be very stable, and proteins by nature are very unstable, much of the initial interest in this field was focused on the possibility that learning might involve a change in the RNA molecule.

Early experiments in this area indicated that learning might result in the synthesis of novel RNA species in portions of the brain that were selectively activated during learning, whereas the mere activation of the same sensory and motor pathways might produce only an increase in the production of existing RNA molecules. This interpretation appeared to be supported by experiments which indicated that RNA-rich extracts from the brains of trained animals seemed capable of transmitting information to untrained animals. Moreover, injections of RNA or of drugs which facilitate its synthesis in the brain seemed to enhance recall. It soon became clear, however, that the RNA molecule is not sufficiently stable to serve as the substrate for long-term memories. Subsequent research further demonstrated that: (1) the apparently positive effects of RNA extracts in the transfer of training experiments must be due to a much smaller molecule; (2) drugs which inhibit RNA synthesis in the brain do not interfere with acquisition or recall; and (3) the facilitatory effects of RNA and of drugs which promote its synthesis may be caused by a general stimulant effect instead of a facilitation of mechanisms specifically related to learning.

In recent years, most of the research in this field has been devoted to the demonstration that changes in protein- rather than RNA-synthesis provide the substrate for memory. A number of experiments have shown that protein synthesis increases during learning in parts of the brain (such as the hippocampus) that are suspected of participating in learning, consolidation, or recall. An inhibition of protein synthesis in these areas has been reported to selectively interfere with access to recent memories. One of the most surprising findings in this field has been the observation that learning proceeds, apparently unimpaired, when protein synthesis in the brain is inhibited by as much as 95 percent. There is some indication that memories established during periods of low protein synthesis are not stable, but even this effect is small. Some drugs which inhibit protein synthesis in the brain produce marked inhibitory effects on recall even weeks or months after training. However, this appears to be caused by an interference with access to perfectly intact memories rather than their destruction. Moreover, the drugs' effects on protein synthesis cannot be responsible for their effect on recall because other protein-synthesis inhibitors do not produce it.

Most protein-synthesis inhibitors produce a delayed inhibitory effect on recall when training or the initial phases of consolidation occur during the period of maximal inhibition of protein synthesis. However, overtraining seems to protect the memory traces from this disruptive effect, indicating that the brain can establish long-term memories when protein synthesis in the brain is inhibited by as much as 95 percent.

Some investigators have attempted to test the hypothesis that the facilitation of synaptic transmission which is assumed to occur as the result of learning may be due to an increase in the availability of a neurohumoral transmitter. After much research, it is now clear that major changes in the efficacy of transmission at central adrenergic or cholinergic synapses do not result in demonstrable changes in the organism's ability to learn. Drugs which modify the concentration or efficacy of adrenergic or cholinergic transmitters do affect behavior in most test situations, but these effects appear to be caused by a modification of attentional or inhibitory processes. Exposure to complex environments, which may provide exceptional opportunities for learning, modify the distribution of acetylcholine or related enzymes, but these effects have not been successfully related to learning or memory storage per se.

Drugs that nonspecifically facilitate neural activity have been reported to enhance recall when given in small doses just before or after learning. These effects are time-dependent, and the pattern of results indicates that drug effects on consolidation-related processes might be responsible for the observed changes in recall. Larger doses of the same drugs produce seizure activity and retrograde amnesia in much the same way as ECS and other disruptive agents.

Bibliography

1. Adair, Linda B., Wilson, J. E., & Glassman, E. Brain function and macromolecules. IV. Uridine incorporation into polysomes of mouse brain during different behavioral experiences. *Proc. Nat. Acad. Sci. U.S.*, 1968, **61**, 917–922.
2. Agranoff, B. W., & Klinger, P. D. Puromycin effect on memory fixation in the goldfish. *Science*, 1964, **146**, 952–953.
3. Agranoff, B. W., Davis, R. E., Gasola, L., & Lim, R. Actinomycin D blocks formation of memory of shock avoidance in goldfish. *Science*, 1967, **158**, 1600–1601.
4. Armitage, S. G. The effects of barbiturates on the behavior of rat offspring as measured in learning and reasoning situations. *J. comp. physiol. Psychol.*, 1952, **45**, 146–152.

5. Babich, F. R., Jacobson, A. L., Bubash, S., & Jacobson, A. Transfer of a response to naive rats by injection of ribonucleic acid extracted from trained rats. *Science*, 1965, **149**, 656–657.

6. Banks, Amelia, & Russell, R. W. Effects of chronic reductions in acetylcholinesterase activity on serial problem-solving behavior. *J. comp. physiol. Psychol.*, 1967, **64**, 262–267.

7. Barnhart, Sharon S., & Abbott, D. W. Dissociation of learning and meprobamate. *Psychol. Rep.*, 1967, **20**, 520–522.

8. Barondes, S. H., & Cohen, H. D. Puromycin effect on successive phases of memory storage. *Science*, 1966, **151**, 594–595.

9. Barondes, S. H., & Cohen, H. D. Comparative effects of cycloheximide and puromycin on cerebral protein synthesis and consolidation of memory in mice. *Brain Res.*, 1967a, **4**, 44–51.

10. Barondes, S. H., & Cohen, H. D. Delayed and sustained effect of acetoxycycloheximide on memory in mice. *Proc. Nat. Acad. Sci. U.S.*, 1967b, **58**, 157–164.

11. Barondes, S. H., & Cohen, H. D. Memory impairment after subcutaneous injection of acetoxycycloheximide. *Science*, 3 May 1968a, **160**, 556–557.

12. Barondes, S. H., & Cohen, H. D. Arousal and the conversion of "short-term" to "long-term" memory. *Proc. Nat. Acad. Sci. U.S.*, 1968b, **61**, 923–929.

13. Barondes, S. H., & Jarvik, M. E. The influence of actinomycin-D on brain RNA synthesis and on memory. *J. Neurochem.*, 1964, **11**, 187–195.

14. Belluzzi, J. D. Long-lasting effects of cholinergic stimulation of the amygdaloid complex in the rat. Ph.D. dissertation, University of Chicago, 1970.

15. Belluzzi, J. D., & Grossman, S. P. Avoidance learning: Long-lasting deficits after temporal lobe seizure. *Science*, 1969, **166**, 1435–1437.

16. Bennett, E. L., Rosenzweig, M. R., & Diamond, M. C. Time courses of effects of differential experience on brain measures and behavior of rats. In *Molecular approaches to learning and memory*. W. L. Byrne, Ed. New York: Academic Press, 1970, pp. 55–89.

17. Berger, B. D., & Stein, L. Asymmetrical dissociation of learning between scopolamine and Wy 4036, a new benzodiazepine tranquilizer. *Psychopharmacologia (Berl.)*, 1969, **14**, 351–358.

18. Bignami, G. Effects of benactyzine and adiphenine on avoidance conditioning in a shuttle-box. *Psychopharmacologia (Berl.)*, 1964, **5**, 264–279.

19. Bogoch, S. *The biochemistry of memory*. New York: Oxford Univ. Press, 1968.

20. Bovet, D., Bignami, G., & Robustelli, F. Action de la nicotine sur le conditionnement à la réaction d'évitement chez le rat. *C. R. Acad. Sci.*, 1963, **276**, 778–780.

21. Bovet-Nitti, F. Facilitation of simultaneous visual discrimination by nicotine in the rat. *Psychopharmacologia* (Berlin-Heidelberg-New York: Springer), 1966, **10**, 59–66.

22. Bowman, R. E., & Strobel, D. A. Brain RNA metabolism in the rat during learning. *J. comp. physiol. Psychol.*, 1969, **67**, 448–456.

23. Breen, R. A., & McGaugh, J. L. Facilitation of maze learning with post-trial injections of picrotoxin. *J. comp. physiol. Psychol.*, 1961, **54**, 498–501.

24. Briggs, M. H., & Kitto, G. B. The molecular basis of memory and learning. *Psychol. Rev.*, 1962, **69**, 537–541.

25. Brown, H. Effect of ribonucleic acid (RNA) on the rate of lever pressing in rats. *Psychol. Rec.*, 1966, **16**, 173–176.

26. Brush, T. R., Davenport, J. W., & Polidora, V. J. TCAP: Negative results in avoidance and water maze learning and retention. *Psychon. Sci.*, 1966, **4**, 183–184.

27. Bureš, J., Bohdanecký, Z., & Weiss, T. Physostigmine induced hippocampal theta activity and learning in rats. *Psychopharmacologia*, 1962, **3**, 254–263.

28. Burešová, O., Bureš, J., Bohdanecký, Z., & Weiss, T. Effect of atropine on learning, extinction, retention and retrieval in rats. *Psychopharmacologia*, 1964, **5**, 255–263.

29. Byrne, W. L., Samuel, D., Bennett, E. L., Rosenzweig, M. R., Wasserman, E., Wagner, A. R., Gardner, R., Galambos, R., Berger, B. D., Margules, D. L., Fenichel, R. L., Stein, L., Corson, J. A., Enesco, H. E., Chorover, S. L., Holt, C. E., III, Schiller, P. H., Chiapetta, L., Jarvik, M. E., Leaf, R. C., Dutcher, J. D., Horovitz, Z. P., & Carlson, P. L. Memory transfer. *Science*, 1966, **153**, 658–659.

30. Cameron, D. E., & Solyom, L. Effects of ribonucleic acid on memory. *Geriatrics*, 1961, **16**, 74–81.
31. Carlton, P. L., & Vogel, J. R. Studies of the amnesic properties of scopolamine. *Psychonom. Sci.*, 1965, **3**, 261–262.
32. Chamberlin, T. J., Rothschild, G. H., & Gerard, R. W. Drugs affecting RNA and learning. *Proc. Nat. Acad. Sci. U.S.*, 1963, **49**, 918–925.
33. Clark, F. C., & Steele, B. J. Effects of d-amphetamine on performance under a multiple schedule in the rat. *Psychopharmacologia*, 1966, **9**, 315–335.
34. Cohen, H. D., & Barondes, S. H. Further studies of learning and memory after intracerebral actinomycin-D. *J. Neurochem.*, 1966, **13**, 207–211.
35. Cohen, H. D., & Barondes, S. H. Puromycin effect on memory may be due to occult seizures. *Science*, 1967, **157**, 333–334.
36. Cohen, H. D., & Barondes, S. H. Effect of acetoxycycloheximide on learning and memory of a light-dark discrimination. *Nature*, 1968a, **218**, 271–273.
37. Cohen, H. D., & Barondes, S. H. Cycloheximide impairs memory of an appetitive task. *Comm. Behav. Biol.*, 1968b, Part A, **1**, 337–340.
38. Cohen, H. D., Ervin, R., & Barondes, S. H. Puromycin and cycloheximide: Different effects on hippocampal electrical activity. *Science*, 1966, **154**, 1557–1558.
39. Cook, L., & Davidson, A. B. Effects of yeast RNA and other pharmacological agents on acquisition, retention and performance in animals. In *Psychopharmacology: a review of progress, 1957–1967*. D. H. Efron, Ed. Washington, D. C.: U. S. Govt. Printing Office, 1968, pp. 931–946.
40. Cook, L., Davidson, A. B., Davis, D. J., Green, H., & Fellows, E. J. Ribonucleic acid: effect on conditioned behavior in rats. *Science*, 1963, **141**, 268–269.
41. Corning, W. C., & Freed, S. Planarian behaviour and biochemistry. *Nature*, 1968, **219**, 1227–1229.
42. Corning, W. C., & John, E. R. Effect of ribonuclease on retention of conditioned response in regenerated planarians. *Science*, 1961, **134**, 1363–1365.
43. Corson, J. A., & Enesco, H. E. Attempts to obtain "information transfer" in rats with brain extracts. *J. Biol. Psychol.*, 1968, **10**, 10–23.
44. Davis, R. E., & Agranoff, B. W. Stages of memory formation in goldfish: evidence for an environmental trigger. *Proc. Nat. Acad. Sci. U.S.*, 1966, **55**, 555–559.
45. Davis, R. E., Bright, Patricia J., & Agranoff, B. W. Effect of ECS and puromycin on memory in fish. *J. comp. physiol. Psychol.*, 1965, **60**, 162–166.
46. Deutsch, J. A. Substrates of learning and memory. *Diseases of the Nervous System*, Monograph Supplement, 1966, **27**, 20–24.
47. Deutsch, J. A. The physiological basis of memory. *Ann. Rev. Psychol.*, 1969, **20**, 85–104.
48. Deutsch, J. A., & Leibowitz, Sarah F. Amnesia or reversal of forgetting by anticholinesterase, depending simply on time of injection. *Science*, 1966, **153**, 1017–1018.
49. Deutsch, J. A., & Rocklin, K. W. Amnesia induced by scopolamine and its temporal variations. *Nature*, 1967, **216**, 89–90.
50. Deutsch, J. A., Hamburg, M. D., & Dahl, H. Anticholinesterase-induced amnesia and its temporal aspects. *Science*, 1966, **151**, 221–222.
51. Domino, E. F. Unpublished paper, 1964. Cited in McGaugh, J. L., & Petrinovich, L. F. Effects of drugs on learning and memory. In *Intern. Rev. of Neurobiology*, Vol. 8. New York: Academic Press, 1965, pp. 139–196.
52. Doty, B., & Howard, S. Facilitative effects of post-trial magnesium pemoline on avoidance conditioning in relation to problem difficulty. *Life Sci.*, 1968, **7**, 591–597.
53. Essman, W. B. Effect of tricyanoaminopropene on the amnesic effect of electroconvulsive shock. *Psychopharmacologia*, 1966, **9**, 426–433.
54. Essman, W. B. Retrograde amnesia in seizure-protected mice: behavioral and biochemical effects of pentylenetetrazol. *Physiol. & Behav.*, 1968, **3**, 549–552.
55. Essman, W. B., & Jarvik, M. E. Impairment of retention for a conditioned response by ether anesthesia in mice. *Psychopharmacologia*, 1961, **2**, 172–176.

56. Fjerdingstad, E. J., Nissen, Th., & Røigaard-Petersen, H. H. Effect of ribonucleic acid (RNA) extracted from the brain of trained animals on learning in rats. *Scand. J. Psychol.*, 1965, **6**, 1–6.

57. Flexner, J. B., Flexner, L. B., Stellar, E., Haba, G. de la, & Roberts, R. B. Inhibition of protein synthesis in brain and learning and memory following puromycin. *J. Neurochem.*, 1962, **9**, 595–605.

58. Flexner, J. B., Flexner, L. B., & Stellar, E. Memory in mice as affected by intracerebral puromycin. *Science*, 1963, **141**, 57–59.

59. Flexner, L. B., & Flexner, J. B. Effect of acetoxycycloheximide and of an acetoxycycloheximide-puromycin mixture on cerebral protein synthesis and memory in mice. *Proc. Nat. Acad. Sci. U. S.*, 1966, **55**, 369–374.

60. Flexner, L. B., & Flexner, J. B. Intracerebral saline: Effect on memory of trained mice treated with puromycin. *Science*, 1968, **159**, 330–331.

61. Flexner, L. B., Flexner, J. B., & Roberts, R. B. Memory in mice analyzed with antibiotics. *Science*, 1967, **155**, 1377–1383.

62. Frey, P. W., & Polidora, V. J. Magnesium pemoline: Effect on avoidance conditioning in rats. *Science*, 1967, **155**, 1281–1282.

63. Gaito, J., Mottin, J., & Davison, J. H. Chemical variation in the ventral hippocampus and other brain sites during conditioned avoidance. *Psychonom. Sci.*, 1968, **13**, 259–260.

64. Gatti, G. I., & Bovet, D. Analysis of the action of the psychotropic drugs in a "lever pressing avoidance" conditioning. In *Psychopharmacological methods*. Z. Votava, M. Horvath, & O. Vinar, Eds. Oxford: Pergamon Press, 1963, pp. 50–57.

65. Girden, E. Cerebral mechanisms in conditioning under curare. *Amer. J. Psychol.*, 1940, **53**, 397–406.

66. Glasky, A. J., & Simon, L. N. Magnesium pemoline: Enhancement of brain RNA polymerases. *Science*, 1966, **151**, 702–703.

67. Glow, P. H., & Rose, S. Cholinesterase levels and operant extinction. *J. comp. physiol. Psychol.*, 1966, **61**, 165–172.

68. Goddard, G. V. Analysis of avoidance conditioning following cholinergic stimulation of amygdala in rats. *J. comp. physiol. Psychol.*, 1969, **68**, Pt. 2, 1–18 (Monograph).

69. Grossman, S. P. Effects of chemical stimulation of the septal area on motivation. *J. comp. physiol. Psychol.*, 1964, **58**, 194–200.

70. Grossman, S. P. The VMH: A center for affective reaction, satiety, or both? *Physiol. & Behav.*, 1966a, **1**, 1–10.

71. Grossman, S. P. Acquisition and performance of avoidance responses during chemical stimulation of the midbrain reticular formation. *J. comp. physiol. Psychol.*, 1966b, **61**, 42–49.

72. Grossman, S. P. Behavioral and electroencephalographic effects of microinjections of neurohumors into the midbrain reticular formation. *Physiol. & Behav.*, 1968, **3**, 777–787.

73. Grossman, S. P. Facilitation of learning following intracranial injections of pentylenetetrazol. *Physiol. & Behav.*, 1969, **4**, 625–628.

74. Grossman, S. P., & Grossman, Lore. Effects of chemical stimulation of the midbrain reticular formation on appetitive behavior. *J. comp. physiol. Psychol.*, 1966, **61**, 333–338.

75. Grossman, S. P., & Mountford, Helen. Learning and extinction during chemically induced disturbance of hippocampal functions. *Amer. J. Physiol.*, 1964, **207**, 1387–1393.

76. Grossman, S. P., & Peters, R. H. Acquisition of appetitive and avoidance habits following atropine-induced blocking of the thalamic reticular formation. *J. comp. physiol. Psychol.*, 1966, **61**, 325–332.

77. Grossman, S. P., Peters, R. H., Freedman, P. E., & Willer, H. I. Behavioral effects of cholinergic stimulation of the thalamic reticular formation. *J. comp. physiol. Psychol.*, 1965, **59**, 57–65.

78. Gurowitz, E. M. *The molecular basis of memory*. Englewood Cliffs, N. J.: Prentice-Hall, 1969.

79. Gurowitz, E. M., Gross, D. A., & George, R. Effects of TCAP on passive avoidance learning in the rat. *Psychonom. Sci.*, 1968, **12**, 293–294.

80. Hamilton, L. W., & Grossman, S. P. Behavioral changes following disruption of central cholinergic pathways. *J. comp. physiol. Psychol.*, 1969, **69**, 76–82.

81. Hearst, E., & Whalen, R. E. Facilitating effects of D-amphetamine on discriminated avoidance performance. *J. comp. physiol. Psychol.*, 1963, **56**, 124–128.

82. Herz, A. Über die Wirkung von Scopolamin, Benactyzin und Atropin auf das reaktive Verhalten der Ratte. *Arch. exp. pathol. Pharmakol.*, 1959, **236**, 110–111.

83. Hudspeth, W. J. Strychnine: Its facilitating effect on the solution of a simple oddity problem by the rat. *Science*, 1964, **145**, 1331–1333.

84. Hudspeth, W. J., & Thomson, C. W. A further study of the facilitative effect of 5-7-Diphenyl-1-3-Diazadamantan-6-01 (1757 I.S.) on maze learning. *Psychol. Rep.*, 1962, **10**, 222.

85. Hughes, K. R., & Zubek, J. P. Effect of glutamic acid on the learning ability of bright and dull rats: I. Administration during infancy. *Can. J. Psychol.*, 1956, **10**, 132–138.

86. Hughes, K. R., & Zubek, J. P. Effect of glutamic acid on the learning ability of bright and dull rats: II. Duration of the effect. *Can. J. Psychol.*, 1957, **11**, 182–184.

87. Hughes, K. R., Cooper, R. M., & Zubek, J. P. Effect of glutamic acid on the learning ability of bright and dull rats: III. Effect of varying dosages. *Can. J. Psychol.*, 1957, **11**, 253–255.

88. Hydén, H. Behavior, neural function, and RNA. *Prog. Nucleic Acid Res. Mol. Biol.*, 1967, **6**, 187–218.

89. Hydén, H., & Egyházi, E. Nuclear RNA changes of nerve cells during a learning experiment in rats. *Proc. Nat. Acad. Sci. U. S.*, 1962, **48**, 1366–1373.

90. Hydén, H., & Egyházi, E. Glial RNA changes during a learning experiment with rats. *Proc. Nat. Acad. Sci. U. S.*, 1963, **49**, 618–624.

91. Hydén, H., & Egyházi, E. Changes in RNA content and base composition in cortical neurons of rats in a learning experiment involving transfer of handedness. *Proc. Nat. Acad. Sci. U.S.*, 1964, **52**, 1030–1035.

92. Hydén, H., & Lange, P. W. Protein synthesis in the hippocampal pyramidal cells of rats during a behavioral test. *Science*, 1968, **159**, 1370–1373.

93. Hydén, H., Egyházi, E., John, E. R., & Bartlett, F. RNA base ratio changes in planaria during conditioning. *J. Neurochem.*, 1969, **16**, 813–821.

94. Jacobsen, E., & Sonne, E. The effect of benzilic acid dethylaminoethylester HC2 (Benactyzine) on stress-induced behavior in the rat. *Acta pharmac. tox. Kbh.*, 1955, **11**, 135–142.

95. Jarvik, M. E. The influence of drugs upon memory. In *Ciba foundation symposium on animal behaviour and drug action.* H. Steinberg, A. V. S. De Reuck, & Julie Knight, Eds. Boston: Little, Brown, 1964, pp. 44–61.

96. Jensen, D. Paramecia, planaria, and pseudo-learning. *Animal Behav.*, 1965, **13**, Suppl., 9–20.

97. Kelsey, J. E., & Grossman, S. P. Cholinergic blockade and lesions in the ventro-medial septum of the rat. *Physiol. & Behav.*, 1969, **4**, 837–845.

98. Krivanek, J., & Hunt, E. The effects of post-trial injections of pentylenetetrazole, strychnine and mephenesin on discrimination learning. *Psychopharmacologia*, 1967, **10**, 189–195.

99. Krivanek, J., & McGaugh, J. L. Effects of pentylenetetrazol on memory storage in mice. *Psychopharmacologia* (Berlin-Heidelberg-New York: Springer), 1968, **12**, 303–321.

100. Kulkarni, A. S. Facilitation of instrumental avoidance learning by amphetamine: An analysis. *Psychopharmacologia* (Berlin-Heidelberg-New York: Springer), 1968, **13**, 418–425.

101. Lashley, K. S. The retention of habits by the rat after destruction of the frontal portion of the cerebrum. *Psychobiology*, 1917, **1**, 3.

102. Latané, B., & Schacter, S. Adrenaline and avoidance learning. *J. comp. physiol. Psychol.*, 1962, **65**, 369–372.

103. Leaf, R. C., & Muller, S. A. Effects of scopolamine on operant avoidance acquisition and retention. *Psychopharmacologia* (*Berl.*), 1966, **9**, 101–109.

104. Leaf, R. C., Dutcher, J. D., Horovitz, Z. P., & Carlton, P. L. Unpublished manuscript referred to in Byrne, W. L. et. al. Memory transfer. *Science*, 1966, **153**, 658–659.
105. Leibowitz, Sarah F. Memory and emotionality after anticholinesterase in the hippocampus: reverse function of prior learning level. Ph.D. dissertation, New York Univ., 1968.
106. Levine, S., & Soliday, S. An effect of adrenal demedullation on the acquisition of a conditioned avoidance response. *J. comp. physiol. Psychol.*, 1962, **55**, 214–216.
107. Lewis, S. Maze acquisition and nucleic acid metabolism: effects of two malononitrile derivatives. Paper presented at Eastern Psychological Association meetings, Boston, 1967.
108. Luttges, M., Johnson, R., Buck, C., Holland, J., & McGaugh, J. L. An examination of "transfer of learning" by nucleic acid. *Science*, 1966, **151**, 834–837.
109. McConnell, J. V. Memory transfer via cannibalism in planaria. *J. Neuropsychiat.*, 1962, **3**, 1–42.
110. McConnell, J. V. Comparative physiology: Learning in invertebrates. *Ann. Rev. Physiol.*, 1966, **28**, 107–136.
111. McConnell, J. V., & Shelby, J. M. Memory transfer experiments in invertebrates. In *Molecular mechanisms in memory and learning*. G. Ungar, Ed. New York: Plenum Press, 1970, pp. 71–101.
112. McEwen, B. S. Cellular dynamics of brain proteins. In *Physiological and biochemical aspects of nervous integration*. F. D. Carlson, Ed. Englewood Cliffs, N. J.: Prentice-Hall, 1968, pp. 361–381.
113. McGaugh, J. L., & Krivanek, J. A. Strychnine effects on discrimination learning in mice: Effects of dose and time of administration. *Physiol. & Behav.*, 1970, **5**, 1437–1442.
114. McGaugh, J. L., & Petrinovich, L. F. Effects of drugs on learning and memory. *International Review of Neurobiology. Vol. 8.* New York: Academic Press, 1965, pp. 139–196.
115. McGaugh, J. L., Thomson, C. W., Westbrook, W. H., & Hudspeth, W. J. A further study of learning facilitation with strychnine sulphate. *Psychopharmacologia*, 1962a, **3**, 352–360.
116. McGaugh, J. L., Westbrook, W. H., & Thomson, C. W. Facilitation of maze learning with posttrial injections of 5-7-diphenyl-1-3-diazadamantan-6-01 (1757 I. S.). *J. comp. physiol. Psychol.*, 1962b, **55**, 710–713.
117. Machlus, B., & Gaito, J. Detection of RNA species unique to a behavioral task. *Psychonom. Sci.*, 1968a, **10**, 253–254.
118. Machlus, B., & Gaito, J. Unique RNA species developed during a shock avoidance task. *Psychonom. Sci.*, 1968b, **12**, 111–112.
119. Machlus, B., & Gaito, J. Successive competition hybridization to detect RNA species in a shock avoidance task. *Nature*, 1969, **222**, 573–574.
120. Margules, D. L., & Stein, L. Cholinergic synapses in the ventromedial hypothalamus for the suppression of operant behavior by punishment and satiety. *J. comp. physiol. Psychol.*, 1969, **67**, 327–335.
121. Mendenhall, M. C. The effect of sodium phenobarbital on learning and "reasoning" in white rats. *J. comp. Psychol.*, 1940, **29**, 257–276.
122. Metzger, H. P., Cuenod, M., Grynbaum, A., & Waelsch, H. The effect of unilateral visual stimulation on synthesis of cortical proteins in each hemisphere of the split-brain monkey. *J. Neurochem.*, 1967, **14**, 183–187.
123. Migdal, W., & Frumin, M. J. Amnesic and analgesic effects in man of centrally acting anticholinergics. *Fed. Proc.*, 1963, **22**, 188.
124. Moroz, M. Effect of pentobarbital sodium on the behavior of rats in the Krech hypothesis apparatus. *J. comp. physiol. Psychol.*, 1959, **52**, 172–174.
125. Moyer, K. E., & Bunnell, B. N. Effect of adrenal demedullation on an avoidance response in the rat. *J. comp. physiol. Psychol.*, 1959, **52**, 215–216.
126. Neill, D. B., & Grossman, S. P. Unpublished observations. University of Chicago, 1971.
127. Oliverio, A. Effects of nicotine and strychnine on transfer of avoidance learning in the mouse. *Life Sci.*, 1968a, **7**, 1163–1167.
128. Oliverio, A. Neurohumoral systems and learning. In *Psychopharmacology: A review of progress, 1957–1967*. D. H. Efron, Ed. Washington, D.C.: U.S. Govt. Printing Office, 1968b, pp. 867–878.

129. Overton, D. A. State-dependent or "dissociated" learning produced with pentobarbital. *J. comp. physiol. Psychol.*, 1964, **57**, 3–12.

130. Overton, R. A. Differential responding in a three-choice maze controlled by three drug-states. *Psychopharmacologia (Berl.)*, 1967, **11**, 376–387.

131. Overton, D. A. Visual cues and shock sensitivity in the control of T maze choice by drug conditions. *J. comp. physiol. Psychol.*, 1968, **66**, 216–219.

132. Palfai, T., & Cornell, J. M. Effect of drugs on consolidation of classically conditioned fear. *J. comp. physiol. Psychol.*, 1968, **66**, 584–589.

133. Paré, W. The effect of caffeine and seconal on a visual discrimination task. *J. comp. physiol. Psychol.*, 1961, **54**, 506–509.

134. Pazzagli, A., & Pepeu, G. Amnestic properties of scopolamine and brain acetylcholine in the rat. *Int. J. Neuropharmacol.*, 1964, 291–299.

135. Pearlman, C. A., Sharpless, S. K., & Jarvik, M. E. Retrograde amnesia produced by anesthetic and convulsant agents. *J. comp. physiol. Psychol.*, 1961, **54**, 109–112.

136. Pechstein, L. A., & Reynolds, W. R. The effect of tobacco smoke on the growth and learning behavior of the albino rat and its progeny. *J. comp. Psychol.*, 1937, **24**, 459–469.

137. Petrinovich, L., Bradford, D., & McGaugh, J. L. Drug facilitation of memory in rats. *Psychonom. Sci.*, 1965, **2**, 191–192.

138. Plotnikoff, N. Magnesium pemoline: Enhancement of learning and memory of a conditioned avoidance response. *Science*, 1966a, **151**, 703–704.

139. Plotnikoff, N. Magnesium pemoline: Enhancement of memory after electroconvulsive shock in rats. *Life Sci.*, 1966b, **5**, 1495–1498.

140. Plotnikoff, N., Will, F., & Ditzler, W. Stimulant activity of pemoline and magnesium hydroxide. *Arch. int. Pharmacodyn.*, 1969, **181**, 441–458.

141. Quinton, E. E. Retrograde amnesia induced by carbon dioxide inhalation. *Psychonom. Sci.*, 1966, **5**, 417–418.

142. Rambourg, A. Détection des glycoprotéines en microscopie électronique: coloration de la surface cellulaire et de l'appareil Golgi par un mélange acide chromique-phosphotungstique. *C. R. Acad. Sci. Paris*, 1967, **265**, 1426–1428.

143. Reiniš, S. Formation of conditioned reflexes in rats after the parenteral administration of brain homogenate. *Activ. Nerv. Super.* (Praha), 1965, **7**, 167–168.

144. Richardson, A. J., & Glow, P. H. Discrimination behavior in rats with reduced cholinesterase activity. *J. comp. physiol. Psychol.*, 1967, **63**, 240–246.

145. Robustelli, F. Azione della nicotina sull' apprendimento del ratto nel labirinto. *Atti Accademia Nazionale dei Lincei. Rend. Classe Sc.fis. mat. e nat.* (Series 8), 1963, **34**, 703–709.

146. Rose, S. P. R. Changes in incorporation of H^3-lysine into protein in rat visual cortex following first exposure to light. *Nature*, 1967, **215**, 253–255.

147. Rosenblatt, F. Induction of behavior by mammalian brain extracts. In *Molecular mechanisms and learning*. G. Ungar, Ed. New York: Plenum Press, 1970, pp. 103–147.

148. Rosenzweig, M. R., Krech, D., & Bennett, E. L. Effects of pentobarbital sodium on adaptive behavior patterns in the rat. *Science*, 1956, **123**, 371–372.

149. Rosenzweig, M. R., Krech, D., & Bennett, E. L. Brain chemistry and adaptive behavior. In *Biological and biochemical bases of behavior*. H. F. Harlow & C. N. Woolsey, Eds. Madison: Univ. of Wisconsin Press, 1958, pp. 367–400.

150. Russell, R. W., Watson, R. H. J., & Frankenhaeuser, M. Effects of chronic reductions in brain cholinesterase activity on acquisition and extinction of a conditioned avoidance response. *Scand. J. Psychol.*, 1961, **2**, 21–29.

151. Shashoua, V. E. The relation of RNA metabolism in the brain to learning in the goldfish. In *The central nervous system and fish behavior*. D. Ingle, Ed. Chicago, Univ. of Chicago Press, 1968, p. 203.

152. Sines, J. O. Reserpine, adrenalin, and avoidance learning. *Psychol. Rep.*, 1959, **5**, 321–324.

153. Solyom, L., & Gallay, H. M. Effect of malononitrile dimer on operant and classical conditioning of aged white rats. *Intern. J. Neuropsychiat.*, 1966, **2**, 577–584.

154. Solyom, L., Enesco, H. E., & Beaulieu, C. Effect of RNA on learning and activity in old and young rats. *J. Gerontol.*, 1967, **22**, 1–7.

155. Stellar, E., & McElroy, W. D. Does glutamic acid have any effect on learning? *Science*, 1948, **108**, 281–283.

156. Stewart, C. N., & Brookshire, K. H. Shuttle box avoidance learning and epinephrine. *Psychonom. Sci.*, 1967, **9**, 419–420.

157. Storm, T., Caird, W. K., & Korbin, E. The effects of alcohol on rote verbal learning and retention. *Psychonom. Sci.*, 1967, **9**, 43–44.

158. Stratton, L. O., & Petrinovich, L. Post-trial injections of an anticholinesterase drug and maze learning in two strains of rats. *Psychopharmacologia*, 1963, **5**, 47–54.

159. Ungar, G. Role of proteins and peptides in learning and memory. In *Molecular mechanisms in memory and learning*. G. Ungar, Ed. New York: Plenum Press, 1970, pp. 149–175.

160. Ungar, G., & Oceguera-Navarra, C. Transfer of habituation by material extracted from brain. *Nature (London)*, 1965, **207**, 301–302.

161. Verhave, T. The effect of d-methamphetamine on avoidance and operant level. *J. exp. Anal. Behav.*, 1958, **1**, 207–220.

162. Votava, Z., Bebesova', O., Metysova', J., & Souskova', M. Drug-induced changes of higher nervous activity in experimental animals. In *Psychopharmacological methods*. Z. Votava, M. Horvath, & O. Vinar, Eds. Oxford: Pergamon Press, 1963, pp. 31–40.

163. Wagner, A. R., Carder, J. B., & Beatty, W. W. Yeast ribonucleic acid effects on learned behavior in the rat. *Psychonom. Sci.*, 1966, **4**, 33–34.

164. Walker, D. R., & Milton, G. A. Memory transfer versus sensitization in cannibal planarians. *Psychonom. Sci.*, 1966, **5**, 293–294.

165. Weissman, A. Effect of electroconvulsive shock intensity and seizure pattern on retrograde amnesia in rats. *J. comp. physiol. Psychol.*, 1963, **56**, 806–810.

166. Weissman, A. Drugs and retrograde amnesia. *Int. Rev. Neurobiol.*, 1967, **10**, 167–198.

167. Westbrook, W. H., & McGaugh, J. L. Drug facilitation of latent learning. *Psychopharmacologia*, 1964, **5**, 440–446.

168. Westerman, R. A. Somatic inheritance of habituation of responses to light in planarians. *Science*, 1963, **140**, 676–677.

169. Wiener, N. I., & Deutsch, J. A. Temporal aspects of anticholinergic- and anticholinesterase-induced amnesia for an appetitive habit. *J. comp. physiol. Psychol.*, 1968, **66**, 613–617.

170. Williams, G. W., & O'Brien, C. The effect of sodium phenobarbital on the learning behavior of white rats. *J. comp. Psychol.*, 1937, **23**, 457–474.

171. Zelman, A., Kabat, L., Jacobson, R., & McConnell, J. V. Transfer of training through injection of "conditioned" RNA into untrained planarians. *Worm Runner's Digest*, 1963, **5**, 14–21.

172. Zemp, J. W., Wilson, J. E., Schlesinger, K., Boggan, W. O., & Glassman, E. Brain function and macromolecules, I. Incorporation of uridine into RNA of mouse brain during short-term training experience. *Proc. Nat. Acad. Sci. U.S.*, 1966, **55**, 1423–1431.

173. Zemp, J. W., Wilson, J. E., & Glassman, E. Brain function and macromolecules. II. Site of increased labeling of RNA in brains of mice during a short-term training experience. *Proc. Nat. Acad. Sci. U.S.*, 1967, **58**, 1120–1125.

174. Zimmerman, F. T., & Ross, S. Effect of glutamic acid and other amino acids on maze learning in the white rat. *A.M.A. Arch. Neurol. Psychiat.*, 1944, **51**, 446–451.

Chapter 20

THEORIES OF LEARNING

Physiological Theories
Molecular Theories of Learning
Anatomical Theories of Memory Storage
Review

PHYSIOLOGICAL THEORIES

General Considerations

Most contemporary physiological theories of learning and memory assume that: (1) learning requires concurrent activation of two or more central pathways; (2) concurrent activation somehow lowers the resistance of synaptic connections between active pathways; and (3) repeated activation of these interconnections produces electrophysiological or anatomical changes which permanently reduce their resistance. The theories differ primarily with respect to: (1) the nature of the influence that is thought to produce the initial facilitation of the synaptic connections; (2) the nature of the physiological and anatomical change that results from the use of these connections; and (3) the site of the storage process.

All contemporary theories share some common problems. Purely functional electrophysiological changes cannot be the basis of long-term memory traces because they are not sufficiently stable and permanent. Most theories attempt to circumvent this problem by postulating anatomical changes, but there is little experimental evidence for morphological plasticity in the adult brain. It is, indeed, difficult to imagine anatomical connections that are, on the one hand, capable of the continuous change or growth necessary for learning and, on the other, sufficiently stable to account for the persistence of memories over a lifetime. The second of these requirements presents few problems since we have ample evidence that the central nervous system of the adult is, in fact, static. What is not so easy to come by is evidence for sufficient plasticity to permit learning.

Neural development is not completed in the fetus but continues for some time after birth. Some early developmental theories suggested, in fact, that specific functional connections between neurons may not be established until environmental stimuli are received and processed by the nervous system.[3, 18] Neural growth and development stops soon after birth, but some observations suggest that at least limited anatomical change can occur in the adult nervous system. Neurons that project long axons to peripheral sensory receptors or muscles retain an ability to regenerate these projections if they are cut not too close to the cell body. Most textbooks of anatomy conclude that regeneration does not take place in the brain, but some experimental findings indicate that there may be exceptions to this rule. Lesions in the cerebral cortex as well as some subcortical and spinal regions are often invaded by fibers of apparently neuronal origin,[41, 30] and fairly extensive regeneration has been reported under unusual experimental conditions.[44, 33] Histological studies of the rabbit cortex[48, 49] have further shown that the number of dendritic terminals on cortical cells continues to increase during approximately half of the animal's lifetime. That this proliferation of neural connections may be related to learning is suggested by the observation[46] that animals reared in "complex" environments have significantly larger brains than animals reared in simple environments. Inferential support for continued neural growth in the mature nervous system can further be adduced from the observation that a continuous movement of protein[19] and other cytoplasmic materials[12] from the cell body toward its axonal and dendritic projections seems to take place.

If neural growth is indeed essential for the development of permanent memory traces, as many theories propose, some intervening process must retain the memory until the slow morphological changes can be completed. It appears unlikely, as we have seen in our discussion of consolidation, that purely functional neural changes such as reverberatory activity can entirely bridge these intervals. A possible additional step is suggested by the finding that neurons[10, 11] as well as glial cells[40] appear to be capable of movement and display slow rhythmic pulsations under some conditions which modify the relationship between neighboring cells. It is possible that these movements may be modified by activation of a cell and that repeated "use" of junctions that are established as the result of such movement may initiate a sequence of events culminating in permanent anatomical growth.

All currently available theories of learning or memory storage share a common weakness with respect to an explanation of the initial activation of previously nonfunctional pathways and the description of the mechanisms responsible for the resulting electrophysiological or anatomical changes. There is, as yet, no evidence for the widely accepted hypothesis that simple "use" of a synaptic junction provides sufficiently prolonged facilitatory effects to account for short-term memory. Many theorists attempt to circumvent this problem by suggesting that some neural networks may be capable of sustained self-excitation once any of their components has been activated. This requires only a brief period of hyperexcitability in any given neuron, since impulses can be returned to the cell that originated them within a few milliseconds via feedback loops. There is some electrophysiological and anatomical evidence for feedback connections in the central nervous system that could subserve such functions. However, sustained reverberatory activity per se, as postulated by these theories, has not been observed in the laboratory.

Nor is it clear that even sustained re-excitation of a neural pathway is capable of inducing whatever structural changes may be required to produce a long-term memory trace. Support for this explanation comes almost entirely from experiments showing that prolonged high-frequency and high-amplitude stimulation of some neural fibers facilitates the response of associated neurons to subsequent single-pulse stimuli.[31] This "post-tetanic potentiation" or PTP may persist for several minutes and decays gradually.[32] Some observations suggest that PTP may result in a temporary swelling of the axon end feet,[16,17] and it has been suggested[4] that this may itself produce a decrease in synaptic resistance and thus facilitate transmission. It has been shown[13] that prolonged excessive stretch of a muscle, which produces maximal discharges in associated stretch receptors, may similarly result in an apparent facilitation in associated motor neurons. It seems nonetheless unlikely that PTP or related facilitatory effects can account for short-term memory because most neurons do not propagate impulses of sufficient amplitude.[51] Moreover, few neurons maintain the high firing rates required to generate this effect. Even if a temporary facilitation similar to PTP occurs in some neural pathways, it could not, as far as we know, persist long enough to sustain the memory trace until permanent morphological changes could occur.

Theories Relying Exclusively on Anatomical Growth

Nearly all of the modern theories of learning and memory are significantly influenced by a model proposed by Tanzi[52] 80 years ago. In essence, this model suggested that the passage of a nerve impulse causes metabolic changes in the neuron that increase the volume of the cell and elongate its projections. Repeated activation of the neuron thus causes its axonal terminations to approach closer and closer to adjoining cells, thereby decreasing synaptic resistance and facilitating the conduction of subsequent impulses. Finally, a firm bond is established, which represents the physical basis of memory.

Another important influence on theoretical thinking in this field was Ariëns Kappers' notion of "neurobiotaxis." Kappers[24,25] suggested that all neurons may be polarized and, upon activation, generate magnetic fields which influence the growth of dendritic and axonal processes in adjacent cells and may induce movement of the cell body. More specifically, neural activity was thought to produce an electrically positive field inside the cell and a compensatory field of negativity outside it. Neurons in the vicinity of such a cell were thought to be attracted by this negativity and to project axons or dendrites towards the active cell. Attempts to demonstrate neural growth in the direction of positively or negatively polarized neurons have not been successful,[34] and the theories of learning (see below) that explicitly rely on neurobiotaxic influences are no longer considered very seriously. The basic proposition—that centers of high neural activity somehow exert an attracting influence on other neural pathways and induce facilitation in connecting pathways—is, however, at the heart of many modern theories of learning.

Most of the theories that have attempted to account for memory explicitly in terms of neurobiotaxic influences have assumed that learning is responsible for the entire functional organization of the brain. One example may help in understanding this intriguing notion. Holt[18] proposed that the nervous system initially consisted of an essentially random network of neurons and that functional connections between specific pathways may be made only when activation of some neurons establishes metabolic gradients that attract dendritic or axonal projections from neighboring neurons. When sensory receptors are initially stimulated, impulses are transmitted to the brain where they follow random paths which are determined by chance fluctuations in synaptic resistance. Eventually the excitation spreads, by chance, to some motor neurons and this elicits an overt response which is entirely random with respect to the environmental stimulus that elicits it. This response, in turn, produces kinesthetic afferents that find their way to the previously active motor neurons, thus setting into motion a feedback between associated efferent and afferent impulses, which results in anatomical growth and the establishment of basic reflex connections. The application of this principle to learning is best described in Holt's words.

Inasmuch as every afferent impulse spreads more or less widely as it traverses the central nervous system, the afferent impulse which is to be conditioned will somewhere come to a synaptic region which forms a part of the sensorimotor tract along which the unconditioned impulses are traveling to a muscle. At this point of conjunction, the conditions requisite for neurobiotaxic growth are realized, and the dendrites on the motor side of the synapse of the junction will be stimulated to grow contracurrently, toward the terminal arborizations of the neurons on which the to-be-conditioned impulses are arriving. This dendritic growth will tend to reduce the extent of non-nervous, and more resistant, tissue across which subsequent nerve impulses arriving on the same to-be-conditioned path must pass in order to reach the motor side (the dendrites) of this synaptic region. Thus will be reduced the resistance which this synapse interposes between the to-be-conditioned impulses and the already established motor outlines of the unconditioned impulses.

Two-Factor Theories

The majority of the contemporary anatomical theories of learning[14, 54, 4] propose that memory traces are initially represented by reverberatory activity and that this, in turn, produces anatomical changes such as an enlargement of existing presynaptic terminals[4] or the development of additional end feet.[14]

One of the first and most influential two-factor theories was presented over 20 years ago by Hebb.[14] This theory proposes that the neurons of the cortical sensory projection areas are randomly connected to cells of the association areas so that excitation of a particular sensory cell results in a random pattern of activity in the association areas. By chance, the randomly propagated impulse returns to the cell that initiated it and begins to retrace its initial path because the previous activation of these neurons has resulted in a temporary synaptic facilitation. In this fashion, a reverberatory circuit or, as Hebb[14] called it, a *"cell assembly,"* is established which represents the original stimulus input long after it has ceased. This persisting activation eventually causes the growth of additional end feet at synapses that are part of the cell assembly. This growth permanently facilitates this particular circuit. The next time the stimulus is presented, the cell assembly is again activated, providing the basis for recognition. More complex memories are thought to be stored in *"phase sequences,"* which consist of several cell assemblies interconnected such that activation of any one of its members produces an orderly sequence of excitation throughout the phase sequence.

Hebb's theory accounts quite elegantly for the initiation of reverberatory activity but fails to explain why it ever stops or how it could be prevented from spreading to all neurons of the brain. Milner[35] has suggested some modifications of the theory that avoid these problems. He proposed that the input to any cell in the association areas may be inhibitory as well as excitatory and that repeated activation of a cell inhibits neighboring inactive cells. These inhibitory influences limit the spread of excitation to cells that happen to have low-resistance excitatory interconnections and prevent subsequent "mushrooming" of the cell assembly. The eventual disappearance of the reverberatory activity occurs, according to Milner, because the prolonged activation of the cells of the cell assembly produces adaptation and fatigue. This reduces the inhibitory effects on neighboring units, which are thus free to fire and, in turn, inhibit the cell assembly.

Hebb's theory was initially designed primarily to account for perceptual recognition. It can be extended to the traditional model of conditioning as follows. The presentation of the CS and the UCS initiates two cell assemblies or phase sequences that are thought to overlap to some extent. In these regions of overlap, both stimuli produce activation, and the connections are consequently strengthened until activation of the CS cell assembly leads to an activation of the UCS cell assembly.

Summary and Review Questions

Most contemporary attempts to describe the physiological and anatomical changes that may occur during learning share a number of common features. They generally assume that activation of a cell (i.e., depolarization) results in a temporary facilitation such that weak impulses that cannot normally produce postsynaptic depolarization and propagation do so if they arrive concurrently or shortly afterwards. Although the temporal relationships do not agree well with the behavioral literature, the CS is thus thought to become initially able to produce excitation in the pathways of the UCS (or UR) because of its arrival at a synapse concurrently or shortly after it has been used by the UCS. Repeated use of a previously inactive synapse is thought to result in an incremental and persisting facilitation, which eventually allows the weak CS signal to cross the synaptic junction to the UCS pathway even when the postsynaptic membrane has not recently been depolarized by the UCS itself.

Most investigators believe that feedback loops that permit self-sustaining "reverberatory" neural activity are responsible for the initial phases of this facilitation. Since there is good evidence that well-established memories are not destroyed by procedures that disrupt such reverberatory activity, it is generally agreed that more permanent structural alterations in the relationship between two cells must eventually occur. Many neurophysiologists favor the hypothesis that repeated use may result in enlargement of the terminal end feet of an axon and that this may (1) increase the area of contact (or otherwise reduce the "resistance" between the two cells) and (2) increase the availability of the neurohumoral transmitter at the end feet.

1. Review some of the experimental findings which suggest that neural growth may occur in the adult brain and that this may be responsible for long-term memory traces.

2. Review the data which suggest that repeated activation of a synapse may result in facilitation.

3. Describe Hebb's theory of learning and Milner's modification of it.

MOLECULAR THEORIES OF LEARNING

General Considerations

Every cell of every living organism performs its functions by a series of chemical reactions. The properties of a visual receptor, muscle fiber, or nerve cell can be fully understood only when we know how these chemical reactions are triggered and how they produce their effects. We have recently begun to understand how different cells of the same organism come to specialize in often quite different functions. All cells are basically equipped to perform all possible functions but are genetically programmed to exercise only part of their potential. The genetic code is contained in molecules of deoxyribonucleic acid (DNA), a complex molecule found in the genes of every cell.

What a cell does and how it interacts with its environment is determined by the type of proteins it produces and by the rate of their synthesis. Protein synthesis occurs on templates of ribonucleic acid (RNA) which, in turn, are faithful replica of the DNA template of the gene. RNA molecules are manufactured in the cell's nucleus and then migrate into the cytoplasm. The structure of the RNA molecule is then used as a model for the combination of several amino acids into complex chains of proteins. Since there are 25 to 30 different amino acids that can be combined in every possible combination or permutation, a vast number of slightly different protein molecules occurs. The type and rate of protein synthesis thus determines the properties of each cell on the basis of genetic information which is encoded in the structure (i.e., the sequence of bases) of the DNA molecule.

The DNA molecule must be extraordinarily stable and resistant to modification if genetic information is to be transmitted faithfully and if proper cellular functions are to be guaranteed over the life-span of an organism. This, of course, is a basic condition for survival. The moment a significant proportion of the total population of a particular type of cells does not function as designed, the organism dies. Fortunately, such mutations occur only rarely and only in response to special forces such as radiation. Yet, when we consider learning, we are assuming that very basic changes in the activity of some nerve cells can occur as a result of seemingly trivial (in a biochemical sense) events such as concurrent activation of adjacent cells. How can we obtain plasticity in a system that appears to be so resistant to change?

It is clear that learning must somehow involve either a change in the nature of the proteins produced by a cell or a change in the relative rate of synthesis of some types of proteins. The big question is how this comes about and how it becomes a permanent feature of the cell's organization.

As we have just discussed, the DNA molecule is very resistant to modification, and it appears unlikely that the minor biochemical or bioelectrical events that occur during learning could produce a true mutation of the DNA template. It has been suggested that the DNA molecule of nerve cells may have unique properties which make it more labile than those of cells in other parts of the organism,[7] but it is difficult to see how nerve cells could then maintain the basic stability of sensory, motor, and various regulatory functions, as well as the faithful transmission of instinctive behaviors and the long-term survival of memory traces. As we shall see in a moment, it may be possible to circumvent this problem by assuming that parts of the gene are repressed or otherwise not maximally active and that learning may involve not a basic change in the DNA structure but a derepression or activation of parts of the gene as it exists.

The RNA molecule appears to be much more easily modifiable, and many investigators have proposed that the process of learning may involve a change in RNA instead of DNA structure. This would lead to the synthesis of novel proteins (or a change in the rate of synthesis of proteins produced during the normal activity of the cell). However, RNA molecules as well as proteins are not very stable, and it is difficult to see how the altered cellular activity (i.e., the memory trace) could be maintained for more than a few days at most. Once the originally changed RNA molecule disappears, new ones are presumably synthesized on the basis of the unchanged DNA template, and cellular function should revert to the "untrained" state. This provides a simple mechanism for forgetting but fails to account for the obvious longevity of some memories.

The last member of the chain—the protein molecule—has similar problems. It is conceivable that the biochemical or bioelectrical events that occur during learning might directly alter the structure of some protein molecules that are part of the cell structure. This, in turn, might render specific portions of the cell membrane more sensitive to bioelectric events or neurohumoral transmitters and thus make the cell selectively responsive to the arrival of impulses at some of the end feet which impinge on it. Alternatively, a change in protein synthesis might increase the availability of a neurohumoral transmitter at some of the cell's own end feet and thus make it more probable that subsequent activation of the cell will be propagated to other cells. Something like this must almost certainly occur as a result of learning. The big question is how such a change in protein synthesis can become permanent. The life-span of protein molecules is even shorter than that of RNA, and forgetting caused by the manufacture of "untrained" proteins or RNA templates should be even more rapid.

Just as it is possible that the DNA of nerve cells might be more labile than that of other cells, it is conceivable, although not likely, that the longevity of RNA or protein molecules is greater in neurons than in other cells. Alternatively, it is possible that RNA or protein molecules that have undergone modification from learning may somehow be able to induce similar changes in the RNA or protein molecules that replace them. Finally, it is conceivable that the change in cellular activity which results from the learning-induced alteration in RNA or protein structure may, itself, perpetuate the conditions that were responsible for the initial change in protein synthesis. There is, as yet, very little evidence for any of these mechanisms and a fair amount of data from research on nonneural tissues which suggests that none of the proposed events are very probable.

As yet there is no satisfactory answer to the riddle how changes in protein synthesis, which almost certainly must occur as part of the learning process, can become a permanent feature of the cell's operations. As we have seen in a previous part of our discussion, there is a great deal of current research which attempts to pinpoint where the crucial changes occur along the DNA-RNA-protein chain and what the nature and critical determinants of these changes might be (see Chapter 19). Until we get some of this information, the specific theoretical models in this field are uniformly open to the challenge that they postulate biochemical events which are unlike those seen in nonnervous tissue. We shall therefore have only a cursory glance at some of the specific models that have been proposed.

There are, basically, two approaches to modeling in this field. Some investigators have proposed that each discrete memory may be represented by a unique protein molecule and that recall somehow involves direct activation of this "tape-recorder molecule." It is not logically impossible that such a specific molecule might result from the unique pattern of bioelectrical or biochemical events which occur during learning if we assume that no two neurons have precisely the same pattern of interconnections. Moreover, the number of possible permutations and combinations of amino acids might be sufficient to account for memory in this fashion. However, it is difficult to understand how this type of model achieves recall of a memory, particularly in view of the fact that the pattern of neural activity which existed during learning is never exactly duplicated and may, in fact, be quite different during recall. Tape-recorder models are still used by investigators who believe that the brain processes information not via discrete connections between neurons but by subtle changes in the electrical "fields" of larger regions of the brain.[28, 15] Most contemporary investigators would, however, agree with Holger Hydén's cryptic statement that the notion of a tape-recorder molecule is "biological nonsense."[22]

More commonly, the theorists in this field attempt to postulate a biochemical mechanism for nonspecific facilitation of synaptic transmission. In the simplest model, concurrent activation of two pathways which are interconnected by nonfunctional junctions produces pre- and/or postsynaptic changes which make a passage of subsequent impulses at the previously nonfunctional junction more probable. The activation of one cell by the UCS may thus increase the sensitivity of its membranes such that the arrival of a CS-related impulse may be able to produce postsynaptic depolarization where the CS-related potential alone could not have done so.

Some Examples of Molecular Models

Biochemical hypotheses of learning or memory storage were first proposed about twenty years ago when it became apparent that some cells can "learn" to synthesize special proteins such as antibodies or enzymes. Monné,[36] for example, suggested that instinctive behavior might be based on genetically determined patterns of protein synthesis and that the essential events responsible for learning might be a change in these innate cellular functions. Katz and Halstead[26] went a step further and proposed that only a few of the neurons of the brain might be joined by connections that are functional at birth. Most, they believed, become functional only when environmental stimuli begin to establish complex patterns of neural activity. According to this model, synapses become functional when the arrival of impulses causes randomly oriented protein molecules to assume a specific configuration. These special proteins then were thought to act as templates for the synthesis of many structurally identical protein molecules which are then incorporated into the cell membrane. This, in turn, results in a selective sensitivity to the type of input that originated the first oriented proteins. A memory trace is laid down when complex neural pathways are "specified" by a diffusion of oriented proteins to concurrently active cells. It has turned out that protein molecules probably cannot reproduce themselves as suggested, but the general outlines of this early hypothesis were remarkably prophetic.

The current interest in biochemical models of learning traces back more specifically to Holger Hydén's[20] suggestion that RNA molecules might be modifiable by cellular activity and that this might be the essential biochemical event in learning. On the basis of rather sketchy experimental data, he suggested that the arrival of a particular spatiotemporal pattern of neural impulses at a cell might create a unique change in the electrochemistry of that cell which results in a structural change in some RNA molecules. He initially suggested that these novel RNA molecules might then be used as templates for the synthesis of proteins which were assumed to have the unique property of dissociating explosively (thus causing the release of neurohumoral transmitters) whenever the pattern of inputs which originated the RNA change is duplicated.

An interesting variation of the RNA hypothesis was suggested by Landauer.[28] His model proposed that the activation of the CS pathway might result in the synthesis of novel RNA molecules not in the directly activated neurons but in associated glial cells. These "CS-specific" molecules were thought to be transferred to neighboring neurons activated by the UCS shortly afterwards. They then become part of that cell's structure and serve as templates for proteins that are selectively sensitive to the pattern of activity in the CS pathway. This model is of particular interest since it avoids a problem common to all other hypotheses in this field—the postulation of concurrent activation of the CS and UCS pathway. The proposed sequence of biochemical events instead fits the established behavioral facts rather nicely. Since the synthesis of CS-specific RNA molecules and their diffusion into the vicinity of neurons of the UCS pathway requires some time, conditioning cannot occur unless the CS precedes the UCS by at least a fraction of a second. Uptake of the RNA molecules into inactive neurons presumably does not occur because these large molecules cannot cross cellular membranes except during the brief period when the transmission of impulses across the synaptic junction has removed the resting potential of the cell membrane.

Subsequent research has indicated that RNA molecules are probably not sufficiently stable to serve as the templates for the continued synthesis of novel proteins. Hydén[21] has consequently abandoned the RNA hypothesis in favor of a model suggesting that the formation of long-term memory traces must involve some modification in the only stable component of the cell—the DNA molecule. Circumventing, to some extent, the problem of DNA stability, Hydén now proposes that stimulation of a cell may activate small areas of the genome that were fully or partially repressed. This would lead to the synthesis of radically altered RNA molecules which, in turn, can serve as templates for the novel proteins believed to be responsible for a general increase in the responsiveness of that cell to any type of input. This hypothesis differs from the original one not only in a shifting emphasis from RNA to DNA but also in abandoning a tape-recorder model and shifting to a mechanism producing only general facilitation.

A similar model has been proposed by Flexner.[6] This hypothesis assumes that learning involves an increase in the synthesis of a particular RNA molecule (not necessarily the creation of a novel one) and a consequent increase in the manufacture of a protein that modifies the cellular wall in the vicinity of the synapse to facilitate the passage of impulses. Permanence is provided in this system by the assumption that the protein also acts as an inducer on repressed aspects of the gene which are responsible for the synthesis of the RNA molecule needed to produce more of the same protein.

Briggs and Kitto[2] earlier proposed an inducer model that tied the process of learning more specifically to an increased availability of a neurohumoral transmitter. They argued that the RNA changes which have been observed during learning (see Chapter 19) might be a by-product of an enzyme induction process. The proposed model rests on the following assumptions. (1) All cells of an organism contain the same genes and each of these genes is capable of synthesizing a specific protein. (2) Cells do not produce the same proteins and synthesize quite different amounts of the proteins which they do produce. (3) The synthesis of a particular protein can be induced by the presence of the appropriate substrate. These considerations are related to the learning process as follows. Whether an impulse is transmitted across a synaptic junction depends, in part, on the quantity of the transmitter released. This, in turn, depends in part on the total quantity available, which is determined by the activity of the related biosynthetic enzymes. If these enzymes are inducible by the presence of their substrates as proposed, each activation of the cell will increase its ability to manufacture and release the transmitter.

Most contemporary molecular models of learning have been content to describe how altered proteins might modify the reactions of cells to particular inputs without worrying about the mechanisms responsible for the continued availability of the modified proteins. Attempts have been made to implicate specific types of proteins in learning- or memory-related processes,[1,53,45] but these often complex chemical considerations do not, at the moment, help us understand the basic problem.

Another development has been the attempt to devise hypotheses that postulate several interrelated processes. Roberts,[42] for instance, has proposed a model that conceives of the basic process in learning as a gradual increase in "connectivity" between adjacent cells and he has postulated several sequentially related processes that might produce it.

The first of these consists of a direct neurohumoral feedback between the pre- and postsynaptic membranes. It is assumed that information transfer occurs by the release of an excitatory transmitter. When this transmitter produces depolarization of the postsynaptic membrane, an inhibitory transmitter is thought to be released which, in turn, acts on the presynaptic membrane to aid in the restoration of its natural state. A relative facilitation of previously active synapses is thought to occur when the inhibitory transmitter acts on adjacent presynaptic membranes that have not recently been depolarized.

This very transient facilitation is believed to lead to the second process—active growth of the presynaptic membrane. Roberts proposes that the biochemical events triggered by the transmission of an impulse include the release of rate-limiting materials needed for biosynthetic reactions. These are believed to be further aided by an exchange of materials between the blood, glia, and synaptic membranes during the concurrent depolarization of the pre- and postsynaptic membranes. The resulting biosynthetic activity results in the development of additional presynaptic tissue and the differentiation of additional vesicles containing neurohumoral transmitters. Subsequent depolarization of the presynaptic membrane thus should be more likely to induce a change in the postsynaptic membrane not only because the distance which separates the site of transmitter release and its site of action is decreased but also because more transmitter is available for release.

The biosynthetic growth reaction is believed to be aided by a third process—the development of specific biochemical "affinities" between the pre- and postsynaptic membranes. Roberts proposes that the concurrent biochemical activity that occurs during the passage of an impulse in the pre- and postsynaptic membranes may permit an exchange of molecules between the two membranes. As a result, their surface structure is believed to become increasingly similar and increasingly likely to "adhere" to each other.

Roberts suggests that these three processes

may interact and form the basis of what has been called consolidation. The transient facilitation caused by the differential effect of the inhibitory transmitter obviously can last at best for a few seconds. It accounts, perhaps, for the transient memories involved in dialing an unfamiliar telephone number without having to look up each digit separately. Processes leading to biosynthesis could conceivably begin within a minute or two after the activation of synaptic mechanisms and might achieve a significant development in several hours. The exchange of molecules between the pre- and postsynaptic membranes occurs during the transmission of the impulse itself. However, the postulated change in the surface structure of the cell would not be expected to become a factor until hours or even days later. This model has many obvious shortcomings, but it is of interest because it attempts to explicitly deal with the problem of multistage memories.

Most contemporary molecular theories of memory attempt to account for the selective facilitation of transmission of impulses between neurons that are concurrently or sequentially active during the learning experience. Galambos[8] suggested some years ago that storage of information might be a function of glia instead of neurons but presented no formal model of such a mechanism. Landauer's[28] RNA hypothesis (see above) postulated the participation of glial cells in the formation of novel molecular structures, but the details of this mechanism were not spelled out. A more complete and general model of a nonneural storage and retrieval mechanism has more recently been proposed.

Robinson[43] suggests that the storage of information may not require structural changes in any cells but merely the movement of molecules from one cell to another. It is assumed that any sensory input produces a complex pattern of neural activity. The memory trace of this activity consists of the information that certain key elements in the chain of active neurons called "pattern neurons" have been concurrently or sequentially active. Each of these pattern neurons contains a reservoir of identical "pattern molecules" that are unique (i.e., different from the pattern molecules of any other cell). When pattern neurons fire, some of these pattern molecules are released into the intercellular spaces. In the vicinity of the pattern neurons, glial "storage cells" are believed to exist which react to the presence of a number of different pattern molecules by incorporating them into their own structure. The storage cells begin to produce novel molecules called comolecules, which are complementary to the pattern molecules they have incorporated. Once this has occurred, the storage unit is said to be "recorded" and is no longer available for storage. Memory retrieval occurs when, because of the activation of one or more pattern neurons that were active during learning, pattern molecules are released into the vicinity of a recorded storage unit which contains, among others, comolecules that are complementary to these pattern molecules. This triggers the release of all comolecules that were formed by the storage unit during learning. These comolecules then interact with the pattern molecules of the pattern neurons that were active during the initial acquisition and thus induce neural activity, which reproduces the essential elements of the original experience.

Summary and Review Questions

Cells are basically biochemical systems, and a change in cellular functions requires a modification of their chemical structure. The functions of each cell are basically determined be genes which consist of deoxyribonucleic acid (DNA). Individual DNA molecules act as models or "templates" for the synthesis of ribonucleic acid (RNA) molecules which, in turn, act as templates for the combination of amino acids into complex protein molecules. Everything a cell does is determined by the type of proteins it synthesizes and by the relative rate of their formation.

If we assume that learning must involve a change in the function of some cells (such as an increased sensitivity to some or all afferent inputs or an increased ability to generate electrical potentials and transmit them to neighboring cells), a change in protein synthesis must almost certainly occur. The major questions which concern molecular biologists today include: (1) what triggers these changes in protein metabolism; (2) are they basically different in different cells or even within the same cell depending on the nature of the afferent input; (3) how do the changes in protein synthesis become translated into the functional changes that represent the memory trace; and (4) how do these changes become permanent.

In order to faithfully transmit essential genetic information and maintain the stability of cellular functions, the mechanisms that control protein synthesis cannot be subject to permanent modification except under very unusual circumstances which result in a mutation of the genetic material itself. To the best of our current knowledge, it is unlikely that the relatively minor disturbances in biochemical activity that occur during activation of a nerve cell can induce such a basic change in the structure of a DNA molecule. Structural modifications in RNA or protein molecules are much more probable, but it is not clear how these can be perpetuated. Both RNA and protein molecules are very unstable and are continually being resynthesized on the basis of the presumably unmodifiable DNA templates.

Some contemporary theorists have attempted to circumvent these problems by suggesting that the bioelectrical events which occur during learning may directly or indirectly "derepress" or otherwise facilitate small segments of the gene and thus result in an expression of potential functions. This is thought not to involve a major structural change or the rearrangement of previously active sites of the gene and thus be more likely to occur in response to relatively minor disturbances in cellular activity.

Other contemporary molecular models of learning ignore this aspect of the problem and concentrate on a description of the events which translate the changes in protein synthesis that are presumed to occur into the gross functional events (i.e., pre- and/or postsynaptic facilitation), which we assume to be responsible for learning on a more molar physiological level. Postsynaptic facilitation is generally thought to be caused by the incorporation of proteins that were formed during learning into the postsynaptic membrane. Presynaptic facilitation could similarly occur as a result of the incorporation of particular proteins into the presynaptic membrane (which might thus become "similar" to the postsynaptic membrane) or to the increased availability of a neurohumoral transmitter.

1. Describe the intracellular mechanisms that determine protein synthesis.

2. Discuss how the bioelectrical events that occur during activation of a nerve cell might modify protein synthesis.

3. Discuss how such a change in protein synthesis might be perpetuated and thus constitute a permanent memory trace.

4. Describe the mechanisms by which a change in protein synthesis might produce the molar changes (pre- or postsynaptic facilitation) which we associate with learning.

Anatomical Theories of Memory Storage

Many investigators are concerned not so much with the details of the mechanisms of memory formation or storage as with the pathways that may be specifically responsible for this function. Pavlov[37] proposed many years ago that learning might involve a direct interaction between the cortical "analyzers" of the CS and UCS, and variations of this interpretation continue to be popular. Hebb[14] as well as many contemporaries[27,4] suggest that memories may be stored in the specific sensory association areas which adjoin the sensory projection areas of the cortex. This interpretation is supported by experimental findings showing that modality specific memory deficits can be produced by damage to the cortical association areas. However, it is not entirely clear to what extent these deficits may be caused by an impairment in complex sensory functions instead of mechanisms specifically related to memory. Simple conditioning does not require cortical influences, and even complex discriminations can often be relearned following damage to the association areas.

Many theorists consequently believe that while the establishment of complex associations may require cortical influences, the process of connection-formation itself must occur subcortically. Because an almost infinite number of associations between stimuli of all modalities are possible, these subcortical mechanisms must have reciprocal connections with all areas of the cortex as well as many subcortical relay stations. This effectively limits our choice to the hippocampus,[38] brainstem reticular formation,[5] or the nonspecific thalamic projection system.[9] Extensive damage to the reticular formation or related thalamic nuclei produces a more or less complete and permanent unresponsiveness to all sensory stimuli, and one can interpret this as a reflection of the interruption of basic memory traces. Reflexes and other simple "instinctive" behaviors tend to be less affected by such lesions and recover sooner than complex, learned reactions. However, there is as yet no proof that the observed impairment is caused by an interference with memory mechanisms rather than sensory, motor, or motivational influences which may be essential for an integration of complex behavior (see Chapter 16).

A number of investigators[38,47] believe that the hippocampus and some associated temporal lobe neocortex may be specifically involved in the storage and retrieval of memory. This view is shared particularly by many neurosurgeons who find that electrical stimulation of the hippocampus and associated temporal lobe structures elicits often very specific and complete memories,[39] whereas tumor growth or surgical damage results in memory loss.[50] Electrical stimulation or damage to the hippocampus or associated temporal lobe structures does not, however, elicit or obliterate the relatively simple memories which can be established in laboratory animals, suggesting that this region may not be essential for basic memory functions. Although species differences cannot be entirely ruled out, it appears more likely that the "memory" deficits seen in man may reflect stimulation or disruption of higher order integrative or reasoning processes not essential to simple conditioning.

It has been suggested[29,23] that memories may not, in fact, be represented by specific geographically identifiable pathways but may reflect, instead, a unique spatiotemporal pattern of activity in neural systems which pervades much if not all of the brain. This "statistical" approach to memory is based largely on the observations that most neurons are spontaneously active, that their response to stimulation is not entirely determined by the parameters of the stimulus, and that most neurons receive inputs from many diverse sources. This suggests that the output of any single neuron cannot reliably carry information, as most theories of neural function and learning assume. It is therefore suggested that information may be processed in the nervous system in terms of the *average* spatiotemporal activity pattern in large neural networks and that learning involves an increase in the probability that the CS alone can elicit an average population response which is similar to that produced by the UCS and CS in combination. Almost any stimulus appears to be capable of eliciting responses from neurons in all parts of the brain, and the statistical approach consequently suggests that learning can take place in any coherent neural network. This interpretation is supported by the demonstration that none of the major anatomical subdivisions of the central nervous system appears to be essential for memory storage or retrieval (see Chapter 17).

Summary and Review Questions

Most contemporary investigators believe that memory traces consist of specific patterns of synaptic facilitation in neural pathways. There are, however, wide differences of opinion concerning the geographic distribution of these pathways. Some investigators believe that memory functions might be uniquely represented in restricted portions of the brain such as the association areas of the cortex, the hippocampus, or the reticular formation of the brainstem or thalamus. Others conceive of memory traces in terms of spatiotemporal patterns of activity that involve much if not all of the brain. There is some evidence in support of the notion that memory-related processes may be preferentially localized in some portions of the central nervous system, but it is also quite clear that no single aspect of the brain is uniquely charged with learning, memory storage, or retrieval.

1. Summarize the evidence suggesting that memory-related processes might be represented in specific parts of the brain.

2. Why do some investigators suggest that most or all parts of the brain may participate in memory storage?

Review

The biological basis of learning has been conceptualized at molar as well as molecular levels. Most neurophysiologists consider learning in terms of gross alterations of synaptic functions which are believed to permit the establishment of novel interconnections between neurons. It is generally assumed that depolarization of a cell membrane produces a measure of facilitation which decays within a short period of time. If an impulse arrives at a nerve terminal that is not, under normal circumstances, capable of propagating the impulse across the synapse, it may be able to do so during this period of facilitation. This is thought to constitute the initial step in the learning process.

The use of a previously inactive synapse is believed to result in a measure of facilitation which increases the probability that subsequent impulses will be able to cross it. Many neurophysiologists believe that this process may be aided by feedback loops which maintain self-sustaining or "reverberatory" activity across such a synapse for some time. This repeated activation, in turn, is believed to produce anatomical growth that permanently decreases the resistance of the synapse and maintains the memory after the reverberatory activity has disappeared because of the gradual development of inhibitory influences.

Some investigators believe that this process of synaptic facilitation occurs only in specific portions of the central nervous system (such as the association areas of the cortex, the hippocampus, or the reticular formation of the thalamus or brainstem). Others suggest that all neural tissue may be capable of learning and that memory traces may be diffusely distributed throughout the brain.

In recent years, we have learned a great deal about the genetic mechanisms that regulate cellular functions, and a number of molecular models for the gross functional changes discussed above have been suggested. Synaptic facilitation can be the result of changes in the activity of the cell that intends to propagate impulses or in the activity of the cell destined to receive them. Molecular models of learning generally suggest that both types of facilitatory influences may be due to the formation of specific protein molecules during learning which are then incorporated into the pre- and/or postsynaptic membranes. Incorporation of a particular protein into the postsynaptic membrane may generally decrease its threshold for depolarization. It might make the membrane selectively sensitive to a particular spatial pattern of input if the novel protein is incorporated selectively into those regions of the postsynaptic membrane that are adjacent to the end feet that participated in the depolarization of the postsynaptic membrane at the time the novel proteins were formed. Incorporation of novel proteins into the presynaptic membrane might increase the availability of a neural transmitter or simply produce some growth which decreases the physical distance between its site of release and site of action. A number of recent molecular models have suggested that the concurrent depolarization of the pre- and postsynaptic membrane might also permit an exchange of molecules between the two membranes such that a degree of structural similarity is achieved which itself might facilitate the transmission of impulses.

The molecular models of learning are, as yet, not sufficiently precise to be of much help in understanding the molar changes in neural activity which occur during learning or the process of learning as the psychologist sees it. However, the molecular approach to other complex biological problems has already been enormously successful, and there seems to be a good chance that its application to the problem of learning might bear fruit in the not too distant future. While we are awaiting such progress, it is important to remember that the molecular models of learning do not compete with more molar interpretations but attempt to provide complementary information which may help us understand the functional changes which occur as a result of learning.

Bibliography

1. Bogoch, S. *The biochemistry of memory*. New York: Oxford Univ. Press, 1968.
2. Briggs, M. H., & Kitto, G. B. The molecular basis of memory and learning. *Psychol. Rev.*, 1962, **69**, 537–541.
3. Coghill, G. E. *Anatomy and the problem of behavior*. New York: Macmillan and Cambridge Univ. Press, 1919.
4. Eccles, J. C. *The neurophysiological basis of mind*. Oxford: Clarendon Press, 1953.
5. Fessard, A. E. Mechanisms of nervous integration and conscious experience. In *Brain mechanisms and consciousness* E. D. Adrian, F. Brenner, H. H. Jasper, & J. F. Delafresnaye, Eds. Springfield, Ill.: Thomas, 1954, pp. 200–236.
6. Flexner, L. B., Flexner, J. B., & Roberts, R. B. Memory in mice analyzed with antibiotics. *Science*, 1967, **155**, 1377–1383.
7. Gaito, J. *Macromolecules and behavior*. New York: Appleton-Century-Crofts, 1966.
8. Galambos, R. A glia-neural theory of brain function. *Proc. nat. Acad. Sci. U.S.*, 1961, **57**, 129–136.
9. Gastaut, H. Some aspects of the neurophysiological basis of conditioned reflexes and behaviour. In *Ciba Foundation symposium on the neurological basis of behaviour*. G. E. W. Wolstenholme & Cecilia M. O'Connor, Eds. London: Churchill, 1958, 255–276.
10. Geiger, R. S. Subcultures of adult mammalian brain cortex. *Exp. Cell Res.*, 1958, **14**, 541–566.
11. Geiger, R. S. The behavior of adult mammalian brain cells in culture. In *International review of neurobiology*. C. C. Pfeiffer & J. R. Smythies, Eds. 1963, **5**, 1–51.
12. Gerard, R. W. Some aspects of neural growth, regeneration and function. In *Genetic neurology. Conference of the international union of biological science*. P. Weiss, Ed. Chicago: Univ. of Chicago Press, 1950, 199–207.
13. Granit, R. Reflex rebound by post-tetanic potentiation. Temporal summation—spasticity. *J. Physiol. (London)*, 1956, **131**, 32–51.
14. Hebb, D. O. *The organization of behavior: a neuropsychological theory*. New York: Wiley, 1949.
15. Hechter, O., & Halkerston, I. D. K. On the nature of macromolecular coding in neuronal memory. *Perspectives Biol. Med.*, 1964, **1**, 183–198.
16. Hill, D. K. The effect of stimulation on the opacity of a crustacean nerve trunk and its relation to fiber diameter. *J. Physiol. (London)*, 1950a, **111**, 283–303.
17. Hill, D. K. The volume changes resulting from stimulation of a giant nerve fibre. *J. Physiol. (London)*, 1950b, **111**, 304–327.
18. Holt, E. B. *Animal drive and the learning process*. New York: Henry Holt, 1931.
19. Hydén, H. Protein and nucleotide metabolism in the nerve cell under different functional conditions. *Nucleic acids: Symposium of the society for experimental biology. Vol. I.*, 1947, 152–161.
20. Hydén, H. Quantitative assay of compounds in isolated, fresh nerve cells and glial cells from control and stimulated animals. *Nature*, 1959, **184**, 433–435.
21. Hydén, H. Biochemical changes accompanying learning. In *The neurosciences, A Study Program*. G. C. Quarton, T. Melnechuk, & F. O. Schmitt, Eds. New York: Rockefeller Univ. Press, 1967, pp. 765–771.
22. Hydén, H. Biochemical aspects of learning and memory. In *On the biology of learning*. K. H. Pribram, Ed. New York: Harcourt, Brace & World, Inc., 1969, pp. 95–125.
23. John. E. R. *Mechanisms of learning*. New York: Academic Press, 1967.

24. Kappers, C. U. A. Further contributions on neurobiotaxis. *J. comp. Neurol.*, 1917, **27**, 261–298.
25. Kappers, C. U. A. Principles of development of the nervous system (Neurobiotaxis). In *Cytology and cellular pathology of the nervous system*. W. Penfield, Ed. New York: Paul Hoeber, 1932, pp. 43–89.
26. Katz, J. J., & Halstead, W. C. Protein organization and mental functions. *Comp. Psychol. Monograph*, 1950, **20**, 1–38.
27. Konorski, J. The physiological approach to the problem of recent memory. In *Brain mechanisms and learning*. J. L. Delafresnaye, A. Fessard, R. W. Gerard, & J. Konorski, Eds. Oxford: Blackwell Scientific, 1961, pp. 115–132.
28. Landauer, T. K. Two hypotheses concerning the biochemical basis of memory. *Psychol. Rev.*, 1964, **71**, 167–179.
29. Lashley, K. S. Cerebral organization and behavior. *Proc. Ass. Res. nerv. ment. Dis.*, 1958, **36**, 1–18.
30. Liu, C. N., & Chambers, W. W. Intraspinal sprouting elicited from intact spinal sensory neurons by adjacent posterior root section. *Amer. J. Physiol.*, 1955, **183**, 640–641.
31. Lloyd, D. P. C. Post-tetanic potentiation of responses in monosynaptic reflex pathways of the spinal cord. *J. gen. Physiol.*, 1949, **33**, 147–170.
32. McIntyre, A. K. Synaptic function and learning. *Proceedings of the nineteenth international physiological congress*, Montreal, 1953, 107–114.
33. Malis, L. I., Baker, C. P., Kruger, L., & Rose, J. E. Effects of heavy ionizing monoenergetic particles on the cerebral cortex. II: Histological appearances of laminar lesions and growth of nerve fibers after laminar destruction. *J. comp. Neurol.*, 1960, **115**, 243–297.
34. Marsh, G., & Beams, H. W. In vitro control of growing chick nerve fibers by applied electrical currents. *J. cell. comp. Physiol.*, 1946, **27**, 139–158.
35. Milner, P. M. The cell assembly: Mark II. *Psychol. Rev.*, 1957, **64**, 242–252.
36. Monné, L. Functioning of the cytoplasm. In *Advances in enzymology. Vol. VIII*. F. F. Nord, Ed. New York: Interscience, 1948, 1–69.
37. Pavlov, I. *Conditioned reflexes. An investigation of the physiological activity of the cerebral cortex*. New York: Oxford Univ. Press, 1927.
38. Penfield, W. Memory mechanisms. *Arch. Neurol. Psychiat. (Chicago)*, 1952, **67**, 178–191.
39. Penfield, W., & Milner, B. The memory deficit produced by bilateral lesions in the hippocampal zone. *Arch. Neurol. Psychiat. (Chicago)*, 1958, **79**, 475–497.
40. Pomerat, G. M. Pulsative activity of cells from the human brain in situ. *J. nerv. ment. Dis.*, 1951, **114**, 430–449.
41. Ramón y Cajal, S. *Degeneration and regeneration of the nervous system*. London: Oxford Univ. Press, 1928.
42. Roberts, E. The synapse as a biochemical self-organizing cybernetic unit. In *Molecular basis of some aspects of mental activity. Vol. I*. O. Walaas, Ed. London: Academic Press, 1966, pp. 37–82.
43. Robinson, C. E. A chemical model of long-term memory and recall. In *Molecular basis of some aspects of mental activity. Vol. I*. O. Walaas, Ed. London: Academic Press, 1966, pp. 29–35.
44. Rose, J. E., Malis, L. I., & Baker, C. P. Neural growth in the cerebral cortex after lesions produced by monoenergetic deuterons. In *Sensory communication*. W. A. Rosenblith, Ed. Cambridge, Mass.: M.I.T. Press, 1961, pp. 279–301.
45. Rosenblatt, F. Induction of behavior by mammalian brain extracts. In *Molecular mechanisms in memory and learning*. G. Ungar, Ed. New York: Plenum Press, 1970, pp. 103–147.
46. Rosenzweig, M. R., Krech, D., Bennett, E. L., & Diamond, M. C. Effects of environmental complexity and training on brain chemistry and anatomy: a replication and extension. *J. comp. physiol. Psychol.*, 1962, **55**, 429–437.
47. Russell, R. W. *Brain, memory, learning*. Oxford: Clarendon Press, 1959.
48. Schadé, J. P. A histological and histochemical analysis of the developing cerebral cortex. *Proc. roy. Acad. Sci. (Amsterdam)*, 1959a, **62**, 445–460.
49. Schadé, J. P. Differential growth of nerve cells in cerebral cortex. *Growth*, 1959b, **23**, 159–168.

50. Scoville, W. B., & Milner, B. Loss of recent memory after bilateral hippocampal lesions. *J. Neurol. Neurosurg. Psychiat.*, 1957, **20**, 11–21.
51. Ström, G. Physiological significance of post tetanic potentiation of the spinal monosynaptic reflex. *Acta physiol. scand.*, 1951, **24**, 61–83.
52. Tanzi, E. I fattie la Induzime ell odierne istologia del sistema nervoso. *Rev. sper. Freniat.*, 1893, **19**, 419–472.
53. Ungar, G. Role of proteins and peptides in learning and memory. In *Molecular mechanisms in memory and learning*. G. Ungar, Ed. New York: Plenum Press, 1970, pp. 149–175.
54. Young, J. Z. Growth and plasticity in the nervous system. *Proc. roy. Soc. (London)*, B, 1951, **139**, 18–37.

AUTHOR INDEX

Numbers in parentheses are reference numbers and show that an author's work is referred to although his name is not mentioned in the text. Numbers in italics indicate the pages on which the complete references appear.

Abbott, D. W., 460(7)
Abe, K., 182(2), 332(8), 347(8)
Abel, S., 259(1)
Abrams, R. M., 214(1)
Adair, Linda B., 442(1)
Adametz, J. H., 332(1), 347(1)
Adams, H. E., 390(1, 2)
Adams, R. D., 406(1)
Ader, R., 280(43), 289(43)
Ades, H. W., 109(38), 399(103)
Adey, W. R., 340(2), 342(84), 343(38), 426(1, 15), 427(16)
Adolph, E. F., 193(2), 228(4, 5), 229(3)
Adrian, E. D., 75(1, 2), 138(2), 139(1), 340(3)
Affani, J., 348(4)
Aghajanian, G. K., 337(5, 6)
Agranoff, B. W., 454(2, 45), 455(44), 456(3)
Ahn, H., 429(36)
Ahumada, A., 403(101)
Ai, N., 138(115)
Ajmone-Marsan, C., 182(15)
Akert, K., 159(33), 283(68), 332(7), 404(134)
Akimoto, H., 182(2), 332(8), 347(8)
Alcaraz, M., 340(73, 77), 348(73, 79)
Alcocer-Cuaron, C., 340(76), 411(48)
Allara, E., 131(3)
Allen, E., 257(3)
Allen, W. F., 400(2, 3)
Alpern, H. P., 388(3)
Altoman, J. A., 348(56)
Amatsu, M., 141(66)
Amoore, J. E., *123*(4, 5, 6, 7, 8, 9, 10), *126*(4, 7, 8, 9), 127(8, 9)
Anand, B. K., 200(3, 6, 9, 134), 202(34), 206(4), 208(5), 212(6, 7, 8), 213(36), 231(6), 291(1)
Anderson, C. H., 263(4)
Andersson, B., 214(10), 232(8, 9,

12, 14), 233(11), 234(10), 240(7, 12, 13), 243(10)
Andy, O. J., 292(2)
Angeleri, F., 139(12, 32)
Apelbaum, J., 340(9)
Appelberg, B., 140(11)
Arden, F., 239(15)
Arduini, A., 160(19), 341(62), 342(62), 343(62), 426(26), 427(26)
Arees, E. A., 212(11)
Aristotle, *69, 226*
Armitage, S. G., 452(4)
Aronsohn, E., 121(13)
Aronson, L. R., 255(102)
Artemyev, V. V., 429(2)
Auleytner, B., 290(3)
Austin, G. M., 179(3)
Avakyan, R. V., 348(56)
Ax, A. F., 280(4)

Babich, F. R., 447(5)
Bagchi, B. K., 340(10)
Bagshaw, M. H., 132(14), 404(4)
Bailey, C. J., 197(110)
Baily, P., 406(5)
Baker, C. P., 472(33, 44)
Balagura, S., 205(12), 316(1)
Baldwin, B. A., 140(15)
Ball, J., 257(8), 258(5), 259(6, 7)
Banerjee, M. G., 213(36)
Banks, Amelia, 449(6)
Barbizet, J., 407(6)
Bard, P., 255(9, 10), 259(9), 264(9), 282(6, 104), *285*(5), 289(7), 291(7), *296*
Bardier, E., 193(13)
Bardós, V., 261(51)
Barker, J. P., 228(5)
Barker, R. G., 254(121)
Barlow, H. B., 75(3, 4)
Barnard, J. W., 157(110)
Barnes, R. H., 212(93)
Barnett, R. J., 197(101), 212(97)
Barnhart, Sharon S., 460(7)

Barondes, S. H., 453(8), 454(9, 10), 455(11, 35, 36, 37, 38), 456(13, 34)
Barraclough, C. A., 261(11, 12, 13, 60), 263(11), 264(13)
Barrera, S. E., 390(57)
Barrett, R. J., 388(49)
Barron, D. H., 156(1)
Barry, J., 404(96)
Bar-Sela, Mildred E., 264(36)
Bartlett, F., 430(40), 443(93)
Bartley, S. H., 79(5)
Bash, K. W., 192(14)
Bates, M. W., 198(15, 16), 212(102)
Batini, C., 180(4), 332(11, 12)
Battig, K., 410(7)
Bauer, D., 263(14)
Baumgarten, R. von, 138(16, 79), 139(79), 181(5)
Baumgartner, G., 83(7, 8, 9, 10, 55), 84(8, 9)
Baumgartner, R. von, 83(6, 54, 55)
Baxter, D., 346(143)
Beach, F. A., 253(24, 29), *254*(18, 19, 23, 28), 255(18), 258(19, 21, 27), 259(15, 17, 20, 22), 260(29), 264(16, 23, 25) *362,* 362(1)
Beams, H. W., 473(34)
Bean, C. M., 128(44)
Beatty, W. W., 295(8), 456(163)
Beaulieu, C., 456(154)
Beaulnes, A., 337(26), 338(25)
Bebesova, O., 459(162)
Beck, E. C., 181(8), 332(35), 347(35), 411(24)
Beck, L. H., *124*(18, 19), *125*(17), 128(19), *132*(18)
Beckwith, W. C., 387(4, 28)
Bedard, P., 201(17)
Behar, A. J., 198(44)
Beidler, L. M., 135(70), 136(20), 141(21)
Bekesy, G. von, 95(2, 3), 100(5), *103*(1, 6), *106, 108,* 108(6)

Bekkering, D., 340(55)
Belding, H. W., 192(92)
Bell, F. R., 140(15)
Bellows, R. T., 228(16, 17), 231(16)
Belluzzi, J., 291(9)
Belluzzi, J. D., 450(14, 15), 451(14, 15)
Benjamin, R. M., 132(23), 141(22, 23, 90)
Bennett, E. L., 444(149), 446(29), 447(29), 452(148), 472(46)
Bental, E., 330(43)
Benussi, V., 279(10)
Berde, B., 169(2)
Berger, B. D., 446(29), 447(29), 460(17), 461(17)
Berger, Hans, *339*(13), *422* (3)
Berlyne, D. E., 360(2)
Bernard, Claude, *227*(18)
Bernhard, C. G., 163(3)
Berry, C. M., 131(24)
Berry, R. N., 73(77)
Bexton, W. H., 360(3)
Bickford, R. G., 433(7)
Bidder, T. G., 290(13)
Biddulph, R., 96(54)
Bignami, G., 449(20), 451(18)
Bihari, B., 330(43)
Birnbaum, D., 198(44)
Bishop, M. P., 312(2), 318(2)
Bivens, L. W., 388(50)
Bizzi, E., 328(21)
Black, A. H., 343(30, 187), 427(12, 92)
Black, S. P. W., 181(39)
Blanchard, D. C., 295(11)
Blanchard, R. J., 295(11)
Blandau, R. J., 259(30)
Blass, E. M., 234(20), 240(19)
Bliss, E. L., 326(14)
Blum, J. S., 404(9)
Boas, E. P., 327(15)
Boeckh, J., 135(25, 26)
Bogacz, J., 344(53)
Bogoch, S., 444(19), 479(1)
Bohdanecký, Z., 387(34), 390(35), 459(27, 28)
Bohm, E., 163(3)
Bohus, B., 280(12)
Boling, J. L., 259(30)
Bond, D. D., 290(13)
Bonnet, Charles, *380*(5)
Booth, D. A., 203(18), 208(18)
Booth, G., *214*(19)
Boren, J. J., 313(11), 317(9)
Boring, E. G., 96(7), 126(27)
Boshes, B., 278(14)
Boswell, R. S., 294(126)
Bouris, W., 431(63)

Bourne, G. H., 125(28, 47, 48), 132 (28, 47, 48)
Bovet, D., 449(20), 451(64)
Bowden, J., 365(17)
Bowden, J. W., 180(20), 280(97), 332(115), 346(115)
Bower, G. H., 311(3), 312(3)
Bowman, K. M., 213(76)
Bowman, R. E., 443(22)
Boyd, E. S., 310(4)
Boyd, T. E., 193(126)
Boyle, *91*
Bozladnova, N. I., 429(2)
Bradford, D., 457(137)
Bradley, H., 433(80)
Bradley, P. B., 332(16), 347(17), 425(44)
Brady, J. V., 280(112), 293(15, 16), 294(15), 307(77), 313(5, 6, 7, 8, 77), 314(6), 317(7, 9), 386(6, 7, 29), 387(8, 9, 10, 18, 30), 409(10)
Branchey, M., 337(18)
Bray, C. W., 100(72), 102(73)
Brazier, Mary A. B., 343(37)
Breder, C. M., 255(31)
Bremer, F., 132(29), 160(5), 161(4), 180(6), *331,* 331(19)
Bremner, F. J., 426(4)
Bridson, W. E., 260(63)
Briese, E., 317(10)
Briggs, M. H., *479* (2)
Bright, Patricia J., 454(45)
Brindley, G. S., 72(79)
Brobeck, J. R., 195(23), 197(20), 198(20, 152), 203(3), 206(4), 208(130), *214*(21, 22, 140, 142), 231(6), 243(90)
Broca, P., 380(11)
Brodal, A., 156(103), 178(46), 346 (20)
Brodie, D., 313(11)
Brodmann, K., *47*
Bromiley, R. B., 398(11)
Brookhart, J. M., 156(6), 263(32)
Brooks, C. McC., 255(33), 264(33)
Brooks, D. C., 328(21)
Brookshire, K. H., 451(156)
Brouwer, B., 81(11)
Brown, B. B., 343(22)
Brown, H., 456(25)
Brown, J. S., 361(4)
Brown, K. T., 74(13), 75(12)
Brown, P. K., 71(88)
Brown, S., *195*(24), 206(24)
Brunswick, D., 279(17)
Brush, T. R., 456(26)
Brust-Carmona, H., 344(23), 365(12), 411(48)
Brutkowski, S., 289(18), 290(3), 291(19)

Brügger, M., 202(25)
Brunn, F., 231(21)
Brusa, A., 160(19)
Brush, E. S., 403(12), 404(12)
Bubash, S., 447(5)
Buchwald, N. A., 158(7, 8, 9, 37), 411(13, 50)
Buck, C., 448(108)
Bucy, P. C., 163(10), 264(83), *290*(90), *291*
Buijs, K., 122(30)
Bulatão, E., 211(26)
Bunch, C. C., 94(8)
Bunnel, B. N., 451(125)
Bureš, J., 398(14, 15), 431(6), 459 (27, 28)
Burešová, O., 398(14, 15), 459(28)
Burford, T. H., 257(3)
Buser, P., 346(163)
Bush, D. F., 389(46)
Butler, R. A., 360(5), 399(16) 400 (16)
Byrne, W. L., 446(29), 447(29)

Caggiula, A. R., 317(12)
Caird, W. K., 461(157)
Cairns, H., 406(17)
Calabresi, P., 124(19), 128(19)
Callens, M., 131(31), 139(31)
Calloway, J. W., 212(93)
Calma, I., 181(27), 343(121), 347 (121)
Cameron, D. E., 456(30)
Campbell, B. A., 198(146)
Campbell, F. W., 72(14, 79)
Campbell, H. J., 168(11), *263* (34)
Campbell, J. F., 310(94)
Campbell, K. H., 131(109), 141(109)
Campbell, R. J., 402(18)
Cannon, W. B., *191*(27), *192* (28), *227*(22), *228, 230, 245, 275*(20), 276(20), *279* (22), *285*(20), *296, 361* (7), *365*(6), *369*
Cant, B. R., 433(7)
Carder, B., 284(23)
Carder, J. B., 456(163)
Cardo, B., 408(19)
Carlson, A. J., *191*(29), 192(156), 193(29), 211(26)
Carlson, P. L., 446(29), 447(29)
Carlton, P. L., 447(104), 451(31)
Carpenter, D., 157(12)
Carreras, M., 131(33), 139(12, 32)
Case, T. J., 327(49)
Caspers, H., 330(24), 433(8)
Caussé, R., 95(9)
Cavanaugh, E. G., 263(105)
Chamberlin, T. J., 456(32)

Author Index

Chambers, W. W., 159(93), 161(13, 14, 92), 178(55), 179(54), 181(7)
Chavasse, P., 95(9)
Chávez-Ibarra, G., 338(80), 347(80),
Cheesman, D. F., 132(46)
Chevalier, J. A., 388(12)
Chhina, G. S., 200(9), 208(5)
Chiapetta, L., 446(29), 447(29)
Chiorini, J. R., 433(9)
Chorover, S. L., 446(29), 447(29)
Chow, K. L., 404(9), 428(10), 431(55)
Christensen, J. H., 190(103)
Churcher, B. G., 94(11)
Cizek, L. J., 240(60)
Clark, F. C., 452(33)
Clark, G., 258(35)
Clark, L. D., 326(14)
Clark, W. E., 130(34)
Clemente, C. D., 206(53), 264(67), 333(171, 172), 347(171, 172), 426(89)
Coates, C. W., 255(31)
Coghill, G. E., 472(3)
Cohen, D., 178(55)
Cohen, H. D., 453(8), 454(9, 10), 455(11, 35, 36, 37, 38), 456(34)
Cohen, J., 433(11)
Cohen, L., 344(34)
Cohen, M. J., 414(26)
Collins, E., 201(30), 206(30)
Collins, G. H., 406(1)
Conner, R. L., 280(169)
Connors, J., 407(100)
Conrad, D. G., 307(77), 313(8, 77), 317(9)
Cook, L., 456(40)
Coombs, C. H., 278(24)
Coons, E. E., 317(13)
Cooper, R. M., 452(87)
Corbit, J. D., 242(24)
Corcoran, A. C., 243(82)
Cordeau, J. P., 337(26), 338(25)
Cornell, J. M., 457(132)
Corning, W. C., 443(41, 42)
Corson, J. A., 446(29), 447(29), 456(43)
Coscina, D. V., 205(12)
Costa, L. D., 433(24)
Coury, J. N., 203(31), 208(31), 235(35)
Cox, V. C., 198(155), 203(154), 231(106)
Cragg, B. G., 139(35)
Craig, C., 214(105)
Crepax, P., 161(16)
Creutzfeldt, O., 330(27)
Critchlow, B. V., 263(105)
Critchlow, V., 264(36)
Crocker, E. C., *126*(36, 37)

Cross, B., 263(86)
Cruce, J. A. F., 317(13)
Cruikshank, Ruth M., 340(90, 91)
Crump, C. H., 327(155)
Crowley, T. J., 337(28)
Cuenod, M., 441(122)
Culler, E. A., 104(12), 413(116, 117)
Cummins, G. M., 192(55), 212(55)
Cunningham, F., 290(27)
Cytawa, J., 200(147)

Dagnon, J., 403(46)
Dahl, H., 459(50)
Dahlström, A., 337(29)
Dalle, Ore G., 264(123), 405(121)
Dallenbach, J. W., 128(38)
Dallenbach, K. M., 128(38)
De Lovenzo, A. J., 130(42, 43)
Dalton, A., 343(30), 427(12)
Daly, C., 213(76)
D'Amato, M. R., 309(88)
Danna, C. L., 285(25)
Darrow, C. W., *280*(26)
Darrow, D. C., 240(26)
Dartnall, H. J. A., 72(16, 17)
Darwin, Erasmus, *191,* 191(32), 239(27)
Davenport, J. W., 456(26)
Davidovich, A., 344(148)
Davidson, A. B., 456(40)
Davidson, J. M., 263(37, 38)
Davies, J. T., *132*(39, 40, 41)
Davis, D. J., 456(40)
Davis, H., 100(13, 57), 106(57), 108(26, 59), 110(26, 27, 61)
Davis, J. D., 210(33)
Davis, R. E., 454(45), 455(44), 456(3)
Davison, J. H., 444(63)
Dawe, A. R., 336(31)
Dax, E., 290(27)
Dean, W., 386(54)
Deecke, L., 433(13, 48), 434(13)
de Groot, J., 206(53)
Delgado, J. M. R., 202(34), 208(94), 214(35), 286(28), 291(107), 306(41), 318(14), 403(105), 410(105)
Dell, P., 327(36)
Delorme, F., 328(101)
Dement, W., 328(32, 33), 332(32, 33), 347(32, 33)
Dempsey, E. W. A., 346(129)
Denniston, R. H., 254(39)
Denny-Brown, D. E., 162(17, 18)
de Quijada, Mary G., 317(10)
Desiraju, T., 213(36)
Desmedt, J. E., 113(17), 114(18)
Deuel, H. J., 259(56)
Deutsch, J. A., 309(17), 314(15, 16, 26), *318*(15, 16), *459,* 459(46, 47, 48, 49, 50, 169)
Deutschman, D., 433(80)
De Valois, R. L., *79*(18, 19, 20, 21)
DeVito, R. V., 160(19)
DeWied, D., 280(29)
Dey, F. L., 263(32)
Diamond, I. T., 114(19, 40), 399(16), 400(16, 20), 401(20, 89), 407(51)
Diamond, M. C., 472(46)
Diddle, A. W., 257(3)
Dill, D. B., 240(28)
Dilworth, Margaret, 182(15)
Di Salvo, N. A., 229(29)
Ditzler, W., 452(140)
Doane, B., 343(152)
Dobelle, W. H., 79(63)
Dobrzecka, C., 205(161)
Domino, E. F., 450(51)
Donchin, E., 344(34)
Dongier, S., 340(55)
Donhoffer, H., 341(61), 426(25)
Donner, K. O., 76(23)
Donoso, M., 344(72)
Dott, N. M., 406(21)
Doty, B., 452(52)
Doty, R. W., 181(8), 332(35), 347(35), 411(24), 412(22, 23)
Douglas, R. J., 292(73), 293(30), 407(52)
Dow, R. S., 161(23)
Drake, C. G., 185(39)
Drezner, N., 259(48)
Dua, S., 200(6, 9, 134), 208(5), 212(6, 8)
Du Bois Reymond, E., 73(24)
Duffy, E., *365,* 365(8)
Dumas, C. L., 230(30), 239(30)
Dumont, S., 327(36), 348(87)
Duncan, C. P., 385(13, 14), 386(14)
Duncan, D. R., 128(44)
Dunlop, C. W., 340(2), 426(1)
Dusser de Barenne, J., 161(20)
Dutcher, J. D., 446(29), 447(29, 104)
Dykman, R. A., 413(25)
Dysinger, D. W., 278(31)
Dyson, G. M., 122(45), 124(45)

Eccles, J. C., 162(21), 473(4), 474(4), 481(4)
Eccles, M., 162(21)
Echeverría, Yolanda, 317(10)
Eckhaus, E., 411(48)
Edwards, D. A., 260(129, 130)
Egan, G., 290(32)
Egyházi, E., 443(93)
Ehrensvärd, G. C. H., 132(46)
Ehrlich, A., 207(37)
Eichelman, B. S., Jr., 282(33)

Eidelberg, E., 343(37)
Einstein, Albert, 64
Eisenstein, E. M., 414(26)
Elazar, Z., 343(38), 426(15), 427(16)
El-Baradi, A. F., 125(47, 48), 132(47, 48)
Elder, J. H., 257(3)
Elder, S. T., 312(2), 316(18), 318(2)
Eleftheriou, B. E., 264(40)
Elkinton, J. R., 240(31)
Ellen, P., 292(36), 295(34, 35, 37), 409(27), 428(53)
Ellison, G. D., 285(39)
Endroczi, E., 280(12)
Enesco, H. E., 446(29), 447(29), 456(43, 154)
Engle, E. T., 258(41)
Engle, J., 431(63)
Epstein, A. N., 192(40), 198(149), 199(148), 200(148), 201(40, 41), 205(128), 212(136), 213(38), 214(41), 231(102), 233(32), 243(33)
Erdheim, J., 194(42)
Ervin, R., 455(38)
Essman, W. B., 456(53), 457(54, 55)
Evans, E. F., 112(20, 21), 113(77)
Evarts, E. V., 327(39, 42), 330(41, 43), 343(40), 404(28)
Everett, J. W., 264(42)
Ewald, J. R., 192(43)

Fadiga, E., 161(16)
Falk, J., 312(19)
Falk, J. L., 241(34)
Farney, J. P., 259(80)
Farrell, G., 234(100)
Faure, J., 265(43, 44)
Favale, E., 327(45), 332(44)
Fazekas, J. F., 213(76)
Fechner, 84, 94
Feder, H. H., 261(45)
Fee, A. R., 255(46)
Feiner, L., 258(47)
Feldman, S. E., 198(44)
Feldman, S. M., 181(9), 340(57)
Feleky, A. M., 279(40)
Fellows, E. J., 456(40)
Felson, H., 259(65)
Fenichel, R. L., 446(29), 447(29)
Fernandez, de Molina, A., 282(4)
Fernández-Guardiola, A., 340(73, 77), 348(73, 79)
Ferrier, D., 289(42), 380(15)
Fessard, A. E., 482(5)
Fetz, E. E., 432(17)

Filler, W., 259(48)
Finan, J. L., 402(29)
Fisher, A. E., 206(159), 235(35, 69), 263(49, 126), 363(27)
Fisher, C., 263(50)
Fisher, G. L., 125(105), 141(105)
Fishman, I. Y., 140(49), 141(21)
Fitzsimons, J. T., 241(36), 242(37, 39, 40), 243(33, 38)
Fjerdingstad, E. J., 447(56)
Fleming, T. C., 327(42)
Flerkó, B., 261(51)
Fletcher, H., 97(22, 23)
Flexner, J. B., 453(57, 58), 454(59, 60), 456(61), 478(6)
Flexner, L. B., 453(57, 58), 454(59, 60), 456(61), 478(6)
Flynn, J. P., 283(168), 285(39)
Fonberg, Elzbieta, 291(19)
Foote, R. M., 259(52)
Forman, D., 158(22)
Foshee, D. P., 292(2)
Fourier, 93
Fox, S. S., 423(18), 430(19, 75), 433(54)
Frank, M. K., 125(105), 141(105)
Frankenhaeuser, M., 449(150)
Franzisket, L., 413(30)
Freed, H., 407(118)
Freed, S., 443(41)
French, J. D., 332(47), 346(47, 48)
Frey, P. W., 452(62)
Frick, O., 340(9)
Friedgood, H. B., 258(53)
Friedman, M. H., 259(93)
Friedman, S. B., 280(43), 289(43)
Fröhlich, A., 194(45)
Frumin, M. J., 457(123)
Fry, F. J., 408(123)
Fry, W. J., 408(123)
Fubini, A., 227(67)
Fujimori, B., 343(186)
Fuller, J. L., 291(44)
Fulton, J. F., 161(23), 178(56), 195(48), 207(46, 47, 157), 289(45, 47), 293(45, 46, 133), 403(31, 32)
Funderbunk, W. H., 327(49)
Fuster, J. M., 346(50), 411(33)
Fuxe, K., 337(29)

Gaito, J., 443(117, 118, 119), 444(63), 476(7)
Galambos, R., 108(26), 109(26), 110(26, 27, 41), 112(28), 114(25), 343(86), 348(52, 134), 387(9), 427(20), 446(29), 447(29), 480(8)
Galen, 226

Gall, F. J., 380(16)
Gallagher, R. J., 210(33)
Gallay, H. M., 456(153)
Gallinek, A., 386(17), 389(17)
Gandelman, R., 314(90)
Garcia-Austt, E., 344(53)
Gardner, L. C., 310(4)
Gardner, R., 446(29), 447(29)
Gasnier, A., 190(49)
Gasola, L., 456(3)
Gassel, M. M., 327(54)
Gastaut, H., 265(54), 340(55), 425(22), 482(9)
Gastaut, R., 131(50)
Gatti, G. I., 451(64)
Gauer, O. H., 242(42)
Gault, F. P., 138(51), 427(72)
Gay, Patricia E., 291(150), 295(150)
Geiger, R. S., 472(10, 11)
Geller, I., 387(8, 10), 409(10)
Gengerelli, J., 309(91)
George, R., 456(79)
Gerall, A. A., 260(55, 104)
Gerard, R. W., 456(32), 472(12)
Gernandt, B. E., 179(11)
Gershuni, G. V., 348(56)
Gesteland, R. C., 133(52), 135(53, 77), 136(53)
Gibson, W. E., 314(20)
Gilbert, G. J., 234(43, 45), 242(44)
Gilden, L., 433(24)
Gilman, A., 239(46)
Gilmour, A., 198(50)
Girden, E., 461(65)
Giurgea, C., 412(35)
Glasky, A. J., 452(66)
Glass, S. J., 259(56)
Glassman, E., 442(1, 173)
Glees, P., 178(56), 405(36)
Glickman, S. E., 340(57)
Glow, P. H., 449(67, 144)
Goddard, G. V., 450(68)
Gold, R. M., 202(51, 52), 206(51), 231(47)
Goldberg, J. M., 109(30), 111(35), 112(35), 114(30)
Goldfarb, W., 213(76)
Goldfrank, F., 327(167)
Goldschmidt, E. F., 327(15)
Goldstein, A. C., 263(57), 264(57)
Goldstone, M., 433(79)
Gollender, M., 431(55)
Goltz, F., 282(48), 380(19)
Goodrich, C. A., 336(149)
Gordon, G., 140(54)
Gordon, M. B., 259(58)
Gorski, R. A., 261(12, 59, 60)
Goto, M., 73(83)
Goy, R. W., 260(62, 63, 104), 263(61)

Author Index

Graber, S., 336(128)
Grady, K. L., 261(64)
Graebler, O., 168(87)
Graf, G., 178(23)
Graller, D. L., 259(65)
Granit, R., *73*(30, 31, 32), 75(30), *76*(23, 26, 28, 30, 31, 37), 152(25), 155(26), 160(25), 179(12), 348(58), 473(13)
Grastyán, E., 341(61), 342(59, 60), 407(56), 411(37), 426(25)
Gravis, D. M., 327(155)
Green, H., 456(40)
Green, J. D., 138(16, 79), 206(53), 263(66), 264(67), 341(62), 342 (62), 343(62), 347(62), 426(26), 427(26)
Green, J. R., 406(5)
Greenblatt, R. B., 258(68), 259(69, 70)
Greenwald, G. S., 263(4)
Gregersen, M. I., 229(62), 239(61)
Griffith, H. B., 405(36)
de Groot, J., 264(67)
Gross, C. G., 403(38, 137)
Gross, D. A., 456(79)
Grossman, Lore, 201(66), 206(65), 207(65), 234(55, 56), 283(57), 450(74)
Grossman, M. I., 192(54, 55), 193 (80), 212(55, 79)
Grossman, S. P., 197(64), 198(61), 199(61, 132), 201(66), 203(57, 58), 205(57, 66), 206(65), 207(57, 65, 67), 208(56, 57, 62), 213(63), 214(68), 232(48, 49, 50), 233(55, 56), 235(49, 50, 51, 52), 282(52, 55, 56, 115, 116, 152), 283(47, 54), 289(61), 291(9, 49), 294(50, 55, 59, 60, 61, 80), 295(81, 115, 116), 306(21), 307(28), 314(28), 318(28), 407(41, 43), 409(42, 59), 410(90), 450(15, 69, 71, 72, 74, 77, 126), 451(15, 69, 70, 72, 76, 80, 97), 455(75), 458(73)
Grota, L. J., 280(43), 289(43)
Gruner, J., 265(44)
Grunt, J. A., 254(72)
Grüsser, O. -J., 74(33)
Grynbaum, A., 441(122)
Gulick, W. Lawrence, 95(31), 100 (15, 16, 31), 180(32)
Gumnit, R., 433(27)
Gurian, B., 73(34)
Gurowitz, E. M., 456(79)
Guth, L., 141(55)
Guzmán-Flores, C., 340(73, 77), 348 (73, 79)

Haba, G. de la, 453(57)

Hagamen, W. D., 131(24)
Hagbarth, K. E., 139(69), 179(13), 348(63)
Hagins, W. A., 72(79)
Hagman, N. C., 198(15)
Hagstrom, E. C., 141(58)
Haider, M., 344(64, 169)
Hakas, P., 83(8, 9)
Hale, H. B., 261(73)
Halkerston, I. D. K., 477(15)
Haller, A., *191* (69), *227* (57)
Halstead, W. C., *477*(26)
Hamburg, M. D., 459(50)
Hamilton, C. L., 214(70, 140), 243(90)
Hamilton, L. W., 289(61), 294(58, 59, 60, 61), 409(44), 451(80)
Hamlin, H., 318(14)
Hammel, H. T., 214(1)
Hammond, J., 258(74, 75)
Hampson, J. L., 160(27)
Hamuy, T. P., 157(108, 109)
Hanai, T., 214(35)
Hanbery, J., 159(28), 182(14, 15)
Hands, A. R., 122(60)
Hanson, D. G., 234(20)
Hardiman, C. W., 141(21)
Harlow, H. F., 235(76), 402(18), 403(46), 404(45)
Harris, G. W., 167(29), *169* (30), 260(77, 79), 263(78)
Harrison, C. R., 160(27)
Hartline, H. K., 74(68), *75*(35, 36, 37, 38), 77(74, 75)
Hartog, J., 403(101)
Hartman, C. G., 257(8)
Hartmann, E., 336(67), 337(66)
Harvey, E. N., 328(117, 118)
Harvey, J. A., 234(58, 89), 294(62, 63), 295(98), 408(124)
Hassler, R., 159(31, 43)
Hatton, R. A., 261(13), 264(13)
Hawkes, C. D., 208(125)
Hawkins, D. T., 312(65), 314(64)
Hawkins, W. F., 408(125)
Head, H., 285(64)
Hearst, E., 451(81)
Heath, R. G., 158(38, 39), 179(16), 312(2), 318(2)
Hebb, D. O., 360(9), 403(47), *474* (14), *481*(14)
Hechter, O., 477(15)
Heller, C. G., 259(80)
Heller, H., 167(32)
Helmholtz, G. L. F. von., *67, 102* (33)
Helson, H., 366(10)
Hemmingsen, A. M., 253(81)
Henderson, L. F., *126* (37)

Hendley, C. D., 158(39)
Hendrickson, C., 292(66)
Hendrix, C. E., 340(2), 426(1)
Hendrix, D. E., 138(63)
Hendry, D. P., 229(59)
Henning, H., *126*(61, 62)
Henry, C. E., 425(45)
Henry, J. P., 242(42)
Henson, C. D., 343(86)
Herberg, L. J., 213(71)
Hering, E., *67, 68,* 380(21)
Heriot, J. T., 386(22)
Hernández-Peón, R., 333(70), 338 (70, 80), 340(73, 74, 75, 76, 77, 78), 344(23, 72, 74, 148), 347(80), 348(69, 71, 73, 78, 79), 365(11, 12), 411(48), 429(41)
Heron, W., 360(3)
Herrmann, D. J., 108(32)
Herz, A., 459(82)
Herz, M. J., 389(23)
Hess, E. H., 279(67)
Hess, R., Jr., 159(33), 332(7)
Hess, W. R., 158(34), 159(35, 36), 283(68), 311(22), 327(81), *331,* 331(81), *332,* 332(81), *335,* 346 (81)
Hetherington, A. W., 195(73), *198,* 198(72, 74, 75)
Heuser, G., 158(7, 8, 9, 37), 411(13)
Hilgard, E. R., 400(77)
Hill, D. K., 473(16, 17)
Himwich, H. E., 213(76)
Hind, J. E., 111(35), 112(34, 35)
Hinsey, J. C., 131(24)
Hippocrates, *226*
Hitzig, E., 380(24)
Hoagland, H., 280(69)
Hobart, G. A., 328(117, 118)
Hobson, J. A., 327(82, 167)
Hodes, R., 327(83)
Hodes, R. S., 158(38, 39, 68), 179 (16), 180(41)
Hodos, W., 317(23)
Hoebel, B. G., 199(77), 283(89), 284(89, 156), 316(1, 24, 25), 317 (12)
Hogberg, D., 310(59)
Holland, J., 448(108)
Holmes, J. E., 342(84)
Holmes, J. H., 229(62, 79), 239(61), 240(60, 63)
Holt, C. E., III, 446(29), 447(29)
Holt, E. B., 472(18), *473*(18)
Holz-Tucker, A. M., 258(27)
Horn, G., 345(85)
Horridge, G. A., 414(49)
Hororitz, Z. P., 446(29), 447(29, 104)
Horvath, F. E., 291(70)

Author Index

Horwitz, N. H., 139(78), 286(108)
Hösli, L., 332(127), 336(127)
Howard, Helen, 340(91)
Howard, S., 452(52)
Howarth, C. I., 314(26)
Hoy, P. A., 228(5)
Huang, K. C., 240(64)
Hubbard, R., 71(39)
Hubel, D. H., 72(42, 44), 81(40, 41, 42, 43, 44, 45, 46), *85,* 113(36), 343(86)
Hudspeth, W. J., 386(25), 390(25), 457(83, 115), 458(84)
Hugelin, A., 348(87)
Hughes, J. R., 138(63, 64, 65)
Hughes, K. R., 452(85, 86, 87)
Hull, C. D., 411(50)
Hull, C. L., *361*(13), *365* (13), *377, 433*(29)
Hunsperger, R. W., 282(41)
Hunt, E., 458(98)
Hunt, E. B., 389(46)
Hunt, H. F., 234(58), 294(62, 63), 386(22, 29), 387(4, 10, 28, 30, 31), 407(51), 408(124)
Hunt, J. McV., 366(14)
Hunter, W. S., 413(102)
Hurvich, L. M., 68(47, 48)
Hutchinson, R. R., 283(71)
Huttenlocher, P. R., 327(42), 330 (43, 88), 347(88)
Huzimori, B., 425(65)
Hydén, Holger, *441*(88, 89, 90), *442*(91), 443(93), *456,* 472 (19), *477*(22), *478*(20, 21)

Ingelfinger, F. J., 192(92)
Ingraham, F. D., 293(46)
Ingram, W. R., 263(50), 428(56)
Irwin, D. A., 433(30, 57)
Isaacson, R. L., 292(73, 76), 407(52)
Ishiko, N., 141(66)
Ito, M., 426(91)
Ivy, A. C., 192(55), 193(78), 212(55), 336(162)
Izquierdo, I., 425(31)

Jackson, T., 402(53)
Jacobs, G. H., 79(20, 21)
Jacobsen, C. F., 289(47)
Jacobsen, E., 451(94)
Jacobson, A., 447(5)
Jacobson, A. L., 447(5)
Jacobson, C. F., 195(48), 402(53)
Jacobson, L. E., 234(58), 294(62, 63)
Jacobson, R., 446(171)
Jacoby, J., 337(179, 180)
Jakob, A., 159(41)
James, William, *274*(74), *275,*

276, 297, 380(32)
Jameson, D., 68(47, 48)
Janowitz, H. D., 193(80), 212(79)
Jansen, J. K. S., 153(42)
Jarrard, L. E., 292(75, 76)
Jarvik, M. E., 386(47), 487(34), 390(35), 446(29), 447(29), 456 (13, 135), 457(55, 95)
Jasper, H. H., 159(28), 163(71), 182(14), 340(90, 91), 154, 164), 343(152), 346(89), 347(89), 407 (54), 425(32)
Jensen, D., 414(55), 446(96)
Jernberg, P., 387(30, 31)
Jewett, R. E., 433(66)
John, E. R., 340(92), *427* (35, 37, 38, 39), 429(35), 430(34, 35, 36, 40), 443(42, 93), 482(23)
Johnson, R., 448(108)
Johnson, R. E., 214(81)
Johnson, R. H., 404(127)
Johnson, V., 211(121)
Johnston, J. W., Jr., 125(67)
Jones, A. E., 79(20, 21)
Jones, C., 294(103)
Jones, F. N., 128(68)
Jones, Lucy E., 280(94)
Jordan, L., 254(28)
Jouvet, M., 327(94), 328(101), 332 (94, 95), *336*(96, 97, 99), *337*(98, 99, 100), *338,* 340, (74, 78), 344(74), 348(78), 349 (93), 429(41)
Jung, R., *83*(6, 10, 49, 50, 53, 54, 55), *84*(51, 52), *85,* 159 (43), 330(27)
Jus, A., 340(55)
Jus, C., 340(55)

Kaada, B., 155(26)
Kaada, B. R., 179(12), 286(77)
Kabat, L., 446(171)
Kakolewski, J. W., 198(155), 203 (154), 231(106)
Kameda, K., 327(135), 330(135), 343(135)
Kamin, L. J., 383(33)
Kamp, A., 340(55)
Kandel, E. R., 432(43, 43)
Kaplan, S. J., 291(135)
Kappers, C. U. A., *473*(24, 25)
Kark, R. M., 214(81)
Karli, P., 291(78)
Karmos, G., 407(56)
Karpman, B., 128(130)
Kasmatsu, A., 330(160)
Katsuki, Y., 108(37), 110(37), 111 (37)
Katz, J. J., *477* (26)
Kaufmann, P., 407(57)

Kavanagh, A. J., 293(100)
Kawakami, M., 162(44, 45)
Kawamura, H., 330(102)
Keane, J., 193(78)
Keesey, R. E., 201(118), 309(27), 317(27)
Kellicutt, M. H., 291(79), 293(151), 295(151)
Kellogg, V., 255(82)
Kellogg, W. N., 413(58)
Kelsey, J. E., 289(61), 294(61, 80), 295(81), 409(59), 451(97)
Kennard, Margaret A., 157(46), 195(48), 290(82)
Kennedy, G. C., 190(82)
Kennedy, J. L., 279(83)
Kent, E., 307(28), 314(28), 318(28)
Kenyon, J., 294(91)
Kerr, D. I. B., 139(69), 179(13), 348(63)
Kessen, M. L., 194(109)
Key, B. J., 425(44)
Kiess, H. O., 284(141)
Kikesi, F., 411(37)
Killam, E. K., 327(103)
Killam, K. F., 327(103), 349(92), *427* (37, 38, 39)
Kimble, D. P., 292(66, 84, 85, 86), 293(87, 136), 407(60), 410(62)
Kimble, R. J., 292(86)
Kimura, D., 407(61)
Kimura, K., 135(70)
King, F. A., 293(88), 294(88)
King, M. B., 283(89), 284(89, 156)
Kirkby, R. J., 410(62)
Kirschbaum, W. R., 207(83)
Kissin, B., 337(18)
Kistiakowsky, G. B., 125(71), 132 (71)
Kitchell, R., 140(15, 54)
Kitto, G. B., *479*(2)
Klee, M., 336(107)
Kleitman, N., 328(32, 33), 329(104), 332(32, 33), 347(32, 33)
Kling, A., 291(147), 409(10)
Kling, J. W., 312(29)
Klinger, P. D., 454(2)
Klüver, H., 264(83), *290*(90), *291,* 400(63)
Knott, J. R., 425(45), 428(56), 433 (30, 57)
Knowles, W. B., 180(21), 332(116), 346(116), 365(18)
Koella, W. P., 159(33), 332(7)
Kogan, A. B., 343(105), 426(46)
Koh, S. D., 141(72)
Köhler, W., 433(47)
Kohn, M., 194(84)
Koller, Th., 336(128)
Kolmer, W., 131(73)

Komisaruk, B. R., 263(84)
Konorski, J., 349(106), 403(68, 69), 481(27)
Kooi, K. A., 181(8), 332(35), 347 (35), 411(24)
Kopp, R., 387(34), 390(35)
Korbin, E., 461(157)
Kornblith, C., 314(30)
Kornhuber, H. H., 433(13, 48)
Kornmüller, A. E., 336(107)
Korsakoff, *407*
Kozhevnikov, V. A., 348(56)
Kramer, R. F., 404(128)
Krasne, F. B., 199(85)
Krech, D., 444(149), 452(148), 472 (46)
Kreickhaus, E. E., 294(91)
Kreindler, A., 411(64)
Krivanek, J., 458(98)
Kroll, F. W., 336(108)
Kruger, L., 124(19), 128(19), 400 (65), 472(33)
Kryter, K. D., 109(38)
Kuffler, S. W., 75(57, 58), 433(49, 71)
Kun, H., 258(119)
Kuypers, H. G. J. M., 177(36), 178 (36), 346(141)

Ladove, R. F., 210(33)
Lafora, G. R., 159(48)
Lammers, H. J., 130(75), 131(50)
Landau, W. M., 156(49, 50)
Landauer, T. K., 477(28), *478* (28), *480*(28)
Lange, Carl G., *274* (92), *275, 276*
Lange, P. W., 444(92)
Langley, L. L., 167
Larochelle, L., 201(17)
Larson, Truns, 280(43), 289(43)
Larsson, B., 214(10)
Larsson, S., 202(86), 232(9), 234 (10), 243(10)
Lasareff, P., 132(76)
Lash, L., 292(93)
Lashley, Karl S., *362*(15), *380, 381*(36), *400*(66, 67), 457(101), 482(29)
Lassek, A. M., 156(52)
Latané, B., 451(102)
Lauprecht, C. W., 158(8, 9), 411 (13)
Laurin, C., 337(26)
Lavin, A., 340(76)
Law, T., 263(85)
Lawicka, W., 403(68, 69)
Lawrence, M., 100(74, 75, 76), 101 (74, 75), 102(76), 104(76)
Leaf, R. C., 446(29), 447(29, 104), 451(103)
Leão, A. A. P., 398(70)
Leaton, R. N., 138(51), 427(50)
Legendre, R., 326(109, 110)
Leibowitz, Sarah F., *204*(87, 88), *232*(65, 66), 459(48, 105)
Leonard, D. J., 390(38)
Lepidi-Chioti, G., 227(67)
Leschke, E., 228(68), 231(68)
Lesse, H., 427(51, 52)
Lettvin, J. Y., 77(60, 61, 67), 81 (61, 66), 135(77)
LeVine, M., 204(139)
Levine, S., 260(79), 280(94, 160), 451(106)
Levitt, M., 286(130), 408(92)
Levitt, R. A., 235(69)
Lewin, I., 312(89), 314(89)
Lewis, D. J., 388(39, 44), 390(1, 2, 44)
Lewis, G. P., 336(111)
Lewis, O. F., 337(28)
Lewis, S., 456(107)
Lewis, T. C., 292(75)
Li, C. L., 330(112)
Liberson, W. T., 428(53)
Lickey, M. E., 433(54)
Lifschitz, W., 340(146), 346(113), 348(113)
Lilly, J. C., 307(31)
Lim, R., 456(3)
Lincoln, D., 263(86)
Lindquist, J. L., 211(120)
Lindsley, D. B., 180(20, 21), *280,* 281(96, 97), 332(115, 116), 344(169), 346(115, 116), *347* (114), *365*(16, 17, 18), *366, 367,* 426(88), 431(55)
Lindy, J., 312(73)
Ling, G., 411(50)
Ling, G. M., 336(184, 185), 338 (185)
Lints, C. E., 234(58), 295(98)
Linzell, J. L., 168(53)
Lisk, R. D., 258(88), 263(87, 88)
Lissak, K., 280(12), 341(61), 411 (37), 426(25)
Liu, C. N., 472(30)
Livingston, R. B., 179(22)
Lloyd, D. P. C., 473(31)
Loeb, C., 327(45), 332(44)
Loeffler, J. D., 113(39)
Long, C. N. H., 168(87), 195(23), 198(152)
Longet, F. A., 227(70)
Loomis, A. L., *328*(117, 118)
Lopez-Mendoza, E., 411(48)
Lorens, S. A., 310(32)
Loucks, R. B., 412(71)

Lubar, J. F., 234(7), 293(99, 100)
Lubin, A., 327(136)
Luckhardt, A. B., 210(90)
Luco, J. V., 414(72)
Lundbaek, K., 190(91)
Lundberg, A., 157(12), 162(21)
Lurie, L. A., 259(89)
Luttges, M., 448(108)
Luttges, M. W., 389(40)
Luttge, W. G., 269(130)
Lux, H. D., 336(107)

McAdam, D., 428(56)
McAdam, D. W., 433(30, 57)
McCann, S. M., 231(88), 232(12), 233(11), 240(12, 13)
McCleary, R. A., 293(101, 102), 294(60, 101, 103), 295(176), 342(119), 407(130), 409(73)
McConnell, J. V., 446(109, 110, 111, 171)
McCulloch, W. S., 77(60, 61, 67), 81(61, 66), 157(46), 160(89) 161(89), 178(23), 181(52)
McDonald, P. G., 263(84)
MacDonald, R. M., 192(92)
McElroy, W. D., 452(155)
McEwen, B. S., 264(131), 444(112)
McGaugh, J. L., 383(41), 386(25), 387(41), 388(3, 41, 43), 389(40), 390(25, 42), 448(108), 457(114, 115, 137), 458(116, 167)
McGinty, D. J., 332(120)
McGregor, P., 337(179, 180)
Machlus, B., 443(117, 118, 119)
Machne, X., 158(84), 181(27), 343(121), 347(121)
Macht, M. B., 282(104)
McIntyre, A. K., 473(32)
McIver, A. H., 294(126)
Mackay, E. M., 212(93)
Mackey, P. E., 108(32)
McLardy, T., 182(24, 25)
MacLean, P. D., 139(78), 208(94), 264(90), 265(91, 92), 286(108), *288*(105), *289,* 291(106, 107), *296*
McMasters, R. E., 178(26)
MacNichol, E. F., Jr., 74(62), 76 (87), 79(63)
MacPhail, E. M., 283(109)
Madaraxz, I., 341(61), 426(25)
Madsen, M. C., 390(42)
Maekawa, K., 330(160)
Magendie, F., 158(55), *194* (95), *227*(73)
Magoun, H. W., 159(56, 79, 80), 160(89), 161(88, 89), 178(23, 28), 179(29, 30), *180*(20, 21, 29, 30, 35, 38), 181(27, 52), 280(97,

122), *331,* 332(115, 116, 133), *335,* 343(121), *346*(115, 116, 133, 170), 347(121), *365*(17, 18, 21)
Maier, N. R. F., 397(74)
Maire, F. W., 208(96)
Makepeace, A. W., 259(93)
Malis, J. L., 313(11)
Malis, L. I., 472(33, 44)
Malmo, R. B., 402(75), 403(76)
Mancia, D., 131(33)
Mancia, M., 131(33), 138(16, 79), 139(79), 337(122), 348(4)
Mandell, A., 337(123)
Manfredi, M., 327(45)
Marantz, R., 337(124)
Marchiafava, P. L., 327(54), 348(4)
Marczynski, T. J., 336(184, 185), 337(184, 185), 338(185)
Margules, D. L., 282(111), 291(110), 311(33, 36), 317(35), 447(29), 451(120)
Marks, W. B., 79(63)
Marquis, D. G., 400(77)
Marsh, G., 473(34)
Marsh, J. T., 345(182), 348(134)
Marshall, F. H. A., 255(94)
Marshall, N. B., 190(103) 212(97)
Marshall, W. H., 81(64)
Martin, G., 389(46)
Maruseva, A. M., 348(56)
Masahashi, K., 182(2), 332(8), 347(8)
Mashayekhi, M. B., 190(103)
Mason, J. W., 280(112)
Masserman, J. H., 285(113), 286 (130, 148), 408(92, 111)
Masson, G. M. C., 243(82)
Massopust, L. C., Jr., 407(126), 408(126)
Masterton, R. B., 114(40)
Matsumiya, Y., 312(29)
Matthews, B. H. C., 340(3)
Matthews, P. B. C., 152(57), 153 (42)
Matthews, R., 75(1, 2)
Maturana, H. R., 77(60, 61, 65, 67), 81(61, 66)
Mayer, A., 190(49), *239*(74)
Mayer, B., 128(80)
Mayer, Jean, 190(103), 197(101), 198(15, 16), *210, 211*(99, 100), *212*(11, 97, 98, 102), *213*(100), *216*
Maxurowski, J., 138(64, 65)
Meagher, W., 263(85)
Means, L. W., 283(142)
Mempel, E., 291(19)
Mendelson, J., 317(37), 318(37)
Mendenhall, M. C., 452(121)

Mersenne, *92*
Meschan, I., 193(104)
Mettler, F. A., 156(59), 158(60), 159(58), 178(31), 290(114)
Metysova', J., 459(162)
Metzger, H. P., 441(122)
Meyer, D. R., 157(108, 109), 400 (79), 404(78)
Mhatre, R. M., 212(8)
Mickelsen, O. S., 214(105)
Miczek, K., 282(115, 116), 295 (115, 116)
Migdal, W., 457(123)
Mihailovic, L., 403(137)
Miles, W. R., *124*(18), *132,* (18)
Milisen, R. L., 340(175)
Miller, A. J., 389(56)
Miller, H. R., 291(158)
Miller, Neal, *309*
Miller, N. E., 194(109), 197(110), *199*(107), 202(106), 203 (108), 229(75), 231(75), 233 (76), 258(95), 283(109), 284 (117), *306*(38, 41), 311(3, 39, 40), 312(3), 318(87), 388 (48), 390(48)
Miller, R. E., 280(118, 123)
Miller, R. R., 388(39, 44), 390(44)
Miller, T. B., 336(149)
Miller, W. H., 74(68), 77(75)
Mills, J. A., 293(171)
Mills, J. N., 326(125), 337(125)
Milner, B., 291(127), 405(93), 406(80, 81, 115), 482(39, 50)
Milner, P., *306*(57), *309,* 407(120)
Milner, P. M., *474* (35)
Milton, G. A., 446(164)
Mirsky, A. F., 408(94)
Misanin, J. R., 388(39, 44), 390 (44)
Mishkin, M., 403(12, 82, 99, 106, 136), 404(12, 83), 410(7, 107)
Mishkin, W., 291(119, 135)
Mita, T., 73(69)
Miyamoto, K., 426(91)
Moefan, J. D., 192(111)
Moefane, P. J., 201(112, 113), *203*(113), 206(112), 234 (81), 309(46)
Moehlig, R. C., 258(96)
Moeuzzi, G., 160(62), 161(61), *180*(4, 35), *181,* 32, 33, 34), 280(122), *332* 12, 132, 133), 346(133, 161), 347(126, 132, 161), 365(21)
Mogenson, G. J., 313(42), 317(44), 318(43)
Mollica, A., 161(61), 181(5, 32),

346(161), 347(126, 161)
Moncrieff, R. W., 121(83), 122(82), 123(81, 83), 128(83), 132(83)
Moniz, E., *289*(120), *290,* 403(84)
Monné, L., *477*(36)
Monnier, M., 332(127), 336(127, 128)
Montemurro, D. G., 231(78)
Montgomery, A. V., 229(79)
Montgomery, M. F., 228(80)
Montgomery, N. P., 316(18)
Mooew, C., 337(179)
Moore, C. R., 258(97)
Moore, R. Y., 292(73), 293(121), 294(121), 407(52), 408(124), 409(85)
Moreau, A., 337(26), 338(25)
Moreno, O. M., 313(11)
Morgan, C. T., 192(111), *362* (19, 20), *364, 365, 367, 369*
Morgane, P., 338(80), 347(80)
Morison, R. S., 346(129)
Moroz, M., 452(124)
Morrell, F., 340(55, 130), 425(58), 431(59, 63), 433(59), 434(60, 61, 62)
Morris, G. O., 326(131)
Mortara, F., 259(70)
Mosberg, W. H., Jr., 406(17)
Motokawa, K., 73(69), 74(70), 425(64, 65)
Mottin, J., 444(63)
Moulton, D. G., 138(84, 85, 86)
Mountcastle, V. B., 289(7), 291(7)
Mountford, Helen, 207(67), 407(43), 455(75)
Mouren-Mathieu, Anne-Marie, 198 (117)
Moushegian, G., 110(41), 348(134)
Moyer, K. E., 451(125)
Mozell, M. M., 133(87), 136(88)
Mulinos, M. G., 211(114)
Müller, G. E., 383(45)
Muller, S. A., 451(103)
Munson, W. A., 95(42)
Murata, K., 327(135), 330(135), 343(135)
Murphy, J. V., 280(123)
Murray, E. J., 327(136)
Myers, G. B., 259(80)
Myers, R. D., 204(135)
Myers, R. E., 109(29)

Näätänen, R., 344(137, 138)
Nagahata, M., 408(86)
Nagao, T., 406(86)
Nairn, R. C., 243(82)
Naitoh, P., 434(62)
Nakagawa, T., 182(2), 332(8), 347(8)

Nakamura, I., 182(2), 332(8), 347(8)
Naquet, R., 161(61), 181(32), 291(124), 340(55), 346(163), 347(126)
Narabayashi, H., 406(86)
Nathan, P. W., 406(87)
Nauss, S. F., 198(15, 16)
Nauta, W. J. H., 177(36), 178(36), 182(37), 293(15, 16), 294(15), 309(48), 311(47, 49), 332(139), 333(140), 346(141), 347(139)
Needham, D. M., 162(63)
Neff, W. D., 109(30, 43), 114(19, 30, 43, 44), 399(16), 400(16, 20), 401(20, 89)
Neil, D. B., 450(126)
Neill, D., 410(90)
Nelson, T. M., 79(5)
Newman, B. L., 317(50)
Newman, E. B., 275(125)
Newton, Sir Isaac, 66
Nice, M. M., 255(98)
Nicholls, J. G., 433(49, 71)
Nielson, H. C., 294(126)
Niemer, W. T., 180(38)
Ninteman, F. W., 310(67)
Nissen, H. W., 254(99), 258(99), 360(22)
Nissen, Th., 447(56)
Noble, G. K., 255(100, 101, 102)
Noble, R. G., 253(29), 260(29)
Norrsell, U., 157(12)
Norton, S., 433(66)
Norton, T., 412(132)
Novin, D., 204(139)
Nulsen, F. E., 181(39)

Oakley, B., 141(89, 90)
Oatley, K., 241(83), 242(40, 83)
O'Brien, C., 452(170)
O'Brien, J. H., 423(18)
Oceguera-Navarra, C., 447(160)
O'Connor, M., 170(107)
Oehme, C., 231(84)
Ogawa, N., 280(118)
Ogawa, T., 346(142)
Ogura, H., 431(90)
Ohma, S., 126(91)
Oikawa, T., 74(70)
Okabe, K., 182(2), 332(8), 347(8)
Okuma, T., 158(7)
Olds, Marianne E., 309(38, 59, 60, 100), 310(61), 432(70)
Oliverio, A., 458(127)
Olsa, J., *306* (57), 307(53), *309* (54, 55, 58, 60, 100), 310(61, 99), 312(51), 313(75), 314(30, 75, 76), 316(52), 317(35, 52, 56), 431(69), 432(67, 68, 70)
Olszewski, J., 177(40)
Olzewski, J., 346(143)
Omura, K., 133(121)
Oppenheimer, M. J., 291(158)
Orbach, J., 291(127)
Orchinik, C. W., 407(118)
Orkand, R. K., 433(71)
Orkand, R. V., 433(49)
Orndoff, R. K., 253(29), 260(29)
Orrego, F., 137(92), 138(93)
Ostenso, R. S., 157(110)
Oswald, I., 336(145)
Otis, L. S., 387(31), 407(122)
Ottoson, D., 133(94, 95), 136(96, 97), 137(96, 97)
Overton, D. A., 460(129, 131)
Overton, R. A., 460(130)

Pagano, R. R., 389(46), 427(72)
Paillas, N., 348(87)
Palestini, M., 180(4), 332(11, 12), 340(146), 344(148), 346(147), 347(147)
Palfai, T., 457(132)
Panksepp, J., 314(90), 315(62, 63)
Paolino, R. M., 388(48), 390(48)
Papez, J. W., *287* (128, 129), *288, 289, 296*
Pappenheimer, J. R., 336(149)
Paré, W., 458(133)
Parent, A., 201(17)
Parks, A. S., 255(46)
Pattison, M. L., 264(40)
Patton, H. D., 152(67), 208(130)
Pavlov, Ivan, *339*(150), *365* (23), *380, 425*(73), 480(37), *481*
Pazzagli, A., 459(134)
Peacock, S. M., 158(38, 68), 179(16), 180(41)
Pearlman, C. A., 456(135)
Pearlman, C. A., Jr., 386(47)
Pechstein, L. A., 449(136), 450(136)
Pechtel, C., 286(130, 148), 408(92, 111)
Peeke, H. V. S., 389(23)
Peele, T. L., 310(98), 317(97)
Peeler, D. F., Jr., 292(2)
Pellegrino, L., 291(131)
Penfield, W., 157(72), *163*(69, 70, 71, 72), 405(93), 406(81), 482(38, 39)
Pepeu, G., 459(134)
Peretz, E., 207(116), 293(132)
Perachio, A. A., 293(100)
Perkins, F. T., 275(125)
Peters, R. H., 408(94), 450(77), 451(76)
Petrinovich, L., 457(114, 137), 458(158), 459(158)
Petrinovich, L. F., 388(43)

Pfaff, D. W., 263(103)
Pffaffmann, C., 125(103, 105), 131(103), 132(23, 100), 135(102, 104), 140(98, 101, 102, 103, 104, 105), 141(23, 58, 105), 263(103)
Pfalz, R. K. J., 114(46)
Phillips, C. G., 138(106), 155(74), 163(73)
Phoenix, C. H., 260(62, 104), 261(61, 64)
Piéron, H., 326(109, 110), 336(151)
Pillard, J., 163(66)
Pilzecker, A., 383(45)
Pitts, W. H., 77(60, 61, 67), 81(61, 66)
Plato, *380*
Pliskoff, S. S., 312(65), 314(64)
Plotnikoff, N., 452(138, 139, 140)
Poirier, L. J., 198(117), 201(17)
Polidora, V. J., 452(62), 456(26)
Poltyrew, S. S., 398(95)
Pomerat, G. M., 472(40)
Pompeiano, O., 160(75, 76), 327(54)
Porter, P. B., 314(20), 400(65)
Porter, R., 155(74)
Porter, R. W., 263(105)
Poschel, B. P. H., 310(66, 67)
Powell, E. W., 295(34, 35, 37), 409(27)
Powell, P. T. S., 138(106)
Powley, T. L., 201(118)
Pribram, Helen B., 404(96)
Probram, K. H., 132(14), 207(46), 291(44, 135), 292(134), 293(133), 402(97), 403(98, 99, 101), 404(4, 9), 407(100), 409(114)
Price, D., 258(97)
Prosser, C. L., 413(102)

Quartermain, D., 388(48), 390(48)
Quigley, J. P., 193(104, 151), 193(104, 119), 211(120, 121)
Quinton, E. E., 457(141)

Raab, D. H., 399(103)
Rabin, B. M., 199(122)
Rabinovich, M. Ia., 425(74)
Racine, R. J., 293(136)
Radionova, E. A., 348(56)
Radley-Smith, E. J., 290(27)
Raiciulescu, N., 412(35)
Rambourg, A., 441(142)
Ramony, Cajal, S., 181(43), 472(41)
Randall, W. L., 114(47)
Randt, C. T., 290(13)
Ranson, S. W., 178(44), 195(73), 198(74), 263(32, 50), 283(137)
Ranson, S. W., Jr., 178(44)
Rapport, M. M., 337(180)
Rasche, R. H., 229(59)

Rasmussen, H., 171(77)
Rasmussen, T., 157(72), 163(72), 291(127)
Ratliff, F., 74(68), 77(73, 74, 75)
Rawson, R. W., 170(78)
Ray, O. S., 312(84), 388(49, 50)
Rebert, C. S., 433(30, 57)
Rechtschaffen, A., 337(124)
Regan, P. F., 280(138)
Regis, H., 340(55)
Reid, L. D., 314(20)
Reilly, J., 280(138)
Reiniš, S., 447(143)
Reitman, B., 290(27)
Reitman, F., 290(139), 403(104)
Renfrew, J. W., 283(71)
Renqvist, Y., 132(107)
Resvold, H. E., 403(12, 105, 106), 404(12), 408(94), 410(7, 105, 107)
Reynolds, R. W., *199* (123, 124), 317(69)
Reynolds, W. R., 449(136), 450 (136)
Rheinberger, M. B., 340(154)
Rhines, Ruth, 159(56, 79, 80), 179(29, 30), 180(29, 30)
Ricci, G. F., 343(152)
Rich, G. J., 96(49)
Richardson, A. J., 449(144)
Richer, Claude-Lise, 198(117)
Richter, C. P., 131(109), 141(108, 109), 208(125), 259(106, 107), 326(153)
Riesz, R. R., 95(50)
Riggs, L. A., 73(34, 77), 75(76)
Rioch, D. McK., 286(148), 408 (111)
Riss, W., 253(125)
Roberts, E., *479* (42)
Roberts, R. B., 453(57), 456(61), 478(6)
Roberts, W. W., 283(142), 248(140, 141), 306(41), 311(70, 71)
Robertson, R. T., 260(130)
Robin, E. D., 327(155)
Robins, R. B., 193(126)
Robinson, B., 263(112), 362(24)
Robinson, C. E., *480* (43)
Robinson, F., 139(78), 286(108)
Robustelli, F., 449(20, 144)
Rocklin, K. W., 312(89), 314(89), 459(49)
Rodgers, W. L., 205(128)
Roger, A., 332(156), 340(55)
Røigaard-Petersen, H. H., 447(56)
Rose, J. E., 111(51, 52), 112(52), 182(45), 472(33, 44)
Rose, S., 449(67)
Rose, S. P. R., 441(146)

Rosecrans, J. A., 337(6)
Rosenblatt, F., 446(147), 447(147), 448(147), 495(45)
Rosenfeld, J. P., 430(75)
Rosenzweig, M. R., 444(149), 446 (29), 447(29), 452(148), 472(46)
Ross, L., 403(101)
Ross, S., 126(110), 452(174)
Rossi, G. F., 178(46), 180(4, 47), 332(11, 12, 44, 156), 346(147), 347(147)
Rosvold, H. E., 207(46), 291(44, 135)
Rothballer, A. B., 337(157)
Rothman, T., 258(47)
Rothschild, G. H., 456(32)
Routtenberg, A., 312(73), *315* (72)
Rowland, V., 290(13), 427(76), *433*(78, 79, 80), 434(78)
Ruch, T. C., 164(81), 208(129, 130)
Ruckmick, C. A., 279(144)
Rudell, A. P., 430(75)
Rullier, J., 227(85)
Runge, S., 258(108)
Rupert, A., 110(41), 112(28), 343 (86), 348(134)
Rushton, W. A., *72* (14, 78, 79)
Rusinov, V. S., 340(158, 159), 434 (81)
Russell, R. W., 390(51), 449(6, 150), 482(47)
Rutherford, W., 102(53), *103*
Rye, M., 316(18)
Rylander, G., 290(145), 403(109)

Sacco, G., 332(44)
Saito, Y., 330(160), 406(86)
Samuel, D., 446(29), 447(29)
Santibañez, G., 340(76)
Sato, Y., 141(66)
Sawyer, C. H., 262(109), 263(38, 84, 105, 109, 110, 111, 112), 330 (102), 362(24)
Sawyer, W. H., *168* (83)
Schacter, S., 276(146), 451(102)
Schadé, J. P., 472(48, 49)
Schaeffer, C. F., 234(71)
Schaefer, E. A., *195* (24), 206 (24)
Scheff, N. M., 433(83)
Scheibel, A. B., 178(48), 346(161), 347(161)
Scheibel, M. E., 178(48, 49), 346 (161), 347(161)
Scheid, P., 433(13)
Scherrer, H., 340(74, 75, 78), 344 (74), 348(78)
Schiff, L., 259(65)
Schiff, M., 192(131), 227(86)

Schiller, P. H., 397(110), 446(29), 447(29)
Schlosberg, H., 279(173)
Schnedorf, J. G., 336(162)
Schneider, A. M., 388(52), 390(52)
Schneirla, T. C., 397(74)
School, P., 433(80)
Schreiner, L., 409(10)
Schreiner, L. H., 178(57), 180(21), 286(130, 148), 291(147), 332 (116), 346(116), 365(18), 408(92, 111)
Schulman, A., 307(77), 313(77)
Schwartzbaum, J. S., 291(79, 149, 150), 293(151), 295(8, 150, 151), 409(112, 113, 114)
Schwartzkopff, J., 112(28)
Sclafani, A., 197(132), 199(132), 233(87), 282(152)
Scott, T. H., 360(3)
Scoville, W. B., 290(153), 292(153), 406(115), 482(50)
Segundo, J. P., 158(84), 340(9), 346(163), 425(31)
Sem Jacobsen, C. W., 307(74)
Sencer, W., 157(108, 109)
Settlage, P. H., 157(108, 109)
Seward, G. H., 254(114)
Seward, J. P., 254(114), 313(75), 314(75, 76)
Shagass, C., 425(32)
Shapiro, H. A., 258(115)
Sharma, K. N., 193(133), 200(9, 134)
Sharp, L. G., 204(135)
Sharpless, S., 340(164)
Sharpless, S. K., 386(47), 456(135)
Shashoua, V. E., 443(151)
Shaw, J. A., 345(165, 166, 174)
Shaw, T., 327(103)
Sheard, M. H., 337(5, 6)
Sheatz, G., 109(29), 348(52)
Sheer, D. E., 427(82)
Shelby, J. M., 446(111)
Shenkin, H. A., 208(129)
Shepherd, G. M., 138(106)
Sherman, W., 388(52), 390(52)
Sherrington, C. S., *151*(85, 86), 162(85), 275(154), 282(174)
Shibuya, T., 133(111, 112, 113, 122, 123, 124), 135(114), 138(115)
Shimokochi, M., 426(91), 430(40)
Shower, E. G., 96(54)
Shurrager, P. S., 413(25, 116, 117)
Sidman, M., 280(112), 307(77), 313 (77), 317(9), 387(18)
Siegel, P. S., 390(53)
Sierra, G., 425(31)
Silva, E. E., 340(9)
Singer, J. E., 276(155)

Author Index

Simmons, H. J., 294(91)
Simon, L. N., 452(66)
Simons, Barbara J., 243(33)
Sines, J. O., 451(152)
Singer, M. T., 326(131)
Singh, B., 200(6, 9, 134), 212(6)
Skramlik, E., 128(117)
Skramlik, E. Von, 136(117)
Slotnick, B., 293(162), 295(163), 408(124)
Smirnov, G. D., 340(158, 159)
Smith, C. J., 199(122)
Smith, D. E., 284(156)
Smith, E., 337(28)
Smith, G. P., 212(136)
Smith, K. R., 104(55)
Smith, M. C., 406(87)
Smith, O. A., Jr., 202(137)
Smith, P. H., 71(88)
Smith, R. W., 231(88)
Smith, R. W., Jr., 168(87)
Smith, W. K., 293(157)
Snider, R. S., 160(89), 161(88, 90), 179(51), 181(52)
Snodgrass, L., 428(56)
Snyder, F., 327(167)
Sokai, M., 314(20)
Sokolov, E. N., 340(177)
Soliday, S., 451(106)
Solomon, E. I., 211(121)
Solyom, L., 456(30, 153, 154)
Sommer, Sally R., 204(139)
Sömmerring, S. T., *191*(138)
Sonne, E., 451(94)
Sorensen, J. P., 234(89)
Soroko, V. I., 348(56)
Sousková, M., 459(162)
Spector, N. H., 214(140), 243(90)
Spence, *377*
Spencer, W. A., 413(129)
Sperry, R. W., 163(91)
Spiegel, A., 407(118)
Spiegel, E. A., 286(158), 291(158)
Spies, G., 312(78)
Spong, P., 344(169)
Spooner, C. E., 337(123)
Sprague, J. M., 159(93), 161(13, 14, 92), 178(55), 179(53, 54)
Sprague, J. W., 181(7)
Spurrier, W. A., 336(31)
Spurzheim, J. G., *380*(16)
Squires, R. D., 240(31)
Stamm, J. S., 403(119)
Stare, F. J., 190(103)
Starzl, T. E., 346(170)
Stebbins, W. C., 387(9)
Steele, B. J., 452(33)
Steggerda, F. R., 228(91)
Stein, D. G., 293(87)
Stein, I. F., 192(54)

Stein, L., 282(111), 309(81, 85, 86), 311(36, 82), 312(84), 313(79), 446(29), 447(29), 451(120), 460(17), 461(17)
Steinach, E., 258(116, 119), 259(117, 118)
Steinbaum, E. A., 318(87)
Steinberg, M. L., 283(142)
Steiner, S. S., 309(88)
Stellar, Eliot, *195*(141), 200(150), 231(103), *363*(25, 26), *364*(25), *365, 367, 369*, 452(155), 453(57, 58)
Sterman, M. B., 332(120), 333(171, 172), 347(171, 172), 426(89)
Stevens, S. S., 94(56), 96(7), 100(57), 106(57)
Stevenson, J. A. F., 190(91), 197(110), 231(78), 233(92)
Stewart, C. N., 451(156)
Stone, C. P., 254(121), 258(120)
Storm, T., 461(157)
Storm Van Leeuwen, W., 340(55)
Stowell, A., 179(51)
Strang, J. M., *214*(19)
Stratton, L. O., 458(158), 459(158)
Strauss, M. B., 240(93)
Stricker, E. M., 241(94, 95, 97, 99), 242(97, 111), 242(94, 96, 98)
Strobel, D. A., 443(22)
Ström, G., 473(51)
Ström, L., 140(54)
Strominger, J. L., 214(142)
Ström-Olsen, R., 279(159)
Stuiver, M., 130(118)
Stumpf, W. E., 263(122), 264(122)
Stutz, R. M., 312(89), 314(89)
Suzuki, J. -I., 327(83)
Svaetichin, G., 74(62, 81)
Swann, H. G., 287(160, 161)
Szwarcbart, M. K., 410(107)

Takagi, S., 138(115)
Takagi, S. F., 133(112, 113, 120, 121, 122, 123, 124, 125)
Takahashi, S., 214(105)
Takenaka, S., 330(160)
Talbott, S. A., 81(64)
Taleisnik, S., 264(127)
Talwar, G. P., 212(8)
Tanzi, E., *473*(52), *474*
Tarnecki, R., 205(161)
Tarozzi, G., 326(173)
Tasaki, I., 108(59, 60), 110(61)
Tasaki, K., 74(70)
Tauc, L., 432(42, 43)
Taylor, Anna N., 234(100)
Taylor, C. W., 346(170)
Taylor, F. H., 132(40, 41)
Tecce, J. J., 433(83)

Teitelbaum, H., 407(120)
Teitelbaum, P., 141(72), 192(40), 197(143), *198*(144, 146, 149), 199(148), 200(144, 147, 148, 150), 201(40, 41, 144, 160), 202(145), 205(128), 206(145), 214(41), 231(102, 103), 235(101), 316(25)
Templeton, R. D., 193(151)
Tepperman, J., 195(23), 198(152)
Terzian, 264(123), 405(121)
Thomas, E., 412(132)
Thomas, G. J., 293(162), 294(91), 295(163), 407(122), 408(123, 124)
Thompson, C. W., 386(25), 390(25)
Thompson, J. B., 293(151), 295(151)
Thompson, R., 386(54), 407(126), 408(125, 126)
Thompson, R. F., *113*(63), 345(165, 166, 174), 404(127, 128), 413(129)
Thomson, C. W., 457(115), 458(84, 116)
Thorn, N. A., 169(94)
Timo-Iaria, C., 338(80), 347(80)
Tinbergen, N., 254(124), 255(124)
Toida, N., 73(83)
Tomita, T., 75(84, 85)
Tomlin, M. I., 254(121)
Torii, H., 182(2), 332(8), 347(8)
Torpin, R., 259(70)
Towbin, E. J., 228(104), 229(105)
Tower, S. S., 156(96), 163(95, 97)
Travis, A. M., 157(108, 109, 110)
Travis, L. E., 340(175)
Travis, R. C., 279(83)
Trowill, J. A., *314*(90), 315(62, 63)
Tsang, Y. C., 192(153)
Tucker, D., 133(126, 127), 135(114), 136(20, 126, 127)
Tunturi, A. R., 112(64, 67), 112(66), 113(65)
Turausky, A. J., 210(33)

Ungar, G., 446(159), 447(159, 160), 448(159), 479(53)
Ungher, I., 411(64)
Uretsky, Ella, 407(130)
Ursin, H., 291(165), 294(103)
Uyeda, A., 309(91)
Uyeda, A. A., 313(75), 314(75, 76)

Valasco, M., 340(75)
Valenstein, E. S., 198(155), 203(154), 231(106), 253(125), 307(93), 310(92, 94), 317(23)
Vanderwolf, C. H., 159(99), 294(166), *342*(176), *343*(176, 181), 427(84)
Vane, J. R., 170(100)

Vanzulli, A., 344(53)
Van Wagenen, W. P., 228(16, 17), 231(16)
Vaughn, E., 263(126)
Vaughn, H. G., Jr., 433(24)
Velardo, J. T., 168(101)
Velasco, M., 426(88)
Velasco, M. E., 264(127)
Venstrom, D., 123(10)
Veress, E., 121(128)
Verhave, T., 451(161)
Verney, E. B., 240(107)
Vernier, V. G., 348(52)
Victor, M., 406(1)
Villee, C. A., 168(102)
Vimont, P., 328(101)
Vitale, J. J., 190(103)
Vloedman, D. A., 193(78)
Vogel, J. R., 451(31)
Volanskii, D., 411(64)
Voronin, L. G., 340(177)
Votava, Z., 459(162)

Wade, Marjorie, 402(131)
Waelsch, H., 441(122)
Wagner, A. R., 412(132), 446(29), 447(29), 456(163)
Wagner, H. G., 76(87)
Walberg, F., 156(103)
Wald, G., 71(39, 88)
Waldeyer, W. von, *381* (55)
Walker, D. R., 446(164)
Wall, P. D., 178(56)
Waller, H. J., 181(9)
Waller, W. H., 159(104)
Walter, W. G., *433* (11, 85, 86), 434(86, 87)
Walzl, E. M., 112(79), 113(78, 79)
Wangenstein, O. H., 192(156)
Ward, A. A., Jr., *293*(167)
Ward, H. P., 310(95, 96)
Ward, I. L., 260(55)
Ward, J. W., 157(105), 158(22)
Warren, H. B., 404(134)
Warren, J. M., 403(133), 404(134)
Washburn, A. L., *192*(28)
Wasman, M., 283(168)
Wasserman, E., 446(29), 447(29)
Watson, R. H. J., 449(150)
Watts, J. W., 207(157)
Wayner, M. A., 73(77)
Weber, *84, 94, 95*
Wegener, J., 433(47)
Weil-Malberbe, H., 279(159)
Weinberger, N. M., 426(88)
Weinstein, G. L., 259(93)
Weinskrantz, L., 292(134), 403(38, 136, 137), 404(83), 409(135)

Weiss, T., 459(27, 28)
Weissman, A., 457(165. 166)
Weitzman, E. D., 337(179, 180)
Wells, D. G., 234(71)
Wells, L. J., 255(128)
Werre, J., 340(55)
Wertheim, G. A., 280(169)
West, C. D., 326(14)
Westbrook, W. H., 457(115), 458(116, 167)
Westerman, A., 446(168)
Wettendorff, H., *239*(108)
Wever, E. G., *94, 95, 100*(71, 72, 74, 75, 76), 101(74, 75), 102(73, 76), *104*(71, 76), *105, 106, 107,* 108(71)
Whalen, R. E., 260(129, 130), 261(45), 451(81)
Whaley, R. D., 327(155)
Wheatley, M. D., 199(158), 282(170), 293(170)
Wheeler, L., 276(146)
Wheeler, R. H., 275(125)
Whishaw, I. Q., 343(181)
White, J. C., 343(37)
White, N. M., 206(159), 363(27)
Whitfield, I. C., 112(21), 113(77)
Whitlock, D. G., 178(57), 182(37)
Whitmoyer, D. I., 263(84)
Wickelgren, W. O., 292(76)
Wiener, N. I., 459(169)
Wiesel, T. N., 74(13), 75(12), 79(44), 81(43, 44, 45, 46), *85,* 113(36)
Wilcox, R. H., 205(12)
Wilkinson, H. A., 310(98), 317(97)
Will, F., 452(140)
Williams, D. R., 201(160)
Williams, G. W., 452(170)
Williams, H. L., 327(136)
Williams, R. H., 170(106)
Wilson, A. S., 292(36), 295(37)
Wilson, J. E., 442(1, 173)
Wilson, W. A., Jr., 407(100)
Wing, K. G., 399(138, 139)
Winkle, K., 336(107)
Winocur, G., 293(171)
Wise, C. D., 309(85, 86)
Woerdeman, M. W., 57
Wolbarsht, M. L., 76(87)
Wolf, A. V., *228*(109, 110), 229(110), 240(109)
Wolf, G., 241(99), 242(97, 111)
Wolf, S., 279(172)
Wolfe, J. B., 402(53)
Wolff, H. G., 279(172)
Wolstenholme, G. E. W., 170(107)
Woodrow, H., 128(130)

Woodworth, R. S., 279(173), 282(174)
Woolsey, C. N., 112(79), 113(79), 157(108, 109, 110), 160(27), 400(79)
Worden, F. G., 345(182)
Wortis, J., 213(76)
Wright, C. A., 259(56)
Wright, J. E., 312(65)
Wright, R. H., 122(131, 132), 124(131, 132)
Wycis, H. T., 407(118)
Wyers, E. J., 158(7, 8, 9, 37), 411(13)
Wyse, G. A., 133(125)
Wurtz, R. H., 310(99)
Wyrwicka, Wanda, 205(161), 232(14), 425(31), 426(89)

Yajima, T., 133(125)
Yamada, K., 140(133)
Yamaguchi, N., 182(2), 332(8), 336(184, 185), 337(184, 185), 338(185), 347(8)
Yamamoto, C., 137(134), 138(134)
Yannet, H., 240(26)
Yokota, T., 343(186)
Yoshida, M., 406(86)
Yoshii, N., 426(91), 431(90)
Young, C. W., 125(135)
Young, G. A., 343(187), 427(92)
Young, J. Z., 474(54)
Young, Thomas, *64, 67*
Young, W. C., 168(111), 253(125), 254(72), 260(62, 63, 104), 261(45)
Yrarrazaval, S., 261(13), 264(13)
Yun, C., 309(100)
Yuwiler, A., 309(100)

Zanchetti, A., 180(4), 332(11, 12), 346(147), 347(147)
Zavala, A., 390(38)
Zeeman, W. C. P., 81(11)
Zeliony, G. P., 398(95)
Zelman, A., 446(171)
Zemp, J. W., 442(173)
Zigmond, R. E., 264(131)
Zimmerman, F. T., 452(174)
Zinkin, Sheila, 389(56)
Zirondoli, A., 180(47), 332(156)
Zotterman, Y., 135(137), 140(54, 136), 229(112)
Zubek, J. P., 452(85, 86, 87)
Zubeck, J. P., 400(140)
Zubin, J., 390(57)
Zwaardemaker, H., 123(139), *125* (138, 139), *126*(140)
Zucker, I., 294(175), 295(176)

SUBJECT INDEX

Abducens nerve, 54
Ablation, technique, 7
Absorption, of light, 65
  of sound, 91
Accommodation, 70
Acetoxycycloheximide, effects on memory, 453
Acetylcholine, change during learning, 444
  effects on, aggression and avoidance behaviors, 291
    drinking, 203, 206, 232
    learning, 448
  neurohumoral function, 24
ACTH, 169
  influence on avoidance behavior, 280
  release during affective reaction, 280
Action potential, 20
Adenohypophysis, 167
ADH, 169
  secretion due to, hypothalamic stimulation, 232
    intrahypothalamic saline, 240
Adipsia, result of lesions in, amygdala, 206
    globus pallidus, 201, 234
    hypothalamus (LH), 200, 231
    midbrain tegmentum, 201
  role of motor deficits, 205
Adrenalectomy, effects on CAR, 451
  metabolic effects, 169
Adrenal gland, 169
Adrenergic mechanisms, role in, drinking, 205, 232
    feeding, 203, 205
    learning and/or recall, 451
    reward, 309
    sleep, 336
Adrenocorticotrophic hormone, 168
  influence on avoidance behavior, 280
  release during affective reaction, 280
Adsorption, role in olfaction, 121
Affective behaviors, influence of, frontal lobe, 289
    hypothalamus, 282
    limbic system, 286
    thalamus, 285
  physiological correlates, 276
  sensory feedback, 275
Afferent pathways, spinal cord, 39
Aggressive behavior, effect of, hypothalamic lesions, 282
    limbic system lesions, 291

Allocortex, 49, 286
Alpha-block, 339
  conditioned, 425
Alpha motor fibers, 53
Alpha motor neurons, 151
Alpha waves (EEG), 29, 424
Amnesia, after drug-induced CNS seizures, 456
  after electroconvulsive shock, 385
  after hippocampal lesions, 405
  after intracerebral acetoxycycloheximide, 454
  after intracerebral puromycin, 453
Amphetamine, effects on learning and/or recall, 451
Amygdala, anatomy, 44
  effects of, chemical stimulation, 207, 234
    electrical stimulation, 206, 234
    lesions on, affective reactions, 290
      drinking, 234
      feeding, 206
      learning and/or recall, 409
      sexual behavior, 263
Anabolic process, 14
Androgens, effects on, development of hypothalamus, 259
    sexual behavior, 257
Androstene dione, role in sexual behavior, 256
Angiotensin, role in thirst, 233, 243
Annulo-spiral endings, 152
Anticholinergics, effects on learning and/or recall, 451, 458
Antidiuretic hormone, 169
  secretion due to, hypothalamic stimulation, 232
    intrahypothalamic saline, 240
Aphagia, result of lesions in, amygdala, 206
    globus pallidus, 201
    hypothalamus (LH), 200
    midbrain tegmentum, 201
  role of motor deficits, 205
ARAS, 180, 331, 346
Arcuate n., 42
Arousal, definition, 339
  EEG, 424
  neuroanatomy, 346
  role of, midbrain reticular formation, 180
    nonspecific thalamic projections, 182
Arousal theory, 365
Ascending reticular arousal system (ARAS), 331, 346

Association areas, 47, 401
    effects of lesions on learning and/or recall, 401
Attack behavior, hypothalamic influences, 282
Attention, effects on evoked potentials, 344, 348
Audition, theories of, 102
Auditory cortex, 112
    effects of lesions on auditory discriminations, 195, 399, 410
Auditory nerve, anatomy, 55
    electrophysiology, 107
Auditory system, anatomy, 55, 109
    auditory nerve potentials, 107
    centrifugal influences, 114
    cochlear n, electrophysiology, 110
    cortical projections, 112, 399
    electrophysiology, 100
    sensitivity range, 94
    thresholds, 94
    transmission in ear, 99
Autonomic nervour system, anatomy, 56
Autonomic responses, correlates of arousal, 276
Avoidance behavior, after lesions in, amygdala, 290
    caudate, 410
    cingulate gyrus, 293
    hippocampus, 291, 407
    hypothalamus, 199, 282
    septal area, 293

Bandwidth of sound, 95
Barbiturates, effects on memory, 456
Basal ganglia, anatomy, 44
    influence on reticular formation, 181
    motor functions, 157
Basis pedunculi, 42
Blind spot, 70
Blocking agents, neurochumoral, 25
Blood pressure, change during arousal, 278
Blood sugar, role in feeding, 211
Body temperature, effect on feeding, 214
Body water, 237
Boundary detectors, vision, 77
Brachium conjunctivum, 41
Brachium pontis, 41
Brainstem, anatomy, 41
Brain temperature, effect on, drinking, 243
    feeding, 214

Carbohydrates, 14
Cardiac muscle, 34
Castration, effects on sexual behavior, 258
Catatonia, result of hypothalamic (LH) lesions, 205
Caudate n., anatomy, 44
    effects of lesions on learning and/or recall, 410
Cell, anatomy, 12
    basic constituents, 13
    basic functions, 14, 16
        conductor, 17, 19
        effector, 18, 33
        energy transformation, 14
        metabolism, 14
    muscle, 33
    receptor, 16, 29
    secretory, 35
Cell assembly, 474
Center frequency, of sound, 95
Central nervous system, gross anatomy, 37
Cerebellum, anatomy, 50
    effects of, electrical stimulation, 160
        lesions, 160
    influences on reticular formation, 181
    motor functions, 159
Cerveau isolé, EEG, 180
Chemical brain stimulation, effects on, avoidance behavior, 291, 294
    drinking, 232
    feeding, 203, 207
    learning, 444, 448, 458
    urine secretion, 233
Chemical stimulation, techniques, 6
Cholinergic mechanisms, role in, avoidance behavior, 291, 294
    drinking, 203, 205, 232, 234
    learning and/or memory, 444, 448, 458
    punishment, 311
Cholinesterase, 25
Cholinesterase inhibitors, 25
Chorda tympani, 131, 135, 139
Choroid, 70
Cingulate gyrus, 46, 49
    effects of lesions on affective reactions, 293
Circumvallate papillae, 131
C.N.V., 433
Cochlear duct, 98
Cochlear n., anatomy, 55
    electrophysiology, 110
Cochlear potential, 100
Colliculi, anatomy, 41
    electrophysiology, 81, 112
Color, blindness, 68
    determinants of, 66
    spectrum, 65
    vision, theories, 67
Compound action potential, 26
Conditioned emotional responses, effects of, ECS, 387
    limbic system lesions, 294
    while working for brain stimulation, 313
Conductors, 17
Cone receptor, 70
Consolidation, EEG correlates, 427
    effects of, drug-induced CNS seizures, 456
        intracerebral acetoxycycloheximide, 354
        intracerebral puromycin, 453
Consonance, of sound, 96
Contingent negative variation, 433
Convulsions, effects on memory, 387, 456
Cornea, 69
Coronal plane, 36
Corpus callosum, 46
Corpus luteum, 256
Corpus striatum, 44

Cortex, anatomy, 45
  association areas, 47, 400
  auditory projections, 112, 399
  effects of spreading depression, 398
  electrophysiology, 340
  frontal lobe, anatomy, 47
    role in, affective reactions, 289
      learning and/or recall, 401
    influence on reticular formation, 181
    motor functions, 47, 156, 157
    olfactory projections, 139
    role in learning and/or memory, 397
    temporal lobe, anatomy, 47
      role in affective reactions, 290
    visual projections, 81, 399
Corti, organ of, 98
Corticospinal tracts, 40
Cranial nerves, 53
Cretinism, 170
Cribriform place, 130
Cycloheximide, effects on memory, 453
Cytoplasm, 13

Dark adaptation, 72
D.C. potentials, 433
Decortication, effects on, learning and/or memory, 397
  pyramidal motor system, 156
Degeneration, peripheral nerve, 53
Delayed response learning, effects of lesions in, frontal lobe, 401
  hippocampus, 407
  striatum, 410
Delta waves (EEG), 29
Dentate, gyrus, 50
Dentate n., 50, 161
Deoxyribonucleic acid (DNA), 13
  role in, cellular activity, 475
    memory, 476, 478
DFP, 25
  effect on learning and/or recall, 449, 459
Diabetes mellitus, 170
Diencephalon, 42
Diffraction, 66, 91
Diffusion, 15
Diisopropyl fluorophosphate, effects on learning and/or recall, 449, 459
Dimming detectors, vision, 77
Direct current potentials (EEG), 433
Dissonance, 96
DNA, role in, cellular activity, 475
  memory, 476, 478
Dominator functions, 76
Dopamine, 25
Dorsal roots, 52
Drinking, classic theories, 226
  effects of, hypothalamic (LH) lesions, 231
    intrahypothalamic saline, 233, 240
  extrahypothalamic mechanisms, 233
  osmotic influences, 239

pharmacology of central pathways, 232
role fo kidney, 233
systemic influences, 226
volumetric influences, 240
Dry mouth, role in thirst, 227

Ear, 97
ECS, 385
EEG, see Electroencephalogram
Effectors, 18, 33
Efferent pathways, spinal, 40
Electrical brain stimulation, effects on, ADH secretion, 232
  aggressive behaviors, 282
  drinking, 203, 231
  feeding, 202, 206, 208
  ovulation, 261
  sexual behavior, 263
  punishing effects, 282, 311
  rewarding effects, 307
  technique, 6
Electroconvulsive shock, effects on memory, 385
Electroencephalogram, during arousal, 280, 339
  during learning, 424
  during movement, 342
  during sleep, 328
  of hippocampus, 341, 426
  of hypothalamus, 200, 212, 263
  of olfactory bulb, 138
  waveforms, alpha, 29, 424
    high frequencies, 427
    recruiting responses, 182
    slow waves, 328, 425
    spindles, 182, 328
    theta, 341, 426
Electromagnetic spectrum, 65
Electromyogram, 279
Electro-oculogram, 73
Electro-olfactogram, 132
Electroretinogram, 73
Emboliform n., 50
Emotions, influence of, frontal lobe, 289
  hypothalamus, 282
  limbic system, 286
  thalamus, 285
  physiological correlates, 276
Encephal isolé, EEG, 180
Endocrine system, 165
Enzyme inhibition, influence on olfaction, 125
Enzymes, 14
EOG, 133
Epinephrine, adrenal secretion, 170
  effects on appetite, 213
  neurohumoral functions, 25
Epithalamus, 43
ERG, 73
Estrogen, 168
  role in sexual behavior, 256, 263
Estrus, 257
Eustachian tubes, 98

Evoked potential, 28, 32
  effects of, attention, 344
    habituation, 348
    learning, 429
Extensors, 150
Extinction, after limbic system lesions, 289
Extrafusal muscle fiber, 151
Extrapyramidal motor system, 40, 157
Eye, anatomy, 53, 69
  electrophysiology, 73

Facial nerve, 54
Fasciculus cuneatus, 39
Fasciculus gracilis, 39
Fastigial n., 50, 161
Feeding, effects of, chemical brain stimulation, 203
    electrical brain stimulation, 202
    hypothalamic lesions, 195, 202
    extrahypothalamic influences, 206
    glucostatic mechanisms, 211
    pharmacology of central pathways, 208
Feminization, 260
Filtration, 15
Finickiness, 197, 200
Flocculus, 50
Flower spray ending, 152
Follicle stimulating hormone, 168
  role in sexual behavior, 256
Fornix, 42, 49
Fourth ventricle, 41
Frequency theory of hearing, 102
Frontal lobe, 47
  effects of lesions on, avoidance behavior, 289
    feeding, 207
    learning and/or recall, 401
Frontal lobotomy, 289
Frustration, response after limbic system lesions, 289
FSH, 169
Fungiform papillae, 131

GABA, neurochumoral function, 25
Galvanic skin response (GSR), 278
Gamma efferents, 53, 153
Gamma motor neuron, 151
Gamma waves (EEG), 29
Gastric motility, change during arousal, 279
  role in hunger, 192
Generator potential, 73
Geniculate body, lateral, electrophysiology, 79
Geniculate n., 43, 54, 55
Glands, 18, 35
Globose n., 50
Globus pallidus, anatomy, 44
  effects of lesions on, drinking, 234
    feeding, 201, 206
Glossopharyngeal nerve, 55
  taste fibers, 131, 135, 139
Glucoreceptors, role in feeding, 211
Glucose, effects, of central administration, 213
  on feeding, 211

Glucostatic theory of hunger, 210
Goldthioglucose, effects on feeding, 212
Gonadotrophic hormones, role in sexual behavior, 256
Gonadotrophins, 168
Gonads, transplants, 259
Growth hormone, 168
GSR, 278
Gustatory system, anatomy, 130
  electrophysiology, 135
  receptors, 131
  stimuli, 121

Habenular n., 43
Habituation, 340, 348
  of EEG, 424
Hair cells, of auditory system, 99, 107
Hearing, theories of, 102
Heart rate, change during arousal, 278
Heat production, effects of hypothalamic (VMH) lesions, 198
Heliocotrema, 98
Hippocampus, 49
  effects of lesions on, avoidance behavior, 291
    feeding, 207
    learning and/or recall, 405, 443
  electrophysiology, 341
Histology, procedure, 9
Hormones, 165
Hunger, classic theories of, 191, 194
  extrahypothalamic influences, 206
  glucostatic mechanisms, 210
  hypothalamic influences, 195
  pharmacology of central pathways, 203
  thermoregulatory influences, 214
Hyperdipsia, result of septal lesions, 234
Hyperglycemia, effects on, EEG, 212
  feeding, 212
Hyperphagia, result of lesions in, amygdala, 206
  frontal lobe, 208
  hypothalamus (VMH), 195, 212
  thalamus, 208
Hypertonic fluids, 239
Hypervolemia, 240
Hypnotoxin, 336
Hypoglossal nerve, 56
Hypoglycemia, effects on, EEG, 212
  feeding, 211
Hypophysis, 167
Hypothalamohypophyseal tract, 168, 169
Hypothalamus, affinity for glucose, 212
  anatomy, 42
  effects of, chemical stimulation, 203, 232
    electrical stimulation on, ADH secretion, 232
      drinking, 231
      feeding, 202
      sexual behavior, 263
    lesions on, avoidance behavior, 282
      drinking, 231
      sexual behavior, 263
      sleep, 332

local heating or cooling, 214
influence of androgen on development, 259
response to local saline injections, 233
RNA synthesis during learning, 442
secretion of releasing factors, 256
sex hormone uptake, 263
Hypotonic fluids, 239
Hypovolemia, 241

ICSH, 168, 257
Incus, 98
Induced waves (olfactory bulb EEG), 138
Infrared absorption, influence on olfaction, 124
Insulin, effects on ,feeding, 211
    stomach motility, 212
    release by pancreas, 170
Internal capsule, 46
Interpositus n., 161
Interstitial cell stimulating hormone, 168, 257
Intrafusal muscle fiber, 151
Intrinsic waves (olfactory bulb EEG), 138
Iodopsin, 71
Ionic mechanisms in neurons, 19
Isometric contractions, 33, 151
Isotonic contractions, 33, 151
Isotonic fluids, 239

Juxtallocortex, 49, 286

Kamin effect, 384
Kidney, role in thirst, 233
Korsakoff's psychosis, 407

Labyrinth, of ear, 98
Lactogenic hormone, 168
Lateral geniculate body, electrophysiology, 79
Lateral hypothalamus, effects of, chemical stimulation, 203, 208, 232
    electrical stimulation, 205, 231, 283, 309
    lesions, 200, 231, 283
Lateral lemniscus, 41
Learning, anatomical substrate, 395
    hippocampus, 405
    neocortex, 197
    subcortical, 409
    behavioral considerations, 375
    brain chemistry, 440
        ACh and AChE, 444
        protein synthesis, 444
        RNA content or composition, 441
        transfer of training, 445
    drug effects on, acquisition, 448, 451, 452
        recall, 453, 456, 458
    electrophysiology, 341
    simple organisms, 413
    state dependency, 460
    theoretical issue, 379
    theories, 471, 473, 475, 481
Lens of eye, 70
Lesion, technique, 7
LH, 168

Lie detection, 276
Light, nature of, 63
Limbic system, 46, 286
Lingual nerve, taste fibers, 131, 135
Locomotion, 162
Locus coeruleus, effects of lesions on sleep, 332
Lordosis, 253
Loudness, 92
Luminosity potentials, 74
Luteinizing hormone, 168, 256
Luteotrophin, 168

Malleus, 98
Mammillary bodies, 42
    effects of lesions on learning and/or recall, 406, 408
Mammillotegmental tract, 42
Mammillothalamic tract, 42
Manubrium, 98
Masculinization, 260
Medial forebrain bundle, 42
    role in, feeding, 201
    rewarding effects of brain stimulation, 309
Medial lemniscus, 132
Medulla, anatomy, 41
Mel, 96
Membrane, permeability, 15
Memory, anatomical substrate, 395
    hippocampus, 405
    neocortex, 197
    subcortical, 409
    chemistry, 440
        protein synthesis, 444
        RNA content or composition, 441
        transfer of training, 445
    consolidation, effects of ECS, 385
    drug effects on, acquisition, 448, 451, 452
        recall, 453, 456
    simple organisms, 413
    state dependency, 460
    temporal characteristics, 380
    theories, 471, 473, 475, 481
Mesencephalon, anatomy, 41
Metrazol, effects on memory, 456
MFB, role in, feeding, 201
    rewarding effects of brain stimulation, 309
Midbrain, anatomy, 41
    motor functions, 159
Midbrain reticular formation, role in arousal, 180, 332, 346
Middle ear, 98
Modulator functions, 76
Molecular models of memory, 477
Molecular vibrations, influence on olfaction, 122, 124
Motor system, 40
    alpha efferents, 53, 151
    cerebellar components, 50, 159
    cortical components, 47, 157
    extrapyramidal aspects, 157

feedback mechanisms, 152
gamma efferents, 53, 151, 153
pyramidal tracts, 155
reflexes, 151
reticular system influences, 179
sensory input, 152
spinal components, 40, 53, 157
Mouth, role in thirst, 228
Movement, complex, 164
EEG correlates, 342
role of servo-mechanism, 163
voluntary, 162
MRF, 180
role in arousal, 346
Multi-unit activity, recording techniques, 4
Muscle, 18, 150
cardiac, 34
extrafual fiber, 151
innervation, 156
intrafusal fiber, 151
mechanisms of action, 33
smooth, 35
spindle, 151
striated, 33

N. reticularis pontis oralis, role in arousal, 181
Nerve conduction, 26
Neural nets, 379
Neural transmitter, 23
Neurobiotaxis, 473
Neurohumor, 23
Neurohypophysis, 168
Neuromuscular transmission, 34
Neuron, afterpotential, 22
basic functions, 19
compound action potential, 26
ionic mechanisms, 19
refractoriness, 21
response to stimulation, 21
Nicotine, effects on learning and/or recall, 449, 458
Nonspecific thalamic projections, 182
role in arousal, 346
Norepinephrine, adrenal secretion, 170
effects of central injections on drinking, 203, 207, 232
neurohumoral function, 24
role in, reward, 309
sleep, 336
Nose, anatomy, 130
Nucleus pontis caudalis, effects of lesions on sleep, 332
Nucleus reticularis pontis oralis, effects of lesions on sleep and arousal, 332, 347

Occipital cortex, 47, 81, 399
Oculomotor nerve, 54
Odor, basic properties, 122
classification, 125
influence on sexual behavior, 255
Odorivector, 122
Olfaction, adaptation, 127

classification of stimuli, 25
receptor anatomy, 131
theories, 126, 132
thresholds, 127
Olfactory bulb, 137
Olfactory nerve, 53, 136
Olfactory system, anatomy, 53, 130
central projections, 139
electrophysiology, 132
Olivocochlear bundle, 114
Ommatidium, 77
On-off responses in, auditory system, 111, 112
olfactory system, 138
visual system, 75, 82
Opponent-process theory of color vision, 68
Opsin, 71
Optic nerve, 54
Organ of Corti, 98
Orienting, 339
Osmometric theory of thirst, 239
Osmoreceptor, hypothalamus, 233, 240
Osmosis, 15
Oval window, 98
Oxytocin, 169

Pancreas, 170
Paradoxical sleep, 328
Parasympathetic nerves, 56
Parathyroid, 171
Parietal lobe, 47
Passive avoidance, effects of limbic system lesions, 289
Pentylenetetrazol, effects on learning and/or recall, 407, 456
Peripheral nerves, 52
Periventricular fiber system, 42
role in punishment, 311
Perseveration, after limbic system lesions, 289
after frontal lobe lesions, 403
PGO spikes, 328, 336
Phase sequence, 474
Photoreceptors, 69
chemistry, 71
electrophysiology, 73
sensitivity range, 65
Physostigmine, 25
Pinna, 98
Pitch, 93, 95
Pituitary, structure and function, 167
Place theory of hearing, 102
Polarity potential of eye, 73
Pons, anatomy, 41
Ponto-geniculo-occipital spikes, 328, 336
Portal blood supply, of pituitary, 168
Posterior commissure, 43
Post-tetanic potentiation, 472
Post-synaptic potentials, 24
Posture, 161
Potassium chloride, effects on cortical functions, 399
Prandial drinking, 231
Preoptic area, 42

role in sexual behavior, 261
Prepyriform cortex, olfactory projections, 139
Priming brain stimulation, 313
Progesterone, 168
  role in sexual behavior, 256
Protein synthesis, role in memory, 444, 453
Protoplasm, 13
Punishment, effects of electrical brain stimulation, 310
  response after, caudate lesions, 411
    limbic system lesions, 289
Pupil, 69
Puromycin, effects on memory, 453
Putamen, anatomy, 44
Pyramidal tracts, 40, 155

Raphe n., effects of lesions on sleep, 332, 337
Rapid eye movement sleep (REM), 328
Receptor, 16
  functions, 29
  potentials, 30
  types, 31
    auditory, 97
    gustatory, 131
    kinesthetic, 152
    olfactory, 130
    visual, 69
Recruiting response, EEG, 182
Red-green potentials, 74
Red nucleus, motor functions, 159
Reflection, of light, 65
  of sound, 91
Reflexes, 151, 179
Refraction of light, 65
Regeneration, peripheral nerve, 53
Reissner's membrane, 98
Releasing factors, 168, 256
REM, 328
Respiration, change during arousal, 279
Restiform body, 41
Resting potential, 19
Reticular formation, afferent and efferent connections, 178
  anatomy, 178
  effects of stimulation or lesions on, arousal, 180, 332, 346
    learning and/or recall, 411
    motor functions, 159, 179
    sensory functions, 178
Reticular n., 43
Retina, 70
Retinene, 71
Retrograde amnesia, 383, 406, 456
Reverberatory activity, role in learning, 379
Reward effects of brain stimulation, 307
Rhinencephalon, 49, 286
Rhodopsin, 71
Ribonucleic acid, changes during learning, 441, 456, 476, 478
  role in cellular activity, 475
RNA, *see* Ribonucleic acid

Rod receptor, 70
Round window, 98

S-potential, 74
Sagittal plane, 36
Saliva, role in thirst, 227
Salt-deficiency, effects on drinking, 240
Satiety, influence of, hypothalamus, 195
  skin or body temperature, 214
  stomach distention, 193
Scala tympani, 98
Scala vestibuli, 98
Sclera, 70
Scopolamine, effects on learning and/or recall, 451, 459
Sensory nerves, terminations, 52
Sensory pathways, spinal cord, 39
Sensory projection areas, cortex, 47, 399
Septal area, 49
  effects of lesions on, avoidance behavior, 293
    drinking, 234
Serotonin, neurohumoral function, 25
  role in sleep, 336
Sex hormones, 256
  effects on brain development, 259
Sexual behavior, definition, 253
  influence of, environment, 254
    hormones, 256
    hypothalamus, 263
    limbic system, 264
    sensory input, 255
Sexual receptivity, 257
Single cell recordings, during "expectancy," 431
  during hyper- or hypo-glycemia, 212
  during learning, 430
  during sleep/arousal, 330, 343
  recording techniques, 3
  response to sex hormones, 263
Sleep, chemistry, 335
  definition, 326
  electrophysiology, 328
  neuroanatomy, 331
Skin potentials, change during arousal, 278
Skin temperature, effect on feeding, 214
Slow wave sleep, 328
Slow waves (EEG), 328, 341, 425
Smooth muscle, 35
Sodium chloride, effects on thirst, 240
Somatosensory association cortex, 47
Sone, 94
Sound, basic properties, 91
Spinal accessory nerve, 55
Spinal cord, 38
Spinal nerves, 52
Spinal reflexes, 151, 179
Spindle receptors, 152
Spindle waves (EEG), 29, 182
Spinothalamic tracts, 39
Spreading depression, 398
Stapes, 98

Subject Index

State dependent learning, 460
Steady potential, 19
Stereochemical factors, influence on olfaction, 123
Stereotaxic procedure, 7
Stomach, contractions, 192
    distention, 229
    removal, 192
Stretch reflex, 152
Stria medullaris, 44
Stria terminalis, 42
Striated muscle, 33
Striatum, 157
Strychnine, effects on learning and/or recall, 457
Subcommissural organ, role in thirst, 234
Subiculum, 49
Substantia nigra, 42, 159
Subthalamic n., 43, 158
Summation potential, of ear, 100
Superior colliculi, 42, 81
Sympathetic nerves, 56
Synapse, 22
Synaptic facilitation, 379

Taste, basic properties, 122
    buds, 131
    classification, 127
    effect of drugs, 135
    electrophysiology, 135, 139
    properties of stimuli, 127
    receptor anatomy, 131
    thresholds, 127
Tectorial membrane, 99
Tectum, 41
Tegmentum, 42, 201, 206, 234
Temperature, effect on, feeding, 214
    sexual behavior, 254
    thirst, 243
Temporal lobe, 49
    role in, affective reactions, 290
    learning, 453
Tendon organs, 152
Testosterone, effects on, development of hypothalamus, 261
    sexual behavior, 256
Thalamus, anatomy, 43
    effects of lesions or stimulation on, affective behaviors, 285
    arousal, 346
    feeding, 208
    motor functions, 159
    sleep, 332
Thermoregulatory influences on feeding, 214
Theta waves, EEG, 29, 341, 426
Thirst, classic theories, 226
    extrahypothalamic mechanisms, 233
    hypothalamic mechanisms, 231
    osmotic influences, 239
    pharmacology of central pathways, 232
    role of kidney, 233, 242
    thermoregulatory influences, 243
    volumetric influences, 241
Thyroid, 170
Thyrotrophin, 168
Thyroxin, 170
Timbre, 97
Tonicity, 239
Transfer of training, 445
Trichromatic theory of color vision, 67
Trigeminal nerve, 54
Trochlear nerve, 54

Vagotomy, effects on food intake, 192
Vagus nerve, 55
Ventral roots, 52
Ventromedial hypothalamus, effects of electrical stimulation or lesions on, avoidance and aggression, 282
    food intake, 195
    sexual behavior, 263
    electrophysiology, 200
Vermis, 50
Vestibular n., 41, 159
Vestibular system, anatomy, 55
Visual cortex, 47, 195, 399
Visual stimulus, 63
Visual system, anatomy, 53
    electrophysiology, 73, 79, 81
    receptor chemistry, 71
Volatility, influence on olfaction, 121
Volley theory of hearing, 104

Water content of body, 225
Water, distribution in body, 237

Yellow-blue potentials, 74

Zona incerta, 43